A Companion to American Thought

A Companion to American Thought

Edited by Richard Wightman Fox and James T. Kloppenberg

BLACKWELL
Publishers

Copyright © Blackwell Publishers Ltd 1995, 1998
Editorial organization © Richard Wightman Fox and
James T. Kloppenberg 1995, 1998

The right of Richard Wightman Fox and James T. Kloppenberg to be
identified as authors of this work has been asserted in accordance with
the Copyright, Designs and Patents Act 1988.

First published 1995
First published in paperback 1998
Reprinted 1998

Blackwell Publishers Inc
350 Main Street
Malden, Massachusetts 02148, USA

Blackwell Publishers Ltd
108 Cowley Road
Oxford OX4 1JF, UK

Library of Congress Cataloging in Publication Data
A Companion to American Thought/edited by Richard Wightman Fox and
James T. Kloppenberg.
Includes bibliographical references and index.
ISBN 1–55786–268–0 — ISBN 0–631–20656–6 (pbk)
1. United States—Intellectual life—Dictionaries.
I. Fox, Richard Wightman, 1945– . II. Kloppenberg, James T., 1951–
E169.1.C685 1995   94—13002
001.1'0973—dc20   CIP

British Library Cataloguing in Publication Data
A CIP catalogue record for this book is available from the British Library

Typeset in 9.5 on 11pt Bembo
by Graphicraft Typesetters Limited, Hong Kong
Printed in Great Britain by Redwood Books

This book is printed on acid-free paper

Contents

Contributors

Edward Abrahams
Brown University

Robert H. Abzug
University of Texas

Guy Alchon
University of Delaware

Frances R. Aparicio
University of Michigan

Jonathan Auerbach
University of Maryland

Edward L. Ayers
University of Virginia

David Barrow
Northern Illinois University

Philip D. Beidler
University of Alabama

Donald C. Bellomy
Arlington, Massachusetts

Thomas Bender
New York University

Paula Bennett
Southern Illinois University

Matthew Berke
First Things, *New York City*

Robert F. Berkhofer Jr.
*University of California,
Santa Cruz*

Dwight B. Billings
University of Kentucky

Casey Blake
Indiana University

David W. Blight
Amherst College

Daniel H. Borus
University of Rochester

Joseph Boskin
Boston University

Paul Boyer
University of Wisconsin

Ann Braude
Macalester College

Paul Breines
Boston College

Howard Brick
University of Oregon

Gillian Brown
University of Utah

JoAnne Brown
Johns Hopkins University

Rachel Buff
University of Minnesota

John Burt
Brandeis University

Jon Butler
Yale University

William E. Cain
Wellesley College

Charles Capper
University of North Carolina

Anne Carr
University of Chicago

Clayborne Carson
Stanford University

John Carson
*The Wellcome Institute for the
History of Medicine, London*

Elizabeth B. Clark
Boston University

Kenneth Cmiel
University of Iowa

Thomas R. Cole
*University of Texas,
Medical Branch*

Gary Collison
*Pennsylvania State University,
York*

Paul Conkin
Vanderbilt University

Stephen A. Conrad
Indiana University

Anthony Cook
Georgetown University

Terry A. Cooney
University of Puget Sound

Saul Cornell
Ohio State University

Nancy F. Cott
Yale University

Elaine Forman Crane
Fordham University

William Cronon
University of Wisconsin

George P. Cunningham
Brooklyn College

Reed Way Dasenbrock
New Mexico State University

Michael Davidson
University of California, San Diego

G. Scott Davis
University of Richmond

Carl N. Degler
Stanford University

Roland A. Delattre
University of Minnesota

Andrew Delbanco
Columbia University

Raymond J. Demallie
Indiana University

John P. Diggins
City University of New York

Ellen Carol Dubois
*University of California,
Los Angeles*

Roger C. Echo-Hawk
University of Colorado

Jean Bethke Elshtain
University of Chicago

Philip J. Ethington
University of Southern California

Michel Fabre
Université de Paris III

Candace Falk
University of California, Berkeley

Paula S. Fass
University of California, Berkeley

William W. Fisher III
Harvard University

Ellen Fitzpatrick
Harvard University

Jane Flax
Howard University

William Flesch
Brandeis University

Barbara Foley
Rutgers University, Newark

William E. Forbath
*University of California,
Los Angeles*

Lacy K. Ford
University of South Carolina

Richard Wightman Fox
Boston University

Jenny Franchot
University of California, Berkeley

Edith Gelles
Stanford University

Dan Georgakis
Queens College

Alexander George
Amherst College

Donald B. Gibson
Rutgers University

Jonathan A. Glickstein
*University of California,
Santa Barbara*

Karla Goldman
Hebrew Union College, Cincinnati

Warren Goldstein
*State University of New York, Old
Westbury*

Linda Gordon
University of Wisconsin

Robert W. Gordon
Yale University

Cheryl Greenberg
Trinity College, Hartford

Katherine Grier
University of Utah

Robert L. Griswold
University of Oklahoma

Richard Grusin
Georgia Institute of Technology

Carl Guarneri
St. Mary's College

Rochelle Gurstein
New York City

Knud Haakonssen
Boston University

David D. Hall
Harvard University

Jacquelyn Dowd Hall
University of North Carolina

Peter Hansen
Brandeis University

Russell L. Hanson
Indiana University

Margaret Mills Harper
Georgia State University

Thomas L. Haskell
Rice University

C. Dallett Hemphill
Ursinus College

Ellen Herman
Harvard University

J. David Hoeveler Jr.
University of Wisconsin, Milwaukee

David A. Hollinger
University of California, Berkeley

Thomas C. Holt
University of Chicago

James Hoopes
Babson College

Howard Horwitz
University of Utah

Nian-Sheng Huang
Bentley College

Jean M. Humez
University of Massachusetts, Boston

Maurice Isserman
Hamilton College

Kathleen B. Jones
San Diego State University

Amy Kaplan
Mount Holyoke College

Cora Kaplan
Rutgers University

Michael Kaufmann
Temple University

Morton Keller
Brandeis University

Mary Kelley
Dartmouth College

Robin D.G. Kelley
New York University

David M. Kennedy
Stanford University

Lori J. Kenschaft
Boston University

Linda K. Kerber
University of Iowa

Elizabeth Keyser
Hollins College

Richard H. King
University of Nottingham

Jordan Kleiman
University of Rochester

John Kloos
Illinois Benedictine College

James T. Kloppenberg
Brandeis University

James F. Knapp
University of Pittsburgh

Jane Knodell
University of Vermont

Isaac Kramnick
Cornell University

Mark Krupnick
University of Chicago

Vera M. Kutzinski
Yale University

Glenn W. La Fantasie
United States Department of State

Ellen Condliffe Lagemann
New York University

Ann J. Lane
University of Virginia

Amy Schrager Lang
Emory University

Christopher Lasch†

Paul Lauter
Trinity College, Hartford

Henry Samuel Levinson
*University of North Carolina,
Greensboro*

Sanford Levinson
University of Texas

David W. Levy
University of Oklahoma

Patricia Nelson Limerick
University of Colorado

Charles Lindholm
Boston University

Amy Ling
University of Wisconsin

Julia E. Liss
Scripps College

Tessie P. Liu
Northwestern University

Ronald Lora
University of Toledo

Drew R. McCoy
Clark University

Lisa MacFarlane
University of New Hampshire

Michael McGerr
Indiana University

Nellie Y. McKay
University of Wisconsin

Jane Mansbridge
Northwestern University

George E. Marcus
Williams College

Joseph Margolis
Temple University

Louis P. Masur
City College of New York

Susan Mizruchi
Boston University

Michael Moon
Duke University

R. Laurence Moore
Cornell University

James H. Moorhead
Princeton Theological Seminary

Victor Navasky
The Nation, *New York City*

Mark A. Noll
Wheaton College, Illinois

Anne Norton
University of Pennsylvania

William J. Novak
University of Chicago

Michael O'Brien
Miami University

Michael Oriard
Oregon State University

Nell Irvin Painter
Princeton University

Thomas L. Pangle
University of Toronto

Peggy Pascoe
University of Utah

Diane B. Paul
University of Massachusetts, Boston

Philip J. Pauly
Rutgers University

Lewis Perry
Vanderbilt University

Mark A. Peterson
Boston University

Joel Pfister
Wesleyan University

Mel Piehl
Valparaiso University

Ellen Pifer
University of Delaware

Amanda Porterfield
*Indiana University-Purdue
University, Indianapolis*

Ross Posnock
University of Washington

Marjorie Pryse
*State University of New York,
Plattsburgh*

Edward A. Purcell Jr.
New York University

Paula Rabinowitz
University of Minnesota

Jack N. Rakove
Stanford University

John Louis Recchiuti
Lawrence Technological University

Henry S. Richardson
Georgetown University

Dana Robert
Boston University

Jon H. Roberts
*University of Wisconsin,
Stevens Point*

David M. Robinson
Oregon State University

Daniel T. Rodgers
Princeton University

Kenneth M. Roemer
University of Texas, Arlington

Nancy L. Rosenblum
Brown University

Lawrence Alan Rosenwald
Wellesley College

Dorothy Ross
Johns Hopkins University

Joan Shelley Rubin
*State University of New York,
Brockport*

Rachel Rubin
Yale University

Lois Palken Rudnick
University of Massachusetts, Boston

Alan Ryan
Princeton University

Robert Blair St. George
University of Pennsylvania

José David Saldívar
University of California, Berkeley

George J. Sánchez
University of Michigan

Mark Seltzer
Cornell University

Robert E. Shalhope
University of Oklahoma

Dmitri N. Shalin
University of Nevada, Las Vegas

David E. Shi
Furman University

Richard Shusterman
Temple University

Reva Siegel
Yale University

Daniel J. Singal
Hobart College

Sheila L. Skemp
University of Mississippi

Kathryn Kish Sklar
*State University of New York,
Binghamton*

Peter Gregg Slater
Mercy College

James Smethurst
Harvard University

Laurence D. Smith
University of Maine, Orono

Rogers M. Smith
Yale University

Mitchell Snay
Denison University

John M. Staudenmaier
University of Detroit Mercy

Robert B. Stepto
Yale University

Louise L. Stevenson
Franklin and Marshall College

John W. Stewart
Princeton Theological Seminary

Shannon C. Stimson
University of California, Berkeley

Stephen H. Sumida
University of Michigan

Brook Thomas
University of California, Irvine

Emory J. Tolbert
Howard University

James Turner
University of Michigan

Thomas A. Underwood
Boston University

Gerald Vizenor
University of California, Berkeley

Candace Waid
Yale University

Priscilla Wald
Columbia University

James D. Wallace
Boston College

Glenn Wallach
Georgetown University

Stephen P. Waring
University of Alabama

Michael Warner
Rutgers University

Kenneth W. Warren
University of Chicago

Robert B. Westbrook
University of Rochester

Richard White
University of Washington

Todd Whitmore
University of Notre Dame

Robyn Wiegman
Indiana University

Sean Wilentz
Princeton University

Joan Williams
American University

Christopher P. Wilson
Boston College

Daniel J. Wilson
Muhlenberg College

Richard Wolin
Rice University

Donald Worster
University of Kansas

Gwendolyn Wright
Columbia University

Bertram Wyatt-Brown
University of Florida

Richard Yarborough
*University of California,
Los Angeles*

James E. Young
*University of Massachusetts,
Amherst*

Viviana A. Zelizer
Princeton University

Christina Zwarg
Haverford College

Introduction

This volume is both a reference work and a book to be read for enjoyment. Our goal is to help students, scholars, and general readers deepen their knowledge of the major concepts and thinkers in the diverse traditions of American thought, and to become acquainted with key debates in the contemporary intellectual life of the United States.

American scholarship in many fields has been transformed over the last generation. As disciplinary boundaries erected a century ago have become permeable or fallen completely, scholars in all fields have sought to reposition themselves and reconceive their disciplines. Many have become, in effect, intellectual historians of their own professions; those, like us, who call themselves intellectual historians have seen their field shift dramatically under their feet over the last two decades. As the importance of language and "textuality" in the shaping of ideas has become evident, so has the impact of social facts such as religion, race, region, gender, ethnicity, and class upon the development of American thought. As a result, the once-standard distinction between "high" and "low" culture has been blurred.

Meanwhile, these very innovations have prompted resistance by some scholars who insist that novel topics and methods of interpretation have contributed to weakening our collective understanding of our central intellectual traditions. The militant version of this resistance, popularly associated with the late Allan Bloom and his bestseller *The Closing of the American Mind* (1987), contends that American scholarship, like American culture as a whole, is succumbing to a pernicious relativism. The militants, including many of the academics in the traditionalist National Association of Scholars, call for a revival of "excellence" and a return to teaching the "truths" contained in the classics of the Western tradition. The moderate version of the resistance, exemplified by E. D. Hirsch's ongoing campaign for "cultural literacy" (also the title of his widely read 1987 book), seeks to promote basic education in the fundamental ideas of our intellectual inheritance. Without a common, historically based language and discourse, according to Hirsch, extensive public deliberation of any kind will be impossible.

With the publication of this *Companion*, we seek to enter this debate in two ways. First, we endorse, and want to contribute to, the moderates' program of cultivating a body of common knowledge. But we also want to provide a forum in which authors of divergent intellectual persuasions can come together and display their differences as well as their agreements. Common knowledge is more complex than some educational critics allow. We believe that common knowledge requires awareness of the multiple standpoints from which knowledge is actually fashioned. We reject Bloom's contention that truth exists timelessly, and we are committed to a broadly pluralistic interpretation of what should count as valuable common knowledge. Knowledge, in our view, is produced by historical communities. This historicist position makes us traditionalists, however, not relativists, since in our view it is particular historical traditions, not some transcendent Reason or Revelation, that provide us with the linguistic, moral, and aesthetic resources for judging value in the realm of thought. Devotion to tradition, moreover, demands, as T. S. Eliot argued in

"Tradition and the Individual Talent," an openness to innovation. It requires debate with and willingness to learn from other traditions and cultures; in that way one's own tradition can remain loyal to its own deepest past insights, some of which over the course of centuries may have been forgotten, camouflaged, or corrupted.

Struggles over canons of thought are as old as the battles fought in ancient religions over the selection of sacred texts. Both the Italian and Northern Renaissances were sparked by the "new" ideas recovered from classical Greek and Roman texts (preserved thanks to Islamic scholars) and insinuated into a medieval synthesis regarded by some of its defenders, then and even now, as timelessly true. In America, the version of truth preached at Harvard College prompted a band of rebels to found Yale. Thomas Jefferson rebelled against himself: having advocated a set of required texts for all students, he later called for an open curriculum to accommodate the "illimitable freedom of the human mind."

Clashes between "ancients" and "moderns" are perennial. The canon of Great Books that dominated American higher education for most of the twentieth century took shape partly in response to university leaders' campaigns to align Americans with Allied struggles against German autocracy in World War I, fascism in World War II, and totalitarianism in the Cold War. That canon was decisively different from the curriculum taught in American universities 100 or 200 years ago. Judgments of intrinsic merit always underlie the selection of texts and writers for canonical status, but those judgments are always shaped by historical contingencies. In constructing this *Companion*, we are aware that we occupy a particular historical moment, one of intense rethinking and restructuring of intellectual discourse. Our volume of several hundred entries will play its own small part in determining which ideas and thinkers are regarded as primary, which as secondary. We cannot escape our time any more than our predecessors could. We fully expect our effort to be revised in the future. Indeed, given the rapid development of ideas and modes of thought in this era, we hope to revise it ourselves.

The end of the Cold War has made it more difficult to discuss the nature of tradition or of canonicity, since these issues have now been systematically politicized and rigidified. It was hard enough to talk about them during the Cold War, when ideological positions on the conflict between capitalism and socialism, or democracy and totalitarianism, exerted a dramatic influence on what counted as a valid intellectual tradition or an appropriate course syllabus. But after the fall of the Soviet Union and the apparent triumph of varieties of capitalism and democracy in many parts of the world, public debate has moved away from economics and politics to culture. To put it another way, cultural topics, including such intellectual issues as canons and curricula, have been requisitioned by political armies of the right and left. Those on the right, deprived of Soviet communism as an object of vilification, have relocated subversion in such cultural practices as abortion and homosexuality, and in such intellectual practices as challenges to the canon of Western classics or to other parts of the college curriculum. Those on the left, deprived of American imperialism as a viable target of scorn, have relocated oppression in such cultural practices as religious fundamentalism and artistic censorship, and in such intellectual practices as the study of "dead, white, European, male" authors.

While the most recent politicizing of cultural and intellectual debate may offer an opportunity to address a volume on American thought to a wider audience than ever before, it also presents the danger that the book will be taken as an ideological weapon on one side of the battle. We intend this book to transcend the terms of the contemporary culture wars. At the simplest level we hope to accomplish this goal by bringing together authors who occupy a full range of viewpoints, traditional and innovative, conservative and progressive, and by giving scholarly attention to new as well as familiar topics in American thought. We have striven to find contributors and formulate topics representative of the full range of contemporary American intellectual life. In our view the most plausible synthesis of American thought at this time is a collaborative effort of this sort, one that foregrounds the vast diversity of intellectual voices while holding each voice to the same standard of responsible and engaging argument. We want our readers to find these essays, whatever their intellectual provenance, so intriguing that upon reading them they will say to themselves not "this author is a canon-buster" or "this essay is too old-fashioned," but "I want to know more about these issues." We have provided cross-references to aid readers in following their curiosity from one part of the book to another. One of the rewards of exploring the *Companion*, we hope, will be the discovery of the different angles of vision from which contributors approach similar topics.

At a deeper level the *Companion* tries to challenge and reconfigure one of the main assumptions that dominate the contemporary culture wars, the view that a "common culture," which supposedly united Americans of earlier generations, is under attack and must be defended. There is a growing feeling among many intellectuals that this is the most urgent question facing the nation: how, in the face of strident demands for the legitimation of ethnic, racial, and cultural diversity, and in the face of declining standards of achievement in secondary and college education, can Americans rebuild or restore a common culture? Without such a culture, according to observers ranging from conservative to liberal and including William Bennett, Lynn Cheney, Diane Ravitch, Robert Hughes, and Arthur Schlesinger Jr., the United States risks degenerating into a mass of atomized, uprooted, uneducated individuals who gather only, if they gather at all, into consumption-oriented 'lifestyle enclaves,' in Robert Bellah's phrase, not into a vibrant, participatory civic culture. When Arthur Schlesinger Jr. describes "the disuniting of America," or Robert Hughes "the fraying of America," as they respectively titled and subtitled their recent books, they are lamenting the centrifugal spin of an American culture threatened by a loss of unifying identity. Irreversible national decline may be expected to follow, they imply, unless Americans renew their pledge of allegiance to the foundational principles of the nation or the essential truths or traditions of the West.

We sympathize with much of this critique, especially when it is marked by a wider democratic or egalitarian perspective. As historians of the United States we share Schlesinger's unhappiness about the tendency of much recent social, cultural, and intellectual history to turn away from the traditional narrative line of American history: the struggle for democracy. That struggle, we believe, can now be much more fully understood thanks to new scholarship in such fields as women's history and African American and other minority-group histories. That research has greatly deepened our grasp of the character of democracy and the obstacles it has faced throughout American history, not least by forcing us to start taking issues of gender as seriously as critical historians of the 1960s began to take issues of race or those of the 1930s began to take questions of class. For that reason we have placed great importance, throughout the *Companion*, on the development of feminist thought, and we have also stressed emerging thinking about American Indian, Latino, and Asian American cultures as well as the more fully matured scholarship on African American cultures. We have chosen to use the labels Indian (rather than Native American) and Latino/Latina (rather than Hispanic) after consulting with specialists in those fields. Recently those terms have become more and more widely used by members of those groups, although both remain contested. Shifting nomenclature is inevitable at a time when identities are subject to profound reexamination.

While we support one part of the quest to bolster a traditional common culture—the part that locates our central cultural tradition in the historic yearning for democracy—we also wish to resist one of the primary assumptions of the larger campaign, the idea that the fundamental problem facing the United States today is too much diversity, not enough commonality. We believe it is more to the point to complain about too much commonality of one kind, too little diversity of another kind. The real problem in our view is not the lack of a common culture but the overbearing presence of a common culture of standardized production and consumption, one that makes memorable cultural creation of any kind—whether old style (based on careful cultivation of the Western classics) or new style (based on opening minds and curricula to new voices and new texts)—harder and harder to achieve.

Alexis de Tocqueville was right: democracy generates its own censorship, its own affably conformist mediocrity. Cultural critique on all sides takes on too much the tone of the publicity handout rather than the reasoned argument. What we may be most in danger of losing is not some common core of beliefs, assuming that such a thing ever existed, but a shared commitment to open intellectual argument. Most of us who work in universities have witnessed verbal exchanges in recent years—perhaps in the classroom, perhaps in a meeting or at a conference—in which one person accuses another of making a personally offensive comment of the sort that no right-minded individual would utter. The most worrisome sign on the intellectual horizon is not diversity, but the closing off of debate through the intense personalizing of issues. The problem is not too much passionate belief, but too little willingness on all sides to engage in discussion with those who hold different passionate beliefs. What we may now need most is not more commonality and less difference, but a renewed practice of engaged, impersonal argument.

Educators in a democratic society have to be vigilant about protecting critical thought, about promoting real excellence in achievement, and they must struggle to open students' and readers' minds to all neglected voices, including both those previously silenced and those of many classic authors whom the most recent generation of students, at any rate, has not read. Who has read Jonathan Edwards lately? Who has read Thorstein Veblen or Henry Adams? Teachers have the dual responsibility of keeping alive the voices of authors, usually male and white, who used to be more widely read, while making sure that students encounter important voices, often female and nonwhite, frequently ignored by earlier as well as many present-day scholars. We want this *Companion* to help rekindle a commitment to broad common knowledge and to pointed intellectual argument.

It should be obvious that American voices are not the only ones to which students and other readers should attend. Indeed, there is some danger of parochialism in producing a book on "American" thought, since it might imply either that citizens of the United States are the only true "Americans" (Canadians as well as Latin Americans take vigorous exception to that presumption, even though they, too, typically use "America" to mean the United States), or that what Americans think has arisen out of some unique American experience. We have chosen to limit this book to American topics and individuals not because Americans are specially chosen or because they have had unique intellectual experiences (although to some extent they have), but because one book cannot do everything and because we wish to emphasize ongoing American intellectual debates. The foreign, especially European, sources and analogues for many of these debates will be evident to the readers of the following essays, since the essays make frequent reference to those sources and analogues.

In order to approach the twin aims of comprehensiveness and depth of treatment in a single volume, we have chosen the imperfect expedient of including entries of different lengths. For the most important individuals and topics we solicited essays of between 1,000 and 2,500 words. Other individuals and topics receive brief treatment in about 100 words, just enough to signal their existence and to suggest their value for further study. Of course our decisions about which entries deserve greater or lesser space are debatable; we debated them ourselves and changed our minds many times. The fundamental criterion that provided general guidance for our choices is the importance of a particular thinker, concept, or movement both to the development of American thought and to contemporary intellectual debate. (For individuals from the colonial period, birth and death dates are given only according to the new calendar instituted in 1752.)

We asked the authors of the longer entries to offer a historically informed assessment of their topic and to suggest how the topic relates to present-day scholarly or intellectual discussion. We know there are severe limits to what can be said in 1,000 or 2,500 words, but we believe the essays demonstrate that something important can be done even in that space: delimiting, identifying, and critically examining topics or thinkers, and positioning them in a continuing debate or set of debates. We encouraged our contributors to avoid the dry style of most encyclopedia offerings and to offer provocative interpretations as well as useful information. They have given us challenging essays that will engage readers in the critical issues of contemporary scholarship and intellectual life.

The primary focus of the *Companion* is upon the debates that occupy humanists, social scientists, and those outside of academia in journalism, politics, law, the ministry, social work, psychology, and other professions. The essays center on key ideas and thinkers in history, literature, religion, philosophy, political theory, and other social sciences. Although the book does not systematically address music, the plastic and visual arts, or the natural and physical sciences, we have included essays on selected artistic and scientific topics and individuals, especially when they cross over into general intellectual debate, as in the case of a scientist who is widely read by a general audience or a group of artists committed to making a statement about social or political ideas.

We have included a wide range of literary figures on the grounds that authors of fiction and poetry have often contributed to thought as well as literature. This is true in the obvious sense that many writers have explicitly joined in general intellectual debate, but also in the less obvious sense that many writers, perhaps especially women and members of minority groups, have produced their thought in fictional or poetic forms (and in journals and diaries). If this were a strictly literary history rather than a volume on American thought, we would have made different choices about which writers and poets to include and which to treat at greater or lesser length. No set of criteria is foolproof. Our method of selection casts a wide net, but our format of a single volume necessitated difficult decisions, which we made with the help of specialists in the literary fields. We welcome suggestions from readers about topics or individuals in all areas of thought that should be considered for inclusion in any future edition of this book.

One of our principal contributors, Christopher Lasch, died while the *Companion* was in production. His eight essays, models of probing, engaged scholarship, are among his last written works. We are grateful for his participation in this project, and with many others mourn his passing, a severe loss for American intellectual life because he had embarked upon a profoundly significant rethinking of American democratic and religious traditions. We want the *Companion* to further the goal to which he was devoted, the clarification of public ideals through critical scholarship.

In preparing this book we depended upon many people for advice and assistance. John Davey and Alyn Shipton at Blackwell Publishers provided splendid suggestions on matters large and small, while also giving us free rein to conceive the book in our own way. For their efficiency in handling the manuscript we thank our editor Halina Boniszewska, our copyeditor Ann Bone, and Mary Riso, who kept track of the typescript in the early stages. Mike Pardee, our first all-purpose assistant, aided us in the initial process of lining up contributors. Our second one, Lori Kenschaft, besides authoring three essays, did first drafts of most of the short entries, along with managing the data base. Her contribution to the *Companion* has been central and she has our profound gratitude. David Shawn gave us valuable help in the final preparation of the manuscript.

A large number of scholars gave us indispensable advice about the overall conception of the project and about which topics to include. For especially helpful counsel we want to thank Tom Bender, Elizabeth Beverly, Casey Blake, Paul Boyer, Alan Brinkley, Paul Conkin, David Brion Davis, Ellen Fitzpatrick, Alexander George, Jacquelyn Dowd Hall, Peter Hall, David Hollinger, Fred Hoxie, Mary Kelley, Linda Kerber, Arnold Krupat, Paul Lauter, Amy Ling, Nellie McKay, Michael O'Brien, Barry O'Connell, Philip Pauly, Tim Peltason, Nancy Rosenblum, Dorothy Ross, Alan Ryan, Jose David Saldivar, Arthur Schlesinger Jr., Kathryn Kish Sklar, Neil Smith, Gerald Vizenor, Robert Westbrook, Joan Williams, and Christopher

Wilson. The editors' families, Rachel and Christopher Fox, and Mary, Annie, and Jay Kloppenberg, sometimes aided this lengthy enterprise directly, but most importantly they gave us the gift of their love.

Lisa Luedtke and Ginny Stroud-Lewis helped us find Michael Dersin, the photographer who provided just the right image, for the front jacket design, of the Library of Congress—an institution worthy of celebration for its historic commitment to the preservation of knowledge and to open, democratic access to its resources. Scholars great and simple have sat at its grand circular tables and reflected on the course of human civilization depicted on the dome. Edwin Blashfield's mural "The Evolution of Civilization," painted in 1895 and 1896, probably signified to most of its viewers over the last century that "America" represented the culmination of a long march that began in Egypt. But the circular design implicitly challenges the metaphor of procession and suggests a second, more complicated meaning: each epoch, each culture, builds as best it can on its inheritance and makes its own distinctive contribution to human thought. America is certainly positioned at the chronological end-point of dynamic traditions of thought bequeathed by the ancients and developed by their successors. But occupying that position is no guarantee of virtue. Inheriting traditions is not a passive activity; it requires a struggle to incorporate their deepest truths, in part by confronting the wisdom imparted by other traditions. America is no closer to the center of the circle than any of the earlier cultures. The sources of human wisdom are plural. Some lie outside the Western European tradition, as in Blashfield's representations of "Egypt" and "Islam." Diversity of perception and inspiration is fully compatible with excellence of achievement.

RICHARD WIGHTMAN FOX
JAMES T. KLOPPENBERG

How to use this book

Each essay is followed by a list of suggestions for further reading. The list also provides the sources for most citations made in the text of the essay. To minimize textual intrusions, we have given only page references in the text when the author of the quotation is already clear; turn to that author's entry in the "further reading" section to get the full bibliographical reference.

Some cross-references appear within the essays (in small capital letters); others follow the essays. Most of the cross-references point to other entries in which the designated topic or individual is discussed. But sometimes the goal is broader: to suggest that intriguing connections may exist between one topic and another. The index can also be used to uncover some of the thematic threads that tie the essays together. We hope that in moving from one entry to another, readers will create their own evolving set of cross-references.

A

Abbott, Edith (b. Grand Island, Neb., Sept. 26, 1876; d. Grand Island, Neb., July 28, 1957). Social worker. The first dean of the University of Chicago's School of Social Service Administration (1924–42), Abbott was committed to the professionalization of social work. She argued that a new stress on scientific knowledge and expertise must replace the charity workers' older reliance upon personality and intuition. She urged both Hoover and Roosevelt to institute a comprehensive system of social insurance. Like her younger sister Grace, head of the Immigrants' Protective League and later of the U.S. Children's Bureau, Edith was particularly concerned about expanding the opportunities available to immigrants and working-class women. Cofounder with SOPHONISBA BRECKINRIDGE of the *Social Service Review* (1927), she wrote more than a hundred books and articles, including *Women in Industry* (1910), *The Real Jail Problem* (1915), *Immigration: Select Documents and Case Records* (1924), and *Public Assistance* (1941).

See also PROFESSION; WELFARE.

FURTHER READING

Ellen F. Fitzpatrick, *Endless Crusade: Women Social Scientists and Progressive Reform* (New York: Oxford University Press, 1990).

abortion The termination of a pregnancy, by the loss or destruction of the embryo/fetus before birth, may be spontaneous or induced. In contemporary usage spontaneous abortions are generally referred to as "miscarriages"; the term "abortion" commonly denotes the intentional termination of a pregnancy.

Since antiquity, there have been numerous techniques for inducing abortion. Women may ingest substances ("abortifacients") or engage in physical activities intended to disrupt pregnancy; they may use surgical implements on themselves or submit to procedures by others. Just as techniques for inducing abortion have varied over time and across cultures, so too have the types of regulation to which the procedure is subject. In the West, political, religious, and medical authorities have each played a role in regulating abortion, subjecting the practice to shifting and, at times, inconsistent regulatory constraints.

State regulation of abortion in the United States has evolved through three phases since the colonial era. Initially, the Anglo-American common law allowed abortion until the moment in pregnancy known as quickening—the first perception of fetal movement, typically during the fourth or fifth month of gestation. But by the mid-nineteenth century, most states in the U.S. had enacted legislation that criminalized abortion, and also contraception, unless prescribed for medical reasons. Finally, in the late twentieth century, the practices were legalized, first by legislative reform and then by constitutional decision; in this period, the United States Supreme Court declared that the constitutional right to privacy was broad enough to protect the practice of contraception (*Griswold v. Connecticut*, 1965) and abortion (*Roe v. Wade*, 1973).

Public law, however, is not an entirely reliable guide to the social status of birth control practices. Throughout the century in which contraception and abortion were subject to criminal prohibition, they were widely practiced, with and without the assistance of the medical profession. Moreover, since decriminalization, abortion and contraception remain subject to persistent forms of social censure that inhibit their practice. This discrepancy between law and social practice is due in part to the influence of religious and medical institutions, which have often proscribed or permitted birth control practices that diverge from those sanctioned by public law. The medical profession, for example, led the movement to criminalize birth control practices in the nineteenth century; it then provided increasing access to the outlawed procedures, and by the 1960s and 1970s generally supported their legalization. By contrast, organized religion played little role in the nineteenth-century movement to criminalize abortion and contraception, but now supplies some of the most vigorous leadership of the antiabortion movement, with many churches continuing to oppose public education concerning matters of contraception and some (notably the Catholic Church) forbidding "unnatural" forms of contraceptive practice altogether.

Regulating the practice of contraception and abortion is commonly justified on the grounds that any effort to prevent or terminate pregnancy threatens the sanctity of human life. This concern is especially pronounced in the case of abortion, where debate focuses on the ontological status of unborn life. One question typically dominates such disputes: Does the embryo/fetus share the attributes of human life (religiously, philosophically, scientifically, or legally defined), so that abortion assumes the character of homicide? Simply put, "when does life begin?" At the moment of conception? At the implantation of the fertilized ovum in the uterus? At ensoulment? At the first sign of brain function? At the moment a pregnant woman first senses fetal movement? At "viability," when the fetus becomes capable of surviving outside the mother's womb? Or at birth? Scientific, religious, philosophical, and legal authorities, each reasoning within their own discursive frameworks, have reached answers to these questions which differ not only from one interpretive community to another, but shift over time within particular communities.

But regulatory conflicts over abortion cannot be understood by analyzing disputes about the ontological status of the embryo/fetus alone. To appreciate why this society both tolerates and condemns the practice of abortion, one has to examine the practice in social context. Consider, for example, the reasons that women attempt to terminate (and to prevent) pregnancies. Women abort pregnancies for reasons rooted in the social conditions of motherhood: because they are concerned that bearing a child will injure their health, impoverish them or their families, impair their education or employment prospects, threaten a troubled relationship, bind them to men who have abused them or from whom they wish to separate, or because they may be left struggling for some two decades as a single parent. Society tacitly condones abortion for many of these reasons, but even under the most socially acceptable circumstances, the act still excites unease because it entails a fundamental breach of gender-role expectations. A woman seeking an abortion is a woman avoiding motherhood, and by violent means: she is destroying her own potential offspring. Moreover, abortion and contraception are practices that release human sexuality from its procreative consequences. It is because abortion and contraception are perceived to liberate human sexuality from procreation and to liberate women from motherhood that the practices and their regulation are the sites of profound social conflict.

Thus the regulation of birth control is shaped, not only by concerns about unborn life, but also by concerns about the structure of family life. Indeed, major epochs in the history of American birth control regulation correlate intriguingly with changes in family size, roles, and work patterns. The nineteenth-century campaign to criminalize birth control practices occurred as family size declined in the wake of the industrial revolution, and coincided with the first

demands from woman's rights advocates for suffrage and for reform of marital status laws. Legalization of birth control practices in the twentieth century occurred as women's participation in the labor force was escalating, and coincided with the so-called "second wave" of feminist agitation for women's equality. (*See also* FEMINISM.) In the nineteenth century, the social anxieties informing the shift in birth control laws were openly expressed. While opponents of abortion and contraception voiced concern about protecting unborn life, they also urged criminalizing birth control practices in order to direct marital sexuality to procreative ends and to ensure that women performed their work as wives and mothers. By contrast, in the twentieth century, those who seek to restrict abortion have, at least in public, stressed the apparently gender-neutral question of when life begins.

But as controversy over the abortion right has escalated, numerous commentators have challenged this fetus-centered framework. The work of Rosalind Petchesky, Kristin Luker, Linda Gordon, Carroll Smith-Rosenberg, and James Mohr offers historical and sociological evidence that in debates about the regulation of abortion, concerns about protecting the unborn are entangled with assumptions about sexuality and MOTHERHOOD. Those who would protect the unborn by prohibiting abortion are willing to enforce the procreative consequences of sexual relations and to compel women who are resisting motherhood to perform the work of bearing and rearing children, whereas those who defend the abortion right are unwilling to impose motherhood upon women in this fashion.

After some two decades of wide-ranging controversy over *Roe v. Wade*, the Supreme Court itself seems to show a fuller appreciation of the gendered character of the abortion conflict. In *Planned Parenthood of Southeastern Pennsylvania v. Casey* (1992), the Court upheld waiting-period restrictions on abortion, insisting that the state has the power to protect the sanctity of human life by requiring women who seek abortions to meditate on the implications of their act. But it also reaffirmed women's privacy right, under *Roe*, to abort such pregnancies after due deliberation. In the *Casey* opinion, the Court identified constitutional reasons for protecting this privacy right not discussed in *Roe*. The Court observed that the state was obliged to respect a pregnant woman's decision about abortion because her

suffering is too intimate and personal for the State to insist . . . upon its own vision of the woman's role, however dominant that vision has been in the course of our history and our culture. The destiny of the woman must be shaped to a large extent on her own conception of her spiritual imperatives and her place in society (p. 2807).

In short, the Court ruled that laws prohibiting abortion offend the Constitution because they use the power of the state to impose traditional sex roles on women.

For similar reasons, the Court struck down a provision of the Pennsylvania statute requiring a married woman to notify her husband before obtaining an abortion. The Court was concerned that, in conflict-ridden marriages, forcing women to inform their husbands about an abortion might deter them from "procuring an abortion as surely as if the Commonwealth had outlawed abortion in all cases" (p. 2829), and it ruled that the state lacked authority to constrain women's choices in this way. The notice requirement "give[s] to a man the kind of dominion over his wife that parents exercise over their children" (p. 2831), and thus reflects a "common-law understanding of a woman's role within the family," harkening back to a time when "'a woman had no legal existence separate from her husband, who was regarded as her head and representative in the social state . . .'" (pp. 2830–1, quoting *Bradwell v. Illinois*, 16 Wall. 130, 141 (1873) Bradley, J., concurring). "These views," the Court observed, "are no longer consistent with our understanding of the family, the individual, or the Constitution" (p. 2831).

Justice Blackmun, who authored *Roe*, endorsed the gender-conscious reasoning of the *Casey* decision, and drew upon it to advance the argument that restrictions on abortion offend constitutional guarantees of *equality* as well as privacy. In this equality argument, Justice Blackmun emphasized that abortion restrictions are gender biased in impetus and impact. When the state restricts abortion, it exacts the work of motherhood from women without compensating their labor because it assumes that it is women's "natural" duty to perform such labor:

> The State does not compensate women for their services; instead, it assumes that they owe this duty as a matter of course. This assumption—that women can simply be forced to accept the "natural" status and incidents of motherhood—appears to rest upon a conception of women's role that has triggered the protection of the Equal Protection Clause (p. 2847; citations and footnote omitted).

Restrictions on abortion do not stem solely from a desire to protect the unborn; they reflect, and enforce, social judgments about women's roles. While the abortion controversy is typically discussed as a conflict between an individual's freedom of choice and the community's interest in protecting unborn life, Justice Blackmun reframes the conflict. The community's decision to intervene in women's lives is no longer presumptively benign; its decision to compel motherhood is presumptively suspect, one more instance of the sex-role restrictions imposed on women throughout American history.

The Court's analysis of the constitutional question in *Casey* presents a challenge to those who would regulate abortion in the name of family and community values. In what ways is it legitimate to use the power of the state to enforce family and community relationships? Can a community express respect for the value of human life by means that constrain and instrumentalize women's lives? In reaffirming constitutional protection for the abortion right, *Casey* thus engaged the core questions of the abortion debate. What vision of family and community best respects, and protects, the value of human life? As long as these questions provoke controversy, so too will the practice of abortion.

R. SIEGEL

See also FEMINIST JURISPRUDENCE; WOMEN'S RIGHTS.

FURTHER READING

Celeste M. Condit, *Decoding Abortion Rhetoric: the Communication of Social Change* (Urbana: University of Illinois Press, 1990).

Linda Gordon, *Woman's Body, Woman's Right: a Social History of Birth Control in America* (New York: Penguin, 1974).

Griswold v. Connecticut, 381 U.S. 479 (1965).

Kristin Luker, *Abortion and the Politics of Motherhood* (Berkeley: University of California Press, 1984).

James C. Mohr, *Abortion in America: the Origin and Evolution of National Policy, 1800–1900* (New York: Oxford University Press, 1978).

Rosalind Pollack Petchesky, *Abortion and Woman's Choice: the State, Sexuality and Reproductive Freedom* (Boston: Northeastern University Press, 1984).

Planned Parenthood v. Casey, 112 S.Ct. 2791 (1992).

Roe v. Wade, 410 U.S. 113 (1973).

Reva B. Siegel, "Reasoning From the Body: a Historical Perspective on Abortion Regulation and Questions of Equal Protection," *Stanford Law Review* 44 (1992): 262–381.

Carroll Smith-Rosenberg, *Disorderly Conduct: Visions of Gender in Victorian America* (New York: Oxford University Press, 1985).

Laurence H. Tribe, *Abortion: the Clash of Absolutes* (New York: Norton, 1990).

abstract expressionism This was the first art movement to reflect a strong American presence in international MODERNISM. American and European émigré artists working in New York City during the 1940s and 1950s reworked several earlier forms of European modernism (expressionism, abstraction, surrealism) into painting concerned with existentialist and psychoanalytic themes of tortured interiority. The popular press seized upon these artists as examples of a particularly modern and vibrant American spirit, critics CLEMENT GREENBERG and HAROLD ROSENBERG championed their work, and abstract expressionism became the sanctioned form in an art establishment now centered in New York. Prominent abstract expressionists included William Baziotes, Willem de Kooning, Adolph Gottlieb, Helen Frankenthaler, Franz Kline, Lee Krasner, Robert Motherwell, Barnett Newman, JACKSON POLLOCK, Mark Rothko, and Clyfford Still.

See also AESTHETICS; CULTURAL CRITICISM.

FURTHER READING

Stephen Polcari, *Abstract Expressionism and the Modern Experience* (New York: Cambridge University Press, 1991).

academic freedom The term usually refers to claims of occupational autonomy advanced as a matter of right by scholars in the distinctly professional setting of the college or university. There are precedents, both customary and legal, for extending academic freedom beyond the professoriate to students, to teachers below the college level, or even to educational institutions as corporate entities, but these can be regarded as derivative cases. Although academic freedom is part and parcel of what might be called the self-conception or occupational ideology of the professoriate, it is widely understood to signify a great deal more than that. In the words of U.S. Supreme Court Justice William Brennan in *Keyishian v. Board of Regents* (1967),

> academic freedom . . . is of transcendent value to all of us and not merely to the teachers concerned. That freedom is therefore a special concern of the First Amendment, which does not tolerate laws that cast a pall of orthodoxy over the classroom. . . . [which is] peculiarly the marketplace of ideas.

Allowing scholars to speak their mind without hindrance undoubtedly serves pluralistic values and fosters a spirit of openness and candor that is vital to the well-being of democratic culture. Yet the claim of autonomy that lies at the heart of academic freedom also reflects the specific interests of the occupational group advancing it. Collegial self-governance and immunity from outside influence are among the defining features of all those occupations that have achieved the comparatively high status and dignity

of professions. The kinship of professors to other professionals is often overlooked because the university relieves professors of the necessity of individually seeking clients or working on a fee-for-service basis, as lawyers and physicians do. But it cannot exempt anyone from the laws of supply and demand: professors, like other workers in a market economy, sell their labor. Most workers sell not only their labor but also the right to command them. The distinguishing feature of professionals, whether they teach in the classroom or hang out their shingle on Main Street, is that they do not sell the right to command them—not, at least, in matters that fall within the domain of their expertise. On that privileged and carefully circumscribed terrain, the professional employee tells the boss what to do.

On this interpretation, the learning the scholar imparts to his students is a form of professional advice, and autonomy is a precondition of its value to the recipient. One cannot expect candid advice from hirelings. Not all expert advice is worth having, of course, and even the best should sometimes be rejected, but once the consumer has decided to seek advice, any effort to dictate its content plainly takes on a contradictory, self-defeating quality. Why seek advice in the first place, if the only acceptable advice is that which conforms to one's own untutored judgment? The medically uninformed patient who instructs his surgeon when and where to insert the scalpel is being unwise; the defendant who tells his attorney how to litigate a case is endangering his own interests. By the same token, it is anomalous to seek the benefits of a teacher's learning while confining what can be taught within predetermined limits.

The temptation to set such limits is immense, however, for the teacher's ultimate "clients" typically are not those who pay the bills, but impressionable young people; and the "advice" teachers give in the form of classroom instruction is not limited to prudential matters of health and legal liability but extends to life's deepest and most controversial questions. Unsurprisingly, then, struggles over academic freedom are virtually coterminous with the history of education itself.

Although there are valid lines of descent linking academic freedom to all those long-term historical processes that have fostered free speech, individualism, tolerance, and pluralism in Western culture, as a practically enforceable right in the United States it is a European import of fairly recent vintage. When George Ticknor, who later introduced the study of modern language and literature to Harvard, visited Göttingen in 1815 he found a cosmopolitan atmosphere that contrasted sharply with that of his home country: "No matter what a man thinks," he reported to Thomas Jefferson, "he may teach it and print it; not only without molestation from the government but also without molestation from publick opinion. . . . If truth is to be obtained by freedom of inquiry, as I doubt not it is, the German professors and literati are certainly on the high road." Friedrich Paulsen, one of the theorists of *Die akademische Freiheit* whose writings growing numbers of visiting American students imbibed in Germany after the Civil War, was typical in making autonomy for both teacher and student an indispensable prerequisite to the effective pursuit of truth.

> The content of instruction is not prescribed for the academic teacher; he is, as searcher as well as teacher, attached to no authority; he himself answers for his own instruction and is responsible to no one else. Opposite him is his student with complete freedom to accept or to reject; he is not a pupil but has the privilege of the critic or the improver. There is only one aim for both: the truth; only one yardstick: the agreement of thought with reality and with no other outside authority.

This curious flowering of liberty within Victorian culture was not without limits, of course. Paulsen held that "scholars cannot and should not engage in politics," lest it compromise their objectivity, and the Prussian Minister of Education did not hesitate to remove a politically active junior professor over the objections of his peers, on the grounds that it was every teacher's duty to "defend the existing order against all attacks" (quotations from Hofstadter and Metzger, *Development of Academic Freedom in the United States*, pp. 389–91).

Emboldened by the glorious achievements of the German universities and encouraged by favorable domestic developments such as the retreat of religious orthodoxy in the face of the Darwinian revolution, the rising prestige of science, and a substantial infusion of funds from a burgeoning industrial economy, the first generation of professional scholars in this country managed between 1875 and 1915 to transform the nation's system of higher education by harnessing it to the ideal of professional autonomy. The heart of this complex transformation was the emergence of "communities of the competent," social contrivances that, like icebergs, remained mostly out of sight, but which manifested themselves most palpably in a swarm of new professional organizations that began to appear in the 1880s. The Modern Language Association (1883), the American Historical Association (1884), and the American Economic Association (1885) set the pattern for a new intellectual division of labor that took shape in the years around the turn of the century. (*See also* PROFESSION.)

These densely interactive communities (not to be equated with the professional associations that formally speak in their name) effectively constitute the specialized universes within which scholarly discourse proceeds today. Their emergence enabled professors to divide their loyalties in a manner well calculated to foster professional autonomy and personal authority. Professors would, of course, continue to be teachers, dependent as always on a particular school for a salary and for provision of the mainly undergraduate classrooms in which they earned their keep. But they would also become research scholars, whose stature was contingent upon membership and reputation within a trans-local community made up of fellow specialists scattered around the country or the world. By keeping up a constant exchange of communications in the form of journal articles and books, the members of these disciplinary communities would police each other's opinions and thus provide a collective warrant for one another's authority.

The first principle of professional autonomy, and hence of academic freedom, is that only one's professional peers are competent to judge one's performance. Wealthy university trustees, who were legally empowered to superintend every detail of university operations, did not bow to this bold claim willingly. The result was a rash of academic freedom controversies during the politically tumultuous decades at the end of the nineteenth century. To mention only one example, when Stanford sociologist Edward A. Ross wrote pamphlets and gave lectures supporting "free silver" and other Populist measures in the presidential campaign of 1896, the widow of railroad magnate Leland Stanford, then the sole trustee of the university, declared herself "weary" of him and demanded his expulsion.

The academic freedom controversies of the 1880s and 1890s gradually created a rough consensus within the academy about the proper limits of advocacy. The degrees and kinds of politically sensitive behavior that the professoriate was willing to defend through collective action finally crystallized in 1915 with the creation of the American Association of University Professors. The founders of the AAUP included some of the most eminent scholars of the day, including philosophers JOHN DEWEY and ARTHUR O. LOVEJOY, and economist Edwin R. A. Seligman. By conducting inquiries into alleged violations, and by acting as friend of the court, lobbyist in the halls of government, and publicist before the nation at large, the AAUP has ever since its founding been the steadiest and most focused of all the forces shaping academic freedom in this country.

From the outset the AAUP moved beyond the German model by calling not only for freedom in research and teaching, but also "freedom of extra-mural utterance and action." The university, it said in its landmark 1915 report on "Academic Freedom and Academic Tenure," should be an "intellectual experiment station" and an "inviolable refuge" against tyrannies of both public opinion and political autocracy. The report specifically denied that the relationship between professor and trustee was merely that of employee to employer, likening it instead to the relation between the federal courts and the President, who appoints judges, but retains no control over their decisions. Both trustees and faculty, the report contended, were answerable to the public. Trustees therefore "have no moral right to bind the reason or conscience of any professor. . . . The responsibility of the university teacher is primarily to the public itself, and to the judgment of his own profession."

The 1915 report also presented "practical proposals" calling for faculty representation on committees considering reappointment; judicial hearings and formulation of explicit grounds in cases of dismissal; and permanent tenure for all positions above the grade of instructor after ten years of service. These practical institutional arrangements underpinning academic freedom were further strengthened in a second landmark AAUP document, the "1940 Statement of Principles on Academic Freedom and Tenure," which continues to enjoy something approaching constitutional status today. Although at that time many professors' contracts were still being renewed annually, the 1940 statement effectively rooted academic freedom in job security by shortening the probationary period to seven years and allowing for termination only at retirement, upon demonstration of adequate cause, or because of extraordinary financial exigencies. The 1940 statement does not have the force of law, but it was jointly authored by scholars in the AAUP and administrators in the American Association of Colleges. Although the premier association of college administrators, the American Association of Universities, never endorsed the 1940 principles, its member institutions uphold them at least as scrupulously as other schools.

How secure is the right of academic freedom today? The AAUP code was severely tested in the patriotic fervor of World War I and placed under heavy strain again in the loyalty controversies of the McCarthy era. On both occasions critics alleged that the association defined academic freedom too narrowly and failed to extend shelter to the untenured radicals who most needed it. On the other hand, had it not been for the AAUP and the specific occupational interests that it mobilizes and articulates, it is difficult to imagine how academic freedom could have achieved the degree of constitutional protection that it now enjoys. As late as 1907, Supreme Court Justice OLIVER WENDELL HOLMES JR., whom we now remember as a pioneering champion of First Amendment rights, was still upholding a conventionally narrow doctrine that prohibited *previous restraint* on expression, but permitted "the subsequent punishment of such [expression] as may be deemed contrary to the public welfare"—an interpretation obviously inimical to any robust conception of academic freedom. Not until 1919, in *Abrams v. United States*, did Holmes argue that open competition in the marketplace of ideas was such a vital "test of truth" that even opinions we "loathe" must be tolerated, thus blazing a trail toward Justice Brennan's *Keyishian* decision of 1967, quoted above, which put academic freedom near the center of an expanding umbrella of First Amendment protections.

Enshrining academic freedom within the inner sanctum of First Amendment rights has undoubtedly strengthened it, yet even favorable developments can have unsettling implications. For example, in *Healey v. James* (1972), Supreme Court Justice WILLIAM O. DOUGLAS invoked the "academic freedom" of militant students as a beneficial corrective to the timidity and narrowness of faculty decisions regarding the curriculum—thus turning academic freedom against the project of professorial autonomy that gave birth to it in the first place. Now that academic freedom is understood as a subset of First Amendment protections, professors with unpopular views have more effective recourse against administrators or trustees who wish to silence them as a condition of employment, but it remains to be seen how much shelter the law will provide for unpopular views that are, say, shouted down by militants in a classroom (arguably a rival exercise of "free speech"). And what of demands for political orthodoxy that originate *within* the professional community and win the endorsement of a well-organized faction of the dissenter's professional peers, pursuing their own sincerely held vision of righteousness? Demands for political orthodoxy are obnoxious whatever their source, yet it is not clear that any existing legal doctrine offers adequate recourse in such a case.

Also worrisome is the emergence during the 1970s and 1980s of a deep skepticism within the academy about the very possibility of truth. The Victorian educators who established communities of the competent and proclaimed academic freedom as a means of ensuring their autonomy were not epistemologically naive. They had learned the lessons of fallibilism and the unavoidable subjectivity of perception. The very idea of relying on the community of the competent implies that truth is no simple matter of solitary minds achieving correspondence with reality, but instead a collective, competitive, culturally mediated enterprise, the results of which remain perpetually open to revision. Still, as we have seen, Friedrich Paulsen could define the aim of academic freedom as the discovery of truth, and speak of truth simply as "the agreement of thought with reality and with no other outside authority." Even so sophisticated a thinker as John Dewey, the founding president of the AAUP, found it only natural to invoke a classic antithesis between power and knowledge and justify academic freedom as a matter of erecting fences around knowledge, so as to shelter it against the intrusions of power. "To investigate truth, critically to verify fact; to reach conclusions by means of the best methods at command, untrammeled by external fear or favor . . . this is precisely the aim and object of the university," declared Dewey in his 1902 essay "Academic Freedom."

Today, in contrast, many scholars have rejected fallibilism for more radical positions that put immense stress on the contingent, perspectival nature of all knowledge and effectively deny that any opinion could ever deserve the label "truth"—except perhaps in quotation marks. Reality, they contend, is something we collectively construct, not discover, and our constructions ineluctably conform, it is said, to our interests. Many now accept the view associated with Michel Foucault that power and knowledge, far from being a natural antithesis, are so deeply entangled with one another that they cannot come into authentic opposition and thus should always be written "power/knowledge," as if two sides of a single coin. By this standard, no line can be drawn between scholarship and propaganda that does not merely reinscribe the political passions that it pretends to erase. The implication is that knowledge innocent of considerations of power—exactly what both Paulsen and Dewey promised as the finest fruit of academic freedom—is but a will-o'-the-wisp. The question to ask about knowledge, some would now contend, is not whether it is true, but which regime it serves, which interests it propagates.

Admitting that the results of inquiry are less than certain is a matter of simple candor that does no harm to the case for academic freedom. Nor does politically committed scholarship do any harm, as long as the scholarly virtues of objectivity and detachment are not thrown out with the bathwater of neutrality and indifference. But if "truth" belongs always in quotation marks, as befits a claim made only halfheartedly, must not the "rights" of academic freedom end up in quotation marks too? If there is no such thing as truth, and if inquiry is merely politics by other means, why should the public defer to the community of the competent, pay for its upkeep, or bend over backwards to be tolerant when its findings are upsetting? These questions had scarcely been asked as the decade of the 1990s began, but they will be in years to come, and the fate of academic freedom—and, quite possibly, of liberal democracy as well—may depend upon the answers.

THOMAS L. HASKELL

See also COLLEGES AND UNIVERSITIES.

FURTHER READING

"Freedom and Tenure in the Academy: the Fiftieth Anniversary of the 1940 Statement of Principles," special issue ed. William W. Van Alstyne, *Law and Contemporary Problems* 53, no. 3 (summer 1990).

Mary O. Furner, *Advocacy and Objectivity: a Crisis in the Professionalization of Social Science in the United States, 1865–1905* (Lexington: University Press of Kentucky, 1975).

Carol S. Gruber, *Mars and Minerva: World War I and the Uses of Higher Education in America* (Baton Rouge: Louisiana State University Press, 1975).

Thomas L. Haskell, *The Emergence of Professional Social Science: the American Social Science Association and the Nineteenth Century Crisis of Authority* (Urbana: University of Illinois Press, 1977).

Richard Hofstadter and Walter P. Metzger, *The Development of Academic Freedom in the United States* (New York: Columbia University Press, 1955).

Ellen Schrecker, *No Ivory Tower: McCarthyism and the Universities* (New York: Oxford University Press, 1986).

"Symposium on Academic Freedom," *Texas Law Review* 66 (June 1988).

Laurence R. Veysey, *The Emergence of the American University* (Chicago: University of Chicago Press, 1965).

Adams, Abigail (b. Weymouth, Mass., Nov. 22, 1744; d. Quincy, Mass., Oct. 28, 1818). The independent reputation of Mrs. Adams derives from the letters that she wrote for over half a century and that have survived, thousands of them. She was an author who composed in the genre available to her in an era before it was socially acceptable for a woman to write in any other medium. Her letters are extraordinary for their range of topics, eloquence, and style, although since she was never formally schooled, her spelling and punctuation frequently reflect the spontaneity of her thought and speech. Despite their rough composition, Adams's letters compare with those of the great correspondents of her age, which explains why they have been in print since her grandson, Charles Francis Adams, first published a selection in 1840.

Often personal, these letters provide unusual access to her private life, but they also capture her age—its social conventions, politics, and people. Her 1776 admonition to her husband JOHN ADAMS to "remember the ladies" has become the most quoted statement from a woman of her time, giving a mistaken impression of her as more radical than she was. An autodidact for her entire life, she became as erudite and wise as any American woman of the late eighteenth century. She was liberal in politics and religion, loyal to her husband's party, positions, and predicaments, and she defined herself primarily by her domestic roles as wife, mother, sister, daughter, and friend.

Born in the Weymouth, Massachusetts parsonage of her clergyman father, the Reverend William Smith, and her mother Elizabeth Smith, who was descended from the first families of the Bay Colony—Nortons, Shepards, Quincys—Abigail married the young lawyer John Adams in 1764. During their first decade of marriage, as events escalated into rebellion, and John was increasingly involved in the developing American Revolution, Abigail bore four children who would survive, Abigail Jr., John Quincy (the sixth president), Charles, and Thomas. As a result of her husband's political career, she presided as the wife of the first American Minister to the Court of St. James, as the first Second Lady, and as the second First Lady, and she is distinguished as the only woman to be both wife and mother of presidents of the United States.

Abigail's personal philosophy was founded on Puritan religious principles as they had been translated by the mid-eighteenth century into secular and enlightened New England values. These values included the personal virtues of family, work, education, and charity. She believed that a better world could be produced by human effort under circumstances of enlightened education, and that this constituted the divine plan. Her belief system and her behavior, furthermore, were remarkably consistent throughout her lifetime. She possessed, as well, an optimistic, sunny temperament that merged well with eighteenth-century enlightened thought.

Adams typified the New England mentality: she understood the human potential for mischief, if not evil. She observed, after all, that it was the decay into which old England had fallen that justified rebellion and revolution. As the Revolutionary War progressed and she noted that opportunism and greed existed among the rebels themselves, she acknowledged that corruption was endemic to all human behavior. Ever hopeful, she believed that religious

principles, translated by liberal education, could prevent degeneracy.

Abigail was drawn toward the liberal theology and rational practice of the philosopher Richard Price, whom she met and befriended during the years she lived in England as wife of the first American Minister to the Court of St. James. She read and quoted biblical texts with ease, but she also cited her favorite poets, playwrights, and historians. She did not separate the worldly from the divine. She disapproved of religious enthusiasm. In her times of personal crisis, however, as with the death of beloved family members, she turned to a more conservative religion, invoking the Trinity and an eternal system of rewards and punishments.

Education, she believed, mediated between religious beliefs and human behavior. Abigail, whose own youthful education at home had been rudimentary, began to read broadly after her marriage to John Adams, using his library to read freely and deeply in literature, history, and political theory. She also requested John to send her books—sometimes medical or scientific, often fictional—from the various cities where he resided. She became an erudite person whose challenging discourse was more than once referenced by John as "saucy," in an affectionate tribute to her intellectual power.

Because Abigail was separated from her husband for many of the 25 years of his public service, the Adams marriage produced a rich correspondence if not an ideal relationship. As a consequence of this separation and her independent functioning as a single parent and household provider during those years, many of Abigail's comments and observations about women appear more modern than they were. She was forced by circumstance of revolution and her husband's absence to take on roles that she considered unnatural. As "deputy husband," a role performed by many wives who took on their husbands' work in their absence, Abigail ran a farm, started a small business enterprise, and speculated in land. She also handled all family accounts after John entered public service. But she always regarded these functions as aberrant for a woman, acceptable only as a part of her "patriotic sacrifice" for her country. Woman's work, she believed, centered on the family, rearing children, serving as companion to her husband, and caring for a household. In the eighteenth century, these roles were dignified both biblically and by enlightened natural philosophy.

Adams believed the "theater of life" for woman to be domestic, but she also expanded the parameters of domesticity to include education, and especially the equal education of female children. She wanted women to be prepared to speak about political theory to husbands and to teach history and Latin to children. She had no premonition of such later feminist agendas as ownership of property or suffrage. Her office and her energies were socially prescribed to serve people. Whereas she understood the grand design to mandate her husband's service on the large theater of nation-building, her service was likewise prescribed at the local level, to individuals, family, community. That role was, she believed, religiously as well as biologically determined. She wrote all of this in her letters, creating a rich historical document of eighteenth-century women's lives, as well as eloquent testimony of one woman's noble life.

EDITH GELLES

FURTHER READING

Charles Francis Adams, ed., *Letters of Mrs. Adams, the Wife of John Adams* (New York: Hurd and Houghton, 1848).
L. H. Butterfield et al., eds., *The Adams Papers: Adams Family Correspondence*, 6 vols. (Cambridge: Harvard University Press, Belknap, 1961–92).
Edith B. Gelles, *Portia: The World of Abigail Adams* (Bloomington: Indiana University Press, 1992).
Phyllis Lee Levin, *Abigail Adams* (New York: St. Martin's, 1987).
Lynne Withey, *Dearest Friend: a Life of Abigail Adams* (New York: Free Press, 1981).

Adams, Brooks (b. Quincy, Mass., June 24, 1848; d. Boston, Mass., Feb. 13, 1927). Historian. Adams's *Law of Civilization and Decay* (1895) revived the republican notion of historical cycles, a view that led many progressive-minded observers to dismiss him as a crank and an anachronism. Pessimistic about the state of American political democracy in the age of industrialism, he argued in *The Theory of Social Revolutions* (1913) that the governing capitalist elite was losing control because of its exclusive focus on money-making and its consequent overspecialization, disrespect for law, and administrative ineptitude, a judgment shared by his brother HENRY ADAMS.

FURTHER READING

Timothy Donovan, *Henry Adams and Brooks Adams: the Education of Two American Historians* (Norman: University of Oklahoma Press, 1961).

Adams, Henry (b. Boston, Mass., Feb. 16, 1838; d. Washington, D.C., Mar. 27, 1918). A polymath, expert in languages, literature, art, architecture, and the philosophy of science as well as in his vocations of history and politics, Henry Adams was also the model of the committed intellectual. Intellectual activity seemed to him absurd unless it accomplished meaningful cultural work. Adams investigated history and politics, philosophy and religion, unity and

multiplicity, order and chaos, motion and change, in order to illuminate "the machinery of society" or more generally "POWER," as he characterizes Madeleine Lightfoot Lee's quest in *Democracy* (1880), one of his two novels. Adams's career constitutes a rarely paralleled inquiry into the relation between the life of the mind and historical patterns and prospects.

Throughout his career, Adams inquired whether experience, history, and natural phenomena exhibit coherence and whether they are comprehensible and therefore manageable by human intelligence. His answer was often ironic. Still, if the caustic "The Rule of Phase Applied to History" (1908) demolishes historians' pretensions to discern progress or even pattern in history, the closing chapters of his best-known work, *The Education of Henry Adams* (1907), acquire a redemptive tone from "the dynamic theory of history" Adams formulates there. Commentators have uniformly sought in Adams's work instruction about whether intellect can apprehend and shape history. We should not, however, forget the cultural specificity of Adams's endeavors. T. S. Eliot called Adams "a sceptical patrician," and Adams was probably even more accurate to call himself after 1895 a "conservative Christian anarchist." Adams sought to revive a cultural disposition to perceive the unity underlying the chaos apparently exhibited by the physical and social worlds.

Adams's intellectual currency begins with his patrician heritage. His entrée to intellectual arenas, he frankly confessed, was his descent from Presidents John Adams and John Quincy Adams. This heritage forms the framing irony of *The Education*. Adams was a diplomatic assistant, political essayist, Harvard professor and editor of the *North American Review*, and finally peripatetic historian and confidant of powerful figures like JOHN HAY, architect of American imperialism while Secretary of State under Presidents McKinley and Roosevelt. Adams notoriously represented his wide-ranging career as a meandering descent from the unambiguous authority of his eighteenth-century ancestors. Nevertheless, Adams's background afforded him intimacy with the powerful and, by his own account, was what made his opinions of interest.

Critical assessment of the implications of Adams's opinions has shifted over time. Contemporary and posthumous reviewers regarded Adams as a "clever" "New England Montaigne." In this view, the range of Adams's experiences and intellect belies his avowed failure in education, as he educates readers about history and the deepest philosophical questions. During the epoch of the new criticism, Adams became a prototypical modernist. A consummate ironist about life's paradoxes, the Adams of R. P. Blackmur's criticism and Ernest Samuels's monumental biography explored the limits of knowledge to help us to glimpse the potential, if elusive, unity of experience. Although he resigned his post at Harvard in 1877 declaring the futility of pedagogy, Adams's sense of failure thus becomes the pedagogical value of his work. He teaches us to examine frailties and pursue ineffable ideals. Recent poststructuralists have refused to redeem Adams's skepticism. John Carlos Rowe and Gregory Jay, for example, characterize Adams, especially in his pose in *The Education* as "manikin," as a proto-postmodernist doubtful of the possibilities of human knowledge and agency. These critics emphasize Adams's own belief that the failure to overcome chaos and glimpse unity is an ontological and epistemological necessity.

For Adams, skepticism—and its concomitant social critique—were also hereditary traits, indeed duties ordained by his eighteenth-century birthright. Adams greatly admired his grandfather John Quincy Adams's suspicion of social developments, and this disposition seemed both to decrease in practical influence and intensify as a family trait after John Quincy's defeat by Andrew Jackson. Henry customarily equated heritage and heredity. He held a typically biologistic, specifically Lamarckian, account of how manners and social ordering are transmitted. Character seemed an effect of breeding. "Roosevelts are born and never can be taught," announces *The Education*, and Adams supposes that he likewise inherited his family's taste, principles—he is "antislavery by birth"—and even its feuds. More generally, "Friends are born, not made." Quality of mind is a birthright shared with others of the same caste. After the Civil War, however, the emergence of a trained rather than hereditary managerial class threatened patricians' authority—this tragedy is incipient in Adams's nine-volume *History of the United States of America during the Administrations of Jefferson and Madison* (1889–91)—and Adams continually explored how the patrician class might reinvigorate its managerial mission.

Reconditioning the authority of birthright was also the goal of Adams's famous critique of historical science. Adams's contemporary historians sought a more developmental and less individualistic model of history than their Romantic predecessors employed. They found one in evolutionary science: any stage of social organization, like a species undergoing modification, succeeds and is prepared for by previous stages. Change is, here, sequential, but the evolutionists, as Adams called them, idealized the principle of sequence as a guarantee of unity. In their millennial vision, Western civilization and America in particular were fulfilling a divine plan for the perfection of man. In *The Education* and the essays his brother BROOKS ADAMS collected in *The Degradation of Democratic Dogma* ("The Rule of Phase," "Letter to American Teachers of History" [1910], and "The Tendency of History" [1894], (which was Adams's presidential address, delivered in absentia, to the American Historical Association), Adams satirized evolutionists' theological conviction of unity and progress. The evolutionists have no evidence for evolution. Fossils like *Terebratula* and *Pteraspis* indicate, respectively, no development and no antecedents. But the evolutionists' lack of evidence for evolution is irrelevant because, finally, they don't believe in evolution. They believe in "natural uniformity"— "unbroken evolution under uniform conditions." Disregarding both contradictory evidence and the merely sequential development implied by natural selection, evolutionists simply impose favored premises on data to confirm foreordained conclusions.

Their empirical mistake was for Adams symptomatic of all knowledge. Scientists Ernst Mach and Karl Pearson had argued that matter is the motion of imperceptible particles and therefore only apparently substantial. Knowledge, finally, simply masks what Pearson called the "chaos behind impressions." Ideas of sequence and order are, then, projections. If the idea of natural selection potentially discredits the idea of a natural aristocracy, Pearson's idea of chaos would seem to threaten any faith in order. In *The Education*, however, Adams uses Pearson's insight to redeem the possibility of order and unity. If humans inevitably project coherence onto phenomena, then unity is in fact the abiding phenomenon of history. Finally, Adams's subjectivism discloses the order beneath anarchy: "order and anarchy were one."

Believing that the perception of anarchy intimates the unity of experience, Adams too, then, was a uniformitarian: "he found no change to record" because history is the record not of change but of the constant impulse to discover order in manifold change. The "Dynamic Theory of History" formalized this vision. Mind is not the autonomous spirit of classical Western philosophy. It is one particle among others, subject to the forces of other particles. But, like all particles, mind keeps trying to realize the force it embodies and thereby fulfill itself; all episodes of what we call history repeat this structure—mind's aspiration toward unity—and therefore history is unity.

What Adams called "empire-building" exemplifies humankind's innate aspiration toward unity, and seemed culminated in John Hay's foreign policy. Hay's "Atlantic system," which Adams helped design, sought to make diplomatic relations a reflection of the will to unity. A "general peace" or "equilibrium" would issue when the major European nations agreed on how the world would be divided and aligned, meaning that they had settled on which master nations would control which subject nations. Adams wrote to Hay that this system expressed a physical equilibrium, "the law of mass."

Adams speculates in *The Education* that the physical necessity of empire-building would fulfill his family heritage and its prior authority. Adams's writings tend to seek the renovation of an intelligible order now dissolved but intuited and perhaps realized in the past. This is the situation faced by the heroine of the novel *Esther* (1884) after her father dies, and it constitutes the tragedy of the royal family of Tahiti in the three versions of its supposed "memoirs" that Adams published after his visit to the island— *Memoirs of Marau Taaroa* (1893), *Memoirs of Arii Taimai* (1901), and *Tahiti* (1902). In Adams's work, the present social order is almost by definition rickety and corrupt. In *Democracy*, Madeleine goes to Washington to apprehend "the great American mystery of democracy," which presumably would manifest "the action of primary forces." She finds, instead, systematic corruption, because governmental power cannot be exercised without politics, and politics is inevitably the effort to realize local and individual interests rather than primary forces. Governance is therefore territorial conflict rather than scientific management. This critique propels the essays that established Adams's career: his two annual "Session" essays on Washington politics, and his controversial exposés of financial intrigues, "The Legal-Tender Act" and "The New York Gold Conspiracy" (all 1869 and 1870). In Adams's view, Reconstruction financial policies encouraged rampant competitive activity in trade markets. But culture cannot serve its citizens when it consists of "feverish" conflicts over resources.

Adams's conservatism here is not simply policy preference. He heartily criticized gold-bugs' support for the gold standard, and was, atypically for the period, respectful of Marx's work. Adams's conservatism consists more profoundly of a distaste for energetic political and cultural activity, conflict that inevitably unsettles social arrangements. The dynamic theory of history purifies history of such conflict by imagining specific events not really as events but as epiphenomena of unity. Adams's willfully paradoxical characterization of himself as a "conservative Christian anarchist" is therefore fitting. Anarchy is, after all, the condition for faith's intimation of unity, and this intimation might reillumine the order that genealogy once manifested and transmitted.

Adams's concern with the disruption of universal order by individual action helps explain his obsession with anonymity, typified by his response to his wife Marian "Clover" Hooper's suicide in 1885: he termed his subsequent work 'posthumous' and commissioned from Augustus St. Gaudens an unmarked monument for the site where Clover and Henry are buried. But even before, *Democracy* was published anonymously, *Esther* under a pseudonym. All three "memoirs" of a member of Tahiti's royal family were published privately and none acknowledged Adams as author. *Mont-Saint-Michel and Chartres* (1905), Adams's paean to thirteenth-century architecture, spiritual devotion, and social organization, was also privately printed; so was *The Education*, which, parodying autobiography, refers to Adams in the third person and characterizes him as a manikin. Order and the mysteries of power, motion, and change are metaphysical truths to be glimpsed by those who, anointed by heritage and purified of individuality, can intuit metaphysical order.

If these true representatives of the spirit of the race were to rule, social order might feel necessary and harmonious rather than contentious. *Mont-Saint-Michel*, Adams's most exquisite achievement, is a devotional to the Virgin largely because the metaphysical ideal of unity that she represents completely organizes life in the thirteenth century, and *The Education* reprises this homage. For Adams, no distinction between the ideal and the social existed in the thirteenth century; order was manifest, not to mention honored, in every act and architectural creation, and, moreover, was so self-evident that it did not feel like an achievement, like ordering, but rather like eternal unity. In the twentieth century, in contrast, the effort—which means individual action —required to convert multiplicity into unity is too palpable.

Adams's professed debt to and confidence in women was part of his fascination with the ordering best supplied by genealogy. Because they are removed from spheres of action, women—meaning women from the leisure class—do not act but rather engage in thought and conversation. Moreover, "women's thought is mostly subconscious"—that is, more closely connected to their biological makeup—and so Adams employs "tricks and devices to disclose it." Adams's "Primitive Rights of Women" (1876) follows what we might call this genealogical logic. This essay does not promote suffragettism; instead it observes that "primitive" societies, unlike modern societies, honored the rights of women because rights and property were based in genealogy. In the primitive epoch, genealogy was matrilineal and equality reigned because "all were one family"; "the instinct of property" attended "natural affections." Later, family structures became organized around the (male) pursuit of property. When property reflects genealogy, social arrangements express natural affections. But when property becomes an artificial institution, arousing interest and activity and therefore intrinsically disturbing traditions, then society must create mechanisms to "inculcate the duties" formerly assured as (birth)rights.

Adams often lamented that arrangements that formerly seemed necessary and transmitted through genealogy had become political achievements. Authority and the distribution of resources seemed no longer manifestations of metaphysics but products of interpretation and conflict. Deeply pessimistic about the prospects for history—Adams saw Western nations marching toward a great war—the conservative Christian anarchist offered the dynamic theory of history idealistically, to presage the vanquishing of politics and purification of history. Equilibrium realized, duties will seem rights rather than rules.

HOWARD HORWITZ

See also AESTHETICS; AUTOBIOGRAPHY.

FURTHER READING

R. P. Blackmur, *Henry Adams*, ed. Veronica A. Makowsky (New York: Harcourt Brace Jovanovich, 1980).

T. S. Eliot, "A Sceptical Patrician," *Athenaeum*, May 23, 1919, pp. 361–2.

Gregory Jay, *America the Scrivenor: Deconstruction and the Subject of Literary History* (Ithaca: Cornell University Press, 1990).

William H. Jordy, *Henry Adams: Scientific Historian* (New Haven: Yale University Press, 1952).

T. J. Jackson Lears, *No Place of Grace: Antimodernism and the Transformation of American Culture, 1880–1920* (New York: Pantheon, 1981).

John Carlos Rowe, *Henry Adams and Henry James: the Emergence of a Modern Consciousness* (Ithaca: Cornell University Press, 1976).

——, ed., *New Essays on "The Education of Henry Adams"* (New York: Cambridge University Press, 1994).

Ernest Samuels, *The Young Henry Adams; Henry Adams: the Middle Years; Henry Adams: the Major Phase* (Cambridge: Harvard University Press, 1948, 1958, 1964).

Adams, John (b. Braintree, Mass., Oct. 30, 1735; d. Quincy, Mass., July 4, 1826). A man of seemingly boundless energy and ambition, Adams was a prominent American Revolutionary, signer of the Declaration of Independence, drafter of the Massachusetts Constitution of 1780, minister plenipotentiary and ambassador to England, and second President of the United States. The sheer quantity of Adams's contributions to and participation in American political life in the revolutionary and founding era is perhaps unrivaled, and certainly not superseded, by the work of any other of the nation's founding fathers. Indeed, Adams has been acutely characterized by colonial historian Bernard Bailyn, in his "Butterfield's Adams: Notes for a Sketch," as "a driven and uneasy man" who felt himself "impelled by a frantic desire for affluence and fame" (p. 243). Adams harnessed his ambitions to a puritan-inspired regimen of self-discipline and a declensionary perspective on his fellow man which effectively shaped both the theoretical foundations and the practical trajectory of his long political career.

Adams's *Diary and Autobiography* record his earliest and formative political experiences as a practicing lawyer in the courts of his "litigious" native Braintree, Massachusetts, and as an outspoken critic of what he perceived to be the increasingly familial and thus corrupted arena of provincial politics. He took his political opponents to be nothing less than the forces of ignorance (in the form of legal quackery) and hereditary power (in the form of the artificial "aristocracy" of overmighty provincial families). With a flair for hyperbole, Adams pledged in his *Diary* of 1760 to "rescue the Souls and Bodies, and Estates" of Braintree "from that Thraldom and slavery, to which these Petty foggers have contributed to depress them; and if I can revive in them a génerous Love of Liberty and sense of Honour" (p. 137). The same *Diary* records Adams's increasing suspicions toward the "amazing ascendency" of one family in Massachusetts—the Hutchinsons—whose appointments to "the most important offices in the Province" he felt threatened to "erect a Tyranny" of royal authority in the province and to "excite Jealousies among the People" (p. 260).

Reacting to the implementation of the Stamp Act of 1765, Adams crystalized these urgent practical concerns into political theory with the publication of a series of letters to his fellow lawyers entitled a *Dissertation on the Canon and Feudal Law*. He interpreted the "restraints and duties" (p. 21) of the Stamp Act as nothing less than an effort to introduce "feudal inequalities" and "hereditary dependencies" (p. 9) to America. More importantly, he claimed a plan was afoot in the British Parliament to "enslave all America" (p. 20) through this act by denying citizens those "Rights that cannot be repealed or restrained by human laws" (p. 5). Adams's argument for the right to be taxed only by one's "own consent in person or by proxy" (p. 23), more clearly articulated in his contemporaneously published "Instructions of Braintree" and developed in the *Novanglus* letters of 1775, established the very core of American revolutionary theory.

However, in the aftermath of the AMERICAN REVOLUTION, Adams's founding-era writings, such as his *Defence of the Constitutions of Government of the United States* (1787–8) and his *Discourses on Davila* (1790), were received with less enthusiasm and at times with bewilderment and hostility by other founders, most notably JAMES MADISON, and by his countrymen at large. On the one hand, Adams's unwavering commitment to a theory of balanced constitutionalism, incorporating an overlapping system of separation of powers and checks and balances, was ultimately adopted in the design of national government. (*See also* DEMOCRACY.) On the other, his equally persistent claim in the *Defence* and later writings that social and economic inequality necessarily resulted from the nature of man and the right to private property, and that political stability required that the great socioeconomic divisions of society be structurally incorporated in a "mixed government" appeared completely out of touch with American realities. In explaining the anomalous character of the *Defence*, Gordon Wood suggested in *The Creation of the American Republic* that American political thought by 1790 rested the logic of constitutional reasoning firmly on the belief that "government was not a balancing of people and aristocracy, but only the distribution and delegation of the people's political power" (p. 584). Adams's concerns with inequality and mixed government thus appeared at best outdated and irrelevant, and at worst dangerously conservative, even monarchical.

Whether Adams's political philosophy actually changed—growing more conservative and less democratic—during the course of his political lifetime, and the nature and extent of any such change, has been the subject of much controversy. From a theorist's perspective, the more supportable position would seem to be that Adams's position did not change. A fundamental tenet of Adams's political philosophy, drawn equally from experience as well as study, was his belief that man's nature comprised a potential balance of private and social passions. The "truths" of men's private and selfish passions painstakingly explored in his later *Political Writings* were there from Adams's earliest days and included the belief "that the first want of man is his dinner, and the second his girl" (p. 206). That this "truth" could be balanced by a second—the social "passion for distinction," "to be observed, considered, esteemed, praised, beloved, and admired by his fellows" (p. 176)— Adams never doubted, and he consistently translated this concern for a balance of corruptions into a political science of government which viewed "simple unchecked government" as "always despotic, whether

it be government by a monarch, by aristocrats, or by the mass of people." In his view, all were potentially "equally intolerant, cruel, bloody, oppressive, tyrannical" (p. 106).

While Adams's concern with the dynamic interplay of social and political power upset his contemporaries of the 1780s, it would seem less certain that his position was thus outdated. In the 1830s, Tocqueville echoed Adams's perceptions of the political instability threatened by the passion to equalize and "level" in the face of comparative social inequalities. And contemporary political theorists as recently as Hannah Arendt in *On Revolution* have seen fit to interpret Adams as theorizing well beyond his own time in his recognition of the politically as well as personally "crippling consequences of obscurity" which compound the misery of those in economic distress (p. 69).

Given his complexity as both a statesman and theorist of government, Adams is perhaps ill-suited to the role in which he has been cast by those seemingly rights-obsessed conservative theorists who would consider him a founder of American conservatism; neither should he be dismissed by egalitarians as a simple-minded champion of hierarchy. Instead Adams, worried about the dangers of aristocracy and corruption but uneasy about equality, accurately reflects the ambivalence and complexity of early American political thought.

SHANNON C. STIMSON

See also ABIGAIL ADAMS.

FURTHER READING

John Adams, *The Political Writings of John Adams*, ed. George A. Peek Jr. (Indianapolis: Bobbs-Merrill, 1954).
——, *Diary and Autobiography of John Adams*, vol. 1 (1755–70), ed. L. H. Butterfield (Cambridge: Harvard University Press, 1962).
Hannah Arendt, *On Revolution* (New York: Penguin, 1963).
Bernard Bailyn, "Butterfield's Adams: Notes for a Sketch," *William and Mary Quarterly* 19 (1962): 238–56.
John R. Howe Jr., *The Changing Political Thought of John Adams* (Princeton: Princeton University Press, 1966).
Shannon C. Stimson, *The American Revolution in the Law* (Princeton: Princeton University Press, 1990).
M. J. C. Vile, *Constitutionalism and The Separation of Powers* (Oxford: Oxford University Press, 1967).
Gordon Wood, *The Creation of the American Republic* (Chapel Hill: University of North Carolina Press, 1969).

Adams, Samuel (b. Boston, Mass., Sept. 27, 1722; d. Boston, Mass., Oct. 2, 1803).   Agitator and strategist. Believing that the commonwealth was the level of society to which ultimate loyalty was due, Adams endorsed active, even violent, opposition to established authority if such resistance was for the good of the whole. He founded the Boston Committee of Correspondence and developed direct action tactics, such as nonimportation agreements backed up by the Boston Tea Party. A delegate to the First Continental Congress, he later supported the Constitution but, persuaded of the corrupting effects of power, he remained wary of centralized government.

See also AMERICAN REVOLUTION.

FURTHER READING
Peter Shaw, *American Patriots and the Rituals of Revolution* (Cambridge: Harvard University Press, 1981).

Addams, Jane (b. Cedarville, Ill., Sept. 6, 1860; d. Chicago, Ill., May 21, 1935).   One of the most influential social reformers in American history, Addams was a settlement house founder, a pacifist, and an insightful social and cultural analyst. The eighth of nine children, and one of only four to reach adulthood, she lost her mother when she was two years old and was cared for by her older sisters. In 1867 her father John Addams married Anna H. Haldeman, a widow with two children of her own, one of whom, George, became a companion to and an important influence on his stepsister. John Addams, a rather stern man of Quaker background who preached self-reliance, honesty, and devotion to duty, prospered as a miller and banker and, later, as an eight-term member of the Illinois Senate. He helped to found the Illinois Republican Party.

John Addams's political heroes were Joseph Mazzini, the Italian patriot and republican, and ABRAHAM LINCOLN. According to Jane Addams, her father was the dominant influence in her life. A serious, earnest child, Addams embraced her father's heroes—particularly the martyred sixteenth President. The childhood ties Addams forged to the legend of Lincoln as a symbol of all that was great and good were reconfirmed throughout her adult life. In the active shaping or her own legend, Addams tied her principles, struggles, and public accomplishments to the legacy of Lincoln. Imbued with driving ambition and a sense of destiny, both for herself and for her country, Addams was a member of the first generation of college women. She entered the Female Seminary in Rockford, Illinois, in 1877, acquiescing in her father's wish that she attend a religious school. Her own goal was to attend Smith College, but that ambition was postponed and later abandoned as Addams found herself immobilized by a deep social, moral, and psychological conflict: the struggle to balance off "the family claim" against her own ambitions and a wider "social claim." In her essay "Filial Relations," which appears in the collection *Demo-*

cracy and Social Ethics (1902), Addams describes this conflict as both necessary and tragic:

> The collision of interests, each of which has a real moral basis and a right to its own place in life, is bound to be more or less tragic. It is the struggle between two claims, the destruction of either of which would bring ruin to ethical life (pp. 76–7).

Addams graduated at the head of her class in 1882. Her college years had been spent in a high-minded, self-critical search for meaning, purpose, and a secure identity. During her Rockford years she met and became fast friends with Ellen Gates Starr, the first of two special female friends and companions in her life. The second, Mary Rozet Smith, joined Addams in 1892 and they remained steadfast companions until Smith's death in 1933. It was with Ellen Starr that Addams shared her early hopes and dreams. Her letters reveal Addams to be idealistic yet determined to forge a direct connection between abstract ideas and concrete actions. The urge to be "useful," to embrace a worthy "vocation," became Addams's torment and passion. Convinced that women had their own claims to authority and knowledge, a thesis she put forward in her graduation-day senior essay and speech, "Cassandra," Addams believed women should enter the world on the basis of those special claims. The education of young women should never lose touch with their active emotional and ethical lives.

In 1881 Addams's father died suddenly at the age of 59. His death paralyzed her will to act. For an eight-year period Addams was frequently bedridden or near collapse, a victim of "neurasthenia," a vague malaise that overtook many young, educated women of the middle classes whose pathways to action were blocked by external impediments, internal conflicts, or both. Addams later described that period, in her masterful autobiography *Twenty Years at Hull-House*, as a time when she was unable to

> formulate my convictions even in the least satisfactory manner, much less . . . reduce them to a plan for action. During most of that time I was absolutely at sea so far as any moral purpose was concerned, clinging only to the desire to live in a really living world and refusing to be content with a shadowy intellectual or aesthetic reflection of it (p. 64).

Addams's period in purgatory ended when she found a way to put her social gospel and piety directly to work on behalf of others with the founding of Hull House in 1889, the joint undertaking of Addams and Ellen Starr. Hull House was a political solution to a nearly overwhelming personal malaise, as Addams notes in her address, "The Subjective

Necessity for Social Settlements," delivered in 1892. Addams made it clear that the settlement house movement was as much for the benefit of idealistic young women, and a few men, of the middle classes as it was for those they aimed to live among and to serve. The constituency for Hull House was Chicago's nineteenth ward, a bustling mix of immigrants. Addams's dream, noted in her autobiography, was to bring "all those adjuncts which the cultivated man regards as good and suggestive of the best life of the past" to the immigrants in the area (p. 94). Hull House was also an experiment in urban sociology. Its activities were shaped by Addams's yearning to improve the quality of life for the disadvantaged by an enthusiastic social engagement, and by a pragmatic faith that the problems of urban life could be ameliorated through cooperative reform. Hull House quickly became the great national symbol of the social gospel in operation. Addams herself was idealized as an American heroine.

Hull House was to be Addams's home base for the next 46 years. At its height, it was a bustling center which included a day nursery, kindergarten, playground, boys' and girls' clubs dedicated to education and refinement, cooperative boardinghouse, theatre workshop, music school, reading groups, handicrafts center, museum of immigrant crafts, courses in cooking and sewing, a butcher shop and a bakery. Addams later wrote in *Twenty Years* that "From the first it seemed understood that we were ready to perform the humblest neighborhood services. We were asked to wash the new-born babies, and to prepare the dead for burial, to nurse the sick, and to mind the children" (p. 109). Addams soon displayed her remarkable gifts as a fundraiser, business woman, organizer, arbitrater, and public relations expert. Her faith in the "scientific study of social life" is reflected in the *Hull-House Maps and Papers*, published in 1895. Addams used data on tenement conditions, the existence of sweatshops, and the abuse of women and child labor to press for dozens of reforms.

Hull House allied with other reform groups in lobbying for labor and housing laws, regulation of employment for women, the eight-hour day, old age and unemployment insurance, as well as drives against prostitution and vice—all aimed at combating the worst abuses of industrial capitalism. Addams's name is attached to every major reform effort of the first four decades of the century. She was also the first woman president of the National Conference of Charities and Corrections (1909), the first woman awarded an honorary degree from Yale University (1910), and the winner of the Nobel Peace Prize (1931). Her name is linked to the creation of the American Civil Liberties Union, the Urban League, the National Association for the Advancement of Colored People, and to the fight for women's suffrage. In addition to her many books, she published hundreds of essays and articles in mass circulation magazines, including *The Ladies Home Journal*, *McClure's*, and *The American Magazine*.

One reason for the enormous success of Hull House as a symbol and focus of reform efforts was the talented group of women and men who, inspired by Addams, joined her there. She had the capacity to inspire long-term loyalty. The names of her associates are a "who's who" of American reform. Three early collaborators were FLORENCE KELLEY, Julia Lathrop, and Alice Hamilton. JOHN DEWEY became an associate, and famous visitors included WILLIAM JAMES and Sidney and Beatrice Webb. By 1915 her public reputation seemed secure as she searched constantly for the middle road between those more zealously uncompromising than herself and those less willing to attack established interests.

But World War I, at least for a time, turned Addams's world upside down. Her defense of radicals and "anarchists," her brave and often lonely opposition to both "the idea of war" and its terrible butchery, not only placed her outside the American mainstream but brought down on her a tide of derision and abuse. When war broke out, but before America entered, Addams helped to create the Woman's Peace Party, which called for "continuous mediation" of the conflict. In articles, speeches, and books, Addams argued that women had a powerful role to play in promoting peace, because they could grasp the imperative to preserve human life. Her understanding of feminism puts it in "unalterable" opposition to militarism. As she wrote in *The Long Road of Woman's Memory*, "It would be absurd for women even to suggest equal rights in a world run solely by physical force, and Feminism must necessarily assert the ultimate supremacy of moral agencies" (p. 129).

Called a traitor, denounced as a Bolshevik, Addams stood her ground. In the decade following the Russian Revolution and the conclusion of World War I, America was gripped by anti-red hysteria and Addams's name appeared regularly on lists of "subversives," but she never reneged on her commitment to civil liberties and to pacifism. As America moved into the 1930s, public hostility toward Addams softened. Her joint recognition (with Nicholas Murray Butler) for the Nobel Peace Prize; her support of prohibition; her endorsement of Herbert Hoover for reelection to the Presidency; her ongoing embodiment of service; and her undying faith in the basic goodness of all people helped to restore her to her earlier niche as America's foremost humanitarian. She died from cancer at the age of 74. Her death prompted an enormous outpouring of public grief. Some, following her own lead, compared her to Lincoln.

In many respects, however, it seemed that history had passed her by. To the flapper generation, she was an asexual, maternal figure from the past. To the rising group of "professional" social workers, her personal methods and determination to see life from the vantage point of the less privileged appeared anachronistic. Of her extraordinary energy, unflagging commitment, and brilliant capacity to forge a pragmatic, eclectic faith out of disparate philosophies there is no doubt. But a full evaluation of her career as social thinker, reformer, and symbol has yet to be written. A complete account will have to see her once again as a citizen and thinker who offered her community a lifelong commitment to democratic possibility. In the meantime, Walter Lippmann's eulogy remains apt:

> She had compassion without condescension. She had pity without retreat into vulgarity. She had infinite sympathy for common things without forgetfulness of those that are uncommon. That, I think, is why those who have known her say that she was not only good, but great. For this blend of sympathy with distinction, of common humanity with a noble style is recognizable by those who have eyes to see it as the occasional but authentic issue of the mystic promise of American democracy (Davis, p. 291).

JEAN BETHKE ELSHTAIN

See also DEMOCRACY; PROGRESSIVISM; WORLD WAR I.

FURTHER READING

Jane Addams, *Democracy and Social Ethics* (New York: Macmillan, 1902).
——, *Twenty Years at Hull-House* (New York: Macmillan, 1910).
——, *The Long Road of Woman's Memory* (New York: Macmillan, 1916).
Allen Davis, *American Heroine: the Life and Legend of Jane Addams* (New York: Oxford University Press, 1973).
Jean Bethke Elshtain, "A Return to Hull House: Reflections on Jane Addams," in *Power Trips and Other Journeys* (Madison: University of Wisconsin Press, 1990).
Christopher Lasch, *The New Radicalism in America, 1889–1963* (New York: Vintage, 1965).
——, ed., *The Social Thought of Jane Addams* (Indianapolis: Bobbs-Merrill, 1965).
Daniel Levine, *Jane Addams and the Liberal Tradition* (Madison: The State Historical Society of Wisconsin, 1971).

Adler, Mortimer (b. New York, N.Y., Dec. 28, 1902).   Educator. Creator of the "great books" edu-cation program, Adler believes that the purpose of education is to prepare students to be intelligent citizens by teaching the great books of Western literature and philosophy. Since one truth—ontological and moral—does exist, discussions should focus on the truths and errors found in each work. Adler has written numerous books on education and philosophy, including *How to Read a Book* (1940, 1972), *The Idea of Freedom* (2 vols., 1958–61), and *Philosopher at Large: an Intellectual Autobiography* (1977). *The Paideia Proposal: an Educational Manifesto* (1982) opposed educational tracking: since all Americans are citizens, Adler argued, every student should receive the same rigorous liberal education.

See also EDUCATION; ROBERT M. HUTCHINS.

FURTHER READING

Edward A. Purcell Jr., *The Crisis of Democratic Theory: Scientific Naturalism and the Problem of Value* (Lexington: University Press of Kentucky, 1973).

aesthetics   The philosopher MORRIS COHEN, surveying the course of American thought at the beginning of the postwar era, prefaced his discussion of aesthetics by explaining that "there can be no doubt that the development of the fine arts amongst us has not shown the energy and pre-eminence of our industrial enterprise" (p. 209). This perennial complaint of modern Western intellectuals has been especially common in the the United States, where self-consciously masculine democracy has often scurried to defend itself against the sensual, the feminine, and the elitist, and against the supposed artificiality and superfluity of art. American aesthetic theory, as a result, has often veered toward a justification of art as "useful," a tendency periodically countered by opponents of utility.

The dominant mode of aesthetic thought in the eighteenth century, both in England and its American cultural provinces, was grounded in the comprehensive moral philosophy of the Scottish Enlightenment (*see* SCOTTISH COMMON SENSE REALISM). In the work of Thomas Reid, Lord Kames, and others, aesthetic "taste" was part of the "moral sense," a system guiding and balancing the mind's rational faculties. Critical judgment was a matter of deciding how well an object corresponded to certain fixed and knowable aesthetic principles, certain rules of beauty which all rational, civilized men perceived. This view was supported by the neoclassicism of the painter Sir Joshua Reynolds, who asserted that participants in aesthetic experience—creator and critic, artist and viewer—realized their moral potential by rearranging certain "natural" codes into a harmonious order of perfection. "Associationist" psychology troubled this scheme by asserting that the beauty of an object depended less on abstract harmony than on intellectual and emotional references in the viewer's memory. This psychological move was significant for the development of Greek Revival architecture in the early republic, as artists like THOMAS JEFFERSON attempted to construct a contemporary public space which would refer to knowledge of classical democracies, and thereby inspire like-minded citizens. But both of these positions rested on the belief that aesthetic understanding or "taste" was an epistemological issue, and as such could be "cultivated" like all applied knowledge. Aesthetic understanding was basic to the formation of the sociable, reflective individual, the basic unit of the bourgeois cultural order of nineteenth-century America.

Put off by this rationalization of beauty, RALPH WALDO EMERSON and MARGARET FULLER resisted the reduction of "imagination" to a functional administration of controlled expression, perception, and normative taste. Their TRANSCENDENTALISM turned from the Scots to the Germans, beginning with Kant. His *Critique of Judgment* (1790) asserted that beauty was the visible symbol of the morally good; by mediating the sensual or phenomenal world and the interior, noumenal seat of universal principles, aesthetic experience represents that which is otherwise unseen, but which we must in some way "know" if we are to function as moral subjects. This basic insight, variously expanded upon by Romantic poets and philosophers, facilitated Emerson's claims about Nature being the symbol of Spirit—not Reynolds's codified Nature, represented in the harmonious "picturesque," but a Nature embodying inherent truths which the individual imagination could tap, thereby experiencing the Absolute through art. While pointing to the subtle materialism of "taste" (in the Scottish sense), the Transcendentalists democratized perception and opened the field of judgment to cover all experience, not merely that prescribed by neoclassical dicta. They therefore encouraged the apotheosis of *American* nature, of American form and expression, over the European. The cultural nationalism they promoted would continue in the twentieth century to inform popular aesthetic understanding as well as major developments in the art world itself.

But Transcendentalist aesthetics became problematic for many Americans as it edged closer to pantheism, and to the mystical sensuality which would foster misunderstanding of the movement as apolitical, antisocial, and vaguely immoral. In this context, the English critic John Ruskin met with great public approval during the middle third of the nineteenth century. Retaining Romantic insights about subject-

ive imagination and the aesthetic purpose of the natural world, Ruskin moved from sensuality to a clear, didactic moralism commensurate with evangelical piety; under this regime—an organic continuum of art, nature, and religion—aesthetic issues could once again be understood as essential to the everyday life of the Christian citizen. Paradoxically, Ruskin's elevation of the Gothic, part of his Tory-radical critique of industrial society, sanctioned that form (and medievalism in general) in what was a frankly anti-Catholic society. The spread of the Gothic, which might have been expected to provoke painful historical associations, shows how deeply nineteenth-century bourgeois Americans were committed to finding a moral aesthetic capable of placing the individual in a communal order held together by organic form. Ruskin's insistence that a society's art revealed its immanent virtue was well suited to the dominant cultural-nationalist sensibilities. The fact that the most important American Ruskinian, CHARLES ELIOT NORTON, was an agnostic and a liberal attests to the plasticity of this aesthetic for Victorian intellectuals. At a time when many thinkers eschewed politics as an arena of corruption, an artistic sensibility permitted participation in public life on a moral basis. Art history could emerge as a mode of moral training. Ruskin's influence on the intellectual life of bourgeois women was particularly important, since they coordinated both the Gilded Age art world and contemporary social reform; from this women's public, Ruskin's moral critique would flow into the mainstream of Progressive social thought.

But as with so much of the intellectual life of the Civil War generation, the Ruskinian aesthetic fell into crisis after the 1880s. The classic statement of this malaise was represented in the later work of HENRY ADAMS, notably his *Mont-Saint-Michel and Chartres* (1905), in which he depicted himself as cut adrift from the earlier aesthetic sensibility. Challenges to this sensibility had come in the form of a new paradigm of nature itself. Ruskin's unitary system linking nature, religion, and art had been in accord with the Victorian "natural theology" which linked observable phenomena to religion, and thereby affixed it to culture. But Darwinism, as Adams realized, undid the tie between aesthetics, morality, and experience. Aestheticians "lost" their claim as readers of nature to the professionalizing scientists.

At the turn of the century two leading aestheticians conceded that art had little bearing on the understanding of nature or the practice of everyday life. Psychologist Henry Rutgers Marshall and philosopher GEORGE SANTAYANA relocated aesthetics in the realm of feeling and emotion. Marshall, whose *Pain,*

Pleasure, and Aesthetics (1894) rejected the idea of any necessary connection between a work's creator and its observer (breaking up the conceptual public formed by artist and critic), found the locus of aesthetic response in a nonrational hedonism. Santayana returned to the early associationists in affirming the psychological nature of aesthetics as the projection of subjective feeling onto objects, but he stressed personal and individual as opposed to historical and public resonances. Santayana was a particularly strong polemicist against Ruskinian moralism. He excoriated the work of people like Norton for perpetuating a gentle, feminine "back-water" of ideas, "while, alongside, in invention and industry and social organization the other half of the [American] mind was leaping down a sort of Niagara Rapids" (p. 39). Santayana's formulation of a retrograde "genteel tradition" helped to isolate and anathematize Victorian-American thought, thus assisting many early twentieth-century American artists and intellectuals in their flight from the moral-practical tradition to the new aesthetic heights of European MODERNISM. Concentrating on the autonomy of artistic form—pure form, distinct from moral purpose and from any history outside its own morphological development—modernist formalism gained strength through the mid-twentieth century, both in American academic letters (through the work of the New Critics) and in the American art world (through the dominant critical voices of such writers as CLEMENT GREENBERG and Michael Fried).

The most complete American aesthetic theory developed in the twentieth century came not from the modernists but from JOHN DEWEY. Though Dewey wrote only one complete work on this topic —*Art as Experience* (1934)—aesthetics is the cornerstone, as Thomas Alexander has argued, of Dewey's general public-philosophical project. Individuals in a community, Dewey held, direct their experience toward meaningful ends through symbolic expression and interpretation. An educated public is "made" through the activity of this communicative exchange. In a Deweyan democracy, experience is itself an aesthetic process whereby a particular context is symbolically transformed by artist-citizens, through what Hans Joas has called "situated creativity" (p. 4). Clarifying this aspect of Dewey's thought—his quest for the artfulness of everyday life—we can see that he was working along lines parallel to the early twentieth-century modernism of Central and Eastern Europe, which asserted a revolutionary linkage between aesthetics and popular political mobilization. Thomas Alexander's emphasis on Dewey's aesthetics helps explain Dewey's emergence in our own day—a postmodern moment when aestheticism has leapt

into new prominence across the human sciences —as the preeminent American philosopher of the twentieth century.

It is even possible to detect a return to the moral-practical in American aesthetic thought. It has become increasingly difficult to speak of aesthetics as an autonomous category of knowledge. Interest in the revolutionary European avant-gardes has led American critics to refocus attention on the processes by which "universal" ideas about art and beauty have been historically generated around nodes of social power. In *The Anti-Aesthetic*, Hal Foster has posited a postmodern "anti-aesthetic" which denies "the idea of a privileged aesthetic realm" (p. xv) and embarks on a search for new modes of political and artistic experience, such as feminist art.

Meanwhile other theorists such as Arthur Danto have attacked the notion of an autonomous aesthetics from another angle. Danto argues that beginning with Marcel Duchamp, and concluding with POP, the issue of the philosophical nature of art—the central topic of aesthetics—has been raised within art itself. Artistic practice becomes, in all its specificity and contingency, a valid form of philosophy in its own right, thus rendering "aesthetics" superfluous. In a cultural context in which any object can be considered art—a urinal, for instance, or a soap box—art becomes that set of objects, however commonplace, which has been transfigured by reflexivity.

PETER HANSEN

See also CULTURAL CRITICISM; NATURALISM; REALISM; ROMANTICISM.

FURTHER READING

Thomas M. Alexander, *John Dewey's Theory of Art, Experience, and Nature: the Horizons of Feeling* (Albany: State University of New York Press, 1987).

Morris R. Cohen, *American Thought: a Critical Sketch* (Glencoe: Free Press, 1954).

Arthur C. Danto, *The Philosophical Disenfranchisement of Art* (New York: Columbia University Press, 1986).

Hal Foster, ed., *The Anti-Aesthetic: Essays on Postmodern Culture* (Port Townsend, Wash.: Bay Press, 1983).

Charles Harrison and Paul Wood, eds., *Art in Theory, 1900–1990: an Anthology of Changing Ideas* (Cambridge: Blackwell, 1992).

Hans Joas, *Pragmatism and Social Theory* (Chicago: University of Chicago Press, 1993).

George Santayana, *The Genteel Tradition: Nine Essays* (Cambridge: Harvard University Press, 1967).

Roger B. Stein, *John Ruskin and Aesthetic Thought in America, 1840–1900* (Cambridge: Harvard University Press, 1967).

Agassiz, Louis (b. Motier-en-Vuly, Switzerland, May 28, 1807; d. Cambridge, Mass., Dec. 14, 1873). Naturalist and educator. Agassiz's *Recherches sur les poissons fossiles* (1833–43) launched the field of paleontology, while his inspired oratory brought natural history to packed lyceum audiences. As a professor at Harvard University (1848–73), Agassiz professionalized natural history by emphasizing experimentation, direct observation from nature, and institutional support for specialized work. He rejected Darwinism as incompatible with religion: since each species represented a thought of God at its moment of creation, species were immutable.

See also DARWINISM.

FURTHER READING
Michael Ruse, *The Darwinian Revolution* (Chicago: University of Chicago Press, 1979).

Agee, James (b. Knoxville, Tenn., Nov. 27, 1909; d. New York, N.Y., May 16, 1955). A poet, journalist, film critic, screenwriter, and novelist, Agee was the son of a genial businessman from the hill country and a very formidable Anglo-Catholic mother. He was deeply affected by his father's death in an automobile accident in 1916, an event over which he brooded for the remainder of his life and recast as fiction in his novel, *A Death in the Family*. Educated at St. Andrews Episcopal School near Sewanee, Tennessee, Phillips Exeter Academy, and Harvard, Agee proved an indifferent student but a talented poet. Upon graduation from college in 1932 he landed a job with *Fortune* magazine, joining ARCHIBALD MACLEISH and DWIGHT MACDONALD in the unorthodox crew of brilliant young writers Henry Luce had assembled to celebrate the accomplishments of American capitalism and trace the course of the New Deal. Agee, Macdonald recalled in his contribution to *Remembering James Agee*, quickly became the "staff specialist in rich, beautiful prose" (p. 124). This began nearly 20 years of unsteady employment by Time Incorporated, a relationship that elicited in Agee a debilitating mix of emotions, from grateful dependence to anguished self-loathing. He could never escape the suspicion that in writing for Henry Luce, impresario of popular journalism, he had sold out the high calling of critical intellectual craftsmanship.

In the summer of 1936 Agee and photographer WALKER EVANS were sent South by *Fortune* to do a story on poverty-stricken tenant farmers. Anticipating a documentary account of lower-class life similar to those (such as Erskine Caldwell and Margaret Bourke-White's *You Have Seen Their Faces*) which loomed large in the cultural landscape of the 1930s, *Fortune* editors instead received a manuscript that, as William Stott has argued, takes the rhetoric and perspective of the liberal reform documentary of the thirties and "explodes it, surpasses it, shows it up"

(p. x). In a powerful combination of cool, detached photographs and extravagant, self-lacerating prose, Evans and Agee starkly portrayed the damaged lives of three white Alabama families, while at the same time calling into question the ethics of documentary "spying." The book challenged the very possibility of adequately describing, let alone explaining or redeeming, the lives of other human beings. Yet it joined this skepticism with a profound appreciation for the sanctity, even divinity, of each person, however ordinary or "backward."

Appalled by Agee's sprawling, unconventional manuscript, *Fortune* rejected it, and Agee labored for three years to transform it into a book, to which he gave the ironic title *Let Us Now Praise Famous Men*. Published in 1941 as preparations for war were finally putting an end to the Depression and to concern for the tenant farmer, the book suffered poor sales and bad reviews and quickly disappeared from sight. Only a few critics such as LIONEL TRILLING saw it for what it was: "the most realistic and the most important moral effort of our American generation" (p. 102). In the 1960s the book was rediscovered and would find a particularly appreciative audience among civil rights activists struggling with moral questions similar to those raised by Agee and Evans.

In 1939 Agee moved from *Fortune* to *Time* as a regular book reviewer. Two years later he assumed the role of the magazine's principal film critic, while at the same time agreeing to write regularly about the movies for the *Nation*. From 1942 to 1948 Agee was the best film critic in America, bringing to the task a deep passion for the movies he had held since he was a schoolboy, as well as the eye of a would-be director for the grammar and syntax of film. Siding with the popular film audience, he sought to educate its vision without succumbing to the pretensions that had already begun to infect film criticism. In a fan letter to the *Nation* in October 1944, W. H. Auden placed Agee's reviews among "that very select class—the music critiques of Berlioz and Shaw are the only other members I know—of newspaper work which has permanent literary value."

Agee gave up film reviewing in 1948 (though his best-known piece of film criticism, "Comedy's Greatest Era," a study of silent film comedians, was published in *Life* in 1949). Determined to concentrate on his own fiction, he found himself free of the constrictions of the Luce empire only to fall quickly into the arms of Hollywood. He was unable to resist the blandishments of those eager to exploit his talents as a screenwriter. He authored several scripts for the movies and television, the most famous of which was the screenplay he coauthored for *The African Queen* (1951) with John Huston, the director whom he most admired. He did publish a novella, *The Morning Watch* (1951), based on his years at St. Andrews, and nearly finished *A Death in the Family* before dying of a heart attack in a New York cab in May 1955 at the age of 45. Published posthumously in 1957, this moving evocation of familial love, boyhood, and bereavement won the Pulitzer Prize and initiated the lionization Agee had been denied in his lifetime.

What Agee said in *Agee on Film* of director D. W. Griffith could be said of him as well: "He was at his best just short of his excesses, and he tended in general to work out toward the dangerous edge" (vol. 1, pp. 315–16). In the end, his excesses—of alcohol, cigarettes, sexual appetite, and frustrated ambition—got the better of him. As Macdonald observed,

> Even for a modern writer, he was extraordinarily self-destructive. He was always ready to sit up all night with anyone who happened to be around, or to go out at midnight looking for someone: talking passionately, brilliantly, but too much, drinking too much, making love too much, and in general cultivating the worst set of work habits in Greenwich Village (pp. 137–8).

Aspiring to the heights scaled by his heroes, Shakespeare, Beethoven, William Blake, and Charlie Chaplin, Agee regarded his literary career and its modest fruits as a failure. Not content to be anything less than a "great" writer, he sketched many lofty projects and accomplished relatively few. Yet he did leave behind a remarkable novel, and his film criticism remains an inviting model of cultural journalism at its best. And, above all, we may be grateful for *Let Us Now Praise Famous Men*, a book indispensable to the student of the modern American moral imagination.

ROBERT B. WESTBROOK

FURTHER READING

James Agee, *Agee on Film*, 2 vols. (1958, 1960; New York: Perigee, 1983).
——, *Letters of James Agee to Father Flye*, 2nd ed. (Boston: Houghton Mifflin, 1971).
Laurence Bergreen, *James Agee: a Life* (New York: Dutton, 1984).
David Madden, ed., *Remembering James Agee* (Baton Rouge: Louisiana State University Press, 1974).
Dale Maharidge and Michael Williamson, *And Their Children After Them: the Legacy of "Let Us Now Praise Famous Men"* (New York: Pantheon, 1989).
William Stott, *Documentary Expression and Thirties America* (New York: Oxford, 1973).
Lionel Trilling, "Greatness with One Fault in It," *Kenyon Review* 4 (1942): 99–102.

Alcott, [Amos] Bronson (b. near Wolcott, Conn., Nov. 29, 1799; d. Boston, Mass., Mar. 4, 1888).

Philosopher and educator. Founder of a series of schools, including Boston's Temple School, Alcott was a leading Transcendentalist. He believed that children are naturally good and need only a stimulating and supportive environment to develop morality and self-expression. He started Fruitlands, a cooperative community with ideals of spiritual asceticism and nonexploitative agriculture, which disintegrated within a year. Alcott later founded the Concord Summer School of Philosophy and Literature in order to encourage a synthesis of St. Louis Hegelianism and New England TRANSCENDENTALISM.

See also UTOPIAS.

FURTHER READING

Anne, C. Rose, *Transcendentalism as a Social Movement, 1830–1850* (New Haven: Yale University Press, 1981).

Alcott, Louisa May (b. Germantown, Pa., Nov. 29, 1832; d. Boston, Mass., Mar. 6, 1888). Upon her death Louisa May Alcott was memorialized as "the children's friend," a soubriquet which has endured for a century. Best known for her children's classic *Little Women* (1868–9), and especially for her tomboy heroine Jo March, Alcott has never, like so many other nineteenth-century American women writers, lapsed into obscurity. The daughters of Transcendentalist philosopher and educator Bronson Alcott, Louisa and her three sisters grew up in Concord, Massachusetts, where they associated with such luminaries as RALPH WALDO EMERSON, HENRY DAVID THOREAU, NATHANIEL HAWTHORNE, and MARGARET FULLER. In this heady atmosphere of spiritual self-culture and social reform, Louisa, as her journals and letters attest, was early affected (and perhaps afflicted) by the moral earnestness and idealistic enthusiasm of her elders. Yet she managed to preserve an irreverent and rebellious spirit. Bronson Alcott's impecuniousness, as well as his strict vegetarianism, sometimes reduced the family to a diet of apples, bread, and water (especially at his short-lived utopian community, Fruitlands, satirized in Louisa's *Transcendental Wild Oats* of 1873). But Louisa found compensation in nature (including berrying parties with Thoreau), reading (especially Shakespeare, Goethe, Hawthorne, and Dickens), and, above all, writing, producing, and acting in amateur theatricals. Having witnessed her parents' frequently stormy marriage and experienced the shame of economic dependence—on the largesse of Emerson and her mother's relatives—Louisa emerged from her teens skeptical of matrimony and determined to support herself, preferably by her pen.

Prior to the appearance of *Little Women*, Alcott published anonymously or pseudonymously a number of stories, which she characterized as "lurid," in sensational weekly newspapers. She also, as recounted in her autobiographical adult novel *Work* (1873), supported herself as governess, nurse/companion, seamstress, and even domestic servant before enlisting as a Union Army nurse. Her experience at the Union Hotel Hospital in Washington was brief, terminated by illness in less than a month, but its impact was profound and led to the publication of her first successful book, *Hospital Sketches* (1863). Its publication enabled her to market an adult novel on which she had been working for several years. Entitled *Moods* (1864), it dramatizes the fatal consequences for many women of society's insistence upon marriage as their sole career. Because of its frank treatment of infidelity and divorce as responses to loveless marriage, the book was censured by many, including the youthful reviewer HENRY JAMES. Discouraged by her novel's reception, Alcott returned to writing "blood and thunder" tales and assumed the editorship of a popular magazine for children, *Merry's Museum*. On being asked to write a girls' story by editor Thomas Niles, Alcott reluctantly consented, for, as she wrote in her journal, "I don't enjoy this sort of thing. Never liked girls or knew many, except my sisters; but our queer plays and experiences may prove interesting, though I doubt it" (p. 166). Alcott later added a postscript to this entry, "Good joke," as it indeed proved to be.

Although Alcott's reputation has never suffered oblivion, literary critics and historians tended until recently to share the opinion of Jenny Blair Archibald, the nine-year-old heroine of Ellen Glasgow's *The Sheltered Life* (1938), who on "reading *Little Women* for the assured reward of a penny a page" complains that "even if Mamma did form her character on Meg and Jo, I think they're just poky old things." The revival of the women's movement in the 1970s, however, gave rise to a new scholarly interest in Alcott's work. This interest was intensified by the reprinting of *Work*, by the publication of a previously unpublished, autobiographical novel fragment *Diana and Persis*, and, especially, by Madeleine B. Stern's editions of Alcott's sensation stories, many of them featuring maniacal, homicidal, and drug-dependent female characters. These works were followed by the appearance of Alcott's full-length sensation novel *A Modern Mephistopheles* (1877), her letters and journals, and finally *Moods*.

Stern's biography of Alcott, first published over 40 years ago and still the standard, protrays her as a lively, energetic, relatively unconflicted individual, who, though committed to women's rights, wrote her dark thrillers for pleasure and profit, her children's books for profit alone. Martha Saxton's "modern biography" swings too far in the other direction, presenting her as a tortured soul, deeply scarred by a materially and emotionally deprived childhood, writing her thrillers out of sexual frustration, her children's fiction as a cynical compromise. Saxton's assessment is the first, and one of the most extreme, of recent interpretations of Alcott as a victim of patriarchy, as an author who wrote one brave novel of protest—*Moods* (or, as some would argue, one great subversive *tour de force*, the sensation story "Behind a Mask")—and then surrendered her authorial ambition and feminist anger to her family's need for financial support.

While literary critics have lately found in Alcott a submerged rage toward the confining conventions of gender in Victorian America, social historians have been reconstructing Alcott as a domestic feminist, one who, in the words of Charles Strickland's *Victorian Domesticity*, "subscribed to the idea that cultured women hold an obligation peculiar to themselves to promote the moral regeneration of society through their influences as wives and mothers" (p. 145). Whereas the literary proponents of Alcott's radicalism tend to focus on *Moods* and the sensation stories, the social historians tend to draw their evidence from *Work* and the children's fiction, especially the *Little Women* trilogy. They interpret Jo March's Plumfield School in *Little Men* (1871) and *Jo's Boys* (1886), despite its repressiveness and gender bias, as a feminist revision of Bronson Alcott's utopian experiment at Fruitlands.

Close examination of Alcott's entire canon—children's fiction, adult domestic fiction, and sensation stories—suggests commitment rather than compromise, a unified rather than a bifurcated career. Situated in a generation between Hawthorne and James, her work, like theirs, abounds in portraits of the artist, and these give rise to the suspicion that Alcott was only masquerading as "Aunt Jo," "the children's friend." Most famous, of course, are the writer and artist sisters Jo and Amy March, based on Alcott and her sister Abigail May. But from the actresses Jean Muir in "Behind a Mask" and Christie Devon in *Work* to the eponymous artist heroines of *Diana and Persis* (both modeled on May Alcott's experience studying art abroad) to the poets Felix Canaris and Jasper Helwyze in *A Modern Mephistopheles*, Alcott produces a gallery of artists, who, whether male or female, present both a composite self-portrait and a portrait of the woman artist in Victorian America. Stories like "Behind a Mask," in which an actress heroine assumes the role of governess and infiltrates in order to disrupt a patriarchal family, and *A Modern Mephistopheles*, in which a poet allows the works of his satanic patron to be published as his own youthful lyrics, support a reading of Alcott as insurgent. Hence to characterize her as either defenseless victim or compromised defender of her culture's values is to slight and oversimplify a surprisingly subtle and complex American artist.

ELIZABETH KEYSER

See also DOMESTICITY; VICTORIANISM.

FURTHER READING

Louisa May Alcott, *The Journals of Louisa May Alcott* and *The Selected Letters of Louisa May Alcott*, ed. Joel Myerson, Daniel Shealy, and Madeleine B. Stern (Boston: Little, Brown, 1987 and 1989).

Sarah Elbert, *A Hunger for Home: Louisa May Alcott's Place in American Culture* (New Brunswick: Rutgers University Press, 1987).

Elizabeth Lennox Keyser, *Whispers in the Dark: the Fiction of Louisa May Alcott* (Knoxville: University of Tennessee Press, 1993).

Ruth K. MacDonald, *Louisa May Alcott* (Boston: Twayne, 1983).

Joy A. Marsella, *The Promise of Destiny: Children and Women in the Short Stories of Louisa May Alcott* (Westport: Greenwood, 1983).

Martha Saxton, *Louisa May: a Modern Biography of Louisa May Alcott* (New York: Avon, 1978).

Madeleine B. Stern, *Louisa May Alcott* (1950; Norman: University of Oklahoma Press, 1971).

Charles Strickland, *Victorian Domesticity: Families in the Life and Art of Louisa May Alcott* (University, Ala.: University of Alabama Press, 1985).

Alger, Horatio (b. Revere, Mass., Jan. 13, 1832; d. Natick, Mass., July 18, 1899). Writer. Author of more than a hundred books for boys, Alger repeatedly returned to the formula he had found in *Ragged Dick, or Street Life in New York with the Bootblacks* (1867–8). His heroes are boys who rise from rags to middle-class respectability by a combination of luck and character. In a world that is deceptive and dangerous, but also full of opportunity, they take advantage of their lucky breaks by being aggressive, charming, clever, and—most importantly—willing to take risks. Although Alger's stories apparently preach that middle-class status is available to anyone who is self-disciplined, they in fact also underline the importance of chance.

See also INDIVIDUALISM; SOCIAL MOBILITY.

FURTHER READING

Carol Nackenoff, *The Fictional Republic: Horatio Alger and American Political Discourse* (New York: Oxford University Press, 1994).

American exceptionalism The idea that America occupies a place in history significantly different from that of any other country in the world stands at the core of nationalist ideology in the United States and at the center of reflection and debate about the American experience.

As nationalist ideology, exceptionalism took shape at the time of the AMERICAN REVOLUTION and the decades following, joining Europeans' utopian projections of the "New World," Puritan faith in America's holy mission, republican hope that the American republic, unlike all previous republics in history, would live forever, and liberal expectations of economic expansion. The successful establishment of republican institutions and the liberal opportunity guaranteed by a continent of uncultivated land appeared to set American history on a millennial course, guarded by divine providence, and this faith was transmuted as secularization proceeded into a civil religion. Exceptionalism is thus one variant among many nationalist versions of special destiny derived from a Christian heritage.

Embedded in exceptionalist ideology is a distinctive, pre-historicist historical consciousness that removes America from the vicissitudes of time. It also defines an optimistic political economy: republican government, with its broad suffrage and relative social equality, and a market economy that offered widespread economic independence, would hold the poverty and class conflict of European history forever at bay. Finally, exceptionalist ideology projects a unique American mission to the world, casting American experience as the model the world is destined to follow.

Exceptionalist ideology was woven into American literature, politics, and social theory until challenged during the Gilded Age, when industrialization and class conflict forced the recognition of change. It was then reworked by attaching America to the modernizing course of Western liberal history. Still, it retained its force by casting America as the vanguard of modernity or as an ideal liberal society. In popular culture and politics, it survived as edifying myth, as calculated mystification, and as chauvinism.

From the early nineteenth century onward, a critical discussion of America's place in history took exceptionalism as a problem, rather than a belief, asking how different the United States is from other countries and what significance that difference has. Since the historical experience of every country is to some degree unique, and since differences are always interwoven with similarities (otherwise no comparison would be possible), the decision to cast American difference as exceptional implies a standard of importance or a norm of historical development against which American experience is measured.

In the ideological formulation of exceptionalism, the standard of importance is the world-historical project of millennial or modernist transformation; the normal or average course of development is set by Europe, but American experience itself sets the ideal norm toward which history moves.

The critical discussion began, and many of its basic terms were set, by ALEXIS DE TOCQUEVILLE in *Democracy in America*. Tocqueville emphasized the absence of a feudal past and the consequent individualism and democratic equality of American society and institutions. Special historical conditions like Protestant religiosity and continental size also figured in his analysis. Although at one point Tocqueville called American conditions "exceptional," (vol. 2, p. 36), his was not an ideological formulation. If he predicted that the principle of democracy would triumph, the principle itself was not essentially American. Adventitious historical conditions allowed Americans to work out its implications, but it would likely take different forms in Europe and, should conditions change, in the United States. American differences were not *sui generis*, but variations on European forms, and were understandable by the same kinds of historical and analytical categories that applied to Europe.

The exceptionalism developed by Marxist writers was differently focused; here the norm of historical development was the transformation of Western nations from capitalism to communism. According to Marxist logic, America's nonfeudal past, bourgeois capitalist institutions, and rapid industrialization should have produced a communist revolution. Werner Sombart, a German sociologist influenced by Marx, raised the issue in his 1905 pamphlet, "Why Is There No Socialism in America?" The term "American exceptionalism" apparently came into use in discussions between American and European communists in the 1920s and 1930s.

Both the Tocquevillean and Marxist analyses influenced American intellectuals from the late 1930s to the 1950s, when America's centrist politics and worldwide power focused attention on American difference. Studies of American literature, politics, history, and national character all claimed uniqueness. Within this context, American Studies formed as a separate academic specialty in the United States and abroad. Under the pressure of intense nationalism during these decades of war and Cold War, the critical discussion of American difference was sharpened to exceptionality and often linked to the ideological framing of America's world-historical role.

During the 1960s, ideological conflict and disillusion with imperialism led writers, particularly on the left, to question the assumption of uniqueness. Since that time, scholars have continued that critique by historicizing the ideology and recovering a wide diversity of experiences among Americans. Critics of exceptionalism deny that so essentializing and totalizing a concept can describe such diverse and changing patterns of behavior and belief. However, the national focus of scholarship keeps the perception of difference alive, and the decline of communism and the breakup of the Soviet Union threaten to revive belief in America's world-historical role. Moreover, some writers, across the political spectrum, think that American exceptionalism is an edifying myth central to American democracy and hence warrants inquiry into and support of American uniqueness. Others believe, against all odds, that inquiry into American uniqueness can be pursued apart from ideology. This writer believes, rather, that a differentiated view of American experience and of its relations to the many peoples and histories in the world will both improve understanding and strengthen democratic values.

DOROTHY ROSS

See also IDEOLOGY; SOCIAL SCIENCE.

FURTHER READING

Sacvan Bercovitch, *The Rites of Assent: Transformations in the Symbolic Construction of America* (New York: Routledge, 1993).
Allen F. Davis, "The Politics of American Studies," *American Quarterly* 42 (Sept. 1990): 353–74.
Michael Denning, "'The Special American Conditions': Marxism and American Studies," *American Quarterly* 38 (1986): 356–80.
Michael Kammen, "The Problem of American Exceptionalism: a Reconsideration," *American Quarterly* 45 (Mar. 1993): 1–43.
Byron E. Shafer, ed., *Is America Different? A New Look at American Exceptionalism* (New York: Oxford University Press, 1991).
R. Laurence Moore, *European Socialists and the American Promised Land* (New York: Oxford University Press, 1970).
Dorothy Ross, *The Origins of American Social Science* (Cambridge: Cambridge University Press, 1991).
Alexis de Tocqueville, *Democracy in America*, 2 vols. (1831; New York: Alfred A. Knopf, 1945).

American Revolution Musing about his nation's past in a letter to H. Niles dated February 13, 1818, JOHN ADAMS asked: "What do we mean by the American Revolution? Do we mean the American war?" He responded:

The Revolution was effected before the war commenced. The Revolution was in the minds and hearts of the people; a change in their religious sentiments of their duties and obligations. . . . *This radical change in the principles, opinions, sentiments, and affections of the people, was the real American Revolution.*

Adams's observations offer profound insight into eighteenth-century America; without an understanding of the transformations taking place throughout the colonies well before the outbreak of the Revolution it is impossible to understand the precipitous collapse of the monarchical culture that pervaded American society prior to 1776. That culture, characterized by inequality, hierarchical social and political arrangements, patronage, and patriarchal socioeconomic relationships, had already suffered decades of erosion from institutions and habits of mind arising spontaneously within the New World environment. The freehold system and the increasingly fluid and competitive nature of colonial society inhibited the solidification of the dependent patron–client associations characteristic of European society at that time. The widespread ownership of land created an uncommonly large body of voters, who elected a wide array of political officials. The extraordinary political awareness and independence of so many ordinary citizens meant that most officeholders in America asked favors rather than granted them. In addition, religious and ethnic groups multiplied throughout the colonies, and the outward thrust of thousands of migrants into wilderness areas shattered traditional communal bonds as well as familiar lines of interest or patronage. Thus, even though the forms and the language of monarchy appeared omnipresent throughout the American colonies, they proved much too insubstantial and superficial to withstand the subtle transmutations taking place throughout American society. Consequently, by 1776, these forms and customs rested upon an essentially republican society. By and large, contractual rather than dependent relationships characterized the colonies on the eve of the Revolution.

As John Adams indicated, the minds and hearts of the colonists underwent great changes prior to the outbreak of the war. And yet the process of change had only begun. In response to British attempts to reorganize the empire in the decade of the 1760s a rationale for revolution and regeneration emerged that contributed greatly to transformations within American society far more fundamental than merely the erosion of monarchical culture.

Based upon the ideas of John Locke and radical opposition figures such as John Trenchard and Thomas Gordon, a comprehensive theory of politics took shape within the colonies that created an ominous pattern out of such British actions as the Stamp Act, the Townshend Duties and the Coercive Acts. This theory focused on the role of power—defined as the domination of some men over others—within American life. Such a perception led colonists to a central, all-important conclusion: the preservation of liberty relied entirely upon the moral strength and vigilance of the people. Many colonists believed that Britain was succumbing to the all-too-familiar tendencies seen throughout history for nations to decline with age, to fall prey to the corruptions of power. Viewed in this way, the measures taken by the British subsequent to the Stamp Act represented not only mistaken or ill-advised behavior, but a deliberately planned attack upon liberty in America that had to be resisted at all costs.

The belief that they faced a ministerial conspiracy against liberty transformed the meaning of resistance in the minds of many colonists from a constitutional quarrel over the legitimacy of Parliamentary legislation into a world regenerative creed. For many Americans the Revolution became more than simply a political revolt; it represented the creation of a fresh world, a republican world. Consequently, REPUBLICANISM came to stand for more than just the substitution of an elective system for a monarchy. It infused the political break with England with a moral fervor and an idealistic depth linked inextricably to the very character of American society. Emphasizing a morality of social cohesion, Americans hoped to create an organic state by joining individual citizens together in an indissoluble union of harmony and benevolence: a true republic. For Americans a commitment to EQUALITY and VIRTUE (defined as the sacrifice of individual interests to a greater common good) comprised both the essence of republicanism and the idealistic goal of the Revolution. Inspired by this outlook, they set out to gain their independence and to establish a new republic.

While most Americans who supported the Revolution considered themselves republicans, what that meant beyond a belief in virtue and equality remained open to question. Some enthusiastically accepted the new world of market relations while others remained deeply anticapitalistic. Some wanted to retain a communal society based on social hierarchy, others desired an open, competitive society without regard for rank or status, while still others preferred a simple, homogeneous society of relative equality held together by deep corporate bonds. These particular desires represented discrete fragments of two larger cultural impulses—republicanism and LIBERALISM—coursing through the lives of late eighteenth-century Americans. At times the two seemed to run parallel to one another, at other times they appeared in direct conflict, and at still other times they blended into a nearly indistinguishable whole.

In recent years historians have attempted to interpret the Revolution in terms of republicanism or liberalism. Advocates of the former view, emphasizing the causal nature of ideas, insist that Americans broke free from Great Britain in order to maintain public and private virtue, social solidarity, and to blunt the scramble for wealth and power beginning to appear within their society. Adherents of liberalism, stressing the social basis of human actions, maintain that aggressive INDIVIDUALISM, optimistic materialism, and interest group politics motivated Americans in the Revolutionary era.

This disagreement among historians threatens to cloud our understanding of the formative years of the American nation's past. Certainly Americans living in these years never felt themselves confronted by two sharply contrasting modes of thought—liberalism or republicanism. Such intellectual concepts are the creation of recent scholars, and when historians insist upon forcing individuals or groups from the past into a particular ideological mold, they distort our ability to reconstruct that past in a way that would be recognizable to people of the time who actually experienced it. Americans living in the late eighteenth century could, quite unselfconsciously, believe simultaneously in the promotion of their own individual socioeconomic and political prospects, as well as in the distinct possiblity that their FREEDOM might be endangered by corrupt forces of power within their governments. By this time classical republican traditions and modern social, economic, and political behavior had blended so thoroughly and so imperceptibly that efforts by historians to force historical participants into one or another static frame of mind simply create a historical anachronism.

In many ways, republicanism—a familiar ideology permeating all walks of life—shaped Americans' thoughts by providing their lives with meaning and identity. Liberalism, more an unarticulated behavioral pattern than a sharply delineated mode of thought, unconsciously shaped their day-to-day activity. Still, most Americans clung to a harmonious, corporate view of themselves and their society even while behaving in a materialistic, utilitarian manner in their daily lives. Thus, while rapidly transforming their society in an open, competitive, modern direction, Americans continued to idealize communal harmony and a virtuous social order.

Such values could not, however, remain inviolate in the decades following the end of the war. Throughout these years social, economic, and demographic forces, fueled by Revolutionary republicanism's emphasis upon equality and popular sovereignty, created a cultural ferment within American society that radically altered republican values. The nation's population grew at an astonishing rate and began to spread out from the original states at a rapid pace. At the same time great numbers of people accustomed only to an isolated, subsistence life became drawn into the market economy. An environment of rising expectations developed that stimulated the acquisitive instincts of innumerable individuals while straining customary paternalistic social relationships. The traditional bonds—gentleman and servant, parent and child, landowner and tenant, master and apprentice, merchant and client—that had joined people together over the years began to unravel. Set loose from such constraints. many Americans took advantage of the expanding opportunities that surrounded them. Since they believed that to get ahead in such an entrepreneurial and individualistic environment required only ingenuity and hard work, thousands of simple folk anticipated that the contours of their society would increasingly be shaped by ordinary citizens like themselves pursuing economic prosperity.

Within such an atmosphere upward mobility no longer hinged on proper breeding and social connections, restricted political privileges, and, least of all, a genteel education. By means of chapbooks, almanacs, broadsides, and pamphlets simple folk began to gain snatches of information about matters that had always been considered solely within the ken of the genteel. Learning had not been rejected; it had been popularized. By far the greatest stimulant to this popularization of knowledge was the increased publication and widespread distribution of newspapers. The number of newspapers published in America increased from 100 in 1790 to over 250 a decade later. With this increase in circulation came a change in the nature of newspapers. Not only did common people read these papers, but they increasingly began to contribute to them. "A Farmer," "A Republican," or "A Friend to Liberty and Equality" replaced classical pseudonyms, and editorial policies changed to meet the demands of a popular constituency. In this environment truth itself gradually underwent a process of democratization: ordinary individuals began to consider themselves capable of discovering and acting upon what was best for their society.

These attitudes accompanied a social disintegration that was taking place within late eighteenth-century American society. As economic and demographic forces at work within that society gradually undermined the aristocratic hierarchies that had for so long provided order and meaning, a pervasive collapse of certainty spread throughout the culture.

Many individuals accustomed to living within deferentially ordered harmonious communities found themselves far more independent than ever before. The ideological and social forces unleashed by the Revolution simultaneously exacerbated this process of social disintegration and provided it with a positive meaning for obscure individuals. For many Americans, Revolutionary republicanism came to mean that no one man or set of men was better than any other. The pursuit of happiness—the achievement of property and wealth—thus became a scramble to get ahead in an increasingly materialistic and acquisitive society.

Not only did Revolutionary republicanism support ordinary farmers, mechanics, and shopkeepers in their belief that they were the equals of gentle folk, it provoked them to challenge the idea that a gentlemanly few should direct and control their society. Throughout the final decades of the eighteenth century, an explicitly egalitarian impetus arose within American society that brought together, in an attempt to shatter the hegemony of gentlemanly elites, those inherently suspicious of power with others who had traditionally been powerless. Quite spontaneously, individuals and groups actively began to challenge the religious, economic, social, and political authority of elites within their society. Their efforts culminated in the creation of a culture quite unlike any the world had ever seen or that republican leaders of the Revolution had anticipated.

Thus it was that Americans, quite inadvertently, quite unselfconsciously, caught up in circumstances over which they had little control and of which they had perhaps even less understanding, brought about a fundamental reordering of society. The enlightened republic envisioned by Revolutionary leaders, in which self-sacrificing citizens would defer to the judgment of a natural hierarchy of disinterested gentlemen, had been displaced by an egalitarian social order composed of ordinary citizens trying to get ahead in their own individualistic, materialistic way. This did indeed constitute a *"radical change in the principles, opinions, sentiments, and affections of the people."* This transformation in beliefs and attitudes regarding the basic organization of society, this destruction of hierarchical principles throughout the last half of the eighteenth century and the first decades of the nineteenth, comprised the real American Revolution.

ROBERT E. SHALHOPE

See also THOMAS JEFFERSON; THOMAS PAINE.

FURTHER READING

Joyce Appleby, *Capitalism and a New Social Order: the Republican Vision of the 1790s* (New York: New York University Press, 1984).

Bernard Bailyn, *The Ideological Origins of the American Revolution* (Cambridge: Harvard University Press, 1967).

Richard Bushman, *King and People in Provincial Massachusetts* (Chapel Hill: University of North Carolina Press, 1985).

Robert E. Shalhope, *The Roots of Democracy: American Culture and Thought, 1760–1800* (Boston: Twayne, 1990).

Gordon Wood, *The Creation of the American Republic, 1776–1787* (Chapel Hill: University of North Carolina Press, 1969).

——, *The Radicalism of the American Revolution* (New York: Knopf, 1992).

ancient Indian history Native American historians have created and maintained a large variety of records about the ancient past. These records preserve a discourse which considers such matters as world origins, human creation, social arrangements, the development of political institutions, medical practices, religious systems, and many other arenas of human activity. There should be no question that for thousands of years, Indian people have shared among themselves stories about the past which have been organized to present a coherent and meaningful picture of human history. But what can Native American oral traditions contribute to the study of ancient Indian history?

John Lawson, an English visitor to the Carolinas in 1700, remarked on the detail, consistency, and depth of Indian historical records, some of which concerned events "that happen'd many Years ago; nay two or three Ages or more" (in Axtell's *The Indian Peoples of Eastern America*, p. 221). The Elizabethan writer Christopher Marlowe even declared that Indian historians had better information about world history than did the Bible—a view which was branded as heresy by less tolerant contemporaries. Marlowe would get an equally unsympathetic reception from most twentieth-century scholars and Christian theologians.

The American academic community has inherited and articulated a broad range of views about Indian oral traditions as a medium of historical discourse. The spectrum of opinion includes some scholars who deny that oral traditions have any value in helping to understand historical events that occurred before "living memory," while other scholars believe that verbal accounts can provide a durable vehicle for moving information across great spans of time. The dominant perspective, however, has treated Indian oral traditions as a dubious source of information about historical events dating back more than two or three centuries.

To some degree, the conquest of Native America by Euro-American invaders has involved the destruction, devaluation, and appropriation of Indian historical discourse about ancient North America. With the arrival of Europeans, the ancient history of the New World crumbled into the dark seas of "pre-history"—a concept which denies the existence of relevant Indian historical discourse. Through such terminology, the American academic community has taught that Indian historical documents are extremely limited in their ability to convey a sense of the true span of human events. Indian historians, in other words, have not succeeded in explaining Indian history, and they have been marginalized by a powerful new community of Euro-American "ethnohistorians" and "prehistorians."

During the nineteenth century, the American academic community embraced ideas which prevented its members from fully appreciating Native American intellectual traditions. Samuel Morton, a leading American scientist of the 1830s and 1840s, sought to develop proof for the assertion that Indians, Africans, and Asians were intellectually inferior to white Europeans; through the study of Indian skulls stolen from graves, Morton argued that Indians ranked below white people in mental capabilities. Indians could never hope to create legitimate intellectual traditions that might rank with European accomplishments. By the end of the century, even members of the academic community who disagreed with these findings of science felt compelled to employ models of cultural inferiority. George Bird Grinnell, for example, argued that Indians were fully capable of grasping the uplifting ideas of civilized human society. Yet Indians could be viewed, in his opinion, as cultural "children."

Grinnell often consulted oral traditions in writing about Indian history; but for members of the American academic community who felt some apprehension at the notion of relying on documents produced by "children," Robert Lowie offered a clear solution to the problem. In 1915 and 1916 he leveled scathing attacks against the use of Indian traditions as historical records. In the pages of the *Journal of American Folk-Lore*, he wondered:

If we do not accept aboriginal pathology as contributions to *our* pathology, if we do not accept aboriginal astronomy, biology, or physics, why should we place primitive history alone on a quite exceptional pedestal, and exalt it to a rank co-ordinate with that of our own historical science? (p. 162)

He went on to "deny utterly that primitive man is endowed with historical sense or perspective." Lowie's extreme views elicited little protest from university history departments, where faculties generally displayed an impressive (and enduring) disinterest in ancient Indian history.

Not everyone in the academic community, however, adopted Lowie's position. Ethnohistorians frequently consulted Indian oral traditions to support evidence from linguistics, archaeology, and other fields of study, but these efforts typically focused on recent centuries, with marginal attention to ancient Indian history. Throughout the twentieth century, folklorists such as Stith Thompson, Anna Rooth, and Andrew Wiget accepted the notion that "legends" can be handed down over many generations from distant antiquity. If "legends" or any other type of oral account can be preserved for millennia, then it should also be possible for oral traditions to preserve *historical* information of similar age.

Perhaps the strongest academic challenge to Lowie has come from archaeologists. During the 1920s and 1930s an increasing number of archaeological investigations throughout the United States began to fill the vacuum left by the banishment of Indian oral traditions from the field of history. Scholars who rejected Indian historians as colleagues discovered that they could accept the credentials of archaeologists. Though most archaeologists, like American historians, tended to ignore Indian historical traditions, a few helped to keep alive the question of the contribution of Indian oral traditions to ancient Indian history.

In 1934 William Duncan Strong presented a group of Indian traditions which he interpreted as referring to the long-extinct mammoth. Though evidence of human coexistence with mammoths had come forward in 1932, this was not confirmed by more careful archaeological study for almost two decades. Strong's ideas were rejected by leading anthropologists and his views never achieved broad acceptance; as recently as 1980, folklorist George Lankford also disagreed with Strong's conclusions. Though he was reluctant to "see mammoths" in Indian oral traditions, Lankford nevertheless endorsed the idea that some "legends" have been preserved as oral documents over countless generations from the first human settlers of the New World.

Other scholars have found areas of unmistakable correspondence between oral traditions and archaeology. Clement Meighan and David Pendergast reported in 1959 on a set of Paiute traditions referring to a period dating back before the thirteenth century. During the 1970s and 1980s, Robert L. Hall, John H. Moore, Karl Schlesier, and others sought to link archaeological evidence with information found in oral traditions, and Indians such as William Tallbull, Ben Rhodd, and Diane Yupe worked with archaeologists on collaborative projects. Archaeology showed that it could work in partnership with

Indians in the study of recent and ancient Native America.

One reason why such partnerships have not been more common is that Indians and archaeologists in the United States have long been divided in their views on ancient history. Throughout the twentieth century, for example, the two groups confronted one another with opposing views on the origins of the first humans in North America. Many Native historians rejected the anthropological model of Asian origins for their distant ancestors, and the entrenched presumption of both Native Americans and archaeologists has been that their stories of Indian "origins" are mutually exclusive accounts of ancient history. Anthropologists have emphasized the cultural dimensions of Indian origin traditions, arguing that these stories are not historical in nature; but many Indians disagreed and continued to accept origin traditions as accounts of history.

Not all Indians, however, have accepted Native American origin traditions as descriptions of actual events. By the mid-twentieth century, Indians across the United States had been subjected for at least several generations to intense pressures to reject their heritage, embrace Christian religious traditions, and accept the teachings of American science and history. The American academic community viewed origin traditions as articulations of culture and as literary works—but not as accounts of history. By the end of the century, a large number of Indian people had come to doubt the historicity of tribal origin traditions.

Many of the few Indians who became prominent members of the academic community during the twentieth century rejected Indian origin traditions as historical documents. Alfonso Ortiz argued during the 1970s that traditions about the underground origins of the first people ought to be viewed as "metaphorical" rather than "historical" in character. In this view, the emergence of Indian ancestors from the earth serves as a metaphor expressing powerful cultural ties which bind Indian people to the earth and to their homelands. Ortiz dismissed the possibility that "metaphorical" origin traditions might describe ancient historical events.

Describing Indian origin traditions as "fanciful" in *They Came Here First*, D'Arcy McNickle felt that Indian people could never have maintained any record of their migrations from Asia, so far off in the distant past. McNickle accepted the anthropological model of Indian origins, in which ancient Asians crossed Beringia, a Pleistocene land bridge connecting Asia to Alaska. Northern Beringia lies above the Arctic Circle, where darkness lingers over the land.

McNickle did not see how the anthropological view of Indian origins might connect to Indian origin traditions, even though he noted that Acoma, Zuni, Tlingit, and Kiowa traditions all associate human origins with a region of darkness. Some of the oldest known "Paleo Indian" sites in Alaska, such as Gallagher Flint Station and Bear Cave, are located above the Arctic Circle, but archaeologists have never recognized the landscape of Beringia in the theme of darkness which runs through many Indian origin traditions.

When oral traditions are rooted in the same "actuality" that gave rise to the archaeological record, then connections should exist between both stories of the past. The persistence of specific artifacts over time also implies the coexistence of oral accounts about manufacturing processes, practical utilization, and symbolic meaning. If we infer the presence of oral traditions by this means, it may be possible to gain insights into the potential longevity of orally transmitted information. The persistence of a particular house form over a period of centuries, for example, would imply that generations of builders successfully passed down verbal information about the house.

It may be possible to argue for the durability of verbal accounts over millennia. Consider, for example, the transmission of knowledge about the production and utility of lithic projectile points. Indians manufactured this class of artifacts in North America for at least 11,200 years, and since the production of such tools is not an instinctive behavior, Native Americans must also have transmitted information about these artifacts over the same span of time. If it is possible for Indians to hand down technical knowledge about lithic projectile points for nearly 12,000 years, then it might also be possible for Indian historians to preserve historical traditions over a similar span of time.

Both archaeology and Indian traditions can work together to shed light on the ancient history of Native North America; but entrenched opinions must first be challenged. The American academic community should acknowledge Native American historians as colleagues, and archaeologists should work in partnership with Indians in exploring the past. The development of cooperative relationships between these groups could introduce dramatic changes in our collective understanding of ancient human history in North America. Arranging these relations will be a challenge for the twenty-first century, but it is a challenge which promises to give us all greater access to both the remembered history and the forgotten past of "prehistoric" America.

ROGER C. ECHO-HAWK

See also INDIAN IDENTITIES.

FURTHER READING

James Axtell, *The Indian Peoples of Eastern America: a Documentary History of the Sexes* (New York: Oxford University Press, 1981).

George E. Lankford, "Pleistocene Animals in Folk Memory," *Journal of American Folklore* 93 (July–Sept. 1980): 293–304.

——, *Native American Legends, Southeastern Legends: Tales from the Natchez, Caddo, Biloxi, Chickasaw, and Other Nations* (Little Rock: August House, 1987).

Robert Lowie, "Oral Tradition and History," *Journal of American Folk-Lore* 30 (Apr.–June 1917): 161–7.

Alfonso Ortiz, "Some Concerns Central to the Writing of 'Indian' History," *Indian Historian* 10 (winter 1977): 17–22.

Anderson, Sherwood (b. Camden, Ohio, Sept. 13, 1876; d. Colón, Panama Canal Zone, Mar. 8, 1941). Writer. Having started out as an advertising copywriter, Anderson was drawn into bohemian Chicago early in the twentieth century. Eager to uncover "authentic" experience, he developed a naturalistic representation of middle-American life based on language forms drawn from folk idioms and his own ad-writing. The classic statement of Anderson's project is the collection *Winesburg, Ohio* (1919), a collection of stories reflecting his preoccupation with primitive, libidinal drives, and with the concealed anguish underlying everyday life in middle America. His other works include *Poor White* (1920), *The Triumph of the Egg* (1921), and his posthumous *Memoirs* (1942).

See also NATURALISM; REALISM.

FURTHER READING

T. J. Jackson Lears, "Sherwood Anderson: Looking for the White Spot," in Richard Wightman Fox and T. J. Jackson Lears. eds., *The Power of Culture: Critical Essays in American History* (Chicago: University of Chicago Press, 1993).

animal Although Americans typically have less firsthand contact with nonhuman animals than their ancestors did, they think and speak about animals all the time. American minds, media, and personal possessions are saturated with narratives and visual images of animals—from traditional stories such as Native American tales of Coyote to television commercials starring virtuous dogs who know how to recycle aluminum foil; from bumper stickers proclaiming "I Love My Labrador Retriever" to the stuffed toys and ceramic figurines of animals that populate interior decor. Our colloquial speech is enriched by a wide range of metaphors employing animals ("dumb as an ox," "blind as a bat"), phrases reflecting either actual work with animals or folk conceptions of animal behavior.

Historically, these varied linguistic and artifactual representations have provided pointed, yet sometimes safely oblique, commentaries on human relationships and society. Folklorists point out that tales about wild animals, from alligators to turkeys, were and are still employed as commentaries on the alien other, articulating and mediating social and sexual boundaries. Today animals are not only the subjects but the symbols of conflict on environmental questions, as when the spotted owl became a metonym for protection at the expense of economic growth during the 1992 presidential campaign. Domestic artifacts depicting or shaped like animals may be totemic, indicating the owner's desire to be identified with the creature's attributes, or they may, in the context of room decor, symbolize where such creatures properly "belong." Placing humans and animals in relation to one another is another key function of symbolic discourse about nonhuman animals.

The possession of animals as pets also reveals a great deal about culture. Maintaining animals for nonutilitarian reasons is a practice found in a variety of world cultures over many centuries, but the form Americans practice is a legacy of the distinctive bourgeois culture that coalesced in North America and Europe in the late eighteenth and early nineteenth centuries. For middle-class Americans, the paradigm for thinking about good animal–human interaction is the pet–owner relationship, where the animal is a recognized, named individual. Thus the pet represents nature controlled by human love rather than brute force; this conception parallels middle-class ideals of parent–child relationships. Still, no matter how deeply embedded in society and culture the pet is, its potentially disturbing biosocial characteristics (pack behavior, sexual activity) can never be fully suppressed.

The same bourgeois culture that encouraged pet-keeping identified animal treatment as a social problem requiring direct intervention. Just as middle-class humanitarians in the nineteenth century rallied to the defense of laborers, slaves, prisoners, and others, so they organized anticruelty organizations and passed legislation against blood sport and cruelty to working animals. But their definition of animal welfare did not question the fundamental "rights" of human beings to use animals. For example, while some humane reformers expressed concern about the treatment of livestock en route to slaughter, most nineteenth-century Americans were fascinated, rather than appalled, by the application of industrial methods to slaughter. This change, along with the advent of "factory farming" in the twentieth century, transformed animal bodies into products and erased the visible link between animal death and food. The exploitation of animals—on farms, in slaughterhouses, in laboratories and other settings—was forgotten as it was industrialized and bureaucratized.

In the late twentieth century, increasing numbers of Americans are uncomfortable with the apparent ethical contradiction that allows us to treasure selected animals (our pets, privileged species such as bottlenose dolphins) while we experiment on, consume, or eradicate others. The richness and complexity of our symbolic discourse employing animals, and the depth of our private relationships with companion animals, contrast starkly with the failure of responsibility evident in our society's relations to them. This discomfort motivates the expanding animal protection movement, which builds upon the Humane Society of the United States founded in the 1950s. In the 1970s, however, the customary orientation of humane groups toward companion animals and the prosecution of individual acts of cruelty was challenged by the emergence of an "animals rights" movement led by groups such as People for the Ethical Treatment of Animals. These new activists found guidance in the thought of ethicists who moved away from older conceptions of stewardship and toward a model of animal rights that paralleled other RIGHTS movements of our time. Utilitarian philosopher Peter Singer provided the touchstone for this development in his book *Animal Liberation* (1975). He contended that most humans were guilty of "speciesism" and that "to discriminate against beings solely on the grounds of their species is a form of prejudice, immoral and indefensible" (p. 225). In Singer's view, the humane movement's appeal to sympathetic concern was inadequate to guarantee appropriate treatment of nonhuman animals; their rights needed to be based on "equal consideration of pain and pleasure" (p. 18).

Such arguments for animal rights have begun to redefine what constitutes cruelty to animals. They have been invaluable in attacking through legal means the most grotesque abuses of medical researchers, product testers, and industries where animal bodies are the raw materials for consumer goods from fur to meat. Yet the full animal rights perspective seems too absolute in its opposition to human intervention in the animal world. The most consistent Singerian position requires the end of traditional animal–human relations, such as the practice of husbandry in traditional communities. It implies an active assault on age-old cultural practices of human groups, in the name of nonintervention in the life of animals. Further, it neglects the fact that animals, despite their creative mental, sensory, and physical adaptations to the often deteriorating conditions of life, are dependent for their individual and species survival not only upon human self-control but on active human stewardship.

On the other hand, the limitations of past definitions of stewardship must also be acknowledged. The "stewardship" toward NATURE defined by religious dissenters in seventeenth- and eighteenth-century England was a departure from the concept of "dominion" based on the Old Testament, where humans ruled the natural world absolutely. Stewardship concurred with dominion in believing that animals were created to serve human beings, but it insisted on a kindly hierarchy; animals must be used carefully and with divine purposes in mind. Rehabilitating stewardship requires reconsidering, and perhaps abandoning, the metaphor of animals as servants, while embracing special responsibilities on the part of humankind. This new stewardship would integrate animal rights positions and older arguments about care and responsibility into a new model for ecological-cultural community. If such a model ever becomes the framework for a new practice, our symbolic discourse about animals, which pervades our speech and our thought, may be fundamentally reshaped. Future generations may shake their heads at the idea that their ancestors spoke easily of "killing two birds with one stone," or about "goring someone's ox."

KATHERINE GRIER

See also DARWINISM; SOCIOBIOLOGY.

FURTHER READING

Angus K. Gillespie and Jay Mechling, eds., *Animal Wildlife in Symbol and Story* (Knoxville: University of Tennessee Press, 1987).

Harriet Ritvo, *The Animal Estate: the English and Other Creatures in the Victorian Age* (Cambridge: Harvard University Press, 1987).

Andrew N. Rowan, ed., *Animals and People Sharing the World* (Hanover, N.H.: The University Press of New England, 1988).

James Serpell, *In the Company of Animals: a Study of Human–Animal Relationships* (Oxford: Blackwell, 1986).

Peter Singer, *Animal Liberation: a New Ethics for Our Treatment of Animals*, 2nd ed. (New York: New York Review of Books/Random House, 1990).

Keith Thomas, *Man and the Natural World: a History of the Modern Sensibility* (New York: Pantheon, 1983).

Anthony, Susan B. (b. Adams, Mass., Feb. 15, 1820; d. Rochester, N.Y., Mar. 13, 1906). Reformer. An early advocate of WOMEN'S RIGHTS to work and to control money, Anthony sought to build a broad political coalition among women. As editor of *The Revolution* (1868–70), she addressed working women's wages and hours, sexual violence, birth control, infanticide, prostitution, and dress reform. An ardent abolitionist, she helped after the Civil War to organize the National Woman Suffrage Association (1869), and devoted the rest of her life to the suffrage movement.

See also ELIZABETH CADY STANTON.

FURTHER READING
Kathleen Barry, *Susan B. Anthony: a Biography of a Singular Feminist* (New York: Oxford University Press, 1988).

Anti-Federalists History invariably favors winners. It has been the prerogative of the victors to write the history of America's great political struggles. It was the Federalists, the supporters of the U.S. Constitution, not the Anti-Federalist opponents of ratification, who triumphed in 1788, and the historical treatment of Anti-Federalism during most of the hundred years after ratification reflected the perspective of the victorious Federalists. Modern American culture, however, has been shaped by a strong current of populist sentiment; the emergence of left-leaning and right-leaning variants of POPULISM has led recent generations of Americans to reassess the contributions of the Anti-Federalists.

The Anti-Federalists were championed by the Progressive historians, who viewed them as the forerunners of Jeffersonian and Jacksonian Democracy, the first spokesmen for the tradition of agrarian democracy. During the Cold War, counter-Progressive historians and political scientists challenged this interpretation. For these revisionists, the Anti-Federalists were "men of little faith," narrow-minded politicians who opposed democracy and trusted neither society's rulers nor the people. Temporarily consigned to the margins of the American political tradition, Anti-Federalists were regarded as provincial politicians, proponents of a paranoid style in American life which made no lasting positive contribution to our political culture.

The emergence of an ideological approach to the study of political culture encouraged scholars to reconsider the nature of Anti-Federalist political thought. The revival of interest in civic REPUBLICANISM led historians and political theorists to examine the crucial role that Anti-Federalists played in the ideological struggles of the early republic. Drawing inspiration from this body of scholarship, a number of political and legal theorists at both ends of the contemporary political spectrum have used civic republican ideas as part of an effort to formulate a critique of postwar liberalism.

The most influential effort to bring Anti-Federalist ideas to bear on modern political and legal issues occurred during the Reagan administration. The doctrine of states' rights, once dismissed as a thinly veiled defense of segregation, was transmuted by the Reagan administration into the more palatable idea of new-federalism. Hostility to centralized government and to high levels of taxation, two other themes central to Reaganism, contained elements of a neo-Anti-Federalist rhetoric. The most explicit connection between Anti-Federalism and Reaganism can be discerned in the doctrine of original-intent jurisprudence, the idea that judges should be bound by the principles articulated by the Founders. Supporters of this philosophy urged judges to consult both the writings of Federalists and Anti-Federalists when seeking to discern the Framers' understanding of the CONSTITUTION and the BILL OF RIGHTS.

The most important scholarly consequence of the Reagan revolution in government is the recognition that discussions of the political thought of the Founders can no longer concentrate exclusively on the Federalists. It is now impossible to ignore the spirited intellectual dialogue between Anti-Federalists and Federalists over the meaning of American constitutionalism.

Supporters of the Constitution refined and elaborated their understanding of that document in response to Anti-Federalist criticism. The classic text for understanding the philosophy of the Constitution, *The Federalist*, was itself occasioned by Anti-Federalist attacks on the Constitution. The fact that the Anti-Federalists did not produce a single text comparable to the *Federalist* has prompted scholars to construct a comparable set of Anti-Federalist papers to match the *Federalist*. This move, dictated by the institutional and intellectual imperatives of modern American legal culture, has exacerbated the tendency to homogenize Anti-Federalist thought.

To speak of an Anti-Federalist party or a single Anti-Federalist agenda would be anachronistic, since the opposition to the Constitution brought together a loose coalition of different political factions. Despite the difficulty of discerning a single Anti-Federalist voice, it is possible to identify a range of common concerns among the Anti-Federalists. Many traditional republican ideas figured prominently in Anti-Federalist writings: hostility to standing armies, opposition to high levels of taxation and government corruption. Anti-Federalist ideology was not, however, uniformly republican in content. Important liberal themes also informed Anti-Federalist criticisms of the new Constitution. Some groups within the Anti-Federalist coalition articulated an interest-oriented theory of REPRESENTATION. Additional evidence for a liberal component to Anti-Federalist thought may be found in the nearly universal support for a written bill of rights as an indispensable safeguard for basic liberties.

The single most important aspect of the Anti-Federalist critique of the Constitution was the charge that the new government was an act of "consolidation," a move designed to weaken the states and endow a new centralized national government with vast powers. Anti-Federalists were localists who defended the individual states as the ideal embodiment of the small republic in which a relatively homogeneous citizenry participated actively in political affairs.

Anti-Federalist discourse allowed the opponents of the Constitution to unite behind what appeared to be a common critique. Yet this shared language disguised deep cleavages within the ranks of the Anti-Federalists. The defense of the small republic, a common Anti-Federalist rhetorical theme, provided a common conceptual vocabulary that allowed wealthy Virginia planters, newly empowered middle-class politicians in the mid-Atlantic, and plebeian farmers and artisans in the backcountry to unite in opposition to the Constitution. Localism was compatible with a number of different views on vital questions like representation. GEORGE MASON, a wealthy Virginia planter, and Elbridge Gerry, a prosperous New England merchant, each defended a decidedly elitist conception of representation. Spokesmen for the middling sort, including Pennsylvania's William Findley and New York's Abraham Yates, supported an egalitarian ideal that held up the rising middling sort as a model of republican virtue. Finally, farmers and artisans like the Carlisle rioters championed a plebeian ideology that embraced a radical majoritarian form of DEMOCRACY.

Anti-Federalist ideology contained nearly all of the tensions and contradictions present in late eighteenth-century political discourse. Many elements of Anti-Federalist ideology, including the tensions between liberal and republican ideals, influenced the evolution of Jeffersonianism. Perhaps the greatest testimony to the continuing vitality of Anti-Federalism has been the ability of modern groups on both left and right to find something of interest in their writings.

SAUL CORNELL

FURTHER READING

Saul A. Cornell, "The Changing Historical Fortunes of the Anti-Federalists," *Northwestern University Law Review* 84 (fall 1989): 39–73.

———, "Aristocracy Assailed: the Ideology of Backcountry Anti-Federalism," *Journal of American History* 76 (Mar. 1990): 1148–72.

Cecelia Kenyon, ed., *The Anti-Federalists* (Indianapolis: Bobbs-Merrill, 1966).

Jackson Turner Main, *The Anti-Federalists: Critics of the Constitution, 1781–1788* (Chapel Hill: University of North Carolina Press, 1961).

Herbert J. Storing, *The Complete Anti-Federalist*, 7 vols. (Chicago: University of Chicago Press, 1981).

Gordon S. Wood, *The Creation of the American Republic, 1776–1787* (Chapel Hill: University of North Carolina Press, 1969).

antislavery As but the lowest and most degrading of a range of labor dependencies and hierarchical social statuses, black slavery provoked little opposition during most of the colonial period—little more opposition, indeed, than slavery had for centuries provoked throughout the Western world. Yet chattel servitude's symbolic power as an extreme example of abject dependence on the will of another increasingly manifested itself during the third quarter of the eighteenth century, as white American colonists denounced the "slavery" into which Britain's arbitrary policies were leading them. Not a few of the patriot leaders went the additional step and accepted the full antislavery implications of their position. Joined by some black Americans, they deplored the contradictions between the Revolutionary case being made for inalienable natural rights and liberty for white men and the toleration of black chattel slavery in their midst.

This willingness to draw the connection between white and black rights took intellectual sustenance from a variety of secular and religious currents that had been converging since mid-century. These included not only John Locke's natural rights doctrine, but Montesquieu's antislavery interpretation of natural law, as well as Quaker and evangelical Christian antislavery themes insisting on universal spiritual equality.

Revolutionary antislavery bore its most tangible fruit in the northern states, which took decisive steps to remove black slavery through gradual emancipation and other measures. Yet the religious and republican antislavery principles referred to above played only a limited role in the emancipation process. In Pennsylvania and New York, slaves generally won their freedom only when it suited their owners' purposes and interests and when it became evident that freedom for blacks would not disrupt the order of white society. Because slavery was less pivotal in the North, both as an economic institution and as a system of racial control, white private property considerations and racial prejudice simply did not pose the formidable obstacles to emancipation that they already did in the late eighteenth-century South (*see also* PROSLAVERY THOUGHT).

Historians continue to debate why the widespread antislavery sentiment of the Revolutionary era eventuated in the compromises of the federal Constitution, rather than in a more serious and effective challenge to slavery in the South. Beyond debate is the dual legacy of the era's antislavery: on the one hand, northern blacks were left as a cheap and dependent labor force, hemmed in by economic, social, and political restrictions. On the other hand, chattel servitude was effectively sectionalized. All subsequent antislavery efforts would confront this dual legacy, including the most dubious of such efforts, the American Colonization Society (1817), a national organization that promoted the voluntary removal of free blacks to Africa. The society's membership included southern slaveholders who wanted to remove the troublesome and growing free black presence, thereby reducing the danger of servile insurrection and securing slavery. But the outlook of other ACS members illustrates the complexity of "antislavery." As David Brion Davis has argued, individuals like the Connecticut Congregational cleric Leonard Bacon, writing in the 1820s and 1830s, were as convinced as any of the new "immediatist" abolitionists that slavery possessed irremediable evils: that it generated the intellectual and moral degradation of the bondsmen, that it corrupted the morals of slaveowners, that it stunted and distorted southern economic development, that the institution itself carried the seeds of bloody race war. Yet in the wake of the Missouri crisis over slavery (1819–21), Bacon and other of the more antislavery colonizationists, concerned with national harmony, defended gradual manumission. Bacon and others believed that given the intractability of racial prejudice in America, blacks could never be successfully amalgamated into American society.

The ACS enjoyed considerable national appeal during the 1820s. Its early critics included not merely the most militant defenders of slavery but also free black Americans who denounced the ACS from an antislavery perspective. Blacks insisted that colonizationists acquiesced in and contributed to white racial prejudice. If free blacks were forced by the worsening racial climate to leave the country, the enslavement of the most unfortunate members of the race would be perpetuated.

Some white advocates of colonization, including the youthful WILLIAM LLOYD GARRISON, listened to these black voices, and the early 1830s witnessed the emergence of an aggressive northern-based, anticolonization crusade for uncompensated and "immediate" abolition, organized and led by Garrison and others. Stripping away the complexities of south-ern slavery that had paralyzed previous antislavery efforts, abolitionists reduced the institution to the level of personal sin. Every individual who engaged in "man stealing" was guilty of blaspheming divine authority by establishing his own absolute dominion over his fellow creatures. Strongly influenced by the tenets of evangelical religion, the early abolitionists saw their task as one of nonviolent "moral suasion": to persuade slaveholders to seek immediate repentance for, and abandonment of, their sin. Antislavery in both America and Britain had in earlier decades included various advocates of immediatist themes. But the ongoing southwestern expansion of slavery had only seemed to further weaken the Enlightenment-inspired premise of gradualists that historical and natural forces, moving in the direction of "progress," would eventually put an end to slavery. Post-1830 immediatism heralded the contrary need for drastic human intervention.

Abolitionists disagreed about how "immediate" emancipation could actually be, but they did envision the eradication of southern slavery within a decade. They also believed their campaign of education could within that period end racial prejudice and discrimination in the free states. Abolitionists' millennial expectations regarding white racial attitudes may now seem naive, but they had imbibed the early nineteenth century's romantic faith in the individual's power to effect change. Immediatists insisted that only by regenerating individuals could they reform or dismantle oppressive social institutions. Chattel slaves themselves, their intellects and souls brutalized and crushed, were the great exception to the abolitionist rule of individual autonomy and power, although even bondsmen might somehow find the mental and spiritual resources to throw off their oppression in bloody revolt.

Through an expanding matrix of transatlantic organizations and literature, American abolitionists largely succeeded in discrediting the ACS. But by 1838, although the American Anti-Slavery Society had grown impressively, it was clear that moral suasion had failed. Slaveholders remained impervious to the appeals of the immediatist "outsiders." Northern churches and other institutions in the free states had not committed themselves either to antislavery or to ending northern racial prejudice and discriminatory practices. Whites feared that "unqualified" as well as "immediate" emancipation would free over two million more blacks to wander as vagabonds and paupers, although many abolitionists supported "benevolent supervision" to help prepare ex-slaves for freedom and civil equality. Frustrated by the North's temporizing, WENDELL PHILLIPS concluded in 1842 that "Northern opinion, the weight of Northern power, is the real slave-*holder* of America" (*Liberator*, Feb. 4, 1842).

Phillips, a leading member of the Garrisonian contingent of abolitionists, urged dissolving the Union; southern masters would be *forced* to give up their human property without the support of the federal government and the people of the free states. Indeed, the various paths taken by antislavery radicalism during the 1840s and 1850s—disunionism, direct political action and appeals to state power, "righteous" violence in support of fugitive and insurrectionary slaves, even the black separatist movement—reflected the failure of abolitionist moral suasion in the previous decade. This is not to deny the genuine, if unintended, impact of the abolitionist crusade during the 1830s. Immediatist denunciations of the "sin" of slavery provoked the animosities of the South, prompting efforts to deny abolitionists the right of petition, use of the mails, and freedom of the press. Although abolitionists remained a more or less "hated minority" in the North throughout the thirties, their agitation goaded the South into suppressing the basic liberties of northern *whites*, which in turn fomented more widespread antisouthern feeling in the North.

The history of antislavery during the 1840s and 1850s illustrates how radical demands need be watered down to win mass acceptance in America. Leading members of the Liberty Party (1839), the first political party based on antislavery principles, continued to oppose slavery on religious and humanitarian grounds, and to focus on the bondsmen as the primary victims of the institution. But by invoking the concept of the "slave power" and attacking slavery as a force destructive to the interests of northern and southern white nonslaveholders alike, the Liberty Party also helped mainstream antislavery become more "white centered" and less concerned with "the wrongs of the negro through slavery." Unlike the Liberty Party and the abolition societies, the Free Soil Party (1848) did not even profess to support "interference" with slavery in the states where it already existed. The party instead ran on the Wilmot Proviso principle that slavery should only be prevented from spreading into newly acquired western territories. And consistent with the racism of many Free Soilers, who would exclude not merely "degrading" slave labor but all blacks from the territories, the party's platform ignored the basic abolitionist demand that blacks in the free states be granted equal rights.

The dilution of antislavery principles in Freesoilism reflected the influence of prominent antislavery insurgents from the Whig and Democratic parties. The Republican Party leadership, like that of the earlier Free Soil coalition, included individuals who sympathized with southern slaves and northern free blacks. The reception accorded *Uncle Tom's Cabin* (1852) showed the reservoir of sentimental and humanitarian feeling for blacks among northern whites. But the Republican Party nonetheless sustained the central antislavery emphases of Freesoilism. By the late 1850s ABRAHAM LINCOLN was warning of a second Dred Scott decision that would legalize black chattel slavery in the free states as well as the territories; he was also publicizing southern proslavery claims that all laboring people, white as well as black, made "natural" slaves. The North's ideological preparation for the CIVIL WAR included an ironic reversal of the pre-Revolutionary War pattern, in which white colonists' republican fears of their own "enslavement" had generated increased sensitivity to the injustice of black chattel servitude. The moral and religious preoccupation of radical abolitionists with the evils that slavery and prejudice inflicted on blacks had been gradually secularized and otherwise transformed into a more palatable antislavery message for the masses of northern whites: the dangers that black slavery and an aristocratic slave power, bent on untenable geographic expansion, posed to their own economic well-being and "republican" liberties.

Whether the Republican principle of restricting chattel servitude to the slave states amounted to a policy of "gradual" abolition was among the many questions mooted by the Civil War. Chattel slavery everywhere within the United States was immediately abolished by the Thirteenth Amendment. But because emancipation came only as a result of armed conflict, and without the transformation in white American racial values sought by abolitionists, blacks made only limited advances in the era of Reconstruction.

Early American feminism provides the clearest example of how the crusade against black servitude was a stimulus for other reform movements that widened the concept of "antislavery" to apply to their own attacks on perceived inequities. Efforts by white middle-class females in the 1830s to participate as equal partners with men in abolition activities acted —in part precisely because those efforts met with resistance from many men both inside and outside the abolition movement—to sensitize these women to their own condition of subordination and "slavery."

Abolitionism's relationship to the tolerance of racial inequalities in the North remains more problematic. The paternalistic attitudes and prejudices of white male and white female abolitionists impeded their cooperation with black abolitionists. Jane and William

Pease have gone so far as to generalize that there were two abolitionisms: a black abolitionism that reflected bitter familiarity with the quasi-freedom that was the lot of northern blacks, and a white abolitionism that tended to conceptualize slavery and freedom as "polar absolutes" and had no comparable antipathy to the existing intermediate conditions of quasi-freedom.

White abolitionism's tendency to conflate legal self-ownership—bare legal freedom—with authentic, substantive freedom raises the most provocative issue in recent antislavery historiography: the issue of abolitionist insensitivity, both in Britain and the United States, to the inequalities of *class* under early industrial capitalism. Abolitionist attacks on chattel slavery established the frame of reference for labor and socialist movements that deplored the "wage slavery" of factory workers and other free laborers under capitalism. But abolitionists themselves characteristically rejected the parallel. Predominantly of the middle class, they exalted the individual self-discipline and autonomy demanded by competitive market societies. They deplored not only the intellectual and moral deprivations and the sexual degradations suffered by slaves, but the bondsmen's lack of incentive to work as diligently and efficiently as workers who owned themselves. The tendency of American antislavery to legitimate the condition and mythologize the opportunities of laborers in the free states grew more pronounced during the escalating sectional conflict of the 1850s, as antislavery became, under the Republicans, more resolutely a doctrine of northern nationalism.

Beyond agreeing that antislavery was scarcely, either in its origins or in its continuing evolution, a consciously cynical attempt to advance capitalist class interests, historians are engaged in a sophisticated debate as to what forces *did* explain abolitionists' selective humanitarianism. Glossing over class inequalities in the North was hardly the exclusive province of abolitionists; there were innumerable privileged and wealthy middle-class northerners who were bitterly hostile to both the objectives and the tactics of abolitionists but who nonetheless shared the abolitionist faith in a competitive economic order. Radical opposition to slavery only reinforced a tendency to sanction emerging relationships between northern capitalists and workers. Conversely, the white artisans and other northern elements who were most critical of those same relationships could, like working-class Britons, themselves embrace antislavery; their antagonism to exploitation fueled hostility toward tyrannical slaveholders, if not necessarily identification with black slaves. But if the northern workers, shopkeepers, and others who signed petitions protesting suppression of the abolitionists' civil rights made up an antislavery "rank and file," their antislavery commitment was hardly so relentless as that of the evangelically inspired abolitionist activists.

As agitators marginalized from the centers of northern power, few American abolitionists remained completely uncritical of northern labor conditions and class inequalities. The fact that abolitionists always considered their greatest antagonists in the North to be the wealthy and influential no doubt facilitated their willingness to make some intellectual concessions to the radical spokesmen for northern labor. Abolitionists argued that restoring self-ownership to black slaves was the basic reform, not the only reform.

By highlighting chattel slavery as an unacceptable form of labor exploitation, antislavery did function to legitimate class inequalities in the North, but one might also speculate, finally, that antislavery was not essential to that process of legitimation. Indeed, if antislavery, and its idealization of the formal autonomy enjoyed by legally free labor, acted in the interests of capitalist hegemony, so in certain ways did the presence of chattel slavery. It was no coincidence that the labor movement was weakest in the antebellum South, where employers could replace restive white workers with bondsmen they either owned or hired. Marx did well to note, writing to François Lafargue in November 1866, a year after the Civil War's end, that "labor in white skin cannot emancipate itself where the black skin is branded" (in Padover, ed., *Karl Marx on America and the Civil War*, pp. 274–5).

JONATHAN A. GLICKSTEIN

See also RACE; RESPONSIBILITY.

FURTHER READING

Thomas Bender, ed., *The Antislavery Debate: Capitalism and Abolitionism as a Problem in Historical Interpretation* (Berkeley: University of California Press, 1992).

David Brion Davis, "Reconsidering the Colonization Movement: Leonard Bacon and the Problem of Evil," *Intellectual History Newsletter* 14 (1992): 3–16.

Martin Duberman, ed., *The Antislavery Vanguard: New Essays on the Abolitionists* (Princeton: Princeton University Press, 1965).

Eric Foner, *Free Soil, Free Labor, Free Men: the Ideology of the Republican Party before the Civil War* (New York: Oxford University Press, 1970).

George M. Fredrickson, *The Black Image in the White Mind: the Debate on Afro-American Character and Destiny, 1817–1914* (New York: Harper and Row, 1971).

Alan M. Kraut, ed., *Crusaders and Compromisers: Essays on the Relationship of the Antislavery Struggle to the Antebellum Party System* (Westport: Greenwood, 1983).

The Liberator (Boston), 1831–65.

Gary B. Nash, *Race and Revolution* (Madison: Madison House, 1990).

Gary B. Nash and Jean R. Soderlund, *Freedom by Degrees: Emancipation in Pennsylvania and its Aftermath* (New York: Oxford University Press, 1991).

Saul K. Padover, ed., *Karl Marx on America and the Civil War* (New York: McGraw-Hill, 1972).

Jane H. Pease and William H. Pease, *They Who Would Be Free: Blacks' Search for Freedom, 1830–1861* (New York: Atheneum, 1974).

Lewis Perry and Michael Fellman, eds., *Antislavery Reconsidered: New Perspectives on the Abolitionists* (Baton Rouge: Louisiana State University Press, 1979).

apocalyptic literature From a Greek term meaning an unveiling of hidden truths, the apocalyptic genre arose in Jewish religious life ca. 200 B.C. and flowed into early Christianity, where it flourished until ca.100 A.D. The best-known apocalypses are those included in the Bible: parts of Daniel, Ezekiel, and Isaiah in the Old Testament; the so-called "Little Apocalypse" ascribed to Jesus in Mark 13, and the awe-inspiring Book of Revelation, the Apocalypse of John, with which the Bible closes.

In diverse guises, the apocalyptic view of history has influenced American thought from the first European contact to the present. Indeed, Christopher Columbus himself, an avid student of prophecy, viewed his voyages as fulfillments of God's plan for human history. A century and a half later, the New England Puritans shared the apocalyptic hopes that pervaded English PURITANISM down to the Stuart Restoration in 1660. INCREASE MATHER, his son COTTON MATHER, and other New England divines immersed themselves in eschatology, sometimes contending that the New Jerusalem (Rev. 21:2) would arise in America. During the Great Awakening, JONATHAN EDWARDS speculated that the revivals sweeping America heralded the onset of the Millennium (see MILLENNIALISM). The American Revolution and the emergence of an independent United States gave rise to a secularized apocalypticism, proclaimed by TIMOTHY DWIGHT and others, in which the new nation would lead the world toward a millennial condition. In various forms, this civic millennialism would shape the American sense of MISSION for the next two centuries.

Meanwhile, in the 1830s, a self-taught itinerant New Yorker, William Miller (1782–1849), on the basis of his reading of the Book of Daniel, began to preach Jesus's Second Coming "about the year 1843." Other Millerites set a precise date: October 22, 1844. The Millerite fiasco discredited date setting, creating a receptive climate for the dispensational teachings of the Britisher John Darby (1800–1882). The present "Church Age," Darby taught, marshalling ingenious

scriptural proofs, will end with the Rapture, when all true believers will meet Christ in the air, followed by Antichrist's seven-year rule (the Tribulation); the Second Coming and the Battle of Armageddon; Christ's thousand-year earthly reign ("the Kingdom Age" or Millennium); and the Last Judgment. Cyrus Scofield (1843–1921) embedded Darby's scheme in his vastly influential *Reference Bible* (1909). While Catholic, Lutheran, and Reformed groups remained firmly amillennial, and liberal Protestant progressives embraced a "postmillennialist" faith in Christ's arrival *after* the thousand-year Kingdom, *premillennialism* (the return of Christ *before* the Millennium) flourished among evangelical, fundamentalist, and Pentecostal groups. After World War II, itinerant evangelists, radio and television preachers, schools like Dallas Theological Seminary and Chicago's Moody Bible Institute, and scores of paperback writers promulgated variants of Darby's scheme. Hal Lindsey's *The Late Great Planet Earth* (1970), a popularization of dispensationalism, was *the* nonfiction bestseller in the United States in the 1970s. Half or more of contemporary Americans, polls suggest, believe that the Bible does indeed provide an explicit plan of history's end.

Prophecy expounders—more often amateurs than trained theologians or settled ministers—use biblical apocalyptic to give meaning and order to history. They find a place in their end-time scenarios for contemporary political entities and social realities: the atomic bomb, Russia, China, Israel, the United States, the European Community, and the rise of a global, computerized economic order (foretold, they teach, in Revelation 13 with its cryptic reference to 666, the number of the "Beast," or Antichrist). A multiplicity of current trends are seen as "signs" of the end. As the twentieth-century nears its close, apocalypticism remains vigorously alive in American popular religion.

Apocalypticism has also influenced ostensibly secular works of U.S. social thought, especially at times of social tension and anxiety about the future. The catastrophist and utopian genres that flourished in the turbulent Gilded Age offer a case in point. For example, *Caesar's Column: a Story of the Twentieth Century* (1891) by IGNATIUS DONNELLY, with its horrific images of a final bloody denouement to American history, is clearly in the apocalyptic tradition, though with class warfare rather than the clash of demonic and heavenly forces as the source of the final conflict. William T. Stead's *If Christ Came to Chicago* (1894), by contrast, with its vision of a purified social order and of Chicago as the shining New Jerusalem, harked back to the millennialist strand of the apocalyptic vision.

Post-World War II writers who warned of imminent nuclear holocaust similarly exploited the apocalypticism latent in American thought. Indeed, Bible passages such as II Peter 3:10 ("[T]he elements shall melt with fervent heat: the earth also and the works that are therein shall be burned up") took on new resonance after 1945. Jonathan Schell's *The Fate of the Earth* (1982), with its vision of earth as "A Kingdom of Insects and Grasses" after World War III, offered a secularized version of John's memorable images of a burning sun, falling stars, bloody seas, hideous sores, and hordes of plague-bearing insects.

As environmental and population concerns intensified in the 1970s, a flourishing secular-apocalyptic industry produced such works as Alvin Toffler's *Future Shock* (1970), Barry Commoner's *The Closing Circle* (1971), Lefton Stavrianos's *The Promise of the Coming Dark Age* (1976), and a spate of similar titles. But despite their structural similarities, the religious-apocalyptic and the secular-apocalyptic genres offered very different messages: in the former, the end is foreordained and one can do nothing to avert it except to assure one's personal salvation and thus escape the horrors to come; in the latter, hope remains—collective human action can still avert the disasters that loom, whether nuclear, environmental, or demographic.

With both religious apocalyptic and a derivative secularized apocalyptic flourishing as the portentous year 2000 approaches, this ancient mode of organizing experience and of finding meaning in history is likely to remain an influential strand in American popular thought for many decades to come.

PAUL BOYER

See also EVANGELICALISM; FUNDAMENTALISM.

FURTHER READING

Michael Barkun, "Divided Apocalypse: Thinking about the End in Contemporary America," *Soundings* 66 (fall 1983).

Ruth H. Bloch, *Visionary Republic: Millennial Themes in American Thought, 1756–1800* (New York: Cambridge University Press, 1985).

Paul Boyer, *When Time Shall Be No More: Prophecy Belief in Modern American Culture* (Cambridge: Harvard University Press, 1992).

Nathan O. Hatch, *The Sacred Cause of Liberty: Republican Thought and the Millennium in Revolutionary New England* (New Haven: Yale University Press, 1977).

Ronald L. Numbers and Jonathan M. Butler, eds., *The Disappointed: Millerism and Millenarianism in the Nineteenth Century* (Bloomington: Indiana University Press, 1987).

Ernest Sandeen, *The Roots of Fundamentalism: British and American Millenarianism, 1800–1930* (Chicago: University of Chicago Press, 1970).

Ernest Lee Tuveson, *Redeemer Nation: the Idea of America's Millennial Role* (Chicago: University of Chicago Press, 1968).

Timothy P. Weber, *Living in the Shadow of the Second Coming: American Premillennialism, 1875–1925* (New York, Oxford University Press, 1979).

architecture Despite considerable attention to stylistic details, architectural debate is primarily concerned with more substantive intellectual issues such as rigor and originality, expression and effect. Questions of national idioms also come into play, even though stylistic fashion usually transcends such boundaries. Some commentators praised an indigenous functionalism or inventiveness in the United States, while others castigated its kitsch or damned the prevalence of tedious mass production. In many minds the country's provincial isolation encouraged ingenuity, unhampered by official culture. Regionalism could flourish, maintained through a diversity of vernacular landscapes. For others, provincial status signified America's exclusion from cosmopolitan culture.

Such contested interpretations affected architects' thoughts about their discipline, which constitutes one definition of "architecture." The history of architecture has long been recounted in semibiblical terms, as a tale of transcendent purpose, godlike genius, and pure form. By this account, architecture is limited to the uncompromised creations of a few exceptional figures. Indeed, many architects today would claim that their art, like painting or sculpture, is primarily a matter of representation, best captured in drawings rather than buildings.

In direct opposition stands a broader, more inclusive definition, one that views architecture as the full spectrum of the built environment. The populist aspect of this approach accepts commercial success and mass appeal, sometimes using them as standards of worth. An aesthetic dimension emerges from this vantage, at times resolutely simple, based on pragmatic problem-solving rather than poetic freedom, but equally capable of lighthearted play. Generations of architects have drawn inspiration from this vernacular tradition, especially the simple shapes of barns, the functional massing of factories, and the exuberant surfaces of roadside commerce. Some even proclaimed the need for a distinctive national character in American design—though only architects, at once educated and independent, were deemed capable of the challenge.

Professional architects are still responsible for only a fraction—perhaps five percent—of the American built environment. They recognize the need to expand both their authority and actual commissions. Yet the discourse of American architects has tended to be narrowly self-referential. With the cultural superiority of a Victorian elite or the self-conscious estrangement of a modernist avant-garde, most architects dismiss the public's preferences. Instead they continue to search for a distinctive architectural culture.

The great majority of American architects has looked to Europe for direction and validation. Europe embodied a theoretically rigorous approach to design, captured not only in buildings, but also in treatises that announced artistic intentions in absolute terms. Such polemics presuppose the prestige of an academy or the single-mindedness of an avant-garde challenge to authority. The polemical manifesto, insisting on a single aesthetic and charging it with singular meaning, is therefore a recent phenomenon in the United States.

Europe also evoked history, seen positively as the mainstay of culture and the canon of architectural precedents, or negatively as the weight of the past. During the nineteenth century, American architects, like their counterparts in Europe, claimed that a precise knowledge of classical, medieval, and Renaissance antecedents distinguished their work from the flamboyant eclecticism of "heathen" builders and amateurs. When professional programs in architecture were established at American universities (beginning with MIT in 1865, then increasing in number at the turn of the century), an extensive history curriculum gave them legitimacy within the liberal arts curricula. Then, with the rise of modernism in the 1930s, history lost its preeminent position—first to the social sciences, especially studies of psychological perception and social interaction, and more recently to literary criticism and deconstructionist philosophy.

To be sure, this pattern is familiar. Themes that reverberate in the larger domain of American culture manifest themselves in architecture as well. Pragmatic aversion to rules and universal principles has generally prevailed, sometimes resulting in the flaunting of idiosyncratic designs, but more often in the insistence on adapting to particular circumstances. American architecture has usually emphasized a tie to the land—the particular site, the idealized garden or landscape, or simply the open road—although the constraints of actual ecologies are all too often given short shrift. Americans have long harbored a belief in the power of the environment to affect (or, more passively, to reflect) people's beliefs and actions, for good or evil. Finally, commercialism is virtually synonymous with American architecture. The profession is loathe to acknowledge the self-promotion of prominent designers, competition for fame and commissions, the strong role of clients, the prevalence of business-oriented commissions, and the building as display—advertising owner and architect—yet these realities are conspicuous.

An extensive literature has presented architecture to the American public. At every stage consumer education preceded artistic rigor. And alongside the handbooks and treatises stands an important legacy of intellectuals and journalists who have used architectural metaphors and descriptions to speak about more general political and cultural issues.

The first American books on architecture, beginning in the late eighteenth century, closely followed the format of English handbooks for builders. Colonial carpenters and master builders were aware of European fashions and scholarship; so too, of course, were potential clients. Yet Americans viewed architecture as a practical "science," even more than an art of refinement. Authors taught basic techniques and encouraged adaptation to function. Empirical information prevailed over abstract theory. Establishment of the republic soon engendered claims of a distinct national character for American architecture. Books further modified presentations of the classical orders to emphasize convenient, economical construction, linking simplification with democratic values.

Both Benjamin Latrobe and his friend, THOMAS JEFFERSON, considered architecture a skilled art and a formative influence on society. Together they represent two poles of Enlightenment thought in America. Latrobe, trained in Europe, is often identified as the country's first professional architect; he also undertook engineering commissions such as the Philadelphia waterworks. The elegant geometries of his buildings reflect the rationalism of late neoclassicism. Jefferson, in contrast, the last of the amateur-gentlemen designers, was an idealist seeking to educate the fledgling nation. His own architectural work, most notably the University of Virginia, encompassed those ambitions within an orderly composition harmoniously set in the landscape.

Westward expansion raised questions about the respective virtues of a coherent unity or multiple variations, rules or invention. Those who worried about the breakdown of social hierarchy and the frenzied pace of life in American cities looked for stability to churches, town halls, and, most emphatically, dwellings. Addressing these issues, the pattern books of Andrew Jackson Downing Americanized the style and theories of English Romanticism, whereby beauty resided in the power of images to provide a succession of mental associations. The intensity of the sublime risked social disruption, he argued, while the merely beautiful could instill order. Downing's Gothic Revival dwellings were accordingly keyed to the appropriate scale of a family's class, with materials that fit harmoniously into their surroundings.

The house, from Downing onward, provided a focus for wide-ranging discourses on design principles and the nature of American life. The decades after the Civil War witnessed a growing interest in the domestic sphere, differentiated by class, glorifying the ideal of individualism, yet suggesting equality through parallel styles. Fashionable architects built grand resort "cottages" in a rambling plan and mixture of materials that has come to be known as the Shingle Style; their city mansions imitated medieval castles and Renaissance palazzi. For middle-class clients, builders produced the first suburban houses that claimed to "express" the family: a gender-based formula that conveyed the status of the man and the domestic refinements of the woman, in both specific and generic terms.

Single-family houses would continue to be the mode through which most architects explored their aesthetic and cultural ideas. In his domestic architecture FRANK LLOYD WRIGHT, this country's most famous architect, extolled the organic ideal of American architecture and experimented with new technologies. While each commission was unique and intensely private, he continued to explore schemes for likeminded communities. With astonishing skill, both architectural and discursive, Wright epitomized a new level of architectural creativity and self-promotion.

Wright's mentor, LOUIS SULLIVAN, brought mystical poetry and artistic elegance to the most technically challenging new type of building, the skyscraper. Again calling for a distinctly national architecture, Sullivan sought to find the correct proportions and embellishments for commercial office buildings of unprecedented height. His formula was eloquent, at once classical and modern: the restraint of the tall "shaft" (likening the structure to a Greek column) would be balanced by ornamentation at the roof (or capital) and the base. More than formal principles were at issue here, for Sullivan hoped to humanize contact with the corporate buildings that were transforming Americans' lives.

Sullivan and Wright, like countless other American architects, claimed to be modern in that they were unimpaired by historical styles, responsive to new technologies and social conditions. During the interwar years the term MODERNISM became more restrictive, codified and made exclusive to a small coterie who asserted dogmatic principles: a rational gridplan, the elimination of all ornament, the expression of structure, and the belief that such architecture would issue in a more egalitarian, less parochial society that transcended differences of place and culture.

A single event crystalized architectural modernism as a narrowly formal paradigm in the United States. In 1932 New York's Museum of Modern Art held an exhibition on "Modern Architecture," curated by Philip Johnson and Henry-Russell Hitchcock. *The International Style* (1932), their short text written in conjunction with the show, suggested a heroic role for architecture as the driving force of a modern society—yet all that mattered was the elegant, metaphoric expression of anonymity and control. This book, along with Sigfried Giedion's *Space, Time, and Architecture* (1941), based on a series of lectures given at Harvard, defined new goals for the American profession. Both texts gave new prominence to museums and schools, rather than the market or the office-apprentice system, as the terms for judging architecture became increasingly abstract, removed from the public's actual experience of buildings or spaces.

Invoking the reductionist imagery of American modernism, postwar urban renewal dramatically changed the face of many American cities. Downtown slums and working-class neighborhoods were demolished, the land transformed into pristine complexes of high-rise office buildings and apartments. Extensive networks of highways connected these enclaves to sprawling suburbs. Validated by government bureaucracy and private business, a rationalized landscape promised to provide the American dream of harmonious equality.

Almost simultaneous with this monotonous postwar landscape came a call for greater expression among architects, as if to deny their growing obligations to corporate clients. Eero Saarinen's TWA terminal, Louis Kahn's Salk Institute, and Mies van der Rohe's Seagram building suggested a new vision of monumentality. Rational structure could become romantic, institutions could assume a public role, and architects could regain their authority as creative form-givers.

The 1960s witnessed further assaults on the complacency of modernism. Jane Jacobs's vehement tract, *The Death and Life of Great American Cities* (1961), blamed modern architecture for the demise of urban neighborhoods (*see also* URBANISM). Some architects also criticized the brutal aesthetic and social sterility of high-rise public-housing projects and vast suburban enclaves. Robert Venturi's *Complexity and Contradiction in Architecture* burst forth in 1966, calling for visual richness and an acceptance of cultural diversity in architectural design. History reentered the architectural curriculum: formal parallels with historical buildings from both vernacular and high art traditions provided "justifications" for modern designs.

Intersecting these trends came the emergence of the movement for historic preservation, which soon gained the legal power to prevent demolition of valuable buildings. Adaptive reuse helped give thematic focus and commercial animation to urban neighborhoods. Design soon followed with a nostalgic fiction of multiethnic history in "festival marketplaces" along inner-city waterfronts or colorful classical imagery in new public buildings. American POSTMODERNISM proclaimed a search for forms that could awaken collective memory.

The past decade has witnessed a flood of books and journals about architecture. Architectural firms underwrite their own hagiographic "monographs," suggesting a new level of self-promotion. Other texts seek to charge the discipline with "theory" that would bolster the self-image of an architectural intelligentsia, hermetically removed from the concerns—indeed, the comprehension—of the public. Deconstructionism has launched an assault on conventional ways of experiencing space and, by association, cultural institutions. Themes of fragmentation, collage, display, transgression, and an ephemeral, often narcissistic *jouissance* dominate the literature, while metaphoric expressions of these qualities characterize recent design.

It would be reductive to insist on a single style or stance in a domain so complex. Architecture is indisputably an art, and as such deserves the freedom to explore formal and poetic concerns. But it can never be entirely the private realm of the designer. The American pragmatic tradition provides a base that should not be readily dismissed. Indeed, the glory of architecture is its dynamic multiplicity: it extends from architect to client to public sphere in unpredictable ways, affecting the lives and expectations of all.

GWENDOLYN WRIGHT

FURTHER READING

Giorgio Ciucci et al., *The American City from the Civil War to the New Deal*, trans. Barbara L. La Penta (Cambridge: MIT Press, 1979).

David Harvey, "Postmodernism in the City: Architecture and Urban Design," in Harvey, *The Condition of Postmoderism* (Cambridge: Blackwell, 1989).

William H. Jordy and William H. Pierson Jr., *American Buildings and Their Architects*, 4 vols. (Garden City: Doubleday, 1972–80).

Leland M. Roth, *A Concise History of American Architecture* (New York: Harper and Row, 1979).

Gwendolyn Wright, *Moralism and the Model Home: Domestic Architecture and Cultural Conflict in Chicago, 1870–1913* (Chicago: University of Chicago Press, 1980).

Arendt, Hannah (b. Hanover, Germany, Oct. 14, 1906; d. New York, N.Y., Dec. 4, 1975). Raised by assimilated, middle-class Jewish parents, Arendt grew up in Königsberg, Kant's city and the capital of East Prussia. Although her parents were committed social democrats, she displayed little interest in politics as a young woman. In the 1920s she studied at three leading German universities—Marburg, Freiburg, and Heidelberg—with the three great German philosophers of that decade, Martin Heidegger (with whom she had a brief love affair), Edmund Husserl, and Karl Jaspers (with whom she wrote a doctoral dissertation on the concept of love in St. Augustine).

Arendt's career, as well as her indifference to politics, was utterly transformed by the rise of Nazism, which led her to an intensified awareness of herself as a Jew and to affiliation with the Zionist resistance to German anti-Semitism. With Adolf Hitler's rise to power, she fled Germany for Paris, where she helped find refuge for young Jews in Palestine. There she also completed a biography (unpublished until 1958) of Rahel Varnhagen and her salon of the Enlightenment period. The book, subtitled *The Life of a Jewess*, was both a historical study and an effort at self-definition.

In Germany in 1929 Hannah Arendt had married Günther Stern, and in Paris she was reunited with him as a fellow exile. But the marriage soon collapsed, and in the mid-1930s Arendt fell in love with a German communist refugee, Heinrich Blücher, a gifted autodidact who was to be her last great teacher and lifelong companion. They were married in 1940, and after a series of harrowing escapes from French internment camps for German nationals, emigrated to New York City, where they took up residence in May 1941.

Arendt worked in relative obscurity in the 1940s, reflecting on the contemporary political catastrophes that would form the context of all her thinking. With the publication of *The Origins of Totalitarianism* (1951), the single most important effort by an American intellectual to interpret and explain the principal horrors of the twentieth century, she was thrust into the public eye, where she remained—sometimes uncomfortably—for the remainder of her life. Often incoherent as history but compelling as cautionary nightmare, *Origins* characterized totalitarianism—Nazism in Germany and Stalinism in the Soviet Union—as a novel form of politics. It was a "radical evil" in which movement leaders deployed manipulation and, above all, terror to transform an atomized mass society of lonely, uprooted, superfluous human beings into the new order envisioned by their ideology.

At the core of Arendt's thinking—implicit in *The Origins of Totalitarianism* and explicit in her most abstract work of political theory, *The Human Condition* (1958)—was what she termed the "love of the world." In the latter volume she advanced her own brand of *Existenz* philosophy centered on human being-in-the-world, particularly its active dimensions (the *vita activa*). Drawing on classical republicanism, Arendt divided human activity into the *labor* necessary to sustain life, which the Greeks confined to the private sphere, the *work* required to fabricate durable objects, and *action* in which the uniqueness and freedom of the human species and of each human individual was manifested in the public speech, deliberation, and heroic deeds of citizens. She used these distinctions not only to celebrate ancient participatory politics but to condemn modernity (and such modernists as Marx) for blurring the boundaries between private and public life. "Labor" was not the source of ultimate value, as Marx held. By allowing such "social" concerns as the material welfare of the poor to dominate politics, Marx had literally domesticated the public arena, deprived it of its distinctive practice of virtue. (*See also* AUTHORITY.)

On the other hand, in *On Revolution* (1963) Arendt applauded modern revolutions, in which she saw momentary reincarnations of classical politics in constitutional conventions, communes, councils, and soviets. She reserved her greatest praise for the American Revolution because it was least preoccupied with social concerns, and in essays such as those collected in *Crises of the Republic* (1972) she sounded an alarm against the squandering of the American revolutionary tradition evident in such documents as the Pentagon Papers. At the same time, she wrote approvingly of the glimmers of participatory citizenship she saw in the civil rights and anti-war movements.

Despite her eminence among American intellectuals, Arendt always regarded herself as a Jewish "pariah"—a stance of self-conscious marginality and resistance. She was a severe critic of the myth of the Jew as eternal victim and bitterly condemned Jewish "parvenus" who eschewed demands for political equality in favor of assimilationism and social ingratiation. This self-conception informed her controversial report on the trial of Adolf Eichmann, *Eichmann in Jerusalem* (1963) (*see also* HOLOCAUST), which elicited outrage from critics—especially Jewish critics. They were angered by her argument that the evil of Nazi desk-murderers such as Eichmann was not willfully malicious but bureaucratically "banal," and they were incensed at her harsh indictment of European Jewish elites for participating in the collaborative Jewish Councils (*Judenräte*) that facilitated deportation to the camps.

At the end of her life, Arendt turned from the *vita activa* to the *vita contemplativa*, to a study of the internal dialogue of thinking, willing, and judging, which given the centrality of Kant to her reflections on these matters brought her full circle to Königsberg. Unfortunately, at the time of her death she had yet to begin the third section of this meditation on *The Life of the Mind* (1978), the consideration of judgment that promised to bridge the realms of contemplation and action.

As Margaret Canovan has said in *Hannah Arendt: a Reinterpretation of her Political Thought*, "Hannah Arendt is one of the great outsiders of twentieth-century political thought, at once strikingly original and disturbingly unorthodox" (p. 1). Few have shared her austere and distant ideal of public life, her Hellenic nostalgia, her contempt for the "social," or her rendering of Jewish identity, yet fewer still can gainsay the originality and durability of the insights to which her unique sensibility led her. In her preface to *Men in Dark Times* (1968), a collection of portraits of writers she admired, Arendt remarked that "even in the darkest times we have a right to expect some illumination" (p. ix). In the dark times after Auschwitz, no American intellectual met this expectation better than Arendt herself.

ROBERT B. WESTBROOK

See also AUTHORITY.

FURTHER READING

Margaret Canovan, *Hannah Arendt: a Reinterpretation of Her Political Thought* (Cambridge: Cambridge University Press, 1992).

Hannah Arendt, *Karl Jaspers Correspondence, 1926–1969*, ed. Lotte Kohler and Hans Saner (New York: Harcourt Brace Jovanovich, 1992).

Jeffrey C. Isaac, *Arendt, Camus and Modern Rebellion* (New Haven: Yale University Press, 1992).

Stephen J. Whitfield, *Into the Dark: Hannah Arendt and Totalitarianism* (Philadelphia: Temple University Press, 1980).

Elizabeth Young-Bruehl, *Hannah Arendt, For Love of the World* (New Haven: Yale University Press, 1982).

Armory show Officially the International Exhibition of Modern Art, held in the Sixty-Ninth Regiment Armory in New York from February 17 through March 15, 1913, the show was one of the pivotal moments in American intellectual and cultural history, exposing artists and critics, as well as a skeptical public, to developments in European MODERNISM. Traveling from New York to Chicago and Boston, the exhibition attracted as many as 500,000 viewers. It inspired a generation of American cultural leaders, and created a media event that focused even provincial opinion on the new aesthetic ideas.

See also ALFRED STIEGLITZ.

FURTHER READING

Martin Green, *New York 1913: the Armory Show and the Paterson Strike Pageant* (New York: Macmillan, 1988).

Arnold, Thurman (b. Laramie, Wyo., June 2, 1891; d. Alexandria, Va., Nov. 7, 1969). Legal scholar and litigator. Arnold argued in *The Symbols of Government* (1935) and *The Folklore of Capitalism* (1937) that beliefs about law, economics, and politics belong to the realm of folklore. People are rarely rational, especially in groups. They are immersed in symbolism and display; they seek comfort and reassurance. Governments should create rational plans for fulfilling people's emotional needs while working behind the scenes to maximize the production and distribution of goods. Arnold considered himself a pragmatist and an experimentalist. He joined the New Deal in 1938 as an Assistant Attorney General in the antitrust division of the Justice Department; he resigned in 1943 to become a judge on the First Circuit Court of Appeals.

See also LEGAL REALISM.

FURTHER READING

Alan Brinkley, "The Antimonopoly Ideal and the Liberal State: the Case of Thurmond Arnold," *Journal of American History* 80 (Sept. 1993): 557–79.

Ashcan School   This movement in American painting centered around the mentor figure of Robert Henri from 1900 through the early 1910s. Inspired by the mid nineteenth-century realism of Gustave Courbet and Édouard Manet, Henri believed that the artist had a role in progressive social reform, and should represent not academic themes but modern life "as it is." Accordingly, Henri and his followers, many of whom had been magazine and newspaper illustrators, took to painting the everyday experience of urban-industrial America in a sympathetic manner analogous to that of their literary MUCKRAKING contemporaries. "Ashcan" artists included Henri, Arthur B. Davies, William Glackens, George Luks, Maurice Prendergast, Everett Shinn, and John Sloan.

FURTHER READING

William Innes Homer, *Robert Henri and his Circle* (Ithaca: Cornell University Press, 1969).

Asian American identity   For Asian Americans, as for all visibly differentiated peoples in the United States, identity is deeply problematic, and the struggle to make sense of one's identity is at the center of intellectual as well as everyday life. What W. E. B. Du Bois noted of the African American in 1903 in his *The Souls of Black Folk* is equally true of Asian Americans: "It is a peculiar sensation, this double-consciousness, this sense of always looking at one's self through the eyes of others, of measuring one's soul by the tape of a world that looks on in amused contempt and pity" (p. 45). While the Asian American family provides emotional support and positive valuation for its children, the larger society designating them as the racial Other, more often than not, devalues and humiliates them.

"Chinky, Chinky Chinaman, yellow-face, pig-tail, rat-eater" were the taunts that Edith Eaton (also known as Sui Sin Far), a Eurasian and a pioneer Asian American writer, heard as a child in Hudson City, New York in the 1870s. Her lifelong battle to uphold racial pride during a period of the most virulent sinophobia is movingly recorded in her 1909 autobiographical essay, "Leaves from the Mental Portfolio of an Eurasian." In the middle of the twentieth century, the popular playground chant was "Chinky, Chinky Chinaman, sitting on a fence/trying to make a dollar out of fifty cents." Today, Asian American children are still taunted on the playground with "Slit eyes!" or the chant: "Chinese (pull corners of eyes up), Japanese (pull corners of eyes down), dirty knees, look at these (point to breasts)." In this atmosphere, to be Asian and to have a sense of pride in one's ancestry is a difficult challenge.

As Asian American children mature, they become infected by what Edward Said has called the "orientalist" discourse of the Western world, a discourse which posits a dichotomy characterizing "western" as normal, rational, technologically advanced and "oriental" (all of the Middle East and the Far East) as synonymous with exotic, quaint, superstitious, and backward. Further refinements of the popular images lead to stereotypes of the Asian male as asexual, effeminate, small, but clever (Charlie Chan) or dangerous, swarthy and wily (Fu Manchu). The Asian female, for the last half-century associated with the treachery or the spoils of war, may be represented as the malevolent, devious Dragon Lady or the shy, desirable (because submissive) Madame Butterfly/Lotus Blossom.

The usual response by Asian Americans to such racist denigration has been to reject the aberrant (and abhorrent) ancestry and wholeheartedly embrace the dominant culture. However, since the racial difference is visible and ineradicable, assimilation is never complete. People with Asian features may be sixth-generation Americans, yet they will be asked where they come from, or they may be bestselling authors and yet complimented on their good English. As even the most assimilated Asian Americans repeatedly discover to their dismay, Asian facial features are still often perceived as foreign.

On the other hand, another kind of imaging has appeared in the media, again at odds with the actual facts: the Asian American as a model minority and therefore a different kind of threat. According to the model minority myth, Asian Americans are superior in science and math; Asians take up too many places in the best colleges and universities. Actual data, however, reveals that with the equivalent education, Asian American males earn approximately 70 percent of the income earned by white males. In large businesses, Asian Americans are hired for their technical expertise but rarely for managerial and decision-making positions. The model minority myth is insidious because it ignores and masks the social and economic problems of many Asian Americans, and it pits Asians against other minorities, condemned as less accomplished, and against whites, fueling envy and resentment on all sides.

Identity is formed not only by the perceptions of others, but also by the differentiating forces of history and culture, forces brought from the Old World as well as encountered in the New. Though certain of the diverse Asian groups gathered under the umbrella of "Asian American" share cultural traits (such as the Chinese written language, Confucianism and Buddhism among the Chinese, Japanese, and Koreans), the diversity within such a large geographical area as Asia is obviously enormous. Since all groups carry separate histories from their country of origin, what finally brings these disparate groups together is their shared history of discrimination within the United States. And yet, within the U.S., the Chinese and Japanese, the longest Asian American residents in America, have preserved a sharp sense of their own distinctive histories.

At the end of the Civil War, Chinese coolie labor became indispensable in the west, but when the railroads were completed and the California swamps drained, the Chinese were, by law, harassed, driven out, and even murdered without legal recourse. Perpetual aliens, Chinese were denied the right to testify in the courts, to own land, to marry whites, to become citizens. Constitutional amendments gave the vote to African American males (in principle) in 1870, to women in 1920, and to American Indians in 1924, but Asians were denied citizenship and the franchise until 1954. The Chinese Exclusion Act denied immigration to Chinese from 1882 until 1943. In order to circumvent this law, the ingenious scheme of the "paper son" was created whereby a Chinese residing in the U.S. would pay a visit to his wife in China (Chinese women were not permitted to immigrate) and officially record, upon his return to the U.S., that he had sired a son, whether that was the case or not. Fourteen years later, a young Chinese boy could gain entry into this country. In the cases where no son had actually been sired, the U.S. entry slot was sometimes sold to the highest bidder, who was then forced to take the name of the ostensible father, creating identity problems for generations to come: an entire family of Wongs, for example, would be aware that their name was originally Ma.

For Japanese Americans, the problem of identity was created by the cultural trait of silence in the face of trauma and misfortune. One cannot know who one is without a history, but the history of Japanese Americans has been so fraught with pain and humiliation that it could not be spoken of until recently. The forced removal from their homes in the western coastal states of 120,000 Japanese Americans, two-thirds of whom were American citizens, to inland desert camps for the duration of World War II was a trauma of such immense proportions that it was not spoken of for several decades. An entire generation grew up ignorant of their family history because of the silence of their elders. Four decades later, through the efforts of the second generation, the wounds suffered by Japanese Americans during World War II have begun to come to light, the stories are being retrieved, and redress has begun.

More recent Asian immigrant groups have carried personal and national identity questions with them from their countries of origin. For Koreans, the defining event was the colonization of their nation by the Japanese from 1910 until 1945, a period of extreme suffering, when Koreans were denied their language, their culture, and their family names as well as their national sovereignty. Again, this legacy of suffering and shame was so intense that it was met by a silence which is only gradually being broken by such books as Richard Kim's *Lost Names* and Sook Nyul Choi's *Year of Impossible Goodbyes*.

Civil wars and international interventions leading to the partition of India and to military regimes in Vietnam, Myanmar, Laos, and Cambodia—all have resulted in a dual legacy of pain and a pride in survival which characterize the refugees from those countries, a legacy passed on to their descendants in the U.S. who are now swelling the numbers of Asian Americans.

Not surprisingly, the question of identity—both the individual identity and that of the community— is one of the major themes in Asian American literature, much of which seeks to answer the questions: Who am I? How do I negotiate the conflicting demands, languages, and values of two disparate cultures? What about me is American? What Asian? Is this a hyphenated condition, a combination of two things, or something else entirely? This question of "authenticity" has been posed forcefully by playwright/editor Frank Chin, who has denounced as "fake" many (mostly female) Asian American writers, those who he believes implicitly endorse a subordinate, exoticized position for Asians in American culture. To these he opposes the "real" Asian American writers, himself and others, who do not cater to what he calls "white supremacist" views.

Although no written work should carry the burden of representing an entire culture or people, three texts may be taken as major expressions of three Asian American experiences: Carlos Bulosan's *America is in the Heart* (1946), John Okada's *No-No Boy* (1957) and Maxine Hong Kingston's *The Woman Warrior: Memoir of a Girlhood among Ghosts* (1976).

Bulosan was the first to write of the Filipino experience of the 1920s and 1930s, of the disillusionment of a young immigrant who finds an enormous gulf between the Jeffersonian ideals he was taught in American schools in the Philippine Islands and the violently hostile reception he receives as a migrant worker on the West Coast during the Depression. He questions what it is to be an American and poignantly concludes that, however badly one is treated, it is a faith and a belief in the worth of one's fellow man that one must hold in one's heart.

No-No Boy by John Okada is an exploration of the psyche of a Japanese American, who, after being interned in a relocation camp, answered "no" when asked to forswear allegiance to any other country and to serve in the United States military. Though now released from prison, the protagonist is tormented by his label of traitor and questions his place in the land that, he now realizes too late, he deeply loves. The book is Okada's effort both to explain the particular forces behind the resistance of the No-No Boys to World War II and to bring a measure of healing to a deep national wound.

In *The Woman Warrior*, MAXINE HONG KINGSTON created a collage which speaks eloquently for Chinese American women, denied a voice because of their sex in a traditional Chinese patriarchy and denied authority because of their race and sex in a Euro-dominant American society. She writes of her bewilderment in trying to sort out what is expected of her as a child simultaneously given the story of a woman warrior as a model and of a silenced, shamed, "no name" aunt. She seeks to know what in her is Chinese, "what is the movies," and what is peculiar to her family.

The national designation of May as Asian American Heritage Month, and the slow but gradual growth of Asian American studies courses being taught at colleges and universities, beginning on the west coast in the 1970s, spreading to the east coast in the 1980s and finally in the 1990s reaching the midwest; the recent efflorescence of Asian American writers in all genres, and of scholars unearthing Asian American history—all attest to an important fact: a formerly silent minority, taking example from African Americans, is discovering its past, is exploring its identity, and is silent no more.

AMY LING

See also ASSIMILATION; CULTURAL PLURALISM AND MULTICULTURALISM.

FURTHER READING

Carlos Bulosan, *America is in the Heart* (1946; Seattle: University of Washington Press, 1981).

Sucheng Chan, *Asian Americans: an Interpretive History* (Boston: Twayne, 1991).

W. E. B. Du Bois, *The Souls of Black Folk* (1903; New York: New American Library, 1982).

Sui Sin Far, "Leaves from the Mental Portfolio of an Eurasian," *Independent* 65 (Jan. 21, 1909): 125–32.

Maxine Hong Kingston, *The Woman Warrior: Memoirs of a Girlhood among Ghosts* (New York: Knopf, 1976).

Lee C. Lee, *Asian Americans: Collages of Identities*, Cornell Asian American Studies Monograph Series, no. 1 (Ithaca, 1992).

John Okada, *No-No Boy* (1957; Seattle: University of Washington Press, 1976).

Edward W. Said, *Orientalism* (New York: Vintage, 1979).

Ronald Takaki, *Strangers from a Different Shore* (New York: Penguin, 1989).

assimilation A powerful ideological force in the United States during the twentieth century, assimilation initially represented a response to extreme positions of nativism. Nativists saw the millions of immigrants, especially those arriving after 1880 from Southern and Eastern Europe, Mexico, and Asia, as outsiders corrupting American culture and threatening the predominantly Anglo Americans already "native" to the United States. Assimilationists countered by theorizing that the immigrant newcomers and their progeny could and would become "assimilated." Playing roles in modernization experienced within industrial, urban, and class-structured environments, immigrants and peoples incorporated into America by slavery and conquest would be socialized to surrender their loyalties to "folk groups" and would conform to dominant "American" cultural norms. Thus "freed" from their historical burdens, they would become the productive laborers American industry needed. This project of assimilation contributed to the development of sociology as a discipline, notably the rise of the "Chicago School."

While use of the term "assimilation"—the process of "making similar"—has late sixteenth-century roots in physiology and concepts about the digestion of foods by the body, the prime symbol for it in twentieth-century America is the "melting pot," a metaphor derived from the refining and alloying of metals. This metaphor was first suggested by MICHEL-GUILLAUME-SAINT-JEAN DE CRÈVECOEUR, who wrote in *Letters from an American Farmer* (1782) of the "American, who, leaving behind him all his ancient prejudices and manners, receives new ones from the new mode of life he has embraced, the new government he obeys, and the new rank he holds." The modern nation in Crèvecoeur's time was transforming immigrants from England, Scotland, Ireland, Holland, France, and Germany into "Americans," which itself was a term British colonists had only begun using to describe themselves in the mid-eighteenth century. In America, Crèvecoeur thought, "all individual nations are melted away into a new race of men." By the metaphor of "melting" it is clear that Crèvecoeur expected the "new race" to be homogeneous, contrary to a common, late twentieth-century confusion that the "melting pot" is a symbol of cultural diversity. In a similar way, and in apparent contrast with Aristotle's concept of a democracy that thrives on heterogeneity, Thomas Jefferson envisioned American democracy as working best in a homogeneous society. That idea received support from two sources: the philosophical universalism of the Enlightenment and the need felt by many of those holding political power in the new nation for a narrowly construed ideological, cultural, and racial unity.

In 1914, Crèvecoeur's expression was echoed and popularized in Israel Zangwill's *The Melting-Pot*, a four-act dramatization of a faith Zangwill believed "the people," the immigrants he characterized, had in the "American crucible." In Dearborn, Michigan, Henry Ford was producing not only autos in his factories but also allegories of assimilation, captured on film, depicting immigrants, at first wearing the tattered clothes of their old worlds, as they march into a melting pot and then re-emerge in the uniform of American industrial workers. Concepts of mass homogeneous culture, mass production, mass consumption of standardized goods, and appeals to "core American values" were all of a piece at this historical juncture.

"Melting" into a "new race" requires either being released from, or letting go of, one's old history. Subcultures are assumed frozen in history at the moment of the emigrant's departure and left behind by change. The host culture alone is understood in terms of historical change, its "traditions" too multidimensional to be fixed in definitions, except in one

crucial respect: when the immigrant assimilates, the image of what she or he is to conform to—that is, what is "American"—assumes an ahistorical and materialist fixity, such that the immigrant cannot simply claim to be "American" by aspiration and by experience within America's boundaries, but must look, act, eat, speak, dress, and even be named like a standard, contemporary "American" as well. Because the dominant culture, however, is simultaneously privileged by being conceived in terms of both constancy and change, timeless "tradition" and modernity, the common notion is that the assimilating immigrant (or the immigrant's child) melts into a culturally "free," fluid new culture. It is thus not unusual to hear self-contradictory expressions of how assimilation, though it requires a measure of conformity, "frees" one to be an individual.

But the difficulty the immigrant has with rejecting old national history, culture, and the narrative that begins in the old country and brings him or her into the new world is reflected in the popular convention of calling not the immigrant but the next, the American-born, generation the "first" generation. By this terminology, the immigrant is cast in the role of a perpetual alien, stuck in an identification with the "tradition" of a "subordinate" or "sub" culture.

Interpretations of assimilation in twentieth-century American literature, some of them powerfully anxious ones, are many. Whether simply replicated or critiqued, the theme and its influence can be seen in Gertrude Stein's story of "The old people in a new world, the new people made out of the old," in her *The Making of Americans* (1908). The theme appears in works by Henry James; and its efficacy is questioned in the (attempted) change of the German-American identity of James Gatz into the assimilationist construct of Jay Gatsby, kept at a distance for the vagueness of his history, in F. Scott Fitzgerald's novel *The Great Gatsby* (1925). Often the greatest expense of assimilation is felt by the assimilated to be the loss of personal, family, and cultural histories when their lack has resulted in failures of self-understanding and, consequently, of social relations. Men and women generally play different roles under assimilation, where the division of labor—the "freeing" of people by assigning them defined tasks and limited responsibilities—is basic and desired. Insofar as women are characterized as bearers of culture while men are divested of their old narratives and associated with the work of creating civilization, women are seemingly tied to the marginal, the buried past, and intuitive, hidden truths. In William Faulkner's *Light in August* (1932), it is the former slave Cinthy who is able to tell the young Hightower the "truth" of his grandfather's ignominious death, contradicting the heroic story which obsesses Hightower. Applicable in different ways to different racial and ethnic groups and their histories, themes of assimilation are so endemic to "ethnic" American literatures that questions, inherent in the concept of assimilation, of the inequality of cultures in the United States, the crossing and recrossing of cultural borders, and relationships between subordinate and dominant cultures, are sometimes treated as being among the definitive elements of an "ethnic" American literature.

When the diversity of European ethnicities of immigrants from 1880 to 1924 melted under Anglo-assimilation, a Caucasian "racial majority" was constructed. This concept works against the political empowerment of other citizens who, even if they and their neighbors were to achieve a "rainbow coalition" which Democratic Party activist the Reverend Jesse Jackson has proclaimed, would still constitute less than 50 percent of the population by race (although currently changing demographics and theories countering assimilationism are overturning the concept of the "racial majority"). Some theorists of assimilation have concerned themselves primarily with what Gunnar Myrdal called "the Negro problem," or the racial problems that elude solutions contained within the melting pot as originally conceived.

But when racial, Anglo-assimilation has been impossible, cultural assimilation has yet seemed possible. Unlike LANGSTON HUGHES, who drew his literary creations from jazz and African American speech, COUNTEE CULLEN wrote in "traditional" forms of English poetry (he called John Keats his greatest literary influence). In his poem "Heritage" (1925), Cullen struggled with questions about his relationships with African civilization in what seemed to be the absence of a mediating African American history. Cullen's distinction between his Anglo literary "culture" and his "race" implied a recognition that assimilation and its aims for social equality could not be complete unless one were Caucasian in race as well as in culture. His presence among poets of an English literary culture might be thought thus to highlight the preeminence, the leading role, played by the English in an American culture defined by assimilation and thus by race. RALPH ELLISON narrates this complex phenomenon in his *Invisible Man* (1952), in the incident where the protagonist, working for Liberty Paints, is ordered to add a tiny and precisely controlled amount of "dead black" liquid into white paint to make the resulting "Optic White" appear whiter than it did without the black "dope." With its invisible yet necessary black ingredient, the batch of Optic White, further, is bound for the painting of a "national monument."

Against the possibility of voluntary assimilation, barriers posed by "scientific," post-Darwinian concepts of RACE can be seen in the history of Asian Americans. Laws of the United States long prohibited Asian immigrants from becoming naturalized. Asians did not come under the category "white," privileged with eligibility in the 1790 Naturalization Act. Between then and 1924, eligibility was established for Mexicans in lands the United States conquered (incorporated under the Treaty of Guadalupe Hidalgo in 1848); "persons of African nativity or descent" (in 1870); Puerto Ricans (acquired from Spain by war, 1898); native Hawaiians (by forceful overthrow and subsequent annexation in 1898) and other Pacific Islander subjects of the United States; and American Indians (1924). In 1922, the United States Supreme Court ruled (*Ozawa v. United States*) that despite his American education and assimilation in ways within his power to choose, Takao Ozawa, who immigrated from Japan in 1894, could not be granted naturalization—explicitly because he was not white. Bhagat Singh Thind, an immigrant from India, was taken to the Supreme Court in 1923, where his United States citizenship was struck down. Thind was among 70 South Asian Americans individually granted citizenship between 1907 and 1923 on the basis of their arguments that being of Indian origin they were "Aryan" and, hence, were Caucasians eligible for naturalization. The decision against Thind resulted in the revoking of those naturalizations. The Court judged that any applicability of the term "Caucasian" to Thind still did not make him a "white person" in the eyes and "language of the common man." Although Filipinos were nationals of, and therefore not "aliens" to, the United States since the 1898 takeover of the islands from Spain, they too were excluded and were labeled by an odd euphemism, "noncitizens."

The conviction that Asians were unassimilable was inscribed everywhere from common opinion to the highest legal discourse of the land. Unlike European newcomers, these immigrants were not committed to America, according to the circular logic of this argument. Significantly, Japanese immigrants recognized their own participation in American history. They called themselves *issei*, the first Japanese American generation. "First" implied more generations would follow, and in their term for themselves the *issei* contradicted the prevailing, assimilationist convention of numbering "American" generations beginning with the next generation. It was not until 1952, however, that the McCarren-Walter Act removed racial prohibitions against their naturalization.

The American legal and social alienation of Asian immigrants made even the cultural assimilation of their children difficult (*see also* ASIAN AMERICAN IDENTITY). Attempts by second and subsequent generations of Asian Americans to assimilate have resulted in the notion of a "dual identity" consisting of a "blend of the East and the West." As successfully as "dual identities" of the children of European immigrants may have been resolved, in assimilationist analyses, the same concept also produced a sharp justification for the World War II internment of the *nisei* (the Japanese American "second generation," who were American citizens by birth). For, added to the volatile claim that behavior is dictated genetically by blood, the notion of the existence in *nisei* of a "blend of the East and the West" meant that a part of the person was thought "Japanese," an "enemy alien," in a hysterical confusion and mistaking of "nationality," "race," and Japanese American "culture" of the *nisei* and their parents. Assimilationist theory was invoked to conceive and justify the social engineering and eventual diaspora attempted by President Franklin D. Roosevelt, the Assistant Secretary of War John J. McCloy, and his subordinates in "relocating" nearly 120,000 Japanese Americans of the West Coast along with over a thousand from Hawaii during World War II.

The internment of Japanese Americans should have proved that assimilation was beyond the reach of Asian Americans and had betrayed them. But the project at the same time was aimed to pressure people, in wartime and afterward, to try all the harder to assimilate. In *Fifth Chinese Daughter* (1950), the autobiography Jade Snow Wong wrote in the third person shortly after World War II, Jade Snow considers her parents "Chinese" regardless of their long residence in America; and although she herself was born in America, she considers herself not "American" until she learns to be one outside her home. In the work, which assumes Western cultural dominance (as assimilation posits by its designation of a "dominant" culture in America), "America" alone stands for a timeless "freedom," despite the process of conformity Jade Snow is subjected to in that culture, and despite social and political ideals of revolution in Chinese history, evidently untaught and unexpressed by her father.

Meanwhile the local, American influences on her parents' stubbornness about being protectively, patriarchically "Chinese" in America go unexamined in the narrative. Directing her criticism against the antifeminism of "the Chinese," represented by her father (a businessman and Christian convert), Wong does not take similar account of American antifeminism, for instance in the immigration laws which from 1882 to the end of World War II established a Chinese American male "bachelor society" and defined peculiarly American roles for those men who had families in America. The fact that Wong sees herself to be "a blend of the East and the West," thus partly "Chinese," is not a proclamation of heterogeneity and hybridity—or dialogics and heteroglossia, in Mikhail Bakhtin's terms—but an expression of belief in cultural homogeneity on either side in her experience of cultural conflict. Since the parents, as immigrants departed from the living history of China but unable to be American by law, see "Chinese" and "American" cultures in monolithic, ahistorical ways, they too share assimilationist assumptions about culture. Entrenched in their "Chinese" otherness, the parents exercise their relative freedom within that space—distinctive to their American experience—to dictate stiff versions of "Chinese tradition" to their children.

Wong is far from alone in Asian American literature and community life. A persistent reinvention of the wheel in the Asian American literature of identity and cultural studies testifies to a continuing assumption that assimilation is fundamental to understanding Asian Americans, no matter how repeatedly it has been twisted to marginalize them and, in circular arguments, to punish them for being marginal. For example, Daniel Okimoto's autobiography, *American in Disguise* (1972), extends Wong's assimilationist thoughts. At his book's conclusion, Okimoto states his hope that, in time, the minor race and culture his body represents will be bred genetically out of his descendants by intermarriage. Okimoto's is a vision of ultimate exclusion. His assimilationist assumptions and predictions about race and culture ironically contribute to the problem, the valorization of racial homogeneity, he is trying to resolve.

Historical studies, book reviews, and literary criticism steeped in assimilationist assumptions usually cannot tell assimilationism apart from cultural pluralism. But for a century a great many Asian American literary works have examined and exposed, with great sophistication, the assimilationist assumptions Wong and Okimoto espouse. Authors of narrative works in this literature include, for example, MAXINE HONG KINGSTON, Sui Sin Far, Carlos Bulosan, Shelley Ota, Monica Sone, John Okada, Kazuo Miyamoto, Louis Chu, Frank Chin, Milton Murayama, Joy Kogawa, Darrell H. Y. Lum, Bharati Mukherjee, Gish Jen, David Mura, and, sometimes in deeply subtle ways, Hisaye Yamamoto. Among poets strongly versed in these themes and their critique are Mitsuye Yamada, Wing Tek Lum, Janice Mirikitani, and Lawson Inada. These are some of the creators and carriers of past and current Asian American literary history, the very existence of which controverts the dehistoricizing powers (and requirements) of assimilation.

Other writers of the literatures of the United States with historical origins in other lands have resisted the lure of assimilation. In contrast to Countee Cullen, his cultural assimilation, and his own concern over a loss of history, ZORA NEALE HURSTON informed her works with an understanding of how African cultural elements entered the Americas with slaves and continue, through changes both practical and metaphysical, to course through the lives of her twentieth-century characters. This view of culture not simply apprehended *in* change but *as* change—and of history not as a preserved past but as narratives with ongoing, many-layered plots—is basic to a "historical constructionist" point of view and a concept of "cultural pluralism," one response to assimilation. Again, as in the example of Jade Snow Wong and her ahistorical view of culture, it is not the mere presence of an alien, "minor," or "ethnic" element within a "larger" or "major" culture that signals pluralism and its dismantling of the politics of racial and cultural majoritarianism. Pluralism concerns histories (themselves multiple), interactions, and consequent changes and dynamics of a multiplicity of cultures—and includes analyses of the rise and effects of assimilation—through time, rather than cultures as defined, synchronically, at the moment the individuals who bear them enter the melting pot. Though pluralism arose in response to assimilationism, their relationship is not of a diametric opposition, in part because pluralism recognizes assimilation as a historical antecedent, and they are but two theoretical areas within what is broadly called "multiculturalism."

STEPHEN H. SUMIDA

See also CULTURAL PLURALISM AND MULTICULTURALISM; ETHNICITY.

FURTHER READING

Robert Blauner, "Internal Colonialism and Ghetto Revolt," *Social Problems* 16 (spring 1969): 393–409.

Sucheng Chan, *Asian Americans: an Interpretive History* (Boston: Twayne, 1991).

Nathan Glazer and Daniel Patrick Moynihan, *Beyond the Melting Pot: the Negroes, Puerto Ricans, Jews, Italians, and Irish of New York City* (Cambridge: MIT Press, 1963).

Milton Myron Gordon, *Assimilation in American Life: the Role of Race, Religion, and National Origins* (New York: Oxford University Press, 1964).

Sucheta Mazumdar, "Race and Racism: South Asians in the United States," in Gail M. Nomura et al., eds., *Frontiers of Asian American Studies: Writing, Research, and Commentary* (Pullman: Washington State University Press, 1989).

Gunnar Myrdal, *American Dilemma: the Negro Problem and Modern Democracy* (New York: Harper, 1944).

Michael Novak, *The Rise of the Unmeltable Ethnics: Politics and Culture in the Seventies* (New York: Macmillan, 1971).

Robert Ezra Park, *Race and Culture* (New York: Free Press, 1950).

Ronald Takaki, *Strangers from a Different Shore: a History of Asian Americans* (Boston: Little, Brown, 1989).

Louis Wirth, *The Ghetto* (Chicago: University of Chicago Press, 1956).

Austin, Mary (b. Carlinville, Ill., Sept. 9, 1868; d. Santa Fe, N. Mex., Aug 13, 1934). Writer. A prolific author of novels, essays, and short stories, Austin won fame for *The Land of Little Rain* (1903) and *A Woman of Genius* (1912). Her work treats many themes: the glory and natural beauty of the American southwest, the suppression of women's individuality by family, culture, and societal norms, the art and culture of American Indians and their fight for land and water rights. A proponent of ENVIRONMENTALISM, WOMEN'S RIGHTS, and FEMINISM, she considered artistic work and direct political action to be complementary aspects of her effort to preserve beauty and promote justice. Aesthetic creativity emerges, she believed, from a mystical wellspring.

FURTHER READING

Esther Stineman, *Mary Austin: Song of a Maverick* (New Haven: Yale University Press, 1989).

authority   A concept in wide circulation, authority is a term found as often in common parlance as in social and political philosophy. We use it to signal the credibility of those experts with whom we consult for advice on subjects as divergent as health and fashion, or to whose judgment we refer when making decisions about the next novel to read or the latest film to view. Yet we also use the same concept to refer to the legitimacy of political rulers, and to justify obedience to them. Although it is connected linguistically both to the Latin noun for author—*auctor*, one who gives meaning—and to the verb *augere*—to augment—it is yet distanced from these two original meanings by layers of interpretations that have renegotiated its signification almost beyond recognition; authority becomes more closely connected to the practice of obedience the more proximate the terrain of its usage is to the realm of governments and politics.

Authority is a remarkably protean concept with an important and contested history in modern philosophy. Any adequate analysis would have to situate the concept in different social and cultural contexts in order to consider the ways that context and history have altered its meaning. Little analysis of this sort exists at present. As a consequence, authority is a concept of considerable mobility, yet remarkable fixity. Most frequently, authority has been conflated with the legitimate power to rule. The result is that although modern political theorists have noticed an implicit tension between authority and autonomy, few have enabled us to think about authority beyond the scope of command–obedience relationships.

In Western political philosophy it has been common to regard authority as a distinctive type of social control or influence. Political theorists have attempted to define authority as a peculiar form of getting people to obey social prescriptions without resorting to overt coercion. Most theorists argue that authority describes a relationship existing somewhere between force and persuasion. Consequently, they contend that authority necessarily entails some sort of surrender of private judgment—at least in the weak sense of submitting to the judgment of another without making conduct dependent on one's assessment of the merits of the command. The implication is that recognition of authority itself is sufficient for accepting the prescriptions produced by authority systems. Put differently, if authority is defined as a consensually established relationship that gives someone the right to command another who has a duty to obey, then any justification of authority depends only on clarification of the criteria whereby authority is recognized as such in the first place. One does not have to be persuaded to obey those in authority, nor is one coerced into obeying. One obeys those in authority because they are entitled to obedience.

The dominant view that authority requires obedience from subjects pits it against democratic notions of self-governance. This is because, as anarchists have argued most forcefully, the belief in absolute individual sovereignty apparently cannot be squared with the notion that someone has the right to command another. Yet, during the seventeenth and eighteenth centuries especially, social contract theorists began to investigate the theoretical possibility of reconciling authority with DEMOCRACY.

Contract theory, complemented by natural rights theory, attempted to provide a logical basis for claiming that every individual remained indirectly self-governing in republics, or representative democracies. Since all individuals had the equal right to represent themselves in authority relations through electoral actions, every individual freely consented to be governed by legitimately elected rulers. Although authority established a relationship of ruler–ruled, no one could claim the right to subordinate others without their consent. Elections represented the voluntary agreement to be governed by someone other than oneself. (*See also* REPRESENTATION.)

Despite the claim that everyone had an equal voice in representative systems, citizenship was strikingly limited throughout the eighteenth century and most of the nineteenth century in Europe and in the United States. Only property-holding white males enjoyed the rights ostensibly won for all through the War of Independence. All slaves and women were not citizens; they were subordinated without their consent. Even when the Fourteenth and Fifteenth Amendments to the U.S. Constitution granted civil and political rights to former slaves, black women remained excluded from the gains that black men had made.

The history of republican systems of authority includes the history of the critique of patterns of exclusion in the definition of those eligible for participation in governance, and the gradual expansion of the range of those who were considered eligible to participate in electing legitimate rulers. Yet instead of questioning the identification of authority with a form of social control, critics of the republican tradition have urged the removal of remaining obstacles that prevent marginalized groups from being integrated into authority relations.

The assumption that liberal democratic authority remains a kind of "control over" the community despite its increase in the number and types of "controllers" links liberalism's apparent shift in thinking about authority—a shift insofar as authority in the liberal tradition is said to be created through the actions of those who will become obligated to it, instead of being instituted from above—with the long tradition of thinking about authority that preceded its modern formulation. Authority remains conceptualized within the structure of command–obedience relations.

Feminist theory represents the most recent effort to criticize the persistence of practices of exclusion within democratic authority structures. Feminist theory falls within the range of democratic social theories that explore the possibility of the empirical realization of a more fully participatory society, that is, one in which individuals are not excluded arbitrarily from sharing in the practice of authority. Feminists have argued that women have been among those who have been arbitrarily excluded and made marginal to politics. Feminist research and theory have explored how the structures of sexual, social, political and economic power have interfered with the goal of radically democratizing decision-making.

Feminist theory shares with liberal theory an interest in investigating barriers to equal access. But unlike traditional liberal theory, which generally insisted on a "natural" separation between public life and private arenas such as domestic life and the economy, feminists have insisted on the contrary. Feminists have documented the internal connections between the articulation of authoritative values in the private realm and the nature and structure of authority in the public realm. Writers such as Carole Pateman, Susan Okin, and others have emphasized the necessity of considering the relationship between nonpolitical (nongovernmental) experience and the development of a participatory authority structure. Consequently, they have been critical of those theories which treat as unproblematic the patterns and norms of "decision-making" in the "private" sphere.

Yet even feminist critics of social contract theories have generally accepted the conceptualization of authority in republican theories. In Western feminist theory, authority remains defined as the exercise of sovereign political control by legitimate rulers on behalf of the public's welfare. As a practice, sovereignty claims to be gender neutral; it is represented as a tool of influence disconnected from sexual politics. Anyone can be in authority. Yet whether authority as the practice of sovereignty can include women warrants further investigation.

A deeply problematic side of democratic theory has been downplayed in contemporary debates about representative systems of governance: how can we reconcile the intensive and extensive "participation" of diverse groups in politics with the requirements of authority? Most feminists theorists, like so many others, have finessed this challenge by supporting implicitly the claim that the foundation of democratic authority in consent balances a concern for individual autonomy with the requisites of rule-governed behavior through the convention of consent to duty. As long as we are all, as individuals, equally bound by the terms of the contract, then the participation of the previously excluded in no way compromises the ability of the system to maintain order, that is, to apply the rules fairly. More extensive participation merely increases the number of those whose consent is required and whose obligations are expected to be fulfilled. Of course, there may be special burdens that certain groups have previously borne privately, such as domestic responsibilities, which will have to be redistributed in order to secure equal access to participatory opportunities. But if redistribution creates new public claims against the state, or additional private claims against individuals or groups who had been previously "excused" from

sharing such responsibilities by virtue of their being members of the privileged sex, race, class or sexuality, these claims need not compromise the principle of equal subjection to the rules.

Those theorists who subscribe to the traditional understanding of authority as the rightful governance of human action by means other than coercion or persuasion have argued nonetheless that modernity has undermined the foundation of authority. Either because truth or custom have been destabilized, or because modern theories of subjectivity have created an irreconcilable tension between individual liberty and public order, modern theorists across the political spectrum from Richard Sennett to Allan Bloom have pointed to a crisis of authority, and have suggested vastly different ways to address it.

The work of HANNAH ARENDT is distinctive among these voices because of her critique of the identification of authority with command. Arendt considered the fact of our plurality, or our relationship to difference, central to the problem of authority. By resisting the temptation to anchor authority in an absolute that would suffocate freedom of political action, Arendt provides a way to think about and construct authority that promotes a repoliticization of public life. More than this, Arendt's specific reflections on the "human condition" as a condition of plurality, or, what she called the "paradoxical plurality of unique beings," sharply distinguished this concept of plurality from the idea of "otherness." Arendt's stress on a model of authority as the process of augmentation that facilitates our living together in a secular world of equality and uniqueness provides a particularly appropriate way to think about reconstructing authority consistent with feminist concerns.

Theorists such as Pateman, Zillah Eisenstein, Martha Minow, and others who have stressed the radically disturbing presence of women in politics contend that women's presence in politics represents not just the acknowledgment of another interest group with the right to share in decision-making, but the presence of a *particular kind* of group whose bodies, and whose values and senses of obligation, have been characterized in Western discourse as antithetical to public life, and as symbolizing that constellation of attachments and duties that citizenship was supposed to transcend.

Women's bodies pose a peculiar problem: they can be menstruating bodies, pregnant bodies, lactating bodies. Women's bodies are the bodies from which we all emerge. Feminist theorists who stress these differences, and the gendered discourse defining their meaning, have argued that public life and political authority have to be rethought so that the menstruating, pregnant, birthing, lactating female body, the dividing and divided body, is taken not as the exception to the rule but as the point of departure.

"Women's values" often have been expressed in the language of nurturance, compassion and care-taking, and women's duties identified with the protection of the familial, the particular and the everyday. It is the *particularity* of women's different interests *as women* that unsettles public order. Recognizing the right of individuals who happen to be women to participate in decision-making—making a gender-neutral claim for inclusiveness, and treating sexual difference as accidental and inconsequential—does not unsettle public life because difference has been neutralized. Yet some contemporary scholars, such as Patricia Hill Collins, Jean Bethke Elshtain, Nancy Hartsock, Kathleen B. Jones, and Sara Ruddick have implied that politics would be transformed if those compassionate concerns associated symbolically with women, those modes of knowledge connected to intuition, insight, and vision, which conjoin the moral with the aesthetic, the rational with the affective, were to be directly woven into the fabric of authority. The work of these scholars draws, in part, on the tradition of Progressive reformism in American history, as well as on studies of different women's political actions. These other modes of knowing to which they refer—moral and aesthetic modes—can be seen as the basis for the construction of different norms of leadership.

The dominant discourse on authority places strict limits on the publicly expressible, restricting critical reflection about the norms and values that structure "private" life, and affecting the parameters and rhythms of public speech. This discourse reduces the meaning of human communication to its ability to transmit information. By rejecting the ambiguities our feelings introduce, we reject a mode of compassionate authority that would remind us that the construction of a harmonious, ordered, rule-governed world is always based on the exclusion and derogation of what does not fit within its neat boundaries. Compassion has the potential to humanize authority. Compassion reminds us of the discipline and responsibility entailed in judgment. It also reminds us that the act of authority is an act of promising enacted not in solitude but in front of the world. As Arendt wrote in *The Human Condition*,

[promising and forgiving] depend on plurality, on the presence and acting of others, for no one can forgive [her]self and no one can feel bound by a promise made only to [her]self; forgiving and promising enacted in solitude or isolation remain without

a reality and can signify no more than a role played before one's self.

KATHLEEN B. JONES

See also HEGEMONY.

FURTHER READING
Hannah Arendt, *The Human Condition* (Chicago: The University of Chicago Press, 1958).
Patricia Hill Collins, *Black Feminist Thought* (New York: Unwin and Hyman, 1991).
Jean Bethke Elshtain, *Power Trips and Other Journeys: Essays in Feminism as Civic Virtue* (Madison: University of Wisconsin Press, 1990).
Richard Flathman, *The Practice of Political Authority* (Chicago: University of Chicago Press, 1980).
Nancy C. M. Hartsock, *Money, Sex and Power: Toward a Feminist Historical Materialism* (New York: Longman, 1983).
Kathleen B. Jones, *Compassionate Authority: Democracy and the Representation of Women* (New York: Routledge, 1993).
John Schaar, *Legitimacy and the Modern State* (New Brunswick: Transaction, 1981).

autobiography This form of imaginative literary discourse is much practiced and widely appreciated in the United States. The steady practice is partly accounted for by the urge of many writers to register themselves as individuals, as democratic American beings. Inscribing one's life in an autobiography can demonstrate that whatever the pernicious forces operating to standardize experience—industrialism, mass culture, even, as Tocqueville feared, the conformity enforced by democracy itself—singularity in an individual is still prized and possible (*see also* INDIVIDUALISM). The classic autobiography *The Education of Henry Adams* (1906) is the crowning moment of this type of text; it caps a tradition that includes the *Autobiography* of BENJAMIN FRANKLIN (written between 1771 and 1790) and the *Narrative* (1845) by FREDERICK DOUGLASS.

Other writers turn to autobiography because the cultural group to which they belong has been unacknowledged. This autobiographical activity may be termed making "invisible Americans visible"; it is an activity especially of the twentieth century, one that the poet Langston Hughes captured in his line (carefully echoing and revising Walt Whitman), "I, too, sing America." But some nineteenth-century texts, such as Harriett Jacobs's *Life of a Slave Girl* (1861), might also be placed in this category.

The American penchant for autobiography can also be traced to the tradition, both religious and secular, of testifying, giving witness. While testimony may take the form of spiritual autobiography, as it often did in centuries past, it may assume the shape of the appeal, the exposé, the call for reform. In this latter mode of testimony, what autobiographers give witness to, through stories of their lives, are the shortcomings—spiritual or otherwise—of American habits or behavior. Jane Addams's *Twenty Years at Hull-House* (1910) is an exemplary instance of this tradition. In his *Autobiography* (1931) LINCOLN STEFFENS manifests but also challenges it.

With its many modes, autobiography attracts and engages a variety of audiences. Personal accounts of achieving material or public success (Lee Iaccoca), gaining citizenship (Edward Bok or Mary Antin), being educated or miseducated (Richard Rodriguez), confronting psychic disorder (Robert Lowell), healing after trauma (Kate Simon or Ron Kovic), battling injustice (Ida B. Wells), arriving at self-definition in the face of imposed identities (MALCOLM X), converting to a new faith or philosophy (Julia Foote or DOROTHY DAY)—each of these has an eager clientele. What binds these various reading constituencies is their willingness to believe that autobiography, unlike poetry or fiction, is inherently truthful in its utterances and grounded in verifiable historical fact. Believing that recollection is rooted in the solidity and reliability of memory is one way to buttress the idea of a stable, continuous self. As BOOKER T. WASHINGTON said in his autobiography, *Up from Slavery* (1901), of his own appetite for reading biography: "I like to be sure that I am reading about a real person."

This commitment to the truthfulness of autobiography has led to certain unspoken pacts between autobiographers and their readers. Ever since the first surge of enthusiasm for Franklin's *Autobiography*, readers have agreed to be pupils to an autobiographer's didacticism, while ignoring ample evidence that the pose of noble instructor sometimes masks the writer's self-interested reconstruction or reinvention of a life. In turn, readers have been granted some masking privileges of their own. Since the early American captivity narratives, tales of women and children seized by Indians, readers have been permitted to construe their voyeurism as useful, even scientific, inquiry. The American practice of autobiography allows authors and readers to appear to

be dispassionately and publicly engaged, while they simultaneously activate their most private desires.

This paradox of autobiographical activity helps explain why, as Paul John Eakin points out, the study of American autobiography has not been institutionalized in the curricula of secondary schools and colleges. It is too unpredictable in its impact, too explosive in its uses. The debate over the admission of autobiography to the curriculum revolves around the issue of whether public truth commingled with personal truth is still truth, and whether autobiography has finally matured to the stature of a literary genre. But these debates ignore how messily human and eccentric autobiographies are. They are too various in their forms and intentions to be the proper study of any one discipline. They have begun to find a secure niche in the interdisciplinary work of American Studies, African American Studies, Women's Studies, and related programs. At a time when scholars in many disciplines have come to stress the perspectival basis of truth, autobiography has a key role to play. Each autobiography becomes a case study in how the truths of a life are imagined and remade as new experience unfolds.

ROBERT B. STEPTO

See also JAMES BALDWIN; BLACK ELK; DIARIES.

FURTHER READING

Shari Benstock, *The Private Self: Theory and Practice of Women's Autobiographical Writings* (Chapel Hill: University of North Carolina Press, 1988).

Elizabeth G. Bruss, *Autobiographical Acts: the Changing Situation of a Literary Genre* (Baltimore: Johns Hopkins University Press, 1976).

G. Thomas Couser, *Altered Egos: Authority in American Autobiography* (New York: Oxford University Press, 1989).

Margo Cullery, ed., *American Women's Autobiography: Fea(s)ts of Memory* (Madison: University of Wisconsin Press, 1992).

Paul John Eakin, ed., *American Autobiography: Retrospect and Prospect* (Madison: University of Wisconsin Press, 1991).

Albert E. Stone, ed., *The American Autobiography* (Englewood Cliffs: Prentice-Hall, 1980).

B

Babbitt, Irving (b. Dayton, Ohio, Aug. 2, 1865; d. Cambridge, Mass., July 15, 1933). Born in the Midwest, Babbitt moved with his family several times and enjoyed travels on his own around the country. His father, a physician and writer, would later represent to his son the undisciplined and speculative thinking that he associated with the ills of a modern romantic culture. Babbitt found his own intellectual nourishment in the ancient classics, which he pursued through his B.A. degree at Harvard University, supplemented by a great interest in the ancient religious literature of the East, a focus of the M.A. degree he received from Harvard in 1892. Two years later he joined the Classics Department at Harvard, but later moved to the Department of Romance Languages, where he remained for the rest of his academic life.

Babbitt's Harvard career marked the effective beginning of an intellectual movement known as the New Humanism. He had met PAUL ELMER MORE in graduate school; More became the other major voice of the New Humanism. More credited Babbitt with changing his whole intellectual outlook, though in personality Babbitt, "the warring buddha of Harvard," contrasted starkly with More, "the hermit of Princeton." One of Babbitt's disciples, the literary critic Stuart Sherman, remembered Babbitt's dynamic classroom teaching at Harvard. Babbitt relished an intellectual skirmish and welcomed even the most boisterous complaints of his opponents. "It shows," he said, "that we've gotten under their skins." And when one student expressed regret to him about the sorry state of traditional literary values, Babbitt replied, "Well, why don't you get out and fight?"

Babbitt published his first book, *Literature and the American College*, in 1908. It outlined a New Humanist critique of American higher education and presented a Humanist philosophy that Babbitt would expand and refine in his later writings. These publications included *The New Laokoon* (1910), *Masters of Modern French Criticism* (1912), and Babbitt's two most important and influential books, *Rousseau and Romanticism* (1919), and *Democracy and Leadership* (1925). Babbitt held consistently to his basic tenets. As More wrote of him in *On Being Human*: "He seems to have sprung up, like Minerva, fully grown and fully armed . . . There is something almost inhuman in the immobility of his central ideas" (p. 29).

Babbitt's Humanism centered on a dualistic description of the human personality. In each individual he posited a principle of expansion, an indefinite reach of will and imagination, lust, and quest for power. Babbitt associated that norm with the Romantic and naturalistic movements in Western culture over the last century. But Babbitt also posited a force of discipline and restraint, of moderation. That element, he believed, had received its most powerful depiction in classical literature, but also in later thinkers like Samuel Johnson. Babbitt defended the great classics of Western literature for their ability to depict, imaginatively, an ideal human nature that was also the basis of an enduring, or universal, common humanity. At worst, Babbitt's intellectual descriptions became parody, as in his understanding of Jean-Jacques Rousseau; at best, Babbitt's reading of the great writers and thinkers showed considerable erudition and shrewd analysis. Always, though, Babbitt's Humanist standards stood out visibly.

However unpopular Babbitt's views were in the major academic and literary centers in America, they always attracted a small but cohesive following. The reminiscences of Babbitt collected in *Irving Babbitt: Man and Teacher* (1941) testify to his influence and persuasion. The establishment of *Modern Age*, a conservative academic journal, in 1957, owed much to Babbitt's influence. For a long time, Babbitt suffered scholarly neglect, but that situation changed in the 1970s and afterward.

Today, Babbitt remains an individual of importance in American intellectual CONSERVATISM for at least three reasons. First, Babbitt has been a major figure for certain Americans who identify their cause with a form of European conservatism. Best articulated by Edmund Burke, this conservatism invokes tradition and historical memory as the stabilizing forces for society and politics and as countervailing influences to utopian and reformist schemes. Babbitt's two chapters on Burke and Rousseau in *Democracy and Leadership* are masterly summaries of particular kinds of conservatism and liberalism. Major American conservatives such as Peter Viereck, Russell Kirk, and George Will, each of whom has outlined this kind of European conservatism, have expressed a debt to Babbitt.

Second, Babbitt addressed the conservative problem of locating order within freedom. Opposed to schemes that would give excessive power to the state but also mistrusting ideologies of individualism, this conservatism looks to principles of internal controls, such as those outlined in Babbitt's Humanism, to supply the discipline and restraint required for social order. Babbitt liked to quote Burke's formulation that the less there was of internal order in society's members, the more must restraints be imposed externally —that is, by the state. Babbitt believed democracy could be saved only by an aristocratic principle within it. It is an idea found variously expressed in the writings of all traditionalist American conservatives.

Finally, Babbitt speaks for those American conservatives who have not been much enamored of its business civilization or its capitalist order. Babbitt himself decried an American mentality that blindly worshipped technology and money and that had made the United States imperialistic in its behavior toward the rest of the world. He also complained bitterly that American higher education had come to reflect the values of a business society. But the corrective to these ills, Babbitt and like-minded conservatives insisted, was not socialism or any extreme reform of the economic system. All useful reform began at the top, he believed. "Our real hope of safety," Babbitt wrote in *Literature and the American College*, "lies in our being able to induce our future Harrimans and Rockefellers to liberalize their own souls, in other words to get themselves rightly educated" (p. 71). Babbitt's efforts thus constituted an uneasy effort to instill conservative notions in American democracy, an essential goal of conservatism in the United States.

J. DAVID HOEVELER JR.

FURTHER READING

J. David Hoeveler Jr., *The New Humanism: a Critique of Modern America, 1900–1940* (Charlottesville: University Press of Virginia, 1977).
Thomas R. Nevin, *Irving Babbitt: an Intellectual Study* (Chapel Hill: University of North Carolina Press, 1984).
George A. Panichas, and Claes G. Ryn, eds., *Irving Babbitt in Our Time* (Washington, D.C.: Catholic University of America Press, 1986).
Claes G. Ryn, *Will, Reason and Imagination: Irving Babbitt and the Problem of Reality* (Chicago: Regnery, 1986).

Backus, Isaac (b. Norwich, Conn., Jan. 9, 1724; d. Middleborough, Conn., Nov. 20, 1806).   Minister. A Baptist and a champion of religious freedom, Backus argued for extending the principle of toleration for dissident groups. Equality is compromised, he asserted, when the majority retains the privilege of determining what will be tolerated. Religious liberty and civil liberty are interdependent, and people have the right to rise against illegitimate authority in any form. Backus's writings include *A Seasonable Plea for Liberty of Conscience* (1773) and *A History of New England, with Particular Reference to the Denomination of Christians Called Baptists* (1777–96).

See also TOLERATION; ROGER WILLIAMS.

FURTHER READING
William G. McLoughlin, *Isaac Backus and the American Pietistic Tradition* (Boston: Little, Brown, 1967).

Baldwin, James [born James Arthur Jones] (b. New York, N.Y., Aug. 2, 1924; d. Saint-Paul de Vence, France, Nov. 30, 1987).   Essayist, novelist, playwright and activist, James Baldwin broke new ground in American writing about both race and homosexuality, themes often entwined in his writing. Baldwin showed himself, especially in his essays, to be one of the great prose stylists of twentieth-century America. As novelist TONI MORRISON says in her memorial to him, "Life in His Language," Baldwin "made American English honest—genuinely international . . . stripped it of ease and false comfort and fake innocence and evasion and hypocrisy . . . un-gated it for black people" so that in his wake they could "enter it, occupy it, restructure it" (p. 76).

Baldwin's gifts were recognized very early by his schoolteachers and schoolmates in Harlem and the Bronx, by poet Countee Cullen, and a little later, by RICHARD WRIGHT. His desire to become a writer intensified in his teens, even during those years between the ages of 14 and 18 when, as a "young minister," he preached regularly at the Fireside Pentecostal Assembly. His Harlem boyhood, his struggles with his preacher stepfather, David Baldwin, and his brief career in the church are *leitmotifs* in his essays and fiction. The church and its influence are at the center of his first novel, *Go Tell It On the Mountain* (1953), and his first play, *The Amen Corner*, and he revisited the experience of his child ministry in his last novel, *Just Above My Head* (1979).

The innovative use of autobiography in Baldwin's essays, as well as its translation into his fiction and plays, is the generic and thematic thread that binds all of Baldwin's writing together. What he called using himself as witness was muted, however, in the essays from his twenties, published in such left-liberal journals as *Commentary*, *New Leader*, *Partisan Review* and *Encounter*. His contributions on topics like "The Harlem Ghetto," Richard Wright and HARRIET BEECHER STOWE ("Everybody's Protest Novel"), and the courting and betrayal of the Negro in Henry Wallace's campaign, have the lapidary authority of his later style, yet the author himself still hovers in the wings. He enters tentatively but powerfully in an extraordinary essay, "Stranger in the Village" (1953), which moves from Baldwin's experience of being black in the Swiss village (where he finished his celebrated first novel *Go Tell It On the Mountain*) to consider the whole condition of the black man in the West. The wider Baldwin's audience became, the more he extended his use of autobiographical polemic, a genre refined between his nonfiction collections *Notes of a Native Son* (1955) and *Nobody Knows My Name* (1961). Many of his most important essays from the mid-fifties onward, such as "Notes of a Native Son," "Fifth Avenue, Uptown," and "Notes from a Region of My Mind" were published in mainstream magazines like *Esquire*, *Harper's* or the *New Yorker*, where his analysis of American racism (joined from the first to a stinging critique of postwar American MASCULINITY) was directly addressed to the white middle class.

White readers were more prepared to listen to and admire his writing on the black experience than his writing on whiteness, miscegenation, and homosexuality. Baldwin's second novel *Giovanni's Room* (1956), set in Paris and first published in England, explored a tragic love affair between a white American expatriate, David, and an immigrant Italian peasant, Giovanni. He returned to a New York setting in his novel *Another Country* (1963), which centered on interracial and homoerotic love, situating both the traumatic failures and utopian possibilities of those relationships as the basic condition of metropolitan modernity. Taken together, Baldwin's fiction, essays and plays from the 1950s and 1960s lay out a stunning critique of actually existing Western humanism, marking its silences, limits and hypocrisies, both between and within cultures, genders, nations and sexualities. Although an agnostic vis-à-vis psychoanalysis, Baldwin's view of both race and sexuality insists on the centrality of psychic life and on its wider social and political effects. This emphasis made him, in this period, a controversial figure for some African American critics. But his original insight into the psychic effects of racism and imperialism remains one of Baldwin's strongest contributions to their theorization; it should be read now in dynamic apposition to the work of Frantz Fanon.

Baldwin's despair over the racism of white America deepened in the mid-sixties. The murders of Emmett Till and Baldwin's friend, Medgar Evers, were the source for *Blues for Mister Charlie* (1964), which dramatizes the racial murder of a young man in the deep South and dares to represent in the immediacy of the theatrical event not only black men and women but the underside of southern white masculinity. *The Fire Next Time* (1963), a jeremiad, had suggested that violence might be averted, but *Blues for Mister Charlie* was a more defiant defense of the black struggle. It provoked attacks from white critics, who claimed that his southern whites were caricatures.

In the novels, essays, and plays written through the mid-sixties in the crucible years of the civil rights movement and his own vertiginous celebrity, Baldwin's writing reached new heights of vigor and innovation. Both *Tell Me How Long the Train's Been Gone* (1968) and *Just Above My Head* (1979) have a successful bisexual artist as their protagonist; these fictions probe, among other things, the painful contradictions of success. But Baldwin's best use of AUTOBIOGRAPHY in his later work remains in his essays, which offer often bleak but always resonant trips through his own (and America's) history. In the book-length *No Name in the Street* (1972) and *Evidence of Things Not Seen* (1985), Baldwin moves skillfully between the personal and the public prophetic voice; his prose mirrors his argument in forcing us to see the intimate connection between individual experience and communal solidarity, even when the community refuses solidarity to the individual. "To be an American black," Baldwin wrote in *No Name in the Street*, "is to be in the situation, intolerably exaggerated, of all those who have ever found themselves part of a civilization which they could in no wise honorably defend—which they were compelled indeed, to attack and condemn—and who yet spoke out of the most passionate love, hoping to make the kingdom new, to make it honorable and worthy of life" (p. 552).

CORA KAPLAN

See also AUTOBIOGRAPHY; EXPATRIATION.

FURTHER READING

James Baldwin, *No Name in the Street*, in *The Price of the Ticket: Collected Nonfiction, 1948–1985* (New York: St. Martin's/Marek, 1985).

——, *Conversations with James Baldwin*, ed. Fred L. Standley and Louis H. Pratt (Jackson: University Press of Mississippi, 1989).

Trudier Harris, *Black Women in the Fiction of James Baldwin* (Knoxville: University of Tennessee Press, 1985).

Toni Morrison, "Life in His Language," in Quincy Troupe, ed., *James Baldwin: the Legacy* (New York: Simon and Schuster, 1989).

Horace Porter, *Stealing the Fire: the Art and Protest of James Baldwin* (Middletown: Wesleyan University Press, 1989).

W. J. Weatherby, *James Baldwin: Artist on Fire* (New York: Dell, 1989).

Bancroft, George (b. Worcester, Mass., Oct. 3, 1800; d. Washington, D.C., Jan. 17, 1891). Historian and public official. Secretary of the Navy when

Polk was president, Bancroft was a Jacksonian Democrat who saw American history as a struggle of the people to free themselves from oppression. With FRANCIS PARKMAN he was in the top rank of ROMANTIC HISTORIANS. Bancroft's ten-volume *History of the United States* (1834–74) was the first comprehensive study of American history. He saw colonial history as leading inevitably to the AMERICAN REVOLUTION, since the American colonies exhibited a vital spirit of liberty and independence from the very beginning. Committed to the careful use of primary sources, he wrote in a majestic narrative style that celebrated America's destiny of leading the world to freedom.

FURTHER READING
Lilian Handlin, *George Bancroft: the Intellectual as Democrat* (New York: Harper and Row, 1984).

Baraka, [Imamu] Amiri [born LeRoi Jones] (b. Newark, N.J., Oct. 7, 1934). As a poet, dramatist, essayist, novelist, editor, anthologist, cultural critic and social critic, with 25 published books and over 20 produced plays to his credit, Baraka is without peer for virtuosity in modern American letters. It is not merely that Baraka writes, and writes well, in so many genres, but that so many of his efforts in these different genres have had a major impact on American culture. A good case could even be made for declaring Amiri Baraka the most important American writer since World War II.

Consider, for example, Baraka's work as editor, anthologist and/or publisher. Baraka's *Yugen*, which as LeRoi Jones he edited with Hettie Jones in the late 1950s and early 1960s, was one of the key journals of the "New American Poetry" scene. His Totem Press, usually in collaboration with Ted and Eli Wilentz's Corinth Books, published works (often the first book) by such key New American Poetry figures as ALLEN GINSBERG, JACK KEROUAC, Frank O'Hara, Philip Whalen, Gary Snyder, Charles Olson and Ed Dorn. The publication of the anthology of African American writing, *Black Fire*, which Baraka edited with Larry Neal in 1968, was one of the defining moments of literary cultural nationalism. The 1983 anthology of African American women's writing, *Confirmation*, which Baraka edited with Amina Baraka, is an important collection of different generations of black women writers ranging from Gwendolyn Brooks and Margaret Walker, who began publishing in the 1930s and 1940s, to Sherley Anne Williams and TONI MORRISON. This abridged list of Baraka's editorial accomplishments leaves out his activities as cultural organizer, such as his key role in creating the Black Arts Repertory Theatre in Harlem-School

in 1965. His efforts on behalf of this shortlived but seminal organization of African American cultural nationalism were followed by other artistic, educational, and political projects after he returned later that year to his native Newark, New Jersey.

Similarly one could cite Baraka's work as a critic and theorist of African American culture, particularly African American music. His early political and cultural criticism collected in *Home* (1966) and *Raise Race Rays Raze* (1971) practically defined the trajectory of the Black Arts Movement during the cultural nationalist era of the 1960s and early 1970s. Now often remembered mostly for its apocalyptic and virulently antiwhite and often antisemitic and misogynist language, it offered too a visionary utopian view of African American destiny. His book *Blues People* (1963), while strongly and famously criticized by such figures as RALPH ELLISON, was one of the first attempts seriously to trace the social development and social meaning of African American vernacular music. His book *Black Music* (1968), largely a collection of articles and columns first published in such journals as *Kulchur*, *Metronome* and *Downbeat*, helped introduce the "new jazz" of such artists as John Coltrane, Ornette Coleman, Archie Shepp and Sun Ra to a wider audience, and to theorize the meaning and cultural significance of their work. Baraka's concept of "the changing same," referring to the cultural adaptations that social conditions in the United States have forced on African Americans, who nonetheless have in Baraka's view maintained a consistent core of meaning, value, and identity, has remained productive in the work of African American literary and cultural critics such as Houston Baker and Deborah McDowell.

Baraka's role as a dramatist was also of crucial importance to the development of the African American theatre. Certainly his plays *Dutchman* and *The Slave* (both 1964) mark not only an increasing engagement with black nationalist thought on Baraka's part, but a new era of African American drama, an era of militant and often violent assertions of black pride. The assertion of black manhood, frequently couched in homophobic, misogynist, and antisemitic language, is thematically central, but it should not be permitted to obscure the formal break with naturalist drama. Baraka adopted many of the techniques and devices of the theatrical avant-garde from Samuel Beckett to the Living Theater. Nearly all dramatic works by black authors since 1964 have reacted with or against these cultural nationalist dramas. While Baraka's postnationalist plays, written after his adoption of Marxism-Leninism in 1974, have not had the impact that his protonationalist and nationaiist plays had, these maintain nonetheless a powerful radical presence in the black theatre.

Baraka's social impact may have been greatest in his roles as editor, publisher, dramatist, theorist, political activist and political role model, but his paramount literary achievement is his poetry. Through all the major stages of his literary career—bohemian, cultural nationalist and Marxist-Leninist—Baraka has continued to create strikingly original poems. His work collected in *The Dead Lecturer* (1964) is his most powerful and disturbing: a vivid record of the black intellectual-artist in torment during a tortured and yet promising moment in African American, and American, history. The pain, the dislocation, the anger, the sense of destiny in these poems find a nearly perfect vehicle in their violent imagery and framentary style and syntax. However, such earlier and similarly broken poems as "Look for You Yesterday, Here You Come Today" and "The Bridge" in his first volume of poetry *Preface to a Twenty Volume Suicide Note* (1961), where the fragmentation is less obviously rooted in the subject's quest for racial identification and assertion and more connected to a relatively race-neutral struggle with personal identity and expression, are also compelling. And Baraka's later poems, during both his cultural nationalist and Marxist-Leninist periods, of which his recent *Why's Wise* poems are notable examples, were crucial in establishing an oral vernacular African American voice as the dominant voice of African American literature.

Baraka remains a controversial and difficult, and for many a repulsive, figure. Certainly, the misogyny, antisemitism and antiwhite rhetoric of his cultural nationalism and the political unpopularity of his Marxist-Leninism have caused Baraka to be generally undervalued despite the relatively large body of critical literature devoted to his works. This devaluation has been explicit, as when Morris Dickstein in his cultural study of the 1960s, *The Gates of Eden*, refused to treat Baraka in a discussion of cultural nationalism because of Baraka's antisemitism—a move equivalent to discussing "high" modernism without considering Ezra Pound because of Pound's antisemitism. It has also been implicit, as signaled by the fact that virtually all of Baraka's books are out of print, or have been out of print for long periods of time. But Baraka's role as a catalyst of the New American Poetry and the Black Arts Movement, his part in establishing the vernacular as the dominant narrative voice of African American literature, his work in establishing a non-naturalistic experimental tradition of African American drama, not to mention the elemental power of his poetry and the artistic excellence of much of the rest of his writing, mark Baraka as a hugely important, however unpalatable, figure in twentieth-century American literature.

JAMES SMETHURST

FURTHER READING
Kimberly Benston, *Baraka: the Renegade and the Mask* (New Haven: Yale University Press, 1976).
——, *Imamu Amiri Baraka (LeRoi Jones): a Collection of Critical Essays* (Englewood Cliffs: Prentice-Hall, 1978).
Joseph Harris, *The Poetry and Poetics of Amiri Baraka: the Jazz Aesthetic* (Columbia: University of Missouri Press, 1985).
Henry Lacey, *To Raise, Destroy and Create: the Poetry, Drama and Fiction of Imamu Amiri Baraka (LeRoi Jones)* (Troy, N.Y.: Whitson, 1981).
Werner Sollors, *Amiri Baraka/LeRoi Jones: the Quest for a "Populist Modernism"* (New York: Columbia University Press, 1978).

Barlow, Joel (b. Redding, Conn., Mar. 24, 1754; d. Zarnowiec, Poland, Dec. 24, 1812). Poet and diplomat. A nationalist, deist, and member of the Hartford Wits, Barlow celebrated American fine arts as a source of patriotic pride and a contribution to human progress. He envisioned a worldwide moral order of peace, beauty, and happiness ushered in by American democracy, literature, science, and public humanistic education. Since reason is the force that structures the universe, he believed, the rational faculty will develop naturally in schoolchildren who are released from the tyranny of inherited rules and authorities. Barlow, who served as U.S. Consul in Algiers in the 1790s, is now remembered for *Vision of Columbus* (1787) and *The Columbiad* (1807), both poetic paeans to America, and *The Hasty Pudding* (1796), a humorous epic poem about New England life.

FURTHER READING
Arthur L. Ford, *Joel Barlow* (New York: Twayne, 1971).

baseball Until Ring Lardner, most American writers and thinkers paid little attention to baseball. And if they did, they risked F. Scott Fitzgerald's famous assessment of his friend offered in "Ring":

> when most men of promise achieve an adult education, if only in the school of war, Ring moved in the company of a few dozen illiterates playing a boy's game. A boy's game, with no more possibilities in it than a boy could master, a game bounded by walls which kept out novelty or danger, change or adventure.... However deeply Ring might cut into it, his cake had exactly the diameter of Frank Chance's diamond. (p. 36)

An exception was Mark Twain, who delivered "Welcome Home" at the 1889 Delmonico's banquet celebrating Albert G. Spalding's return from an around-the-world baseball tour. Although his paean to the game—"the very symbol, the outward and visible expression, of the drive and push and rush and struggle of the raging, tearing, booming nineteenth century" (p. 244)—strikes today's reader as a better description of football, it suggests that our modern notions of baseball's pastoral power have less to do with the game as it was played and watched than with where it resides in our imaginations.

While baseball has been the favorite sport of American intellectuals for most of the twentieth century, and is the most historically self-conscious of American sports, its history has proved peculiarly elusive. That is because fans of the sport, a category including most of the people who have written about it, as well as those who play and watch the game, are less interested in the history of baseball than they are in the ways in which baseball has intersected with and helped frame their own childhoods.

Particularly for men, baseball has provided a framework for emotional exploration and discovery, a language and an arena within which intense emotional expression is sanctioned, even encouraged. It has served twentieth-century poets, novelists, and essayists both as a bridge carrying emotional cargo back and forth across generational boundaries, and as an imaginative home base from which they venture out into the world, and to which they can circle back. The best-known and finest books written about the game, therefore—Roger Kahn's *The Boys of Summer*, Lawrence Ritter's *The Glory of Their Times*, Roger Angell's *The Summer Game*, for example—combine memoir and descriptions of games and well-known players. Perhaps more than most subjects, baseball forces intellectuals to declare their emotional connection to the material up front; it turns a fine mirror on the writer.

But the game promises more than sentimental or psychoanalytic self-regard. Even more than writing about the movies, writing about baseball has been an arena in which intellectuals can both demonstrate and experience immersion in the American crowd, a respectable giving up of themselves to an undeniably popular culture. One thinks of the dandyish George Will or A. Bartlett Giamatti, or George Plimpton, or of the scientist-essayist Stephen Jay Gould.

For many, the game has been a touchstone to worlds—purer, less materialistic, more pastoral—elsewhere. No writer fails to mention its anticapitalist sense of time, its respect for craft done well and gracefully for its own sake, its charming uselessness. Few see, and fewer still care, that since its origins baseball has been thoroughly implicated in and structured by the "material" worlds of American social and cultural history: cities and political machines, transportation and communication, labor conflict, immigration, and racial and sexual discrimination.

Because baseball has been played by children as well as adults for nearly a century and a half, it has managed by and large to escape debates about its contributions to capitalist hegemony and working-class accommodation or resistance. Political interest in the game has generally revolved around four issues: the exclusion and inclusion of African Americans by "organized baseball"; the reserve clause (virtually invalidated in 1975, but which earlier tied players to bosses for life); the influence of the television industry on the structure and play of the game (divisional playoffs, indoor stadiums, astroturf, the designated hitter, night World Series games); and the "perfidy" of Walter O'Malley, whose decision to move the Brooklyn Dodgers to Los Angeles in 1958 ignited a generation's hostility to baseball capitalism.

Still, the question of the audience remains as open in ballparks as it does in movie theatres and living rooms. Does baseball somehow "mirror" other patterns in the society, or does it offer some liberation from the bureaucratized routines of the workaday world? For fans as well as commentators, the answer is clearly both, even as the major league game increasingly "manages" the spectators with almost as much zeal as the field manager directs the players.

Nearly every social current and eddy shows up in the ballpark, whether it be athletes' fundamentalist Christianity, struggles between middle-aged managers and young players over hair length and jewelry, front-office racism, player alcoholism and drug use, or sexual violence. Major league baseball is a multibillion dollar entertainment business, and the men who run it are quite naturally far more concerned about selling their product than guarding the integrity of a national treasure. Players demonstrate little sense of their game's history, and particularly in the 1990s, have begun to earn the gargantuan salaries of other superstars in the entertainment industry.

At the same time, the game on the field is probably played as well as it ever has been (some think better), and each day during the season, fans experience moments of astonishing, transcendent beauty and grace. How to grasp or balance, intellectually and emotionally, these two competing sides of the game, has proved as difficult for fans as for intellectuals. Each wants to choose one and suppress or ignore the other. The great Giant center-fielder Willie Mays tried the same trick: "I don't make history," he said once. "I catch fly balls." In point of fact he did both.

If F. Scott Fitzgerald was rough on Ring Lardner,

his standard for intellectuals suggested in *The Crack-Up* was also demanding: "the test of a first-rate intelligence is the ability to hold two opposed ideas in the mind at the same time, and still retain the ability to function" (p. 69). Understanding baseball requires of fans and intellectuals the ability to grasp a complex, contradictory set of events, feelings, and experiences. Most of us fail the test most of the time. So, of course, do most batters. But there is evidently something irresistible about standing in and taking one's cuts.

WARREN GOLDSTEIN

See also PLAY.

FURTHER READING:
Roger Angell, *The Summer Game* (New York: Viking, 1984).
Gai Ingham Berlage, *Women in Baseball: the Forgotten History* (Westport, Conn.: Praeger, 1994).
F. Scott Fitzgerald, "Ring," in *The Crack-Up*, ed. Edmund Wilson (1937; New York: New Directions, 1956).
Roger Kahn, *The Boys of Summer* (New York: Harper and Row, 1972).
Steven A. Riess, *Touching Base: Professional Baseball and American Culture in the Progressive Era* (Westport, Conn.: Greenwood, 1980).
Richard Skolnik, *Baseball and the Pursuit of Innocence: a Fresh Look at the Old Ball Game* (College Station: Texas A&M, 1994).
Mark Twain, *Mark Twain Speaking*, ed. Paul Fatout (Iowa City: University of Iowa Press, 1976).
George F. Will, *Men at Work: the Craft of Baseball* (New York: Macmillan, 1990).

Beard, Charles A. (b. near Knightstown, Ind., Nov. 27, 1874; d. New Haven, Conn., Sept. 1, 1948). This prolific scholar/activist was raised in a well-to-do family on a farm near Knightstown, Indiana. Beard graduated from DePauw College in 1898 and attended Oxford and Cornell universities before receiving his Ph.D. from Columbia University in 1904. An independent-minded intellectual, he regarded political concerns as paramount. While living in England, he helped found Ruskin Hall, a workers' college, at Oxford. In December 1905, in New York, he joined the American Socialist Society (ASS). He served on the committee that wrote the society's bylaws and on the society's board of directors for seven of the next eight years. The objectives of the ASS were "to study and discuss political science" and "to expound the theories of modern socialism by lectures and publications." He maintained his interest in workers' education by teaching at the Society's Rand School for Social Science, by helping to found the New School for Social Research (1918), and through his involvement with the Workers' Education Bureau in the early 1920s. Beard also led the movement to reform municipal government. He edited the *National Municipal Review*, served as director of the New York Bureau of Municipal Research's Training School for Public Service, and traveled to Japan, where he advised the Japanese government on municipal issues during 1922 and 1923.

Beard taught at Columbia University from 1904 until 1917. In 1917, amid the turmoil of World War I, he resigned from the university over issues involving ACADEMIC FREEDOM. At Columbia, Beard wrote books on history and political science and developed, along with JAMES HARVEY ROBINSON, the New History. The New History sought to stimulate reform by interpreting the past in relation to the present.

In 1913, Beard created a national sensation with the publication of his *An Economic Interpretation of the Constitution of the United States*, in which he argued that "the concept of the Constitution as a piece of abstract legislation reflecting no group interests and recognizing no economic antagonisms is entirely false" (p. 188). His thesis, that the Founding Fathers represented the interests of capital (manufacturers, shippers, traders, and those who held public securities) as opposed to the interests of the majority of Americans who were small farmers, hinted at intrigue and has been alternately attacked and praised. The book intimated that the Founding Fathers conceived the CONSTITUTION as a bulwark against democracy. While much of Beard's evidence and argument has been subsequently found wanting, the book was a milestone in the development of Progressive historiography.

In 1927, Charles and his wife MARY RITTER BEARD published their multivolume *The Rise of American Civilization*. The book continued Beard's earlier approach of interpreting U.S. history in terms of a dialectic between rural agrarian interests and urban capital. The Beards characterized the Civil War as a conflict in which "capitalists, laborers, and farmers of the North and West drove from power in the national government the planting aristocracy of the South." The war, they argued, resulted in "vast changes in the arrangement of classes, in the accumulation and distribution of wealth, in the course of industrial development, and in the Constitution." They concluded that "the so-called civil war was in reality a Second American Revolution and in a strict sense, the First" (vol. 2, pp. 52–4). Praised for including elements of social, economic, and women's history, their work has been faulted for under-emphasizing the role of slavery in bringing about the war.

In the 1930s and 1940s, Beard expressed concern repeatedly that the executive branch of the federal government was gaining too much power; he wrote on foreign policy, urged a "continentalism" of the Western hemisphere, became an isolationist, and supported increased state planning of the domestic economy.

In his presidential address before the American Historical Association in 1933, Beard delivered his "Written History as an Act of Faith." In this, and in a number of other brief essays, Beard elaborated his theory of historical interpretation. Influenced by the New History, issues of relativity in modern physics, the work of William James and John Dewey, and careful reading of Benedetto Croce and Karl Mannheim, Beard dismissed the quest for OBJECTIVITY in history writing as an illusory "noble dream." He argued, instead, for *subjective* historical interpretation. Writing history is an act of interpretation that depends upon the historian's "angle of vision," itself influenced by the "biases, prejudices, beliefs, affections, general upbringing, and experience, particularly social and economic" (p. 220) that each author brings to his or her subject. Beard's view of historical interpretation resonates with philosophical PRAGMATISM and perspectivalism. He dismissed the crude relativistic view that every belief is as good as every other, stating that the historian ought not to embrace "the fleeting shadow of relativity" (p. 225). He stressed, instead, the importance of influencing present-day politics. His personal hope was that his own writing was part of a general movement toward "social democracy." He nevertheless held to a correspondence theory on questions of fact. That is, he believed that there is an "actuality," or "physical world," outside the "thinker" and that historians can discern "true" statements about "facts" (pp. 225–8). Interpretations are the narratives or analyses that a particular author imposes upon facts.

Beard wrote or edited scores of articles and more than 40 books. Throughout his adult life he was an exemplar of the social scientist as political reformer.

JOHN LOUIS RECCHIUTI

FURTHER READING
Howard K. Beale, *Charles A. Beard: an Appraisal* (Lexington: University of Kentucky Press, 1954).
Charles A. Beard, *An Economic Interpretation of the Constitution of the United States* (1913; New York: Macmillan, 1961).
——"Written History as an Act of Faith," *American Historical Review* 39 (Jan. 1934): 219–29.
——"That Noble Dream," *American Historical Review* 41, no. 1 (Oct. 1935): 74–87.
Charles Beard and Mary Beard, *The Rise of American Civilization* (1927; New York: Macmillan, 1930).
"By-laws of the American Socialist Society, Adopted February 23, 1906," Rand School for Social Science Papers, New York University.
Ellen Nore, *Charles Beard: an Intellectual Biography* (Carbondale: Southern Illinois University Press, 1983).
Peter Novick, *That Noble Dream: the "Objectivity Question" and the American Historical Profession* (New York: Cambridge University Press, 1988).

Beard, George (b. Montville, Conn., May 8, 1839; d. New York, N.Y., Jan. 23, 1883). Neurologist and writer. Beard was instrumental in popularizing the idea of neurasthenia. A wide variety of symptoms, he explained in *American Nervousness* (1881), were caused by nervous exhaustion resulting from the hectic pace of American life. Intense emotion and sexual repression were also pathogenic. Although he believed that psychological illness operated through a physiological intermediate (depletion of nervous energy), he emphasized the preventive importance of anxiety reduction and sex education. As a cultural critic Beard was influential in pointing to the psychic costs of "civilized" existence and in calling for therapeutic intervention to help restore individual and social equilibrium.

FURTHER READING
Tom Lutz, *American Nervousness, 1903* (Ithaca: Cornell University Press, 1991).

Beard, Mary Ritter (b. Indianapolis, Ind., Aug. 5, 1876; d. Phoenix, Ariz., Aug. 14, 1958). Suffragist, independent scholar, and historian, Mary Beard was reared in comfort in Indianapolis. She was one of six children of Narcissa and Eli Ritter, both from Southern families. High school valedictorian, she went on to Methodist-affiliated DePauw University, where she obtained the Ph.B. (1897), and met CHARLES BEARD. In 1900 they married and departed for Oxford University. Two years in England introduced Mary Beard to working-class poverty and promoted her allegiance to cooperative socialism and workers' education. Influenced by her neighbor in Manchester, Emmeline Pankhurst (soon to become world-renowned for suffrage militance), she became deeply interested in the lives and problems of women wage-earners and committed to women gaining the ballot as a form of leverage.

The Beards returned to New York City shortly after the birth of a daughter, Miriam, in 1901. After brief graduate study in political science at Columbia University, Mary Beard combined care and education of her children (a son, William, was born in 1907) with voluntary activities. Between 1907 and 1912 she worked with such groups as the Rand School of Social Science, the American Socialist Society (which promoted workers' education), the Equality League for Self-Supporting Women (a suffrage group), and the

New York Women's Trade Union League. During 1910–11 she edited *The Woman Voter*, published by the New York state Woman Suffrage Party, then worked to develop a Wage-Earners' Suffrage League. Meanwhile, she collaborated with her husband on a high-school civics text, *American Citizenship* (1914), which gave particular attention to girls' and women's preparation for participation in the polity. In 1913 Alice Paul and Lucy Burns recruited Beard for the inner circle of the Congressional Union, a new militant suffrage group (later the National Woman's Party), in which she served avidly, forming strong attachments. Never satisfied with concentrating on suffrage alone, however, Beard eased herself from the top leadership in 1915 and completed her first book, *Women's Work in Municipalities* (1915), an overview of the accomplishments of contemporary women's voluntary associations. After New York women got the ballot by state referendum in 1917, she left the suffrage movement, and wrote a second book, *A Short History of the American Labor Movement* (1920), for the Workers' Education Bureau that she and her husband had helped found.

After World War I and the family's permanent move to Connecticut, Mary Beard became known as a historian. She collaborated with Charles Beard on the much-acclaimed and very widely read two-volume *The Rise of American Civilization* (1927), a panoramic history that stressed the natural and industrial resources of the nation and its democratic culture—and paid more attention to women than any other survey written prior to the 1970s. The sequels *America in Midpassage* (1937), treating the 1920s and 1930s, and *The American Spirit; a Study of the Idea of Civilization in the United States* (1942), which especially showed Mary Beard's hand, followed. Although her husband unfairly received the lion's share of the credit for the joint works, there is reason to believe that Mary Beard introduced into the series the broad-ranging "civilization" concept which so distinguished *Rise* from preceding national histories. She believed it necessary to go beyond the narrowly political, to "widen the frames" of history and "comprehend the wide course of civilization," in order to achieve a fully human history, that is, one that included women. These convictions, which had been developing for several decades, emerged in her book on women's part in the history of Western civilization, *On Understanding Women* (1931).

Using her increasing renown to speak up for women's history, Beard published *America through Women's Eyes* (1933), an anthology of women's documents of U.S. history; *Laughing Their Way* (1934), a collection of women's humor co-edited with Martha

Bruere; a syllabus of study topics and questions published for the American Association of University Women called *A Changing Political Economy as it Affects Women* (1934); and a number of articles on women's relation to the economic crisis of the Depression. Having left socialism behind, she remained a sharp critic of capitalism. Her Depression-era works showed not only her rejection of economic individualism, but also her disenchantment with the feminist goal of "sex equality," which meant to her "pure imitation" of men, rather than the exercise of social leadership of which she believed women capable. Between 1935 and 1940 she headed an effort to found a World Center for Women's Archives, to collect documents and thus record women's constructive and vital social roles. Although unsuccessful, the project was the progenitor of major archives founded at Radcliffe and Smith colleges during the 1940s. Her attempt to revise the *Encyclopedia Britannica* to include women's part in culture and history also met frustration.

Admittedly "obsessed" with women, Beard had an ambivalent relation to FEMINISM. She retained ex-suffragist friends, and moved in circles of women activists, but did not join women's organizations and did not support the Equal Rights Amendment advocated by her former Congressional Union colleagues. She raged against what she called the feminist version of history because, by stressing women's subjection to men, it hid, in her view, their historical achievements. She, in contrast, saw women as "co-makers" of civilization, sustaining a creative, if underacknowledged, partnership with men throughout world history. Her most ambitious and best-known work, *Woman as Force in History* (1946) elaborated that viewpoint, along with acid criticism of male historians for their disregard of women's past. Her research agenda—to show that equity courts enabled married women to escape the disabilities imposed on them by the Anglo-American common law—continued to fuel historiographical debate almost a half-century later.

Substantially founding the modern field of women's history, Mary Beard left it an awkward legacy. Her rejection of sex equality as an adequate goal for women was disconcerting for later historians who adopted a feminist viewpoint. Yet she alone in her generation refused to allow men to be the measure of human accomplishment and was persistently determined to put women on the historical record. She made a start on reconstructing history by looking at it "through women's eyes," and seeking out women's contributions to public as well as private life. If her perspective downplayed the social construction of gender hierarchy, her emphasis on the persistent agency of women throughout history had lasting influence on subsequent historians of women. In line with her life-long belief that learning was sterile unless aimed at social use, she tried to supply her contemporaries, and future generations of women, with a past to inspire rather than defeat them.

NANCY F. COTT

See also WOMEN'S RIGHTS.

FURTHER READING

Berenice A. Carroll, "Mary Beard's *Woman as Force in History*: a Critique," *Massachusetts Review* 13 (winter–spring 1972): 125–43.
Nancy F. Cott, *A Woman Making History: Mary Ritter Beard through Her Letters* (New Haven: Yale University Press, 1991).
Ann J. Lane, *Mary Ritter Beard: a Sourcebook* (New York: Schocken, 1977).
Bonnie Smith, "Seeing Mary Beard," *Feminist Studies* 10 (fall 1984): 399–416.
Barbara K. Turoff, *Mary Beard as Force in History*, Wright State University Monograph Series (Dayton, Ohio, 1979).

Beat Generation Referring to a community of writers who began their careers in the 1940s and who achieved national attention in the 1950s, the phrase also evokes the bohemian lifestyle represented in works like Allen Ginsberg's "Howl" (1956) and Jack Kerouac's *On the Road* (1957), in which the social and psychological repression of the postwar period are decried and an alternative participatory ethos is celebrated. The explosion of the atomic bomb over Japan, the revelations about the prison camps of the Soviet gulag, the new corporate mentality of the Eisenhower cabinet, the effects of McCarthyism and redbaiting by the House Un-American Activities Committee, the new "joiner" mentality of suburban life all contributed to a feeling of rootlessness that as yet had no expression. The Beat writers responded to this malaise by living at the margins of American life, satirizing middle-class conformism by refusing its institutions and social mores. The media, sensing a lively alternative to the Eisenhower doldrums, seized upon Beat lifestyles and created a cartoon creature, the "beatnik," a comic alternative to the man in the grey flannel suit.

The origins of the term "beat" have been debated by many of the movement's participants, but it is clear that its use as a cultural marker began in conversations among WILLIAM BURROUGHS, ALLEN GINSBERG, Neal Cassady, JACK KEROUAC, Herbert Huncke and Carl Solomon in New York during the late 1940s. Jack Kerouac is usually described as being if not the term's inventor, at least its most subtle genealogist. Writing in *Esquire* of March 1958, Kerouac stated that "beat" referred to world-weariness, being "down

and out but full of intense conviction" (p. 24). Many in the urban underclass, he wrote, were "beaten down" by circumstance, yet capable of a kind of mystical "beatitude." His models for beatitude were the "felaheen people"—hobos, black jazz musicians, religious mystics, petty criminals—whom he encountered first around New York's 42nd Street bars and cafeterias and later on his cross-country trips with Neal Cassady. The Beats, he claimed, were

solitary Bartlebies staring out the dead wall window of our civilization . . . subterranean heroes who'd finally turned from the "freedom" machine of the West and were taking drugs, digging bop, having flashes of insight, experiencing the "derangement of the senses" . . . free from European influences (p. 24).

Although the Beat writers regarded themselves as the heirs of HERMAN MELVILLE and WALT WHITMAN, their invocation of Rimbaud's linguistic experimentalism ("derangement of the senses") suggests that they were not entirely free of European influence. The prophetic mode of British Romantics like Blake and Shelley could be felt in the work of Gregory Corso, Allen Ginsberg and Michael McClure, while the spirit of Dada experimentation continued in the cut-up novels of William Burroughs. Other members of the movement like Gary Snyder and Philip Whalen drew from classical Chinese poetry and Native American folklore. French and Spanish Surrealism made their appearance in the work of Lawrence Ferlinghetti, Philip Lamantia and Bob Kaufman. Many of the writers acknowledged the inspiration of jazz improvisation, and one of the period's more enduring legacies was the phenomenon of poetry and jazz collaborations. Finally, one finds a populist strain in all of the writers, whether through the street poetry of Bob Kaufman and Ray Bremser or in Kerouac's celebration of the urban proletariat.

Whatever literary sources influenced individual styles, Beat poets sought compositional models outside of the New Critical aesthetics then reigning. Nothing could be further removed from the artisanal poetics of late MODERNISM than Jack Kerouac's theory of "spontaneous prose," which recommended writing "from jewel center of interest in subject of image at *moment* of writing" and which rejected any impulse to "afterthink" or censor one's initial inspiration (Parkinson, p. 66). Kerouac's practice of writing while high on marijuana or benzedrine and his famed use of a teletype roll to compose parts of *On the Road* hardly lent themselves to those qualities of aesthetic distancing advocated in the classic essay by T. S. ELIOT, "Tradition and the Individual Talent."

The same could be said for Ginsberg, whose long

Whitmanian line and bardic voice were the antithesis of the reflective, metaphysical lyric that was the model for so many poems published in the academic quarterlies:

I saw the best minds of my generation destroyed by
    madness, starving hysterical naked,
dragging themselves through the negro streets at
    dawn looking for an angry fix,
angelheaded hipsters burning for the ancient heavenly
    connection to the starry dynamo in the machinery
    of night

"Howl" brought the author's personal life and contacts directly before the reader, describing sexual acts, moments of illumination, and drug experiences in a nonstop, hallucinatory catalogue. It was a poem written for oral performance in front of an audience, not for quiet contemplation in the private study. When *Howl* was seized by customs officials in 1956 for obscenity, the pornography trial that ensued validated many of Ginsberg's warnings about police surveillance and censorship. Thus Ginsberg's voice was extended off the page and into the public sphere—a position he has occupied continuously since the mid-fifties.

The *Howl* trial brought national attention to the Beats, as did the publication of Kerouac's *On the Road* in 1957 and the *Evergreen Review*'s 1957 "San Francisco Scene" issue. The Beat movement quickly became the centerpiece of the "San Francisco Renaissance" occurring in the city's North Beach area, where many of the New York writers had moved. They joined West Coast poets such as Kenneth Rexroth, Robert Duncan, William Everson (then Brother Antoninus), Jack Spicer, Gary Snyder, Philip Whalen and Michael McClure. Local bars, galleries and coffeehouses provided a supportive social network, and public poetry readings became a standard literary venue. With the opening of Lawrence Ferlinghetti's City Lights Bookstore in 1953 and the formation of his Pocket Poets Series in 1957 (which published *Howl* among other titles), the small press revolution was inaugurated.

This lively ambience was heightened by local media coverage of North Beach bohemia, including an exposé written by a reporter from the *San Francisco Chronicle* who went "undercover" in North Beach pads and bars. *Life* and *Fortune* featured Greenwich Village and North Beach lifestyles, while beatnik characters made cameo appearances on television sitcoms. Such media attention seldom addressed questions of literary value and focused instead on drugs, sex, and offensive behavior. Paul O'Neil, writing for *Life* (Nov. 30, 1959), noted that many of the beats are "talkers, loafers, passive little con men, lonely eccentrics, mom-haters, cop-haters, exhibitionists with abused smiles and second mortages on a bongo drum." Local columnist Herb Caen, building on anxieties produced by the Sputnik crisis, when the Soviets launched their first satellite, coined the term "beatnik," thereby linking antisocial behavior on the domestic front to the (perceived) threat of world communism.

While the popular media sneered at the Beats for various affronts to bourgeois manners, the intellectual establishment attacked them for their lack of decorum. Writers like John Hollander, John Ciardi, and Herbert Gold scoffed at their poetics of immediacy and spontaneity, while cultural critics like LIONEL TRILLING, IRVING HOWE, and NORMAN PODHORETZ mocked their pretense to social disaffiliation. Howe, writing in the *Partisan Review* (summer 1959), saw the Beats as the pale reflections of their bohemian forebears: "In their contempt for mind they are at one with the middle class suburbia they think they scorn" (p. 435). Norman Podhoretz regarded Kerouac's celebration of spontaneity and primitivism as arising "from a pathetic poverty of feeling" (Parkinson, p. 211). Such attacks attempted to undercut whatever cultural critique the Beats might offer by seeing them as an emanation of rather than alternative to mass society.

Many of these criticisms came from members of the Old Left who regarded the younger generation's rejection of traditional Marxism and its elevation of lifestyle politics as an oedipal challenge to stable parental authority. In this view, the Beats were an extension of the antisocial behavior and juvenile delinquency being mythologized in Hollywood films like *The Wild One* and *Rebel Without a Cause*. The Beat generation, according to these critics, was a bohemianism that lacked a critique, a spirituality that lacked doctrinal authority, a politics that lacked a party. Worse, by espousing the virtues of MASS CULTURE—its folk heroes, musicians, media celebrities and pulp literature—the Beat generation had allegedly sold out to the culture industry.

The Beats paid a price for the media scrutiny and public attention they cultivated. By constantly having to embody the lifestyle fictionalized in their literary works, certain figures—Kerouac in particular—had difficulty separating public and private lives. In public forums they felt called to dramatize the "energy" of the present rather than provide an analysis *of* it, a constraint that limited the force of their critique of middle-class values. And while the model of the bourgeois nuclear family was often the object of their scorn, the communal alternatives they offered were often no more emancipatory, especially for women. The Beat Generation was masculinist in temperament and ideology, relegating women to the role of sexual surrogates or family providers. But as Barbara Ehrenreich points out in *The Hearts of Men*, the very fact that the Beats projected alternative modes of family, sexuality, and community helped break down the model of the nuclear family with its wage-earner male and unpaid domestic servant female. And because many of the Beats were gay or lesbian, their open (and often defiant) expression of sexual orientation served as a significant step towards gay liberation.

During the 1950s, the Beat generation was often linked to other forms of intellectual dissent—from Britain's Angry Young Men to France's existentialists. While such parallels articulate a general sense of postwar disaffection, they tend to blur the movement's distinctly American forms. The Beats' rejection of white-collar suburbia came from having grown up in urban, middle- to lower-middle class urban families. Although several of them entered college, most dropped out and made their living in low-paying jobs or through the largesse of friends and family. They identified themselves with those marginalized communities untouched by the postwar economic boom and idealized their cultural products, especially the African American music of Charlie Parker, Billie Holliday, and John Coltrane. Where their more academic counterparts turned to Anglicanism or Catholicism, they turned to esoteric Jewish religion and Zen and Tantric Buddhism as spiritual alternatives to doctrinal religion. Their faith in personalism and process in art was a direct response to the narrow application of neo-Kantian aesthetics promulgated in the classroom and literary periodicals. If the Beat generation often gesticulated wildly, it was because so many others in America spoke in measured, reasonable sentences and pursued the politics of rational consensus.

Although the energy of the Beat movement died out by the early 1960s, it lived on in many of the countercultural values of the next generation. The Beat belief in the personal as political reached new audiences among women, gays, ethnic minorities and students who formed the basis of the New Left. The politics of disaffiliation continued within the anti-Vietnam War movement where coalition-building and decentralized organization challenged traditional political activism. Sexual openness and alternative spiritual practices, so much the objects of ridicule by mainstream media during the 1950s, flourished within the youth-culture movements of the next decade. And although the Beat apocalyptic voice gave way to a cooler, more cosmopolitan tone in American poetry,

it lived on in Europe, where Ginsberg and his peers continue to attract a mass following. A relatively short-lived phenomenon, the Beat movement left a powerful legacy of cultural resistance that has continually found new audiences throughout the world.

MICHAEL DAVIDSON

FURTHER READING

Donald Allen, ed., *The New American Poetry* (New York: Grove, 1960).

Ann Charters, ed., *The Beats: Literary Bohemians in Postwar America*, vol. 16, parts 1 and 2 of *Dictionary of Literary Biography* (Detroit: Gale Research, 1983).

——, *The Portable Beat Reader* (New York: Penguin, 1992).

Bruce Cook, *The Beat Generation* (New York: Scribners, 1971).

Michael Davidson, *The San Francisco Renaissance: Poetics and Community at Mid-Century* (Cambridge: Cambridge University Press, 1989).

Barry Miles, *Ginsberg: a Biography* (New York: Simon and Schuster, 1989).

Gerard Nicosia, *Memory Babe: a Critical Biography of Jack Kerouac* (New York: Grove, 1985).

Thomas Parkinson, ed., *A Casebook on the Beat* (New York: Crowell, 1961).

John Tytell, *Naked Angels: the Lives and Literature of the Beat Generation* (New York: McGraw-Hill, 1976).

Becker, Carl (b. near Waterloo, Iowa, Sept. 7, 1873; d. Ithaca, N.Y., Apr. 10, 1945). Historian. A scholar of American intellectual history and the Enlightenment, Becker argued that historical facts emerge from and are shaped by particular contexts of interpretation. Although he remained committed to the ideal of accuracy, Becker disputed claims that history could be completely objective; he shared William James's and John Dewey's conception of truth as open-ended and subject to continuing debate. Author most notably of *The Heavenly City of the Eighteenth-Century Philosophers* (1932), Becker articulated his pragmatic approach to history in his controversial 1931 presidential address to the American Historical Association, "Everyman His Own Historian" (published in the *American Historical Review* in 1932).

See also CHARLES BEARD; OBJECTIVITY; PRAGMATISM.

FURTHER READING

Peter Novick, *That Noble Dream: the "Objectivity Question" and the American Historical Profession* (New York: Cambridge University Press, 1988).

Beecher, Catharine (b. East Hampton, N.Y., Sept. 6, 1800; d. Elmira, N.Y., May 12, 1878). The oldest child of LYMAN BEECHER, the most prominent Evangelical clergyman of the 1820s and 1830s, Catharine Beecher rose to prominence in the decades before the Civil War because her writings effectively expressed new views about the expanded power of women in family life. Those views broke with outdated eighteenth-century notions and set the stage for modern assumptions about the place of women in American society.

Beecher's adult achievements were rooted in her childhood, during which she absorbed her father's phenomenal energy. She also inherited his ability to use popular modes of communication to foster new communal values capable of sustaining yet restraining the exuberant spirit and culture of the young Republic. Her father harvested souls. She cultivated new domestic affections. Both were responding to the growing power of middle-class values in American life and the waning authority of traditional elites.

At the age of nine Catharine Beecher moved with her family from isolated and rural East Hampton, Long Island to fashion-conscious and class-conscious Litchfield, Connecticut. Catharine acquired the ornamental accomplishments of her well-born status. When her mother, Roxanne Beecher, died of consumption in 1816, Catharine had to take on extra responsibility for her young siblings, including Harriet and Henry, and her father's remarriage bred a spirit of independence on account of her dislike for her stepmother. In the pivotal event of her young adulthood she resisted her father's pressure to undergo religious conversion, for conversion required a submission to external authority that Catharine could no longer accept. That self-assertion, together with the independence thrust upon her when her fiancé, a young professor at Yale, perished in a sea wreck, led her to seek a career in the world. She channeled her energies into the only respectable work open to women of her social standing—teaching.

Beecher's career as an educator and as a publicist for new attitudes towards women flourished in the dynamic cultural environment of pre-Civil War America. In 1823 she founded one of the new nation's most rigorous academies for higher education for women, the Hartford Female Seminary, and hitched her own star to the rising status of women as educators. In 1832 she followed her father and siblings to Cincinnati, where, like them, she championed the dominance of New England evangelicalism in the multicultural environment of the American West. By hiring others—including Harriet—to teach in her newly founded Western Female Institute, Catharine freed herself to write a series of popular books that established her reputation for astute social commentary on the place of women in American society.

Although she did not use the term, Beecher's writings advocated "domestic feminism"—that is, expanded power for women within domestic life, and ancillary power in the wider society. She was best known for *A Treatise on Domestic Economy. A Treatise* was first published in 1841, reprinted annually through 1856, and greatly expanded in a version coauthored with Harriet Beecher Stowe widely reprinted between 1869 and 1873, *The American Woman's Home.* Beecher's advice to women reflected contemporary economic changes that were relocating male labor and much of what had formerly been household production outside the household. She advised married women to exercise greater control over domestic life, including family finances, and to value their work as an honorable calling with great significance for the future of American democracy. "While woman holds a subordinate relation in society to the other sex," she said, "it is not because it was designed that her duties or her influence should be any the less important, or all-pervading." In other domestic writings, especially *Letters to Persons Who Are Engaged in Domestic Service* (1842), *Letters to the People on Health and Happiness* (1855), and *Physiology and Calisthenics for Schools and Families* (1856), Beecher reinforced her authority as a delineator of middle-class social mores and personal development.

Beecher's domestic writings provided her with a modest income between 1840 and 1860, but more important to her (if less lucrative) were her efforts to feminize the teaching profession and to justify women's greater access to higher education through their "calling" as teachers. The future of American democracy, she argued, depended on "the intellectual and moral character of the mass of the people," and the shaping of that character within family life was "committed mainly to the female hand." Thus women needed to gain access to higher education so they could bring to the nation the same benefits as teachers that they brought to family life as mothers. This theme, which also justified her own public activities, first appeared in her 1829 pamphlet, *Suggestions Respecting Improvements in Education*, and was subsequently orchestrated in such works as *An Essay on the Education of Female Teachers* (1835) and *The Duty of American Women to their Country* (1845). The success of the National Board of Popular Education, which she founded in the late 1840s to place eastern women teachers in western communities, showed that her ideas were sustained by two of the most fundamental processes of change underway in nineteenth-century America—geographical expansion and the empowerment of women as the chief agents of childhood socialization. Patriarchy, defined as the rule of the father, was still alive and well in courts and other arenas of public life, but the basic shift from male to female rule in family matters was, thanks in part to Catharine Beecher's formidable influence, well launched by 1850.

Beecher's domestically based expansion of women's influence competed for the loyalties of American women with the natural-rights views forged in the antislavery movement. A debate between the two perspectives occurred when, in response to the public activity of antislavery women, especially Angelina Grimké's *Appeal to the Christian Women of the Southern States* (1836), Beecher published *An Essay on Slavery and Abolitionism with Reference to the Duty of American Females* (1837). Later, her book *Woman's Profession as Mother and Educator with Views in Opposition to Woman Suffrage* (1872) insisted "that the evils it is hoped to cure by the ballot would continue" until women's domestic labor was granted the respect accorded to male labor outside the home.

To a considerable degree Catharine Beecher's authority on matters pertaining to education and to family life derived from her facility as an interpreter of American religious life. In an age dominated by grass-roots religious fervor, she deftly channeled spiritual anxieties into commonsense moralism. Her *Elements of Mental and Moral Philosophy, Founded upon Experience, Reason and the Bible* (1831) was the first in a series of her writings that turned away from doctrinal controversies and stressed a moral system based on self-sacrifice. An ethic of self-sacrifice would permit society to develop its material wealth and at the same time remain moral. Seeking to replace her father's theology with "sure and universal principles that will evolve a harmonious system in which we shall all agree," she identified "self-conquest" and service to others as the highest good. Through service to others—especially as "infallible teachers of what is right and true"—women occupied the center of her moral universe. Theories of morality and religion, she thought, "are especially to be examined and decided on by woman, as the heaven-appointed educator of infancy and childhood."

KATHRYN KISH SKLAR

See also DOMESTICITY; VIRTUE; WOMEN'S RIGHTS.

FURTHER READING

Jeanne Boydston, *Home and Work: Housework, Wages, and the Ideology of Labor in the Early Republic* (New York: Oxford University Press, 1990).

Jeanne Boydston, Mary Kelley, and Anne Margolis, eds., *The Limits of Sisterhood: the Beecher Sisters on Women's Rights and Woman's Sphere* (Chapel Hill: University of North Carolina Press, 1988).

Nancy F. Cott, *The Bonds of Womanhood: Woman's Sphere in New England, 1780–1835* (New Haven: Yale University Press, 1976).

Nancy Hoffman, ed., *Woman's "True" Profession: Voices from the History of Teaching* (Old Westbury, N.Y.: Feminist Press, 1981).

Kathryn Kish Sklar, *Catharine Beecher: a Study in American Domesticity* (New York: Norton, 1976).

——"Catharine Beecher's *A Treatise on Domestic Economy: a Document in Domestic Feminism*," in Earl A. French and Diana Royce, eds., *Portraits of a Nineteenth-Century Family* (Hartford, Conn.: Stowe–Day Foundation, 1976).

Beecher, Henry Ward (b. Litchfield, Conn., June 24, 1813; d. Brooklyn, N.Y., Mar. 8, 1887). Son of renowned churchman LYMAN BEECHER, and younger brother of CATHARINE BEECHER and HARRIET BEECHER STOWE, Henry Ward became a preacher of unsurpassed power in Victorian America. From the 1850s to the 1880s he occupied a position of cultural significance that we can scarcely comprehend today, since he was above all else an orator, and ours is no longer a culture that cherishes the art of RHETORIC and public speech. He wrote no memorable books, and the vast run of his published sermons and lectures do not convey the full impact he made as an elocutionist. In his own time Beecher was widely hailed as the "Shakespeare of the pulpit," and the phrase was not meant idly: Beecher's imaginative and topical range, his luxuriant and inventive language, were legendary. Abraham Lincoln chose him to deliver the address at Fort Sumter when the Union flag was raised there on April 14, 1865. Beecher's jubilant and mournful speech preceded Lincoln's assassination by a few hours: "noon and midnight," Beecher remarked afterwards, "without a space between" (Rugoff, p. 394).

Lincoln is alleged to have remarked that if a foreigner needed a quick introduction to America, he should go to Plymouth Church in Brooklyn to listen to Beecher, the representative American man. Many twentieth-century writers have followed Lincoln's advice. They have viewed Beecher as a living document of his era. Those like Paxton Hibben, eager to distance themselves from the alleged complacency of the Victorian bourgoisie, have fixed on Beecher as exemplary sentimentalist, florid rhetorician, and baptizer of things as they are. Those like William McLoughlin, awed by the transformation of middle-class values that took place over the course of the nineteenth century—from the fixed moral proprieties of the early industrial order to the increasingly open-ended and therapeutic consumerism of the turn of the century—have grasped Beecher as a key mirror and instigator of a massive cultural shift.

There is no question that in retrospect Beecher reveals a great deal about the development of the American bourgoisie in the late nineteenth century. He was a latter-day Romantic in his craving for intense feeling, and he sought to make the quest for effusive feeling respectable within middle-class culture. As a Protestant clergyman of notable lineage he was in a special position to effect change. His marriage of ROMANTICISM and liberal Protestant evangelism was a potent force in discrediting formal dogmas and impersonally enforced norms of behavior. He wanted Americans to cultivate themselves as individuals—a standard moralist's theme—but he saw individuality as an eruptive, explosive "personality." He undertook the delicate task of encouraging uncustomary transgressive impulses, yet keeping them safely domesticated, circumscribing them as feeling, not permitting them the full outlet of action. In his own life he cultivated a special friendship with Elizabeth Tilton, one of his parishioners, and they paid a heavy price for their experiment in pushing back that boundary between feeling and behavior. Although Beecher was acquitted by a hung jury in the sensational "adultery trial" of 1875, he and Tilton were severely reprimanded for giving free reign to individual feeling and implicitly mocking the moral system that restricted intense, cross-gender, adult love to the marital bond.

But Beecher was no libertine. In his *Yale Lectures on Preaching*, delivered in the early 1870s, he made plain that his plea for the individualizing of personality was all in the interest of greater social cohesion. Like many social observers of his day, he sensed that an urbanizing, industrializing America was skirting the edge of an abyss. The (supposedly) stable communities of earlier generations were now rent by sudden economic reversals and by class and ethnic antagonisms. Rather than call in conservative fashion for a reassertion of "order" or "discipline" in the face of social chaos, he urged a "spiritual engineering" that would release dammed-up springs of personality but direct them in socially productive paths. Charismatic preachers could stir the masses to new heights of feeling yet also bind them together in a new collective life. Ann Douglas was on the right track when she argued in *The Feminization of American Life* (1977) that Beecher's religion of solidarity through expressive individuality was a pivotal preparation for the twentieth-century culture of consumption—a culture in which social order was grounded not in disciplined austerity or rigid codes, but in ceaseless innovation and the making-over of tastes and lifestyles. But she overlooked Beecher's conviction that the good society—one that encouraged yet managed each person's flights of feeling—was not the Christian's only or noblest goal. For Beecher, the first concern of life was to follow Jesus in loving God.

From a late twentieth-century vantage point, Beecher can represent the seismic shift of sensibility and socialization that took place in nineteenth-century America: a new individuality beyond inherited convention, and a newly conventional social order based on the cultivation of safely liberated emotion. But in the nineteenth century he could stand for America itself in its headlong rush toward self-creation. He was such a memorable preacher, Yale Divinity School professor Lewis Brastow wrote in 1904, because

he was so distinctively American in his qualities. . . . It is precisely this sort of personality, individualistic, unique, transcendent in power though it be, that becomes representative of the national temperament, of its intensity, force, self-assertion, independence, emancipation from bondage to tradition and convention and custom. (pp. 100, 106)

He could stand for the nation because he literally stood before the nation as orator and translated its religious and secular experience into language and gesture that moved men and women to applause and to tears. Oratory was entertainment in the world before film, but it was also combat, instruction, celebration, and stock-taking. Audiences were discriminating and attentive, trained to expect compelling, virtuoso speech, and northern audiences between the 1850s and the 1880s found their hero in a gifted wordsmith who on the platform could excoriate his enemies or whisper of love and intimacy. "Deeper than all qualities of character," intoned Beecher's obituary writer in the *Andover Review* in 1887, "there is the indescribable something, baffling still to the philosophers, which we call personality, the mixture of the qualities that make up one's peculiar manhood." Beecher was the master of personality in an era which saw it (as Beecher did) not only as a useful social glue but as a depth of being that bonded a person to others and prepared a person for the sudden encounter with God.

RICHARD WIGHTMAN FOX
See also LIBERAL PROTESTANTISM; VICTORIANISM.

FURTHER READING
Lyman Abbott, *Henry Ward Beecher* (1903; New York: Chelsea House, 1980).
Lewis O. Brastow, *Representative American Preachers* (New York: Macmillan, 1904).
Marie Caskey, *Chariot of Fire: Religion and the Beecher Family* (New Haven: Yale University Press, 1978).
Clifford E. Clark Jr., *Henry Ward Beecher: Spokesman for a Middle-Class America* (Urbana: University of Illinois Press, 1978).
Paxton Hibben, *Henry Ward Beecher: an American Portrait* (New York: George H. Doran, 1927).

William G. McLoughlin, *The Meaning of Henry Ward Beecher: an Essay on the Shifting Values of Mid-Victorian America, 1840–1870* (New York: Knopf, 1970).

Milton Rugoff, *The Beechers: an American Family in the Nineteenth Century* (New York: Harper and Row, 1981).

Halford R. Ryan, *Henry Ward Beecher: Peripatetic Preacher* (New York: Greenwood, 1990).

Beecher, Lyman (b. New Haven, Conn., Oct. 12, 1775; d. Brooklyn, N.Y., Jan. 10, 1863). Minister and revivalist. An inspired preacher and president of Lane Theological Seminary (1832–50), Beecher linked revivalism and moral reform, and expected spiritual redemption to transform both individuals and society. America, he held, is part of God's design: if the country survives its temptations of passion and greed, its reformation will spread throughout the world. What is needed is sincere conversion—which happens by God's grace, not human potency—and a commitment to embodying God's will in the social order. His sermons attacking such evils as intemperance and Catholicism were frequently published, but his main intellectual legacy was not his preaching but his 13 children, who included CATHARINE BEECHER, HARRIET BEECHER STOWE, and HENRY WARD BEECHER.

FURTHER READING

Vincent Harding, *A Certain Magnificence: Lyman Beecher and the Transformation of American Protestantism, 1775–1863* (Brooklyn: Carlson, 1991).

behaviorism The intellectual roots of behaviorism can be traced to such European sources as Descartes's theory of reflexive behavior, British associationist philosophy, Russian reflexology, Ernst Mach's positivistic philosophy of science, and Darwinian notions of organismic adaptation and continuity between species. But as an explicit school of psychological thought and a program for social reform, behaviorism has been a characteristically American movement ever since its formal founding by JOHN B. WATSON in 1913. An outgrowth of the functionalist psychology, pragmatist philosophy, and social meliorism of WILLIAM JAMES and JOHN DEWEY, behaviorism stresses the functions served by behavior in the process of an organism's adjustment to an environment. For behaviorists, it is overt actions, not internal cognitions, that make a difference in this process; as Watson put it, behaviorism is the only consistent functionalism. (*See also* SCIENTISM AND COGNITIVISM.)

Behaviorism emerged at a time when the social dislocation caused by rapid urbanization of American society demanded new means of social organization and control to replace the Victorian mores of small-town rural life. During this period, progressivists such as Walter Lippmann called on psychologists to help formulate those means, and the newly established science of psychology, eager to justify its status as an independent discipline, responded by aggressively promoting itself in terms of social utility. Alongside its sibling movements of mental testing and scientific management (see MANAGERIALISM), behaviorism proclaimed itself a scientifically respectable means of grounding social technology in the rigors of laboratory science. During its formative period, behaviorism was warmly endorsed by such notables as Dewey and Bertrand Russell, and one reviewer of Watson's 1924 *Behaviorism* found himself "blinded with a great hope" for the future of a scientifically managed society.

Privileged by its dual rhetoric of pure science and social technology, behaviorism enjoyed preeminent status in American psychology from the 1930s until it was challenged by a resurgence of cognitive psychology in the 1960s. Though no longer in a position of hegemony, it remains an active and influential approach to theory and application. As a tradition of scientific research, behaviorism comprises a loose family of theories sharing certain assumptions about the environmental determination of behavior, the malleability of human nature, and the generalizability of laboratory research with animals to real-world human problems. Classical behaviorists, including Watson, tended to conceive behavior as chains of simple Pavlovian conditioned reflexes. But, in the 1930s and 1940s, neobehaviorists revived Edward L. Thorndike's "law of effect," treating behavior as a function of its consequences—reinforcers and punishers—rather than its antecedent causes in the form of eliciting stimuli.

The best-known architect of this less mechanistic version of behaviorism was B. F. SKINNER, whose principles of operant conditioning proved powerful enough to be applied in a variety of settings. Sometimes grounded in elegant mathematical theories of learning, but more often based on intuitive rules of thumb, behavioral techniques were applied to education, psychotherapy, medicine, business, advertising, childrearing, and the management of prisons and mental hospitals. Given its inevitable likening of humans to lower animals and its assertive infiltration into such traditionally humanist realms as the healing arts and education, it is not surprising that behaviorism has long provoked controversy.

Nowhere has this debate been so heated as in response to the behaviorists' explicit social philosophies. Like Watson before him, Skinner proposed a behaviorist utopia, publishing an account of the fictional Walden Two community in 1948. Embodying strains of Henry David Thoreau's anarchistic skepticism toward political action, Walden Two is a small-scale collectivist community marked by an absence of political institutions, harmony with the natural environment, carefully restricted consumption of resources, and an egalitarian sharing of labor. As an experiment in behavioral technology, the community is managed by experts who arrange the practices of day-to-day life, including childrearing and the allocation of goods, in line with scientific principles of behavior. The rationale for cultural engineering was later elaborated in Skinner's 1971 bestseller *Beyond Freedom and Dignity*, which, like *Walden Two*, drew sharply divided reactions. Skinner's social views were hailed as a means of cultural salvation by his cultlike following and by many disaffected youths, but they were also denounced on the floor of Congress and attacked by humanist scholars as totalitarian. The philosopher Karl Popper, writing in the "secular humanist" journal *Free Inquiry*, attacked Skinner as a "megalomaniac" defender of a behaviorist "dictatorship," while the linguist and social critic NOAM CHOMSKY, in *For Reasons of State*, warned of a totalitarian state with "gas ovens smoking in the distance" (p. 344).

However, as Skinner himself and a number of commentators have realized, behaviorist social philosophy is in many respects well within the Western tradition, displaying marked affinities with Hobbes's attempt to ground political organization on principles of psychological hedonism and Condorcet's Enlightenment dream of rational social engineering. And, as an extension of the Progressivists' vision for social order and efficiency, behaviorist social philosophy poses technological solutions of the sort that give it a continuing appeal in a technocratic American culture otherwise repelled by its reductionistic depiction of human nature.

If behaviorism has a truly radical side, it is found in its rejection of the Western—and quintessentially American—ideal of the autonomous individual. In behaviorism's deterministic ontology of the individual, a person is regarded as a pure process of on-going interaction with the environment—as what Skinner called a "locus of variables." Simply put, the organism is what the organism does; nowhere in the locus of variables is there to be found any self, ego, or directing agency that stands outside the stream of natural events. On this construal, the concept of praise or blame for individuals becomes meaningless—as does the notion of legal responsibility—for there are only good or bad environments in which the individuals operate. The behaviorist concept of the egoless individual bears a striking resemblance to the Buddhist metaphysics of no-self. Indeed, Skinner's autobio-

graphy concludes with the acknowledgment that the West's extension of scientific determinism to human affairs has led behaviorism to embrace the no-self doctrine of Eastern mysticism as one of its central themes.

Those who view behaviorism as an exaggerated relic of Enlightenment scientism foresee no place for it in a postmodern world where grand narratives of science-based progress are widely dismissed as outmoded. Nonetheless, many of behaviorism's precepts remain well entrenched in American cultural practices, and it has more than once survived the death notices posted by its critics. In its denial of the autonomous individual, moreover, it continues to pose a vexing challenge to American political and legal traditions, as well as providing a source of alternative images of human nature and social planning for a culture that finds itself increasingly engaged with the collectivist cultures of the East and the challenges of global survival.

LAURENCE D. SMITH

FURTHER READING
Robert Boakes, *From Darwin to Behaviourism: Psychology and the Minds of Animals* (Cambridge, U.K.: Cambridge University Press, 1984).
Kerry W. Buckley, *Mechanical Man: John Broadus Watson and the Beginnings of Behaviorism* (New York: Guilford, 1989).
Noam Chomsky, *For Reasons of State* (New York: Pantheon, 1973).
John M. O'Donnell, *The Origins of Behaviorism: American Psychology, 1870–1920* (New York: New York University Press, 1985).
Paul T. Sagal, *Skinner's Philosophy* (Lanham: University Press of America, 1981).
Barry Schwartz and Hugh Lacey, *Behaviorism, Science, and Human Nature* (New York: Norton, 1982).
B. F. Skinner, *Walden Two* (1948; New York: Macmillan, 1976).
——, *Beyond Freedom and Dignity* (New York: Knopf, 1971).
——, *A Matter of Consequences: Part Three of an Autobiography* (New York: Knopf, 1983).

Bell, Alexander Graham (b. Edinburgh, Scotland, Mar. 3, 1847; d. Cape Breton Island, Nova Scotia, Aug. 2, 1922). Inventor and educator. Bell was committed to integrating deaf people into general society. He opposed the development of sign language, residential schools, and the evolving deaf subculture, for fear that deaf intermarriage and defective children would result. Instead, he argued, deaf people should use speech and lip reading. His search for mechanical devices to help deaf people communicate with hearing people led to his invention of the telephone (patented 1876) and a lifetime of technological innovation related to communication and education.

See also TECHNOLOGY.

FURTHER READING
Robert V. Bruce, *Bell: Alexander Graham Bell and the Conquest of Solitude* (Boston: Little, Brown, 1973).

Bell, Daniel (b. New York, N.Y., May 10, 1919). Sociologist, journalist, and intellectual activist, Bell was raised in New York City by his mother, a widowed garment worker. He joined the Young People's Socialist League (the Socialist Party youth wing) as a teenager and quickly drifted to the movement's more conservative, anticommunist faction. He graduated from City College of New York, took a master's degree in sociology at Columbia University, and during World War II edited the *New Leader*, a social democratic weekly. After teaching social science at the University of Chicago from 1945 to 1948, he returned to New York and worked ten years as labor columnist for *Fortune*. In these years, he also helped lead the American Committee for Cultural Freedom, a group of liberal anticommunist intellectuals affiliated with the international Congress for Cultural Freedom, and published *Marxian Socialism in the United States* (1952), which argued that a streak of moral purism had robbed the American socialist movement of political influence. At the end of the decade, Bell collected his essays on labor and society, social theory, and intellectual life to compose *The End of Ideology: On the Exhaustion of Political Ideas in the Fifties* (1960). In the 1960s, he was a sociology professor at Columbia University; in 1969 he moved to Harvard.

The phrase "the end of ideology" had been used by Edward Shils, Raymond Aron, and Seymour Martin Lipset to connote the postwar disenchantment of Western intellectuals with fervent political doctrines of the far left and right and the apparent CONSENSUS in the West on the legitimacy of a "welfare state" combining market mechanisms and government intervention (*see also* IDEOLOGY). After publication of Bell's book, the phrase served as a lightning rod for young radicals, who identified it with the quiescent mood of the 1950s and the liberal proposition that American society had "matured" to the point where only technical adjustments, not substantial social change, were required to meet common goals. It was clear that Bell had dismissed the relevance of Marxian socialism and supported Cold War containment policy, but charges of liberal or technocratic triumphalism were misplaced. His *End of Ideology* manifested more uncertainty than confidence in the well-being of American society or the potency of social science; he believed that most traditional perspectives in social thought failed to understand the dynamics of contemporary society or to respond to

the real dilemmas of the time. Bell's early purpose and abiding concern was not so much the celebration of the status quo as a diagnosis of discontinuity, an insistence that society and culture—and the relation between them—had taken on a distinctive, unheralded form in the West since World War II.

The core of Bell's analysis appeared in a pair of books, *The Coming of Post-Industrial Society* (1973) and *The Cultural Contradictions of Capitalism* (1976). For Bell, postindustrial society was still only emerging, but it had its "birth years" in the period 1945–50. It was defined by the primary role that formal knowledge and computer techniques played in production, the social centrality of institutions devoted to producing knowledge, and the growing weight of "services" as a component of the economy. To manage its resources, such a society had to orient itself toward a long-range future and adopt a new "sociologizing" mode of judgment that grasped an array of social conditions and outcomes, including education, health and environmental quality, more comprehensively than conventional market-based cost accounting did. Such demands put government in the lead, or "cockpit," of postindustrial society, though Bell believed markets remained necessary means of allocating resources.

The poignancy of Bell's analysis emerged more clearly in *The Cultural Contradictions of Capitalism*, one of the earliest American works to examine POSTMODERNISM—the peculiar amalgam of styles and attitudes which fused the modernist avant-garde with MASS CULTURE while spurning elements of modernity associated with the "rational cosmology" of the ENLIGHTENMENT. In Bell's view, the deep hostility to social institutions and the promotion of limitless appetites implied by these trends helped erode the social solidarity and common norms needed to give direction to postindustrial society. Construction of what Bell called a "public household," a political consensus to extend a just share of resources, rights, and responsibilities to all members of the civic community, seemed doomed by the antinomian ethos of late capitalist consumerism.

Much of Bell's sensibility stemmed from his participation during the late 1940s in a kind of religious revival among Jewish intellectuals, who shared a new interest in theology, respect for religious experience, and the sentiment of belonging to a people having a trans-historical identity. Without claiming a personal conviction of faith, Bell came to voice a deep appreciation for the value of tradition, a sense of depending on larger things, and the need to accept constraint on impulse and personal gratification. This disposition carried over to social affairs as he insisted on the role that AUTHORITY—that is, respect due to professional, political and cultural elites—played in granting society continuity and stability, a precious achievement, he believed, in a world of many atrocities. Bell's call in the 1970s and 1980s for the "restoration of authority" in American life, combined with his bitter denunciations of 1960s radicals and their legacy, constituted a genuinely conservative element of his thought.

Still, it was a mistake to associate Bell with NEOCONSERVATISM. He refused to follow the rightward current that led some postwar liberals, like his friend IRVING KRISTOL, to join the Reagan coalition of the 1980s. Reaganism, for Bell, connoted an "ideologizing" of capitalism (which he still regarded as ethically bankrupt), an outburst of crabbed religious moralism that threatened rights of privacy, and a desecration of the public household. In articles of the 1980s and 1990s, often published in the social democratic journal *Dissent*, Bell continued to probe the social and political implications of recent technological and economic innovations, particularly the "problem of scale" that rendered the modern nation-state unfit either to manage a new economy of global range or to foster local participatory institutions that could give people a stake in civil society.

Bell's work helped spark reflections by other writers on the problems and promise of postindustrial society. The sociologist Fred Block, a New Left veteran, picked up Bell's theme of discontinuity in a 1990 book, *Postindustrial Possibilities*, which argued that contemporary trends in the techniques and organization of production rendered conventional economic reasoning (particularly the free-market ideology of the 1980s) obsolete. Greater income equality, fuller provision of public goods, and "expand[ed] popular sovereignty over all critical social and economic decisions" (p. 194) were, according to Block, not only feasible but also in some sense necessary to foster the fullest development of productive capacities. Postindustrial development, in other words, was full of radical promise. Bell, in contrast, seemed to evade the implications of his own diagnosis. His cautious, anti-utopian temperament led him to resist calls for radical change, even though he argued that the distinctive conditions of life in a postindustrial age posed radically new challenges to society and polity.

HOWARD BRICK

See also NEW YORK INTELLECTUALS.

FURTHER READING

Daniel Bell, *The End of Ideology: On the Exhaustion of Political Ideas in the 1950s* (1960; Cambridge: Harvard University Press, 1988).
——, *The Coming of Post-Industrial Society: a Venture in Social Forecasting* (New York: Basic, 1973).
——, *The Cultural Contradictions of Capitalism* (New York: Basic, 1976).
——, *The Winding Passage: Essays and Sociological Journeys* (New York: Basic, 1980).
——, "The Revolt Against Modernity," *Public Interest* (fall 1985): 42–63.
——, "The Cultural Wars: American Intellectual Life, 1965–1992," *Wilson Quarterly* (summer 1992): 75–107.
Fred Block, *Postindustrial Possibilities: a Critique of Economic Discourse* (Berkeley: University of California Press, 1990).
Howard Brick, *Daniel Bell and the Decline of Intellectual Radicalism: Social Theory and Political Reconciliation in the 1940s* (Madison: University of Wisconsin Press, 1986).

Bellamy, Edward (b. Chicopee Falls, Mass., Mar. 26, 1850; d. Chicopee Falls, Mass., May 22, 1898). The most significant of American utopian writers, Edward Bellamy lived most of his life in the small industrial village in which he was born. He was descended on both sides of his family from leading New England clergy, including the formidable disciple of Jonathan Edwards, Joseph Bellamy. As a boy coming of age during the Civil War, he dreamed of a military career, but he failed to pass the physical examination for West Point. He attended Union College, and after a brief legal career turned to journalism, working first for the New York *Evening Post* and then editing the Springfield, Massachusetts *Daily Union* (1872–7).

In the late 1870s Bellamy launched a successful career as a novelist, publishing six romances in six years. Though he is seldom remembered as the author of such tales as *Six to One* (1878), *The Duke of Stockbridge* (1879), *Dr. Heidenhoff's Process* (1880), or *Miss Luddington's Sister* (1884), Bellamy's stories were well regarded by such contemporary critics as William Dean Howells. His early fiction often took the form of science fiction and fantasy, and anticipated his later utopian novels in their preoccupation with such parapsychological phenomena as somnambulism, hypnotic states, hysteria, hallucinations, and ventriloquism.

Looking Backward (1888), Bellamy's first utopian tale, propelled him to sudden fame. The book tells the story of a young man, Julian West, who awakens in the year 2000 from a state of suspended animation to find himself not in the strife-ridden, class-bound Boston of 1887 in which he went to sleep, but in the placid, egalitarian utopia of a city without divisions. Propelled forward (at what modern readers invariably consider a snail's pace) by a predictable romance between West and Edith Leete, daughter of his late twentieth-century host Dr. Leete, the novel is primarily a series of didactic lectures by Leete designed to convince West of the superior virtues of the new order. Convinced that market competition was the source of a corrupt consciousness that blinded capitalists and workers alike to their common brotherhood, Bellamy imagined an alternative society modeled on the republican fraternity of Sparta. He envisioned a utopia in which the whole of American society was recruited into a single "industrial army" working for a single state monopoly of all the means of production and distribution. This utopian nation would be administered by an elite of old men, the "alumni" of the industrial army, and social order would be sustained not by the coercive power of this elite, but by the "religion of solidarity" shared by all its citizens. (*See also* UTOPIAS.)

Looking Backward was a huge bestseller, and spawned a reform movement, Nationalism, which enjoyed considerable success in the early 1890s. By 1890, 162 Bellamy clubs had been established in 27 states, and in Massachusetts Nationalists waged an effective campaign for the municipal ownership of public utilities. Bellamy himself initially kept his distance from the Nationalists, who were led by such venerable, genteel Bostonians as Edward Everett Hale and THOMAS WENTWORTH HIGGINSON and dominated by Theosophists. But in 1891 Bellamy assumed a much more active role in the movement, editing its principal journal, the *New Nation*, and pressing fellow Nationalists to extend their influence beyond the middle class. Bellamyite Nationalists were a significant element in the People's Party, and the movement collapsed in the wake of the Populist debacle of 1896 and Bellamy's death from tuberculosis in 1898. Many Nationalists found their way into the Debsian wing of American SOCIALISM.

In the face of criticism of *Looking Backward* and his own awakening to the attractions of democratic politics, Bellamy began to modify many (if not all) of the more authoritarian features of his utopian vision. In *Equality* (1897), a novel even more didactic than *Looking Backward*, he eschewed military analogies for those of civil service, substituted a confederation of self-sufficient regional economies for the centralized planning of his earlier ideal, and added a measure of local participatory democracy to his vision of the good society. But, despite the support of such critics as Peter Kropotkin and JOHN DEWEY, who both thought *Equality* the better of Bellamy's utopias, it has languished unread. *Looking Backward*, on the other hand, lived on for decades as an influence on such turn-of-the-century American radicals as EUGENE DEBS, THORSTEIN VEBLEN, and CHARLOTTE PERKINS GILMAN, and on various stripes of progressives in the twentieth century, including Al Haber, a founder of Students for a Democratic Society in the 1960s. Over the last century it has also found significant audiences abroad.

Critics of *Looking Backward* have tended, especially in the wake of fascism and Stalinism, to portray Bellamy's utopia as a totalitarian nightmare. But one might just as easily see in the novel an anticipation of many of the lineaments of twentieth-century American society and culture. For all his talk of a religion of solidarity, Bellamy's ideal Boston is a city without public life, in which families live their lives in privatized cubicles of consumption. For all his criticisms of market competition and his call for "selflessness," he imagined an exemplary industrial army of men animated by status striving and competition for such badges of honor as the favor of the nation's most winsome women. Bellamy's improved Boston is less terrifying than boring, the sort of place that led a critic of socialized mediocrity like WILLIAM JAMES to clamor half seriously for *anything* vital, even war or tumult, as an alternative to mind-numbing half-heartedness.

ROBERT B. WESTBROOK

FURTHER READING

Sylvia E. Bowman, *The Year 2000: a Critical Biography of Edward Bellamy* (New York: Bookman, 1958).

Arthur Lipow, *Authoritarian Socialism in America: Edward Bellamy and the Nationalist Movement* (Berkeley: University of California Press, 1982).

Arthur E. Morgan, *Edward Bellamy* (New York: Columbia University Press, 1944).

Daphne Patai, ed., *Looking Backward, 1988–1888* (Amherst: University of Massachusetts Press, 1988).

John L. Thomas, *Alternative America: Henry George, Edward Bellamy, Henry Demarest Lloyd and the Adversary Tradition* (Cambridge: Harvard University Press, 1983).

Bellow, Saul (b. Lachine, Quebec, June 10, 1915). The son of Russian Jews who emigrated from St. Petersburg to Canada in 1913 and subsequently moved to the United States, Bellow was raised in Chicago. He was educated at the University of Chicago and Northwestern University, from which he graduated in 1937.

At the beginning of his writing career, Bellow supported himself by teaching and working at various odd jobs. In 1948 he won a Guggenheim Fellowship and travelled to Europe, where he spent two years living and writing in Paris. After returning to the United States in 1950, Bellow took up residence in New York City. At different periods he taught at the University of Minnesota, New York University, and Princeton. In 1962, Bellow moved back to his hometown of Chicago, the setting of many of his novels, where he served on the University of Chicago's Committee on Social Thought.

Awarded the Nobel Prize for Literature in 1976, Bellow is the only novelist to have won three National Book Awards—for *The Adventures of Augie March* (1953), *Herzog* (1964), and *Mr. Sammler's Planet* (1971). Other honors include the French Croix de Chevalier des Arts et Lettres (1968) and the Pulitzer Prize (1975).

Spanning half a century, Bellow's literary output features ten novels, two collections of short stories, three novellas, and a vivid memoir of his 1975 trip to Israel; it also includes a few stage plays and numerous published essays, interviews, and lectures. While his earliest novels, *Dangling Man* and *The Victim*, were written in a deliberately compressed style, Bellow's third novel marked a bold departure from their tight formal construction. Echoing the title of Mark Twain's nineteenth-century American classic *The Adventures of Huckleberry Finn*, *The Adventures of Augie March* celebrates the freedoms of the picaresque form. Giving free rein to a narrator who recounts his "adventures" in a style at once spontaneous and lofty, colloquial and poetic, Bellow introduced a fresh voice into mid-century American fiction. Most of Bellow's subsequent novels partake of the hybrid language, expansive style, and exuberant comic vision he forged in *Augie March*. In such masterpieces as *Henderson the Rain King*, *Herzog*, and *Humboldt's Gift*, however, the blatant excesses of Augie's style have been curbed and honed.

That Bellow never abandoned his interest in the shorter forms of fiction is evinced by his highly praised short novel, *Seize the Day* (1956), and two major collections of short stories published in 1968 and 1984. More recently, since achieving the age of 75, Bellow has expressed renewed dedication to the standard of linguistic economy. In 1989 he published the first of three consecutive novellas that have since been collected in a single volume, *Something to Remember Me By*. In his foreword to this 1991 collection, Bellow confesses his former propensity for writing "fat book[s]," but now declares himself in agreement with Anton Chekhov, the Russian playwright and short story writer who developed a "mania for shortness." The "modern taste for brevity and condensation," Bellow explains, is a way of surviving the demands made on one's attention by advertising and the media. "The modern reader," he adds, "is perilously overloaded." If the contemporary writer expects to be heard, he "will write as short as he can" (pp. vi–x).

Although this latest phase of Bellow's career marks a bold departure from past practice, his most recent fiction does not abandon the ambitious interrogation of twentieth-century American life that his first novels set in motion. Finding themselves in Chicago or New York, Bucharest or Jerusalem, Bellow's heroes suffer the peculiar dilemmas and contradictions of twentieth-century life. Dispossessed of traditional values and codes, torn between faith and cynicism, affection and contempt for their fellow creatures, they are driven to question the premises by which human beings live. Bellow's vision is more radically searching than is commonly recognized. Penetrating beneath the noisy distractions of the American city and its diverse inhabitants, his fiction challenges the conventional ideas and values that drive the engine of urban life.

From the outset of his career Bellow has been characterized as a realist writer—as a novelist who defines the individual's relationship to his social environment and employs traditional narrative techniques to fix that relationship in concrete detail. For this reason, his novels are often linked to their nineteenth-century predecessors and relegated by some critics to the category of "old-fashioned." What such critics tend to ignore, however, is the way that Bellow's exhaustive depiction of the material and social environment subverts old notions of reality—undermining the faith in material causes and explanations that inspired traditional forms of literary realism.

The paradoxical effects of Bellow's special brand of REALISM have been astutely appraised by his younger contemporary, the novelist John Updike. Writing in the *New Yorker*, Updike deems Bellow "one of the rare writers" who take "mimesis a layer or two deeper than it has gone before" (p. 127). Driven by intellectual curiosity and emotional restlessness, Bellow's heroes, like their author, are determined to penetrate appearances and discover a meaningful fate. In order to carry out their quest they leave home literally or figuratively, in search of mental and spiritual territory.

The most successful of Bellow's seekers arrive, like Albert Corde in *The Dean's December* (1982), at a new and liberating vision of reality. At the Mt. Palomar observatory in California, Albert Corde gazes into outer space and reads, beneath all the human as well as atmospheric "distortions," a message encoded in "the very blood and the crystal forms inside [one's] bones" (p. 311). Similarly, the elderly narrator of Bellow's latest work, the title story in *Something to Remember Me By*, recalls the formative influence of certain contemplatives on his youthful mind, philosophers who wrote "that the truth of the universe was inscribed into our very bones. That the human skeleton was itself a hieroglyph" (p. 221). The "message" encoded in each individual's "blood" and "bones" is only obliquely relayed in Bellow's fiction, but it hints at the profound bond linking each human being's private existence to the furthest reaches of the cosmos.

ELLEN PIFER

FURTHER READING
Saul Bellow, *The Dean's December* (New York: Harper and Row, 1982).
——, *Something to Remember Me By: Three Tales* (New York: Viking, 1991).
Malcolm Bradbury, *Saul Bellow* (New York: Methuen, 1982).
Daniel Fuchs, *Saul Bellow: Vision and Revision* (Durham: Duke University Press, 1984).
Ellen Pifer, *Saul Bellow Against the Grain* (Philadelphia: University of Pennsylvania Press, 1990).
Irwin Stock, *Fiction as Wisdom* (University Park: Pennsylvania State University Press, 1980).
Stanley Trachtenberg, ed., *Critical Essays on Saul Bellow* (Boston: G. K. Hall, 1979).
John Updike. "Toppling Towers Seen by a Whirling Soul," review of *The Dean's December*, *New Yorker*, Feb. 22, 1982, p. 127.

Benedict, Ruth Fulton (b. New York, N.Y., June 5, 1887; d. New York, N.Y., Sept. 17, 1948). An influential twentieth-century anthropologist and public intellectual, Benedict was raised in the Midwest and northern New York. Her college education at Vassar led her to abandon the Baptist faith, but it deepened her religious and aesthetic sensibilities. She embraced the humanism of Walter Pater, wrote poetry under the pseudonym of Anne Singleton, and then studied anthropology. She taught at girls' schools in California before returning to New York to marry Stanley Benedict, a chemist. Her early writings on Mary Wollstonecraft indicate feminist leanings, and an unhappy marriage and her emerging homosexuality led Benedict to seek new realms of self-expression. Deafness contributed to the sense of marginality which she shared with other anthropologists, such as her mentor, FRANZ BOAS, and her student, MARGARET MEAD. A relatively new discipline, concerned with private as well as public life, anthropology was more open to women than any other social science. Nonetheless, advancement was slow: Benedict spent almost ten years as a lecturer in anthropology at Columbia, becoming an assistant professor in 1931 and an associate upon Boas's retirement in 1936; she was passed over as chair of the department and named a full professor only four months before her death.

Benedict came to anthropology rather late in life. After taking courses with Boas's students Elsie Clews Parsons and Alexander Goldenweiser at the New School for Social Research, Benedict completed a Ph.D. under Boas at Columbia in 1923. Her dissertation "The Concept of the Guardian Spirit in North America" stressed the importance of religious experience over theological dogma and raised the issue of cultural patterns for which she would be famous. After earning her degree, Benedict did fieldwork in the American Southwest, primarily among the Zuñi, Cochiti, and Pima. This research provided the basis of her continuing work on cultural configurations, published in 1934 as *Patterns of Culture* and elaborated as part of the culture and personality movement in *The Chrysanthemum and the Sword: Patterns of Japanese Culture* (1946). Through these two books Ruth Benedict left her mark on anthropological theory and American social thought. (*See also* CULTURAL ANTHROPOLOGY.)

Patterns of Culture is one of the most important books in the history of anthropology, a bestseller when it was reissued in paperback in 1946, and translated into at least 14 languages. A prime example of the culture and personality movement, Benedict's work influenced psychologists such as HARRY STACK SULLIVAN and Karen Horney (*see also* NEO-FREUDIANISM). As Mead said in her preface to the 1959 edition, the familiarity of "the modern world . . . with the concept of culture . . . is in very great part due to this book" (p. vii). In this comparative study of the "Apollonian" Pueblos, the treacherous Dobu of Melanesia, and the "Dionysian" Indians of the Northwest Coast, Benedict had two main objectives: to establish how each culture demonstrated a "personality writ large," and to examine how individuals function within such cultures. In other words, this book articulated most effectively the dual trends developing in anthropology since the 1920s. First, cultures "tend to be integrated. A culture, like an individual, is a more or less consistent pattern of thought and action" (p. 46). Second, anthropological work should be devoted to "the study of cultures as articulated wholes" (p. 48). At the same time, Benedict paid attention to those deemed "abnormal . . . individuals whose native responses are not reaffirmed by society . . . person[s] unsupported by the standards of [their] time and place and left naked to the winds of ridicule . . ." (p. 270). In her conclusion, Benedict called on Americans to be "culture-conscious," to turn their critical abilities "on the dominant traits of our own civilization" (p. 249), and asked for tolerance of "the coexisting and equally valid patterns of life which mankind has created for itself out of the raw materials of existence" (p. 278). With these words, Benedict summarized the principles of cultural relativism.

The critiques of Benedict's argument were almost as important as the book itself. Fellow anthropologists found much greater variation within the cultures she described than Benedict acknowledged. The linguist EDWARD SAPIR argued that her equation of individual with cultural personality reified culture as something apart from the individuals who create it. Although largely ignored by contemporaries, these criticisms offered the most important challenge to the Boasian concept of culture, particularly the tendencies toward functionalism and toward substituting cultural for racial and biological generalizations.

The problems of Benedict's approach are apparent in *The Chrysanthemum and the Sword* (1946). Written under the aegis of the Office of War Information, the book sought to "understand the Japanese," the "most alien enemy" of the United States (p. 1). Utilizing the perspective of the cultural anthropologist, Benedict looked for the way "the most isolated bits of behavior have some systematic relation to each other . . . [and] fall into over-all patterns" (pp. 11–12). Despite her efforts to humanize the Japanese for her American readers, it is hard to know where cultural introspection leaves off and generalizations about national character begin. What started as a way to understand the internal workings of a culture and to query the relationship between individual and society ultimately took as its premise the existence of cultural integrity. After Hitler and Hiroshima, and in the wake of the Cold War, when cultural relativism came under attack and consensus reigned, anthropology's cultural critique was eclipsed by the triumphalism of national character studies, including the emergence of American Studies. Much of Benedict's contribution has been submerged beneath this wave. Like Boas before her and Mead after her, Benedict's anthropology cast a sharply critical look at American society itself: its materialism, excessive individualism, and rootlessness. The contrasts she wished to draw were most revealing concerning her contemporary world, and her works should be read as testimony of American cultural and intellectual life, not primarily as revelations of the Zuñi, Dobu, Kwakiutl, or Japanese. Benedict's writings teach most, as Clifford Geertz has written in *Works and Lives*, by "look[ing]-unto-ourselves-as-we-would-look-unto-others" (p. 107).

JULIA E. LISS

FURTHER READING
Ruth Benedict, *Patterns of Culture* (1934; Boston: Houghton Mifflin, 1959)
——, *The Chrysanthemum and the Sword: Patterns of Japanese Culture* (Boston: Houghton Mifflin, 1946).
Margaret M. Caffrey, *Ruth Benedict: Stranger in this Land* (Austin: University of Texas Press, 1989).
Clifford Geertz, *Works and Lives: the Anthropologist as Author* (Stanford: Stanford University Press, 1988).

Richard Handler, "Vigorous Male and Aspiring Female: Poetry, Personality, and Culture in Edward Sapir and Ruth Benedict," in George W. Stocking Jr., ed., *Malinowski, Rivers, Benedict and Others: Essays on Culture and Personality*, vol. 4 of *History of Anthropology* (Madison: University of Wisconsin Press, 1986).
George E. Marcus and Michael M. J. Fischer, *Anthropology as Cultural Critique: an Experimental Moment in the Human Sciences* (Chicago: University of Chicago Press, 1986).
Margaret Mead, *An Anthropologist at Work: Writings of Ruth Benedict* (Boston: Houghton Mifflin, 1959).
Judith Schachter Modell, *Ruth Benedict: Patterns of a Life* (Philadelphia: University of Pennsylvania Press, 1983).

Berle, Adolf (b. Brighton, Mass., Jan. 29, 1895; d. New York, N.Y., Feb. 17, 1971).   Lawyer and public official. While teaching law at Columbia University, Berle coauthored, with his colleague Gardiner Means, *The Modern Corporation and Private Property* (1932). Sponsored by the Social Science Research Council, the book was deeply influential in public debate about alternatives to a recently collapsed economic system. Building on THORSTEIN VEBLEN, Berle and Means argued that ownership of corporations no longer coincided with the control of them: power was now in the hands of a new class of managers, thus opening up the possibility of efficient direction of economic life in the public interest. A member of Franklin Roosevelt's circle of advisers during the Depression, Berle was an assistant Secretary of State during World War II. His other books include *The Twentieth Century Capitalist Revolution* (1954) and *Power* (1969).

See also MANAGERIALISM.

FURTHER READING
Jordan A. Schwarz, *Liberal: Adolf A. Berle and the Vision of an American Era* (New York: Free Press, 1987).

Bernstein, Richard J. (b. Brooklyn, N.Y., May 14, 1932).   Philosopher. Against the prevailing currents of twentieth-century Anglo-American academic philosophy, Bernstein has insisted that philosophy must provide more than the logical analysis of language or science: it must assess cultural habits, political action, and ethical dilemmas as well as investigate linguistic phenomena. Emphasizing praxis as well as theory, Bernstein advocates a "nonfoundational pragmatic humanism" that acknowledges its own contingency and fallibility as it engages in conversation with both the Continental European and the Anglo-American traditions. Together with RICHARD RORTY and Hilary Putnam, he is one of the leading contemporary philosophers of PRAGMATISM. He has done perhaps more than anyone else to forge a link between American philosophy and current developments in German and French thought. His writings include *John Dewey* (1966), which helped reawaken philosophers' interest in Dewey's pragmatism; *Praxis and Action: Contemporary Philosophers of Human Activity* (1971); *The Restructuring of Social and Political Theory* (1976); *Beyond Objectivism and Relativism: Science, Hermeneutics, and Praxis* (1983); and *The New Constellation: the Ethical-Political Horizons of Modernity/Postmodernity* (1992).

FURTHER READING
Hans Joas, *Pragmatism and Social Theory* (Chicago: University of Chicago Press, 1993).

Berrigan, Daniel (b. Virginia, Minn., May 9, 1921). Poet and social activist. Founder, with his brother Philip, of the Catholic Peace Fellowship (1964), Berrigan led a campaign of direct-action "witnessing" against the VIETNAM War. His antiwar protests included marches, fasts, civilian international diplomacy, and such symbolic acts as pouring blood on draft files (in Baltimore in 1965) and setting draft cards on fire with napalm (in Catonsville in 1968). With his brother, also a Catholic priest, Berrigan was instrumental in the development of a Catholic left in the last third of the twentieth century. Daniel authored, among many works, *The Trial of the Catonsville Nine* (1970) and Philip wrote *Prison Journals of a Priest Revolutionary* (1970). Over the last quarter century they have remained involved in social action, including antinuclear and AIDS work.

See also CATHOLICISM.

FURTHER READING
Ross Labrie, *The Writings of Daniel Berrigan* (Lanham: University Press of America, 1989).

Bettelheim, Bruno (b. Vienna, Austria, Aug. 28, 1903; d. Silver Spring, Md., Mar. 13, 1990). Psychologist. An Austrian emigrant to the United States (after a year spent as a prisoner in German concentration camps), Bettelheim sought to create a humanistic psychology as a foundation for and defense of human dignity. Individual and social psychologies, he believed, are mutually reinforcing: a child's dysfunctions, for example, may be adaptations to a detrimental environment. Racial prejudice, which reduces anxiety by externalizing feared characteristics, is a response to emotional and physical deprivations. Better childrearing and institutional structures can nurture responsibility and tolerance. Bettelheim's writings include *Love Is Not Enough: the Treatment of Emotionally Disturbed Children* (1950), *The Uses of Enchantment: the Meaning and Importance of Fairy Tales* (1977), and *Freud and Man's Soul* (1982).

See also CHILDHOOD.

FURTHER READING
Paul Roazen, "The Rise and Fall of Bruno Bettelheim," *Psychohistory Review* 30 (spring 1992): 221–50.

biblical criticism This scholarly discourse seeks to provide a nuanced understanding of the Hebrew and Christian Scriptures. It includes a variety of methodological principles and interpretative techniques and often encompasses scholarly studies in philology, archaeology, textual criticism, hermeneutics, and exegesis. While adherents of Jewish and Christian communities often look to their Scriptures as sacred sources of divine revelation and religious practices, biblical critics address and interpret the Scriptures as historical and literary documents. Most modern biblical criticism is now located in academic institutions. The American Society of Biblical Literature, founded in 1880, lists a current membership of over 5,500.

The Bible was an important ingredient in the early American ethos and myth, and the academic study of the Bible was present at the beginning of American institutions of culture. In 1636 half of John Harvard's library, the foundation of Harvard College's holdings, was books about the Bible. In "Biblia Americana," an unpublished manuscript of 6,000 pages (ca.1720), COTTON MATHER offered elaborate comments on biblical passages, Jewish antiquities, harmonies of parallel biblical passages, and European scholarship.

Biblical scholarship in America took a decidedly secular turn after the Enlightenment era. Samuel Miller's *A Brief Retrospect of the Eighteenth Century* (1803) surveyed American scholarship about the Bible, noting its desacralization in many publications. In 1810 Samuel Dexter endowed Harvard College with $5,000 to promote "a critical knowledge of the Holy Scriptures." Within a few decades the American reading public became aware of the emerging issues in modern biblical scholarship and its primary impetus in German and English universities. *The Biblical Repository* (Andover), *The Biblical Repertory and Princeton Review* (Princeton) and *Bibliotheca Sacra* (New York) all began appearing in the antebellum period. In general, more radical positions were tolerated at universities like Harvard, Yale and Pennsylvania, while more traditional positions were endorsed at seminaries such as Andover and Princeton. Apparently, scholars in the South were unimpressed until later in the nineteenth century. Roman Catholic critical scholarship did not blossom until after the founding of the Catholic Biblical Association in 1936.

By the mid-nineteenth century, a plethora of critical issues surfaced and chafed; the Mosaic authorship of the Pentateuch, the dating of the Psalms, the nature of Hebrew poetry, the multiple authorship of the book of Isaiah, the external influences on Jewish cultic practice, the variants in early Hebrew and Greek texts, the literary relationships of the four Gospels, controversies about authorship of New Testament (NT) books. Particularly controversial were D. F. Strauss's *Life of Jesus Critically Examined* (1842 in its English translation) and W. M. L. De Wette's *Critical and Historical Introduction to the Canonical Scriptures of the Old Testament* (translated in America in 1843). Strauss compelled Protestantism to face questions about the historicity of the NT by insisting that the NT was a collection of myths and a product of early Christian consciousness. De Wette's revisionist history of Israel was at radical variance with the narratives of the Hebrew Scriptures; he argued that little if any historical information in a modern sense could be obtained from the Pentateuch.

Julius Wellhausen's *Prolegomena zur Geschichte Israels* (1883) applied to the biblical sources a "scientific-historical criticism" based upon Hegelian evolutionism. He concluded, among other things, that neither Moses nor the Patriarchs were monotheists, that the Levitical laws were actually very late in Israel's development, and that much of Israel's cultic life derived from other cultures. Similar radical revisions of the NT circulated in scholarly circles. Some critics irrevocably placed NT ideas within the cultural milieu of first-century Hellenistic and Gnostic thought, often insisting that the NT's Jesus was the creation of his followers in the early Church. Other critics denied the historical existence of Jesus altogether.

By the early twentieth century, historical questions about the Bible were overlaid with social concerns and various literary techniques. ELIZABETH CADY STANTON published *The Woman's Bible* (1895–8) and initiated a new feminist interpretation, and Albert Schweitzer's famed *The Quest of the Historical Jesus* (1906) also pleaded for fresh approaches. One new technique, pioneered by German scholars like Herman Gunkel and Ruldolf Bultmann, sought to identify the oral sources behind biblical documents and simultaneously examined the literary forms (tales, laws, poetry, myths) employed by the biblical writers. This "form history" (*Formgeschichte*) exercised substantial influence among American critics.

By the middle third of the twentieth century, an indigenous biblical criticism emerged in American universities and seminaries. Shirley Jackson Case of the University of Chicago Divinity School refined a "socio-historical" method which viewed biblical personages and commitments as products of their social settings. This attention to "social location" continues into the

present in the works of Robert Grant, Wayne Meeks, and Robert Wilson. Feminist biblical scholars, such as Rosemary Ruether, Elisabeth Schüssler Fiorenza and Letty Russell, offer alternative assessments.

A second mode of American biblical criticism, which coincides with the rise of Protestant neo-orthodoxy, is that of William F. Albright of Johns Hopkins University. Albright sought to place biblical criticism on an empirical base by linking biblical studies and the archaeology of the Middle East. Albright mentored a generation of influential scholars, including George E. Wright, Frank Cross, George Mendenhall and David N. Freedman (Protestants); Nelson Glueck (Jewish); and Joseph Fitzmyer and Raymond Brown (Catholic). The monumental *The Anchor Bible* commentaries are testimonies to the ecumenical influence of this school. American contributions to the critical study and publication of the Dead Sea Scrolls are also substantial.

A third cluster of recent American biblical criticism derives its clues from numerous schools of contemporary literary criticism. One such branch, "narrative criticism," approaches the biblical narratives not as historical sources but as literary texts that may be analyzed in literary terms (plot, characterization, rhetorical devices, etc.) like any other work of literature. Prominent in this contemporary field are the works of Robert Alter (*The Art of Biblical Narratives*, 1981) and Robert Tannehill (*The Narrative Unity of Luke-Acts*, 1986). Another contemporary literary technique applied to the Bible, "rhetorical criticism," was pioneered by James Muilenburg and extended by Phyllis Trible (*God and The Rhetoric of Sexuality*, 1978). Trible employs "rhetorical criticism" as a methodological clue for her feminist hermeneutics. Other postmodern literary approaches, such as "reader response" criticism, are in current use by some critics, while the "canonical criticism" of Brevard Childs and James Sanders is still another literary-critical variant. American scholars have also contributed seminal studies in textual criticism and lexicography. Prominent in this technical field are Jewish and Protestant scholars, including Max Margolis, J. C. Greenfield, Harry Orlinski and Bruce M. Metzger.

Biblical criticism is one field of study in which vigor of scholarship does not seem to produce consensus of interpretation. This is nothing new. Virtually every Protestant, Catholic, and Jewish community has been rent by disagreements about the Bible during the nineteenth and twentieth centuries. Disputes between evangelical traditionalists and modernists, and between Orthodox and Reformed Jews, continue to this day. But equally contentions are the disagreements between those scholars whose critical orientation is cultural and contextual, and those who stress the Bible's textual structures. In that way biblical scholars mirror the wider intellectual currents of the 1990s.

JOHN W. STEWART

See also TEXTUALITY.

FURTHER READING

Jerry W. Brown, *The Rise of Biblical Criticism in America, 1800–1870: the New England Scholars* (Middletown, Conn.: Wesleyan University Press, 1969).

Cambridge History of the Bible, 3 vols. (Cambridge: Cambridge University Press, 1963).

Gerald P. Fogarty, *American Catholic Biblical Scholarship: a History from the Early Republic to Vatican II* (San Francisco: Harper and Row, 1989).

David N. Freedman et al., eds., *The Anchor Bible Dictionary*, 6 vols. (New York: Doubleday, 1992).

R. J. Goggins and J. L. Houlen, eds., *A Dictionary of Biblical Interpretation* (London: SCM Press, 1990).

Mark Noll, "Review Essay: the Bible in America," *Journal of Biblical Literature* 106 (1987): 493–509.

Mark A. Powell, *The Bible and Modern Literary Criticism* (New York: Greenwood, 1992).

S. David Sperling, *Students of the Covenant: Studies of Jewish Biblical Scholarship in North America* (Atlanta: Scholars, 1992).

Bill of Rights When the U.S. Constitution was submitted to the state conventions for ratification, it contained no bill of rights. Anti-Federalists claimed that this omission was one of the most significant defects of the new frame of government. Rather than concede that the absence of a bill of rights was a serious problem, Federalists attacked proposals for amendments as unnecessary. Indeed, the supporters of the CONSTITUTION went even further, arguing that the inclusion of a bill of rights might actually be detrimental to American liberties.

Federalists maintained that the new government created by the Constitution was one of delegated authority. Except for those powers assigned to the new government, all essential rights and liberties were still retained by the people and the states. Supporters of the Constitution also feared that an enumeration of rights might inadvertently exclude some fundamental liberties from a bill of rights. Federalists argued that written declarations of rights were "mere parchment barriers," ineffectual safeguards for liberty. Rather than look to a bill of rights to guard liberty, Federalists believed that three structural elements of the Constitution would prevent encroachments on rights: the principle of representation embodied in the legislative branch; the checks and balances provided by the separation of powers among the legislative, executive, and judicial branches of government; and the distribution of sovereign power within the federal system.

Anti-Federalists disputed the Federalist claim that the new government was one of limited delegated authority. The text of the Constitution contained a number of elastic clauses that seemed to provide the new government with enormous legislative powers. If the Federalists believed that a partial enumeration of rights threatened liberty, why did the Constitution include some provisions for basic rights, like the prohibition on ex post facto laws? In the minds of many Anti-Federalists, the logic of the Federalist position seemed inconsistent. Anti-Federalists also maintained that a bill of rights served the indispensable function of educating the people in the basic principles of republican government.

During ratification a number of state conventions voted in favor of the new frame of government with an implicit understanding that amendments would be made to the Constitution. JAMES MADISON, an opponent of the original call for a bill of rights, shifted his position and assumed a leading role in securing amendments to the new Constitution. Pressure from the Baptist community in Virginia had persuaded Madison of the need for a set of amendments that would assuage the fears of those who believed that the Constitution threatened individual rights. Madison also hoped that a set of amendments designed to protect individual liberty would preempt those Anti-Federalists who desired to restore greater authority to the individual states. An additional impetus for a bill of rights was provided by THOMAS JEFFERSON, who forcefully argued that a properly framed set of amendments would do little harm and might actually provide the judiciary with additional authority to safeguard liberty.

Madison studied the various state proposals for amendments and consciously blocked any effort to use the amendment process as a means of weakening the new central government. Madison also recommended that the individual states be prohibited from violating the core freedoms of speech, press, religion, and the equally crucial right of jury trial. This recommendation was defeated in the First Congress during a heated debate in which several ANTI-FEDERALISTS argued against granting the Federal government any additional power to police the internal affairs of the states. The ten amendments to the Constitution that Congress adopted became the Bill of Rights.

Two traditions have dominated modern scholarship on the origins of the Bill of Rights. Some historians consider the Bill of Rights a testimony to the presence of a strong tradition of LIBERTARIANISM in early America. Other historians interpret the Bill of Rights as a political document cynically manipulated by both Federalists and Anti-Federalists for their own partisan agendas. Neither of these one-dimensional accounts captures the complexity of Federalist and Anti-Federalist views of the relationship between American constitutionalism and the problem of liberty. While each side in the ratification debate defended the concept of liberty, neither Federalists nor Anti-Federalists were modern libertarians. Any account of the origins of the Bill of Rights must acknowledge that eighteenth-century conceptions of liberty were articulated within the context of RE-PUBLICANISM. Liberty was set against the right of self-governing polities to legislate on behalf of the common good. Anti-Federalists continued to adhere to the Revolutionary republican belief that the greatest threat to liberty was posed by a distant government. Federalists believed that the excessive powers of the individual states were more likely to trample on individual liberty.

Although it would be an exaggeration to say that the Bill of Rights remained dormant for the first hundred years of its existence, there is a strong scholarly consensus that the Bill of Rights did not exert a profound influence on the course of constitutional law for much of the nineteenth and early twentieth centuries. The period after 1920, however, witnessed an expansion of constitutional jurisprudence based on the authority of the Bill of Rights. In part the explosion of litigation was facilitated by the emergence of the doctrine of incorporation, which allowed the federal judiciary to use the authority of the Fourteenth Amendment to apply various provisions of the Bill of Rights to internal state matters.

There has been an enormous expansion of rights-oriented jurisprudence in modern America. This growth is both a reflection and a consequence of a pervasive RIGHTS consciousness in our culture. One consequence of these developments is the dominance of "rights talk" in public life—a tendency to frame public policy debates in terms of legal questions about competing rights claims. In response to this trend, communitarian critiques of rights have emerged at both ends of the political spectrum. These challenges to "rights talk" have attempted to strike a new balance between individual liberty and the rights of self-governing communities to legislate on behalf of the common good. The tensions between libertarian and communitarian impulses in American constitutionalism, a legacy bequeathed to us by the Founders, continues to shape our public discourse.

SAUL CORNELL

FURTHER READING

Saul Cornell, "Moving Beyond the Canon of Traditional Constitutional History: Anti-Federalists, the Bill of Rights and the Promise of Post-Modern Historiography," *Law and History Review* 12 (Spring 1994): 1–28.

Jon Kukla, ed., *The Bill of Rights: a Lively Heritage* (Richmond: State Library Archives, 1987).

Michael J. Lacey and Knud Haakonssen, eds., *A Culture of Rights: the Bill of Rights in Philosophy, Politics, and Law, 1791 and 1991* (Cambridge: Cambridge University Press, 1991).

Leonard Levy, *Original Intent and the Framers' Constitution* (New York: Macmillian, 1988).

Bernard Schwartz, *The Great Rights of Mankind: a History of the American Bill of Rights* (New York: Oxford University Press, 1977).

David Thelen, ed., *The Constitution and American Life* (Ithaca: Cornell University Press, 1988).

Black, Hugo (b. Harlan, Ala., Feb. 27, 1886; d. Bethesda, Md., Sept. 25, 1971).   Supreme Court Justice (1937–71). A strict constructionist, Black believed that judges must not grant new rights (such as privacy) or allow their own moral or political views to shape constitutional interpretation. The "preferred freedoms" of religion and speech were not to be compromised—even for communists or purveyors of obscenity. A firm defender of civil liberties and civil rights, Black argued that the Fourteenth Amendment extended the Bill of Rights to the states and insisted on the principle of one person, one vote for districting. Lauded by liberals for his strong defense of free speech, he nevertheless took some positions that appalled them, such as his dissent in *Bergen v. New York* (1967), in which he upheld wire-tapping.
    See also LAW.

FURTHER READING

Howard Ball, *Of Power and Right: Hugo Black, William O. Douglas, and America's Constitutional Revolution* (New York: Oxford University Press, 1992).

Black Elk [later baptized Nicholas] (b. Little Powder River, now Wyo., Dec. 1863; d. Manderson, S. Dak., Aug. 19, 1950).   An American Indian, a member of the Oglala division of the Teton Sioux (Lakota), Black Elk experienced the Indian wars of the 1860s and 1870s, the extinction of the buffalo herds in the early 1880s, adjustment to life on Indian reservations, and the ushering in of modern times symbolized by Sioux involvement in World War II. He was raised to be a hunter and warrior, but Black Elk was also a religious visionary.

In most regards, Black Elk's life experiences differed little from those of his contemporaries among the Sioux. What makes him historically exceptional, however, is the written record of his life. In 1931 he related an autobiography to John G. Neihardt, poet laureate of Nebraska, who used the material to write *Black Elk Speaks, Being the Life Story of a Holy Man of the Oglala Sioux.* Originally published in 1932, the book attracted an enormous readership after it was reprinted in 1961. Black Elk's life story is representative of the Plains Indian experience, and through *Black Elk Speaks* has come to symbolize the American Indian experience at large.

Neihardt interviewed Black Elk again in 1944, and based a historical novel, *When the Tree Flowered* (1951), in part on these later interviews. The transcripts of both sets of interviews represent Black Elk's words as translated by interpreters into English, then recast in grammatical sentences and recorded in writing by Neihardt's daughters, Enid and Hilda. Although the transcripts are considerably removed from the original Lakota, they are the most primary sources for Black Elk's story. In 1984 they were published as *The Sixth Grandfather: Black Elk's Teachings Given to John G. Neihardt,* edited by Raymond J. DeMallie. As a historical source, these interview transcripts present invaluable data on Lakota culture and allow for a critical evaluation of Neihardt's portrayal of Black Elk.

Among scholars, as for the general public, it is Black Elk's traditional religious life that has attracted the greatest attention. At the age of nine he received a vision from the Thunder-beings, the powers of the west, and was taken to meet the Six Grandfathers, the spiritual embodiments of all the powers of the universe—the four directions, the sky, and the earth. In the vision he was offered powers to heal and to destroy. At the age of 16 Black Elk felt himself called by the Thunder-beings to use the vision powers. He began to publicly enact his vision, the traditional means for validating and activating vision powers. In 1881, at the camp of the Sioux refugees who at the end of the Indian wars had returned from Canada and surrendered to the U.S. Army at Fort Keogh, Montana, Black Elk sponsored a Horse Dance, dramatizing, by riders on variously colored horses, the vision of the Six Grandfathers. The following spring, now settled at Pine Ridge, which would become the Oglalas' reservation, Black Elk fasted and sought another vision. Again the Thunder-beings came to him, following which he began his career as a medicine man. (*See also* INDIAN–WHITE RELATIONS.)

Black Elk's account is invaluable as a first-person narrative of religious experience. The visions, the vision enactments, and Black Elk's experiences as a healer are explicated from his own perspective and contextualized in his own terms. His narrative is unique in the literature on Plains Indian religions.

The context of changing times led Black Elk to question his religious beliefs and practices. He decided to learn about the Euro-Americans' world. In

1886 he joined Buffalo Bill's Wild West Show, which provided the opportunity to tour and study the ways of the white people. During an odyssey that took Black Elk to New York, England, France, and Italy, he embraced Christianity and came to find value in its teachings. But when he returned to Pine Ridge in 1889 he discovered that some of his people were practicing a new religion, the Ghost Dance, a millenarian movement that promised the return of the dead and of the buffalo, and the destruction of non-Indians. What attracted Black Elk to the new religion was not these beliefs, however, but the ritual—a dance in which men and women circled a sacred pole, experiencing visions in which they saw the dead and learned about the coming millennium. For Black Elk, the dance seemed the actualization of the sacred tree and hoop of the people that he had seen in his great vision. He was convinced that he should return to his vision experiences for religious guidance.

The Ghost Dance was short-lived among the Sioux. The unprovoked massacre of nearly one hundred Sioux men, women, and children at Wounded Knee by members of the Seventh U.S. Cavalry on December 31, 1890, ended hopes for the millennium. Peace quickly returned to Pine Ridge, and the people went back to learning about how to make a living under changed conditions.

Black Elk continued to perform healing ceremonies using his vision powers. In 1904, however, he abandoned these practices and joined the Roman Catholic Church, in which he was baptized Nicholas. His decision to join the Church was likely to have been motivated in part by a sense of the necessity to adapt to the realities of reservation life; churches provided access to money, goods, and services. At the same time, Black Elk's earlier acceptance of Christianity may have led him to choose this as the better path for his growing family to follow. He quickly developed in his knowledge of Catholicism and served as a missionary, visiting other Indian groups to prepare the way for the establishment of churches.

When Black Elk decided to tell his life story to Neihardt, it seems to have been a way of unburdening himself of a responsibility left unfulfilled. By giving the visions to Neihardt to put into a book, Black Elk managed a different kind of enacting, one that had the potential to spread his traditional religious knowledge throughout the world. Neihardt told him, too, that he would try to have the great vision enacted as a motion picture. Black Elk was especially concerned that non-Indians understand that the traditional Sioux religion was legitimately a religion, not the work of the devil. To this end, beginning in 1935, he oversaw summer pageants in the Black Hills, in which parts of sacred ceremonies were reenacted for the edification of tourists.

In old age Black Elk dictated one more set of teachings. In 1947–8 he related to Joseph Epes Brown detailed descriptions of Lakota religious rituals. As a synthetic account of American Indian religious practices, Brown's *The Sacred Pipe: Black Elk's Account of the Seven Rites of the Oglala Sioux* (1953) is an unparalleled masterpiece. At the same time that it embodies the fundamentals of traditional Sioux religion, it may also be interpreted as bringing together fundamental Christian concepts with native ones.

Since the emergence of Black Elk as a popular literary figure, and especially since the publication of Neihardt's interview transcripts, there has been considerable scholarly debate concerning Black Elk, the legitimacy of Neihardt's portrayal, and the sincerity of Black Elk's conversion to Christianity. The silence of both Neihardt and Brown, Black Elk's amanuenses, on the topic of his practice of Catholicism, laid the basis for interpretative mystique. Having accepted the stereotyped holy man of *Black Elk Speaks*, uncontaminated by Christianity, many writers seem to feel betrayed to discover the actual complexity of the historical Black Elk. In *Black Elk's Story* (1991), Julian Rice attempts to disentangle Black Elk's Lakota religion from his Christian teachings. Michael Steltenkamp's *Black Elk* (1993), on the other hand, presents the reminiscences of Black Elk's daughter and argues for the sincerity of Black Elk's conversion to Catholicism and the impossibility of distinguishing the strands of Lakota and Christian religions in Black Elk's thought. Since no native religious system by the late nineteenth century was pristinely isolated from Christian influences, to search for purely native religion is necessarily a pointless quest.

Black Elk's position as a representative of American Indian religion and as a source for the study of Lakota religion, culture, and history seems secure. Because of his remarkable experiences, his genuine religiosity, and the humane quality that comes through even in translation, the written record of his teachings will stand as an invaluable source for the future.

RAYMOND J. DEMALLIE

See also AUTOBIOGRAPHY; INDIAN IDENTITIES; TRANSLATION.

FURTHER READING

Joseph Epes Brown, recorder and ed., *The Sacred Pipe: Black Elk's Account of the Seven Rites of the Oglala Sioux* (Norman: University of Oklahoma Press, 1953).
Raymond J. DeMallie, ed., *The Sixth Grandfather: Black Elk's Teachings Given to John G. Neihardt* (Lincoln: University of Nebraska Press, 1984).
John G. Neihardt, *Black Elk Speaks: Being the Life Story of a Holy Man of the Oglala Sioux* (1932; Lincoln: University of Nebraska Press, 1979).
——, *When the Tree Flowered: the Story of Eagle Voice, A Sioux Indian* (1951; Lincoln: University of Nebraska Press, 1991).
Julian Rice, *Black Elk's Story: Distinguishing Its Lakota Purpose* (Albuquerque: University of New Mexico Press, 1991).
Michael F. Steltenkamp, *Black Elk: Holy Man of the Oglala* (Norman: University of Oklahoma Press, 1993).

Blackwell, Antoinette Brown (b. Henrietta, N.Y., May 20, 1825; d. Elizabeth, N.J., Nov. 5, 1921). Reformer and pastor. The first female pastor in the United States, Blackwell wrote and lectured for over half a century on a broad range of reforms including abolitionism, temperance, education and WOMEN'S RIGHTS. The Bible does not, she insisted, endorse women's subordination. Appointed to a Congregationalist church, she came to doubt orthodox views of human sinfulness and divine justice. DARWINISM proved, she thought, that nature and society evolve toward cooperation and unity, that personality is immortal, and that the sexes are equal though different.

FURTHER READING

Elizabeth Cazden, *Antoinette Brown Blackwell: a Biography* (Old Westbury, N.Y.: Feminist Press, 1983).

Blackwell, Elizabeth (b. Bristol, England, Feb. 3, 1821; d. Hastings, England, May 31, 1910). Physician. The first certified female physician, Blackwell believed that women should be treated by women doctors. She urged all physicians to cultivate the nurturance and holistic approach to health that she traced to women's maternal instinct. With her younger sister Emily, also a physician, she opened the New York Infirmary for Women and Children, which specialized in the care of poor women. They also helped found women's medical schools in New York and London, insisted on high academic standards in women's professional education, and discouraged educated women from contemplating marriage.

See also MEDICINE.

FURTHER READING

Margaret Forster, *Significant Sisters: the Grassroots of Active Feminism, 1839–1939* (New York: Knopf, 1985).

Boas, Franz (b. Minden, Westphalia, July 9, 1858; d. New York, N.Y., Dec. 21, 1942). An ethnologist, physical anthropologist, and linguist, Boas was a founder of American academic anthropology, pushing the discipline away from armchair theorizing into the emerging world of university-dominated social science. His students, including Alfred Kroeber, Robert Lowie, EDWARD SAPIR, RUTH BENEDICT, MARGARET MEAD, ZORA NEALE HURSTON, and Melville Herskovits, dominated the discipline for over a generation. Through this institutional empire-building, Boas achieved a revolution in American social thought, challenging the evolutionary notions of race and culture, advancing a "concept of culture" that was holistic, relativistic, and pluralistic.

Boas was educated at Heidelberg, Bonn, and Kiel, where he was influenced by neo-Kantians in psychophysics and geography. He completed his doctorate in physics at Kiel in 1881. A Jew and political progressive, Boas felt marginalized by the increasing nationalism and anti-Semitism of Wilhelmine Germany. Although he claimed to be raised free of the "shackles of dogma" of his father's religion, he bore a famous set of scars from duels he fought to become part of the masculine culture of his student days and to challenge anti-Semitic insults. After his first field trip among the Eskimo of Baffin Island in 1883, Boas immigrated to the United States in 1887, working briefly at Clark University and in Chicago at the World's Columbian Exposition of 1893. He finally settled among a family circle of German immigrants in New York, where he affiliated with the American Museum of Natural History (1895–1905) and Columbia University, where he taught until his retirement in 1936.

Central to Boas's conception of anthropology was a cosmopolitan view of science which would transcend differences and allow the creation of a world without particulars. More than the "culture concept," which was important primarily after World War I in the work of his students (*see also* CULTURAL ANTHROPOLOGY), Boas's cosmopolitanism focused on the problem of migrations, contact, and interrelationships, problems that paralleled his own experience of immigration and exile. Through his study of cultural contact, linguistic borrowing, and racial intermixture, Boas based his relativism on two connected principles: people are related, and values are contingent. The role of anthropology was to illuminate this contingency and provide emancipation from the cultural values that bind us.

Although he would probably not have sympathized with the hermeneutic turn in anthropology—he believed too much in the empirical foundations of the discipline—Boas challenged the normative basis of culture on methodological and epistemological grounds. In "The Occurrence of Similar Inventions in Areas Widely Apart" (1887) and "On Alternating Sounds" (1889), he argued against *a priori* assumptions. In the first essay he opposed evolutionism

in favor of a method that would determine the history of contact and diffusion. In the second, he determined that sounds are misheard according to the phonetic system of the listener. Both arguments would have wide-ranging implications for the future of ethnological work. Similarly in physical anthropology, *Changes in Bodily Forms of Descendants of Immigrants* (1911) documented the plasticity of physical types, undermining the fundamental assumptions about racial categories. Boas popularized these conclusions in *The Mind of Primitive Man* (1911), where he argued that values we assume to be absolute are culturally determined, and in *Anthropology and Modern Life* (1928), where he criticized racism, nationalism, and eugenics. Stressing the bias implicit in judging societies different from one's own, Boas emphasized the lessons anthropology offered for "civilized" society and placed particular responsibility on intellectuals to provide a rational understanding of cultural difference.

The institutional setting for Boas's work illustrates some of the contradictions inherent in the claims to a cosmopolitan enterprise. Although for Boas the difficulties of marginality were the primary filter for his anthropological vision, a different kind of cosmopolitanism among New York elites—one primarily concerned with cultural authority—attracted the heads of the city's museums and universities. This particular and uneasy alliance provided Boas with the opportunity in New York that he had not found elsewhere, an alliance that inevitably would fracture. As part of the struggle for hegemony over his profession, crises of authority, in which intellectual views clashed with institutional powers, punctuated Boas's career. Among these were his resignation from Clark University, losing his position after the World's Columbian Exposition in Chicago, his rift with the American Museum of Natural History, and his censure by the American Anthropological Association over his opposition to World War I. In each case, Boas characterized his position as scientific principle and contrasted it to the political machinations of his opponents. Thus Boas's view of science—as disinterested inquiry above power politics—was tied up with his own struggle for institutional power. In addition, the conflicts were ideological, placing Boas's critique of racialism and evolutionism against those whom George Stocking Jr. has called the "racial formalists," the old guard of anthropologists and New York elites.

Critiques of Boas increased after World War II, with the revival of evolutionism and cultural materialism. Marvin Harris and others challenged his relative neglect of economic factors, while Leslie White criticized the "Boas school" for favoring Jews and

Eastern Europeans within the discipline. Although he collected massive amounts of data, Boas never wrote an ethnological monograph, leading some observers to criticize his preference for blueberry pie recipes over systematic theorizing and his tendency to snipe at others instead of making positive assertions of his own.

Despite these internal conflicts within anthropology, Boas is one of those rare academic intellectuals whose name holds some currency outside the academy. Mostly due to his persistent fight against racism, this notoriety is ironic, considering his constant battles for institutional authority and his wariness of exceeding what he saw as the legitimate purview of science. With the exception of moments of particular crisis, such as the two world wars when Boas fought for intellectual freedom and international cooperation, he was careful about, even jealous of, using his scientific authority for public causes. This caution, combined with the conservatism of tradition about which Boas so often wrote, meant that although Boas ultimately won the fight within the profession, battles over the relative importance of culture would continue well into our own time.

JULIA E. LISS

FURTHER READING
Franz Boas, *Race, Language and Culture* (1940; Chicago: University of Chicago Press, 1982).
Douglas Cole, " 'The Value of a Person Lies in His *Herzensbildung*': Franz Boas' Baffin Island Letter Diary, 1883–84," in George W. Stocking Jr., ed., *Observers Observed: Essays in Ethnographic Fieldwork*, vol. 1 of *History of Anthropology* (Madison: University of Wisconsin Press, 1983).
Carl N. Degler, *In Search of Human Nature: the Decline and Revival of Darwinism in American Social Thought* (New York: Oxford University Press, 1991).
Richard Handler, "Boasian Anthropology and the Critique of American Culture," *American Quarterly* 42 (June 1990): 252–73.
Julia E. Liss, "The Cosmopolitan Imagination: Franz Boas and the Development of American Anthropology," Ph.D. diss., University of California, Berkeley, 1990.
——, "Patterns of Strangeness: Franz Boas, Modernism, and the Origins of Anthropology," in Elazar Barkan and Ronald Bush, eds., *Prehistories of the Future: The Primitivist Project and the Culture of Modernism* (Stanford: Stanford University Press, 1995).
George W. Stocking Jr., *Race, Culture and Evolution: Essays in the History of Anthropology* (1968; Chicago: University of Chicago Press, 1982).
——, ed. *A Franz Boas Reader: the Shaping of American Anthropology, 1883–1911* (Chicago: University of Chicago Press, 1974).

body Nothing is more visible, across the range of work in recent cultural studies, than "the return of the body." But what such a turn or return to the body itself makes visible is perhaps less self-evident. As one of the great communicators of the problem of the body and bodily practices in contemporary culture, the novelist J. G. Ballard, expresses it in *The Atrocity Exhibition* (1969): "As you and I know, the act of intercourse is now always a model for something else" (p. 77). The body, one might say, always becomes visible as a model for something else.

For one thing, the emergence of the body means the emergence of the body as problem. Consider, for example, how the popular preacher Josiah Strong registers the matter of the American national body at the turn of the century in *The Times and Young Men* (1901): "Evidently, getting the most good out of life, which is getting the most service into it, raises the problem of *The Body*" (p. 125). What raises the problem of the body for Strong is the body's incorporation into new economic relations. The natural body appears as the transit point between getting and servicing, in effect as the relay between an ethos of physical, material production and an emergent culture of consumption. The very notion of a culture of *consumption* is bound up with the double logic of the body: one of the basic paradoxes of the culture of consumption is the manner in which a style of life characterized by the exceeding or disavowing of mere physical and natural and bodily needs is nevertheless understood on the model of the natural body and its needs, on the model of hunger or eating. If the equivalences between the bodily and the economic —the body as leading economic indicator—have become familiar enough, so too has this paradoxical economy by which the corporeal becomes visible in the process of its material, social, and technological *incorporation*.

The problem of the body—the body in its fascinating concreteness and its shifting historicality—is thus inseparable from the uncertain assemblages of nature and culture, biology and history, deep materialism and sheer culturalism. "The body" is the name given to these relays in our contemporary world. Hence it is not simply a matter of *historicizing the body*, although a good deal of recent work (following Michel Foucault, among others) has proceeded along the lines of writing the histories of bodies, sexualities, and forms of racialized and gendered embodiment. If there has been a sort of naughty thrill in historicizing bodies—a thrill that may by now be going—this is because "the body" signals something like a limit point of the historical: the problem of the body and the problem of historicization or periodization have come to indicate or stand in for, and test out, each other.

The governing models of the American national

body have been the model of possession (bio-economics), the model of the machine (the body-machine complex), and the model of writing or code (the biotext). These variant genre fictions of the body entail in turn variant genre fictions of the individual. It is possible to trace a series of uneven transitions, from the later eighteenth century on, from market society and possessive INDIVIDUALISM to machine society and disciplinary individualism to the control society and cybernetic "dividualism." The shifting determinations of the individuality of the individual are inseparable from transformations in economic, technological, and biological arrangements, in short, shifting models of the body.

Bio-economics "There's a truly strange incoherence in saying—man *has* a body," the psychoanalyst Jacques Lacan concisely observes, and yet "for us it makes sense" (p. 72). What makes sense of the body as possession—as something one *has* rather than something one *is*—is the understanding of the body as *prosthesis*, or self-extension. The links between WORK and self-realization, for example, are the Lockean prosthetics binding the natural body, labor, and property in the self. The history of contract, as OLIVER WENDELL HOLMES JR. traces it in *The Common Law* (1880), is a process of translation between the bodily and the economic. If one first "looked to the body of the contracting party as the ultimate satisfaction," or ground of exchange, the understanding of body as possession makes possible a different sort of satisfaction: one "no longer paid with his body . . . but his liability was translated into money"(pp. 198, 205). The relations of possessive individualism involve what HARRIET BEECHER STOWE, instancing the slave's body, called "living property" and what THORSTEIN VEBLEN, instancing the aura accorded to possession and possessive individuals in the culture of conspicuous consumption, invidiously referred to as "the radiant body."

The Body-Machine Complex For Veblen, among others, the wearing out of the model of possessive individualism mandates the progressive replacement of the radiant body by dispassionate mechanisms of efficient production. This is the achievement of systematic management and comprehensive incorporation of the body in the machine process: the regimes of corporeal discipline, productivism, rationalization, and standardization that make up the body-machine complex. Such an achievement might be represented diversely by the "medicalization" of late nineteenth-century American society, the rise of therapeutic practices, eugenics, euthenics, "scientific motherhood" and "physical culture"; by the statistical and biomet-

rical mapping of natural bodies and the establishment of standardized body sizes—for instance, Daniel Edward Ryan's codification, in 1880, of the "human proportions in growth." It might be represented by the consumer's *model body*, at once individualized and standardized in practices of consumption. The making of statistical persons and bodies extends from calorie counting and ergonomics to the privilege of relative disembodiment or weightlessness in rituals of consumption. And it extends to the weightiness or deep embodiment of those bodies (the laboring body, the visibly gendered body, the racialized body) against which that privilege is measured.

More generally, systematic management makes visible a very different, even opposed, sense of the body as prosthesis. Consider, for example, the small fantasy that appears in Henry Ford's autobiography *My Life and Work* (1923). The production of the Model T required 7,882 distinct work operations, but, Ford observed, only 12 percent of these tasks—only 949 operations—required "strong, able-bodied, and physically perfect men." Of the remainder—and this is clearly what Ford saw as the central contribution of his method of production—"we found that 670 could be filled by legless men, 2,637 by one-legged men, two by armless men, 715 by one-armed men and ten by blind men" (pp. 108–9). From one point of view, this fantasy projects a violent dismemberment of the human body and emptying out of human agency in the work process; but, from another, it projects a transcendence of the natural body and the extension of human agency through the forms of TECHNOLOGY that supplement it. Hence the double logic of technology as prosthesis makes visible the twin operations of the body-machine complex. This involves the mechanization of bodies and the vitalization of technologies. It involves, above all, the *coupling* of bodies and machines.

The Biotext The coupling, or miscegenation, of nature and culture, bodies and machines, effectively collapses the difference between the life process and the machine process. What is then progressively elaborated is a general processing system, correlating biological and mechanical forms of reproduction. The coupling of the life process and the machine process as integrated processing and control systems centers the second industrial revolution—the "control revolution"—from the turn of the century on. And these biotechnologies of control are inseparable from information or writing technologies: the biotext. Hence time–motion studies of the natural body and writing technologies indicate each other from the start—for instance, in the "graphic method" of the pioneer in bio-engineering Étienne-Jules Marey. This is how Marey represents the prosthetic language of the body: "When the eye can no longer see, the ear cannot hear, or touch cannot feel, or even when the senses appear to deceive us, these instruments perform like a new sense with astonishing precision" (p. 108). The intimacy of bodies and machines here becomes the technical and automatic inscription of bodily forces and motion: not merely bodies writing themselves but bodies as writing technologies. The problem of the body, from Marey or Taylorization to cybernetics, from *Dracula* to *Neuromancer* or *Terminator*, is bound up through and through with these media of information and registration, with the "literal technologies" (*see also* TAYLORISM).

There is no simple sequence in these transformations in models or logics of the body: economic, machinic, textual. The violences and pleasures induced by the unstable arrangements of possession, mechanics, and mediation are the landmarks of corporeality in our culture.

MARK SELTZER

See also GENDER; REPRESENTATION; SOCIOBIOLOGY.

FURTHER READING
J. G. Ballard, *The Atrocity Exhibition* (1969; San Francisco: Re/Search, 1990).
Jonathan Crary and Sanford Kwinter, eds., *Incorporations* (New York: Zone, 1992).
Michel Feher, Ramona Naddaff, and Nadia Tazi, eds., *Fragments for a History of the Human Body*, 3 vols. (New York: Zone, 1989).
Michel Foucault, *Discipline and Punish: the Birth of the Prison* (New York: Pantheon, 1977).
Donna Haraway, *Primate Visions: Gender, Race, and Nature in the World of Modern Science* (New York: Routledge, 1989).
Oliver Wendell Holmes Jr., *The Common Law*, ed. Mark DeWolfe Howe (1880; Boston: Little, Brown, 1963).
Jacques Lacan, *The Seminar of Jacques Lacan: Book II*, ed. Jacques-Alain Miller, trans. Sylvana Tomaselli (New York: Norton, 1988).
Étienne-Jules Marey, *La Méthode graphique dans les sciences expérimentales et principalement en physiologie et en médecine* (Paris: G. Masson, 1878).
Mark Seltzer, *Bodies and Machines* (New York: Routledge, 1992).

Boorstin, Daniel (b. Atlanta, Ga., Oct. 1, 1914). Historian. Best known for his three-volume work *The Americans* (1958–73), Boorstin exemplifies one version of the "consensus" approach to history most prominent in the early post-World War II period. The "genius of American politics," he believes, is its "pragmatic" rejection of European ideologies. Americans developed a shared national identity because of their common experience in solving practical problems. They inherit not so much a democratic philosophy as a longstanding democratic practice.

See also: AMERICAN EXCEPTIONALISM; CONSENSUS.

FURTHER READING
Robert Skotheim, *American Intellectual Histories and Historians* (Princeton: Princeton University Press, 1966).

Bourne, Randolph S. (b. Bloomfield, N.J., May 30, 1886; d. New York, N.Y., Dec. 22, 1918). Bourne has exercised a powerful hold over the imagination of the American intelligentsia since the publication of his first book, *Youth and Life*, in 1913. As a prophet of a new generation of young intellectuals, Bourne spoke with a distinctive voice, at once intensely personal and politically committed. He insisted that radical intellectuals explore the subtle connections between private life, culture, and politics. Bourne's searing attacks on JOHN DEWEY and the prowar liberal intelligentsia, and his death at 32 in the influenza epidemic of 1918, transformed the youth prophet into a martyr and mythic figure for later generations of intellectuals. Forever immortalized in John Dos Passos's *1919* as a ghost haunting the American conscience with the refrain, "War is the health of the State," the memory of Bourne survived the years of postwar disillusionment to inspire such radical critics of liberalism as LEWIS MUMFORD, DWIGHT MACDONALD, DOROTHY DAY, C. WRIGHT MILLS, NOAM CHOMSKY, and CHRISTOPHER LASCH. The most recent wave of "Bourne-again" criticism has seized upon Bourne's 1916 essay, "Trans-national America," as a multicultural manifesto for a new American national identity. (*See also* CULTURAL PLURALISM AND MULTICULTURALISM.)

The terrible circumstances of Bourne's birth and childhood undoubtedly contributed to the preoccupation with personal identity in his work. A forceps delivery that mangled his face was followed a few years later by spinal tuberculosis, which left Bourne a hunchbacked dwarf forced to tolerate steady pain, labored breathing, and the visible discomfort of most every new acquaintance. Whatever marginality Bourne felt as a result of his disability was deepened by his unsettled family life. His father's alcoholism, business failures, and abandonment of his family came to symbolize for Bourne the collapse of masculine dreams of entrepreneurial self-reliance in an age of giant industry. Meanwhile, his mother's desperate attempts to maintain genteel standards in the face of the family's deepening economic crisis suggested to Bourne the bankrutcy of a feminized culture removed from practical life—a recurrent theme in his later polemics against the genteel tradition and (Matthew)

Arnoldian conceptions of culture. Bourne drew repeatedly on his early feelings of being "truly in the world, but not of the world"—as he wrote in "The Handicapped"—to speak for a generation of young people from educated Protestant backgrounds who found little moral sustenance in either their parents, traditions, or the new corporate order of the twentieth century (p. 76).

Upon entering Columbia in 1909, Bourne immediately won the admiration of a circle of students who embraced his initial writerly attempts at self-expression as prophetic tracts for their generation. Among these students were many second-generation Jewish immigrants in flight from their parents' Old World culture. Bourne saw in their encounter with Protestant student refugees from the genteel tradition a thrilling opportunity for a vital popular culture and an intellectual life infused with democratic values. The friendships Bourne made at Columbia informed his quest for what he might rightly have called "identity politics": the building of wider and wider circles of fellowship patterned on the model of personal companionship. (*See also* YOUTH.)

Historians have been hard pressed to find coherence in the dizzying range of subjects Bourne addressed in the 1910s, among them youth culture, modern art and literature, progressive education, PRAGMATISM, and war. A recurrent scholarly complaint is the apparent contradiction between Bourne's "apolitical" writings on selfhood and culture, and the vivid antiwar polemics for which he is best known. But such a contradiction relies on a stark distinction between public and private that Bourne took pains to criticize. Bourne's essays traced his generation's crisis of selfhood back to its social roots in the rise of corporate industry and other large-scale institutions. Faced with a choice between an anachronistic ideal of self-reliance and a bureaucratic ethos, Bourne and his friends preferred not to choose at all. Instead, they believed that a meaningful private life could only be found in the democratic reconstruction of social and political institutions: "the good life of personality lived in the environment of the Beloved Community" (p. 264).

As a leader of Greenwich Village's prewar "Little Renaissance," Bourne staked out a role for intellectuals that kept in close tension two apparently contradictory impulses. On the one hand, Bourne embraced his marginality in order to subject mainstream institutions and assumptions to scathing, ironic criticism. On the other, Bourne scoured the American landscape for concrete examples of mutual aid, friendship, and common purpose that might model a new indigenous, democratic culture and politics.

The first project led him to Nietzsche, psychoanalysis, and other currents in continental modernism, while the second brought him to the cultural criticism of VAN WYCK BROOKS, the new liberalism of WALTER LIPPMANN and HERBERT CROLY, and, above all, the pragmatism of John Dewey. In *The Gary Schools* (1916) and *Education and Living* (1917), and in essays on education for THE NEW REPUBLIC, Bourne wrote as a full-fledged Deweyan, heralding the progressive classroom as a seedbed of democratic community. Bourne's admiration for Dewey turned to rage as he watched his mentor endorse American intervention in World War I. His famous antiwar essays of 1917–18 in *The Seven Arts* moved rapidly beyond the diplomatic issues of the war to a bitter indictment of Dewey, Lippmann, and other prowar progressives for succumbing to a fascination with power and technique over the intellectual's responsibility as creator and clarifier of values.

Bourne's last writings leave no single legacy for his many admirers. Embittered by the liberal intelligentsia's enthusiasm for the war, Bourne was prone at the end of his life to entertain a Nietzschean fantasy of "malcontents" gathering to combat America's complacent optimism and resist its "herd mentality." But Bourne's apparent dismissal of the mindless masses contained within it a sympathetic assessment of their powerlessness in the face of war and wartime propaganda. Beneath their acquiescence Bourne discerned the tenacious force of loyalties to friends, family, and place, loyalties that a democratic movement must build on. But at the time of his death, he had not resolved the conflicting images of the people's lethargy and loyalty, or the correspondingly conflicting vocations for intellectuals—detached critics or communally based interpreters. His successors among the radical intelligentsia have not done much better. In the end, Bourne's profoundly honest ambivalence about his own vocation may be his greatest legacy to twentieth-century intellectuals.

CASEY BLAKE

See also CULTURAL CRITICISM; PROGRESSIVISM.

FURTHER READING

Edward Abrahams, *The Lyrical Left: Randolph Bourne, Alfred Stieglitz, and the Origins of Cultural Radicalism in America* (Charlottesville: University Press of Virginia, 1986).

Casey Nelson Blake, *Beloved Community: the Cultural Criticism of Randolph Bourne, Van Wyck Brooks, Waldo Frank, and Lewis Mumford* (Chapel Hill: University of North Carolina Press, 1990).

Paul F. Bourke, "The Status of Politics, 1909–1919: *The New Republic*, Randolph Bourne and Van Wyck Brooks," *Journal of American Studies* 8 (Aug. 1974): 171–202.

Randolph Bourne, *The Radical Will: Selected Writings,*

1911–1918, ed. Olaf Hansen (Berkeley: University of California Press, 1992).

Bruce Clayton, *Forgotten Prophet: the Life of Randolph Bourne* (Baton Rouge: Louisiana State University Press, 1984).

David A. Hollinger, "Ethnic Diversity, Cosmopolitanism, and the Emergence of the American Liberal Intelligentsia," in Hollinger, *In the American Province: Studies in the History and Historiography of Ideas* (Bloomington: Indiana University Press, 1985).

Christopher Lasch, *The New Radicalism in America, 1889–1963: the Intellectual as a Social Type* (New York: Knopf, 1965).

John Adam Moreau, *Randolph Bourne: Legend and Reality* (Washington, D.C.: Public Affairs Press, 1966).

Bradford, William (baptized Austerfield, England, Mar. 29, 1590; d. Plymouth, Mass., May 19, 1657). Governor of Plymouth Colony. One of the framers of the Mayflower Compact, Bradford sought to create a Christian community based on reason and goodwill. When the colony was charged with doctrinal looseness, he answered that only God is infallible: all churches err, and it is arrogant to think one has so thoroughly understood God that others cannot differ. Bradford nevertheless justified violence against Indians by asserting that any resistance against God's people was the work of the devil. His *History of Plymouth Plantation, 1620–47* is an invaluable source for the settlement's early history.

See also PURITANISM.

FURTHER READING

Perry D. Westbrook, *William Bradford* (Boston: Twayne, 1978).

Bradstreet, Anne (b. Northampton, England, ca.1612; d. Andover, Mass., Sept. 16, 1672). Poet. Bradstreet preached a simple piety as she sought to submit herself to God's will and see God's presence and purpose in everyday things. Her love poems to her husband stylistically resemble the Song of Solomon, while her desriptions of children and motherhood are unusually realistic. Although she acknowledged male superiority, Bradstreet defended women's desires to use their talents and looked to Queen Elizabeth as a model of female worth. Her poems were first published in England as *The Tenth Muse Lately Sprung Up in America* (1650).

FURTHER READING

Jeffrey Hammond, *Sinful Self, Saintly Self: the Puritan Experience of Poetry* (Athens: University of Georgia Press, 1993).

Brandeis, Louis D. (b. Louisville, Ky., Nov. 13, 1856; d. Washington, D.C., Oct. 5, 1941). Brandeis has been lionized, in his day and ours, for his achievements as a liberal Supreme Court Justice (1916–39)

and, before that, as the nation's first "public interest lawyer" or, as the Progressive era press dubbed him, the "People's Attorney." Famous for his briefs and dissenting opinions freighted with facts and statistics, Brandeis brought "sociological jurisprudence," with its emphasis on "experience" over formal doctrinal logic, into the courtrooms and case law. As he pioneered this modern liberal approach to LAW, Brandeis also championed a thoroughly traditional reformist outlook. He was among the last great defenders of the republican producerist tradition, which ran through Progressives like Brandeis back to POPULISM and to THOMAS JEFFERSON and THOMAS PAINE— and, for Brandeis, to its roots in republican Athens. "Two interacting themes dominated Brandeis's talk," Dean Acheson, one of his first Supreme Court law clerks, recalled wryly, "the Greek genius and the curse of Bigness" (Strum, p. 242).

A vision of a vigorous, decentralized DEMOCRACY of active and independent citizen-producers lent Brandeis's thought its much-celebrated unity. Brandeis's own insistent independence, as gadfly, adviser, and then life-tenured jurist, unbound to client, party or elected office, enabled him to sustain this coherent vision of reform, even as his ideas fell increasingly out of step with prevailing economic developments, social movements, and reform ideals.

Such independence requires a material basis. While still a young man, Brandeis built up a substantial fortune as a business and corporation lawyer in Gilded Age Boston. As his generation's brightest Harvard Law graduate, Brandeis might have expected to find the city's great financiers and railroad magnates among his clients. However, his Jewishness barred him from a practice counseling the Brahmin business elite. Brandeis's clients were mostly small and medium-sized manufacturing firms, along with prominent Jewish wholesalers and retailers such as the Filenes. After his fortune was made, and Brandeis shifted from business lawyer to people's advocate, assailing the life insurance industry, the "corporate tyrants" like Standard Oil and U.S. Steel, and the "money trust," he was not biting the hand that had fed him.

Indeed, Thomas McCraw, a leading historian of business regulation, has suggested that even as a reform advocate and foe of the "trusts," Brandeis was not really "the people's lawyer"; instead, he remained "the advocate of the small businessman." McCraw sharply criticizes Brandeis for failing to see that bigness was inevitable because it was efficient; it yielded economies of scale and thereby produced savings for the nation's consumers. As other historians have taken up this view of Brandeis's economic thinking, it has become commonplace to assert that Brandeis and his followers had no solutions to the problems of technological change, economic instability, overproduction, price and wage gouging—all of which were addressed by those Progressives, like THEODORE ROOSEVELT, who accepted the inevitability of bigness and sought to regulate trusts rather than undo them.

This picture is wildly one-sided, revealing more, perhaps, about late twentieth-century economic thought than about Brandeis. First, Brandeis, no less than the pro-corporate reformers around Roosevelt, railed against the evils of unregulated competition. He too sought to legitimate administered markets, but he envisioned market administration under the looser cooperation of many small firms. Second, Brandeis actually had much to say about the efficiency claims made on behalf of large corporations, pointing out the irrationalities and perverse motivations generated by the administrative hierarchies that large-scale corporations require to coordinate production. He also anticipated the potentially fatal rigidities that afflicted such units in comparison to smaller, more flexible firms.

Brandeis's support for trade unionism explains why small businessmen's organizations and spokesmen consistently assailed him as a dangerous radical. Brandeis prized smaller firms because he valued the independent entrepreneur, but, equally, he prized them because he understood that such firms were far less able than trusts to defeat workers' efforts at organizing and gaining a strong voice in the workplace. Faced with labor law reforms that protected workers' freedom of association and right to strike—reforms that Brandeis championed and associations of small and medium-sized firms opposed—those firms would be constrained to deal with unions. By contrast, even with such reforms, Brandeis believed that the giant, hierarchical corporations were far less likely to evolve in the direction of genuine worker participation in "the decisions about how the business shall be run."

In testimony before the U.S. Senate Committee on Industrial Relations in 1915, Brandeis insisted that without such participation, without the "sharing of responsibility and profits," there could be no "fullgrown industrial democracy," and the world of work would continue to impede the development of "responsible, democratic individuals," which Brandeis saw as the goal of American law and life. Unlike defenders of corporate capitalism who take for granted that allocative efficiency and "consumer welfare" are the sole valid criteria for assessing economic good sense, Brandeis demanded that industry do more than produce goods enough to meet Americans' material needs. He wanted American industry to be organized so that it would help produce democratic citizens.

As with industry, so with government: Brandeis's famous devotion to federalism, his preference, where possible, for local and state-based rather than national law reform, flowed from two sources. First, he insisted that the states were well-suited to serve as "social laboratories" where divergent reform initiatives could be tested and refined. Second, he believed that every increase in the scale of politics contributed to reducing informed, active citizens to mere voters.

Finally, Brandeis's conviction that the law should shape democratic individuals inspired his most eloquent and enduring contributions to constitutional law. The basic ideas and metaphors underlying contemporary First Amendment doctrine derive largely from a handful of dissenting opinions by Justices Holmes and Brandeis during the 1920s. Characteristically, the contributions from OLIVER WENDELL HOLMES JR. had a skeptical as well as negative cast. Brandeis, by contrast, turned not to the liberal marketplace but to the ancient republican ideal of civic courage for scaffolding to support broad constitutional protection for "subversive advocacy" and for associations accused of such advocacy. So doing, in *Whitney v. California* (1927), he set out a rare—and doctrinally generative—affirmative vision of the goals of the First Amendment.

> Those who won our independence believed that the final end of the State was to make men free to develop their faculties; and that in its government the deliberative forces should prevail over the arbitrary. They valued liberty both as an end and as a means . . . they knew that order cannot be secured merely through fear of punishment for its infraction; that it is hazardous to discourage thought, hope, and imagination; that fear breeds repression; that repression breeds hate; . . . and that the fitting remedy for evil counsels is good ones . . .

> Those who won our independence by revolution were not cowards. They did not fear political change. [Instead, they had] confidence in the power of free and fearless reasoning applied through the processes of popular government . . .

What separates us from Brandeis, what places him on the far side of an ideological gulf, may be less his supposedly wrong-headed economics or his ignorance of the "inevitability" of corporate capitalism, and more his profound and austere faith in the capacity of citizens and the "processes of popular government" to produce and sustain such robust democracy.

WILLIAM E. FORBATH

See also PRAGMATISM; PROGRESSIVISM.

FURTHER READING

Vincent Blasi, "The First Amendment and the Ideal of Civic Courage: the Brandeis Opinion in *Whitney v. California*," *William and Mary Law Review* 29 (summer, 1988): 653–97.

Louis D. Brandeis, *The Social and Economic Views of Mr. Justice Brandeis*, ed. Alfred Lief (New York: Vanguard, 1930).

——, *The Curse of Bigness: Miscellaneous Papers*, ed. Osmond Fraenkel (New York: Viking, 1935).

Thomas K. McCraw, *Prophets of Regulation: Charles Francis Adams, Louis D. Brandeis, James M. Landis, Alfred E. Kahn* (Cambridge: Harvard University Press, 1984).

Clyde Spillenger, "Reading the Judicial Canon: Alexander Bickel and the Book of Brandeis," *Journal of American History* 79, (June 1992): 125–51.

Phillippa Strum, *Louis D. Brandeis: Justice for the People* (Cambridge: Harvard University Press, 1984).

Breckinridge, Sophonisba (b. Lexington, Ky., Apr. 1, 1866; d. Chicago, Ill., July 30, 1948). Social worker and educator. Promoting the idea that government, at the state and especially federal levels, must be engaged in social welfare programs, Breckenridge brought empirical social science research to the cause of progressive social reform. She argued that social and economic conditions bred truancy and crime, and that racism and systematic discrimination locked African Americans into poverty. She taught in the University of Chicago's Graduate School of Social Service Administration, although her own reformist sensibilities were increasingly inconsistent with the ethos of professional social work that emerged in the 1920s. She also cofounded the *Social Service Review* (1927) and wrote 12 books, including *The Delinquent Child and the Home* (with EDITH ABBOTT, 1912) and *The Family and the State* (1934).

See also SOCIAL SCIENCE; WELFARE.

FURTHER READING

Ellen Fitzpatrick, *Endless Crusade: Women Social Scientists and Progressive Reform* (New York: Oxford University Press, 1990).

Brooks, Van Wyck (b. Plainfield, N.J., Feb. 16, 1886; d. Bridgewater, Conn., May 2, 1963). Brooks's reputation has suffered one of the most thorough reversals of fortune of any intellectual in the twentieth century. Historians have typically divided his work into two periods: the penetrating critic of the 1910s, who explored the fatal division between cultural values and practical life in American history, and the Depression and World War II era champion of his country's resilient traditions in art and literature. Many observers who praise the youthful scourge of the genteel tradition dismiss the mature Brooks as a genteel dispenser of liberal bromides, indifferent to politics and ignorant of the rigors of academic literary criticism.

Brooks was born into a family that maintained the trappings of Victorian culture amid inescapable evidence of its decline. Brooks's grim family life stood in stark distinction to the cheery professions of Republican, liberal Protestant, and middle-class self-assurance that permeated his suburban environment. His mother's aspirations to a cultured domesticity ran aground after his father's business failures, which left the elder Brooks emotionally broken, a ghost haunting his own household. His father's demise, followed many years later by the suicide of Brooks's brother—a closet poet laboring on Wall Street—seared Brooks's imagination: the masculine world of commerce was a Moloch that devoured creative personalities. Meanwhile, his mother's frantic efforts at respectability made Brooks look sourly on genteel moralism. Even as a high school student and undergraduate at Harvard (1904–7), Brooks was seeking a way of overcoming the antagonistic split between (male) business and (female) culture, neither of which, in gendered isolation, offered the prospect of a fulfilling life.

Brooks's earliest essays explored two different paths toward reconciling the warring tendencies in American life. In his private diaries, and in such early works as *The Soul* (1910) and *The Malady of the Ideal* (1913), he indulged fantasies of spiritual, interpersonal communion, imagining a mystical resolution to the fragmentation of the self. But mysticism was double-edged: it promised complete deliverance, yet the deliverance was strangely akin to a disintegration of the self—a fear made palpable for Brooks with the deepening of a manic-depressive condition that had plagued him since adolescence. He spent much of his life tempted by mysticism, but trying to keep its terrors at bay.

Brooks's second early response, in *The Wine of the Puritans* (1908), *America's Coming-of-Age* (1915), and the essays in *The Seven Arts* (1916–17) published in *Letters and Leadership* (1918), was to embark on a campaign of CULTURAL CRITICISM: he inveighed against the split between an airy "highbrow" idealism and a thoughtless "lowbrow" commercialism. On the one hand, Brooks hoped to "remasculinize" culture, bring it into contact with labor and politics, rescue it from decadent sentimentalization by genteel critics and readers alike. On the other, he condemned masculine enterprise as the enemy of "personality," an ideal of selfhood that Brooks endowed with such valuable "feminine" traits as mutuality and intuition. With these essays, which made him a leading figure in the American literary renaissance of the 1910s,

Brooks established cultural criticism as a hybrid of literary history and social criticism. With his friend RANDOLPH BOURNE and the other editors of *The Seven Arts*, Brooks believed that America would only "come of age" through the interaction of two separate movements: a renewal of an indigenous American artistic tradition, and a new radical politics. Brooks's project was more than a campaign against the division between "high" and "low" culture, as later authors have mistakenly argued. It was political as well as cultural advocacy, culminating in an indictment of capitalism reminiscent of William Morris's English Romantic radicalism.

Brooks's early essays played a crucial role in expanding Americans' understanding of the meaning of "culture." Like Matthew Arnold, Brooks was inclined to emphasize the didactic content of cultural expression and to praise great art and literature as "the best that has been thought and said in the world." But during the Gilded Age, he argued, Arnoldian critics capitulated to commercial pressures by relegating culture to an other-worldly realm remote from social experience or political concerns. Brooks anticipated the anthropological redefinition of culture that occurred in the thirties: culture as an "entire way of life." At the same time he used Arnold's idealism as a vantage point for his critique of American business and politics. Playing an Arnoldian conception of culture off against an ideal of culture as lived experience, Brooks sought to promote an art and literature steeped in the colloquial idiom of American life even as he held Americans accountable to their professed moral and democratic ideals.

The problem for Brooks was that American history offered so few examples of the sort of interplay between dissenting popular and artistic traditions that sustained Morris's cultural criticism in England. In the aftermath of Randolph Bourne's death in 1918 and the war-inspired hysteria that destroyed the American left, Brooks felt increasingly isolated from the remaining fragments of an intellectual or political opposition. Beginning with his call for a "usable past" in *The Dial* in 1920, and continuing with his essays for the *Freeman* in the twenties, Brooks's critical vision narrowed decisively. He intended his trilogy of biographical studies of Twain, James, and Emerson, which appeared in the 1920s, as a development of his critical project, but they marked instead a retreat from his early ambitions. He was scouring the past for a literary hero whose life would single-handedly resolve the deep contradictions in American history. That search became ever more desperate as Brooks slipped into depression and madness in 1926.

Brooks literally wrote his way back back from the abyss by inverting his early critical stance and proclaiming that the United States had long enjoyed a "middle ground" of humanistic art and literature that reflected its frontier egalitarianism and democratic sensibility. His "Makers and Finders" series (1936–52) completely abandoned the tough dialectic of his early work for a curatorial solicitude toward the web of friendships and social relations that sustained great and not-so-great writers from the Revolution to his own era. The best of these books—*The Flowering of New England* (1936) and *The World of Washington Irving* (1944)—offered compelling portraits of the new nation's Jeffersonian culture, but Brooks's work had lost its edge. Brooks's cultural nationalism fitted well with the shallow populism of the Popular Front, which Brooks served as an officer of the League of American Writers until the Hitler–Stalin pact. Brooks's work in the thirties won him a large audience outside of left-liberal circles: *Flowering* remained on the bestseller list for 59 weeks. When Brooks joined ARCHIBALD MACLEISH during World War II in nationalistic attacks on T. S. ELIOT and other modernists as deracinated expatriates, he sealed his fate with younger critics at the *Partisan Review*, many of whom had cut their teeth on his early essays and emulated his then-prophetic voice.

Brooks continued writing until his death in 1963, producing more and more testaments to his country's literary vitality and three remarkably self-aware volumes of autobiography. But in an echo of his father's fate, Brooks roamed postwar American literary culture as a living ghost, ignored by Marxist critics and New Critics alike. He lived long enough to see a distinguished lineage of writers—from MALCOLM COWLEY, EDMUND WILSON, and F. O. Matthiessen to ALFRED KAZIN, Richard Chase, and Sherman Paul—claim his legacy, but he had to suffer the indignity of watching virtually every one of these men seize upon the dialectical method of his early essays to attack the complacent nationalism of his later work. Just as Brooks read Twain and James as exemplars of a riven culture, current critics are more likely to read Brooks for insights into the precarious place of the critical imagination in America than as a model for contemporary cultural criticism.

CASEY BLAKE

See also AESTHETICS.

FURTHER READING

Steven Biel, *Independent Intellectuals in the United States, 1910–1945* (New York: New York University Press, 1992).

Casey Nelson Blake, *Beloved Community: the Cultural Criticism of Randolph Bourne, Van Wyck Brooks, Waldo Frank, and Lewis Mumford* (Chapel Hill: University of North Carolina Press, 1990).

Van Wyck Brooks, *An Autobiography* (New York: E.P. Dutton, 1965).

James Hoopes, *Van Wyck Brooks: In Search of American Culture* (Amherst: University of Massachusetts Press, 1977).

T. J. Jackson Lears, *No Place of Grace: Antimodernism and the Transformation of American Culture, 1880–1920* (New York: Pantheon, 1981).

Raymond Nelson, *Van Wyck Brooks: a Writer's Life* (New York: E.P. Dutton, n.d.).

Claire Sprague, ed., *Van Wyck Brooks: the Early Years, a Selection from his Works, 1908–1921* (New York: Harper and Row, 1968).

William Wasserstrom, *The Legacy of Van Wyck Brooks: a Study of Maladies and Motives* (Carbondale: Southern Illinois University Press, 1971).

Brown, Charles Brockden (b. Philadelphia, Pa., Jan. 17, 1771; d. Philadelphia, Pa., Feb. 22, 1810). Writer. The first professional American novelist, Brown wrote stories that abound in psychological terror, crime, and paranormal phenomena. In *Wieland* (1798) and *Arthur Mervyn* (1799–1800), appearances are deceptive, neither sensory impression nor rational analysis is trustworthy, and reliance on emotion or human benevolence leads to violence and tragedy. Preoccupied by the relationship between society and the individual, Brown suggested that communal structures of authority must protect society from the destructive tendencies individuals direct toward themselves and others.

FURTHER READING

Steven Watts, *The Romance of Real Life: Charles Brockden Brown and the Origins of American Culture* (Baltimore: Johns Hopkins University Press, 1994).

Brownson, Orestes (b. Stockbridge, Vt., Sept. 16, 1803; d. Detroit, Mich., Apr. 17, 1876). Raised as an orthodox Calvinist, Brownson experimented with several varieties of Presbyterianism, Universalism, free thought, and Unitarianism, before scandalizing his staunchly Protestant friends by converting to Catholicism in 1844. Since his political views were equally unstable, he gained a reputation for inconsistency and flightiness that has dogged him ever since. An Owenite socialist in the 1820s, he later embraced the cause of working-class radicalism, briefly called himself a Jacksonian Democrat, soured on democracy after the log-cabin, hard-cider campaign of 1840, allied himself for a time with JOHN C. CALHOUN, and finally settled down as a Catholic conservative in the last 25 years of his life (*see* CATHOLICISM).

If Brownson had been the kind of man to keep his thoughts to himself, the checkered pattern of his career might not have prompted the "sneer," characteristically reported by himself, that his "versatil-

ity and frequent changes of opinion" made him an unreliable commentator on politics or any other subject. Unfortunately for his reputation, Brownson was incurably loquacious; he conducted his self-education in public, in the pages of magazines written entirely by himself. Arthur Schlesinger aptly subtitled his life of Brownson, *A Pilgrim's Progress*, since Brownson invested his journeyings, religious and political, with spiritual significance of the highest order. It was this sense of large issues at stake, rather than vanity or self-importance, that caused him to assume that his "progress" was of interest to readers far beyond his immediate circle.

It is a pity that he never found the wider audience he hoped for. He was a remarkably astute and penetrating thinker, with a knack for going to the heart of an issue. Few intellectuals, moreover, can be said to have sacrificed themselves so completely to the service of the nation. It was as if he had appointed himself its conscience, identified his own spiritual struggles with America's search for its soul.

Two central preoccupations gave unity and direction to the seemingly meandering course of Brownson's thought. The first, his insistence that "religion and politics run perpetually into one another" and could not be separated without doing violence to both, put him at odds with the dominant view that liberal democracy required precisely the relegation of religion to private life. Brownson opposed this commonplace position not because he wanted the state to impose religious uniformity but because he understood that even liberalism requires a minimum of moral agreement. Efforts to promote such agreement by means of a secular, quasi-official public piety—what later came to be called civil religion—were not enough. They would reduce religion to its lowest common denominator and encourage a bland, platitudinous form of public discourse. The public arena needed the provocation and judgment that only biblical religion could provide.

Brownson believed, moreover, that the state has an obligation to educate its citizens in the broadest sense—to teach them not just civility but the essential requirements, spiritual as well as material, of a good life. These views made Brownson by far the most discerning critic of the system of education promoted by HORACE MANN—which already, by virtue of Mann's zeal to eliminate political and religious subjects, contained the seeds of the moral and intellectual disaster that American education has become. They also gave rise to a critique of the "comforting system" that rivalled that of William Cobbett, who coined the phrase—the system of philanthropy that makes communities depend on the state to do the things they ought to do for themselves. Brownson took self-government more seriously than most of his contemporaries. Hence his observation that humanitarianism—just because its intentions appeared so impeccably virtuous—is "more dangerous in principle" than selfishness itself: the devil's work, at its most insidious.

The other concern that animated Brownson's entire career was his impatience with INDIVIDUALISM and his search for a politics that would do justice to the fact of human solidarity. "All that was destructible had been destroyed, and it was time to begin the work of reconstruction—a work of reconciliation and love." In these words, Brownson described the leitmotif of his life as a writer.

Because he refused to see enlightened self-interest as the be-all and end-all of the political order, Brownson sometimes sounded like a socialist, even a communist. In his famous essay of 1840, "The Laboring Classes," he denounced industrial capitalism with a vehemence hardly equaled eight years later by *The Communist Manifesto*. What he advocated, however, was proprietorship, not communism. He proposed to abolish the "distinction between capitalists and laborers," the "factory system," the "banking and credit system"—the whole structure of modern progress, in short. For progressives, Brownson understandably remains what he always was—"a man of unbalanced mind," as Theodore Parker once called him. But for those who believe that DEMOCRACY and PROGRESS (or the spirit of "improvement," as Brownson called it) are related more often as adversaries than as allies, he appears a model democrat, one whose writings deserve to be read more widely than they have been in the past.

CHRISTOPHER LASCH

FURTHER READING
Orestes Brownson, review of Horace Mann's Second Annual Report, *Boston Quarterly Review* 2 (Oct. 1839): 394–434.
——, "The Laboring Classes," *Boston Quarterly Review* 3 (July 1840): 358–95.
——, *The Convert* (New York: Sadlier, 1857).
——, *The American Republic* (New York: O'Shea, 1866).
Americo P. Lapati, *Orestes A. Brownson* (New York: Twayne, 1965).
Thomas R. Ryan, *Orestes A. Brownson* (Huntington, Ind.: Our Sunday Visitor, 1976).
Arthur M. Schlesinger Jr., *Orestes Brownson: a Pilgrim's Progress* (Boston: Little, Brown, 1939).

Bryan, William Jennings (b. Salem, Ill., Mar. 19, 1860; d. Dayton, Tenn., July 26, 1925). Democratic politician and orator. Known as "The Great Commoner," Bryan rallied farmers and workers in a common campaign against big business and monopolies. A perennial presidential candidate and eloquent speaker famous for his "Cross of Gold" address in 1896, Bryan is remembered today as much for his celebrated role at the Scopes "Monkey" trial of 1925 (when a Tennessee high-school teacher was convicted for teaching the Darwinian theory of evolution) as for his producerist populism of the 1890s. He is one of the last exemplars of the evangelical reform tradition which until the 1920s joined liberal politics with evangelical religion.

See also EVANGELICALISM; LIBERAL PROTESTANTISM; POPULISM.

FURTHER READING
LeRoy Ashby, *William Jennings Bryan: Champion of Democracy* (Boston: Twayne, 1987).

Bryant, William Cullen (b. Cummington, Mass., Nov. 3, 1794; d. New York. N.Y., June 12, 1878). Poet, critic, and journalist. Bryant's lyrical descriptions of natural beauty evoke the possibility of union with a God indwelling in nature. Joining the widespread commitment to creating a distinctively American literature with a reliance upon European poetic traditions, his romantic standpoint stressed simplicity, originality, and the emotional and suggestive nature of poetry. As editor of the New York *Evening Post* (1827–78), Bryant supported labor organization, free trade, abolition, and other reforms.

See also ROMANTICISM.

FURTHER READING
Albert F. McLean, *William Cullen Bryant* (Boston: Twayne, 1989).

Buckley, William F. Jr. (b. New York, N.Y., Nov. 24, 1925). As a young man in the early postwar period, Buckley enjoyed a prominence that made him one of the most familiar and controversial conservative intellectuals in the United States. His acquiring this status seems the more remarkable when one considers that Buckley always defied easy categorization as a conservative. His journalistic commentary made him at various times a libertarian, a traditionalist, a nationalist, a localist, an elitist, and a democrat. Some conservative critics faulted Buckley for a failure of ideology, a want of intellectual cohesiveness, and they found his opinions too "ad hoc."

But these qualities do, in turn, help explain Buckley's role in the conservative intellectual movement over more than four decades. His launching of the *National Review* in 1955 had the singular effect of bringing diverse, and sometimes divergent expressions of conservatism into one journalistic household.

The magazine welcomed anticommunists, free-market economists, Roman Catholic apologists, but also moral libertarians and agnostics. These groups did not always sit comfortably with each other. Those who departed the review often cited its heavy religious atmosphere as cause. Yet Buckley managed to function as a kind of paterfamilias to American conservatism. And beyond the readership of *National Review*, Buckley became known to many Americans through his television program "Firing Line," which enjoyed the greatest longevity of any offering on national public television. The program also gave visibility to Buckley's signature traits—his wit and sarcasm, his expansive lexicon, his affected pensiveness, and his erudition.

If Buckley's role as conservative eluded ideological consistency, it nevertheless displayed a style and perspective that gave Buckley a special identification as a conservative. Buckley came from a large Catholic family. His father, William Frank Buckley, made his money in Texas oil and carried both his financial interests and his Catholic loyalties into Mexican politics. Buckley's mother, Aloise, influenced her children through her strong Catholic pietism. But the Buckleys often felt themselves to be outsiders—Catholics in a Protestant country, and later southerners among northerners. The Buckley siblings developed a cohesive loyalty among themselves and eventually nine of the ten contributed writing to the *National Review*. Buckley's conservatism always reflected a familial loyalty, a tribal cohesiveness, that marked off in strict boundary lines the faithful within and the enemies without.

The Buckley style became evident in his first book. Published upon his graduation from Yale University in 1950, *God and Man at Yale* broadcast Buckley's combativeness. The book recounted an institutional betrayal—the subversion of traditionalist Yale by liberal economics and secular moral relativism. To Buckley, defense of traditionalist Yale coincided with loyalty to traditionalist America. A major influence in shaping these loyalties came from Whittaker Chambers, the accuser of Alger Hiss in one of the great controversies in the domestic Cold War. Chambers's celebrated memoir *Witness* (1952) outlined a great spiritual battle between those committed to freedom and God, and those who would enslave humanity through an atheistic materialism. Buckley became a friend and correspondent of Chambers and published their exchanges in *Odyssey of a Friend* (1964).

This categorizing habit also described the book that Buckley wrote with his brother-in-law L. Brent Bozell, *McCarthy and His Enemies* (1954). Their defense of the Wisconsin senator's anticommunist pro-gram rested on a majority's prerogative to defend what Buckley called its "folkways and mores" against any who would subvert them. Buckley in turn showed little patience for what he perceived as a prevailing laxness or indifference toward American principles. His book *Up From Liberalism* (1959) excoriated liberals for their moral relativism. Buckley charged that liberals' pragmatic and accommodating spirit, in the midst of an ominous rivalry with the Soviet Union, weakened the national will. But Buckley was also afraid that conservatism, under the too temperate Eisenhower Presidency, similarly reflected America's growing anemia. Eisenhower, he believed, did not take the Cold War seriously, thinking he might dissolve the Soviet threat with a beneficent smile.

Buckley believed that conservatives must constitute a vigilant minority in liberal America. He saw them as embattled outsiders whose coming together in *National Review* would solidify their tribal bonds against the enemy without. Buckley particularly sounded these notes regarding the Cold War and warned against any accommodation with the Soviet Union. In a 1970 *Playboy* interview, when asked what he thought was most important in the decade just passed, he replied, "the philosophical acceptance of coexistence by the West." To this extent, Buckley thrilled to the writings of the Russian emigré novelist Alexander Solzhenitsyn, for they evoked dramatically, he believed, the monstrous evils of communism. Moreover, they helped preserve the kinship bonds of conservatism. By Solzhenitsyn's works, Buckley wrote in *A Hymnal* (1975), "we are annealed into a brotherhood, with a sense of mission." "I feel differently in the company of men who have read Solzhenitsyn" (pp. 24–5).

Buckley's aristocratic demeanor and his Catholic loyalties partly link him with the Old Right intellectual conservatives who disparaged mass democratic society and upheld certain theological and metaphysical standards against modern secular life. But Buckley also anticipated a direction in American CONSERVATISM that became more visible with the NEOCONSERVATISM of the 1970s and 1980s. By then American conservatism had assumed a majoritarian bias and articulated an anti-elitist animus against the "New Class" of allegedly leftist or liberal influences in academia, the media, the professions, and the government bureaucracies. Buckley anticipated these prejudices in his 1950 vendetta against the Yale professoriat. Buckley's views sometimes bordered on conservative populism, as suggested by his familiar quip that he would rather live in a society governed by the first two thousand names in the Boston telephone directory than in a society governed by the Harvard University faculty.

Buckley's tribal conservatism effectively cautioned his readers against misconceiving the realities of the Soviet Union. But it also carried an intransigence that made Buckley inflexible. He seemed never to forget an offense. On other matters, this character of his thinking gave a hit-and-miss quality to his conservatism. At one point in the 1960s he celebrated black pride and black community control as a mode of racial loyalty; in the 1980s, he accused the followers of Jesse Jackson—African American candidate for the Presidency—of an alienating tribalism that set them off from the rest of the nation.

But by this decade Buckley as conservative could no longer posture as the outsider. In Ronald Reagan he could claim a President who many times acknowledged Buckley's influence on him. That fact may be a measure of Buckley's influence and success, but it deprived him of the strategic vantage that had given his conservatism its effective critical edge.

J. DAVID HOEVELER JR.

FURTHER READING

J. David Hoeveler Jr., *Watch on the Right: Conservative Intellectuals in the Reagan Era* (Madison: University of Wisconsin Press, 1991).

John B. Judis, *William F. Buckley, Jr.: Patron Saint of the Conservatives* (New York: Simon and Schuster, 1988).

George H. Nash, *The Conservative Intellectual Movement in the United States: Since 1945* (New York: Basic, 1976).

Mark Royden Winchell, *William F. Buckley, Jr.* (Boston: Twayne, 1984).

Bunche, Ralph (b. Detroit, Mich., Aug. 7, 1904; d. New York, N.Y., Dec. 9, 1971). Diplomat and political scientist. Bunche's Harvard dissertation, never published, focused on trusteeship and decolonization in the international arena, issues that would preoccupy him as a diplomat. Author of many published articles, he also wrote a steady stream of official reports and speeches. A gifted conciliator, he received the 1950 Nobel Peace Prize for his work in promoting an armistice to end the Arab–Israeli war of 1948.

FURTHER READING

Brian Urquhart, *Ralph Bunche, an American Life* (New York: Norton, 1993).

Burke, Kenneth (b. Pittsburgh, Pa., May 5, 1897; d. Andover, N.J., Nov. 19, 1993). A critic, philosopher, poet, and fiction writer, Burke was educated at—though he did not graduate from—Ohio State and Columbia. He spent the years from 1918 to 1922 in Greenwich Village, leaving it to settle on a farm

in Andover, New Jersey. Burke was a member of the editorial board of *The Dial* from 1921 to 1929, and its music critic from 1927 to 1929, and he published stories in two other important little magazines, *Broom* and *Secession*. He lectured and wrote extensively while remaining outside the professional networks of the academy, though he did hold a special appointment at Bennington College from 1943 to 1963.

Burke's main contribution has been to describe and assess literature as a form of symbolic action that must be understood in relation to the psychology of both author and audience. Key influences on Burke's ideas include Coleridge, Marx, Freud, and WILLIAM JAMES, but he drew from a host of writers, fields, and disciplines as he sought to integrate literature, history, philosophy, sociology, and history in complex, intricate acts of synthesis and system. His major books include *Attitudes Toward History* (1937), *The Philosophy of Literary Form* (1941), *A Grammar of Motives* (1945), *A Rhetoric of Motives* (1950), and *Language as Symbolic Action* (1966).

Burke is still sometimes classified as a New Critic, but he is only loosely linked to the New Critical revolt against positivist historical scholarship and to the modern reform of literary studies. Burke has appeared to many readers to lack the aesthetic taste and discrimination that a true critic should possess: he is not really *literary* in his interpretations. R. P. Blackmur, for example, noted in *A Double Agent* that Burke's "method could be applied with equal fruitfulness either to Shakespeare, Dashiell Hammett, or Marie Corelli" (p. 294). As Blackmur indicates, Burke's criticism is weakened by an arbitrariness of literary judgment, however admirable its exploratory verve.

Burke's ideals have nevertheless proven attractive to those dismayed by the narrowness of the New Criticism and its rival formalist schools. In his best book, *The Philosophy of Literary Form*, Burke suggests fruitfully that critics should ask leading questions and hence actively structure the text or field they investigate. Literary texts, Burke adds, reveal the same concerns that motivate other texts: all texts can be treated in terms of their strategies and designs on audiences. The interpretative tools employed in analyzing aesthetic phenomena can be applied to the analysis of social and political questions. Literary criticism cannot be separated from cultural criticism; art and society are fatefully entwined.

In this judgment Burke was typical of the generation of writers formed by the political and ideological battles of the 1930s. In his important address to the left-wing League of American Writers in 1935 he asserted the reality and indispensability of "myths" in social life. The crucial question, he told his largely communist audience, was to promulgate the symbols and myths most serviceable for revolutionary advance. By that standard the communists' own symbolic "worker" and "masses" were inferior to the "people" because the latter symbol, "closer to our folkways," could mobilize the lower-middle class as well as the proletariat. It drew emotional power from its association with the admittedly outdated symbol of the "nation," while it asserted the ideal future of a classless society beyond nationalism. (Aaron and Bendiner, p. 315.)

But Burke's validation of propaganda and myth-making as serious pursuits for writers was offset by his simultaneous assault on the "anti-intellectualism" of the proletarian movement, which implied that "there is some disgrace attached to things of the mind." He could understand such anti-intellectualism, since so many "channels of thought are in control of reactionaries." But "to turn against thought for such a reason would be like advocating illiteracy because people that read are exposed to the full force of our newspapers and magazines" (p. 316). The tension in his position was typical of a generation of writers devoted to art and politics alike, though Burke was more self-conscious and articulate about the dilemma than most. His wrestling with that tension has been inspiring to some contemporary writers, such as Frank Lentricchia, as they debate the proper relation between politics and art.

In his major works Burke tried to articulate the theoretical underpinnings of a perspective that could restore the connections between literary criticism on the one hand, and culture and politics on the other. He sought to reconceive the relations between literature and society, and between different kinds of texts—enterprises scuttled by the New Criticism in its quest to grasp the dense particularity of each text. Burke believed he was also a practitioner of that close textual criticism, but except for several good essays on Shakespeare, Burke's commentaries on specific literary works are awkward, eccentric, brilliant in flashes but unpersuasive as a whole. René Wellek points out that Burke can be "grossly unfair and absurdly farfetched," as in his judgment that in *Faust* Goethe "anticipated Hegel and thereby anticipated both communism and nazism" (p. 253).

Burke was unquestionably a gifted, original, and pleasure-giving writer. His interpretive claims ultimately matter less than the ingenuity of his smart, cogently crafted sentences. Only Burke could concisely portray Volumnia, the mother of Coriolanus in Shakespeare's play, as "a pugnacious virago of

whom the son became a responsive masculine copy." Burke's distinction lies in such local displays of compact insight.

WILLIAM E. CAIN

See also NEW LITERARY HISTORICISM; TEXTUALITY.

FURTHER READING

Daniel Aaron and Robert Bendiner, eds., *The Strenuous Decade: a Social and Intellectual Record of the 1930s* (Garden City, N.Y.: Anchor, 1970).

R. P. Blackmur, *The Double Agent: Essays in Craft and Elucidation* (1935; Gloucester: Peter Smith, 1962).

Kenneth Burke, *The Philosophy of Literary Form: Studies in Symbolic Action* (Baton Rouge: Louisiana State University Press, 1941).

Paul Jay, ed., *The Selected Correspondence of Kenneth Burke and Malcolm Cowley* (New York: Viking, 1988).

Frank Lentricchia, *Criticism and Social Change* (Chicago: University of Chicago Press, 1983).

William Rueckert, ed., *Critical Responses to Kenneth Burke: 1924–1966* (Minneapolis: University of Minnesota Press, 1969).

René Wellek, *A History of Modern Criticism: 1750–1950*, vol. 6: *American Criticism, 1900–1950* (New Haven: Yale University Press, 1986).

Hayden White and Margaret Brose, eds., *Representing Kenneth Burke: Selected Papers from the English Institute* (Baltimore: Johns Hopkins University Press, 1982).

Burnham, Daniel H. (b. Henderson, N.Y., Sept. 4, 1846; d. Heidelberg, Germany, June 1, 1912).   Architect and city planner. Promoting an orderly and dignified neoclassical aesthetic, Burnham sought to design cities as unified wholes. His plans for Chicago, including the 1893 Columbian World Exposition, for the center of Washington, D.C., and for other cities featured rational progressions of public spaces and attention to both aesthetic effect and practical use. Critics charged that his plans left little room for the changes that cities inevitably underwent, or for savoring the rich street life of urban cultures. But his monumental vision had a decisive impact on American city planning.

See also ARCHITECTURE; URBANISM.

FURTHER READING

Thomas S. Hines, *Burnham of Chicago, Architect and Planner* (New York: Oxford University Press, 1974).

Burnham, James (b. Chicago, Ill., Nov. 22, 1905; d. Kent, Conn., July 28, 1987).   Political philosopher. A Trotskyist in the mid-1930s, Burnham became a leading conservative and anticommunist after he concluded that communist revolution leads naturally to totalitarianism. Capitalism and socialism are not, he argued in *The Managerial Revolution* (1941), the only alternatives. Stalin's communism, Hitler's fascism, and Roosevelt's New Deal are all examples of the modern managerial economy, which is characterized by central planning boards, state ownership of major industries, goals of efficiency and rationalization rather than profit, and an executive ruling class.

See also MANAGERIALISM.

FURTHER READING

John Patrick Diggins, *Up from Communism: Conservative Odysseys in American Intellectual History* (New York: Harper and Row, 1975).

Burroughs, John (b. near Roxbury, N.Y., Apr. 3, 1837; d. on a train to New York, N.Y., Mar. 29, 1921).   Writer. Burroughs's popular essays described the beauty of the natural world in lyrical prose. Carefully observant, they were nevertheless more literary than scientific or philosophical. Though he recognized the value of Thoreau's meditations on nature, Burroughs sharply criticized writers who injected nature writing with moralizing or saw the natural world only as a backdrop for human striving. His tribute to his close friend WALT WHITMAN, *Notes on Walt Whitman as Poet and Person* (1867), helped bring the poet to the public's attention.

See also NATURE.

FURTHER READING

Edward Renehan, *John Burroughs: an American Naturalist* (Post Mills, Vt.: Chelsea Green, 1992).

Burroughs, William S. (b. St. Louis, Mo., Feb. 5, 1914).   Writer. Loosely linked to the Beat Movement through his friendship with ALLEN GINSBERG and JACK KEROUAC, Burroughs emerged with *The Naked Lunch* (published in the U.S. in 1962) as one of the most important and disruptive figures in American literature. Drawing on the Surrealist tradition of collage and irrational "play," Burroughs's books fashioned an image repertoire of mythological proportions. They combined satirical readings of American academic and popular culture with his own experiences on the margins of Western society as drug addict, fugitive, and homosexual. An icon of American POSTMODERNISM, Burroughs was influential for those artists, both of his own and subsequent generations, working in a number of different media from poetry to film to musical performance.

See also BEAT GENERATION.

FURTHER READING

Robin Lyndenberg, *Word Cultures: Radical Theory and Practice in William S. Burroughs' Fiction* (Urbana: University of Illinois Press, 1987).

Bushnell, Horace (b. Bantam, Conn., Apr. 14, 1802; d. Hartford, Conn., Feb. 17, 1876).   Minister and theologian. Bushnell's liberal theology emphasized religious experience, environmental influences, doctrinal flexibility, and the immanence of God. His *Christian Nurture* (1847) rejected the belief that children are sinful: since children raised in a Christian family need never know a time before being Christians, conversion in their case was unnecessary. Revivals, he thought, overemphasized the individual "personality" and threatened to undermine the order of a community based on the slow growth of "character." Christian nurture in family and church was a lifelong deepening in Christian understanding. In *God in Christ* (1849), he rejected the orthodox doctrine of substitutionary atonement and argued that since language is essentially evocative, poetic, and imprecise, it is futile to seek a literal understanding of creeds.

See also LIBERAL PROTESTANTISM.

FURTHER READING

David L. Smith, *Symbolism and Growth: the Religious Thought of Horace Bushnell* (Missoula, Mout.: Scholars, 1980).

Byrd, William, II (b. Virginia Colony, Mar. 28, 1674; d. Westover, Va., Aug. 26, 1744).   Planter and public official. Byrd's diaries and historical writings, never published in his lifetime, reveal an unsentimental eye and a sometimes caustic wit. Byrd granted that human reason could not always control human passions, yet that did not stop him from satirizing the backcountry poor for their laziness, which he traced to an overly fertile environment. Sympathetic to the Indians and their ways, and critical of slavery's dehumanizing effects, he saw human beings as fundamentally similar but was resigned to slavery's sway.

See also SOUTHERN INTELLECTUAL HISTORY.

FURTHER READING

Kenneth A. Lockridge, *On the Sources of Patriarchal Rage: the Commonplace Books of William Byrd and Thomas Jefferson and the Gendering of Power in the Eighteenth Century* (New York: New York University Press, 1992).

C

Cable, George Washington (b. New Orleans, La., Oct.12, 1844; d. St. Petersburg, Fla., Jan. 31, 1925). Writer. Usually viewed as a charming local-color writer about Creole life, Cable in fact portrayed the tragedies that stalked a society stratified by RACE and CLASS. The stories collected in *Old Creole Days* (1879) and the novel *The Grandissimes* (1880) show that the problems of race are not simply the inheritance of slavery, but stem from deep, persistent patterns of prejudice. Himself a son of slaveholders, Cable insisted there was a "silent South" of thoughtful people who would not deny justice to blacks, a belief that alarmed many white southerners. In 1885 he left New Orleans for Northampton, Massachusetts, and became an established interpreter of the South to northern readers and lecture audiences.

FURTHER READING
Eric J. Sundquist, *To Wake the Nations: Race in the Making of American literature* (Cambridge: Harvard University Press, 1993).

Cage, John (b. Los Angeles, Calif., Sept. 5, 1912; d. New York, N.Y., Aug. 12, 1992). Composer, artist. One of the most influential figures of late twentieth-century culture, Cage developed "musics" inspired less by the European classical tradition than by Eastern harmonies, Surrealist collage, and Zen Buddhism, all of which led him to value chance, irrationality, and even silence in the construction of performance works of various kinds. Such essay collections as *Silence* (1961) and *A Year from Monday* (1967) presented his ideas in written form, but writing could not convey the radical innovation of his art. Indeed, much of his music could not be written down in conventional notation. Cage reimagined the boundaries of both "music" and "performance."
See also POSTMODERNISM.

FURTHER READING
David Revill, *The Roaring Silence: John Cage, a Life* (New York: Arcade, 1992).

Calhoun, John C. (b. Abbeville District, S.C., Mar. 18, 1782; d. Washington, D.C., Mar. 31, 1850). A ubiquitous figure in antebellum southern politics, Calhoun served as state legislator (1808–9), Congressman (1811–17), Secretary of War (1817–25), Vice President of the United States (1825–32), United States Senator (1832–43, 1845–50), and Secretary of State (1844–5). The son of a prosperous Scotch-Irish planter and local political leader, Patrick Calhoun, and his wife Martha Caldwell Calhoun, the young Calhoun received his early education in rural academies before he entered Yale College at age 20, graduating in two years. Later, Calhoun attended Litchfield Law School and read law in Charleston before returning to his native Abbeville District, where he soon entered the practice of law. Calhoun disliked law and quickly turned his attention to politics, winning election to the lower house of the South Carolina legislature in 1808. During his one term as a state legislator, Calhoun supported white manhood suffrage (adopted in 1810) and earned a reputation as a legislative prodigy. In 1810, Calhoun ran successfully for Congress as a Jeffersonian Republican, beginning a long, remarkable, controversial, and ultimately frustrating career in national politics.

During his distinguished national career, Calhoun evolved from War Hawk nationalist to independent states' rights nullifier to strong southern rights advocate. Calhoun's tortuous political odyssey followed his changing assessment of the relationship between the nation and its component sections. Throughout his long career, Calhoun believed that the success of the republican experiment depended on maintaining the proper equilibrium between the new nation's various sections as well as between the states and the national government. Responding to the War of 1812, Calhoun worked to "bind the republic together" through mildly protective tariffs to help infant industry, a second national bank to stabilize commerce, and an ambitious system of federally financed internal improvements designed to foster economic interdependence among sections. By the late 1820s, however, Calhoun's youthful optimism waned as he witnessed the emergence of a persistent factional majority favoring high tariffs which the South Carolinian believed injurious to the southern economy. Calhoun no longer feared the centrifugal pull of divergent sectional forces nearly as much as he did the gradual consolidation of power in the national government and the corruption of the executive branch by extensive federal patronage. To stop this steady accretion of power by the national government, Calhoun proposed nullification, an innovative constitutional doctrine which allowed an individual state, falling back on its original sovereignty as a party to the Constitution, to suspend operation of a federal law it deemed unconstitutional unless or until three-fourths of the states decided otherwise. President Andrew Jackson discredited nullification by equating it with disunion and isolating Calhoun from the southern wing of the emerging Democratic Party.

During the 1840s an older Calhoun emerged as a thoroughgoing sectionalist, defending the South and its slaveholding society against criticism from a northern majority increasingly antagonistic toward the so-called Slavepower (the South). Calhoun now feared that the too-powerful national government would fall into the hands of an antislavery sectional majority. Calhoun's remedy centered on the restoration of sectional political equilibrium through the adoption of a constitutional amendment allowing a sectional minority to veto federal legislation. Calhoun failed to unite the South, however, because most southerners thought that slavery was best defended through continued southern influence on national parties. With partisan differences still dividing the South internally, and the controversy over the expansion of slavery rapidly coming to a head, Calhoun died in 1850 from tuberculosis and respiratory complications.

Calhoun's chief contribution to American political thought lay in his provocative reconsideration of the republican wisdom received from the Founding Fathers. The Founders had satisfied themselves that Madison's theory of extended republics had solved the problem of majoritarian tyranny in a democratic republic. JAMES MADISON argued that the multiplicity of factions included in a large republic and the geographic distance separating them would render the formation of a durable and oppressive majority impossible. Plausible as this argument seemed in the 1780s, Calhoun recognized that the rise of partisan politics left it outmoded by the 1840s. Political parties, taking advantage of transportation and communication improvements and using expanding federal patronage aggressively, had easily overcome the barriers of distance and diversity which Madison believed would block the formation of lasting majorities.

Beginning with his major writings and speeches of the nullification era, and culminating with his two most systematic political treatises, *A Disquisition on Government* and *A Discourse on the Constitution of the United States*, both published posthumously, Calhoun proposed to check the power of potentially tyrannical numerical majorities by giving significant minority interests in the body politic effective veto power over majority actions. The true expression of the political will of any given community, Calhoun argued,

was not the opinion of a simple numerical majority but the consensus which emerged when all of the community's component interests were consulted. This process of governing through the common consent of the body politic's conflicting interests Calhoun called government by concurrent majority, and whether expressed through nullification or sectional veto, the power of the concurrent majority served as a check on the power of renegade numerical majorities. In an era of democracy, Calhoun sought to check the power of one kind of majority (numerical) with that of another (concurrent).

Undeniably rooted in the South Carolinian's desire to protect the minority interests of his section, Calhoun's theory was dismissed by many critics as special pleading. The differing interests protected in Calhoun's scheme always seemed geographic or sectional, and it was unclear how minority interests within sections would be protected. The consensus and harmony Calhoun thought government by concurrent majority would produce seemed likely to prove illusory, with stalemate and paralysis their likely surrogates. And, to Americans swept up in the democratic vortex of the Age of Jackson, Calhoun's government by concurrent majority smacked ominously of minority rule. But if Calhoun's remedy seemed cumbersome and unworkable, his indictment of the excesses of Jacksonian Democracy, and his exposition of a conservative, post-Madisonian republicanism which highlighted the obsolescence of much of the Founders' logic, earned him a deserved reputation as one of nineteenth-century America's foremost political thinkers. The problem Calhoun pinpointed, the difficulty of protecting the rights of political minorities against the power of elected majorities, remains one of the most vexing problems of modern democracy.

Since World War II, scholars have debated Calhoun's proposition that the actions of a truly representative government should reflect not simply the will of the majority but a broad consensus among all the major interests of society. Some scholars see Calhoun's theory as a recognition of the legitimacy of interests as forces shaping government and hence as a sharp break with classical republican tradition. Thus Calhoun emerges as both a "modern" political thinker and an architect of interest-group pluralism, reflected in the post-New Deal broker state, as a proper system of republican government. In recent years, revisionists have sharply disputed these claims, arguing that Calhoun's theory merely recognized the inevitability, not the legitimacy, of interests and that the concurrent majority was a political mechanism designed to produce a stalemate among interests and force the search for a broad consensus closely attuned to the common good. Thus, while Calhoun conceded more to interests than most previous thinkers, he had hardly abandoned the notion of civic virtue. In contemporary times, some version of the concurrent majority is often discussed as a possible solution for problems facing multiethnic nation-states, and it is used in the United Nations where the "superpower" veto in the Security Council gives concurrent majority rights to individual nations. But, in practice, the worldwide ascendancy of "one person, one vote" as the dominant democratic creed, and the prospect that powerful elites as well as relatively powerless minorities could seek refuge in the exercise of concurrent majority rights, have pushed Calhoun's ideas to the margins of modern political debate.

LACY K. FORD

See also PROSLAVERY THOUGHT.

FURTHER READING

Richard K. Cralle, ed., *The Works of John C. Calhoun,* 6 vols. (Columbia, S.C., and New York, 1851–7).

Lacy K. Ford, "Republican Ideology in a Slave Society: the Political Economy of John C. Calhoun," *Journal of Southern History* 54 (1988): 405–24.

William W. Freehling, "Spoilsmen and Interests in the Thought and Career of John C. Calhoun," *Journal of American History* 52 (1965): 25–42.

Robert O. Meriwether, Edwin W. Hemphill, and Clyde N. Wilson, eds., *The Papers of John C. Calhoun,* 20 vols. to date. (Columbia: University of South Carolina Press, 1959–).

Merrill D. Peterson, *The Great Triumvirate: Webster, Clay, and Calhoun* (New York: Oxford University Press, 1987).

Clyde N. Wilson, *John C. Calhoun: a Bibliography* (Westport: Meckler, 1990).

Charles M. Wiltse, *John C. Calhoun,* 3 vols. (Indianapolis: Bobbs-Merrill, 1944–51).

Calvinism   The distinctive features of the Calvinist Reformation derived from John Calvin's refusal to write off politics as an activity unredeemed by ethics. Unlike Martin Luther, Calvin did not regard government merely as a necessary evil, a purely coercive institution made necessary by man's fallen state. He took the position that political power had a moral and educative as well as a coercive dimension. In his *Institutes of Christian Religion,* he argued that the state served, among other things, "to adapt our conduct to human society, to form our manners to civil justice, to conciliate us to each other, to cherish common peace and tranquility" (IV:xx:2). Its existence reflected humanity's social rather than its sinful nature. Strictly speaking, the church alone could deal with sin; the function of the state was not so much to punish sin, much less to enforce order through repression, but to cultivate habits of neighborliness

and civility. Civic virtue was by no means to be confused with salvation, but neither were they to be regarded as antithetical.

The Calvinist state has often been described as theocratic, but Calvin did not advocate government by the church. His point was that a community of believers required political as well as ecclesiastical institutions and that state and church were complementary structures, neither identical nor fundamentally opposed. His refusal to accept either the sectarian critique of politics or the subordination of the church to the state (the practical upshot of the Lutheran Reformation) helps to explain the rapid spread of Calvinism, in the sixteenth and seventeenth centuries, in parts of the world where the redefinition of political authority was emerging as a major issue: Scotland, the Netherlands, England, America. The tension between sectarianism and subordination, rebellion and submission, made Calvinism the natural ally of those who wished to impose legal and moral limits on the state without undermining political authority altogether.

The tension proved extraordinarily difficult to maintain, however, as the history of Calvinism in New England quickly made clear. The secession of ANNE HUTCHINSON threatened the newly established community of saints from the sectarian side, while the Salem witch trials dramatized the danger of an excessively intimate identification of political and religious authority. The long controversy over the so-called half-way covenant, an arrangement that admitted unconverted children of saints to partial membership in the church, showed how hard it was to balance Puritan "tribalism" (as Edmund Morgan calls it) against the priority assigned, in Calvinist theology, to the individual's direct relation to God. Strict qualifications for church membership had the effect of excluding many prominent and respectable citizens, the very people on whom the continuity of the community had to depend. To relax the requirement of conversion, on the other hand, encouraged a confusion of social standing and political power with true virtue, the measure of which, as JONATHAN EDWARDS explained when he revoked the half-way covenant in his Northampton church, was the inner state of one's soul, not one's service to the community.

The same issue—the tension between civic priorities and the theological individualism inherent in the doctrine of justification by faith alone—found theological expression in the conflict between Arminianism and antinomianism, the most persistent division within American Calvinism. The primacy of faith over works was never easy to explain to sober, upstanding, industrious citizens who led what appeared to be exemplary lives and expected to be rewarded not only on earth but in heaven. Such people were attracted, in growing numbers, to the ideas of the Dutch theologian Jacobus Arminius, who attached more importance to good works than orthodox Calvinists did. On the other hand, those who insisted on faith alone invited attacks on the Calvinist synthesis from the opposite direction. Hutchinson, ROGER WILLIAMS, and other antinomians argued that the only reliable source of religious authority was the inner light of faith. This claim, pushed to its limits, undermined religious as well as political institutions. It also had anti-intellectual implications. Early Calvinism had its roots not only in the Reformation but in the humanist revival of learning. The antinomian impulse, by contrast, encouraged a type of revivalism that dispensed with learned arguments and finally came to rest on sheer emotion.

Edwards, at once a revivalist and a theologian of immense learning, proved to be the last exponent of a tradition that sought to negotiate the treacherous ground between Arminianism and antinomianism. After his death, American Calvinism split in two. The learned classes, with a few exceptions, carried Arminianism in the direction of religious liberalism, while the antinomian revivalists ended up in the twentieth century as fundamentalists, expending most of their energy on denunciations of Darwin, Freud, and other enemies of "Jesus." LIBERAL PROTESTANTISM and FUNDAMENTALISM both can be said to descend from Calvinism, and the descent has been not only a genealogical linkage, but a falling off of moral insight and intellectual rigor.

CHRISTOPHER LASCH

See also EVANGELICALISM; PURITANISM.

FURTHER READING

John Calvin, *Institutes of the Christian Religion* (1536, 1559), trans. Henry Beveridge (Grand Rapids: Eerdmans, 1957).
Andrew Delbanco, *The Puritan Ordeal* (Cambridge: Harvard University Press, 1989).
Joseph Haroutunian, *Piety versus Moralism: the Passing of the New England Theology* (New York: Henry Holt, 1932).
Perry Miller, *The New England Mind*, 2 vols. (Cambridge: Harvard University Press, 1939, 1953).
Edmund Morgan, *The Puritan Family*, rev. ed. (New York: Harper and Row, 1966).
Sheldon Wolin, *Politics and Vision* (Boston: Little, Brown, 1960).

Cardozo, Benjamin (b. New York, N.Y., May 24, 1870; d. Port Chester, N.Y., July 9, 1938).   Judge and Supreme Court Justice (1932–38). A proponent of pragmatic and sociological jurisprudence, Cardozo believed that the law is an ongoing engagement with changing social, economic, and psychological conditions. In *The Nature of the Judicial Process* (1921) and *The Paradoxes of Legal Science* (1928) he explained that judges should seek unity, clarity, and impartiality, but also equity and responsiveness to current needs. After a career as a judge on the New York Court of Appeals, he was appointed to the Supreme Court, where his decisions defended free speech, supported New Deal legislation, and interpreted commercial common law for an industrial society.

See also LEGAL REALISM.

FURTHER READING

Morton J. Horwitz, *The Transformation of American Law, 1870–1960: the Crisis of Legal Orthodoxy* (New York: Oxford University Press, 1992).

Carey, Henry C. (b. Philadelphia, Pa., Dec. 15, 1793; d. Philadelphia, Pa., Oct. 13, 1879).   A publisher, economist, and essayist, Carey was one of the most visible, original, and influential intellectuals in mid nineteenth-century America. The son of Matthew Carey—an Irish immigrant, a successful Philadelphia publisher, and a close friend of Alexander Hamilton—young Henry inherited both wealth and social standing. At his Philadelphia estate he later entertained a steady flow of famous visitors, such as RALPH WALDO EMERSON. He became an early founder and supporter of the Republican Party, a close friend and advisor of ABRAHAM LINCOLN, and an intellectual architect of Republican tariff policies. In the post-Civil War years he became disillusioned with restrictive Republican monetary policies and monopolistic industrial policies, and joined the inflationist Greenback Party. By the time he died he was disillusioned by economic policies that favored large cities, the Northeast, and monopolistic firms, and which hurt the Midwest and South, small farmers and manufacturers, and all debtors.

In 1835, Carey relinquished his responsibilities as president of the publishing house founded by his father. For the rest of his life Carey devoted most of his talents to political economy. Gradually, he broke away from the dominant free market model of David Ricardo and Thomas Malthus, in time to become its bitterest enemy. His optimistic system, which promised unending growth however rapid the increase of population, entailed not diminishing returns but ever ascending ones. He worked out a replacement labor theory of value (the value of any product is not the labor that produced it but the labor needed to reproduce it). This generally meant that, with invention and greater specialization of labor, with population growth and a fuller form of association or cooperation, the value of existing capital goods would steadily fall. An ever larger share of the total product would thus go to wages and less to profits, eliminating any basis for class conflict.

Carey denied any natural scarcity, and thus any access costs (rent) for land or other natural resources in an economy without politically anchored land monopolies. He even denied any advantages to those who gained land with greater fertility or better location. Instead of a historical progression from the use of the best lands to more marginal ones (and thus a rent value for those who came first and gained the most fertile land), Carey argued that the natural progression was from the barren and often forbidding hilltops (accessible to lonely, culturally deprived frontier people with low skills) to fertile but forested or swampy low lands (exploitable only by clustered, specialized, skilled populations). This meant that latecomers really ended up with the best land. Also, since the costs of creating farms steadily declined, no net advantages accrued to those who grabbed first. He acknowledged the greater market value of well-located land, such as in cities, but attributed this value, not to any natural scarcity, but to the types of labor that improved land or, more often, that created forms of public capital (surveys, roads, schools, government facilities). Anticipating HENRY GEORGE, he admitted that such publicly established values, since unearned by those who occupied the land (they did not do the work), were proper subjects of taxation, but he did not advocate a single tax.

Carey's growth model had conditions. It required public policies that encouraged local commerce and discouraged distant trade. This usually meant protective tariffs, particularly for commodity-exporting countries such as the United States. Great Britain had used free trade doctrines to help anchor its advantages in the production of finished manufactured goods, and to keep outlying areas of the world in a dependent position. America could move to a free trade position only when it largely exported refined, manufactured goods. Carey wanted, so far as possible, to eliminate distant trade in bulk commodities, which drained away unreplenishable American resources. He favored a type of intense, local development, with much local trade and specialization of tasks, so that everyone could develop their special talents and interests.

A second foundation of growth was a steadily growing supply of money. This required easy credit and moderate monetary inflation. Money, a necessary lubricant of exchange, facilitated growth when its supply was slightly ahead of need. When credit or monetary growth lagged behind the normal growth of production, it had a drastic, inhibitory effect, for it penalized debtors and dampened down the demand for goods among the largest class of consumers.

Healthy economic growth required an integration of intensive agriculture and small manufacturing. Carey wanted a truly scientific agriculture in America, not the soil-mining that had heretofore characterized farming. To him, the ideal farm was only ten acres and given over to fruits and vegetables. He was a vegetarian, and believed meats, and the type of grain farming that supported such a diet, both wasteful and unhealthy. Factory manufacturing, which he glorified, best flourished when decentralized and fully integrated with both farms and shops. He thus celebrated small towns and cities, and in later years came to hate large, commercial cities, for they fostered both waste and monopoly.

Above all, sustained growth mandated the retention at home and the recycling of all waste products, or what he called manure. People had to respect the great earth mother. One problem with commodity exports was that Americans shipped abroad a large share of their greatest resource—the fertility of their soils. Great trading empires, and large commercial cities, fostered such reckless resource waste. But if respected, if it received its needed manures, then the great earth was like a bank that paid more dividends the more humans invested in it and used it.

Carey's anti-Malthusian model of unending economic growth, and his celebration of ever more people (the greatest economic asset of all), had its share of sophistries. Despite all his efforts, he never quite abolished rent. His hilltop version of early land exploitation was more disingenuous than historically accurate. But Carey's system, however perverse it seemed to contemporary economists, has continued to offer hope to developing countries, and it anticipated almost all of the environmental concerns of the late twentieth century.

PAUL CONKIN

FURTHER READING
Henry C. Carey, *The Past, the Present, and the Future* (Philadelphia: Carey and Hart, 1848).
——, *Principles of Social Science*, 3 vols. (Philadelphia: J.B. Lippencott, 1858–60).
Paul K. Conkin, *Prophets of Prosperity: America's First Political Economists* (Bloomington: Indiana University Press, 1980).
Rodney J. Morrison, *Henry C. Carey and American Economic Development* (Philadelphia: American Philosophical Society, 1986).

Carnap, Rudolf (b. Ronsdorf, Germany, May 18, 1891; d. Santa Monica, Calif., Sept. 14, 1970). Philosopher. A student of the relations between language and logic, Carnap was an early advocate of logical positivism as a member of the "Vienna Circle," and continued to preach the anti-"metaphysical" faith after emigrating to America in 1935. Trying to give philosophy the rigor and precision of a science, he believed that philosophy is properly the logic of science—that is, of scientific language. In *Der logische Aufbau der Welt* (1928) (published as *The Logical Structure of the World* in 1967), he argued that all sensical statements can be "reduced" to sentences that contain only logical relationships and references to physical sense-data. Metaphysical speculation is nonsensical. In his later work Carnap tried to develop a systematic understanding of inductive logic as a theory of probability.

See also POSITIVISM.

FURTHER READING

Laurence C. Smith, *Behaviorism and Logical Positivism: a Reassessment of the Alliance* (Stanford: Stanford University Press, 1986).

Carnegie, Andrew (b. Dunfermline, Scotland, Nov. 25, 1835; d. Lenox, Mass., Aug. 11, 1919). Industrialist and philanthropist. Carnegie made his fortune in the steel industry through strategies of vertical integration, technical innovation, methodical administration, and minimizing wages while maximizing work. His most noted article, "Wealth" (in the June 1889 *North American Review*), propounded what came to be known as the "gospel of wealth." Unfettered individualism and competition benefit the race, Carnegie argued, by directing money and power to people of great ability, thus promoting the survival of the fittest. The wealthy, therefore, should live modestly and regard most of their income as a trust that they manage for the good of the community.

See also SOCIAL DARWINISM.

FURTHER READING

Joseph F. Wall, *Andrew Carnegie* (Pittsburgh: University of Pittsburgh Press, 1989).

Carson, Rachel (b. Springdale, Pa., May 27, 1907; d. Silver Spring, Md., Apr. 14, 1964). The American movement to preserve the natural world from human abuse, a movement with roots in nineteenth-century Romanticism and transcendentalism, and early twentieth-century conservation, was redefined after World War II to assume its modern form. No individual was more important than Rachel Carson in that achievement. Scientist, writer, and environmentalist, she taught the public how to think about nature in new ways and was the first to warn of a new generation of toxic substances that were polluting the earth. Translated into more than two dozen languages, her work inspired a global environmental consciousness.

Carson grew up on the rural outskirts of Pittsburgh and with the aid of a scholarship attended the Pennsylvania College for Women (now Chatham College), then went on to Johns Hopkins University for an M.A. degree in genetics. Her most important scientific training, though, came in summers spent at Woods Hole Marine Biological Laboratory on Cape Cod, where she discovered the power of the sea. She felt drawn to it emotionally as well as scientifically and devoted most of her life to its study and enjoyment. What she found in the sea was a vast untouched realm in which living organisms had evolved in an environment quite unlike the land surface. The sea seemed an unspoiled part of nature, whereas the North American continent had by the 1920s been explored, settled, and manipulated extensively. Had Carson lived in earlier days, she might have longed to go westward and alone into the wilderness. Instead, she became a marine biologist prowling the wild oceanic world of the East Coast, peering into tide pools, wading at night onto mudflats with bucket and flashlight in hand, diving into deeper waters with a snorkel or pressurized helmet. No one would do more than she to direct American thinking to the ocean environment, which comprises three-fourths of the planet's surface.

The decade of the 1930s was not a propitious one for a woman seeking a career in the natural sciences. She had become her mother's sole financial support and, in 1936, found it necessary to accept a job as junior aquatic biologist with the Bureau of Fisheries. She worked there until 1952, when income from her writings allowed her to be independent. Her first book was *Under the Sea Wind* (1941), but it was her second, *The Sea Around Us* (1951), that brought her fame and a small fortune; it was on the bestseller lists for more than 80 weeks and won the National Book Award. A third title, *The Edge of the Sea*, appeared in 1955. By that point Carson had moved far beyond the empirical work of the laboratory scientist and found a new career of searching for beauty and inspiration in the stories of the sea.

World War II left an unintended but destructive legacy for nature. Carson's own government agency was mobilized to learn more about the marine environment and help devise means to exploit it for food, navigation, and defense. Although her own work was confined to editing government publications, she was disheartened by the agency's narrowness of vision. In a second edition of *The Sea Around Us*, published in 1961, Carson noted the dramatic impact of nuclear technology on the world's oceans. Both Americans and Russians were dumping radioactive wastes in the sea, and fallout from the testing of bombs was settling over the waters. The effects of those substances on the whole chain of living organisms, from the smallest diatoms to the largest marine mammals, and on human beings, could not be foretold.

Carson subsequently turned her attention to another deadly poison falling from the sky, the pesticides like DDT that had also come out of the war years and were spreading through terrestrial food chains and draining into the sea, affecting even penguins at the South Pole. After years of gathering all the scientific data she could find on the ecological consequences of pesticides, she brought out in 1962 a very different book from any she had written heretofore; *Silent Spring*, a measured but severe indictment of modern agriculture, the chemical industry, and applied entomology. The message of the book, still controversial, was that humans were endangering their own lives through an arrogant, manipulative attitude toward other forms of life. Carson assembled enough facts to persuade Congress to restrict use of the more persistent chemicals, but her deeper message was the need for ethical change, away from a spirit of conquest and toward a respect for all forms of life and an acknowledgement of our dependence on them.

Recent feminist scholars have argued that Carson's moral critique of the conquest of nature emerged out of a "women's culture" that had long emphasized cooperation and nurturance instead of the pursuit of power and wealth. Certainly, Carson drew on many women for support during what became a storm of criticism, much of it belittling to her as a woman. But the chief intellectual influences on her life were men like Albert Schweitzer and HENRY THOREAU, and millions of men as well as women looked on her as the prophet of a new ethic toward nature. When she died of cancer at age 56, she had neither organized a political movement nor seen that new environmental ethic become common; however, she had helped make ecology a familiar word and ENVIRONMENTALISM a growing international cause.

DONALD WORSTER

See also NATURE.

FURTHER READING

Paul Brooks, *The House of Life: Rachel Carson at Work* (Boston: Houghton Mifflin, 1972).
Rachel Carson, *The Sea Around Us* (1951; rev, ed., New York: Oxford University Press, 1961).
——, *Silent Spring* (Boston: Houghton Mifflin, 1962).
Thomas R. Dunlap, *DDT: Scientists, Citizens, and Public Policy* (Princeton: Princeton University Press, 1981).
H. Patricia Hynes, *The Recurring Silent Spring* (New York: Pergamon, 1989).
Vera Norwood, *Made From This Earth: American Women and Nature* (Chapel Hill: University of North Carolina Press, 1993).

cartooning The cartoon has long been an important popular art in America, framing an intersection of entertainment, public satire, and even moral dissidence. Cartooning has self-consciously challenged the separation between "high" and "low" art while being fully engaged in the capitalist marketplace of images that often relied upon just that separation. Cartoonists are the artisans of MASS CULTURE, and their history reflects the irony of that apparently oxymoronic status. Cartooning, moreover, has been a very significant forum for the expression and spreading of ideas; it must be seen as a potent mode of thought.

Keyed by the critical style of English satirists like William Hogarth, cartoonists in the eighteenth century actively embraced the polemical melee of ideology and libel located at the margins of democratic revolution on both sides of the Atlantic. But by the 1840s, with the popularity of Honoré Daumier in France and the introduction of London's *Punch* weekly, the cartoon had been well integrated into bourgeois political culture. In the United States the form matured after the Civil War. Thomas Nast's caricatures of Gilded Age public life in *Harper's Weekly* not only affected contemporary politics, but also developed a vocabulary of images (signifying "machine" politics, "bossism") about which there was much discussion in later reform thought.

While the editorial cartoon established its legitimacy in political discourse, news entrepreneurs like Joseph Pulitzer expanded their use of illustration, and by the mid-1890s newspapers featured single-panel comics with continuing characters. Many of these cartoonists, such as Richard Felton Outcault of Pulitzer's New York *World*, appealed to a popular audience with slapstick send-ups of the *haute bourgeoisie*. In 1896 Pulitzer used Outcault's popular "Hogan's Alley" to experiment with yellow ink, marking the gown of the cartoon's central character to create "The Yellow Kid," the first modern comic. The same year, William Randolph Hearst responded with an eight-page comic section, the *American Humorist,* and the Sunday funnies were born. The Yellow Kid represented much more than a big advance in color reprographics: it unveiled the true potential of the cartoon in industrial mass culture. While drawing readers and advertisers to Pulitzer's paper, it also became a *marketed image* in its own right, appearing on consumer products with no apparent connection to either Outcault's satire or the *World* itself. The Kid also left a deeper mark by furnishing a name for the sensationalist "yellow journalism" that dominated contemporary news production. Transcending its own restricted context, the cartoon opened a door between public life and what would come to be called the "culture industry."

In the early twentieth century, thanks to the distribution strategies of national syndication networks, cartoons contributed to the standardization of mass-produced representations of American life. The early work of Outcault, which expressed an awareness of class divisions, gave way to politically benign (if often violent) parodies of middle-class mores like Rudolph Dirks's "Katzenjammer Kids" and George McManus's send-up of 1920s *nouveaux riches*, Jiggs and Molly. Frank King's "Gasoline Alley" (1919) and Harold Gray's later "Little Orphan Annie" (1924) established continuing narrative structures, arguably fashioning a transition between the dime novel and the television situation comedy. At the same time, the aesthetic potential of comic form and modern reprographics was explored by artists like Windsor McCay ("Little Nemo in Slumberland") and George Herriman ("Krazy Kat"), who were concerned with many of the same issues—dream states, aggressively absurd humor—which interested contemporary European avant-gardes. The notion that "real art" could be produced *within* mass culture, however, would remain undeveloped for at least another generation.

From the mid-twenties, with the increased corporatization of a national culture industry, cartoons became ubiquitous and powerful mechanisms in the development of popular consciousness and American self-image. Following the publication of *Funnies on Parade* in 1933, "comic books" became a major commodity on the youth market. By 1936, more than 75 comic books were in production by six publishers. No longer merely reproducing syndicated Sunday features, comic books began to generate their own canon of horror, humor, and adventure—again carrying on the tradition of the dime novel in more purely *visual* terms. Initially dominated by "true detective" stories (elaborating the fetish for contemporary crime), comic books found in "Superman" (1938) a character type that bred the fantasy of H. G. Wells and Jules Verne with the spectacle of the cinema. Dramatically expanding the audience for science fiction, the numerous cartoon "superheroes" supplied a frenetic conflation of patriotism, technology, and distended masculinity.

The incursion of cartoon images into national consciousness was propelled by the establishment of cinematic animation as a staple of modern American expression. Short features by Walter Lanz ("Popeye"), Max Fleischer ("Betty Boop"), and the artist/producers at Warner Brothers studios, represented best by Chuck Jones, became daily fare in moviehouses at a time when film was the dominant medium of public exchange. Towering over them all was Walt Disney, whose *Steamboat Willie* (1928) introduced Mickey Mouse—perhaps the single most recognizable image, throughout the world, of twentieth-century American culture. Disney not only pushed the cartoon toward acceptance as "serious" art (especially with the middlebrow classic *Fantasia* of 1940), he also developed a postindustrial megacomplex of image production (film, television, and tourism) which continues to sit atop the global culture industry as a moral beacon for a well-scrubbed corporate ethos.

At the same time, a rougher vision of popular entertainment—marked by the violence, open sexuality, and adolescent humor present in cartooning since well before Hogarth—came under attack. Frederic Wertham's 1954 study *Seduction of the Innocent* linked comic books to the "crisis of juvenile delinquency" which had become a favorite topic of social commentary. Not unlike crusades against "TV violence" later in the century, when unregulated mass-cultural production would yet again play scapegoat for deeper patterns of social conflict, pressure from Capitol Hill and threats from an opinion-sensitive advertising industry drove cartoon publishers to establish a Comics Code Authority, armed with a "seal of approval," to monitor representations of violence and sexuality.

While the pages of the *New Yorker* continued the *Punch* tradition of light social satire (notably with the work of Charles Addams and JAMES THURBER), political cartoons remained part of the machinery of public opinion, both in the mainstream press and its radical counterpart. In the pages of *The Masses* (1911–17) and its successors, many artists of the left had followed Art Young and John Sloan in returning to democratic critique and provocation through cartoon images. This comic activism eventually merged with an always present, always hidden, tradition of cartoon pornography, which had been driven underground by the atmosphere of the Comics Code and nurtured by segments of the youth culture. With the public crises of the 1960s, the underground cartoon was mobilized as polemical advocate for alternative lifestyles. The *East Village Other*, the Berkeley *Barb*, the Los Angeles *Free Press*—publications at the center of the counterculture—became training grounds for a new generation of cartoonists. The best-known figure of this vanguard, Robert Crumb, initiated the first underground comic book *Zap!* in 1968 and, with a Disney-like deftness, created such generational icons as "Mr. Natural" and "Fritz the Cat." Crumb also helped open an "alternative" market further developed by artists like Garry Trudeau ("Doonesbury") and Matt Groening ("Life in Hell," "The Simpsons").

Also during the 1950s and 1960s, cartoons were revaluated by the established art world and by a critical intelligentsia interested in effacing the rigid line between "high" and "low" art. POP artists, particularly the early Andy Warhol and, above all, Roy Lichtenstein, challenged conventions of aesthetic "seriousness"—so important to the ghettoization of popular arts generally and cartoons in particular—by reconfiguring the comic image as both museum piece and luxury commodity. While the hegemony of pop sensibilities in subsequent American art has tended to conceal the radical nature of this shift, there is no doubt that the dismantling of the high/low barrier changed ideas about the nature of mass culture and allowed cartoons to emerge in the United States, as they have in Europe, as a recognized art form. Artists following Art Spiegelman have successfully recast the comic book as "serious" literature, the "graphic novel." Spiegelman's *Maus* (1989), a pastiche of comic-book traditions and earnest humanism wrapped in a story of the Jewish Holocaust, has been widely hailed as a major event in late twentieth-century American letters. The comic book *Raw*, founded in 1980 by Spiegelman and Françoise Mouly, features post-punk images of technology and supplies a forum for cartoonists far less optimistic about contemporary society than those of the Disney persuasion. Yet it is the mainstream cartoonists of the Disney or Superman variety who continue to shape the aesthetic vocabulary, and often the commercial ambitions, of younger artists.

PETER HANSEN

See also AESTHETICS; JOURNALISM.

FURTHER READING
Stephen Becker, *Comic Art in America* (New York: Simon and Schuster, 1959).
Mike Benton, *The Comic Book in America: an Illustrated History* (Dallas: Taylor, 1989).
Kirk Varnedoe and Adam Gopnik, *High and Low: Modern Art and Popular Culture* (New York: Museum of Modern Art, 1990).

Cather, Willa (b. near Winchester, Va., Dec. 7, 1873; d. New York, N.Y., Apr. 24, 1947). Writer. Best known for *O Pioneers!* (1913), *My Ántonia* (1918), and *One of Ours* (1922), which won her the Pulitzer Prize, Cather celebrated the strength and simple piety of pioneer women and men, immigrant and native-born, in Nebraska and other parts of the West. Highly critical of the mechanization and materialism of modern life, Cather increasingly turned to the past for a vision of moral simplicity and stability. *Death Comes for the Archbishop* (1927) expresses that yearning in its account of the Catholic Church in New Mexico.

See also REGIONALISM.

FURTHER READING
Sharon O'Brien, *Willa Cather: the Emerging Voice* (New York: Oxford University Press, 1987).

Catholicism George Bernard Shaw quipped that a Catholic university was a contradiction in terms, and some have felt the same about American Catholic thought. Thirty years ago RICHARD HOFTSTADTER complained in *Anti-Intellectualism in American Life* (1963) that American Catholicism, which might have brought to American thought a different sense of the past and of the human condition, had failed to do so. Echoing Catholic historian John Tracy Ellis's indictment in the Jesuit journal *Thought* (1955), Hoftstadter charged that American Catholicism had failed to produce an intellectual class or vision capable of mediating between the Catholic tradition and the American Protestant and secular mind. More than a generation later, the American Catholic intellectual landscape seems far from the wasteland Hofstadter depicted, although a historian's eye can still detect some of the old deserts and salt flats in the distance. If Catholic thought in America has still not attained the depth, maturity, and imaginative scope that might be wished, it has increasingly engaged American culture in lively and provocative ways. And while many Catholic and non-Catholic writers have traditionally been preoccupied with the question of how Catholicism might be Americanized, the more interesting question may be what happens to American thought when it is seriously Catholicized.

Before assaying Catholic thought in America, three signposts are in order. First, for Catholic intellectuals—no less than for other Catholics—Catholicism means faith, prayer, liturgy, doctrine, morality, and ultimately a way of living and dying in community, more than it means cogitation as such. The relation among all these elements is complex and controverted, but any separation of Catholic thought from its necessary religious environment is artificial.

Second, Roman Catholic thought, conceived by members of the institutional Catholic Church, is only one part of what may be called the broader tradition of catholic reflection shared by all Chalcedonian Christians and sustained beyond the splits of 1054 and 1521. Polemical focus on controverted questions and an understandable fascination with religious sociology, Protestant–Catholic differences, and "pluralistic" denominational proliferation—especially in religiously exotic America—have long obscured this shared doctrinal and intellectual heritage. Even before Vatican II brought them into deeper conversation, Catholics, Protestants, and Orthodox in America drew on a common heritage of biblical and ecumenical religious thought. Today, a catholic historical work such as Lutheran Jaroslav Pelikan's multivolume *The Christian Tradition* is both a sign and promoter of this shared heritage. In what follows, "Catholic thought" is defined as the work of self-identified Roman Catholic writers, but it must be kept in mind that Catholic intellectual influences of all sorts have operated far beyond these bounds.

Finally, American Catholic thought cannot be viewed as an isolated phenomenon occurring within borders of the republic. The Catholic Church has been and is an international community of faith and learning, and American Catholic writers have been shaped by currents abroad even more than is usually the case. Indeed, much of the interest of Catholic intellectual history in this country lies in observing the intersection of distinctly American developments with non-American Catholic movements, whether coming from Rome, Paris, Louvain, Tübingen, Montreal, or—increasingly—Lima, São Paulo, Manila, and Nairobi.

The stance of politically authoritarian, Counter Reformation, antirevolutionary, ultramontanist Roman Catholicism was never a serious presence in the historical experience or outlook of American Catholics, who cherished American freedom from the beginning, especially because they were a conspicuous minority in a Protestant land. But the *ancien régime* of European Catholicism did make itself felt as a powerful ideological symbol in American thought and culture, fascinating even to those who fervently attacked it. American popular opinion, and even many American Protestant and secular intellectuals, have periodically detected the shades of Torquemada, Richelieu, and de Maistre behind one or another of the Roman Church's postures, and suspected all American Catholics of being the cat's-paws of a reactionary clerical hierarchy. Much of historic American Catholic thought was thus preoccupied, not to say obsessed, with this opposition. Most of the vast resulting apologetic literature, from the time of Bishop John Carroll, founding bishop of the American church, to that of Father JOHN COURTNEY MURRAY, who wrote the final chapter, took the form of endless analysis of the particular problem of Catholicism and American political republicanism (or democracy). From our present perspective, this "American problem" seems far less significant than

it appeared to contemporaries, for it is abundantly evident that almost all articulate American Catholics have been deeply devoted to the American polity, with all that implies about church–state relations, republican virtue, the role of reason in social order, and the like. Moreover, at Vatican II the universal church essentially declared that on this issue the American church—and Murray—were right.

The nineteenth-century Catholic engagement with the "American problem" came in two major forms. First, there was an elite Anglo-American Catholic Enlightened outlook represented by John Carroll, Bishop John England, Bishop John Lancaster Spaulding, historian Peter Guilday, and others, who discerned in liberal America an expression of profoundly "Catholic" principles that they identified with a universally "reasonable religion." Dissent from this stance appeared in the militantly defensive-aggressive outlook derived mostly from an immigrant Catholicism—represented by the Jesuits and others—that denounced alleged American Protestant and secular bigotry, fanaticism, immorality, and individualism, while professing fervent devotion to a higher Americanism that was to be most fully realized within the dogmatically defined perfect society of the Roman Church.

While much of the triumphalist stance was sub-intellectual and often aggressively anti-intellectual, the deeper questions it raised about the relation of Catholicism's ancient spiritual and intellectual traditions to American culture were and are more provocative than the narrower church–state political questions. This inquiry found its most provocative initial exploration in the writings of the convert ORESTES BROWNSON. Brownson's career as a controversialist after his conversion to Catholicism in 1844 was nearly as erratic as it had been in his earlier incarnations. But beneath his polemical posturing and vacillations, Brownson was a penetrating philosopher and social critic who ably employed metaphysical dialectics in an attempt to integrate the "subjective" intuition of divinity he had learned from American transcendentalism with the "objective" religious truths taught by the universal church. Although laden with Romantic organicism and a typically Catholic idealization of medieval social forms, Brownson's grasp of the underlying tendencies of American thought and culture led him toward some unusually provocative criticisms of American worldviews. For example, Brownson saw in the nervous individualistic perfectionism and utopian social passions of many American intellectuals (such as himself in the earlier stages of his career) an essentially spiritual impulse that could be satisfied only by religious truth and community. He criticized American democratic capitalism and materialism, not primarily from distributionist perspectives, but because of its seductive deflection of the most authentic human spiritual aspirations into lower pursuits. He argued that the harshness of American poverty, for example, reflected the callousness of a culture that acknowledged no values higher than the acquisition of wealth.

Brownson's idiosyncratic critique of major trends in American thought was rejected by most of the tiny band of liberal Catholic intellectuals, including Brownson's equally romantic but more optimistic and irenic friend and fellow convert ISAAC HECKER, who developed a near-Whitmanesque mystical vision of an American democracy being subtly led by the Holy Spirit into the bosom of the Catholic faith, where Americans' profound intuitions of human fellow-feeling and progress would find their natural home. But such elevated reflections on the meaning of Catholicism and American culture—along with Catholic intellectual life in general—were crushed in the years 1895 to 1910 by the grinding of much larger wheels. The nascent efforts of Catholic modernists to engage contemporary intellectual currents in science (especially the work of Notre Dame biologist Father John Zahm), literature, and biblical scholarship (particularly in the journal *New York Review*) ran afoul of the increasingly reactionary politics and authoritarian anti-intellectualism at the Vatican. The papal condemnations of "Americanism" in *Testem Benevolentiae* (1899), and of "modernism" in *Pascendi Dominis* (1907), cast a pall over free American Catholic inquiry on almost all major intellectual questions—as it did throughout the Western world—while most modern thought unfortunately lost serious contact with the spiritual, moral, and intellectual traditions from which it had originally derived.

The result, in America, is best described as a tragedy with a comic subplot, though sensitive and thoughtful contemporary Catholics seldom saw the humor. The American church—swelled by millions of immigrants eager to buy up shares in the American Dream—adopted a general posture that combined large doses of patriotism, moral authoritarianism (fixed especially on sexual matters), and dogmatic devotion to an abstract conception of omniscient and eternal Rome. While native American intellectuals such as HENRY ADAMS, VIDA SCUDDER, and T. S. ELIOT pursued personal quests for spiritual meaning amidst medieval cathedrals and Anglo-Catholic liturgy and poetry, American Catholics were largely reducing the rich intellectual heritage of their church to a catechetical battering ram. Scholarly and reflective

clerics such as John Lancaster Spaulding disappeared, replaced by flamboyant, vulgar bishops such as Boston's Cardinal William O'Connell, who has been described as "authority's answer to intellectual curiosity." In literature and the arts, Catholicism became the patriotic defender of "American innocence" (that is, naive moralism and representationalism) against the intrusions of a purportedly cynical and immoral modernism.

This phase of American Catholic life—roughly from 1900 to 1960—is wonderfully rich in postimmigration ethnic sociology, urban politics, labor activity, devotional Catholic piety, sexual inhibition, and the building of ecclesiastical and social institutions—not to mention Notre Dame football and Bing Crosby movies—but seemingly thin in institutionally sponsored higher thought. The first *Catholic Encyclopedia* (1907–13) stands as one permanent monument to intellectually undernourished immigrant-era American Catholicism, as full of narrow polemics, partisan history, and casuistic moralism as it is empty of critical engagement with contemporary thought, religious or otherwise.

Accurate as this portrait is in the main, however, a closer look reveals a somewhat more complicated picture. While American Catholics of that period operated within defined boundaries, some of them did so in intellectually arresting ways that defy the common stereotypes, especially after the 1930s. Indeed, American Catholic intellectuals of that time are often intriguing precisely because of the subtlety, courage, and imagination with which they engaged a defined order. Here, we can cite a few notable Catholic thinkers in three broad areas: social thought, theology and philosophy, and imaginative literature. All were orthodox and most, by general American standards, "conservative," standing in some ways outside the dominant pragmatic liberal tradition—and perhaps more interesting today for just that reason.

In social thought, as in all other areas, American Catholics were formally obliged to adhere to neo-Thomism, promulgated in the late nineteenth century by Leo XIII as the "official" and all-embracing Catholic philosophy. Neo-Thomism was slow to take hold in America, but when it did it yielded what historian Philip Gleason has called a "search for unity" everywhere in American Catholic thinking. By the 1920s, Catholic scholars and educators began producing elaborate systematic codifications of Catholic moral teaching in practically every area of culture. Most of this work was rigid, parochial, and dogmatic. But serious neo-Thomism was an entirely respectable intellectual position, and in a few cases its American proponents produced interesting results. William Kerby and JOHN A. RYAN developed lively syntheses of neoscholasticism, papal social teaching, and American-style liberal reform theory: Ryan's argument for the minimum wage has been described as the scholastic proof for progressivism. While lacking the philosophical rigor and speculative bent of Brownson and Hecker, this encounter of Catholic moralism with the traditions of American liberalism first blossomed in the Bishops' Program of Social Reconstruction (1919), and eventually produced many New Deal activists and pro-labor reformers such as Raymond McGowan, Philip Murray, and Robert Wagner. Vigorously revived in the 1960s and after, it is strongly evident in the American bishops' pastoral letters on nuclear weapons (1983) and the economy (1986), and in the work of many contemporary liberal Catholic social critics. A strong strand of religiously inspired liberal Catholic reform runs from the early twentieth-century progressives to present-day activist intellectuals such as J. Bryan Hehir, John C. Cort, David J. O'Brien, and George Higgins (who helped promote the farm workers' union of CÉSAR CHÁVEZ among Catholics).

Much of the wider interest in Catholic social thought in the 1930s and 1940s came as a result of the search for coherent faiths strong enough to resist fascist and communist appeals. In the hands of the French philosopher Jacques Maritain, whose later career was carried on in the United States, and others —including immigrants such as Waldemar Guriar, founder of the *Review of Politics*, converts such as historians Ross Hoffman and Carlton J. H. Hayes, as well as American cradle Catholics such as John Courtney Murray—this work had at least a minority impact and appeal in the United States. Most Catholic intellectuals were democratic liberals in the broad philosophical sense, but conservatives in American political terms, as were William F. Buckley and the Catholic neoconservatives such as Michael Novak, George Weigel, and Richard John Neuhaus, who appeared in the 1970s and after. Others, such as the aristocratic Jesuit John La Farge, *Commonweal* editors George Shuster and John Cogley, writer Abigail Quigley McCarthy, and politician Eugene McCarthy, integrated an intellectually refined Catholic faith and philosophy with more standard left-liberal politics.

A somewhat different type of Catholic social thought that appeared in the 1930s and 1940s was more self-consciously Catholic and even "integralist," less connected to the traditions of American liberalism, and often strongly influenced by European currents of thought—especially those associated with the interwar Catholic intellectual revival. Writers such as

Karl Adam, Georges Bernanos, Emmanuel Mounier, Romano Guardini, G. K. Chesterton, Ronald Knox, and Christopher Dawson were all important figures. The numerically small movements of this sort, which defy conventional categorizations of right and left, strongly emphasized the distinctive role of the laity in bringing Christian values to American society at large, and so departed from the oppressive clericalism of much Catholic life of the time. Among socially and intellectually conscious movements that followed this path are the Grail, Catherine de Hueck's Friendship House movement, the various "specialized Catholic action" groups like the Young Christian Students and the Young Christian Workers, the Christian Family movement, and the group around the magazine *Integrity*. The Catholic Worker movement, founded in 1933 by convert DOROTHY DAY and French peasant philosopher Peter Maurin, also fits this description, although Day brought to her movement some of the distinctive outlook and traditions of native American radicalism.

Many of these "integralist" or "personalist" American critics gradually slipped out of the scholastic straitjacket, and began to draw on the more biblical and evangelical currents of thought then appearing on the margins of the church. Many took their greatest theological inspiration from the American branch of the liturgical movement led by the Benedictine Virgil Michel, with its emphasis on the doctrine of the Mystical Body of Christ, which had closely linked the liturgical renewal to the Christian reform of society. Because they took a religious point of departure more distant from ordinary American thought and culture, these movements tended to see a greater gap between prevalent American social values and those upheld by the church and the gospel, to operate on the margins of mass society and institutional intellectual life, and to develop countercultural moral and spiritual communities that emphasized demanding personal religious transformation and discipline as the first steps toward deeper Christian commitment and reform of both the American church and American culture. In the case of the Catholic Worker movement, at least, these efforts attracted considerable attention from figures as diverse as CLAUDE McKAY, W. H. Auden, Caroline Gordon, DWIGHT MACDONALD, and THOMAS MERTON.

In philosophy and theology, most original work in the 1940s and 1950s occurred in Europe and only slowly filtered into American circles. The publishing house of Sheed and Ward, run by Australian immigrant Frank Sheed and his British wife Maisie Ward, was the major vehicle for the importation of advanced Catholic thought from abroad. By the early 1950s similar work was taken up by Joseph and Sally Cunneen's *Cross Currents*, a journal that has played a central role in the cross-fertilization of American and international Catholic thought ever since. Until the 1950s, most Catholic reflection remained within the neo-Thomist framework, though with increasing sophistication and daring in the work of Maritain, Etienne Gilson, and their later American and Canadian descendants, notably the Jesuits Bernard Lonergan and Walter Ong. A curious but enduring strand of Catholic neo-Thomist and Aristotelian influence sprouted at the University of Chicago in the late 1930s and after, where figures such as ROBERT M. HUTCHINS, MORTIMER ADLER, and Richard McKeon attempted to promote it as an alternative to American pragmatism and standard academic objectivism. This controversial and not entirely successful effort was full of cronies and oddities: Chicago was, the saying had it, the place where ex-Protestants taught Catholic philosophy to Jewish students. Nevertheless, the Chicago school represented one major breakthrough of generally subcultural Catholic thought into broader American currents.

Among American Catholics, the neo-Thomist hegemony began to fracture in the 1950s and was largely swept away in the 1960s, as American Catholicism exploded amidst a chaotic encounter with every imaginable cultural and intellectual force, serious and otherwise. Thomas Merton was perhaps the weightiest American figure in this transformation, especially for his reintroduction of pre-Augustinian patristic spiritual and intellectual traditions into the American church, and his Thoreau-like capacity to link native American outlooks with a range of biblical, monastic and Buddhist ideas. His vast corpus is uneven, and falls into several distinct phases. But at his best, Merton suggested what a truly Catholic version of American thought might involve, and how it could connect with diverse areas of culture, as Merton, for example, influenced the mystical abstract painter Ad Reinhardt. In figures like Merton and Dorothy Day, both converts, one may thus discern the maturing of a critical perspective, both deeply Catholic and deeply American, that Hofstadter failed to find in 1963.

Defining a modern and distinctively North American Catholic intellectual tradition would also involve tracing the influences on a wide range of contemporary committed Catholic thinkers. At the very least, such an inquiry would include discussion of critics and writers such as J. M. Cameron, Charles Taylor, Philip Gleason, Garry Wills, and Robert Coles; theologians such as Avery Dulles and Joseph Komonchak; as well as the growing numbers of American Catholic women such as Sally Cunneen, Mary Jo Weaver, Elisabeth Fiorenza, and Margaret O'Brien Steinfels; African Americans such as Albert Raboteau; and Hispanic figures such as Jaime Vaidal. These writers, and many others, have continued to draw on the central core of Catholic tradition while addressing modern intellectual problems in provocative ways.

No assessment of contemporary Catholic reflection can ignore the growing company of American Catholic imaginative writers, some but not all of them converts. Leaving aside lapsed Catholics THEODORE DREISER, EUGENE O'NEILL, F. SCOTT FITZGERALD, MARY McCARTHY, James Farrell, Wilfrid Sheed, Mary Gordon, and others whose work nevertheless strongly reflects a continued engagement with their religious tradition, the roster of important self-consciously Catholic American writers would include at least ALLEN TATE, Flannery O'Connor, Robert and Sally Fitzgerald, Harry Sylvester, Caroline Gordon, J. F. Powers, and Walker Percy. In their imaginative and critical work one sees best those incarnational and sacramental perspectives central to any Catholic vision of human life and society, often combined with a humorous sensibility fostered by their love-hate relationship with the peculiar surroundings of American Catholic (and, in the case of the southerners like O'Connor and Percy, Protestant) piety and life.

The dramatic transformations in American and global Catholicism since the 1960s have caused intense ferment and controversy among Catholic intellectuals. Strangely enough, there are probably more nominally Catholic but alienated American thinkers in the present environment than there were in the supposedly repressive pre-Vatican II church. The academization of intellectual life has tended to suppress or privatize confessional stances in the secular academy, whether Jewish, Catholic, Protestant, Orthodox, or Muslim. Many contemporary Catholic scholars in theology and religious studies appear to function defensively, worrying more about potential church repression and secular dismissal than about finding points of creative engagement between faith and culture. The furious controversies over sexual ethics and abortion preoccupy many Catholics and non-Catholics alike, while Rome's occasional heavy-handed and largely ineffectual interventions help sustain comfortable intellectual and popular stereotypes of secular freethinkers and unorthodox Catholic progressives endlessly battling a repressive Catholic hierarchy.

The truth is far more complex and elusive than this old melodrama would have it. Among those American thinkers who are seriously practicing Catholics and who do continue to share broadly defined common premises of faith, the differences in theology, philosophy, politics, aesthetics, moral theory, feminist theory, and sexual ethics are nearly as great as among secular thinkers. The Catholic belief that unites Charles Taylor, Avery Dulles, Garry Wills, and Michael Novak hardly guarantees their agreement on controverted issues of American politics and culture. The strong recent interest generated by the philosophical work of ALASDAIR MACINTYRE, essentially a new brand of more historically conscious Catholic neo-Aristotelianism, demonstrates that at least some overtly Catholic perspectives have attained a general standing in American thought unimaginable a hundred years ago. But however forceful his arguments, MacIntyre's final vision of American intellectuals as new monks preserving virtue and culture amidst vast barbarian hordes, armed this time with credit cards and VCRs rather than clubs and torches, probably appeals to a traditional American intellectual (and Catholic) romanticism as much as it does to rigorous rationalism or a distinctly Catholic vision of truth.

Fortunately, American Catholics and other religious thinkers are no longer required to subscribe to particular intellectual formulations of their faith tradition. Equally fortunately, there may be more non-Catholics who welcome a diversity of intelligent Catholic voices into the common conversation.

MEL PIEHL

FURTHER READING

Patrick Carey, ed., *American Catholic Religious Thought* (New York: Paulist Press, 1987).

Jay Dolan, *The American Catholic Experience: a Social History from Colonial Times to the Present* (Garden City: Doubleday, 1985).

Virginia Geiger and Stephen Viccio, eds., *Perspectives on the American Catholic Church, 1789–1989* (Westminster, Md.: Christian Classics, 1989).

Philip Gleason, *Keeping the Faith: American Catholicism Past and Present* (Notre Dame: University of Notre Dame Press, 1987).

William Halsey, *The Survival of American Innocence: American Catholicism in an Era of Disillusionment* (Notre Dame: University of Notre Dame Press, 1980).

James Hennesey, *American Catholics: a History of the Roman Catholic Community in the United States* (New York: Oxford University Press, 1981).

David J. O'Brien, *Public Catholicism* (New York: Macmillan, 1989).

Mary Jo Weaver, *New Catholic Women* (New York: Harper and Row, 1985).

Catlin, George (b. Wilkes-Barre, Pa., July 26, 1796; d. Jersey City, N. J., Dec. 23, 1872). Painter and writer. Convinced that Indians were doomed to destruction, Catlin determined to preserve a record of their ways. His exhibits and writings, notably *Letters and Notes on the Manners, Customs, and Condition of the North American Indians* (1841, illustrated with numerous engravings), contrasted mercenary Euro-American society with the Indians' allegedly carefree and colorful lives and condemned the greed that was destroying both the buffalo and Plains cultures. Although Catlin complained that white vices were "contaminating" Indians, he also wanted to convert Indians from "barbarism" to civilized Christian virtue. His admiration and reformatory aspirations were both overshadowed by his sense of the Indians' imminent demise.

See also INDIAN–WHITE RELATIONS.

FURTHER READING

William H. Goetzmann, *The West of the Imagination* (New York: Norton, 1986).

Cavell, Stanley (b. Atlanta, Ga., Sept. 1, 1926). After studying music at Berkeley and the Juilliard School, Cavell turned to philosophy at Harvard Graduate School, where first J. L. Austin, and later Wittgenstein's *Investigations* shaped his unique sense of what philosophy is about. His striking essays of the 1950s and 1960s juxtapose epistemology and ethics in probing the philosophical depths of literature and art, themes central to all Cavell's work.

Skepticism is natural to us, he holds, when we bump up against the limits of language. The more we know of the world the more afraid we may become that our knowing has gone awry, and with it our proper relation to the world. The philosophical fear of skepticism provokes both Descartes and Kant. In Shakespeare it leads to tragedy. On Cavell's reading, *King Lear* illuminates the human condition by taking the urge to abdicate, to free oneself from cares, as the temptation provoked by the pressures of human engagement. Our urge to be recognized and loved pushes us to become involved in the world, while at the same time we seek to insulate ourselves from uncertainty and refuse to acknowledge genuine love, preferring an inhuman counterfeit that, when embraced, leads to blindness and destruction. But, like Lear with his dead Cordelia, the attempt to avoid engagement costs us no less than what we had attempted to secure.

The temptation to avoid the self motivates *The Senses of Walden* (1972) as well. In Cavell's reading of the classic text by HENRY DAVID THOREAU, Thoreau goes out to Walden to test himself, recognizing that there are genuine alternatives to the life we lead and that the pretense of being trapped by society and life's necessities is just that, pretense. But for Cavell *Walden* also attempts a distinctively American way of interpreting our place in history and in the community we should try to create. Thoreau's cabin is the new dwelling that needs to be built up and made a home, and the responsibility belongs to the builder. Thoreau acts out Emerson's critique of the stultifying religious and intellectual establishment, embarking on an already modern version of the Puritans' flight from the old world and errand into the wilderness. Here philosophy becomes something that tends toward, and bids to replace, religion.

Toward the end of *The Claim of Reason* (1979) Cavell asks, "Is the cover of skepticism—the conversion of metaphysical finitude into intellectual lack —a denial of the human or an expression of it?" (p. 492). The skeptic flees the ordinary because it just doesn't seem enough. Tragic figures deny its sufficiency out of fear that they are too exposed, too vulnerable to weightlessness or the erosion of vitality. But in distancing ourselves from the everyday we make impossible demands on ourselves and others, and risk descending into the shared pathology of Othello and Desdemona. When Wittgenstein tries to nudge his interlocutor out of a strangling picture of language and back to the everyday, his goal is to return us our speech so we may encounter and give ourselves to our friends and lovers. The task is a chore because we are always tempted into flattering self-images and deceptive social myths.

Deflating these images and myths is also what comedy is about. What, in *Pursuits of Happiness* (1981), Cavell calls the comedy of remarriage shows us we can overcome our enforced distances, acknowledge what counts, and give up the quest for unilateral control.

> In *It Happened One Night* Clark Gable is not interested in a $10,000 reward but he insists on being reimbursed in the amount of $39.60, his figure fully itemized . . . Thoreau claimed to have spent in building his house, $28.12½. The purpose of these men in both cases is to distinguish themselves, with poker faces, from those who do not know what things cost, what life costs, who do not know what counts. (p. 5)

If Wittgenstein tries to liberate us from our slavery to myth, the Hollywood comedy shows us why this is important.

Cavell has turned ever more to RALPH WALDO EMERSON himself as the architect of this philosophical alternative. The end of writing is to return to us the everyday, the ordinary. Emerson now becomes the precursor of Wittgenstein and Heidegger and if we could be brought round to the everyday, as this Emersonian tradition tries to make possible, then life needn't be either melancholy or tragic.

Music, movies, the sense of being sundered from ourselves and others, Wittgenstein, our Puritan origins: Cavell resembles no one in contemporary American letters so much as Thomas Pynchon. Critics complain of Cavell's often convoluted, sometimes mannered and occasionally self-indulgent style, but like Pynchon's, Cavell's prose is not simple game-playing, but an attempt to work through what kind of thinker, or artist, it's possible to be in a modern world. Both fear that at any moment the individual may be co-opted by dehumanizing powers that are themselves a manifestation of what it can mean to be human. For all his brilliance, Pynchon seems ever more tempted to admit defeat, but Cavell retains a reservoir of moral strength in acknowledging a shared world of human experience that may be tragic, but remains human for all that. In Pynchon's early novel *V.*, McClintic Sphere, a saxman, like Cavell, comes to see that life is

> obviously slow, frustrating and hard work. Love with your mouth shut, help without breaking your ass or publicizing it: keep cool, but care. He might have known, if he'd used any common sense. It didn't come as a revelation, only something he'd as soon not've admitted. (p. 343)

To acknowledge the *lacrimae rerum*, the sorrow of things, without giving in to despair is what Cavell, in *Conditions Handsome and Unhandsome* (1990), takes Emerson to be about: "Emerson seems to take despair not as a recognition of [life], but as a fear of life, an avoidance of it. I persist in thinking this is correct, then and now. Call this my (American) faith" (p. 130).

G. SCOTT DAVIS

FURTHER READING

Stanley Cavell, *The World Viewed: Reflections on the Ontology of Film* (1971; enlarged ed., Cambridge: Harvard University Press, 1979).

——, *The Senses of Walden* (1972; expanded ed., San Francisco: North Point, 1981).

——, *The Claim of Reason: Wittgenstein, Skepticism, Morality, and Tragedy* (Oxford: Oxford University Press, 1979).

——, *Pursuits of Happiness: the Hollywood Comedy of Remarriage* (Cambridge: Harvard University Press, 1981).

——, *Conditions Handsome and Unhandsome: the Constitution of Emersonian Perfectionism* (Chicago: University of Chicago Press, 1990).

Michael Fischer, *Stanley Cavell and Literary Skepticism* (Chicago: University of Chicago Press, 1989).

Richard Fleming and Michael Payne, eds., *The Senses of Stanley Cavell* (Lewisburg, Pa.: Bucknell University Press, 1989).

Thomas Pynchon, *V.* (1963; New York: Bantam, 1964).

Channing, William Ellery (b. Newport, R.I., Apr. 7, 1780; d. Bennington, Vt., Oct. 2, 1842). As Unitarianism emerged from Calvinist Congregationalism in the early nineteenth century, Channing became recognized on both sides of the Atlantic as the voice and conscience of the new denomination. His Federal Street Church in Boston grew into the most prestigious Unitarian congregation in America. In his Baltimore Sermon of 1819 and elsewhere, he provided lucid statements of the basic tenets of UNITARIANISM, in the process unleashing withering attacks on Calvinist doctrines of innate depravity, atonement, and election. Although later in his life Channing's relations with his own congregation soured over his controversial antislavery stand, contemporaries elevated him to something like sainthood for his wide-ranging, high-minded treatises on religion, education, literature, culture, and social reform. THEODORE PARKER, who was something of a protégé, captured the nineteenth-century reverence toward Channing when he observed that no United States President, except Jefferson, had influenced Americans' minds as profoundly as had Channing.

Awkward in his social and pastoral relations (Emerson, who admired Channing, found his stiffness and propensity to pontificate unbearable), Channing excelled as a preacher and lecturer. Though on the printed page Channing's sermons and lectures appear tame in comparison with the verbal fireworks of RALPH WALDO EMERSON or HENRY DAVID THOREAU, it was reason, not imagination, that Channing appealed to. His intense, logical, spare, carefully structured prose embodies the Unitarians' idealized view of themselves as Christian inheritors of the Enlightenment. Despite the restraint that in Channing is both method and message (he insisted on deep religious feeling or "sentiment," but always chaperoned by reason), he could still achieve considerable pungency of thought and expression. In his lectures on war, he wrote, Thoreau-like, that the common soldier "hires himself to be shot at for a few cents a day" and that "men acting in masses shift off responsibility on one another. Multitudes never blush" (*Works*, pp. 656, 677).

Much of the limited interest in Channing in the post-World War II era has come from literary scholars who tend to see him (rather narrowly) as a transitional figure leading to Emerson and TRANSCENDENTALISM. Clearly Channing gravitated toward the extremes of Unitarian liberalism and became something of a spiritual godfather to the young Transcendentalists. By humanizing not merely Christ (whom he saw as the perfect human mind/conscience) but God (a divine "philanthropist"), and by deifying the human mind (to which he gave authority over Scripture and conceptions of the deity), Channing helped make more radical positions possible. He made the mind and particularly the conscience the only truly important "evidence" of Christianity and indeed the "Likeness to God," as he titled one of his most famous sermons.

Channing also shared the views of Emerson, Parker, and other Transcendentalists on other philosophical and social issues. His criticism of capitalist culture and its monied aristocracy reverberates with the same social idealism that led some Transcendentalists to create the utopian Brook Farm experiment and that also expressed itself in interest in working-class issues and in other social reforms. Even more fundamentally, Channing's emphasis on mental development, especially as expressed in his lecture "Self-Culture," linked him with the Transcendentalists' deepest urges toward ROMANTICISM. Delivered more than a year after Emerson's "American Scholar" and deriving, in part, from his continuing conversations with the Transcendentalist group, "Self-Culture" contains many passages about progressive self-creation and the sovereignty of the individual mind that strike the same chords of Romantic individualism as Emerson's work in the period. Like Emerson, he warned that even the best influences "may harm us, by bowing us to servile acquiescence and damping our spiritual activity" (*Works*, p. 24), though unlike Emerson, he balked at including Christ and the Bible among the potential dangers.

Despite his many similarities with the Transcendentalists, Channing held back from their most extreme positions. He criticized both Parker's theism and Emerson's mystical pantheism, insisting (with less than complete consistency) on the "evidences" of the biblical miracles and on the centrality of Jesus and the historical Christian experience. Although numerous claims have been made about Channing's contribution to theology, Daniel Walker Howe has argued persuasively that Channing needs to be understood principally as a Christian-humanist moral philosopher grounded in SCOTTISH COMMON SENSE REALISM (as adapted by Harvard-based Unitarians in the early nineteenth century).

It is easy to see why the elite New England Unitarians were attracted to Channing, for he reinforced their self-important view of themselves when their status was being challenged by democratic culture. But if a posthumous collection of his works could reach a nineteenth edition by 1859, his appeal obviously cut across denominational and class lines as well as local boundaries. D. H. Meyer has argued that Channing provided the right mix of elements to soothe middle- and upper-class anxieties during a time of enormous political and social change. His confidence in education and individual development, and his example of leadership in an age of declining clerical influence, made the increasingly secular, materialistic culture of the nineteenth century seem less threatening and even controllable. At the same time, by turning inward to a religious psychology, Channing provided a sophisticated, intellectually palatable version of Christianity when science had eaten away at the traditional underpinnings of belief.

What is yet needed is a broader-based study of Channing that charts the complex cultural origins of both his thought and his enduring popular appeal throughout the nineteenth century. Further explorations of his life, work, and influence will show the full extent to which Channing participated in creating and fostering the culture of VICTORIANISM—particularly the culture of sentiment—in America.

GARY COLLISON

FURTHER READING

Lawrence Buell, *New England Literary Culture from Revolution through Renaissance* (New York: Cambridge University Press, 1986).

William Ellery Channing, *The Works of William Ellery Channing, D.D., With an Introduction. New and Complete Edition, Rearranged* (Boston: American Unitarian Association, 1898).

Andrew Delbanco, *William Ellery Channing: an Essay on the Liberal Spirit in America* (Cambridge: Harvard University Press, 1981).

Daniel Walker Howe, *The Unitarian Conscience: Harvard Moral Philosophy, 1805–1861* (Cambridge: Harvard University Press, 1970).

D. H. Meyer, "The Saint as Hero: William Ellery Channing and the Nineteenth Century Mind," *Winterthur Portfolio 8* (Charlottesville: University of Virginia Press, for the Winterthur Museum, 1973): 171–85.

Theodore Parker, *The American Scholar*, ed. George Willis Cooke, vol. 6 of the centenary ed. (Boston: American Unitarian Association, 1907).

David Robinson, "The Legacy of Channing: Culture as a Religious Category in New England Thought," *Harvard Theological Review* 74, no. 2 (1981): 221–39.

Conrad Wright, "The Rediscovery of Channing," in Wright, *The Liberal Christians: Essays on American Unitarian History* (Boston: Unitarian Universalist Association, 1970).

Chase, Stuart (b. Somersworth, N.H., Mar. 8, 1888; d. Redding, Conn., Nov. 16, 1985). Economist. Convinced that industry had largely solved the problem of production, Chase turned to the problems of distribution and consumption. He argued that the inefficiencies and inequities of capitalism caused the Great Depression by reducing purchasing power. Cooperative economic planning that aimed to provide goods, not profits, would rely on technocratic expertise to render both capitalism and communism obsolete. A broad-ranging writer, Chase also produced important cultural criticism, as in his *Mexico: a Study of Two Americas* (1931), which contrasted organic traditionalism to mechanical modernity. His thought was a potent endorsement of the social power of professional managers, who he believed could be mobilized to serve the public interest. His other writings include *The Tragedy of Waste* (1925), *Men and Machines* (1929), *A New Deal* (1932), and *The Tyranny of Words* (1938).

See also MANAGERIALISM.

FURTHER READING

Robert Westbrook, "Tribune of the Technostructure: the Popular Economics of Stuart Chase," *American Quarterly* 32 (fall 1980): 387–408.

Chávez, César (b. Yuma, Ariz., Mar. 31, 1927; d. San Luis, Ariz., Apr. 23, 1993). Labor organizer. Following the example of MARTIN LUTHER KING JR., Chávez, head of the United Farm Workers, used techniques of non-violent resistance—strikes, boycotts, marches, and hunger fasts—to call attention to farm workers' substandard working and living conditions. Like King, too, he embraced a prophetic vocation rooted in the Christian tradition, the vocation of self-sacrificial witness to justice. Chávez's effort to connect his Catholic spirituality to the earlier American tradition of radical agrarian protest contributed to the notable leftward swing in Catholic social thought after the 1960s.

See also CATHOLICISM; LATINO AND LATINA CULTURES.

FURTHER READING

J. Craig Jenkins, *The Politics of Insurgency: the Farm Worker Movement in the 1960s* (New York: Columbia University Press, 1985).

Chesnut, Mary Boykin (b. near Camden, S.C., Mar. 31, 1823; d. near Camden, S.C., Nov. 22, 1886). Diarist. Devoted to the slaveholding planter class, Chesnut was nevertheless troubled by some of the consequences of slavery. Her diary of the Civil War, which she repeatedly revised but never herself published, sought to provide an objective account of historical events. That goal did not keep her from bemoaning white women's incapacity to prevent their husbands from making sexual use of their slaves. Nor did she hesitate to suggest that women deserved a share of the power exercised by men. Her diary offers a reminder that the thought of many articulate writers, women in particular, was recorded in unpublished forms.

See also DIARIES.

FURTHER READING

Elisabeth Muhlenfeld, *Mary Boykin Chesnut: a Biography* (Baton Rouge: Louisiana State University Press, 1981).

Chesnutt, Charles W. (b. Cleveland, Ohio, June 20, 1858; d. Cleveland, Ohio, Nov. 15, 1932). Writer and lawyer. The first successful black American fiction writer, Chesnutt used magical motifs in *The Conjure Woman* (1899) to show the courage and heroism that slaves needed simply to survive. *The Wife of His Youth and Other Stories of the Color Line* (1899) contained contemporary stories describing the ironies of racism, the horrors of white discrimination and violence in the South of the post-Reconstruction period, and the social and professional aspirations, as well as prejudices and pettinesses, of light-skinned blacks in the northern, middle-class, mixed-race communities of Chesnutt's birth. After three subsequent novels met with a lukewarm reception, he gave up writing to return to the law.

FURTHER READING

William L. Andrews, *The Literary Career of Charles W. Chesnutt* (Baton Rouge: Louisiana State University Press, 1980).

Child, Lydia Maria (b. Medford, Mass., Feb. 11, 1802; d. Wayland, Mass., Oct. 20, 1880). In 1833 Child was hailed by the *North American Review* as America's foremost female writer. Her publication that year of *An Appeal in Favor of That Class of Americans Called Africans*, one of the earliest and most influential abolitionist texts, put her at the forefront of the abolitionist movement, and from 1841 to 1843 she edited the *National Anti-Slavery Standard*. During her prolific career Child wrote or edited 58 books, including fiction for adults and children, domestic manuals, biographies, a freedmen's textbook, and polemical works on Indians' rights, religion, women's condition, and, above all, slavery. Throughout her life she moved easily among interests and issues and sought to balance her literary leanings with her passionate commitment to racial and economic justice.

Child consistently argued that any classification that makes groups more significant than individuals is both inaccurate and dangerous. This theme unified her opposition to racism, sexism, and slavery, her radical antisectarianism in religion, and her political theory. She believed, for example, that slavery would be eliminated by awakening the moral conscience of the country, in both the North and the South. Any political activity that pitted one group against another, even for the best of purposes, she saw as a form of coercion. "Politics and war both arise from want of faith in spiritual weapons," she wrote to a colleague. "Both start with the ideas that the outward can *compel* the inward" (*Selected Letters*, p. 158). Child thus held to the old New England ideal of a community in which difference of opinion would not degenerate into faction. Rather, individuals would debate among themselves, and out of that debate would emerge a consensus that represented the will of the people as a whole. Child did not abjure politics altogether, but she argued that the tactics of "moral influence" were not only more ethical than the alternatives, but also more effective.

In 1843 Child resigned from organized abolitionist activity. The movement's bitter internecine battles had disillusioned her, and she vowed never to belong to any association again. "My own appropriate mission is obviously that of a writer," she concluded, "infusing, as I must necessarily do, *principles* in favor of peace, universal freedom, &c into all I write" (*Selected Letters*, p. 228). This sense of mission was apparent even in her first novel, *Hobomok* (1824), which had described a relationship between a Puritan woman and an Indian man. With its daring treatments of race, sex, and religion, the novel was praised as one of the first attempts to define a specifically American literature. Child's later work, both fiction and nonfiction, addressed a full range of social, ethical, and political themes. At every opportunity she published stories of fugitive salves and their northern allies, in which she showed personal courage and cleverness triumphant over an evil but ultimately self-destructive system. Her goal, explicitly stated, was to shape the great forces of public opinion by creating works of beauty that would appeal to both intellect and emotions.

As a female leader of the abolitionist movement, Child was inevitably engaged in discussions about the proper roles of women. In the 1830s she had tried to avoid the issue. "It is best not to *talk* about our rights," she argued, "but simply go forward and *do* whatsoever we deem a duty. In toiling for the freedom of others, we shall find our own" (*Selected Letters*, p. 123). She was not deterred when her understanding of duty challenged others' ideas of appropriate behavior: if a woman had an ability to write or to speak, to edit a newspaper or to organize a petition drive, she should follow her own conscience in using that God-given gift. Child thus found herself on both sides of the debate about women's rights that helped split the abolitionist movement. While she certainly believed that women's talents and energies should be fully utilized on behalf of the slaves, she did not want antislavery organizations to adopt a feminist agenda: their goal should be to end slavery by pulling as many people as possible into a broad coalition, not to advocate (or oppose) other reforms that could undermine that effort. Yet Child's political theory almost went to the extreme of making women's constraints a virtue. Since individuals were more important than organizations, and moral persuasion more powerful than political meetings, women already had abundant power and needed only to choose to use it.

As she grew older, however, Child increasingly resented women's subordination and men's misuse of their privileges. She articulated the limits that being a woman had placed on her creativity and productivity: the brain-numbing domestic work and duties to husband and father, as well as the political and legal structures that excluded women. With the Civil War approaching, Child's frustration flared in a letter to Charles Sumner: "At times, my old heart swells almost to bursting, in view of all these things; for it is the heart of a man imprisoned within a woman's destiny" (*Selected Letters*, p. 283). Through her writings, Child had attained the status of an elder cultural sage, but her influence never amounted to actual authority, and she chafed at its limited reach.

Despite the growing social and economic radicalism of her later years, Child continued to call for mutual understanding as well as ethical passion. She decried "ultraism" and asked people to respect the inherited wisdom of the past without clinging to its prejudices. Her *Progress of Religious Ideas* (1855), a history of the world's religions through early Catholicism, aimed to promote a universal faith beyond sectarianism. "No portion of truth ever did die, or ever can die," she wrote. "Its *spirit* is eternal, though its *forms* are ever changing" (vol. 3, p. 419). Social and political as well as religious changes were therefore not to be feared. The quest for justice embodied an eternal truth that had always inspired seekers of equality, peace, and beauty, and this truth would eventually find full expression in human societies. Later generations would find this conviction overly optimistic, but it motivated Child and her colleagues to try, with occasional success, to transform their world.

LORI J. KENSCHAFT

See also ANTISLAVERY; WOMEN'S RIGHTS.

FURTHER READING

Lydia Maria Child, *The Progress of Religious Ideas*, 3 vols. (New York: C. S. Francis, 1855).
——, *Lydia Maria Child: Selected Letters, 1817–1880*, ed. Milton Meltzer and Patricia G. Holland (Amherst: University of Massachusetts Press, 1982).
Deborah Pickman Clifford, *Crusader for Freedom: a Life of Lydia Maria Child* (Boston: Beacon, 1992).
Carolyn L. Karcher, "Introduction," in Lydia Maria Child, *Hobomok and Other Writings on Indians* (1824; New Brunswick: Rutgers University Press, 1986).

childhood The history of ideas about childhood splits into two largely disconnected chapters: one from an adult perspective, the other from a child's point of view. The bulkier chapter describes, documents, and debates changing adult conceptions of children. Starting with Philippe Ariès' seminal book, *Centuries of Childhood*, historians have been primarily occupied with two tasks: first, tracking down when, where, and if a social "discovery" of childhood took place; and then tracing the history of parental sentiment. Traditionalists—drawing on such evidence as the portrayal of children as small adults—claim that the concept of childhood as a separate stage began only in the seventeenth century and that intense parental emotion is a modern creation made possible by lowered infant mortality. Revisionists contend that childhood was recognized at least by the sixteenth century and that parents cared deeply about their children well before our own time.

A much sketchier chapter examines the actual social life of children. We have a meager record of children's activities, and only scattered evidence on the social differentiation of childhood by class, gender, race, ethnicity, or region. In principle, information on children's demographic experience and economic activities could fortify our understanding of children's social life. But the interest in childhood of demographers and economists remains framed by an adult perspective, concerned primarily with parental motivation for childbearing and its relation to fertility patterns and population policy.

Even sociologists (who pride themselves on their empathy with the underdog) have neglected children's social experiences. While child psychology has thrived, the sociology of childhood has only begun to explore the social life of children. Most notably, family sociology has been for the most part adult sociology: the study of courtship, marriage, parenting, and divorce, not childhood. Socialization literature does focus directly on children, but chiefly on their channeling into adult behavior, not their social life. Curiously, even feminist sociologists retain this adult orientation. As they set about revolutionizing notions of gender, feminist scholars still kept children in their invisible place.

The two chapters of children's history need binding together. Studying children's economic activities provides a splendid opportunity for just this junction. Consider the dramatic shift in the working patterns of American children between the 1870s and 1930s. For all of American history prior to the late nineteenth-century, children played a significant part in the productive activities of American households. Working-class urban families in the late nineteenth century still depended on the wages of their older children and the household assistance of younger ones. Although child labor did not totally vanish (children still worked in rural areas, in street trades, as actors), by 1930 child labor laws and compulsory education had put most children out of work; working-class children joined their middle-class counterparts in a new nonproductive world of childhood.

Children's social life moved into an increasingly age-segregated, supervised, privatized sphere of lessons, games, sports, and consumption. Children's acceptable "jobs"—baby-sitting for neighbors, mowing lawns, or selling newspapers—were defined primarily as educational tasks, not "real" work. Children's token household contributions became a form of moral training rather than material assistance to their parents. Earlier generations of children had been given responsibility for regular supervision of younger siblings. Now, especially in the middle class, children within a family were increasingly segregated from one another as paid babysitting took older children outside the home to learn responsibility in the marketplace.

For adults, the transformation of children's economic activities involved a profound redefinition of childhood, from an economically useful to an economically useless but emotionally "priceless" child. While the working child had been a legitimate participant in the nineteenth-century household economy, twentieth-century critics recast the child laborer as the victim of ruthless employers or mercenary parents. True parental love could exist only if the child was defined exclusively as an object of sentiment and not an agent of production.

Changes in children's social life and adult conceptions of children interacted in multiple ways, redefining for instance monetary exchanges between parents and children. As the consumer society was being established—with many products targeted for children—what was to be the unemployed, "useless" child's source of income? The weekly allowance took shape as a legitimate form of child money, not a wage but an educational currency designed to turn children into competent consumers.

The dual transformation of childhood transcended the household, shaping social welfare policies such as mothers' pensions legislation as well as adoption and foster care practices. For instance, while nineteenth-century foster families took in useful—usually older—children, expecting them to help out with chores, twentieth-century adoptive parents searched only—and were willing to pay for—an adorable infant to love.

At the turn of the twenty-first century, both chapters in children's history are being rewritten. A series of social changes strongly affects them. The place of children in the home has become newly unsettled as women's paid employment spreads, as home-based employment on commission or contract reappears, as divorce results in more single-parent families, as remarriage creates new kin networks, and as unmarried—heterosexual or homosexual—couples have or adopt a child. Outside of households, childhood is being reshaped by advertising and merchandising focused on children, by debates over public child-care arrangements and family leaves for new parents, by contestation over welfare payments for mothers and children, and by concern with child abuse or kidnapping.

At the same time the debate over the utility or uselessness of children has reignited. Once again, as at the turn of the twentieth century, two views of childhood are being disputed, but this time the reform group proposes to selectively increase children's useful adultlike participation in productive activities, while traditionalists cling to the Progressive ideal of a separate domestic domain for children.

VIVIANA A. ZELIZER

See also FATHERHOOD; MOTHERHOOD; PLAY.

FURTHER READING

Philippe Ariès, *Centuries of Childhood* (New York: Vintage, 1962).

Bruce Bellingham, "The History of Childhood Since the 'Invention of Childhood': Some Issues of the Eighties," *Journal of Family History* 13, no.3 (1988): 347–58.

Sarane Spence Boocock, "Children in Contemporary Society," in Arlene Skolnick, ed., *Rethinking Childhood* (Boston: Little, Brown, 1976).

Gary Alan Fine and Jay Mechling, "Minor Difficulties: Changing Children in the Late Twentieth Century," in Alan Wolfe, ed., *America At Century's End* (Berkeley: University of California Press, 1991).

Linda Pollock, *Forgotten Children: Parent–Child Relations from 1500–1900* (Cambridge: Cambridge University Press, 1984).

Barrie Thorne, "Re-Visioning Women and Social Change: Where Are the Children?" *Gender and Society* 1 (Mar. 1987): 85–109.

Viviana A. Zelizer, *Pricing the Priceless Child: the Changing Social Value of Children* (New York: Basic, 1985).

Choate, Rufus (b. Ipswich, Mass., Oct. 1, 1799; d. Halifax, Nova Scotia, July 13, 1859). Lawyer and politician. Next to DANIEL WEBSTER the most powerful and popular Whig orator, Choate expressed a romantic nationalism that celebrated the organic growth and spiritual distinction of the United States. Florid effusions about distinctive national destiny were typical of ROMANTICISM in Europe as well as America. Choate's invocations of national identity were also designed to stimulate political support for the Whigs' vision of nationalization. Like other conservative Whigs, he could on the one hand endorse the entrepreneurial ethos exemplified by the railroad interests he served as counsel, and on the other moralize about the universal virtues of self-restraint and social order.

FURTHER READING

Jean V. Matthews, *Rufus Choate: the Law and Civic Virtue* (Philadelphia: Temple University Press, 1980).

Chomsky, Noam (b. Philadelphia, Pa., Dec. 7, 1928). The twentieth century's most influential linguist and one of the most incisive radical critics of United States foreign policy, Noam Chomsky received his B.A. degree in 1949 from the University of Pennsylvania, where he studied under the eminent structural linguist, Zellig Harris. Chomsky subsequently received his doctorate from the same university in 1955, the year he took up a position at MIT, where he was made Institute Professor in 1976.

Chomsky's written output has been torrential, with some dozen books on linguistics to his credit, an approximately equal number on international affairs, and hundreds of articles, essays, and reviews in the two areas. He also travels frequently and extensively to give public interviews and talks, and is one of the most powerful speakers of his day, frequently drawing vast crowds to hear him.

Chomsky's major intellectual contribution was to revolutionize the scientific study of LANGUAGE, setting it off in new and deep directions that continue to be fruitfully explored today. The central task of linguistics, he has insisted, is to explain the everyday phenomenon of language acquisition. Once we come to appreciate its nature, we will see that nothing like the once dominant behaviorist models of learning will do. The knowledge that children come to acquire upon learning a language is so rich and the basis on which they acquire it so poor that we must conclude, he argues, that children are born knowing a great deal about the possible forms natural languages can take. Chomsky holds that, despite their great surface variety, at a deeper level natural languages must in fact be very closely related to one another, and, furthermore, that knowledge of how languages are at root identical is part of the genetic endowment of the child. The language-learning child is not attempting to construct from scratch the language of others; rather, the child comes into the world in possession of a short list of candidates, as it were, and is trying to identify which of those languages on the list to select. Characterization of the child's innate knowledge will help solve the central problem of linguistics, where linguistics is now understood as that branch of human psychology that focuses on the acquisition of a distinctive domain of knowledge: knowledge of language.

Chomsky's theoretical articulation of this conception and his technical development of it opened up ever richer veins of exploration. His creative use of modern formal methods, developed earlier in the century by logicians and other students of formal languages, enabled him to provide descriptions of natural languages that far exceeded in explicitness, detail, and depth all that had come before.

Moreover, Chomsky's conception not only established a new way of pursuing linguistic research, but it also posed challenges to dominant practices and views in psychology and philosophy. First, Chomsky's work encouraged rejection of the view that innate knowledge is either incoherent or useless for the purposes of scientific explanation. Second, it fostered skepticism regarding the intimate relation on which behaviorism insists between observable behavior and unobservable posits, in particular mental states like linguistic knowledge. According to Chomsky, linguistic knowledge is not only in large part innate, but it is also irreducible to complexes of behavioral abilities, though to be sure it makes our use of language possible. Rather, this knowledge is to be understood as consisting in an as yet unknown state of the speaker's neurophysiology. A far-reaching effect of this move is to weaken the link between central notions employed in linguistic explanations and the observable behavior of speakers.

On the polemical side, these shifts of orientation led Chomsky into famous disputes with the psychologist B. F. SKINNER and the philosopher W. V. O. QUINE. On the positive side, they provided a framework for the so-called cognitive revolution that greatly influenced, if not inaugurated, inquiry into such diverse areas as child development, the visual system, arithmetical competence and mental imagery. Research in these and other areas became characterized by a willingness to explore the possibility that explanatory accounts would have to make reference to highly specialized principles (modularity), which are taken to be known by the subject without the benefit of experience (nativism), and knowledge of which is not to be understood in terms of the subject's behavioral abilities, but rather is to be taken to explain them (mentalism). In these ways, Chomsky's views have had a major impact on work in the philosophy of language and mind, and in psychology generally.

Chomsky's political writing began during the Vietnam War, providing impassioned, yet well-documented and carefully reasoned, analyses of U.S. foreign policy towards Southeast Asia. While always focusing on current events, he increasingly sought to explain Washington's conduct in the context of its behavior throughout the twentieth century and to reveal the motivating dynamics of actions he considered brutal, immoral, and hypocritical. Though his writing gradually encompassed many facets of American foreign policy (*see also* COLD WAR), his primary focus has been its impact on the peoples of Southeast Asia, Central America and the Middle East, areas in which, he argues, America's actions, while often cloaked under the guise of furthering humanitarian goals and of promoting democracy, instead have predictably led to tremendous misery in the attempt to make the world safer for U.S. capitalism. This radical critique has been carried on in his work concurrently with an examination of the means by which U.S. citizens have been kept largely ignorant about their government's activities. The result has been perhaps this century's most sustained and trenchant exposé of the manner in which the mass media and intellectuals in the United States have abandoned their responsibility as objective seekers after the truth and instead have become purveyors of the state's ideological perspective and promoters of its domestic and international policy objectives.

Chomsky's brilliance and articulateness, together with his iconoclastic tendencies and the breadth of his interests, have generated strong responses of all kinds. His towering reputation and enormous impact within the academy, wider intellectual circles, and the general population (of his own country and beyond) are comparable to that of the greatest engaged intellectuals of the century. Most importantly and enduringly, the body of his work has substantially deepened our understanding of ourselves and of the world in which we live.

ALEXANDER GEORGE

FURTHER READING
Noam Chomsky, *Syntactic Structures* (The Hague: Mouton, 1957).
——, *Aspects of the Theory of Syntax* (Cambridge: MIT Press, 1965).
——, *American Power and the New Mandarins* (New York: Pantheon, 1969).
——, *For Reasons of State* (New York: Pantheon, 1973).
——, *Reflections on Language* (New York: Pantheon, 1975).
——, *Rules and Representations* (Oxford: Blackwell, 1980).
——, *The Fateful Triangle: the United States, Israel, and the Palestinians* (Boston: South End, 1983).
——, *Knowledge of Language* (New York: Praeger, 1986).
——, *Deterring Democracy* (New York: Verso, 1991).
Carlos Otero, ed., *Noam Chomsky: Critical Assessments*, 4 vols. (London: Routledge, 1994).

Chopin, Kate (b. St. Louis, Mo., Feb. 8, 1851; d. St. Louis, Mo., Aug. 22, 1904).   Writer. While Chopin's stories of Creole Louisiana frequently depicted independent women in unsatisfying marriages, she is best known for her novel *The Awakening* (1899), in which she portrayed a woman who is frustrated as a wife and mother and seeks to find her own life through painting, two love affairs, and ultimately even in suicide. Chopin's descriptions of a woman's passion, power, and sexuality reveal a complex web of desire for both deep connection with another and for the solitude of separation.

See also FEMINISM.

FURTHER READING
Emily Toth, *Kate Chopin* (New York: Morrow, 1990).

cinema   Now a century old, cinema originated in the work of inventors and scientists seeking to analyze physical movement. These early recording efforts, such as Edison's *Fred Ott's Sneeze* (1889), credited as the first filmed closeup, centered on human and animal physiology. But in depicting movement through time, they inevitably constructed narratives and exhibited aesthetic choices, thus establishing motion pictures as both documentary tools and artistic forms. Because film could be manipulated—slowed down or speeded up, reversed, or overshot—cinema was a potent medium of fantasy, imaging worlds unseen by the human eye. Public exhibition of films began in the mid-1890s and the commercial release of shorts to storefront arcades was widespread by 1905. Within the first few years of film's emergence its entire range—mass-produced entertainment, documentary newsreel, scientific tool, abstract and fantastic visuals—had been explored. Almost immediately, an array of critics had emerged to debate film's status as art form, commercial venture, propaganda, scientific evidence, and historical record.

By the middle of the next decade, after Carl Laemmle moved West to open Universal Pictures, Hollywood had become the center of American film production. Universal's lengthy film, D. W. Griffith's inflammatory *Birth of a Nation* (1915), sparked censorship fights and racial violence across the country. But most early commercial films were short two-reelers and relied heavily on the melodramatic theatricals, which were extremely popular throughout the world, to assure immediate audience recognition and response. Griffith perfected their use in film. In 1922, Lillian Gish was able to persuade Griffith to film *Orphans in the Storm* after she discovered that the play *Two Orphans* had had successful runs in over 40 countries. Griffith set the tearjerker against the background of the French Revolution, in much the same way that he had used the battle scenes of the Civil War to energize *Birth of a Nation*'s melodrama. The combination of melodrama and spectacle, firmly in place within decades of film's invention, continues to mark most Hollywood blockbusters.

Griffith used large numbers of extras—virtually the entire town of Marmaroneck, New York, where he filmed *Orphans*—to stage his historical scenes. In that way, cinema presented itself as a mass art form. But, as Walter Benjamin would point out, the impact of film was much broader. It virtually called forth a MASS CULTURE: not only were there crowds in its images and crowds at each theatre, this pattern could be replicated as many times as there were prints of the film. At each site, cinema actually represented the masses to themselves. For Benjamin this doubled process of mass culture—its simultaneous creation of mass viewing and representation of mass society—meant that film had the capacity to forge and mobilize new political alliances: it could either serve fascism as had Leni Riefenstahl's *Triumph of the Will*, or promote revolution as had Eisenstein's *October*.

Because film was associated with the masses, respectable people initially viewed it as a lower-class form of amusement, appropriate only for the vaudeville houses and penny arcades located in working-class neighborhoods. In the 1920s, studios began designing movie palaces in more upscale neighborhoods attracting middle-class audiences. But the taint of working-class entertainment clung to movies, and the endless debates—beginning as early as the 1910s (Vachel Lindsay's *Art of the Moving Picture* appeared in 1915)—about whether cinema was high art or debased commodity were exacerbated when the studio system established itself as a powerful monopoly controlling production and distribution. Just what did the studios sell—moving pictures or tickets to movie palaces? Clearly the latter; hence the more cheaply and quickly a picture could be produced and distributed, the more tickets could be sold, insuring the reign of Hollywood's studio system.

Although early film's appeal was international— the Lumière brothers, French inventors, filmmakers, and distributors, sent their cinematograph traveling across continents filming and showing moving pictures—cinema became deeply implicated in nationalism by helping people to envision communities of solidarity. Film served vital political ends, especially among illiterate populations; within days of the October Revolution, the Bolsheviks nationalized the film industry and established film schools. Following the Soviet model, in the mid-twentieth century, Cuba inspired Latin American and Caribbean radicals to study and exhibit films; France helped newly independent African states develop their film industries. Today the Indian film industry produces most of its films for export to its diasporic population. Not until the 1930s, with the Resettlement Administration's funding of Pare Lorentz's films, *The Plow That Broke the Plains* (1936) and *The River* (1937), did the U.S. government begin major film production. Its original goal of selling New Deal policies continued throughout World War II, when Hollywood directors were enlisted to make films for the army and for audiences at home. But Hollywood, with its vast resources and power, has dominated American filmmaking throughout the century. As a result, as Stuart Hall aptly claims, "the world dreams itself to be 'American.'" Under transnational corporations, most films now are bankrolled by conglomerates fusing Japanese, American, and European capital. The resulting blockbusters are designed to appeal to international audiences, hence the retreat from intricate and rapid-fire dialogue, which characterized Hollywood films during its heyday, to action-packed stories filled with special effects.

Cinema's apparatus—the projection of light onto a large screen—propels its highly stylized vision of the real. Yet its conventions of illusion and verisimilitude result from a complex layering of narrative and visual formulas already in use elsewhere: adaptations of novels and theatricals dominated early filmmaking as much as they do today, and cinematography is indebted to photography and painting. However, the mechanics of movement—flickering light, advancing celluloid, persistence of vision—add another dimension of realism. The reality effect of cinema is achieved through mise-en-scène, which fills the screen with objects evoking a sense of plenitude; editing techniques smooth transitions, producing temporal continuity; depth of field, shot length, and camera angle connote three-dimensional space. One looks on at the evolving visual display of a story whose characters and settings are uncannily familiar; yet the sheer fact that they are effects solely of light patterns means cinema remains deeply strange.

The experience of film viewing gave birth to theoretical discussions of film's relation to consciousness and the unconscious. The cinematic apparatus was said to resemble Plato's cave in which shadows flickered, the keyhole through which one spied one's parents, the dark chamber in which one dreamt nightly. Moreover, psychoanalysis provided clues to the psychosexual workings of voyeurism at the heart of the pleasures of viewing. Early pornographic films indicate just how closely film watching is associated with illicit viewing—they reveal a "frenzy of the visible," as Linda Williams calls it in *Hard Core* (1989). Thus it is not surprising that within decades of cinema's invention, book-length analyses of film's language, such as Hugo Münsterberg's *The Photoplay: a Psychological Study* (1916), argued that film was closely akin to dreams and the unconscious—not only of individuals but of nations, according to Siegfried Kracauer's view of German expressionist films. It was not accidental that cinema should be linked with social psychology and psychoanalysis since these modes of visualization and interpretation developed almost simultaneously; and the language used to describe the processes of national consciousness and of the individual unconscious, especially the workings of dreams, resembled descriptions of cinema. Films, like dreams or nations, were windows through which reality could be glimpsed or onto which fantasies could be projected. Each revealed the narratives derived from recognition and refusal, each fostered a sensation of knowing through seeing.

The popularity of classic Hollywood narrative cinema results from its reliance on genre and formula to shape and fulfill audience expectations; from its staple of characters and stars embodying the fantasy life of the fans; its orderly timing of the film-watching experience, first codified into two-reelers then longer sequences, establishing patterns of visual pleasure and routine; its extravagant spectacle; and especially, according to feminist critic Laura Mulvey, its fetishistic display of female sexuality. Each aspect—technological, historical, ideological, psychological—prods the seemingly endless outpouring of writings about all aspects of cinema: about screenwriting, directing, acting, star biographies, criticism, and theory. Film's easy accessibility and its mysterious power (as Benjamin observed) to produce mass cultural experiences make its viewers, too, feel equipped to judge it. Despite the consolidation of film studies in the academy since the 1960s, the notion of a film expert is problematic; as a popular commodity, film endows its consumers with taste, making everyone into a critic. Still, as a complex semiotic system, cinema demands rigorous critique to unpack *how* films express meaning as individual texts, historical artifacts, and ideological formations.

Since the early years of filmmaking, documentary films have existed side-by-side with fictional narratives. Like the still camera, the motion picture camera was understood as a scientific device capable of recording evidence and maintaining historical truth. Carted to battlefields and factories, the camera revealed the horrors (and majestic beauties) of mass dying or mass production. The sense of vast scale was crucial to the effects of truth documentaries produced. Robert Flaherty's shots of the emptiness of the Hudson Bay region in *Nanook of the North* (1922) gave viewers a sense of the distant spaces beyond the screen. He defined another genre of filmmaking, the ethnographic, as anthropologists used the camera to record the ritual practices and everyday lives of faraway peoples. MARGARET MEAD and Gregory Bateson's films of Samoa brought another dimension to the spectacle of the cinema, that of exoticism. The uses of film—as propaganda, imperialist survey, commercial entertainment, scientific record, and manipulation—opened cinema to critiques for its complicity with and aid in conquest and exploitation, spurring a movement for "counter-cinema," as Claire Johnston named it.

With the post-World War II plethora of army surplus 16mm film equipment and stock, practically everyone could afford to make movies. Home movies became popular among the 1950s middle class, while a growing underground of independent filmmakers, rejecting the restricting notions of cinema imposed by Hollywood, pushed cinema into new forms. Like their European predecessors, American avant-garde filmmakers explored alternative sexualities, expanded consciousness through trance films, ritualized vision by breaking down the elements of film. For instance, by exposing the formal aspects of bourgeois ideology underpinning narrative film—with its conventions of verisimilitude achieved through continuity editing and causal logic—structuralist filmmakers such as George Landow pushed viewers to become active participants in what Malcolm Le Grice called "the pure politics of perception," rather than passive consumers of conventional genre films. The phenomena of cult films like *Rocky Horror Picture Show* suggests that moviegoers produce diverse interpretations of even the most formulaic films offered to them.

What do spectators do with films? Avant-garde and cult films suggest that audiences are not the static receptacles of ideology posited by Frankfurt School critical theorists and eerily repeated in the construct of the spectator theorized by psychoanalytic film studies. Hollywood grasps that multiple responses to a film ensure its popularity. Contemporary blockbusters open-endedly allow audiences the pleasure of taking contradictory positions: *Terminator II* can be read both as a New Right vigilante fantasy *and* as a feminist morality tale. Audience members' experiences as subjects differentiated by race, class, gender, sexuality, age, and geography create varied and conflicting uses of film. A movie that initially shocked its audience, as *The Exorcist* did when first released in Boston, might amuse those seeing it dubbed in French with Arabic subtitles in Marrakesh. A film documenting the exploitation of women in the pornography industry, like the Canadian film, *Not a Love Story*, might get wide distribution precisely because Canada's restrictions on pornography make this exposé one of the few X-rated films available.

Audiences are vital and unpredictable elements of cinema. Hollywood does extensive marketing research to predetermine which films will be successful, but they are often wrong. Its reliance on tried and true genres employing stars whose bodies and faces are manufactured to please suggests that it needs to rein in the various diverse audiences. Yet Hollywood films have always segmented their audiences by race, class, gender, and age. This segmentation has inspired newly empowered political movements to use film to redress the abuses perpetrated by a dominant culture—racist, sexist and homophobic stereotypes. Recent African American films have pushed the boundaries of classic narrative to explore the racism of urban America. Women's counter-cinema has resurrected film noir and melodrama to reinscribe the female subject in narrative; and the new queer cinema defies the heterosexual logic of the romantic plots policing desire.

PAULA RABINOWITZ

See also CARTOONING; REPRESENTATION.

FURTHER READING

Walter Benjamin, "The Work of Art in the Age of Mechanical Reproduction," *Illuminations: Essays and Reflections*, trans. Harry Zohn (New York: Schocken, 1968).

David Bordwell, Janet Staiger, and Kristin Thompson, *The Classical Hollywood Cinema: Film Style and Mode of Production to 1960* (New York: Columbia University Press, 1985).

Gilles Deleuze, *Cinema 1: the Movement-Image*, trans. Hugh Tomlinson and Barbara Habberjam (Minneapolis: University of Minnesota Press, 1986).

Mary Ann Doane, *Femmes Fatales: Feminism, Film Theory, Psychoanalysis* (New York: Routledge 1991).

Richard Harpole, ed., *History of American Cinema*, 4 vols. (New York: Charles Scribner's Sons, 1990).

Teresa de Lauretis and Stephen Heath, eds., *The Cinematic Apparatus* (New York: St. Martin's, 1980).

Malcolm Le Grice, *Abstract Film and Beyond* (Cambridge: MIT Press, 1977).

Bill Nichols, *Representing Reality: Issues and Concepts in Documentary* (Bloomington: Indiana University Press, 1991).

citizenship   The men who made the AMERICAN REVOLUTION created American citizenship. It was a significantly new political and legal status that at once reflected their most longstanding traditions, their deepest conflicts, and their most daring hopes for the common life they strove to create. Those hopes were far from universally shared. Most colonial inhabitants were British loyalists, or slaves, servants, or members of native tribes, much more concerned with securing freedom for themselves than with the revolution. Hence American citizenship had to be achieved and sustained by force.

But the revolutionary leaders would never have prevailed if they had not also offered a new civic identity that promised to advance the ambitions and aspirations of many less privileged Americans. Subsequently, changes in the power, the traditions, and the hopes of various American elites, relative to each other, to international pressures, and to the nation's less endowed inhabitants, have worked major changes in American citizenship. The process is political, unending, and unpredictable. Yet some dominant patterns can be discerned, and they are not quite the ones American leaders and scholars have often proclaimed.

The political status the revolutionaries created was so novel, and so imperfectly conceptualized, that they lacked fit terminology for it. They spoke of "citizenship" and "naturalization," as we still do. But "citizenship" originally meant membership in self-governing city-states, like those of ancient Greece and Rome and Renaissance Italy. "Naturalization" meant a subject's voluntary acquisition of the perpetual allegiance to a sovereign that men ordinarily attained by being born under their "natural" sovereign's protection. Yet neither the new states nor the successive federal regimes were city-states, and the American revolutionaries often denounced the idea that people were born natural subjects of any rulers. They claimed legitimate governments originated in popular consent.

They did so to deny that they must perpetually be British subjects. Instead Americans made popular self-governance, without hereditary aristocracy or monarchy, a core principle of their state and national governments. Stretching old words, they called these governments "republican," and themselves "citizens." And they sought support, at home and abroad, by proclaiming republican citizenship to be the political partner of modern strivings for emancipation and enlightenment. America, they promised, would test whether men could truly be self-governing equals.

Their civic experiment was indeed bold. The learned had long proclaimed that if republican governments could thrive at all, it could be only in small city-states, where citizens could learn to know and trust each other. Yet the United States was to be something new, an extended republic. From the outset many contended such a regime could not remain republican, rather than elite-dominated and imperial. Tenacious beliefs that the states were the true homes of republican citizenship eventually had to be repudiated by civil war. Even so, longings for smaller, purer democracies remain powerful today, as the vast modern American state makes opportunities for meaningfully self-governing citizenship seem vanishingly small.

Many of the Constitution's framers worried about the American experiment for quite different reasons. They believed republican governments were prone to become "elected despotisms," in Jefferson's phrase. Masses of debtors would legislate violations of the economic rights and freedoms of the affluent; intolerant religious majorities would persecute rival sects; incumbents would suppress political dissidence. The framers created innumerable restraints on direct popular rule. Many, like ALEXANDER HAMILTON, espoused a vision of American civic life that esteemed vigorous political participation far less than industrious pursuit of one's "private" economic and spiritual interests.

Writers throughout American history have produced narratives in which the nation's development is seen as driven by conflicts among Americans most attached to their heritage of DEMOCRACY and those who have stressed protection for individual RIGHTS in order to achieve FREEDOM and wealth, admittedly accompanied by inequality. Many recent scholars have reprised these narratives as contests between communitarian "civic republican" and individualistic "liberal" traditions of citizenship, although most now acknowledge that virtually all American political figures have espoused some combination of these themes. (See also REPUBLICANISM and LIBERALISM.)

Although these narratives have captured driving tensions in American civic life, there is much they have neglected. Just as Americans tried to adopt older terms not really appropriate to their purposes to define the new political status they were creating, they also retained in it adapted forms of established political hierarchies. These civic hierarchies were ascribed, not consensual, and hence they were not truly "liberal" or "republican," though to many they were quintessentially "American."

The revolutionaries did not simply tell their fellow Americans they ought to be experimenters in the causes of republican governance and human rights. They also told them that Americans were a people chosen by Providence and especially equipped by their Protestant and Anglo-Saxon cultural inheritances to be exemplars of political and religious liberty. American lawmakers also accepted, then and for the next century and a half, that most persons not so designated and equipped by God and nature might not be eligible for full American citizenship. In 1790 Congress proclaimed that only whites could be naturalized. Blacks could legally be ruled as slaves, Indians as conquered subjects. Women were assigned the citizenship of their fathers or husbands. Only white men could exercise political power. Most of the domestic population was ineligible, on grounds of race, ethnicity, or gender, for the full rights and powers American citizenship conferred. That would remain explicitly true until women received the vote 130 years later, and it would remain functionally true until the successes of the civil rights and women's movements in the 1960s.

For some Americans, this legal structuring of American citizenship represented efforts to achieve the homogeneity among citizens successful republics allegedly required. But for many, these were arrangements ordained by God, written into human natural capacities, and affirmed both by scientific evidence and historical experience. Hence they were far better grounded than the still novel causes of egalitarian republicanism and universal human rights. For those so minded, such ascriptive hierarchies, as much or more than republican self-governance or liberal rights, were the central components of American citizenship.

The question of why these ascriptive conceptions of "Americanism" have always had great power needs much more scholarly attention, but some reasons are likely. Liberal and republican conceptions of civic membership have always had political liabilities. Liberal visions of citizenship risk encouraging divisive self-absorption; they prod all to progress through difficult individual striving, within market economies in which success is bound to be highly unequal; and their implicit endorsement of equal rights for all has not sat well with defenders of traditional American social and political arrangements. Republicanism requires time-consuming commitment to public service, and can also spark expansive popular claims to greater political power. Hence both liberal and republican traditions have always had great potential to disturb elites by their transformative implications, especially in combination. They can also demoralize those who cannot live up to their demanding standards for good citizenship, or who find meaning in social forms these traditions refuse to sanctify.

In contrast, the religious, intellectual, and cultural traditions that have proclaimed the superiority of

Christianity, Anglo-Saxon civilization, the white race, and male governance have had obvious legitimating value for those who sat atop traditional hierarchies. And they have assured many Americans that, simply because of who they are, they have a secure and worthy place within a meaningful, indeed sacred, natural order. As a further edge over liberalism and republicanism, those affirmations have extended not just to Americans' lives in this world but also the next.

Hence American elites have always had reason to advocate ascriptive conceptions of American citizenship, and many other Americans have had reasons to embrace them. And because such views have shaped American life since before the nation was born, scholarly investigators long found it easy to provide empirical evidence for their presuppositions: blacks, women, Indians, Chinese laborers, and others did appear to conform significantly to their stereotypes. The imprimatur of scientific truth granted to theories of natural hierarchy, especially by the American school of ethnography in the 1830s and 1840s and the racial Darwinists of the 1890s and early 1900s, helped reinforce these aspects of American political culture. But siren songs of how true Americans are the deserving favorites of nature, history, and God have resonated more or less powerfully through all the epochs of American life.

Yet these ascriptive categories of civic identity always fit even less well with the consensual rhetoric of the creators of American citizenship than the terms "citizenship" and "naturalization" did. Enlightenment political theories preached that all minimally rational humans possessed certain rights, and despite heroic efforts, scientists could not really show that nonwhites and women did not possess basic rational capacities. The heart of republican citizenship was supposed to be political participation, and it was never easy to explain why all women and free blacks could be citizens and yet be denied the franchise, explicitly or tacitly.

The contradictions have mattered, because liberal and republican themes have always remained potent in American life, with religious dispensations lending support to them as well as to ascriptive "Americanist" views. Despite their drawbacks, liberal and republican conceptions of civic identity offered attractive promises of freedom from oppression, opportunities for success in one's preferred pursuits, and the dignity of personal and political self-governance. Thus leaders of both powerful and weak American communities have virtually always tried to attract support by offering visions of America that blended liberal, republican, and ascriptive elements in ways that were politically serviceable, if rarely intellectually consistent. Jacksonian Democrats, for example, stood for "republican" democratic self-governance, equal "liberal" property rights and religious pluralism, and "ascriptive" white supremacy over blacks and Indians. Whigs advocated "liberal" vested rights and recognition of the basic, if primitive, humanity of blacks and Indians; fervent "republican" patriotism; and "ascriptive" immigration and educational laws favoring Protestant Anglo-Saxon culture. Antebellum protest leaders, including African Americans and women, claimed to be entitled to the individual rights proclaimed in the Declaration of Independence, to equal republican citizenship, and to recognition as equal children of God. The Jacksonian vision held sway for a time, but antislavery protesters succeeded in fragmenting the nation sufficiently so that, within the new Republican Party, they could gain power in alliance with former Whigs. The result was a major transformation in the nation's civic laws, the postwar amendments affirming not only the supremacy of the national republic but also the eligibility of African Americans for at least the minimal prerequisites of civic membership.

That forcible reshaping of American citizenship did not mean that the influence of ascriptive notions of political community faded thereafter. Just the opposite: postwar Republicans found they could retain supremacy only by forging a new coalition that jettisoned the cause of racial equality and sanctioned not only Jim Crow but, eventually, massive race-based immigration exclusions and new imperial ventures. Many pragmatic theorists of the Progressive Era openly disavowed older appeals to transcendental standards in favor of reliance on democratic judgments guided by technically competent instrumental rationality. In so doing they seemed to take the revolutionary demand that all be governed by their own collective reason to its fullest expression. But other Progressives saw people as profoundly constituted by their social communities, in ways few could alter. Hence many agreed that those who appeared culturally distinct, such as immigrants and African Americans, should be subjected to special restrictions in America or barred from further immigration.

The historical tendency of Americans to try to shape their citizenship in ways that harmonize logically inconsistent consensual and ascriptive elements has not ended. Most Americans still wish for their nation to provide rights and powers so that they can shape their own destinies, domestically and internationally, *and* for their forms of civic life to express a higher moral order that guides, but is beyond, human choice. Thus in the early 1990s Republicans still stood for expansive economic liberties; the ardent, sometimes militaristic patriotism characteristic of republicanism; and the traditional Christian or "Judeo-Christian" cultural values that some advocates see as divine mandates. Democrats advocated expansive civil liberties, along with further democratization of political processes. They also invoked social gospel reform traditions espoused by religious Progressives and modern civil rights activists to sanction their vision of America's special character. Both, then, continued to blend versions of liberal, republican and ascriptive Americanist themes.

All those themes were, to be sure, significantly modified by twentieth-century political and intellectual developments, especially after World War II. Most importantly, overt racial and gender hierarchies became widely discredited and more directly democratic forms of self-government gained prestige. The resulting changes in American citizenship were again momentous: the outlawing of all public and some private racial discrimination, greater protection for voting rights, the end of national origins quotas in immigration and of many legal discriminations against women, and other reforms, largely enacted during the 1960s. American citizenship laws looked more fully liberal and democratic, less ascriptive and hierarchical, than ever before.

Yet, even as Americans have moved away from doctrines holding that only one biological race and gender fit people to be full American citizens, many have increasingly accepted the view that people are shaped by cultural forces giving them distinct, largely unalterable identities, as African Americans, Asian Americans, Latinos, fundamentalist Christians, or scarred members of an "underclass." Most Americans profess to favor equal respect for all cultural communities within the U.S. but many exhibit rising concern that their community may be eclipsed or harmed by others. Controversies over CULTURAL PLURALISM AND MULTICULTURALISM, affirmative action, bilingualism, immigration restriction, gay rights, the role of women, the place of religion in schools and public policies, and the transparent racial appeals made by prominent extremists such as Pat Buchanan and Louis Farrakhan all suggest that Americans may long struggle over the transformations in American civic life wrought by the reforms of the 1960s. American conflicts over civic membership have also never failed to be affected by international trends. Disturbingly, the post-Cold War international environment at least initially provided fertile ground for various forms of religious fundamentalism and exclusionary nationalism.

These persistent problems show that Americans have yet to succeed fully even in conceiving of citizenship in ways that supply all they wish their political identities to provide. To do so, it seems, American citizenship would have to be at once a continual product of collective political choices that genuinely promotes a wide range of opportunities for all, and an embodiment of transcendental standards that give it worth above and beyond its possessors' always uncertain decisions and achievements.

That bill remains hard to fill. Yet ironically, American citizenship has in fact been both an ongoing, partly conscious and consensual collective creation (shaped by far more participants than the old textbooks acknowledged), and a product of historical traditions and imperatives that extend before and beyond the lives of any of its members. Perhaps through full recognition of that reality, Americans and other peoples might perceive how they can choose to shape their political destinies in ways that fulfill what appear on reflection to be the deepest, wisest, and most enduring values discernible in the world in which they find themselves.

ROGERS M. SMITH

See also ASSIMILATION.

FURTHER READING

Joyce Appleby, *Liberalism and Republicanism in the Historical Imagination* (Cambridge: Harvard University Press, 1992).

Kenneth L. Karst, *Belonging to America: Equal Citizenship and the Constitution* (New Haven: Yale University Press, 1989).

James H. Kettner, *The Development of American Citizenship, 1608–1780* (Chapel Hill: University of North Carolina Press, 1980).

H. Mark Roelofs, *The Tension of Citizenship: Private Men and Public Duty* (New York: Rinehart, 1957).

Judith N. Shklar, *American Citizenship: the Quest for Inclusion* (Cambridge: Harvard University Press, 1991).

Rogers M. Smith, "Beyond Tocqueville, Myrdal, and Hartz: Multiple Traditions in America," *American Political Science Review* 87 (Sept. 1993): 549–66.

civil rights The intellectual dimensions of the civil rights movement have been relatively neglected for at least two reasons: first, some scholars suspect that intellectual history is intrinsically elitist and that the history of the movement should be written as "history from the bottom up"; and second, some prefer to distance a predominantly African American movement from "white" and "bourgeois" modes of thought. Although theoretical issues arising from the movement provide one of the central elements of CRITICAL LEGAL STUDIES, and the intellectual development of MARTIN LUTHER KING JR. has received considerable attention, this problem persists. Keith Miller's *Voices of Deliverance* (1992), for example, argues that black southern religious culture, not formal political and theological training, was the primary force in the shaping of King's thought.

Such a claim, however, depends on rigid oppositions between (white) European and Afro-American cultures, between "high" intellectual systems and folk-cultural traditions. A more fruitful approach is to stress the ways in which political concepts were implemented through movement activities, while showing how motifs in the cultural experience of movement participants were articulated as ideas as the movement developed. From this perspective, a figure such as King would be a representative voice, mediating between the two sites of intellectual and cultural experience.

To reconstruct the conceptual genealogy of the movement, attention should fall, first, upon what Vincent Harding has called the "great tradition" of secular RIGHTS theories from the eighteenth-century revolutionary traditions of America, France, and Haiti, along with the African American transformation of the Exodus story into an explicitly political narrative of collective chosenness and group liberation. As with the abolitionist movement, the civil rights movement—and not just King—appealed to rights, stated or implied in the Declaration of Independence and the Constitution, particularly the First Amendment and the Reconstruction Amendments. Central themes of American legal and political culture were obviously crucial to the arguments of lawyers of the National Association for the Advancement of Colored People against "separate but equal" as a constitutional principle and to King's "Letter from Birmingham Jail" (1963). Such themes also pervade the testimony given by grass-roots participants in the movement concerning their own experience. The rhetoric of freedom in the movement derived also from the biblical tradition's emphasis upon collective liberation from the bondage of slavery and then segregation. Spirituals were translated into "freedom songs," which became vehicles for collective self-understanding, manifestos of political action set to music.

Yet another intellectual tradition was also powerfully at work in the movement. The libertarian notion of civil disobedience articulated by Thoreau was later taken up by Gandhi and given collective form. The idea of civil disobedience then reentered the intellectual and strategic arsenal of the movement, first through the efforts of pioneers of nonviolent direct action such as A. J. Muste and Bayard Rustin, and then later thanks to Martin Luther King and the college students who made up the Student Nonviolent Coordinating Committee (SNCC). If the idea of collective civil disobedience was crucial in the early

stages of the movement, the work of Frantz Fanon (as well as the personal example of MALCOLM X) had a considerable impact on movement radicals beginning in the mid-1960s. It was then that the ideology of nonviolent direct action gave way to the idea of redemptive and therapeutic violence in the black liberation struggle.

Finally, again through King and student activists, contemporary theological and philosophical ideas often informed movement thought and practice. The Social Gospel and Protestant neo-orthodoxy, as found in the writings of REINHOLD NIEBUHR, created a fruitful tension in King's thinking about the political relevance of Christianity and the coercive dimension of nonviolence. Marxism played a relatively small role in movement thinking, at least in its early phases. More important were traditions of sociology and social policy deriving from the work of E. Franklin Frazier and W. E. B. DU BOIS, as well as from Gunnar Myrdal's social democratic analysis of America's dilemma, all of which were part of an emerging intellectual consensus in the postwar world as to the causes of and cures for America's racial divisions. Finally the existentialist writings of Jean-Paul Sartre and Albert Camus offered a vocabulary in which to formulate ideas of action and identity, violence and nonviolence, that proved particularly attractive to many students involved in the movement.

Although much of this intellectual background has been acknowledged, if not closely analyzed, less has been written about the intellectual legacy of the movement. Future intellectual historians will need, for instance, to pay more attention to the ideological continuities between the movement and the black power/consciousness/aesthetic nexus. Simply counterposing Martin Luther King and Malcolm X does little to illuminate this issue. One crucial connection was the emphasis upon black self-respect and collective self-transformation; this will require careful examination.

There is a clear, if undeveloped, link between the civil rights experience and the explosion of Afro-American historiography beginning in the late 1960s. August Meier and Elliot Rudwick's *Black History and the History Profession, 1915–1980* (1986) is a valuable beginning in this area. But much work remains to be done on the traditions of black history and black sociology in black colleges and universities (and the segregated black school systems) in the South in the 1950s and 1960s. Indeed, the importance of movement citizenship and freedom schools as instruments of political education (including the teaching of black history) remains a largely untold story.

Most neglected have been the implications of

the civil rights movement for mainstream political theory. Black power ideologies have made ample use of Marxist and nationalist ideologies. In addition, African American thinkers such as Cornel West, Bernard Boxill, Adolph Reed, and Laurence Thomas have drawn upon, as well as analyzed, the ideological legacy of the movement in general terms. But the full potential of the civil rights movement (along with the other radical movements of the 1960s) to enrich contemporary liberal and communitarian political thought has scarcely been realized. JOHN RAWLS did acknowledge King's importance in *A Theory of Justice* (1971), while Ronald Dworkin's *Taking Rights Seriously* (1977) is unimaginable without the example of movements which had done just that. But generally, ideas central to "bourgeois" political theory—rights, equality, justice, and especially freedom—could gain in specificity if informed by the history of the civil rights movement. Indeed, the same could be said, even more forcefully, about the "process" concepts of political theory—solidarity, self-respect, participation, and even politics itself. In sum, the civil rights movement presents an opportunity to see the central ideas of liberal political theory operate oppositionally, while closer attention to the civil rights experience might also go a long way toward counteracting what Richard Rorty has referred to as the "terminal wistfulness" of recent communitarian thought.

RICHARD H. KING

FURTHER READING

John Ansboro, *Martin Luther King, Jr.: the Making of a Mind* (Maryknoll, N.Y.: Orbis, 1982).

Clayborne Carson, *In Struggle: SNCC and the Black Awakening in the 1960s* (Cambridge: Harvard University Press, 1981).

V. P. Franklin, *Black Self-Determination* (Westport, Conn.: Lawrence Hill, 1984).

Vincent Harding, *There is a River* (New York: Vintage, 1981).

Leonard Harris, *Philosophy Born of Struggle: an Anthology of Afro-American Philosophy from 1917* (Dubuque: Kendall Hunt, 1983).

Richard H. King, *Civil Rights and the Idea of Freedom* (New York: Oxford University Press, 1992).

August Meier and Elliott Rudwick, *Black History and the History Profession, 1915–1986* (Urbana: University of Illinois Press, 1986).

Keith Miller, *Voice of Deliverance: the Language of Martin Luther King, Jr. and Its Sources* (New York: Free Press, 1992).

Civil War Americans have long expected their Civil War to produce profound art and thought. "A great literature will yet arise out of the era of these four years," Walt Whitman predicted in 1879, "an inexhaustible mine for the histories, drama, romance and even philosophy, of peoples to come—indeed the vertebrae of poetry and art for all future Americans." But even as histories, novels, and films by the hundreds have been mined from the Civil War, Americans wait still for the Homer or Shakespeare that Whitman confidently expected to emerge. Despite the mountain of words written about the years of conflict between 1861 and 1865, the Civil War somehow seems unconsummated in the American imagination. A visitor to a battlefield in the title story of Bobbie Ann Mason's 1982 collection, *Shiloh*, cannot help but think that the landscape "looks like a subdivision site." He "tries to focus on the fact that thirty-five hundred soldiers died on the grounds around him. He can only think of that war as a board game with plastic soldiers" (pp. 15–16).

Although such feelings of disconnection are apparently widespread—many high school students, polls show, cannot tell within a quarter century the date of the war—in some ways the Civil War has never been more popular. Historians, indeed, may look back on the late 1980s and early 1990s as a golden age for portrayals of the war. James McPherson's *Battle Cry of Freedom* scaled the bestseller lists; Ken Burns's Civil War series pulled in the largest audience in the history of public television; the film *Glory* introduced millions to the gallantry of black soldiers. Colorful monthly magazines pore over the military aspects of the war as if they were today's news; men and women go to elaborate lengths to reenact battles and camp life; Civil War roundtables meet across the country to debate one campaign or maneuver yet again. The interest of these passionate amateurs shows no sign of flagging.

Coincidentally or not, for several decades the Civil War has been something of a scholarly and artistic backwater. The sentimentality with which the war has long been presented discredits it in the eyes of many intellectuals; the military aspects appeal little to thinkers of the avant-garde; the profusion of popular scholarship challenges and annoys professionals used to unquestioned authority. No important visual artists and no major writers of innovative fiction have recently turned their energies toward the war. The trends of historical scholarship since World War II have largely bypassed the Civil War, the focus on social structures and long-term processes leading many young historians to view the war with an indifference bordering on contempt. The work that has been undertaken is cautious in style and content.

Such a state of affairs stands in sharp contrast to previous eras. The war was, of course, refought in sectional terms from the day the guns stopped, the North glorying in its moral virtue, the South seeking solace in battlefield bravery and high-minded devotion to a lost cause. But there were other voices as well. Ambrose Bierce's *Tales of Soldiers and Civilians* (1891) and Stephen Crane's *Red Badge of Courage* (1895) brought skepticism to bear on the holy events of 30 years earlier, casting them in a light far harsher than the sentimental glow of other contemporary accounts. The era between the world wars saw novels such as Evelyn Scott's *The Wave* (1929) and William Faulkner's *Absalom, Absalom!* (1936) explore the Civil War through multiple perspectives and narrative invention. In the 1930s and early 1940s historians such as James G. Randall and Avery O. Craven brought the aims and value of the war into question, challenging the inevitability of the conflict and the efficacy of any warfare to solve social problems. Such revisionist views exerted great influence in the years between the Versailles Treaty (1919) and the Potsdam Conference (1945). The film version of *Gone with the Wind* seemed to fit this mood quite well, supplying sympathy for a paternalistic southern elite and condemnation of an intrusive Reconstruction.

All but this most sentimental mode of revisionism, however, came under attack as World War II blurred into the Cold War. Americans' experience with Hitler and Stalin made questioning the war appear misguided, unpatriotic. In a 1949 article in *Partisan Review*, Arthur Schlesinger Jr. chastised the revisionists, whose vogue, he suggested, was "the offspring of our modern sentimentality which at once evades the essential moral problems in the name of a superficial objectivity and asserts their unimportance in the name of an invincible progress" (pp. 969–81). Whether out of a deeper sense of the tragedy and limits in history or because of an atrophied historical imagination, the question of the Civil War's inevitability or value no longer seemed debatable. Hitler's horrific use of "race" as the measure of human worth recast the way many educated Americans thought about the Civil War, making it appear less about INDUSTRIALISM versus agrarianism, less about modernity versus tradition, than about slavery versus freedom. The events of the early CIVIL RIGHTS movement sharpened that perspective, suddenly forcing white attention to black aspiration, a facet of the war that had been subordinated in white memory since the days Reconstruction ended. Together, the twin themes of nationalism and racial progress bestowed on the war an aura of destiny and benevolence it had not enjoyed in prior years.

Those who write for a wide readership now seem to assume that the war was inevitable, that it grew out of deeply rooted divisions between ANTISLAVERY in the North and PROSLAVERY THOUGHT in the South, that a unified American nationalism was ultimately worth the sacrifices made in its name, that the war, rather than a mere political victory for the North, was morally redemptive for the nation as a whole. Debate has come to focus on important but subordinate issues: the timing of the war's outbreak, the depth of the North's opposition to slavery, the relative importance of various battles, generals, or fronts, the reason the South lost. The white South is still permitted praise for its courage on the battlefield, a certain quixotic idealism, a high-mindedness of a deluded sort, but is discredited in virtually every other respect. The South lost whatever claim it had on the nation's sympathy when distinctions between quality folk and plain folk no longer seemed to matter, when paternalistic masters seemed not much better than callous ones.

Within the limits of these ideas, repeated so often as to have become virtually unquestioned, people have written powerful works of imagination and scholarship. Historians began preparing for the centennial of the war in the early 1950s, turning out numerous books of military history. Authors such as Bruce Catton and T. Harry Williams wrote popular histories of Northern armies and leaders, histories that sold in enormous numbers; Bell Wiley's pioneering 1943 social history of *The Life of Johnny Reb* was followed by a companion piece on Billy Yank in 1952. So great was the outpouring of books in the late 1950s and early 1960s, in fact, that the public's interest in the centennial seems to have peaked a bit too early, leading to disappointing sales later in the decade. Independent thinkers such as David Potter began to test the waters of revisionism again in the 1960s, but more cautiously than their predecessors, more wary of appearing unappreciative of what had been won in the war.

Shelby Foote, a novelist who planned a brief history of the Civil War for the centennial, found his subject far deeper and wider than he had anticipated; an enterprise that he had envisioned taking a few years ended up taking twenty, the expected few hundred pages growing tenfold. Foote, a white Mississippian, published the first volume of his *The Civil War: A Narrative* in 1958; the second volume appeared in 1963 and the third in 1974. Foote wove the most complex and subtle narrative of events on the battlefield that has been written. Blending his own voice with those he found in the records, Foote dramatized the stories of every major battle and many lesser ones. The organizing principle was time itself, events following one another in the logic and illogic of sequence, accident, and personality. Foote's narrative was one, by and large, of the battlefield, his interpretation inseparable from description. Foote's work won a wide audience early and maintained its appeal through the tumult of the 1960s and 1970s. The writing—evenhanded, restrained, and focused tightly on the military aspects of the war—contained little to date it.

A steady flow of books and articles on the Civil War continued through the 1970s and 1980s, though the subject proved at first an unappealing topic to historians attuned to the *Annales* school, to family reconstruction, to social science history, to cliometrics, to women's history. David Potter's masterpiece, *The Impending Crisis*, completed by Don Fehrenbacher after Potter's death and published in 1976, was widely recognized as a culmination of an older tradition of political narrative; people admired Potter's book but showed no desire to emulate it. Even the exciting advances in the study of the Old South did not lead to a broad reconsideration of the Civil War. Indeed, as historians such as Eugene Genovese revealed just how integral slavery was to every aspect of the white South, the war came to seem inevitable, necessary. Genovese scoffed at the notions that white Southerners felt guilty, or that anything other than slavery could have accounted for the white South's suicidal war. Eric Foner's complementary portrayal of the power of free labor ideology in the North buttressed the view that North and South were fundamentally different, that war could hardly have been avoided. A widespread and heated debate raged over C. Vann Woodward's portrayal of defeat and emancipation as fundamental breaks in the South's history, but the war itself did not come in for much reconsideration. Historians such as J. Mills Thornton and Michael Holt, who focused on the political events of the 1850s, proved more skeptical of sharp dichotomies between the regions, as did postrevisionist students of Reconstruction. Historians found wartime societies on both sides of the conflict deeply at odds with themselves, ridden with class, ethnic, and political conflict.

Few historians, then, would have anticipated that the Civil War volume in the Oxford History of the United States, appearing in 1988, would quickly climb to the very top of the nation's bestseller lists. Its author, James McPherson, a northerner teaching at Princeton, presented a one-volume history of the Civil War that fell comfortably within the contours of the post-World War II interpretation. The North appeared as a pioneering modern society, the South as a backward place retarded in every aspect by its dedication to slavery; the title, *Battle Cry of Freedom*, carried little irony. McPherson's book was a masterful account of events on the battlefield and, to a lesser

extent, events in the capitals of North and South; it had little to say about life on the home front, about women, or about the slaves who slowly became the focus of the war. It was just what many readers wanted, apparently, an authoritative and relatively unproblematic account of the war.

Even the success of McPherson's book was overshadowed by what is certainly the most remarkable event in contemporary treatments of the Civil War: Ken Burns's ten-part series of the Public Broadcasting System, televised in 1990. Millions of people appeared to be transfixed by the images, music, and voices on the screen. The war took on an immediacy for many people it had never had before; the plastic soldiers of the country's imagination became flesh and blood. An American people lonely for a living history welcomed the soldiers and civilians of Burns's series into their homes. One key to Burns's success was his technique of panning slowly over a photograph as an actor read words the person on the screen had spoken or written. Others were his focus on a few relatively anonymous men and women, his searing portrayal of slavery, his unflinching view of the horrors of the battlefields, hospitals, and prisoner-of-war camps.

"Historians delight in telling us what our history is and what it means," Burns commented in the introduction to Ward's *The Civil War: an Illustrated History*, the bestselling book drawn from the series. "The documentarian, on the other hand, as often delights in recording and conveying the simple fact that we have had a history at all: that there was a time when people looked like this, or sounded like that, or felt these ways about such things" (p. xvii). Some professional historians complained that the series had made the "simple facts" of the Civil War too simple, reducing complexities and ambiguities to false clarity, reducing ideology and culture to personality. Indeed, the complex events that led to sectional estrangement and the Southern decision to secede were reduced to a straightforward moral conflict over slavery. All questions of interpretation, both in the series and in the book, were left to professional historians. Shelby Foote became a national celebrity, his spots on the show becoming for many the most memorable moments; his own trilogy, completed 16 years before, became a bestseller once again. Barbara Fields, a historian from Columbia University, emerged as a mesmerizing presence as well, speaking with unrehearsed eloquence on the way the war became a struggle for black freedom.

Recent scholarly accounts of the Civil War take a darker view of its causes and consequences than appear in the works of McPherson and Burns. Phillip

Paludan's account of the killing of Unionists in the southern mountains, Michael Fellman's account of brutal guerrilla warfare in Missouri, Iver Bernstein's account of the New York City draft riots, Grace Paladino's account of the conflicts surrounding the Pennsylvania coalfields, George Rable's and Catherine Clinton's accounts of women during the war—all complicate the images of the nationalist school. The year after the PBS series, Charles Royster published *The Destructive War*, a book that cast the conflict in an especially troubling light. Royster, elaborating on themes enunciated in earlier decades by Robert Penn Warren and others, emphasized Americans' refusal to accept limits, their great impatience, their unquestioning allegiance to ideas and expectations rather than experience, their quick recourse to violence, their belief that history could be bullied into the course they thought it should follow. Royster found a widespread longing for bloody and vengeful destruction throughout the northern and southern populace as the war began. The mass killing of the war, rather than being isolated from what came before and after, seemed to grow out of a strain of violence endemic in American life, its butchery showing the failure rather than the success of highly touted generals, its fascination with technology and the delusions of national righteousness and invincibility shaping American foreign policy and war-making ever since. The most recent studies of both the North and the South, in sum, do not portray self-confident, unified civilizations on collision courses, but rather ambivalent, almost neurotic, societies filled with unresolved conflicts thrown into motion and visibility by the war.

Such views are a necessary corrective. While the nationalist perspective rightly insists upon the centrality of slavery to the Southern cause, it tends to foreshorten and simplify the moral and political complexities of the war. The effect of that simplification is to simplify other conflicts as well, defining good and evil with a dangerous certainty, identifying the United States as the agent of God's will, as the beneficiary of the inevitable course of history. Even as we recognize the greatness of the freedom won in our Civil War, we might be wary of the tendency to find redemption for the American nation in its bloodiest years.

EDWARD L. AYERS

See also ABRAHAM LINCOLN.

FURTHER READING
Shelby Foote, *The Civil War: a Narrative*, 3 vols. (New York: Random House, 1958, 1963, 1974).
James McPherson, *Battle Cry of Freedom: the Civil War Era* (New York: Oxford University Press, 1988).
Bobbie Ann Mason, *Shiloh and Other Stories* (New York: Harper and Row, 1982).
Charles Royster, *The Destructive War: William Tecumseh Sherman, Stonewall Jackson, and the Americans* (New York: Knopf, 1991).
Kenneth Stampp, ed., *The Causes of the Civil War* (New York: Simon and Schuster, 1991); also reprints the 1949 article by Arthur Schlesinger Jr.
Geoffrey C. Ward, *The Civil War: an Illustrated History* (New York: Knopf, 1990).

Clark, John Bates (b. Providence, R.I., Jan. 26, 1847; d. New York, N.Y., Mar. 21, 1938).   Economist. One of the founders of the American Economic Association (1885), Clark brought some German historical methods to a field previously dominated by rigidly abstract thinking. *The Philosophy of Wealth* (1885) expressed a vigorous reformist orientation, while his major work, *The Distribution of Wealth* (1899), contributed significantly to the emerging science of economics. Applying the theory of diminishing marginal returns to the factors of production (labor and capital/land), he concluded that as one factor increases relative to others, its additional productivity per unit declines. In a static state, factors distribute themselves to maximize productivity.

See also SOCIAL SCIENCE.

FURTHER READING
Dorothy Ross, *The Origins of American Social Science* (New York: Cambridge University Press, 1991).

class   The term acquired its modern meaning between 1770 and 1840, as a concept to make sense of the social groupings spawned by the industrial revolution. In Marxist theory, one's class derived from one's relationship to the means of producing socially necessary goods; class conflict within capitalism pitted factory owners, who controlled the means of production, against workers, who had only their labor power to sell. But Marx also distinguished between class "in itself" (an economic category) and class "for itself" (a formation that emerges when people become conscious of their situation and develop the organization to deal with it). In common usage class refers both to objective categories and subjective states. This ambiguity has led to ongoing arguments over the difference between class and class consciousness and over the significance of solidarities that may not manifest themselves in common political aims. More recently, debate has swirled around the question of how class is conditioned by RACE, ETHNICITY, and GENDER.

Until the 1960s, most mainstream scholars in the United States took their cues not from Karl Marx but from Max Weber, who emphasized the importance of social rankings that did not necessarily correspond to economically determined classes. In a country where abundant land, social mobility, and a devotion to Lockean liberalism blunted class consciousness, they argued, social divisions rested on perceived status rather than on relationships of production. In the Weberian view American workers, content with climbing incrementally up the status ladder, lacked the class consciousness that inspired socialist revolutions, labor parties, and powerful trade union movements around the world. The counter-tradition of Marxism, which flourished mainly in the 1930s, reached its nadir in the 1950s, under the combined pressures of prosperity and Cold War ideology. Its revival in the 1960s, in turn, owed much to that era's social strife.

Rejecting liberal assumptions about a consensual, classless society, New Left activists and scholars looked to a humanistic Marxism purged of the economic determinism they associated with their predecessors on the left. For many university-based radicals, the work of the British labor historian E. P. Thompson provided just such a revisionist model. Class, Thompson argued in *The Making of the English Working Class*, is "something which in fact happens . . . in human relationships" (p. 9). It is a way of perceiving oneself in relation to others, not an economic category or an automatic outcome of economic relations.

Feminists, meanwhile, offered their own revisions of Marxist theory. They pointed out that Marx's concept of class could not explain the virtually universal, yet historically variable, subordination of women. The problem lay partly with Marxists' emphasis on production, which led them to ignore conflicts over the socially necessary work of childbearing and rearing. Introducing the concept of social reproduction, feminists argued that the cultural creation of human beings was as important to the social order as the production of things. Yet because under capitalism this traditional form of women's labor took place largely outside the marketplace, it did not appear to be real work. Both capitalists and male workers benefited from this arrangement— capitalists because women served as a reservoir of cheap labor and because their unpaid work in the home made it possible for working-class families to survive on subsistence wages, working-class men because they were freed both from domestic responsibilities and from job competition with women. For women, the sexual division of reproductive labor had a circular effect. It put them at a disadvantage in the paid workforce, and that disadvantage reinforced their subordination to men. Women whose wage labor

consisted of performing domestic tasks in the homes of others were particularly marginalized by the distinction between the reproduction of people and the production of things.

The "new labor history" that emerged out of this intellectual ferment produced rich empirical studies of diverse working-class communities, cultures, and radicalisms, but the forest was soon obscured by the trees. In search of a synthesis, labor historians seized on "republicanism" as their unifying theme. In the United States, they argued, class conflict grew not just from economic exploitation but from a clash between, on the one hand, the ideals of independence, mutuality, and virtue that had animated the American Revolution and, on the other, the authoritarian work discipline imposed by capitalism.

In the 1990s this emphasis on republicanism as the key to American working-class consciousness attracted critical scrutiny from several quarters. John Diggins reasserted the view that American workers, for all their use of republican rhetoric, had always been acquisitive individualists. Feminists pointed out that the republican emphasis on manly independence and productivity excluded women, who were by definition dependent and relegated to the realm of reproduction. Similarly, historians emphasized republicanism's racist effects. Barbara Fields, building on the work of Edmund Morgan, argued that slavery was a means of class exploitation; the ideology of race arose later, as a way of justifying enslavement in a society officially based on republican ideals. Students of white working-class racism asserted that in the United States class identity was intimately bound up with whiteness: working-class manhood was construed in opposition to black servility as well as to female dependency. Blacks and women thus served as negative reference groups; compensated by the public deference they enjoyed on account of their race and sex, white male workers tended not to see wage labor itself as degradation.

This disillusionment with republicanism dovetailed with a more general flight from class analysis. Faith in traditional working-class movements crumbled along with the decline of SOCIALISM and the waning of organized labor, and leftists looked increasingly to popular social movements organized around issues of race, gender, or sexuality as the best hope for progressive change. At the same time, the circulation of theories broadly captured by the term poststructuralism armed scholars with a panoply of new conceptual tools. Especially challenging to economistic approaches was the work of Michel Foucault, who traced modern forms of domination not so much to the spread of capitalism as to the emergence of new types of knowledge. Power, in Foucault's formulation, was not concentrated in the hands of a bourgeois ruling class; exercised through techniques of surveillance perfected by the social sciences, it was diffused throughout society and anchored in everyday social practices.

Feminist scholars, drawing on poststructuralism and discouraged by Marxists' persistent inattention to gender, became less interested in what has been termed a "dual systems approach"—the attempt to trace the interaction between patriarchy and capitalism, or between the sexual division of reproductive labor and job segregation by sex—and more concerned with how symbolic representations of gender differences shape all hierarchical relationships. Joan Wallach Scott, for example, attacked labor historians for their allegiance to the notion that class was, at bottom, immanent in productive relations. Despite their efforts to distance themselves from economic determinism, she believed, even Thompsonian post-Marxists had left Marx's base/superstructure, production/reproduction dichotomies intact. They continued to assign gender to the ideological superstructure and thus to marginalize women, and they underestimated the degree to which class itself was created by language and systems of discourse.

Such criticisms and defections notwithstanding, advocates of class analysis by no means conceded the field. Feminist scholars such as Louise Tilly reasserted the importance of materialist perspectives. Labor historian Bryan Palmer called for resistance to poststructuralist theories that ignore the material effects of economic power. Essayist Benjamin DeMott insisted that government regulations and programs in every area of social life "ordain class advantages and disadvantages" (p. 230). Sociologists Reeve Vanneman and Lynn Weber Cannon marshaled extensive survey data to dispute the assumption that contemporary Americans lack class consciousness. Workers, they found, draw clear distinctions between themselves and a middle class that includes not only those who own productive property—the bourgeoisie of classic Marxist theory—but also the salaried managers and professionals who enjoy the advantages of supervisory authority, mental labor, and control over the design of work.

Much of this discussion about the place of class in American history and society was confined to the academy. The question of how class figures in the African American experience, however, sparked heated public debate. In *The Declining Significance of Race* (1978), William Julius Wilson claimed that African Americans in the late twentieth century comprise an "underclass" disabled more by social pathologies and structural economic problems than by discrimination. His ideas were taken up by commentators such as Jim Sleeper who minimized the salience of racism in American life. They argued that the Democratic Party had forfeited its white middle-class and blue-collar base by kowtowing to the special interests of blacks and women. In order to wrest power from the Republicans, they insisted, the Democrats should abandon the rhetoric of racial liberalism and pursue race-blind policies of economic regeneration.

Cornel West and other radical black intellectuals, on the other hand, rejected both the underclass theory and the dichotomizing of class and race. In the African American community, they maintained, racial discrimination and class inequality reinforce one another; insisting on the centrality of race does not require a disregard for class, nor does it entail ignoring the class oppression suffered by many whites. Indeed, the presumption that in America only blacks are poor has had pernicious effects. It discourages poor whites from making common cause with blacks and invites whites in general to blame the plight of the poor on racial inferiority or a "culture of poverty" rather than on public policies and economic forces. "Perhaps Americans will never overcome their endemic pathology of race," David Brion Davis concluded in "The American Dilemma," "until they are finally able to confront both the underlying reality of class divisions in America and the destructive myth of a classless society" (p. 17).

It is difficult to predict the future of class—as a determinant of life chances, a basis for political conflict, or a category of analysis. Taken together, however, the decline of blue-collar labor and the rise of service and sales occupations, the numerical domination of the work force by women and ethnic and racial minorities, and the globalization of the economy seem certain to render some older forms of class action and class analysis obsolete. New ways of theorizing power relations will have to take those profound transformations into account, as will new progressive coalitions.

Recent developments in narrative theory may help to forward that project. Carolyn Steedman, in *Landscape for a Good Woman*, an evocative working-class memoir, contends that class is a "structure of feeling that can be learned in childhood" (p. 7). Class, viewed from this perspective, is a complex subjective identity, rooted in material relations but also created through dialogue, through the stories people tell about themselves. How, then, are feelings of difference, deprivation, and desire "storied" and thus transmitted? How do they figure in the narratives that construct identity and inspire social action? And how are those narratives linked to the discursive and institutional networks in which we find ourselves, networks that stretch from particular families, workplaces, and communities to international capital–labor arrangements? The emergence of such questions in cultural studies, just as poststructuralism seemed to trump class analysis, suggests that class issues will retain their urgency, whatever the vicissitudes of labor movements and academic debates.

JACQUELYN DOWD HALL

See also INDUSTRIALISM; POSTMODERNISM; REPUBLICANISM; SOCIAL MOBILITY.

FURTHER READING

David Brion Davis, "The American Dilemma," *New York Review of Books* 39 (July 16, 1992): 13–17.

Benjamin DeMott, *The Imperial Middle: Why Americans Can't Think Straight About Class* (New York: William Morrow, 1990).

Barbara J. Fields, "Slavery, Race and Ideology in the United States of America," *New Left Review* 181 (May–June 1990): 95–118.

Bryan D. Palmer, *Descent into Discourse: the Reification of Language and the Writing of Social History* (Philadelphia: Temple University Press, 1990).

David R. Roediger, *The Wages of Whiteness: Race and the Making of the American Working Class* (London: Verso, 1992).

Joan Wallach Scott, *Gender and the Politics of History* (New York: Columbia University Press, 1988).

William H. Sewell Jr., "Introduction: Narratives and Social Identities," *Social Science History* 16 (fall 1992): 479–88.

Carolyn Kay Steedman, *Landscape for a Good Woman: a Story of Two Lives* (New Brunswick: Rutgers University Press, 1987).

E. P. Thompson, *The Making of the English Working Class* (1963; New York: Vintage, 1966).

Reeve Vanneman and Lynn Weber Cannon, *The American Perception of Class* (Philadelphia: Temple University Press, 1987).

William Julius Wilson, *The Declining Significance of Race: Blacks and Changing American Institutions* (Chicago: University of Chicago Press, 1978).

Clay, Henry (b. Hanover County, Va., Apr. 12, 1777; d. Washington, D.C., June 29, 1852). Political leader. Repeatedly elected to the Senate and the House of Representatives from Kentucky, Clay sought to unify the nation through an aggressive program of industrial development. His "American System" included a protective tariff, national bank, and federal financing of internal improvements, especially transportation. The resulting regional interdependency would, he hoped, make the nation independent of foreign trade. Although himself a slaveholder, Clay endorsed gradual emancipation and colonization of blacks in Africa. His primary commitment, however, was to the preservation of the Union, and he became known as "the Great Compromiser" for his efforts to reduce regional antagonisms through political means. He was a major advocate of the Missouri Compromise (1820) and the Compromise of 1850.

FURTHER READING

Robert Remini, *Henry Clay: Statesman for the Union* (New York: Norton, 1991).

Cohen, Morris (b. Minsk, Russia, July 25, 1880; d. Washington, D.C., Jan. 28, 1947). Philosopher. A dominant figure in New York intellectual life during the 1920s and 1930s, Cohen was a founding father of the Jewish American intelligentsia so pivotal to twentieth-century American thought. His work in philosophy of science (such as *Reason and Nature*, 1931) and philosophy of law (*Law and the Social Order*, 1933) had considerable influence among contemporaries. For Cohen, liberalism was a protoscientific cognitive style—a *method* rather than an ideology. It provided a normative middle path between totalitarianisms of left and right, both of which displayed the triumph of politics over free inquiry.

See also LIBERALISM; NEW YORK INTELLECTUALS.

FURTHER READING

David A. Hollinger, *Morris R. Cohen and the Scientific Ideal* (Cambridge: MIT Press, 1975).

cold war The recent novelty of considering the Cold War to be past history allows us to grasp it as a central—perhaps *the* central—mode of national self-definition in the United States during the second half of the twentieth century. Fear of Soviet imperialism abroad and un-Americanism at home permeated American society and severely constricted political, economic, cultural, and intellectual possibilities. During the decades that followed World War II, complex problems of domestic and foreign policy were either neglected or distorted by an obsession with the conflict between the "Free World" and the "International Communist Conspiracy."

Such terms denote sharp polarization and, from the outset, the Cold War was defined as ideological combat without compromise. President Eisenhower, for example, pronounced it a battle over mutually exclusive concepts of human nature, a "war for the minds of men." Analysts of the conflict's origins and history were hardly immune from the pressure to choose sides in this war, a fact that turned interpreters into soldiers and their ideas into ammunition. From denunciations of Soviet authoritarianism in the late 1940s to the revisionism and neorevisionism of recent decades, Cold War scholarship has been forced into the Cold War mold, needlessly replicating its Manichaean vision and its metaphors of loyalty and treason. As a result, the complex historical meanings of capitalism, DEMOCRACY, and SOCIALISM have been caricatured rather than studied. Independent, critical thought about the Cold War was perhaps the Cold War's first and most serious casualty.

In the immediate aftermath of World War II, many liberal "realists" joined conservatives in applying to the Soviet Union the lesson learned in the war against fascism: aggression must never again be appeased or met with halfway measures. Because the Soviet Union was apparently bent on fomenting worldwide revolution, the appropriate response was a long-term military buildup, a willingness to go to war (as in Korea and Vietnam), and a wide-ranging ideological onslaught against Soviet tyranny. In 1947 GEORGE KENNAN framed this Cold War orthodoxy with his influential analysis of the deep historical roots of the Soviet imperial appetite. The United States, he predicted in "The Sources of Soviet Conduct," could hope for little beyond "firm and vigilant containment of Russian expansive tendencies" (p. 119). Pockets of resistance to the dominant view persisted among the Henry Wallace "Progressives," but they were roundly denounced by most respectable opinion.

Twenty years later, deep divisions over the Vietnam War revived doubts about the orthodox version of the Cold War. A revisionist school on the left, inspired by the work of diplomatic historian William Appleman Williams, recast the origins of superpower conflict. It emphasized the domestic and economic sources of American foreign policy and called into question the idea that America's actual international mission had been to defend democratic freedoms. Instead, American support for a series of repressive regimes in Vietnam and elsewhere in the Third World suggested that control over markets and access to foreign resources was the overriding factor shaping American foreign policy. This position turned rhetoric about the "free world" on its head. The postwar United States aimed to counter revolutionary impulses that threatened American economic hegemony, even when they promised democratization.

Linguist NOAM CHOMSKY has been an ardent proponent of the revisionist position for a quarter century. The Cold War, he argues, was a largely mythological war that afforded American policy-makers a convenient rationale to impose their will around the world while shielding their underlying political and economic strategy from open debate. John Lewis

Gaddis, representing a neorevisionist effort at even-handedness, has called for an end to the assignment of blame. He concludes nevertheless that the international order managed from Washington was less nefarious than the one managed from Moscow. American hegemony was, he asserts, "invited," whereas the Iron Curtain crashed down without regard for local sentiments (Hogan, p. 27).

Unable to agree on who was to blame for the Cold War, scholars now dispute the question of who, if anyone, won it and why. Scholars such as Samuel F. Wells Jr. have argued that the United States won the war because of the aggressive defense policies of Presidents Reagan and Bush during the 1980s, which provoked Gorbachev's reforms and the ultimate disintegration of the Soviet Union. But this view is contested by others—including even such conservatives as Richard Pipes—who accord Soviet domestic developments more salience than American sabre-rattling in explaining the demise of the Soviet state.

Whatever the role of American military policy in contributing to the end of the Cold War, some scholars wonder whether the outcome can be considered a "win." Among others, Richard Barnet (in Hogan) suggests that the notion of victory may not apply. The national security state developed to fight the Cold War jeopardized democratic political institutions, while huge defense budgets weakened the domestic economy. According to this view, Japan and Germany, vanquished in 1945 and barred from creating warfare states, may well emerge as the Cold War's ironic victors. But the unstable and dangerous international situation that has evolved during the early 1990s, founded on resurgent religious, ethnic, and national animosities, suggests that victory may have as hollow a ring for Germany and Japan as it does for the United States.

Surprisingly little work connects the vast literature on American foreign policy since World War II to examinations of the Cold War at home. Historians of McCarthyism and the old and new lefts have, of course, noticed congruities between geopolitics and the domestic exercise of power. Holding the global line against communism required rooting out communists on university campuses, as Ellen Schrecker has shown. And Maurice Isserman has argued that it led to the repression of movements, such as the Communist Party-USA and Students for a Democratic Society, which advocated either mild economic planning or radical redistribution, and to suspicion of campaigns for racial and gender equality.

Scholars interested in gender and sexuality have documented how even the private lives of citizens became weapons in the Cold War. Elaine Tyler May has illustrated that patriarchal domesticity promised to bolster national security by "containing" the unruly sexual energies that supposedly menaced the country's backbone. And John D'Emilio has shown how the "moral turpitude" of homosexuals focused the glare of superpower rivalry on the most intimate of relationships. President Truman's executive order banning gays from federal employment turned sexual conduct into a referendum on patriotism, compromised the civil liberties of millions, and blurred the distinction between private pleasure and public power.

The culture and politics of the Cold War have deeply molded all adult Americans. Now that the war is over, historians and other scholars can finally turn in earnest to the study of its causes and consequences. It is possible, however, that doing so may produce another major Cold War irony: the intellectual generation whose lives and ideas were most profoundly shaped by the Cold War era may be the one that ends up judging it to have been a noisy detour from the main line of history: the development of free-market states in an international order both stabilized and unsettled by economic competition and nationalistic rivalry.

ELLEN HERMAN

See also CONSENSUS; VIETNAM.

FURTHER READING

Noam Chomsky, *American Power and the New Mandarins* (New York: Vintage, 1967).

John D'Emilio, "The Homosexual Menace: the Politics of Sexuality in Cold War America," in D'Emilio, *Making Trouble: Essays on Gay History, Politics, and the University* (New York: Routledge, 1992).

John Lewis Gaddis, *The Long Peace: Inquiries into the History of the Cold War* (New York: Oxford University Press, 1987).

Michael J. Hogan, ed., *The End of the Cold War: Its Meanings and Implications* (New York: Cambridge University Press, 1992).

George F. Kennan, "The Sources of Soviet Conduct," in Kennan, *American Diplomacy*, expanded ed. (Chicago: University of Chicago Press, 1979).

Ellen W. Schrecker, *No Ivory Tower: McCarthyism and the Universities* (New York: Oxford University Press, 1986).

Elaine Tyler May, *Homeward Bound: American Families in the Cold War Era* (New York: Basic, 1988).

Samuel F. Wells Jr. and Robert S. Litwak, eds., *Strategic Defenses and Soviet–American Relations* (Cambridge: Ballinger, 1987).

colleges and universities   Throughout American history, colleges and universities have been among the nation's more important institutions of higher learning. In the eighteenth and nineteenth century,

learned societies, such as the American Philosophical Society, and in the twentieth century private or government-funded research institutes, such as the Carnegie Foundation and the National Institute of Health, have organized and promoted the dissemination and advancement of knowledge. Unlike European institutions of higher education, American colleges and universities of the past did not belong to a centralized, national system of EDUCATION. Until the present, they have been local institutions depending on regions or states (colonies until 1776) and their particular religious groups for students and financial support. Before the last part of the nineteenth century, the university was defined as an institution comprising several degree-granting faculties of higher learning, often called colleges or schools. In the twentieth century, the term university may apply as well to an institution that promotes higher learning in various fields by supporting research and the advancement of knowledge.

During the colonial period and through much of the nineteenth century, colleges that granted the B.A. degree were the primary institutions of formal higher education for a select portion of American young men. Before 1860, fewer than 1 percent of white men attended college, and these men might have been as young as 12 or as old as 24. Before the American Revolution and into the early nineteenth century, the colleges modeled their organization and curriculum after British universities. The required curriculum of classical languages, mathematics, natural philosophy, philosophy, ethics, and rhetoric prepared all graduates to play a leading role in public affairs, and about half of the graduates of colonial colleges entered the ministry. Colonial colleges drew students and faculties from their home colonies. From Harvard (1636) in Massachusetts to William and Mary (1693) in Virginia, colleges taught the doctrines and beliefs of the colony's dominant religious group through organized religious life and required courses.

The Enlightenment beliefs and republican ideas of the age of the American Revolution had a profound impact upon the older colleges and inspired as well the founding of numerous new colleges, including Dickinson (1773) in Pennsylvania, Bowdoin (1794) in Maine, and Williams (1800) in Massachusetts. At all colleges, professors adjusted course readings to support Patriot or Loyalist positions, and after the Revolution colleges often became bastions of belief for a political faction; for example Yale for the Federalists and the University of Virginia (1819) for Jeffersonian Republicans. Professors and presidents expected that colleges would educate young men in republican virtue, the knowledge that they should place national interest before self-interest. Despite the small percentage of white men attending college in the late eighteenth century, many graduates were influential in the founding of the new nation. Of the 55 men attending the 1787 Constitutional Convention, 33 had graduated from college.

At many late eighteenth-century colleges, especially those influenced most strongly by the Scottish Enlightenment, the more fervent religious beliefs of the colonial period yielded before the new spirit of liberalizing science; practical subjects such as agricultural science, modern history, and mathematics replaced or more usually modified the established curriculum. For instance, the anthem sung at the founding of Franklin College (1787) in Lancaster, Pennsylvania, proclaimed that "science" would join "with mild Religion." In other words, organized rational knowledge would coexist with faith. By 1800 only about 9 percent of college graduates were entering the ministry, while 50 percent were becoming lawyers.

During the nineteenth century, college founding continued in the East and in the newly settled western states, for example Wesleyan (1831) in Connecticut and Grinnell (1846) in Iowa. Most often these new colleges were sponsored by Protestant denominations inspired by the evangelical belief and energy of the antebellum years. Faculty and trustees wanted colleges to educate citizens who would help secure the Millennium, the second coming of Christ. While denouncing sectarianism in education, college professors nevertheless promoted their own religious beliefs. Students were required to attend chapel daily, and sometimes twice on Sundays, faculty members usually had to be members of a certain denomination, and the curriculum, both in its explicitly religious courses and in its secular courses, taught lessons supportive of that denomination's religious teachings. As in the colonial period, the largest number of college graduates pursued postgraduate theological study and entered the ministry, but many graduates, between 40 percent and 60 percent, also pursued postgraduate study of law or medicine, and a college degree gradually became a prerequisite for entry into these professions. Colleges often attracted young men from rural backgrounds and then sent graduates forth across the nation into various professions. Thus, in the nineteenth century, colleges joined the many forces making the United States a more unified country.

Meanwhile young men wishing to pursue college teaching as a profession learned that they had to pursue advanced studies in fields other than theology to participate in the transatlantic world of learning. Many aspiring professors traveled to Europe to pursue advanced studies in its universities. From 1840 to 1860, German scholarship, especially in the fields of biblical history, philology, and philosophy powerfully influenced prospective American scholars. From 1830 through 1860 almost every young professor at Yale College attended a German university for at least one year.

The late eighteenth-century debate about the desirability of a required college curriculum centering upon study of classical languages extended through the antebellum years and into the 1870s. On the one side, advocates argued that a college curriculum should include Latin and Greek as well as courses in the natural sciences, English literature, and European history. These advocates claimed such a curriculum was liberal because it transformed students into men of culture. Because college graduates would think broadly, and not narrowly according to the views of one political party or religious sect, they would be prepared to provide the political and cultural leadership for American democracy. On the other side, opponents of a curriculum based upon Latin and Greek said that college studies should become more practical, directly related to graduates' vocational ambitions. Short-lived reforms at the University of Virginia, Harvard, Amherst, and the University of Vermont fed this educational debate.

The proponents of practical education rejoiced when the Morrill Land Grant Act (1862) provided funding for state institutions of higher education that included schools of agriculture or the mechanic arts. The federal grants gave impetus to the founding or reform of many state universities. In Pennsylvania, the state transformed its agricultural college into Pennsylvania State University in 1874. In New York, Cornell University (1865) became the state land-grant institution. Cornell President Andrew Dickson White argued that pursuit of any studies, whether natural sciences or classical languages, could provide the basis of a liberal and liberalizing education.

The 1860s and 1870s were decades of significant change for American higher education. Until these decades a mere handful of institutions of higher education had admitted women and African Americans to their student bodies. These changes show that late nineteenth-century American educational leaders believed that African Americans should have their own professional class, and that colleges should prepare women either for professional employment thought appropriate for their womanly natures or for marriage to a professional. Also during these years educational leaders including Daniel Coit Gilman, G. STANLEY HALL, and James B. Angell proposed that American universities should have a higher purpose than the mere organization of learning; they could also promote the advancement of knowledge.

Before 1860 the few coeducational and women's colleges, for example Oberlin in Ohio (1833) and Georgia Female (1838), usually offered women students a course of literary studies. Then in the 1860s, the Civil War and Morrill Act encouraged both the admission of women to state universities, for instance Wisconsin in 1867 and Minnesota in 1869, and the founding of women's colleges, most notably Vassar (1861), Wellesley (1870), and Smith (1871). By 1872, women could attend 97 colleges and universities, and by 1880 women constituted one-third of all college and university students in the United States.

At both coeducational and single-sex institutions women followed curricula conforming to the gender conventions of the late nineteenth century, which expected them to become nurturers. Many pursued courses of study preparing them to be teachers, and about 70 percent of women graduates before 1900 held teaching positions. Male students and professors did not always welcome women to campus. Campus organizations usually were segregated by sex, and college rules limited women's access to libraries and chapels. By the first decades of the twentieth century these barriers to women's higher education were falling, although until the 1960s many presidents of women's colleges maintained that students should prepare themselves for the profession of MOTHERHOOD.

Before 1860 only 28 African Americans had earned B.A. degrees. With the end of the Civil War, African Americans and their northern abolitionist supporters started a campaign of college and university founding. Among the first institutions of higher education to focus on African Americans were Lincoln University (1865), first founded in 1854 as an academy, Fisk University (1866), and Atlanta University and Howard University (both 1867). Most of the new universities had preparatory schools to compensate for the minimal formal schooling that students had received in the South, where most states had banned the teaching of reading and writing to slaves. The universities also comprised undergraduate colleges and schools of medicine, law, and theology. While institutes such as Hampton in Virginia and Tuskegee in Alabama offered vocational programs for African American students, the university colleges offered a traditional liberal arts curriculum resembling that of other leading colleges. The new colleges were supposed to supply the professionals to serve and lead a free African American community. These universities primarily employed whites as professors and administrators until the 1920s, when that situation began to reverse itself.

When most people refer to "the American university" today, they are usually referring to the American research university. Early universities such as the University of Pennsylvania (1740) and University of Georgia (1785) had been universities in the sense that they were degree-granting institutions comprehending various colleges or schools, usually an undergraduate college, a medical school, and a law school. But with the founding of the Johns Hopkins University (1876) and Clark University (1887), and the redirection of other state institutions of higher education such as the University of Michigan, aspects of the German university were adopted and adapted to the United States. Both Hopkins and Clark, privately endowed universities, were founded with the expressed purpose of advancing knowledge in the humanities, nascent social sciences, and natural sciences. While each university contained an undergraduate college, its graduate school or faculty was its heart. In these schools, professors taught their research specialties to graduate students in seminars. They also pursued research and published in discipline-specific journals read by specialists.

At the undergraduate colleges of the new universities and reformed colleges, the traditional curriculum, centered upon study of classical languages, vanished as students specialized by electing courses and fields of concentration. No longer meant as preparation for public life, the undergraduate degree program now was intended to prepare students for eventual entry into a profession within American public life.

Since the 1920s, the research university has been the dominant secular institution of American middle-class life. By the third decade of the twentieth century, organized religion had a role only at the periphery of college life, for example in benedictions at commencement. Daily chapel and weekly church attendance were not required, faculty members might belong to any organized religion or none at all, and the curriculum might contradict religious teachings. Starting in the post-World War II period, religious studies departments came to be responsible for the teaching of knowledge about religion, and they did so in a nondenominational way.

As the number of high school graduates increased in the 1920s, so did the number of college graduates. The percentage of 22-year-old Americans holding the B.A. degree increased dramatically. In 1920 3.5 percent of American men and 1.7 percent of American women held the degree, while in 1940 9.7 percent of American men and 6.6 percent of American women did. An undergraduate degree then started to be a prerequisite for white-collar employment. Today about 52 percent of American young people between 18 and 24 pursue an undergraduate degree. Of these, 9.2 percent are African Americans, 5.7 percent are Hispanics, and 4.2 percent are Asian Americans. The proportion of women is 53 percent.

In 1990 American institutions of higher education enrolled almost 14 million students, including 258,000 students at historically black colleges and 2.2 million undergraduates at private colleges. Since World War II, the federal government has supported university-based research with ever larger proportions of the national product. Universities are increasingly tied to federally funded programs of research in agriculture, education, health, defense, and social problems. As universities have defined the advancement of knowledge as their primary function, the expertise required for research has become even more highly valued, and undergraduate education has followed the universities' research agenda. While early American colleges reflected the cultural diversity of American regions and religions, today's universities increasingly are national institutions supported by the national government and integral to the nation's prosperity.

LOUISE L. STEVENSON

See also ACADEMIC FREEDOM.

FURTHER READING

James D. Anderson, *The Education of Blacks in the South, 1860–1935* (Chapel Hill: University of North Carolina Press, 1988).
James Axtell, *The School upon a Hill: Education and Society in Colonial New England* (New Haven: Yale University Press, 1974).
Roger L. Geiger, *Research and Relevant Knowledge: American Research Universities since World War II* (New York: Oxford University Press, 1993).
——, *To Advance Knowledge: the Growth of American Research Universities, 1900–1940* (New York: Oxford University Press, 1986).
W. Bruce Leslie, *Gentlemen and Scholars: College and Community in the "Age of the University," 1865–1918* (University Park: Pennsylvania State University, 1992).
David W. Robson, *Educating Republicans: the College in the Era of the American Revolution, 1750–1800* (Westport, Conn.: Greenwood, 1985).
Barbara Miller Solomon, *In the Company of Educated Women: a History of Women and Higher Education in America* (New Haven: Yale University Press, 1985).
Louise L. Stevenson, *The New Haven Scholars and the Transformation of Higher Learning in America, 1830–1890* (Baltimore: Johns Hopkins University Press, 1986).
Laurence R. Veysey, *The Emergence of the American University* (Chicago: University of Chicago Press, 1965).

Commons, John R. (b. Hollandsburg, Ohio, Oct. 13, 1862; d. Madison, Wis., May 11, 1945).   Econom-ist. The spiritual nucleus of the "Wisconsin School" of American labor history from his arrival in Madison in 1904, Commons assembled a massive *Documentary History of American Industrial Society* (1910–11) and a comprehensive *History of Labor in the United States* (1918–35). He felt social scientists could play an active role in the formulation and administration of public policy, a vision shared by ROBERT LA FOLLETTE, the Progressive governor of Wisconsin. Commons felt that an active, rationally organized government could mediate the conflict between labor and capital, thereby fostering greater equity and social justice.

See also PROGRESSIVISM.

FURTHER READING

Lafayette G. Harter, *John R. Commons* (Corvallis: Oregon State University Press, 1962).

community   The concept of community is at once descriptive and normative. One might say that Euro-Americans have been in flight from community from the moment of settlement, but they have as consistently longed for it. The quest is not only a recurring theme in American writing; generations of seekers after community in America have founded their own UTOPIAS, from the seventeenth-century Puritans, to nineteenth-century Fourierists, to twentieth-century "hippies."

The invocation of community is almost always nostalgic; community is posed as a richer and more humane alternative to liberal INDIVIDUALISM. For left critics of LIBERALISM, community has a Rousseauian cast, egalitarian and conducive to free consensus, while champions of CONSERVATISM (of the romantic sort, not market-oriented individualists) imagine a hierarchical social body knit together by memory in a fixed place.

Despite numerous attempts in the literature of philosophy and the social sciences to give a bounded meaning to the idea of community and to the experience of community, no common usage has developed. Community remains a term of enormous emotional appeal and remarkable vagueness. It is sometimes used very loosely to designate a unified society, something perhaps better understood as a political community or commonweal. Robert MacIver developed this meaning in *Community: a Sociological Study* (1917). He referred to community as a unity of interests, something instrumental, created by an act of political will rather than by tradition. Not far from MacIver is a liberal pluralist definition of community that refers to a society made up of many partial communities (such as the academic community). Depending upon one's sense of the relations among these various organized interests, one has either liberal fragmentation or the negotiated community of interests envisioned by MacIver, one out of many (*e pluribus unum*).

More commonly, community is defined in terms of location. In this view, a quarter of a city or a whole town or village might be referred to as a community. For many Americans, the New England town of fond memory represents community. Others would not necessarily deny that community might be realized spatially, in a place, but they would emphasize a quality of relationship as the special attribute of community. At times, place coincides with this emotional bonding. But community without propinquity is possible (as in scattered networks of friends), and in modern cities one often finds physical proximity without community.

A community is most rigorously defined as a network of social relations marked by mutuality and emotional bonds. It involves a limited number of people in a somewhat restricted social space or network, held together by shared understandings and a sense of obligation. There is a distinct "we-ness" in such a community. Perhaps because the concept is so entangled in nostalgia, there is a tendency to assume that within a community conflict is absent and power is not structured or exercised. But communal conflict and power are real, though differing from, say, market competition in being mediated by emotional bonds. Finally, a community in this sense is an end in itself, not a means to some other end. Distinctively communal actions are based upon affection, not rational calculation of self-interest.

All formal reflections on community assume a history, a process of change leading to a moment when community became threatened or transformed into something else. The social sciences were born of the attempt to gain intellectual and social control over the modernizing transformations associated with the democratic revolutions and the industrial capitalism of the nineteenth century. Community, thus threatened with destruction, became a focus of social analysis; it became one of the unit-ideas, to use Robert Nisbet's phrase in *The Sociological Tradition* (1966), of modern social theory.

The most widely influential sociological formulation of the nature of the great transformation derives from the work of the German sociologist Ferdinand Tönnies, whose *Gemeinschaft und Gesellschaft* was published in 1887. *Gemeinschaft*, usually translated as community, is characterized, he wrote, by "intimate, private, and exclusive living together." *Gesellschaft*, usually translated as "association" or "society," is identified with the city. It is an "artificial construc-

tion of an aggregate of human beings," characterized by instrumental values, competition, and impersonality. Summing up the difference between the two, Tönnies observed that in *Gemeinschaft* people "remain essentially united in spite of all separating factors, whereas in *Gesellschaft* they are essentially separated in spite of all uniting factors" (p. 65). These distinctions were incorporated into American SOCIAL SCIENCE early in the twentieth century; later, after World War II, they undergirded MODERNIZATION theory, a unified theory of SOCIETY and social change associated with TALCOTT PARSONS in sociology but elaborated in all the social science disciplines.

The *Gemeinschaft–Gesellschaft* transformation was particularly central to the development of urban theory at the University of Chicago, the preeminent center for social science research in the interwar years. W. I. Thomas in social psychology, Louis Wirth in urban studies, and Robert Redfield in anthropology all worked with dichotomies derived from Tönnies's distinction. This notion of community and social change also found its way into historical scholarship, most clearly and influentially in the work of Oscar Handlin, especially in *Boston's Immigrants* (1941) and *The Uprooted* (1951).

These scenarios of community collapse, so common in modern American social thought, derive from Tönnies, but they do not (save for the later work of Redfield) accurately represent the argument Tönnies actually made. He did not argue a community-breakdown thesis; rather he argued that society became bifurcated. People in modern times were compelled to live their lives in two modes and contexts: *Gemeinschaft* and *Gesellschaft*. Community and society were not places, nor were they historical sequences. They were distinct forms of human interaction that constitute distinct but interlinked social forms in modern society. Tönnies indicated that *Gesellschaft* was gaining significance in people's lives, but he did not believe that all communal relationships would disappear. Life, once more or less fully contained in local communities, was in modern times inevitably and rather directly integrated into larger structures of society. But, he concluded, "the force of *Gemeinschaft* persists, even within the period of *Gesellschaft*" (p. 232).

Instead of assuming the demise of community, the issue for scholarship—and for life—is to know where to look for community. One must be prepared to recognize its various forms and locales. Most important of all, one must acknowledge that one cannot live a modern life entirely within the confines of community. And that need not be an occasion for regret.

Unease with American competitive individualism

and despair over group conflict nourishes the dream of a community that is whole, providing a complete and sustaining surround. Such a desperate need for community can blind one to the way in which the impulse to community invites a quest for sameness, thus representing an exclusive idea in a democracy ideally inclusive. The desire to make the spirit of community universal risks parochialism and threatens the cosmopolitan spirit necessary in a modern heterogeneous society.

Some recent proponents of community, most notably CHRISTOPHER LASCH in his *The True and Only Heaven* (1991), recognize the parochialism of their rejection of Enlightenment universalism and cosmopolitanism, but insist that is a price they will pay. More worrisome are calls to renew a presumed common culture uniting all Americans. *Habits of the Heart* (1985), a best-selling book by Robert Bellah and several colleagues, is a compelling diagnosis of contemporary America: the authors argue that Americans lack a language for expressing mutual respect and concern. But when the authors call for revitalizing biblical and republican languages from the American past, they imply that "community" must in principle mean "commonality." That inplication works against the best insights of the book, which documents a diversified pursuit of public goods by various groups of citizens. In *The Good Society* (1991), Bellah and colleagues respond in part to this worry, recognizing that a society-wide communal solidarity cannot be achieved in a pluralistic society. A recent neo-Progressive movement calling itself communitarian, seeking to recapture the broader spirit of community articulated by MacIver, has emphasized social responsibility as part of the liberal tradition. In a book titled *The Spirit of Community* (1993), Amitai Etzioni balances rights with responsibilities, seeking to establish a new and shared moral order without moralizing. (*See also* RESPONSIBILITY.)

Other arguments for American pluralism, past and present, envision a landscape of many communities, each distinct and exclusive, the whole making up a diverse modern society. To some extent, this is precisely how intense feelings of community were achieved in seventeenth-century New England, but it can work only if these islands are isolated from one another. If they are not, and Tönnies insisted that in modern times such communities cannot pretend to be self-contained, then one must have a social category greater than community, and it must be defined by its accommodation of difference, by its cosmopolitanism.

The dominant myths of American life, the New England town tradition and the Jeffersonian ideal of agrarian democracy, tend to favor communalism and avoid the complexity of cosmopolitanism. Both of these traditions are identified with distinct regions. Both emphasize sameness; neither can accommodate difference. The lay sermon delivered by JOHN WINTHROP aboard the *Arbella* in 1630, upon the arrival of the Puritans in Massachusetts Bay, is the most powerful statement of community in American literature. Yet it is also a demand for sameness under God. "We must," Winthrop urged his party, "be knitt together in this worke as one man" (in Bender, p. 63). He envisioned a single moral community that acknowledged no distinction between private and public values.

Jeffersonian Democracy is far from Winthrop's religious utopia. Yet beneath the confident democratic professions of THOMAS JEFFERSON lay the assumption of an underlying harmony of society and values. He feared immigration and cities for the diversity of values that attended both, and his inability to imagine a postslavery biracial American society reflected his belief that no natural harmony of interests united —or could unite—the former masters and former slaves. He feared, as he wrote in his *Notes on the State of Virginia* (1784), that emancipation would culminate in "the extermination of one or the other race" (p. 138).

There is, however, another historical tradition, identified with another region, the middle colonies. Here, in contrast to the experience of Massachusetts Bay and the Chesapeake, diversity marked society. Various groups, especially in New York City, regularly interacted with each other across lines of difference, and they created a political culture that not only acknowledged diversity of interests and values but affirmed these differences as a basis for liberty. The lessons of experience in the middle colonies were articulated by the middle of the eighteenth century. William Livingston, writing in *The Independent Reflector* (1753) with reference to the founding of a college in New York, argued that since the colony was divided by different religious and cultural traditions, the college ought not be identified with any one community. He argued that the institution must be equally accessible to and equally the possession of the various groups of the larger society by means of control by the colonial legislature. He grasped the relation of homogeneous communities to a heterogeneous public. "For as we are split into so great a Variety of Opinions and Professions; had each Individual his Share in the Government of the Academy, the Jealousy of all Parties combating each other, would inevitably produce a perfect Freedom for each particular Party" (p. 195).

The conditions of modernity compromise community and bring it into relation with a heterogeneous public culture. Part of modern experience is lived in small, *gemeinschaftlich* worlds of sameness, but they cannot be all-inclusive or global. They inevitably must relate themselves to a larger public world, where neither intimacy nor sameness is a bond. The collective meaning of the public culture is not preordained; it is constantly made and remade from a discourse of difference, even while a belief in sameness sustains a particularistic sense of "we-ness," a sense of intimacy real but necessarily with permeable boundaries in modern society. The appeal of sameness can be acknowledged, and its appeal ought not be begrudged anyone. Yet it must be limited in its reach. Small circles of "we" characterized by sameness and even parochialism nourish and secure part of everyone's identities, but everyone is also engaged in a broader and more public sense of the "we." The problem of community in modern society is to understand the interplay, personally and politically, of the smaller homogeneous circles of "we" and the more inclusive and cosmopolitan world of public culture.

THOMAS BENDER

See also INDUSTRIALISM; URBANISM.

FURTHER READING

Robert Bellah, Richard Madsen, William M. Sullivan, Ann Swidler, and Steven M. Tipton, *Habits of the Heart* (Berkeley: University of California Press, 1985).

Thomas Bender, *Community and Social Change in America* (Baltimore: Johns Hopkins University Press, 1982).

Amitai Etzioni, *The Spirit of Community* (New York: Crown, 1993).

Thomas Jefferson, *Notes on the State of Virginia*, ed. Willean Peden (Chapel Hill: University of North Carolina Press, 1955).

Christopher Lasch, *The True and Only Heaven* (New York: Norton, 1991).

William Livingston, *The Independent Reflector*, ed. Milton M. Klein (Cambridge: Harvard University Press, 1963).

Robert M. MacIver, *Community: a Sociological Study* (New York: Macmillan, 1917).

Robert Nisbet, *The Sociological Tradition* (New York: Basic, 1966).

Ferdinand Tönnies, *Community and Society*, trans. Charles P. Loomis (New York: Harper, 1963).

Conant, James B. (b. Dorchester, Mass., Mar. 26, 1893; d. Hanover, N.H., Feb. 11, 1978).   Educator. Trained as a chemist, Conant was president of Harvard and, during World War II, a leading figure in organizing scientists for the war effort. An active proponent of liberal arts EDUCATION, he authored *On Understanding Science* (1947) and *Science and Common Sense* (1951) for a general audience. He also headed the research team that produced *The American High School Today* (1959), a study that promoted comprehensive high schools as instruments of social equality.

FURTHER READING

James G. Herschberg, *James B. Conant: Harvard to Hiroshima and the Making of the Nuclear Age* (New York: Knopf, 1993).

consensus   As a term in American historical discourse, consensus refers to a set of interrelated ideas that characterized the politico-cultural tone of the two decades from World War II to the early 1960s. Reacting to worldwide turmoil and war in the 1930s and 1940s, American intellectuals—led once more by the indefatigable JOHN DEWEY—rallied to the defense of three causes they revered and saw endangered: science, democracy, and America. In the heat of successive crises, they fused those causes into the fervent belief that the special and enduring strength of the United States grew from a socially unifying national culture which embodied practices, attitudes, and values that uniquely nourished both scientific inquiry and democratic government.

Condemning the evils of Nazism, fascism, and then communism, American intellectuals understood those movements as originating in the spread of antiscientific political "ideologies"—nonempirical sociomoral belief systems that claimed to possess absolute truth and consequently drove fanatical "true believers" to attempt to remake the world according to their mandates. Contrasting the moral and political absolutism of those movements to the mundane practical compromises that marked American politics, such scholars as the historians DANIEL BOORSTIN and ARTHUR M. SCHLESINGER JR. and the political scientists Robert A. Dahl and Gabriel A. Almond, readily saw the latter as the product of pragmatism, social tolerance, and openness to diverse interests. Those admirable qualities, many intellectuals came to believe, could not have developed from "ideological" faiths, including rationalist philosophies and supernaturalist religions. Rather, such qualities must have grown from practical and nondogmatic habits and attitudes embedded in a distinctive and pluralistic national culture. Inculcating TOLERANCE, pragmatism, and openness as norms of social interaction, the national culture inoculated Americans against ideological fanaticism and created the social conditions that enabled diverse groups to live together peacefully and cooperatively. Similarly, those same characteristics of the national culture also nourished the tentative, open-minded, and experimental attitudes that ideally characterized scientific inquiry. Hence, American culture uniquely supported both DEMOCRACY and SCIENCE. In turn, science—the ultimate intellectual authority for most American intellectuals—provided a rational justification for democratic government and demonstrated as well the de facto virtue and superiority of American culture.

In the postwar context of American world leadership, pervasive anticommunism, and unparalleled national prosperity, belief in such a normative cultural consensus led many intellectuals, including the sociologists DANIEL BELL, Seymour Martin Lipset, and Edward Shils, to embrace the status quo. It induced some to contend that the United States had successfully resolved its major internal social problems and, in particular, that it had transcended the economic conflicts and inequities that had marked the preceding age of industrialization. The practices and attitudes that purportedly composed the American cultural consensus became for them political and moral norms by which to judge the world. At the root of the consensus orientation lay a half-conscious and all-encompassing politico-moral dichotomy that helped for more than two decades to shape the way American intellectuals both perceived and interpreted their world: one side linked moral good with America, democracy, science, relativism, pluralism, compromise, and existing social institutions; the other side linked moral evil with Nazi Germany and the Soviet Union, totalitarianism, ideology, absolutism, repression, command, and significant social change.

The consensus orientation had its strengths as well as its weaknesses. Its virtues included, first, an insistence that political thought and action be constantly chastened by the tests of pragmatic analysis and empirical confirmation and, second, an emphasis on the need for toleration and compromise to nourish the cultural values and practices that undergird democratic government. Its flaws included a simplistic equation of the threats posed by Nazism and communism, a Panglossian view of American society and politics, confusion between descriptive and prescriptive levels of analysis, and a failure to recognize the extent to which the consensus orientation itself was historically contingent and apologetic.

The consensus era ended and the orientation itself came under increasingly hostile attack in "the sixties," the legendary cultural era that peaked between 1965 and 1974. Challenges to basic American policies and values and the emergence of activist "liberation" movements based on race, gender, sexual orientation, and new or newly insistent religious faiths combined to highlight the nature of the heralded American consensus as narrow and oriented to the status quo. Equally important, new approaches in philosophy, linguistics, history, and the sciences—exemplified and inspired by the work of such diverse American scholars

as THOMAS S. KUHN, Carl Rogers, and C. WRIGHT MILLS and, subsequently, by the writings of such French intellectuals as Jacques Derrida and Michel Foucault—challenged the fundamental idea of "objective" truth itself. Those explosive developments combined to undermine the implicitly normative and ostensibly scientific foundation of the consensus orientation and, in the minds of many at least, to justify and legitimate one or more of the proliferating new liberation movements. The "sixties" fragmented the consensus orientation because that tumultuous cultural era witnessed the combined mass impact of three divergent and transforming developments: the globalization of pivotal ideas and institutions, multiplying domestic ethnic and cultural conflicts, and a profound intellectual upheaval that challenged the nation's underlying Enlightenment faith in human reason.

The mutually reinforcing relationship between the postwar era and the development of the consensus orientation suggests the complex dynamics that operate today between the nation's escalating cultural conflicts and the contemporary intellectual debate over the nature of human knowledge. The power of that explosive mix of cultural conflict and intellectual fragmentation illuminates the recent celebrity of the term POSTMODERNISM, the now-accepted label used to lump together the divergent developments of the twentieth century that have since the 1960s insistently pressed intellectuals to confront what they perceive as the insoluble problematics of human knowledge. That volatile mix also helps us understand some of the forces driving current efforts to find a replacement for the idea of a normative American cultural consensus by developing such purportedly suprasubjective normative concepts as the market, rights theories, original intent, wealth maximization, traditional values, religious fundamentals, civic republicanism, and communities of the competent. If our current absorption with the problematics of knowledge helped undermine the intellectual foundations of the consensus orientation, however, that dilemma should not detract from the still vital goals of those who spoke for the alleged American consensus: preserving democratic values and practices, identifying the nation's strengths with openness, tolerance, and diversity, and affirming a sustaining faith in the possibilities of human self-government based on some combination of reason, decency, and humility.

EDWARD A. PURCELL JR.

See also COLD WAR.

FURTHER READING

Daniel Boorstin, *The Genius of American Politics* (Chicago: Chicago University Press, 1953).

Robert A. Dahl, *A Preface to Democratic Theory* (Chicago: Chicago University Press, 1956).

John P. Diggins, *The Proud Decades: America in War and Peace, 1941–1960* (New York: Norton, 1988).

John Higham, "Beyond Consensus: the Historian as Moral Critic," *American Historical Review* 67 (1962): 609–25.

Peter Novick, *That Noble Dream: the "Objectivity Question" and the American Historical Profession* (Cambridge: Cambridge University Press, 1988).

Richard H. Pells, *The Liberal Mind in a Conservative Age: American Intellectuals in the 1940s and 1950s* (New York: Harper and Row, 1985).

Edward A. Purcell Jr., *The Crisis of Democratic Theory: Scientific Naturalism and the Problem of Value* (Lexington: University of Kentucky Press, 1973).

——, "Social Thought," *American Quarterly* 35 (1983): 80–100.

conservatism American history has conspired against the flourishing of conservative thought. To make that point, however, one must distinguish between two expressions that in Europe have always registered different meanings, but that in the United States have seemed almost synonymous. "Conservatism" in modern European history begins with Edmund Burke in the late eighteenth century. It suggests a suspicion toward change, reform, and philosophies of PROGRESS. It registers a bias toward TRADITION and the past and a deference toward the social order as found. It sees human nature as deficient, if not innately sinful, and seeks a variety of checks against it through the influence of social institutions or by some redemption in culture or religion. Conservatism values the organic society, its collective experience and memory, over its autonomous units. Generally, conservatism sits comfortably with rank and order in society and judges them to be the necessary conditions of stability and responsible change. It accepts the state as the symbolic unity of the people. It thus does not disparage notions of aristocracy or elitism. It often renders a profound, aesthetic distaste for radical DEMOCRACY and mass society.

The term "right wing," on the other hand, has in Europe signified various forms of nationalist movements, often based in mass politics, as in the fascist movements of the twentieth century. Whereas earlier rightist politics may have suggested forms of monarchism or Catholicism, in the era of the modern nation-state they express patriotic loyalty to the nation, often against a perceived, subversive influence, such as Jews or communists.

The origins and development of the United States have not favored the first kind of conservatism. America was born in the celebration of its independence from the old world. The Puritans fled a historical Christianity they perceived as wrought with corruption and error. The republican culture of the revolutionary era idealized the virtue, simplicity, and innocence of the New World citizenry. And the romantic literature of the nineteenth century found in the biblical Adam a prototype of the American, bereft of history and happily unburdened by its constraints.

For much of its history the United States thrived as a FRONTIER society. Growth and expansion, rebirth and renewal, seemed to be the norms of existence as the frontier assumed a mythic status in the American imagination. The frontier experience, as Frederick Jackson Turner said, meant a continual evolution from the past, the sloughing off of old world ways, the intensification of an Americanizing process. This condition of mind gained reinforcement from the industrial revolution and its impressive material impact. Dynamic growth and change in even the most mundane aspects of life seemed the essence of American reality. A landscape that elsewhere reflected—in castles or cathedrals—the temporal depth of human experience, in the United States registered the momentous power of the present.

Nor has conservatism's admiration for rank and its habit of social deference found much favor in American democratic culture. From the ideology of the Revolution, through various populist movements, even into the commercial culture of the television era, the assumption of an innate, intuitive wisdom in the collective mass of ordinary men and women has gained an axiomatic credibility.

Other normative American values have also hindered conservative thinking. The American celebration of the individual has the corollary effect of dichotomizing the state and the citizen, society and the individual. American political philosophy, it seems, often begins with an assumption of the autonomous self, which it poses against the collective whole. Government, or the state, becomes a conspiracy against personal liberty, or at best, a pragmatic necessity, the functional sphere of drab and dreary bureaucracies. Thus, the American state has lacked those trappings of crown and throne, ritual and tradition, that symbolize a nation and give it an imaginative coherence.

What has passed for conservative in America is what one might otherwise call "right wing." Probably most Americans would define conservatism by reference to the business community, to the free market, and to the rights of property. That identification, of course, connects conservatism to the most revolutionary force for change over the last century and a half—the technological and commercial impact of capitalism. Others would identify conservatism with certain right-wing political movements—those led, for example, by Joseph McCarthy, Barry Goldwater, George Wallace, or Ronald Reagan. That identification links conservatism to mass movements, often emphatically populist in style, and manifestly anti-elitist in their attitudes toward government and intellectuals.

Against these realities, conservatism has made certain adaptations to American conditions and these various expressions have created a viable conservative intellectual tradition in the United States. Seldom has any one conservative writer's thought fallen within a precise category; nonetheless, one can glimpse the tradition, with its many varieties, by looking at some basic themes.

One form of conservatism has accepted the libertarian ideal of personal liberty and applied it to economic theory. This conservatism endorses the free market and the competitive system of capitalism, stressing the priority of the individual entrepreneur, or the corporation, against the regulatory powers of the state. In its earliest expressions, laissez-faire economics represented a form of democratic radicalism, as in the works of THOMAS JEFFERSON and in the economic programs of the Jacksonians, authored by WILLIAM LEGGETT and Theodore Sedgwick, for example. Laissez-faire economic theory also enjoyed a long hegemony in the colleges. Often, partisans of this position linked their ideology to the "natural system" of universal laws as formulated in the Enlightenment. Most of the exponents stood variously in the tradition of Adam Smith. Leggett wrote that his economics sought to institute the "natural system" in all matters both of politics and political economy.

Libertarian conservatism gained later reinforcements. Under the influence of evolutionary theories, those of Herbert Spencer or Charles Darwin, some American writers celebrated the capitalist order as the competitive system that alone could assure progress in the struggle for survival. WILLIAM GRAHAM SUMNER (*What Social Classes Owe to Each Other*, 1883) and ANDREW CARNEGIE ("The Gospel of Wealth," 1886) most emphatically expressed these notions. But Sumner, however much he celebrated the virtues of the successful businessman, consistently defended the market system and strongly criticized protective tariffs. Later still, free market theory acquired a major impetus from the "Austrian" school of economists, which attacked the reigning Keynesian ideology. Ludwig von Mises (*Human Action*, 1944) and his student FRIEDRICH A. HAYEK (*The Constitution of Liberty*, 1960) warned the West of its drift toward a state

tyranny prepared by policies of central economic planning. Hayek's *The Road to Serfdom* became a surprising bestseller after its publication in 1944. In the 1960s and 1970s the writings of MILTON FRIEDMAN, a winner of the Nobel Prize, kept free market ideology in the foreground of economic discussion.

LIBERTARIANISM, interestingly, has seldom gained full ideological support among American conservative thinkers. Instead, conservatives accept the principle of liberty in economic policy, but not in moral and cultural considerations. While liberals have tended to champion personal First Amendment freedoms and personal discretion in morals and "lifestyles," the opposite has been true for conservatives. Many conservatives, Sumner for example, have conjoined their libertarian economics to a traditional "Protestant ethic" stressing personal self-discipline, thrift, and frugality. Only occasionally have conservatives, such as Murray Rothbard, embraced a complete system of liberty. Mises' instructive paradox that "a successful free society will always in a large measure be a tradition-bound society" bespeaks a general conservative consensus on mixing freedom and constraint.

Other conservative thinkers have approached the question of liberty with greater skepticism. They have viewed the United States as a nation lacking the direction and stabilizing influence of tradition, a nation of autonomous, uprooted individuals. The American system of liberty, they have further argued, has unleashed natural human lusts for sensual gratifications and has thus created the dominant materialism of American culture. Conservatives have sought to contain the libertarian impulses in American life without pursuing an alternative course of statist controls. At one level, conservatives have sought to define an intellectual order based in religion or metaphysics and have made obedience to that order a necessary check on discretionary morals or behavior. The New Humanists, particularly in the writings of IRVING BABBITT (*Rousseau and Romanticism*, 1919 and *Democracy and Leadership*, 1925) and PAUL ELMER MORE (*Shelburne Essays*, 1904–21), appealed to the neoclassical standards of a universal human nature posed against the individualistic ethic of Rousseau and other romanticists. In his powerful polemic of 1955, *Essays in the Public Philosophy*, WALTER LIPPMANN rendered the ideas of his former teacher Babbitt more emphatically in terms of natural law. In 1948, Richard Weaver provided the most influential formulation of the intellectual problem in his book *Ideas Have Consequences*. Weaver described a long period of intellectual decline in Western thinking, beginning with the decline of realism in medieval philosophy and the triumphs of nominalism, which led in his view to pragmatism and other forms of materialistic and relativistic thinking. Weaver traced the many ills of modernity back to this intellectual lapse, insisting that "our conception of metaphysical reality finally governs our conception of everything else" (p. 51). Other efforts to secure a principle of order by appropriating select aspects of the intellectual past include the work of LEO STRAUSS (*Natural Right and History*, 1953) and his numerous academic followers, and ERIC VOEGELIN (*The New Science of Politics*, 1952). Another surprising bestseller, Allan Bloom's *The Closing of the American Mind* (1987), expanded this literature.

For conservatives, the problem of liberty relates critically to the problem of capitalism. Capitalism, they have recognized, fuels those appetites that bring change and uproot human lives. Capitalism, in short, has not always sat well with conservative preferences for organic communities. The manifesto of SOUTHERN AGRARIANISM, *I'll Take My Stand* (1930), made that case forcefully by surveying the social wreckage of the industrial revolution and showing its effect on the dominant materialistic culture of the United States. Russell Kirk (*The Conservative Mind*, 1953; *A Program for Conservatives*, 1954) protested against the "assembly-line civilization" of Henry Ford and the blight of the industrial revolution around the rural Michigan of his youth. In the 1970s and 1980s, George Will, who described himself as a "European conservative," warned that capitalism is a relentless engine of change; it inflates appetites and expectations, and it takes its toll most heavily on those things that conservatives hold dear—family farms, traditional craftsmanship, local neighborhoods, historic homes and buildings. Many American conservatives in that "European" tradition have endorsed the state's role in welfare programs that preserve the organic community, and they have cited Benjamin Disraeli and Otto von Bismarck as model conservatives.

Conservatives have often linked capitalism with democracy. Both make room for the exercise of people's individual wants. But with respect to both democracy and capitalism, conservatives have tended not to reject these American ideals but to accommodate them. Thus socialism, or any strongly statist economic system, has not, in conservatives' judgment, presented itself as a viable alternative to capitalism. Although conservatives from H. L. MENCKEN and Irving Babbitt to IRVING KRISTOL have faulted American businessmen as an unworthy leadership class, they have not abandoned the effort to define aristocratic principles within American democracy. Sometimes that effort has yielded a nostalgia for the Old South or a fondness for medieval influences in American life. By invoking an intangible aristocratic spirit, conservatives have sought to pose an aesthetic counterforce to the blandishments of democratic taste and mass society. Peter Viereck wrote in *Conservatism Revisited* (1949) that "democracy is the best government on earth when it tries to make all its citizens aristocrats" (pp. 34–5).

Nonetheless, democratic ideals and democratic rhetoric have occasionally shaped conservative sentiments. As the United States, in the judgment of conservatives, moved toward excessive state controls and lapsed in its commitment to fight communism, conservatives appealed to what they believed was a majority in America that opposed these trends. Increasingly, conservatives charged that a liberal elite in government and in the universities had co-opted American politics for its own subversive purposes. This habit of thought became dramatically clear in 1950, when WILLIAM F. BUCKLEY JR. published *God and Man at Yale*. Buckley in effect charged that his venerable alma mater had become socialist and atheist. Four years later, in *McCarthy and His Enemies*, written with L. Brent Bozell, Buckley defended the anti-communist crusade of the Wisconsin senator, upholding the right of the American majority to defend its "folkways" against alien influences.

In the 1970s and 1980s the movement of so-called NEOCONSERVATISM reinforced a putatively democratic conservatism. The neoconservatives consisted heavily of (often secular) Jewish intellectuals, almost all of them with backgrounds in the American left. Most, since the 1950s, had been loyalists of the Democratic Party, but by the late 1960s they were breaking ranks. They charged that the party had fallen under NEW LEFT influences and had absorbed the utopian ideologies of the 1960s. They especially lamented the Democratic Party's alienation from its major constituencies—labor leaders and working-class people, city machines, and European ethnic groups. Neoconservatives used the label New Class to describe a reigning, liberal elite in the United States, whose values and political agenda differed emphatically from democratic opinion. In the neoconservative description, the New Class of government bureaucrats and academics had been reinforced by a liberal media of television, radio, and the eastern, urban newspapers. Neoconservatives sought to relocate power from the undemocratic judiciary and government regulatory agencies and into the popularly elected legislatures.

Conservatism in the United States, then, has been a history of accommodation. Often it has preserved the standards and biases that shaped an old world conservatism, but it has also incorporated ideals of democracy and liberty more appropriate to New World conditions.

J. DAVID HOEVELER JR.

FURTHER READING

David Hoeveler Jr. *Watch on the Right: Conservative Intellectuals in the Reagan Era* (Madison: University of Wisconsin Press, 1991).

Ronald Lora, *Conservative Minds in America* (Chicago: Rand-McNally, 1971).

George H. Nash, *The Conservative Intellectual Movement in America: Since 1945* (New York: Basic, 1976).

Constitution Two centuries after its adoption, disputes over the original meaning and proper interpretation of the Federal Constitution continue to roil American politics and jurisprudence, and thus to generate further debates beyond the sphere of government. Far from being relegated to the status of a quaint if justly revered symbol of our national origins—the American equivalent, say, of the English Magna Carta or the Declaration of Rights of 1689—the Constitution remains an active source of controversy. Much of this controversy has been sparked by the labors of the Supreme Court to apply the BILL OF RIGHTS of 1789 and the Fourteenth Amendment of 1868 to dismantle the edifice of racial segregation and discrimination, to enlarge the rights of those accused or convicted of crimes, and to protect the reproductive liberty of women. But important questions also continue to arise in other areas that lie closer to the problems of institutional design that preoccupied the framers of 1787. From the American intervention in Vietnam to the liberation of the emirate of Kuwait in 1991, for example, the relative authority of the executive branch and Congress in matters of foreign relations and war has been a subject of repeated wrangling. These and other disputes have helped to give constitutional discourse a striking vitality, and to forge links between public debate and the academic fields of law, history, and political science.

Even as this scholarship continues to flourish, one older work retains a striking influence over popular impressions of the origins of the Constitution. In *An Economic Interpretation of the Constitution* (1913), CHARLES BEARD argued that its framers acted as a coherent class of propertyholders who had a special interest in creating a national government capable of redeeming the public debt created during the Revolutionary War. While recognizing that the framers did indeed represent a propertied elite alarmed over what JAMES MADISON described as the "multiplicity," "mutability," and "injustice" of state legislation, contemporary scholars tend to view the Philadelphia convention of 1787 as the culminating achievement of a "republican experiment" than had actually begun with the drafting of republican constitutions for the states a decade earlier.

In recent years, however, the most publicized debate about the Constitution has concerned the authority that modern interpreters should give to the "original meaning" of its text and the original intentions and understandings of its framers and ratifiers. In reaction to the leading decisions of the Supreme Court under Chief Justices Earl Warren and Warren Burger, such conservative writers as Raoul Berger and Robert Bork argue that the true task of interpretation is to fix the meaning of the text at the moment of its adoption, and not to impose by judicial fiat other preferences, however appealing, grounded only in notions of policy or moral principle. The idea that federal judges may recognize or even create rights not explicitly mentioned or protected by the Constitution is regarded by these commentators as a particular heresy whose acceptance would turn the judiciary into a class of Platonic guardians of the public weal.

Critics of this position argue, on the other hand, that the Bill of Rights and the Reconstruction amendments embody deeper and more principled ideas of RIGHTS than their mere textual formulations can express. A Constitution whose meaning was so constrained by the dead hand of the past could never meet the challenge of adapting to the enormous changes that have occurred since 1787, transforming the country in ways that the gentry-statesmen who gathered at Philadelphia in that year did not foresee. While conceding that some deference to original meaning must be part of any process of adjudication, these writers question whether the original intentions of the adopters can ever be conclusively known, and if known, should be binding in themselves.

Both theories rest on democratic foundations—but of very different kinds. For the advocates of "originalism," the crucial proposition is that the Constitution acquired its supreme authority through the extraordinary procedures required for ratification and subsequent amendments by Article V, and that these make the text an expression of popular sovereignty to a degree that no decision by a politically unaccountable judiciary can ever equal. By contrast, the critics of "originalism" contend that the appeal to the binding authority of a distant past is undemocratic; the same conviction inspired Thomas Jefferson to ask, in a letter to James Madison of September 6, 1789, "whether one generation of men has a right to bind another."

Where issues of rights are at stake, the usual axis of division in these debates has pitted politically conservative opponents of the judicial expansion of rights against liberals who have supported the Court in most of its landmark decisions. But to reduce these disputes to a political quarrel between the political right and left obscures more than it explains. Because the Constitution and its crucial amendments were themselves the product of intense debates conducted during periods of profound political transformation, it is illusory to think that any appeal to the evidence of the past can tidily resolve current disputes. In any controversy, both parties may readily find statements to support their arguments. On some issues, such as the allocation of authority over war and foreign relations, the weight of historical evidence actually falls on the side of the position that would conventionally be characterized as liberal. On other issues, such as the separation of church and state, scholars have come to recognize a spectrum of original positions, ranging from those who joined Jefferson and James Madison in believing that religion could be safely privatized to others who thought that the states could continue to play an active role in supporting religion (though not particular denominations) more generally.

In rhetorical terms, then, the appeal to original meaning may be either liberal or conservative according to the politics of a given issue. In cultural terms, however, it remains an essentially conservative idea. What still needs explaining, then, is why a society not otherwise known for its deference to patriarchal authority finds it so useful to couch its constitutional discourse in the language of appeals to the wisdom of its Founding Fathers. An answer to this question may lie in recognizing that the Constitution functions not only as a superlegal text but also as a legitimating symbol of national origins. Even if the Civil War redeemed the Union the Fathers sealed in 1787 from their original sin of slavery, its bloodshed and strife make it too painful a symbol of national division to enable it to operate as a consensual source of political authority. But along with the Declaration of Independence, the Constitution offers the one symbol of American nationality to which all parties can appeal, and this in turn guarantees that the struggle to control the interpretation of its original meaning will remain a fruitful source of public controversy and scholarly inquiry.

JACK N. RAKOVE

FURTHER READING

Walter Berns, *Taking the Constitution Seriously* (New York: Simon and Schuster, 1987).
Robert Bork, *The Tempting of America: the Political Seduction of the Law* (New York: Free Press, 1990).
Michael Kammen, *A Machine That Would Go of Itself: the Constitution in American Culture* (New York: Knopf, 1987).

Leonard Levy, *Original Intent and the Framers' Constitution* (New York: Macmillan, 1988).
Jack N. Rakove, ed., *Interpreting the Constitution: the Debate over Original Intent* (Boston: Northeastern University Press, 1990).

Cooley, Charles Horton (b. Ann Arbor, Mich., Aug. 17, 1864; d. Ann Arbor, Mich., May 8, 1929). Sociologist. One of the first professional sociologists, Cooley made a major contribution to social psychology. In *Human Nature and the Social Order* (1902) and *Social Organization* (1909), he stressed the interdependence of self and society. Selfhood emerges through social interaction, he believed, and communal bonds, similarly, derive from individuals' primary relationships. The common experience of human interaction in small groups suggested to him that all societies shared certain fundamental experiences.

See also SOCIAL SCIENCE.

FURTHER READING

Marshall J. Cohen, *Charles Horton Cooley and the Social Self in American Thought* (New York: Garland, 1982).

Cooley, Thomas M. (b. Attica, N.Y., Jan. 6, 1824; d. Ann Arbor, Mich., Sept. 12, 1898). Jurist. Named in 1859 to the law faculty at the University of Michigan, Cooley was elected to the Michigan Supreme Court in 1864 and served until 1885. In his influential *Treatise on the Constitutional Limitations which Rest Upon the Legislative Power of the States of the American Union* (1868), Cooley provided the principal statement in constitutional LAW of the principles of laissez-faire. Writing at the height of post-Civil War activism, Cooley's work provided a brake on reform-minded legislatures and judges. He championed limited government, criticized the regulation of business, and proclaimed the supremacy of the judiciary over the legislatures in the shaping of the law.

FURTHER READING

Alan R. Jones, *The Constitutional Conservatism of Thomas McIntyre Cooley: a Study in the History of Ideas* (New York: Garland, 1987).

Cooper, James Fenimore (b. Burlington, N.J., Sept. 15, 1789; d. Cooperstown, N.Y., Sept. 14, 1851). In his novels, essays, and histories Cooper helped shape Americans' emerging sense of their national culture. Son of the Federalist judge who founded Cooperstown, N.Y., Cooper attended Yale but was expelled for blowing up a classmate's door. At 21 he resigned a commission in the U.S. Navy to marry Susan De Lancey, daughter of an old Tory family. Cooper converted to Jeffersonian principles but tried to live as an eighteenth-century gentleman while the fevers of Jacksonian Democracy swept the land. After the decisive success of *The Last of the Mohicans* (1826), he took his family to Europe for a seven-year stay, and upon his return to Cooperstown in 1833 he began a series of lawsuits meant to enforce the sanctity of private property and truth in journalism.

In both fiction and nonfiction Cooper acutely analyzed American political and cultural life and engaged in controversy. In Europe he wrote *Notions of the Americans* (1829) and the journals that would become his travel books: *Sketches of Switzerland* (1836), *Gleanings in Europe* [France] (1837), *Gleanings in Europe: England* (1837), and *Gleanings in Europe: Italy* (1838). *A Letter to His Countrymen* (1834) assailed American provincialism, and *The American Democrat* (1838) was meant to tutor high school students in their political and social responsibilities. Cooper's fine naval histories included *The History of the Navy of the United States of America* (1839), *The Cruise of the Somers* (1844), and *Lives of Distinguished American Naval Officers* (1846). All these nonfiction works reveal Cooper's interest in the effects of DEMOCRACY on manners and morals. He insisted that Americans were better Christians, made more rational citizens, and treated women better than did any other people. At the same time he was critical of the American susceptibility to demagoguery, inflammatory gossip, and the sway of the popular will. He was sympathetic to the plight of Native Americans, but he justified the Jacksonian policy of removing all Indians to reservations west of the Mississippi; he condemned populist attacks on the patroon system that had granted huge tracts of land in New York to a few well-placed families; he loathed slavery but conceded that it had been recognized by the Constitution of the U.S. and was a necessary evil; he stressed the importance of class differences and ridiculed the American habit of calling all women "ladies" and men "gentlemen." Outspoken and truculent, Cooper managed at one time or another to antagonize nearly all his readers.

But it is for his fiction that Cooper is best known, especially for the mythic sweep and power of his five Leatherstocking novels (*The Pioneers*, 1823, *The Last of the Mohicans*, 1826, *The Prairie*, 1827, *The Pathfinder*, 1840, and *The Deerslayer*, 1841). D. H. Lawrence called the series "a *decrescendo* of reality, and a crescendo of beauty," and certainly *The Pioneers* is most concerned with the recovery of the past of Cooper's youth. He drew on his experience growing up in a frontier village to probe what it meant to inherit the American history of conflict over possession of the American landscape, setting the claims of Native Americans, British loyalists, American patriots, roaming hunters, and forest-clearing farmers against each other. If the novel rather wistfully resolved all these conflicts in the marriage of the children of all the contending forces, it nevertheless succeeded brilliantly as a thoroughly *American* fiction, not least in its invention of the Leatherstocking, Natty Bumppo, as Cooper's essential American hero. But all Cooper's novels engaged historical themes and helped to form the popular sense of American history and romantic historiography in the nineteenth century. Among the abiding themes of the Leatherstocking Tales are race relations among white, black, and Native Americans, the course of "historical progress," the shaping (especially through violence) of the national character, romantic religious enlightenment, and the importance of an almost Hemingwayesque personal "code."

From *The Spy* (1821) to *The Ways of the Hour* (1851), Cooper's other novels similarly (and sometimes as successfully) engaged American history. In *The Spy*, as in *The Pilot* (1823), *Lionel Lincoln* (1825), and *Wyandotté* (1843), Cooper treated, with increasing skepticism, the patriotic fervor of the American Revolution; *The Wept of Wish-ton-Wish* (1829) was set in Connecticut in the period of King Philip's War; the "Littlepage trilogy" (*Satanstoe*, *The Chainbearer*, and *The Redskins*, 1845–6) chronicled events of the "Anti-Rent Wars" in New York (1839–46) virtually as they occurred.

The weaknesses of Cooper's fiction are famous. James Russell Lowell, in his "A Fable for Critics" (1848), called attention to Cooper's own undemocratic class-consciousness and to the limitations of his female characters: "And the women he draws from one model don't vary, / All sappy as maples and flat as a prairie." Mark Twain hilariously skewered the excesses of Cooper's romanticism in "Fenimore Cooper's Literary Offenses" (1895), claiming that in two-thirds of a page of *The Deerslayer* Cooper had "scored 114 offenses against literary art out of a possible 115. It breaks the record." Twain expressed the exasperation of many readers when he argued that Cooper's diction was grotesquely inflated and imprecise, his incidents absurd and repetitive, his characters more dead than alive. *Deerslayer*

has no invention; it has no order, system, sequence, or result; it has no lifelikeness, nor thrill, no stir, no seeming of reality; its characters are confusedly drawn, and by their acts and words they prove that they are not the sort of people the author claims that they are; its humor is pathetic; its pathos is funny; its conversations are—oh! indescribable; its love-scenes odious; its English is a crime against the language.

Other readers have chafed, justifiably, at Cooper's annoying didacticism, and several critics would agree with Donald Darnell that "Above all else Cooper's theme is Know Your Place." But Cooper's work is too complex for that formula, and his characters (including the women) are often more richly developed than is usually recognized, constituting a remarkable gallery of American types—not only Natty Bumppo, the essential frontiersman, but Yankee peddlers, Puritan sectarians, Dutch patroons, Irish laborers, self-reliant women, slaves, free blacks, sailors, farmers, Native Americans of many nations and kinds, Virginian horsemen, western beehunters, pretentious scientists, quack doctors, ministers, lawyers, immigrants from all over Europe, and more. For all their sterilities and excesses, Cooper's novels teem with his acute sense of the variety of American life. They also constitute a valuable record of American custom and society (for instance, the account of the Pinkster Festival of New York slaves in *Satanstoe*), and at their best they present a richness, depth, and complexity that was unsurpassed in American fiction before the works of Hawthorne and Melville. In particular, Cooper (unlike Hawthorne) was unwilling or unable to rationalize the contradictions and incoherencies of American cultural life. This stubborn honesty not only was the key to his own character, but his most valuable contribution to our understanding of the history of American culture.

JAMES D. WALLACE

See also ROMANTIC HISTORIANS.

FURTHER READING

Charles Hansford Adams, *"The Guardian of the Law": Authority and Identity in James Fenimore Cooper* (University Park: Penn State University Press, 1990).

James Fenimore Cooper, *The Letters and Journals of James Fenimore Cooper*, ed. James Franklin Beard, 6 vols. (Cambridge: Harvard University Press, 1960–8).

Donald Darnell, *James Fenimore Cooper: Novelist of Manners* (Newark: University of Delaware Press, 1993).

James Grossman, *James Fenimore Cooper: a Biographical and Critical Study* (1949; Stanford: Stanford University Press, 1967).

John P. McWilliams Jr., *Political Justice in a Republic: James Fenimore Cooper's America* (Berkeley: University of California Press, 1972).

Warren Motley, *The American Abraham: James Fenimore Cooper and the Frontier Patriarch* (New York: Oxford University Press, 1987).

Geoffrey Rans, *Cooper's Leatherstocking Novels: a Secular Reading* (Chapel Hill: University of North Carolina Press, 1991).

Mark Twain, "Fenimore Cooper's Literary Offenses," in Edmund Wilson, ed., *The Shock of Recognition: the Development of Literature in the United States Recorded by the Men Who Made It* (1943; New York: Modern Library, 1955).

James D. Wallace, *Early Cooper and His Audience* (New York: Columbia University Press, 1986).

Cooper, Thomas (b. London, England, Oct. 22, 1759; d. Columbia, S.C., May 11, 1839). Philosopher and scientist. After emigrating from England in 1793, Cooper practiced medicine and law in Pennsylvania and then taught chemistry at the University of Virginia and at South Carolina College, where in 1821 he became president. But his views antagonized the clergy and he eventually had to resign. In *On the Connection between Geology and the Pentateuch* (1833), Cooper insisted that geology does not support the biblical account of creation. Physical phenomena, he believed, can explain all mental processes: the soul does not exist before or after the body. A staunch liberal individualist, Cooper argued for free trade and states' rights, including the right of a state to secede from the Union. He was a strong supporter of nullification in 1832.

FURTHER READING

Charlotte M. Porter, *The Eagle's Nest: Natural History and American Ideas, 1812–1842* (University, Ala.: University of Alabama Press, 1986).

Corwin, Edward S. (b. near Plymouth, Mich., Jan. 19, 1878; d. Princeton, N.J., Apr. 29, 1963). Constitutional scholar. Hired to teach at Princeton by Woodrow Wilson in 1905, Corwin remained there for four decades, most of that time as Professor of Jurisprudence. Author of *The Constitution and What It Means Today* (1920) and *The President: Office and Powers* (1940), among many other volumes, Corwin argued that the Constitution must develop to keep pace with modern needs. A strong booster of the New Deal, he held that the Constitution permits social and economic powers to shift from states to the federal government, a necessary shift in an increasingly global economy. He therefore deemphasized judicial review and called for an active Congress with strong Presidential leadership.

See also LAW.

FURTHER DETAILS

Kenneth D. Crews, *Edward S. Corwin and the American Constitution* (Westport, Conn.: Greenwood, 1985).

Cotton, John (b. Derby, England, Dec. 4, 1584; d. Boston, Mass., Dec. 23, 1652). Although John Cotton was a powerful and beloved minister in both England and New England, he is perhaps best remembered today as the man who banished ROGER WILLIAMS and ANNE HUTCHINSON. Held to current literary and political standards, Cotton's sermons seem dry and technical, his politics intolerant and elitist. Yet in his own day he was admired as a preacher of enormous inspiration; indeed, members of his congregation in England traveled across the Atlantic to continue to hear him preach. And, compared to his more extremist colleagues on both the right and the left of the political spectrum, Cotton's politics were almost always tempered by his gift for moderation and compromise. Unless we appreciate these contexts we cannot understand what made Cotton the most important Puritan minister in the New World.

Cotton's rise to prominence began long before he set sail for New England. In his home country he was educated at Trinity College and Emmanuel College, Cambridge, where he studied with the brightest lights of English reform. He eventually became vicar of St. Botolph's Church in Boston, Lincolnshire, where Anne Hutchinson and ANNE BRADSTREET were among those who heard him preach. For nearly 15 years Cotton not only survived but thrived in a political climate marked by tensions between the established and dissenting branches of the Church of England. His success was due, in part, to his willingness to make certain concessions on church rituals (for example, he allowed marriage ceremonies in his church although he did not perform them himself) while never wavering on the fundamental tenets of belief.

His tenure in England was not without turmoil, however. He was twice suspended from his post for nonconformity, and was eventually summoned to appear before William Laud and the High Court in 1632. Previously, Cotton had supported migration to the New World—in, for example, his famous sermon to JOHN WINTHROP and the *Arbella* fleet, "God's Promise to His Plantation" (1630)—but he himself never desired to leave England. But Laud's rise to power and Cotton's own reputation eventually made it impossible for him to remain in Lincolnshire unpersecuted. Again, Cotton compromised. He resigned his vicarship, went first into exile and then migrated to Boston, New England, in 1633. However, he refused to separate from the Church of England, preferring instead to think of the colonial churches as "nonseparating congregations": laboratories in which to formulate an ecclesiastical polity that, when the time was right, would be transplanted back to England. Thus, for Cotton at least, migration was a means to an end, not an end in itself.

In New England, Cotton was quickly appointed teaching elder of the First Church of Boston. Through his explications of scriptures such as Ecclesiastes, Canticles and Revelation, and in major works such as his *Treatise of the Covenant of Grace*, Cotton aimed to clarify and to expand his theory of spiritual conversion. The majority of the Puritan ministry in New England—most notably Thomas Hooker—held that individual believers could partially prepare themselves to receive grace from God by following a carefully defined set of behaviors. This theory led to what we now think of as the stereotypical Puritan: rigid, overly scrupulous, anxiously attentive and hard working. Cotton was different. He believed that the individual could do almost nothing to affect the state of his or her soul; that there was no direct correlation between outward behavior and inner spirituality. Instead, one receives grace from God in an overwhelming, immediate, almost sensuous influx of the spirit. Moreover, Cotton preached his brand of conversion in a rhetoric different from that of most of his peers. While Hooker marched to the rigid lockstep of Ramist logic, Cotton's sermons were organized along the emotional contours of the doctrines and experiences he described. Readers today may prefer Hooker's fire and brimstone, but listeners in Cotton's own time may have heard something we no longer hear in sermons that were quietly attuned to their fears and anxieties, that struck a proper balance between urgency and nurturance.

While we have no way to capture the effect of Cotton's preaching on the vast majority of his audience, we do know that at least one congregant—Anne Hutchinson—was so moved by his sermons that she followed him to the New World. The Antinomian crisis of 1636–8 has come to be viewed almost exclusively in terms of the patriarchal oppression of Hutchinson and her followers. This interpretation is in many ways valid, but we should not lose sight of the importance of the special and complicated relationship between minister and congregant. Throughout the trials Hutchinson singled out Cotton as one of the few ministers who preached a true covenant of grace: that is, that good works (or justification) may be a sign of conversion, but they do not cause salvation. Even before the trials, Hutchinson and other members of Cotton's congregation would often disrupt sermons of other ministers to correct their doctrine. Thus, ministers and magistrates alike, perhaps jealous of Cotton's renown, used the Antinomian crisis as a way to challenge his preeminence. He was relentlessly questioned in print and in person: he was censured by the court for allowing Hutchinson to persist in her doctrinal "errors." Although Cotton never altered these doctrines to meet the demands of the court, he did finally abandon Hutchinson, first by failing to come actively to her defense, then by supporting her excommunication and banishment. Later in life Cotton publicly attempted to depict the trials as an example of the efficiency of the congregational way; privately, he viewed the crisis as a defeat of his view of conversion.

After the Antinomian crisis Cotton worked to codify and defend his plans for Congregationalism in New England. In works such as *The Keyes of the Kingdom of Heaven* and *The Way of the Churches of Christ*, Cotton sketched out what amounts to a compromise between high church presbyterianism and radical separation. Each church (or congregation) was to consist of visible saints: those who had testified to the experience of conversion. These members, in turn, elected their ministers and elders. While each congregation governed itself independently and was not subjected to an overarching hierarchy of bishops or presbyters, churches were nevertheless encouraged to associate voluntarily in the form of synods. Moreover, Cotton posited a theocratic relationship between church and state: ministers and magistrates would consult on matters spiritual and civil.

The articulation of the New England Way became increasingly important for Cotton in the mid to late 1640s for a variety of reasons. News from abroad, particularly the execution of Charles I and the early successes of Cromwell, seemed to indicate that England would soon be ready to institute a fully reformed church polity. Cotton also responded to events in New England, especially the challenges mounted by Roger Williams. In recent times, Williams has been championed as one of the few Puritans to advocate toleration of dissent and separation of church and state. The motivations for these arguments, however, are better understood in the context of his infamous debates with Cotton than in light of post-Enlightenment ideals of liberal democracy. Cotton was always willing to tolerate the possibility that some hypocrites would gain admission to the church; Williams insisted that the true church should consist purely of those who were absolutely, unequivocally saved. Consequently, the unregenerate many should be tolerated, almost by default, as long as they remained outside the church. Similarly, while Cotton argued that alliances between church and state in both England and New England would be mutually beneficial in bringing about reform, Williams held that since the state was generally corrupt and unreformed, it must be kept separate to preserve the absolute purity of the church.

Scholars interested in issues of gender, rhetoric, politics and toleration in the colonial era have focused most of their attention on Williams and Hutchinson and have tended to push Cotton to the periphery. Since Cotton was so intimately involved in these debates, however, we cannot gain a full understanding of their complexity without an appreciation of his life and work.

MICHAEL KAUFMANN

See also PURITANISM.

FURTHER READING
Everett Emerson, *John Cotton* (New York: Twayne, 1965).
Ann Kibbey, *The Interpretation of Material Shapes in Puritanism: a study of Rhetoric, Prejudice, and Violence* (New York: Cambridge University Press, 1986).
Larzer Ziff, *The Career of John Cotton: Puritanism and the American Experience* (Princeton: Princeton University Press, 1962).

Cowley, Malcolm (b. Belsano, Pa., Aug. 24, 1898; d. New Milford, Conn., Mar. 27, 1989). Literary critic. Literary editor of THE NEW REPUBLIC (1929–44), Cowley ranged widely across the artistic and political landscape and urged a socially engaged interpretation of literature. With *Exile's Return* (1934), he issued a pivotal statement of the intellectual's fate in the twentieth century: seeking immersion in the vitality and immediacy of "real life," intellectuals find themselves, for all their ostensible bohemianism, locked into bourgeois patterns of life and thought. Critical of efforts to romanticize the "lost generation" of artistic exiles of the 1920s, Cowley nevertheless helped establish that myth all the more firmly in American historical memory.

See also NEW YORK INTELLECTUALS.

FURTHER READING
Hans Bak, *Malcolm Cowley: the Formative Years* (Athens: University of Georgia Press, 1993).

Crane, Stephen (b. Newark, N.J., Nov. 1, 1871; d. Badenweiler, Germany, June 5, 1900). Writer. In *Maggie: a Girl of the Streets* (1893) and *The Red Badge of Courage* (1895), Crane expressed his fascination with the psychological realities of life in degrading or dangerous circumstances. His impressionistic techniques created vivid depictions of internal emotions and liminal experiences. As a war correspondent in Greece and Cuba in the late 1890s, he contributed to the image of the intellectual as the reporter of "real life" as it is lived on the edge. His poetry, journalism, and stories all helped constitute a new realism in American literature—not because he "documented" reality but because he labored to find a new language for the experiencing of reality.

See also NATURALISM; REALISM.

FURTHER READING
Michael Fried, *Realism, Writing, Disfiguration: On Thomas Eakins and Stephen Crane* (Chicago: University of Chicago Press, 1987).

Crèvecoeur, Michel-Guillaume-Saint-Jean de

[pen name J. Hector St. John Crèvecoeur] (b. near Caen, France, Jan. 31, 1735; d. Sarcelles, France, Nov. 12, 1813). Essayist. Best known for his *Letters from an American Farmer* (1782), Crèvecoeur claimed that the American landscape had created a new American with a distinctive way of thinking and acting. Characterizing America as a land of small agrarian freeholds, he praised its social equality, economic liberty, and freedom from the tyranny of church or state. He described it as a melting pot of different (European) stocks, and lauded the independence and vigor of frontier life. At the same time, he warned of the threat posed to an egalitarian society by violence, greed, and other vices.

See also AMERICAN EXCEPTIONALISM; ASSIMILATION.

FURTHER READING
Gay Allen Wilson, *St. John de Crèvecoeur: the Life of an American Farmer* (New York: Viking, 1987).

critical legal studies In 1977, a group of young, iconoclastic American legal scholars formed the Conference on Critical Legal Studies. During the succeeding decade the organization grew rapidly. Large numbers of law teachers, law students, and practicing lawyers attended its annual meetings, and the scholarship produced by its members quickly came to rival in volume and influence the work associated with LAW AND ECONOMICS, the other coherent movement in legal theory during the period. In the late 1980s, critical legal studies appeared to be losing novelty and force, but in the early 1990s it was reenergized through its association with a cluster of scholarly initiatives it had helped spawn: CRITICAL RACE THEORY, FEMINIST JURISPRUDENCE, and (most recently) legal theories concerned with sexuality and sexual orientation.

The backgrounds and interests of the original organizers of the critical legal studies movement were diverse. Some—especially those affiliated with the Law and Society Association—were committed to the study of the actual operation of legal rules and, in particular, the ways in which they reinforce inequalities of wealth and power. Others—especially those steeped in continental social and literary theory —were interested primarily in the structure of legal doctrine and consciousness and cared little about the law in action. The political orientation of all of the organizers was left of the center of the American ideological spectrum, but the extent to which they were committed to radical restructuring of American society varied considerably. To these differences in outlook were added the variety of perspectives brought to the movement during the 1980s by growing numbers of women and members of racial and ethnic minorities. The results were fractiousness, fun, and scholarly fecundity.

The history and character of the movement make it impossible to summarize concisely the contributions it has made to American legal thought, but one can identify three lines of argument that thus far have been most influential.

First, drawing on structuralist theory, several members of the group have sought to demonstrate that American legal doctrine is both organized around and destabilized by fundamentally contradictory aspirations or commitments. This aspect of critical legal studies represents an extension of the work of the legal realists, the most influential group of American legal scholars during the 1920s and 1930s. The adherents of LEGAL REALISM contended that many fields of law are beset with tensions and inconsistencies. The critical theorists make similar assertions on a grander scale. Conflicts of the sort identified by the realists between individual rules or canons of interpretation are merely manifestations, they claim, of more general and durable antinomies. Brought to the surface, most of these antinomies turn out to be related in some way to classical LIBERALISM. For example, the notion that both social welfare and justice are best served if disputes are resolved through the mechanical operation of clear rules wars with the notion that only the discretionary administration of flexible standards can accommodate the idiosyncrasies of persons and conflicts; the familiar principle that values and desires are arbitrary and subjective is undercut by a yearning to identify stable social and ethical truths; the idea that human action is the product of will is in constant tension with the idea that human action is largely determined by environment. Duncan Kennedy, in a seminal study of the history of American legal thought, has contended that underlying each of these antinomies is a deeper trauma experienced by most participants in American culture —a painful sense that "the goal of individual freedom is both dependent on and incompatible with the communal coercive action that is necessary to achieve it" (Boyle, p. 5).

The critical theorists do not content themselves, of course, with merely reciting these contradictions; in long articles rich in doctrinal and historical detail, they seek to show how a struggle to come to terms with them—or, more often, to postpone facing them—has shaped field after field of the law. To be sure, some of the essays in this vein (especially the later ones) are formulaic and tiresome, but most are illuminating, and a few are brilliant.

The second of the three arguments is commonly known as the "indeterminacy thesis." Most legal principles, the critical theorists contend, are far less effective as guides to decision-making than is conventionally assumed. For example, Mark Tushnet argues that the "right to equal concern and respect" (a favorite among liberal legal theorists) is incapable of generating answers to real problems (such as the scope of parents' and children's entitlements against one another) because the meaning of the right depends on matters of social context (such as whether children need their biological parents in order to develop into autonomous persons) about which Americans are in profound disagreement.

A common misconception of critical legal studies is that arguments of this sort lead inexorably to the conclusion that legal decision-making is unpredictable in practice. The reason most critical theorists do not make that inference is that they are sensitive to the grip exerted on judges by two related aspects of legal culture: tacit agreements concerning the most appropriate meanings of contested concepts; and conventions concerning which of the terms in each of the fundamental contradictions that undergird legal doctrine ordinarily should be privileged. But—and here is the nub of this line of argument—those agreements and conventions are sufficiently tenuous that the subordinate term of each of the dyads is always available to overturn or confound the dominant term and to prompt judges to alter dramatically their responses to particular sorts of cases. No objective, neutral canons of reasoning and no integrated justificatory system stabilize the legal order as a whole.

The subject of the third kind of argument is the ideological function of legal discourse. Drawing on the work of Antonio Gramsci, the FRANKFURT SCHOOL, and the general tradition of Critical Marxism, several scholars associated with critical legal studies have sought to show how legal doctrine and discourse have hidden injustice, obscured the contradictory impulses in the legal system, reduced popular appreciation of the indeterminacy of legal norms, and disabled participants in legal culture from envisioning truly radical departures from the status quo. For example, Alan Freeman contends that modern antidiscrimination law, by focusing attention upon and limiting relief to circumstances in which particular defendants can be shown to have engaged in purposeful discrimination, "has served more to rationalize the continued presence

of racial discrimination in our society than it has to solve the problem" (Kairys, p. 97). Similarly, Peter Gabel argues that the ubiquitous vocabulary of "rights" encourages us to pretend that we currently enjoy both as much autonomy and as much community as we desire and inhibits our efforts to imagine and establish a less alienated form of social relations.

Such arguments have been highly controversial. Traditional legal scholars have reacted to critical legal studies sometimes with curiosity, sometimes with condescension, sometimes with rage. Struggle continues within many American law schools over what role if any critical theory should play in law teaching. This situation, combined with the effervescence of the movement itself, makes the future of critical legal studies uncertain.

WILLIAM W. FISHER III

FURTHER READING
James Boyle, ed., *Critical Legal Studies* (New York: New York University Press, 1992).

"Critical Legal Studies Symposium," *Stanford Law Review* 36 (Jan. 1984): 1–674.

Morton Horwitz, *The Transformation of American Law*, vols. 1, 2 (New York: Oxford University Press, 1977, 1992).

David Kairys, ed., *The Politics of Law: a Progressive Critique*, rev. ed. (New York: Pantheon, 1990).

Mark Kelman, *A Guide to Critical Legal Studies* (Cambridge: Harvard University Press, 1977).

Duncan Kennedy and Karl E. Klare, "A Bibliography of Critical Legal Studies," *Yale Law Journal* 94 (1984): 461–90.

"Symposium on Feminist Critical Legal Studies and Postmodernism," *New England Law Review* 26 (summer 1992): 639–891, 1173–537.

Roberto Unger, *The Critical Legal Studies Movement* (Cambridge: Harvard University Press, 1986).

critical race theory The latest addition to the postrealist smorgasbord of jurisprudence, critical race theory is uniquely situated because its diverse subject matter traverses the boundaries that separate other critical movements along the lines of class, gender, and ethnicity. It has the opportunity to immerse itself in the particularity of its own historical experience and aspirations while simultaneously providing insight for others whose horizons are darkened by the clouds of oppression.

So many struggles for inclusion and liberation in the American context have been inspired by the resistance movements and critiques of black people. From Nat Turner and Denmark Vesey, through HARRIET TUBMAN and SOJOURNER TRUTH, to FREDERICK DOUGLASS and MARTIN DELANY, to W. E. B. DU BOIS, BOOKER T. WASHINGTON and MARCUS GARVEY, to A. Philip Randolph and Angelo Herndon, to Rosa Parks and Fannie Lou Hamer, to MARTIN LUTHER

KING JR. and MALCOLM X, we are heir to a tradition of struggle that has vacillated between the poles of particularism and universalism, nationalism and integration, the struggle to acknowledge both the difference and the sameness of our experiences with others. My hope is that critical race theory will be in the forefront of developing a powerful synthesis of particularist and universalist strategies of liberation from the context of our own experiences—a synthesis that will continue to light the flame for liberation struggles around the world.

The dichotomy between abstract universalism, that is assimilation masquerading as integration, and concrete particularism, separatism masquerading as nationalism, is false. The choice is not an either/or dilemma but a both/and possibility that expunges the most debilitating dimensions of these polar opposites and incorporates their most liberating qualities. Any abstract universalism that denies the particularity of the black experience and uncritically assimilates it to others' experiences is problematic. Equally, any concrete particularism that denies the possibilities of more universal connections that might bridge the gulfs that separate black men from black women, the black poor from its middle class, and the black race from other groups who themselves have similar histories and trajectories is problematic as well. Critical race theory can provide a critical process of talking across these spaces that define our separateness in ways that treasure the best of our separateness.

Critical race theory has two goals in this regard. The first is to elucidate the ways in which those in power have socially constructed the very concept of RACE over time, that is, the extent to which white power has transformed certain differences in color, culture, behavior, and outlook into hierarchies of privilege and subordination. As Winthrop Jordan put it in *White Over Black* (1968), American history has been one predicated on the ideological assumption that white is superior to black.

Theories of black inferiority have all embraced some real or contrived differences between the two groups as the basis of deducing a social arrangement that legally, economically, and culturally subordinated blacks to whites. The opinion written by ROGER TANEY in the *Dred Scott* case (1857) is the most notable legal expression of this naturalist or essentialist approach. Some black intellectuals have responded uncritically to this racist history by denying both the negative and positive meanings attributed to difference, while arguing for some universal conception of humanity thought to transcend the politics of difference. In so doing, they reject one essentialism for another. The essentialism of difference, identity politics, is rejected for the essentialism of sameness, abstract universalism.

The second goal, apparently in tension with the first, acknowledges differences between blacks and whites that are "sufficiently" real, differences in experience, outlook, and response. That is, while the meanings attributed to those differences may be socially constructed meanings, as Jacques Derrida and Michel Foucault, for example, have argued, those social constructions have constituted identities in very deep and structural ways. Indeed, a critical understanding of and deference to those identities may be essential to the group's survival and liberation. Some black intellectuals have opted for an uncritical acceptance of racial essentialism based on the socially constructed meanings of difference. In so doing, this tradition also rejects one essentialism for another. Here the essentialism of universal sameness is rejected for the essentialism of an identity politics rooted in the particularity of black experience. If accepted uncritically, both kinds of essentialism are problematic. If critically appraised and revised, both are necessary for the project of critical race theory.

Critical race theory thus faces a dilemma. On the one hand, blacks have had to vindicate standards of sameness (colorblind universalism) when difference (race-conscious particularism) is used as an instrument of oppression. This is what much of the ANTISLAVERY and CIVIL RIGHTS struggle was about. On the other hand, blacks have had to sing the praises of difference (race-conscious particularism) when sameness (colorblind universalism) is the instrument of oppression. This is what much of the Black Power struggle was about.

Critical race theory contends that both essentialisms are simultaneously right and wrong because it sees the partial truth of each. Critical race theory sees the problem in terms of the ways in which blacks have been dominated and oppressed. It discloses the power of one group to realize through the rhetoric of sameness and/or difference the dominance of another on the basis of that group's perceived inferiority. This historical backdrop has at different times necessitated different modes of response that are only contradictory if abstracted from that historical context and examined as mere ideas in the intellectual history of African Americans.

In other words, vital to an understanding of how critical race theory hopes to have its cake and eat it too is the acknowledgment that the dominance of one group by another can be achieved through two different ideological constructs—one overtly racist, the other ostensibly race neutral. *Dred Scott* and *Plessy v. Ferguson* (1896), which upheld the constitutionality of racial segregation, vindicated white cultural standards that blacks were thought incapable of attaining. While *Dred Scott* explicitly stated this belief of inferiority, *Plessy* clearly assumed it in its contention that the inequality of separate facilities was but a figment of blacks' imagination.

The decisions challenging segregation, especially *Brown v. Board of Education of Topeka*, (1954) and its progeny, on the other hand, also vindicated white cultural norms. Only this time blacks were permitted, indeed encouraged, to strive for these standards in a newly desegregated social order. In the first era, the white standard was a "my standard" to which blacks were thought incapable of conforming because of natural inferiority. In the second era, the white standard was recast as an "our standard" to which blacks were invited to conform against the backdrop of undisturbed allocations of wealth and power created by a racist history that made conformity, for most, practically impossible. While the first era predicated subordination on difference, the second predicated subordination on sameness. Neither questioned the standards or paradigms themselves; that project lies at the very core of critical race theory. It is this depthful critique of norms, background assumptions, and paradigms within which black progress and regress take place that gives critical race theory its critical bite.

I have argued in the *Harvard Law Review* (1990) that a full critical praxis contemplates four interrelated critical activities: theoretical deconstruction, experiential deconstruction, reconstructive theorizing, and transformative social struggle. The first two embody critiques of the two forms of essentialism discussed above. They are space-clearing activities that help prepare the way for the third and fourth critical practices. While the first two activities are often antiessentialist in tone, since they challenge traditional ways of viewing the world, the second two are essentialist in orientation, since to reconstruct theoretically and to struggle to realize one's vision assumes a degree of certainty and fixity about the real world. The first activities are admittedly in tension with the latter.

Theoretical deconstruction examines binary concepts like colorblindness and race-consciousness, discriminatory intent and discriminatory effect, and public and private space, for purposes of delineating their differences and mutual dependencies and demonstrating that either/or dilemmas might be recast as both/and possibilities. Theoretical deconstruction shakes one from one's intellectual stupor and exposes as socially contrived and susceptible to change what people have been socialized to see as natural and un-

alterable. For example, the logically fastidious lines dividing the public from the private in the late nineteenth century are blurred as one discovers that the public has shaped the private and that the private has perennially transgressed the public. Thus, private property is incomprehensible independent of a public sphere that defines and enforces property rights, while the sociocultural and geopolitical influence of private concentrations of property on public space seems incontrovertible.

Theoretical deconstruction diligently searches for the socially constructed qualities of society's supposed objective realities and encourages it to envision different social constructions and realities more liberating than those presently endured. The danger is that critique of logical closures and distinctions always threatens to undo the done, to destabilize the stable, and to undermine any constructive theory or narrative of oppression that replaces the old with the new. It raises the specter of radical relativism and heightens to feverish delirium the fear of living in a state of theoretical flux.

Theoretical deconstruction must be linked to experiential deconstruction, or analysis of the material reality of oppression, if it is to be more than a string of meaningless destabilizing abstractions. Experiential deconstruction chooses narrative as a mode of communication, because in the narratives of marginality and difference, the cries of oppression are more clearly heard. Voices silenced by the tyranny of "logical" argumentation, and realities obscured by the mystifications of elaborate abstractions find space for expression and recognition in the theater of voices and experiences that makes us.

The historicist's turn to narrative provides no guarantees, however, for history can yield conflicting stories and interpretations that lead away from, rather than toward, what might be deemed a just society. Thus, not all stories can be told, and fewer still can be recognized or affirmed, in a society characterized by scarcity of resources and time. One is compelled, then, to tell a story about the story one is telling that accounts for how and why it is privileged over others. It is in this regard that both theoretical and experiential deconstruction must be linked to the enterprise of reconstructive theorizing. Reconstructive theorizing talks explicitly about values and priorities, that is, the kind of community envisioned. It refuses to assume, with liberal process theory, that a perfected *process*, whether it is one embracing reasoning by precedent or by narrative, will be itself yield a just society.

Finally, each of these dimensions of critical activity must be seasoned and informed by a commitment to transformative social struggle—an attempt to actualize what has been visualized through the processes of deconstruction and reconstruction just outlined. In this way, theory and praxis are always engaged in a dialectic of mutual dependency, in which each learns from and teaches the other in the pursuit of JUSTICE.

Certain dimensions of this critical praxis influence one of the central projects of critical race theory: negotiating the tension between universalism and particularism in our struggles for Justice. Critical race theory's commitment to deconstruction highlights the problematic nature of either/or frameworks and encourages a synthesis of the most enabling dimensions of oppositionalized identities like nationalism and integrationism. It is the creative synthesis encouraged by the critique of either/or frameworks that moves us from deconstruction to reconstruction with a certain orientation to the spiritual movement toward Justice.

The Supreme Court's exclusive focus in *Brown* was on the ways in which segregation had affected the hearts and minds of Negro children in ways they were not likely to overcome. The Court made no reference to the ways in which segregation and historic forms of racism had inculcated false feelings of racial superiority in the hearts and minds of white children that they were not likely to overcome. We have, of course, paid dearly for the oversight; the promised program of integration has turned out to be one of ASSIMILATION in which the racist assumption of white superiority was left unchecked.

Thus, those in our intellectual tradition who have been uncritical in their acceptance of a universal and fundamentally assimilationist norm of colorblindness have not fully understood the workings of racism in the American context. Similarly, those who have been uncritical in their acceptance of a particularist and fundamentally separatist norm of race consciousness have not fully understood the authoritarianism often engendered by their uncritical essentialism.

The preceding account of the tension between nationalist and integrationist strands shows why critical race theory must in some sense remain marginal. Marginality requires a critical self-consciousness about one's position that is sacrificed by one's unreflective absorption into either of the two polar camps. Operating from the margins, or the edge of historically constituted identities, provides invaluable insight into problems often distorted because of one's inability to see the forest for the trees. The orientation of an African-American or Black-American critical theory must be the full exploration of the hyphenated space that lies between the supposed particularism

and avowed universalism of African"-"American or Black"-"American. It is in the interstices of the space between African and American that we will find the true stuff of life rather than the simplistic responses of crude assimilationists and nationalists. It is in that space, often signaled by the use of a hyphen, that the marginality of our existence becomes clear and a moral light emanating from the particularity of our own experience provides vision for those in darkness. It is quite fitting that the hyphen both denotes a separation and unity. It is both barrier and bridge. Its duality demands a respect for the particularity of historical experiences that assimilationist narratives dismiss and requires a willingness to connect with experiences different from our own in ways that insular nativisms prohibit.

This critique is well prepared then to explore the role of race in culture as a hegemonic ideology and to thus lay bare its relationship to gender, ethnicity, class and other forms of identity oppression. It is this critical exploration of the hyphenated space that embodies in abstract form the spirituality that must be integrated into our emerging critiques and reconstructive visions.

This spirituality must constitute a vital part of our critique and vision for it is the cry of human anguish across the chasms of class, gender, race and ethnicity. This spirituality is the longing for understanding based on, yet not wholly defined by, the particularities of our own identities and experiences. It is an attempt to balance the uneasy tension between a unifying universalism and a parochial particularism. This spirituality is an understanding that when all is said and done and the final act of our struggle for Justice is played upon the stage of life, our legacy must be one of Love, of a faithful struggle to mend the broken humanity of our fractured existence, a legacy of Love that tried to heal the wounds inflicted on those marginalized within our own race as well as the races of others, a legacy of Love that flows outward from the basin of our own experiences, intellectual histories and cultural traditions to connect with other tributaries that flow once again into the gulf of common concern.

The implications of this spirituality for critical race theory are clear. We must be outward-looking in our introspection; as we look to and study with great detail our histories and traditions, we must understand how these histories connect with the histories of other dominated groups within our own race and in the society at large. We must continue to explore the ways in which the dominant culture has developed canons of interpretation cloaked by science, religion and a socially constructed common sense that continue to relegate us to a subordinate status. But let us also be careful to understand that these very same cultural conventions have likewise relegated others also deemed inferior to varying degrees of subordination.

Spirituality is the sincere *striving* for unalienated and unfractured human connection. Spirituality is understanding the limits of our knowledge and allowing the humility fostered by such understanding to open us to the possibilities of knowledge once impeded by the arrogance of our self-contained worlds. The spirituality that flows from a critical and open engagement with the hyphenated space is one that focuses our attention and concern on those less fortunate—the least of these—the wretched of the earth—the despised, dejected, and downtrodden. In understanding our own marginality, we are enabled to understand the marginality of others who, because they are not forgotten in our critiques, are neither forgotten in our visions of a better tomorrow.

The spiritual movement towards Justice, then, is one that searches out the otherness of self and the context of being, that is, the ways in which we all are heir to common hopes, dreams, and fears. It holds out the possibility that even in our separate struggles for self-understanding we might glimpse the commonality of our particular alienation and oppression and seek collectively to overcome them yet.

ANTHONY COOK

See also CIVIL RIGHTS; CULTURAL PLURALISM AND MULTICULTURALISM.

FURTHER READING

Anthony Cook, "Beyond Critical Legal Studies: the Reconstructive Theology of Dr. Martin Luther King, Jr.," *Harvard Law Review* 103 (1990): 985–1044.
Kimberlé Crenshaw, "Race, Reform and Retrenchment: Transformation and Legitimation in Antidiscrimination Law," *Harvard Law Review* 101 (May 1988): 1331–87.
Patricia J. Williams, *The Alchemy of Race and Rights* (Cambridge: Harvard University Press, 1991).

Croly, Herbert (b. New York, N.Y., Jan. 23, 1869; d. Santa Barbara, Calif., May 17, 1930). Political philosopher and editor Herbert Croly was the son of two prominent journalists: his mother, Jane Cunningham Croly, was known all over the country as "Jennie June," a prolific commentator on women's topics and an organizer of women's clubs; his father, who began instructing his son at an early age and exerted a lifelong influence on his thought, was David Goodman Croly, a veteran New York newspaperman, a writer of quite unorthodox books and articles, and perhaps America's leading disciple of the French philosopher Auguste Comte. Thus Herbert was raised in a home where thinking, writing, and publishing were routine.

After a year at City College in New York, he began an erratic stay at Harvard in 1886; his student career ended in 1899 without his having earned a bachelor's degree. He returned to New York, the only place he considered suitable for the intellectual life and thus the only place he ever considered home. From 1900 to 1906 he edited the *Architectural Record*, a trade magazine founded by his father. By 1905, however, he found his mind drawn to the swirling political ferment that turned out to be the beginnings of the Progressive movement. He loosened his connection with the magazine and began to work on a book of social and political analysis that was to embody his best thought and provide the basis for his reputation as the man WALTER LIPPMANN (in his contribution to "Herbert Croly, 1869–1930") called "the first important political philosopher who appeared in America in the twentieth century" (p. 250).

Despite its ponderous style, *The Promise of American Life* (1909) received numerous complimentary reviews and was read by many political, intellectual, and reform leaders. The book conveyed Croly's views on a dozen current questions—everything from taking the Philippines to taxation policy, from the Australian ballot to municipal corruption, the merits of the closed shop and reciprocity with Canada. He also evaluated the leading political figures of the day. These judgments of issues and men, however, were scarcely random observations; they were embedded within a thoughtful and comprehensive general framework.

Before the Civil War, Croly argued, the American character took shape under the influence of three powerful faiths: a belief in unhampered and ambitious pioneer individualism; an insistence upon the strictly limited central government that Thomas Jefferson had advocated; and a confidence in the "promise of American life," a promise of ever-increasing democracy, freedom, and prosperity. During the nation's youth, these three beliefs existed in relative harmony: in order to develop its abundance, America needed free citizens unrestrained by an interfering central government. But, Croly continued, in the modern world of corporations, cities, and industry, the three elements in the American credo had begun to rub up against one another dangerously. Suddenly it appeared that ambitious individualism and a passive government were no longer adequate instruments for the achievement of the American dream—indeed, if Americans persistently adhered to these two principles, they would put the dream in jeopardy. Croly hoped to replace the stereotypical free and selfish individual with a new sort of American—one who valued community, accepted social responsibility, and felt loyalty to the nation. For the weak Jeffersonian government of antebellum America, Croly proposed to substitute a Hamiltonian government of substantial powers and the will to use them in unprecedented but democratic ways. *The Promise of American Life* was also notable because Croly opposed attempts to break down trusts into competing units, favoring instead a policy of regulation by the central government.

Historians have disagreed about the sources of Croly's beliefs. There is certainly present a large dose of the Comtean positivism he inherited from his father. In addition, it is possible to detect the influence of his philosophy professors at Harvard, a range of contemporary American and European social thinkers, and a novel by Robert Grant that Croly himself thought to be an important trigger for his thinking. No doubt the political and intellectual agitation of PROGRESSIVISM itself played a part in the book's focus and tone.

After THEODORE ROOSEVELT read and praised Croly's work, many doors opened for him. Mark Hanna's family hired him to write a biography of the political boss. Harvard gave Croly his degree in 1910 and invited him to deliver the Godkin lectures in 1913–14. Those lectures became his second book of political commentary, *Progressive Democracy* (1914). Although critical of Wilson's program, the new book drew encouragement from the wave of reform sentiment sweeping over the nation, put less faith in an elite of social experts and heroic leaders and more in an awakened populace, and reflected on every page the pragmatic and optimistic teachings of WILLIAM JAMES and, especially, JOHN DEWEY. Despite the book's penetrating analyses, and despite the many favorable reviews it received, it never achieved the fame or exerted the influence of *The Promise of American Life*.

In 1913, Croly was invited by Dorothy and Willard Straight, two idealistic and progressive philanthropists, to establish and edit a weekly "journal of opinion." After a year of preparation, which included gathering a brilliant staff of young contributors and fellow editors, the first issue of THE NEW REPUBLIC appeared in November 1914. From that moment on, Herbert Croly's life was tied intimately—one might even say exclusively—to the enterprise. He edited the magazine until a stroke in 1928 ended his public career. From 1914 until 1919, Croly's *New Republic* was the country's leading journalistic voice of progressivism. Although its circulation was always rather modest, its impact was enormous. In those golden years of influence, the journal broke with Roosevelt, struck an alliance with WOODROW WILSON (the editors

claiming that the President had transformed himself into a truly national reformer), supported military preparedness and then war, and advocated the whole array of liberal reform measures. The Treaty of Versailles at the end of World War I was a crushing blow to Croly himself and to his magazine. The journal forthrightly condemned the treaty and blasted Wilson in strident and uncompromising terms.

The last decade of Croly's life was unhappy. He continued to defend progressive measures, but, like many of the old reformers, felt on the defensive in an America that had turned away from reform and plunged into political conservatism, rank materialism, and business ascendancy. Despite momentary flashes of hope in 1924 with Robert La Follette and in 1928 with Al Smith, Croly turned the *New Republic* increasingly to literary and cultural questions, and he himself spun off into a flirtation with religious mysticism. Although the journal continued to attract illustrious contributors and maintained the allegiance of old progressive subscribers, the number of readers declined and its influence dwindled. Croly's own despair can be traced in his articles (many of them on religious topics), in an unpublished manuscript entitled *The Breach in Civilization*, and in an unpublished autobiographical fragment which was, he said, "an obituary of a past world of opinion and aspiration" and a confession that his early hopes for improving society had been "a mistake." The paralyzing stroke cut short his disappointment in America's wrongheadedness, and his death in 1930 came three years before the next flowering of centralized national reform and energetic social purpose.

Croly was extraordinarily shy and had almost to force himself to resist the life of a recluse. He dreaded speaking in public, and even casual conversation with strangers was painful. Ideas were everything to him, and his thought was his world. These obstacles to friendship notwithstanding, he managed to maintain a small circle of companions who respected his motives, admired his intelligence, and valued his integrity.

Herbert Croly was one of the principal intellectual founders of twentieth-century LIBERALISM. In his two major books and in his weekly journal, he put forward a penetrating critique of laissez-faire capitalism and offered a compelling description of what a wise and vigorous central government might achieve. He also left a lasting vision of a society that could combine scientific efficiency, individual fulfillment, and social justice, and do so by genuinely democratic means. His thought encompassed, defined, and illuminated a great many of the concerns of modern reform movements.

DAVID W. LEVY

FURTHER READING

Herbert Croly, Autobiographical fragment, Felix Frankfurter MSS, Box 215, Library of Congress.

Iris Dorreboom, *The Challenge of Our Time: Woodrow Wilson, Herbert Croly, Randolph Bourne and the Making of Modern America* (Amsterdam: Rodopi, 1991).

Charles Forcey, *The Crossroads of Liberalism: Croly, Weyl, Lippmann and the Progressive Era, 1900–1925* (New York: Oxford University Press, 1961).

"Herbert Croly, 1869–1930," *New Republic* 63 (July 16, 1930): 241–71.

James T. Kloppenberg, *Uncertain Victory: Social Democracy and Progressivism in European and American Thought, 1870–1920* (New York: Oxford University Press, 1986).

David W. Levy, *Herbert Croly of The New Republic: the Life and Thought of an American Progressive* (Princeton: Princeton University Press, 1985).

David W. Noble, "Herbert Croly and American Progressive Thought," *Western Political Quarterly* 7 (1954): 537–53.

Edward A. Stettner, *Shaping Modern Liberalism: Herbert Croly and Progressive Thought* (Lawrence: University Press of Kansas, 1993).

Cullen, Countee (b. probably Louisville, Ky., May 30, 1903; d. New York, N.Y., Jan. 9, 1946). Poet. Insisting on the artist's transcendence of racial categories, Cullen sought recognition as a poet, not a "black" poet. A central figure of the HARLEM RENAISSANCE, he used traditional forms and themes, endorsed a poetic romanticism that he equated with artistic quality, and emphasized that the "double obligation of being both Negro and American" does not mean the same thing for every African American. *Color* (1925) and *The Black Christ and Other Poems* (1929) contain powerful descriptions of African American race consciousness that range from militant optimism to disillusioned despair.

FURTHER READING

Houston A. Baker, *Modernism and the Harlem Renaissance* (Chicago: University of Chicago Press, 1987).

cultural anthropology A uniquely American creation, cultural anthropology has no clear disciplinary mandate aside from the anthropologist's participatory study of "culture"—an abstraction notoriously difficult to clarify. The resultant freedom to "do anything and call it anthropology" (as Clifford Geertz once said) is both exciting and confusing. However, cultural anthropology does have a certain coherence, if only in the tensions which underlie its intellectual history.

The first great American anthropologist was the New York lawyer and amateur ethnographer LEWIS HENRY MORGAN, whose mid nineteenth-century research on Iroquois kinship systems culminated in his brilliant and hugely influential cross-cultural typologies of kinship structures and social organization. Morgan thus began an American tradition of empiricist, problem-oriented comparative ethnographic research, aimed at discovering historical evolutionary processes and coupled with a concern for the material bases of social life.

Another tradition, however, originated at the turn of the century with FRANZ BOAS, who infused his graduate students at Columbia University with the German romantic concern for the uniqueness of all cultures. Boas taught that the job of the anthropologist was to learn in depth both the language and the cultural repertoire of rapidly vanishing American Indian groups. The mission of these fieldworkers was to preserve as much of this dwindling world as possible—all data, including hair styles, clothing, tool types, as well as myths, social structure, and rituals, were equally valuable.

Thus, from its very beginnings, American anthropology, drawing on fieldwork with American Indians, had at its base a double commitment: the discovery of laws of comparative social structure, and the preservation or recreation of unique cultural worlds. Furthermore, the image of the detached observer stood in contrast to that of the participant fieldworker. These incompatible models of the discipline remain salient, and cultural anthropologists waver in their general allegiance to one or the other, usually trying to combine both. This tension generates a continued and creative intellectual ferment in the discipline.

The 1930s and 1940s, for instance, were the heyday of the Culture and Personality school identified with the dominant figures of MARGARET MEAD and RUTH BENEDICT, both former students of Boas. Culture and Personality bravely attempted to connect personal experience with larger cultural processes, though the effort sometimes seemed to reflect the ethnographer's political agendas as much as any cultural reality.

Alongside Culture and Personality was the empirically oriented neo-Durkheimian structural-functionalism espoused by the British anthropologist A. R. Radcliffe-Brown. The general principle here was that cultural acts and beliefs could be understood as contributing to the continued functioning of society. But the implicit assumption that everything in a society worked harmoniously made it impossible to understand either social power, social conflict or social change.

Later materialist and Marxist analysis attempted to maintain scientific rigor and also to remedy the difficulties of functionalism, but tended to reduce symbolic worlds to derivative "superstructures." A turn toward the analysis of just such superstructural elements was inspired by Claude Lévi-Strauss, whose linguistically influenced structuralism promised a new universal science of comparative symbol systems.

In a recent reaction to the scientific pretensions of functionalism, materialism and structuralism, American interpretive and symbolic anthropologists, led by CLIFFORD GEERTZ, denied all forms of comparison in favor of literary "thick description" of other cultural worlds. The balance, at present, lies with this school of interpretive anthropologists, who are clearly direct descendants of Boas.

The movement away from comparison and the tradition of Morgan, however, is not simply another pendulum swing in anthropological theory; it is also a result of a wider change in the conditions faced by anthropologists in their fieldwork and in their classrooms. While early American fieldworkers had little reason to question the value of their research on supposedly disappearing cultures, modern anthropologists now have to deal with criticisms from the very people they have made their subjects. Margaret Mead's pioneering work in Samoa, for example, recently elicited a disparaging response from literate Samoans who say her ethnography created imprisoning stereotypes. Clearly, "they" are now wondering what the anthropologist is doing to "them"; and anthropologists too have begun to wonder the same thing—especially when they find themselves questioned by students who are members of so-called minority cultures.

Simultaneous with growing self-awareness among the "natives," the small-scale isolated societies that formed anthropology's main subject population have, as Boas feared, almost completely disappeared. Most anthropologists now work in complex, literate social worlds, and even those living in remote regions are likely to find their informants watching reruns of "I Love Lucy" on local television. The romance of the exotic that was so much a part of early anthropology has given way to a concern with the transformation of indigenous cultures and the global spread of capitalism and consumerism.

Anthropologists, as fieldworkers who have traditionally felt a strong identification with the people they have lived among, see the effects of this transformation firsthand, and are naturally concerned about the position they will take as representatives of the West. In this context, scientific observation seems too unresponsive a stance for many, who wonder if instead they should document their own reactions to the confrontation with those who are always called "the Other." Some anthropologists even worry whether they should participate in fieldwork at all, claiming it reduces the people studied to "objects." The present sense of insecurity about the anthropologist's privileged position thus corresponds with an increasing fear of analysis, and a tendency toward solipsism. These crippling attitudes can only be understood as reflections of the present systemic and intellectual crisis of the West.

Yet, despite considerable inner turmoil, anthropology has never had such high intellectual standing as it does today. Historians, philosophers, literary theorists, theologians, psychologists all cite anthropological literature in their own work. Perhaps this is because American cultural anthropology has always listened to the voices of those who are excluded from the cultural mainstream. Presently, as that cultural mainstream threatens to be engulfed, or at least diluted, by an ocean of other modes of experience, the struggle of anthropologists to do credit to divergent visions offers instructive examples for disciplines just now discovering their own contingency.

CHARLES LINDHOLM

FURTHER READING
James Clifford, *The Predicament of Culture* (Cambridge: Harvard University Press, 1988).
Jonathan Friedman, "The Past in the Future: History and the Politics of Identity," *American Anthropologist* 94 (1992): 837–59.
Richard Handler, "An Interview with Clifford Geertz," *Current Anthropology* 12 (1991): 603–13.
Marvin Harris, *The Rise of Anthropological Theory* (New York: Thomas Y. Crowell, 1968).
Sydel Silverman, ed., *Totems and Teachers: Perspectives on the History of Anthropology* (New York: Columbia University Press, 1981).
George Stocking, *Race, Culture and Evolution: Essays in the History of Anthropology* (New York: Free Press, 1968).
Thomas Trautmann, *Lewis Henry Morgan and the Invention of Kinship* (Berkeley: University of California Press, 1987).
Albert Wendt, "Novelists, Historians and the Art of Remembering," in A. Hooper et al., eds., *Class and Culture in the Pacific* (Auckland: Institute of Pacific Studies, 1987).

cultural criticism In the eighteenth-century notion of a bourgeois public sphere or "civil society," the sociopolitical and the cultural tended to be represented as two distinct, if mutually referential, arenas of experience: the former the realm of commerce and governance, the latter a field of individual expression and symbolic order. Cultural knowledge became an important part of subjectivity, a component of the individual's "moral sense" manifested in "civility" and the "cultivation" of taste. An ability to read for signs of moral value in art, literature, and other aesthetic or ritual objects was the marker of the cultural citizenship that betokened a "civil-ization," the highest stage in a progressive hierarchy of human development.

In the late eighteenth and early nineteenth centuries, certain Romantic theorists, beginning with J. G. Herder in Germany, reconfigured these terms to accommodate their own critiques to bourgeois society. To Herder, "civilization" tended to signify the processes of social and material "progress," and "culture" meant aesthetic production and moral speech. A cultural critic examined images of morality in a people or an age and held them up for indictment or example. In nineteenth-century England and its cultural provinces, where "civilization" came increasingly to mean the norms and attainments of Protestant, free-trade bourgeois democracies, "culture" could become even more closely aligned with "criticism" of everyday thinking. For Matthew Arnold the function of criticism was to preserve and develop "the best that is known and thought" in the history of the West.

Until the twentieth century, these were the terms of cultural-critical debate available to American intellectuals. In nineteenth-century New England, where the *North American Review* began publication in 1815, a Whig-Unitarian cultural order emerged as the foundation of bourgeois-liberal public life. The practice of cultural critique was easily assimilated into a region where intellectual elites had for nearly two centuries claimed leadership by virtue of their interpretive mediation over symbolic experience and sacred texts. RALPH WALDO EMERSON, the most important American critic of this period, reasserted the stark separation between cultural and sociopolitical experience by depriving the latter of its animating principle—"progress"—and instilling it instead in the individual. Culture was individual moral growth against injustice and vulgarity; public life depended upon "domestication of the idea of Culture"—that is, its instantiation in every subject. The critic's role, Emerson explained in his précis for "The American Scholar" (1837), was to undertake the "public labor" of clarifying cultural knowledge, to work as "the world's eye" and "the world's heart." By "preserving and communicating heroic sentiments, noble biographies, melodious verse, and the conclusions of history," the critic guarded aesthetic and moral expression against the "barbarism" of "vulgar prosperity" (p. 46).

In the generation after the Civil War, cultural criticism expanded into cultural politics. Frustrated by the destabilization of public life through industrialization and immigration, Northeastern intellectuals asserted that cultural citizenship was incompatible with unmediated, unreflective popular democracy. Inspired by their English counterparts, particularly Arnold, these "mugwump" critics insisted on the linkage between culture and cultivation. While their position has often been ridiculed as an effeminate "genteel tradition," mugwump cultural critics were among the few champions of cosmopolitanism in a provincial age. Devoted to aesthetic achievement as much as they were to moral probity, they helped prepare the way for a twentieth-century MODERNISM that built on Victorian AESTHETICS while splitting it off from Victorian moral inquiry.

Cultural criticism in the early twentieth century took several major competing forms, but each of them stressed its distance from VICTORIANISM by arguing for a reintegration of "culture" and "civilization," for an end to the conventional bourgeois idea of culture as an autonomous moral ground. The dominant "progressive" view attempted to reconcile "art" with "life," and envisioned cultural production as a model for "creative" public interaction, for the kind of democratic citizenship espoused by JOHN DEWEY in *Art and Experience* (1934). Another current, the cultural revolutionism associated with the sensibilities of European modernism, and exemplified by the community around the periodical *The Masses* (1911–17), sought to reconstruct subjectivity through "liberation" from repressions of class, race, and gender in bourgeois life. A third perspective, naturalist or positivist, sought to give "scientific" representations of cultural knowledge an institutional dominance over previous, humanist versions. Whereas Dewey's democratic criticism preserved a central place for moral inquiry—though it could no longer be seen as separate from social, political, or even scientific endeavor—the cultural revolutionists forged an implicit alliance with the positivists in rejecting moral inquiry. For the former it reeked of moralism; for the latter it smelled of a priori reasoning.

At least since the work of the English anthropologist E. B. Tylor (*Primitive Culture*, 1871), evolutionary NATURALISM had been used to critique the conventional humanist culture-concept: culture as the privileged haven of value, the secularized sphere of soul. With the emergence of a descriptive ethnographic "science," "culture" referred not to a scheme of moral instruction but to a complex totality of all human artifacts and social processes. Cultural criticism shifted from "discrimination," a matter of judgment and taste, to a supposedly nonjudgmental "investigation," a posture that encouraged the emergence of professional "experts," some of whom sought actively to apply knowledge to the reform of society. Thus "culture," hitherto conceived as an alternative to social life, was increasingly drawn into it.

The status of cultural criticism as an American public institution was dramatically enhanced after the second decade of the twentieth century. Excitement over critical debate in the Progressive years eventuated in the establishment of "opinion making" as a crucial element in an increasingly mass-mediated polity. As evidenced in THE NEW REPUBLIC, this mode of cultural criticism followed the mugwump sensibility in calling for reflective public discourse, but sought to exert a utilitarian *power*, rather than merely moral leadership. (*See also* JOURNALS OF OPINION.) Meanwhile, the ideological utility of cultural knowledge was made plain by the arrival of "Western Civilization" in American higher education. "Culture" was reified as a canon, a normative iconograghy of the aesthetic and moral codes in the "classics" of Western cultural history. This institutionalization of cultural knowledge was part of a post-World War I adaptation of the national public to its identity as a global cultural, as well as military-political, force.

Nevertheless, independent critics held to their self-image as the moral adversaries of bourgeois society. VAN WYCK BROOKS, in *America's Coming-of-Age* (1915), had reinvoked the split between the cultural and the social in his categories of "highbrow" and "lowbrow," which ranged the mugwump's cosmopolitan, aesthetic elitism and *theoretical* knowledge (highbrow) against mass society and the "distinctively American spirit" of *practical* knowledge (lowbrow). For critics such as H. L. MENCKEN and those in Harold Stearns's landmark collection *Civilization in the United States* (1922), this great divide isolated the American intellectual in the cultural sphere. Conservative critics still working in the Arnoldian tradition—IRVING BABBITT, T. S. ELIOT—saw this isolation of the cultivated and reflective subject from the rest of society as a form of life particular to modern experience. Still others, like LEWIS MUMFORD or the exemplars of SOUTHERN AGRARIANISM, remained convinced of potential moral and social unity; the function of criticism was to them the discovery of adequate formulas of reintegration.

Marxism offered the most important alternative vision of unity, one that paradoxically preached an organic "renewal" of cultural expression and social relations through a provisional act of negation, the destruction of bourgeois life. The Stalinist Granville Hicks, writing in *The New Masses* (1926–48), pushed the "proletarianization" of culture, that is, the nullification of aesthetic and moral autonomy (*see* PROLETARIANISM). Less parochial thinkers like EDMUND WILSON and Meyer Schapiro—social democrats drawn to Marx from the cultural radicalism of the original *Masses*—built a more nuanced position based on the writing of Leon Trotsky. For Trotsky, cultural production was *ultimately* rooted in the "real life" of social conditions, yet was capable of a type of autonomy through aesthetic transgression. Under bourgeois capitalism, modernism could constitute a refusal or disruption of cultural norms. Its characteristic irony and disjuncture of form could stand as a kind of "moral" negation.

Through Trotsky, American cultural critics thus rediscovered the idea of culture—avant-garde culture, at least—as a criticism of life, a semi-autonomous, particularly modern critique of sociopolitical experience. Concurrently, in the work of Sigmund Freud, they found a conception of humanist subjectivity which they considered adequate to the task of grounding such a monumental project. The psychoanalytic subject, or "Freudian man," LIONEL TRILLING explained in *The Liberal Imagination* (1950), was the truly modern self, "an inextricable tangle of culture and biology" (p. 57). For Trilling, who led his contemporaries back to a version of Matthew Arnold, modern literature—in its account of human "variousness, possibility, complexity, and difficulty"—stood against a bourgeois liberalism that organized life, yet denied the "primal" or "moral imagination" (p. xv). The function of criticism was to explore and clarify this internal contradiction; the critic as analyst and liberal culture his analysand.

This theoretical development was in turn integrated into one central ideological discourse that drove public debate from the late 1930s: modern, anxiety-ridden cultural expressions were icons of autonomous individuals in the Free World, while, as Arthur Schlesinger Jr. put it in *The Vital Center*, "totalitarian man remained ruthless, determined, extroverted, free from doubts or humility" (p. 56). Thus the pathologies of modernism could serve both as civilization' ultimate critique and its last great hope. As the community of NEW YORK INTELLECTUALS largely responsible for these formulations assumed center stage from the late 1940s through the early 1960s, their cultural criticism came to define the character of modern civilization in the West. CLEMENT GREENBERG wrote that the "main premises of Western art have at last migrated to the U.S., along with the center of gravity of industrial production and political power" (Wood, p. 125).

But the social and political unrest of the sixties and seventies—from the civil rights movement to feminism—brought major revaluations of the nature of cultural production and knowledge. A nascent youth culture dismissed reflective cultural knowledge in favor of immediate sensual experience, and distinctions between "high" and "low" art collapsed along with the whole category of "taste." With this paradigmatic shift in the conditions of cultural knowledge, the role of the critic as moral mediator became highly problematic. SUSAN SONTAG challenged the idea that cultural production had any necessary public message. In her collection *Against Interpretation* she described moral criticism as a vulgar "revenge of intellect upon the world," an effacement of the sensuous by "a shadow world of 'meaning'" (p. 7).

For HERBERT MARCUSE the sensual became a new moral standard in itself, a total "negation of the entire Establishment, its morality, culture." In his *Essay on Liberation* (1969), criticism was true praxis, transcending bourgeois consciousness through the "*moral* rebellion" of an "aesthetic ethos" (pp. 25, 62). Alarmed by such doctrines, neoconservative cultural critics like Hilton Kramer, editor of the *New Criterion*, argued for a return to "excellence" in cultural performance. Critics on the left, by contrast, built on Marcuse and his Frankfurt School colleague Theodor Adorno by stressing the role of power in the constitution of cultural knowledge. Cultural works were not disclosures of "humanity," as traditionalists imagined, but revelations of particular empowerments and deprivations. French poststructuralist ideas further suggested that a "politics" was to be found in any mode of representation, particularly in a narrative—such as the developmental story of "civilization."

With "power" replacing "morality" as the preferred framework of cultural judgment, American critics sought a more "interested," less detached role in public life. The critique of "cultural difference" —uncovering the symbolic reproduction of sociopolitical categories like race, class, and gender—has become a major concern of the pluralistic field of "cultural studies," the form of cultural criticism institutionalized in the university. Meanwhile, opponents of this decentering of cultural discourse, usually themselves based in universities, have sought to restore confidence in the traditional canon or in the distinctive wisdom of the West.

PETER HANSEN

FURTHER READING

Ralph Waldo Emerson, "The American Scholar," in *Ralph Waldo Emerson*, ed. Richard Poirier (New York: Oxford University Press, 1990).

Giles Gunn, *The Culture of Criticism and the Criticism of Culture* (New York: Oxford University Press, 1987).

Herbert Marcuse, *An Essay on Liberation* (Boston: Beacon, 1969).

Arthur Schlesinger Jr., *The Vital Center: the Politics of Freedom* (1949; New York: Da Capo, 1988).

Susan Sontag, *Against Interpretation and Other Essays* (New York: Farrar, Straus, and Giroux, 1966).

Lionel Trilling, *The Liberal Imagination: Essays on Literature and Society* (New York: Charles Scribners' Sons, 1950).

Raymond Williams, *Culture and Society: 1780–1950* (1958; New York: Columbia University Press, 1983).

Paul Wood, Francis Frascina, Jonathan Harris, and Charles Harrison, *Modernism in Dispute: Art since the Forties* (New Haven: Yale University Press, 1993).

cultural pluralism and multiculturalism   The idea that the United States should be home to a number of distinctive cultures defined largely in ethno-racial terms has been advanced in the twentieth century under two labels, "cultural pluralism" and "multiculturalism." The first was introduced by the philosopher HORACE KALLEN in *Culture and Democracy in the United States* (1924). The second, which has never been identified with the name of any individual, came into vogue in the 1980s. But the basic idea advanced under both labels draws upon a commitment to plurality that predates both the term ETHNICITY and the modern notion of "culture." The national motto, *e pluribus unum*, displayed from the Republic's start a sense that whatever singularity the nation achieved was to be constructed out of diverse materials. This appreciation for multiplicity derived in large part from the fact that 13 different sovereignties needed to be incorporated into a single political authority. But it derived also from the new nation's social and religious heterogeneity, especially as lived and sometimes celebrated in the colonial past of polyglot Pennsylvania and New York.

Not everyone shared this appreciation for diversity. But neither those who sought to circumscribe it nor those who sought to expand it bequeathed to the twentieth century any carefully elaborated theory of "pluralism." Hence the formulation of cultural pluralism took place in the context of ambiguities inherited from the eighteenth and nineteenth centuries. These ambiguities created openings, invited contentions, and fostered confusions that affected the shape and character of cultural pluralism, and eventually of multiculturalism.

One ambiguity was at the heart of the very idea of a pluralistic society. Just what human properties served to distinguish people from one another, and thereby to define the "many" (*pluribus*) to be incorporated into "one" (*unum*)? Was religious affiliation the salient property? Or was it language, biological ancestry, prior nationality, geographic locality, political ideology, economic interest, or perhaps all of the above? Some references to plurality even in the eighteenth and nineteenth centuries took for granted that the relevant distinctions were those then called "racial" or "national," distinguishing "Germans," "English," "Swedes," "Irish," etc., from one another. But other references to plurality invoked religious denominations, political factions, states of the Union, and property interests. That an appropriate form of pluralism was "cultural," and that cultural meant ethno-racial, was determined by Kallen and his contemporaries, not by prior convention.

A second ambiguity had to do with the scope of diversity, even when discussants assumed that ethno-racial distinctions were the stuff of which diversity was made. Did that multiplicity embrace persons of all ethno-racial groups? In practice, the obvious answer to this question was "no." The privileged status of British, and later of Western European, and still later of any European ancestry is now one of the most widely recognized themes in the history of the United States. Several prominent advocates of cultural pluralism considered themselves radical for appreciating the cultural contributions of Irish Catholics, Jews, and various Eastern European peoples, but were slow to conceive of the possibility that pluralism might provide legitimacy to peoples known today as African American, Asian American, Native American and Latino. But in theory, cultural pluralism meant something different. The privileged status of certain "stocks" was informal in character, thereby inviting contest by an ever-expanding number of marginalized groups in the name of the Enlightenment abstractions implanted in the nation's political charters.

Yet a third ambiguity lay in the extent to which ethno-racial identity implied affiliation with an autonomous and enduring social aggregate. American political ideology and constitutional doctrine so emphasized individuality that the pluralists of the early twentieth century inherited very few tools for talking about the claims of groups. The notion of legally protected territorial enclaves for nationality groups was rejected by Congress—first for Irish immigrants in Ohio, and later for German immigrants in Texas—but informal clustering and a measure of legally sanctioned residential segregation were facts of American demographic life. It was possible to construe ethno-racial groups as internally coherent subsocieties expected to perpetuate themselves and to warrant some measure of recognition as groups. Yet it was more common to regard these groups as fluid, contributing to American diversity by serving as temporary homes for individuals whose descendants would eventually "assimilate." Uncertainty about the character of ethno-racial groups and their place in the larger American society was even displayed, as Philip Gleason has demonstrated, in constructions of the

"melting pot." The chemistry of this cauldron served in the first major instance—the play by Israel Zangwill, *The Melting Pot* (1908), which wrote this figure of speech into the American political language—to transform not only the immigrants, but everyone, including the Mayflower descendants, who were to be improved through a dynamic mixing with immigrants. The term also became associated, however, with an antithetical, conformist impulse to melt down the peculiarities of immigrants in order to pour the resulting liquid into preexisting molds created in the self-image of the Anglo-Protestants who claimed prior possession of America. The significance of ethno-racial groups for American society was radically unresolved when taken up by the men and women who would eventually be remembered as "cultural pluralists."

Chief among these was Kallen, who in magazine articles published as early as 1915 set forth the ideas that in 1924 he named "cultural pluralism." Kallen envisioned the life of the United States as analogous to a symphony orchestra: each instrument was a distinctive group transplanted from the Old World, making harmonious music with other groups. He emphasized the integrity and autonomy of each descent-defined group. But Kallen's cultural pluralism was defined less sharply as a positive program than as a negative reaction to conformist versions of the "melting pot." The massive immigration from Eastern and Southern Europe since the 1880s had generated an increasingly hostile movement to "Americanize" the immigrants according to norms favored by the nation's old, Protestant elite. This movement intensified after 1914, when the outbreak of war in Europe rendered suspect the "dual loyalties" perceived in immigrants from the German and Austrian empires. Kallen, a Jew born in Germany, defended the right of immigrants to resist ASSIMILATION, and to maintain cohesive communities devoted to the perpetuation of ancestral religious, linguistic, and social practices. Hence the vision of America as a political canopy providing protection for a variety of descent-defined groups was the dialectical product of a distinctive historical moment: a moment at which unprecedented ethno-racial diversity collided with an Anglo-conformist movement made more aggressive by World War I.

Kallen's constitutionally vague references to the United States as a "federation" of enduring ethno-racial groups located him at the protoseparatist extreme of cultural pluralism, but his celebration of group differences appealed to a number of liberal intellectuals who shared his opposition to forced assimilation. The critic RANDOLPH BOURNE, for example, acknowledged Kallen as the inspiration for "Transnational America" (*Atlantic Monthly*, 1916), the essay of Bourne's destined to become the period's most remembered appreciation of cultural diversity. Bourne celebrated the deprovincializing effect of immigrants on the native-born population, and hailed a new, "cosmopolitan" America as superior to the more homogeneous societies left behind by the immigrants. Bourne himself was of Anglo-Protestant ancestry, as were JOHN DEWEY, JANE ADDAMS, and a number of the others who defended a vision of America in which immigration-derived cultural diversity was an asset rather than a problem. This vision was also shared by the Supreme Court Justice LOUIS BRANDEIS, a Zionist who proclaimed that one could maintain strong simultaneous identities as a Jew and as an American.

The simple, unelaborated insistence that American nationality need not entail the suppression of diversity and of multiple identity turned out to be the primary legacy of the cultural pluralism of the 1910s and early 1920s. This critique of "intolerance," "prejudice," and "ethnocentrism" was routinely advanced by liberal and radical intellectuals in the 1930s and 1940s, and was taken up by the popular media during World War II when its propaganda value was recognized by a government eager to mobilize Americans of all ethno-racial identities against the Axis powers. Yet the classic "foxhole society" of wartime movies—consisting of an Anglo-Protestant soldier surrounded by comrades representing Irish, Jewish, Italian, and other ethnic groups—did not really challenge the individualist and ultimately assimilationist presuppositions that Kallen's formulation of cultural pluralism had begun to call into question. In the meantime, Kallen himself had lost interest in these issues, and from the late 1920s until his death in 1974 did almost nothing to clarify cultural pluralism as a positive program. Some of the most ambitious and probing theoretical work of the 1930s on the culture of American ethno-racial groups was produced by the philosopher ALAIN LOCKE, but his work, including "The Negro's Contribution to American Culture" (*Journal of Negro Education*, 1939), attracted little notice outside the circle of African American intellectuals.

An ideology of cosmopolitan tolerance remained a prominent feature of American intellectual life from World War II through the 1960s, but this ideology's ties to cultural pluralism became more attenuated. Neither Kallen's name nor the term he contributed were invoked significantly during this era, when advocates of racial equality directed their energies increasingly against a specific target that had been of little concern to the cultural pluralists of the 1910s and 1920s: antiblack racism and the political and social inequalities resulting from it. Any movement to replace "segregation" with "integration" had little incentive, moreover, to embrace the pluralist emphasis on the autonomy and durability of ethnoracial groups.

Cultural pluralism had thus become "ancient history" by the end of the 1960s, at which time a number of historic turns produced a new willingness to explore pluralist ideas. Among these turns were an extensive reconsideration of integrationist goals and strategies by frustrated black leaders, the "backlash" against affirmative action on the part of "white ethnics" suddenly eager to proclaim the solidarity of their own groups, and the dramatic increase in immigration from Asian and Latin American countries facilitated by Congressional action taken in 1965. The revision of immigration legislation not only increased the number of diverse ethno-racial groups substantially present in the American population, but, by maintaining a steady flow of immigrants fresh from each source, provided such groups with identity reinforcement absent for most groups since Congress had curtailed massive immigration in 1924. (*See also* ASIAN AMERICAN IDENTITY.) An interest in maintaining the integrity of ethno-racial communities was also stimulated, less directly, by the Vietnam War, which generated among many American intellectuals a deep skepticism about the society into which peoples of all ethno-racial affiliations had been encouraged to assimilate.

These and other distinctive matrices were conducive to the initiatives of the 1970s and 1980s that eventually came to be called "multiculturalism." Prominent among these initiatives were educational reforms designed to foster appreciation for the achievements of African Americans, Asian Americans, Native Americans, and Latinos. A truly national debate on these curricular initiatives gave the concept of multiculturalism much more prominence than the concept of cultural pluralism had ever enjoyed. The two movements differed even more dramatically in their relation to perceived political and economic inequalities, which cultural pluralists had tended to overlook, but multiculturalists examined explicitly and extensively. Indeed, its champions offered multiculturalism as a means of empowering young people said to be psychologically victimized by a "Eurocentric" curriculum that displayed few achievements by members of their own ethno-racial groups. (*See also* CRITICAL RACE THEORY; INDIAN IDENTITIES; LATINO AND LATINA CULTURES.) Whereas cultural pluralism, as developed by Kallen and Bourne, was exclusively European in scope, from the perspective of multiculturalism Europe was just one of many sources for the culture of the United States. The cultural pluralists' lack of attention to African Americans, in particular, renders ironic the fact that it was a black contemporary of theirs, W. E. B. DU BOIS, who elaborated in *The Souls of Black Folk* (1903) the notion of dual identity that would become influential among multiculturalists. As an intellectual movement, multiculturalism thus took on a shape and character rather different from that of cultural pluralism.

The most striking difference of all was the triumph of the ideal of multiculturalism: the basic doctrine that the United States ought to sustain, rather than to diminish, a great variety of distinctive cultures carried by ethno-racial groups. Although some remained suspicious of this classically cultural pluralist idea, a sea-change had taken place since 1924, when Kallen named and then quickly abandoned this idea at the crest of the tide of Anglo-Protestant nativism. By the early 1990s this idea had become so widely accepted that most of the debates over multiculturalism turned less on its soundness than on its implications. About these there was plenty of argument. Multiculturalism was often associated with highly particularist projects, such as "Afrocentrism," which sought to reinforce African American identity even at the expense, its critics complained, of a broader education. Yet those who made this complaint often claimed for themselves the banner of multiculturalism, as did some defenders of a frankly Europe-centered curriculum who insisted that the Western tradition was profoundly multicultural from the beginning.

Multiculturalism was an occasion for renewed attention to a number of questions that had been discussed episodically in relation to "Americanization" and "cultural pluralism" early in the century, but which had become, by the last decade of the century, the basis for a vast and multilayered discourse embracing local school boards and philosophers of the stature of Charles Taylor and Michael Walzer. To what extent is "America" assigned any cultural identity, beyond its function as a container of cultures defined by ethno-racial communities? How autonomous and how enduring are the ethno-racial communities credited with producing the nation's many "cultures"? Are all of these cultures of equal value, and demanding of equal attention in education? What are the limits of any cultural program for dealing with political and economic inequalities? To what extent can an emphasis on the differences between people promote the goal of human equality?

One prominent theme in this lively discourse has been a recognition of the diverse character of the ethno-racial communities creating and sustaining the several cultures at issue. These communities have assumed their present shape in response to very different historical forces—enslavement, conquest, and immigration under widely varying socioeconomic conditions—and differ one from another in the extent of their internal homogeneity and in the clarity of their external boundaries. It has proved harder and harder to represent the society as an expanse of internally homogeneous and analogically structured units, each authorized by an ancestral charter and each possessed of a singular mythology of diaspora. Indeed, the sensitivity to diversity fostered by multiculturalism has had the ironic result of diversifying diversity to the point of challenging multiculturalism's prior assumptions about the foundations and integrity of ethno-racial groups. Kallen's primordialist notion that one can never change one's grandparents was replaced, in some quarters, by resistance to the idea that one's grandparents should be assigned the authority to determine one's primary identity within American society. This resistance sometimes took the form of a "postethnic" perspective, the view that affiliation on the basis of shared descent should be more voluntary than ascribed.

The ideal of postethnicity that emerged out of the multiculturalist debates was just that, an ideal, and one vividly at odds with the reality of ethno-racial ascription still widespread in the United States of the 1990s. Postethnicity builds upon the recognition and appreciation of diversity fostered by multiculturalism, but seeks to protect individuals from the confinements of ascribed social distinctions. A virtue of the term *post*ethnic is to distinguish the new perspective's appreciation for ethno-racial communities from the *pre*ethnic perspective—insisting on a monolithic society, and on the abolition of ethnic enclaves—against which the cultural pluralists of Kallen's generation revolted. Postethnicity looks to the national community of the United States as a potential mediator between the species and the ethno-racial varieties of humankind found within this national community. Hence the postethnic ideal embodies the hope that the United States can develop a democratic and egalitarian culture enabling it to be more than a site for a variety of diasporas and of projects in colonization and conquest.

DAVID A. HOLLINGER

FURTHER READING
American Quarterly 45 (June 1993), special issue on multiculturalism.

Philip Gleason, *Speaking of Diversity: Language and Ethnicity in Twentieth-Century America* (Baltimore: Johns Hopkins University Press, 1992).

John Higham, "Ethnic Pluralism in American Thought," in Higham, *Send These To Me: Immigrants in Urban America*, 2nd. ed. (Baltimore: Johns Hopkins University Press, 1984).

David A. Hollinger, "How Wide the Circle of the We: American Intellectuals and the Problem of the Ethnos Since World War II," *American Historical Review* 98 (1993): 317–37.

David A. Hollinger, "Postethnic America," *Contention 2* (1992): 79–96.

Wendy Katkin, ed., *Beyond Cultural Pluralism* (Urbana: University of Illinois Press, 1995).

Werner Sollors, *Beyond Ethnicity: Consent and Descent in American Culture* (New York: Oxford University Press, 1986).

Charles Taylor, *Multiculturalism and "the Politics of Recognition"* (Princeton: Princeton University Press, 1992).

Michael Walzer, "What does It Mean to be an American?" *Social Research* 57 (1990): 591–614.

D

Darrow, Clarence (b. near Kinsman, Ohio, Apr. 18, 1857; d. Chicago, Ill., Mar. 13, 1938). Lawyer and orator. Famous for championing the underdog against large, powerful forces, Darrow specialized in labor cases, most notably the defense of EUGENE DEBS and other union leaders in the Pullman strike. An opponent of capital punishment, he saved many clients from execution and was among the first lawyers to make successful use of psychological evidence to influence sentencing. His public shaming of WILLIAM JENNINGS BRYAN at the Scopes trial of 1925 dramatically increased the polarization between adherents of EVANGELICALISM or FUNDAMENTALISM on the one hand, and secular and religious liberals on the other. Darrow's writings included *An Eye for an Eye* (1905) and *The Story of My Life* (1932).

FURTHER READING

John Livingston, *Clarence Darrow: the Mind of a Sentimental Rebel* (New York: Garland, 1988).

Darwinism For much of its career, the term Darwinism has been used by scientists and nonscientists alike to refer to the theory of organic evolution. Charles Darwin was not the first thinker to embrace a transmutation hypothesis, but his *On the Origin of Species by Means of Natural Selection, or the Preservation of Favoured Races in the Struggle for Life* (1859) was decisive in convincing most nineteenth-century natural historians that the history of life was the result of "descent with modifications." According to Darwin, individuals within every species possessed hereditable differences—variations—that arose in "random" fashion. Because it is generally the case that more individuals within a species are born than can survive on the available resources, these variations are of crucial importance in fostering evolutionary change. Organisms that happen to possess variations best adapted to their environment are most likely to survive long enough to leave offspring, while organisms that are less "fit" are relentlessly eliminated. Over vast periods of time and in the face of a dynamic environment, this process of natural selection gradually leads to divergences sufficiently great to generate new varieties and eventually new species.

By 1875 the vast majority of natural historians had come to view the history of life as the result of the gradual change of species over time rather than the separate creation of individual, essentially fixed species. Ironically, however, during the late nineteenth and early twentieth centuries few committed evolutionists accepted Darwin's view that natural selection was the primary mechanism of organic evolution. Although most were willing to concede that it helped to eliminate the unfit, they insisted that the adaptive mechanism of Lamarckism—whereby changes in behavior could lead to changes in inherited characteristics—and a variety of nonadaptive mechanisms such as orthogenesis and "mutation pressure" were more important than natural selection in accounting for the gradual change of species. Not until after 1920, when evolutionary biologists constructed the "modern evolutionary synthesis" by combining the insights of Mendelianism, whereby inherited characteristics are determined by the particular combinations of genes, with the sophisticated statistical techniques of population genetics and insights concerning geographical factors derived from field biologists, did most evolutionists become convinced that natural selection was paramount in determining the relative frequency of genes within species populations. Although the pace and mode of the evolutionary process continue to be controversial issues, natural selection remains central to the way in which that process is conceived.

In attempting to place the acceptance of Darwinism within the context of broader cultural concerns, some historians have linked Darwin's theory to the ethos of competitive capitalism. For many years, however, the mechanism of natural selection, the most competitive element in the theory, was the object of a great deal of vilification from capitalism's friends as well as its foes. Indeed, any explanation of Darwinism emphasizing the salience of socioeconomic factors must grapple with the fact that evolutionism has been invoked to support a wide range of social and political ideologies, from the most progressive to the most reactionary. Explanations that center on the congeniality of Darwinism with the naturalistic thrust of modern science are more promising. Since the seventeenth century, the effort to account for natural phenomena in terms of natural, "secondary" causes has been central to the scientific enterprise. Darwin's claim that the origin of species was the product of secondary agencies more clearly accorded with this effort than the concept of "special" creations by an unknown power. In addition, the theory of organic evolution subjected the relationships of organisms through time to scientific investigation, thereby seeming to represent a more "scientific" account of the history of life than the doctrine of separate creations. (*See also* NATURALISM.)

The growing authority of science within American culture, coupled with the fact that the implications of Darwinism extended well beyond the boundaries of natural science, impelled nonscientists to come to grips with Darwinism. During the late nineteenth century, efforts to respond to the implications of evolutionary theory led to significant changes in the way in which psychology, the social sciences, literature, philosophy—virtually every field of human inquiry—were viewed. During the early twentieth century American intellectuals began to place greater emphasis on the significance of human culture and its independence from biology. This shift was instrumental in weakening and in some cases even eliminating links between Darwinism and other areas of scholarly investigation. Nevertheless, the relationship between Darwinism and other realms of thought has remained contested and problematic.

In no area has the impact of Darwinism been more traumatic and lasting than Christian theology. The transmutation hypothesis not only undermined the credibility of arguments for God's existence based on the design of organisms, but it also challenged the veracity of many of the prevailing formulations of Christian doctrine. By 1900 most intellectuals within the American religious community had come to believe that evolution was God's way of doing things and that the Bible could be reinterpreted to bring it into harmony with the implications of evolutionary thought. A sizable minority of religious thinkers, however, remained convinced that a gracious God had revealed the scheme of redemption to human beings through an inerrant Bible. These thinkers continued to reject the theory of organic evolution. In the period since 1960, many of these conservative Christians have engaged in an offensive against that theory in the name of "creation science." Thus far, their efforts have met with relatively little institutional success, but the evidence of recent polls, which indicate that almost half of all Americans remain committed to creationist perspectives, suggests that popular views concerning Darwinism are decidedly different from those of American intellectuals.

JON H. ROBERTS

See also SOCIOBIOLOGY.

FURTHER READING

Peter J. Bowler, *The Non-Darwinian Revolution: Reinterpreting a Historical Myth* (Baltimore: Johns Hopkins University Press, 1988).

Charles Darwin, *On the Origin of Species by Means of Natural Selection, or the Preservation of Favoured Races in the Struggle for Life* (1859; facsimile ed., Cambridge: Harvard University Press, 1964).

Carl N. Degler, *In Search of Human Nature: the Decline and Revival of Darwinism in American Social Thought* (New York: Oxford University Press, 1991).

Adrian Desmond and James Moore, *Darwin* (New York: Warner, 1991).

Ronald L. Numbers, *The Creationists* (New York: Knopf, 1992).

William B. Provine, *The Origins of Theoretical Population Genetics* (Chicago: University of Chicago Press, 1971).

Jon H. Roberts, *Darwinism and the Divine in America: Protestant Intellectuals and Organic Evolution, 1859–1900* (Madison: University of Wisconsin Press, 1988).

Cynthia Eagle Russett, *Darwin in America: the Intellectual Response, 1865–1912* (San Francisco: W. H. Freeman, 1976).

Davis, Katharine Bement (b. Buffalo, N.Y., Jan. 15, 1860; d. Pacific Grove, Calif., Dec. 10, 1935). Penologist. Superintendent (1901–14) of the State Reformatory for Women at Bedford Hills, N.Y., and Commissioner of Correction (1914–18) for New York City, Davis was at the forefront of the prison reform movement. An advocate of individualized treatment of inmates, she initiated the use of psychological and intelligence testing to identify "mental defectives" and commit them to long-term custodial care. She also put female inmates into work previously restricted to male prisoners, including outdoor labor and manual trades. Her belief that medical techniques would cure social ills culminated in her efforts to eliminate prostitution by defining it as a public health problem.

FURTHER READING

Estelle B. Freedman, *Their Sisters' Keepers: Women's Prison Reform in America, 1830–1930* (Ann Arbor: University of Michigan Press, 1981).

Day, Dorothy (b. Brooklyn Heights, N.Y., Nov. 8, 1897; d. New York, N.Y., Nov. 29, 1980). An influential and inspirational journalist, religious social critic, communitarian leader, and cofounder of the Catholic Worker movement, Dorothy Day was the daughter of a sports writer who worked for newspapers in New York, San Francisco, and Chicago. Her parents were of conventional nonpracticing Protestant background, but from early childhood the precocious Day displayed a keen interest in religious and social matters. Her formal education ended after two years at the University of Illinois. She always read widely in social commentary and fiction, especially Dickens and Russian literature of the nineteenth century. Although she had no taste for abstraction, eventually she became thoroughly versed in religious and social literature of all kinds.

In 1916 Day moved with her family to New York, where she became caught up in radical social movements and journalism, writing for *The Call*, *The Masses*, and *The Liberator*. A disastrous love affair, an abortion, and a failed rebound marriage left her disillusioned with bohemia and discontented with social protest as a basis for life. Increasingly drawn to religion, she long resisted it as socially reactionary and a sign of weakness in herself. But a new love and the birth of her daughter Tamar Teresa convinced her that she was drawn to faith not by weakness but by "love and gratitude to God," as she put it in her autobiography *The Long Loneliness* (p. 139). Her conversion to CATHOLICISM in 1927 cut her off from radical friends, but she retained her social commitments. The French peasant philosopher Peter Maurin finally introduced her to Catholic social thought, and on May Day 1933 they launched *The Catholic Worker*, a penny tabloid that quickly became a Depression phenomenon with a circulation of nearly 200,000. The Catholic Worker movement soon followed. By 1940 it operated over 40 communitarian Houses of Hospitality where Day and other Catholic Worker volunteers promoted their cause, practiced "voluntary poverty," and provided free food and shelter to the poor.

Day and the Catholic Workers agitated for a "personalist revolution in self and society," unions, racial justice, communitarian anarchist production, the dignity of physical labor, and nonviolence, among other causes. The movement declined in the 1940s because of Day's pacifism, but revived in the 1950s and 1960s, all the while spawning numerous other forms of Catholic social criticism. It remains vital today, with over a hundred Houses of Hospitality and numerous publications.

As writer and activist, Day integrated a fervent orthodox Catholicism with radical social thought. Where many saw contradiction, she discovered inner harmony, with the divine *caritas Christi* impelling Christians toward "personalist" commitment to "see Christ in His poor," and toward a radical transformation of bourgeois society and economy through a nonviolent "revolution" in spiritual and social values. For this proposed "revolution" a critical but unyielding loyalty to the church was essential. In *The Long Loneliness* she wrote, "I loved the Church for Christ made visible, not for itself, because it was so often a scandal to me" (pp. 149–50). She sustained her consistent stance as "the angry but obedient daughter of Holy Mother Church" (as she put it in *By Little and By Little*, p. xviii) for nearly 50 years by constantly uncovering the spiritual and social treasures apparently hidden beneath the institution, and by appealing to Catholics to live out the vision of the gospel they professed. Day retained much of the free-form libertarianism and anarchism of native American radicalism, but also drew on the traditions of Catholic social thought, ancient and modern, as the basis for her attempt to "revolutionize" complacent, bourgeois American society. The gospels, the communitarianism of the Book of Acts, the church fathers, the saints, the religious orders (especially the Benedictines and Franciscans), and the liturgical movement led by Father Virgil Michel were all important influences on Day and the Catholic Worker movement. Day also adopted and spread the spiritual and social perspectives of many Catholic and Orthodox writers and intellectuals: Emmanuel Mounier, the English Distributists G. K. Chesterton and Hilaire Belloc, Luigi Sturzo, Feodor Dostoevsky, Nikolai Berdyaev, Romano Guardini, Charles Péguy, and Jacques Maritain, among others. Day consistently practiced and promoted the voluntary spiritual disciplines of prayer, worship, retreat, and fasting, insisting on "the primacy of the spiritual" as the necessary foundation of any lasting personal and social transformation.

The charismatic Day's vision was complex and her legacies diverse. Even among those who do not share her social views, she is today regarded, as historian David J. O'Brien wrote in *Commonweal*, as "the most significant, interesting, and influential person in the history of American Catholicism." As a social thinker and activist, she enjoyed a small but significant success, as Catholic Worker principles became admired if not imitated among American Catholics and others. Ex-Catholic Workers MICHAEL HARRINGTON, Jacques Maritain, DWIGHT MACDONALD, THOMAS MERTON, DANIEL BERRIGAN and his brother Philip, Robert Coles, and the evangelical Sojourners community, along with many ordinary people, have testified to her impact. As a religious figure, she moved from the scorned margins of society and church (many Catholics originally thought of her as a communist infiltrator) to her current status as the somewhat nervously honored pioneer of contemporary social Catholicism. As a writer, she produced some ephemeral journalism, but her best writing, collected in *By Little and By Little*, is warm, engaging, and rich in religious and moral insight. Like her autobiography *The Long Loneliness*, it displays a keen ability to see the mundane world of self and society *sub specie aeternitatis*. Finally, as a woman, Day has attracted a small but growing interest among people who find her alternative model of female servant leadership attractive or challenging.

Day's achievement as a religious social thinker remains provocative and controversial. Some secular and religious radicals admire her social perspectives but discount her moral and religious traditionalism, while many religious conservatives acknowledge her piety but disdain her politics. Among some American Catholics and other Christians, including Christian intellectuals, Day's fervent recovery of the social imperatives of orthodox faith have struck deeper chords than the earlier liberal Protestant Social Gospel, and revived ancient debates about the relation between the radical ethical demands of the gospel and the constraints of sin and society. Day's "harsh and dreadful love" escapes many of the strictures leveled by REINHOLD NIEBUHR and others against sentimental Christianity, and points toward the deeper paradoxes of Dostoevsky's Grand Inquisitor. The strongest Augustinian criticism is that Day and the Catholic Worker movement sometimes tended mistakenly to set the love, freedom, and service of the gospel against the necessary order of power in state and society. Her most compelling critical insights concern the relation between inner spiritual condition and external states of wealth and poverty, a species of religious social criticism almost unknown in America, yet highly relevant to it.

Besides her social thought, Day's greatest significance may be that she represents, within the modern American context, a figure of great religious imagination and intense devotion and moral commitment, who challenges the Enlightenment's equation of religious fervor with fanaticism, intolerance, and reaction. Day's person and work displayed the most orthodox Catholic Christianity coexisting with openness to diverse religious and nonreligious people and ideas, traditional religious social thought linked to free service rather than control, and the ancient Christian spiritual disciplines and moral practices harnessed to the spirit of American liberty. There is enough here to challenge the easy assumptions of many secularists and religious folk alike. The fading of secular faiths and the increasing implausibility of permanent secularization as the fate of American culture make the question of religion's social impact of growing importance to believers and nonbelievers alike. Day's life and writing ought to weigh heavily in the discussion.

MEL PIEHL

FURTHER READING

Robert Coles, *Dorothy Day: a Radical Devotion* (Reading, Mass.: Addison-Wesley, 1987).
Dorothy Day, *The Long Loneliness* (New York: Harper and Row, 1952).
——, *Loaves and Fishes* (New York: Harper and Row, 1963).
Robert Ellsberg, ed., *By Little and By Little: the Selected Writings of Dorothy Day* (New York: Knopf, 1983).
Anne Klejment and Alice Klejment, *Dorothy Day and the Catholic Worker: a Bibliography and Index* (New York: Garland, 1986).
William Miller, *Dorothy Day: a Biography* (New York: Harper, 1982).
David J. O'Brien, "The Pilgrimage of Dorothy Day," *Commonweal* 107 (Dec. 19, 1980): 711–15.
Mel Piehl, *Breaking Bread: "The Catholic Worker" and the Origin of Catholic Radicalism in America* (Philadelphia: Temple University Press, 1982).
Nancy L. Roberts, *Dorothy Day and "The Catholic Worker"* (Albany: State University of New York Press, 1984).

De Leon, Daniel (b. Curaçao, Netherlands Antilles, Dec. 14, 1852; d. New York, N.Y., May 11, 1914). Political leader. An orthodox Marxist, De Leon believed that America, with its advanced industry, could expect a socialist revolution—through the democratic process, not through violence—that would destroy capitalism and establish a cooperative industrial democracy. He served the Socialist Labor Party as editor of the *People*, its newspaper, and as a political candidate. He also helped found the Industrial Workers of the World in 1905.

See also SOCIALISM.

FURTHER READING

L. Glen Seretan, *Daniel De Leon: the Odyssey of an American Marxist* (Cambridge: Harvard University Press, 1979).

Debs, Eugene (b. Terre Haute, Ind., Nov. 5, 1855; d. Elmhurst, Ill., Oct. 20, 1926). Political leader. Imprisoned for his role in the Pullman strike (1894), an unsuccessful effort by his American Railway Union to reverse the decline in Pullman workers' wages, Debs turned from unionism to SOCIALISM. Though he continued to support labor organization, he doubted unions could hold their own against the power of capital. Instead, he put his energy into building a specifically American socialism that would eventually bring about true political and economic democracy. He ran for the Presidency five times as the candidate of the Socialist Party. An unyielding pacifist, Debs was again imprisoned for his opposition to World War I. Among his best-known writings are *Unionism and Socialism* (1904) and *Walls and Bars* (1927).

FURTHER READING

Nick Salvatore, *Eugene V. Debs: Citizen and Socialist* (Urbana: University of Illinois Press, 1982).

deconstruction The term—often bandied about loosely and polemically—denotes a style of analytical reading suspicious of the manifest content of texts for reasons which it typically discovers in those texts. In France, beginning in the 1960s, Jacques Derrida (b. 1930) combined the linguistic ideas of Ferdinand de Saussure and their extension in Claude Lévi-Strauss's structuralism (ideas whereby significance cannot reduce to simple individual intention but resides in larger differential structures) with the psychological accounts of the vexation that can befall acts of conscious meaning to be found in Nietzsche and Freud. Saussure had argued that LANGUAGE consists of difference without positive terms (an idea with roots that are very old), and that we only know a word by contrast with everything that it is not: it is limned by the system which differentiates and distinguishes it, a system composed only of other likewise differentiated and distinguished terms. Lévi-Strauss argued that social structures were also formed around systematic oppositions and differentiations. Derrida (in this somewhat like the psychoanalyst Jacques Lacan) equated this systematic production of meaning through differentiation with the Freudian concept of repression. For Freud, too, conscious meanings, manifest intentions, are the products of repression, and Derrida argues that any apparently univocal human intention, like any apparently simple word, is in fact the product of its differentiation from everything it is not, its repression or denial of what in it is equivocal or complex. It is the product of this differentiation and indeed depends on differentiation, and so depends on everything that it denies itself to be dependent on in any essential way. Derridian reading looks to uncover the repressions that make meaning possible, first and foremost the repression of the ruinous fact that repression makes meaning possible.

It is the repression of this fact that allows a deconstructive reading of a text to turn into a theoretical brief for deconstruction. Any text, in order to sustain the illusion of univocal coherence, must repress what deconstruction uncovers, viz. the fact that this repression is taking place at all. Deconstruction operates by looking for the inevitable symptoms of repression, inevitable since meaning itself is such a symptom. Texts elaborate themselves by a constant practice of self-correction; deconstruction notes that such series of correction are the very being of the text itself, no matter how much the text would claim to be univocal and present all at once. And so deconstruction looks first of all for places where texts claim the full presence of their meaningfulness and it asks why, if not out of a kind of textual anxiety, such a claim is being made. To the extent that any text claims to have a univocal and complete meaning, deconstruction will find repeated (though under repression) its own claim—that meaning is differen-

tial and produced only by repression. Like Freud, Derrida finds his theory already known by the unconscious of the targets of his analysis, already known by Plato and Husserl and Rousseau, and like Freud he merely attempts to bring to light a fully formed but repressed knowledge. (Typically for Derrida the name for the illusion of presence will be voice, as opposed to the clearly differential, iterated system of writing; writing's foundational status is repressed by a host of theorists of meaning who see writing as merely the representation of voice rather than the best model of how all language, including acoustic language, works.)

Derrida, in using the psychoanalytic language of repression and symptom formation, tends to treat anything a writer says, in any attested work, as symptomatic, and thus he continues to rely on (even as he reveals its arbitrariness) some sort of unified idea of the writer's psyche (he relies on it in order to reveal its arbitrariness). For this reason he tends to write on philosophers, who have particular claims to make, though the readings he gives them, his attention to imperfectly resolved psychic dramas, has much in common with literary criticism.

Derrida's ideas were not as novel in France as in America, and part of his extraordinary cult may be due to the paradoxical fact that on this new ground he became something like the unique voice of a dialectically oriented philosophical tradition pretty much neglected in the United States, especially among literary critics. Still, many of those critics were quickly receptive to Derrida since his work dovetails nicely with the technique of extremely close reading developed by the New Criticism. (*See also* ALLEN TATE and ROBERT PENN WARREN). Those critics glamorized such close reading as the profoundest mode of investigation into society, culture, and the mind.

American deconstruction proper, however, is largely the invention of Paul de Man (1919–1983). De Man eschews Derrida's analysis of the fraught conditions of the production of the text, reproves Derrida's psychoanalytic language, and looks not at the process of writing but at that of *reading*. (Of course in his accounts of particularly influential readings de Man treats the written texts that present them, and this overlaps considerably with Derrida's procedure.) It is thus understandable that de Man's main interest should be literary texts: where Derrida reads philosophical texts literarily, de Man reads literary texts philosophically. For de Man the text represents a resistance to the readings that would endow it with meaning, the author's reading included. Such readings, de Man claims, evade the flat austerity of what he calls the text's materiality, and seek through a kind of universal personification to phenomenalize, to make part of a human phenomenality and so to humanize, what confronts us as sheer sequence or articulation: language as the inhuman, something as alien as all those aspects of the material world, including our own bodies, which we wishfully attempt to render meaningful and humanize. De Man praises a very few texts for knowing this about themselves, and his readings of these texts (Shelley's "The Triumph of Life," Kleist's "On the Marionnette Theatre," for example) tend not to claim any repression within the text but to be the most lucid and inevitable results of pure exegesis.

As the word "knowing" in the previous sentence might imply, de Man's claims cannot be made utterly consistent, but they are extremely attractive nevertheless—attractive because they seem to go beyond a relation to literature which would be simply one of attraction, or aesthesis. De Man claims that a truth far more fundamental and disquieting is most visible in literature's refusal of lifelikeness, of phenomenality. Yet de Man's critique of phenomenality itself has phenomenal attractions, and it is difficult to see what besides those attractions might make persuasive a skeptical stance so thoroughgoing as to claim that even skepticism is a self-deluding philosophical stance. De Man's project, from the standpoint of the rigor he keeps invoking, can never be made consistent, and it is finally as an aesthetic phenomenon that his anti-aesthetic commitment recommends itself. Still it is no small thing to have promulgated a new aesthetic experience, even if the experience is constituted by the denial that it *is* an aesthetic experience.

It should be stressed, against most received opinion, that far from claiming the equal validity of all interpretation deconstruction is tirelessly vigilant in pointing out errors in interpretation (especially the author's own errors in the process of self-correction), errors that it tries to demonstrate by using and exploding their own claims for being merely clarifications or corrections. The political valence of deconstruction (a vexed issue, made even more so by the recent discovery, irrelevant to his mature ideas, of de Man's collaboration with Nazis in wartime Belgium from 1940–2) is not obvious, but certainly its demands do not make reading and interpreting easier but harder. Its authentic ability to unsettle is a great merit.

WILLIAM FLESCH

See also POSTMODERNISM; SEMIOTICS.

FURTHER READING

Harold Bloom, Paul de Man, Jacques Derrida et al., *Deconstruction and Criticism* (New York: Seabury, 1979).

Cynthia Chase, *Decomposing Figures: Rhetorical Readings in the Romantic Tradition* (Baltimore: Johns Hopkins University Press, 1986).

Paul de Man, *Allegories of Reading: Figural Language in Rousseau, Nietzsche, Rilke, and Proust* (New Haven: Yale University Press, 1979).

——, *Blindness and Insight: Essays in the Rhetoric of Contemporary Criticism*, 2nd ed. (Minneapolis: University of Minnesota Press, 1983).

——, *The Rhetoric of Romanticism* (New York: Columbia University Press, 1984).

Jacques Derrida, *Of Grammatology*, trans. Gayatri Chakravorty Spivak (1967; Baltimore: Johns Hopkins University Press, 1976).

——, *Writing and Difference*, trans. Alan Bass (1967; Chicago: University of Chicago Press, 1978).

——, *Dissemination*, trans. Barbara Johnson (1972; Chicago: University of Chicago Press, 1981).

Neil Hertz, *The End of the Line: Essays on Psychoanalysis and the Sublime* (New York: Columbia University Press, 1985).

Barbara Johnson, *The Critical Difference: Essays in the Contemporary Rhetoric of Reading* (Baltimore: Johns Hopkins University Press, 1981).

Delany, Martin (b. Charles Town, Va., May 6, 1812; d. Wilberforce, Ohio, Jan. 24, 1885). Physician and journalist. Delany encouraged American blacks to take pride in African civilizations, to join Africans in a pan-African nationalism, and to emigrate to Africa. A land belongs to those who hold economic and political power, he argued in *The Condition, Elevation, Emigration and Destiny of the Colored People of the United States Considered Politically* (1852). As a visually recognizable minority in North America, blacks in his view could never expect full citizenship. After the Civil War Delany worked for the Freedmen's Bureau, served as a justice of the peace, and wrote *Principia of Ethnology: the Origins of Race and Color* (1879), in which he urged the preservation of racial purity.

See also RACE.

FURTHER READING

Cyril E. Griffith, *The African Dream: Martin R. Delany and the Emergence of Pan-African Thought* (University Park: Pennsylvania State University Press, 1975).

Dell, Floyd (b. Barry, Ill., June 28, 1887; d. Bethesda, Md., July 23, 1969). Writer and editor. A prominent participant in the Greenwich Village intellectual community of the 1910s and 1920s, Dell was an editor of *The Masses* (1914–17) and the *Liberator* (1918–24). Also a playwright and a novelist, he argued for the importance of joining artistic and political radicalism. A harsh critic of bourgeois provincialism, he rebelled against sexual repression and moralistic codes as well as outmoded aesthetic conventions and oppressive economic structures.

See also MODERNISM.

FURTHER READING
John Hart, *Floyd Dell* (New York: Twayne, 1971).

democracy This political ideal now commands nearly universal approbation, but only because it means different things to different people. For some it means no more than choosing political representatives through universal suffrage, for others it means universal participation in social and economic as well as political decision-making. Current disagreements are rooted in the complex and ironic process of democratization that has swept the world during the last two centuries.

The history of democracy in America is a history of frustrated hopes. The ideal of popular sovereignty, which promises that the people might control the laws that govern them, has foundered upon the ideal of individual autonomy, which promises that each citizen might shape his or her own life. The concept of legitimate AUTHORITY, grounded on ancient desires to enforce the good and the right, has confronted the steadily rising demands of individuals to decide for themselves how to define virtue and responsibility.

American civic institutions derive from the colonists' commitment to popular consent as the underlying principle guaranteeing political legitimacy. The Puritans cited God's covenant with his people; Virginians invoked the natural rights of Englishmen. Despite their different inflections, Americans throughout the colonies spoke the language of popular sovereignty. Yet they also took for granted the necessity of hierarchy and obedience, since they inherited the Christian and classical republican fear of social disequilibrium and political anarchy. The recurrent conflicts between Puritans seeking to preserve order, and dissidents such as ROGER WILLIAMS who challenged their authority, indicate the intensity of the conflict between the dual imperatives of divine law and popular will. Southern planters legitimated their colonies' representative institutions by contrasting their prerogatives as citizens to the dependency and depravity of their slaves, an alternative response to the problem of hierarchy and the pervasive desire to establish authority. Americans seldom invoked "democracy," which they understood as the rule of the mob. But by the end of the seventeenth century the ideal of REPUBLICANISM, government for the public good, had become a pervasive theme in American political discourse.

Republican government required VIRTUE, and virtue required balance. Political theorists since the Greeks had agreed that masses of dependent people could not be trusted to exercise good judgment because they could be corrupted by those with power. Different social orders of autonomous citizens had to be balanced in governments to ensure JUSTICE. Thanks to the availability of land and the economic and geographic mobility of the American population, the number of autonomous citizens swelled steadily. By 1763 these independent Americans clamored for a voice in shaping the future of their towns and their colonies. When England attempted to assert its authority over matters of taxation, the colonists drew on more than a century of political experience and ideas to justify their resistance.

Americans achieved independence because they successfully united beneath a banner stitched from various traditions. Twentieth-century historians, bewitched by social contract theory and the now common conception of individuals as bearers of RIGHTS, have seen conflicts between the ideas of republicanism and LIBERALISM, but those who made the Revolution and consolidated the Republic operated in a different conceptual universe from our own. They saw no need to choose between their rights as Englishmen to self-government and their rights as Christian individuals to economic freedom.

Republican virtue required autonomy and underwrote popular sovereignty. Because citizens were independent they were incorruptible; because they were constrained by moral and religious imperatives, their pursuit of self-interest was unproblematical. Partisan political scheming and unchecked personal aggrandizement were equally unacceptable to American republicans during the late 1770s. Just as they sought to balance the distinct orders of society by institutionalizing the separation of powers, so republicans sought equilibrium between FREEDOM and RESPONSIBILITY.

That balance was quickly upset. Older systems of hierarchy collapsed in the wake of the Revolution, and new tensions arose immediately between those Americans who sought to reinstate legitimate authority and those who now suspected that all authority was illegitimate. In the new Constitution he wrote for Massachusetts in 1779, JOHN ADAMS drew on the doctrine of popular sovereignty and the ideal of autonomy to establish the principle that government is "instituted for the common good . . . and not for the profit, honor, or private interest of any one man, family, or class of men." Moreover, Adams explicitly endorsed public education for a moral as well as civic purpose, to "inculcate the principles of humanity and general benevolence" among the people of his state (*Political Writings*, pp. 96–7, 103).

THOMAS JEFFERSON had similar objectives in mind when he sought to reform the laws of Virginia. In addition to advocating land grants to secure independence for individuals, he advocated a general scheme of education to enlighten popular sensibilities. As Adams did, Jefferson invoked the principle of popular sovereignty to justify indirect elections, because he wanted to protect government from the dangerous instability he associated with popular passion.

The United States Constitution also reflected the desire of JAMES MADISON to reconstitute authority; the challenges that greeted the Constitution revealed how quickly that concept had become controversial. Madison's contributions to *The Federalist*, in which he attempted to persuade Americans to ratify the Constitution, have become perhaps the most familiar texts in American political thought. Legions of interpreters have incorrectly characterized Madison as a liberal pluralist who took for granted—and deemed legitimate—the pursuit of individual interest and the balancing of demands of competing factions as the heart of American politics. *Federalist* number 10 may present that appearance to some late twentieth-century American political scientists unacquainted with eighteenth-century thought. But Madison's speeches on behalf of the Constitution in the Virginia Ratifying Convention reveal doubts about trusting the structure of government to ensure justice. Elected representatives could not be trusted to underwrite virtue. (*See also* REPRESENTATION.) The fate of the republic must rest with the character of its people. Only their virtue, not that of their "rulers" or the design of their institutions, could ensure liberty and happiness. Yet Madison, a partisan of popular government, shared with Adams and Jefferson the conviction that a stable society requires legitimate authority; this standard republican commitment faced a new and bewildering challenge in the democratic America that emerged in the first three decades of the nineteenth century.

The earlier world of balance, virtue, and restraint vanished in the midst of tempestuous change. The Enlightenment ideal of benevolence was rooted in confidence that man's innate moral sense would provide an ethical compass when the older restraints imposed by hierarchy were removed. But for nineteenth-century Americans self-interest displaced self-discipline as the central cultural value. Democracy, now nearly universally acclaimed, came increasingly to mean only the unbridled pursuit of wealth and power. Virtue was relocated in the sphere of women, who embodied it in domestic life and sought to perpetuate it through the moral education of their children. Largely unencumbered by concern with the protests of African Americans, women, and

other dependent groups (such as wage workers), independent white males—their status, however fragile, secured by the presence of subservient groups beneath them—were free to seek their fortune in the hurly-burly world of commerce and politics.

In this chaos lay a certain grandeur. ALEXIS DE TOCQUEVILLE, who shared the American founders' misgivings about the democratic forces that had swallowed his own aristocratic culture in France, displayed remarkable sympathy for the new world of egalitarianism in both volumes of *Democracy in America* (1835, 1840). Despite notable differences between his first volume, in which he stressed the vitality and volatility of democracy, and the second, in which he stressed the danger of cultural suffocation beneath the weight of a tyrannical majority, Tocqueville consistently revealed his own ambivalence regarding the disappearance of hierarchy and the cultural consequences of Americans' passion for EQUALITY. Only religion or authority could check the materialism of people obsessed with getting ahead, and both were increasingly vulnerable.

Tocqueville distinguished the ancient vice of egoism from the democratic virtue of INDIVIDUALISM, and he argued that in America widespread participation in voluntary associations might prevent individualism from devolving into egoism by enlarging private sensibilities to encompass the welfare of the community. Such "self-interest properly understood" could prevent the preoccupation with property from strangling all further reform and stifling innovation. But that outcome was hardly preordained. The peculiar dynamic of democratic egalitarianism, Tocqueville warned, threatened to consume the original desire for freedom. Having dismantled inherited hierarchies, democrats were tempted to enthrone an even more ominous power, sanctioned by the doctrine of popular sovereignty, enforced by the state, and all but invisible: the tyranny of public opinion.

Democracy in America worked, Tocqueville understood, because no fundamental disagreements divided citizens, at least not as they did, for example, in France. For that reason all Americans agreed to accept the outcome of elections, which a disgruntled Henry David Thoreau likened to participating in a game of chance. But on slavery there could be no consensus; ultimately too many Americans cared too much to gamble on its fate. To the South, Abraham Lincoln's election signaled an alarming assault on their cherished institution of slavery. The principle of popular sovereignty had collided with slaveholders' conception of their prerogatives as autonomous citizens, and only war could compel the South to accept—grudgingly and, as it turned out, only briefly—the demand, institutionalized in the Fourteenth and Fifteenth Amendments, that African Americans be treated as citizens. (*See also* PROSLAVERY THOUGHT.)

The diverse reforms championed at the turn of the twentieth century can also be seen as attempts to extend the privileges of autonomous CITIZENSHIP to other Americans. Farmers, industrial workers, immigrants, blacks, partisans of woman suffrage, and other citizens who felt stampeded by the force of organized capitalism tried through cooperatives, unions, organizations of ethnic, racial, and gender solidarity, and especially through reliance on government regulation, to seize control of public authority and resist the reign of laissez-faire. Wielding various democratic slogans, conceiving themselves grandly as "the people" at war with "the interests," reformers tried but failed to transform the public sphere. Despite their efforts to resurrect notions of the common good or the public interest, they remained divided factions, unable to unite against enemies that seldom assumed human shape as villains and too often remained invisible abstractions such as "property rights" or "the laws of supply and demand." The reformers' most cherished achievements, the instruments of government regulation created to oversee the workings of the marketplace, usually functioned as wrist slaps rather than effective long-term restraints on corporate power. Again Tocqueville's analysis of American democracy proved incisive: because the state continued to labor under popular suspicion that it was a dangerous threat to individual freedom, legitimating public authority to challenge private power remained enormously difficult.

Some progressives believed they could resolve that problem by reorienting America toward social democracy. Philosophers of pragmatism such as WILLIAM JAMES and JOHN DEWEY argued that the untenable dogmas propping up laissez-faire individualism should be replaced by a flexible, experimental approach to problem-solving in the economic, political, and cultural spheres. Reformers such as WALTER RAUSCHENBUSCH, RICHARD T. ELY, JANE ADDAMS, W. E. B. DU BOIS, LOUIS BRANDEIS, WALTER LIPPMANN, and HERBERT CROLY, persuaded by James and Dewey to exchange inherited assumptions for the radical embrace of contingency and uncertainty, tied their pragmatism to a broadened conception of democracy. Their open-ended attitude toward knowledge was congruent with the open-endedness of democratic decision-making, which they sought to extend from the voting booth to social institutions such as schools and workplaces, and to the realm of law and political administration. If citizens could participate more fully in shaping a democratic culture, and if

civil servants shared their commitment to the public interest instead of petty partisanship, then state power would no longer loom as a threat to the people but might instead serve as their ally. Against the forces of entrenched reaction, such progressives launched their campaign for pragmatic social democracy. Their hopes were among the casualties of World War I.

American suspicions of the state, coupled with a new fear of the irrationality and untrustworthiness of public opinion even darker than Tocqueville's, emerged in the wake of the war. Disillusioned by reformers' failures—and even more by war-makers' success—erstwhile democrat and progressive Walter Lippmann, in *Public Opinion* (1922), indicted the myth of "the omnicompetent citizen" that Americans had inherited from Jefferson. Not only were citizens easily manipulated, Lippmann claimed, they were incapable of the careful critical thinking required for responsible public decision-making. Only when instructed by experts could the people be trusted.

John Dewey's *The Public and Its Problems* (1927), his most searching analysis of democratic theory, presented an eloquent response to Lippmann. But Dewey's criticism of experts' presumptions and his confidence in the public's capacity were both out of step with popular sentiment in the 1920s. Feminists noted that the legitimacy of democratic judgment fell under suspicion at just the moment when women won the right to vote. Other frustrated radicals noted that reactions against democratic and egalitarian reforms coalesced in the shape of prohibition, nativism, and Ku Klux Klan-style racism.

By the middle of the twentieth century, having weathered the storms of depression and global war, many thinkers believed that American democracy looked better than the alternatives. Theorists such as David Truman, Robert Dahl, DANIEL BOORSTIN, and LOUIS HARTZ argued that American pluralism, moderation, and even America's lack of interest in ideology accounted for its success—or at least for its unique stability. If America had lost sight of any conception of the common good such as that animating American revolutionaries and many progressives, thinking of justice as nothing more than the sum of individual choices seemed a welcome relief from grander myths that had sparked so much tragedy. For many Americans, surveying the ruined hopes of rival dreams, democracy could be equated with the existing American balance between popular sovereignty and autonomy, a consensus from which few dissented during the 1950s.

But the consensus was precarious, because the promise of equality remained empty for millions of Americans. First the CIVIL RIGHTS movement riveted attention on the injustice of segregation. Then the NEW LEFT challenged the anemic conception of democracy that equated participation with voting and equality with the chance to consume. Radicals in the 1960s either consciously invoked or more often unknowingly echoed Dewey's arguments for democracy. With him they conceived of democracy as an ethical concept, a way of life, a development of selfhood in community. In the Port Huron Statement (1962) of Students for a Democratic Society, Tom Hayden drew directly on Dewey's arguments in *The Public and Its Problems*.

Unknowingly resurrecting arguments advanced earlier in the twentieth century, radicals in the 1960s demanded that the principle of democracy, one person one vote, be extended from the voting booth to social and economic institutions large and small, so that all individuals would participate in making the decisions that affect their lives. Unintentionally resurrecting Tocqueville, they maintained that full participation could prevent self-interest from degenerating into self-centeredness. A participatory culture could also shield self-realization from the tyranny of standardized, mass-produced experience.

Recent discussions of democracy have continued to center on the questions of participation, autonomy, and authority. Whereas conservatives, neo- and otherwise, still fear that "power to the people" means anarchy, two developments have weakened their position. First, calls for more democracy are difficult to resist now that radical democrats can no longer be tied to communist subversion engineered by self-styled "people's democracies" in the former Soviet bloc. Second, management gurus and economists alike have demonstrated that worker involvement is not only more attractive to American workers, it is also more profitable for American corporations. It is not clear whether such experiments culminate in industrial democracy or a well-adjusted, compliant workforce willingly doing management's bidding. But the principle of worker involvement, at least potentially a democratic lever, has become almost as pervasive among American business people as it has long been among American political theorists.

Several recent developments reflect the continuing vitality of democratic discourse in contemporary America. Prominent analysts of American politics such as William Schneider, Kathleen Jamieson, and E. J. Dionne have written incisive accounts of contemporary politics that illuminate its artificial and antidemocratic dimensions. Feminist theorists such as Joan Williams and Kathleen Jones, and critical race theorists such as Cornel West and Patricia Williams, have shown how current conceptions of gender and

race inhibit the development of democratic participation and individual autonomy by constricting the options available to women and nonwhites. Communitarians such as William Galston and Mary Ann Glendon have revealed the shallowness of American "rights talk" and urge a return to substantive issues of justice and personal responsibility. All of these thinkers seek to develop an ideal of "deliberative democracy" that moves beyond the electoral process to the ways we shape our communities and our lives. Finally, philosophers from JOHN RAWLS and ALASDAIR MACINTYRE to RICHARD RORTY and RICHARD J. BERNSTEIN now acknowledge that we must debate political principles within the historical context of "our tradition" rather than attempting to frame our discussions in universal human terms.

Democracy is not now, nor has it ever been, primarily a question of representative institutions, which are a necessary but not sufficient condition for a democratic culture. Democracy, particularly in the multicultural America of the late twentieth century, requires a profound ethical commitment to an ideal of reciprocity that has been present as an undercurrent in Western philosophy since Plato's dialogues. Participation makes sense, and produces results, only if it goes beyond acknowledging the clash of interests to probe the question of how interests emerge, how the self is constituted through the process of interacting with others and seeking to understand them. Only if Americans accept the challenge of an explicitly ethical conception of discursive democracy, democracy conceived as a way of life rather than a way of simply managing conflict and preserving order, can the original democratic promise, the reconciliation of popular sovereignty with individual autonomy, be fulfilled.

JAMES T. KLOPPENBERG

FURTHER READING

John Adams, *The Political Writings of John Adams*, ed. George A. Peek Jr. (Indianapolis: Bobbs-Merrill, 1954).

Benjamin Barber, *Strong Democracy* (Berkeley: University of California Press, 1984).

Russell Hanson, *The Democratic Imagination in America* (Princeton: Princeton University Press, 1985).

James T. Kloppenberg, *Uncertain Victory: Social Democracy and Progressivism in European and American Thought, 1870–1920* (New York: Oxford University Press, 1986).

——, "The Virtues of Liberalism: Christianity, Republicanism, and Ethics in Early American Political Discourse," *Journal of American History* 74 (1987): 9–33.

Jane Mansbridge, *Beyond Adversarial Democracy* (Chicago: University of Chicago Press, 1980).

Edward A. Purcell Jr., *The Crisis of Democratic Theory: Scientific Naturalism and the Problem of Value* (Lexington: University Press of Kentucky, 1973).

Daniel T. Rodgers, *Contested Truths: Keywords in American Politics Since Independence* (New York: Basic, 1987).

Robert Wiebe, *Self-Rule* (Chicago: University of Chicago Press, forthcoming).

Gordon S. Wood, *The Radicalism of the American Revolution* (New York: Knopf, 1992).

Dew, Thomas (b. King and Queen County, Va., Dec. 5, 1802; d. Paris, France, Aug. 6, 1846).   Historian and political economist. In his *Review of the Debate in the Virginia Legislature of 1831 and 1832* (1832), later reprinted as *The Pro-slavery Argument*, Dew argued that an expanding population inevitably makes free labor cheaper than slave labor. The outcome—laborers at a subsistence level with no protection against periods of starvation—is both morally unacceptable and politically destabilizing. Slavery is therefore necessary both to provide minimum security to laborers and to ensure that some people will have the economic, political, and intellectual freedom required for participating in a republican government and for fostering economic and technological progress.

See also PROSLAVERY THOUGHT.

FURTHER READING

Eugene Genovese, *The Slaveholders' Dilemma: Freedom and Progress in Southern Conservative Thought, 1820–1860* (Columbia: University of South Carolina Press, 1992).

Dewey, John (b. Burlington, Vt., Oct. 20, 1859; d. New York, N.Y., June 1, 1952).   The most significant American philosopher of the first half of the twentieth century, John Dewey had a career that spanned three generations. He developed a philosophy that called for the unity of theory and practice and exemplified this unity in his own work as a critical intellectual and political activist. His thinking was grounded in a commitment to DEMOCRACY as a moral ideal, and he devoted much of his life to the construction of a persuasive philosophical argument for this ideal and to an activism that would secure its practical realization.

The son of a storekeeper, Dewey graduated from the University of Vermont in 1879, and after a brief stint as a schoolteacher in western Pennsylvania and Vermont, he enrolled as a graduate student in the department of philosophy at Johns Hopkins University. There he came under the influence of George S. Morris, a neo-Hegelian idealist. Receiving his Ph.D. in 1884 with a dissertation on "Kant's Psychology," Dewey followed Morris to the University of Michigan, and assumed leadership of the philosophy department there following the latter's untimely death in 1889.

At the heart of Dewey's work at Michigan was an effort to put liberal Christianity on a neo-Hegelian foundation and thereby to protect it from the threat of modern, especially Darwinian, science. His principal contribution to this project was a bold, controversial, and, for many, unconvincing merger of idealist metaphysics and recent developments in experimental psychology. At Michigan, he met and married Alice Chipman, a young teacher from a reform-oriented family who effectively urged him to turn his attention to matters of ethics and politics. He began in the late 1880s to advance a thoroughly democratic version of the idealist ethics of his intellectual hero, T. H. Green, and in his first major statement on "The Ethics of Democracy" (1888), he declared that "Democracy and the one, the ultimate, ethical ideal of humanity are to my mind synonyms" —a conviction to which he would remain wedded throughout his career.

In 1894 Dewey left Michigan for the newly founded University of Chicago. There during the 1890s he moved steadily away from absolute idealism toward a new philosophy that WILLIAM JAMES would in 1898 label PRAGMATISM. Dewey's attachment to neo-Hegelianism was at bottom less religious than moral: he feared that without the Absolute the world would be denuded of purpose and hence of ethical possibility. But drawing on a functional psychology that owed much to James's magisterial *Principles of Psychology* (1890), he became convinced that one could formulate a Darwinian naturalism that provided if not for a purposeful universe at least for the emergence of human beings as a purposeful species, which was all that the moral life required. From this perspective, the mind was not the repository of a transcendent Reason or a passive receptacle of sense impressions but *intelligence*: an active, mediating, problem-solving function that had evolved in order to serve the interests of human survival and welfare.

At Chicago Dewey also began to devote himself to EDUCATION and school reform, interests that had emerged during his Michigan years. Believing that the classroom was an ideal setting in which to test the new philosophy and psychology he was formulating, he persuaded the university to establish a Laboratory School in 1896 for this purpose. In the curriculum of this school, as well as in such widely read books as *The School and Society* (1899), *The Child and the Curriculum* (1902), and later *Democracy and Education* (1916), Dewey criticized both traditionalist advocates of a "studies-centered" curriculum and reformers given to romantic "child-centered" pedagogy. In *Democracy and Education* he called upon educators to build upon the impulses that children brought with them to school, but he attacked those who would merely give these impulses free rein. Rather than leave children to their own devices as romantics recommended, or impose subject-matter on pupils as traditionalists advised, Dewey proposed constructing an environment in which the child, engaged in familiar activity, would be confronted with a problem solvable only with the aid of the knowledge and skills supplied by the traditional subjects. This task, Dewey admitted, required teachers of extraordinary skill and learning. His was not so much a child-centered as a "teacher-centered" pedagogy.

The Laboratory School and educational theory were also home to Dewey's democratic thought in these years. In his ethical writings, he argued that individuals achieved self-realization by utilizing their peculiar talents to contribute to the well-being of their community and that democratic communities were those that best fostered this coincidence of individual and public good. Hence the critical task of democratic education was to help children develop the character that would enable them to achieve self-realization as members of society. If the school was to foster the social spirit in children and develop democratic character, Dewey argued, it had to abandon individualistic methods and be organized itself as a cooperative community.

Dewey hoped for schools that would not reproduce but reconstruct the existing social order, and throughout his career, he was a sharp opponent of proposals for vocational education that would replicate the class structure of capitalism within the schools. Perhaps the most radical feature of the Laboratory School curriculum was the effort to build social relationships between students and teachers that prefigured a democratized industrial workplace. Until World War I, Dewey naively believed that the school could serve as the principal agency for social change, even contending in his "Pedagogic Creed" (1897) that the teacher would be "the usherer in of the true kingdom of God" (p. 95). Although he would abandon this faith, as well as the language of the Social Gospel, Dewey remained certain that the remaking of public schools was a necessary if not sufficient condition for a more profound American democracy.

Dewey resigned from the faculty at Chicago in 1904 following a bitter dispute with university president William Rainey Harper over Alice Dewey's role in the administration of the Laboratory School. He was quickly hired by the philosophy department at Columbia University, where he taught for the remainder of his career. Much of Dewey's work in the first two decades of the twentieth century centered on a complicated three-way epistemological debate between idealists, realists, and pragmatists. Dewey attacked both idealism and realism as species of "intellectualism" which, by regarding man in the first instance as a spectatorial "knower" detached from the rest of the nature, created all sorts of unsolvable problems and insurmountable dualisms of mind and world. These difficulties could be overcome, he argued, by recognizing that knowing was a second-order, functional, mediating activity that occurred at problematic moments within a larger, more immediate realm of noncognitive experience and that truth was the predicate of judgments that resolved such problems. He contended that this was the way both ordinary men and women and modern scientists thought about knowledge and truth, and philosophers would do well to follow their example. Philosophers, Dewey urged in a pivotal essay on "The Need for a Recovery of Philosophy" (1917), ought to abandon the pseudo-problems of epistemology that they had created for themselves and devote their attention to the "problems of men" (p. 46).

Dewey's own most significant venture into the problems of men in these years was an unhappy one, according to his own later judgment. He threw his support behind American intervention in World War I, hoping against an abundance of evidence to the contrary that the war could help make the world safe for a democracy even more thoroughgoing than that envisioned by WOODROW WILSON. This shortsightedness occasioned an acute polemic by his former student RANDOLPH BOURNE, who charged Dewey with a failure of pragmatic intelligence only slightly less disastrous than the belligerent enthusiasm of younger progressives who had made of "pragmatism" little more than the exercise of technical reason on behalf of the demiurge of war.

After the war, at an age at which he might well have contemplated retirement, Dewey embarked on three more decades of intense labor as a philosopher and activist. In a series of public lectures and magisterial volumes—*Reconstruction in Philosophy* (1920), *Experience and Nature* (1925), *The Quest for Certainty* (1929), *Art as Experience* (1934), *A Common Faith* (1934), and *Logic: the Theory of Inquiry* (1938)—he reiterated his critique of the Western "spectatorial" theory of knowledge and truth and elaborated his pragmatic alternative. But he also, most significantly, offered his view of the noncognitive realms of experience and of the "consummatory experiences" of art, religion, and everyday activity which made life worth living. In these books Dewey brought his democratic moral convictions together with his pragmatism and metaphysical naturalism, trying, as he said in "Philosophy and Democracy" (1918), to see if one could not persuasively conceive of nature in such a way as to give democratic hopes and aspirations "an encouraging nod" (p. 48).

Dewey spent most of the years 1919–21 in China, where he was lionized by Chinese liberals who were struggling unsuccessfully amidst revolutionary turmoil to democratize their culture and society. Upon his return to the United States, he devoted much of his energy to playing a leading role in the Outlawry of War movement headed by an old Chicago friend, S. O. Levinson. In advancing outlawry arguments, Dewey began to articulate a view of war as an uncontrollable and counterproductive means of democratic social action, a view very close to the one held by Bourne in his dispute with Dewey during World War I.

Distressed upon his return from Asia in the early 1920s by the retreat of many social scientists and such fellow liberals as WALTER LIPPMANN from fully participatory democracy, Dewey offered a powerful ethical defense of democratic ideals and the local public sphere in *The Public and Its Problems* (1927). Unfortunately, he failed to meet the challenge of the withering skepticism Lippmann so effectively voiced in *Public Opinion* (1922) and *The Phantom Public* (1925) about the practical likelihood or wisdom for modern societies of pursuing anything other than a profoundly constricted democratic politics. For the remainder of his career, Dewey remained on the defensive in the face of such "democratic realists" wary of government by the people.

With the collapse of American capitalism in 1929, Dewey began to articulate his own peculiar version of democratic socialism in such books as *Individualism Old and New* (1930), *Liberalism and Social Action* (1935), and *Freedom and Culture* (1939). He assumed a leading role among critics of the New Deal and as a spokesman for radical third-party politics. At the same time, he voiced vigorous opposition throughout the 1930s and 1940s to the terrors of the Soviet regime and to the antidemocratic politics of the American Communist Party. He walked the difficult ideological tightrope of the anti-Stalinist left more adroitly than many of his younger contemporaries, balancing his anti-communism with a sustained criticism of American society seldom evident in their Cold War liberalism.

Following his death in 1952, Dewey's stock among American philosophers fell rapidly with the ascendancy of analytical philosophers who regarded him, as James Gouinlock has said, as "a nice old man who hadn't the vaguest conception of real philosophical rigor or the nature of a real philosophical problem" (p. xi). He fared no better among educators, many of whom blamed him for the woes wrought by progressive reforms he opposed, or among leading political theorists (such as the followers of Reinhold Niebuhr) given to hard-boiled realism about the limits of democratic horizons. But the last decade has witnessed a considerable revival of interest in Dewey's thinking. Much of it has taken the form of "neopragmatisms" such as that of Richard Rorty, which reiterates and applauds Dewey's dismantling of "foundational" metaphysics. Rorty's perspective needs to be balanced by one that is equally appreciative of Dewey's reconstructive metaphysics, ethics, and democratic hope.

ROBERT B. WESTBROOK

See also ACADEMIC FREEDOM; AESTHETICS; CULTURAL CRITICISM.

FURTHER READING

Neil Coughlan, *Young John Dewey* (Chicago: University of Chicago Press, 1975).

John Dewey, *The Collected Works of John Dewey*, 37 vols. (Carbondale: Southern Illinois University Press, 1968–92). References to Dewey's writings above are to this edition.

George Dykhuizen, *The Life and Mind of John Dewey* (Carbondale: Southern Illinois University Press, 1975).

James Gouinlock, *John Dewey's Philosophy of Value* (New York: Humanities, 1972).

Katherine Camp Mayhew and Anna Camp Edwards, *The Dewey School* (New York: Atherton, 1966).

Steven Rockefeller, *John Dewey: Religious Faith and Democratic Humanism* (New York: Columbia University Press, 1991).

Robert B. Westbrook, *John Dewey and American Democracy* (Ithaca: Cornell University Press, 1991).

diaries A history of the diary would have to do what histories of other forms of expression do: describe the movement of the genre from one local and transient form to another, and situate individual diarists in the context of the precepts, models, and audiences available to them. It would also need to take as its principal subject not merely diaries as the raw materials of history and literature but also diarists as historians and literary artists.

At present, studies of American diaries have accomplished those tasks only for the period reaching from the New England Puritans to the New England Transcendentalists. The history of that period begins with the Puritan diary of spiritual experiences. This was the normative diary of the Puritans, to which they gave public recognition and public sanction. Precepts for keeping such a diary were expounded in the English Puritan writer John Beadle's 1656 *Journal or Diary of a Faithful Christian*, and no doubt in unpublished sermons; examples of it were widely available in the numerous biographies and autobiographies in which such diaries were quoted, though living diarists were unlikely to have their diaries read by audiences outside their families. The subject of these diaries is the diarists' experiences of their own sinfulness and of what they felt as God's grace, and the states of mind these experiences evoke. The characteristic entry is an account of difficult perception, of the arduous labor necessary to see oneself clearly; the diary as a whole is the highly self-conscious dramatization of the process of spiritual self-examination, aimed both at open investigation of the health of the soul and at creating an *exemplum* of that process for descendants and biographers.

This diary became in its turn one of the models for the Transcendentalists, especially through the influence of Mary Moody Emerson's (1774–1863) journal on that of her nephew RALPH WALDO EMERSON. The other model was the Lockean commonplace book, a scheme for organizing insights into publicly usable categories. The ingenious and surprising combination of the two models made for the excellence of the best Transcendentalist diaries. Often these were their authors' best work; this is clearly true for Charles King Newcomb (1820–94) and BRONSON ALCOTT (1799–1888), and arguably true for Emerson, MARGARET FULLER, and HENRY DAVID THOREAU. The prestige of the form was correspondingly high; hence Thoreau's question in his *Journal*, "is there any other work for the poet than a good journal?" (vol. 10, p. 115) and the regular interchange of journals among members of Emerson's circle. The Transcendentalist diary is the highly self-conscious dramatization of the process of having insights, and at the same time an efficiently organized repository of those insights, available to be drawn on at need for essay and oration; it is the Transcendentalist intellectual "savings bank," in Emerson's phrase (*Journals*, vol. 4, p. 251), and at the same time the Transcendentalist autobiography, presenting diverse insights in a contingent, autobiographical form reflecting the Transcendentalist concern with personhood, sincerity, and inspiration. (*See also* TRANSCENDENTALISM.)

So far as it goes, such an account is fine; it makes good sense of the texts it focuses on, and the models it describes retain influence throughout the history of the American diary. The diary of ALICE JAMES (1848–92), for example, though distinctly stamped by her rejection of the narcissistic grandiloquence of the French diarists Henri-Frédéric Amiel and Marie Bashkirtseff, also drew on the Transcendentalist model; like those diaries it is part commonplace book and part AUTOBIOGRAPHY, and dramatizes the process of having insights. Its indebtedness to the Transcendentalist model extends even to its rejec-

tions of it: of its unironic sincerity, of its reluctance to situate insights in the context of the petty events that give rise to them, of its amplitude, of its ethereal exclusion of gossip.

But such an account hardly goes far enough. It does not describe very well even the temporal and geographic territory it circumscribes; it leaves out, for example, the almanac-diaries of the Puritans, which are mostly minimalist chronicles of secular life modeled on the almanac itself but which include the marvelously precise comic scenes and anecdotes of SAMUEL SEWALL (1652–1730). It leaves out the antiquarian diaries of Ezra Stiles (1727–1795) and William Bentley (1759–1819), the *philosophe*-like diary of Aaron Burr (1756–1836), and the scrupulous, public-spirited chronicles of the Adams family.

New England from the Puritans to the Transcendentalists is, moreover, too small a territory even if treated comprehensively, because the real territory of the diary is, as several recent bibliographies make clear, enormous. Women's diaries of the westward journey and Civil War diaries have been at least identified as subjects; but no study even of the greatest known Civil War diary, that of MARY BOYKIN CHESNUT (1823–1886), adequately describes Chesnut's pointillistic, contingent sense of history or her extended heroic narratives, or sets her in the context of other southern diaries or of the historical memoirs she read in such abundance. No study, that is, takes her seriously as a diaristic historian. Beyond these two subgenres the territory is pretty much uncharted except by bibliographers and by editors of diary anthologies and individual diarists. But even from these preparatory studies we can see how apt the diary was in its ease of access and production for the uses of women (*see also* ELIZABETH SANDWITH DRINKER), minority women not least among them, and so can look forward to studies of such diarists as, to name a few among many, the reformer Charlotte Forten Grimké (1837–1914), the writer Alice Dunbar-Nelson (1875–1935), the bohemian intellectual Mary Maclane (1881–1929), and the teacher and literary historian Joyce Mary Horner (1903–1980).

LAWRENCE ALAN ROSENWALD

FURTHER READING

Laura Arksey et al., eds., *American Diaries: an Annotated Bibliography of Published American Diaries and Journals* (Detroit: Gale Research, 1983).

Sharon Cameron, *Writing Nature: Henry Thoreau's "Journal"* (New York: Oxford University Press, 1985).

Margo Culley, ed., *A Day at a Time: the Diary Literature of American Women from 1764 to the Present* (New York: Feminist Press at the City University of New York, 1985).

Ralph Waldo Emerson, *Journals and Miscellaneous Notebooks*, 16 vols., ed. William Gilman et al. (Cambridge: Harvard University Press, 1960–82).

David Hall, "The Mental World of Samuel Sewall," *Proceedings of the Massachusetts Historical Society* 92 (1980): 21–44.

Lawrence Rosenwald, "Cotton Mather as Diarist," *Prospects* 8 (1983): 129–61.

——, *Emerson and the Art of the Diary* (New York: Oxford University Press, 1988).

Lillian Schlissel, *Women's Diaries of the Westward Journey* (New York: Schocken, 1982).

Henry David Thoreau, *Journal*, 14 vols., ed. Bradford Torrey and Francis H. Allen (Boston: Houghton Mifflin, 1906).

C. Vann Woodward, ed., *Mary Chesnut's Civil War* (New Haven: Yale University Press, 1981).

Dickinson, Emily (b. Amherst, Mass., Dec. 10, 1830; d. Amherst, Mass. May 15, 1886). Poet. Famous for her apparently reclusive withdrawal from the world, Dickinson in fact engaged in a rich, dense social existence within the chosen confines of her private life. She produced 1,775 poems and fragments that possess a haiku-like intensity of imagery. Her sensuous and often startling descriptions of small details of the natural world, her concern with death and immortality, her idiosyncratic use of metaphor and symbol, her innovative rhymes, and the immediacy of her language can all be traced to transcendentalist roots, but her vision is unique and her poetry and her life defy easy categorization. Only seven poems were published during her lifetime, but she carefully prepared her work for posterity. Not a thinker in any conventional sense, she offered a voice and vision that challenge conventional modes of expression and thought.

FURTHER READING
Judith Farr, *The Passion of Emily Dickinson* (Cambridge: Harvard University Press, 1992).

Dobzhansky, Theodosius (b. Nemirov, Ukraine, Jan. 25, 1900; d. Davis, Calif, Dec. 18, 1975). Population geneticist. An architect and publicist of modern evolutionary theory, Dobzhansky argued that the properties of an individual or population are produced by interactions between genes and the environment. Successful species exhibit substantial genetic diversity. Organisms' adaptation to their environment is explicable neither as chance (because mutation and selection have causes) nor as predetermination (because many results are possible). Inorganic, organic, and social evolution all follow similar laws, but two transcendent events have occurred: the emergence of life and of human consciousness. Dobzhansky

authored many books for general readers. His *Genetics and the Origin of Species* (1937) established evolutionary genetics as a field, while *Mankind Evolving* (1962) presented his views on human evolution.

See also DARWINISM; HEREDITY.

FURTHER READING
Ernst Mayr and William B. Provine, *The Evolutionary Synthesis: Perspectives on the Unification of Biology* (Cambridge: Harvard University Press, 1980).

domesticity In general American parlance today, domesticity is a seldom-used term indicating homelike qualities or circumstances. In the study of nineteenth-century American culture, however, the word has taken on enormous explanatory power because new attention has been paid to women, the family, and GENDER. In "The Cult of True Womanhood" (1966), historian Barbara Welter first identified domesticity as a principal characteristic (along with PIETY, purity and submissiveness) demanded of antebellum middle-class women if they were to merit devotion from suitors, husbands, and children. Now it seems clear that domesticity was both a daily practice and a cardinal value, the hallmark of the ascendant bourgeoisie, shared by men and women, although the roles of each sex in sustaining the attributes of domesticity differed. The word did not appear before the 1720s, according to the *Oxford English Dictionary*, and most uses date from the nineteenth century. From Dutch genre painting which focused sensuously on the icons and ordinary items of the home, through paeans to "home, sweet home" in American and British prose and song, domesticity was a prime means by which men and women of the commercial and then industrial bourgeoisie understood themselves and presented themselves to the world.

In the United States, the material preconditions for dwelling on the value of home life did not appear for any significant proportion of the population until the revolutionary period. As late as 1775 only half of the middling households in Massachusetts, for example, had forks and knives, much less the chairs, tables, beds, pillows, tea sets, books, musical instruments and other accoutrements requisite to making the home the center of sociability and restorative personal relations that domesticity would promise. The ascendancy of marketplace relationships, commodity consumption, and partisan politics in a liberal state were contemporaneous and complementary with the constellation of ideas and ideals called domesticity. An ability to imagine needs and provide goods for the home and an understanding of the world of business and politics outside the home as competitive, turbulent, and soul-withering were equally necessary to the strong hold of domesticity in bourgeois life.

Domesticity was an ideological presumption that the home ought to serve as a haven of PRIVACY from the stresses of public life and commerce—a domain well-furnished physically and morally, which would be comforting and serviceable to a hardworking man, and also a nursery of spiritual and civic values in children, presided over by a calm, devoted, effective yet self-abnegating wife and mother. The spirituality and moralism of late eighteenth and early nineteenth-century evangelical Protestantism animated Anglo-American visions of domesticity. As evangelicals preferred concern for the immortal soul over the tawdry "world" of mortal goods, they contrasted the soul-refreshing home to the corrupting arenas of business and politics. But the rhetoric of domesticity was not limited to them. It was welcomed by a whole generation that saw the household devolve from being *the* central institution of daily life, work, collectivity, and sociability to being a residual site of family economy and reproduction set among many (often new) institutions—the factory, office, shop, school, saloon, club, hospital, and government bureau. Comfort, crusading zeal, and nostalgia mixed in the recipe for domesticity. To what degree the great middling ranks of families (or even the smaller numbers of the prosperous bourgeoisie) actually sustained an idyllic haven at home is of course another matter. The rhetoric of "home, sweet home" often thinly papered over paternal or parental tyranny, domestic violence, slavery, and other evils, as well as gilding husbands' legal rights of ownership of the bodies and work of wives and children. (*See also* WOMEN'S RIGHTS.)

The ideology of domesticity served social order and CLASS solidarity in the nineteenth century. Among the bourgeoisie it acted as a code for identity and mutual recognition. As a code that could be learned and also lost (if financial reverses occurred), it allowed for class fluidity. It was most visibly incarnated in (indeed, often indistinguishable from) a system of gender conventions, which assigned to men the role of providers, who went out to work and earn and therefore deserved to be dutifully served, loved, and replenished at home. Women's complementary role of loving, serving and replenishing took place only in the home, their work site—but since the home could not be figured as a site of work while also being a haven from it, women's actual labor was eclipsed, transmuted into a domestic way of being. It was the genius of the nineteenth-century bourgeoisie to make this very contingent family pattern seem necessary—and, without acknowledg-

ment of contradiction, to accept it as natural while trumpeting it as the height of civilization.

It may appear that domesticity as a normative construct affected only the private life of middling and well-to-do whites, but it figured prominently in reform, in the very maintenance of constitutional order, in intercultural contact, and in relations between the United States and other nations. For instance, moral and social reformers at mid-century attacked the problem of urban poverty in the language of domesticity. In their view, the poor who peddled and scavenged on city streets needed above all to learn that children should be off the streets, that the wife/mother should be at home, and the husband/father/provider at work. Similarly, immigrants' adherence to standards of domesticity was judged as a principal criterion of their fitness for American life. Native Americans' divergence from the values of domesticity was consistently cited as justification for intervention, renovation, or coercive actions by both Christian missionary and state authorities. Likewise American foreign missionaries applied their own domestic values to the "heathen" abroad, and often saw Christianization and the attainment of domesticity as virtually one and the same.

Having been a value and a sign of a particular class (forwarded by that class as a universal norm), domesticity evolved in the half-century of national consolidation after the Civil War into a national standard and way of life, used to understand, measure, invite in, or cast out, cultural and racial groups such as Mormons, Asians, freed blacks, Northern Europeans and Southern Europeans. Middle-class women seeking to exert social power through reform organizations redeployed domesticity by adopting rather than rejecting its presumptions of maternal goodness and guidance and turning these toward social and public goals. Groups denied access to the material conditions of domesticity have sought its prerogatives as a form of resistance to the preponderant power of the propertied classes: thus workers in the late nineteenth century asserted their right to a family wage earned by the male head of household, and freed slaves (male and female) collaborated in denying white landowners the use of black women's field labor, so that wives could work in their own homes. These intended subversive as well as dominant uses had the ironic effect of deepening the hold of domesticity as an American practice and worldview. Usually invoked to explain women's roles, domesticity equally ensnared men, shaping the powers and limitations of American manhood well into the mid-twentieth century.

NANCY F. COTT

See also FATHERHOOD; MOTHERHOOD; VIRTUE;
WELFARE.

FURTHER READING
Jeanne Boydston, *Home and Work: Housework, Wages, and the Ideology of Labor in the Early Republic* (New York: Oxford University Press, 1990).
Joan Brumberg, "Zenanas and Girlless Villages: the Ethnology of American Evangelical Women, 1870–1910," *Journal of American History* 69 (Sept. 1982): 347–71.
Nancy F. Cott, *The Bonds of Womanhood: "Woman's Sphere" in New England, 1780–1835* (New Haven: Yale University Press, 1977).
James Horton, "Freedom's Yoke: Gender Conventions among Antebellum Free Blacks," *Feminist Studies* 12 (spring 1986): 51–76.
Linda Kerber, "Separate Spheres, Female Worlds, Woman's Place: the Rhetoric of Women's History," *Journal of American History* 75 (June 1988): 9–39.
Mary P. Ryan, *Cradle of the Middle Class* (New York: Cambridge University Press, 1981).
Christine Stansell, *City of Women: Sex and Class in New York, 1789–1860* (New York: Knopf, 1986).
Barbara Welter, "The Cult of True Womanhood," *American Quarterly* 18 (summer 1966): 151–74.

Donnelly, Ignatius (b. Philadelphia, Pa., Nov. 3, 1831; d. Minneapolis, Minn., Jan. 1, 1901). Politician and writer. A Republican member of Congress from Minnesota from 1863 to 1869, Donnelly went on to become a peripatetic activist for numerous third-party movements in the late nineteenth century—Liberal Republican, Greenbacker and Granger, and finally Populist. In his weekly *Anti-Monopolist* (1874–9), Donnelly criticized the rapid corporatizing of American society and blasted the refusal of the regular party system to mount a challenge to it. His most significant works were the technological dystopia *Caesar's Column: a Story of the Twentieth Century* (1889) and the preamble to the Populist Party's "Omaha Platform" (1892), often considered the classic statement of the western insurgency.

See also POPULISM.

FURTHER READING
Martin Ridge, *Ignatius Donnelly: the Portrait of a Politician* (Chicago: University of Chicago Press, 1962).

Doolittle, Hilda [pen name H.D.] (b. Bethlehem, Pa., Sept. 10, 1886; d. Zurich, Switzerland, Sept. 27, 1961). Poet. Doolittle's early poems, first published in *Sea Garden* (1916), inspired the Imagist movement with their spare precision and unusual meters. Her later epic poems used classical myths to explore religious and philosophical themes from the viewpoints of a variety of active, intelligent female protagonists. She continued to experiment with form as she examined the roles of symbols, tradition, and the unconscious in the human psyche and soul. Herself a patient of Freud, she published *Tribute to Freud* (1956) among other prose works, including a recollection of Ezra Pound entitled *End of Torment* (1958).

FURTHER READING
Barbara Guest, *The Poet H.D. and Her World* (Garden City, N.Y.: Doubleday, 1984).

Dos Passos, John (b. Chicago, Ill., Jan. 14, 1896; d. Baltimore, Md., Sept. 28, 1970). Writer. Horrified by the waste of World War I, Dos Passos gave voice to the disillusionment of the "lost generation." Best known for his trilogy *U.S.A.* (1930–6), he used disjointed narratives—snippets from newspapers and popular songs, autobiographical fragments, parallel stories of characters picked up then dropped again—to create a panoramic impression of an era. His radical criticism of the hypocrisy and shallowness of American institutions later gave way to a conservative embrace of the unique virtues of American democracy. Like many other mid-century migrants from the political left to the political right, he was a perennial critic of liberalism, which he viewed as limp and temporizing in the face of dire threats to liberty.

FURTHER READING
Virginia Carr, *Dos Passos: a Life* (Garden City, N.Y.: Doubleday, 1984).

Douglas, Stephen A. (b. Brandon, Vt., Apr. 23, 1813; d. Chicago, Ill, June 3, 1861). Politician and orator. A Democratic Congressional leader and firm believer in America's manifest destiny, Douglas supported territorial expansion with local self-determination. Claiming to fear a loss of individual and local liberty from a concentration of power in the federal government, he tried to defuse the slavery controversy by advocating the doctrine of "popular sovereignty," which would allow each state or territory to enact its own position on the question. His debates with Lincoln during their 1858 Senate battle not only made Lincoln a national figure but framed the issues that would split the Union. Douglas portrayed Lincoln and the Republicans as proponents of racial equality; Lincoln focused on Douglas's failure to confront the moral evil of slavery. National politics thereafter pivoted on the slavery question and helped set the nation on the path to war.

See also ABRAHAM LINCOLN.

FURTHER READING
Harry V. Jaffa, *Crisis of the House Divided: an Interpretation of the Issues in the Lincoln–Douglas Debates* (Chicago: University of Chicago Press, 1982).

Douglas, William O. (b. Maine, Minn., Oct. 16, 1898; d. Washington, D.C., Jan. 19, 1980). Supreme Court Justice (1939–75). After a brilliant scholarly career as a partisan of LEGAL REALISM, Douglas served as chairman of the Securities and Exchange Commission before being named to the Supreme Court. His opposition to monopoly practices and defense of civil liberties—especially the rights to free speech and privacy—earned praise from liberals and disdain from conservatives, who sought to impeach him in 1970. In addition to defending democratic politics against judicial supremacy in *We the Judges* (1955), Douglas wrote many books on civil rights, the importance of conservation, and the regenerative power of wilderness experience.

See also ACADEMIC FREEDOM.

FURTHER READING
Howard Bell, *Of Power and Right: Hugo Black, William O. Douglas, and America's Constitutional Revolution* (New York: Oxford University Press, 1992).

Douglass, Frederick (b. Tuckahoe, Md., probably Feb. 1818; d. Washington, D.C., Feb. 20, 1895). The most important African American leader and intellectual of the nineteenth century, Frederick Douglass lived for 20 years as a slave and nearly nine years as a fugitive slave. From the 1840s to his death in 1895 he attained international fame as an abolitionist, editor, orator, and the author of three autobiographies which are classics of the slave narrative tradition. Douglass lived to see emancipation and to make a major contribution to interpreting its meaning. He worked actively for women's rights long before they were achieved, and he labored for the civil rights triumphs and witnessed their many betrayals during Reconstruction and the Gilded Age. Today, his work receives widespread critical attention in the fields of literature and history.

Douglass is significant in American history first for his heroic life, as a slave who escaped to freedom, fashioned a dramatic career as an activist and later as a sagelike statesman, and emerged as a true "representative man" in the century that so admired such figures. Second, he is important as an artist, a writer and an orator of uncommon skill and penetrating analysis of America's struggle over slavery and race, and as the narrator of his own story, the first two versions of which, *Narrative of the Life of Frederick Douglass* (1845) and *My Bondage and My Freedom* (1855), are now treated as masterpieces of the American Renaissance. Third, he endures as a thinker, important for his insights and as an interpreter of events and social conditions, if not for his philosophical originality. He was a unique voice of humanism, Romantic individualism, political and reform ideology, and the jeremiadic tradition. Because of his bitter experience as a slave, telling his own personal story was at the core of much of Douglass's work. He never stopped seeking the meanings in the transformations of his own life. Although his life was full of anguish and struggle, and many people helped and influenced his career, Douglass embraced "self-reliance" as much as Ralph Waldo Emerson, albeit for different reasons, and he endlessly probed, like Walt Whitman, the meaning of the self in relation to society and history. Moreover, like Abraham Lincoln and many other contemporaries, Douglass believed in a providential view of history, and in America as a nation with a special destiny and unique obligations.

Douglass matured as a thinker during his career as an abolitionist. In the early 1840s he was an adherent of the doctrines of WILLIAM LLOYD GARRISON: antipolitics, anticlericalism, and moral suasion. But of necessity and temperament, Douglass eventually broke with the Garrisonians and advocated the antislavery interpretation of the Constitution, participation in political parties that opposed slavery's expansion, and the use of violence against slavery when it might prove effective. As a black editor and orator who had no elective sanction, and who spoke for an almost entirely disenfranchised or enslaved people, Douglass came to be a fierce activist at the same time as he embraced practical politics. By the eve of the Civil War he came to believe that slavery would be abolished in America only by some kind of violent reckoning, and that blacks should favor whatever slaveholders and their northern sympathizers opposed. Hence, he lent his qualified support to the Republican Party in the late 1850s, and identified with it increasingly during Reconstruction. At heart, Douglass was a reformer who yearned for a revolution he could help to shape. Above all, he was a master of political and moral language, and in an age that mixed sacred and secular thought, he became a spiritual prophet for black aspirations in America.

In the I-narrative form, from countless platforms, and in his newspapers which he edited for 16 years (1847–63), Douglass found his voice as a critic of American racism and hypocrisy, as a master ironist, and as an advocate of the country's oldest creeds derived from the natural rights tradition. In *The Life and Times of Frederick Douglass* (1881), Douglass remembered his newspaper as "the best school possible for me . . . it obliged me to think and read, it taught me to express my thoughts clearly." This was liberation through the acquisition and mastery of language. The newspapers, he said, gave him "an audience to speak to every week," and provided the "motive power" for his life (p. 264).

Douglass welcomed the Civil War in 1861, and interpreted the process of disunion, total war, and emancipation as a second American Revolution. He imagined himself as one of the new founders of a reinvented Union, rooted in the fact of black freedom and the promise of equality. Moreover, Douglass made a major contribution to the broad, biblical apocalypticism through which Americans, North and South, made sense of the war. In the crucible of such a bloody conflict, Douglass saw a regenerative power for American society. "We are all liberated by this [emancipation] proclamation," he said in an 1863 editorial. "It is a mighty event for the bondman, but it is a still mightier event for the nation at large" (*Douglass Monthly*, Feb. 1863). Douglass's personal religious outlook changed over time, moving from a Christian millennialism early in his career to a postwar religious liberalism and humanism. But biblical imagery, metaphor, and traditions informed Douglass's rhetoric and his view of history throughout his life, and he never ceased his attacks on religious hypocrisy.

During Reconstruction and beyond, Douglass's leadership became more emblematic and less activist as he sought and received functionary appointments from the federal government. Douglass's ideas on Reconstruction aligned with the Radical Republicans' efforts to remake the South on the cornerstone of black suffrage, and to guarantee that the Old South's leadership would never attain power again. But framed by classic liberal political ideology, Douglass's vision of Reconstruction lacked a thoroughgoing economic analysis. Political and moral phenomena dominated Douglass's mind and caused several unresolved contradictions in his postwar thought: he professed a strong belief in the sanctity of private property while demanding land for the powerless freedmen; he coupled laissez-faire individualism and black self-reliance with demands for federal aid to the freedmen; and he implied that political liberty was a sufficient as well as a necessary cause of economic independence and social equality. Although such inconsistencies might have limited his effectiveness, they were typical of the age, and consistent with Douglass's understanding of his own experience as a fugitive slave rising to fame as a reformer. A self-made life had always seemed to him an intensely individualistic affair.

Finally, Douglass's varied writings are significant for their searching analysis of the alienation caused by racism. They offer a striking description of the concept of "double consciousness" framed by W. E. B. Du Bois in *Souls of Black Folk* (1903). Had Douglass lived to read the famous passage about the African American dilemma of being "an American, a Negro; two souls, two thoughts, two unreconciled strivings, two warring ideals in one dark body . . . ," it might have struck him as an astute description of his own inner life. Douglass lived and analyzed what Du Bois would call the "double-aimed struggle" between national and racial identity. The reconciliation of such dualities was one of the central challenges of Douglass's personal and public life. In an 1853 editorial, Douglass described the mid-nineteenth century black intellectual as "isolated in the land of his birth— debarred by his color from congenial associations with whites . . . equally cast out by the ignorances of the blacks" (*Frederick Douglass Papers*, Mar. 4, 1853). Like virtually all black thinkers in the nineteenth century, Douglass never fully resolved his simultaneous beliefs in special racial gifts and the Enlightenment notion of a common human nature. Sometimes he asserted black uniqueness, at least as the product of experience if not of nature, but he never relinquished his faith in human unity. In an 1884 interview, Douglass declared that

there is no division of races. God Almighty made but one race. I adopt the theory that in time the varieties of races will be blended into one. . . . You may say that Frederick Douglass considers himself a member of the one race which exists. (*Frederick Douglass Papers*, vol. 5, p. 147)

As a former slave, born of his black mother and, in all likelihood, her white master, Douglass's life and work provide perhaps the most compelling indictment of racism and the most probing reflection on the meaning of being black in nineteenth-century America.

DAVID W. BLIGHT

See also ANTISLAVERY; AUTOBIOGRAPHY; RIGHTS.

FURTHER READING

William L. Andrews, ed., *Critical Essays on Frederick Douglass* (Boston: G. K. Hall, 1991).

David W. Blight, *Frederick Douglass' Civil War: Keeping Faith in Jubilee* (Baton Rouge: Louisiana State University Press, 1989).

Frederick Douglass, *The Frederick Douglass Papers*, 4 vols., ed. John W. Blassingame and John McKivigan (New Haven: Yale University Press, 1979–92).

William S. McFeely, *Frederick Douglass* (New York: Norton, 1991).

Waldo E. Martin, *The Mind of Frederick Douglass* (Chapel Hill: University of North Carolina Press, 1984).

Dickson J. Preston, *Young Frederick Douglass: the Maryland Years* (Baltimore: Johns Hopkins University Press, 1980).

Eric J. Sundquist, ed., *Frederick Douglass: New Literary and*

Historical Essays (Cambridge: Cambridge University Press, 1990).

Peter F. Walker, *Moral Choices: Memory, Desire, and Imagination in Nineteenth Century American Abolition* (Baton Rouge: Louisiana State University Press, 1978).

Draper, John W. (b. near Liverpool, England, May 5, 1811; d. Hastings-on-Hudson, N.Y., Jan. 4, 1882). Scientist, historian, and philosopher. Trained in medicine, Draper roamed widely through the sciences—he held professorships in chemistry, physiology, and natural philosophy—and also wrote history. His *Human Physiology, Statical and Dynamical* (1856) and *History of the Intellectual Development of Europe* (1860) emphasized the ordered processes of change and development. Both nature and society, Draper believed, obey natural laws of growth, differentiation, and division of labor. Since society is shaped by the environment and by the racial characteristics of its population, history can become a predictive science by studying the effects of such factors as climate, immigration, and political ideas. In his *History of the Conflict between Religion and Science* (1874), Draper argued that religion and science are inherently at odds: though Christianity had hindered the emergence of scientific truth, modern SCIENCE had fought back and proven its superiority over religious superstition.

FURTHER READING

Donald Fleming, *John William Draper and the Religion of Science* (Philadelphia: University of Pennsylvania Press, 1950).

Dreiser, Theodore (b. Terre Haute, Ind., Aug. 27, 1871; d. Hollywood, Calif, Dec. 28, 1945). Novelist. A primary proponent of literary NATURALISM, the grittily "factual" presentation of social existence, Dreiser expressed a fatalistic vision popularly associated with Darwinism. In *Sister Carrie* (1900), *The Financier* (1912), *The Titan* (1914), and *An American Tragedy* (1925), he portrayed a world in which people are driven by external forces and internal compulsions beyond their control. His characters possess a will toward power or mastery, sex or money that is doomed to failure in an impersonal universe where people rise or fall to a level predetermined by their nature and position.

FURTHER READING

Walter Benn Michaels, *The Gold Standard and the Logic of Naturalism* (Berkeley: University of California Press, 1987).

Drinker, Elizabeth Sandwith (b. Philadelphia, Pa., Feb. 27, 1735; d. Philadelphia, Pa., Nov. 24, 1807).

Relatively few people recognize the name of Elizabeth Sandwith Drinker. She was neither a political figure (in the traditional eighteenth-century sense), nor a literary personage (in terms of highly regarded and widely read publications). Drinker was not illuminated by the limelight of her husband's activities, for he was no more than one of many prominent Philadelphia merchants. Yet Elizabeth Drinker deserves recognition nonetheless, because she produced a diary so extensive and rich in content that it must be acknowledged as the single most important document written by a woman in eighteenth-century America.

Drinker did not intend her diary for publication. She recorded details as a reminder of the sequence of events in her life, so that she could refer back to them as necessary. Who called on her? What medicines were effective? How much blood was taken? Which servant misbehaved? Who died from yellow fever? Yet despite the seemingly unrelated incidents, the diary is a narrative, and a well-written one at that. Drinker's respect for the English language, her concern for detail, and her recognition that her children, at least, would examine the journal, make it a highly readable chronicle, and one of the few that describe a world where the female perspective is central rather than peripheral to the story.

Elizabeth Sandwith was the second daughter of an Irish Quaker family. She spent her entire life in Philadelphia, eventually as the wife of Henry Drinker, mother of five adult children, and grandmother of 19. Her world, not surprisingly, was shaped by her class and religion, as well as by eighteenth-century Anglo-American cultural assumptions. Drinker's diary reflects that time and place, and thus invites us into a world which, until recently, historians have reconstructed from the perspective of Drinker's male contemporaries.

The diary, spanning 49 years (1758–1807) and 2,000 printed pages, is a journal of record at its most elementary level, and a perceptive and observant commentary at its most sophisticated. It reaches far beyond the life of its author, and permits exploration of a multitude of topics: medicine, urban growth, master–servant relations, public health, and revolutionary activities. Indeed, in addition to the traditional and selective topics of historical inquiry, the Drinker diary encourages consideration of eighteenth-century society as a whole.

A focus on the broader view indicates that most of Drinker's family and friends were subject to chronic ill health. While Drinker did not dwell on the implications of this phenomenon, it is likely that these ailments affected personal relationships, economic productivity, and individual identity. At the very least it created a constant insecurity; it may also have been one of the decisive forces that shaped early American culture and society. The diary suggests that eighteenth-century society was also molded by the conjunction of home and production for income. In Philadelphia, as elsewhere, fathers as well as mothers interacted with children during the day, and the lack of privacy due to the constant flow of people in the household conditioned attitudes and relationships. According to Drinker, rumor and gossip were rampant —and no wonder, considering that few actions went unnoticed and few words unheard.

Most important in the context of current historical debate, however, is what the diary discloses about gender and society—which in turn suggests a need for the reassessment of roles played by women and men 200 years ago. Eighteenth-century cultural constraints created middle- and upper-class women who saw themselves first and foremost as wives and mothers, an expectation probably shared by the less affluent as well. This is not to say that women did not consider themselves as economic beings, but rather that their economic contribution was inseparable from their socially constructed private roles within the family circle.

Elizabeth Drinker subscribed to and accepted the domestic quality of her life, as did her friends and relatives. Yet the eighteenth century also demanded that women be timid, submissive, obedient, selfless, and pious—subcharacteristics of the more general category entitled "virtue." Drinker accepted these attributes as they applied to women, but her daily journal entries suggest that she and other women were only partially successful in meeting the standards set for and by them. Consider timidity. Drinker may have eschewed horseback riding, and she may have been startled by the sound of loud thunder, but her timidity was, like everything else, socially defined. It was hardly timid to make a life-or-death decision during a health crisis, and as primary care-giver such decisions often confronted Drinker. It was not submissive to urge powerful politicians to release a group of imprisoned Quakers (including Drinker's husband). Drinker did not show obedience when she rebuffed the request of an army officer for quartering during the occupation of Philadelphia. As Drinker advanced in age, her selflessness waned in proportion to the amount of time spent pursuing her favorite activity, reading. And if piety was measured (at least in part) by the amount of time a Quaker spent in the meeting house, perusing the Bible, or reflecting on God's works, Elizabeth Drinker was not especially pious.

This is not to say that Drinker saw herself as anything other than a representative of her generation, a woman who measured her life by contemporary definitions and expectations. It is rather that her diary requires us to confront the paradox of a world which defined permissible female attributes so narrowly as to deny women recognition for qualities that were applauded in men—even when women exhibited those qualities in socially acceptable behavior.

Elizabeth Drinker would be surprised to learn that her diary has earned her recognition. But even as she prized her private thoughts, she would accept this public notice with the same equanimity that she tried to exhibit throughout her life, and she might even be pleased to know that she has influenced our perception of her world.

ELAINE FORMAN CRANE

See also DIARIES; DOMESTICITY; VIRTUE.

FURTHER READING

Elizabeth Sandwith Drinker, *The Diary of Elizabeth Sandwith Drinker,* ed. Elaine Forman Crane, 3 vols. (Boston: Northeastern University Press, 1991).

Linda K. Kerber, *Women of the Republic: Intellect and Ideology in Revolutionary America* (Chapel Hill: University of North Carolina Press, 1980).

Mary Beth Norton, *Liberty's Daughters: the Revolutionary Experience of American Women, 1750–1800* (Boston: Little, Brown, 1980).

Du Bois, W[illiam] E[dward] B[urghardt] (b. Great Barrington, Mass. Feb. 23, 1868; d. Accra, Ghana, Aug. 27, 1963). One of the true "renaissance men" of the modern era, Du Bois pursued simultaneous careers in university teaching, academic scholarship, and political activism. His writings— which encompassed 17 books of sociology, history, fiction, and poetry, editorial contributions to four journals, and countless newspaper columns—made possible new ways of thinking about America and African America; enabled new articulations of the complexities and nuances of our national and racial identities; and offered new ways of analyzing our present and of imagining a future.

Du Bois attended public schools in Great Barrington before going on to Fisk, a black college in Nashville, Tennessee, and then to Harvard, from which he received a B.A. in 1890 and Ph.D. in 1895. He studied and traveled in Germany between 1892 and 1894, and upon his return to the United States he taught for two years at Wilberforce University. Du Bois then conducted a pioneering urban research study under the auspices of the University of

Pennsylvania in 1896–7, after which he undertook the first of two teaching stints at Atlanta University. He left Atlanta in 1910 to accept a position with the newly organized National Association for the Advancement of Colored People, where he edited the organization's journal, *The Crisis*.

Du Bois used *The Crisis* to rally black support for the NAACP's challenge to the philosophy of accommodation associated with the southern black leader and educator, BOOKER T. WASHINGTON. Through legal suits, legislative lobbying, and propaganda, the NAACP uncompromisingly attacked lynching, the segregation and discrimination of Jim Crow, and disfranchisement. Moreover, in an era of increasing black literacy and expanding media of communication, Du Bois's journal constituted a vital public arena for African American self-expression. Its pages were a forum for the coherent representation and enactment of black intellectual and cultural life. There one found discussions and emblems of black religious, cultural, and social life; poetry and song; and visual images of the richness and diversity of the black presence in America. As an appreciative NAACP would note years later, Du Bois virtually created a politically engaged black intelligentsia.

Following a bitter dispute over the NAACP's direction and policies in 1934, Du Bois resigned from that organization and returned to Atlanta University, where he taught sociology, studied Marx, founded and edited a new scholarly journal, and authored two more books of social commentary and a history of Reconstruction. He would return to the NAACP in 1944 to study and devise responses to the coming postwar settlement, especially as it affected black peoples in Africa and the diaspora. Representing the NAACP, he was a consultant to the U.S. delegation at the founding of the United Nations, and in 1947 he prepared and presented to it an antiracist appeal. Meanwhile, he continued his pan-Africanist activities and wrote two books on colonialism and world peace. His outspoken radicalism led to his second forced departure from the NAACP in 1948 and his trial and acquittal in 1951 on federal charges of being an "unregistered foreign agent." Subject to continuous political harassment, including denial of a passport between 1952 and 1958, he vigorously defended the Soviet and Chinese communist regimes and joined the American Communist Party in 1960. In that same year he moved to Ghana, where he remained until his death.

Throughout a life that spanned many of the crucial transitions of the modern era, Du Bois remained a profound and politically committed thinker, a determined interrogator of practically all that was taking place around him. His oeuvre ranges from poignant essays to political novels to children's stories, but fundamental to all of them is the puzzle of the concept of race, the investigation into the causes of racism, and strategies for resistance to it. The place of these issues in his life and thought is signaled by the prophetic words opening the second essay in *Souls of Black Folk* (1903): "The problem of the twentieth century is the problem of the color-line,—the relation of the darker to the lighter races of men in Asia and Africa, in America and the islands of the sea." This essay linked the contemporary color-line to the nineteenth-century aftermath of slavery, emancipation, and Reconstruction. Together with the opening chapter on modern black identity, it framed conceptually just what "the problem of the color-line" was all about. The problem was first of all that of comprehending identity and difference in the modern world, a world profoundly shaped by slavery, emancipation, and imperialism. It was also a problem of overcoming labor exploitation, of people being able to claim not only their cultural birthright but the very fruits of their labor.

"The Conservation of Races," an essay written for presentation to the American Negro Academy in 1897, was one of his earliest efforts at elaborating a theoretical and political analysis of the race concept. Aimed at a primarily black audience, the essay sought to establish not only the intellectual and moral validity of the race concept but the indispensability of race consciousness for black progress. As the paper's very title suggests, he wanted to *conserve* the "race idea" and racial integrity. Yet most of the essay actually sketches a historical and at root materialistic process of "race-making." From the age of nomadic tribes to the development of settled communities and cities, common economic and social needs broke down the barriers of blood *within* communities, while at the same time new differences—ones also based initially on a diversity of material interests—developed *between* communities. That "deep and decisive" historical process was repeated in the formation of nations, and of supranational entities like civilizations and language groups. In this account the ultimate roots of race consciousness were socioeconomic; therefore, even as he affirmed the centrality of the race concept, Du Bois shifted the emphasis from a biologistic to a social conception of race, emphasizing the historical and material grounding of racial identity and thus its embeddedness in concrete relations of power.

Some readings of this essay, as well as of Du Bois's work generally, have emphasized how much he was still entangled in nineteenth-century ideas about race and nation. But much more noteworthy are the strides he had already made, even at the outset of his career, toward a late twentieth-century conception of race as a social and historical construction. This conception became more and more evident in his writings over the course of the first half of the twentieth-century, especially during the World War I era, and is fully evident in *Dusk of Dawn: an Essay Toward an Autobiography of a Race Concept* (1940).

The core texts among Du Bois's writings make plain that racial identity is no a priori, fixed category. It is something one discovers. "Very gradually," he wrote in *Darkwater* in 1918, "—I cannot now distinguish the steps, though here and there I remember a jump or a jolt—but very gradually I found myself assuming quite placidly that I was different from other children" (p. 11). His coming of age at Fisk and Harvard added other experiences that furthered his education about the material and ideological basis of group identities and differences. And during his sojourn as a student in Germany, he came to understand that the men and women he met there were "not white folks, but folks" (p. 16). Very soon thereafter, especially after his return to "'nigger'-hating America," he also realized that race is not only learned from one's environment, but can be externally imposed. Racial violence in Georgia and elsewhere at the *fin de siècle* definitively reshaped his consciousness of self and ultimately his career commitment; he left the university for the NAACP to undertake a "hot and indignant defense" of his race.

But the learning process by which one takes on an identity—willingly or unwillingly—is not confined to the excluded and oppressed. If "black" is socially constructed, so too is "white." "The discovery of personal whiteness among the world's peoples is a very modern thing," he wrote in *Darkwater* (pp. 29–30). In his analysis of the causes of the 1917 race riot in East St. Louis, Du Bois expanded upon this insight. A war-induced boom had produced a historic conjunction in that city of northern capitalists, eastern poor white labor, and southern impoverished blacks. The latter two groups might have logically found common cause in their similar relations to northern capital; but instead white labor—led on by mass media—came to see itself, and its interests, as fundamentally different from black labor. They learned a discourse of race that allowed them not only to conceive of themselves as "white" but to engage in and justify barbarous deeds of racial violence.

In many ways World War I powerfully transformed Du Bois's conception of race, deepening his commitment to a materialist analysis of, and socialist solution to, racism. The terrible carnage of the war itself—

which he blamed on imperialism and colonialism—discredited any claims Europeans might have had to a superior culture and civilization. He came to see race as a phenomenon of the modern era, and of the vast transformation of human life which that era had witnessed. The origins of modernity he dated from the expansion of Europe and its subsequent accumulation of capital on a world scale. At this point, his rejection of nineteenth-century idealist conceptions of race was quite explicit: "There are no races," he wrote in the September 1917 edition of *The Crisis*, "There are great groups, now with common history . . . common interests . . . common ancestry . . . common experience." It became increasingly clear to him that race must be understood in relation to class formation. It was also clear that, despite the high correlation between class and color, one could not successfully analyze racial oppression solely in racial terms. But contrary to many of his socialist contemporaries who emphasized *only* class, Du Bois continued to insist that race was a central structural feature of this global, hegemonic system. European expansion and colonialism had racialized class. Capital ruled, and the capitalists were white. Consequently, any socialist reform, he argued, must be accompanied by the destruction of race prejudice.

Du Bois's rigorous analysis of the deep-seated obstacles to such reform did not prevent him from remaining a spirited idealist to the end. What was most important about socialism, he wrote in the 1917 issue of *Crisis*, was its spirit: "the Will to Human Brotherhood of all Colors, Races, and Creeds; the Wanting the Wants of All." Indeed, his final years were spent at work on the *Encyclopedia Africana*—a work similar to one he had envisioned a half-century before, and moreover one that underscored his fundamental faith that knowledge and liberation were intimately linked. At least since *Souls of Black Folk* he had insisted that exploring the lived experience of black peoples in America could open the unique knowledge, special insights, and prophetic visions that that experience embraced. Such understanding, he believed, might lend itself to the common struggle to create a world that was both democratic and tolerant of the diversity of humankind.

THOMAS C. HOLT

See also CLASS; RACE.

FURTHER READING

Anthony Appiah, "The Uncompleted Argument: Du Bois and the Illusion of Race," *Critical Inquiry* 17 (summer 1991): 773–97.

W. E. B. Du Bois, *Darkwater: Voices from within the Veil* (1920; Harcourt, Brace, 1921).

Thomas C. Holt, "The Political Uses of Alienation:

W. E. B. Du Bois on Politics, Race and Culture, 1903–1940," *American Quarterly* 42 (June 1990): 100–15.

Gerald Horne, *Black and Red: W. E. B. Du Bois and the Afro-American Response to the Cold War, 1944–1963* (Albany: SUNY Press, 1986).

Manning Marable, *W. E. B. Du Bois: Black Radical Democrat* (Boston: Twayne, 1986).

Arnold Rampersad, *The Art and Imagination of W. E. B. Du Bois* (Cambridge: Harvard University Press, 1976).

Dubos, René (b. Saint-Brice-sous-Forêt, France, Feb. 20, 1901; d. New York, N.Y., Feb. 20, 1982). Microbiologist and environmentalist. A major figure in the development of ecological thought, Dubos held that an understanding of organic entities—from microbes to human beings—requires a grasp of their symbiotic interaction within an ecosystem. These views led Dubos from a revisionist understanding of "disease" as an integral part of any organic system to a broad ecological humanism. That humanism transcended the dualism of "man" and "nature" by focusing on interactions of human beings with their environment, interactions capable of transforming the human-natural nexus.

See also ENVIRONMENTALISM; NATURE.

FURTHER READING

Osborn Segerberg Jr., *The World of René Dubos* (New York: Henry Holt, 1990).

Dulles, John Foster (b. Washington, D.C., Feb. 25, 1888; d. Washington, D.C., May 24, 1959). Lawyer and public official. Born to a family of diplomats, Dulles brought his Christian faith to bear upon his diplomatic career, which began during World War I and ended with his service as Eisenhower's Secretary of State (1953–9). In two books—*War, Peace, and Change* (1939) and *War or Peace* (1950)—Dulles placed foreign policy in the context of Christian stewardship and called for a revival of American righteousness on the world stage. As a strategist he is responsible for introducing concepts like "massive retaliation" and "brinkmanship" into the COLD WAR lexicon. One of the more public members of the Eisenhower administration, Dulles was a mass media figure, pioneering the use of television as an engine of opinion management.

FURTHER READING

Townsend Hoopes, *The Devil and John Foster Dulles* (Boston: Atlantic-Little, Brown, 1973).

Durant, Will[iam James] (b. North Adams, Mass., Nov. 5, 1885; d. Los Angeles, Calif., Nov. 7, 1981). Writer. A teacher and administrator at the Labor Temple School in New York from 1917 to 1927, Durant authored the bestselling *Story of Philosophy* in 1926 and thereafter turned to full-time writing. Criticized by some scholars for oversimplification, and by some defenders of high culture as a purveyor of the middlebrow, Durant saw himself as making the fruits of Western civilization available to all the people. With his wife Ariel Durant, he produced the multivolume *Story of Civilization* (1935–75). In Durant's story, civilization tended to lead to the inevitable triumphs of twentieth-century American society.

See also MIDDLEBROW CULTURE.

FURTHER READING

Joan Shelley Rubin, *The Making of Middlebrow Culture* (Chapel Hill: University of North Carolina Press, 1992).

Dwight, Timothy (b. Northampton, Mass., May 14, 1752; d. New Haven, Conn., Jan. 11, 1817). Clergyman and poet. Grandson of JONATHAN EDWARDS, Dwight defended orthodoxy but meanwhile stressed individual human potency more than most Calvinists. His sermons and lectures defended Federalist order against the anarchy of Jeffersonian republicanism and the French Revolution: unrestrained by law and religion, he argued, people become beasts of prey. Though he regarded human knowledge as inherently incomplete, Dwight supported scientific study (to support religious truths) and better education for women. A wide-ranging writer, he produced, in addition to his poetry, the four-volume *Travels in New England and New York* (1821–2). From 1795 to 1817 he was the president of Yale University.

FURTHER READING

Annabelle S. Wenzke, *Timothy Dwight* (Lewiston, N.Y.: E. Mellen Press, 1989).

E

Eastman, Crystal (b. Marlborough, Mass., June 25, 1881; d. Erie, Pa., July 8, 1928).   Lawyer and journalist. Eastman helped write the first workers' compensation law and the Equal Rights Amendment, and helped found the American Civil Liberties Union and the Women's International League for Peace and Freedom. A socialist and pacifist, she asserted that women should be able to combine marriage and motherhood with satisfying paid work. She campaigned for the redistribution of wealth and against the suppression of civil liberties during wartime. Equality for women, she insisted, meant access to daycare centers and birth control as well as the vote. A flamboyant and energetic organizer, speaker, and writer for the periodical press, she also wrote *Work Accidents and the Law* (1911) and coedited *The Liberator* (1918–1922).

FURTHER READING
Mari Jo Buhle, *Women and American Socialism, 1870–1920* (Urbana: University of Illinois Press, 1981).

Eastman, Max (b. Canadaigua, N.Y., Jan. 4, 1883; d. Bridgetown, Barbados, Mar. 25, 1969).   For roughly the first quarter of the twentieth century Max Eastman was the most important intellectual figure on the American Left. During the third quarter, beginning with the 1950s, he surprised many of his old comrades when he turned toward conservatism and associated with McCarthyism and the anticommunist Right. Whether championing Bolshevism or capitalism, Eastman was a splendid writer of lively, witty prose, one of the few intellectuals who actually reached the masses when he later became a contributor to *Reader's Digest*.

Raised by devout Congregationalist parents who imbued in him both the spirit of moral idealism and a lust for life, Eastman graduated from Williams College and did graduate work in philosophy with John Dewey at Columbia University. In the pre–World War I years he became famous as editor of *The Masses*, a publication unique in the annals of American radicalism for combining not only art and politics but sardonic humor along with serious reportage on the struggles and miseries of the working class. Leaving the religion of his parents behind, Eastman's passions ran in many directions as he invoked poetry, philosophy, and science to support such causes as anarchism, feminism, socialism, and pacifism. With the October Revolution of 1917, Eastman rushed off to the new Soviet state, learned Russian, translated Lenin and Trotsky, and became one of the leading exponents of Bolshevism in the West, the first to claim that Leninism dramatized a willful defiance of Marxism and not merely a deviation from its doctrines. Because of press censorship in much of eastern and southern Europe, Eastman's writings during the red scare of 1919–20 provided some of the only reports coming out of Russia and influenced the young Italian communist, Antonio Gramsci.

Like his friend JOHN REED, Eastman grew critical of the dictatorial direction taken by the Bolshevik party. In 1924, Eastman smuggled out of Russia Lenin's deathbed will and testament warning against Stalin's succession to power. Eastman published the document in the *New York Times*, assuming that Trotsky and other old revolutionaries would now move against Stalin and the rapidly growing bureaucratic state. The failure of the anti-Stalinists to offer an effective opposition continued to disappoint Eastman, and in the thirties he incurred the wrath of many communist-leaning American intellectuals for exposing, in his book *Artists in Uniform*, the suppression of cultural freedom in Russia.

Eastman also carried on a decade-long debate with SIDNEY HOOK over the philosophical foundations of Marxism. Hook had denied that Marxism had metaphysical foundations and instead had explicated its pragmatic dimensions in order to emphasize action and experimentation. Eastman insisted that Marx had sublimated German philosophy and read into matter and motion all the inexorable forces that Hegel had identified as the unfolding of "Spirit." Eastman's conviction that Marxism was more myth than science, that it was a rhetorical construction based on little more than the language of dialectics, influenced such eminent writers as EDMUND WILSON. Today debates continue over Hegel's legacy in the school of thought known as Critical Theory, which seeks to restore the "dialectical imagination" to politics and society in order to sustain belief in the goals of the Left. (*See also* FRANKFURT SCHOOL.)

In his later conservative years Eastman introduced the works of Austrian economists and became a proponent of free enterprise. As an atheist as well as an anarcho-libertarian, Eastman resigned from the *National Review* and broke with editor WILLIAM F. BUCKLEY over religion. Although Eastman's politics went through significant changes, he remained consistent in some cultural issues, especially feminism. Brother of the Greenwich Village heroine CRYSTAL EASTMAN, Max fought for such issues as suffrage, birth control, and women's entry into the professions.

Tall and handsome, an eloquent orator as well as writer, Eastman left a striking impression on generations of young American activists who heard him speak or debate. He "looked Beauty and spoke Justice," recalled one of his admirers. He wrote with verve and insight on many topics, and in *Great Companions* (1959) he offered vivid recollections of such figures as Freud, Santayana, Dewey, Hemingway, Einstein, Bertrand Russell, and Edna St. Vincent Millay. Eastman's description of Hemingway as offering "a literary style . . . of wearing false hair on the chest" led to a brief fight between the two in the office of Scribner's. Of St. Vincent Millay, Eastman wrote:

> She was not voluptuously beautiful like her sister. She had the legs and, at times, the expression of a maiden aunt. But the eyes were of an incredible wild gray-green out of the forest, and they had bewitching crinkles around them. Her torso was shapely, and her voice as thrilling as a violin. She could indeed in moments of high animation become beautiful, almost divinely so . . . but then all the more she seemed—to me at least—in some strange way remote. Her determination to be a poet, and not some man's woman or even some child's mother, was absolute—and absolutely necessary, I'm afraid, if a woman is to rival men in creative art.

Admiration for Eastman dropped off drastically during the early Cold War years. American intellectuals were dismayed by Eastman's support, however conditional, of Joseph McCarthy. Eastman's anticommunism was deeply personal. He could never forget the fate of friends and relatives. The family of his third wife, Eliena Krylenko, was murdered by Stalin's assassins. He tried unsuccessfully to publicize the Soviet Union's gulag labor camps while other intellectuals in America and Europe denied their existence. In 1989, with the fall of the Berlin Wall, Eastman's prescient anticommunism received historical vindication.

JOHN P. DIGGINS

See also NEW YORK INTELLECTUALS; SOCIALISM.

FURTHER READING

Daniel Aaron, *Writers on the Left: Episodes in American Literary Communism* (New York: Harcourt, 1961).

John P. Diggins, *Up From Communism: Conservative Odysseys in American Intellectual History* (New York: Harper, 1975).

Max Eastman, *Enjoyment of Living* (New York: Harper, 1948).

——, *Love and Revolution: My Journey Through an Epoch* (New York: Random House, 1964).

William L. O'Neill, *The Last Romantic: a Life of Max Eastman* (New York: Oxford University Press, 1978).

Eddy, Mary Baker (b. Bow, N.H., July 16, 1821; d. Chestnut Hill, Mass., Dec. 3, 1910). Founder of the Church of Christ, Scientist, Eddy published the first edition of *Science and Health* in 1875 (the subtitle *Key to the Scriptures* was added in 1883). That event marked the beginning of a new religious movement that would make an indelible mark on the landscape of American religion.

Few dispassionate voices have entered the discussion of Christian Science. Most available literature emanates either from ardent admirers or from zealous detractors. The two groups agree on only one point—the enormous power of Mary Baker Eddy's personality and the centrality of her role in the church she founded. In his book *Christian Science* (1907) Samuel Clemens devoted 362 pages to his accusation that Eddy exercised "a despotism . . . more absolute than the Russian Czarship" (p. 343). The closest approximation to an official history of Christian Science—Robert Peel's three-volume biography of the church's esteemed founder—rejects Clemens's animus, but offers a similar estimation of Eddy's stature and authority. However she is viewed, there is no question that Eddy exercised a degree of religious authority unprecedented for an American woman, and that the impact of her personality continues to be felt today. She articulated an unorthodox metaphysical theology that implied the rejection of conventional medical practice, and built a tightly organized church structure to promote the thought of its founder.

According to her own account, Eddy discovered the principles of Christian Science when she found, following a fall on the ice in 1866, that she could heal herself through the application of mental principles based on the New Testament. She began teaching her new system of healing and published the first edition of *Science and Health* in 1875. Eddy asserted the absolute power of Spirit over matter, of Mind over body. Christian Science recognized no objective physical reality, but only the reality of Spirit, an infinite, all-encompassing principle of goodness, also called God. The physical world and all evidences of evil resulted from the workings of Mortal Mind, the opposite of Spirit. Mortal Mind had no ultimate reality, since it was created by human thoughts.

Christian Science perceives a great divide between

the perfect thoughts of Infinite Mind, and the finite thoughts of human minds that have not yet realized their union with all-encompassing Principle. Our perception that we each possess individual physical bodies, for example, results from our failure to recognize that we are in fact Spirit, and that nothing real separates us from the Divine Mind. Thus all pain, suffering, and misfortune arise not from external causes, but rather from false beliefs on the part of the sufferer. Even death was considered to result from errors in thinking. The false belief in mortality, rather than physiological inevitability, prevented human beings from realizing their potential for immortality.

This view led to one of Eddy's most controversial tenets—the rejection of conventional medicine in favor of mental healing. In this Eddy built on the views of her early teacher Phineas Parkhust Quimby (1802–1866), whose influence also blossomed in the New Thought movement. In Christian Science the nature of Spirit and of its opposite, Mortal Mind, are revealed to individuals through experiences of illness and healing. Healing lay at the core of Eddy's teaching, and much of the church's efforts went into training practitioners to treat sick patients according to the principles of Christian Science. These benign mental treatments offered a healthful alternative to the more invasive medical practices of the day, especially for women, for whom conventional medicine could be punitive as well as dangerous. This may explain the special appeal of Christian Science to middle-class urban women. Having survived an early widowhood, 20 additional years of unhappy marriage, and decades of occasional invalidism, Eddy knew from experience the limited options available to women in a culture that assumed woman's role to be dictated by her reproductive system. Eddy ingeniously assaulted the notion that biology was destiny without attacking conventional gender roles. Instead she asserted that the body did not exist. With the biological basis of gender difference out of the way, she was free to abrogate the very norms of femininity that she exempted from criticism.

In *A Religious History of the American People*, Sydney Ahlstrom coined the term "harmonialism" to describe a widely accepted cosmological outlook which can be traced from Swedenborgianism through SPIRITUALISM to Christian Science and New Thought. Theologically, these movements are distinguished by the view that the universe is fundamentally in harmony with itself, and by the belief that individual well-being depends on recognition of one's own inherent harmony with the cosmos. Eddy agreed with other harmonialists that human beings are good by

nature, and thus joined in departing from orthodox Protestantism. In a general way, Christian Science was part of the nineteenth-century liberal revolt against Calvinism.

The Christian Scientist historian Stephen Gottschalk takes issue with Ahlstrom's inclusion of Christian Science in the category of "harmonialism," arguing that Christian Science should be seen as a more orthodox Christian expression which acknowledges the need for salvation through Christ, although understood in a distinctive way. Gottschalk tends to minimize Eddy's historical roots in the harmonial stream, which are evident in the central role she assigned to concepts developed within it. The "Father Mother God," the "Christ Principle," and the definition of God as principle rather than person, which became quite important in Christian Science, would have been familiar to nineteenth-century spiritualists from the works of Andrew Jackson Davis and others. Likewise, Swedenborgians would have agreed with Eddy's assertion that the Bible contains an inner spiritual sense different from its mundane meaning.

But Gottschalk is right to stress that Christian Science, unlike other harmonial groups, put great emphasis on evil. Eddy had no doubt that human life expressed the total depravity that stemmed from Adam. She did contend that evil had no ultimate existence, but she was alarmed by the potency of evil in everyday life. It was powerful because people believed in its power. From her conviction that mind could control matter Eddy concluded that if thoughts could heal, they could also harm. She harbored deep personal fears of "mental malpractice" by those who wished her ill, and attributed the death of her third husband to arsenic placed in his body by the malicious thoughts of her enemies.

In Christian Science worship, selections from *Science and Health* take the place of sermons, and those who preside are called "readers" rather than "ministers," because their function is to read the words of Mary Baker Eddy, not to interpret scripture on their own. This ritual practice, and the highly centralized and tightly structured organization of the Church of Christ, Scientist, ensure that the institution Eddy founded will continue to be an effective vehicle for the perpetuation of her thought.

ANN BRAUDE

See also LIBERAL PROTESTANTISM; RELIGION.

FURTHER READING

Sydney Ahlstrom, "Eddy, Mary Baker," in Edward T. James, Janet Wilson James, and Paul Boyer, eds., *Notable American Women*, 3 vols. (Cambridge: Harvard University Press, 1975).
Mary Baker Eddy, *Science and Health with Key to the*

Scriptures (1875; Boston: Trustees under the Will of Mary Baker G. Eddy, 1934).

——, *Retrospection and Introspection* (Boston: Trustees under the Will of Mary Baker G. Eddy, 1910).

——, *Miscellaneous Writings* (Boston: Trustees under the Will of Mary Baker G. Eddy, 1910).

Stephen Gottschalk, *The Emergence of Christian Science in American Religious Life* (Berkeley: University of California Press, 1973).

——, "Christian Science and Harmonialism," in Charles H. Lippy and Peter W. Williams, eds., *The Encyclopedia of the American Religious Experience* (New York: Charles Scribner's Sons, 1988), vol. 2.

Robert Peel, *Mary Baker Eddy*, 3 vols. (New York: Holt, Rinehart and Winston, 1966–77).

education Few aspects of American history reveal more contradictions between "rhetoric" and "reality" than the history of American education. Celebrated as the means by which Americans have offered equal opportunity to all people, education has in actuality been deeply involved in allocating different opportunities to different groups within the population. Cherished as a means for liberating individual talent and creativity, education has in fact been a primary means for socializing people to the norms of a community, including, most importantly, the attitudes and behaviors associated with the world of WORK. Most telling of all, however, Americans have assigned high value to education, but have been consistently unwilling to support education sufficiently in material ways. That education is expected to fulfill a host of essential social functions, while Americans demean teaching as an occupation and consistently provide insufficient funds for educational projects and institutions, raises difficult questions about the depth of American commitment to a viable, democratic communal life.

Not surprisingly, the contradictions apparent in the history of American education have been reflected in the literature of educational history. Indeed, there has been a clear, repeated division between those historians who have stressed the positive aspirations of educators, often in the process failing equally to stress the degree to which these have fallen short of realization, and those historians who have stressed the illiberal underside of education, again without balancing that judgment with attention to real idealism and concern for social betterment.

In addition, the literature of educational history has been characterized by important differences of definition. Some historians have viewed the topic narrowly, as nothing more than the history of schools and colleges; others have viewed it very broadly, as all that has been involved in the transmission of culture across generations. Some have focused on thinkers and thinking about education; others have focused on institutions and their changing functions over time. Whether, as some historians would now contend, recognition of ethnic, class, and gender differences renders it impossible to speak generally of "American" educational history, there is no doubt that recent interest in diversity and in finding ways sensibly to revise standing interpretations to take fuller account of diverse experiences has begun to enlarge the purview of the field. To include the educational experience of women and groups that have been marginalized, one must move beyond the history of schooling to consider as well the educational significance of religious institutions, the popular media, and fraternal and labor organizations. Whether a more comprehensive and diverse history can shed new light on the gaps between rhetoric and reality sketched above remains to be seen.

Although the history of education in North America actually begins with the arrival of the very first settlers, the "native American" peoples who came to the continent from Asia long before the arrival of Europeans, the origins of modern institutions of education date from English colonization in the seventeenth century. Spurred by religious zeal, and encouraged by patterns of colonization that brought entire families to the new world, the English moved promptly to establish churches, schools, and even a college. Other colonizing groups, for example the Dutch in what is today New York, the English Quakers in Pennsylvania, and the Catholics in Maryland, followed suit. The result, even before independence, was an unusually high rate of literacy among white males.

African Americans who were forcibly brought to the North American colonies, often by way of the Caribbean, were generally denied access to formal institutions of education, their educational disenfranchisement growing as the formal institution of slavery was increasingly codified during the seventeenth century. Despite barriers of language and cultural tradition, however, which initially separated African Americans from one another as well as from Anglo Americans, African Americans slowly evolved their own mechanism for educating young people and sustaining a sense of community. Central among these were religious celebrations, music, and FOLKLORE, all of which often had origins in African beliefs and ceremonies.

After the Revolution, the nature of education in the new republic became an important topic for debate, especially among learned patriots. Many agreed with the Pennsylvania doctor and statesman, BENJAMIN RUSH, when he wrote in a letter of May 1786:

We have changed our forms of government, but it remains yet to effect a revolution in our principles, opinions, and manners, so as to accommodate them to the forms of government we have adopted. This is the most difficult part of the business of the patriots and legislators of our country (*Letters*, vol. 1, p. 388).

Some argued that public schooling based on a common religion would be a necessity in the new nation; others, notably the Connecticut lawyer NOAH WEBSTER, insisted that it was a common language that was most important to democracy and union. Rush himself claimed that, along with schooling, education within families was essential, virtuous citizens requiring the nurture of "Republican mothers."

Whether discussions of education in the new Republic initiated or confirmed actual institutional arrangements, schooling was well established in the new nation by the first decades of the nineteenth century. Locally controlled and supported common schools, open to all white children, male and female (and on a few occasions to free black children as well), were prevalent throughout the Northeast and populated areas of the Middle West even before the so-called common school movement of the 1830s and 1840s. Led by such prominent "friends of education" as HORACE MANN, CATHARINE BEECHER, and Henry Barnard, the common school movement helped win more regularized public support for schools, advocated reliance on (less expensive) female teachers, popularized pedagogical and architectural innovations, and, most important, extended earlier rationales for schooling to include economic and civic arguments, in the process establishing a logic, a rhetoric, and a coalition-style of politics that has continued to mark the politics of education to the present day.

Importantly, however, the common school movement did not foster uniformity in school arrangements for all groups throughout the nation. Common schools did not become well established in the South until after the Civil War, and public schooling in that region (for whites and especially for African Americans) was relatively poorly supported until well into the twentieth century. School arrangements in the South were also legally segregated until 1954 and de facto racial segregation, or "racial isolation," persists in many schools throughout the nation to this day. Finding the public schools more Protestant than their supposedly nondenominational character might have suggested, Catholics (and some other religious groups) also felt compelled to organize their own separate ("parochial") school system, which meant in effect that Catholic parents were taxed twice, once

to support the public schools, and once to support the private schools they had created. This phenomenon came subsequently to characterize the experience of other groups with particular educational demands, groups as various as upper-class WASP New Englanders, who wanted their children to experience an American equivalent of the English "public" school, and middle-class religious fundamentalists, who wanted their children exposed to a "creationist" curriculum instead of one based on evolutionary science.

In the process of providing instruction in the elementary subjects of reading, writing, and arithmetic, the common schools of the Northeast and Middle West purveyed a *paideia* or civic creed, rooted in the skills, sensibilities, values, and prejudices of Protestant EVANGELICALISM combined with REPUBLICANISM. Typified by the rhymes, stories, and expository essays of the famed McGuffey Readers, this *paideia* reinforced messages conveyed by the actual organization of schools. Though still small in size, and often housed in one-room buildings, with small windows, little heat in winter, and uncomfortable wooden benches and chairs, antebellum schools were divided into grades and based on strict discipline. Physical punishment and humiliation, as in the instance of caning or forcing a child to sit in a corner wearing a dunce cap, were commonplace.

Although the early common schools were essential in establishing the work disciplines necessary to an expanding capitalist economy, the schools did not operate in a vacuum. The messages they transmitted resonated with and were reinforced by the values explicitly trumpeted by newspaper editors like Horace Greeley, lyceum lecturers like RALPH WALDO EMERSON, and museum masters like P. T. Barnum. If the young women who moved from New England hill towns to work in the textile mills of Lowell, Massachusetts, in the 1830s and 1840s were prepared to work by the norms and behaviors they had been taught at home, in church, and in the common schools, that preparation was purposefully sustained, and labor militancy for a time contained, by employer-enforced residence in dormitories and attendance at church and lyceum.

At the same time that common schools were becoming widespread, colleges and academies were also increasing in number. In an era when few high schools existed, academies were a frequent choice as a final, often vocationally oriented, setting for formal education. Having finished the curriculum of an academy, young men could enter directly upon professional training, which in law or medicine typically involved an extended apprenticeship and in engineering, employment on a canal, bridge, or road-building project; or they could move directly into business. Some female academies were nearly on a par with their masculine equivalents, offering sufficient academic instruction for entrance into teaching, while others "finished" the education of young women with instruction in sewing, drawing, and dancing.

Colleges were relatively numerous and likely to be small and local in character. Daniel Boorstin labeled them "booster" institutions, the founding of which might justify a town's name change from Dry Gulch or Far Valley to Aberdeen, Oxford, or Athens. Colleges offered varied instruction in the sciences, classics, and liberal arts, the final course usually being the president's course in moral philosophy. Some colleges prepared ministers, others merely offered one or several years of advanced learning, the assumption being that professional instruction would be sought elsewhere. Despite a few anomalies, such as Oberlin College, which admitted African Americans and women as early as the 1830s, almost all colleges restricted admission to white men. Most activities that would now be designated as "research" were carried on under private auspices or in association with a learned society, literary circle, club, or museum.

After the Civil War, there were many important modifications in the institutional arrangements of education. High schools multiplied in number, becoming by the 1890s common adjuncts to local elementary schools. A sequential order of study or academic career path became standard for students progressing from elementary school, through high school or an academy, to college. Increasingly after the 1870s, professional education also moved within the enlarging precincts of formal institutions of education, which now also began to sponsor research and knowledge dissemination via the publication of scholarly journals. With the establishment and growth of land-grant colleges and universities, most initially founded with appropriations authorized by the Morrill Act of 1862 (a wartime bill passed in part to help keep wavering states in the Union), coeducation spread from the common schools to the state universities, with single-sex education continuing at the private, mostly eastern institutions. African Americans in the South also began to gain access to the colleges and institutes founded and operated by white missionaries and philanthropists, often following the plan for vocational education pioneered by BOOKER T. WASHINGTON at Hampton Institute.

Generally speaking, all these developments and many more were related to one of the two central tendencies of the post-1870 period, increasing comprehensiveness and centralization of control. Comprehensiveness involved enrolling more people in schools, colleges, and universities, for a greater variety of purposes, and over longer periods of time. An important legacy of PROGRESSIVISM in education, a central assumption of which was that schools should be multifaceted community institutions, comprehensiveness meant that public schools were asked to add many nonacademic activities to their original scholastic functions. Between 1890 and 1918 the National Education Association moved to embrace a conception of schooling in which the worthy use of leisure time, responsible family membership, and other nonacademic goals were accorded equal priority with the mastery of fundamental processes—reading, writing, and arithmetic. Despite intermittent waves of enthusiasm for "back-to-basics" reform—most notably after the Soviet Union launched Sputnik, the first orbiting satellite, in 1957—schools continued throughout the twentieth century to be assigned more and more responsibility for community well-being. Concern about child health, child labor, communism, automobile accidents, teen pregnancy, and AIDS all fostered new programs of social service and education. Over time, newly identified needs and capacities for learning also found manifestation in educational programs—to wit, the establishment of kindergartens as a consequence of the child-study movement of the early twentieth century, and the later organization of adult education courses as a consequence of the psychological study of adult learning.

That the failure to complete high school, an unremarkable occurrence only 40 years earlier, had come to be called "dropping out" by the 1980s, and was considered a major social and educational problem, revealed the greatly expanded place of schooling in the expectations of American society. It was a matter for debate, however, whether that expanded place derived from a firm commitment to effective and equal universal education or a reluctance to support other more specific, targeted social interventions. It was also not clear whether reliance on schools to redress problems ranging from racial desegregation, to economic inequality, to declining economic competitiveness represented a slow but enduringly effective attack on these problems or a hesitancy to address those problems more directly through changes in zoning laws, taxation, and corporate organization.

Centralization, the second major tendency of post-1870 educational developments, involved both the growth of bureaucracy within schools and colleges and the subordination of local institutions to external authorities, public and private. Centralization was evident in turn-of-the-century school board reforms across the country. More often than not, centralized school boards replaced local neighborhood boards, which often represented immigrant working people, with smaller boards, often dominated by wealthy professional elites. At roughly the same time, the administrative personnel operating within schools multiplied, as supervisory, curriculum planning, and guidance functions were separated from those involving direct instruction. Centralization was also evident at the collegiate and university levels, where internal administrations underwent notable growth and bureaucratization. Importantly, too, while colleges and universities came increasingly under the influence of such powerful and purposive standardizing agencies as the Carnegie Foundation for the Advancement of Teaching, schools fell more and more under the sway of testing and accrediting agencies such as the North Central Association, the College Entrance Examination Board and, later, the Educational Testing Service.

Over time the federal government joined accrediting agencies and private philanthropic foundations as an important force for centralization. First at the collegiate and university levels, and then at the lower levels, the federal government provided significant financing for specific objectives, for example, under the auspices of the National Defense Education Act of 1958, for foreign area and language studies, and eventually, after 1965, for the promotion of general goals like equity in education. Whether in the form of the Servicemen's Readjustment Act of 1944 (the G.I. Bill), or the Elementary and Secondary Education Act of 1965, federal involvement in education advanced centralization by virtue of the assistance and regulation provided.

In the 1990s, a long-simmering debate about school choice became a topic of national concern. Highly controversial, but largely nonpartisan, discussion of the pros and cons of allowing parents to choose among an array of competing schools once again revealed the contradictory tendencies that seem always to have been present in educational history in the United States. Described by school-choice advocates as a reform that would not only improve schools, but also equalize educational opportunity (wealthy parents already having the "right" to choose out of public schools through the purchase of private education), school choice in practice seemed to handicap those children whose parents were less able as a result of cultural difference or social stress to make an informed and prudent choice of school for them. In a very real sense, therefore, one of the major educational issues of the 1990s underscored questions evident throughout American educational

history, questions having to do with relations between educational aspirations and actualities. It is these questions about ideals and realities that make the study of education important not only for policy makers but for students of American culture.

Among the large company of men and women who have influenced expectations for education as well as public policies toward education—a company that would include THOMAS JEFFERSON, LYMAN BEECHER, JANE ADDAMS, W. E. B. DU BOIS, CHARLES W. ELIOT, Abraham Flexner, and JAMES B. CONANT, among many others —none is better known than the philosopher JOHN DEWEY. Often presented as the father of child-centered pedagogy, Dewey was, in fact, an exponent of educational efforts that sought to mesh the psychological needs of children with the social needs of their society. A wide-ranging thinker, who wrote about psychology, politics, aesthetics, and logic as well as education, Dewey is the most important modern American philosopher. His thought fits within a tradition that can be traced from Jonathan Edwards through Ralph Waldo Emerson and William James. He was a person of powerful mind and deep social convictions, who believed education was a necessity for a democratic way of life. Whether his ideas were, in fact, as influential as popular wisdom would suggest, Dewey did capture in his voluminous writings over a life stretching over more than 90 years some of the educational aspirations that have long been central to American ideals. Most of all, he understood that education has been relied upon to improve society and to solve a host of social imperfections since at least the 1600s. If there is any single characteristic of "American" education, it is that reliance.

ELLEN CONDLIFFE LAGEMANN

See also COLLEGES AND UNIVERSITIES; LITERACY.

FURTHER READING

James D. Anderson, *The Education of Blacks in the South, 1860–1935* (Chapel Hill: University of North Carolina Press, 1988).

John Hardin Best, ed., *Historical Inquiry in Education: a Research Agenda* (Washington, D.C.: American Educational Research Association, 1983).

Lawrence A. Cremin, *American Education*, 3 vols. (New York: Harper and Row, 1970–88).

Michael B. Katz, *Class, Bureaucracy, and Schools: the Illusion of Educational Change in America* (New York: Praeger, 1971).

Ellen Condliffe Lagemann, *The Politics of Knowledge: the Carnegie Corporation, Philanthropy, and Public Policy* (1989; Chicago: University of Chicago Press, 1992).

Diane Ravitch, *The Troubled Crusade: American Education, 1945–1980* (New York: Basic, 1983).

Rush, Benjamin, *Letters of Benjamin Rush,* ed. L. H.

Butterfield, 2 vols. (Princeton: Princeton University Press, 1951).

Barbara Solomon, *In the Company of Educated Women: a History of Women and Higher Education in America* (New Haven: Yale University Press, 1985).

David B. Tyack, *The One Best System: a History of American Urban Education* (Cambridge: Harvard University Press, 1974).

David B. Tyack and Elizabeth Hansot, *Learning Together: a History of Co-education in American Public Schools* (New Haven: Yale University Press, 1990).

Robert B. Westbrook, *John Dewey and American Democracy* (Ithaca: Cornell University Press, 1991).

Laurence Veysey, *The Emergence of the University* (Chicago: University of Chicago Press, 1965).

Edwards, Jonathan (b. East Windsor, Conn., Oct. 5, 1703; d. Princeton, N.J., Mar. 22, 1758).   The son and grandson of Puritan ministers, Edwards became the greatest American theologian and philosopher before the Civil War, a leading participant in, but also a most discerning critic of, religious awakenings. Edwards studied and tutored at Yale before accepting a pastorate in Northampton, Massachusetts, first as assistant to his distinguished maternal grandfather Solomon Stoddard, then for 23 years as his successor until he was dismissed by his congregation in 1750. Edwards then served a mission church at Stockbridge, Massachusetts, where he did much of his most important writing, until called to the presidency of the College of New Jersey, where he died within weeks of his arrival.

Jonathan Edwards is a seminal and benchmark figure in American intellectual and religious life, perhaps the brightest luminary among the heirs to John Calvin (*see* CALVINISM). His reputation has waxed and occasionally waned, but American interpreters have generally treated him as our greatest theologian and one of our two or three greatest philosophers, especially if one includes under philosophy the range of subjects it included in Edwards's day. Later generations have turned to him with a variety of agendas, seeking to be illuminated by his work or to shed fresh light on it from a number of different directions. Scholarship of this kind became especially exciting after fresh interest in Edwards was generated by Perry Miller's provocative *Jonathan Edwards* (1949), in which Miller emphasized Edwards's naturalism and protomodernism and his role as a contributor to democratic nationalism.

Those who have appropriated Edwards for our own time have stood mainly in the Reformed (Calvinist) tradition. Those who come to Edwards with an agenda of their own, lifting Edwards out of his own time and into ours, have not always avoided the dangers of presentism. Yet Edwards is such a

seminal thinker that, however distant his universe of discourse sometimes seems to us late in the twentieth century, his voice is still proving strong and his thought illuminating even when not entirely persuasive. Many find it profitable to draw Edwards into contemporary discussions, and even to draw out implications of his thought that may be instructive today even if not explicitly present in his writings.

Central themes of Edwards's thought are laid out in two early sermons, most readily available in Winslow's edition of Edwards's *Basic Writings*. "God Glorified in the Work of Redemption" (1731) gives a distinctively Edwardsean flavor to the Calvinist doctrine of humanity's complete dependence upon God's sovereignty and grace. What the redeemed receive is not only something *from* God but something *of* God, "spiritual excellency and joy by a kind of participation of God" (p. 115). "God puts his own beauty, i.e. his beautiful likeness, upon their souls," such that the saints are empowered to find in "the glorious excellencies and beauty of God" their greatest pleasure, all other things being enjoyed for "what shall be seen of God in them" (p. 115)—that is, according to their relationship to God.

Three years later "A Divine and Supernatural Light" shows that all this is made possible by a "spiritual and saving conviction of the truth and reality" of divine things consisting in a sight, taste, and "true sense" (p. 128) immediately communicated to the saints by God. This "sense of the heart" is drawn to the beauty or excellency of God and "necessarily feels pleasure in the apprehension" (p. 129). Edwards identifies this new sense with the will or disposition or inclination of the soul, rather than with merely notional or speculative knowledge, so that it is "attainable by persons of mean capacities and advantages, as well as those that are of the greatest parts and learning" (p. 132). This saving light or sense "changes the nature of the soul" and "assimilates our nature to the divine nature," and thus "turns the heart to God" (p. 134) and liberates all the human faculties for their proper and free exercises.

In his major treatises, Edwards develops and amplifies these and related themes into a distinctive system of theological, philosophical, and moral ideas. In *A Treatise Concerning the Religious Affections* (1746), his most thorough analysis of the religious experiences manifest in the Great Awakening, he observes that people act in all matters only as they are affected and that therefore "true religion, in great part, consists in holy affections" (*Works*, vol. 2, p. 95). Since not all religion is true, and since Edwards questioned the validity of some of the "experiences" produced by the revivals, he sets himself to distinguish between true and false spiritual affections by 12 carefully examined signs. The most important sign of holy affections is that they "have their exercise and fruit in Christian practice" (p. 383), but the first sign he discusses is that they arise from the "new spiritual sense"—"infinitely more noble" than any of the natural senses—given by God as "a new foundation laid in the nature of the soul" (p. 206) for a new kind of exercise of both understanding and will. Another sign is that "the beginning and spring of all holy affections" is "a love to divine things for the beauty of their moral excellency" (p. 256). Indeed, "from this sense of spiritual beauty" arises "all true experimental knowledge of religion" and a whole "new world of knowledge" (p. 275). This new sense and its proper object are so important that "he that sees not the beauty of holiness" is "in effect ignorant of the whole spiritual world" (p. 275).

In his treatise *Freedom of the Will* (1754), the key formula of which is that "the will always is as the greatest apparent good is" (*Works*, vol. 1, p. 144), Edwards develops systematically his rejection of every kind of determinacy (and indeterminacy!) of the will (indeed, the whole language of determinism), arguing that people are free because they always act according to their own pleasure—that is, according to their perception and conviction of their own apparent good. Who could ask for greater freedom? What goes with it is that God can therefore hold human beings responsible for their actions. That the human will is free but corrupted, finding its greatest apparent good in self and other lesser goods or attachments rather than in God, is the subject of Edwards's treatise *Original Sin* (1758). Here Edwards appeals both to empirical evidence of humanity's governing inclination as he knew and observed it, and to a less persuasive metaphysical theory about God's regarding all humanity as one in Adam, according to which God's judgment justly condemns every sinner for his own sin and not for the sin of Adam imputed to him. Only by the interposition of God's grace can that judgment be avoided. The fulfillment of that gracious interposition is central to God's aim in the work of redemption.

Edwards's untimely death left unfulfilled his intention to make a *History of the Work of Redemption* the framework for a major theological treatise, so that we are left with only a shadow of that treatise in the form of a frequently republished set of sermons bearing that title. We quite naturally ask: Why has a sovereign God's purpose not been accomplished? Edwards's answer is essentially that God governs the moral world not by force but by the attractive power of beauty—of humanity's real good made visible and apparent in the figure of Christ and infused as holy or virtuous affections by an indwelling of the Holy Spirit.

His *Dissertation on the End for Which God Created the World*, and a companion essay on *The Nature of True Virtue*, were not published until after his death. In *The Ethical Writings* (edited by Paul Ramsey), volume 9 of the new Yale edition of the *Works*, these two essays are now for the first time published together, as Edwards intended, and together as well with the 15 sermons of 1738 on *Charity and its Fruits*, which Ramsey has rightly called Edwards's "most important treatise on Christian ethics" (p. 64). All three of these works are also committed to the development of themes present in the two early sermons discussed above. For example, God's end in the creation of the world is "the emanation of God's glory; or the excellent brightness and fullness of the divinity diffused, overflowing, and as it were enlarged; or in one word, *existing ad extra*" (p. 527). Because "God's respect to the creature's good, and his respect to himself, is not a divided respect" (p. 533), humanity participates in this outpouring of the divine fullness "consisting in the knowledge of God, love to him, and joy in him" (p. 531).

Without pretending to cover Edwards's systematic thought, or to display the unity most interpreters find in his thought, I want to identify a few of the most distinctive and characteristic themes. Perhaps the most striking feature of Edwards's thought is the way beauty and the perception of beauty stand at the center of what is most distinctive and challenging in his philosophy, theology, and ethics. This may seem strange to anyone unfamiliar with Edwards scholarship over the past 40 years, but the place of beauty and of aesthetic experience has figured importantly in several contemporary studies of Edwards. Where else in orthodox Christian theology do we find all of the perfections of God reduced very explicitly and repeatedly to these three: beauty, love, and joy? It is by God's beauty that God is distinguished from all other beings, and God governs the creation by the attractive power of God's own beauty, offering redemption to sinful creatures by presenting in Christ the real human good become most visible as our apparent good.

A second distinctive theme that runs throughout Edwards's thought is his relational, dynamic, even dispositional ontology. Here we see most forcefully the unity of his theology and his philosophy of being, according to which the first principle of being is beauty—the primary form of which Edwards defines as being's cordial consent to being. God is essentially identical with being in general or Being as such, and reality—whether in God or God's creation—is, for Edwards, radically relational. One alone cannot be, for without plurality there can be no consent. Thus, that plurality (Trinity) is an essential feature of the divine being, and everything that exists is constituted in being by its relations. One can rightly call Edwards a pan-en-theist (meaning all things are in God), though not in the manner of modern process theology, for both creation and redemption are understood by Edwards as a continuing process by which it is only by virtue of the overflowing fullness of the divine fountain of being (as he sometimes puts it) that anything subsists, and not by virtue of any imagined relation to some preceding condition or cause. The most provocative interpretation of these relations is in terms of the Edwardsean concepts of habit and disposition in Sang Lee, *The Philosophical Theology of Jonathan Edwards.*

These two themes inform Edwards's lifelong interest in the dynamics of the moral and spiritual life, the moving power of which resides in the relations between the affections and their objects. Accordingly, as noted above, the will or self always is as its greatest apparent good is. The dynamics of the moral and spiritual life are traced back to the relations among the persons of the Trinity and the creative, dispositional, self-communicating nature of God. God is immediately present in every relationship, since it is only by virtue of the overflowing fullness of the divine being that anything has being. The Christian life, a life of holiness or true virtue, consists in a cordial participation in the life of God. Such a life is not so much beautiful as it is actively beautifying.

Edwards is further distinguished by his philosophical (not to be confused with a moral) idealism. Reality exists in the mind, in perception. For example, true virtue or holiness begins with God's gracious infusion of a "sense of the heart," an active and transforming perception of the beauty of divine things, from which everything follows that is distinguishing about the Christian life.

Finally, I call Edwards an actualist, since I do not want to distract from his philosophical idealism by calling him a realist. He was always in relentless pursuit of a better grasp and perception of the real. He both preached and wrote with the aim of bringing others to share and experience as real whatever was actual or real for him. And the actuality of something could not be properly understood until perceived in relation to God.

Many modern readers are disturbed and put off by the unflinching actualism or realism of Edwards's views on *Original Sin* and in such sermons as "Sinners in the Hands of an Angry God" (*see also* GUILT).

But it may be by just such a radically theocentric voice as his that light may be shed on a path to renewal through the landscape of violence, destruction, and alienation by which humanity and the earth itself is daily defaced. He sought to make the fires of hell vividly apparent to his parishioners, not in the hope that he could frighten them into virtuous living, but in order that they might experience more powerfully the contrasting attractive beauty he perceived as manifest in God, in the world, and in a life of true virtue.

ROLAND A. DELATTRE

See also APOCALYPTIC LITERATURE; EVANGELICALISM; PIETY; PURITANISM.

FURTHER READING

James Carse, *Jonathan Edwards and the Visibility of God* (New York: Charles Scribner's Sons, 1967).

Conrad Cherry, *The Theology of Jonathan Edwards: a Reappraisal* (1966; Bloomington: Indiana University Press, 1990).

William A. Clebsch, *American Religious Thought: a History* (Chicago: University of Chicago Press, 1973).

Roland A. Delattre, *Beauty and Sensibility in the Thought of Jonathan Edwards* (New Haven: Yale University Press, 1968).

Jonathan Edwards, *Works* (New Haven: Yale University Press, 1957–), 10 vols. in print to date.

——, *Basic Writings*, ed. Ola E. Winslow (New York: New American Library, Signet Classic, 1966).

Norman Fiering, *Jonathan Edwards's Moral Thought and its British Context* (Chapel Hill: University of North Carolina Press, 1981).

Nathan O. Hatch and Harry S. Stout, eds., *Jonathan Edwards and the American Experience* (New York: Oxford University Press, 1988).

Robert W. Jenson, *America's Theologian: a Recommendation of Jonathan Edwards* (New York: Oxford University Press, 1988).

Sang Hyun Lee, *The Philosophical Theology of Jonathan Edwards* (Princeton: Princeton University Press, 1988).

Eggleston, Edward (b. Vevay, Ind., Dec. 10, 1837; d. Lake George, N.Y., Sept. 4, 1902).   Clergyman and writer. Best remembered for his vivid descriptions of backwoods Indiana in *The Hoosier Schoolmaster* (1871), Eggleston called for a "new history" that would chronicle the lives of all Americans, however ordinary. History, he argued, should be a record of culture: it should explore people's daily actions and the ideas that underlie them. An early president of the American Historical Association, Eggleston authored, in addition to his many novels, two volumes of his projected History of Life in the United States (1896, 1900).

FURTHER READING

William Peirce Randel, *Edward Eggleston* (New York: King's Crown Press, 1946).

Eliot, Charles W. (b. Boston, Mass. Mar. 20. 1834; d. Northeast Harbor, Maine, Aug. 22, 1926). Educator. Long-time president of Harvard University (1869–1909), Eliot believed education should serve the nation by promoting both variety and depth of intellectual interests. An advocate of academic freedom of thought, he encouraged specialized study and faculty scholarship by developing an elective curriculum. He also created Harvard's graduate program and helped found Radcliffe College. Author of *Educational Reform: Essays and Addresses* (1898) and editor of the 50-volume *Harvard Classics*, he argued that society is best served by a liberal education of its leaders.

FURTHER READING

Hugh Hawkins, *Between Harvard and America: the Educational Leadership of Charles W. Eliot* (New York: Oxford University Press, 1972).

Eliot, John (baptized Widford, England, Aug. 5, 1604; d. Roxbury, Mass., May 21, 1690). Missionary. Eliot converted Indians by learning their languages, translating the Bible, and settling believers into English-style "praying towns." Convinced that Indian cultures and worldviews were incompatible with Puritan Christianity, he sought to replace them with European values, beliefs, and behaviors. He tried to "restrain" and "humble" Indians in order to lead them to righteousness, hard work, and fixed residence, but also protested racial violence and tried to preserve Indians' lives if not their ways of life. His writings include *The Christian Commonwealth* (1659) and *The Harmony of the Gospels* (1678).

FURTHER READING

James Axtell, *The Invasion Within* (New York: Oxford University Press, 1985).

Eliot, T[homas] S[tearns] (b. St. Louis, Mo., Sept. 26, 1888; d. London, England, Jan. 4, 1965). A native-born American, T. S. Eliot moved to England and became a major literary figure from the 1920s on. Though best known as a poet, he first gained fame and influence as a literary critic. As his poetic development led to a career as a dramatist, so his literary criticism came increasingly to emphasize more general cultural issues and generated a significant body of social criticism. Eliot combined an acute sensibility to difference and fragmentation with a deep longing for unity. His social criticism has a distinctly conservative, Christian flavor because he thought that this tradition offered the best means to guide the West through modernity's discontents and provide harmonizing unity in, as he put it in *The Sacred Wood*, "a formless age" (p. 64). Eliot's critical reputation has greatly suffered because new generations of theorists have been unable to see past his religious faith and conservative politics to his actual arguments about literature, criticism, and culture, which are largely independent of specific theological or political presuppositions. Tying him to his early objectivist views on poetry and criticism, which Eliot himself transcended but which were erected by his New Critical epigones into the established dogma, contemporary theorists, in revolt against the New Criticism, mistakenly condemn him as a formalist critic with no philosophical depth. This could not be further from the truth.

In fact, Eliot first pursued a philosophical career, studying at Harvard with JOSIAH ROYCE and the visiting Bertrand Russell, spending a year at the Sorbonne where he attended Henri Bergson's lectures, and moving to Oxford in 1914 to pursue his Harvard doctoral dissertation on F. H. Bradley. Though the dissertation was completed in 1916 and hailed as "the work of an expert," Eliot never returned to Harvard for his oral examination. Yet he continued for several years to publish articles and reviews in professional journals of philosophy, while pursuing his new career as poet and critic. This change of career was encouraged by EZRA POUND, who first discovered and promoted Eliot's poetic genius. Eliot was also discouraged from returning to America by his parents' disapproval of his sudden marriage in 1915 to Vivian Haigh-Wood, a young English woman. Her unstable mental condition caused Eliot much suffering, which, by his own account, contributed to his poetry. Unable to live on his poetry and journalistic criticism, Eliot supported himself first by teaching school and then by working at Lloyds bank for eight years, until his literary fame got him an appointment in publishing as an editor at Faber and Faber, where he helped develop such younger poets as W. H. Auden and Stephen Spender.

By 1919, Eliot had published two small volumes of poetry (which include such now-famous works as "The Love Song of J. Alfred Prufrock" and "Gerontion"). But he first won literary renown through a collection of critical essays called *The Sacred Wood* (1920). Here Eliot formulates the four theories which made him probably the most influential Anglo-American critic of the century: the doctrines of impersonality and of TRADITION, the objective correlative, and the theory of the dissociation of sensibility. The first two insist that the more perfect and original a poet the less he concentrates on displaying his particular personality, and the more he expresses objective images, feelings, and the progressive direction of his age and the continuing poetic tradition.

Tradition, Eliot claimed, was a creative developing project which structured the individual artist's efforts but was reciprocally further shaped by them. Critics should likewise curb their personal feelings and concentrate on the facts and techniques of the work. Of course, literature was not thereby deprived of feeling. It simply was not to be expressed directly as subjectivity, but instead had to be conveyed through an objective correlative, that is, an objective structure of images, thoughts, or events embodying feeling to be expressed. Such objective expression was hard to achieve in poetry after the bifurcation of sensibility in the seventeenth century when strong emotional feeling came to be dissociated from strenuous thinking and acutely scrupulous observation. The result was a gushy romanticism which Eliot attacked and hoped to replace by a new classicism, though a good case can be made for the presence of romantic themes in his work.

All these theories emphasize the ideal of OBJECTIVITY, whether in poetry or in its criticism. Eliot's objectivist ideal and emphasis on unified sensibility were very influential for the New Criticism which dominated American academic criticism until it was displaced in the late 1960s and 1970s by structuralism and poststructuralism. In advocating objectivism as theory, Eliot hoped to make his own objectivist style of poetry and criticism all the more convincing. His poetic and critical stature were greatly strengthened in 1922 by his founding of a new quarterly *The Criterion*; its first issue contained *The Waste Land*, which established Eliot both as a modernist innovator of form and as the voice of a disillusioned generation facing a fragmented world whose traditional meanings had been shattered by modern PROGRESS. This disillusionment led Eliot to a religious reawakening; in 1927 he joined the Church of England (and became a British subject). His new religious perspective was combined with a move from objectivist technical criticism to a greater interest in the complexities of hermeneutical, historicist understanding and a greater focus on "the relation of poetry to the soul and spiritual life" (*Sacred Wood*, p. viii) and on poetry's social uses and constitution. Eliot pursued these interests in his critical writings, most notably in *The Use of Poetry and The Use of Criticism* (1933), which argues for a socially determined historicist pluralism with respect to poetry's nature and function. His poetry also increasingly turned to religious themes, especially in "The Journey of the Magi," "Ash Wednesday," and the culminating vision of *Four Quartets* (1944). Later he turned to drama, because he thought that through this form poetry could have a greater social effect by reaching a larger, more diversified audience. His plays include *Murder in the Cathedral* (about St. Thomas Becket), *The Cocktail Party*, *The Confidential Clerk*, and *The Elder Statesman*. His book of children's verse, *Old Possum's Book of Practical Cats*, was adapted for the stage as the musical *Cats* in 1981 and had great success. "Old Possum," we should note, was Eliot's nickname, alluding to his desire for privacy.

Believing that poetry and criticism were largely the product of more general forces and structures of society and culture, Eliot also devoted considerable attention to CULTURAL CRITICISM. His theory of tradition, which originally concentrated on art, was expanded in *After Strange Gods* (1934) and *Notes Toward the Definition of Culture* (1948) to cover culture as a whole, emphasizing its unconscious as well as conscious workings. Eliot's conservative social and political perspective was distinctly communitarian. He was a sharp critic of bourgeois liberalism's emphasis on the individual and of its faith in human PROGRESS through free experimentation and technology. Insisting on the social construction of the self, Eliot argued that individuals are only as strong and coherent as the society which forms them and that today's fragmented society (the product of liberal individualism) cannot yield strong selves. Attacking our excessive faith in SCIENCE, he argued that TECHNOLOGY cannot in itself solve our problems and needs to be guided by practical wisdom informed by developing tradition. Eliot recognized the communitarian appeal of Marxism, but felt that Christianity still provided the best global communal tradition for a Western civilization whose social fabric and value structures were already disintegrating through excessively rapid change. Eliot's sincere religious faith contained a strong element of PRAGMATISM; he advocated Christianity as a social solution. Pragmatism likewise formed an important, often overlooked, dimension of his later critical theory with its emphasis on historicist, fallibilist practical wisdom.

RICHARD SHUSTERMAN

See also COMMUNITY; CONSERVATISM.

FURTHER READING

T. S. Eliot, *The Sacred Wood*, 2nd edn. (1920; London: Methuen, 1968).

——, *Notes toward a Definition of Culture* (1948; London: Faber, 1962).

——, *Selected Essays*, 2nd ed. (1950; London: Faber, 1976).

Roger Kojecky, *T. S. Eliot's Social Criticism* (London: Faber, 1971).

A. D. Moody, *Thomas Stearns Eliot: Poet* (Cambridge: Cambridge University Press, 1979).

Richard Shusterman, *T. S. Eliot and the Philosophy of Criticism* (New York: Columbia University Press, 1988).

Stephen Spender, *Eliot* (London: Fontana, 1972).

Ellison, Ralph (b. Oklahoma City, Okla., Mar. 1, 1914; d. New York, N.Y., Apr. 16, 1994). Despite having published only one novel, Ellison is one of the most anthologized African American writers. He is the American writer most responsible for putting jazz into the novel and for theorizing the relationship of jazz to American belle-lettres. His aesthetic is most usefully approached within this historical and formal framework of jazz. The particular qualities of South-western Territory jazz (also called Kansas City jazz), which had a profound influence on at least two other African American writers, LANGSTON HUGHES and Melvin Tolson, provide a key for reading Ellison and confronting his critical perspective.

Ellison's interaction with Territory jazz is considerable. From the start of the big band and swing era in the late 1920s through the beginnings of be-bop in the 1940s, a thriving Midwestern jazz scene had immense impact on American music. Besides launching a large number of outstanding musicians, including Big Joe Turner, Jay McShann, Pete Johnson, Jimmy Rushing and Mary Lou Williams, as well as the classic swing band in the form of the Count Basie Orchestra, the Territory scene produced Charlie Parker, Lester Young and Coleman Hawkins, the three musicians who made the saxophone the dominant solo instrument of jazz. Ellison came of age in this vital musical center. He had himself planned to be a musician, and studied trumpet at Tuskegee Institute from 1933 to 1936.

Both of Ellison's collections of essays, *Shadow and Act* (1964) and *Going to the Territories* (1986), emphasize his ongoing relationship with music. In addition, Ellison's early journalism and criticism (largely uncollected), published in mostly left-wing journals while he worked for the Work Projects Administration in the thirties, foreground "folk forms" such as blues, spirituals, and folk tales in the creation of African American literature.

The structure of jazz provides an understanding of the syncretic quality that is a hallmark of Ellison's prose. Jazz is by nature intertextual and amalgamated, but the riff-based Kansas City jazz is particularly so; in his book *Goin' to Kansas City* Nathan Pearson describes the creole nature of its development as blues migrated north to mix with more or less indigenous Midwestern musical styles—brass band music, church music, black vaudeville, tent show, minstrel show and carnival music and ragtime. In a similar fashion, Ellison's great novel *Invisible Man* (1952) invokes and revises innumerable works of literature by writers black and white, American and European, among them Feodor Dostoevsky, W. E. B. Du Bois, James Joyce, Ralph Waldo Emerson, Richard Wright,

Rudolph Fisher, and Mark Twain. Indeed, a substantial portion of the existing criticism on Ellison is devoted to examination of his various rewritings of the literary canon. Ellison specifically discusses intertextuality in relation to jazz performance, noting in *Going to the Territory* that "the jazz musician . . . is nothing if not eclectic" and observing that the "snatching of phrases" from various sources by T. S. Eliot is something "which one got in jazz" (p. 40).

Ellison's notions about what constitutes an American audience are also illuminated by an understanding of Kansas City jazz. The Territory jazz bands followed a circuit that had largely been mapped by the bands traveling with carnival, tent and minstrel shows and the Theater Owners Booking Association shows. They had to be able to play a huge repertory of music according to the race and region of their audiences. As the musicians played everything from polkas to square dances to blues to ragtime, cobbling together a new kind of music as they performed, a dialogic creation of meaning and tradition took place. Ellison considers this active, disparate audience to be a quintessentially American phenomenon—in American history "everyone played the appropriation game," he writes in *Going to the Territory* (p. 28). Thus, in *Shadow and Act* he places music in the context of community:

> For who knew what skinny kid with his chops wrapped around a trumpet mouthpiece and a far-away look in his eyes might become the next Armstrong? Yes, and send you, at some big dance a few years hence, into an ecstasy of rhythm and memory and brassy affirmation of the goodness of being alive and part of the community? Someone had to: for it was part of the group tradition (p. 192).

Jazz performance is again signaled at the start of *Invisible Man*. The novel opens with a reference to none other than Louis Armstrong. *Invisible Man* is anchored by jazz throughout, opening with an invocation of Armstrong's "Black and Blue" and ending with a reference to radio. In Harlem, the Invisible Man meets a character named Peter Wheatstraw (in another incarnation a well-known blues singer), as well as being mistaken repeatedly for a man called Rinehart, who seems to be all things to all people, operating as a kind of combination trickster figure and African American Everyman. Ellison explains in *Shadow and Act* that his source for the name Rinehart is Oklahoman Jimmy Rushing's song "Harvard Blues," which made him think of "a character who was a master of disguise, of coincidence" (p. 181). According to Mort Goode's liner notes to the Basie/Rushing album "Blues by Basie" on which "Harvard

Blues" appears, Rinehart was a Harvard undergraduate who used to stand under his dormitory window and call his own name to create the illusion of popularity.

Rinehart's Harlem is also many things to many people; one does better to speak of the Harlems of the novel in the plural. The Harlem of *Invisible Man* is the Harlem of books more than of maps; Ellison uses copious references to the function and character of Harlem in other periods of literature. For instance, the Invisible Man encounters and debunks the notion of Harlem as refuge (as in Claude McKay's *Home to Harlem* or Rudolph Fisher's "City of Refuge"); as cultural mecca for the New Negro of the Harlem Renaissance; as a focus for the communists during the thirties. Again, as he raises and rejects a litany of possibilities for selfhood, Ellison self-consciously riffs on multiple literary traditions—the African American flight motif, the European education of the naïf, the classical American romance of the frontier.

Besides garnering him an array of awards including the National Book Award, Ellison's work has profoundly influenced American literature. *Invisible Man* has achieved resounding visibility in the work of a breathtaking range of American writers and critics who concern themselves with American vernacular music, with the possibility and limitations of the frontier, with the relationships among various narrative and linguistic traditions—rendering nearly superfluous the question whether a major second novel, left nearly complete at his death, will ever be published.

RACHEL RUBIN

FURTHER READING
Kimberly W. Benston, ed., *Speaking for You: the Vision of Ralph Ellison* (Washington, D.C.: Howard University Press, 1987).
Ralph Ellison, *Shadow and Act* (1964; New York: Signet, 1966).
——, *Going to the Territory* (New York: Random House, 1986).
William Grimes, "Did Ralph Ellison Leave a 2nd Classic?," *New York Times*, April 20, 1994, p. C13.
Alan Nadel, *Invisible Criticism: Ralph Ellison and the American Canon* (Iowa City: University of Iowa Press, 1988).
Robert G. O'Meally, *The Craft of Ralph Ellison* (Cambridge: Harvard University Press, 1980).
Nathan Pearson, *Goin' to Kansas City* (Chicago: University of Illinois Press, 1987).
Joseph Trimmer, ed., *A Casebook on Ralph Ellison's "Invisible Man,"* (New York: Thomas Y. Crowell, 1972).

Ely, Richard T. (b. Ripley, N.Y., Apr. 13, 1854; d. Old Lyme, Conn., Oct. 4, 1943). Economist. Ely, a founder of the American Economic Association (1885), led the revolt against the classical theory of laissez-faire economics in favor of the German historical school and the Social Gospel. He accepted the basic structures of capitalist competition and private property, but urged trade unionism, public ownership of natural monopolies, and legislation to protect workers and consumers. Economics and ethics, he argued, should be unified in a humane social vision; government, religion, and science should each contribute to social welfare and class harmony. His many writings, which include *The Labor Movement in America* (1886), *The Social Aspects of Christianity* (1889), and *Monopolies and Trusts* (1900), disclose the intimate connection, in the early years of professional social science, between the new academic scholarship and Christian reform sentiment.

FURTHER READING
Benjamin G. Rader, *The Academic Mind and Reform: the Influence of Richard T. Ely in American Life* (Lexington: University of Kentucky Press, 1966).

Emerson, Ralph Waldo (b. Boston, Mass., May 25, 1803; d. Concord, Mass., Apr. 27, 1882). John Jay Chapman's remark that "Emerson represents a protest against the tyranny of democracy" (p. 601) gets to the heart of Emerson's identity both as writer and as citizen. It suggests how Emerson represents the perennial protest of artists and thinkers against the social pressures that suppress and conventionalize art and thought; but it also invites us to look at Emerson's life and work as a series of particular resistances against particular, democratically exerted pressures to hold certain beliefs or take certain actions.

Emerson's shaping of the first 40 years of his life reveals a thoughtful, comprehensive, and remarkably successful search for freedom in a democracy: freedom of finances and vocation, of artistic form, of dwelling place, and of thought. On finding himself unwilling to administer communion on the ground that it was an outgrown form of religion, he was in 1832 amiably but inexorably constrained to resign his promising job as junior (and probably soon senior) pastor of the Second Church in Boston, and began in 1833 his long career as a freelance lecturer, constrained to please and instruct his audiences but not to share their opinions or to perform any regular function for them, and free to move from one audience to another. By 1834 Emerson had also produced his first great artistic invention, namely the form of his journal. He had begun his journal in 1821 as a commonplace book after the model of John Locke, that is, as an ordered storehouse of insights for public discourses; but under the influence of his aunt Mary Moody Emerson he would sometimes use the intended commonplace book as a Puritan diary of spiritual experiences, and the tension between the two prescriptive models cramped him as a diarist. In 1834, however, just as he was finding his vocation as a lecturer, he also found his form as a diarist, and delivered himself from the constraints of both models by fusing them together into a form brilliantly expressing the Transcendentalist aspiration that the work of art be an integral part of the life of the artist. Also in 1834, Emerson completed this first stage of his emancipation by moving from the metropolitan complexities of Boston to the rural, Jeffersonian independence of Concord, not then linked even by railroad to the city of which it is now a suburb. Unlike his disciple HENRY DAVID THOREAU, Emerson was not seeking the perfect autarchy of the hermit; he saw in that mirror image of society a mirror image of social constraint rather than a deliverance from it. He was seeking not to escape democracy but to find a space for free work within it, and so moved to Concord rather than to Walden Pond.

In his three great proclamations of the 1830s Emerson strove to add freedom in thought to his already found freedom in vocation and in private artistry. The treatise *Nature*, published anonymously in 1836, was among other things Emerson's manifesto of idealism, his emancipation from what he felt as the debasement of human capacity, and the constrained intellectual passivity, of British empiricism. The 1837 "American Scholar" was, as Oliver Wendell Holmes said, "the American intellectual declaration of independence"; that is, it proclaimed the American intellectual's freedom, and thus Emerson's freedom, from European tradition and from tradition generally. It was well received, partly because that freedom was not, really, a very controversial one; calls for an American literature emancipated from European influence were common enough that Emerson's address seems in their context a passionately dramatized commonplace, resembling in that respect the Declaration of Independence itself. The 1838 Divinity School Address, on the other hand, was not well received; the eminent divine Andrews Norton called it "the latest form of infidelity," and after giving it, Emerson was barred from speaking at Harvard till after the Civil War. Emancipating oneself from Locke was necessary but unexciting, emancipating oneself from Europe was exciting but uncontroversial; but emancipating oneself from the special authority of Jesus meant, in 1838 New England, emancipating oneself from any conceivable authority; anticipating the Nietzsche he would later influence, Emerson had as good as proclaimed, "God is dead."

The three great proclamations of the 1830s marked three intellectual emancipations, but all of them were composed according to prefabricated organizations, and certainly in none of them had Emerson evolved an authentic public mode of writing. He had begun to do this in some of his poems, which show the charged, plain-spoken diction that distinguishes a lot of the best subsequent American verse. But he did not exhibit his characteristic public prose until the 1841 *Essays, First Series*, above all in "Self-Reliance," the greatest of Emerson's essays. In that essay Emerson gives his sharpest, most surprising account of his central topic, what a journal entry from April 1840 calls "the infinitude of the private man." Emerson has the nerve in "Self-Reliance" to give that infinitude the disreputable name of "whim," realizing that "freedom" is already too civic-minded a name for it, and to proclaim, in explicit dismissal of every social constraint, that whim may for all he cares be wicked, so long as it is authentic. And in describing the deepest ontological truths about whim he also describes the form he has found for his prose. "Life only avails," he writes, "not the having lived. Power ceases in the instant of repose; it resides in the moment of transition from a past to a new state, in the shooting of the gulf, in the darting to an aim." There is no better account of the infinitude of the private man, but also no better account of an Emerson essay's unpredictable, abrupt, transitionless movement in thought from one epiphany to another.

The remainder of Emerson's long life was a sustained attempt to maintain individual whim against the pressures of experience, sometimes a successful attempt and sometimes not. One failure, both personal and artistic, centered around his 1840 encounter with MARGARET FULLER. Fuller sought intense personal intimacy in her friendship with him, and he refused it as he did in other friendships also, always conceiving of intimacy as a constraint. His essays on "Love" and "Friendship" attempt a justification of that conception and way of being, but in fact give lifelessly schematic accounts of the richest of human relations; Chapman is right when he says that "an inhabitant of another planet . . . would receive . . . a truer notion of human life by attending an Italian opera than he would by reading Emerson's volumes. He would learn from the Italian opera that there were two sexes" (p. 644). On the other hand, Emerson's refusal in 1840 to join the Transcendentalist utopian community at Brook Farm seems in retrospect a right recognition that a Concord burgher had more writerly freedom than a utopian laborer did, and the essays that came out of that and similar encounters are as sharp and knowing a conservative commentary on utopian and reformist thought as is Nathaniel Hawthorne's *Blithedale Romance*.

The death of Emerson's five-year-old son Waldo in 1842 devastated him, and some of his most evocative work got written in his grappling with that event: poignant passages of the journal, the poem "Threnody," and the other great essay, "Experience." "Experience," first published in the 1844 *Essays, Second Series*, is a great essay partly because it evokes so vividly the constraints and uncertainties of empirical reality, and students of Emerson have sometimes pointed to that essay as the refutation of "Self-Reliance." But in fact Emerson in "Experience" retains the fundamental opposition of his thought and diction even while weighting it differently; in "Experience" we are more abjectly the victims of temperament and habit and illusion than in "Self-Reliance," but still the opposition between the constraints of the empirical world and the infinitude of the private man remains the central opposition, and it is the opposition rather than the weighting that distinguishes Emerson's thought and writing.

The railroad linked Concord with Boston in 1844, and after the 1844 publication of *Essays, Second Series* Emerson's writing accordingly gained in urbanity. But it also lost something in energy. Emerson did in the 1850 *Representative Men*, in the 1856 *English Traits*, and in the 1860 *The Conduct of Life* write as a shrewd social, psychological, and historical observer. But set in the context of Emerson's fundamental concerns, these works do little more than consolidate the achievement of "Self-Reliance," teaching in adroitly articulated detail how intelligent and responsive men can function in, and serve as models for, a democratic society. Emerson was not here reshaping his thought to take account of how this rapidly industrializing democratic society was becoming a nation of classes.

It was also becoming a nation increasingly and irreparably split over the question of slavery. And in some of his other writings of the 1850s, Emerson did acknowledge that his society not only tyrannized individuals but had also enslaved an entire people. He writes in a wonderfully candid passage of the journal for 1852,

> I waked at night, & bemoaned myself, because I had not thrown myself into this deplorable question of Slavery, which seems to want nothing so much as a few assured voices. But . . . I have quite other slaves to free than those negroes, to wit, imprisoned spirits, imprisoned thoughts, far back in the brain of man,—far retired in the heaven of invention, & which, important to the republic of Man, have no watchman, or lover, or defender, but I (August 1, 1852, in vol. 13, p. 80).

No passage in Emerson better dramatizes the limits inherent in conceiving of individual freedom as a deliverance from the intellectual and spiritual constraints a society imposes. Emerson's characteristic trust in "a few assured voices" misconstrues the actual need of 1852 America, the need not of a few voices but of many, and not in any case voices alone but also votes and actions and laws, and the Underground Railroad and the Emancipation Proclamation. The fundamental and equally characteristic error of the passage, however, is its assimilation of slaves to imprisoned thoughts and spirits, an assimilation that reveals Emerson's inability to conceive of civic, collective action, of individual freedom as won not from, but in, the communities people inhabit. Later, in the furor over the Fugitive Slave Law and then in the Civil War itself, Emerson wrote and spoke eloquently: against the Fugitive Slave Law and Daniel Webster, for John Brown and the Union and the war. But this is eloquence without much curiosity or reflection; Emerson has not integrated the idea of collective action into his thought, he has simply surrendered to it.

The stakes in judging Emerson are high, because he claimed to be a teacher and guide not only to the practice of art but also to the conduct of life. The second, more general claim is tenuous. Emerson was of little use to slaves in the struggle against slavery, and has been of little use to workers in the struggle against exploitation; he is of generally little use to those in our time who seek a collective deliverance from a collective oppression, and for whom, therefore, the cult and cultivation of the individual are at best self-indulgent and at worst pernicious. The first claim, however, is indisputable; in support of it we may adduce his empirical influence on artists and thinkers from Thoreau and Walt Whitman through Nietzsche and Louis Sullivan and John Jay Chapman to Ralph Ellison and Robert Musil, or Harold Bloom's magisterial characterization of Emerson as "the inescapable theorist of virtually all subsequent American writing" (p. 19). The writer's freedom *is* in a sense the individual's freedom from convention, from the tyranny of the majority; Emerson understood brilliantly how deeply that freedom cut, and shaped an exemplary if still sometimes disturbing life and work of writerly freedom.

LAWRENCE ALAN ROSENWALD

See also AESTHETICS; CULTURAL CRITICISM; DIARIES; INDIVIDUALISM.

FURTHER READING

Quentin Anderson, *The Imperial Self* (New York: Knopf, 1971).

Harold Bloom, "Mr. America," *New York Review of Books* 31 (Nov. 22, 1984): 19–24.

John Jay Chapman, "Emerson," in Edmund Wilson, ed., *The Shock of Recognition* (New York: Doubleday, 1943).

Ralph Waldo Emerson, *The Journals and Miscellaneous Notebooks*, ed. William Gilman et al. (Cambridge: Harvard University Press, 1960–82).

Henry James, "Emerson," in James, *Literary Criticism: Essays on Literature, American Writers, English Writers*, ed. Leon Edel (New York: Library of America, 1984).

F. O. Matthiessen, *American Renaissance* (London: Oxford University Press, 1941).

Barbara Packer, *Emerson's Fall* (New York: Continuum, 1982).

Lawrence Rosenwald, *Emerson and the Art of the Diary* (New York: Oxford University Press, 1988).

Stephen Whicher, *Freedom and Fate* (Philadelphia: University of Pennsylvania Press, 1953).

Enlightenment   Denoting the celebration of human reason in eighteenth-century American and European culture, the Enlightenment has, however, also become a symbol for excessive confidence in the capacity of reason. Ever since Romantic poets and critics faulted Enlightenment rationalists for their failure to appreciate the depths of cultural tradition and the heights of creative intuition, the Enlightenment has been blamed for flattening human experience. Much of intellectual life in America and Europe since the eighteenth century can be seen as a pitched battle between champions and critics of the Enlightenment's commitment to reason in general and to SCIENCE in particular.

In America, Christianity provided the framework within which, rather than against which, the Enlightenment emerged. The pervasiveness of RELIGION, whether manifested in varieties of orthodox or LIBERAL PROTESTANTISM or reformulated by deists such as Thomas Jefferson, shaped the reception of European ideas in America. Advocates of philosophical skepticism such as David Hume, and wide-ranging cultural critics such as Voltaire, attracted fewer Americans than did less radical thinkers. Champions of empiricism, science, and moderate politics such as John Locke, Isaac Newton, and Montesquieu were especially revered, as were spokesmen of the dissenting Whig tradition, such as Algernon Sidney, and Scottish moral philosophers who followed Francis Hutcheson and Adam Ferguson.

Distinct forms of Enlightenment emerged in New England, the Middle Atlantic, and the South, although there was some variation within each region. In New England the tension between the experience of democracy and Calvinists' views of man's depravity—a tension heightened by the Great Awakening of the mid-eighteenth century—could be eased, if not resolved, through the idea of the moral sense. This innate capacity, according to JONATHAN MAYHEW,

enabled human beings, although flawed by sin, to discern the difference between right and wrong. Calm confidence in the human ability to identify and comply with the demands of morality, while hardly consistent with Puritan doctrine, became the backbone of the Scottish-inspired and New England dominated genteel tradition that emerged in the early nineteenth century. (*See also* CALVINISM; SCOTTISH COMMON SENSE REALISM.)

In the more heterogeneous, commercial, and urban Middle Atlantic region, such accommodations with the ideas of free will and perfectibility came more easily. BENJAMIN FRANKLIN, the kite-flying scientist and smooth-talking statesman who embodied the American Enlightenment, scorned the Puritan divines' faith in God's absolute sovereignty. His fellow Philadelphians BENJAMIN RUSH and JAMES WILSON joined Franklin in tying divine providence to the moral sense of sympathy; humans were capable of progressing to ever greater heights through education and republican politics.

In the South, most champions of Enlightenment were members of the planter oligarchy; for them Enlightenment meant refinement in manners as well as philosophy. But their frequently and fervently professed commitment to reason stopped at the boundary of race. Jefferson, like other members of the southern gentry, expressed deep misgivings about slavery consistent with his ideals of freedom and equality and his conception of an innate moral sense rooted in sympathy. But most planters were willing to compromise those principles in order to preserve their way of life. Many of them understood that their unwillingness to repudiate slavery contradicted every value they claimed to embrace.

The Enlightenment passed through three phases in America. Before 1763 Americans borrowed and adapted European ideas about the desirability of using reason, and the undesirability of relying on authority and tradition, to solve human problems. Between 1763 and 1789 came a burst of creativity, as enlightened ideas and American experience coalesced. Finally, during the postcolonial decades the Enlightenment was assimilated in the dual ideas of individual autonomy (restrained within the boundaries of responsibility as understood by the moral sense) and popular sovereignty (restricted by a mechanism of government enabling the many to select as representatives those few with exceptional wisdom and virtue).

Instead of challenging power fruitlessly from the outside, as many European partisans of Enlightenment were forced to do, some of America's philosophers eventually exercised cultural and political authority themselves. The presidents of the two leading American learned societies at the close of the eighteenth century, the American Academy of Arts and Sciences and the American Philosophical Society, were also the second and third Presidents of the United States, JOHN ADAMS and THOMAS JEFFERSON. Succeeding them as President was Jefferson's Secretary of State, JAMES MADISON, author of two of the most important documents of the American Enlightenment, the Constitution and the *Federalist Papers*.

These statesmen tried to construct the institutions of the republic on the basis of Enlightenment ideas, with mixed results that by the middle of the nineteenth century revealed the limits of their creed of reason, refinement, and moderation. Their experiment built upon the century-old experience of religious dissent, self-government, and the traditions of common law, natural RIGHTS, and REPUBLICANISM. Some European philosophers hailed that experience and those traditions as living models of Enlightenment; Americans likewise concluded that the culture and institutions of the new nation provided an ideal environment for Enlightenment ideas. Slavery was the one issue that could not be resolved through calm, rational deliberation. It was a problem only muddied by the elaborate federal structure and the separation of powers. The struggle over slavery gradually revealed that the ideals of individual autonomy and popular sovereignty were inconsistent. Slaveholders' conception of their autonomy could not be reconciled with the expression of popular sovereignty in the 1860 Presidential election. As a result, the American Enlightenment dissolved into CIVIL WAR.

Enlightenment conceptions of universality, nature, and reason have frequently served as targets rather than ideals for cultural critics in the last two centuries. As was true in Europe, where the chaos of the French Revolution and dissatisfaction with the perceived sterility of rationalism in philosophy and neoclassicism in aesthetics fed the rising streams of ROMANTICISM, so in America nineteenth-century critics of Enlightenment emphasized the salience of TRADITION, intuition, and emotion. Twentieth-century modernists reformulated and extended those arguments, accenting the themes of disorder and irrationality. If Romantics often longed for transcendence of alienation through artistic creation, the modernist sensibility took a step further away from the Enlightenment's dream of order by revaluing chaos. The fiction of GERTRUDE STEIN, the early poetry of T. S. ELIOT, and the paintings of the American pioneer of abstraction Arthur Dove all manifested the modernist dissatisfaction with both classical and Romantic sensibilities and the desire to find revolutionary forms of expression.

Despite the long lineage of such critiques, the goal of a science of humanity that animated many *philosophes* has persisted. American analytic philosophers and empirical social scientists, continuing the eighteenth-century quest for clarity of expression and reliability of knowledge, have demonstrated the continuing lure of a value-free positive science that reached its logical conclusion in the behaviorism of B. F. SKINNER.

Yet attacks on the Enlightenment, inspired by the horrors of fascism and the technologies of modern war, have also grown more strident. Some twentieth-century critical theorists, taking their cue from Max Horkheimer and Theodor Adorno's *The Dialectic of Enlightenment* (1947), contend that the impulse toward science and social engineering derives from Enlightenment rationalism and culminates logically and historically in the horrors of Nazi death camps. (*See also* FRANKFURT SCHOOL.) REINHOLD NIEBUHR expressed a widely held mid twentieth-century viewpoint when he charged pragmatists such as JOHN DEWEY and SIDNEY HOOK with overlooking tragedy and sin in human experience. Dewey and Hook were overly impressed with the power of reason and education to remake the world. Modern history had demonstrated, Niebuhr believed, that reason was the servant of interests as well as ideals. Dewey and Hook responded that reason was indeed beleaguered, but insisted that there was no alternative: "science," understood as free inquiry and the spirit of experimentation, was far superior to "faith" as a social resource and instrument.

At the end of the twentieth century, debate still rages not only over the adequacy of reason and science, but over the Enlightenment ideals of cosmopolitanism and humanity. Taking their cue from the provocative writings of French theorists such as Michel Foucault, Jacques Derrida, Luce Irigaray, and Julia Kristeva, American critics have attempted to topple what they perceive to be oppressive ways of thinking. In current skirmishes over multiculturalism, champions of ethnic particularism scorn Enlightenment universalism as a sham masking white male hegemony. Some feminist postmodernists charge that the very concepts of order and reason are gendered male and reinforce illegitimate hierarchies. It is possible to admit the historical reality of domination, however, and still point out that critics who invoke the notions of oppression and illegitimacy necessarily rely on their own rational capacity as critics, and on implicit ideals of freedom and legitimacy whose lineage runs directly back to the Enlightenment.

ALASDAIR MACINTYRE has argued, in *After Virtue*

(1981) and in *Whose Justice? Which Rationality?* (1988), that because the Enlightenment project culminates in a Nietzschean dead-end of nihilism, we should admit the inadequacy of purely secular rationalist strategies and return to the Aristotelian tradition of the virtues. RICHARD RORTY, especially in *Philosophy and the Mirror of Nature* (1979) and in *Contingency, Irony, and Solidarity* (1989), has dismissed the Enlightenment ideals of rationality and progress as chimeras we chase only because we have been deluded into thinking our philosophy can be about something other than the conventions we cherish and the words we use. Both MacIntyre and Rorty share the belief that reason yields no transhistorical, universal warrant for the values we embrace.

Against such criticism, some philosophers still embrace modified versions of Enlightenment ideals. JOHN RAWLS in *Political Liberalism* (1993) continues to advance, although recently in a somewhat chastened, pragmatist tone, Kantian themes of autonomy and justice that can be traced directly back to the Enlightenment. Drawing on the ideas of GEORGE HERBERT MEAD, JOHN DEWEY, and Jürgen Habermas, RICHARD J. BERNSTEIN argues eloquently in *The New Constellation: the Ethical-Political Horizons of Modernity/ Postmodernity* (1992) for the continuing importance of the regulative ideal of undistorted communication. Even when we acknowledge the force of the most far-reaching postmodernist challenges, and even when we admit that the grandest Enlightenment hopes for universality, unanimity, and certainty have dissolved, the ideal of understanding endures, in Bernstein's view, as a necessary condition for human communication.

Those who dismiss the Enlightenment sometimes ignore—or perhaps are innocent of—its variety and its complexity. Enlightened thinkers in Europe and America understood that reason was potent but not all-powerful. Many American thinkers, from Adams and Madison to Rawls and Bernstein, have stressed the importance of reason while acknowledging its limitations. Rejecting both the conservative quest for timeless, foundational truths and the radical postmodern search for liberation from the prison house of totalizing reason, they have counseled turning to aesthetic, religious, and social experience as a means of tying reason to the actual problems, material or spiritual, it can successfully address, however provisionally. That Deweyan course is fully consistent with the sober optimism of the American Enlightenment, which rarely took flight in the grandiose visions of individual or social progress that sometimes characterized its French counterpart.

JAMES T. KLOPPENBERG

FURTHER READING

Joseph Ellis, ed., "An American Enlightenment," *American Quarterly* 28 (1976): 147–271.

Henry F. May, *The Enlightenment in America* (New York: Oxford University Press, 1976).

Donald H. Meyer, *The Democratic Enlightenment* (New York: G. P. Putnam's Sons, 1976).

J. R. Pole, "Enlightenment and the Politics of American Nature," in Roy Porter and M. Teich, eds., *The Enlightenment in National Context* (Cambridge, U.K.: Cambridge University Press, 1981).

Richard J. Bernstein, *The New Constellation: the Ethical-Political Horizons of Modernity/Postmodernity* (Cambridge: MIT Press, 1992).

environmentalism The environmental movement made a very recent appearance in the 1960s. For generations technological development had progressed on the premise of transforming, even replacing, the natural world. Environmentalists contended that human beings, no matter how impressive their technology, need to protect the surrounding biophysical world to survive or live well. Environmentalism focused on describing a critical relationship: humans netted together with other forms of life with which they must maintain a healthy symbiosis. That network set limits on social development.

In the earlier part of this century the word "environment" referred mainly to the external social influences working on the individual (as opposed to genetic endowment). "Environmentalism" itself, as the *Encyclopedia of the Social Sciences* defined it in 1931, meant the belief that "physical, biological, psychological or cultural environment" was a crucial factor shaping "the structure or behavior of animals, including man" (vol. 5, p. 561). But increasingly, as the heredity versus environment battle lost saliency after World War II, environment came to mean the *natural* influences surrounding people, including flora, fauna, climate, water and soil, the biosphere. At the same time the environment came to seem highly vulnerable to human activity; it was no longer only an influence but an endangered source of sustenance. By the late 1960s that perspective began to take on political form in and out of government. In 1967, for example, a group of scientists founded the Environmental Defense Fund, which sought to get the chemical pesticide DDT banned by the courts as a threat to both human life and natural ecosystems. (Five years earlier RACHEL CARSON, in her book *Silent Spring*, had criticized the contamination of the environment by DDT.) In 1969 Congress passed the National Environmental Policy Act, which set up a federal regulatory agency, the Environmental Protection Agency, and required an "environmental impact statement" for any federally funded project that might cause damage to the earth. The new federal posture, the banning of DDT in 1972, and the passing of many new laws (including the Clean Water Act in 1960 and the Clean Air Act in 1963) sprang from the conviction that the everyday relationship between humans and NATURE was more essential than Americans had heretofore understood, and that what happened to one vitally affected the other.

Environmentalism, to be sure, did not appear suddenly on the scene with no precedents or intellectual preparation. Rachel Carson acknowledged an indebtedness to such nineteenth-century figures as HENRY THOREAU and JOHN MUIR, who had celebrated nature in its wilder state and sought to reestablish a direct personal relationship with the nonhuman. Both men devised private strategies for getting outside the cocoon of civilization and into the woods or mountains. But in a nation of over 200 million people, with a far denser web of artifice obscuring the natural order, that kind of private quest had become difficult. Environmentalism was, therefore, not a private relationship, a kind of retreat, but a decidedly public one—a strategy pursued in the courtroom and legislative chamber to defend a relationship found even in the heart of the largest megalopolis.

Other precedents include the conservation movement, which gained momentum in the early twentieth century under the leadership of GIFFORD PINCHOT, Chief Forester during the Theodore Roosevelt administration. But that movement had aimed at preserving national parks and wildlife refuges, setting up a national forest system under sustained-yield management, and protecting the nation's soils and minerals. Typically, conservation had been a movement to put the government in charge of managing and even owning the land. Activists like Pinchot certainly understood that American society could not endure without a permanent supply of natural resources, and they feared that a shortsighted consumption might threaten the nation's security. On the other hand, conservationists tended to look on nature as a series of discrete places needing defense—a Yosemite Valley, a redwood forest, an eroded farm on the Great Plains. When environmentalism emerged, its proponents took over some of that same program. For example, they supported the Wilderness Act of 1964.

But even as that Act was passed, the core of the movement was shifting: more and more activists sensed that the human–nature umbilical itself was under attack and that defending it required a different way of thinking. The "environment" had to be seen holistically. Nature is not a realm set apart from humans, like another country that one visits from time to time, but instead is a vast, intricate community, a system of connections and interchanges. One cannot move away from that condition.

The emergence of the new viewpoint owed much to a relatively obscure group of thinkers in the two or three decades that preceded the age of environmentalism, most of them academics in such fields as ecology and geography. They were the first to see the environment as a set of interactive relationships between humans and the rest of nature. Many of them thought about those relations on a global scale, transcending dramatically the highly nationalized consciousness of the conservationists. Their ideas often came from abroad: for example, from the Russian geologist V. I. Vernadskii, inventor of the concept of the biosphere; from French and German geographers, who had long debated the question of nature as a limiting factor on human activity; and from a succession of English naturalists, including Charles Darwin, Charles Elton, and Arthur Tansley (the last of whom suggested the idea of the ecosystem). A key American figure in this emerging body of thought was Aldo Leopold, a wildlife expert in the Midwest, who introduced many readers to the science of ecology through his outdoor essays, *A Sand County Almanac*. By the 1950s those influences had all come together in a new integrative and interdisciplinary point of view that united the natural and social sciences, a view that might be called human ecology. Avoiding the extremes of environmental determinism, which had tried to reduce cultures to their physical circumstances, and of a technological optimism that was blind to its side-effects, the new view taught that human life must be lived within natural constraints, both physical and moral.

Examples of that emerging human ecology run all through the late 1940s and the 1950s. Among anthropologists of the period Betty Meggers and Julian Steward, one working in Amazonia, the other in the desert Southwest, laid the foundations for "cultural ecology." Among historians James Malin argued for an ecological approach and applied it in his own studies of the relations of plants, animals, soils, climate, and people on the Great Plains. Among geographers Carl Sauer was the crucial figure, with a broad-ranging mind, producing a number of influential studies of people living in close contact with nature. In 1956 several of those same scholars, and many more from many disciplines, came together in Princeton for a symposium on the state of the human–nature relation. As much as any event, that gathering prepared the intellectual ground for the environmental movement.

Take, for example, the contribution by Paul B. Sears, a botanist and chairman of the conservation program at Yale University, entitled, "The Processes of Environmental Change by Man." Sears reviewed the global impact of human population growth, the intensification of agricultural land-use, water and air pollution in industrial areas, noting along the way that the United States, with less than a tenth of the world's population, was consuming more than half of the mineral production. "Man is dependent," he argued, "upon other organisms both for the immediate means of survival and for maintaining habitat conditions under which survival is possible." Neither Sears nor the others at the 1956 conference called themselves environmentalists, but their focus on the place of humans in the global environment, and their general concern about the state of that environment, all helped give environmentalism a set of defining ideas. In 1972, when environmentalists from poor and rich countries alike assembled in Stockholm to resurvey the global situation, they drew on the same perspective worked out by those pioneering minds. Today their ideas have become widely popularized in the United States, and ecology has become a part (however large or small) of the daily thinking of masses of people here and abroad.

What recent environmentalism subsequently added to the fertile ideas of human ecology was a sense of urgency, bordering at times on apocalyptic fear. The environment was, by the 1960s, in a condition of "crisis." Rachel Carson's 1962 nightmare of a springtime when no birds sang, all dead from poison, introduced a tone of anxiety missing from the writings of Paul Sears or Aldo Leopold. Following Carson, another biologist, Paul Ehrlich, warned of a population bomb that "keeps ticking," and still another, Barry Commoner, began alerting the country to the death of Lake Erie from pollutants, and the death of people from radioactivity, smog, and ground water contamination. In his book *The Closing Circle*, published in 1971, Commoner explained that he had first learned about the environmental crisis from the Atomic Energy Commission, which during the fifties had exposed Americans to the dangers of strontium 90 through a series of atmospheric nuclear tests and then failed to let the public know the full consequences of that exposure. The great need, in his view, was for an awakened public, led by informed scientists, to force powerful institutions in government and business to develop less threatening technologies. The specter haunting each of these environmentalists was death—the death of birds, of ecosystems, of nature itself, and, because of our dependence on nature, the death of humans as well.

Only a little less apocalyptic were the environmentalists who, by the 1970s, were calling for an end to economic growth. In their view, an economy expanding at a constant geometric ratio, using ever more energy, land, minerals, and water, must eventually run up against the limits of the earth. Looked at as a set of interdependencies rather than as a storehouse of commodities, the environment was not merely a set of things to be used. Here the environmentalists confronted deeply seated attitudes among economists, business leaders, politicians, and the public about the virtues of economic growth, attitudes underlying the modern economic system and indeed the whole materialistic ethos of modern culture. It is still too early to gauge the popular response to that challenge, though polls show a growing tilt toward environmentalist views in all the industrial countries and greater willingness to make economic sacrifices to reduce pollution, preserve species, and use less energy.

During the 1980s, as American national politics turned very conservative, a rising chorus of anti-environmentalists insisted that the environment was neither indispensable, nor fragile, nor a real constraint on human ambition. Environmentalists countered by seeking alliances with other groups demanding cultural change: with feminists, some of whom insisted that women were more attuned to grasping ecological interdependencies than men; with ethical radicals who wanted to extend rights to animals, trees, and the rest of nature; with advocates for poor nations, who demanded protection from environmental damage and toxic dumping caused by rich nations. Environmentalists, above all, tried to temper their apocalyptic tendencies with a more hopeful and politically acceptable emphasis on a "green future" in which cities, economies, and productive technologies would all be reembedded in the tangled web of life.

DONALD WORSTER

FURTHER READING

Stephen Fox, *The American Conservation Movement: John Muir and his Legacy* (Madison: University of Wisconsin Press, 1981).

Samuel P. Hays, *Beauty, Health, and Permanence: Environmental Politics in the United States, 1955–1985* (New York: Cambridge University Press, 1987).

Carolyn Merchant, *Radical Ecology: the Search for a Livable World* (New York: Routledge, 1992).

Robert C. Paehlke, *Environmentalism and the Future of Progressive Politics* (New Haven: Yale University Press, 1989).

Joseph M. Petulla, *American Environmentalism: Values, Tactics, Priorities* (College Station: Texas A&M University Press, 1980).

Paul B. Sears, "The Processes of Environmental Change by Man," in William L. Thomas Jr., ed., *Man's Role in Changing the Face of the Earth*, vol. 2 (Chicago: University of Chicago Press, 1956).

Bob Pepperman Taylor, *Our Limits Transgressed: Environmental Political Thought in America* (Lawrence: University Press of Kansas, 1992).

Donald Worster, *Nature's Economy: a History of Ecological Ideas* (New York: Cambridge University Press, 1977).

equality   Inequalities of any kind are difficult to justify in the modern world, since the dispossessed are inclined to demand a larger share of the benefits of social life, and fewer of its risks, pains, and losses. Equality summarizes these calls for JUSTICE and fair treatment; it is the rallying cry of the downtrodden and their sympathizers.

It was not always so. Until quite recently, historically speaking, masses of people tolerated great and apparently permanent inequalities. For the most part, they did not openly challenge the power and perquisites of their "social betters." Threats to rulers and prominent individuals came primarily from other elites, who encouraged insurgency when it suited their political purposes, but condemned it once they obtained power. Violent repression was the usual reward for those unfortunates who embraced the idea of equality too warmly and failed to respect distinctions of rank.

One reason for the long acceptance of inequality was a widespread (or at least widely propagated) notion that inequality was both natural and inevitable. According to this belief, men differed enormously in their capacity for leadership, and women had no capacity at all. Given this inequality, it seemed obvious that men of superior breeding, and therefore political virtue, should rule, while those of humble origin, and hence no political competence, ought to follow. Any other arrangements were perverse; in varying degrees, they wasted the talents of exceptional individuals and gave authority to those who were most likely to abuse positions of power and influence.

English immigrants brought these ideas to North America in the seventeenth century. Distinctions of social rank were a prominent feature of settlements in the New World, just as they were in the old, where the Great Chain of Being justified extraordinarily complex social hierarchies. Nothing so elaborate emerged in the colonies, but "free men" clearly ranked higher than mechanics, indentured servants, sailors, and other classes of men. Of course, women were subordinated to men in all ranks, and slaves were confined to the lowest station of all.

Rank had its privileges, and in the English colonies political RIGHTS were reserved for free men, male property holders who were entitled to vote, hold office, and frame laws within the terms of colonial charters. Everyone else lived under laws enacted by free men. Free men were no less subject to these laws, however; in keeping with English legal tradition there was supposed to be "equality under the law." Thus the 1641 Massachusetts Body of Liberties ordained that "every person within jurisdiction, whether inhabitant or foreigner shall enjoy the same justice and law, that is general for the plantation, which we constitute and execute towards another, without partiality or delay."

Equality under the law is not the same as having an equal say in making the law, as even free men had learned by 1776. Colonial demands for representation in Parliament were based on the presumption that Englishmen in the colonies were the equal of Englishmen in Britain, and were therefore entitled to the same rights and liberties. These included a say in policy-making, and when Parliament rejected the colonists' demands, radicals pushed for independence and the right to govern themselves.

"All men are created equal," THOMAS JEFFERSON wrote, and "are endowed by their creator with certain inalienable rights," and that "among these are life, liberty and the pursuit of happiness." The purpose of government is to secure these rights, and the people who hold rights decide which form of government is best suited to this purpose. These "self-evident truths," were put forth without qualification in the Declaration of Independence. And while the object of criticism was the political "enslavement" of the colonies, the inclusive language of independence certainly implied that all men—including chattel slaves—had equal rights, if Garry Wills's interpretation of Thomas Jefferson's meaning is correct.

Ultimately, the Civil War tested the truth of Jefferson's proposition, but not before many leading Americans denied the radically egalitarian thrust of his words. For example, in his debates with STEPHEN A. DOUGLAS in 1858, ABRAHAM LINCOLN took the Declaration of Independence to mean only that the black man has the "right to eat the bread, without leave of anybody else, which his own hand earns" (p. 53). That is, the black man's economic freedom was entitled to equal protection under the law. But like the free men who preceded him, Lincoln refused to concede any role for racial minorities in the making or application of laws under which all Americans lived.

Lincoln's reading of the Declaration was still too radical for Douglas, an opponent of slavery who nevertheless insisted that the signers of the Declaration manifestly intended to establish a government "on the white basis, by white men, for the benefit of white men and none others" (p. 127). ROGER TANEY made the same point in the infamous *Dred Scott* decision, and he was probably right insofar as the intentions of the founders were concerned. For as soon as the War for Independence was concluded, ALEXANDER HAMILTON, JAMES MADISON and others who became Federalists campaigned against the idea that all men are equal and ought to be treated as such.

The Federalists observed that among the swelling ranks of free men were individuals of superior wisdom, talent, and political vision. These individuals constituted a "natural aristocracy" born to rule. Unfortunately, under the Articles of Confederacy natural aristocrats were being displaced by individuals of dubious merit, men who flattered the electorate to win office and used their power in ways that were harmful to property, or so said the Federalists. To halt the decline a new framework of government was needed, one that would lessen the influence of the common sort of man and restore superior men to positions of influence.

Thus, only 11 years after independence was declared, Federalists recoiled from revolutionary notions of equality. Their Constitution aimed to place natural aristocrats in high office by electoral arrangements designed to produce what Madison called "a filtration of talent." Once in office, men of exceptional ability could use the separation of powers to frustrate majorities bent on undermining property. The whole system was undemocratic, the Federalists admitted, but that was assumed to be a point in its favor, since democracy was not then a widely admired form of government. A republican government was what was needed, in the Federalists' view, and that is what the Constitution provided.

The Federalists won the battle for ratification, but they lost the war for the hearts and minds of American citizens. As Gordon Wood shows, revolutionary ideas about equality could not be contained; they fueled an "assault on aristocracy" equivalent in ferocity to that which toppled the *ancien régime* in France. Hence the Federalists were defeated at the hands of the more democratically inclined Jeffersonian Republicans in the election of 1800. The Jeffersonians maintained their grip on power until the Jacksonian Democrats permanently installed "the common man" as the equal of any natural aristocrat with ruling pretensions, setting the stage for Tocqueville's commentary on American culture.

The assault on aristocracy was noticed by ALEXIS DE TOCQUEVILLE, whose *Democracy in America* gave a trenchant account of equality and its historical progress. The inexorable leveling of status was evident throughout Christendom, according to Tocqueville, and he wanted to know where the widespread movement for equality might lead. His interest was piqued by the early ascendance of equality in the new world, and he thought its future might be glimpsed in the United States. So he "saw in America more than America; it was the shape of democracy itself which I sought, its inclinations, character, prejudices and passions; I wanted to understand it so as at least to know what we have to fear or hope therefrom" (p. 19).

As it happened, the advance of DEMOCRACY brought hope *and* fear in its train. Hope derived from democratic people's "natural taste for liberty; left to themselves, they will seek it, cherish it, and be sad if it is taken from them" (p. 506). The fear arose from democrats' "ardent, insatiable, eternal and invincible" passion for equality (p. 506). Tocqueville was certain this passion would cause citizens to place great powers in the hands of a government charged with eradicating inequalities. But the amelioration of inequality by government would be insufficient, for "the more equal men are, the more insatiable will be their longing for equality" (p. 538). Consequently, government would be invested with still more powers, and liberty would eventually succumb to a kind of democratic despotism, unless the passion for equality was balanced by other considerations or values.

There are some who believe that Tocqueville's prediction came to pass, though not with the despotic consequences he feared. During the past 150 years or so, a passion for equality inspired ANTISLAVERY activists and legitimated the most significant exercise of governmental power in the nineteenth century: the maintenance of the Union by force of arms, and the legal reconstruction of the plantation economy in the South. A segregated society remained, but a hundred years later it, too, was dismantled in what may have been the most significant domestic undertaking of the twentieth century.

Thus the push for racial equality was accompanied by a vast expansion of political authority. Under pressure from CIVIL RIGHTS advocates, the national government played a leading role in desegregating schools, public accommodations and workplaces. The exercise of power was extraordinary, and required special justification. Champions of civil rights, such as the Southern Christian Leadership Conference and the National Association for the Advancement of Colored People, supplied the necessary authorization, crafting their demands for equality in terms that could not be denied by whites, unless they were willing to resort to openly racist arguments (as members of the Ku Klux Klan and Aryan Nation were).

Racial inequalities have not been the only target of government action. Under the Fourteenth Amendment, persons are entitled to equal protection under the laws, regardless of their creed, ethnic origin or race. Recently, this has been extended to include gender, as part of a broader attack on discrimination by such groups as the National Organization of Women. (*See also* FEMINIST JURISPRUDENCE.) Responding to these demands for equal rights, agencies of the national government have been made the chief guarantors of civil rights, regulating interactions between persons, and between individuals and corporate entities, such as state and local governments, employers, business organizations, and some private clubs and associations.

The progress of equality has met with resistance, some of it openly violent, much of it furtive and private. To overcome this resistance, the power of government has been increased, just as Tocqueville predicted it would be. Yet the majority of Americans welcomed these changes; few saw the zeal for equality in the civil rights movement as excessive, so long as it confined itself to combating discrimination and stopped short of affirmative action. Nor did many sense "democratic despotism" at work in the expansion of political power, when that power was used to protect the rights of individuals who have been the victims of majority rule, not its authors.

Still, there is one important sense in which the passion for equality has generated opposition, not so much from those who defend the old idea of natural inequality, but from rival conceptions of equality itself. After all, the meaning of equality is far from settled; it is quite obviously a matter of political dispute. Various interpretations of equality and its demands have been expressed in American politics, usually in the course of debates over the appropriate role of government in reducing inequality. As a result of these political contests, the passion for equality has been diffused somewhat, preventing it from having the effects dreaded by Tocqueville.

The current controversy over affirmative action is instructive in this regard. Supporters of affirmative action welcome the achievement of legal equality for women and people of color. Arbitrary restrictions have been struck down, and "second-class citizenship" no longer exists, at least in theory. Everyone now has the right to equal protection under the laws, and most citizens have the right to participate in collective decision-making, unless they lack reason or are convicted felons.

Backers of affirmative action admit this, but insist that certain forms of discrimination or harassment still exist, in spite of legal gains. Moreover, they argue that even if discrimination disappeared, it might be impossible for many women or minorities to use their new-found opportunities effectively. That is because the effects of discrimination persist long after the abolition of oppressive institutions and practices; for progress to occur these effects must be counteracted.

Hence proponents of affirmative action want policies that give preferential consideration to qualified women and racial minorities, especially in employment. They argue that only in this way is it possible to overcome the dark legacy of unfair treatment. As Justice Harry Blackmun opined in *Regents of University of California v. Bakke* (1975),

> In order to get beyond racism, we must first take account of race. There is no other way. And in order to treat some persons equally, we must treat them differently. We cannot—we dare not—let the Equal Protection Clause perpetuate racial supremacy.

Underlying this stance is a view of equality that wants differences taken into political consideration. Some who hold this conviction believe that racism and sexism are so pervasive that it would be unjust to ignore their consequences, even if the goal is a society in which human differences are irrelevant. Others go further, wanting to preserve differences by protecting identities based on RACE, GENDER, ETHNICITY, and language which are in danger of being swamped by the cultural mainstream. Both groups support government policies that address the particular needs of special populations, creating a form of social life in which all differences are respected, and none are subordinated. Diversity without domination is the essence of this notion of equality, which owes much to the philosophy of HORACE KALLEN and JOHN DEWEY, and echoes Madison's admiration for an "extended republic" capable of taming the mischief of faction. (*See also* CULTURAL PLURALISM AND MULTICULTURALISM.)

Opponents of affirmative action, and there are many, reject this whole line of reasoning. For them, affirmative action is simply a form of reverse discrimination. As Justice Powell insisted in *Regents of University of California v. Bakke*, "The guarantee of equal protection cannot mean one thing when applied to one individual and something else when applied to a person of another color. If both are not accorded the same protection, then it is not equal."

Those who share Powell's opinion believe that the interests of men and whites are subordinated to those of women and racial minorities whenever the latter are accorded preferential treatment. Therefore, affirmative action contradicts a basic responsibility of government, which is to reduce or eliminate variation in the treatment of different races and genders. Only policies that are color-blind and gender-blind should be pursued, since neutral policies are the best means of establishing a society in which arbitrary differences play no role in determining the life chances of individuals.

Sustaining this position is a belief that governments ought to ensure all citizens an equal opportunity to earn a living or otherwise express themselves. This now includes making education available to all, without regard to race, gender or income, and it has come to entail combating discriminatory actions. Beyond this governments should not go, and in particular they should not try to produce equal outcomes for all, according to commentators like George Will (and Republicans of almost every persuasion). These conservatives hold that "leveling" undermines individuals' sense of responsibility by guaranteeing benefits and services without regard for desert or effort. "Social engineering" also prevents others (chiefly taxpayers) from enjoying fully the fruits of their labor, and ultimately threatens economic prosperity and even the institution of private property upon which individual liberty rests.

Similar arguments are sometimes made against public WELFARE programs, especially when they are financed by progressive forms of taxation. Such programs favor the poor at the expense of the middle and upper classes, whose tax dollars provide the indigent with public housing, food stamps, health insurance, and cash allowances. Thus welfare programs transfer income from one group to another in the name of equality, and are far from neutral in their impact on the lives of different citizens.

Redistributive policies have generally met stiff resistance in the political sphere. In the early years of the nation, some republicans favored policies for equalizing wealth, but as modern LIBERALISM came to the fore Americans' tolerance for disparities of income grew. Income differentials are not arbitrary, in the eyes of many Americans; they reflect individual differences in talent, effort and luck. As such, income differentials are viewed as a legitimate form of inequality, and a large number of citizens think it is wrong to equalize incomes by government fiat. They would probably agree with WILLIAM GRAHAM SUMNER, who concluded in 1874 that the rich owe nothing to the poor, and that laissez-faire really is the best policy where the distribution of wealth is concerned.

Radical egalitarians challenge this position, portraying great income disparities as an arbitrary (and therefore illegitimate) form of inequality. The starting point for this particular vision of equality is the proposition that all human beings are moral agents, at least potentially. On the basis of this fundamental similarity, radical egalitarians hold that every citizen's interests deserve equal consideration in collective decision-making. No position should be privileged in politics; every point of view ought to be represented equally in the councils of state. This would seem to require that all citizens must participate in political decision-making, either directly or through elected representatives. Then political equality would mirror the fundamental moral equality of individuals, and the preservation of individual autonomy would be the proper object of government policy.

In particular, government would guarantee basic necessities to all members of society, regardless of income. The necessities include employment, shelter, and health care, in the absence of which it is difficult to understand how anyone could be autonomous. Thus, radical egalitarians believe that individuals are entitled to goods and services necessary for them to be effective moral agents in today's society. If people cannot obtain these goods and services on their own, it is the responsibility of government to help them become autonomous, or else act as the provider of last resort. Consequently, this version of egalitarianism points in the direction of a welfare state much more extensive than anything Americans have known heretofore.

Radical egalitarianism has many precedents in American history; for every Sumner defending inequality there was an EDWARD BELLAMY or HENRY DEMEREST LLOYD touting the superiority of commonwealth over wealth. Traces of radical egalitarianism may also be found in the PROGRESSIVISM of social workers during Woodrow Wilson's administration, when workers' compensation, unemployment insurance, and widows' pensions were in vogue. Similarly, the social welfare programs of the New Deal and Great Society built on egalitarian notions of entitlement, though they did not fully embrace radical egalitarian principles, which would have taken them well down the road toward the SOCIALISM of EUGENE DEBS or NORMAN THOMAS, or the sweeping participatory vision of the NEW LEFT.

Radical egalitarianism is a minority opinion, not least because it breaks with conventional wisdom, which tends to see equality and liberty at odds with each other. That is, reductions in the personal FREEDOM of some are thought to be necessary to the achievement of greater equality for others. Defenders of affirmative action embrace this sacrifice and opponents do not, yet both assume there is a trade-off between liberty and equality. Politics is thereby reduced to making trade-offs, which in the American case seem to favor liberty, disproving Tocqueville's prediction that the "invincible passion for equality" would overwhelm the "natural taste for liberty."

Against this tendency, radical egalitarians point to the convergence of liberty and equality. They argue that individuals are at liberty when they are free to do as they choose, and are not dependent on the will of others. However, that assumes citizens are all more or less equal in power, for wherever power (of whatever sort) is distributed unequally, some are at the mercy of others. Equality is therefore a condition of liberty, just as liberty results from the enjoyment of equality.

If radical egalitarians are right, it is not necessary to choose between two different kinds of community, one oriented toward liberty, the other animated by egalitarian values. Both values can be served by institutions which emphasize self-determination or personal autonomy, and a form of politics that places such important constitutional concerns at the very center of public debate.

RUSSELL L. HANSON

See also CITIZENSHIP; CLASS; JUSTICE; REPUBLICANISM; WOMEN'S RIGHTS.

FURTHER READING

Charles Beitz, *Political Equality: an Essay in Democratic Theory* (Princeton: Princeton University Press, 1989).

Celeste Michelle Condit and John Louis Lucaites, *Crafting Equality: America's Anglo-African World* (Chicago: University of Chicago Press, 1993).

Russell L. Hanson, *The Democratic Imagination: Conversations with Our Past* (Princeton: Princeton University Press, 1985).

Abraham Lincoln and Stephen A. Douglas, *The Lincoln–Douglas Debates of 1858*, ed. Robert W. Johannsen (New York: Oxford University Press, 1965).

Edmund S. Morgan, *Inventing the People: the Rise of Popular Sovereignty in England and America* (New York: Norton, 1988).

Kai Nelson, *Equality and Liberty: a Defense of Radical Egalitarianism* (Totowa: Rowman and Allanheld, 1985).

J. R. Pole, *The Pursuit of Equality in American History*, 2nd expanded ed. (Berkeley: University of California Press, 1993).

Alexis de Tocqueville, *Democracy in America*, ed. J. P. Mayer, trans. George Lawrence (Garden City: Doubleday, Anchor Books, 1969).

Garry Wills, *Inventing America: Jefferson's Declaration of Independence* (New York: Vintage, 1978).

Gordon S. Wood, *The Radicalism of the American Revolution* (New York: Vintage, 1991).

Erikson, Erik (b. Frankfurt am Main, Germany, June 15, 1902; d. Harwich, Mass., May 12, 1994). Psychologist. A student of the relationship between culture and psychology, Erikson argued in *Childhood and Society* (1950) that the growing ego has eight developmental stages, each characterized by a conflict between an impulse toward a new mastery and a desire for a former simplicity. While the general structure of these conflicts—such as the infant's need to trust, or the adolescent's need for identity—is universal, they also reflect their social context. Biographical studies can therefore, in his view, illuminate the psychosocial conflicts of particular historical moments. *Young Man Luther* (1958) and *Gandhi's Truth: On the Origins of Militant Nonviolence* (1969) are his own major contribution to this genre of psychosocial biography.

FURTHER READING

Richard Stevens, *Erik Erikson: an Introduction* (Milton Keynes, U.K.: Open University Press, 1983).

ethnicity The term has become hotly contested across all academic disciplines, yet at the beginning of the century, when SOCIAL DARWINISM was at its height, probably no concept was more rigid or determined more forcefully Americans' perceptions of life chances and opportunities. Ethnicity—or RACE, which had a broader meaning than it does today—placed the individual in a specific biological category to which were ascribed certain fixed intellectual, emotional, and social characteristics (*see* HEREDITY).

The development of the SOCIAL SCIENCES in the age of progressive reform helped to undermine the Darwinian notion of ethnicity and race. The Chicago School of sociology, particularly the work of ROBERT E. PARK and William Thomas, challenged the notion that ethnic origins determined social position, and introduced the idea that gradual ASSIMILATION broke down social barriers and eventually led to the abandonment of immigrant cultures. Focusing on European immigrant groups in large urban areas like Chicago, their work linked ethnicity to spatial arrangements in the city. The urban ghetto was viewed as the arena for a largely unchanged ancestral culture in the United States, and social mobility was determined by how quickly migrants abandoned this tight community and culture of origin. (*See also* URBANISM.)

The causal link between the decline of ethnicity and SOCIAL MOBILITY continued to dominate the thinking of historians and social scientists well into the post–World War II period. In the 1950s, they added an obsessive fixation on the elusive tenets of "Americanism." Oscar Handlin, to cite a prominent example, argued in his classic work *The Uprooted* that writing a history of immigration was, in fact, writing about all of American history. Handlin's account emphasized the loss of European peasant roots, the arduous journey across the Atlantic, and the painful, yet to him inevitable, process of absorption into American society. Yet, as effective as he was in demonstrating the importance of the immigrant experience, Handlin mistakenly assumed that every immigrant shared the same process of cultural adaptation. Indeed, he later extended his thesis regarding the disintegration of peasant cultures in the New World even beyond his European subjects to include African Americans and Latinos.

In the last three decades revisionist historians have argued that Handlin's habit of collapsing the migration experiences of all groups into one story belittles the diversity of such events and distorts history. Moreover, they have especially taken exception to the notion that much was inevitably lost in the transition to life in the United States. They have pointed instead to the retention of Old World culture by many different groups of Americans and to its persistence and resiliency. Unlike Handlin and his contemporaries, later revisionist historians, beginning with Rudolph Vecoli's essay "*Contadini* in Chicago: a Critique of *The Uprooted*," viewed cultural persistence not only as something which had occurred throughout American history, but celebrated the fortitude of ethnicity in contemporary American life.

This "new ethnicity" paradigm, in fact, came to dominate historical writing about immigration in the 1970s and 1980s. Unlike earlier works, which concentrated on the immigrant generation itself, much of the emphasis placed on what Michael Novak called the "rise of the unmeltable ethnics" in the 1970s centered around the second and third generations. Others, such as Virginia Yans-McLaughlin in her important work *Family and Community: Italian Immigrants in Buffalo, 1880–1930* (1977) argued that the immigrants themselves had become simply "old wine in new bottles," essentially utilizing their old habits in a new environment. Emphasizing this continuity of culture, John Bodnar called his 1985 synthesis of the recent historical literature on immigration to the United States *The Transplanted*. There was to be no doubt that most immigrants had maintained their cultural roots, even when planted in different soil.

Historians of the racial minority experience in the United States entered this debate in the late 1960s and early 1970s at the height of the revisionist reinterpretation. Powerfully influenced by the struggles for national liberation in the Third World and the civil rights movements of both African Americans and Chicanos in the United States, particularly by calls for cultural nationalism, minority historians emphasized the retention of ethnic culture throughout the United States, but also distinguished distinct peoples who often identified themselves in opposition to the majority Euro-American society.

Not surprisingly, most historical writings reflecting this nationalist commitment emphasized cultural continuity in almost all geographical settings. Cultural retention was framed not necessarily as a conscious act of resistance, but rather as a condition of the racial and class separation inflicted on minority populations. Following earlier thinkers such as W. E. B. DU BOIS, who had long been interested in the nature of African American culture, investigations of antebellum black life by scholars such as George Rawick and John Blassingame focused less on the intrusion of white culture into slave quarters, and more on the richness of a distinct African American culture. According to these works, the ghetto or the barrio, though circumscribing social and economic possibilities for residents, made cultural survival possible in the twentieth century. Central to this position was the argument that the histories of racial minorities in the United States, and therefore the possibilities of their assimilation into American life, are qualitatively different from the experiences of European immigrants. For racial minorities, the integrating process of assimilation was blocked and their culture reflected their exclusion.

Ironically, though positioning themselves in opposition to cultural assimilation, most revisionist interpretations in the post-civil rights era accepted the terms of the cultural debate set out by the scholars of the 1950s. In the view of both generations of scholars, cultural adaptation occurred in a linear fashion, with strict distinctions made between "traditional" and "modern" cultures, with little in-between. Both poles were depicted largely as static, impermeable, and always in opposition, with individuals constantly pushed or pulled in one direction or the other. Largely accepting this model of bipolar cultural opposites, most minority historians set out to document the cultural persistence of things ethnic in new American surroundings.

Though noting the severity of racial and class discrimination, some immigrant historians began to highlight cultural change in the ethnic population, particularly among the children of immigrants and within the middle class, but they continued to place these changes within a bipolar model of opposing cultures. Chicano historians, such as Albert Camarillo and Mario Garcia for example, have described a variety of experiences among Mexican immigrants divided by age, nativity, and generation, which together resulted in a unique border culture, neither completely Mexican nor American. While most Chicano scholars recognized that change did occur on the northern side of the border, Mexican American culture remained a tenuous site of cultural exchange, always a prelude to the attractions of a "purely" Mexican or "purely" American stance. As anthropologist Renato Rosaldo has pointed out in *Culture and Truth*, this "classic concept of culture seeks out the 'Mexican' or the 'Anglo-American,' and grants little space to the mundane disturbances that so often erupt during border crossings" (pp. 28–9). (*See also* LATINO AND LATINA CULTURES.)

Recently, however, new perspectives offered by scholars working in the field of cultural studies force us to reexamine such static assumptions, and not only along the border. Across a variety of disciplines, scholars such as George Lipsitz, in *Time Passages: Collective Memory and American Popular Culture* (1990), have challenged the very language used to describe the particularistic experiences of individuals—culture, ethnicity, identity, gender and race. Any notion that individuals have occupied one undifferentiated cultural position has been abandoned in favor of the possibility of multiple identities and contradictory positions. Moreover, the strictly nationalist position of earlier historians has been questioned, not only by cultural theorists such as Stuart Hall, exploring the complicated historical allegiances in the ethnic past, but also by feminists such as Evelyn Brooks Higgenbotham, who claim that a single standard of ethnicity largely left women out of historical constructions.

If one looks at the changing language in anthropology, for example, a discipline that has claimed "culture" as its primary focus (*see also* CULTURAL ANTHROPOLOGY), one can see how volatile definitions themselves can become. Once having hoped to understand the "most complex whole," anthropologists have lately come to recognize the myriad contradictions inherent in cultural systems. Ethnographers who have drawn from the perspective of textual analysis and cultural studies have questioned the ability of anthropologists to lay claim to being "scientists of culture." As James Clifford, one of the leading practitioners of this new approach, contends in *Writing Culture*, "culture, and our views of 'it,' are produced historically, and are actively contested" (pp. 18–19).

Literary critic Werner Sollors has gone so far as to emphasize that ethnicity is more a matter of "consent" to belonging in a particular group than "descent" from an identifiable ethnic heritage. He and other scholars have perpetuated an intellectual tradition rooted in an earlier belief in AMERICAN EXCEPTIONALISM. Their argument emphasizes the freedom of Americans to choose their identities. This reasoning follows on the heels of critiques of the "new ethnicity" school by social scientists Herbert Gans and Stephen Steinberg, who question the "fictive ethnicity" of second and third generations of ethnic Americans. Each of these writers emphasize that the creation of boundaries between groups is often as important as the actual practices and beliefs within groups in defining ethnicity. Yet an emphasis solely on "consent" does not fully describe the ethnicity of groups which have encountered widespread and consistent discrimination throughout American history, groups such as African Americans.

Recently, other scholars in the humanities have begun to develop notions of "transcreation" to describe the process of cultural formation among ethnic Americans. The movement between cultures yields not so much a world of confusion, but rather a place of opportunity and innovation. To be betwixt and between, in effect, is to be an ethnic American. In the United States, the new cultural identity of immigrants was forged within the context of a hostile environment seeking to deny them full participation in society. Constrained by their lack of economic and political resources, immigrants drew strength from family networks and fellow countrymen who lived nearby. Through the daily struggle to survive in an often hostile environment, newcomers constructed a world for themselves, shaped both by past memories and present realities.

According to earlier immigrant historians, the comforting presence of a home nation was sufficient to produce a unified cultural concept to which newcomers could turn. Yet nations, too, had to be "imagined" into existence, according to Benedict Anderson and to Eric Hobsbawm. Not only was culture never static in countries of origin, but the construction of a national identity was ferociously pursued by those very nations whose emigrants left for the United States. These efforts reflected attempts by sovereign states to create social cohesion in turbulent times by implementing what Etienne Balibar has called, in *Race, Nation, Class: Ambiguous Identities* (1991), the "fictive ethnicity" of the nation-state. In the United States, as well, new "traditions" had to be invented and older customs discarded or radically transformed.

Immigrants played their part in this drama. Ethnicity was not a fixed set of customs packed in a suitcase with other belongings brought from the mother country, but rather a collective identity that emerged from daily experience in the United States. Cultural identity increasingly has been viewed as a matter of both "becoming" and "being." Moreover, ethnicity arose not only from interaction with fellow countrymen and women, but also through dialogue and debate with the larger cultural world encountered in the United States. Strategies of accommodation, resistance, or indifference marked every individual immigrant's stance towards American culture.

For those who chose to stay in the United States, their cultural adaptations had important implications for American society. As immigrants acclimated themselves over time, they did not remain foreigners simply living in the United States; they became ethnic Americans. They assumed a new ethnic identity, a cultural orientation which accepted the possibilities of a future in their new home. As anthropologist Michael M. J. Fischer observes in *Writing Culture*, "ethnicity is not something that is simply passed on from generation to generation, taught and learned; it is something dynamic, often unsuccessfully repressed or avoided" (p. 195).

In the twentieth century, political participation and labor mobilization often created the context for a new identity. Rather than culture serving as a substitute for politics, it became a way to enter the political arena. This "oppositional potential" of ethnic culture has not only been increasingly studied in relation to the various civil rights movements of the 1960s, but also, by George Sánchez and Lizabeth Cohen, with regard to the radicalism of labor agitation and political organization of the New Deal era. Ironically, it was not the search for ethnic nationalism that engendered political radicalism for large numbers of immigrants and their descendants, but the forging of a new identity as ethnic Americans.

Clearly these recent perspectives have much to offer when considering the emergence of new forms of ethnicity in the United States. Immigrant Italians, for example, were more likely to think of themselves in terms of particular regions than in broad national categories, but life in the United States forged a common Italian identity. Even more has this been true of the new "pan-ethnicities" of the late twentieth century, such as "Indians" or "Asian Americans" (*see* INDIAN IDENTITIES; ASIAN AMERICAN IDENTITY). These groups were formed as collective responses to persistent discrimination in the United States, discrimination which did not respect national or tribal barriers.

Other approaches are sure to emerge in analyzing ethnicity in the late twentieth century. As has been the case throughout the century, these new approaches are likely to continue to be steeped in contemporary cultural politics. Because ethnic identities and politics are prone to constant change and adaptation, the theories used to explain the phenomenon of ethnicity will undoubtedly be transformed in the process. Once considered simply a lasting legacy of the premodern era, ethnicity has reemerged in the late twentieth century as one of the most potent and dynamic forces for understanding the future of the nation and the world.

GEORGE J. SÁNCHEZ

See also CULTURAL PLURALISM AND MULTICULTURALISM.

FURTHER READING

Benedict Anderson, *Imagined Communities: Reflections on the Origin and Spread of Nationalism*, rev. ed. (1983; London: Verso, 1991).

James Clifford and George E. Marcus, eds., *Writing Culture: the Poetics and Politics of Ethnography*, (Berkeley: University of California Press, 1986).

Lawrence H. Fuchs, *The American Kaleidoscope: Race, Ethnicity, and the Civil Culture* (Middletown, Conn.: Wesleyan University Press, 1990).

Renato Rosaldo, *Culture and Truth: the Remaking of Social Analysis* (Boston: Beacon, 1989).

George J. Sánchez, *Becoming Mexican American: Ethnicity, Culture, and Identity in Chicano Los Angeles, 1900–1945* (New York: Oxford University Press, 1993).

Werner Sollors, *Beyond Ethnicity: Consent and Descent in American Culture* (New York: Oxford University Press, 1986).

Stephen Steinberg, *The Ethnic Myth: Race, Ethnicity, and Class in America* (Boston: Beacon, 1982).

Stephan Thernstrom, ed., *Harvard Encyclopedia of American Ethnic Groups* (Cambridge: Belknap Press, 1980).

etiquette   Although this subject has only recently attracted the attention of historians, sociologists and anthropologists have long recognized the significance of etiquette. They may call it by different names (such as ceremonial behavior, social ritual, interaction ritual, politeness, or manners, to name a few in past or current use), but these terms all describe essentially the same thing: the rule-bound and symbolic behaviors that we perform in the presence of others. Indeed, sociologists have been developing what amounts to a theory of etiquette from the very birth of their discipline. From Herbert Spencer to Erving Goffman, scholars have demonstrated that etiquette serves three social functions. First, it constitutes a pervasive system of social regulation or control, a form of AUTHORITY that underlies all other forms. Second, etiquette has a creative function in that the prescribed actions help generate the feelings of RESPONSIBILITY that hold people to their social roles. Third, as Goffman has shown, manners serve a communicative function (*see* LANGUAGE). Acts governed by etiquette tell people about each other and their situation (*see* HONOR). They also symbolize the not readily apparent structure of society.

All of these functions may be illustrated by a single example: the act of bowing, which began as a gesture performed by an inferior to a superior, helps one to feel deferential, and expresses deference to another. Conceived sociologically, the "big rules" of social life—our systems of law, morality, and religion—are necessary if humans are to live in groups; the "little rules" of etiquette are necessary to enact the social order in every situation, and to keep the social order constantly in view.

Students of CULTURAL ANTHROPOLOGY have contributed to the study of etiquette through their study of ritual. They have attributed to ritual in primitive and modern societies the same regulatory, creative, and communicative functions that sociologists have attributed to etiquette. Indeed, some scholars from both disciplines have acknowledged that etiquette is a form of ritual. Anthropologists, most notably Mary Douglas, have recognized that specific rituals and the complexity of the code vary from culture to culture. Douglas has speculated on both the cultural conditions that call for an elaboration of ritual and the types of societies that have less need and concern for ceremonial behavior.

Despite the richness of their work, most social scientists have ignored the question of change over time. The sole exception was Swiss sociologist Norbert Elias's path-breaking work, *The History of Manners*, the first volume of his three-volume *The Civilizing Process* (1939). Overlooked by English-speaking scholars for several decades, Elias's work sparked the interest of British and American historians after it was translated in 1978. In sweeping terms, Elias linked the revolution in Western manners in the early modern era with the process of civilization itself, by pointing out and exploring the theme of self-control that ran through the seemingly petty rules for behavior.

In general, historians have only just begun to make use of these insights; the one exception is the short study by Arthur Schlesinger Sr. of etiquette literature in America, published in 1968. Heavily influenced by Elias, Goffman, and Douglas, American historians have begun to ask questions of this "micro-order" of society in order to understand how individuals might have experienced and upheld the larger social order in past time. Three prominent examples in relation to American history are the works of Karen Halttunen (1982), John Kasson (1990) and Rhys Isaac (1982). Halttunen uses etiquette literature along with other sources in her study of middle-class culture in mid nineteenth-century America. Kasson's book expands on her work by focusing exclusively on nineteenth-century etiquette works and showing how they guided Americans in a new urban and industrial environment. Both carry Elias's story forward in time by showing the use the emerging middle class made

of formerly genteel manners in its quest for self-definition and HEGEMONY. Working with behavioral evidence rather than conduct literature, Isaac is sensitive to the communicative role of face-to-face performances throughout his work on colonial Virginia. Isaac also offers a valuable discourse on method which explores some of the historical possibilities of the work of social scientists.

Historians confront several distinctive challenges in studying etiquette. Discussions of these small symbolic performances are limited in diaries and letters or other such records of actual behavior; generally these rituals are taken for granted once mastered. The use of prescriptive literature raises new questions for each that it answers. Undoubtedly both kinds of sources will have to be explored to decipher the codes of behavior actually followed by various groups of Americans. The inquiry has great potential. For example, the study of etiquette can offer new perspectives on ongoing debates about CLASS, age, GENDER, and ETHNICITY. More importantly, it allows comparison of these subjects, a useful antidote to the chief disease of social history, the fragmentation which has led to distortions as historians examine one variable to the exclusion of others. Most importantly, inquiry in this area suggests that etiquette itself has played a crucial role in American history, as it offered mediating rituals that allowed Americans to live with evolving cultural conflicts, chiefly those between social ideals and material realities. Seventeenth-century Americans lived in fairly equal material circumstances with less social and spatial segregation of age groups and the sexes (all relative to later periods), yet they believed strongly in the inequality of social ranks, age groups, and the sexes. Nineteenth-century middle-class Americans, on the other hand, claimed to revere EQUALITY while scrambling successfully to become as unequal as possible. Changing codes of etiquette provide enticing clues showing how Americans resolved such cultural contradictions by proclaiming certain ideals aloud while acting out, often nonverbally, a rather different reality.

C. DALLETT HEMPHILL

FURTHER READING

Mary Douglas, *Purity and Danger: an Analysis of the Concepts of Pollution and Taboo* (1966; London: Routledge and Kegan Paul, 1978).

Norbert Elias, *The Civilizing Process* (1939), one-vol. ed., trans. Edmund Jephcott (Oxford, U.K. and Cambridge, Mass.: Blackwell, 1994).

Erving Goffman, *The Presentation of Self in Everyday Life* (New York: Doubleday, 1959).

——, *Behavior in Public Places: Notes on the Social Organization of Gatherings* (New York: Free Press, 1963).

——, *Interaction Ritual: Essays on Face-to-Face Behavior* (1967; New York: Pantheon, 1982).

Karen Halttunen, *Confidence Men and Painted Women: a Study of Middle-Class Culture in America, 1830–1870* (New Haven: Yale University Press, 1982).

Rhys Isaac, *The Transformation of Virginia, 1740–1790* (Chapel Hill: University of North Carolina Press, 1982).

John Kasson, *Rudeness and Civility: Manners in Nineteenth-Century Urban America* (New York: Hill and Wang, 1990).

Arthur M. Schlesinger, *Learning How to Behave* (New York: Cooper Square, 1968).

evangelicalism The term "evangelical" has many legitimate meanings, but it is primarily used to describe a tradition of mostly white, Protestant heirs of the English Reformation who share a basic set of religious convictions. D. W. Bebbington summarizes them well: "conversionism, the belief that lives need to be changed; activism, the expression of the gospel in effort; biblicism, a particular regard for the Bible; and what may be called crucicentrism, a stress on the sacrifice of Christ on the cross" (pp. 2–3). The American movement sharing these convictions was conceived in revival and brought to birth with the formal disestablishment of religion. From the 1730s onwards—with the spellbinding preaching of the British itinerant, George Whitefield, and the learned theology of the Massachusetts minister, JONATHAN EDWARDS—revivalism became the foremost means of defining an American Protestant experience. Colonial awakenings, in turn, became the model for the even more influential revivals early in the history of the United States known as the Second Great Awakening. (*See also* GREAT AWAKENING.)

The effect of revivalism on the life of the mind lay in its antitraditionalism. American revivalism was activistic, immediatistic, even anticlerical in its distrust of settled, educated churchmen. Putting results first and doctrinal niceties last, it was able to mobilize great numbers for the cause of Christ. With its scorn for tradition, its concentration on individual competence, and its distrust of mediated knowledge, revivalism turned evangelical thinking from doctrine to practice, from the consideration of first principles to the search for useful wisdom. By the early nineteenth century, American evangelicals also enjoyed an unprecedented degree of religious freedom. This liberty, formalized in the Constitutional separation of church and state, compelled the churches to compete for adherents, rather than, as in Europe, being assigned responsibility for parishioners. The combination of revivalism and disestablishment gave the American churches a new vitality in shaping the country by norms of Christian civilization. But it meant that pragmatic concerns prevailed over principle. The churches required new adherents, or they would go out of business. This history explains at least one major intellectual conundrum—how it was that the greatest evangelical mind in America, Jonathan Edwards, could promote a program that led to the decline of evangelical thinking. Edwards's philosophically sophisticated defense of supernatural Christianity was used to defend a movement in which philosophical sophistication, including his own, had little cash value.

Evangelical thought was also decisively influenced by the ways evangelicals exploited the founding of the American nation. Their eagerness to embrace REPUBLICANISM transformed their thinking. Evangelicals looked on freedom as liberation from sin, republicans as liberation from tyranny. To American Protestants good and evil were represented by Christ and anti-Christ; to republicans, by liberty and tyranny. In the crisis of empire after the mid-1750s, evangelical and republican convictions consummated a union with long-lasting effects. Unhesitating identification with the American political experiment meant that the evangelical mind lent a moral, even distinctly Christian, tone to that experiment. In the process evangelical thinking on political questions became derivative, circumscribed by nationalism. As American missionaries took the gospel to other cultures, and as more and more non-Protestants made their home in the United States, evangelicals had difficulty adapting their thought to new conditions. (*See also* MISSION.)

Even as they became republicans, evangelicals also become democrats. But when they adopted the voice of "the people," evangelicals also made intellectual sacrifices. Unlike their Protestant counterparts in Europe, American evangelicals retained the confidence of ordinary people, contributed more than their share to the United States's relatively high levels of church participation, and so remained a visible factor in the nation's public life. But democratized religion soon had little room for scholarship, scant respect for intellectual complexity, and (at least after the mid-nineteenth century) almost universal preference for building up voluntary societies rather than institutions of higher learning.

In the early years of the nation, evangelicals, when they turned for guidance to the thought of eighteenth-century Scottish philosophers like Francis Hutcheson and Thomas Reid, also became philosophical "realists" in questions of ethics and epistemology. Learned minister-professors, like TIMOTHY DWIGHT at Yale and Samuel Stanhope Smith at Princeton, put the new intellectual system to use in their lectures, as did effective frontier preachers like Barton W. Stone and Alexander Campbell, the two most important leaders in the Disciples or "Christian" movement.

For such thinkers, the AMERICAN REVOLUTION cemented a bond between evangelical theology and Scottish common sense philosophy. When the patriotic rejection of Old World political traditions broadened out into a more general dismissal of Old World traditions in all areas, Protestants in America needed new ways to defend their faith. No longer was simple appeal to authority sufficient. The philosophy of SCOTTISH COMMON SENSE REALISM provided an ideal way to defend the traditional faith without requiring reliance on discredited European traditions. Hence as American evangelicals called on principles of Common Sense philosophy to defend their faith and promote social order, they were able to keep in step with general national feelings about personal liberty, self-determination, and the need for all men (and soon women as well) to think for themselves.

The antebellum entente between evangelicalism, REPUBLICANISM, and Common Sense realism could not withstand the cultural changes of the post-Civil War period. The reorganization of American COLLEGES AND UNIVERSITIES was one of the most important of the new developments. The new university institutionalized an increasingly empirical approach to science and a reform Darwinist spirit that sundered the old synthesis of evangelical convictions and American ideals. The collapse of that synthesis signaled a momentous defeat for American evangelicals.

The aura of intellectual weakness that evangelicals communicated during the transformation of the American university was heightened by the fundamentalist–modernist controversy. Fundamentalists, who are best described as militant antimodernist Protestants of the revival tradition, did sustain a vigorous intellectual life. Their study of Scripture was intense, and they conveyed their convictions to ordinary people much more effectively than did the nation's intellectual elites. But FUNDAMENTALISM, in the persuasive view of those elites, was obscurantist on science and blinded, by its focus on supernatural causation, to the mundane workings of politics, economics, and society.

Reverses for fundamentalists in the 1920s, like the humiliation of WILLIAM JENNINGS BRYAN at the Scopes trial, seemed to signal the end of evangelical intellectual vitality. Before too long, however, ambitious young fundamentalists were finding sectarianism and separation distasteful. Edward John Carnell (1919–1967), after completing doctorates at both Harvard and Boston universities, championed an "orthodoxy" shorn of fundamentalist excesses at the new Fuller

Theological Seminary in California. Carl F. H. Henry (b. 1913), also a professor at Fuller and then the founding editor of *Christianity Today* (1956), called fundamentalists to a new engagement with American society and a new concern for theological reflection.

They were joined in this call by some within the major American denominations who, though never fundamentalists, had preserved evangelical convictions. And they were aided by immigrant communities seeking assimilation, especially members of the largely Dutch Christian Reformed Church. Evangelicals offered the Dutch Reformed an important reference point as their immigrant community moved closer to American ways. The Dutch Reformed, in turn, provided their American counterparts a heritage of serious academic work and experienced philosophical reasoning. They also offered a flourishing network of publishers. By the late 1940s, Eerdmans and several firms in Grand Rapids, Michigan, a center of Dutch immigration, were bringing out the books of Carl Henry, E. J. Carnell, and other American evangelicals. Eerdmans also brought a significant British influence to bear in America by distributing the work of the British Inter-Varsity Fellowship.

The most important force in renewing evangelical thought after World War II was the evangelist Billy Graham. Graham never claimed to be an intellectual, but he did support evangelical institutions (*Christianity Today*, Fuller Seminary, Gordon-Conwell Theological Seminary, Wheaton College) that took the life of the mind seriously. And by dropping opposition to evolution, by eventually downplaying the communist menace, and by promoting books of general Christian orthodoxy (like those of Britain's C. S. Lewis), Graham's popular work also took evangelicals into new intellectual territory.

Since the era of the fundamentalist–modernist controversy the quality of and the reception given to evangelical scholarship have improved considerably. Yet recent gains must be kept in perspective. The overall impact of evangelical thinkers on even the *evangelicals* of the United States, much less on learned culture, is slight. The best-known evangelical spokespersons—Jerry Falwell, Billy Graham, Jimmy Swaggert, Tim LaHaye, Bill Gothard, Kenneth Hagin, Oral Roberts, Chuck Swindoll—owe their influence to practical media skills rather than to theoretical ability or formal thought. These most visible evangelicals are still more likely to express their thought in idioms from the antebellum period than in language familiar to modern intellectuals, religious or secular.

The Lebanese Orthodox Christian, Charles Malik,

once put the case even more starkly in an address to an evangelical audience:

> Who among the evangelicals can stand up to the great secular or naturalistic or atheistic scholars on their own terms of scholarship and research? Who among the evangelical scholars is quoted as a normative source by the greatest secular authorities on history or philosophy or psychology or sociology or politics? (pp. 33–4)

A few academics who might be classed as evangelicals in a general sense do now speak with such authority in their fields. But such examples, including historian George Marsden and philosophers Alvin Plantinga, Nicholas Wolterstorff, and Robert Adams, remain rare.

The "evangelical mind" in America has been rich in practical intelligence but relatively poor in theoretical intelligence. After Jonathan Edwards, a host of sturdy thinkers—SAMUEL HOPKINS, Joseph Bellamy, and John Witherspoon in the eighteenth century; NATHANIEL W. TAYLOR, John W. Nevin, CHARLES HODGE, Edwards Amasa Park, Henry Boynton Smith, and A. H. Strong in the nineteenth century; J. Gresham Machen, E. Y. Mullins, and Carl Henry in the twentieth century (to mention just a few)— have provided intellectual labor of commendable quality. But for every Edwards in the history of American evangelicalism there has been a more widely visible Whitefield; for every patient scholastic like B. B. Warfield of Princeton Theological Seminary a more compelling purveyor of celestial common sense like D. L. Moody. In the course of American history it has been the canny shrewdness of the latter types much more than the creative brilliance of the former that has characterized evangelical thought. It is no accident that the highpoint of evangelical influence in the United States was reached during the decades between the Revolution and the Civil War when practicality and rapid cultural mobilization were emphasized above all else.

The "evangelical mind" has always been profoundly paradoxical; it has deeply influenced America, and been deeply influenced by America. American evangelical thinkers have excelled at translating a Protestant vision of the Christian gospel into the evolving languages of American popular culture. The thoroughness of that translation explains both the strength and the weakness of evangelical thought in America. Evangelicals have excelled in resisting the tendency of liberal Christians to reduce the divine to the human, but they have been less successful in resisting the inclination to identify the divine with the national.

MARK A. NOLL

See also APOCALYPTIC LITERATURE.

FURTHER READING

D. W. Bebbington, *Evangelicalism in Modern Britain: a History from the 1730s to the 1980s* (1989; Grand Rapids: Baker, 1991).

Edith Blumhofer and Joel Carpenter, eds., *Evangelicalism in Twentieth-Century America: a Guide to the Sources* (New York: Garland, 1990), esp. section 3, "Life of the Mind."

Nathan O. Hatch, *The Democratization of American Christianity* (New Haven: Yale University Press, 1989).

Charles Malik, *The Two Tasks* (Westchester: Cornerstone, 1980).

George M. Marsden, "The Collapse of the Evangelical Mind," in Alvin Plantinga and Nicholas Wolterstorff eds., *Faith and Rationality: Reason and Belief in God* (Notre Dame: University of Notre Dame Press, 1983).

——, *Reforming Fundamentalism: Fuller Seminary and the New Evangelicalism* (Grand Rapids: Eerdmans, 1987).

Mark A. Noll, *Between Faith and Criticism: Evangelicals, Scholarship, and the Bible in America*, 2nd ed. (Grand Rapids: Baker, 1991).

Mark A. Noll, David W. Bebbington, and George A. Rawlyk, eds., *Evangelicalism* (New York: Oxford University Press, 1994).

Evans, Walker (b. St. Louis, Mo., Nov. 3, 1903; d. New Haven, Conn., Apr. 10, 1975). Photographer. Rejecting photography's aspirations to artistic beauty and commercial success, Evans reconceived photography as literature, as a creative engagement between artist and subject. Emphasizing the dignity of his subjects, his work relied on significant details and the juxtaposition of images and texts to suggest meanings larger than the photographic frame. In 1934 the Museum of Modern Art in New York featured Evans in its first one-person show for a photographer. Collected in *American Photographs* (1938) and *Let Us Now Praise Famous Men* (1941, with text by JAMES AGEE), Evans's photographs of Depression-era farmers captured both their endurance and the viewer's own dilemma: how to "see" the farmers when, thanks to Evans's art, it was no longer possible to reduce them to types or to romanticize them as stalwart victims.

FURTHER READING

J. A. Ward, *American Silences: The Realism of James Agee, Walker Evans, and Edward Hopper* (Baton Rouge: Louisiana State University Press, 1985).

Evarts, Jeremiah (b. Sunderland, Vt., Feb. 3, 1781; d. Charleston, S. C., May 10, 1831). Advocate of Indian land rights. Editor of the Congregationalist newsletter, the *Panoplist* (1810–21), and a founder of the American Board of Commissioners for Foreign Missions, Evarts tried to block the forced removal of the Cherokees and other tribes from Georgia. In numerous speeches, articles, and his *Essays on the Present Crisis in the Condition of the American Indians* (1829), he argued that the federal government was legally and morally obligated to recognize the Cherokees' right to remain on the land possessed by them for generations and guaranteed to them by treaties. Removal, he believed, would deny the southern tribes the cultural autonomy necessary for their continued progress toward civilization and Christianity. Drawing on religious, moral, legal, and constitutional sources, he advanced compelling arguments for gradual acculturation and against dispossession and forced assimilation, arguments later used by Indians and their supporters.

See also INDIAN–WHITE RELATIONS.

FURTHER READING

John A. Andrew, *From Revivals to Removal: Jeremiah Evarts, the Cherokee Nation, and the Search for the Soul of America* (Athens, Ga.: University of Georgia Press, 1992).

Everett, Edward (b. Dorchester, Mass., Apr. 11, 1794; d. Boston, Mass., Jan. 15, 1865). Clergyman, educator, politician, orator. Everett's career was unusually wide-ranging; minister of Boston's prestigious Brattle Street congregation, editor of the *North American Review*, member of Congress, Secretary of State, vice-presidential candidate, professor and later President of Harvard College. He was a major figure in the Whig-Unitarian elite that dominated American intellectual life in the early nineteenth century. He held the first chair in Hellenic studies at Harvard, and established himself as the leader of the American Greek Revival. Despite Everett's reputation as a conservative "Cotton Whig" and his presence with John Bell on the Constitutional Union Party ticket in 1860, he committed himself fully to the Union cause once the war was underway. Exploiting his reputation as the nation's greatest living orator, he conducted propaganda tours around the North. He capped his oratorical career by delivering the lengthy primary oration at Gettysburg in 1863, the occasion now remembered for the brief Address by ABRAHAM LINCOLN, which followed Everett's.

FURTHER READING

Paul A. Varg, *Edward Everett: the Intellectual in the Turmoil of Politics* (Cranbury, N.J.: Associated University Press, 1992).

expatriation The term "expatriate" still conjures up for most Americans the writers of the "lost generation" nursing drinks at Montparnasse cafés between the world wars. But attention has increasingly turned to Americans who settled all over the world, including black expatriates who have commonly chosen to live not in Europe but in Africa.

Americans in Europe were already visible in the days of Benjamin Franklin and Thomas Jefferson; they were not expatriates but visitors or temporary residents. In the late nineteenth century, traveling "the grand tour" increasingly led to the prolonged residence in England, France, and Italy of such writers as HENRY ADAMS and HENRY JAMES. They often behaved like pilgrims in quest of the fountainhead of their culture and occasionally contrasted the ways of the "innocents abroad" with those of the worldly wise, calculating Europeans. Soon a handful of women played a pioneering role: EDITH WHARTON chose France; GERTRUDE STEIN and Natalie Clifford Barney followed and established avant-garde literary salons, and Sylvia Beach kept a well-attended bookstore cum lending library on the Left Bank. After World War I, many writers impatient with small-town provincialism, "Puritan" taboos, prohibition, and philistinism in the U.S. moved to the Old Continent. A survey conducted by *transition* in 1933 listed the major reasons for living in Europe: the freer, bohemian atmosphere, together with institutions and attitudes conducive to aesthetic creation, not to speak of the advantageous rate of exchange.

The participants in this large-scale literary migration included a who's who of major American writers (the most notable exceptions being William Faulkner and Robert Frost): poets like T. S. ELIOT, Stephen Vincent Benet, ARCHIBALD MACLEISH, EZRA POUND, E. E. Cummings, COUNTEE CULLEN, LANGSTON HUGHES; novelists like ERNEST HEMINGWAY, F. SCOTT FITZGERALD, Louis Bromfield, JOHN DOS PASSOS, CLAUDE MCKAY, Djuna Barnes, HENRY MILLER; musicians like George Gershwin, Virgil Thompson, and George Antheil, artists like Man Ray and Thomas Hart Benton. Gertrude Stein, who presided over the "lost generation," could claim that "Paris was where the twentieth century was."

After World War II, many American writers established themselves in Europe in order to escape the Cold War climate of McCarthyism. Many black expatriates had the additional goal of experiencing a culture freer from racial discrimination. The black writers RICHARD WRIGHT, Chester Himes, JAMES BALDWIN, and William Gardner Smith, cartoonist Ollie Harrington, and conductor Dean Dixon all found in European capitals, mostly in Paris, a setting propitious for self-realization. So did such white writers as Irwin Shaw, James Jones, William Styron, John Ashbery, the *Paris Review* group and poets of the BEAT GENERATION—notably Lawrence Ferlinghetti, WILLIAM BURROUGHS, and Brion Gysin.

During the Vietnam War, while aspiring writers sat out the draft in Canada and Europe, several African Americans preferred for other reasons to relocate to newly independent African nations. Communist W. E. B. Du BOIS chose to die a Ghanean citizen in Accra, and Ghana's president Kwame Nkrumah also welcomed William Gardner Smith, William Sutherland, Maya Angelou, Julian Mayfield and others who worked in education and the media. This movement was the resurfacing of an old tradition, as expatriation has been an enduring dimension of the African American experience in the United States. Not only were slaves forcibly expatriated from their homelands in the first place. The dream of return was never totally extinguished, and was periodically rekindled by such leaders as MARTIN DELANY, Alexander Crummell, and MARCUS GARVEY.

The exclusion of blacks from the American social and cultural scene, although lessened in recent years, has long favored the trend toward "exile" abroad. White American artists have traditionally studied in Europe and many have remained. African American artists have increasingly sought fame and fortune there. Antebellum tragedian Ira Aldridge blazed a trail from England to Russia, while French-speaking New Orleans free men of color, like dramatist Victor Séjour, and composers Edmond Dédé and Lucien Lambert, achieved success in Paris. Hoping their works would be "judged on their own merits," composer Samuel Coleridge-Taylor later settled in London and painter Henry O. Tanner in France. Still later, several musicians found fame in Brazil; novelist Willard Motley sought refuge in Mexico, Frank Yerby in Madrid and William Demby in Italy; painters William H. Johnson and Herbert Gentry thrived in Scandinavia. The notion that social acceptance and success can be achieved more easily in European countries than in the U.S. consistently appears in the attitudes of African Americans, from William Wells Brown to Countee Cullen, from Josephine Baker to Sidney Bechet and Jessye Norman. Euro-Americans, by contrast, tend to stress the sophisticated, free, stimulating atmosphere of European capitals.

Today, expatriation has simply become "living abroad" and many of those concerned prefer to be called "transatlantic commuters." There are now few self-designated American exiles. But the writings of those authors who lived and worked abroad over the last two centuries are still compelling documents for the student of American identities and of the social and political forces that shape intellectual life. These writings reveal the profound effect of place on writing and on the formation of the self. The time has come to explore all the facets of expatriation: the impact of the American creative presence upon the expatriates' countries of election, the influence of those countries upon the writers' sensibilities, the dynamics of race and ethnicity among the expatriates themselves and between them and the cultures that received them.

MICHEL FABRE

FURTHER READING

John Bainbridge, *Another Way of Living: a Gallery of Americans Who Chose to Live in Europe* (New York: Holt, Rinehart and Winston, 1968).

Sylvia Beach, *Shakespeare and Company* (New York: Harcourt, Brace, 1959).

Ernest Dunbar, *The Black Expatriates* (New York: Dutton, 1968).

Michel Fabre, *From Harlem to Paris. Black American Writers in France, 1840–1980* (Urbana: University of Illinois Press, 1991).

Janet Flanner, *Paris Journal, 1944–1965* (New York; Atheneum, 1965).

J. Gerald Kennedy, *Imagining Paris* (New Haven: Yale University Press, 1993).

Herbert Lottman, *The Left Bank* (Boston: Houghton Mifflin, 1982).

Christopher Sawyer-Lauçanno, *The Continual Pilgrimage: American Writers in Paris, 1944–1960* (New York: Grove, 1992).

F

fatherhood American fatherhood has a long history and a short historiography. Until recently, few historians have given the subject sustained attention, a situation that seems to be changing as scholars, influenced by work in women's and family history, turn attention to men's lives. Over the next decade, a fuller picture of American fatherhood that embraces the subject in all of its historical, racial, ethnic, and class complexity will likely emerge. Nevertheless, enough work has already been done to suggest the broad outlines of the story.

For most of the first two centuries of European settlement, fatherhood and patriarchal power were inseparable. Men dominated society and were the titular heads of families. Fathers had not only primary responsibility for providing economic support for their families but in most instances represented their families' political and legal interests before the state. Their power extended to more personal realms as well. Moralists directed child-rearing prescriptions toward fathers who, in turn, guided the family's moral and religious development. Fathers also oversaw their children's education and courtship rituals, and their sons' occupational "callings." Given the rural nature of American society, fathers spent many hours in the company of, or in close proximity to, their children, a fact that no doubt augmented fathers' power and influence. Men directed the work of the family, introduced their sons to farming or craft work, and generally lived among neighbors who held fathers responsible for the good order of their families. (*See also* AUTHORITY.)

Although modes of fatherhood within these communities ranged from evangelical will-crushing to genteel indulgence, patriarchal dominance held until the late eighteenth century. Sometime after 1750, however, a variety of forces transformed fatherhood in ways that shaped men's lives for the next two centuries. At least among the middling classes, family relations became both more companionate and more segmented. The former stemmed from complex religious, political, and economic ideas that gave rise to INDIVIDUALISM, the latter from basic changes in the structure of the economy itself. The result was that mutuality, romance, and personal happiness played a larger role in family life, but so too did male breadwinning, female nurture, and CHILDHOOD innocence. Especially among middle- and upper-class families, mothers increasingly assumed the care of their children while fathers took on the task of earning a living. (*See also* MOTHERHOOD.)

Some of these trends were already evident by the time of the American Revolution, and by the nineteenth century the ideology of fatherly breadwinning and motherly nurture dominated the cultural landscape. At the heart of this transformation lay the decline of the corporate household economy and the emergence of a commercial-industrial world in which increasing numbers of men commuted between their place of WORK and home while their wives assumed direction of child-care and home maintenance. Men's contact with both sons and daughters became more attenuated. Boys might follow their fathers into the factory, but the ability of craftsmen to pass skills to their sons declined as mechanization rendered the skills of fathers obsolete. So, too, with middle-class office workers who had nothing to pass on to their children but access to education and whatever business contacts they could muster. In short, the occupational ties between fathers and sons were gradually giving way. Men's absence from home also undermined father–daughter relations. A virtual apprenticeship system developed as young girls learned the craft of DOMESTICITY and the rituals of female friendships from other women, and over time close psychological and emotional ties among women became one of the defining characteristics of the nineteenth century. These bonds left little room for fathers.

Such broad generalizations obscure important variations. Black sharecroppers and Polish immigrants did not experience fatherhood in the same way. The former had to cope with a racist society that undermined their fatherly status, the latter with a culture that constantly tugged at the cultural allegiances of their children. Nevertheless, both found themselves living in a rapidly industrializing society in which breadwinning was becoming increasingly important to male identity. This cultural emphasis on breadwinning lay at the root of father–children alienation, and the recognition of this alienation prompted a host of writers in the early twentieth century to try to refashion men's sense of their paternal responsibilities. Social scientists, psychologists, and family-life educators urged fathers to spend more time with their children and to establish closer emotional relations with them. By the 1930s these same experts had elaborated a theory of sex-role identity that gave fathers a prominent role in shaping the psychological development of their sons and daughters.

Central to this theory was the belief that the family was "drifting," an analysis made most forcefully by Ernest Groves in The Drifting Home (1926). Swept along by urbanization, materialism, individualism, oversexualization, and changing GENDER relationships, family members found their bonds weakening and the influence of fathers diminishing. Men's roles as religious guides, educators, counselors, and disciplinarians were being undercut by the anonymity of the city, the rise of the state, and a heightened emphasis on consumption; consequently, fathers' influence relative to that of mothers was declining and any hope of restoring lost power through stern discipline seemed destined for failure. Instead, experts argued that fathers had a new role to play. Conceptualizing the family as "a unity of interacting personalities," theorists of family life like Ernest Burgess (The Adolescent in the Family, 1934) suggested that fathers needed to play a central role in promoting proper personality development and individual adjustment, tasks best accomplished in tolerant, nonauthoritarian, flexible families that put the emotional fulfillment and sex-role development of the children first.

By the 1930s, sociologists and psychologists like Lewis Terman and Catherine Miles (Sex and Personality, 1936) had worked out a theory of sex-role identity that persisted more or less unchanged until challenged by FEMINISM in the 1970s and 1980s. Rejecting instinct theory and drawing on Ernest Burgess's theory of the "unity of interacting personalities," academics as well as popular writers emphasized the importance of fathers to sex-role socialization. In a culture threatened by excessive maternal influence, fathers played a vital role in exhibiting proper conceptions of MASCULINITY to their sons and daughters. This task could not begin too early or end too late: infants and toddlers needed a masculine presence, but so too did teenagers. If all went well, sons would grow up to exhibit proper masculine characteristics and daughters would know just what traits to look for in a husband. It was a theory of elegant simplicity and maintained a tenacious hold on American culture.

The "new fatherhood" of the 1920s and 1930s quickly became linked to a therapeutic culture heavily dependent upon expert advice and parent education. Common sense was no longer enough: from the 1920s to the present, a host of books, workshops, radio shows, advice columns, and parent edu-

cation programs have sought, with limited success, to make men into more capable, better informed fathers. Men, especially middle-class men, took advantage of some of these opportunities. Survey data from the late 1920s and early 1930s revealed that middle-class men were far more likely than those from the working class to read child-rearing advice, to listen to radio shows on child-care, and to join a child-study group. Such efforts, insisted experts like Sidonie M. Gruenberg, director of the Child Study Association of America, not only enhanced the personality development of children but redounded to the benefit of fathers as well. Men who spent time with their offspring opened up their more nurturing sides and found that there was more to life than catching the morning commuter train. Fatherhood was well on its way to becoming a "growth experience," a destination reached in the heady therapeutic climate of the 1970s and 1980s.

Yet reaching this destination was, and continues to be, fraught with hardship. With breadwinning a full-time job and a crucial element in men's identity, those who failed found that the consequences could be devastating. The poignant testimonials left by men in the 1930s suggest the high psychic costs of "breadlosing." Men without work blamed themselves for their failures and suffered acute guilt for the hardships they caused their wives and children. Their children, in turn, often lost respect for their fathers and faulted them for their inability to find work.

But even men who succeeded as breadwinners found father–child companionship elusive. As children's employment became less common, youngsters became part of a growing peer culture with standards and values often at odds with those of their parents. Whether it was the working-class immigrant father who watched his son go off to the Rialto Theater or the middle-class father who handed the roadster's keys to his teenage son or daughter, men often witnessed the tug of the YOUTH culture on the arm of their offspring. Likewise, the same culture that called men to the home also extolled the liberating possibilities of consumption. Men's very success as breadwinners required that they meet an ever-rising standard of living characterized by segmented consumption patterns. In the consumer culture of the twentieth century, children needed and wanted both love and money. Mothers supplied healthy doses of the former, while fathers found their responsibilities increasingly driven to the latter. Breadwinning and companionship were thus constantly at odds, a fact that contributed mightily to the alienation between fathers and children.

For most of this century, calls for greater fatherly

involvement in family life did not challenge in any sustained way the gender-based division of labor that made breadwinners of fathers and child-rearers of women. Men's involvement with children was important, but it was a "gift" men made to their children and not part of a restructured conception of manhood that required involvement in the less glamorous aspects of child-rearing. In asking that men be companions and buddies of their children, not co-parents, this message was apolitical, nonfeminist, and dependent upon the good intentions of men. It took more profound changes in American economic life and culture to change fatherhood significantly, and the two changes that finally did so were the reorganization of the household economy and the emergence of feminism that occurred after World War II.

Although both the Great Depression and World War II prompted public debate about fatherhood—the former because it laid bare the psychological costs of breadlosing, the latter because it provoked discussion about the indispensability of fathers and the meaning of wartime sacrifice—the terms of the debate did not change significantly until after World War II. But as mothers steadily made their way into the workforce after 1950, men's claim to the privileges that came with sole breadwinning began to wane. After all, if mothers worked for wages outside the home, how could fathers legitimately avoid assuming more of the day-to-day care of the children? The second great engine of change was the reemergence of feminism in the 1960s. Modern feminists challenged the gender-based division of labor, questioned the belief that women were innately more nurturing than men, and insisted that men perform routine child-care. To feminists and their sympathizers, the male privileges and prerogatives that came with breadwinning seemed suspect in a world in which both mothers and fathers left the home each day to earn a living.

As fathers slowly lost their hold on the privilege, power, and responsibility that accompanied their monopoly on breadwinning, analysts of American culture have sought to understand the meaning of these changes. Self-help enthusiasts have made fatherhood into another form of therapy. "Wildmen" have searched for lost fathers by creating ritual spaces under the tutelage of poet Robert Bly. Conservatives have called for a reinvigoration of male breadwinning, while worrying about the implications of millions of children growing up in fatherless families. Feminists have brought attention to the "second shift," analyzed the politics of housework, and asked why women but not men reorder their lives to rear children. Some men resist, some beat on drums, and some have answered the feminist call and have made genuine efforts to become co-parents. What seems clear is that fatherhood has become politicized. Its meaning is no longer stable: superfather Ted Kramer in *Kramer vs. Kramer* shares cultural space with traditional breadwinners, "Deadbeat Dads," and single, absent, and gay fathers. The cultural coherence about fatherhood that once prevailed has been replaced by fragmentation and controversy.

ROBERT L. GRISWOLD

FURTHER READING

John Demos, "The Changing Faces of Fatherhood: a New Exploration in Family History," in Stanley H. Cath, Alan Gurwitt, and John Munder Ross, eds., *Father and Child: Developmental and Clinical Perspectives* (Boston: Little, Brown, 1982).

Robert L. Griswold, *Fatherhood in America: a History* (New York: Basic, 1993).

Joseph H. Pleck, "American Fathering in Historical Perspective," in Michael Kimmel, ed., *Changing Men: New Directions in Research on Men and Masculinity* (Newbury Park, Calif.: Sage, 1987).

E. Anthony Rotundo, "American Fatherhood: a Historical Perspective," *American Behavioral Scientist* 29 (Sept.–Oct. 1985): 7–25.

Faulkner, William (b. New Albany, Miss., Sept. 25, 1897; d. Byhalia, Miss., July 6, 1962).   Ever since 1950, the year he received the Nobel Prize for Literature, William Faulkner's reputation as one of America's foremost twentieth-century novelists has seemed secure. Literary critics have marveled at his productivity (22 novels and nearly 90 short stories, along with two published books of verse), his technical virtuosity, and his uncanny ability to capture and hold a reader's attention. Those who enter his fictional county of Yoknapatawpha rarely want to leave. Yet debate continues to rage about whether Faulkner was anything more than a skilled storyteller who had the good sense to tap into the rich oral tradition of his native South. Can one find any consistent meaning or message in his work, or any connection to the currents running through American thought during his lifetime? These are among the questions Faulkner scholars have been asking.

Faulkner himself carefully cultivated the image of the simple country bumpkin from rural Mississippi who received minimal schooling and never read much beyond the Bible and Shakespeare. In interviews and public talks he would refer to himself as a farmer, not a writer. To a certain extent, the first generation of Faulkner critics capitalized on this mythic self-presentation. Led by Cleanth Brooks, a southerner with close ties to the movement of SOUTHERN AGRARIANISM, scholars from the 1940s through the 1960s put forth a Faulkner who functioned as an authentic voice of southern tradition. Deeply rooted in village life and thus uncontaminated by the intellectual demimonde found in cities like New York, the creator of Yoknapatawpha, it was said, was at bottom a staunch moralist who championed the oldtime virtues of HONOR, personal heroism, religious faith, and COMMUNITY.

By the early 1970s, this initial view of Faulkner came under challenge for a variety of reasons. A prime factor was the magisterial biography by Joseph Blotner, published in 1974, which provided the first public glimpse of the complex realities of Faulkner's life. While it was true that Faulkner had grown up in the South, it was also the case that Oxford, Mississippi, was a university town with a more sophisticated literary and cultural atmosphere than the standard stereotype of the South would suggest. Most important, Faulkner read extensively, first on his own and then under the tutelage of his friend Phil Stone, a recent graduate of Yale College, who saw to it that Faulkner acquired a thorough background in both classical and modern literature. Close criticism of Faulkner's works confirmed the remarkable range of his learning, making it impossible any longer to depict him as an isolated rural original.

The new portrait of Faulkner that soon emerged from scholars such as John Irwin and Andre Bleikasten was that of a man who, far from subscribing to a few simple moral precepts, was rent by a series of powerful tensions. This Faulkner was caught, among other things, between an underlying loyalty to the aristocratic Old South and a commitment to a more up-to-date "New South" (whose nature was not always well defined). He was a racist and at the same time a racial liberal, a localist and a cosmopolitan, a traditionalist and a novelist who worked on the extreme edge of the avant-garde. The more investigators probed his masterpieces of the prewar era, including *The Sound and the Fury* (1929), *As I Lay Dying* (1929), *Light in August* (1932), *Absalom, Absalom!* (1935), and *Go Down, Moses* (1942), the more they discovered unresolvable paradoxes. The critic's task, then, became one of elucidating those underlying tensions, alerting the reader to the ambivalence that lay at the heart of Faulkner's consciousness.

It would be inaccurate to claim that we have entered a clearly delineated third phase of Faulkner scholarship. Rather, the past decade or so has witnessed the development of a number of divergent tendencies in making sense of Faulkner. Poststructuralist critics such as John T. Matthews and Richard C. Moreland have offered intricate analyses of Faulkner's language, while avoiding the effort to explain what the author actually intended to convey. Other scholars, including John N. Duvall and Minrose C. Gwin, have attempted to pin down Faulkner's attitudes toward race, class, and gender. As a rule, they have been impressed by how far ahead of his times he was on these issues, though they have also typically noted the way he continued to harbor less progressive views alongside his more advanced ones. For example, although he frequently exposed sexist stereotypes of women in a manner that late twentieth-century feminists would strongly approve, one can also find moments of misogyny in his work.

But perhaps the most important new approach in Faulkner scholarship has involved the effort to move beyond the puzzle of endless paradoxes by setting Faulkner within his intellectual context. One such approach views him as a man in the process of transition from the belief system of VICTORIANISM in which he was raised toward the brave new world of cultural MODERNISM that arrived in the South just as he began his career. In effect, this mode of interpretation posits not one Faulkner but two—a nineteenth-century self and a twentieth-century self competing within his mind for predominance, with neither ever fully winning out, but with a gradual, continuous shift toward the modernist self. Critics working along these lines, notably Donald M. Kartiganer, have also found in Faulkner's thought a well-developed existential philosophy that viewed life as a struggle against the inevitable tensions brought about by social and cultural change, with heroism measured by the degree to which individuals are willing directly to engage those tensions.

Whatever meanings may ultimately be ascribed to Faulkner's work, it seems safe to predict that this unlikely man of letters from the Deep South, who was initially written off as a cheap purveyor of sensationalism when he was not pronounced indecipherable, will continue to mesmerize many future generations of readers both in this country and abroad.

DANIEL J. SINGAL

See also SOUTHERN INTELLECTUAL HISTORY.

FURTHER READING

Andre Bleikasten, *The Ink of Melancholy: Faulkner's Novels from "The Sound and the Fury" to "Light in August"* (Bloomington: Indiana University Press, 1990).

Joseph Blotner, *Faulkner: a Biography*, 2 vols. (New York: Random House, 1974).

Cleanth Brooks, *William Faulkner: the Yoknapatawpha Country* (New Haven: Yale University Press, 1963).

Thadious M. Davis, *Faulkner's "Negro": Art and the Southern Context* (Baton Rouge: Louisiana State University Press, 1983).

Michael Grimwood, *Heart in Conflict: Faulkner's Struggles with Vocation* (Athens, Ga.,: University of Georgia Press, 1987).

John Irwin, *Doubling and Incest/Repetition and Revenge: a Speculative Reading of Faulkner* (Baltimore: Johns Hopkins University Press, 1975).

Donald M. Kartiganer, *The Fragile Thread: the Meaning of Form in Faulkner's Novels* (Amherst: University of Massachusetts Press, 1979).

Gary Lee Stonum, *Faulkner's Career: an Internal Literary History* (Ithaca: Cornell University Press, 1979).

femininity "Throughout history people have knocked their heads against the riddle of the nature of femininity," writes Freud in his vexing 1933 essay "Femininity," where he refuses to "describe what a woman is" in favor of "enquiring how she comes into being" (pp. 100, 103). In this refusal, Freud seems strangely in agreement with Simone de Beauvoir's later assertion that woman is made, not born—constituted, that is, by the narrative of her becoming. But the differences between Freud's and de Beauvoir's understanding of how woman "comes into being" are ultimately quite deep, revealing the chasm of sexual difference that feminism in the twentieth century, both in the U.S. and Europe, has simultaneously foregrounded and sought to heal. At issue is indeed the meaning of "woman" or, to be more precise, the cultural and ideological practices that narrate her becoming, that make claims on her body and translate those claims into a sacrosanct ontology: "femininity."

As the primary political discourse dedicated to unraveling the systemic logic of femininity as ontology, FEMINISM in twentieth-century America owes a debt, however contradictory, to the theoretical suppositions inaugurated by Freud and subsequently elaborated upon by his various feminist opponents on both sides of the Atlantic. (*See also* FREUDIANISM.) While by no means the only discourse feminism has grappled with, psychoanalysis nonetheless has been crucial in the American context, as evinced by the many theorists (Dorothy Dinnerstein, Shulamith Firestone, Kate Millet, Nancy Chodorow, Juliet Mitchell, Jane Gallop, and Judith Butler) who have engaged with it in the past 30 years to further the aims of feminism. But the impact of psychoanalysis for American feminism cannot be limited to a narrowly isolationist rendering, for the cross-nationality and interdisciplinary nature of feminism pressures the very logic of borders on which concepts of "nation," like sexual difference, dwell. To frame "femininity" through a reading of de Beauvoir's rethinking of Freud excavates the primal scene of gender instruction in twentieth-century Western culture.

While Freud was right, in his own way, to forgo describing "what a woman is," those embodied under the sign "women," whether feminist or not, have much at stake in the transitivity of the verb "is." For, as de Beauvoir points out, what always lurks behind the linguistic relation that gives woman her meaning, that being in whose reference she can be said to exist, is man. From this perspective, Freud's refusal to describe can be read as an attempt to ward off his masculine privilege, and yet, one must recognize the declination of privilege as the mark of privilege itself. For de Beauvoir, on the other hand, there is nowhere else to begin: "first we must ask: what is a woman?" (p. xv). The answer to this question, she suggests, lies in distinguishing between biological sex (the female) and social GENDER (the feminine), and it is femininity that serves as the governing term for linking the two. "Every female human being is not necessarily a woman; to be so considered she must share in that mysterious . . . reality known as femininity" (p. xvi). But what comprises this reality? What is the content of femininity that ushers the human female into feminine being? What, in short, is woman?

For Freud, she is the culmination of a developmental process tied to sexuality and organized within the framework of the nuclear family. Here, the possibilities of woman begin with the little girl who, like the boy, moves through a series of libidinal phases, initially the oral and anal, followed ultimately by the genital (a.k.a. the phallic), where boys "derive pleasurable sensations from their small penis" while girls "do the same thing with their still smaller clitoris" (p. 104). In time, however, the girl's erotogenic zone must shift away from the "penis-equivalent" to the "truly feminine vagina," a shift described by Freud as "the change to femininity" (p. 104). For the boy, of course, it is a straightforward trajectory from infantile masturbation to sexual maturity, since the penis remains the center of his sexuality. But "a girl's development is burdened" by the necessity of translating pleasure from the clitoris to the vagina (p. 104). And it is burdened as well by the girl's need to transfer her initial identification and erotic attachment from the mother to the paternal figure. In Freud's narrative, this transformation is accomplished through the castration complex, where the girl's simultaneous recognition of her own and her mother's castration makes possible the necessary rerouting of desire from clitoris to vagina and from mother to father. Penis envy, in short, initiates and sustains the transition to femininity.

Because of his conceptualization of the castration

complex as engineering the libidinal shift from clitoris, that "atrophied" (p. 100) penis, to the feminine vagina, the highly influential French feminist theorist Luce Irigaray (a psychoanalyst herself) has argued, "Freud does not see *two sexes*.... The 'feminine' is always ... the other side of the sex that alone holds a monopoly on value: the male sex" (p. 69). His burdened narrative of woman's becoming, caught in a developmental story premised on masculine sexuality, thus turns always toward an implicit conclusion: woman is simply "not man." As such, she can only regard herself as a mutilated and alienated version of the primary form. As Kate Millett writes, Freud's "entire psychology of women ... is built upon an original tragic experience—born female" (p. 254).

But what convinces woman of man's sexual supremacy, of her own arresting lack? In the Freudian story, it is simply the sight of male genitals: girls "at once notice the difference and, it must be admitted, its significance too" (p. 110). De Beauvoir nearly two decades later retorts, "this outgrowth, this little rod of flesh can in itself inspire [girls] only with indifference, or even disgust" (p. 46). And Millett in 1970 queries, "why is the girl instantly struck by the proposition that bigger is better? Might she just as easily ... imagine the penis as an excrescence and take her own body as norm?" (p. 256). To the extent that Freud grounds his theory of femininity on this pivotal visible moment, on the girl's instantly assumed inferiority, one can only ask, as do de Beauvoir and Millett, whose desire has been invested in the girl's looking? Is Freud's narrative of femininity's emergence not a lovely tale of displacement, a way of assigning to women masculine obsessions with sexual diminishment, thereby affirming through the very narrativization of woman the phallus's social and symbolic priority?

For feminist thinkers in the latter part of the twentieth century, Freud's psychoanalytical excursion serves as just such a scene of negative instruction, revealing "the nature of femininity" to be the phantasm of a masculine imaginary, a discursive production that locates the social, economic, and political articulations of masculine supremacy in the realm of woman's sexual and psychical development. As de Beauvoir explains, "the phallus assumes such worth as it does because it symbolizes a dominance that is exercised in other domains" (p. 54). The relations of domination that she notes, those involving law, education, religion, politics, as well as the more abstract realm of ideology, far exceed the Freudian mythology of the penis's natural, visible superiority. As such, the personality traits associated with femininity—

narcissism, envy, vanity, shame, instinctuality—are not immutable qualities emanating from an essential feminine core, but elements of an elaborate signification system whereby sexual differences simultaneously embody and sanction the logic of patriarchal organization. While Freud is right that femininity, as the process of woman's becoming, entails an internalization of masculine supremacy, it is only through a refusal to posit that supremacy as self-evident and natural that any critical understanding of femininity can be forged.

But the knowledge that women are quite literally constituted in service to masculine representations does little to explain either their acquiescence to this becoming or, indeed, their often vigilant defense of it. Ironically, early feminist investigations into femininity often reproduced, albeit in a different register, a passive female subject reminiscent of Freudian theory by positing women as, in all cases, unwitting victims of a coercive social order. Such a reading certainly failed to explain the feminist, who was very much in active resistance to femininity, and it denied as well the complicated processes in which power is articulated within the social. As bell hooks and other African American feminists have pointed out, any claim for women's common victimization failed to recognize the differences among women based on race and class—differences that have important effects for the analysis of gender. Contemporary feminist theory has thus found it necessary to understand that while the category of woman is constructed within masculine narratives of desire, women are nonetheless —and to varying degrees—agents within the historicizing processes of their own socialization. They act in ways that move complexly along axes of compliance and resistance to the dominant requirements of femininity. And quite importantly, they may even garner the accroutrements of social power (wealth and prestige) by mobilizing those aspects of femininity, such as the sexualization of the BODY, that feminism once saw women only as victims of.

In the 1987 *Female Sexualization*, a key text in Women's Studies courses in the United States, a collective of German feminists explores the self-constructed nature of femininity by focusing on the cultivation of the body that accompanies, in culturally differentiated patterns, every female's process of feminine becoming. Autobiographical narratives explore the ways various aspects of the body not usually thought of as sexual are indeed sexualized by the discourse of sexual difference, including hair, legs, height, stomach, weight, and posture. In understanding feminine identity to be culturally organized around the body, the collective finds the social conventions of femininity "anchored within ourselves," where a culturally induced "preoccupation with self-examination" polices the woman's psychical relationship to her body and its sexualization (p. 161). Importantly, the ideals of femininity are not historically constant, but mutable, thereby necessitating repeated performance. In this sense, the production of femininity is a process of ceaseless becoming.

But it is also a process, the German feminists contend, that can be contested, though they hesitate to offer any simple or singular program on which one can model femininity's dissolution. Instead, they complete their exploration with a catalogue of political aims: to create a new politics of the body where it is not "the means and also the end of our socialization," where women can "live a life of resistance," can "perceive in different ways" (p. 283). In this, they are in league with a great many American feminists who desire not to escape the body, but to disrupt and undo the psychical violence underlying femininity's corporeal regime. The radically utopian hope for the end of femininity carries with it the necessary and not to be lamented end of Freud's "woman" as well.

ROBYN WIEGMAN

FURTHER READING
Judith Butler, *Gender Trouble: Feminism and the Subversion of Identity* (New York: Routledge, 1990).
Nancy Chodorow, *The Reproduction of Mothering: Psychoanalysis and the Sociology of Gender* (Berkeley: University of California Press, 1978).
Simone de Beauvoir, *The Second Sex* (1949, New York: Random House, 1974).
Sigmund Freud, "Femininity," in *New Introductory Lectures on Psychoanalysis* (1933; New York: Norton, 1965).
Frigga Haug, ed., *Female Sexualization* (London: Verso, 1987).
bell hooks, *Feminist Theory: From Margin to Center* (Boston: South End Press, 1984).
Luce Irigaray, *This Sex Which Is Not One* (1977; Ithaca: Cornell University Press, 1985).
Kate Millett, *Sexual Politics* (New York: Ballantine Books, 1970).
Juliet Mitchell, *Psychoanalysis and Feminism* (London: Allen Lane, 1974).

feminism   What unites feminists, who have always disagreed among themselves on many issues, is their opposition to sexual hierarchy. One's sex, they have insisted, must be allowed to make a difference only in those arenas of life where it really does make a difference. Faced with a society that has gratuitously maintained and even deepened the sway of sexual difference, thus restricting women's options and experiences, feminists have claimed for women a range of possibilities bounded only by the limitations of their fully human existence.

While twentieth-century feminists look back to eighteenth- and nineteenth-century predecessors for inspiration, their concerns have been somewhat different from those of earlier activists, and the word "feminism," fittingly, is a twentieth-century creation. Beginning in the 1840s, the "woman movement" sought to establish women's legal and economic existence. Opposing the principle of coverture, which declared a married woman dead in the law, activists demanded the civil abilities to earn money, control property, and make contracts. In later decades, women fought for a wide range of reforms, including the freedom to seek an education and to practice a profession, the right to vote, the power to dissolve an abusive marriage, the liberty of wearing more comfortable and healthful clothing, and the right to refuse sexual contact and unwilling motherhood. The word "feminism" emerged in the 1910s, when many of these basic goals had been achieved (albeit often in limited form) and a few women had gained significant power in government and the professions. The word met a need: just a few years after its introduction, it was used widely to signify a new sense of women's ambitions, aspirations, and rebelliousness. Its denotation, never tightly circumscribed, was less significant than its connotations. As Nancy Cott has pointed out, feminism avoided the uniform, archetypal idea of "woman" typical of the "woman movement" and favored a more multiplicitous vision of women's lives and potentials. Sharing a sense of optimism and open horizons, these early feminists embraced the "double aims" of celebrating women's individuality while promoting women's solidarity, and affirming women's equality with men while cherishing women's sexual difference (p. 50).

Since the 1960s, feminism has flowered into a many-branched movement that defies summary or taxonomy. Even a superficial survey reveals a huge variety of feminisms: liberal feminism, socialist feminism, radical feminism, black or womanist feminism, lesbian feminism, ecofeminism, cultural feminism, separatist feminism, Marxist feminism, etc. The differences among these perspectives are profound, but the various viewpoints are bound together by their faith that society can improve and their belief that reshaping the relations between women and men as groups is central to that improvement. Feminist thought, therefore, is deeply tied to feminist activism. Much feminist thought has focused on identifying and analyzing the forces that have created and altered the sexual status quo. In this effort, feminists have given particular attention to five areas of social life and ideology: economics, motherhood, sexuality, religion, and ideas about nature.

According to many feminists, economic structures are at the base of women's subordination. From the starvation wages paid to nineteenth-century "factory girls," to the contemporary sweatshops operated by multinationals in the Third World, and to the recent "feminization of poverty" and the continuing patterns of job segregation and wage and salary differentials in the United States, gender-based economic practices have persistently and systematically exploited women. Many feminist activists have therefore focused on equalizing women's access to well-paid employment, improving the pay and working conditions of traditionally female occupations, and changing the surrounding structures (such as educational discrimination, lack of child-care, and cultural expectations) that have made women economically vulnerable. Some have adopted a more-or-less Marxian analysis of the expropriation of labor to explain women's longstanding lot of hard work and economic marginality. More recently, feminists such as bell hooks have linked sexual and racial oppression, arguing that the intersection of the two is peculiarly effective in maintaining a privileged caste. While feminists disagree about the degree of reorganization needed—from those who seek a gender-blind equal access to existing institutions, to those who insist that equality is unattainable in a profit-driven capitalist system—most believe that women require and deserve better access to economic resources.

Many feminists also point to the heavy toll exacted upon women by the cultural expectation that they will take primary responsibility for child-rearing. While pregnancy and breast-feeding occupy at most two years per child in modern Western societies, the expectation that mothers will be more involved than fathers in child-rearing continues for many more years of the child's life. Women are expected to organize their lives around parenting responsibilities, and to bear the double burden of domestic and paid work if they are employed outside the home. In *The Dialectic of Sex* (1970), Shulamith Firestone argued that women cannot be fully liberated until technology frees them from the biological burdens of pregnancy and childbirth. Most feminists, however, believe that cultural changes can minimize the social penalties of MOTHERHOOD by some combination of paternal involvement in parenting, quality child-care outside the home, flexible work arrangements, and a financial safety net that makes individual mothers of young children less dependent on, and therefore less vulnerable to, individual men. If, as Nancy Chodorow has argued, the childhood experience of being cared for by adults of only one sex has a profound impact on human psychology, such changes

would have far-reaching social and cultural effects. (*See also* FATHERHOOD.)

Other feminists insist that sexual inequality is so deeply embedded in the cultural fashioning of sexuality that economic or child-rearing reforms will have only minor effects. While the overt violence of rape, they argue, is very effective at limiting and punishing women's actions, rape is only an extreme manifestation of a system that ensures women's sexual availability to men on men's terms. Women are psychologically manipulated to believe that their purpose is to please men, kept economically dependent in order to enforce their compliance (as wives or prostitutes), and punished by social ostracism or physical violence if they rebel. The influential 1980 article by ADRIENNE RICH, "Compulsory Heterosexuality and Lesbian Existence" (reprinted in her *Blood, Bread, and Poetry*, 1986), argued that women's bonds with other women have been systematically destroyed in order to enforce women's allegiance to individual men and the patriarchal order. Feminists, Rich believes, should therefore reaffirm a "lesbian continuum" of female love and loyalty, which includes but is not limited to lesbian sexuality. Catherine MacKinnon further argues that contemporary women can never experience sexuality outside the system of men's sexual objectification of women and women's learned pleasure in that objectification. Since pornography is a primary means of perpetuating a sexual ideology that is intrinsically dehumanizing, degrading, and violent to women, its eradication, in her view, is basic to any feminist progress. Other feminists fear, however, that even antipornography legislation based on civil rights arguments, as MacKinnon and Andrea Dworkin propose, will be used to silence women's already nascent but still threatened explorations of their own sexuality.

Some feminists argue that the fundamental source of gender inequality lies not in particular economic and social arrangements, but in deeper cosmological beliefs that devalue femaleness. Pointing to the exclusively male language used to describe the divine and the numerous biblical texts that diminish women, many feminists hold that sexism has shaped the core of Judaic and Christian traditions. Judith Plaskow, for example, argues in *Sex, Sin, and Grace* (1980) that women's experience has been excluded from theological thinking. Male theologians such as REINHOLD NIEBUHR typically see pride as "man's" fundamental sin. But while pride may be the preeminent sin of men, Plaskow suggests, self-abnegation may be the primary sin of women. Some feminists have concluded that a new religious vision is necessary. As Carol Christ argues in her article titled "Why Women

Need the Goddess," the predispositions and motivations established by patriarchal religions cannot be eradicated by women's refusal to endorse them. Rather, they must be replaced by equally rich and satisfying symbolic systems that affirm women's spiritual and social power. Other feminists have sought to reshape their traditions from within by turning to liberating principles found in Jesus's ministry, in the Torah, or in their experience of religious communities. Many have joined women's religious groups that articulate often radical critiques of their traditions while remaining within those traditions. Why, they ask, should women cede to men all the accumulated wealth, power, and authority of religious institutions? These varied analyses and activities reflect a basic belief that social reforms, while necessary, will be piecemeal palliatives unless both women and men experience a spiritual transformation in their understandings of themselves and the world.

Taking a more secular, but equally comprehensive, approach, some feminists point to ideas about nature as the ideological basis for women's subordination. NATURE, in Western society, is usually construed as static, unchanging, and unchangeable. Women are seen as "closer to nature" because of their menstrual cycles and their capacity to give birth: women, it is asserted, are more connected to their bodies than men are. Women must therefore devote their time and energy to the physicality of reproduction, while men are more free for cultural creation. Because they are supposedly "natural," the biological differences between women and men are used to justify a wide range of differences in behaviors and practices. Women, for example, are "naturally" nurturant and affectionate, while men are "naturally" aggressive and violent. Since the 1970s, feminists have challenged this naturalization of "sex difference" by distinguishing between sex, which is a relatively small chromosomal and phenotypic dimorphism, and GENDER, which is the enormously significant social construction of sex. More recent writings, however, have argued that this distinction obscures the amount of social construction inherent in what we see as biological. Biology, Ruth Hubbard points out, is affected by many cultural factors, including exercise, nutrition, and our efforts to adjust widely varying body types to fit normative female and male images. Donna Haraway has explored how representations of nature not only inscribe systems of domination based on sex, but also naturalize race, class, sexuality, family, and colonialism. Ecofeminists argue that the equation between nature and femaleness has had disastrous effects for nature: if the earth is our mother, then our growing ecological crisis reflects our belief that we can endlessly exploit anything that is encoded female. Many feminists now argue that we must stop expecting nature to provide norms or justifications for human behavior.

Some feminists, however, believe that natural differences between women and men do exist, and that the proper response to those differences is to recognize and value women's "different voice." Describing differences in women's and men's moral thinking, Carol Gilligan suggests that society has much to gain by embracing women's ethic of care and responsibility. While Gilligan herself seems to think that sexual differences originate in the psychodynamics of a young child's relationship with a female caretaker, the more deterministic strains in her writing encourage many of her readers to infer that these differences actually reflect male and female nature.

Since the 1970s all of these types of feminist thinking have generated a huge literature and helped shape new social patterns and habits. Ironically, however, feminists in the 1990s are forced to confront the question of whether feminism is becoming an anachronism. As in the 1920s, a younger generation of women has grown up with the belief that since women's options are far less restricted than they used to be, militance on gender issues is passé. Many have adopted the "postfeminist" stance that feminism has achieved its goals and has little further to contribute. Rather than dividing society into female and male components, they suggest, one should see the human race as crisscrossed by a multitude of overlapping social groupings and emphasize the potency and idiosyncrasy of individuals.

The question of addressing multiple differences is indeed one of the most significant challenges facing feminism today. Feminist responses to this increasing awareness of individual and group variation have fallen into two broad categories. On the one hand, feminists have underlined the ways in which all women are vulnerable simply because they are female. The resulting focus on rape, incest, sexual harassment, involuntary pregnancy, and women's health issues highlights the intersections between female bodies and systems of power (*see also* ABORTION). On the other hand, feminists have sought a wider understanding of differences among women and among men. While the second wave of the feminist movement in the 1960s and 1970s did largely emerge among white, heterosexual, middle-class women, and contained a resultant measure of racism, homophobia, and class bias, many feminist scholars and activists have come to consider a critique of racism, compulsory heterosexuality, economic exploitation, and/or colonialism to be an intrinsic part of a feminist agenda. Both types of response represent an attempt to place sex/gender oppression in a fuller perspective on human experience, while retaining a commitment to improving all women's lives. The ongoing debates about the meanings and implications of feminism's quest for women's equality and dignity—debates taking place not just among self-declared feminists, but also in innumerable kitchens, workplaces, legislatures, and bedrooms—indicate that feminism, for all its reexaminings, continues to be a powerful and pervasive influence in American life.

LORI J. KENSCHAFT

See also FEMINIST JURISPRUDENCE; WOMEN'S RIGHTS.

FURTHER READING

Nancy Chodorow, *The Reproduction of Mothering* (Berkeley: University of California Press, 1978).

Carol P. Christ, "Why Women Need the Goddess: Phenomenological, Psychological, and Political Reflections," in Carol P. Christ and Judith Plaskow, eds., *Womanspirit Rising: a Feminist Reader in Religion* (San Francisco: Harper and Row, 1979).

Nancy F. Cott, *The Grounding of Modern Feminism* (New Haven: Yale University Press, 1987).

Carol Gilligan, *In a Different Voice* (Cambridge: Harvard University Press, 1982).

Donna Haraway, *Primate Visions: Gender, Race, and Nature in the World of Modern Science* (New York: Routledge, 1989).

bell hooks, *Feminist Theory: From Margin to Center* (Boston: South End Press, 1984).

Ruth Hubbard, *The Politics of Women's Biology* (New Brunswick: Rutgers University Press, 1990).

Catherine A. MacKinnon, *Feminism Unmodified* (Cambridge: Harvard University Press, 1987).

feminist jurisprudence A branch of feminist theory within the law, this is one of the interdisciplinary fields that grew up in legal scholarship in the 1980s together with LAW AND ECONOMICS, CRITICAL LEGAL STUDIES, and CRITICAL RACE THEORY. Notable accomplishments in feminist jurisprudence include the principle that in similar situations women should be treated the same as men; that sexual harassment that creates a hostile work environment violates federal discrimination law; and that women who kill their batterers may claim self-defense in certain circumstances where such claims traditionally would be prohibited.

The first round of feminist theory within the LAW posed constitutional challenges to statutes that treated women differently from similarly situated men. A key player was Ruth Bader Ginsberg, now a Supreme Court Justice, who headed the American Civil Liberties Union's Women's Rights Project from 1972 to 1980. In cases that challenged traditional stereotypes and advocated gender neutrality, ACLU litigation established that distinctions based on GENDER would be subjected to heightened constitutional scrutiny. A typical case involved a young widower who wanted to stay home to care for his child, but was denied Social Security survivor's benefits, which at the time were available only to widows. The Supreme Court held that this practice violated equal protection. In other cases, the ACLU challenged sex distinctions relating to military benefits, disability programs, administration of decedents' estates, parental support obligations, as well as other traditionally gender-based practices.

The ACLU "equality" approach was shrewdly designed to frame women's issues in ways most easily heard within the American constitutional tradition. The approach also reflected the life experience of Ruth Bader Ginsberg's generation. Ginsberg herself provides a preeminent example. At the top of her class at Harvard Law School and then at Columbia Law School, she was turned down for a Supreme Court clerkship by FELIX FRANKFURTER, who said he was not ready to take on a woman; ultimately no law firm offered her a position. Her experience suggested that women's disadvantage could be remedied simply by treating women the same as men—an approach reflected in her belief (restated during her Supreme Court confirmation hearings) that a person's sex is almost never a relevant consideration.

Issues involving pregnancy benefits presented a challenge for ACLU feminists because they involved "real" sex difference rather than irrational distinctions based on sex. The conceptual challenge of pregnancy came to a head in three cases involving pregnancy benefits, *Geduldig v. Aiello*, *General Electric v. Gilbert*, and *California Federal Savings & Loan Association v. Guerra* (*CalFed*). *Geduldig* and *Gilbert* both involved benefits plans that covered all common disabilities except pregnancy; in each case, the Supreme Court held that the programs did not discriminate against women because the relevant distinction was not drawn on the basis of gender, but rather (to quote *Geduldig*) between "pregnant women and nonpregnant persons." Congress responded in 1978 by passing the Pregnancy Discrimination Act (PDA), which required that pregnant workers be treated the same as other workers. The *CalFed* case arose when an employer challenged a California statute that mandated leave and reinstatement for pregnant workers, claiming that it violated the PDA.

CalFed proved a divisive case for feminists. The ACLU contingent, notably Wendy Webster Williams, opposed "special treatment" and argued that the PDA required that men and women be treated the same. Other feminists supported the California law. Some (notably Herma Hill Kay and Sylvia Law) argued that pregnancy was one of the few "real" differences between men and women. Others (notably Christine Littleton) argued that work places are designed around the life patterns of men, so that giving women so-called "special" treatment was the only path to true EQUALITY.

Widespread dissatisfaction with the ACLU position in *CalFed* converged with the growth of a new brand of FEMINISM, often called "difference" feminism (in contrast with ACLU feminism, often called "sameness" or "equality" feminism). Its single most influential source in the 1980s was the work of developmental psychologist Carol Gilligan, whose *In a Different Voice* (1982) argued that women have a different style of moral reasoning than men. Whereas men focus on a hierarchy of RIGHTS, Gilligan argued, women focus on a web of relationships; whereas men value self-development and self-interest, women value an implicit norm of selflessness.

In a Different Voice made two distinct, and fundamentally incompatible, arguments. In some passages, Gilligan argued the ACLU line that the "different voice" and the mainstream voice both constrained human potential and both needed changing. This was not the message picked up in the tremendous surge of popularity surrounding Gilligan in the 1980s. Gilligan's followers focused on her other message: women's "different voice" represented an ideal toward which society should strive. This (predominant) strain of "different-voice" feminism was a modernized version of the ideology of DOMESTICITY, which described women as the selfless guardians of a superior morality that could save society from the aggressive, competitive, hierarchical and self-interested norms of modern capitalism.

Feminist legal scholars applied this activist strain of domesticity to the law. In "Excluded Voices," published in the *University of Miami Law Review* in 1987, Carrie Menkel-Meadow argued that women seek justice through healing and empathy, and hence often prefer alternative dispute resolution to combative litigation. In "Jurisprudence and Gender," which appeared in the *University of Chicago Law Review* in 1988, Robin West posited that women are "connected" to others, while men (and the ideology of LIBERALISM) celebrate separateness; she argued that women's approach could transform the basic liberal structure of the law. In "Feminist (Re)Torts," published in the *Duke Law Journal* in 1990, Leslie Bender examined how tort law can be changed to emphasize the values of human interdependence, COMMUNITY, and caregiving.

What *CalFed* was to ACLU feminism, *Equal Employment Opportunity Commission v. Sears, Roebuck and Co.* was to different voice feminism. *Sears* was a sex discrimination suit in which the EEOC charged Sears, Roebuck with discrimination against women. The EEOC pointed to statistics showing that women were underrepresented in commission sales positions that paid roughly twice as much as the noncommission sales jobs in which women predominated (Schultz, p. 1752). Sears, which won the case, argued that the paucity of women in commission sales was due not to discrimination, but to women's lack of interest; women preferred the friendly atmosphere of noncommission sales and disliked the "dog-eat-dog" competition of commission sales. Sears cited Gilligan's work and that of historians of women (as well as other studies) to support its image of women as focused on relationships at home and at work, and averse to competition and other supposedly "male" values.

Sears prompted a bitter and agonized reassessment of different-voice feminism by both legal feminists and historians of women. Whereas in the early 1980s few articles criticizing Gilligan appeared in law reviews, recently that has changed. Different voice feminism remains a potent influence in feminist jurisprudence, but today the antiessentialist critique presents an important challenge to its sweeping claims about women in general.

Both the *CalFed* controversy and the *Sears* controversy are commonly lumped together under the rubric of the "sameness/difference debate." This terminology is misleading, however, since "sameness" feminists never pretended that men and women are the same. To do so, they would have had to deny the existence of gender, whereas the most basic belief of ACLU feminism is that women have been disadvantaged by sex role stereotyping. The term "difference feminism" is confusing for a different reason. It seems to lump together "different-voice" feminists with a diverse group of feminists who reject the "sameness" strategy, and supported the California statute in *CalFed*, but do not accept Gilligan's description of the "different voice."

A second major strain in feminist jurisprudence is the work of Catharine MacKinnon. Whereas Gilligan carries on the tradition of cultural feminism, MacKinnon carries on the radical feminist tradition. MacKinnon starts from a Marxist model, with its central focus on power differentials, and substitutes sex for Marx's emphasis on the relations of production: "sexuality is to feminism," she writes, "what work is to Marxism" (p. 48). Her image of sexuality as the locus of powerlessness and victimization accurately reflects the experience of some women, but her bleak imagery of heterosexual intercourse as akin to rape (because women are so disempowered by the conditions of patriarchy they are incapable of true consent) leaves many women shaken, insulted, or simply persuaded that MacKinnon misunderstands the character of their lives.

MacKinnon's analysis of sexuality led to her advocacy (with Andrea Dworkin) of an ordinance giving women a cause of action for damages against anyone who produces, distributes, or sells pornography. The pornography ordinance, adopted in Minneapolis but later struck down as an unconstitutional attempt to limit free speech, rested on several assumptions: that the construction of sexuality is the key to women's oppression, that pornography plays a central role in the construction of sexuality, and that pornography depicts and incites violence against women. The pornography ordinance held little appeal to ACLU feminists, who vigorously opposed it as unconstitutional, and it remains very controversial; the Feminist Anti-Censorship Task Force, a diverse group of feminists, united against it. Some critics view the pornography ordinance as an unholy alliance with conservative forces, reminiscent of the female moral reform campaigns of the nineteenth century, which they view with distaste. Many feminists object that the ordinance encapsulates a repressive view of sex at odds with their own view of sexuality as a locus of free experimentation and self-expression. (*See also* OBSCENITY.)

By the late 1980s the "antiessentialist" critique swept feminist theory both inside and outside the law. The critique began experientially, as lesbians and women of color articulated their sense that feminism ignored their experiences. The main contention of the critique was that traditional feminism assumed an "essential woman" who was white, straight, and professional-middle class.

Both MacKinnon and Gilligan were vulnerable to the antiessentialist critique because of their confident assertions about "women's voice" or "women's point of view." In an influential article Angela Harris argued that "MacKinnon rediscovers white womanhood and introduces it as universal truth" (p. 592). Harris pointed out how MacKinnon's analysis of rape left out the experience of black women, whose response to rape draws on the history of free sexual access to black women, and on the history of rape charges used to justify racial terrorism against black men. This criticism joined critiques from lesbian feminists, notably Patricia Cain, who argued that feminists have glossed over the lesbian experience. Antiessentialism also gave ACLU feminists and others a new language in which to challenge Gilligan's "dif-

ferent voice," as feminists became (as they had been in the 1970s) instinctively suspicious of claims about "all women."

By the early 1990s, feminist jurisprudence had become an established field, heralded as one of the most vibrant areas of feminist theory. Not only do law schools increasingly offer courses treating feminist issues; perspectives from feminist jurisprudence are wending their way slowly into mainstream law courses such as family law, torts, contracts, constitutional law, civil procedure and property. Yet questions remain about the depth and effectiveness of the feminist challenge. The popular media often present Gilligan's defense of the norms of traditional FEMININITY as further evidence that domestic gender ideology represents women's natural "voice." And MacKinnon's voice of feminist anger is at once her greatest strength and her greatest weakness. Inspiring to many, particularly to abused women, MacKinnon's white-hot rhetoric may reinforce for others the uneasy feeling that "I believe in equal rights, but I'm not a feminist." The growing interest in the intersection of feminism and PRAGMATISM, exemplified in the work of such scholars as Margaret Jane Radin, may help reframe feminist arguments to avoid both of these pitfalls.

JOAN WILLIAMS

FURTHER READING

Katherine T. Bartlett and Rosanne Kennedy, eds., *Feminist Legal Theory: Readings in Law and Gender* (Boulder: Westview, 1991).

Patricia A. Cain, "Feminist Jurisprudence: Grounding the Theories," *Berkeley Women's Law Journal* 2 (1988): 191–214.

Paul M. George and Susan McGlamery, "Women and Legal Scholarship: a Bibliography," *Iowa Law Review* 77 (1991): 87–177.

Angela P. Harris, "Race and Essentialism in Feminist Legal Theory," *Stanford Law Review* 42 (1990): 581–616.

Catharine A. MacKinnon, *Feminism Unmodified: Discourses on Life and Law* (Cambridge: Harvard University Press, 1987).

Vicki Schultz, "Telling Stories about Women and Work: Judicial Interpretations of Sex Segregation in the Workplace in Title VII Cases Raising the Lack of Interest Argument," *Harvard Law Review* 103 (1990): 1749–843.

Patricia Smith, ed., *Feminist Jurisprudence* (New York: Oxford University Press, 1993).

Joan Williams, "Domesticity as the Dangerous Supplement of Liberalism," *Journal of Women's History* 2 (1991): 69–88.

Field, David Dudley (b. Haddam, Conn., Feb. 13, 1805; d. New York, N.Y., Apr. 13, 1894).   Lawyer. Field was the hero of the late nineteenth-century legal codification movement, which sought to replace the chaos of the common law with simpler comprehensive codes. Spurred by the success of his Code of Civil Procedure, adopted in whole or in part by states across the country, Field drafted a series of criminal, civil, penal, and political codes. He also sought to standardize court procedures and envisioned a system of international law. Given the diversity of American local and state laws, however, and the reluctance of judges and lawyers to yield authority to legislatures, Field's proposed codification schemes met with less success in substantive than in procedural law.

FURTHER READING

David Van Ed, *David Dudley Field and the Reconstruction of the Law* (New York: Garland, 1986).

Finney, Charles Grandison (b. Warren, Conn., Aug 29, 1792; d. Oberlin, Ohio, Aug. 16, 1875). Clergyman. A leading revivalist and liberal religionist, Finney was President of Oberlin College (1851–66). Rejecting the Calvinist doctrine that God preordains human destiny, Finney asserted that people can choose to be converted and saved. Revivals are not a miracle of God's grace, but a predictable result of human techniques. Sin is avoidable and sanctification humanly possible. Finney insisted, however, that believers exhibit moral commitment after conversion. He thus helped spur the growth of abolitionism, temperance, and other reform movements. His writings include *Lectures on Revivals* (1835) and *Lectures on Systematic Theology* (1847).

See also LIBERAL PROTESTANTISM.

FURTHER READING

Keith Hardman, *Charles Grandison Finney, 1792–1875: Revivalist and Reformer* (Syracuse: Syracuse University Press, 1987).

Fisher, Irving (b. Saugerties, N.Y., Feb. 27, 1867; d. New Haven, Conn., Apr. 29, 1947). Economist. Author of numerous books, including *The Purchasing Power of Money* (1911), Fisher argued that economic problems reflect money's fluctuating purchasing power. Credit availability exaggerates expansions and contractions in the money supply, thus causing booms and busts. Government should manage the gold content of currency to create a "compensated dollar" that stabilizes purchasing power without fixing individual prices. Believing that economists should seek useful knowledge that serves the public good, Fisher also promoted health reforms, conservation, eugenics, prohibition, and the League of Nations.

FURTHER READING

Robert Loring Allen, *Irving Fisher: a Biography* (Cambridge: Blackwell, 1993).

Fiske, John (b. Hartford, Conn., Mar. 30, 1842; d. Gloucester, Mass., July 4, 1901). Historian and philosopher. Fiske combined a Spencerian understanding of natural selection and a progressive theistic cosmology into an integrated view of science, religion, and history. He believed that nature, like human life, is unfolding between unknown eternities: through scientific study, we apprehend the divine. Theology benefits from understanding pain as part of the evolutionary process, while evolution has taken a psychological and social turn that moderates the harsher effects of the "survival of the fittest." A popular lyceum speaker and prolific author, Fiske presented his ideas most clearly in *Outlines of Cosmic Philosophy* (1874) and *The Critical Period of American History: 1783–1789* (1888).

See also SOCIAL DARWINISM.

FURTHER READING

Milton Berman, *John Fiske: the Evolution of a Popularizer* (Cambridge: Harvard University Press, 1961).

Fitzgerald, F. Scott (b. St. Paul, Minn., Sept. 24, 1896; d. Hollywood, Calif., Dec. 21, 1940). Writer. Celebrated as spokesman for, and embodiment of, the excesses and desperation of the Jazz Age, Fitzgerald by his own account squandered much of his talent writing formulaic short stories for the magazines that supported his extravagant tastes. But at his best the imagistic concision of his writing revealed him as a master of modernist techniques. Edmund Wilson's edition of Fitzgerald's memoirs, containing letters and passages from his notebooks, disclosed that Fitzgerald's fiction derived not only from a rich imagination but from a meticulous observation of American life. His novel *This Side of Paradise* (1920) and especially his masterpiece *The Great Gatsby* (1925) brought a new poignancy and depth to popular fictional treatments of pivotal American experiences.

FURTHER READING

Matthew J. Bruccoli, *Some Sort of Epic Grandeur: the Life of F. Scott Fitzgerald* (New York: Harcourt Brace Jovanovich, 1981).

Fitzhugh, George (b. Prince William County, Va., Nov. 4, 1806; d. Huntsville, Tex., July 30, 1881). Writer. In *Sociology for the South; or, the Failure of Free Society* (1854) and *Cannibals All! or, Slaves without Masters* (1857), Fitzhugh argued that slavery is the most humane social order and attacked northern capitalism for exploiting workers without giving them security. People are not born equal in abilities or status, he argued, so social equality is impossible. Liberal "freedom" therefore means a bitter and unproductive competition between strong and weak, while slavery, like feudalism, unifies the interests of rich and poor and allows the wealthy ruling class to act for the good of all.

See also PROSLAVERY THOUGHT.

FURTHER READING

Robert J. Loewenberg, *Freedom's Despots: the Critique of Abolition* (Durham: Carolina Academic Press, 1986).

folklore Like other fields of study, folklore has its own cultural and intellectual history. At least since the founding of the American Folklore Society in 1888 by scholars including William Wells Newell and FRANZ BOAS, "folklore" has meant a vast pool of accumulated myths and legends, tall tales and life stories, jokes and riddles, British ballads and the counting-out rhymes of American children. When the "Folklife Studies" movement gathered steam in America in the disciplinary ferment of the 1960s, another ambitious inventory was added to folklore's territorial claim: domestic architecture, costume, alternate medical therapies, "unofficial" religious beliefs, and foodways, to name but a few. "Folklore" in this sense includes all those items that, to paraphrase folk singer Arlo Guthrie's song "Alice's Restaurant," have been inspected, (endlessly) collected, (sadly) neglected, (spiritually) dejected, (psychically) introjected, and (only rarely) rejected.

This meaning of folklore developed over the last century alongside another idea: that certain small, consensual human communities, often located at the margins of Western European imperialist expansion, harbored nuggets of local knowledge or "lore." The 1888 foundation document of the *Journal of American Folklore* specified groups of this sort as "targets" for early folklore collectors: American Indians, African Americans, Mexican Americans, and Quebec-French living in the remote northern fringes of Yankee New England. Collecting projects would be "salvage" operations, since these cultures were thought to be "dying" or about to disappear, a view that bespeaks a cultural nostalgia forged from both Romanticism and Social Darwinism.

Since the mid-1960s, a new approach to folklore has emerged. Instead of hunting for "traditional" cultures—those marginal groups bypassed by modernity because their exchange-value potential had eroded—folklorists began to explore the whole process of human agency in cultural production and material processes. The legitimate subject-matter was no longer an ever-growing inventory of decontextualized "items," but the more general problem of how people actively construct meaning through the manipulation of symbolic codes, especially in what folklorists call "framed" moments of public artistic communication. An occasion is "framed" when it is lifted beyond the course of quotidian interactions, set off from usual routines by, for example, the use of sacred places, or a distinctive ritual speech, or a heightened sense of moral accountability on the part of participants.

Contemporary folklorists have developed a new methodology to accompany their interest in communicative process. They have tried to approach cultures without preconceptions. Rather than ask, for example, whether a certain categoric view of myth is fulfilled by native speakers, they are liable to ask if those speakers even recognize such a genre as "myth" in their own cognitive map. This concern for "ethnic genres" therefore challenges the ethnocentric, comparativist assumptions of the traditional scholar's imposed "analytic genres."

The current interest in communication has led to a major focus on cultural *performances*, or framed passages of high affect and reflexive knowledge that may resemble one another from culture to culture. Performances stand out from typical experiences because they are marked by a self-referencing style: of talk, body movement, gustation, exaggeration, parody, inversive laughter. Performances constitute intensifications of experience that draw public attention to pivotal social values. Performances also recognize the mutability of social group formations and the multiple roles that individuals can play in any single configuration of COMMUNITY. As a result, the polysemous and theatrical quality of contemporary social life informs the playful, role-reversing, and alternative configurations of such public spectacles as New Orleans Mardi Gras, Carnival in Brooklyn's Trinidadian community, or the Mummer's Parade in Philadelphia. Performances help keep social, psychological, and epistemic systems open-ended and transformative in potential.

Performances also interest folklorists because they frequently center on known texts—whether verbal, aural, kinesic, or material—in either canonical versions or in emergent variants. In their "recurrence" and "repeatability," such texts both conserve known values and work new material onto a cultural matrix. They make performance one of the key frames through which people "traditionalize" (a verb of active process) ideas and materials in the world around them. Performances, in other words, are one means by which people publicly perfect a semiotic of critical style that permits repeatable (and therefore predictable) address to: (1) claims on authority by those in positions of power; (2) the inversive, destabilizing nature of transgressive tropes and actions at cultural boundaries; and (3) the potential for epistemic renewal, or the possibility of alternative "ways of knowing" emerging through situated symbolic communication, in shifting social formations. As a method of analysis and as an interpretive strategy, contemporary folklore concentrates its efforts on these dynamic, framed moments of intense cultural reflexivity. Folklorists currently are less focused on stories *per se*, than on the "ethnography of storytelling" in various places and times; they are less attracted by recipes than they are by the "making of a meal" in poetic and social terms.

As trained folklorists bear down on questions related to performance, its inner dynamics and outer masks, they broaden their disciplinary and interdisciplinary ties. Folklore as practiced today in both university and public agency organizations has broken down the artificial separations between students of oral literature and material culture—differences glossed in the now specious distinction between "folklore" and "folklife." In most instances, the distinction falls apart rapidly: An Amerindian basket is "sung" into existence; is that basket an artifact? music? lyric? The native peoples of Australia "called" the world into existence, naming the rocks, titling the trees, mapping the dreamlines of ancestral imagination and contemporary identity; is the outback a landscape? a poem? Perhaps the answer is "both." Or neither.

Productive ties now extend also to many other disciplines, chief among them the combined fields of sociolinguistics and SEMIOTICS. To sociolinguistics folklore contributes a sensitivity to speech play and analyses of verbal style, and from it folklorists reap an awareness of speech acts and speech communities as meaningful social formations. The context of any given utterance takes on new depth. Texts may be seen as whole symbolic statements dependent on a situated understanding of "who said what to whom, under what conditions, and why?" Folklorists have learned the great lesson of semiotics: meanings are not fixed but delicately negotiated, usually contested, and always provisional. Any performance needs to be grounded in a close contextual ethnography for its meaning even to be imagined, let alone interpreted. (*See also* TEXTUALITY.)

The centrality of contextually situated meanings in folklore has led to a new appreciation for *social difference*—as opposed to the older consensus assumption of "face-to-face, shared values"—as the basis of performance. Folklore is indebted to contemporary poststructural feminist discourse, recent reconceptions of race and ETHNICITY, and various projects on postcolonial subjectivity, but a critical awareness of social difference as a problem with poetic and political dimensions has come from two projects within folklore as well.

One is academic, the other tied to public advocacy and education work that folklorists have undertaken since the 1930s in government agencies, labor unions, and museums. The academic tributary leads back to the University of Texas at Austin, where by the mid-1960s folklorists AMÉRICO PAREDES, Roger Abrahams, Richard Bauman, Beverly Stoeltje, John McDowell, and others had begun ethnographic work on performances along the Texas-Mexican border. The "boundary" issue, crucial in energizing the Chicano cultural rights movement, made *social difference* central to an interpretation of corridos, Mexican Polka, and the contested, doubled meaning of the word "Chicano" itself. (*See also* LATINO AND LATINA CULTURES.) The tributary flowing from the role that folklorists and folklore have played in questions of public policy, rights advocacy for ethnic groups and oppressed peoples—a protest stance from which most of the so-called "folk music" of the 1960s emerged—has led to folk festivals, museum installations, and critical work on the "production of heritage." Heritage, as a commodified reduction of history that can blur lines and "present difference" to tourists and politicians alike, derives power and authority from proper packaging. Heritage productions, like tourist attractions, rely on a representational strategy which, as folklore is abstracted from actual life and transformed into a marketable fetish of vanished social engagement, is termed "folklorism" by European scholars and "folklorization" by South American and Latin American scholars, including Américo Paredes.

Both currents of folklore reveal a fundamental fact about the field: a critical reincorporation of history. In part because of lingering antiquarian obsessions with this ballad version or that proverb variant, and in part because enthusiasm in the 1960s for the synchronic precision of structural anthropology came at the expense of broader diachronic movements, history was largely written out of folklore, even as it embraced performance as an organizing rubric in the early 1970s. Now, however, perhaps driven by the historical precision of museum exhibitions and material culture studies, folklorists are integrating history more fully into their work. Attention turns, for example, to the ways in which a pageant or religious procession selectively references and defines a past through the specific events or characters it offers to public view via "quotation"; one can term this the "performance–of–history" approach. Less common are folklorists who actually bring to the study of past events—of effigy-burnings in the streets of colonial Boston, or labor protest parades in antebellum

Philadelphia—an awareness of how performance might fundamentally redefine how history is researched and written.

Important to both these efforts, however, is the need to examine symbolic performances as actually set in history. All texts are historically specific, all framing or metanarrative devices are set in broader chronologies of causality and, as Max Weber and then Antonio Gramsci noted, all "tradition" is tightly implicated in IDEOLOGY and the twin hegemonic strategies: domination through the cultivation of consent, and charisma through the gendered fabrication of desire. Thus, folklore cuts a much more central figure in human culture than the epitomizing or epiphenomenal role that the "performance of history" approach suggests; indeed, folklore actually shapes—at the concrete level of the overlooked but always preexistent quotidian task, the poetic use of the spoken word, the flash of wit and wisdom in bodily style—the larger, more elusive flow of history and determination. As a result, the idea that folklore actually *does* something in the world positions it in close proximity to current work on linguistic pragmatics and in critical cultural geography. Emerging from and conditioned by situated meanings, the project of contemporary folklore is threefold. As it maps the zone between context and creativity, folklore combines a sensitivity for communicative process as constitutive of social life, a rigorous but reflexive ethnographic method, and a scholarly discipline both philosophical and applied.

ROBERT BLAIR ST. GEORGE

See also HUMOR; ZORA NEALE HURSTON; INDIAN IDENTITIES.

FURTHER READING
Richard Bauman, *Folklore, Cultural Performances, and Popular Entertainments: a Communications-Centered Handbook* (New York: Oxford University Press, 1992).
Charles L. Briggs, *Competence in Performance: the Creativity of Tradition in Mexicano Verbal Art* (Philadelphia: University of Pennsylvania Press, 1988).
Henry H. Glassie, *Passing the Time in Ballymenone: Culture and History of an Ulster Community* (Philadelphia: University of Pennsylvania Press, 1982).
Dell Hymes, "Breakthrough into Performance," in Dan Ben-Amos and Kenneth S. Goldstein, eds., *Folklore: Performance and Communication* (The Hague: Mouton, 1975).
J. E. Limón and M. J. Young, "Frontiers, Settlements, and Development in Folklore Studies, 1972–1985," *Annual Review of Anthropology* 15 (1986): 437–60.
Margaret A. Mills, *Rhetorics and Politics in Afghan Traditional Storytelling* (Philadelphia: University of Pennsylvania Press, 1991).
Américo Paredes and Richard Bauman, eds., *Toward New Perspectives in Folklore* (Austin: University of Texas Press, 1972).

David E. Whisnant, *All Things Native and Fine: the Politics of Culture in an American Region* (Chapel Hill: University of North Carolina Press, 1983).

Frank, Jerome (b. New York, N.Y., Sept. 10, 1889; d. New Haven, Conn., Jan. 13, 1957).   Legal philosopher. Associated with the movement known as LEGAL REALISM, Frank focused on the psychological dynamics of law. In *Law and the Modern Mind* (1930), he used psychoanalytic theory to suggest that the search for absolute certainty in law is a childish desire for paternal authority. The lower courts' original fact-finding efforts count for more than the appellate courts' legal formulations. Consistency is an unattainable goal; the best we can achieve is a careful attention to facts, an approach Frank associated with OLIVER WENDELL HOLMES JR.

FURTHER READING
Robert Glennon, *The Iconoclast as Reformer: Jerome Frank's Impact on American Law* (Ithaca: Cornell University Press, 1985).

Frankfurt School   An illustrious group of German-Jewish social theorists who came of age during the tumultuous years of the Weimar Republic, the Frankfurt School included Theodor Adorno, Walter Benjamin, ERICH FROMM, Max Horkheimer, Otto Kirchheimer, Leo Lowenthal, HERBERT MARCUSE, Franz Neumann, and Friedrich Pollock. Many of them came to enjoy a considerable measure of intellectual renown in the U.S., where they had fled following Hitler's 1933 seizure of power (of course, in the case of Benjamin, who took his own life in 1940 while fleeing Nazi-occupied France, such renown would come posthumously).

The Frankfurt School's organizational base was the Institute for Social Research, established by Felix Weil in the liberal milieu of Frankfurt in 1923. The institute was originally conceived as an intellectual ally of the German working-class movement, whose *Räte* (council) revolution of 1918–19 had been brutally subdued by the reigning social democratic government and its right-wing allies. As such, the institute's commission was to undertake research on working-class politics in order to facilitate the eventual triumph of the progressive social forces that had been defeated in Weimar's early years. However, the Frankfurt School as we know it today was given its definitive shape under the directorship of Max Horkheimer, who succeeded the original director, Carl Grünberg, in 1930.

Horkheimer articulated a new program in his inaugural address as director, "The Present State of Social Philosophy and the Tasks of an Institute for

Social Research." The new approach centered around a research methodology defined by Horkheimer as "interdisciplinary materialism." By this concept he sought to map out a research program that would steer clear of the two prevalent extremes afflicting the human sciences: philosophical speculation that was ungrounded in fact, and social scientific fact-gathering that was ungrounded in theory. The initial collaborative research project intended to implement this program was *Studies on Authority and the Family*, in which the social psychology of Fromm played a key theoretical role. The study's thematic focus revealed one of the institute's dominant empirical concerns in the 1930s and beyond, concerns that reflected the increasingly precarious status of Weimar democracy: the cultural transmission of authoritarian character structures—above all, via the institution of the family—which undermined republican sentiment and paved the way for the totalitarian dictatorships that would soon cast their net over the whole of Europe. (Many of the concepts and research methods employed in this project were also used in the well-known 1950 study edited by Adorno and colleagues, *The Authoritarian Personality*, which was sponsored by the American Jewish Committee as part of its Studies in Prejudice Series.)

But Hitler's seizure of power put an end to the research program. Institute offices and property were rapidly confiscated by the Gestapo; even if they had been left alone, empirical research of the sort Horkheimer imagined had become ideologically impossible. In 1933 the institute relocated to New York, where it established a loose affiliation with Columbia University. Until 1940 its members continued to publish in German, for the sake of preserving those German intellectual and cultural traditions that had been effaced by Nazism. Institute studies appeared in the *Zeitschrift für Sozialforschung* (Journal of Social Research), a repository of some of the most innovative work in cultural criticism, social philosophy, and sociology of its day.

As before, the institute focused on the economic, political, cultural, and psychological preconditions behind the rise of European fascism. But in his own programmatic contributions (such as "Traditional and Critical Theory"), Horkheimer also sought to outline the theoretical foundations of "critical theory," a term that had become a deliberate euphemism for "critical Marxism." Unlike orthodox Marxism, critical theory had shed all vestiges of economic determinism in order to remain sensitive to the multifarious causalities of "the total social process." And unlike "traditional theory" (that is, the "bourgeois" disciplines that Horkheimer sought to integrate) *critical*

theory refused the positivist maneuver of taking bourgeois society in its sheer immediacy as its normative point of departure. Instead, by casting its lot with the "progressive forces of society," it sought to further a process of social emancipation, which Horkheimer would allusively characterize as the "rational organization of society."

Yet, as prospects for social emancipation receded with the triumph of fascism in Europe and "state capitalism" (the New Deal) in the U.S., the discourse of critical theory became increasingly philosophical and speculative. In a number of his essays from the 1930s, Horkheimer began to rely on the ideal of "philosophical reason" (the Greek *nous*, Hegelian *Vernunft*, etc.) as a trans-historical touchstone of humanity's hopes for emancipation. According to Horkheimer, by identifying the constant tension between the "real" and the "rational," philosophical reason tried to highlight the deficiencies of social reality in the present. Thus, by emphasizing the ways in which reality failed to measure up to the sublimity of reason's demands, philosophy held out the prospect of a different, higher order of reality (an intellectual strategy that would also characterize Marcuse's important 1940 study of Hegel, the aptly titled *Reason and Revolution*).

Horkheimer presided over the institute's dissolution (apparently due to financial constraints) in 1940. He and Adorno then moved to Pacific Palisades, California, where they coauthored *Dialectic of Enlightenment* (1944), a key elaboration of the Frankfurt School's philosophy of history. Yet Adorno's philosophical influence clearly predominated, insofar as the new outlook on "reason" was a highly critical one. The authors now believed that it was the very process of human ratiocination or intellection itself—the attempt to make the dissimilar similar by subjecting it to the abstract imperatives of logical thought—that lay behind the modern totalitarian impulse. Despite its fascinating observations on Enlightenment, Homer's *Odyssey*, Sade and morality, and modern anti-Semitism (in a chapter coauthored by Leo Lowenthal), the book never addressed important objections to its argument. The original methodological promise of "interdisciplinary materialism" had been abandoned for an extremely schematic and at times reductive philosophy of history. Horkheimer and Adorno had concluded that the rise of totalitarianism revealed the inner logic of Western cultural development. The possibility that European fascism may have instead represented a last-ditch effort to eliminate the legacy and values of enlightened modernity—as embodied in the republican "ideas of 1789"—was never explored.

But one of the important, while still controversial, innovations of the book was the first systematic, critical treatment of the phenomenon of MASS CULTURE ("The Culture Industry: Enlightenment as Mass Deception"). Remarkably similar ideas concerning the same phenomenon would be expressed by American critics such as DWIGHT MACDONALD, CLEMENT GREENBERG, and IRVING HOWE in ensuing years. Yet here, too, one cannot help but suspect that despite the unquestionable analytical brilliance of their critique, Horkheimer and Adorno had too readily transferred the experience of European totalitarianism to the American situation. As a result, their analysis of the "culture industry" became too monolithic: they assumed too readily that mass culture, as a new form of IDEOLOGY, resulted in the total integration of American society. The distinctiveness of American political traditions—liberalism, federalism, public opinion—as a counterweight to culture-industry conformity played practically no role in their account.

In 1950, Horkheimer and Adorno returned to Frankfurt to accept teaching positions. But other former Institute members—Kirchheimer, Lowenthal, Marcuse, and Neumann (who died unexpectedly in 1952)—remained in the U.S., where they enjoyed distinguished university careers. Though the major philosophical works of Horkheimer and Adorno were first translated into English in the 1970s, the standpoint of critical theory was introduced to the American public in the immensely influential works of Herbert Marcuse. Books such as *Eros and Civilization* (1955) and *One-Dimensional Man* (1964) served as an obligatory intellectual rite of passage for many members of the NEW LEFT during the 1960s and 1970s. Marcuse's critique of the repressive nature of advanced industrial society, predicated on the rechanneling of human desire in accordance with the conformist strictures of mass consumption (a process he famously characterized as "repressive desublimation"), was a remarkably prescient theoretical anticipation of the new "politics of emancipation" that a generation of student radicals would make their own.

Thus, although the Frankfurt School's critique of social domination was first elaborated in the 1930s and 1940s, the reception of its doctrines took place under a very different, yet propitious, set of social conditions. As a result of this unexpected confluence of German social thought and indigenous U.S. radicalism, a generation of younger American scholars (inspired in part by Martin Jay's pioneering history of the School, *The Dialectical Imagination*, in 1973) has sought to renew and adapt the discourse of critical theory to the changed political and social realities of the post-Vietnam era. As such, the discourse of the Frankfurt School has become very much a part of contemporary American intellectual discourse.

The same judgment applies to the philosophical and cultural criticism of the Frankfurt School's heir apparent, Jürgen Habermas. Habermas, who was Adorno's "assistant" in Frankfurt during the 1950s, has continued to build on Adorno's legacy, while distancing himself from his teacher's mid-century preoccupations. Above all, he has taken exception to the inverse historical teleology of *Dialectic of Enlightenment*, its assumption of unilinear decline. Unlike Horkheimer and Adorno, whose work was in no small measure conditioned by the German *Kulturkritik* fashionable during the interwar period, Habermas has been eager to locate and analyze the redeeming features of Western political modernity: the values of civil society, the public sphere, liberalism, human rights, and participatory democracy. Yet he shares his mentor's critical verdict on the deleterious consequences of "instrumental reason" in Western modernity: the technocratic imperatives of economic management and state administration have taken precedence over our capacities for undistorted communicative agreement in political and social life. In his major work, *The Theory of Communicative Action*, he has coined the phrase "administrative colonization of the lifeworld" to describe the process through which the formal imperatives of economic and administrative rationality increasingly subsume modes of informal human interaction in the "lifeworld." Moreover, unlike his intellectual forbears, he has sought to reconcile the emancipatory thrust of critical theory with contemporary developments in philosophy and the social sciences. Hence, his theory of "universal pragmatics" (the philosophical basis for the theory of communicative action) was developed via an encounter with linguistic philosophies of J. L. Austin and John Searle. Similarly, the theory of communicative action has a strong sociological component, which Habermas derives (negatively) from a critique of systems theory and (positively) by building on American PRAGMATISM and the symbolic interactionism of GEORGE HERBERT MEAD. Habermas's own work, which has had a profound and extensive impact on a variety of intellectual fields, is itself telling testimony to the creative power of the original Frankfurt School vision.

RICHARD WOLIN

See also ENLIGHTENMENT.

FURTHER READING

Richard J. Bernstein, ed., *Habermas and Modernity* (Cambridge: MIT Press, 1985).

S. Bronner and D. Kellner, eds., *Critical Theory and Society: a Reader* (New York: Routledge, 1989).

E. Gebhardt and A. Arato, eds., *The Essential Frankfurt School Reader* (New York: Continuum, 1978).

Max Horkheimer, *Critical Theory* (New York: Herder and Herder, 1972).

Martin Jay, *The Dialectical Imagination: a History of the Frankfurt School and the Institute for Social Research, 1923–1950* (Boston: Little, Brown, 1973).

Leo Lowenthal, *An Unmastered Past*, ed. Martin Jay (Berkeley: University of California Press, 1987).

Thomas McCarthy, *The Critical Theory of Jürgen Habermas* (Cambridge: MIT Press, 1978).

Richard Wolin, *The Terms of Cultural Criticism: the Frankfurt School, Existentialism, Poststructuralism* (New York: Columbia University Press, 1992).

Frankfurter, Felix (b. Vienna, Austria, Nov. 15, 1882; d. Washington, D.C., Feb. 22, 1965). Legal scholar and Supreme Court Justice (1939–62). As professor of administrative law at the Harvard Law School, Frankfurter stressed the potential contributions of expert administrators to democratic reform. In *The Public and Its Government* (1930) he argued for using social scientific expertise in government; a number of his students tried to do just that as administrators of New Deal programs established by Frankfurter's friend Franklin Roosevelt. After the 1930s Frankfurter's faith in administrative solutions waned, as did the liberal enthusiasm that had led him to become one of the founders of the American Civil Liberties Union in 1920. On the Supreme Court Frankfurter opposed the notion that laws restricting rights are presumed unconstitutional unless proven otherwise. He urged instead a strict constructionist approach to the Constitution. A man of wide-ranging intellectual interests, Frankfurter published a bitter indictment of the Sacco-Vanzetti trial in 1927 and *Mr. Justice Holmes and the Supreme Court* (1938). *See also* LAW.

FURTHER READING

Michael E. Parrish, *Felix Frankfurter and His Times: the Reform Years* (New York: Free Press, 1982).

Franklin, Benjamin (b. Boston, Mass., Jan. 17, 1706; d. Philadelphia, Pa., Apr. 17, 1790). A figure with a unique place in the American pantheon, Benjamin Franklin was unusually versatile: he was a printer, writer, publisher, newspaper journalist, almanac compiler, inventor, scientist, practical philosopher, civic leader, assembly clerk, postmaster, colonial agent, and philanthropist. Growing up at a time when the influence of PURITANISM remained predominant, he later became an eye-witness to the GREAT AWAKENING, a representative of the transatlantic ENLIGHTENMENT, and ultimately a leading figure in the AMERICAN REVOLUTION. His encyclopedic career reflected the history of North America during the eighteenth century, when the British colonies were transformed into a new republic.

Unlike many colleagues of the distinguished Revolutionary generation, however, Franklin's profound impact on American society was not politically or ideologically oriented. Rather, the model of his personal achievement played a significant role in shaping the American way of life. As one of the most illustrious self-made men, his rise from obscurity to eminence exemplified the American dream of individual success and SOCIAL MOBILITY.

Franklin was born and raised in Boston, the tenth and youngest son in a family with 17 children. His pious parents, Josiah and Abiah Franklin, considered sending him to the ministry, but were unable to provide him with more than two years of elementary education. Exceedingly fond of reading, the boy was indentured to his older brother James, a printer. A few years later, at the age of 17, he broke with his brother, ran away from Boston, and arrived in Philadelphia. Quickly emerging as a diligent tradesman and shrewd competitor, he formed the Junto, a discussion group that spawned America's first subscription library in 1727, and then began revitalizing the *Pennsylvania Gazette* in 1729. He married Deborah Read in 1730. His most popular publication, *Poor Richard's Almanac*, was launched in 1732 and continued for more than two decades. Its sales reached as many as 10,000 copies annually. The preface to the last issue for 1758, generally known as *Father Abraham's Speech* or *The Way to Wealth*, was reprinted hundreds of times and translated into a dozen foreign languages.

Franklin retired from active business in 1748 and devoted much of his time and energy to natural observations and scientific experiments, particularly in the area of electricity. His famous kite experiment, conducted in 1752, proved that lightning was electricity. A series of his discourses and correspondence with friends were collected in *Experiments and Observations on Electricity*, which was first published in England between 1751 and 1754. Because of his outstanding scientific achievement and discovery, the Royal Society of London awarded him the Copley Medal in 1753 and elected him Fellow in 1756. Harvard, Yale, William and Mary, the University of St. Andrews in Scotland, and Oxford University awarded him honorary degrees.

Energetic, practical, and resourceful, Franklin gradually became an influential figure in his adopted city. Few of his contemporaries contributed as much civic and cultural improvement to the community. He successfully helped to found the Library Company of Philadelphia in 1731, the American Philosophical Society in 1743 (the first learned society), the Philadelphia Academy in 1751 (later the University of Pennsylvania), and the Pennsylvania Hospital in 1752.

After his election to the Common Council of the city in 1748, Franklin was frequently asked to serve the public. A delegate to the Albany Congress of 1754, he drafted a plan of union for the colonies. Between 1757 and 1762 he was sent by the Pennsylvania Assembly to England in order to press the colony's claims to tax the proprietary estates. Back in London again in 1764 as agent, first for Pennsylvania and then for Georgia, New Jersey, and Massachusetts as well, he was unable to reconcile the increasing differences between the mother country and the colonies. Realizing that separation was imminent, he returned home in May 1775. Immediately chosen as delegate to the Second Continental Congress, he later became one of the five committee members to draft a Declaration of Independence, and restyled the negative in Thomas Jefferson's "(we hold these truths to be) sacred and undeniable" to the positive "self-evident." Before the end of 1776 Franklin was appointed commissioner to the court of Louis XVI. Because of the victory of American troops at Saratoga and because of Franklin's patience, diplomacy, and immense popularity in France, the United States officially formed its alliance with the French by signing two treaties in 1778.

At the age of 81, Franklin was the oldest delegate at the Constitutional Convention in 1787. On the basis of his motion, a Grand Committee reached the crucial compromise: the election of members of the House in proportion to population and the election of two members of the senate by each state. At the closing of the convention Franklin carefully prepared a written speech calling for mutual understanding, harmony, and unity. In November 1789, five months before his death, he signed a public announcement as president of the Pennsylvania Society for Promoting the Abolition of Slavery, proposing a national policy of emancipation.

Throughout the eighteenth century few Americans won as much international renown as Franklin. His caustic colleague JOHN ADAMS acknowledged that in Europe "his reputation was more universal than that of Leibnitz and Newton, Frederick or Voltaire, and his character more beloved and esteemed than any or all of them." The Scottish empiricist and historian David Hume proclaimed that he was the first philosopher from the New World. The verse of the French statesman and economist Turgot epitomized his countrymen's passionate affection for Franklin:

"He snatched the lightning from heaven, and the scepter from tyrants."

Nevertheless, skeptical observers believed that Franklin's ideas represented the materialistic tendency of human nature, that his life lacked aesthetic value and spiritual aspiration, and that his thoughts were too practical to qualify him as a great philosopher. With a few exceptions, literary critics remained ambivalent about him. Ralph Waldo Emerson and Nathaniel Hawthorne were reserved about his legacy. Herman Melville in *Israel Potter* (1855), Henry David Thoreau in *Walden* (1854), and Mark Twain in "The Late Benjamin Franklin" (1870) expressed their disenchantment with Franklin's mind and philosophy. Beginning in this century, Franklin was simultaneously characterized by the German sociologist Max Weber as a classic embodiment of capitalistic spirit, and condemned by the English novelist D. H. Lawrence as "the first dummy American." Van Wyck Brooks regarded him as typical of the lower category of American thought, in contrast with the "highbrow" intellectual rigor represented by Jonathan Edwards. William Carlos Williams (*In the American Grain*, 1925) lamented Franklin's influence on the perpetuation of the acquisitive mood in American society. The literary critic Charles Angoff, in the *Literary History of the American People*, insisted as late as 1931 that "the vulgarity he spread is still with us."

Yet his champions insisted that Franklin's life represented the best of American values and experiences. Franklin's ingenuity and competence exemplified American know-how. His common sense and practicality pointed toward the embryonic stage of American pragmatism. His ever-present wit, expressed in essays, satires, homespun sayings, bagatelles, and conversation, was an indispensable contribution to the development of American HUMOR. His energy and entrepreneurship categorically demonstrated the dynamics of the middle class. His constant thirst for knowledge and natural inclination for science represented his fellow countrymen's persistent drive for PROGRESS. While his overt pursuit of personal wealth and happiness exemplifies one dimension of American individualism, his numerous philanthropic endeavors manifested the commitment of many Americans to civic duty and social improvement of the community. His widely acknowledged tolerance and benevolence highlighted America's democratic tradition; his lifelong efforts to defend and preserve his independent mind and free spirit reflected one of the very cornerstones of American self-government.

The accomplishments of many distinguished heroes, from George Washington and Thomas Jefferson to Abraham Lincoln, were indissolubly linked with a cause, be it the American Revolution or Emancipation and the Civil War. Their reputations were officially promoted by political organs. Franklin has always been the people's hero. Decade after decade, they regarded him as one of the most inspiring examples of American INDIVIDUALISM. His legacy survived in the memories and hearts of average citizens, not in political campaign slogans, party platforms, or governmental institutions. He was one of the few famous Americans whose greatness rested primarily on his personal merits, and whose own AUTOBIOGRAPHY served as his best advertisement.

In fact, both admirers and critics in the past closely identified Franklin's life with his exceedingly popular *Autobiography*; after no less than 400 editions over the last two centuries, it is still in print. Modern scholars emphasized that his seemingly straightforward autobiography did not always reveal his more complex historical identity. Verner W. Crane asserted in *Benjamin Franklin and a Rising People* that Franklin had "a charm which few could resist, the charm that beguiles us still in all that he said and wrote." The celebrated biographer Carl Van Doren, in his *Benjamin Franklin*, stressed that Franklin "seems to have been more than any single man: a harmonious human multitude" (p. 782).

Contemporary scholars and writers, such as J. A. Leo Lemay, James A. Sappenfield, Melvin H. Buxbaum, John Griffith, Ormond Seavey, John Updike, and Esmond Wright, all insisted in one way or another that Franklin was a man with many disguises. Using various literary and psychological techniques, they concluded that the *Autobiography* was a carefully designed mask which shielded its author's true identity. They suggested that there were in essence two different Franklins, one public and the other hidden or private. The familiar picture of a hard-working, frugal, candid, and modest Franklin was an invention by the author himself in his autobiography. In spite of its enormous popularity, the self-portrait in the book did not reveal the characteristics of the real Franklin, who was hiding behind his self-created images. The public's general assumption of Franklin, therefore, was not altogether reliable because it was based on a noncritical acceptance of his self-presentation. By the same token, precisely because the wide acceptance of his self-image has obscured the real Franklin, only persistent efforts and penetrating analyses might recapture him.

Despite the considerable output of recent scholarship, several areas need further investigation. After the continuous publication of Franklin's papers by the American Philosophical Society and Yale University for more than three decades, few Franklinists have thoroughly explored these documents, and no major biography has been written or rewritten based on the enormous amount of information in this monumental modern edition. Scant attention has been given to the fact that although he was often perceived as a self-made man, Franklin carefully cultivated patronage, a principal way to get ahead in his time. Literary critics have for years scrutinized the style, structure, text, vocabulary, plot, conceit, dramatization, and rhetoric of his writings. But one of the unanswered challenges to all Franklinists is how to reconstruct him as a conversationalist. Increasingly fascinated by his personal traits and domestic life, few scholars have asked why so many personae in his writings were female, such as Silence Dogood, Polly Baker, Bridget Saunders (Poor Richard's wife), and the nameless old mistresses. Even fewer have seriously examined some of the apparently more feminine elements in his personality, such as his tolerance, compromise, benevolence, humanity, and sympathy, as well as his remarkable sensitivity, subtlety, and perception.

Finally, numerous monographs have delineated Franklin's experience in a number of Western nations, such as England, France, Scotland, Ireland, Canada, Italy, and Germany. But scholars have generally ignored his influence on other parts of the world, such as South America, Russia, China, and Japan. A new generation of scholars must address these areas to do justice to Franklin, who remains a giant in world history because his thirst for knowledge, his keen interest in science and humanity, and his universal renown as a great American have always transcended national boundaries.

NIAN-SHENG HUANG

FURTHER READING

I. Bernard Cohen, ed., *Benjamin Franklin's Experiments: a New Edition of Franklin's Experiments and Observations on Electricity* (Cambridge: Harvard University Press, 1941).

Nian-Sheng Huang, *Benjamin Franklin in American Thought and Culture, 1790–1990* (Philadelphia: American Philosophical Society, 1994).

Leonard W. Labaree et al., eds., *The Papers of Benjamin Franklin*, 30 vols. to date (New Haven: Yale University Press, 1959–).

——, et al., eds., *The Autobiography of Benjamin Franklin* (New Haven: Yale University Press, 1964).

J. A. Leo Lemay, ed., *Benjamin Franklin: Writings* (New York: Literary Classics of the United States, 1987).

Claude-Anne Lopez, *Mon Cher Papa: Franklin and the Ladies of Paris* (1966; New Haven: Yale University Press, 1990).

Carl Van Doren, *Benjamin Franklin* (1938; New York: Bramhall House, 1987).

Esmond Wright, *Franklin of Philadelphia* (Cambridge: Harvard University Press, 1986).

freedom Within the class of inherently contested concepts, freedom occupies a special place. Equivalently ample terms, like happiness or EQUALITY, can be defined without recourse to their opposites, but freedom is an idea whose very meanings lie nested in oppositions and antitheses. Its rhetoric works, not by making freedom vivid in itself, for freedom bare and alone proves maddeningly difficult to envision, but by pointing the rhetorical finger of freedom at the nightmares and reversals which, in making freedom urgent, in the same breath define it. Open to virtually every user, the idea of freedom was never one thing—either *in esse* or in embryo—but a string of competing ideas and contested practices.

From the beginnings of English-speaking America, several different understandings of freedom (and its sister term, liberty) jostled against each other in the Americans' minds. At one end of the spectrum was the notion of freedom as privilege: a grant from the sovereign's stock of power. Medieval in origin, the assumption carried over in the bracketing together of the liberties, powers, and franchises granted under the colonial charters, until the Revolutionary crisis made it, suddenly, urgent to pry liberty apart from the rest and place it beyond sovereign whim or favor.

At the other extreme was the philosophers' construction of freedom as the absence of constraint upon action and will. From Hobbes through Dewey, the riddles of the will's freedom—vis-à-vis the constraints of God, fate, or deterministic science—monopolized vast amounts of sermon and seminar discussion of freedom. "Natural liberty" the philosophers called it, and its operational terms were its antonyms: hindrance, determinism, constraint. But the core of common talk about freedom, from the seventeenth century onward, has been about "civil liberty," the liberties of human beings in their relationships to one another, and it has turned on more tangible and urgently freighted antitheses than hindrance in itself. Slavery and freedom, tyranny and liberty, captivity and exodus: these formed the essential repertoire of freedom.

The oldest of these pairs was slavery/freedom. One need not accept *in toto* Orlando Patterson's claim that preoccupation with freedom is the peculiar cultural production of slaveholding societies to recognize how tightly the terms were, from classical Greece onward, wrapped around each other. New World slavery, with its stark racial divisions and intensified exploitation, radically sharpened the polarity. As mastership, with its invasions of body, mind, and person, was personal and possessive, so freedom, its antonym, was personal and possessive: a condition of the self.

Christianity, to be sure, took the dichotomy of free and slave and knotted them in paradox; it made the condition of freedom the condition of more perfect obedience. From John Winthrop's insistence that Christian liberty could only be "exercised in a way of subjection to authority," through Charles Grandison Finney's warning that a Christian, in casting off the slavery of sin for the freedom of Christ, did not escape the "principle of bondage," the paradox of emancipation through more perfect submission ran powerfully through churched America from the Puritan settlements onward. (*See also* PURITANISM.) Libertines behaved as they willed, but the saint, in Finney's words, was the "slave of righteousness." What Isaiah Berlin, in a famous essay on the "two concepts" of liberty, called the idea of "positive liberty"—that freedom consists in throwing off a bad master (sin, one's baser self, class prejudices, or imperfect desire) for submission to a good one (history, the state, the revolutionary will, or, most powerfully, God)—was no stranger to Americans, even if they were more likely to have acquired it from Calvin or Augustine than from Hegel or Rousseau.

By the seventeenth century, however, there ran, alongside the Christian response to the nightmare of slavery, a quite different inversion of slavery, focused not on righteousness but on barriers. A lawyers' notion of freedom, it reared its head early, even in Winthrop's Boston. As slavery raised specters of the self's naked vulnerability to another's power, so, by inversion, the key to "negative" freedom was the armor of RIGHTS and protections free status bestowed. Immunities, in this version, were at freedom's heart. The free self was the moated self, as John Stuart Mill was to crystallize the point in 1859, surrounded by a "sphere" of liberty, the broader each circle of unopposed thought and action the greater the public store of freedom. (*See also* LIBERALISM.)

Not all freedom talk, however, was hinged in these ways to the self. Distinct from both freedom/slavery pairings was a second antithesis—tyranny and liberty—which was as public and political as the former were private and personal. Where the nightmare which energized freedom was dispossession of the self, liberty's nightmare, as it came to a head in the controversies over royal prerogative and authority in the seventeenth and eighteenth centuries, was despotism: public authority run amok into arbitrary decree, extortion, or suppression. The imaginative thrust of the liberty/tyranny pair ran, accordingly, toward neither obedience nor immunities but toward governance, politics, the people's weal and sovereignty.

Yet a third historically important pair—captivity/exodus—crystallized freedom, still differently, as collective deliverance: the movement of a people across space or out of time. No particular form of governance or congeries of rights defined the freedom which was the antithesis of captivity. In a land which was a magnet for escape, the exodus motif was often employed to nationalize freedom and freeze it in time, crowning America with the halo of a city upon a hill, the promised nation. (*See also* AMERICAN EXCEPTIONALISM.) Among African Americans, however, radical exodus dreams, both messianic and secular, at times yoked to freedom beyond death, at other times to the north star of escape, at still others to the elaboration of an internal nation, have run hard from the African captivity into the present day.

These historic forms of freedom talk (and there were still more) sometimes slid into one another; as often, they were pulled apart. "Freedom all winged expands," Emerson exulted in the fall of 1863; but the idea of freedom did not, like an unfurling umbrella, simply enlarge. From circumstance to circumstance, freedom talk has moved by analogy, leapfrog fashion: these conditions, it is said—though others rush in with denials—show but another face of tyranny, those are akin to slavery. Open to radically different uses, freedom's history is the history of its mostly hotly contested employments and embattled boundaries. In that sense, the sites of sharpest contest have moved from liberty to freedom, with the obedience and exodus motifs as constant, complicating backgrounds.

With their liberty poles, liberty trees, "liberty and property" slogans, and "liberty or death" hyperbole, late eighteenth-century Americans left no doubt about the symbolic motor of their Revolution. Seizing the liberty/tyranny polarity which had been a fixture of English politics since the end of the fifteenth century, they turned it, with accelerating urgency, on the managers of their empire. Nothing defined a patriot more quickly by the 1770s—or more strongly shaped the counterlanguage of liberty—than conviction that the decisions emanating from London were designed to subsume the colonists' representative bodies into an "absolute tyranny." At times, the patriots also pushed the theme of personal enslavement as tyranny's ultimate project. Their bills of rights included private rights as well as public guarantees: common law immunities and new, invented rights. Still, the equanimity with which most patriots contemplated African American slavery, the casual way in which they treated dissenting political expression, and their endorsement of religious tests for public office all suggest how much, despite the pressure of legalists and dissenters, the dominant Revolutionary notion of liberty was public and political rather than private and individual. Even the First Amendment rights—of assembly, petition, speech, the press, and religion—were, in the main, public rights. Rights enumeration notwithstanding, eighteenth-century liberty was not fundamentally partible, distributable into personal possessions. Liberty, not liberties, was the iconographic genius of the Revolution. Liberty pole in her arm, the broken shackles of tyranny at her feet, she represented arbitrary power brought to law, constitutional constraint, the people's rule. (*See also* AMERICAN REVOLUTION; BILL OF RIGHTS; CONSTITUTION.)

That view, of course, left immense areas of disagreement. Into the middle of the nineteenth century, the site of most frequent and heated contest was the structure of AUTHORITY compatible with public liberty. Taxation and REPRESENTATION, the standing of person and property in apportionment and suffrage, federalism and the states' reserved powers, legislative and executive authority, court review and presidential veto, the sphere of legitimate state action: it was in struggles over these issues that the practice of liberty was determined.

The sectional crisis was, in one sense, a conflict on that same field of struggle. White southerners took a version of eighteenth-century political liberty and (with Lincoln as despot-in-chief) made a second independence movement out of it (*see* PROSLAVERY THOUGHT). But long before secession, ANTISLAVERY publicists had succeeded in wedging into the destabilized center of political debate the person-centered polarity of bondage and freedom. Neither Lincoln's promised "new birth of freedom" nor the actions of the Reconstruction Congress gave the South's freed people a particularly firm or generous stock of immunities, as the persistence of the exodus motif was painful witness. But in the crisis over slavery, the abolitionists succeeded in working a far-reaching reconstruction of the core of freedom talk, from preoccupation with public authority to preoccupation with the vulnerabilities and immunities of the self.

Within the self's sphere of immunities, which protections were fundamental, which merely secondary? Upon that issue, more than any other, were to turn the post-emancipation contests over freedom. Through the Great Depression, the issue at freedom's epicenter was property. Part of property's salience was the unexpected way in which the slavery crisis had economized the discourse of freedom. By pitching slavery against contract as rival systems of labor, the antislavery publicists brought ownership—of property, labor, and self—into the very eye of freedom. Set loose in the context of the ferocious economizing of social relations which late nineteenth-century capitalism effected, the results were substantial. It would be an exaggeration to say that the concept of liberty was narrowed to the property protection clause of the Fourteenth Amendment; but it is true that property's diverse representatives, with judicial review as their engine, worked extremely successfully to appropriate the language of freedom to insulate property from governmental incursion or restraint. Taxation and business regulation, income and inheritance levies, the sphere of entrepreneurial and employer immunities, the property rights of workers in their own labor and the injustice of "wage slavery": this was the terrain of fiercest contest, littered with the rhetoric of the slavery controversies.

The boundaries of possessive, not expressive freedom, commanded these debates. The lynching epidemic in the turn-of-the-century South, the cultural battles of the 1910s and 1920s over sex and proprieties, and the whiff of totalizing war ambitions in 1917–18 all helped spur, to be sure, a minority's interest in freedoms of dissent. But even the American Civil Liberties Union, formed to defend the war's resisters, took labor politics as its principal terrain through the 1930s. In the same fashion, Franklin Roosevelt's heroic effort to socialize the terms of debate—as the antithesis between collective want and the economic security that made free action possible —took property, labor, and ownership as freedom's key arena.

The term which was to dominate the politics of freedom after World War II, however, was to be neither property nor (still less) want, but person. The nature of the Nazi terror, seeking to reach into the very consciousness of its subjects, helped fuel the new emphasis on personhood. So did the Supreme Court's readiness to redeem its past, abandoning much of its property-centered activism to drive a new conceptual line, consciously ahistoric, between property and distinctly human rights. Most compelling of all was the eruption of an African American protest movement with "freedom now" at its rhetorical core. As the CIVIL RIGHTS movement played on analogies with slavery, so the liberation movements which spun off in its wake pressed the slavery analogy into other uses: to highlight the subjection of women, the closeting of gays, or the oppression of Native Americans, Chicanos, Asian Americans, and others. Exodus visions of a freed black (or gay, or woman's) nation ran hard through all these movements of liberation. But sensitive to the dominant strains of post-World War II politics, their leadership chose, on the whole, to hitch their cause to an agenda of freedoms which, if not person-centered in essence, tacitly became so: equal opportunity, accommodation, and treatment of persons before law; rights of equal pay and equal schooling (to begin each person

fairly at life's starting line); rights of voting (not to give minority groups defined powers but so each individual's voice would finally count on the great electoral tally board).

"Freedom is the right to choose," Archibald MacLeish announced soon after the war in the terms which, as ownership was eased out of the inner metaphors of freedom, now moved into its place. The epigram had sufficient resonance to be quickly appropriated for everything from Cold War anticommunism to the indictment of anticommunist mental conformity that MacLeish himself had in mind, from a strategy for delay in the school integration battles, to defense of mass-consumption supermarket capitalism, to a feminist rallying cry. Amidst these contradictory appropriations, the main effect of the reconstruction of freedom around an axis of choice was to mine expressive personhood, as never before, with freedom controversies. ABORTION (with its explosive confrontation between choice and righteousness), censorship and self-expression, a common culture or a multitude of lifestyle and sexual options: by the 1990s these were the issues at freedom's most contested center.

From both the political left and right, this latest turn inward upon the isolated, expressive self has been cause for second thoughts about freedom talk itself. To those who value comity and deliberation, the exaggerated polarities integral to the rhetoric of freedom sometimes seem too heavy a burden for a polity short on integrative forms of discourse to bear. Others have bemoaned the inability of freedom talk to find its point of equipoise, its fixed and stable form. Still others—though with far too weak a sense of history to sustain the point—have posited an inherently limiting INDIVIDUALISM in the language of freedom itself. The first objection bears more weight than the second or third. From public despotism to private mastership, from property to person, from obedience to choice, from polities to selves, the center of freedom talk has skidded from one dichotomy-mined arena to another in the American past. As with every contested concept, malleability and conceptual power have been inseparably conjoined. But to ask the repertoire of freedom to be any less multiform than the hydra-headed oppositions at its core is to ask for something freedom cannot provide. Yoked to its antitheses of slavery, tyranny, and captivity, freedom has always been less an idea than an accusation, less a definable concept than a democratically open field of argument, less a thing in itself than a nightmare, a rejection, and a hope.

DANIEL T. RODGERS

See also JUSTICE; LIBERTARIANISM.

FURTHER READING

Isaiah Berlin, *Four Essays on Liberty* (Oxford: Oxford University Press, 1969).

Mary Ann Glendon, *Rights Talk: the Impoverishment of Political Discourse* (New York: Free Press, 1991).

Michael Kammen, *Spheres of Liberty: Changing Perceptions of Liberty in American Culture* (Madison: University of Wisconsin Press, 1986).

Richard H. King, *Civil Rights and the Idea of Freedom* (New York: Oxford University Press, 1992).

John Stuart Mill, *On Liberty* (London: J. W. Parker, 1859).

Orlando Patterson, *Freedom*, vol. 1: *Freedom in the Making of Western Culture* (New York: Basic Books, 1991).

Hannah Fenichel Pitkin, "Are Freedom and Liberty Twins?" *Political Theory* 16 (1988): 523–52.

John Phillip Reid, *The Concept of Liberty in the Age of the American Revolution* (Chicago: University of Chicago Press, 1988).

Daniel T. Rodgers, *Contested Truths: Keywords in American Politics since Independence* (New York: Basic Books, 1987).

Freudianism The arrival of Sigmund Freud's work in North America is a classic case of the idiosyncrasies of cross-cultural reception. For it could be said that nowhere was there an intellectual climate less suited to Freud's pessimistic reflections on themes such as hysteria, the unconscious, and human sexuality than in the United States.

With the triumph of Hitler in 1933, the prospects for a creative expansion of Freudian perspectives in the German-speaking world were effectively blocked, since the Nazis dismissed psychoanalysis as a "Jewish science." Freud's thought did enjoy a fruitful development in England. Expelled from Vienna in 1938, Freud died in England the next year, and it was in England that the "object relations" school of psychoanalysis blossomed in the work of Melanie Klein, Donald Winnicott, and others. But it is one of history's strange ironies that Freudian concepts would have their greatest impact in the upbeat and pragmatic cultural climate of the United States. By the 1950s Lionel Trilling could remark that the argot of psychoanalysis had become "the slang of our culture."

Yet America also had a tremendous impact on psychoanalysis. Freudianism could exert so much influence in America in part because Americans made it their own. This process began with such early twentieth-century psychologists as James Jackson Putnam, who after Freud's (single) visit to the United States in 1909 became an avid devotee of psychoanalysis, which he regarded as a salutary alternative, in its attention to dreams and the unconscious, to the dominant somatic and physiological paradigms of American psychology and neurology. But as Freud himself noted in his 1914 "History of the Psychoanalytic Movement," American culture was so prudish

that the physicians who discussed his theories in private had to be reticent about them in public. Putnam could hail Freud's work only if he downplayed its focus on adult and especially childhood sexuality.

The process of accommodation accelerated in the 1930s, as psychoanalysts, many of them Jewish, emigrated en masse from Europe to America to seek refuge from fascism. Once in the United States, they were freed from the domineering influences of the movement's father. This textbook Oedipal revolt against the master's orthodoxy resulted in a radical transformation of psychoanalytic theory.

Freud's original theory of drives (*Trieblehre*) had emphasized the irreducibility of human instinctual conflict. It was *depth psychology* that held the key to character formation. As an interpretive tool, it focused on the mysterious workings of the human unconscious, the ultimate determinant of conscious life. The theory of infantile sexuality showed just how early such ontogenetic conflicts emerged, and, correspondingly, how intractable they could be to resolve. Freud's contention that children too had a sexual life had even in Europe been one of the most scandalous aspects of his theory of mental functioning. Given the refractory character of human instinctual life, Freud's clinical prognoses were far from optimistic. In a remark that has since become well known, he once described the goal of psychoanalysis as an attempt to transform "hysterical misery into normal unhappiness" (*Studies on Hysteria*, p. 305).

It was precisely the depth-psychological dimension, the very hallmark of the analytic approach to mental functioning, that would fall out of account in the continuing Americanization of psychoanalysis after the 1920s. Once the primacy of the unconscious, the drives, and human sexuality had been jettisoned, what remained was a more easily assimilable, "affirmative" version of psychoanalytic theory. It would not be far from the truth to say that in its American incarnation the disturbing truths of Freud's original approach—many of which had been preserved by the first generation of American psychoanalysts—underwent a "repression."

The groundwork for neo-Freudian revisionism was laid in the dispute between Freud himself and Alfred Adler in 1911. Adler, foreshadowing American "ego-psychology," designated his own approach "individual psychology." As Freud put it in the *New Introductory Lectures on Psychoanalysis*, Adler sought to attune psychoanalytic theory to a common sense which "recognizes no complications . . . which knows nothing of the unconscious, which gets rid at a single blow of the universally oppressive problem of sexuality." Thus, "what is selected . . . with Adler [is] egoistic motives. What is left over, however, and rejected as false is precisely what is new in psychoanalysis and peculiar to it . . . the revolutionary and embarrassing advances of psychoanalysis" (p. 142).

The foregoing criticisms could be applied, *mutatis mutandis*, to the case of the American neo-Freudians: among them, Karen Horney, Clara Thompson, and HARRY STACK SULLIVAN. In their vanguard stood eminent émigré revisionists, such as Heinz Hartmann and ERICH FROMM, who, as H. Stuart Hughes observes in *The Sea Change*, "in the ideologically open and welcome atmosphere of the United States . . . became militant optimists."

With the move toward ego-psychology, psychoanalysis had turned into a theory of adaptation. It came to represent the standpoint of the well-adjusted person who strove diligently to keep neurosis in check. It became a crucial ideological and institutional bulwark of the post-World War II therapeutic culture of consumption. By omitting the depth-psychological components of psychoanalytic theory in favor of more "humanistic" nostrums, neo-Freudian revisionism systematically underplayed the tensions between civilization and happiness that Freud stressed in his later reflections on the development of culture. Viewed in analytic terms, ego-psychology had, by collapsing the pleasure principle (the id) into the reality principle (the ego), divested Freud's theory of its deepest insights.

Other adaptations of Freudian precepts proved far more fruitful. In the 1950s, for example, an impressive literature attempted to put psychoanalytic concepts at the service of social criticism. Beginning in the 1930s, in such works as *Studies on Authority and the Family* (1936) and *The Authoritarian Personality* (1950), the FRANKFURT SCHOOL had utilized Freudian concepts to analyze the changing nature of authority under conditions of advanced capitalism. "Critical theorists" Max Horkheimer and Theodor Adorno sought to demonstrate that new forms of social organization had engendered new personality types. Their investigations found that with the eclipse of laissez-faire capitalism and the concomitant rise of a monopolistic, state-managed economy, the relatively "autonomous" personality-type of liberal capitalism had yielded to the "conformist" individual of bureaucratic capitalism.

In the 1950s a number of American critics engaged in a similar attempt to apply Freudian concepts to the understanding of "mass society." Building on the pre-Freudian views of ALEXIS DE TOCQUEVILLE, they feared that rampant consumerism and fanatical anticommunism had produced a culture of conformity that threatened the integrity of traditional American political values. Perhaps the most influential book addressing such themes was *The Lonely Crowd* (1950) by DAVID RIESMAN. In a 1969 preface, Riesman explicitly situated his work in relation to the neo-Freudian social psychology of Fromm, with whom he had studied. The major conceptual opposition guiding Riesman's work was that of "inner-directed" versus "other-directed" personality types. Inner-directed individuals resembled the self-sufficient entrepreneur of the nineteenth century; they developed their personal values and character structure by looking inward, becoming independent-minded and self-reliant.

Other-directedness, conversely, was the fate of the individual subject to the pressures and constraints of mass society. The internal "gyroscope" of the inner-directed person had given way to the external antennae of the conformist who takes a reading of the expectations of others. Ironically, Riesman's proposed alternative to other-directedness—the development of the "autonomous" personality—depended in his view on the embrace of creative acts of consumption in the very mass culture which gave rise to other-directedness in the first place. But whatever the deficiencies of Riesman's position, he had deftly identified something essential about the changing fabric of American society. And he had shown that Freudian and neo-Freudian perspectives helped address pressing questions concerning American "social character." The Yale University Press book became a huge success in the popular marketplace, one of the scholarly works which every so often comes to size up and stand for a cultural moment.

Other attempts to adapt Freudian concepts to the ends of social analysis attempted to historicize Freud's biological theory of "drives." In this way, they sought to counteract the master's own pessimist philosophical anthropology. In his later works, such as *Civilization and Its Discontents*, Freud concluded that civilization and human happiness were instinctually incompatible. Whereas the idea of happiness suggested unrestricted libidinal gratification, civilization was predicated on the repression or sublimation of libidinal drives.

HERBERT MARCUSE took up these themes in *Eros and Civilization* (1955), arguing that the drives Freud described as biological were socially conditioned. Consequently, the lack of gratification that characterized society at present was the result of historical deficiencies subject to alteration by the powers of human consciousness and will. For Marcuse, contemporary capitalism, a society that prized the ends of "production for production's sake," was predicated on the "performance principle." There was no reason to assume a priori that performance had everywhere to take precedence over gratification as a social principle. A future society might be based on the life instincts or Eros, and the repressive features of civilization would recede. Marcuse's "emancipatory" reading of Freud—now, in a complete reversal, reinterpreted as a genial apostle of Eros—would have an immense cultural impact on the generation of the 1960s, which discovered the attractions of sexual liberation and the imperatives of sexual politics.

In *The Culture of Narcissism* (1978), another book that, like *The Lonely Crowd*, came to stand for an era, CHRISTOPHER LASCH held that the modern era was marked by the emergence of narcissistic personality types. Whereas in Freud's day the predominant personality disorders were of the neurotic/hysterical variety, psychologists of the postwar era agreed on the prevalence of narcissistic disturbances. The latter were characterized by self-absorption, coupled with vague sentiments of meaninglessness and the lack of a stable self. These symptoms propelled narcissists toward a constant pursuit of recognition and self-affirmation, though no amount of either would satisfy their quest. *The Culture of Narcissism* represented a return to Freud's stoicism about the human prospect for happiness, and a rejection of Riesman's or Marcuse's neo-Freudian sensibility.

The national fascination with Freud was so considerable that a variety of intellectual disciplines made it de rigueur to experiment with psychoanalytic methods. In history, interest in the use of Freudian analysis was spurred by books such as *Young Man Luther* (1958) by ERIK ERIKSON. Though many would follow in Erikson's footsteps (such as Robert Jay Lifton and Kenneth Kenniston), efforts to apply Freudian concepts to historical study also reaped much criticism. After all, since psychoanalytic theory itself seemed to be in such flux, how was one to know precisely which concepts were still serviceable? Many historians feared that there was something fadlike about the use of Freudian analysis: that it proceeded in reductive, oversimplifying fashion and was thus a poor substitute for traditional, empirical approaches to historical study. In 1985, Peter Gay concluded that "psychohistory is highly visible, but mainly as a target" (p. 17).

Left Freudians such as Marcuse and Wilhelm Reich believed that Freud's theory of sexuality could be used for emancipatory ends. During the 1960s, however, others came to view the institutional uses of psychoanalysis as fundamentally repressive. Such sentiments were reflected in a burgeoning antipsychiatry movement, which sought to reverse the terms of the psychoanalytic theory of neurosis. Spurred by a growing mood of cultural and political radicalism, the anti-Freudians contended that psychoanalysis was little more than an insidious mechanism of societal normalization. Symptom formation and a failure to adapt, far from being disorders in need of a "cure," represented a valid response to a sick society. Freud was a man of science who had given his "talking cure" the famous motto "where id was, there ego shall be," thereby implying that desire and uncontrolled libidinal urges should be forced to submit to the demands of rational consciousness. The imperatives of psychoanalytic theory harmonized well with an authoritarian American society bent on the mastery of both inner and outer nature. (*See also* GUILT; SHAME.)

These were the circumstances that paved the way for the vaunted arrival in the 1970s and 1980s of the "French Freud," the Freud of Jacques Lacan and his disciples. Their reading of Freudianism had an enormous impact on American feminism, literary theory, and cultural studies. According to Lacan, Freud was a revolutionary *theorist of the unconscious*, and ego psychologists had systematically repressed this dimension of his work. For Lacan, the ego perpetrated an imaginary and duplicitous unification of impulses and drives in order to constitute one's supposedly "real" self, but such a self was a fiction. The task for analysis was to minimize the deceit and artifice perpetrated by rational ego consciousness in order to reacquaint the self with its vital, unintegrated, somatic-libidinal origins. (For his efforts, Lacan was expelled from the French Psychoanalytic Association.)

Freud's masculinist biases, his conception of the "dark continent" of female sexuality as defined by a "lack," an "absence" rather than by a "presence," had raised strong suspicions about his theories among American feminists (*see* FEMININITY). In the 1980s there arose a major fusion of feminism and postmodernism, thanks to the mediation of the "French Freud." Jacques Derrida's critique of Western rationalism was joined to the feminist critique of patriarchy. He coined the term "phallogocentrism" to indicate that in the Western tradition the predominance of reason went hand in hand with the values of masculinity. Femininity was conceived as the repressed other of male, "logocentric" thinking. Whereas the latter emphasized the values of mind, unity, and coherence, postmodern feminism stressed the values of the body, difference, and plurality. The work of Luce Irigaray (*The Sex Which Is Not One* and *Speculum of the Other Woman*, both translated in 1985) played an important role in this amalgamation of feminism, philosophy, and psychoanalytic theory.

Yet a contrary perspective also emerged within the feminist camp. Rights-oriented, egalitarian feminists believed that the new emphasis on "difference," by laying such stress on women's distinctiveness, marginalized them and threatened the significant gains that had been made by the women's movement. Postmodern feminism's relentless critique of reason and subjectivity risked leaving the women's movement without an effective concept of human agency. (*See also* FEMINISM, WOMEN'S RIGHTS.)

Throughout these debates, thanks to Lacan, Freud remained an indispensable point of reference. But Freud himself drew increasing fire; his theories were viewed as the product of particular (and limited) central European circumstances. Freud's "biologism," his transhistorical theory of the instincts, seemed out of step with the newly dominant culturalist and contextualist approaches to social criticism. After all, feminism arose in opposition to the profound patriarchal cultural biases inherent in Freud's view that "biology is destiny." For Freudianism to become intellectually acceptable once again, it would have to be presented in a radically altered form.

Concerning the American infatuation with Freud, Americans might ask: Which is the cause and which is the effect? Did Freud and his views come to shape our culture and the way we see ourselves? Or did we embrace Freud because we saw our "selves" reflected in his work—selves that were anxious, lonely, and preoccupied, selves that, in an age skeptical of traditional religion, sought consolation by leaping from one type of PSYCHOTHERAPY to the next. Has the self been so widely cultivated and so intricately analyzed precisely because it is so precarious? As Philip Rieff argued in *The Triumph of the Therapeutic* (1966), Freud and Freudianism have come to serve as a secular religion. They purvey solace and meaning, which have become scarce resources in a harsh, disenchanted, late modern world.

RICHARD WOLIN

See also NEO-FREUDIANISM.

FURTHER READING

Sigmund Freud, *New Introductory Lectures on Psychoanalysis*, trans. J. Strachey (New York: Norton, 1965).
Sigmund Freud and Joseph Breuer, *Studies on Hysteria*, in *The Standard Edition of the Complete Psychological Works of Sigmund Freud*, vol. 2, trans. J. Strachey (London: Hogarth Press, 1953).
Peter Gay, *Freud for Historians* (New York: Oxford University Press, 1985).
Nathan G. Hale Jr., *Freud and the Americans: the Beginnings of Psychoanalysis in the United States, 1876–1917* (New York: Oxford University Press, 1971).
H. Stuart Hughes, *The Sea Change: the Migration of Social Thought, 1930–1965* (New York: Harper and Row, 1975).
Russell Jacoby, *Social Amnesia: a Critique of Contemporary Psychology from Adler to Laing* (Boston: Beacon, 1975).
Mary Johoda, "The Migration of Psychoanalysis," in D. Fleming and B. Bailyn, eds., *The Intellectual Migration: Europe and America, 1930–1960* (Cambridge: Harvard University Press, 1969).
Herbert Marcuse, "Epilogue: Critique of Neo-Freudian Revisionism," in Marcuse, *Eros and Civilization* (Boston: Beacon, 1966).

Friedan, Betty (b. Peoria, Ill., Feb. 4, 1921). The name of Betty Friedan and the emergence of the second wave of American FEMINISM are virtually coextensive. Author of the bestselling *The Feminine Mystique* (1963) and founder of the National Organization of Women (NOW), Betty Friedan has been widely credited with launching the contemporary reassessment of gender relations. Friedan's early years were atypical of her generation only in her decision to follow her mother's example and go to college. After graduating from Smith and studying psychology for a year at the University of California at Berkeley, Friedan became a journalist. At the end of World War II, she lost her job with a news service to a returning G.I., an experience shared by millions of other American women who learned a consequential lesson about female employment: it was socially rewarded during, but not after, military emergencies. In 1947 she married Carl Friedan and embraced the life of a middle-class housewife and mother. She had three children and was eventually divorced in 1969.

During the 1950s, Friedan pursued freelance writing, a choice that promised creative work not in conflict with her full-time domestic duties. She specialized in articles like "I Was Afraid to Have a Baby" for women's magazines. When she surveyed her Smith classmates in 1957, she expected to write an inspiring story about the virtues of higher education for women. Instead, she found that her 200 respondents, 87 percent of them housewives, felt profoundly troubled about their postcollege lives. They articulated a syndrome, a "problem that has no name," that Friedan later named "the feminine mystique." Educa-tion, she concluded in dismay, had failed miserably to prepare her generation for their adult roles. Editors at *McCalls* and *Redbook* refused to publish the piece.

The Feminine Mystique expanded on her findings and argued that femininity was a "comfortable concentration camp" in which procreation was obligatory and other opportunities for fulfillment were foreclosed. The book struck a responsive chord among men as well as women, established Friedan as an advocate of balancing MOTHERHOOD and paid work, and became a bestseller. In 1966, Friedan founded NOW and served as its first president. Since then, she has been active in many causes, from the National Women's Political Caucus and the First Women's Bank to abortion rights and the Equal Rights Amendment (ERA).

By the late 1960s the mobilization of a younger generation of educated women made Friedan's brand of feminism appear tame. "Women's liberationists" denounced male supremacy and the patriarchal nuclear family and called for a radical transformation in the subjective experience and structural deployment of gender. Theorist Shulamith Firestone, for example, ridiculed maternal instinct, declared pregnancy barbaric, and went so far as to call for a revolution in reproductive technology as a prerequisite for gender EQUALITY.

As varieties of feminist radicalism proliferated, Friedan's quest for legalistic forms of equality in the professions and in politics appeared too "liberal" (that is, inadequate). Her denunciation of lesbians as a "lavender menace" in NOW earned Friedan low marks among the youthful rank-and-file. By 1980, charges that the "white-middle-class-women's-movement" systematically ignored the concerns of women of color and others caused Friedan's influence to ebb even further.

Friedan's second book, *The Second Stage* (1981), renewed the controversy about her political vision and strategic thinking. Published on the heels of Ronald Reagan's election as President and just before the defeat of the ERA, the book castigated extremists for conducting a reactionary "sexual war against men" that was "irrelevant" and "self-defeating" (p. 201). Feminists, she warned, must heed the new right's message: heterosexual love and maternity were "the life-serving core of feminine identity" (p. 16).

It is indisputable that Friedan represents the moderate "women's rights" tendency within contemporary feminism. She also embodies, however, another strain within feminist theory and activism, a tradition of preoccupation with the psychological aspects of women's condition. This element of her thought has often been overlooked, perhaps because it is more difficult to characterize politically.

In *The Feminine Mystique* Friedan blamed FREUDIANISM and the "new psychological religion" of adjustment for endowing a self-destructive form of FEMININITY with social and scientific authority. On the other hand, she employed the ideas of psychological experts—especially humanistic psychologists like Abraham Maslow—in her passionate call for change. Women were doomed to a psychological hell, Friedan suggested, because gender conformity required them to renounce their natural tendencies toward growth and the realization of their fullest

selves. Femininity was a travesty because it contradicted the liberating process of "self-actualization." NOW's statement of purpose explicitly incorporated this psychological concept: "NOW is dedicated to the proposition that women first and foremost are human beings, who . . . must have the chance to develop their fullest human potential."

This paradoxical stance—psychology as both problem and solution—pervades contemporary feminism. The feminist slogan "the personal is political" implies that sexism must be addressed on the psychological level if it is ever to be eradicated, yet psychologizing poses the danger of turning women away from political analysis and collective action in hopes of achieving individual change. However flawed, Friedan's effort to grapple with this basic dilemma is being echoed today among younger and more radical feminists, marking the psychology of GENDER as a persistent and unavoidable challenge in the achievement of full equality between women and men.

ELLEN HERMAN

See also WOMEN'S RIGHTS.

FURTHER READING

Alice Echols, *Daring to Be Bad: Radical Feminism in America, 1967–1975* (Minneapolis: University of Minnesota Press, 1989).

Sara Evans, *Personal Politics: the Roots of Women's Liberation in the Civil Rights Movement and the New Left* (New York: Random House, 1979).

Shulamith Firestone, *The Dialectic of Sex: the Case for Feminist Revolution* (New York: Bantam, 1971).

Betty Friedan, *The Feminine Mystique* (New York: Dell, 1974).

——, *It Changed My Life: Writings on the Women's Movement* (New York: Random House, 1976).

——, *The Second Stage* (New York: Summit, 1981).

Abraham H. Maslow, *Motivation and Personality*, 2nd ed. (New York: Harper and Row, 1970).

Gloria Steinem, *Revolution from Within: a Book of Self-Esteem* (Boston: Little, Brown, 1992).

Friedlaender, Israel (b. Wlodwa, Poland, Sept. 8, 1876; d. near Yarmolinetz, Ukraine, July 5, 1920). Religious leader. The founder of Conservative Judaism, Friedlaender believed that the Jewish faith is more a culture than a creed or set of ceremonies. America's political and cultural freedom nurtures Judaism, itself committed to those freedoms. Judaism can preserve its distinctiveness while also opening itself to, and even incorporating some elements of, surrounding cultures, secular and religious. A Zionist, Friedlaender believed that a Jewish nation would foster self-reliance and cross-generational unity among Jews. His many books include *The Political Ideal of the Prophets* (1910), *Jewish Arabic Studies* (1910–13), *The Jews of Russia and Poland* (1915), and *Zionism and the World Peace* (1919).

FURTHER READING
Baila Round Bhargel, *Practical Dreamer: Israel Friedlaender and the Shaping of American Judaism* (New York: Jewish Theological Seminary of America, 1985).

Friedman, Milton (b. Brooklyn, N.Y., July 31, 1912). Economist. Winner of the 1976 Nobel Prize in Economics and author of *A Monetary History of the United States, 1867–1960* (1963), Friedman argues that the business cycle is more responsive to money supply and interest rates than to the fiscal measures favored by Keynesians. Even monetary policy cannot affect interest or employment rates in the long term, however, so the Federal Reserve should commit itself to increasing the money supply at a steady rate. Government should not interfere in the free market, since both poor data and lag times make intentional intervention destabilizing. In *Capitalism and Freedom* (1962, with Rose D. Friedman), Friedman argued for a negative income tax, or guaranteed income, to replace the service-oriented welfare bureaucracy.

FURTHER READING
Abraham Hirsch and Neil de Marchi, *Milton Friedman: Economics in Theory and Practice* (New York: Harvester Wheatsheaf, 1990).

Fromm, Erich (b. Frankfurt am Main, Germany, Mar. 23, 1900; d. Muralto, Switzerland, Mar. 18, 1980). Psychoanalyst and writer. A well-known psychoanalyst in Germany before his emigration to the United States in 1934, Fromm held positions at Columbia University and Bennington College before moving to the National University of Mexico in 1951. His version of psychoanalysis, like that of other proponents of Neo-freudianism, deemphasized the role of childhood sexuality in shaping adult identity. Fromm stressed instead the adaptive power of human beings to grow in healthy relation to others. His writings roamed far beyond psychoanalysis as he assayed broad cultural and social trends of the mid-century. Among his most influential books were *Escape from Freedom* (1941), *Man for Himself* (1947), *The Sane Society* (1955), and *The Art of Loving* (1956).

See also Freudianism.

FURTHER READING
Daniel Burston, *The Legacy of Erich Fromm* (Cambridge: Harvard University Press, 1991).

frontier In an average day at Frontierland, not a soul approaches a Disneyland employee to request a definition of the word "frontier." For the general public, the meaning of this word is one of the clearest ideas on earth. The frontier, everyone with any exposure to American popular culture knows, was the edge of settlement, the place where white Americans struggled to master the continent. The frontier was populated by a colorful and romantic cast of characters—mountain men, cowboys, prospectors, pioneer wives, saloon girls, marshals, and outlaws. Tepees, log cabins, and false-front stores were the preferred architecture of the frontier; coonskin caps, cowboy hats, bandannas, buckskin shirts and leggings, moccasins, boots, and an occasional sunbonnet or calico dress constituted frontier fashion; canoes, saddle horses, covered wagons, and stagecoaches gave Americans the means to conquer the rivers, mountains, deserts, plains, and other wide open spaces of the frontier; firearms, whether long rifles or six-shooters, were everywhere and in frequent use. These images are matters very well understood. Tourists do not need any assistance in defining Frontierland.

As one moves from the terrain of popular culture to the turf of academic historians, one of the clearest terms in the English language becomes one of the most confusing. In 1893 the famed historian Frederick Jackson Turner declared that one could not understand the United States without understanding the frontier. Turner said that the frontier was the most important factor in American history; he characterized it with a number of colorful, even poetic phrases; and yet he refused to say exactly what he meant by the word. Perhaps his most memorable suggestion was this one: "the frontier is the outer edge of the wave [of settlement], the meeting point between savagery and civilization." But what exactly was savagery, and what was civilization, and what was the nature of their meeting? Did settlement really occur in "waves," with "edges"? "The term [frontier] is an elastic one," Turner wrote "and for our purposes does not require sharp definition" (p. 3). "Elastic" it was, and "elastic" it has remained. Even though many historians have relied heavily on the concept in their narrating and interpreting of American history, those who have used it most regularly have often matched Turner in his reluctance to offer a sharp definition.

The word originated from the Latin *frons*, meaning "forehead, brow, front." Moving from Late Latin to Old French to English, frontier came to mean "the marches, or border of a country." This was a border with human occupation on either side; nothing in this definition suggested a people confronting vacancy, wilderness, or a lesser stage of civilization. In his *Dictionary of the English Language* (1755), Dr. Samuel Johnson defined frontier as "The marches; the limit; the border: properly that which terminates not at the sea, but fronts another country." The American dictionaries published in the late eighteenth century and through much of the nineteenth century either followed this definition or, in a striking number of instances, did not list the word at all.

In the late nineteenth century, dictionaries recorded a consequential new variation in the term. An entry in Funk and Wagnalls' *Standard Dictionary of the English Language* (1893), for instance, reaffirmed the old definition ("The part of a nation's territory that abuts upon another country . . ."), but also set forth a new one: "That portion of a country between a civilized and an unsettled region . . ." At this moment in shifting lexicography, Frederick Jackson Turner weighed in, drawing a dramatic contrast between European and American definitions of the word. "The American frontier," he declared, "is sharply distinguished from the European frontier—a fortified boundary line running through dense populations." European frontiers, Turner believed, marked a division between two human populations; the American frontier, by contrast, marked a division between civilized settlement and what Turner called "free land" (p. 3).

As an essayist, Turner employed a style of confident assertion that gave even his more questionable statements an air of authority and persuasive power. Drawing his distinction between the European and American meanings of frontier, Turner seemed to be setting forth an established fact. And yet in 1966 the historian John Juricek made a persuasive case for the proposition that when Turner drew this distinction, he misrepresented earlier American usage of frontier. White Americans before 1890, Juricek argued, left a full record of their recognition of the presence and importance of INDIANS, as well as of French and Spanish colonists. Contrary to Turner's assertion, the traditional American meaning of the word frontier was quite compatible with the European sense of a border between countries or peoples. Neither in the colonial nor the national period did white Americans imagine that their settlements bordered on emptiness; on the contrary, they bordered on Indian countries. Turner, according to Juricek, was imposing a late nineteenth-century assumption—the frontier as an outer strip of thinly settled territory—on earlier generations.

Similarly, when Turner turned to a statistical definition for the frontier, he was adopting a very recent innovation in thought. In 1882, a geographer and special agent in the Census Office named Henry Gannett wrestled with the question of how mapmakers could represent frontier territory. He decided to call "frontier" any area containing between two and six people per square mile. Of course this definition nearly eliminated the presence and power of Indian people as a significant factor in defining the frontier. The approach seemed, nonetheless, to lend the whole idea scientific certainty. In fact, the statistical definition was packed with unexamined and confusing implications, even beyond its dismissal of Indians. If, for instance, an area ceased to be a frontier when the population rose above two to six people per square mile, then what was the frontier historian to make of a mining rush? Once news of a gold or silver discovery spread, the local population immediately exceeded six people per square mile; in mining, then, the frontier closed the instant it opened. The statistical definition thus eliminated mining camps, as well as towns and cities of any sort, from the category of frontier. Inadvertently or not, Turner had imposed stern, rural limits on the idea of the frontier, even though towns and cities were often the beachheads of American expansion.

The quantitative definition led Turner to impose equally strict limits on the chronology and duration of the frontier. In 1890, the Director of the Census had found that "the unsettled area had been so broken into by isolated bodies of settlement that there can hardly be said to be a frontier line" (Turner, p. 1). Embracing this statement, Turner announced that "the frontier has gone, and with its going has closed the first period of American history (p. 38). If one accepted Turner's claim that the frontier had formed American character and served as the source of American democracy, then this was a very gloomy conclusion, with historical change forcing the nation to surrender the foundation of its distinctive identity and strength.

Turner thus left his followers a curious intellectual legacy: a ringing declaration of the vital influence of the frontier, but a declaration resting on a vague, shifting, and finally terminal definition of his key concept. In the 1920s and 1930s, Turner's frontier thesis was a popular target for critical reappraisal; few of its premises or conclusions remained standing after these exercises. Nonetheless, the frontier thesis underwent an extraordinary rehabilitation in the years after World War II. The project manager of this reconstruction was the historian Ray Allen Billington. In a number of books, beginning with *Westward Expansion* in 1949, Billington took up Turner's campaign to promote a recognition of the importance of the frontier. Attempting to offer a more precise definition than Turner's, Billington came up with this: the frontier was "a series of contiguous westward-migrating zones, each representing a different stage in the development of society from elemental to complex forms." The orderliness of "this standardized zonal process," as it passed over the physical terrain of the continent, bore very little resemblance to the complex events of colonization in America north of the Rio Grande (p. 3). But Billington persevered in defining six sequential frontier "zones": first, fur traders; second, cattlemen; third, miners; fourth, "pioneer farmers"; fifth, "equipped farmers"; and finally the "urban pioneers" whose presence closed the frontier (pp. 3–7).

Over the next 30 years, Billington and his colleagues in frontier history wrestled with this definition, and with others just as improbable, trying to find some area of compatibility between their loyalty to the idea of frontier and the complicated reality of the historical record. Consider, for instance, the results of Billington's hope that he could classify frontiers by occupation. This construction gained the support of a surprising number of frontier historians. Many titles of books, chapters, and lectures coalesed around some version of "the mining frontier," "the cattle frontier," or "the farming frontier." These were not logically consistent or parallel concepts. In a mining frontier, for instance, pioneers extracted and exported a resource put in place by nature; by contrast, in a cattle frontier, pioneers imported and introduced an exotic animal into a natural environment where domesticated livestock had never existed.

Still, the most striking feature of the occupational classification of frontiers was the number of important economic activities it ignored. Historians wrote voluminously about the mining frontier and the cattle frontier, while the logging frontier, the fishing frontier, the tourism-promoting frontier, and the investing-in-real-estate-and-mortgages frontier, to name a few, remained very much understudied. Grain-based agriculture dominated the category of the farming frontier; no book appeared under the title *The Vegetable Frontier* or *The Fruit Frontier*. Few of the important economic enterprises resting on women's labor registered in the occupational frontier model: *The Poultry Frontier, The Laundry Frontier, The Sewing Frontier, The Boardinghouse Frontier,* and *The Sexual Services Frontier* all await their authors. Similarly, since conventional historians still rigorously observed the Turnerian deadline for frontier topics, enterprises that started late—what might be called the copper, coal, petroleum, movie-making, skiing, atomic-weapons-developing, and defense-spending frontiers—could not qualify for study.

The rehabilitated school of frontier studies was equally restrictive when it came to matters of ethnicity. The attention of frontier historians was firmly focused on the activities of Anglo-American pioneers;

indeed, it was the timing of the American arrival that determined when a place was a frontier and when it was not. Spanish, French, and Russian colonization could hardly register in this framework. The northward movement of Spanish colonists, and the permanent presence of their descendants in New Mexico, Texas, Arizona, and California could be at best a kind of frontier sidebar or appendix, secondary to the main story of the westward-moving American frontier.

Of the many important subjects of the history of America's West, conventional frontier historians thus excluded far more than they included. Narrow as their approach now appears, these writers had great influence. Into the 1990s nearly every college-level American history textbook followed a plot true to the preferences of Ray Allen Billington, tracking the westward-moving frontier through to its closure in the 1890s.

Nonetheless, by the 1960s a campaign was underway to liberate the term frontier from the control of the traditional scholars. In a spirited article published first in 1962, the historian Jack D. Forbes tried to dislodge the term from its Turnerian and Billingtonian meaning as "the edge of the westward movement." Forbes wanted to see the frontier as a place of intercultural contact where the salient processes included acculturation, assimilation, and miscegenation as well as conquest, imperialism, and colonialism. Viewing the frontier once again as a border and a zone of cultural encounter, Forbes argued, could strike a blow against exaggerated faith in AMERICAN EXCEPTIONALISM, and restore American history to the context of world history. American frontiers would now stand ready for comparison with all the places in the world where different groups converged.

In a collection of essays comparing colonization in North America and southern Africa, published in 1981, historians Howard Lamar and Leonard Thompson joined the campaign for a transformed definition of the frontier "not as a boundary or line, but as a territory or zone of interpenetration between two previously distinct societies." What marked the beginning or ending of such a condition of interpenetration? "The frontier 'opens' in a given zone when the first representatives of the intrusive society arrive," Lamar and Thompson explained; "it 'closes' when a single political authority has established hegemony over the zone" (p. 7).

Forbes, Lamar, and Thompson had provided the clearest, and certainly the most culturally inclusive definition, that the word frontier had ever received. And yet this one, too, was most convincing when it kept its distance from concrete historical developments. Consider, for instance, the application of this definition to New Mexico. When did New Mexico's frontierhood begin, and when did it end? Did the frontier open when Athapascan people, traveling from the north, intruded into Pueblo Indian territory, sometime in the first half of the second millennium? Or did the frontier really open in 1540, with the arrival of the first Spanish conquistador, Francisco Vasquez de Coronado? If so, did it close, or simply pass into dormancy, two years later when Coronado gave up and returned to Mexico? Did the frontier reopen in 1598, with the arrival of seemingly permanent Spanish settlements, and then close in 1680, when the successful Pueblo Revolt drove all Spaniards from the province? Was the reconquest of the 1690s a reopening of the frontier, or was it the permanent closing, since the Indians never again succeeded in expelling the Spanish? Or was all this irrelevant to the arrival of the *real* frontier—when American traders entered New Mexico in 1821? Was the arrival of American soldiers in 1846, and the consummation of an official military conquest, the beginning or end of the frontier? If official military conquest is the measure of established hegemony, did the defeat of the Apaches in the 1880s signify the final closing of this frontier? Or did the twentieth-century growth in Mexican immigration into the Southwest reopen a once-closed frontier, as American officials struggled to control the border that, to Spanish-speaking people, carries the resonant name *la frontera*? Where in this enormously complex story could one locate the moment when a single political authority was established and gave this unevenly punctuated, four-or-five-century-long frontier episode its closure?

While a zone of cultural interaction was certainly a more expansive definition than a meeting line between civilization and vacancy, it too had a tough time keeping its grip on an intractable historical reality. In the 1980s the search for a scholarly definition of the frontier was just as confusing as it had been when Turner refused to give a "sharp definition." And yet all the academic squabbling had remarkably little effect on the term's career in popular culture. When writers of headlines in newspapers and magazines used the word frontier, they gave clear evidence that they were not thinking of a zone of complex cultural interaction and struggle over hegemony. In late twentieth-century publications, frontiers—defined in what resembled Turnerian and Billingtonian terms—were everywhere: frontiers of robotics, frontiers of cable TV, frontiers of lasers, and frontiers of Velcro. Every usage indicated that,

for readers and writers of headlines, frontier still carried the meaning of a place of undeveloped resources, open possibilities, opportunity, adventure, and profit.

The pioneers, the personnel in charge of advancing these frontiers, carried a comparably unambiguous, positive affect. In a quick survey of national headlines from 1989 and 1990, one could encounter a fast-food pioneer, a frozen potato pioneer, and a pasta pioneer; a junk-bond pioneer, a polyester pioneer, and a root canal pioneer; a Jazzercize pioneer, a psychedelic pioneer, and a sex-change pioneer. Each of these varied usages still carried a common suggestion of innovation and achievement, spunk and pluck.

As valiantly as academic loyalists to the idea of frontier have sought to give deeper meaning to the reality of pioneering, popular thinking has not done much shifting. In the very urbanized state of Alaska, each automobile sports a license plate with the words, "Alaska: the Last Frontier." It seems very unlikely that any of the drivers understand this to mean "Alaska: the Last Zone of Cultural Interaction and Contested Hegemony." The popular understanding of the word frontier and the scholarly effort to reckon with a complex history share virtually no common ground.

The irony of the pattern of change here is worth noting. Until the late nineteenth century, many white Americans thought that the term frontier referred to a place where groups of people—usually Anglo Americans and Indians, but sometimes also Spanish and French people—met and struggled for dominance. In the 1890s, academic historians led by Frederick Jackson Turner embraced a very different definition of the frontier, in which participants who were not Anglo-American pioneers virtually faded from view. Then, over a century, popular usage retreated from the earlier sense of the frontier as a contested border, and moved much closer to the Turnerian vision of the frontier as a place where pioneers found open opportunity, abundant resources, and a chance to develop a vigorous, new American character. And now, in our time, scholars struggle to reverse the achievements of their predecessors, and to return the definition to its earlier meaning of a border between peoples, or a place of political, economic, and social contest.

On the Fourth of July, 1982, greeting the return of the space shuttle to Edwards Air Force Base, President Ronald Reagan delivered a set of cheerfully Turnerian remarks. "The quest of new frontiers for the betterment of our homes and families," he said, "is a crucial part of our national character." Well received in his many statements in praise of the nation's pioneer values, the President was, in effect, ratifying the scholarly wisdom of the 1890s. If the velocity of the movement of ideas from frontier historians to Presidential speechwriters remains constant, sometime around the year 2072 a President may deliver a well-received address on the cultural and moral complexity of the American frontier. If this does happen, that Presidential address—more than many other manifestations of public behavior—will be the measure of an enormous change in this nation's understanding of its own origins.

PATRICIA NELSON LIMERICK

FURTHER READING

Ray Allen Billington, *Westward Expansion: a History of the American Frontier* (New York: Macmillan, 1949).

William Cronon, George Miles, and Jay Gitlin, "Becoming West: Toward a New Meaning for Western History," in Cronon, Miles, and Gitlin, eds., *Under an Open Sky: Rethinking America's Western Past* (New York: Norton, 1992).

Jack D. Forbes, "Frontiers in American History and the Role of the Frontier Historian" (1962), *Ethnohistory* 15 (spring 1968).

John Juricek, "American Usage of the Word 'Frontier' from Colonial Times to Frederick Jackson Turner," *Proceedings of the American Philosophical Society* 110 (Feb. 18, 1966).

Howard Lamar and Leonard Thompson, eds., *The Frontier in History: North America and Southern Africa Compared* (New Haven: Yale University Press, 1981).

Patricia Nelson Limerick, *The Legacy of Conquest; the Unbroken Past of the American West* (New York: Norton, 1987).

Fulmer Mood, "Notes on the History of the Word *Frontier*," *Agricultural History* 22 (Apr. 1948).

Frederick Jackson Turner, "The Significance of the Frontier in American History" (1893), in *The Frontier in American History* (New York: Henry Holt, 1947).

Frost, Robert (b. San Francisco, Calif., Mar. 26, 1874; d. Boston, Mass., Jan. 29, 1963).   Poet. Frost's poetry started with a place: the countryside of northern New England. He focused on ordinary people and events, and used familiar language to reveal beauty and tragedy within the commonplace. Though he adopted the words and tones of everyday speech, he infused both nature and people with ambiguity and mystery: daily life took on a rich luminosity sometimes suggestive of transcendence. His poems were collected in several volumes, including *A Boy's Will* (1913), *North of Boston* (1914), *Mountain Interval* (1916), and *New Hampshire* (1923).

FURTHER READING

Richard Poirier, *Robert Frost: the Work of Knowing* (New York: Oxford University Press, 1977).

Fuller, [Sarah] Margaret (b. Cambridgeport, Mass., May 23, 1810; d. at sea off Fire Island, N.Y., July 19, 1850).   Beginning her career as a translator of German texts, notably Goethe's "Tasso" (1833), Eckermann's *Conversations with Goethe* (1839), and Bettina von Arnim's *Günderode* (1842), Fuller was a famous conversationalist and educator of women. She also edited *The Dial*, the transcendentalist periodical, before giving the task over to her close friend RALPH WALDO EMERSON. Among the writing contributed by Fuller to the *Dial* was her controversial feminist essay "The Great Lawsuit; Man vs. Men, Woman vs. Women" which her friends quickly encouraged her to expand into book form as *Woman in the Nineteenth Century* (1844). She also worked as a journalist and critic for Horace Greeley's *New York Daily Tribune*, contributing well over 350 essays on a variety of topics during the course of her tenure with the paper, including a series of dispatches from Italy during the Risorgimento.

Fuller was a true comparativist and her continued insistence that we focus upon (and accept) differences both between and within cultures has significance for contemporary feminism(s) and critical theory alike. Ironically, the fact that Fuller did not write novels made it difficult to situate her among the various women writers recovered in the feminist revision of the nineteenth-century "American" canon. When Bell Gale Chevigny published her landmark edition entitled *The Woman and the Myth: Fuller's Life and Writings* (1976), she made a point of establishing the diversity of Fuller's writerly career. Yet it would take still more time for literary criticism to establish a suitable frame through which to appreciate the complexity of Fuller's work.

Along with Robert Hudspeth's important edition of Fuller's extensive correspondence, Chevigny's book remains one of the most effective tools for understanding the strange turns in the critical reception of Fuller and her work. Far too often a curiosity about Fuller's dramatic public life drew critical interest away from her writing. Many factors contributed to this sustained biographical focus, including the famous men Fuller became close to in this country and abroad, and Fuller's radical political leanings which grew increasingly explicit as her thinking slowly incorporated the theories of French utopian Charles Fourier and other European socialists. Her sympathy for one cause in particular, the Italian revolution of 1848, distinguished her from many of her famous male counterparts, as Larry Reynolds makes clear in his recent study, *European Revolutions and the American Literary Renaissance* (1988).

At the time of her tragic death by shipwreck in

1850 many people viewed Fuller as an outspoken, daring woman; because of her high visibility and popularity, Fuller's return to America from Italy threatened to unsettle a host of orthodoxies. Critics have often speculated that NATHANIEL HAWTHORNE allegorized Fuller's death in *The Blithedale Romance*. Hawthorne appears to have been obsessed with what Henry James would later call the "ghost" of Margaret Fuller, refiguring her in a variety of his novels from *The Scarlet Letter* to *The Marble Faun*. The James quote reveals that Hawthorne was not alone in his response to this powerful woman. Though not yet fully explored in scholarship, Whitman's indebtedness to Fuller is no less significant than that of Edgar Allan Poe, HERMAN MELVILLE and Henry James. (A review of *Moby-Dick* with Fuller's shipwreck in mind offers new insight: the brief chapter on Bulkington reads like Melville's tribute to Fuller.) And Fuller's impact on women writers proves even more pervasive if more subtle, though this influence also awaits critical examination. Fuller's example emboldened authors like LYDIA MARIA CHILD, EMILY DICKINSON, LOUISA MAY ALCOTT and EDITH WHARTON.

Fuller's close relationship with Emerson may have been the most problematic one for critical history: scholars early on described Fuller as a dutiful disciple of Emerson and rarely paused to consider how a mutual influence may have structured the relationship between them. Certainly the large body of letters written by Emerson to Fuller reveals Emerson's extraordinary indebtedness to Fuller. Feminist critics were no doubt correct in first showing how our appreciation of Fuller should be separated from our appreciation of Emerson. Yet in making the separation complete, the initial feminist readers took away one vital element of Fuller's power: her influence over Emerson's work and her impact upon the intellectual debates and trends that developed in conversation with Emerson's thinking. These trends in the Emersonian tradition are not incidental; indeed, we continue to find ourselves locked into patterns formalized by them. According to critics like Richard Poirier, STANLEY CAVELL and Cornel West, Emerson's influence is essential not only to the complex tradition of American pragmatism, but to European developments, especially the stream traceable from Nietzsche through Heidegger to contemporary deconstruction. Yet today's theoretical climate suffers precisely because the interpretation of Emerson and writers influenced by him remains a reading stripped of crucial feminist influences within their work. Refiguring Fuller's influence over Emerson supplies a way to place American feminism in conversation with a number of important intellectual movements.

The history of the critical study of Fuller's work not only reflects the all-too-familiar undervaluation of a woman's accomplishment by traditional scholarship, but also provides an interesting lesson in the history of feminist criticism. Early feminist readers came to her work with an interest in recovering the "experience" of women, and sought evidence in Fuller's biography of her concern for the daily lives of women. These critics were unable to make sense of her intense literary focus and theoretical emphasis. New work on Fuller shifts the intellectual frame. It suggests that Fuller initiated her "feminism" precisely through her reading—which is to say, through the activity of TRANSLATION and literary criticism. And her theoretical concerns, far from detaching her from real women, strengthened her understanding of their actual place in history. Bridging the gap between Fuller's life and work helps to overcome the schism between theoretical and historical concerns in contemporary feminist criticism.

CHRISTINA ZWARG

See also AESTHETICS; TRANSCENDENTALISM.

FURTHER READING

Charles Capper, *Margaret Fuller: an American Romantic Life, the Private Years* (New York: Oxford University Press, 1992).

Bell Gale Chevigny, *The Woman and the Myth: Margaret Fuller's Life and Writings* (New York: Feminist Press, 1976).

Julie Ellison, *Delicate Subjects: Romanticism, Gender and the Ethics of Understanding* (Ithaca: Cornell University Press, 1990).

Ralph Waldo Emerson, William Henry Channing, and James Freeman Clarke, eds., *Memoirs of Margaret Fuller Ossoli* (Boston: Phillips, Sampson, 1852).

Robert N. Hudspeth, ed., *The Letters of Margaret Fuller*, 5 vols. (Ithaca: Cornell University Press, 1983–).

Joel Myerson, *Critical Essays on Margaret Fuller* (Boston: G.K. Hall, 1980).

Jeffrey Steele, ed., *The Essential Margaret Fuller* (New Brunswick: Rutgers University Press, 1992).

Christina Zwarg, *Feminist Conversations: Fuller, Emerson and the Task of Reading* (Ithaca: Cornell University Press, 1994).

fundamentalism Fundamentalist intellectual life is not nearly the oxymoron that many assume it to be. Although the term is now sometimes used in a generic sense for all conservative religious movements resisting the supposedly irresistible tide of modernity, "fundamentalism" was once a clearly demarcated segment of Protestant Christianity in the United States. According to its most perceptive student, George Marsden, the fundamentalism that emerged during the first decades of this century was "militantly anti-modernist Protestant evangelicalism"

(p. 4). It was rooted in American popular revivalism and in the proprietary custody that English-speaking Protestants had exercised over public life during the first two-thirds of the nineteenth century. Fundamentalism overlaps many other Protestant traditions, but its zealous defense of an idealized nineteenth-century American Christianity makes it distinct (at least conceptually) from more generic Protestant EVANGELICALISM, and also from European immigrant pietism, pentecostalism, Calvinist or Lutheran confessionalism, Baptist traditionalism, the holiness movements emerging from Methodism, and other denominational orthodoxies.

Toward the end of the nineteenth century, a growing number of irritants exercised those Protestant evangelicals who would soon become fundamentalists. Foremost among them was the new higher criticism of Scripture, which treated the Bible as a book of religious consciousness studied like any other ancient text (*see also* BIBLICAL CRITICISM). Hardly less disquieting was the way modern science was eating away at traditional belief in divine creation. (Not all evangelicals opposed evolutionary theory, however. James Orr and B. B. Warfield, two of the contributors to "The Fundamentals: a Testimony to the Truth" [1910–15]—a series of pamphlets devoted to the defense of historic doctrines—considered evolution a viable explanation for the development of the earth and even the human body.)

Strife in the 1920s among Baptists and Presbyterians in the northern United States marked the debut of a well-defined fundamentalist movement. In the early phases of this conflict, a Baptist editor, Curtis Lee Laws, first used the term "fundamentalists" for those who opposed doctrinal accommodation to modernity. The denominational conflicts pitted doctrinal conservatives agitated about cultural changes—especially the spread of moral relativism—against those who preferred tranquility to ideological warfare. The inclusivists won. When the agnostic CLAR-ENCE DARROW thrashed WILLIAM JENNINGS BRYAN at the well-publicized Scopes Trial in 1925, fundamentalism's time in the sun was over. Or so it seemed to national commentators like H. L. Mencken.

But fundamentalists, however discredited in northern denominations and the elite media, did not pass away. They regrouped in powerful regional associations, publishing networks, preaching circuits, and Bible schools. The tumults of the 1960s and following decades brought these cultural conservatives back into the public arena. Since the mid-1960s, fundamentalists and their allies have sustained a series of impressive actions. A conservative movement with many parallels to fundamentalism solidified its con-

trol of the Lutheran Church-Missouri Synod. Self-styled fundamentalists have emerged victorious from a painful intramural struggle in the Southern Baptist Convention, the nation's largest Protestant denomination. Fundamentalists have founded hundreds of private schools and several large colleges, while increasingly turning to home-based instruction as a means of circumventing the educational monopoly of the public schools. Most of all, liberal judicial decisions on issues of morality and religion—including the legalization of abortion-on-demand and the ban on school prayer—created a "New Religious Right" in which fundamentalist themes have been prominent.

Fundamentalist intellectual life has been decisively shaped by its ambivalence toward modern America. Fundamentalists oppose much of the secular, liberal worldview that has become entrenched in elite universities and national media. But they are also expert exploiters of marketing and eager users of radio and television, the most modern means of mass communication.

The fundamentalist life of the mind also bears the strong imprint of a theological system first brought to America in the mid-nineteenth century by John Nelson Darby, an early leader of the Plymouth Brethren. This theology is premillennial dispensationalism. Its method is a biblical literalism heavily dependent upon nineteenth-century notions about the goals and systematizing purposes of science. Its content emphasizes the prophetic parts of Scripture. By studying biblical prophecy, dispensationalists make sense of events in ancient times, discern the meaning of current events, and look toward the early return of Christ in an apocalyptic Last Day.

Dispensationalism has been propounded in a series of phenomenally successful books. Cyrus I. Scofield's annotated edition of the King James Bible—first published in 1909 by Oxford University Press and reedited on several subsequent occasions—has spread dispensational interpretations throughout the world. The single bestselling book in the United States during the 1970s (except for the Bible) was a dispensational description of the end of the world, *The Late Great Planet Earth*, by Hal Lindsey. Several evangelical or fundamentalist publishers sold millions of copies of a number of premillennial interpretations of the 1991 Gulf War.

The positive contribution of fundamentalism to American thought in the twentieth century has been that, while other Christian groups were nervously clearing their throats about traditional Christian beliefs, fundamentalists insist unabashedly that Christianity is still a supernatural religion. As early as 1948 a liberal churchman, Nels F. S. Ferré, recognized this fact clearly:

Fundamentalism as the defender of supernaturalism has . . . a genuine heritage and a profound truth to preserve. . . . We shall some day thank our fundamentalist friends for having held the main fortress while countless leaders went over to the foe of . . . a shallow naturalism. ("Present Trends," p. 336)

The other side of the story, however, is well described by evangelical historian Nathan Hatch:

The heritage of fundamentalism was to Christian learning for evangelicals like Chairman Mao's "Cultural Revolution" for the Chinese. Both divorced a generation from mainline academia, thus making reintegration [into larger worlds of learning] a difficult, if not bewildering task. (p. 12)

Fundamentalists of recent decades have only been following their cultural and educational betters when, in purest American fashion, they have translated their private beliefs into public political programs. Since, however, they reject the scientific naturalism that has become axiomatic to many others, a nearly total disengagement has come about between fundamentalists and the elite intellectual culture of late twentieth-century America.

MARK A. NOLL

See also CALVINISM; RELIGION.

FURTHER READING

David O. Beale, *In Pursuit of Purity: American Fundamentalism since 1850* (Greenville, S.C.: Unusual Publications, 1986).

Paul Boyer, *When Time Shall Be No More: Prophecy Belief in Modern American Culture* (Cambridge: Harvard University Press, 1992).

Joel A. Carpenter, ed., *Fundamentalism in American Religion, 1880–1950: a 45-Volume Facsimile Series* (New York: Garland, 1988).

Nels F. S. Ferré, "Present Trends in Protestant Thought," *Religion in Life* 17 (1948).

Nathan O. Hatch, "Evangelical Colleges and the Challenge of Christian Thinking," *Reformed Journal* (Sept. 1985).

George M. Marsden, *Fundamentalism and American Culture . . . 1870–1925* (New York: Oxford University Press, 1980).

——, *Understanding Fundamentalism and Evangelicalism* (Grand Rapids: Eerdmans, 1991).

Ronald L. Numbers, *The Creationists: the Evolution of Scientific Creationism* (New York: Knopf, 1992).

G

Galbraith, John Kenneth (b. Iona Station, Ontario, Oct. 15, 1908). Economist. Galbraith's iconoclastic writings have earned him a wide readership, especially outside the field of professional economics. In *American Capitalism: the Concept of Countervailing Power* (1952), Galbraith claimed that the competition of powerful oligarchies brought stability to the American economy. He began retreating from that rosy view in *The Affluent Society* (1958), where he noted the persistence of poverty amid a flood of consumer goods. In *The New Industrial State* (1967) and *Economics and the Public Purpose* (1973), he posited a "technostructure" of elite managers who, thanks to the emergence of huge, vertically integrated corporations, need no longer fret over the old market constraints of supply and demand. His memoir *A Life in Our Times* (1981) recounts a life in government and politics as well as academia: during the New Deal he served in the Department of Agriculture, during World War II he was director of price controls, and he was thereafter a perennial adviser to Democratic politicians.

FURTHER READING
Loren J. Okroi, *Galbraith, Harrington, Heilbroner: Economics and Dissent in an Age of Optimism* (Princeton: Princeton University Press, 1988).

Garland, [Hannibal] Hamlin (b. near West Salem, Wis., Sept. 14, 1860; d. Los Angeles, Calif., Mar. 4, 1940). Writer. In the stories collected in *Main-Travelled Roads* (1891) and his autobiographical *A Son of the Middle Border* (1917), Garland recorded the harsh realities of midwestern farm life: isolation, drudgery, and economic exploitation by banks and corporations. His characters verge on fatalism but possess a moral strength that enables them to resist oppressive natural and economic forces. Active in the Populist movement and a supporter of Henry George's single tax, Garland regarded monopolistic power as the most insidious threat to liberty. In *Crumbling Idols* (1894), he advocated "veritism," a literary approach that combines the social consciousness of REALISM with attention to individual consciousness.

FURTHER READING
Joseph B. McCullough, *Hamlin Garland* (Boston: Twayne, 1978).

Garnet, Henry Highland (b. New Market, Md., Dec. 23, 1815; d. Monrovia, Liberia, Feb. 13, 1882). Minister and abolitionist. A leading radical African American abolitionist, Garnet supported the Liberty and Republican parties and condemned the Constitution as a proslavery document. Slaveholding and submission to slavery were both sinful, he contended, for both destroy God's seed of liberty. Garnet gained notoriety for his 1843 *Address to the Slaves*, in which he exhorted slaves to resist slavery—preferably by direct moral and economic appeals or work stoppages, but if necessary by a violent uprising. Garnet later endorsed voluntary emigration as a means of building a center of black power in West Africa.
See also ANTISLAVERY.

FURTHER READING
Joel Schor, *Henry Highland Garnet: a Voice of Black Radicalism in the Nineteenth Century* (Westport: Greenwood, 1977).

Garrison, William Lloyd (b. Newburyport, Mass., Dec. 10 or 12, 1805; d. New York, N.Y., May 24, 1879). If we are to measure abolitionism's influence by the degree to which it provoked the Old South into identifying northern society with a variety of "fanatical" impulses, then William Lloyd Garrison was the most influential of all American abolitionists. With a number of other white and black abolitionists, Garrison was also instrumental in identifying ANTISLAVERY with the cause of racial justice and equality.

He was the self-made man as moral reformer, the foremost counterexample to the prominent interpretation of the abolitionists as members of a declining social elite whose hatred of southern slavery served as an unconscious outlet for their status anxieties. The status of the young Garrison could hardly have declined further. When he was three years old, his father, a frequently out-of-work and intemperate sailing master, abandoned his family. By the age of 13, Garrison had already entered into his third apprenticeship, that of beginning printer for the *Newburyport Herald*. Garrison soon came to view his new trade as a providential act of good fortune; printing and journalism were to be for him, as it had been for Benjamin Franklin, the route out of poverty. But Garrison never sought purely worldly success. Although he rejected the ministry as unsuitable for his ambition and intellectual talents, the Baptist piety of his mother continued to push him toward spiritual fulfillment.

The 1820s was the age of the Benevolent Empire, a loose network of missionary organizations dedicated to improving public morals and stabilizing American society by uplifting its criminals, drunkards, and other deviant and downtrodden groups. Although lacking the elite New England background of leading members of these organizations, Garrison shared their moralistic leanings, and he threw his growing journalistic skills into attacking the same vices—liquor, prostitution, and vulgar entertainment. By the end of the 1820s, and largely owing to his friendship with the Quaker Benjamin Lundy, with whom he coedited *The Genius of Universal Emancipation*, Garrison had embraced two other causes dear to the Benevolent Empire: the gradual emancipation of southern slaves and the colonization (return to Africa) of free blacks.

With the British abolitionist attacks on West Indies bondage providing further inspiration, antislavery quickly became Garrison's dominant reform passion, although he lacked direct contact with the institution of slavery. On some deep, personal level Garrison identified with the black bondsman. The slaveholder's absolute tyranny and freedom to indulge his greed and lust, and the slave's commensurate loss of all free agency, offended Garrison's own quest for social independence and spiritual self-discipline and purity.

Increasing familiarity with the arguments of northern blacks, moreover, soon led Garrison to abandon his belief that relocating free blacks to areas outside the United States would encourage antislavery organization and voluntary manumissions within the South. In the early issues of *The Liberator*, the Boston newspaper he launched in January 1831, and then in his landmark book, *Thoughts on African Colonization*, Garrison hammered home the contrary argument. Not merely were the "master spirits" behind the American Colonization Society ineffective in battling slavery; their covert *design* was to stabilize and perpetuate slavery in the South. One of Garrison's major achievements was to harness time-honored conspiratorial thinking to the antislavery cause. "Ye crafty calculators!" he wrote in *Thoughts*. "Ye hardhearted, incorrigible sinners! ye greedy and relentless robbers!" (p. 103).

But in substance as well as tone Garrison launched antislavery in new, more radical and uncompromising directions. He demanded immediate, unconditional, and uncompensated abolition because he insisted that every slaveholder, together with all who sanctioned or merely acquiesced in slaveholding, was guilty of a personal crime against both his human property and divine authority. Garrison further held that this personal crime was sustained by the curse of racial prejudice, in the North and in the South; he rhetorically inquired whether white Americans would have countenanced for a moment the chattel servitude of members of their own race.

In contrast to earlier antislavery evangelicals, Garrison and his doctrines aroused opposition and hatred from the outset. Outraged southerners mistakenly found in Garrison's rhetorical militancy a primary cause of the Nat Turner slave insurrection. (*See also* PROSLAVERY THOUGHT.) The South also believed, just as inaccurately, that Garrison had a substantial body of northern opinion behind him. In fact, sentiment in the free states throughout the 1830s may have remained almost as intensely and uniformly anti-Garrison as that in the South, a reflection of the threat that Garrison's doctrines posed to national political stability, North–South economic relations, and white supremacy in the free as well as the slave states.

Garrison's doctrines, together with his often abrasive personality, gradually generated serious opposition among abolitionists themselves. The American Anti-Slavery Society, which Garrison helped form in 1833, split in 1840, in part because Garrison made an unpopular cause more unpopular by associating the abolition crusade with radical pacifism and advocacy of WOMEN'S RIGHTS, and also because other abolitionists urged the direct political action that Garrison opposed in principle.

Like other abolitionists Garrison realized after the mid-1830s that appeals to the consciences of slaveholders and their northern sympathizers were ineffective. Disappointed with timid Protestant institutions in the North, Garrison moved toward anticlericalism and the doctrines of perfectionism and nonresistance: all who would be pure disciples of the religion of abolition, Garrison proclaimed, should shed the oppressive influences of church and state. Garrison's rejection of organized religion deeply antagonized abolitionists who remained evangelicals and was another basic cause of the 1840 abolitionist schism. He also repudiated some of the nation's dominant secular institutions, including its political and electoral system, as bastions of slavery and other forms of unGodlike force, which led him a few years later to the principle of disunion. In peacefully seceding from the South, the North might at last begin to purify itself, while at the same time weakening slavery by removing its federal supports. Until the North seceded, Garrison argued, the United States Constitution would remain a proslavery "Covenant with Death, an Agreement with Hell."

By the early 1840s, Garrison's hatred of chattel slavery had evolved into a radical disaffection with an array of American institutions, which, as suggested by his quasi-anarchic calls for "no human government," put him on the far left of the American abolition movement. Yet Garrison's alienation never became so absolute as to erode his interest in achieving concrete reform. Notwithstanding the paternalistic attitude toward blacks he sometimes exhibited, Garrison collaborated with them in the effort to desegregate public schools and other institutions in the North.

With respect to perhaps the most fundamental American institution of all, private property in a capitalist labor market, Garrison never became alienated at all, but tended to retain the orthodox views of his youth. Although Garrison did evidence growing sensitivity toward the struggles of British Chartists and other labor movements, he remained antagonistic to all radical social theories that, in his view, trivialized and distorted the meaning of "slavery" by claiming comparable victimization for laborers who were not formally owned. Garrison's own ability to rise from humble beginnings no doubt contributed to his conviction that fair and open economic competition, with significant SOCIAL MOBILITY as a consequence, remained singularly characteristic of the free states.

During the 1840s and 1850s Garrison's role diminished, as he and his circle shared antislavery initiatives not merely with rival abolitionist camps but with growing numbers of mainstream political leaders. Garrison showed much more tolerance for the Free Soil and Republican antislavery extension coalitions than for political abolitionism, in part because they maintained no pretense of antislavery purity, and in part because they did represent new, albeit imperfect, additions to the antislavery ranks—an expression of the welcome if belated development of northern public opinion.

In the late antebellum years Garrison himself was in significant ways pulled into the antislavery mainstream. Although he had never unequivocally denied the legitimacy of slave violence, Garrison had nonetheless once firmly looked to the nonviolent transformation of white American moral values and racial attitudes as the essential means of eradicating slavery. Now, albeit reluctantly, he endorsed violent tactics to achieve antislavery ends. In justifying such developments as John Brown's Harpers Ferry raid and the decision of ABRAHAM LINCOLN to crush southern secession through CIVIL WAR, Garrison modified his doctrines of individual nonresistance and peaceable disunion to the point of near meaninglessness.

With the impending passage of the Thirteenth Amendment, Garrison led the call for the dissolution of the American Antislavery Society, insisting that the rationale for the organization's existence had now been removed. Garrison was one abolitionist whose concern for the civil equality and economic security of the freedman did fall short of his hatred for slavery. Psychological exhaustion partially explained this relative indifference. Whereas for years Garrison drew sustenance from identifying the abolitionist minority with the early Christian martyrs, he had by the mid-1860s tired of the role of outsider and agitator for unpopular causes. He now more highly craved that public acceptance and respect which was in fact coming to him as antislavery prophet and pioneer.

JONATHAN A. GLICKSTEIN

FURTHER READING
George M. Fredrickson, ed., *William Lloyd Garrison* (Englewood Cliffs: Prentice-Hall, 1968).
Wendell Phillips Garrison and Francis Jackson Garrison, *William Lloyd Garrison, 1805–1879: the Story of His Life Told by His Children*, 4 vols. (1885; New York: Negro Universities Press, 1969).
William Lloyd Garrison, *Thoughts on African Colonization* (1832; New York: Arno, 1968).
Aileen S. Kraditor, *Means and Ends in American Abolitionism: Garrison and His Critics on Strategy and Tactics, 1834–1850* (New York: Vintage, 1967).
Walter M. Merrill and Louis Ruchames, eds., *The Letters of William Lloyd Garrison*, 6 vols. (Cambridge: Harvard University Press, 1971–82).
Truman Nelson, ed., *Documents of Upheaval: Selections from William Lloyd Garrison's The Liberator, 1831–1865* (New York: Hill and Wang, 1966).
James Brewer Stewart, *William Lloyd Garrison and the Challenge of Emancipation* (Arlington Heights: Harlan Davidson, 1992).
R. Jackson Wilson, *Figures of Speech: American Writers and the Literary Marketplace, from Benjamin Franklin to Emily Dickinson* (New York: Knopf, 1989).

Garvey, Marcus (b. St. Ann's Bay, Jamaica, Aug. 17, 1887; d. London, England, June 10, 1940). A political activist and publisher who became the foremost proponent of black nationalism among the peoples of the African diaspora, Marcus Garvey reached the peak of his influence during 1918–25 when from his headquarters in Harlem he organized a mass movement with over 100,000 dues-paying members and many more sympathizers. Out of his effort came the symbols of black nationalism that reappeared among black populations around the world during the apex of the black power movement of the 1960s and during the current revival of Afrocentric thought: the red, black, and green flag, the wearing of African attire, and the general "back-to-Africa" cultural trend. During its most successful years the Garvey movement included over one thousand local units (divisions and chapters) in locations throughout the United States, and in the West Indies, Africa, South America and Europe.

Early on, Garvey worked as a printer in Kingston, Jamaica, where he joined the National Club, an organization of native-born Jamaicans who supported home rule. His activism in the National Club and in the printers' strike of 1907 left Garvey in bad standing with the colonial government and with local printers, forcing him to leave the country. Garvey's travels in Central America and the West Indies were a turning point in his life. While traveling among black plantation workers, a mobile working force that harvested the crops in several nations, he first grasped the international nature of the race problem. He published newspapers in Costa Rica and Panama that exposed conditions among the black workers he encountered, leading to his expulsion from both places. A two-year stint in London, during which he worked for the Egyptian black nationalist Duse Muhammed Ali's international newspaper *The African Times and Orient Review*, introduced him to the works of Edward Wilmot Blyden, the black activist from the Danish West Indies who emigrated to Liberia and eventually became that nation's leading educator and diplomat. Blyden was one of the originators of the pan-Negro idea.

On his return to Jamaica in 1914, Garvey set up the Universal Negro Improvement Association and African Communities League (UNIA and ACL). His goals were black self-improvement through emulation of the Jamaican elite; modernization and Christianity in Africa; and educational opportunities for the poor. Progress was slow since many of Jamaica's coloreds and blacks saw no need for a "Negro" organization in a nation where public acknowledgement of rampant color prejudice was rare. A speaking tour of the United States convinced him that his ideas would reach receptive ears in this new environment. When he settled in New York City in 1916, Garvey found himself among a large influx of immigrants from the Caribbean. By 1920 about one-quarter of Harlem's population was West Indian. The wartime ferment in black American communities, exacerbated by lynchings and antiblack riots, provided a better setting than Jamaica for Garvey's race-conscious organization. UNIA emerged as Harlem's most dynamic organization in 1920, when it hosted an international convention that drew over 25,000 delegates, members and sympathizers.

In the militant atmosphere of postwar Harlem, young Garvey polished his already impressive speaking style. He warned of dire results if blacks around the world failed to claim their share of the planet in light of the reorganization of Europe and its colonies at the end of World War I. Garvey prophesied that postwar European immigration into the United States would overwhelm the black population, making the labor and the presence of black people unnecessary and unwanted. The revival of the Ku Klux Klan in the 1920s seemed to give Garvey's argument greater credibility. "One hundred percent Americanism" seemed to be the wave of the future, with blacks relegated to a questionable status at best. Believing that the Klan was the "invisible government" of the United States, Garvey met with its acting leader in 1922 to end the conflicts between Klan members and UNIA members around the nation. Garvey's willingness to negotiate with racist whites on the ground that they represent all "true whites" was his most controversial act. His black American critics were especially incensed.

African American leaders who opposed Garvey's programs nevertheless shared his concerns about the future of blacks worldwide. A. Philip Randolph, the black socialist who would later become an important labor organizer, predicted continued oppression in the absence of unity among the black and white working classes. The National Association for the Advancement of Colored People (NAACP), and its most visible black leader, w. e. b. Du bois, lost its important campaign to pass a federal law against lynching in 1920, further weakening its claim that lobbying and court action were the best strategies for African Americans in the struggle for equality.

The center of Garvey's philosophy was the belief that blacks worldwide could expect equality only when they proved themselves to be equal in a competitive political and economic environment. The amassing of power and influence by Europeans was a deed accomplished by human beings, not superior creatures. He supported his claim that blacks could compete successfully with Europeans and others by citing the glories of ancient Egypt and Ethiopia, advanced civilizations built by black-skinned people.

Relying on themselves and spurning aid from whites, blacks who followed Garvey's plan would develop an independent trade between people of African descent in the Western hemisphere and those on the African continent. To implement the project, Garvey established the Black Star Line in 1919. Of course, this goal could not be reached while Europeans colonized almost all of the African continent. Therefore, armed struggle would be necessary to destroy European domination and ensure that Africa would be for the Africans, including those in the diaspora. All of the colonial governments with substantial black populations took the threat of

Garveyism quite seriously. British and French colonies in Africa and the West Indies outlawed the sale and sometimes even the possession of the *Negro World.*

None of these events went unnoticed by federal authorities in the United States. Beginning in 1919, J. Edgar Hoover pursued strategies aimed at neutralizing Garvey's impact or deporting him back to Jamaica. Garvey's opposition also included black political activists. Acrimonious exchanges characterized his relationships with black integrationists. Separatism was especially controversial among the leaders of integrated civil rights organizations like the NAACP and the Urban League. Black socialists advocated working-class unity rather than racial nationalism. In 1922 the efforts of J. Edgar Hoover and other government agents resulted in federal charges of mail fraud against Garvey, based on the alleged sale through the mail of stock in the financially distressed Black Star Line. He was convicted by an all-white male jury and sentenced to five years in prison.

Garvey's emphasis on the purchase of ships created a mythology around the movement long after its decline. Popular media depicted Garvey as an advocate of mass black migration to Africa, supposedly on his ships. Political opponents and critics used his conviction for mail fraud to create the impression that Garvey's entire movement had been a scheme to persuade poor blacks to part with their meager funds in exchange for a trip to a mythical kingdom in Africa. None of these notions fairly represented the man or the movement. Garvey's intention, it appears, was to recruit skilled blacks from the Western hemisphere to establish colonies in Liberia. Ultimately, Liberia would develop into a nation with sufficient economic and political strength to become the foundation of a greater African nation. Eventually it would expand beyond its present borders to include more and more of the continent. The ships, therefore, were part of an ambitious plan to establish a greater African community, along with trade and passenger travel between major black population centers.

The United States government made sure that Liberia, then in desperate need of a loan from the U.S., did not pursue early cordial exchanges with Garvey. After losing his last legal appeals, Garvey was deported to Jamaica in 1927, with the agreement that he would not be allowed to reenter the United States. Biographers usually treat the remainder of Garvey's career as a postscript. In fact, Garvey's return to Jamaica and his activities there were an important part of that nation's progress toward independence. Later, in London, Garvey published an international newspaper, *The Black Man*, while he attempted to keep his fragmented worldwide following. News of his death rekindled interest in his movement. African leaders, notably Kwame Nkrumah, cited him as a direct influence. His vision of self-direction and racial pride is even more influential among today's black diaspora than during his lifetime.

EMORY J. TOLBERT

FURTHER READING
Amy Jacques Garvey, *Garvey and Garveyism* (Kingston: Amy Garvey, 1963).
Robert Hill, Emory J. Tolbert, Deborah Forscek, and Barbara Bair, eds., *The Marcus Garvey and Universal Negro Improvement Association Papers*, vols. 1–7 (Berkeley: University of California Press, 1983–92).
Rupert Lewis, *Marcus Garvey: Anti-Colonial Champion* (Trenton: African World Press, 1988).
Tony Martin, *Race First: the Ideological and Organizational Struggles of Marcus Garvey and the Universal Negro Improvement Association* (London: Greenwood, 1976).

gay and lesbian identities "The homosexual" is a relatively new character on the historical stage. Though homosexual *acts* appear in every known human culture, most scholars now agree with Michel Foucault that homosexual *identities* evolved in Western societies in the nineteenth century. Before then, homosexual behaviors existed but did not mark a person as belonging to a specific type or group. To claim a homosexual identity, therefore, or impute it to someone else, is to participate in a relatively recent cultural construction of sexuality.

Even those who consider themselves homosexual disagree about the nature and meaning of homosexuality. Similarly, they disagree about the best strategies for securing political rights and societal acceptance, and these practical disputes often turn on the more theoretical question of the causes, or origin, of homosexuality. Many gay men and lesbians hope, for example, to protect their civil rights by establishing homosexuality as genetically predetermined, no more a cause for discrimination than green eyes or dark skin. Others fear that evidence of a genetic origin would be used to brand homosexuality as a pathology that should be cured (or, in the most disturbing scenario, eliminated through prenatal testing and selective abortions). They prefer to view sexual orientation, like religion, as a private choice deserving public protection. Either perspective can also be used to justify restrictive policies: whether homosexual people are sick (in the genetic view) or corrupted (in the private choice model), some argue that they should not be entrusted with such key responsibilities as military service or the education of children.

Competing interpretations of homosexuality reflect a long history of different ways of thinking about and experiencing homoerotic attraction. Contemporary laws prohibiting "sodomy," for example, are inherited from colonial statutes, which considered homosexual and other nonreproductive sexual acts both sinful and criminal: as voluntary deviations from the social order, such acts were punishable, sometimes by death. Sodomy laws thus reflect the historical focus on acts rather than identity. Although erratically enforced, they typically make heterosexual and homosexual couples equally culpable for the same acts.

The word "homosexual" is a medical term coined in the 1880s. Sexologists of the time sought to decriminalize homosexuality by attributing it to an inborn condition they called "inversion": a woman who loved another woman, for example, was actually animated by a male soul. As a fluke of nature, a biological abnormality, the invert was not criminally culpable for homosexual desires. This congenital invert became dangerous, however, when he or she seduced a person who would otherwise have been heterosexually normal, a risk particularly feared in such single-sex institutions as women's colleges. The idea of inversion was popularized through medical texts, advice books, and novels, the most famous of which is Radclyffe Hall's *The Well of Loneliness* (1928). Its protagonist, Stephen Gordon, is the archetypal female invert: masculine in build and dress and name, she courts a more feminine woman whom she meets in an all-female ambulance corps. Ultimately, however, she is doomed to a life of bitter isolation.

A number of working-class women apparently welcomed the medical model of inversion as they donned men's clothes, took men's higher-paying jobs, and courted and married women. Carroll Smith-Rosenberg argues, however, that this new identity represented a loss for middle-class women. Nineteenth-century bourgeois culture had expected intimate friendships between women: in a "female world of love and ritual," women found emotional closeness, physical affection, and support for their domestic responsibilities and/or professional aspirations. As the sexologists' ideas were popularized, however, same-sex love became suspect. Women's physical and emotional intimacy was reinterpreted as perverted and pathological. Because "unfeminine" behavior was seen as a sign of inversion, women were increasingly accused of sexual deviancy when their educational and professional goals challenged GENDER codes. Smith-Rosenberg suggests that bourgeois women accepted this redefinition of women's sexuality because it promised them (hetero)sexual liberation, but the price was political and economic impotence.

When FREUDIANISM streamed into American thought in the 1920s, it introduced a more psychological, less biological, view of homosexuality. Suggesting that all people have both heterosexual and homosexual potentials in the original "polymorphous perversity" of infancy, Freud believed that a man becomes a heterosexual adult by transferring his primal erotic interest in his mother onto other women, while a woman must undergo the more difficult transformation of switching her erotic interest from her mother to the male sex. In each instance, homosexuality represents a failure of psychological development. Homosexuals are made, not born.

Freud himself doubted that an adult's sexual orientation could change, yet Freudian therapists made many attempts to "cure" homosexuality. By mid-century, aversion therapy and shock therapy had joined psychoanalysis as methods to reverse the effects of a childhood misfortune and usher the client into a full, productive, and happy adulthood. Psychological norms of personal growth were applied to homosexuals, who were urged to look forward to a satisfying heterosexuality in the future and to terminate current friendships and romantic relationships. The psychologists' profile of "the homosexual" assumed that sexual pathology pervaded the entire personality: homosexual people were both defined by and obsessed with their sexuality.

While the criminal, medical, and psychological models all portray homosexuality as an individual condition, after 1940 homosexuality increasingly became associated with membership in a socially recognized group. Although small groups of homosexual people, primarily male, had existed since at least the eighteenth century, a real homosexual subculture did not emerge until after consumer capitalism succeeded, by around World War II, in making individual adults (rather than the family) a true unit of economic production and consumption. As women's wages rose to the subsistence level, it became increasingly possible for women as well as men to envision a future without marriage. The result was an increasingly large and visible homosexual community.

The war itself accelerated the formation of homosexual communities. For the first time, psychologists questioned all new inductees about their sexual proclivities. For some, these questions provided a new name for previously undefined inclinations. At the same time, military service provided unusual opportunities for same-sex intimacies. The war also brought large populations of women into cities, gave them economic independence, and encouraged them to engage in behaviors previously stigmatized as unfeminine. The end of the war did not necessarily disrupt homosexual relationships or circles of friends, since many civilians and military personnel chose to remain in port cities, such as San Francisco, that had developed active homosexual communities.

After the war, Joseph McCarthy's charges that homosexuals were working in the State Department kept homosexuality in the public eye. His accusations reinforced the idea that "a homosexual" is an alien and dangerous entity. Like communists, homosexuals were powerful enough to corrupt the national mission, yet shrewd enough to avoid easy detection. In a Cold War world, Americans were urged to scrutinize their neighbors and colleagues for signs of homosexuality, and even to examine themselves for signs of "latency." Homosexuality was one of many internal and external enemies that needed to be contained, isolated from American society. The result was that homosexuality became a broader preoccupation. The widespread anxiety about homosexuality, combined with the social fact of expanding homosexual communities, made it increasingly likely that people with homoerotic feelings would ascribe a homosexual identity to themselves—even if only privately.

The oppression of the McCarthy years also stimulated the founding of the first formal homosexual organizations. The predominantly male Mattachine Society published the first issue of *ONE* in 1953. Daughters of Bilitis, an explicitly all-lesbian group, followed two years later with *The Ladder*. Rejecting the term "homosexual" because it put too much emphasis on sex, these people referred to themselves as "homophiles." The magazines, which quickly gained a combined circulation of several thousand, sought to give isolated individuals a sense of community support. They also tried to convince readers to appear "normal." This effort was unpopular among many women (often working class) who held "men's" jobs and celebrated the butch lesbian's strength and autonomy. Nevertheless, the homophile associations did succeed in building effective middle-class social and political networks. Arguing that their members differed from heterosexuals only in their choice of romantic partners, they tried to convince the general public that homophiles were no less mature, stable, and respectable than anyone else and so should not suffer discrimination.

A more rebellious mood emerged in the 1960s as an increasing number of gay men and women affirmed a gay sensibility that they felt differed fundamentally from the heterosexual, or "straight," worldview. The term "gay" had existed for decades as a code word known to many "in the life" but to few outside; it was used to identify oneself to another discreetly. Now it was chosen as a preferred name by a self-declared minority who insisted on public knowledge and recognition. Drawing direct parallels to the black CIVIL RIGHTS and nationalist movements, activists launched a gay liberation movement. Gays, they insisted, are a minority, not a pathology, so discriminatory practices and policies should be abolished. Nor should gays be expected to be just like everybody else: their distinct history and culture should be recognized as a vibrant tradition that enriches American pluralism. "Coming out"— declaring one's gay identity—became a political act intended to demonstrate the ubiquitous presence of a gay minority.

Gay identity began to be expressed in community rituals, especially in the annual Gay Pride marches commemorating the Stonewall riots of June 1969. These riots, in which drag queens turned against police who were once again raiding a gay bar, are now seen as a turning point in gay consciousness; "before Stonewall" and "since Stonewall" are the primary demarcations of gay folk history. This formative event is reenacted each year as groups of gay men and lesbians (tens of thousands in some cities) take to the streets in a jubilant display of individual self-assertion and group solidarity. Such events reinforce the sense that gay identity is a collective heritage similar to racial or ethnic identity.

With the new wave of FEMINISM, however, many lesbians began to argue that differences between men and women are more fundamental than those between homosexuals and heterosexuals. Noticing that the standard image of a gay person is a gay man, they rejected "gay" as a false generic that is no more inclusive than "man." In a formative essay, ADRIENNE RICH argued that patriarchy tries to divide and diminish women by obscuring the "lesbian continuum" of female love and loyalty, which includes but is not limited to lesbian sexuality. The love of women, she suggested, is natural to women, whose first experience of human relationship is at their mothers' breasts. Heterosexuality is what needs to be questioned and explained. Like Rich, other lesbian feminists celebrate lesbian relationships as a source of strength and nurturance for women who resist patriarchal oppression. Some suggest that women should choose lesbianism as a political tactic and preferred way of life.

By the late 1980s, the idea that sexuality is constructed had considerable impact even outside feminist circles. Often influenced by postmodernist thought, many academics and writers for the gay and lesbian press suggested that erotic attraction is multivalent, fluid, and charged with symbolic meanings. There is no such thing, they argued, as a "natural" sexuality: heterosexuality, like homosexuality, is a cultural product, and these are only two of the many possible variants. Returning to the idea that all humans have both homoerotic and heteroerotic impulses, more and more people claimed bisexual identities. (*See also* POSTMODERNISM.)

For these postmodernists, sexual expression is an appropriate realm of human self-creation. Phrases like Queer Nation's "We're here, we're queer, get used to it" aggressively deny the significance of the question of origin. Sexuality, in this view, is always both a given and a becoming. It is a fallacy to believe that because sexuality is cultural it is easily changed. Rather, sexuality is ever-changing, sometimes because of conscious choices, but often in unpredictable ways. It is a rich pool of experience fed by an individual's lifelong interactions with the world. In everyday life, sexuality is performed: people play out roles, seeking pleasure and self-definition in the mysteries and ambiguities of desire.

Earlier models of sexuality continue, however, to influence current thinking. Although the American Psychological Association removed homosexuality from its diagnostic manual in 1973, many people continue to see homosexuality as a psychological deviation. A statement of homosexual identity is frequently greeted with the response that "it's just a stage." Those who argue that adolescent homosexuality should be accepted as a "normal" part of sexual life inadvertently reinforce the idea that adult homosexual interests are a symptom of arrested development or disordered family relations. Many liberal-minded people who assert their tolerance for homosexuality continue to subscribe to essentialist psychological definitions of the self: a person is either "a homosexual" or "a heterosexual." This stark dichotomizing has shown tremendous staying power in the face of postmodern and feminist critiques. (*See also* FEMININITY; MASCULINITY.)

Modern medical research depends upon and reinforces this dichotomy. Sexologists continue to seek a truth within—this time in the genes. Studies of brain structure and chromosomal markers try to discover a single cause for homoerotic desire, which is construed as a simple deviation from heteroerotic desire. Most of these studies use male subjects. This is partly because AIDS has focused medical attention on gay men, but it also reflects a widely held view that male sexuality is more directed, more driven, than female sexuality. Men's sexual behavior is therefore more amenable to biological explanations, while women's sexual behavior is seen as more contextual and more influenced by such intangibles as affection and love.

Postmodernist ideas, on the other hand, have been enormously influential in the gay and lesbian community, where bitter "constructivist" versus "essentialist" debates raged in the 1980s. The spread of constructivism poses a problem for those who want to portray gay people as one of a number of minorities fighting for their civil and human rights. While minorities often find it useful to highlight their "essential" characteristics, unchanging over generations, this option is not available to postmodernists, for whom sexuality—like race, ethnicity, and gender—is always evolving. Gay people of color face the further dilemma of being asked to choose between two affiliations. If being gay is an ethnicity, how does one belong to two ethnicities? Is "gay" unavoidably white? Many gay people still draw cultural and political strength from the essentialist image of an ethnic group. Nevertheless, the new political groups that emerged in the late 1980s (such as Act Up and Queer Nation) are more likely to insist that sexual expression be protected not in terms of the civil rights of a minority, but as the freely, even flamboyantly, chosen self-creation of the individual. It is not enough, they insist, to ask for toleration of involuntary deviation from a white heterosexual norm; that norm must itself be shattered.

Academic interest has recently turned towards gay and lesbian studies, which has been redefined under the influence of postmodernism. Early gay scholarship was heavily shaped by a sense of responsibility to the gay community: believing academic work cannot be disconnected from its political roots, scholars nurtured self-respect and other survival skills needed in a hostile world. Later work questioned the boundaries of the gay community itself. No longer taking heterosexuality for granted, scholars reexamined the classic accounts of American history and showed that homoeroticism is not as marginal in the American past as we have believed. Now they are exploring the cultural, political, intellectual, and economic ramifications of the homo–hetero split in American thought and life. The relationship between sexuality and gender has become a particularly fruitful field of exploration as both are recognized as highly contested systems of representation. Seeking a proper balance between viewing individuals as autonomous agents and as shaped by social forces, scholars are trying to grasp the connections between subjective experience, material conditions, and cultural ideologies.

An explosion of general public interest in homosexuality has also occurred in the 1980s and 1990s. Motivated in part by AIDS, this discussion goes to the heart of American thoughts and feelings about "difference." The historical connection between homoeroticism and gender transgression means that homosexuality is charged with the fears and tensions brought about by changes in what it means to be a man or a woman. The claim that homosexual identity is equivalent to ethnic identity has challenged Americans to define the terms, and possible limits, of cultural pluralism. In a single decade, gay, lesbian, and bisexual people have gained much more visibility and social acceptance, yet political attacks continue to be effective and physical attacks continue to be fatal. In a time of shifting political and economic allegiances, when cultural and "family" issues are central to both individual and collective self-definitions, we can expect sexuality to remain a key arena of social debate and intellectual exploration.

LORI J. KENSCHAFT

FURTHER READING

John D'Emilio, *Sexual Politics, Sexual Communities: the Making of a Homosexual Minority in the United States, 1940–1970* (Chicago: University of Chicago Press, 1983).

Lillian Faderman, *Odd Girls and Twilight Lovers* (New York: Columbia University Press, 1991).

Michel Foucault, *The History of Sexuality*, vol. 1: *An Introduction* (New York: Random House, 1978).

Radclyffe Hall, *The Well of Loneliness* (New York: Doubleday, 1928).

Shane Phelan, "(Be)Coming Out: Lesbian Identity and Politics," *Signs: Journal of Women in Culture and Society* 18 (summer 1993): 765–90.

Adrienne Rich, "Compulsory Heterosexuality and Lesbian Existence" (1980), reprinted in Rich, *Blood, Bread, and Poetry* (New York: Norton, 1986).

Eve Kosofsky Sedgwick, *Epistemology of the Closet* (Berkeley: University of California Press, 1990).

Carroll Smith-Rosenberg, *Disorderly Conduct* (New York: Oxford University Press, 1985).

Geertz, Clifford (b. San Francisco, Calif., Aug. 23, 1926). Undoubtedly modern America's best-known and intellectually most influential figure in CULTURAL ANTHROPOLOGY, Geertz is head and founder of the prestigious School of Social Sciences at Princeton's Institute of Advanced Studies, author and editor of many often-cited books and articles, winner of the National Book Critics Circle award and numerous other honors, and contributor to important intellectual journals. He has found an admiring audience in disciplines as diverse as history, literary theory, and philosophy—but within his own field his work has become ever more debated and controversial.

Geertz attended Antioch College, where his early ambition to write fiction was set aside in favor of philosophy. In 1950, seeking something "more empirical," he entered graduate school in anthropology in the short-lived multidisciplinary Social Relations Department at Harvard. There he studied with TALCOTT PARSONS, who was bringing the work of Max Weber and Émile Durkheim together into a new kind of systematic American sociology. Geertz found little to admire in Durkheim, and Parsons's own system left him cold, but he took Weber to heart—especially the notion of *Verstehen*, understanding the other's point of view.

In favoring a Weberian approach, Geertz opposed the functionalist paradigm dominating American anthropology of the 1950s. He argued that the task of anthropology was not the discovery of laws, patterns, and norms, but rather was the interpretation of "webs of significance" which people both spin and are caught up in. These symbolic webs were taken by Geertz to be the essence of culture. They legitimized power structures and channelled unruly human desires by offering believers a sense of purpose within a meaningful world. "The trick," Geertz wrote, "is to figure out what the devil they think they are up to." The only way this trick could be accomplished was through what Geertz famously called the "thick description" of another culture—that is, through writing ethnography.

Most of Geertz's work is indeed ethnographic. His first fieldwork was two-and-a-half years in eastern Java. From this research came a series of books, including *The Religion of Java* and *Agricultural Involution*. These works portrayed the pluralistic Javanese society as an inwardly turned and mystically oriented culture in which many different traditions mingled harmoniously. This halcyon picture was tarnished by the later massacre of Indonesian "communists," but Geertz's studies nonetheless won acclaim not only among anthropologists but also among economists and development specialists.

In 1960 he joined the faculty of the anthropology department at the University of Chicago, where he read Herder, Humboldt and Dilthey. Geertz, like RUTH BENEDICT, to whom he has often been compared, was inspired by the emphasis the German Romantics placed on an aesthetic appreciation of other cultures. His youthful ambition to be a writer of fiction could now be realized within the realm of anthropology; fictional artifice was recast as interpretation of the culturally formed symbolic worlds of others, which existed separately from, yet in dialectical relationship with, social action. For Geertz, the Weberian effort to establish a comparative sociology was now set aside; comparison, he argued, serves to show that societies are, in fact, incomparable—each is unique, and the anthropologist's job is to make the reader appreciate that uniqueness via authorial leaps of informed and artful imagination into the "webs of significance" inhabited by exotic others.

Concentrating on creating a new kind of anthropological writing, Geertz began to move beyond professional journals in hopes of reaching a wider audience. His prose now assumed a twisting syntactical structure replete with multiple clauses, lengthy lists, and erudite allusions to philosophy, literature, and popular culture. Those who found this style irritatingly self-referential and low on content were in the minority. Two highly successful collections of essays, *The Interpretation of Cultures* and *Local Knowledge*, contained Geertz's best-known occasional pieces, and introduced the intellectual public to his romantic and writerly version of anthropology. His increasing fame coincided with his appointment in 1970 to Princeton's Institute of Advanced Studies, where he asserted tremendous influence on the Princeton history department, which became the leading exponent of the symbolic study of everyday life in the past.

Meanwhile, Geertz also undertook extensive new fieldwork, first in Bali, and then in Morocco. The latter culminated in his *Islam Observed*, which attempted to demonstrate the distinctiveness of Muslim practice and belief in Indonesia and Morocco. Most influential, however, was his writing on Bali, in which he portrayed Balinese people as passionless aesthetic performers in a vast and timeless cultural play. This portrait has since been strongly challenged. The surface calm of the Balinese, Unni Wikan argues in *Managing Turbulent Hearts*, is a consequence not of an absence of passion, but of deep fears that revealing one's true emotions incites aggressive attacks by witches. Nor, other critics claim, does Geertz's image of Bali recognize the stark disparities of power within the society.

Problems some anthropologists have had with Geertz's later writings are well illustrated in his most famous essay: "Deep Play: Notes on the Balinese Cockfight," in which Geertz asserts that the cockfight is a moral text teaching the Balinese lessons about subjectivity and human action. This may be so, but the Balinese themselves are not consulted about this reading—it remains Geertz's own. Nor does he note that cockfights prevail in many very different cultures besides Bali. We are left, then, with evocative prose that tells us a great deal about the author's sensibility, but may tell us very little about Bali.

In response to these types of critique, Geertz lately has moved toward an even more self-conscious concern with the role of the anthropological author constructing and defining culture, producing CULTURAL CRITICISM rather than scholarship. His most recent, award-winning book, *Works and Lives*, is an analysis of several famous ethnographies as literary texts. However, even though Geertz, using his own considerable poetic talents, has painted the anthropologist, and especially himself, as an artist of culture, most practitioners still consider it their job to help their subjects to speak, not to speak for them.

CHARLES LINDHOLM

FURTHER READING
Clifford Geertz, *The Religion of Java* (Glencoe: Free Press, 1960).
——, *Agricultural Involution* (Berkeley: University of California Press, 1963).
——, *Islam Observed: Religious Development in Morocco and Indonesia* (New Haven: Yale University Press, 1968).
——, "Deep Play: Notes on the Balinese Cockfight," in Geertz, ed., *The Interpretation of Cultures* (New York: Basic Books, 1973).
——, *Local Knowledge: Further Essays in Interpretive Anthropology* (New York: Basic Books, 1983).
——, *Works and Lives: the Anthropologist as Author* (Stanford: Stanford University Press, 1988).
Paul Shankman, "The Thick and the Thin: On the Interpretive Theoretical Program of Clifford Geertz," *Current Anthropology* 25 (1984): 261–70.
Unni Wikan, *Managing Turbulent Hearts: a Balinese Formula for Living* (Chicago: University of Chicago Press, 1990).

gender Although the term dates back to at least the fourteenth century, it has probably never been more popular than it is in the United States today. Certain older usages (gender meaning "kind or sort"; gender meaning "to beget" or "to breed") no longer roll off modern tongues, but new ones have arisen. In the 1990s everyone seems to be talking about gender: scholars study "gender as a category of analysis"; activists challenge discrimination based on "race, class, and gender"; political pundits analyze "gender gaps" in voting patterns; postmodern teenagers champion "gender-bending." About the only thing these phrases have in common is that they refer, in a very general way, to sexual distinctions. Beyond that, popular usage is hopelessly vague, so vague as to suggest there is a pressing cultural demand for a term capable of both signaling and obfuscating a topic of intense contemporary concern: changing definitions of, experiences of, and relations between, the sexes.

The term "gender" is every bit as popular among U.S. intellectuals as it is among the American public. In academic circles, though, gender carries a distinctive—yet no less far-reaching—meaning. Its contemporary scholarly use dates largely from the 1970s, when path-breaking feminist scholars began to distinguish between the biological characteristics they labeled "sex" and the attitudes, behaviors, and social structures they labeled "gender." As they explained it, the concept of sex was limited to the physical distinctions between men and women. The concept of gender, however, was much wider: it stretched from attitudes ("women's place is in the home") to behaviors (rape, sexual harassment) to institutional practices (corporations discriminating against women in hiring, or governments denying women entrance into the armed forces). What the many disparate aspects of gender had in common was that, while they were ordinarily described as "natural" outgrowths of the physical distinctions between men and women, they did not, in fact, bear any necessary relation to biology. In this sense, gender was said to be socially constructed rather than biologically determined.

Once sex and gender had been distinguished from each other, the key question for scholars was why people ordinarily assumed that they were the same thing, why, in other words, so many people regarded socially constructed gender as if it were a naturally biological phenomenon. As anthropologist Gayle Rubin framed it, the task was to examine the ways in which biological sex was transformed and reprocessed into social gender. Scholars in a variety of disciplines took up Rubin's challenge. Feminist psychologists studied the process by which "gender identities" were inculcated in individuals. (*See also* FEMININITY and MASCULINITY.) Feminist historians traced modern notions of women's place to their roots in Victorian society, then contrasted Victorians to their colonial predecessors. Feminist anthropologists compared the "gender systems" of entire societies across time and space. Stunned by both the universality and the remarkable variety of gender distinctions, feminist scholars set themselves the task of outlining gender differences, gender relations, and gender dynamics on both macro and micro levels. Their work laid the basis for the establishment of women's studies programs and departments, and it also opened up vast areas for new research in the humanities and social sciences.

Emerging as it did during the remarkable social and intellectual ferment of the 1960s and 1970s, the feminist definition of gender provided scholars with a striking example of a phenomenon once thought to be entirely natural, but now revealed to be cultural in origin. The distinction between sex and gender echoed, of course, the nature versus nurture debate that runs through the history of Western cultures. In much the same way that another version of this debate, the race versus culture conflict of the 1920s, had moved intellectuals away from biological under-

standings of racial difference in the early twentieth century, the development of the concept of gender set a pattern for contemporary scholars. As a model critique of biological determinism, it has been widely influential. Since the 1970s, theorists have applied it to a variety of other concepts, including sexuality, race, and even sex difference itself.

Take, for example, sexuality. For most of the twentieth century, scholars considered sexuality to be an innately biological phenomenon. So widespread was this consensus that it extended to both sides of controversial political issues. It was, for example, the position taken by conservatives, who defended the "naturalness" of traditional heterosexual family structures. But it was also the assumption made by many gay and lesbian activists, who insisted that conservative attempts to divert homosexual desire into heterosexual channels were doomed to failure because sexual preference was instinctual, not elective. (*See also* GAY AND LESBIAN IDENTITIES.)

This kind of thinking, which Gayle Rubin came to refer to as "sexual essentialism," was sharply challenged by the feminist critique of biological determinism. As one of the scholars most responsible for the rise of the concept of gender, Rubin's own work shows that it was only a small step from the social construction of gender to the social construction of sexuality. In an article entitled "Thinking Sex," Rubin applied to sexuality the language that she might once have used to explain gender. "Sexuality," she wrote, "is impervious to political analysis so long as it is primarily conceived as a biological phenomenon or an aspect of individual psychology." In her mind, the challenge for scholars was to recognize that "sexuality is as much a human product as are diets, methods of transportation, systems of etiquette, forms of labor, types of entertainment, processes of production and modes of oppression" (p. 277).

Contemporary scholarly concepts of RACE have followed a similar trajectory from the biological to the social. Comparisons between race and gender have been commonplace in scholarly analysis and political rhetoric since at least the 1960s, but the relationship between them can be—and has been—conceptualized in dramatically different ways. One way is to offer an analogy between race and sex in which both stand as biological markers used to form the bedrock of systems of social inequality. This is the analogy that was offered by proponents (and opponents) of the civil rights legislation of the 1960s and 1970s; it is embedded in laws which prohibit discrimination on the basis of race and sex.

After feminist scholars began to distinguish social gender from biological sex, however, a new analogy emerged. In a recent article on "African-American Women's History and the Metalanguage of Race," historian Elizabeth Higginbotham makes use of it. Comparing race to gender in the hope of persuading her readers that both are social constructions rather than biological givens, she argues that it is necessary to "define the constructions and 'technologies' of race as well as those of gender and sexuality" (p. 252).

Scholars who have tried to do this have discovered that racial categorizations have more to do with the social and historical traditions of white supremacy —and black resistance to it—than they do with biology. There is, for example, no biological reason why the children of one white and one black parent should be categorized and legally and socially treated as black. Although this happens routinely in the United States, such a child could just as logically be categorized as white. The same point could be made in a much larger sense. Although most people today assume that race is defined by the biological characteristic of skin color, it turns out that in different contexts and time periods, race has been variously described as a matter of skin color, identity, ancestry, or even the mystical quality of "blood."

The most recent—and most daring—extension of the feminist critique of biological determinism has been put forth by scholars who would apply it to sex difference itself. Building on more than two decades of challenges to the foundations of phenomena once thought to be biological in nature, some theorists have begun to argue that human conceptions of biological "sex" are themselves socially constructed (or, to use a current—and revealing—modifier, "gendered"). An intriguing example can be drawn from Thomas Laqueur's book *Making Sex*, which is a study of medical textbook drawings of male and female anatomy from the sixteenth to the twentieth century. These drawings, which purport to represent physical sexual characteristics, change dramatically over time. Early drawings reflect a one-sex model, in which women's genitals are depicted as if they were men's genitals turned inward, with "the vagina . . . imagined as an interior penis, the labia as a foreskin, the uterus as scrotum, and the ovaries as testicles" (p. 4). Later drawings, however, reflect a two-sex model, in which physical differences between the sexes are so dramatic as to make comparisons seem impossible. According to Laqueur, the shift from the one-sex to the two-sex model corresponds more closely to changing cultural ideas of gender than to advances in scientific anatomical knowledge. If Laqueur is right, even physical sexual distinctions must be understood to be the product of gendered assumptions.

The argument that sex is socially constructed is a very recent development. While it is both logically consistent and theoretically ingenious, it is not yet widely accepted. Like the arguments that race, sexuality, and gender are socially constructed, it goes against many people's "common sense." In some respects, the emergence of this argument reflects the coming of age of a new generation of feminist theorists. In her book *Gender Trouble*, postmodern feminist Judith Butler makes the case for the social construction of sex in language saturated with the terminology of poststructuralism. "Perhaps," she writes, "this construct called 'sex' is as culturally constructed as gender; indeed, perhaps it was always already gender, with the consequence that the distinction between sex and gender turns out to be no distinction at all" (p. 7).

Like Butler, other proponents of this argument emphasize their differences with feminist scholars of the 1970s, tracing their intellectual inspiration to poststructuralist theory instead. From a historical point of view, however, the significant point is not that early feminists might have been wrong to define sex as a biological phenomenon, but that their pathbreaking definition of gender as socially constructed has proved so influential that its expansion to concepts like sexuality, race, and sex now presents new challenges for feminist theory. One of these challenges is definitional: if gender can no longer be defined in contrast to sex, how should it be defined?

Some recent work suggests that the answer to this question might involve returning to a part of early feminist analysis that has been overshadowed by the expansion of social construction thinking, and that is the critique of patriarchy. For the feminists who first advanced the contemporary definition of gender, the power of the social construction argument lay not in its logical consistency or its theoretical ingenuity but in its potential to challenge male dominance. The concept of gender could, in theory, be applied to men and boys as well as to women and girls; indeed, masculinity is frequently conceived as the opposite of femininity and defined in relation to it. But gender is not symmetrical for men and women; in fact, gender distinctions form a primary axis of dominance and subordination, a hierarchy as well as a relationship between men and women. As feminist sociologist Dorothy Smith puts it, gender distinctions are arranged into powerful "relations of ruling." By dislodging gender from its supposedly natural roots in sex, feminist theorists had forged a powerful link between scholarship and social action: if gender were socially constructed rather than biological, male dominance and female subordination might be deconstructed, reconstructed, or abandoned altogether.

Adopting the social construction argument allowed feminists to tear down one of the building blocks of twentieth-century relations of ruling—the argument that male dominance was inevitable because it was biologically natural. As we have seen, this feminist deconstruction project was highly effective in persuading scholars in and outside of feminist circles to adopt social construction arguments. It has, however, been much less successful at ending male dominance. In the past two decades, biological determinism has fallen on hard times, but male dominance has proven a wilier opponent, one quite capable of maintaining itself even without explicitly biological arguments.

Challenging patriarchal structures has proved difficult not only because male dominance has demonstrated extraordinary staying power but also because of a dynamic largely internal to feminist theory. One way that scholars dislodged gender from its biological moorings was to show that ideas about womanhood varied enormously in different locations and in different time periods. The effect of this development has been to subdivide the concept of gender into a multiplicity of genders. Spurred by critics who quite correctly pointed out that early feminists' descriptions of supposedly universal gender systems relied almost exclusively on evidence taken from the lives of white, middle-class women, later scholars focused more attention on women in the many social groups previously ignored. As a result, information about the gender systems that shape the lives of women in racial and ethnic minority groups, of working-class women, lesbians, and others has proliferated.

Scholars who pursue this work have raised crucial questions. Can the lives of African American women be understood as variations on a single theme of gender analysis? Or are they so fundamentally different from the lives of white women that they should be analyzed as different "genders"? The same kind of argument has recently been advocated by those who emphasize divisions of sex and sexual preference as well as race. Should a lesbian who adopts a "feminine" role be considered a different gender from a heterosexual woman who adopts a "feminine" style? And what about a gay man, or a heterosexual one, who adopts a "feminine" style? Following this line of analysis suggests that there may be an unlimited number of very particular genders. This splintering of feminist analysis into multiple genders creates much-needed specificity, but does so at the cost of losing sight of the larger systemic nature of gender distinctions. One indication of this shift of vision can

be found in language: while in the 1990s the term "gender" seems to be everywhere, the term "patriarchy," once a staple of feminist scholarship, has all but disappeared.

Of course, studying systemic dominance would involve examining not just patriarchy, but much wider "relations of ruling." Each of the major social categories discussed here—gender, sex, sexuality, race—has been historically associated with a pervasive system of social power: sex and gender with male dominance, sexuality with heterosexual privilege, and race with white supremacy. Analyzing gender in a way that will apply to more than just white middle-class women involves studying all these systems. Understanding the relationships between them will require a complex long-term effort to trace what the theorist Chandra Mohanty has called "cartographies of struggle." (*See also* AUTHORITY.)

The past two decades have shown that, despite the enormous growth of interest in gender analysis and despite continual calls to widen its already enormous scope, there is a central irony embedded in the notion of gender as a social construction. Its very success has not only expanded the range of feminist thought but also brought it full circle. Now that not only gender but also sexuality, race, and sex may be conceived as social constructions, the crucial—and as yet unanswered—question remains that of the relationship between them.

PEGGY PASCOE

FURTHER READING

Judith Butler, *Gender Trouble: Feminism and the Subversion of Identity* (New York: Routledge, 1990).

Evelyn Brooks Higginbotham, "African-American Women's History and the Metalanguage of Race," *Signs* 17 (winter 1992): 251–74.

Thomas Laqueur, *Making Sex: Body and Gender from the Greeks to Freud* (Cambridge: Harvard University Press, 1991).

Chandra Talpade Mohanty, "Cartographies of Struggle: Third World Women and the Politics of Feminism," in Mohanty et al., eds., *Third World Women and the Politics of Feminism* (Bloomington: Indiana University Press, 1991).

Gayle Rubin, "The Traffic in Women: Notes on the 'Political Economy' of Sex," in Rayna R. Reiter, ed., *Toward an Anthropology of Women* (New York: Monthly Review Press, 1975).

——, "Thinking Sex: Notes for a Radical Theory of the Politics of Sexuality," in Carol S. Vance, ed., *Pleasure and Danger: Exploring Female Sexuality* (Boston: Routledge and Kegan Paul, 1984).

Joan Scott, "Gender: a Useful Category of Historical Analysis," *American Historical Review* 91 (Dec. 1986): 1053–75.

Eve Kosofsky Sedgwick, *Epistemology of the Closet* (Berkeley: University of California Press, 1990).

Dorothy Smith, *The Everyday World as Problematic: a Feminist Sociology* (Boston: Northeastern University Press, 1987).

George, Henry (b. Philadelphia, Pa., Sept. 2, 1839; d. New York, N.Y., Oct. 29, 1897).   Writer, orator, newspaperman, self-taught economist, polemicist, and prophet, Henry George probably did more to fasten his contemporaries' attention on the "social question" than any other writer, including Karl Marx and John Ruskin. *Progress and Poverty*, published in 1879 in an edition of 500 copies, was soon reprinted in cheap editions, translated into all the major languages, and serialized in newspapers. By 1905 it had sold more than two million copies. Fifty thousand mourners attended George's funeral in 1897. Nor was his influence confined to the United States. George Bernard Shaw, who became a socialist after reading *Progress and Poverty*, later wrote that "five-sixths of those who were swept into the great Socialist revival of 1883 . . . had been converted by Henry George" (Thomas, p. 196).

George's influence on the socialist movement testified both to the success and to the failure of his project. Though he aimed to awaken a sense of social justice, it was no part of his intention to convert people to socialism or social democracy. The single tax, as he conceived it—a tax on rent, designed to attack the problem of inequality at its source—presented itself as the only feasible alternative to a socialist attack on the problem. "You must choose," he told his countrymen, "between the single tax, with its recognition of the rights of the individual, . . . and socialism" (Thomas, p. 325). Marx, who predictably dismissed *Progress and Poverty* as an "utterly backward" book, at least understood the fundamental opposition between socialist collectivism and George's program of land reform (Thomas, p. 181). Now that socialism has had its day, we might well take that opposition as a point in George's favor, not as a reason to consign him to the garbage dump of history. His "backward" analysis of modern society, it turns out, tells us more about the decline of democracy than the work of those who saw the collectivist future, jumped to the premature conclusion that it "worked," and embraced it without reservation.

Three interlocking principles, each of them deeply rooted in American tradition, lay at the center of George's thought; his originality consisted in the radical conclusions he drew from them. The first —that democracy rests on a broad distribution of property—was so widely shared in the first half of the nineteenth century that it might well be considered the very basis of democratic thought. But democrats also understood the second principle, that property rights were not unconditional, that individuals were entitled to no more than what they brought into being by mixing their labor with na-ture's bounty. Property rights were limited by a third principle as well, according to which the earth is given to mankind in trust, each generation inheriting the obligation to improve it and to pass on the accumulated fruits of human ingenuity and toil, in the form of culture, as a legacy to future generations.

Progress and Poverty can be read as the concrete application of these ideas to the overriding issue of his time, as George saw it—the alarming concentration of wealth in the hands of the great capitalists, financiers, and speculators in particular. The great fortunes based on land speculation struck George as an especially blatant example of the private appropriation of wealth the value of which depended on collective effort. It was the progress of civilization—specifically the settlement of the wilderness—that caused land values to rise, and the rise in land values, which underlay the rising value of every other commodity, properly belonged to the community as a whole. George therefore proposed to tax the "unearned increment" on land ownership—the excess, beyond improvements made by proprietors, that derived simply from the "vast social organism that has grown up from the germ of the first settlement" (p. 240).

The beauty of the single tax, George argued, was that it would promote equality without creating a vast governmental bureaucracy. "We should reach the ideal of the socialist, but not through government repression" (p. 456). His ability to demonstrate that "simplicity" in government was by no means incompatible with social justice helps to explain George's appeal and influence (p. 454). But it was above all the moral urgency of *Progress and Poverty* that attracted followers, together with its prophetic insight into the "rise and fall of nations" (p. 544). History, George insisted, did not support the "current view" that "improvement tends to go on unceasingly, to a higher and higher civilization" (p. 481). The modern world owed its wealth and power to the transmission of skills and knowledge from one generation to the next; but the delicate mechanism of cultural transmission had broken down many times in the past and could easily break down in the future. Growth and decay were not only the general rule but the "*universal rule*" (p. 485). In the modern world, as in the great civilizations of the past, specialization and the concentration of wealth widened the gap between the rulers and the ruled. Advanced civilizations accordingly had to devote more and more of their resources to the maintenance of an idle ruling class. Previous civilizations had collapsed under the strain, and modern nations would succumb to the same fate unless they found a way to assure a more equitable distribution of wealth and to revive the virtues associated with small proprietorship.

The passage of time, which has brought us a widening gulf between wealth and poverty, a massive growth of bureaucracy, and a corresponding decline of the civic virtues, has done nothing to diminish the force of this warning.

CHRISTOPHER LASCH

See also PROGRESS.

FURTHER READING

Henry George, *Progress and Poverty* (New York: Robert Schalkenbach Foundation, 1981).

George R. Geiger, *The Philosophy of Henry George* (New York: Macmillan, 1933).

Edward J. Rose, *Henry George* (New York: Twayne, 1969).

John L. Thomas, *Alternative America: Henry George, Edward Bellamy, Henry Demarest Lloyd and the Adversary Tradition* (Cambridge: Harvard University Press, 1983).

Gibbs, Josiah Willard (b. New Haven, Conn., Feb. 11, 1839; d. New Haven, Conn., Apr. 28, 1903). Mathematical physicist. A preeminent theoretical scientist, Gibbs used the second law of thermodynamics—energy always moves from a higher to a lower level—to develop a new understanding of the behavior of mixtures of substances. His formulas for statistically predicting when a system of liquids and gasses will be at equilibrium (first published in "On the Equilibrium of Heterogeneous Substances," 1876) allowed scientists and industrialists to calculate mathematically, rather than determine empirically, what proportions, concentrations, temperatures, and pressures would efficiently produce a desired product.

FURTHER READING

Albert E. Moyer, *American Physics in Transition: a History of Conceptual Change in the Late Nineteenth Century* (Los Angeles: Tomash, 1983).

Gilman, Charlotte Perkins (b. Hartford, Conn., July 3, 1860; d. Pasadena, Calif., Aug. 17, 1935). A unique and compelling presence in the history of American women, Gilman is also a major figure in the history of American thought. Her reputation as a feminist theorist was enormous from the 1890s to the 1910s, went into decline as enthusiasm for FEMINISM and SOCIALISM, two of her primary goals, eroded in post-World War I America, and has come back again, initially in the late 1960s and most vigorously in the last ten years. It is not by chance that her work has undergone a revival. Most of the trenchant observations and analyses she made, most of the themes she stressed in her books, articles, speeches, essays, and poems, apply as well today as they did when she wrote them. Her entire body of writing constitutes

a legacy for the 1990s. She offered a perspective on the major issues of gender with which we still grapple: the origins of women's subjugation; the struggle to achieve autonomy and intimacy in human relationships; the central role of WORK as a needed definition of self for women as well as for men; and new strategies for rearing and educating future generations to create a humane and nurturing world.

Even Gilman's limitations, serious as they were, should not mar the importance, the boldness, the power of the prodigious work she left behind. Those limitations are easy to identify, if not to justify. She often neglected issues of class, race, and ethnicity and their complex interaction with gender. She believed in laws of racial development which today are viewed as racist and ethnocentric. Her private correspondence and journals indicate that she was anti-Jewish and racist. She never questioned the superiority of a heterosexual, monogamous nuclear family structure. While it is true that these views were widely accepted in her day, we may rightly wonder why, when she was able to transcend many other biases and conventions, she was not able to transcend these. What we learn from that limitation is that it is harder to free ourselves of cultural biases than we usually acknowledge. Her example conveys the harsh truth that we too are probably unable to free ourselves as thoroughly as we think we have from our own cultural limitations, even when we are certain we are doing so.

If Gilman's flaws are easy to identify, so too, I believe, are her strengths, and there are more of them. She sought to create a general theory of men and women in history from the perspective of gender. She raised and tried to answer within her theoretical construct all the questions to which she wanted answers and found none and so addressed the questions herself: sexual identity and how it is formed; the evolution of male/female roles and the origin of female subordination; the nature of work in society; the significance of child-rearing; the relationship between private and public spheres; the limitations imposed by institutions of DOMESTICITY; the use of technology in bringing about change. All such questions were designed to make her audience understand how the structures of society came to be and therefore how to build upon principles of collectivity and community to make them just and equitable.

By making GENDER the center of her analysis in a way no one had done before, she made gender oppression visible. To deny that centrality meant denying the entire body of her work, and so it came to be after World War I that her work was rendered invisible, in the same way that the subordination of women was made so pervasive and so seemingly natural as to be unnoticed and invisible. Her work became unavailable, as much of it remains today.

However much we now acknowledge her significance, the scope and range of what she was trying to accomplish has yet to be appreciated adequately. She was most known in her lifetime as the author of *Women and Economics: the Economic Relation Between Men and Women as a Factor in Social Evolution* (1898), and she is best known in ours for her fictional pieces, "The Yellow Wallpaper" (1892) and *Herland* (1915). But neither then nor now has she had an audience to assess the full body of her work, and without that we have not heard what she has to say to us.

In her first book, *Women and Economics*, she asserted that the economic dependence of women on men was the key to understanding the subordination of women. In her next two books, *Concerning Children* (1900) and *The Home: Its Work and Influence* (1903), she built on that central thesis by arguing that the home was the source of that oppression and that the rearing of children replicated the social system. In Victorian America she stripped the sentimentality from marriage and motherhood and exposed the power relations that imprison women and children, although she did not lump them together. Each was examined separately, the institution of marriage and the institution of motherhood. The home is an institution like any other, she said to a world that revered and idealized it. It is an institution owned by man, in which wife and children are forcibly held, forcibly by virtue of economic dependence and ideological power.

In her study of children, she asserted that children should not be treated as part of a family, but as individuals, vulnerable individuals, who are citizens of the larger world. No private person, no parent, should be permitted to administer justice in secret and alone; it is reprehensible to place the child in the power of the parents without appeal, without a defense, and without witnesses. She insisted that personal relationships (mother–child/husband–wife) are always social relationships and that the apparent privacy of the home should not prevail over social justice. She was building upon, although she probably did not know it, Mary Wollstonecraft's earlier effort to apply the same standards of citizenship to the domestic sphere that were applied to the public sphere.

Gilman then moved on, in *Human Work* (1904), to a sociological analysis of work, arguing that it is through the work we do that we receive a social definition of ourselves. She examined the implications of that idea for women, who are socially defined, whatever other work they may do, primarily as wives and mothers, that is, unlike men, first and foremost by their gender. She argued that INDIVIDUALISM, especially in its extreme version in the United States, was a severe liability for progressive change. She challenged the notion of AMERICAN EXCEPTIONALISM, seeing it as a negative exceptionalism, one that retarded change and led to American backwardness among industrial nations. She sought her humanist roots not in a liberal or individualist tradition of the Enlightenment but in a collectivism located in her views of maternalism, views that were echoed in the wide-ranging women's movement of the nineteenth century.

Two important ideas of Gilman's run counter to, indeed challenge, much of feminist thinking today. It is easy to be gleeful as Gilman pokes fun at many of the cultural artifacts that we also ridicule, such as the notion that half of the adult population should devote its life to feeding and caring for the other half. But our teeth may begin to clench a bit when she pokes fun at some aspects of our culture that many of us still uphold. For example, she did not think much of what today we call female culture. Her eye was sharply focused on the oppression to which women were subject and the effect of that oppression, which she saw as negative and damaging to women. The unhappy result of subjugation through the ages, she suggested, was an inferior product. For Gilman, oppression had consequences. It made us less than we could be. Gilman had no doubt what women were capable of achieving. She wrote three utopian novels to demonstrate her confidence in women's potential. She believed that women were once equal to men; she believed that in the future women would again be equal to men. She allowed for many exceptions, herself probably among them, and she placed great hope in the rising of the women's movement of the nineteenth century.

But throughout our androcentric history men have had power, which meant they had access to learning, to possibilities for growth and development, to the ability to pass on their knowledge to each other through the written record. Men used that power, she insisted, to deny to women the resources *they* enjoyed. Women did the best they could with what they were given, and that effort must be acknowledged and applauded. Gilman understood how male power also has corrupted men in important ways. We need both male and female qualities to be fully human, she argued, but throughout most of time women have been denied opportunities, and it matters and it shows.

Men's work is in general more important than women's work, Gilman believed. The standard markers of a "civilization"—trade, crafts, arts, manufactures, inventions, political institutions, technology —are almost exclusively masculine since women are prevented from participation. If she underestimated the importance of women's culture, her words are important reminders that we must not forget the larger patriarchal world and the negative impact it has had on women. These are not comfortable ideas for women to acknowledge, especially feminists, and so most of us do not confront these handicaps most of the time. But Gilman did not write her books in order to make anyone—critics or supporters—comfortable.

In her later years she addressed the question of ideology and its role in perpetuating what she believed to be the primary inequity, gender subordination. *His Religion and Hers: the Faith of Our Fathers and the Work of Our Mothers* ended the intellectual journey begun with *Women and Economics*. Published in 1923, *His Religion and Hers* is little known, but it is essential to an understanding of Gilman's intellectual legacy. In *Women and Economics*, Gilman had turned her great aunt CATHARINE BEECHER on her head: Beecher saw the domestic sphere as the foundation of woman's vocation and power; Gilman located the home as the place of women's oppression. In *His Religion and Hers* Gilman took another step away from the Beecher clan by dismissing her religious heritage. She asserted that religion has done more disservice to humanity than any other institution or ideology. Religion stressed blind obedience and self-sacrifice, focused on death rather than birth, and concentrated on the individual's life in the hereafter rather than the community's life in subsequent generations.

Gilman was not without a spiritual sense, but her faith was not in what we would today describe as "women's way of knowing." For that notion Gilman had little respect. She had a deep belief in reason and a deep suspicion of "intuition." Relying on emotion has kept women enslaved, she believed, because emotions are no less learned than any of our other socialized learning. We "fall in love" with the kind of person we are socialized to believe is the kind of person we are supposed to love—and we are often wrong. Women need to learn from men to value and use reasoned thinking, for only in that way can we free ourselves from the beliefs we accept as natural but that are, in reality, learned: the legitimacy of obedience and self-sacrifice rooted in religion; the validity of blind, transcending love; the existence of maternal instinct in all women. Gilman believed in what she called the female principle of nurturance and cooperation, but she just as firmly believed that this principle was embedded in rational thinking.

Despite the contemporary acceptance of Gilman as a major thinker, we are only now beginning to explore fully the full and rich body of her work and its implications for our time.

ANN J. LANE

FURTHER READING
Larry Ceplair, ed., *Charlotte Perkins Gilman: a Nonfiction Reader* (New York: Columbia University Press, 1991).
Carl Degler, "Charlotte Perkins Gilman on the Theory and Practice of Feminism," *American Quarterly* 8 (spring 1956): 21–39.
Catherine Golden, ed., *The Captive Imagination: a Casebook on "The Yellow Wallpaper"* (New York: Feminist Press at the City University of New York, 1992).
Mary Armfield Hill, *Charlotte Perkins Gilman: the Making of a Radical Feminist, 1860–1896* (Philadelphia: Temple University Press, 1980).
Ann J. Lane, To "Herland" and Beyond: the Life and Work of Charlotte Perkins Gilman (New York: Pantheon, 1990).

Ginsberg, Allen (b. Newark, N.J., June 3, 1926). Poet. A leading figure among the BEAT GENERATION, Ginsberg has long stood for the alienation and spiritual experimentation of postwar avant-garde art. His poem *Howl* (1956) spoke of a generation destroyed by American society's materialistic and dehumanizing values. In his play *Kaddish* (1961), he mourned his mother's insanity, institutionalization, and death. Ginsberg rejected aesthetic as well as social convention and tried to make his written voice as direct and unmediated as his conversations with friends. He was an early advocate of what became the counterculture's preferred virtues: feeling and impulse, spontaneity and originality, pleasure and sensation, sex and drugs, Zen Buddhism and transformation of consciousness.

FURTHER READING
Michael Schumacher, *Dharna Lion: a Biography of Allen Ginsberg* (New York: St. Martin's, 1992).

Gladden, Washington (b. Pottsgrove, Pa., Feb. 11, 1836; d. Columbus, Ohio, July 2, 1918). Minister and journalist. Gladden was an early exponent of the Social Gospel; like other secular and religious progressives, he sought to correct the worst abuses of an individualist capitalist culture. Social salvation, he argued, was as important as the salvation of individuals; in his conception, practical reform tended to displace prayer as the center of Christian action, and ethics displaced theology. Gladden's LIBERAL PROTESTANTISM was a significant contributor to the general program of socialization favored by late nineteenth- and early twentieth-century reformers. Among his many books are *Applied Christianity* (1887) and *Social Salvation* (1901).

FURTHER READING
Richard Wightman Fox, "The Culture of Liberal Protestant Progressivism, 1875–1925," *Journal of Interdisciplinary History* 23 (winter, 1993): 639–60.

Glasgow, Ellen (b. Richmond, Va., Apr. 22, 1873; d. Richmond, Va., Nov. 21, 1945). Writer. Rejecting romantic and sentimental visions of southern life, and especially southern womanhood, Glasgow created in her fiction a social history of the South since the Civil War. Her novels, including *The Voice of the People* (1900), *Virginia* (1913), *The Sheltered Life* (1932), and *Barren Ground* (1925), portrayed the decay of aristocratic planter culture, the rise of an industrial middle class, and women's rejection of an ornamental role defined by purity and self-sacrifice. Glasgow called for a New South with new leaders and new values, but later criticized modern culture for its superficiality and modern industry for the dislocations it caused.

FURTHER READING
Julius Raper, *From the Sunken Garden: the Fiction of Ellen Glasgow, 1916–1945* (Baton Rouge: Louisiana State University Press, 1980).

Godkin, E[dwin] L[awrence] (b. Moyne, Ireland, Oct. 2, 1831; d. Brixham, England, May 21, 1902). Journalist. As editor of the New York *Evening Post* (1883–99) and founding editor of THE NATION (1865–81), Godkin battled political corruption, fought for the gold standard, advocated civil service reform, and conducted a long campaign against what he called "chromo-civilization"—a culture of gossip, sensationalism, and exposure. Deeply distrustful of the passions of the masses, he opposed organized labor and bemoaned the democratization of taste. Excellence in politics as in culture depended upon education and a sensibility attuned to modesty and reticence.
See also JOURNALS OF OPINION; PUBLICITY.

FURTHER READING
William M. Armstrong, *E. L. Godkin: a Biography* (Albany: State University of New York Press, 1978).

Gold, Mike [born Itzok Isaac Granich] (b. New York, N.Y., Apr. 12, 1893; d. Terra Inda, Calif., May 14, 1967). Writer. Impassioned and acerbic, Gold believed that all literature should contribute to the goal of communist revolution. He exhorted his comrades to avoid the liberals' caution and the intellectuals' abstractions, and to embrace the hearty, virile sensibility of the proletarian culture. Adherence to Communist Party policy, he argued, gave writers a creative self-discipline far superior to the ad hoc eccentricities of bourgeois individualism. A writer or editor for several leftist journals, including the *New Masses*, Gold also wrote *120 Million* (1929), *Jews Without Money* (1930), *Change the World* (1937), and *The Hollow Men* (1941).
See also PROLETARIANISM.

FURTHER READING
James D. Bloom, *Left Letters: the Culture Wars of Mike Gold and Joseph Freeman* (New York: Columbia University Press, 1992).

Goldman, Emma (b. Kovno, Lithuania, June 27, 1869; d. Toronto, Ontario, May 14, 1940). In spite of the remarkable public attention which the American anarchist Emma Goldman received during her lifetime, her influence has been mostly ignored in historical scholarship. A bias against anarchism and its adherents, and a neglect of the role of women and of Jews in American political thought, accounts for this disturbing oversight. Scholarly work on radicalism and the left in the United States has been devoted almost exclusively to histories of the Communist and Socialist parties. Deported to Soviet Russia from the United States in 1919 as an alien anarchist for her stand against conscription, Goldman has also, in effect, been exiled from the historical record.

Ironically, the general dismissal of the significance of Goldman's critique is often based on a misconception of her definition of anarchism. Goldman never repudiated violence outright, but she did stress that social justice depended upon a significant change in popular attitudes and beliefs. A self-appointed professor of the streets, Goldman functioned as a public intellectual as well as an organizer. Goldman linked elements of European anarchist thought with American utopianism, and tapped into growing public concern at the turn of the century about the threat of big government to individual freedom. She addressed the political dimension of personal issues usually consigned to the private realm; her lectures challenging customary social practices were often perceived as more dangerous than those on the usual political topics.

Goldman's critique of the institution of marriage focused primarily on its false promise of security for women, and its sometimes stultifying effect on human relationships. She insisted on the importance of sexuality, and of sexual freedom, including homosexuality. She criticized laws that regulated birth control, prostitution, and marriage because they enforced limitations on women's control of their bodies and, ultimately, on their personal freedom. Goldman always included an economic and social critique of the conditions which prompted such restrictive laws, distinguishing herself from more pragmatic, single-issue birth control advocates. She saw herself as speaking for the moral conscience of society, but was portrayed by her opponents as a licentious rabble rouser. The twentieth-century movement for freedom of expression in the United States can be traced, in part, to Emma Goldman. Her oratorical skill distinguished her from other political activists who waged the battle in streets and courtrooms that eventually led to the enforcement and protection of the right of free expression. Many who did not agree with her anarchist ideas were swayed by her eloquence and supported her right to speak openly; most prominent among her advocates was Roger Baldwin, cofounder of the American Civil Liberties Union, who named her as his primary inspiration. Goldman's stand in 1917 against the military conscription of young men, in her view a denial of their individual rights, and her analysis of the economic factors that fueled World War I, placed Goldman at the forefront of antimilitarism in America. The deportation order that sent her into exile was telling testimony to her persuasive power.

In exile from the United States, Goldman continued to judge international movements on the basis of how much freedom of expression they allowed. She not only warned the world of the dangers of fascism and Nazism, but explored the implications for Soviet communism of the suppression of dissent and examined the contradiction of anarchist cooperation with communists during the Spanish Civil War.

In part because Goldman has been eclipsed from history, there has been little scholarly debate about her ideas or her influence. Scholarship on Goldman has been devoted to establishing the factual record of her life through the retrieval of primary documents and the writing of several biographies. Although her ideas on a multitude of political and cultural issues were not original, her synthesis and persuasive presentation could not be matched, and it warrants serious appraisal.

Goldman's lectures and writings reveal a creative fusion of ideas. She incorporated the concept of mutual aid from Russian anarchist Peter Kropotkin; and, following Michael Bakunin, who believed that property should be owned communally, she identified herself as a "communist-anarchist." Empathy with the plight of labor attracted her to the anarcho-syndicalists. Her early exposure to European Malthusians prompted her to incorporate the campaign for birth control into her work for women's freedom; at the same time she deemphasized the place of eugenics in her formulation. Goldman heard Sigmund Freud lecture, read the various sex theorists of her time including Edward Carpenter and Magnus Hirschfeld, and argued for extending their work by taking women's sexuality seriously. She concluded that male and female creativity were rooted in the expression of sexual impulses, not dependent, as in Freud's thought, on their suppression or sublimation. The philosopher most exciting to Goldman was Friedrich Nietzsche, whom she considered "the intellectual storm center of Europe." Her literary heroes included Leo Tolstoy and Walt Whitman, whose writings she believed captured the essence of Eastern European and American anarchism. She saw modern drama as a usefully indirect vehicle for political expression during periods when radicals were subjected to extreme government and police suppression. Goldman grasped the utility of artistic expression for political transformation, and in writing on art stressed the social significance of theatrical works of her time, especially the plays of Henrik Ibsen and August Strindberg.

With the resurgence of the women's movement in the 1960s and 1970s, Goldman was rediscovered as a foremother of the battle for women's personal and political freedom. Her autobiography and selected essays were republished and circulated widely among the scholars and activists who came to shape the intellectual framework for the study of women's history. Her emphasis on the political aspects of personal life provided the basis for the new feminist scholarship. Many feminists whose ideas were formed in the period of student mobilization against the war in Vietnam also embraced Goldman's anarchist anti-authoritarian stance. Feminists in the 1990s, however, are more likely to extract elements from Goldman's essays that focus exclusively on women's issues.

Although feminist scholarship has evolved, and the drive to gather biographical data on (and to celebrate) early freedom fighters has become less central, critical scholarship on Goldman's ideas and influence has not yet taken hold. It is possible, however, that the end of the Cold War will lift the veil of scholarly prejudice against anarchism in American history and spark an interest in her work. As students of the American past begin to look seriously at the range and depth of radical commitment in nineteenth- and twentieth-century America, they will inevitably come face to face with the imposing figure of Emma Goldman.

CANDACE FALK

See also LIBERTARIANISM; SOCIALISM.

FURTHER READING

Paul Avrich, *Anarchist Portraits* (Princeton: Princeton University Press, 1988).

Richard Drinnon, *Rebel in Paradise: a Biography of Emma Goldman* (Chicago: University of Chicago Press, 1961).

Richard Drinnon and Anna Maria Drinnon, eds., *Nowhere at Home: Letters from Exile of Emma Goldman and Alexander Berkman* (New York: Schocken, 1975).

Candace Falk, ed., *Emma Goldman: A Guide to Her Life and Documentary Sources* (Alexandria, Va.: Chadwyck-Healey, 1995).

——, *Love, Anarchy, and Emma Goldman: a Biography*, rev. ed. (1984; New Brunswick: Rutgers University Press, 1990).

Emma Goldman, *Living My Life*, 2 vols. (1931; New York: Dover, 1970).

Alice Wexler, *Emma Goldman in America* (Boston: Beacon Press, 1986).

——, *Emma Goldman in Exile: From the Russian Revolution to the Spanish Civil War* (Boston: Beacon Press, 1989).

Gompers, Samuel (b. London, England, Jan. 27, 1850; d. San Antonio, Tex., Dec. 13, 1924). Trade union leader. As first president of the American Federation of Labor (1886–94, 1896–1924), Gompers was long lionized by labor historians for his successful organization of American labor. Gompers believed that trade unions enable workers to prevent unjust expropriation of their labor and to share in American prosperity. He urged skilled workers to act together, using strikes and boycotts, to secure higher wages, shorter hours, better work conditions, and job security. Because he distrusted social change through legislation, and because he was unconcerned about the fate of unskilled workers, Gompers opposed a labor party. Convinced that government, corporations, and intellectuals were inevitably paternalistic in their dealings with labor, he rejected cross-class alliances of the sort that labor movements in some other nations have relied on to secure power. Gompers' conception of "pure and simple" unionism triumphed over the ideal of workers' cooperatives envisioned by the Knights of Labor, over the revolutionary syndicalism of the Industrial Workers of the World, and over the ideal of industrial democracy endorsed by many intellectuals and some labor dissidents.

See also DEMOCRACY; SOCIALISM.

FURTHER READING

David Montgomery, *The Fall of the House of Labor: the Workplace, the State, and American Labor Activism, 1865–1925* (New York: Cambridge University Press, 1987).

Goodman, Nelson (b. Somerville, Mass., Aug. 7, 1906). Philosopher. A specialist in epistemology, Goodman has stressed the difficulty of arriving at certain knowledge. He has made especially significant contributions to inductive theory: inductive modes of reasoning, he argues, are flawed by their failure to note that any sequence of events is consistent with multiple hypotheses about their future course. In his later work, Goodman has pursued the elemental constructedness of all forms of knowledge, including scientific knowledge. A professor at Brandeis University, then at Harvard, Goodman published such works as *Fact, Fiction, and Forecast* (1965), *The Structure of Appearance* (1966), *Ways of Worldmaking* (1978), and *Of Mind and Other Matters* (1984).

FURTHER READING

Mia Gosselin, *Nominalism and Contemporary Nominalism: Ontological and Epistemological Implications of the Work of W. V. O. Quine and N. Goodman* (Boston: Kluwer Academic, 1990).

Goodman, Paul (b. New York, N.Y., Sept. 9, 1911; d. Northstratford, N.H., Aug. 2, 1972). Psychologist and writer. One of the most wide-ranging cultural critics in post-World War II America, Goodman published fiction and poetry in addition to the social criticism for which he is best known. *Communitas: Means of Livelihood and Ways of Life* (1947), written with his brother Percival, was a moral exploration of urban and community planning. *Growing Up Absurd* (1960), a bible for many who came of age in the 1960s, shared in the widespread existentialist critique of modern society. But unlike PAUL TILLICH or Albert Camus, who emphasized the anxieties stemming from the human condition, Goodman stressed the stultifying impact of institutions such as schooling on youthful impulse and curiosity. His other writings include *Compulsory Mis-education and the Community of Scholars* (1964) and *New Reformation: Notes of a Neolithic Conservative* (1970), which criticized the anti-intellectualism of much of the youth movement.

See also BEAT GENERATION.

FURTHER READING

Peter Parisi, ed., *Artist of the Actual: Essays on Paul Goodman* (Metuchen, N.J.: Scarecrow Press, 1986).

Gray, Asa (b. Sauquoit, N.Y., Nov. 18, 1810; d. Cambridge, Mass., Jan. 30, 1888). Botanist. A leading scientific advocate of Darwinian theory, Gray argued that evolution does not contradict Christian doctrine: science is impossible without faith in order, which implies faith in an orderer. Design pervades the universe, and natural selection is simply the Creator's chosen means of action. Gray's position helped many scientists accept DARWINISM while rejecting a materialist philosophy. Author of the comprehensive taxonomy *Manual of the Botany of the United States from New England to Wisconsin and South* *to Ohio and Pennsylvania Inclusive* (1848), Gray promoted both the professional and the popular study of botany.

FURTHER READING

A. Hunter Dupree, *Asa Gray: American Botanist, Friend of Darwin* (1968; Baltimore: Johns Hopkins University Press, 1988).

Great Awakening   History happens. And sometimes "history" happens because historians create it. The "Great Awakening," a term signifying massive religious revivals that seemingly "swept" the American colonies in the three decades before the American Revolution, first emerged as a "historical" event in 1842 when the Protestant minister Joseph Tracy coined the term in the title of his book, *The Great Awakening: a History of the Revival of Religion in the Time of Edwards and Whitefield*, which he wrote to provide historical justification for antebellum Protestant revivals. The contrast between the actual events of the 1740s and 1750s and the powerful but deceptive label coined in Tracy's 1842 book reveals much about the powerful attraction of historical precedents in a nation whose founding fathers had imagined it as "the new order of the ages."

The actual religious revivals of eighteenth-century America, which were numerous, defied the cohesion implied in Joseph Tracy's memorable term. Revivals appeared episodically in different colonies and different decades and never occurred at all in others. New England witnessed the most intense revivals, which occurred between 1690 and 1710, 1735 and 1750, and 1770 and 1790. In the middle colonies, New York rarely experienced revivals except when the itinerant Anglican, George Whitefield, visited New York City. Revivals in New Jersey, Pennsylvania, and Delaware usually affected only English, Scottish, and Dutch colonists, seldom occurred outside the 1740s, and almost wholly skipped the region's increasingly large German population, whether German Lutherans, Reformed (Calvinists), Baptists, Mennonites, or Moravians. In the southern colonies, significant revivalism did not occur until after 1750 and peaked in the late 1760s. The seven preaching tours that the evangelist Whitefield conducted between 1740 and his death in Newburyport, Massachusetts in 1770 linked some of these revivals, although others did not depend on Whitefield's efforts at all.

Nor did the scattered eighteenth-century revivals exhibit theological and denominational consistency. In New England, CALVINISM—"New Side" Congregationalists and "New Light" Baptists—dominated the revivals. In the ethnically mixed middle colonies, Scottish Calvinistic Presbyterians divided over the revivals, English Baptists (also Calvinists) and Quakers ignored them, and Dutch Reformed revivalists imbibed "Koelmanism," a form of Dutch pietism named after the theologian Jacobus Koelman. (*See also* PIETY.) In the southern colonies, the revivals of the 1760s occurred largely among Calvinistic Presbyterians and Baptists who often focused more on challenging the dominance of the Church of England in their region than on theology.

The revivals proved nonrevolutionary, despite cries from critics. Certainly, they attracted more spectators than converts. Whitefield drew enormous crowds. Perhaps 10,000 heard him in Philadelphia in 1740, and even BENJAMIN FRANKLIN contributed money to his cause. But only a few listeners converted—easily less than 1 percent—a pattern that has dogged revivalists ever since, whether CHARLES FINNEY in the nineteenth century or Billy Graham in the twentieth. In the wake of such revivals, membership quickly fell back, the number of young male converts declined, and older members again outnumbered the young.

Moreover, the eighteenth-century revivals centered largely on spiritual issues and bore none of the social and political themes that characterized either liberal revivalism in antebellum America or conservative EVANGELICALISM in the late twentieth century. George Whitefield publicly criticized the harshness of some slaveholders, and the South Carolina evangelical layman, Hugh Bryan, predicted that both slavery and slaveholders would be crushed in an apocalyptic preface to the millennium. But Whitefield also quietly wrote an anonymously published tract that vigorously supported slavery and demanded slaves' absolute obedience to owners, while Bryan quickly recanted his alarming prediction after the South Carolina Assembly angrily censured him. Elsewhere, the revivalists not only ignored slavery but sometimes owned slaves themselves, as did New Englanders JONATHAN EDWARDS and James Davenport.

Nor did the revivals promote democracy, antiauthoritarianism, or social leveling. Critics frequently linked revivalists to London's notorious "French prophets" of the 1710s, who proclaimed miracles, raised the dead, and promoted women's preaching. However, the colonial American revivals actually proved remarkably staid. Presbyterian revivalists formed a new, more authoritative presbytery to manage denominational affairs in the middle colonies, which increased rather than decreased the importance of the clergy and vested no new power in the laity. Claims for miracles occurred in only one place, the Freehold, New Jersey, congregation of the Scottish Presbyterian, William Tennent Jr. And women did not march to the pulpit but remained in the pews, a pattern that changed in America only after the Revolution, and then modestly.

Ironically, Joseph's Tracy's "Great Awakening" won little attention among nineteenth-century American historians. George Bancroft, for example, wrote his magisterial ten-volume *History of the United States* (1834–74) without even mentioning Tracy's term or assigning any special importance to colonial revivals. However, beginning in the 1930s, then accelerating after 1950, historians began to ascribe an importance to Tracy's "event" that might have surprised even Tracy himself. As a consequence, recent histories have variously described the Great Awakening as a means of early American lower-class protest, a new avenue of mass communications through extemporaneous preaching, the principal movement that linked the colonies together before the AMERICAN REVOLUTION, a major source of pre-Revolutionary anti-authoritarian protest rhetoric—indeed, even as a major key to the Revolution.

The truth of these descriptions often depends on accepting the accuracy of partisan critical accounts of the eighteenth-century revivals and the validity of the memorable label Joseph Tracy coined one hundred years later to describe those revivals. Both not only provide poor foundations for understanding eighteenth-century events but suggest how easily subsequent depictions—whether by obscure ministers like Joseph Tracy (of colonial revivals) or by well-known novelists like JAMES FENIMORE COOPER (of native Americans) and NATHANIEL HAWTHORNE (of the Puritans)—indelibly but often chimerically shape our remembrances of the past.

JON BUTLER

FURTHER READING

Patricia U. Bonomi, *Under the Cope of Heaven: Religion, Society, and Politics in Colonial America* (New York: Oxford University Press, 1986).

Jon Butler, *Awash in a Sea of Faith: Christianizing the American People* (Cambridge: Harvard University Press, 1990).

Joseph Conforti, "The Invention of the Great Awakening, 1795–1842," *Early American Literature* 26 (1991): 99–118.

Edwin S. Gaustad, *The Great Awakening in New England* (New York: Harper, 1957).

Alan Heimert, *Religion and the American Mind from the Great Awakening to the Revolution* (Cambridge: Harvard University Press, 1966).

William G. McLoughlin, "'Enthusiasm for Liberty': The Great Awakening as the Key to the Revolution," in Jack P. Greene and William G. McLoughlin, eds., *Preachers and Politicians: Two Essays on the Origins of the American Revolution* (Worcester, Mass.: American Antiquarian Society, 1977).

Harry S. Stout, *The Divine Dramatist: George Whitefield and the Rise of Modern Evangelicalism* (Grand Rapids, Mich.: Eerdmans, 1991).

Joseph Tracy, *The Great Awakening: a History of the Revival of Religion in the Time of Edwards and Whitefield* (Boston: Congregational Board of Publication, 1842).

Greenberg, Clement (b. Bronx, N.Y., Jan. 16, 1909; d. New York, N.Y., May 7, 1994). Art critic. One of the most influential cultural critics of the Cold War decades, Greenberg led the highly successful movement to establish MODERNISM as the dominant aesthetic code of the West, with New York succeeding Paris as its cultural capital. He championed ABSTRACT EXPRESSIONISM as the culmination of "progress" in painting: this style, Greenberg claimed, privileged formal qualities over the illusion of "content," thus completing a historical tendency toward antirepresentational "flatness" that began in nineteenth-century France and constituted an important part of modern intellectual experience. Art critic of the *Nation* and a contributor to the *Partisan Review*, his collected essays were published in *Clement Greenberg* (ed. John O'Brian, 1986).

See also AESTHETICS; CULTURAL CRITICISM; MASS CULTURE.

FURTHER READING

Donald B. Kuspit, *Clement Greenberg: Art Critic* (Madison: University of Wisconsin Press, 1979).

Grimké, Sarah (b. Charleston, S.C., Nov. 26, 1792; d. Hyde Park, Mass., Dec. 23, 1873) and **Angelina** (b. Charleston, S.C., Feb. 20, 1805; d. Hyde Park, Mass., Oct. 26, 1879). Reformers. Born to an aristocratic slaveholding family of planter politicians, the Grimké sisters became Quakers and Garrisonians. Although Sarah's *An Epistle to the Clergy of the Southern States* (1836) and Angelina's *An Appeal to Christian Women of the South* (1836) urged southerners to use moral suasion to eradicate slavery, the sisters also believed that women, as citizens, had both a right and responsibility to undertake political action. Both were powerful public speakers who vividly described the degradations inherent in slavery.

See also ANTISLAVERY.

FURTHER READING

Gerda Lerner, *The Grimké Sisters from South Carolina: Rebels against Slavery* (Boston: Houghton Mifflin, 1967).

Gropius, Walter (b. Berlin, Germany, May 18, 1883; d. Boston, Mass., July 5, 1969). Architect. A central figure in the history of modern ARCHITECTURE and MODERNISM generally, Gropius founded the Weimar Bauhaus (1919), the first educational institution founded on self-consciously modernist precepts. He envisioned the integration of all arts and crafts in an atmosphere of communal interaction. A rational marriage of art and technology, he believed, could produce a new environment, a truly modern public space. Gropius emigrated in 1934, finally settling at Harvard University in 1937. His functionalism had a strong influence on the International Style advocated by Ludwig Mies van der Rohe and Philip Johnson— a style which came to define the physical landscape of American corporate culture and which, in its association with private power, represented the ideological antithesis of the Bauhaus ideal.

FURTHER READING

Klaus Herdeg, *The Decorated Diagram: Harvard Architecture and the Failure to the Bauhaus Legacy* (Cambridge: MIT Press, 1983).

guilt   It is customary to distinguish between guilt and SHAME; but the distinction, though necessary, proves unexpectedly elusive. Theoretical investment in this question seems curiously misplaced, leading to the trivialization of both concepts. When the distinction is overemphasized, guilt begins to lose the suggestion of conscientious self-condemnation, while the element of self-condemnation in shame comes to be viewed merely as an unfortunate byproduct of unrealistic expectations.

The most recent phase of speculation about the difference between shame and guilt dates from the 1930s, when cultural anthropologists began to distinguish between shame cultures and guilt cultures. Shame, they argued, derives from a purely external sanction for good conduct, whereas guilt internalizes a sense of right and wrong. Psychoanalysts soon demolished this distinction, pointing out that shame was just as deeply internalized as guilt. Whereas guilt internalized the fear of punishment, in their view, shame internalized the fear of rejection—the parent, say, who simply turns away in disgust. If the unconscious image of the castrating father haunted the guilty conscience, shame rested on the even more terrifying threat of abandonment. Guilt issued from defiance of the father, shame from the failure to live up to his internalized example.

This plausible distinction, which in one form or another continues to inform discussions of these subjects, has a twofold effect: it robs shame of its transgressive dimension, now reserved for guilt alone, and it encourages a legalistic understanding of transgression itself. This diminished conception of guilt reduces it to the fear of retaliation that follows violation of community standards, themselves trivialized and partially discredited as "taboos." The troubled conscience disappears from discussions of guilt, now seen simply as condemnation by "society."

That guilt follows some kind of disobedience is clear enough; the question is how broadly we should construe disobedience. If we see it simply as the violation of a specific rule or commandment, we lose the richer meaning of guilt as it was understood in the religious traditions that once shaped American life. Guilt undeniably has legal overtones, but we would do well to remember that the Protestant Reformation—for a long time the dominant influence in America's moral culture—originated in a rejection of legalism in the name of faith. In Reformation theology, observance of the moral law was not enough to assure salvation. The doctrine of justification by faith—the core of that theology—registered an awareness that men and women can outwardly conform even to the most rigorous moral standard and still lack the inward spirit of obedience and gratitude that defines a true Christian. Formal obedience to the letter of the law can mask a wilful, ungrateful, unforgiving heart. The natural, unredeemed disposition of mankind, as the early Protestants viewed it, is one of rebellion not just against divine commandments but against divine governance in general, since the existence of evil and suffering is hard to reconcile with images of God's benevolence and mercy. To acknowledge dependence on a God who allows humans to suffer and die does not come easily. It comes more naturally to human beings, unless their hearts are softened by grace, to curse the conditions of their existence, to attempt to arrange things to their own satisfaction without any reference to God's will, and even to set themselves up as gods in their own right, replacing God's judgment with their own.

The idea of original sin referred to this rebellious inclination of the will, symbolized by Adam's defiance in coveting the godlike powers conferred by knowledge of good and evil. In their natural state—such was the Protestant view of human nature—human beings listen not to God but to the seductive promise of the serpent: "Ye shall be as gods, knowing good and evil."

The inner meaning of Reformation theology, once it was challenged by the new views of guilt and punishment encouraged by the Enlightenment, became increasingly obscure even to the orthodox. The last-ditch defense by JONATHAN EDWARDS of the "great Christian doctrine of original sin" proved incomprehensible not only to his opponents but to most of his followers, who took a more literal-minded and legalistic view of Adam's transgression but then found it difficult to explain how his guilt could be "imputed" to his descendants. Why should anyone else be damned for Adam's insubordination? Why should insubordination be considered a sin in the first place?

Enlightened men and women, raised on theories of constitutional monarchy, no longer considered *lèse majesté* a civil crime, and they found completely repugnant a conception of sin that seemed to make God into an absolute monarch, touchy about his authority and willing to condemn his subjects to hellfire for a remote ancestor's dubious offense. It was no use for Edwards to insist that sin was "original" in the sense that "hardheartedness," "obstinacy," and "perverseness" were defining traits of unredeemed human nature. Since when were people justly tried and punished for obstinacy and hardheartedness?

Children of the Enlightenment, more and more inclined to equate sin with crime, found it hard to reconcile the seemingly arbitrary justice dispensed by Edwards's angry God with the ideas of justice that now prevailed in politics. They rejected the suggestion that "vindictive retribution," in the rather unfortunate phrase employed by Calvinists, played any part in the administration of justice, human or divine. Calvinists meant that PUNISHMENT is the natural and fitting sequel of disobedience or rebellion. As the climate of nineteenth-century opinion turned against them, they no longer attempted to defend the principle of "vindictive retribution" in the home or the school, but they still maintained that it should inform our conception of civil justice as well as our conception of God. Humanitarians, however, found retribution incompatible with any kind of justice; and it was humanitarians who now set the terms of moral debate.

As God dropped out of the picture, the debate came to concern itself almost exclusively with questions of criminal justice. The idea that criminals owe a "debt to society," which preserved some of the older understanding of punishment and its significance, gradually gave way to more thoroughly secularized ideas of punishment emphasizing prevention or rehabilitation. Those who remained skeptical about the claim that enlightened penology could turn hardened criminals into model citizens defended harsh punishments not as a form of "vindictive retribution" but as the only effective deterrent against crime. In the second half of the nineteenth century, this became the standard argument for capital punishment, and it has remained the standard argument down to our own day. It is a poor argument, not only because the deterrent effect of the death sentence is hard to prove but, more important, because it robs punishment of moral significance and weakens our understanding of guilt. Historically, the concept of guilt has always been closely associated, in penology and for that matter in theology as well, with indebt-

edness. Lawbreakers gain an advantage over those who obey the law and thus incur an obligation to repay whatever was unfairly gained in this way, unless those charged with upholding the law choose to "forgive" the debt when the debtor shows signs of contrition and repentance. Both the "collection" and the forgiveness of debts have unmistakable ethical implications: they right the balance, restore the moral order the disruption of which is the true meaning of guilt. When punishment is conceived as deterrence, however, it loses its moral resonance and becomes purely instrumental—ineffective at that, since the fear of punishment notoriously fails to guarantee good conduct.

The therapeutic critique of guilt, which eventually dissolved the category of guilt and replaced it with the category of sickness, originated in the perception that fear, especially when turned inward in the form of a punitive superego, seldom has the salutary effects envisioned by those who call for strict enforcement of the laws. From this point of view, a guilty conscience does not necessarily make people law-abiding, let alone healthy and happy; to the extent that it rests on fear rather than on contrition and remorse, it may actually make them sick. Nietzsche and Freud, the great debunkers of "civilized morality," insisted that guilt is a pathological condition brought on by the repression of healthy animal instincts. In their more somber moments, they wondered, to be sure, whether humanity could get along without some such system of moral terror—a mental reservation that distinguishes them from most of their followers. The subsequent popularization of a therapeutic sensibility, one that refuses to hold anyone accountable and misunderstands "compassion"—its favorite slogan—as the permanent suspension of moral judgment, might be taken as a confirmation of their misgivings.

Precisely because a permissive morality invites the misguided corrective of a return to rigor and severity, it is necessary to remind ourselves that it was a debased view of moral rigor that gave rise to therapeutic criticism in the first place. The rigor of the older morality did not lie in the deterrent value of punishment—a dubious addition to the discourse on guilt and punishment that appeared only in the nineteenth century. Moral rigor lay in the understanding that retribution (not deterrence) is the only way of dealing with guilt that also leaves open the possibility of mercy. The whole debate between punitive and permissive conceptions of guilt, which occupies so much attention today, is deeply misleading. Both these conceptions need to be rejected in favor of the richer understanding of guilt that began to be lost in the Enlightenment.

CHRISTOPHER LASCH

See also RESPONSIBILITY.

FURTHER READING

Jacob Abbott, *Gentle Measures in the Management of the Young* (New York: Harper, 1872).

Ruth Benedict, *The Chrysanthemum and the Sword* (Boston: Houghton Mifflin, 1946).

Jonathan Edwards, *The Great Christian Doctrine of Original Sin Defended*, ed. Clyde A. Holbrook (1757; New Haven: Yale University Press, 1970).

Sigmund Freud, *Civilization and Its Discontents*, trans. Joan Riviere (1930; Garden City: Doubleday, 1958).

Herbert Morris, *On Guilt and Innocence* (Berkeley: University of California Press, 1976).

Friedrich Nietzsche, *On the Genealogy of Morals* (1887), in Walter Kaufmann, ed. and trans., *Basic Writings of Nietzsche* (New York: Modern Library, 1968).

Gerhart Piers and Milton B. Singer, *Shame and Guilt: a Psychoanalytic and Cultural Study* (Springfield, Ill.: Charles C. Thomas, 1953).

H

Hale, Sarah Josepha (b. Newport, N.H., Oct. 24, 1788; d. Philadelphia, Pa., Apr. 30, 1879). Author and editor. As editor of *Godey's Lady's Book* (1837–77), Hale elaborated the doctrine of separate spheres and claimed for women the vital powers of motherhood, domesticity, and moral influence. Emphasizing female solidarity, she exhorted women to redeem the male world of pecuniary competition through their purity and selflessness. Although she underlined the danger of women's neglecting their domestic obligations, she also supported women writers and championed women's education because of mothers' enormous power over developing minds. In *The Ladies' Wreath* (1837) she collected poetry by English and American women, while *Woman's Record: or, Sketches of All Distinguished Women from "the Beginning" till AD 1850* (1853) contained 2,500 biographical entries about accomplished women.

See also DOMESTICITY.

FURTHER READING

Sherbrooke Rogers, *Sarah Josepha Hale: New England Pioneer, 1788–1879* (Grantham, N.H.: Tompson and Rutter, 1985).

Hall, G[ranville] Stanley (b. Ashfield, Mass., Feb. 1, 1844; d. Worcester, Mass., Apr. 24, 1924). Psychologist and educator. An imaginative student of the stages of human development, especially adolescence, Hall welcomed Freud's emphasis on unconscious drives and early childhood and arranged Freud's visit to America in 1909. Though he helped establish experimental and physiological methods in psychology, thus distancing himself from his teacher William James's methodological eclecticism, he criticized materialist reductionism and emphasized the significance of feelings and emotions as well as consciousness. A leading professionalizer in psychology, he was the first president of the American Psychological Association in 1891. His writings include *Adolescence* (1904), *Senescence, the Last Half of Life* (1922), and *Jesus, the Christ, in the Light of Psychology* (1917).

FURTHER READING

Dorothy Ross, *G. Stanley Hall: the Psychologist as Prophet* (Chicago: University of Chicago Press, 1972).

Hamilton, Alexander (b. Nevis, British West Indies, Jan. 11, 1755 or 1757; d. New York, N.Y., July 12, 1804). American Revolutionary, delegate (New York) to the Constitutional Convention of 1787, principal author of the *Federalist Papers*, and first Secretary of the Treasury (1789–95), Hamilton was an influential theorist as well as a shrewd political strategist.

His political writings have been characterized as "paradoxical" by more than one American historian. Lynton Caldwell argued in *The Administrative Theories of Hamilton and Jefferson* (1944) that Hamilton expressed a desire "above all things to see the equality of political rights, exclusive of all hereditary distinction, firmly established," and believed such equality to be "consistent with the order and happiness of society." Hamilton's political contemporaries nevertheless described him as "a monarchist who hated republican government and feared democracy" (p. 21). A virulent critic of public opinion, Hamilton also recognized it as the governing principle in political life. He informed the New York Ratifying Convention of 1788, as Syrett records in Hamilton's *Papers*, that "in the general course of things, the popular views, and even prejudices will direct the actions of the rulers" (vol. 5, p. 37). At the same time, while labeled "Hobbesian" by modern commentators for his commitment to the ultimate legitimacy of positive law, Hamilton was thoroughly convinced, as he told the Federal Constitutional Convention in 1787, of the Lockean claim that the "voice of the people" was the superior power within the state. Yet it was not the "voice of God" (vol. 4, p. 200).

Perhaps ironically, Hamilton's answers to the dilemmas of popular rule and the threat of majority tyranny were developed at length in his contributions to that great and much analyzed effort to sway popular opinion, *The Federalist Papers*. Here too, the nature of Hamilton's contribution has sparked debate. As Garry Wills has noted in his introduction to *The Federalist Papers*, it is "part of our folk wisdom" both that the CONSTITUTION is intended to limit governmental power through checks and balances and that this system reflects Hamilton's own view of the political struggle between the few and the many. However, as Wills notes, the texts of Hamilton's more than 50 contributions to *The Federalist* contain only one reference (in no. 9) to a scheme of "legislative balances and checks" (p. 38) and no suggestion of the legislative branch checking another branch of government.

In fact, from Hamilton's perspective, no mechanical structure "checking and balancing" orders of men (such as JOHN ADAMS proposed) could alone save a factious people from destroying itself. Nor could men rely, as THOMAS JEFFERSON seemed to suggest, on the improvement of human nature through technological progress and education. Rather, on Hamilton's understanding, conducting "self-government" within an expanded national sphere, which necessarily entails political cooperation in the absence of shared communal values, requires both a set of rules or laws of sufficient generality to achieve assent, and a politically "independent"—that is, neutral between contending parties—public adjudicator to interpret and apply these rules in particular cases. Thus, in a series of arguments beginning with *Federalist* 78, Hamilton sought to justify publicly the need for such judicial power within a scheme of self-government. In so doing, he provided the foundation for that singularly original contribution of American constitutional theory—the notion of a Supreme Court exercising powers of judicial review over legislative enactment. Courts, in general, play an important role in Hamilton's theory of state, which he preferred to characterize as "limited constitutionalism."

Hamilton's articulation of what he characterized in *Federalist* 11 as "the great American System" (p. 55) was as much an economic as a purely constitutional vision, and these two strands of his larger political thinking are deeply intertwined. Had Hamilton never contributed to the *Federalist*, his significant legacy as a political as well as economic thinker could easily be sustained by the four seminal "Reports"—on Public Credit, on the Establishment of a Mint, on the Establishment of a National Bank, and on Manufactures—which he presented to Congress between 1790 and 1791 as the nation's first Secretary of the Treasury. These reports concern themselves most directly with the interplay between the nation's prospects for growth and unity—for "empire" as Hamilton conceived of it—and the new nation's financial and economic institutions. They articulate a relationship between public and private interests, and between politics and markets, that is in marked contrast to the political economy of his Scottish contemporary Adam Smith, whose imputed laissez-faire principles have often been assumed to underpin America's eighteenth-century Constitution. In contrast, Hamilton's "Report on Manufactures," as contained in his collected *Papers*, registers his direct rejection of the Smithian premise that "private interest will, if left to

itself, infallibly find its own way to the most profitable employment: and 'tis by such employment, that the public prosperity will be most effectually promoted" (vol. 10, p. 232). The "Report on Manufactures" is dominated by the strong and recurring theme that economics is interdependent with state power. Hamilton rejected Smith's *Wealth of Nations*, with its strong formal attack on the economics of state intervention, on the empirical grounds that "the fact does not uniformly correspond with the theory" (vol. 10, p. 285). Hamilton was willing to speculate that if all restraints on European trade were dropped—"if the system of perfect liberty to industry and commerce were the prevailing system of nations" (vol. 10, p. 262)—then such a free market ideology might be safely practiced in America. Hamilton quickly dismissed this idea, however, because it rested on an equally dubious empirical proposition "that Industry, if left to itself, will naturally find its way to the most useful and profitable employment" (vol. 10, p. 266).

Some interpreters have argued that Hamilton's economic writings reflect a strand of mercantilist thought prevalent in America at the time, but Hamilton's reports position him as a successor to, rather than a predecessor of, Adam Smith. What clearly differentiates Hamilton's thought from both mercantilism and from the economists of the Scottish Enlightenment is not so much his recognition that manufacturing growth could be the key to national prosperity. On that, they all agreed. Hamilton's point of departure was rather his belief that the state had an important part to play in underwriting and sustaining this process. In addition, Hamilton never doubted that the economic prosperity of such a system could, in principle, be directed politically in order to pursue a "general welfare" beyond the aggregate wealth of the individual citizens. While Hamilton cannot be transformed through historical "revision" into a proponent of extensive social welfare policies, he never denied—as some contemporary economic libertarians have—that "society," in fact, existed. Nor did he deny that the nation could have economic needs beyond market "externalities," which government could be directed to address. Rather, Hamilton's political and economic writings combined to produce what might be thought to be singularly lacking among other early American theorists of politics—a strong and coherent theory of the state.

SHANNON C. STIMSON

FURTHER READING
Samuel H. Beer, *To Make a Nation: the Rediscovery of American Federalism* (Cambridge: Harvard University Press, 1993).

Lynton K. Caldwell, *The Administrative Theories of Hamilton and Jefferson* (Chicago: University of Chicago Press, 1944).

Alexander Hamilton, *The Papers of Alexander Hamilton*, ed. Harold C. Syrett et al., 26 vols. (New York: Columbia University Press, 1961–79).

Alexander Hamilton, James Madison and John Jay, *The Federalist Papers*, ed. Garry Wills (New York: Bantam, 1982).

Forrest McDonald, *We The People: the Economic Origins of the Constitution* (Chicago: University of Chicago Press, 1958).

——, *Novus Ordo Seclorum: the Intellectual Origins of the Constitution* (Lawrence: University of Kansas Press, 1985).

Cathy D. Matson and Peter S. Onuf, *A Union of Interests: Political and Economic Thought in Revolutionary America* (Lawrence: University of Kansas Press, 1990).

Shannon C. Stimson, *The American Revolution in the Law: Anglo-American Jurisprudence before John Marshall* (Princeton: Princeton University Press, 1990).

——, "Reflections on the Economic interpretation of the Constitution," in V. Hart and S. C. Stimson, eds., *Writing a National Identity: Political, Economic and Cultural Perspectives on the Written Constitution* (Manchester: Manchester University Press, 1993).

Hansen, Alvin (b. Viborg, S.Dak., Aug. 23, 1887; d. Alexandria, Va., June 6, 1975). Economist. An influential Keynesian, Hansen was a key government adviser throughout the New Deal. His *Fiscal Policy and Business Cycles* (1941) strongly supported Keynes's interpretation of the Great Depression and warned that capitalist countries were entering a prolonged period of economic stagnation. Capitalism, Hansen explained, requires growth in production and demand. With decreased population growth and increasing technological productivity, capitalism is no longer self-sustaining, since it cannot use its full investment and production potentials. Only deficit spending by the government can stimulate demand, stabilize incomes, and prevent unemployment. Hansen's other works include *Monetary Theory and Fiscal Policy* (1949), *Business Cycles and National Income* (1951, 1964), and *A Guide to Keynes* (1953).

See also KEYNESIANISM.

FURTHER READING

Alan Brinkley, "The New Deal and the Idea of the State," in Steve Fraser and Gary Gerstle, eds., *The Rise and Fall of the New Deal Order* (Princeton: Princeton University Press, 1989).

Harlem Renaissance This movement of the 1920s marked a major turning point in the history of African American and American culture. Not since Reconstruction had African Americans participated in significant numbers in a mainstream arena of American cultural debate. Self-styled as "New Negroes,"

New York's black writers enacted their own dramas of cultural rupture and discovery as part of the cultural moment also symbolized by F. Scott Fitzgerald's "Jazz Age" and Malcolm Cowley's "Lost Generation." In New York, as elsewhere, blacks and whites moved passionately into an artistic urban world already shaped by the blues of Bessie Smith, the jazz of Louis Armstrong, the musical theater of George Gershwin and Lew Leslie, and the painting of Aaron Douglass and Weinold Reiss. As was true of the Reconstruction era, blacks and whites of the 1920s were uneasy allies in their attempts to reconceive American culture. Yet for writers both black and white, jazz, the blues, and African American dance became symbols of transformation to be used as wedges of modernism against their genteel and Victorian predecessors.

The Harlem Renaissance was the moment when the wider society called upon African Americans to move beyond nineteenth-century minstrelsy, to replace the various benign and malevolent masks of blackness worn by white local-color and regional writers, to portray themselves as they really were. All African Americans gave enthusiastic support to these goals. But the Renaissance was also the moment when some African Americans began to demand that black performers and artists help create a sense of community and continuity within the race, and this campaign caused deep fissures in the African American Community.

Symbolically, Harlem embedded itself in the American cultural imagination of the 1920s as the metaphor for racial rebirth. At the beginning of the twenties, Harlem was already the capital of black America, but its ascendancy was largely political; by the end of the decade Harlem became known as the "cultural capital of black America." New York was the home of the Urban League, the National Association for the Advancement of Colored People, and the Universal Negro Improvement Association. Along with MARCUS GARVEY, W. E. B. DU BOIS, and A. Philip Randolph, most of the race's leaders with national reputations lived there, and they turned to the arts as an important site for redefining the place of blacks in American life. In the first half of the 1920s, the NAACP's *Crisis* and the Urban League's *Opportunity* published poetry and prose, held literary contests, and sponsored award dinners to promote the work of African American writers. For W. E. B. DU BOIS, Jessie Fauset, JAMES WELDON JOHNSON, and Walter White at the NAACP, all of them creative writers as well as political spokesmen, and for Charles S. Johnson at the Urban League, the recognition of African American creative talent was crucial to their broader political and economic agenda. Their promotional activity was in many ways strikingly successful; in the early twenties blacks were being published by major New York houses, and a younger generation of writers had found the necessary support and audiences for their work. With their success, traditional race men and women predicted that the recognition given to African Americans as creative artists would, by extension, break down race barriers in other areas.

This early outpouring of work did not constitute a literary movement as such, since there was no guiding aesthetic principle. Of the early novels, for example, only *Cane* by JEAN TOOMER (1923) was a truly innovative portrait of African American southern life; more typical were works like Walter White's *Fire in the Flint* (1924), a melodramatic study of black middle-class life that was reminiscent of the nineteenth-century African American novel. By the middle of that decade, however, writers began to define themselves by assembling their disparate work under a single banner and viewing themselves as part of a larger cultural movement toward racial redefinition. The Renaissance was their own name for that larger movement.

The anthology created by ALAIN LOCKE, *The New Negro: an Interpretation* (1925), played a key role in defining this group of young writers. Appropriating the title "New Negro" from political discourse, Locke labeled the movement the "Negro Renaissance." His essays in that volume helped to map aesthetic boundaries that separated the younger generation of African American writers from their predecessors. The new group defined an ideal of racial expression that drew on African American folk life, incorporating its "flavor of language, flow of phrase, accent of rhythm in prose, verse and music, color and tone of imagery, idiom and timbre of emotion and symbolism" (p. 51). No matter how uneasy the fit between his critical structures and the diversity of the writers themselves, Locke established the basis for a sense of mission and collective identity.

LANGSTON HUGHES was the prototypical "New Negro." His work brought to African American writing a sense of youthful rebelliousness that was essential to its ethos. His first volume of poetry, *The Weary Blues* (1926), brought the blues musician and the cabaret into the realm of poetry. He based the poetry in his second volume, *Fine Clothes to the Jew* (1927), upon the formal structure of the 12-bar blues, and he emulated spirituals and gospel music. His 1926 essay "The Negro Artist and the Racial Mountain" served as the manifesto for his generation of writers. Extending Locke's aesthetic criteria of self-definition

into the broad realm of racial culture, Hughes declared his independence from cultural assimilation— "Nordic manners, Nordic faces, Nordic hair, Nordic art (if any), and an Episcopal heaven." He also proclaimed his allegiance to the "folk" (the urban and rural proletariat), "his racial individuality, his heritage of rhythm and warmth, and his incongruous humor" (Gayle, pp. 176, 177). Most importantly, Hughes insisted that both a distinctive racial art and a distinctive racial identity were found among the folk, not among the middle class.

An unspoken assumption of Hughes's manifesto was the task of separating African American creative art from the hegemony of the political metaphor of racial uplift, and of establishing independent, primarily aesthetic, grounds for nurturing African American literature. Inheriting a literary tradition in which the poetical and the artistic were fused and subordinated to political language and institutions, Hughes and other writers rebelled against their assumed role in a larger political discourse that staked its own claim to them and their work. By disentangling their writing from the language of politics, these artists hoped to participate in politics *as artists* whose vision of the world was as authentic and transformative as that of the politicians.

These notions of the Harlem Renaissance constructed by Locke, Hughes, and others create a difficult legacy for subsequent critics. Critics may want to honor the writers' quest to build a movement, but critical examination reveals no stable movement. Instead we find that the Renaissance image obscures a highly contested and unstable terrain. Post-World War I African American culture was split. Novelists such as Jessie Fauset, W. E. B. Du Bois, and Nella Larsen were symbolically relegated to the cultural rearguard because the protagonists of their novels were middle class. This rearguard dominated the major racial institutions that responded to the challenge of youth throughout the late 1920s. *Crisis* and *Opportunity*, and the editorials in most African American newspapers, became less generous in their support of the younger writers as the twenties progressed. The *Crisis* symposium on "The Negro in Art, How Shall He Be Portrayed" led the debate that was waged in most of the major African American periodicals. Yet the criticism that was leveled against the Harlem Renaissance writers was a marker of the success with which they articulated an alternative view of race and representation, and of the roles of the creative artist and cultural expression in African American life.

The internal debate among blacks was made immensely more complex by the increased white interest in African American writers. Black writers began to publish in major American magazines, their books were reviewed in major periodicals, and they began to compete for the spotlight with traditional racial leaders. They also attracted important white patrons. Carl Van Vechten, a novelist and music critic at *Vanity Fair*, published a series of articles on the blues, conducted tours of Harlem for visiting dignitaries, and gave interracial parties throughout the 1920s. Others worked more quietly. Amy and Arthur Spingarn, long associated with the NAACP, sponsored a literary award and helped Langston Hughes through college. Mrs. R. Osgood Mason was perhaps the most generous, giving substantial financial support to Langston Hughes, ZORA NEALE HURSTON, and Alain Locke, and intermittent support to many others. The support which black writers of the Renaissance received from whites in the late 1920s led many black critics of the movement to view it as part of the general "vogue of the Negro" and, therefore, as a pandering to the quest for exoticism among whites. The legacy of that criticism still haunts the reputation of the Renaissance. Whatever we may think of the white sponsorship, there is no question that much of the most innovative work of the Renaissance was created with that support, and that much of the work now taken as representative of the movement was only mildly endorsed by the majority of African Americans at the time.

The independence of Harlem Renaissance writers reached its apogee with the publication of *FIRE !!!: a Quarterly Devoted to Younger Negro Artists*, a "little magazine" edited by Wallace Thurman in 1926. In *FIRE !!!*, Langston Hughes, Zora Neale Hurston, Aaron Douglass, Gwendolyn Bennett, John Davis, and Bruce Nugent risked becoming an African American avant-garde by questioning the constructions of class, race, gender, and sexuality that comprised the ideals of the educated African American bourgeoisie. Their work in *FIRE !!!* strained the sensibilities of their contemporary audience, and the experiment was short lived. But it remains a guidepost of the cultural rebellion of the 1920s since it defined the limits of the movement.

The new textual emphasis of contemporary African American criticism allows us to conceptualize the Harlem Renaissance more broadly than earlier models, based on social context, permitted. Viewed as a genealogy of texts, the Harlem Renaissance elaborated tensions that had already begun to surface at the turn of the century. The counterpoint between dialect and conventional verse that runs through Paul Laurence Dunbar's corpus, and the division between traditional realistic narratives and the stories built around conjure in Charles Chesnutt's short fiction, anticipates the central debates that shaped the Renaissance. Du Bois, who began as an advocate and ended as a critic of much of the work of the 1920s, gave these tensions their most articulate formulation when he described the double consciousness of African Americans in *The Souls of Black Folk* (1903). Looking forward, the lines of continuity between the Harlem Renaissance and the Black Arts Movement of the 1960s and 1970s, and contemporary vernacular criticism, reveal a legacy of sustained cultural productivity among African Americans throughout the twentieth century.

Similarly, the renaissance of African American women's literature and criticism has redefined the gender constructions of the Harlem Renaissance. Feminist scholars including Hazel Carby and Gloria T. Hull have fashioned a new genealogy based upon the works of women writers of that period. Alice Walker's paradigm of rediscovering Hurston as the significant foremother of contemporary black women writers in the late 1970s marked the beginning of a continuing rereading of earlier twentieth-century black women's writing. The writings of other African American women during the 1920s were formerly assigned to the conservative "rearguard" of the period because most of them seemingly failed to tie the new freedom of the black artist to formal innovation, and because they often used conventional, middle-class heroines as protagonists. But however conventional the writings of such novelists and poets as Nella Larsen and Jessie Fauset may seem, their carefully crafted discourses of community and rebellion firmly address the problem of gender construction within racial ideologies.

The issue of sexuality also sunders the boundaries that traditionally defined the Harlem Renaissance simply as the rebirth of a "race literature." Many of the leading male and female writers and critics of the Renaissance can be reexamined now as gay or lesbian or placed in a more ambiguous sexual category. This development offers the possibility of rereading the ideological nature of individual works and the movement as a whole. Feminist critics have suggested that Alain Locke's homosexuality may have led him alternately to exclude or to be more sympathetic to women writers. The aesthetic tensions in the poetry of COUNTEE CULLEN can easily be read as sexual, not only racial. Likewise the works of Langston Hughes, CLAUDE McKAY, Wallace Thurman, Alice Dunbar Nelson and Mae V. Cowdery can be considered for possible inclusion in an American and African American gay and lesbian literary tradition.

A reexamination of the boundaries that traditionally

define the Harlem Renaissance also must lead toward a reexamination of the boundaries that define the American literary tradition. The Harlem Renaissance evokes an American literary and cultural history beyond that represented by the canonical writers. Not only are the works of many African American authors of the 1920s marginalized in the American canon, but the extensive and rich tradition of white American writing on race—a tradition that black writers engaged and contested—is also generally excluded. Renaissance writers drew not only on the modernists, and on black folk patterns, but on such nearly forgotten white writers as Carl Van Vechten, the author of seven novels, now best remembered for his "Negro novel," *Nigger Heaven* (1926). Another influential figure was Julia Peterkin, who wrote within the still thriving tradition of southern local colorists and regionalists, and won the Pulitzer Prize in 1928 for her folk comedy *Scarlet Sister Mary*. Du Bose Heyward, whose novel *Porgy* (1926) became the basis for George Gershwin's *Porgy and Bess*, earned his reputation as a writer for his portrayal of southern blacks. African American writers and critics of the 1920s often placed their work within the framework of these neglected writers. During the Harlem Renaissance the literary and artistic conventions of American and African American culture were less rigid and exclusionary than they had been before or have been since.

GEORGE P. CUNNINGHAM

See also CLASS; GAY AND LESBIAN IDENTITIES; RACE.

FURTHER READING
Houston A. Baker, *Modernism and the Harlem Renaissance* (Chicago: University of Chicago Press, 1987).
Hazel V. Carby, *Reconstructing Womanhood: the Emergence of the Afro-American Woman Novelist* (New York: Oxford University Press, 1987).
Addison Gayle, ed., *The Black Aesthetic* (Garden City, N.Y.: Doubleday, 1971).
Nathan I. Huggins, *Harlem Renaissance* (New York: Oxford University Press, 1971).
Gloria T. Hull, *Color, Sex, and Poetry: Three Women Writers of the Harlem Renaissance* (Bloomington: Indiana University Press, 1987).
Abby A. Johnson and Ronald M. Johnson, *Propaganda and Aesthetics: the Literary Politics of Afro-American Magazines* (Amherst: University of Massachussets Press, 1979).
Alain L. Locke, ed., *The New Negro, an Interpretation* (New York: Albert and Charles Boni, 1925).
Cary D. Wintz, *Black Culture and the Harlem Renaissance* (Houston: Rice University Press, 1988).

Harper, Frances (b. Baltimore, Md., Sept. 24, 1825; d. Philadelphia, Pa., Feb. 22, 1911). Writer and poet. Harper lectured throughout the South for the abolitionist cause and, after the war, for black education, temperance, and moral uplift. As a black woman, she appealed to white women not to pit their rights, especially suffrage, against those of black men, but to recognize how both suffered from injustice. Her popular verse denounced Christians who supported slavery and portrayed strong, defiant women who refused to bow to abusive power. Her writings include *Poems on Miscellaneous Subjects* (1854), *Sketches of Southern Life* (1872), and the novel *Iola Leroy, or, Shadows Uplifted* (1892).

FURTHER READING
Frances Smith Foster, "Introduction," in *A Brighter Coming Day: a Frances Ellen Watkins Harper Reader* (New York: Feminist Press, 1990).

Harper, William Rainey (b. New Concord, Ohio, July 24 or 26, 1856; d. Chicago, Ill., Jan. 10, 1906). Educator and biblicist. First president of the University of Chicago (1891–1906). Harper recruited renowned scholars, such as JOHN DEWEY, to create a Rockefeller-funded research university. Originally a professor of Semitic languages, Harper supported the controversial position that the words of the Bible had evolved through history. He was a leading liberal Protestant biblical authority and was active in popular biblical education. His writings include *Religion and the Higher Life* (1904), *A Critical and Exegetical Commentary on Amos and Hosea* (1905), *The Prophetic Element in the Old Testament* (1905), and *The Trend in Higher Education* (1905).

See also COLLEGES AND UNIVERSITIES.

FURTHER READING
Richard J. Storr, *Harper's University: the Beginnings* (Chicago: University of Chicago Press, 1966).

Harrington, Michael (b. St. Louis, Mo., Feb. 24, 1928; d. Larchmont, N.Y., July 31, 1989). The best-known socialist writer and activist of his generation, Harrington achieved national prominence in 1962 with the publication of *The Other America*, a study of poverty in the United States. Of Harrington's 16 books, *The Other America* was certainly the most influential. The book helped shape an era of liberal reform. Harrington's expectations when writing the book were rather more modest. The year before it came out, he told *New York Post* columnist James Wechsler he would be pleased if the book sold as many as 2,500 copies. Instead, two years after its publication *The Other America* had sold 125,000 copies in the United States, and had been translated into seven languages. Its sales are now nearing 1,300,000.

Little in Michael Harrington's early career suggested he would become a champion of SOCIALISM or exert such influence on the debate about poverty in the United States. Born to comfortable circumstances in Saint Louis, and educated at Holy Cross, Yale, and the University of Chicago, the youthful Harrington succeeded at virtually every goal he set himself. But for much of his early adulthood he strenuously pursued the cultural and political margins of American life. Moving to New York City in 1949 he soon made his mark, both in the bohemian drinking circles of Greenwich Village and in the fierce internecine battles of the anti-Stalinist left. After a stint on the Lower East Side as one of the Catholic Workers led by DOROTHY DAY (where, characteristically, he rose within months to editorship of the *Catholic Worker* newspaper), Harrington left the church and joined the socialist movement. In the later 1950s he criss-crossed the country as a radical organizer, while turning out a steady stream of reviews and articles for JOURNALS OF OPINION such as *Dissent*, *Commonweal*, and the *New Leader*. In 1959 he wrote an article on poverty entitled "Our Fifty Million Poor: Forgotten Men of the Affluent Society" for *Commentary* magazine. That led to a second *Commentary* article on "Slums, Old and New" in 1960, and then to a book contract with Macmillan.

The Other America was a short book which made two simple points. Despite the prevailing consensus about the arrival of the "affluent society," there was "another America" of 40 to 50 million inhabitants living in the United States, "the unskilled workers, the migrant farm workers, the aged, the minorities, and all the others who live in the economic underworld of American life" (p. 10). This "invisible land" of the poor existed in rural isolation or in crowded urban slums where middle-class visitors seldom ventured. "That the poor are invisible," Harrington argued, "is one of the most important things about them" (p. 14).

Harrington's second point, for which he acknowledged his debt to anthropologist Oscar Lewis, was that "poverty is a culture." Poor Americans were not simply distinguishable by their lack of adequate income. Rather, they were "people who lack education and skill, who have bad health, poor housing, low levels of aspiration and high levels of mental distress. . . . Each disability is the more intense because it exists within a web of disabilities" (pp. 158–9). It was thus a delusion to believe that poverty could be solved by exhortations to the poor to lift themselves up by their own bootstraps. "Society," Harrington concluded, "must help them before they can help themselves" (p. 159).

Harrington's book came out at the right moment. The CIVIL RIGHTS movement and John Kennedy's assassination created the opportunity for President Lyndon Johnson to push an ambitious program of domestic reform through Congress. Harrington was summoned to Washington in 1964 to take part in the early planning sessions for WELFARE programs central to the "war on poverty."

The Other America established Michael Harrington's credentials as a social commentator and public policy expert. But his intellectual interests were much broader, and he sometimes grew frustrated with his reputation as "the man who discovered poverty." His next book, *The Accidental Century* (1965), drew on the insights of Freud, Camus, Nietzsche, and other thinkers to explore the theme of "decadence" in contemporary capitalist society. Harrington argued that "political and social imagination" had not kept pace with the technological transformations of the twentieth century, and it was time to impose intelligent and humane planning on society to bring an end to scarcity and the degradation of labor. The book received respectful but sometimes mystified reviews, and enjoyed only a fraction of the sales of *The Other America*. That would be the pattern for the rest of Harrington's career, as he published books on topics ranging from contemporary political issues (*Toward a Democratic Left: a Radical Program for a New Majority*, 1968) to the "death of God" (*The Politics at God's Funeral: the Spiritual Crisis of Western Civilization*, 1983). He also published two more books on poverty (*The Vast Majority: a Journey to the World's Poor*, 1977, and *The New American Poverty*, 1984), as well as two works of autobiography (*Fragments of a Century*, 1973, and *The Long Distance Runner*, 1988).

Perhaps Harrington's most important work after *The Other America* was *Socialism* (1972). A wide-ranging survey of socialist history and theory, *Socialism* argued that at the core of classical Marxism lay a deep commitment to working-class democracy, which had been perverted in the twentieth century by communist totalitarianism. The "socialist vision," Harrington insisted, could still "be made relevant to the twenty-first century," by restoring its democratic content. Harrington's reading of Marx as a nondogmatic political pragmatist was one of the more original and controversial elements of the book. "The true radicalism of Marx," Harrington contended, "was that he was courageous enough to be outrageously moderate when that was what the times required" (p. 72). That description, some critics felt, was more accurate as a self-portrait of Michael Harrington than as a portrait of the real Karl Marx.

Harrington remained politically active throughout his life. He campaigned for Eugene McCarthy and Robert Kennedy in the 1968 presidential primaries. In 1973 he founded a new organization, the Democratic Socialist Organizing Committee (DSOC), which changed its name to Democratic Socialists of America (DSA) in 1982. Determined to be the "left wing of the possible," DSOC and DSA activists worked within the Democratic Party, trying to win it back to its fading New Deal liberal ideals. A freelance intellectual throughout the formative years of his career, Harrington joined the political science department at Queens College in 1972. Stricken with cancer in 1985, Harrington continued to speak and write and teach as long as he could. His final book, *Socialism: Past and Future* was published in July 1989, the month he died.

MAURICE ISSERMAN

FURTHER READING

Michael Harrington, *The Other America: Poverty in the United States* (New York: Macmillan, 1962).

——, *Socialism* (New York: Saturday Review Press, 1972).

——, *Fragments of the Century* (New York: Simon and Schuster, 1973).

——, *The Long-Distance Runner: an Autobiography* (New York: Henry Holt, 1988).

Loren J. Okroi, *Galbraith, Harrington, Heilbroner: Economics and Dissent in the Age of Optimism* (Princeton: Princeton University Press, 1988).

Harris, William Torrey (b. North Killingly, Conn., Sept. 10, 1835; d. Providence, R.I., Nov. 5, 1909). Philosopher and educator. Founder of the *Journal of Speculative Philosophy* in 1867 (while serving as St. Louis public school superintendent), Harris was a devotee of Hegelian idealism. Since every finite object gets its activity from some other object, Harris argued, the ultimate source of activity must be infinite self-activity, which Harris identified with the Christian trinitarian God. As United States Commissioner of Education (1889–1906), Harris continued to publish in philosophy: his works included *Hegel's Logic* (1890) and *The Psychological Foundations of Education* (1898).

FURTHER READING

Elizabeth Flower and Murray G. Murphey, *A History of Philosophy in America* (New York: Capricorn, 1977).

Hartz, Louis (b. Youngstown, Ohio, Apr. 8, 1919; d. Istanbul, Turkey, Jan. 20, 1986). Political scientist. In *The Liberal Tradition in America: an Interpretation of American Political Thought since the Revolution* (1955), Hartz argued that America is inherently liberal. Settled by European liberals, it lacks a feudal or aristocratic heritage and consequently did not develop a strong oppositional socialist movement. Liberalism's obsolete Lockean belief in private property rights makes it inherently conservative, he believed, while its overly optimistic faith in human reason makes it vulnerable to leftist appeals to human perfectability. Hartz's sense of inexorable liberal hegemony in American thought (a hegemony challenged only by the southern slaveholding power) was persuasive in the CONSENSUS period of American historiography —the 1950s and 1960s—but has been decisively challenged in the last generation by efforts to recover the traditions of CALVINISM, REPUBLICANISM, and POPULISM.

See also LIBERALISM.

FURTHER READING

John Patrick Diggins, "Knowledge and Sorrow: Louis Hartz's Quarrel with American History," *Political Theory* 16 (Aug. 1988): 355–77.

Hawthorne, Nathaniel (b. Salem, Mass., July 4, 1804; d. Plymouth, N.H., May 19, 1864). It is rare enough for a writer to be considered great in a single era. Hawthorne has the unusual distinction of being the only American writer of fiction to have been enshrined as classic in both the nineteenth and twentieth centuries. Yet successive generations, concurring on his elevated place in the literary pantheon, have used him to promote different forms of literary greatness. The nineteenth century's Hawthorne was often cherished for the moral, domestic, spiritual, sentimental, and "exquisite" qualities of his writing. In his review of *Twice-Told Tales* (1837), the Reverend Andrew Peabody gushed over Hawthorne's "garlands of poetic feeling" and praised "The Gentle Boy" for its description of "an adopted child . . . as 'a domesticated sunbeam.'" Jane Tompkins has pointed out that Hawthorne was frequently lauded in the same language that nineteenth-century reviewers applied to the works of female sentimental writers, and that only in the twentieth century was the writing of these women devalued as subliterary. The spread of Freudian assumptions in the twentieth century, in her view, led critics to praise Hawthorne anew as a master of psychological "depth."

No doubt the dominance of psychotherapeutic discourse in twentieth-century culture can be correlated with the critics' stress on Hawthorne's psychological insight, but this critical line was in fact well established in the nineteenth century. Metaphors of psychological surface and depth appear in many discussions of Hawthorne's work in the 1850s and 1860s, as well as in Henry James's *Hawthorne* (1879), in which James approves of his predecessor's "deeper psychology." Hawthorne's eminence was bolstered in the nineteenth century by two powerful traditions —sentimentality and psychology. When the first was discarded, the other remained, and the veneration of his greatness persisted.

In the post-Civil War decades Hawthorne was

much admired and elevated by William Dean Howells and other literary luminaries as a pioneer not only of psychological romance but of realism and of regionalism. However, by the 1910s and 1920s Van Wyck Brooks and Randolph Bourne—with their interest in cultural reform and their disdain for Victorian "puritans"—took Hawthorne to task for having belonged to a literary establishment that ignored the likes of Walt Whitman. Similarly, Vernon Parrington's *Main Currents in American Thought* (1927) upbraided Hawthorne for his brooding absorption with the "inner life," an individualistic preoccupation that in Parrington's mind went hand in hand with Hawthorne's detached, seemingly smug skepticism toward social reformers.

The two influential moderns who breathed new life into Hawthorne were F. O. Matthiessen and D. H. Lawrence. As Richard Brodhead puts it, Matthiessen's *American Renaissance* (1941) made Hawthorne's experimentation with form, symbolism, and allegory a textual "centerpiece" for the kind of close reading that would distinguish the New Critics in the 1950s. Lawrence's *Studies in Classic American Literature* (1923) hailed Hawthorne as a complex protomodernist depth psychologist whose "blood knowledge" throbbed beneath the surface graced by the "sunbeams" which charmed so many nineteenth-century readers. Hawthorne's work and his life assumed the status of psychological case studies in Frederick Crews's *The Sins of the Fathers* (1966), an important, trend-setting book which lends support to Tompkins's contention that psychiatry reshaped critical views on what is "deep" about Hawthorne.

Critics have continued to be drawn to Hawthorne partly because few mid nineteenth-century authors are as provocative as he is in their cultural understanding of the emergence of middle-class *forms* of subjectivity. Recent Hawthorne scholars have established a rich dialogue with new theories of ideology (Sacvan Bercovitch, Lauren Berlant) and new contributions to a more expansive study of history that now encompasses such matters as the cultural encoding of gender difference, sexuality, the emotions, and the body (T. Walter Herbert, Joel Pfister). What James termed the "deeper psychology" and what readers such as Lawrence and Crews saw as Freudian in Hawthorne's fictions can now be recontextualized as a historically specific cultural *production* of the antebellum middle class rather than a literary discovery of a universal "psychological self" later "explored" by modernists.

Thus, in his disturbing allegories, such as "The Birth-Mark" (1843) and "Rappaccini's Daughter"

(1844), Hawthorne parodied male monomaniacs—author figures—who are obsessed with controlling the way women imagine their creativity and sexuality, and suggested that psychological tension between the sexes was one cultural effect of the extreme separation of feminine and masculine roles. In Hawthorne's nightmarish domestic tales of compulsion, women who merely look unfeminine—too powerful, too creative, too sexual—are liable to be feminized (to death). In his novels of the 1850s and 1860s the heroines are classified as toxic—unfeminine—because of their artistic or political commitments. These depictions suggest that Hawthorne saw mid-century efforts to regulate the female body—gynecology, advice books, campaigns against prostitution—as cultural displacements of masculine anxieties about "monstrous" women. Zenobia, a charismatic women's rights orator (partly based on MARGARET FULLER) in *The Blithedale Romance* (1852), is branded a "monster" by a male "reformer" who spurns her for her half-sister, Priscilla. In retaliation, Zenobia characterizes the pale, thin, feminized, stereotyped Priscilla as "the type of womanhood such as man has spent centuries in making."

Hawthorne's "psychological" fiction, in the attention it pays to the social *making* of domesticated, privatized, and deeply gendered identities, may actually have helped prepare a path for the reception of the Freudian psychology that would later, in turn, lead critics to praise Hawthorne. The remark of Charles Hale, a contemporary reviewer of *The Scarlet Letter* (1850), that the book was "an awful probing into the most forbidden regions of consciousness," suggests that Hawthorne's probings may have helped loosen the soil that would later receive Freud's. Hawthorne's middle-class fictions contributed to the cultural appearance of a middle-class "psychological self" that twentieth-century Freudians and other psychologists would come to regard as "human" and "universal."

Hawthorne's journals, letters, sketches, and fictions demonstrate how devoted he was to middle-class domestic femininity; yet his fictions could also shed critical light on the very norm he so adored. *The House of the Seven Gables* (1851), for example, exhibits how the seemingly innocuous femininity of Phoebe can create a middle-class privatization so sentimentally appealing that a would-be radical like Holgrave will eagerly abandon his desire to reform a "republican country . . . in which somebody is always at the drowning point." While Hawthorne strains in his final novel *The Marble Faun* (1860) to make Hilda, the uptight copyist, into an admirable "angel in the house," it is Miriam's original and passionate, unfeminized art that is intellectually intriguing.

Brodhead concludes *The School of Hawthorne* (1986) by observing that Hawthorne will "survive" as long as each generation sees in his works "the image of its living concerns and needs." Late twentieth-century critics, moving beyond psychological interpretation and toward historical and semiotic strategies, beyond the notion of a universal, essential self and toward a culturally specific, constructed self, continue to draw inspiration from Hawthorne, now lauded for his self-reflexive experimentalism. He is a writer, it appears, for the American ages, continually re-earning his privileged position in the literary canon.

JOEL PFISTER

FURTHER READING

Sacvan Bercovitch, *The Office of the Scarlet Letter* (Baltimore: Johns Hopkins University Press, 1991).

Lauren Berlant, *The Anatomy of National Fantasy: Hawthorne, Utopia, and Everyday Life* (Chicago: University of Chicago Press, 1991).

Richard H. Brodhead, *The School of Hawthorne* (New York: Oxford University Press, 1986).

Michael J. Colacurcio, *The Province of Piety: Moral History in Hawthorne's Early Tales* (Cambridge: Harvard University Press, 1984).

Julian Hawthorne, *Nathaniel Hawthorne and His Wife: a Biography*, 2 vols. (Cambridge, Mass.: The University Press, 1884).

T. Walter Herbert, *Dearest Beloved: the Hawthornes and the Making of the Middle-Class Family* (Berkeley: University of California Press, 1992).

Joel Pfister, *The Production of Personal Life: Class, Gender, and the Psychological in Hawthorne's Fiction* (Stanford: Stanford University Press, 1991).

Jane Tompkins, *Sensational Designs: the Cultural Work of American Fiction, 1790–1860* (New York: Oxford University Press, 1985).

Hay, John (b. Salem, Ind., Oct. 8, 1838; d. Newbury, N.H., July 1, 1905).   Diplomat and writer. As a young man, Hay was an assistant private secretary to Abraham Lincoln, an experience which led to his massive, ten-volume *Life of Lincoln* (1874–90), written with John Nicolay. The White House experience also placed Hay at the center of the process of national development, and his subsequent career as a diplomat spanned a major epoch in the emergence of American international power. As Secretary of State under McKinley and Theodore Roosevelt, Hay formulated the "open door policy," a plan to guarantee free commerce and native "territorial integrity" in China. In the midst of his diplomatic work he published poetry, travel writing, and fiction, including the novel *The Bread-winners*, issued anonymously in 1884.

FURTHER READING

Robert L. Gale, *John Hay* (Boston: Twayne, 1978).

Hayek, Friedrich A. (b. Vienna, Austria, May 8, 1899; d. Freiburg, Germany, Mar. 23, 1992).   Hayek is widely recognized for clarifying the meaning of liberal society and for reopening the road to capitalism after governments had turned to central planning in the twentieth century. Economist, social theorist, philosopher of law, and historian of ideas, Hayek was born in turn-of-the-century Vienna into a family that included many academicians and scientists. After serving as an Austro-Hungarian army officer in World War I, he earned doctorates in law and political science from the University of Vienna, where he began teaching in 1929. There followed nearly two decades at the University of London (1931–50) and a dozen years at the University of Chicago (1950–62) before Hayek returned to Europe to teach in Germany and Austria. In the course of a long and distinguished career, Hayek wrote and edited nearly 30 books and 150 articles. His contribution to the theory of business cycles brought him the Nobel Prize in Economics in 1974.

When Hayek emerged on the international scene in the 1940s and 1950s, governments were steadily augmenting their powers over the economy. The social-economic consensus held that by pursuing full employment and distributive policies, governments could stimulate new levels of abundance. Opposition to this interventionist philosophy arose on both sides of the Atlantic after World War II, slowly at first, more rapidly after the mid-1960s. In the United States the voices of LIBERTARIANISM and CONSERVATISM found outlets in publications such as the *Freeman*, *Human Events*, and the *National Review* edited by WILLIAM F. BUCKLEY JR. Besides Buckley's, other prominent voices included those of Frank Chodorov, Henry Hazlitt, Felix Morley, Frank Meyer, and one of Hayek's mentors, Ludwig von Mises, whose *Omnipotent Government* and *Bureaucracy* both appeared in 1944. Hayek was well equipped to lead the revolt against statism, having honed his skills first in pure economic theory as fascism progressively enslaved his native Central Europe and then in polemical analysis while writing the transatlantic tour de force *The Road to Serfdom* (1944).

Hayek's intellectual roots can be traced to eighteenth- and nineteenth-century classical LIBERALISM as developed by Locke, Hume, and Adam Smith, and later expressed by Richard Cobden and John Stuart Mill. The former artillery officer was trained in the Austrian School of Economics founded by Carl Menger, who had employed marginal utility analysis in defense of capitalist value theory. Building on this foundation, Hayek won the respect of his peers with studies in formal economic theory and became one of the most systematic defenders of economic INDIVIDUALISM. But it was *The Road to Serfdom* that brought him worldwide attention as a warning voice against dangers posed by collectivist economics. In what was then a distinctly minority view, Hayek held that governments could not curtail economic freedom without jeopardizing other human rights. Moreover, little intellectual difference separated fascism and communism, he argued, for both were rooted in an anti-individualist mentality that undermined FREEDOM. The most rational and sophisticated of plans produced unforeseen consequences, unwanted even by socialist planners. Economic growth slowed, and people became different psychologically, displaying less initiative and practicing less RESPONSIBILITY.

Near the end of his tenure at the University of Chicago, Hayek published *The Constitution of Liberty* (1960), which spelled out the entire framework of a liberal economic and social order and drove home a central motif of his work: governments could maximize liberty by reversing the trend to the welfare state. Yet he could not fully subscribe to rationalistic laissez-faire doctrine. He emphasized in his Nobel Memorial Lecture "The Pretence of Knowledge" that although government planners could not determine social and economic results, they could cultivate growth as gardeners do with their plants.

Hayek's political and economic philosophy centered on liberty, a condition achieved when the coercion of some people by others is reduced as much as possible. For economic individualists this meant an economy based on private property that operates spontaneously through a market system, a flexible price mechanism, and the perceived self-interest of producers and consumers. But Hayek opposed encroaching government for another reason as well. In many places, notably in *The Counter-Revolution of Science* (1952) and *The Sensory Order* (1952), Hayek's antistatism reflected a Kantian sense of the limitations of human knowledge that also incorporated his friend Karl Popper's stress on human fallibility. Individuals pursue self-interest in economic decision-making, but do so with limited knowledge. Difficult as it is for individuals to understand the totality of circumstances surrounding their own lives, it is even more difficult for central planning authorities, unable to ascertain all the particular facts about market participants, to devise a system consistent with individual self-interest and freedom. It is a conceit of those adept in algebraic equations to assume that the measurable factors are also the most relevant ones.

The way out, in Hayek's philosophy, lay in the rule of LAW, that is, fidelity to general principles that have evolved because they permitted survival and

prosperity without sacrificing certain RIGHTS, especially the right to private property and the sanctity of contracts. Such rules—abstract, nondiscriminating, and understood beforehand—permitted history to unfold as an undesigned process in which men and women with different values and beliefs could in harmony seek to improve their lot in life. It is this self-generating order that the welfare state, in search of distributive JUSTICE, threatened to disrupt.

Hayek's eloquent defense of a free market society was much maligned. Critics argued that it embraced a constricted notion of privilege, of advantages conferred by the state but not by the economic system. Others saw a cold-blooded theoretical approach that resonated mostly with the strong and the comfortable, and a model of minimal government inapplicable in an era of mammoth military establishments. Yet Hayek's admirers pointed to the broader canvass. On it they observed that three and a half decades after *The Road to Serfdom* appeared, a disciple of Hayek (Margaret Thatcher) became prime minister of Britain and Ronald Reagan carried the counter-offensive against KEYNESIANISM to Washington. Among the countries and republics of Eastern Europe and the Soviet Union, one after the other cast off the fetters of communism and abandoned the vision of an economic world of preconceived order.

RONALD LORA

FURTHER READING

Norman P. Barry, *Hayek's Social and Economic Philosophy* (London: Macmillan, 1979).

Eamonn Butler, *Hayek: His Contribution to the Political and Economic Thought of Our Time* (1983; New York: Universe, 1985).

John Gray, *Hayek on Liberty*, 2nd edn. (1984; New York: Blackwell, 1986).

Friedrich A. Hayek, *The Road to Serfdom* (Chicago: University of Chicago Press, 1944).

——, *The Counter-Revolution in Science* (Glencoe: Free Press, 1952).

——, *The Constitution of Liberty* (Chicago: University of Chicago Press, 1960).

——, *The Essence of Hayek*, ed. Chiaki Nishiyama and Kurt R. Leube (Stanford: Hoover Institution Press, 1984).

Fritz Machlup, ed., *Essays on Hayek* (New York: New York University Press, 1976).

Hecker, Isaac (b. New York, N.Y., Dec. 18, 1819; d. New York, N.Y., Dec. 22, 1888). Religious leader. After briefly associating with ORESTES BROWNSON and various Transcendentalist communities in Massachusetts, Hecker converted to CATHOLICISM, prepared for the priesthood, and in 1849 was ordained a Redemptorist missionary. Troubled by the prevailing Catholic emphasis on authority, he won approval from Pope Pius IX to establish his own order of missionaries for America, the Paulist Fathers, in 1858. As founding editor of the Paulists' *Catholic World* in 1865, and in his books *Questions of the Soul* (1855), *Aspirations of Nature* (1855), and *The Church and the Age* (1887), he advanced an American version of Roman Catholicism. He minimized the role of external structure, reason, and ceremony, and emphasized the workings of the Holy Spirit in inner religious impulses and personal regeneration.

FURTHER READING

John Farina, *An American Experience of God: the Spirituality of Isaac Hecker* (New York: Paulist Press, 1981).

hegemony The term is commonly used to refer to the preponderance of influence or power, particularly among nations. But the theoretical concept of hegemony, especially as developed in the sociological thinking of the Italian Marxist Antonio Gramsci (1891–1937), is far more subtle and robust, amounting to nothing less than an entire theory of social order. For Gramsci, "hegemony" refers to the moral and intellectual leadership exercised in society—whether for liberation or oppression—by dominant groups whose authority is grounded in economic, political, cultural, and social institutions. Far from being simply an automatic occurrence reflecting power in any one of these arenas, hegemony, according to Gramsci, denotes the relatively rare political accomplishment of a ruling class whose society-wide dominance rests ultimately upon the consent of those over whom they rule. Thus he contrasted the successful accomplishment of hegemony by the French bourgeoisie during the French Revolution with the failure of the Italian bourgeoisie to achieve a comparable position of leadership during the period of Italy's national unification in the nineteenth century. And he looked forward to a time when the working classes would exercise hegemony in Western democratic societies.

Gramsci, a founder of the Italian Communist Party, was a younger member of the generation of Marxists, including V. I. Lenin (1870–1924) and Rosa Luxemburg (1871–1919), who believed that socialist revolution would result from political and cultural struggles rather than economic crises alone. These Marxists rejected the mechanistic assumption, prevalent among earlier Marxist determinists such as Karl Kautsky (1854–1938), that revolution would occur "naturally" as a consequence of mounting tensions within capitalism. Unlike Lenin and Luxemburg, however, Gramsci rejected the Bolsheviks' capture of the Russian state in 1917 as an appropriate model for successful socialist struggle in Western democracies. Instead, he pointed to civil society—institutions outside the formally organized spheres of state and economy—as the most significant arena of political struggle for the hearts and minds of the citizenry of Western democracies. And, in contrast to Lenin's stress on the role of a vanguard party in bringing revolutionary consciousness to the proletariat, and to Luxemburg's stress on the spontaneity of the working class, Gramsci theorized the importance of cultural contestation and political education in building oppositional or counterhegemonic cultures.

Gramsci's most mature thinking was expressed in *The Prison Notebooks*, a series of essays written cryptically to evade censorship during the years 1926 to 1937 when he was imprisoned by the fascist government of Italy for his political activities. Here he contrasted the Bolshevik's sudden "war of maneuver" that had captured state power to the long-term battles for hegemony within civil society that he likened to the "war of position" that had occurred in the trenches of Europe during World War I. He pointed to the central role that intellectuals play in "wars of position" by formulating political worldviews that articulate the needs and interests of subaltern classes, thereby winning their consent to be governed by hegemonic classes.

In thinking about the prospects for socialist revolution in Western industrial societies, Gramsci stressed that left-wing parties must create autonomous cultural spaces in which "organic intellectuals"—those who arise within the context of working-class life—can gain valuable experiences that will enable them to exert counterhegemonic moral and intellectual leadership ("education") within civil society and to forge political alliances ("historical blocs") in order to build a new society. But Gramsci also warned about societal tendencies such as technocratic management and consumerism ("Fordism") that promote passive consent to new forms of bourgeois domination.

When New Left political forces began to distance themselves from Old Left parties after the abortive student and worker revolt in France in 1968, Gramsci's theory of hegemony became an increasingly important source of ideas for scholars and activists. It enabled Marxist intellectuals to go beyond the narrow confines of the traditional base/superstructure model, which postulates consciousness as a passive reflection of economic influences, and to grasp the active relations of social power that operate in the creation of culture. One of the most influential applications of the theory of hegemony by an American historian is Eugene Genovese's *Roll, Jordan,*

Roll, a study of the hegemonic power of American slaveholders and of the forms of accommodation and resistance to that power that African American slaves used in constructing an oppositional culture and identity. A provocative essay published by T. J. Jackson Lears in the *American Historical Review* shows how profoundly the theory of cultural hegemony can transform the historical understanding of dominance and subordination in capitalist society. Within literary studies, Edward Said has fruitfully combined Michel Foucault's discourse theory with Gramsci's theory of hegemony to examine the social construction of *Orientalism* as a powerful ideological and material force in Western thinking, and Paul Bove has used Gramsci's approach to probe the underlying ideology of New Criticism in American literature.

The theory of hegemony also continues to influence political theory. In a book entitled *Free Spaces*, populist intellectuals Sarah Evans and Harry Boyte stress the importance of autonomous cultural institutions in nurturing grassroots democratic struggles in America. Ernesto Laclau and Chantal Mouffe's *Hegemony and Socialist Strategy*, a post-Marxist theory of the democratic struggle for socialism, argues that the struggle for hegemony is more important than organizing social classes as a strategy for progressive social change. By emphasizing how a diversity of "basic articulatory principles"—including feminism, antiracism, anticolonialism, environmentalism, antimilitarism, and economic democracy—can be interwoven politically to form new historical blocs dedicated to the further democratization of state and economy (p. 67), Laclau and Mouffe contend that the concept of struggles for hegemony remains potent even after the demise of the specific political context, such as workers' parties, that first gave rise to the idea of hegemony. The plurality of social movements in the late twentieth century need not be taken as a sign of the marginalization and fragmentation of emancipatory democratic forces. It may be that struggles for hegemony by such movements will continue to define the horizon of progressive politics.

DWIGHT B. BILLINGS

See also IDEOLOGY; SOCIALISM.

FURTHER READING

Paul A. Bove, "Agriculture and Academe: America's Southern Question," *Boundary 2* 14 (Spring 1986): 169–95.

Sarah Evans and Harry Boyte, *Free Spaces: the Sources of Democratic Change in America* (New York: Harper and Row, 1986).

Eugene Genovese, *Roll, Jordan, Roll: The World the Slaves Made* (New York: Vintage Books, 1976).

Antonio Gramsci, *Selections from the Prison Notebooks*, edited and translated by Quintin Hoare and G. N. Smith (New York: International Publishers, 1971).

Ernesto Laclau and Chantal Mouffe, *Hegemony and Socialist Strategy* (London: Verso, 1985).

T. J. Jackson Lears, "The Concept of Cultural Hegemony: Problems and Possibilities," *American Historical Review* 90 (June 1985): 567–93.

Chantal Mouffe, "Hegemony and Ideology in Gramsci," in Chantal Mouffe, ed., *Gramsci and Marxist Theory* (London: Routledge & Kegan Paul, 1979).

Edward Said, *Orientalism* (New York: Vintage Books, 1979).

Hellman, Lillian (b. New Orleans, La., June 20, 1906; d. Vineyard Haven, Mass., June 30, 1984). Writer. As a playwright Hellman met critical as well as popular success during the 1930s and 1940s. *The Children's Hour* (1934) portrayed two female teachers ruined by their community's nasty response to a schoolgirl's accusation that they were "overly affectionate." *The Little Foxes* (1939) depicted a southern family's battle to adjust to the industrial world, while *Watch on the Rhine* (1941) probed the menace of fascism. As a memoirist Hellman produced *An Unfinished Woman* (1969), *Pentimento* (1973), and *Scoundrel Time* (1976). The latter work, a treatment of McCarthyism in the 1950s, caused a furor in intellectual circles when MARY MCCARTHY and others accused Hellman of falsely remembering herself as a valiant opponent of official repression. Hellman's libel suit against McCarthy was halted by Hellman's death in 1984.

FURTHER READING

Carl E. Rollyson, *Lillian Hellman: Her Legacy and Her Legend* (New York: St. Martin's, 1988).

Helper, Hinton Rowan (b. Rowan County, N.C., Dec. 27, 1829; d. Washington, D.C., Mar. 9, 1909). Writer. Helper's *The Impending Crisis of the South: How to Meet It* (1857) argued that slavery hurts poor southern whites by depressing wages and impeding economic and cultural progress. Appealing to his fellow white southerners' self-interest through statistics that contrasted southern and northern agriculture, industry, communications, and land values, Helper urged poor whites to refuse to cooperate with slaveholders. The book was widely banned in the South, and Helper himself left for the North, where the book was widely praised. Concerned solely with the plight of poorer whites, Helper was no racial egalitarian. After the Civil War he advocated the forcible deportation of African Americans.

FURTHER READING

Louis Filler, *The Crusade against Slavery* (New York: Harper and Row, 1960).

Hemingway, Ernest (b. Oak Park, Ill., July 21, 1899; d. Ketchum, Idaho, July 2, 1961). Writer. Among the most popular twentieth-century American writers, Hemingway developed a bare-bones style that has attracted both imitators and parodists. Wounded in World War I, Hemingway returned from Europe professing his alienation from American culture and his intention to become a writer. Returning to France with his wife as an expatriate, he joined Gertrude Stein, Ezra Pound, Sherwood Anderson, T. S. Eliot, and F. Scott Fitzgerald, a group he portrayed in his posthumously published memoir *A Moveable Feast* (1964). His novels *The Sun Also Rises* (1926) and especially *A Farewell to Arms* (1929) established Hemingway as a literary star, one who eventually came to embody the writer as swaggering celebrity.

FURTHER READING
Jeffrey Meyers, *Hemingway: a Biography* (New York: Harper and Row, 1985).

Henry, Joseph (b. Albany, N.Y., Dec. 17, 1797; d. Washington, D.C., May 13, 1878). Scientist. The first person to record the phenomenon of electromagnetic induction, Henry invented an effective electromagnet, an electric motor, relays, transformers, and a primitive telegraph. Believing that good scientific work requires institutional support and effective communication, he became the first secretary of the Smithsonian Institution (1846), where he promoted collective work and the growth of scientific societies and publications.

FURTHER READING
Robert V. Bruce, *The Launching of Modern American Science, 1846–1876* (New York: Knopf, 1987).

Herberg, Will (b. Liachovitzi, Russia, June 30, 1901; d. Chatham, N.J., Mar. 27, 1977). Theologian and sociologist. Author of *Judaism and Modern Man: an Interpretation of Jewish Religion* (1951) and *Protestant, Catholic, Jew: an Essay in American Religious Sociology* (1955), Herberg was raised an atheist and socialist but under the influence of REINHOLD NIEBUHR came to advocate a neo-orthodox Jewish theology. The religious impulse, he concluded, had become diffuse, idolatrous, and excessively optimistic about human nature. The denial of God's lordship fostered social injustice, while secular cults such as communism, liberalism, fascism, and scientism were responsible for the horrors of the twentieth century. Modernism and traditionalism, Herberg predicted, could be reconciled in a new biblical faith marked by a sense of paradox, irony, risk, and divine transcendence.

FURTHER READING
Harry J. Ausmus, *Will Herberg: From Right to Right* (Chapel Hill: University of North Carolina Press, 1987).

Herbst, Josephine (b. Sioux City, Iowa, Mar. 5, 1892; d. New York, N.Y., Jan. 28, 1969). Writer. Good writing, Herbst believed, comes from an author's active engagement with the social order: it instructs and illuminates but is not dogmatic. As a radical journalist she reported on Russia, Cuba, the rise of Nazism, the Spanish civil war, and domestic labor and farmer movements. Her fiction—including the autobiographical *Nothing Is Sacred* (1928) and a chronicle of a black family since Reconstruction entitled *Pity Is Not Enough* (1933)—explored the complicated intersections of history, social transformation, and human happiness.

FURTHER READING
Elinor Langer, *Josephine Herbst* (Boston: Little, Brown, 1984).

heredity In his 1859 *Origin of Species*, Charles Darwin (1809–1882) admitted a near-total ignorance of the laws of heredity. However, he shared the prevailing "Lamarckian" assumption that external conditions both directly and indirectly induce heritable variation. In the latter case, environmental change generates new needs, which organisms alter their habits to satisfy. The resultant use and disuse of organs elicits physiological changes, which eventually become heritable. (*See also* DARWINISM.)

Nineteenth-century physicians and natural historians, as well as the public, generally assumed that acquired characters were heritable. But the import of that principle for evolution was hotly disputed. Darwin considered Lamarckian processes supplementary to the much stronger force of natural selection, while Herbert Spencer (1820–1903) thought them central. In the view of Spencer and his followers (known as "neo-Lamarckians"), evolution occurred primarily through the active adaptation of organisms to their environment. Notwithstanding this dispute, Darwinians and neo-Lamarckians shared a common view of heredity.

In the 1880s, that consensus was challenged by August Weismann (1834–1914), a German cytologist who argued that the reproductive cells in the gonads were completely isolated from the cells in the rest of the body. The hereditary units, embedded in the reproductive cells, would thus be impervious to changes in environment. Weismann and his followers (known as "neo-Darwinians") denied that acquired traits could be inherited. It followed that natural selection was the sole evolutionary force. Thus the late nineteenth century was characterized by sharply competing views of heredity, linked to different perspectives on evolution.

It was also marked by the widespread assumption that traits making for social success and failure were heritable. In 1865, Darwin's cousin, Sir Francis Galton (1822–1911), had shown that high achievement runs in families, and concluded that professional eminence was largely due to natural ability. By the late nineteenth century, it was taken for granted that most differences in intelligence, talent, and character were inherited—and that the least able members of society produced the most offspring. Numerous family studies, such as Richard Dugdale's "*The Jukes*" (1877) and Henry H. Goddard's *The Kallikaks* (1912), seemed to demonstrate that mental and moral defectives bred at an alarming rate. Bad heredity provided an increasingly popular explanation for the problems besetting post-Civil War America.

There was no consensus on the *nature* of heredity, however, and thus on the proper response to this threat. Many nineteenth-century family studies were conducted by neo-Lamarckians like Dugdale who believed that impoverished environments produced physically and mentally weak individuals. They tended to argue for social reform. Thus Dugdale insisted that "public health and infant education . . . are the two legs upon which the general morality of the future must travel" (p. 119). Primitive hereditary tendencies could be reversed by education and experience (especially when the environment changed early and was constantly reinforced). In contrast, Neo-Darwinians like Goddard or Charles B. Davenport (1866–1944), the respected geneticist director of the Eugenics Record Office (ERO) at Cold Spring Harbor, New York, believed that poor heredity was immutable. Thus the only effective solution was to breed from the fitter stocks. As Davenport wrote in the ERO bulletin, *How to Make a Eugenical Family Study*, "Apart from migration, there is only one way to get socially desirable traits into our social life, and that is by reproduction; there is only one to get them out, by preventing their reproduction through breeding" (p. 4).

By the close of the century, degeneracy theorists had lost considerable ground to the eugenicists. The eugenic cause was further reinforced by two turn-of-the-century events: the rediscovery of monk-botanist Gregor Mendel's laws and the inception of intelligence testing. The former made it possible, at least in theory, to predict the effects of particular matings—and thus to exert eugenic controls. It also reinforced the view that traits making for social success and failure were heritable. The newer family studies seemed to demonstrate that inheritance of mental and moral traits followed a simple Mendelian pattern. Thus Goddard contrasted the effects of a liaison between "Martin Kallikak, Sr." and a barmaid with those resulting from his later marriage to an upstanding Quaker woman. From the illicit union there ostensibly issued 480 descendants, only 46 known to be normal. All the offspring of the second union, however, were respectable members of their communities. Goddard concluded that feeble-mindedness resulted from a single, recessive gene.

Recessive genes are hidden in apparently normal carriers. Thus the problem of feeble-mindedness (which was viewed as the root cause of many asocial behaviors) was apparently much worse than had been thought. Most bad genes would be invisible, even to the carriers themselves. Martin Kallikak Sr. was the scion of a middle-class family of old English stock, which for generations, according to Goddard, had maintained "a reputation for honor and respectability" (p. 50). But Martin Kallikak must have possessed a hereditary taint, for he had sired an appalling line of mental defectives. Feeble-mindedness thus came to be seen as a kind of infectious disease, which could be unknowingly spread. Moreover, it affected not just immigrants and other urban poor, but rural families of seemingly good blood. The Jukes, Kallikaks, Pineys, Dacks, and Yaks were all hillbilly families who lived in places like "Hog Hollow." (A recent collection of these studies is titled *White Trash*.)

The menace of the feeble-minded was also underscored by the results of the Binet-Simon INTELLIGENCE tests, which Goddard brought to America in 1908. The tests were soon administered to potential immigrants, inmates of institutions, and, in 1917, army recruits. It now appeared that different grades of mentality could be rated with scientific precision. If the instruments did measure native ability, as the testers claimed, the nation was clearly in trouble. The average white army draftee scored a mental age of 13 years; the average black a mental age of ten.

Intelligence tests were also thought capable of identifying the subtly affected. "Low-grade idiots" rarely reproduced, but the more intelligent moron (with a mental age of eight to twelve) was alarmingly prolific. Mental tests could ferret them out. Thus at least one stream of "defectives" could be eliminated through rigorous programs of segregation or sterilization. In 1907, Indiana enacted the first statute authorizing compulsory sterilization of confirmed "criminals, idiots, rapists, and imbeciles." Another 29 states eventually followed suit.

The massive influx of immigrants from Southern and Eastern Europe heightened the sense of threat. Mental tests seemed to indicate that at least two of every five immigrants were feeble-minded. Calvin Coolidge had declared in *Good Housekeeping* in 1921 that "America must be kept American. Biological laws show . . . that Nordics deteriorate when mixed with other races" (Kevles, p. 97). Three years later, as President, he signed the Immigration Restriction Act into law.

Newspapers, popular magazines, exhibits at state fairs, and college and high-school textbooks warned of the economic burden of bad heredity. "The cost of caring for those who cannot care for themselves because of their breeding is very heavy—perhaps two hundred million or more a year," cautioned William Castle and his coauthors in *Heredity and Eugenics*, a standard textbook. They also warned students that "from one thousand Roumanians today in Boston, at the present rate of breeding, will come a hundred thousand two hundred years hence to govern the fifty descendants of Harvard's sons!" (p. 309).

By the 1920s, Lamarckism was in retreat. Opponents of eugenics now rarely argued that better nutrition and housing would improve heredity. They asserted instead that the role of genes in explaining individual and group differences had been exaggerated and that poverty and crime resulted from social conditions, not bad genes. These claims were bolstered by the Depression, which undermined the equation of social status with genetic worth. Revelations of Nazi atrocities strongly reinforced the environmentalist turn. Reports of extermination camps and euthanasia programs produced a sharp rejection of biological explanations of human differences. "Hereditarian" thinking went out of fashion, among social scientists, journalists, and most of the public. Heredity might be fixed, but in the now dominant view, genes did not explain human mental and moral differences. Culture did.

Many geneticists continued to assume that human social institutions were strongly influenced by the distribution of genotypes (*see also* SOCIOBIOLOGY). But in the changed climate, these thinkers often retreated from public view. In the 1980s, a return to conservative politics coincided with a renewal of academic and popular interest in genetic explanations of human behavior. As they had before World War II, many social scientists and journalists, as well as geneticists, once again sought biological explanations for social ills. The postwar triumph of environmentalism,

while nearly complete, was perhaps superficial and certainly brief.

DIANE B. PAUL

FURTHER READING

William E. Castle et al., *Heredity and Eugenics* (Chicago: University of Chicago Press, 1912).

Charles B. Davenport and Harry H. Laughlin, *How to Make a Eugenical Family Study*, ERO Bulletin 13 (New York, 1915).

Carl N. Degler, *In Search of Human Nature* (New York: Oxford University Press, 1991).

Richard L. Dugdale, *"The Jukes": a Study in Crime, Pauperism, Disease, and Heredity* (New York: G. P. Putnam's Sons, 1877).

Steven A. Gelb, "Degeneracy Theory, Eugenics, and Family Studies," *Journal of the History of the Behavioral Sciences* 26 (1990): 242–5.

Henry H. Goddard, *The Kallikak Family: a Study in the Heredity of Feeble-mindedness* (New York: Macmillan, 1912).

Daniel J. Kevles, *In the Name of Eugenics: Genetics and the Uses of Human Heredity* (New York: Knopf, 1985).

Nicole Hahn Rafter, *White Trash: the Eugenic Family Studies, 1877–1919* (Boston: Northeastern University Press, 1988).

Charles E. Rosenberg, "The Bitter Fruit: Heredity, Disease, and Social Thought," in *No Other Gods: On Science and American Social Thought* (Baltimore: Johns Hopkins University Press, 1976).

Higginson. Thomas Wentworth (b. Cambridge, Mass., Dec. 22, 1823; d. Cambridge, Mass., May 9, 1911). Clergyman and writer. While a Harvard divinity student, Higginson was converted to the social and philosophical idealism of Emerson and the Transcendentalists. From his pulpit he assumed a leadership role in the reform movements of the 1840s and 1850s. He led demonstrations against the Fugitive Slave Law, and was part of the "Secret Six" cabal behind John Brown. After the war, in which he commanded a regiment of freedmen, he became a vocal feminist as coeditor of *Woman's Journal* (1870–84). His *Common Sense about Women* (1881) argued for gender equality as an essential feature of true civilization. Higginson was also a "man of letters" in the broad Victorian mode, a critic, a prominent literary-biographer, and editor. His most notable editorial act was his co-editing of the first two volumes of Emily Dickinson's poetry (1890–1), with Mabel Loomis Todd.

FURTHER READING

Tilden G. Edelstein, *Strange Enthusiasm: a Life of Thomas Wentworth Higginson* (New Haven: Yale University Press, 1968).

Hodge, Charles (b. Philadelphia, Pa., Dec. 27, 1797; d. Princeton, N.J., June 19, 1878). The best-known confessional Calvinist and one of the most formidable polemical theologians in the United States during the middle third of the nineteenth century, Hodge taught theology at Princeton Seminary for more than 50 years. At the time of his death he had personally instructed more students than had attended any other postgraduate educational institution of any kind in the United States. About 40 of his students became college presidents, over 200 were college instructors, and about 45 were professors in theological seminaries. Hodge's commanding influence was not, however, a result of simple longevity so much as the product of a tireless pen, forceful theological views, and deep personal piety.

Hodge, whose father was a Philadelphia physician and mother a descendant of New England patriots, entered the College of New Jersey (later Princeton University) in 1812, where the president was the redoubtable confessionalist, Ashbel Green. Even more influential than Green on Hodge's intellectual development, however, was Archibald Alexander, who also in 1812 had come to Princeton as the first professor at the new Presbyterian theological seminary. Alexander befriended Hodge as a collegiate undergraduate, directed the course of his seminary studies, invited him along on preaching tours in Virginia, and then persuaded the seminary directors to hire the young graduate as a professor of biblical languages. From Alexander, Hodge learned the singular combination of commitments that defined his own exposition of "the Princeton theology"—heartfelt piety, commitment to the inspiration of Scripture, devotion to the Westminster Confession and Catechisms, confidence in the European Calvinism of savants like François Turretin, and intuitive reliance upon Scottish Common Sense moral philosophy.

Hodge was ordained to the Presbyterian ministry in November 1821, but his entire career was spent as an instructor at the seminary. Early in that career he took a two-year study tour of European universities, where he thoroughly enjoyed firsthand exposure to the rigors of German scholarship, but where he also deepened his wariness, learned from Alexander, against what the Princetonians called "rationalism," "mysticism," and "ritualism." Upon his return to Princeton in 1829, Hodge transformed the seminary's theological journal (which he had established in 1825) into the *Biblical Repertory and Princeton Review*. For nearly a half-century thereafter, Hodge poured his energy into this periodical. It became the major outlet for Hodge's advice to the Presbyterians, the major vehicle for his searching criticisms of contemporary theological trends in Europe and North America, and the organ through which, especially

during the American Civil War, he discussed the momentous political events of the day. In 1871 a writer in the *British Quarterly Review* called this journal "beyond all question the greatest purely theological Review that has ever been published in the English tongue." (A. A. Hodge, p. 257).

Hodge's theological reputation arose from the skill (or, as his opponents would have it, the obduracy) with which he defended confessional CALVINISM. In the pages of the *Princeton Review* he chastised NATHANIEL TAYLOR and the "New Haven" theology for departing from the high Calvinism of JONATHAN EDWARDS. He attacked the revivalism of Charles Finney for promoting a presumptuous confidence in human potency. He called to account the Mercersburg theologians, John W. Nevin and Philip Schaff, for wandering into mysticism. He directed telling shafts at England's Oxford Movement and German neologisms. He defended a high view of the Bible's inspiration against both Roman Catholic arguments for apostolic hierarchy and the first waves of Continental biblical criticism. And he offered encouragement to Calvinist theological movements in other places (especially, after 1843, the Free Church of Scotland) and, more generally, to expressions of Protestant confessionalism (as in many warm, if not entirely comprehending, commendations of Lutheranism).

In a particularly momentous exchange of learned essays with Edwards Amasa Park of Andover Seminary in 1850 and 1851, Hodge defended the capacity of language to communicate theological truth propositionally. This debate, which had been sparked by Horace Bushnell's famous "Dissertation on Language" (1849), marked the high-water mark of public intellectual life in a Christian America that receded rapidly after the Civil War.

In his polemics Hodge sometimes exploited historical arguments casually; for someone whose thought was extraordinarily sophisticated on other matters, he could be quite naive on questions of theological method; and he sometimes did not discriminate well between the minor errors of nearby allies and the major weaknesses of theological adversaries. Yet for all the admitted gaps in his polemical writings, they also displayed a breadth of learning, grasp of basic Christian teaching, cohesive understanding of Scripture, forcefulness of prose, and greatness of soul that was rarely, if ever, matched in the nineteenth century.

The historian Bruce Kuklick has compared the theologians at Princeton Seminary unfavorably with the more adventuresome Christian thinkers of Congregationalist New England. Compared to the intellectual subtlety of Yale's N. W. Taylor, Kuklick held that "Hodge and his peers . . . were never able to see that . . . [Princeton] . . . could profit from German philosophy," and that the Princeton theologians "labored under a ponderous lack of imagination and creative insights" (pp. 77, 204). In strictly philosophical terms, Kuklick may be right. In a broader view, however, Hodge's achievement was remarkable. In an age filled with enthusiasm for the unfettered potential of human action, Hodge recalled the more sober message of Edwards, Pascal, Luther, Augustine, and St. Paul—that humanity's worst enemy is itself and its surest hope a word of divine salvation. At a time of growing estrangement between objective science and romantic inwardness, Hodge strove to keep piety and intellect together. In an age soon to pose scientific knowledge against religious traditions, Hodge argued that theologians had as much to learn from scientists as scientists from theologians. Hodge's attack on modern evolution, *What Is Darwinism?* questioned not change in species over time, nor even Darwin's construction of natural selection, but what he thought was the randomness built into Darwin's scheme. Of this book the modern historian of science, Neal C. Gillespie, has said that Hodge "was, and remains, one of the most astute writers on the theological implications of Darwin's work" (p. 112).

It is regrettable that Hodge is today known more through his books than through his contributions to the *Princeton Review*, which better illustrate his joining of piety and learning. Yet his books—especially a commentary on the Book of Romans (1835), a winsome introduction to Christianity written for the American Sunday School Union (1841), and a massive systematics (1872–73)—were important in their day and have been appreciated by many readers ever since. Hodge once claimed that "a new idea has never originated in this Seminary," but it was an ambiguous claim. Hodge was correct in describing the intent of his long and influential career, but wrong in short-changing the freshness of his own defense of Augustinian Protestant orthodoxy.

MARK A. NOLL

See also EVANGELICALISM.

FURTHER READING

Neal C. Gillespie, *Charles Darwin and the Problem of Creation* (Chicago: University of Chicago Press, 1979).
Archibald Alexander Hodge, *The Life of Charles Hodge* (New York: Charles Scribner's Sons, 1880).
Charles Hodge, *The Way of Life* (1841), ed. Mark A. Noll (Mahwah, N.J.: Paulist Press, 1987).
——, *Essays and Reviews: Selected from the Princeton Review* (1857), ed. Bruce Kuklick (New York: Garland, 1987).
——, *Systematic Theology*, 3 vols. (1872–3; Grand Rapids: William B. Eerdmans, n.d.).

William A. Hoffecker, *Piety and the Princeton Theologians* (Grand Rapids: Baker, 1981).
Bruce Kuklick, *Churchmen and Philosophers: from Jonathan Edwards to John Dewey* (New Haven: Yale University Press, 1985).
Mark A. Noll, ed., *The Princeton Theology, 1812–1921* (Grand Rapids: Baker, 1983).

Hofstadter, Richard (b. Buffalo, N.Y., Aug. 6, 1916; d. New York, N.Y., Oct. 24, 1970). Raised in Buffalo, but very much reared intellectually in New York City at the height of its post-World War II cultural importance, Hofstadter was the most influential American historian during the 1950s and 1960s. Although his professional career was firmly anchored in one place, Columbia University, where he received his Ph.D. and spent almost his entire professional life, his interests ranged broadly throughout American history and over its vast intellectual, political, and cultural landscape.

Hofstadter began publishing early, while he was still a graduate student, when in 1938 he challenged his great predecessor Charles Beard in a brief note, "The Tariff Issue on the Eve of the Civil War," published in the *American Historical Review*. His first book, *Social Darwinism in American Thought* (1944), which was immediately recognized in reviews as "important," brought into question the dominant disdain for the significance of ideas in history, and introduced the concept of SOCIAL DARWINISM into the historian's repertoire. Hofstadter continued as a prolific, brilliant, provocative, and witty interpreter of the American experience into the last years of his life. His last book, *America at 1750: a Social Portrait* (1971), the first of a projected three that aimed at a panoramic view of American society at the mid-century marks of 1750, 1850, and 1950, was published posthumously.

Hofstadter's most significant intellectual engagement was with American political culture, with how democratic traditions are created and challenged, and his concern was not with reverent preservation but with continued critical revitalization of that tradition. Hofstadter's commitment to democratic life often led him to question the heroes and categories that had been conventionally enshrined as markers in the evolution of a liberal society, such as the Jeffersonian tradition, Jacksonian Democracy, and Populism. He began this assault in *The American Political Tradition and the Men Who Made It*, published in 1948 when Hofstadter was 32 years old. Already his second book, it catapulted him to fame and has become a classic in American historiography, still read and enjoyed by students and the public. Marked by brilliant writing and extraordinary insight into personality as well as society, the book challenged assumptions about America's leaders and specifically the Beardian-Progressive interpretation of the conflict between democratic-popular traditions and business interests. As significantly, the book revealed the workings of a mind that was independent and rigorous in analysis, a talent for elegant and penetrating portraits of men and their times, and a refreshing sense of humor.

These qualities were once again displayed in *The Age of Reform* (1955), which was awarded the Pulitzer Prize in 1956. Hofstadter, now a prominent historian, revealed the underside of POPULISM and PROGRESSIVISM, the commonly revered progenitors of modern liberalism, criticizing especially their intolerance of outsiders and those whose culture was other than middle class, Protestant, and small town in its tastes and habits. Hofstadter's central contention was that Populism and Progressivism were as much conservative traditions as reform movements. Each was marked by nostalgia for the past; their reform strategies were circumscribed by the dominant American commitment to free enterprise, INDIVIDUALISM, and equality of opportunity. Rather than a continuation of these movements, the New Deal was, according to Hofstadter, a new and wholly pragmatic response to emergency conditions, unhampered by reverence for the past and unconfined by inherited traditions. Hofstadter's interpretation was strenuously challenged by many, but he had dismantled the secular reverence that had shielded the shibboleths of the "liberal" past from close scrutiny. (*See also* CONSENSUS.)

Hofstadter's irreverence was always balanced by an insistence on complexity in the past and in its interpretation. His vision was usually strongly etched by irony and paradox as he sought to demonstrate how human actions could have multiple consequences and meanings. His thought was always subtle, complex, and nuanced, though his style was limpid and precise. This combination allowed him to reach a wide audience; he was always a popular historian as well as a highly regarded professional. He was also an active participant in the vibrant intellectual life of New York in the 1950s and 1960s. To the end of achieving greater complexity and insight, Hofstadter also often employed the concepts gained from other social science disciplines, especially sociology and psychology. In the mid-1950s he was actively involved in fertile cross-disciplinary exchanges at Columbia, where he helped to inject history into the social science dialogues of the period as well as into the larger intellectual discourse of the time. He soon became well known for his psychologically oriented inquiries into the politics of the Radical Right of the 1950s and 1960s, which Hofstadter identified as de-

fined by a paranoid style of thought rather than true conservatism. Many of the essays he wrote on contemporary politics and his similarly inclined historical essays are collected in *The Paranoid Style in American Politics* (1965).

At his best, Hofstadter balanced his shrewd, complex insight and often acidic criticism with an empathetic, even tragic understanding of the limitations imposed by circumstance and character, as in his portraits of Abraham Lincoln and Woodrow Wilson in *The American Political Tradition*. This perspective was especially prominent in his penultimate book, *The Progressive Historians* (1968), where Hofstadter directly confronted an earlier generation of historians, the dominant thinkers of the Progressive tradition, especially CHARLES BEARD, whose popular interpretation of American history Hofstadter had so actively sought to undermine. Toward the end of his life, Hofstadter's sense of the precariousness of the human condition, once captured in irony, was transmuted into a profound sense of sadness. This transformation can be seen by contrasting *Anti-Intellectualism in American Life* (1964), for which Hofstadter was awarded a second Pulitzer Prize, and in which he identified the elements of an insidious tradition of anti-intellectualism created by an excessive reverence for popular beliefs, and *America at 1750*, in which the lives of ordinary people, usually hard and filled with contradiction, form the ground and substance of the democratic impulse. Hofstadter had struggled all his life with the challenge of revitalizing DEMOCRACY through the critical and unsentimental reading of the past. In his last two books, Hofstadter moved beyond criticism to recapture that past.

PAULA S. FASS

See also NEW YORK INTELLECTUALS.

FURTHER READING

Stanley M. Elkins and Eric L. McKitrick, "Richard Hofstadter: a Progress," in Elkins and McKitrick, eds., *The Hofstadter Aegis: a Memorial* (New York: Knopf, 1974).

Paula S. Fass, "Richard Hofstadter," in Clyde D. Wilson, ed., *Twentieth-Century American Historians*, vol. 17 of *Dictionary of Literary Biography* (Detroit: Bruccoli Clark, 1983).

Daniel Walker Howe and Peter Elliott Finn, "Richard Hofstadter: the Ironies of an American Historian," *Pacific Historical Review* 43 (1974): 1–23.

Daniel Joseph Singal, "Beyond Consensus: Richard Hofstadter and American Historiography," *American Historical Review* 89 (1984): 977–1004.

Holmes, Oliver Wendell, Sr. (b. Cambridge, Mass., Aug. 29, 1809; d. Boston, Mass., Oct. 7, 1894).   Physician and writer. Usually remembered as a literary figure, Holmes was also a leading medical professionalizer from his position at Harvard Medical School (1847–82). He sought to exclude alternative practitioners, institute scientific methods, and convince (unsuccessfully) his colleagues that "puerperal fever" could be prevented by sanitation. Best known today for his novel *Elsie Venner* (1861), he was venerated in his own day for his humorous "breakfast table" essays (first collected in *The Autocrat of the Breakfast Table*, 1858) and poems (best known are "Old Ironsides," 1830, "The Chambered Nautilus," 1858, and "The Deacon's Masterpiece, or 'The Wonderful One-Hoss Shay,'" 1858), all of which reflect his freethinking Unitarianism and his genial wit.

FURTHER READING

Edwin Palmer Hoyt, *The Improper Bostonian: Dr. Oliver Wendell Holmes* (New York: Morrow, 1979).

Holmes, Oliver Wendell, Jr. (b. Boston, Mass., Mar. 8, 1841; d. Washington, D.C., Mar. 6, 1935). Soldier, legal theorist, and historian, as well as modern America's most prominent jurist, Holmes served as Justice of the Massachusetts Supreme Judicial Court (1882–1902) and on the U.S. Supreme Court (1902–32). A patrician Bostonian, grandson of a judge and son of Dr. OLIVER WENDELL HOLMES (the medical researcher and man of letters), the younger Holmes attended Harvard College, became an abolitionist, and fought in the CIVIL WAR, where he almost died of his wounds. The war experience may have laid the foundations of Holmes's bleakly skeptical outlook, according to which rights and morals were only the systems imposed by whatever groups emerged as dominant in the struggle for existence.

After graduation from Harvard Law School, Holmes practiced law in Boston, but determined to make his reputation as a legal thinker. He helped found the Metaphysical Club, a discussion group including WILLIAM JAMES and C. S. PEIRCE that gave birth to the philosophy of PRAGMATISM. As editor and revisor of James Kent's *Commentaries on American Law* (12th edn., 1873) and co-editor of the *American Law Review*, he wrote a series of path-breaking articles on legal theory and history, whose principal themes came together in his cryptic masterpiece *The Common Law* (1881). His earliest writings carried on the mission of John Austin's analytical jurisprudence, to clarify the chaotic miscellany of common law doctrines by gathering them under abstract and general principles. After long immersion in historical study, he overlaid the analytical with a historicist perspective. As he wrote in *The Common Law*,

It is something to show that the consistency of a system requires a particular result, but it is not all. The life of the law has not been logic: it has been experience. The felt necessities of the time, the prevalent moral and political theories, intuitions of public policy, avowed or unconscious, even the prejudices that judges share with their fellow men, have had a good deal more to do than the syllogism in determining the rules by which men should be governed. (p. 5)

In 1881 he became a professor at Harvard Law School, but resigned almost immediately to become a judge of the highest court in Massachusetts. There he sat for 20 years.

Still mostly unknown when THEODORE ROOSEVELT appointed him to the U.S. Supreme Court in 1902, Holmes became nationally famous by his retirement in 1932, especially for his dissents. Most often he dissented (with Justice LOUIS BRANDEIS) when the Court read laissez-faire economic theory into the Constitution to strike down social legislation: "The Fourteenth Amendment does not enact Mr. Herbert Spencer's *Social Statics*" (*Lochner v. New York*, 1905, 198 U.S. 45, 75). Other celebrated dissents came in free speech cases, where he argued that the First Amendment protected freedom even "for opinions that we loathe", and that "the best test of truth is the power of the thought to get itself accepted in the competition of the marketplace" (*Abrams v. U.S.*, 1919, 250 U.S. 616, 630). Holmes's skepticism towards the formalist jurisprudence of his Court's conservative majority made him a hero to young Progressive intellectuals such as FELIX FRANKFURTER, WALTER LIPPMANN, JEROME FRANK, and Harold Laski; and to the antiformalist movement known as LEGAL REALISM. After his death his reputation suffered as revisionists revealed his illiberal side: his disdain for democracy and contempt for social reform and humanitarian sentiment; his Malthusian economics, SOCIAL DARWINISM, and enthusiastic acceptance of force as the root of morals. Yet the originality of his legal theory, his philosophic breadth, cosmopolitan learning and aphoristic brilliance have ensured his undisputed place as the greatest of American jurists.

The many tensions in Holmes's thought make him difficult to pin down intellectually. He has been called a pragmatist, scientific positivist, utilitarian, historicist, Nietzschean, and Emersonian transcendentalist. In truth he was all of those. In his analytic mode, he synthesized general legal principles from timeless sociobiological traits (revenge or territorial instincts) or long-established precedents. Yet unlike his formalist contemporaries he doubted that such principles could ever determine results ("General propositions do not decide concrete cases"), and viewed legal norms as transitory and repeatedly contested by rival social groups. His work sought to de-moralize legal analysis, to see legal rules provisionally as a "bad man" would, not as moral precepts but as objective consequences, "prophecies of what the courts will do in fact," as he put it in "The Path of the Law" in 1897 (p. 173). (*See also* LAW.) This pragmatic heuristic led him to the insight that most rules of civil liability were merely "prices on conduct": a railroad could continue to injure, so long as it compensated accident victims; a contract was only an option to perform or pay damages for breach. Yet he also believed law was the "witness and external deposit of our moral life," and that, although law had evolved toward "objective" standards, away from concern with personal moral fault, it reflected an increasing communal morality. He often analyzed law in utilitarian terms, as a set of incentives to maximize social welfare. In this mode he called history useful only for ridding the law of useless "survivals"—"It is revolting to have no better reason for a law than that it was laid down in the time of Henry IV" (p. 187)—so as to enable lawmakers, including judges, to devise more efficient rules. Yet he thought the scope for rational improvement always small, since lawmaking like all social action was a situated, tradition-bound activity. As a judge Holmes was slow to innovate. In 'Law and Science" (1899), he wrote, "I believe that the claim of our especial code to respect is simply that it exists" (p. 239).

Holmes's Constitutional thought is likewise paradoxical. Here his central tenet was judicial restraint: on the Supreme Court he voted to sustain Progressive social legislation against claims that it was unconstitutional, though privately he thought minimum-wage laws and progressive taxation self-defeating folly. He voted to sustain repressive laws as well. Yet his free-speech dissents pioneered a robust theory of Constitutional limits on government power to punish dissident speech merely for its "bad tendency." He argued that since "every idea is an incitement" (*Gitlow v. New York*, 1925, 268 U.S. 652, 673), subversive advocacy should be protected unless it posed an imminent "clear and present danger" of harm.

Holmes was an atheist who believed that the notion of a special destiny for the human race was an anthropocentric conceit. But he was also a romantic who wrote in "The Soldier's Faith" that "it is true and adorable" for a "soldier to throw away his life in obedience to a blindly accepted duty" (in *The Essential Holmes*, p. 89). Holmes brought that same existential

passion to his legal craft and that same mystical commitment to the discharge of his civic obligations.

ROBERT W. GORDON

FURTHER READING
Robert W. Gordon, ed., *The Legacy of Oliver Wendell Holmes, Jr.* (Stanford: Stanford University Press, 1992).
Oliver Wendell Holmes Jr., *The Common Law* ed. Mark DeWolfe Howe (1881; Boston: Little Brown, 1963).
——, "The Path of the Law" (1897) and "Law in Science" (1899), in Holmes, *Collected Legal Papers* (Boston: Little, Brown, 1920).
——, *The Essential Holmes: Selections from the Letters, Speeches, Judicial Opinions and Other Writings of Oliver Wendell Holmes, Jr.*, ed, Richard A. Posner (Chicago: University of Chicago Press, 1992).
Mark DeWolfe Howe, *Justice Oliver Wendell Holmes: the Shaping Years, 1841–1870* and *The Proving Years, 1870–1882* (Cambridge: Harvard University Press, 1957, 1963).
G. Edward White, *Justice Oliver Wendell Holmes: Law and the Inner Self* (New York: Oxford University Press, 1994).
Thomas C. Grey, "Holmes and Legal Pragmatism," *Stanford Law Review* 41 (1989): 787–870.
Edmund Wilson, "Justice Holmes," in Wilson, *Patriotic Gore: Studies in the Literature of the American Civil War* (New York: Oxford University Press, 1962).

Holocaust   In 1964, when a group of Jewish American survivors of the Warsaw Ghetto Uprising submitted a design for a Holocaust memorial to New York City's Arts Commission, they were turned down for three reasons. The proposed monument was too big and aesthetically unappealing, the commission decided, but there were two deeper problems. Such a monument might inspire other "special groups" to seek similar representation on public land, and the city had to ensure that "monuments in the parks . . . be limited to events of American history." The Holocaust was not an American experience.

For the Jewish survivors of the Holocaust who had immigrated to America after World War II, and who regarded themselves as Americans, the commission's response was painfully nonsensical. It asserted a distinction between "events of American history" and those of "Americans' history." Did American history begin and end within the nation's geographical borders? Or did it, as most of the survivors believed, begin in the experiences abroad that drove these immigrants to America's shores? With the recent dedication of the U.S. Holocaust Memorial Museum in Washington, D.C., it could be said that America has recognized the survivors' experiences as part of a national experience—and has in this way made the Holocaust part of American history. At the same time, the Holocaust museum asserts forcefully that the Holocaust belongs in American history not only because it lives in the memory of one religious group, but because it was a central event for all Americans. In the American government's failure to respond actively to the destruction of the Jews, in the failure of American intellectuals, with few exceptions, to speak out in defense of the Jews, America is revealed to itself.

News of the Nazis' mass murder of Jews, and of the brutal internment of political prisoners, Poles, Soviet prisoners of war, homosexuals and others, was appearing in American newspapers as early as 1943, when the death camps were operating at full capacity. But the reports were often buried in the back pages of newspapers full of military battles and political struggles, and according to historians like David Wyman and Deborah Lipstadt, the response to the stories by both Jewish and non-Jewish communities in America was woefully inadequate. For the most part, the Jewish American leadership feared that calling special attention to the plight of their brethren, while American soldiers were fighting and dying, would alienate the broader public. Meanwhile, the great majority of non-Jews, including the government and military hierarchies, regarded mass murder and concentration camps as further justification for the total war they were already fighting desperately to win, but not as emergencies requiring the diversion of resources or the shifting of priorities.

The Jewish American community began to grasp the full horror of the destruction of European Jewry immediately after the war, but for most Americans the Holocaust remained submerged in the larger memory of World War II. Where it had already been named as a singular event in the Jewish community (as Shoah or Churban), it remained unnamed—and thus unmarked—in America at large until the late 1950s, when scholars began using the term Holocaust to distinguish this mass murder from the rest of the killing during the war.

If there was a single watershed of Holocaust consciousness in America as a whole, it came during the televised 1960 war-crimes trial of Adolph Eichmann in Jerusalem. Though a small number of Holocaust memoirs and diaries had appeared in the intervening 15 years, much of the survivor community in both Israel and America seemed to prefer rebuilding their lives in their new homelands to recalling the tragedy of the war years. In fact, even with half of Israel's 1948 population comprised of survivors, an unspoken understanding between the state and its new citizens discouraged survivors from looking back to what was regarded as the shame of diaspora Jewry. But with the riveting spectacle of the Eichmann trial, all this changed. A parade of hundreds of survivors were now invited to testify to the crimes committed against them by the Nazis, pouring out stories of experiences that shocked the world, stories which received the judicial imprimatur of testimony. The floodgates of memory had lifted.

American Jews and non-Jews began to look anew at their survivor neighbors, who still numbered tens of thousands. Experiences that the survivors once feared would set them apart from their compatriots were now sanctioned, their telling encouraged. Since 1960, when Eichmann was tried, hundreds of survivor memoirs have appeared, including Elie Wiesel's *Night* (1960) and Primo Levi's *Survival in Auschwitz* (1969). American poets such as Sylvia Plath and John Berryman invoked the pain of the Holocaust as a metaphor for their own inner anguish; other poets such as William Heyen and Irving Reznikoff attempted to represent the Holocaust itself in their verse. Novelists like Leon Uris (*Mila 18*, 1962) and William Styron (*Sophie's Choice*, 1979) wrote best-selling stories of the Warsaw Ghetto Uprising and Auschwitz.

Jewish and Christian religious thinkers and philosophers, including Richard Rubinstein and Robert McAfee Brown, began radical reappraisals of their traditions. Jewish émigré philosopher HANNAH ARENDT analyzed Eichmann himself: he represented a new sort of evil, "banal" and bureaucratized. Remarkably, he did not hate Jews. He simply perfected a system for slaughtering them, a system that depended, in Arendt's controversial view, on eliciting the cooperation of the victims. Her formulation provoked the widespread criticism that she was blaming the victims for their own extermination.

By the middle 1970s, knowledge and images of the Holocaust had permeated nearly all sectors of American life and letters, art and politics. This broad diffusion culminated in the 1978 television docudrama "Holocaust," which resembled in its monumental sweep the film version of Alex Haley's celebrated work on the African American experience, *Roots*. The Holocaust had become a fully assimilated icon in American popular culture—even if, as with *Roots*, some viewers had to remain skeptical as to whether the full story had been comprehended or ever could be comprehended. Steven Spielberg's much-praised film *Schindler's List* (1993) convinced some skeptics that much of the story could indeed be told in a manner that combined art, realism, and reverence.

The Holocaust has become such a readymade locus of Jewish identity that it has generated a new debate in the Jewish American community. All agree upon the power of a painful past to bind a group together, but some fear the tendency to isolate group members in the separateness of their own memories.

By the 1960s, as African Americans recalled their enslavement and Native Americans their genocide, Jewish Americans came increasingly to rely on the Holocaust as the crux of their common heritage. Yet while the memory of mass suffering was a potent bond for members of each community, it set the stage for invidious competition between the various histories of victimization, each group implicitly asserting the primacy of its own tragic past.

The challenge facing all Americans is to allow each people's history to be known in its fullness and singularity. No historic experience needs to be put on a balance scale that measures amounts of evil and suffering. Comparison need not be a rating game. Each experience, however, can be better understood in its particularity as we grasp it in relation to the others. In the end, each memory of travail and courage will be unique, while disclosing dramas of similarly inexplicable horror. The Holocaust—the application of industrial efficiency to the systematic destruction of a people and a culture—will always hold a special place in human history and Jewish history. The enormity of it, like the enormity of the decimation of Native American civilizations and the forced enslavement of Africans, is beyond our powers of human reckoning.

JAMES E. YOUNG

See also JUDAISM.

FURTHER READING

Hannah Arendt, *Eichmann in Jerusalem: a Report on the Banality of Evil* (New York: Viking, 1964).

Robert McAfee Brown, *Elie Wiesel: Messenger to All Humanity* (Notre Dame: Notre Dame University Press, 1983).

Deborah Lipstadt, *Beyond Belief: the American Press and the Coming of the Holocaust* (New York: Free Press, 1986).

Richard Rubinstein, *After Auschwitz: Radical Theology and Contemporary Judaism* (Indianapolis: Bobbs-Merrill, 1966).

Art Spiegelman, *Maus: a Survivor's Tale*, 2 vols. (New York: Pantheon, 1986, 1991).

David Wyman, *The Abandonment of the Jews: America and the Holocaust, 1941–1945* (New York: Pantheon, 1984).

honor The concept of honor has played a major and often overlooked part in American life, but its nature has shifted dramatically because of national changes in social and ethnic composition, laws, sentiments, and manners from colonial times to the current era. Indeed, honor stands today very low on the ladder of virtues, probably somewhere near chastity. Even the definition has altered drastically. When honor was a salient attribute which men and women cherished, it was defined, even as recently as 1932, in the *Encyclopedia of the Social Sciences*, as "a strong personal sense of socially accepted dignity or socially expected conduct" (vol. 7, p. 456). (*See also*

ETIQUETTE.) Historians have lately adopted a more anthropological and psychological approach to defining the term. They claim that the code involved much deeper social, racial, and political issues than simply a profession of refinement and gentility. The ethic of honor may serve as a mediator between individual and group aspirations and the judgment of the watching world. Anthropologist Julian Pitt-Rivers, writing in the *International Encyclopedia of the Social Sciences* (1968), observes that "honor felt becomes honor claimed, and honor claimed becomes honor paid" (vol. 6, p. 503). In other words, an American's sense of identity was at one time less determined by a self-sustained sense of individual worth than by a perception of one's public reputation. As institutional life grew more complex and a middle class developed, this older notion of a kin-based and rigidly hierarchical ethic declined.

A notion of honor founded upon such a personal and community reputation has been evident in American politics. A community or even nation might regard an act of political aggression as an attempt to insult, conquer, and humiliate. During Bacon's Rebellion of 1676 in Virginia, for instance, Governor William Berkeley, whose policies had aroused the unrest, insisted that to back down would not "satisfie his honour," and Nathaniel Bacon, his adversary, rallied his unruly forces with the cry, "Come on, my hearts of gold, he that dies in the field lies in the bed of honor" (*Southern Honor*, pp. 80, 82). A century later, the Boston Whig leader John Hancock declared, in *An Oration*, "I conjure you by all that is honourable that you break in sunder with noble disdain the bonds with which the Philistines have bound you" (p. 18). As Hancock implied, slavery represented the very opposite of honor as well as of liberty. References to the disgrace of slavery were designed to appeal to the ideal of MASCULINITY, for to submit to an enemy was to incur the risks of shame and be perceived as womanish and weak.

The gendered character of honor was essential to its simple clarity: honor in men was an active force, but in women it consisted in passive or constrained behavior—the virtues of chastity, modesty, submission to all authorities, particularly men under whose protection they found themselves. Moreover, honor was equally hierarchical with regard to race (white over black); status (free over slave and dependent); class (rich over poor); age (old over young); and ancestry (old wealth over new). These were all part of an ethic widely shared in all sectors of the country (especially among older and richer white men and women), and it was best suited to small, face-to-face communities, such as those from which most

Americans had originally come, in both Europe and Africa. Although slaves were denied many attributes of honor—self-dependence, freedom of movement, the rights of ownership—within their own quarters bondsmen participated in its claims, particularly with regard to possession of their women, jealously guarded from other slaves and sometimes from encroaching masters.

Throughout the early years of the American Republic, economic and demographic forces—the fast development of northern commerce, industry, and urban life along with heavy immigration—eroded the principles of a rural-based ethical system. Northern and southern sections rather diverged in their understanding of what honor meant. In the South the old hierarchies continued, although religious prescriptions altered male habits regarding duels and other forms of the code. The preservation of slavery, however, almost required that the antique ideals of martial honor should survive by endowing all whites with authority over all blacks. (*See* PROSLAVERY THOUGHT.) In the North, honorable behavior took on urban characteristics: reliability in one's personal transactions, a more internalized notion of personal dignity than southern truculence might permit.

The coming of the CIVIL WAR cannot be easily explained without reference to the differing interpretations of the basic polarities between honor and SHAME. Whereas southerners still thought in terms of older units—families, communities, and states—northerners were beginning to conceptualize their culture in relation to ties greater than family and local loyalties. Individuals, particularly in the upper and middle classes, were perceived to be governed less by their blood affiliations and more by their level of education and professional status. In moral terms, conscience replaced honor, guilt replaced shame, that is, inner self-controls rather than public opinion were supposed to govern how one acted. Unlike shame, GUILT did not involve public exposure and therefore was less ruinous to self-regard. Northerners were thus likely to perceive liberty as the right to pursue one's conscience wherever it directed, but in the South liberty has group meaning—the protection of the demos against outsiders or any who might infringe upon long-settled habits, customs, and laws. When white southerners found themselves accused of sin for holding slaves, their reaction was indignation for which the only answer could be violent refutation. In no other fashion could honor be vindicated. "If we fail," declared James Jones, a secessionist hothead from South Carolina, described in my *Yankee Saints and Southern Sinners*, "we have saved our honour *and lost nothing*" (p. 241.)

After the Civil War, the southern cult of the Lost Cause, as it was often called, perpetuated the values of the old regime, but increasingly the South fell under the influence of northern concepts of commerce, industry, and institutional allegiances—professional standards and other forms of nonfamilial exigencies. (*See also* SOUTHERN INTELLECTUAL HISTORY.)

Honor continues to shape American life. From the domain of the Mafia to the modern ghetto, repute for manliness brings special respect. Without it, mere survival becomes problematic. In politics and international affairs, honor or "saving face" is still a powerful motivation. Likewise, the rationale for President Lyndon Johnson's persistence in Vietnam—the dread of military defeat and humiliation—was based on the old code. Jimmy Carter's failure to achieve a second term as President in 1980 might be partly attributed to humiliation over the hostage crisis with Iran. Both Ronald Reagan and George Bush frequently invoked national honor to justify American military action. As a candidate for the Presidency in 1992, Bill Clinton had to struggle against doubts about his personal honor, both because of nationally publicized allegations of earlier sexual misconduct, and because his disapproval of the war in Vietnam and failure to serve in the armed forces were construed by some Americans as a sign of cowardice. The debate in the 1990s over gays in military service reveals that many people still identify military courage with heterosexuality, and cowardice with effeminacy. Although the concept of honor may be less prominent now than it was in the past, the echoes of the old code continue to resonate in American cultural and political life.

BERTRAM WYATT-BROWN

FURTHER READING

Edward L. Ayers, *Vengeance and Justice: Crime and Punishment in the Nineteenth-Century South* (New York: Oxford University Press, 1984).

Kenneth S. Greenberg, *Masters and Statesmen: the Political Culture of American Slavery* (Baltimore: Johns Hopkins University Press, 1985).

John Hancock, *An Oration Delivered March 5, 1774, at the Request of the Inhabitants of the Town of Boston: To Commemorate the Bloody Tragedy of the Fifth of March 1770* (Boston: Edes and Gill, 1774).

Julian Pitt-Rivers, "Honor," in David L. Sills, ed., *International Encyclopedia of the Social Sciences* (New York: Macmillan, 1968).

Julian Pitt-Rivers and J. G. Peristiany, eds., *Honor and Grace* (Cambridge: Cambridge University Press, 1992).

T. V. Smith, "Honor," in Edwin R. A. Seligman, ed., *Encyclopedia of the Social Sciences* (New York: Macmillan, 1932).

Bertram Wyatt-Brown, *Southern Honor: Ethics and Behavior in the Old South* (New York: Oxford University Press, 1982).

———, *Yankee Saints and Southern Sinners* (Baton Rouge: Louisiana State University Press, 1985).

Hook, Sidney (b. New York, N.Y., Dec. 20, 1902; d. Stanford, Calif., July 12, 1989). If the life of the mind were a street fight, Sidney Hook would be without peer among modern American intellectuals. Hook came by his pugnacity in the Brooklyn slum where he grew up, following his birth to Eastern European Jewish immigrant parents in New York City's Lower East Side. Many of his early battles were occasioned by his youthful politics, for he was persecuted by teachers and classmates for the antiwar and socialist convictions that he had adopted by the age of 13.

Like many poor, bright Jewish boys at the time, Hook enrolled at City College, where he was exhilarated by the philosophy courses he took from the legendary MORRIS COHEN. Following his graduation in 1923, Hook taught in the New York public schools and enrolled as a part-time graduate student in philosophy at Columbia University, where his Cohen-inspired efforts to refute PRAGMATISM resulted instead in his conversion to the version of that philosophy articulated by JOHN DEWEY. Under Dewey's direction, he received his Ph.D. in 1927 with a dissertation on *The Metaphysics of Pragmatism* (1927), which was quickly published. He landed a job at New York University, and in 1928 won a Guggenheim fellowship that permitted him a year of study in Germany researching post-Hegelian philosophy, which he followed with a summer in Moscow exploring the archives of the Marx–Engels Institute. Hook's political interests, submerged for much of the twenties, were reignited and henceforth political and ideological combat always complemented his formidable philosophical learning.

Hook returned to the United States and New York University in 1929 and became chair of his department in 1934 (a post he would hold for 35 years). He quickly established himself as the nation's most imposing radical philosopher in a bitter and interminable debate with MAX EASTMAN about the meaning of Marxism. In 1933 he published his most important book, *Towards the Understanding of Karl Marx*, which, as he said in his autobiography, was an attempt "to develop a kind of Americanized Marxism, strengthened by John Dewey's activist theory of mind and knowledge" (p. 177). In the fashion of several other "Western Marxists," Hook offered a fresh reading of Marx that owed a substantial debt to a "bourgeois" philosophy—in his case, Deweyan pragmatism. Drawing on Dewey's conception of science as an experimental, fallible enterprise and identifying it

with Marx's dialectic, Hook's pragmatic Marxism posed a challenge to the dialectical materialism of both orthodox social democrats and orthodox communists. On the one hand, he rejected as unscientific the determinism and reformism of the social democrats, in favor of a politics of revolutionary praxis. On the other hand, the link he forged between dialectical science and radical democracy in the philosophy of Dewey and Marx raised serious questions about the authoritarianism of the Soviet Union and the American Communist Party.

Until 1933 Hook remained a close if contentious ally of the Communists, but by 1934 his heresies had become too much for the party, which denounced him as a "counterrevolutionary reptile." He then became active in the organization of the American Workers Party (AWP), led by A. J. Muste, which put Hook's conception of "workers' democracy" at the heart of its platform. That idea, which represented the full flowering of Hook's libertarian Marxism, was an effort to reinterpret the "dictatorship of the proletariat" as the rule of workers' democratic councils and distinguish it from the rule of a Communist Party dictatorship (which Hook characterized as "dictatorship *over* the proletariat"). Now a fiery anti-Stalinist, Hook nonetheless remained a revolutionary socialist and Leninist through the mid-1930s. He produced a second masterful work of scholarship on Marx's engagement with the Young Hegelians, *From Hegel to Marx* (1936), and he worked closely with American Trotskyists, helping to arrange their merger with the AWP and then (when that coalition collapsed) with the Socialist Party.

The terrors of the Moscow trials initiated a steady transformation of Hook's thinking and set him on the road from anti-Stalinist radicalism to anticommunist liberalism. First to go were his revolutionary convictions, as he began in the late 1930s to tar Lenin and Trotsky as well as Stalin with the brush of totalitarianism. He then abandoned Marxism in the late 1940s on the grounds that if his Marx was the real Marx then he was the only Marxist left in the world. He insisted that he was still a socialist, but his socialism evolved into little more than welfare-state liberalism. In the 1960s, he condemned the New Left and student radicalism as dire threats to academic freedom, and left NYU in 1973 for a senior fellowship at the Hoover Institution at Stanford University. For the next 15 years, he issued pronouncements from that right-wing think tank on affirmative action, academic politics, and other topical issues, articulating views which differed little from those of the neoconservatives with whom he refused to his dying day to be identified.

From the late 1930s onward, Hook argued that the key conflict dividing the world was not between capitalism and socialism but between political freedom and totalitarianism. A ferocious anticommunism moved to the center of his life, coloring nearly everything he wrote. A leading light in such organizations as the American Committee for Cultural Freedom and the international Congress for Cultural Freedom, he launched sharp forays in the 1950s against the beleaguered remnants of American communism and the anti-anticommunists who defended the communists' civil liberties; at the same time he attacked Senator Joseph McCarthy for crude tactics damaging to the anticommunist cause. Of particular note was the argument he advanced in *Heresy, Yes—Conspiracy, No* (1953) that membership in the Communist Party constituted a prima facie case for the dismissal of teachers and professors. Hook was, in short, the quintessential COLD WAR liberal, and it is perhaps fitting that his passing roughly coincided with that of the Soviet Union.

Hook's anticommunist polemics were not without their merits, yet his postwar writing lacked the mix of partisan zeal with subtle philosophy and deep scholarship which made his youthful Marxism so impressive. As Irving Howe said of the latter-day Hook in 1982, "Within that first rate mind there had formed a deposit of sterility, like rust on a beautiful machine" (p. 211). At its best, the life of the mind is more than a street fight.

ROBERT B. WESTBROOK

FURTHER READING
Alexander Bloom, *Prodigal Sons: the New York Intellectuals and Their World* (New York: Oxford University Press, 1986).
Sidney Hook, *Out of Step: an Unquiet Life in the Twentieth Century* (New York: Harper and Row, 1987).
Irving Howe, *A Margin of Hope: an Intellectual Autobiography* (New York: Harcourt, Brace, Jovanovich, 1982).
Neil Jumonville, *Critical Crossings: the New York Intellectuals in Postwar America* (Berkeley: University of California Press, 1991).
Paul Kurtz, ed., *Sidney Hook: Philosopher of Democracy and Humanism* (Buffalo: Prometheus, 1983).
Alan M. Wald, *The New York Intellectuals: the Rise and Decline of the Anti-Stalinist Left from the 1930s to the 1980s* (Chapel Hill: University of North Carolina Press, 1987).

Hoover, Herbert (b. West Branch, Iowa, Aug. 10, 1874; d. New York, N.Y., Oct. 20, 1964). President of the United States, 1929–33. Hailed as a peerless progressive for his resourceful administration of relief during and after World War I, Hoover became an energetic Secretary of Commerce and envisioned an efficient economic system buoyed by government-sponsored coordination of private enterprise. Author of *American Individualism* (1922), Hoover opposed not government intervention in the economy, but direct federal relief, which he feared would undermine individual responsibility. Among his other works are his three-volume *Memoirs* (1951–2) and *The Ordeal of Woodrow Wilson* (1958).

FURTHER READING
David Burner, *Herbert Hoover: a Public Life* (New York: Knopf, 1979).

Hopkins, Pauline (b. Portland, Maine, 1859; d. Cambridge, Mass., Aug. 13, 1930). Educated at the Girls High School in Boston, Hopkins was raised by her mother and stepfather in an atmosphere that nurtured her considerable artistic talents. Indeed, in her youth she performed with the Hopkins Colored Troubadours, a theatrical group made up of her family members, and she produced a musical drama entitled *Slaves' Escape; or the Underground Railroad*, which the Troubadours presented in the Boston area in the mid-1880s.

As was the case with numerous early black authors, Hopkins's literary productivity was not restricted to any one genre. Over a period of roughly 15 years, she wrote biographical and historical sketches, journalistic articles, and several novels and short stories. The common thread uniting all her work was her belief in the political and cultural use of literature: she sought to improve the image of the African American not only in the eyes of whites, but in the self-perception of blacks as well. The continued progress of African Americans depended, Hopkins felt, on seeing their diverse achievements and rich potential fairly presented. Her ongoing commitment to a black readership led to her active support of the African American periodical press.

Hopkins began writing for the *Colored American* in 1900, the year it was founded in Boston. She had been supporting herself as a stenographer, but after becoming involved with the *Colored American* she labored full-time to keep it afloat. In 1903 Hopkins became the *Colored American*'s literary editor, and she remained a key member of its staff until late 1904, after the magazine had been taken over and moved to New York by BOOKER T. WASHINGTON, who successfully sought to mute its criticism of his political program. Despite this setback, Hopkins continued to write, producing among other pieces a pamphlet on African American history. Then in 1916 Hopkins began editing a magazine called *New Era*, in which she published more of her fiction and essays. However, she was eventually forced for want of income to give up her literary efforts and to return to stenography.

In the course of her affiliation with *Colored American* Pauline Hopkins wrote four novels—three of them serialized in the magazine—and numerous short stories and articles. Although her biographical and historical pieces merit far more attention than they have received, it is Hopkins's fiction—and most notably her ambitious first novel, *Contending Forces*—that has established her as a crucial figure on the black literary landscape.

Released in 1900 by the Colored Co-operative Publishing Company (which also produced the *Colored American*), *Contending Forces: a Romance Illustrative of Negro Life North and South* offers a compelling look at black middle-class life in the late nineteenth century. Indeed, as the title and subtitle of the book suggest, Hopkins sought to use the literary conventions of the popular romance to dramatize not just the domestic world of her black characters but also the major ideological conflicts in the African American community at the time. Here, and throughout her fiction, she depicts a personal or domestic sphere that is laden with public and political issues. Black women at a sewing circle discuss the peculiar trials confronting them in a racist society. And two characters represent implicitly the opposing ideologies of Booker T. Washington and w. e. b. Du bois. Although Hopkins favors the more assertive stance of the Du Boisian figure, she is nonetheless careful to portray both leaders in a sympathetic fashion.

In her fiction Hopkins also emphasizes the power of past events to shape—and disrupt—the present. Slavery's brutal assault on the family leaves a traumatic heritage for her characters. Yet Hopkins makes plain that one's past can ultimately be overcome—a crucial claim for a black middle class only a generation or two after Emancipation. Hopkins maintains an abiding faith in the resilience and nurturing force of the black family, and in the potential of romantic love to transcend even the most shameful of victimizations.

Stylistically, *Contending Forces* embodies a variety of conventions and narrative strategies. Hopkins shifts from sentimental romance to slapstick burlesque to sober political debate, and this switching of forms creates structural and tonal dissonance. But the diversity of literary form in *Contending Forces* (as in much of the work of Hopkins's contemporary CHARLES W. CHESNUTT) reminds us that the African American fictive tradition was undergoing major transition at the turn of the century. Hopkins's work constitutes both a culmination of the nineteenth-century form of the sentimental romance—which

dominated African American fiction as it did the rest of popular American fiction—and a first sign of the shift toward REALISM on the part of twentieth-century black authors, particularly those of the New Negro Renaissance of the 1920s and 1930s.

Until recently, scholars neglected Pauline Hopkins just as they neglected most black literary women who wrote before World War I. However, with the upsurge of interest in early African American women writers such as Harriet Jacobs, FRANCES HARPER, and Anna Julia Cooper, critics are also now turning to Hopkins. Contemporary feminist readings of nineteenth-century women's sentimental fiction as more complex, and often more subversive of mainstream gender ideologies, than previously acknowledged have contributed to a growing recognition of Hopkins's importance. These developments are long overdue, for we have a great deal still to learn about this talented author whose contributions to the traditions of African American fiction and journalism have been so underappreciated.

RICHARD YARBOROUGH

FURTHER READING

Elizabeth Ammons, *Conflicting Stories: American Women Writers at the Turn into the Twentieth Century* (New York: Oxford University Press, 1992).

Jane Campbell, "Pauline Elizabeth Hopkins," in Trudier Harris and Thadious M. Davis, eds., *Afro-American Writers before the Harlem Renaissance*, vol. 50 of *Dictionary of Literary Biography* (Detroit: Bruccoli Clark, 1986).

Hazel V. Carby, *Reconstructing Womanhood: the Emergence of the Afro-American Woman Novelist* (New York: Oxford University Press, 1987).

——, "Introduction," in *The Magazine Novels of Pauline Hopkins* (New York: Oxford University Press, 1988).

"Pauline Elizabeth Hopkins," in James P. Draper, ed., *Black Literature: Criticism*, vol. 2 (Detroit: Gale, 1992).

Ann Allen Shockley, ed., *Afro-American Women Writers: an Anthology and Critical Guide* (Boston: G. K. Hall, 1988).

Claudia Tate, *Domestic Allegories of Political Desire: the Black Heroine's Text at the Turn of the Century* (New York: Oxford University Press, 1992).

Richard Yarborough, "Introduction," in Pauline E. Hopkins, *Contending Forces: a Romance Illustrative of Negro Life North and South* (New York: Oxford University Press, 1988).

Hopkins, Samuel (b. Waterbury, Conn., Sept. 17, 1721; d. Newport, R.I., Dec. 20, 1803). One of the five most influential theologians in American history, Hopkins became, by the American Revolution, the symbol of an older CALVINISM. The most influential disciple of JONATHAN EDWARDS, he developed the first systematic theological system in America, a system that came to symbolize the outlook of about one hundred ministers who tried to follow in the footsteps of Edwards and whose outlook gained the label "New Divinity."

A dutiful child and first son of a prosperous farmer, Hopkins had the privilege of attending Yale. As an undergraduate in 1741 he was caught up in the great revival of religion. Sermons by George Whitefield and Gilbert Tennent plunged him into despair and guilt. Out of his agony came eventual comfort and peace, gained in intense religious experiences which he later identified as regenerative. The awakening led Hopkins into the ministry. After hearing a sermon by Jonathan Edwards, he decided to apprentice to him, and lived much of the time from 1741 to 1743 in the Edwards's household at Northampton.

As an insecure young minister, Hopkins gained a pulpit at Great Barrington in western Massachusetts. His location was significant in American theological history. After Edwards lost his pulpit at Northampton in 1750, Hopkins successfully urged him to take a position at the nearby Stockbridge Indian mission. Although a near-failure as a minister (his sermons were dull and abstract, his moral demands rigorous), Hopkins and a neighboring minister Joseph Bellamy were able to meet regularly with Edwards from 1751 to 1757. Their meetings constituted the first and, in caliber of professor and students, the most distinguished theological seminary in America.

By Edwards's death Hopkins was prepared to lead a battle against increasingly self-denominated liberals among fellow Congregational ministers. He once suggested that one should love God so completely as to be willing to praise him even for one's damnation. He frankly admitted that God willed that sin exist in the world because it contributed to God's glory and to the greatest general good. He deplored the old halfway covenant, denied any true virtue or benevolence in the unsaved, emphasized a complete disjunction between the selfish motives of the unregenerate and the complete benevolence that marked a Christian, and denied any efficacy in any of the means of grace. Such bold and uncompromising positions embarrassed even the orthodox and, joined with his somber personality and his frequent jeremiads, made him, as he ruefully admitted, a symbol of a caricatured and cruel form of Calvinism.

In 1769 an unemployed Hopkins accepted a call to the First Congregation of Newport, Rhode Island. If Hopkins had a golden period, it was the next five years. He now had a sophisticated and appreciative audience. He finally had the time to edit the works of Edwards, which appeared after Edwards died, to write the first biography of Edwards, and to publish his own book on moral philosophy. He also confronted a terrible moral evil. Newport owed its prosperity to the triangular trade, exchanging its distilled rum for African slaves for sale in the West Indies or along the American coast. Hopkins launched a crusade against this evil. He ministered to more blacks than any other minister in New England, denied membership to anyone involved in the slave trade, trained two Negroes for mission trips back to Africa (the Revolution disrupted this plan), and soon advocated immediate and unqualified emancipation. He saw slavery as a horrible blemish on Americans, a mockery of their claim to be a covenanted people. Until his death he confidently predicted God's judgment upon the young nation. It did not deserve freedom when it denied such to the Africans. (*See also* ANTISLAVERY.)

During the Revolution Hopkins had to flee an occupied Newport. After the war ended, during the 1780s and 1790s, he ministered to a very small, aged flock. An uncompromising Hopkins now seemed an antique survival of a past age, almost comical for his seriousness and his denunciatory sermons. He kept the faith, wrote essays and books, and in 1793 completed his theological magnum opus, a two-volume *System of Doctrines Contained in Divine Revelation*. In a farewell sermon (he anticipated an early death), possibly written in 1801, Hopkins gave a deeply pessimistic appraisal of the apostasies that dominated his age, consoled only by his vision of a millennial age that would most likely begin by 2,000. In descending order he looked at the world (few true Christians), America (cursed by slavery), New England (once the glory of Christianity but now cursed by every heresy imaginable), and Newport (damned for its ill-gotten wealth and a resumed slave trade). His feeble and faithful congregation was a saving remnant in an awful age when the seventh vial of Revelation was now poured out. (*See also* MILLENNIALISM.) This was only a prelude to divine wrath and destruction, which a dying Hopkins, crippled by a stroke, seemed to relish, for the millennium lay just ahead. In these last sermons a beloved African American disciple, whom Hopkins had trained for the African mission, helped steady him in the pulpit. When Hopkins died in 1803 many assumed that this was also the death of Calvinism. Few shed a tear at its passing.

What his disciples, as well as his enemies, overlooked were the more novel and the more humanistic elements in Hopkins's mature theological system. Even more than Edwards he emphasized God's benevolence. He gave a very moralistic twist to conceptions of faith (love and consent to God), and justified natural and moral evil as a necessity within the system of moral government that God chose for the world. The amount of evil was only that minimally necessary to uphold divine justice. Hopkins violated traditional Calvinism by denying that God chose his elect arbitrarily (those chosen had certain traits that God needed in his kingdom), by stressing the common identity of sinful humans with Adam rather than adhering to a rigid doctrine of imputation, and by his irenic and quasi-universalist expectation that an overwhelming majority of humans would be saved (almost all people would become loving Christians in the millennial age). These moralistic, humanistic, and universalist themes made Hopkins, and his theological system, anathema to more rigid and confessional Calvinists, including most southern Presbyterians. Ironically, in the years after Hopkins died he became a symbol, not of a rigid and inflexible Calvinism, but of dangerous and heterodox revisionism.

PAUL CONKIN

FURTHER READING

Allen C. Guelzo, *Edwards on the Will: a Century of American Theological Debate* (Middletown: Wesleyan University Press, 1989).

Joseph Haroutunian, *Piety Versus Moralism: the Passing of New England Theology* (New York: Henry Holt, 1932).

Samuel Hopkins, *The System of Doctrines Contained in Divine Revelation* (Boston: Isaiah Thomas, 1793).

——, *The Works of Samuel Hopkins*, 3 vols. (Boston: Doctrinal Tract and Book Society, 1854).

Howe, Irving (b. New York, N.Y., June 11, 1920; d. New York, N.Y., May 5, 1993).   He was chronologically the last of the important literary critics and political writers who have come to be known, thanks to a famous essay by Howe himself, as the NEW YORK INTELLECTUALS. During his early years Howe wrote as the political conscience of this group; in his later years he was its historian, indeed its elegist.

Howe was born in the Bronx to working-class Jewish parents whose lives were deeply unsettled by the Depression of the 1930s. He became a socialist at an early age and was one of a gifted group of undergraduates at the City College of New York who argued the merits of Trotsky versus Stalin and other urgent issues of the late 30s. After uneventful war service and a short stint as a book reviewer at *Time* magazine, Howe became a professor of English at Brandeis in 1953. He spent most of a long academic career at the City University of New York, but unlike most of his professional peers in post-World War II America, he embraced a very wide-ranging vocation as a man of letters and public controversialist.

During the 1950s Howe distinguished himself from other New York critics by his refusal to believe that postwar America had become "God's country and mine," the title of a book by the cultural historian Jacques Barzun that summed up a new mood among liberal intellectuals. Howe insisted on his continuing alienation from American culture in an essay, "This Age of Conformity," which attacked his more accommodating contemporaries in their favorite magazine, *Partisan Review*. In the same year (1954) he founded *Dissent*, a quarterly journal of democratic socialist opinion that he edited until his death. Howe's book *Politics and the Novel* (1957) worried the question of the relationship between art and ideology; and another book he published in that year, *The American Communist Party: a Critical History*, gave Howe the chance to denounce Stalinist ideology, which had seduced so many liberal intellectuals in the 1930s and 1940s.

The 1950s and early 1960s were difficult years for writers like Howe who defined themselves chiefly in relation to political issues. They found themselves suddenly without a vocation in a complacently privatized society which no longer had room for radical ideology. But if Howe was unhappy about the depoliticization of the 1950s, he was much more unhappy about the return of radical politics in the student movement of the late 1960s. Howe was seen as a scold and curmudgeon by the young activists of the New Left. Nor was he treated any better by the more aesthetically oriented exponents of what, in a famous manifesto, Susan Sontag called "the new sensibility."

This phase of Howe's career came to a climax with his long essay "The New York Intellectuals," which appeared in *Commentary* magazine in 1968 and two years later, in expanded form, in Howe's very influential collection of literary essays *Decline of the New* (1970). Howe's central theme was the corruption and betrayal of the tradition of modernism, especially the great writers and artists of the early part of the twentieth century. Howe's purpose was to celebrate those early modernists, writers like Yeats and T. S. Eliot, Kafka and Mann, Proust and Joyce, by contrasting their complexity and tragic ironies with a new and (in Howe's view) vulgar art of outrage that we can now see as an early phase of literary postmodernism. Howe's targets were younger writers, like Sontag, who seemed to Howe to be calling for an art of pure sensory experience "as unarguable as orgasm." Other exemplars of this new movement were writers and philosophers as different as Philip Roth, Norman O. Brown, and Herbert Marcuse, grouped together by Howe as apostles of a new cult of desublimation.

In his major decade, from about 1966 to 1976, Howe's program came fully into view. First, and probably most important to Howe himself, there was the political agitation: anticommunist, antiradical, but stubbornly loyal to the tradition of democratic socialism. Even during the years that Howe was publishing his literary polemics and his excellent anthologies on modernism, he was also editing collections of essays with titles like *The Radical Papers* (1966), *Student Activism* (1967), and *Poverty: Views from the Left* (1968). The best survey of Howe's political development is his memoir *A Margin of Hope: an Intellectual Autobiography* (1982). Since Howe makes no great claims for himself in this memoir, any future biographer ought certainly to pay homage to Howe's phenomenal productivity. No New York intellectual comes close to his achievement of more than 50 substantial books authored and edited.

Howe was devoted to his lifelong dream of socialism, but he was better known as a literary critic and reviewer. In addition to able book-length monographs on Sherwood Anderson (1951), William Faulkner (1952), and Thomas Hardy (1967), he published several collections of essays, the best of which, besides *Decline of the New*, are *The Critical Point* (1973) and *Celebrations and Attacks* (1979). The most interesting of his essays are the polemical ones. In many ways Howe was less interested in literature itself than in cultural "episodes," grand battles about the ideals of self and society that works of art imply or promote. A sampler of essays of this kind would include Howe's pieces on the confessional poet Sylvia Plath, the African American novelist Ralph Ellison, the Philip Roth of *Portnoy's Complaint*, the critic George Steiner, and of course the "New York Intellectuals."

The third element in Howe's agenda may yet turn out to have been the most promising for seeding the intellectual terrain of the future. That is the element summed up in *World of Our Fathers* (1976), Howe's major work of cultural history on the lost world of the Yiddish-speaking immigrant Jews of New York. The revival of Yiddish as language and literature owes a great deal to Howe's project of retrieval. That project began in the early 1950s, when Howe began a collaboration with the Yiddish poet Eliezer Greenberg that led to the publication of five collections of Yiddish poetry and prose in translation. If we add Howe's edition of Sholom Aleichem, his edition of Saul Bellow's novel *Herzog*, and his excellent collection *Jewish-American Stories* (1977), it may yet seem that Jewishness (more precisely "Yiddishkeit," the structure of feeling of the Jews of East Europe, many of whom emigrated to America) was as important an element of continuity in Howe's career as his politics and criticism.

MARK KRUPNICK

FURTHER READING

Alexander Bloom, *Prodigal Sons: the New York Intellectuals and Their World* (New York: Oxford University Press, 1986).

Irving Howe, *A Margin of Hope: an Intellectual Autobiography* (New York: Harcourt, Brace, Jovanovich, 1982).

Alan M. Wald, *The New York Intellectuals: the Rise and Decline of the Anti-Stalinist Left from the 1930s to the 1980s* (Chapel Hill: University of North Carolina Press, 1987).

Leon Wieseltier, "Remembering Irving Howe," *New York Times Magazine*, May 23, 1993.

Howells, William Dean (b. Martin's Ferry, Ohio, Mar. 1, 1837; d. New York, N.Y., May 11, 1920). The son of an itinerant printer, Howells apprenticed in the newspaper trade until the *Atlantic Monthly* accepted one of his poems for publication in 1856. Several other acceptances and a highly successful trip to Boston, where he earned the acclamation of the city's leading literary lights, convinced him that a career in letters was viable. Campaign service to Lincoln in 1860 earned him a consulship to Venice, which afforded him the time to try his hand at sketches and short fiction. Assuming the editorship of the *Atlantic* in 1866, he began his career as literary patron to promising authors, publishing both Mark Twain and Henry James. Other U.S. authors whom Howells either brought to public attention or championed vigorously during his lifetime included Hamlin Garland, Frank Norris, Stephen Crane, Paul Dunbar, Henry Blake Fuller, Charlotte Perkins Gilman, and Thorstein Veblen.

In these writers Howells found proof of the validity of his own theory of literature. Honing his position in a series of polemics written during his 1886–91 tenure in the "editor's study" in *Harper's Monthly* and published as *Criticism and Fiction* (1891), Howells declared his opposition to the prevailing aesthetic belief that literature should be concerned only with the transcendentally beautiful rendered in eloquent or polite language. Such a stance, he contended, obfuscated actualities, separated literature as something "superfinely aloof" from life, and flattered the pretensions of the elite. True literature should instead dedicate itself to "the simple, the natural, and the honest" and take as its standard "fidelity to experience and probability of motive" (p. 15). Accurate, truthful depiction required a narrative form in which all the author's references to the make-believe, invented character of the novel were eliminated in favor of a genuine, unstudied prose that reproduced in language readers' own experience of the world. Adherence to these realist tenets, Howells concluded, would free American literature from obedient compliance to inappropriate European models.

Howells's call for REALISM had its problematic aspects. Its sometimes naive empiricism, its inability to dispense completely with literary conventions of narration or with stock endings, and its difficulty in locating the "simple" and the "natural" in social life all restricted its full implementation. Yet understood as an attempt both to recreate direct literary communication in an age of mass-market commodities and to make fiction relevant, Howellsian realism opened to literary portrayal realms previously uninvestigated.

Howells's own fiction of the 1880s displayed both realism's virtues and limitations. Foremost among his voluminous output from those years were *A Modern Instance* (1882), a disquieting depiction of the deteriorating marriage between the daughter of a New England small-town squire and a young journalist on the make; *The Rise of Silas Lapham* (1885), an examination of the comic and tragic facets of the efforts of a *noveau riche* mineral-paint king and his family to enter respectable Boston society; and *A Hazard of New Fortunes* (1890), a panoramic account of the launching of a new magazine that revealed the class and social tensions in New York City. In mapping how industrial capitalism rearranged the social terrain, these novels along with *The Minister's Charge* (1887) and *Annie Kilburn* (1889) construed the "social problem" not only as a matter of working-class suffering and oppression, but of middle-class complacency. Convinced that moral living demanded both cooperation and personal responsibility for the fate of others, Howells's fiction in this period demonstrated that well-meaning men and women did not always achieve the fellow feeling they sought.

Howells always considered realism to be democratic, and his own political activity reflected his animus against individualism and privilege. Almost alone among leading literary practitioners, he protested vigorously the 1887 execution of the Haymarket martyrs, promoted Henry Demarest Lloyd's *Wealth Against Commonwealth*, an exposé of the machinations of Standard Oil, and supported the Populist Party. In the mid-1890s, when many non-Marxist socialists were recanting their SOCIALISM, Howells grew even more insistent that American capitalism both betrayed the original national promise of equality and encouraged an egoistic conspicuous consumption that devalued the contributions of honest toil.

It is a measure of Howells's centrality to American literature that critics have used him as the repository of the sins that they aspire to overcome. Contemporaries, dismayed by his venture into territory previously reserved for comedy or farce, decried the ordinariness of his characters, charging that they were without distinction or interest. The genteel critic Hamilton Wright Mabie contended that Howells was so enamored of the scientific method that he allowed observation to do the work of imagination. Howells's successors indicted him as a timid Victorian frightened by real experience. Frank Norris dismissed Howellsian realism as "the tragedy of the broken teacup" and Sinclair Lewis compared Howells to an old maid whose complacency had stifled American literary expression. Recent academic criticism has fastened upon Howells's belief in an underlying moral order, his failure to create viable working-class characters, and his "last, best hope" American exceptionalism to conclude that his realism was actually a species of romance. The middle-class desire to preserve order in the face of social upheaval, it is charged, remained the paramount concern of his fiction.

There is some truth in each of these positions, but Howells's legacy is not so easily categorized. Those who emphasize his timidity and reticence in sexual matters rarely consider the highly charged scenes in *A Modern Instance* and *Silas Lapham*, in which Howells delineates sexual obsession with an economy of detail. Nor do they account for Howells's refusal to provide happy endings, especially after his own torment and despair following the death of his daughter Winifred at the age of 15 in 1892. Those who consider him a self-satisfied bourgeois seldom note that his famous "smiling aspects" passage in *Criticism and Fiction*—in which he argued that a truthful portrayal of American life must register its comparative advantages—was qualified by his conviction that the present course of the country was distressing. Few critics allow that Howells's ironic tone criticized and undercut bourgeois complacency.

Howells's vigorous defense of realism in the 1880s has made his novels of that decade the ones by which he has been evaluated. His post-1890 career has often been remembered almost exclusively for the Altrurian romances—utopian literature that explicitly laid out his version of socialism. But in *The Shadow of a Dream* (1890), *The Quality of Mercy* (1892), and *The Landlord of Lion's Inn* (1897), Howells moved in new directions which he never fully articulated and which critics have often not acknowledged. In his experiments with subjective narration, the presentation of a fragmented self, and symbolism, all of which contradicted realist dicta on the nature of a stable and transparent reality, Howells proved more supple and complicated than his immediate champions and detractors realized.

DANIEL H. BORUS

FURTHER READING

Daniel H. Borus, *Writing Realism: Howells, James, and Norris in the Mass Market* (Chapel Hill: University of North Carolin• Press, 1989).

Edwin Cady, *The Realist at War: the Mature Years, 1885–1920, of William Dean Howells* (Syracuse: Syracuse University Press, 1958).

John Crowley, *The Black Heart's Truth: the Early Career of W. D. Howells* (Chapel Hill: University of North Carolina Press, 1985).

——, *The Mask of Fiction: Essays on W. D. Howells* (Amherst: University of Massachusetts Press, 1989).

William Dean Howells, *Criticism and Fiction* (1891; New York: Hill and Wang, 1967).

Henry James, "William Dean Howells," *Harper's Weekly* 30 (June 19, 1886): 394–5.

Amy Kaplan, *The Social Construction of American Realism* (Chicago: University of Chicago Press, 1988).

Randy Olsen, *Dancing in Chains: the Youth of William Dean Howells* (New York: New York University Press, 1991).

Hudson River School A group of American landscape painters active circa 1825–75. Working throughout the Northeast, these artists reflected Romantic ideas about the "power of nature." They created a sublime nationalism that for generations inspired American conceptions of a transcendent wilderness. Major figures in this movement included Thomas Cole, Thomas Doughty, and Asher B. Durand.

FURTHER READING

Angela Miller, *The Empire of the Eye: Landscape Representation and American Cultural Politics, 1825–1875* (Ithaca: Cornell University Press, 1993).

Hughes, [James Mercer] Langston (b. Joplin, Mo., Feb. 1, 1902; d New York N.Y., May 22, 1967). A primary figure of the HARLEM RENAISSANCE, Hughes had shown unusual poetic gifts as a teenager, and after a young adulthood spent wandering through America and Europe, established himself as a writer of plays, fiction, and nonfiction as well as poetry. He belongs, with WALT WHITMAN, Stephen Vincent Benet, Vachel Lindsay, and ALLEN GINSBERG, in that company of poets who articulate—who announce and analyze—a vision of America. Their poems on American identity are alike in their aporetic character, in their use of the form of the jeremiad, and in their reliance on difference: to convey the *res Americana*, they depend on differences in historical time, in geographic space, in the activities and forms of the body, in the features of a broad and varied land.

For these poets, and many others who have written America, African Americans have been "the American heartbreak" and the "dream deferred." And a few of these poets have seen America in the feminine. Langston Hughes, however, writes not only of but as an African American, and he writes not only of, but as a woman. As Alberta K. Johnson, "Madam to you," he quarrels with the landlord and remembers the pleasures—and the faults—of old lovers. As the Negro Mother Hughes finds himself "carrying in my body the seed of the free."

Lindsay and Ginsberg, IMAMU AMIRI BARAKA and Walt Whitman saw their poetry as political texts. All refer to specific political events, all served, in their time, to impel political action. Yet when these poets are read, they are read as artists subject to the political analysis of the critic, not as analysts themselves. The distinction between art and politics, frequently used to determine who writes with political authority, becomes indefensible when one reads "Freedom's Plow." In this poem, Hughes provides a commentary on the nation's canonical texts, enriches W. E. B. Du Bois's concept of double consciousness, and constructs a definition of nationality as immanence.

In "Freedom's Plow," Hughes captures the power of American longing. The poem counterposes dreaming and building, the idea and the work, the utterance of words in a historical context and the meaning immanent within them. Hughes quotes the Declaration of Independence and observes that "there were slaves then," but that the slaves "silently took for granted / That what he said was also meant for them." Hughes measures the distance between the "great thoughts" of the people and the manner in which they "faultily put them into practice," but he counsels,

> If the house is not yet finished,
> Don't be discouraged, builder . . .
> The plan and pattern is here
> Woven from the beginning
> Into the warp and woof of America

The poem ends in an aporia that captures the constitutive power of the longing for America: KEEP YOUR HAND ON THE PLOW! HOLD ON!

All Americans know two nations as their own. The first is the nation we inhabit in the flesh, the nation of our experience, the nation of our memory. History has made itself material in this present, providing the hierarchies we know, the laws we obey or disobey, the rent we owe, the money we borrow, the floors we scrub, the places we can have, the places we are denied. This history has imprinted our bodies, marking us with the past. The second nation is the nation of our imagining, of our aspirations. American letters, rather than merely lauding the achievements of the past, or evoking the grandeur of the present, calls up this absent nation, this state of grace we have yet to achieve. "This is not a perfect party," Jesse Jackson declared at the 1984 Democratic convention. "We are not a perfect people. But we are called to a perfect mission." We are made Americans not in our allegiance to the present, but in our longing—and in our work—for the absent nation. In this understanding, American history is, to appropriate Nietzsche's phrase, "how one becomes what one is."

Like W. E. B. DU BOIS, Hughes recognized that African Americans are blessed and cursed with a double consciousness. In Hughes's poetry that double consciousness is not a black but an American thing. The doubled consciousness of the African American becomes a kind of second-sight, the capacity to see, at once, the present and the absent nation. In Hughes's poetry, African Americans are at once the proof of American inadequacy and those who, in need and pride and anger, will fulfill the American promise.

People have recognized, before and after Hughes, that America was incomplete. Others, before and after him, linked that incompleteness to the places occupied by blacks and women. For most, however, blacks and women serve merely as signs of a fault. For Hughes, they are the prophets and the builders. They are those who are most mindful of the American dream. For Hughes, the subaltern are significant not because they mark the defects of the present nation, but because their place away from the table, in the kitchen, invests them with the national mission. When Hughes writes "Alberta K. Johnson— American that's me," he makes this African American woman the author as well as the exemplar of what it is to be American.

Hughes took the exhortation "Keep your hand on the plow" from a slave song. These songs have been the work songs of the American mission. They conveyed the means and the ends of resistance to slavery in the antebellum era. W. E. B. Du Bois placed a bar from "the Sorrow Songs" at the opening of each chapter of *The Souls of Black Folk*. They were the anthems of the civil rights movement, and for many who grew up in the sixties, the songs of their youth.

Sacvan Bercovitch, echoing Max Weber, called on us to see the MISSION as an aspect of the Protestant ethic in the spirit of capitalism. Mindful of Hegel, we have looked upon the Puritans and their successors as impelled by a sense of their world historical importance: through them, the scriptural ideal would make itself real in the world. In Hughes, the mission comes from other mouths, in the words of men and women whose names are lost to us.

Langston Hughes placed his prophecy of the absent nation in the mouths of men and women working in the fields, embodied and enslaved. In conveying

his sense of American identity as incomplete, as "promises that will come true," Hughes found a way to speak the truth about the American present, recall the promise of the past, and call for an America whose time is yet to come.

ANNE NORTON

FURTHER READING
Sacvan Bercovitch, *The American Jeremiad* (Madison: University of Wisconsin Press, 1978).
Langston Hughes, *Selected Poems* (New York: Vintage, 1974).
Arnold Rampersad, *The Life of Langston Hughes*, 2 vols. (New York: Oxford University Press, 1986–88).
Steven C. Tracy, *Langston Hughes and the Blues* (Urbana: University of Illinois Press, 1988).

humor The fundamental force of humor in American society has been an axiomatic belief among observers over the centuries. E. B. White once reflected that "Whatever else an American believes or disbelieves about himself, he is absolutely sure he has a sense of humor" (*Essays*, p. 245). Evidence that American language and mores were enmeshed with humorous connections, and that humor was employed as a means of furthering political and cultural objectives, came from many European travelers throughout the nineteenth century.

Recognition of humor's salience produced a series of treatises in the early decades of the twentieth century, one of the most fascinating being Max Eastman's popular work *Enjoyment of Laughter* (1936). Eastman grandly maintainted that humor "is not only the origin but the main achievement of our imaginative culture in so far as it has been distinctively American" (p. 169). The first major scholarly study to grapple with humor's role, however, was *American Humor: a Study of the National Character* (1931) by Constance Rourke, who argued that a primary unconscious objective of humor was to create "fresh bonds, a new unity, the semblance of a society and the rounded completion of an American type" where none had previously existed. "Humor has been a fashioning instrument in America, cleaving its way through the national life, holding tenaciously to the spread elements of that life" (p. 297). Rourke concluded that no single literary type had emerged from this history; rather, humor reflected and perpetuated cultural diversity.

Yet the subject of humor remained largely unexamined by other scholars until the post-World War II period. At mid-century a number of studies highlighted American humor's hyperbole, its penchant for overstatement and exaggeration, its irreverent and spoofing quality, and its occasional tastelessness.

Nonetheless, as late as 1973 Louis D. Rubin Jr., in "The Great American Joke," protested that more effort had been spent in exploring American tragedy than comedy.

In the last two decades there has been a scholarly outpouring of works in a variety of disciplines, including classical and comparative literature, romance languages, folklore, and eventually the social sciences. Not only have scholars tackled the fundamental issue of humor's function in culture, they have also scrutinized the underlying basis of humor itself. Mahadev L. Apte's treatise, *Humor and Laughter* (1985), drawing on the perspectives of sociology, anthropology, and psychology, was the first systematic analysis of humor to offer historical insight and a comprehensive overview of ethnic humor. New vistas in the field of folklore opened with Alan Dundes's provocative work on joke cycles. "I have come to believe," he argued in *Cracking Jokes* (1987), "that no piece of folklore continues to be transmitted *unless* it means something—even if neither the speaker nor the audience can articulate what that meaning might be" (p. vii). Victor Raskin provided in his *Semantic Mechanisms of Humor* (1985) the preeminent semantic analysis. Significantly, in the 1970s, an interdisciplinary group of scholars established a humor studies association and created *HUMOR*, a scholarly journal.

Recent thinkers have singled out the incongruity between the ideal and real as a particular paradigm in American laughter. The tension of opposites, of optimism and despair, expectation and failure, rationality and anarchy, irreverence and blackness, mirror contradictions inherent in American culture. Thus classic American cartoons portray a man painting himself into a corner, pruning a tree limb while perched on the end of the branch, alone on a desert island with a copy of Bartlett's famous quotations for his prospective audience. Such incongruity has led to the formidable array of good news/bad news jokes, such as the failure to create a pollution-free environment:

Did you hear the good news/bad news about drinking water in the year 2000? The bad news is that the only water left to drink will be recycled sewage. The good news is that there won't be enough to go around.

Contradiction and incongruity have especially informed the humor of racial, ethnic and gender groups. The humor of these groups—virtually ignored by scholars until the force of the civil rights, black power, and women's movements seriously undermined the notion of cultural consensus—has assumed center stage in humor studies. Consequently, analyses of Jewish, black, and women's humor have focused on cultural HEGEMONY, positing that humor refracts the nexus of power relationships. Studies concentrating on protest, adaptation, and resistance as the means by which marginalized groups have survived and retaliated have resulted in a deeper comprehension of humor's operative function in enabling both separateness and assimilation.

Jewish humor has long been recognized for its pivotal role in transforming American comedy in the twentieth century. Women's humor, on the other hand, has existed in obscurity. In the 1980s and 1990s came a stream of works that explored the history and context of women's humor, the most encompassing being Nancy A. Walker's *A Very Serious Thing: Women's Humor and American Culture* (1988). There she noted:

The established tradition in American humor is replete with tall tales, political satire, and absurdity; women's humor presents not boasters but victims of cultural expectations . . . the absurdity they present is the fundamental absurdity of oppression. (p. 12)

More than any other ethnic group, blacks were forced to hone their humor into a weapon of survival by fusing African with North American motifs. Denied access to written culture during slavery, African Americans turned to memory orally transmitted. "If we pass through any cluster of black people at that magical time when 'lying and crying' commences," wrote John A. Williams and Dennis A. Williams in *If I Stop I'll Die: the Comedy and Tragedy of Richard Pryor* (1991), "the story-telling begins, we can find Richard Pryor on every corner, in every barbershop or pool hall, combining humor and folklore" (p. 3).

Minority laughter, in short, reinforces the notion that American humor's vitality derives much of its potency from its ability to convey contradictions: "laughing wild amid severest woe," as Samuel Beckett put it in *Happy Days* (1961).

JOSEPH BOSKIN

FURTHER READING

Mahadev L. Apte, *Humor and Laughter: an Anthropological Approach* (Ithaca: Cornell University Press, 1985).

Alan Dundes, *Cracking Jokes: Studies of Sick Humor Cycles and Stereotypes* (Berkeley: Ten Speed Press, 1987).

Max Eastman, *Enjoyment of Laughter* (New York: Simon and Schuster, 1936).

Victor Raskin, *Semantic Mechanisms of Humor* (Boston: D. Reidel, 1985).

Constance Rourke, *American Humor: a Study of the National Character* (New York: Harcourt, Brace, 1931).

Louis D. Rubin Jr., "The Great American Joke," *South Atlantic Quarterly* 72 (winter 1973): 82–94.

Nancy A. Walker, *A Very Serious Thing: Women's Humor and American Culture* (Minneapolis: University of Minnesota Press, 1988).

Mel Watkins, *On the Real Side: Laughing, Lying, and Signifying—The Underground Tradition of African-American Humor that Transformed American Culture from Slavery to Richard Pryor* (New York: Simon & Schuster, 1994).

E. B. White, *Essays of E. B. White* (New York: Harper and Row, 1977).

John A. Williams and Dennis A. Williams, *If I Stop I'll Die: the Comedy and Tragedy of Richard Pryor* (New York: Thunder's Mouth Press, 1991).

Hurston, Zora Neale (b. Eatonville, Fla., Jan. 7, ca.1901; d. Fort Pierce, Fla., Jan. 28, 1960). A key figure in the HARLEM RENAISSANCE, Hurston is widely known as the author of the novel *Their Eyes Were Watching God* (1937). But she was also known in her time—and is increasingly known today—for her work in African American and African Caribbean folklore. She published two collections of folklore, *Mules and Men* (1935) and *Tell My Horse* (1938), accounts of her collecting ventures in her native Florida and in Haiti and Jamaica. Hurston found her way from Eatonville, Florida, the all-black town that is the setting for much of *Their Eyes*, to Howard University and eventually Barnard College, where she studied with Columbia University anthropologist FRANZ BOAS. "Papa Franz," as she called him, was at once charmed and dismayed by the presentation of the material she gathered, as his introduction to the first edition of *Mules and Men* makes evident. Irresistibly drawn to storytelling, Hurston characteristically blurred the distinction between fiction and ethnography in her seven published books and numerous shorter pieces, including essays, short stories, and journalism.

Hurston was already a published fiction writer when she began to study anthropology at Barnard in 1925, less than a year after her arrival in New York City. Her studies did not prevent her from joining in the aesthetic debates that marked black intellectual life; after all, she had originally come to New York to write. A symposium sponsored by W. E. B. DU BOIS in *The Crisis* in 1926 asked the crucial question of the moment: "The Negro in Art: How Shall He Be Portrayed?" Du Bois endorsed a propagandist art as the best answer to the racism encountered by black writers in the United States. But Hurston, a committed individualist, believed that the artist's unfettered self-expression would do more to promote interracial understanding, and thereby combat racism, than the programmatic art advocated by Du Bois. In this belief, she followed ALAIN LOCKE, with whom she had studied at Howard, and she appeared in his anthology *The New Negro* (1925). But Hurston went further than Locke in her efforts to free her work from the constraints on style and subject-matter that she felt "the race question" imposed. An early draft of her autobiography *Dust Tracks on a Road* (1942) ended with a chapter entitled "Seeing the World as It is," in which Hurston declared "Race Pride and Race Consciousness . . . to be . . . the root of misunderstanding and hence misery and injustice" (p. 326). The folk culture of the black South of her youth, however, haunted her imagination and provided the idiom for most of her work. Both her articulated disavowal of race consciousness and her unflagging commitment to black folk culture troubled intellectuals such as Du Bois, Locke, and RICHARD WRIGHT, whose critical review of *Their Eyes* deplored Hurston's reluctance to challenge an unjust social order.

Recently, Hurston has surfaced at the center of a similar controversy. Her return to prominent circulation, following several decades of relative obscurity, came largely through efforts of African American womanists, such as Alice Walker and Mary Helen Washington, whose efforts gained Hurston's *Their Eyes* a place on the reading lists of white feminists. But the feminist framework for Hurston's recent reception has thrown disproportionate attention upon her treatment of gender issues, leading some critics to allege that her current popularity stems from her avoiding the most pressing concerns of black America, especially those of the urban black proletariat, which so centrally engaged writers such as Wright. Yet gender is only one among many of Hurston's concerns. Social critique emerges most effectively, she argued, when multiple expressions of difference are set in conjunction with each other. Many of her short essays and journalistic pieces suggest that the feminist Hurston of *Their Eyes* must be supplemented not only by Hurston the folklorist, but by Hurston the critic of racism and inequality.

Her social critique grew out of the concept of "jagged harmony" that she developed in her study of "the Negro spiritual" in "Spirituals and Neo-Spirituals." The key to the spiritual, for Hurston, lay in its irreproducibility. Irregular and "bound by no rules," it is the dissonant, spontaneous sound produced by "a group bent on expression of feelings and not on sound effects." The "true spiritual" has little in common, she noted, with the music popularized during this period by glee clubs at Fiske, Hampton, and Tuskegee—"all good work and beautiful," she conceded, "but *not* the spirituals" (*The Sanctified Church*, p. 80).

Jagged harmony became social critique in Hurston's hands because it called for attending to authentic voices often excluded in other aesthetic models, including even one of the most pluralistic of her day, that of HORACE KALLEN. In "Democracy versus the Melting-Pot: a Study of American Nationality" (1915), Kallen advocated a confederation of ethnic groups as the basis for United States culture, a vision that he expressed through the metaphor of "a chorus of many voices each singing a rather different tune." Assuming the undesirability of this "cacophony," he wondered how to "get order out of" it in the form of "a unison or a harmony?" (p. 217). Hurston's jagged harmony, by contrast, celebrated cacophony and thus challenged the classically European notion of proportioned beauty underlying Kallen's metaphor. She gave priority to the unprocessed vitality of oral culture, produced anew by each teller. In the face of potent cultural forces determined to impose cultural uniformity—all the way from virulent anti-immigrant and racist propaganda to the homogenizing imperatives of the agencies of mass culture—Hurston's appeal constituted a critique at once social and aesthetic.

Although the importance of unreproducibility to jagged harmony makes its adoption as an aesthetic principle for written work paradoxical, Hurston strove to incorporate it formally into her writing. In *Mules and Men*, she anticipated contemporary anthropological strategies by inserting herself into the narrative in a less-than-privileged position, as a character in her own story. This method itself became one of her most characteristic themes: the self changes with each telling of the tale. Indeed, her "self" comes into being in the first place only because stories have been told about it. And it is continually modified in her work, from a journalistic piece such as "How It Feels to Be Colored Me" (1928) through *Mules and Men* and *Their Eyes* to *Dust Tracks*. Unintegrated, even contradictory, "selves" emerge from this endless retelling.

In trying to translate her formal experiments into a political program, Hurston encountered some of the inconsistencies of her own philosophy. Determined to prevent the black folk culture from being subsumed into and denatured by a black middle class that she thought mimicked white culture, she found herself preferring right-wing white separatists to white liberal desegregationists. She resented the liberal insinuation that not only black schools but black culture needed upgrading. Even segregation was more palatable than the cultural homogenization that she saw as the outcome of liberal initiatives. (*See also* ASSIMILATION.) Yet she also knew that the segregationists had no use for black culture either. She was left without a political outlet for jagged harmony,

for the full and cacophonous expression of all human voices. Art would have to stand in for politics.

PRISCILLA WALD

See also CULTURAL PLURALISM AND MULTICULTURALISM.

FURTHER READING
Michael Awkward, ed., *New Essays on "Their Eyes Were Watching God"* (Cambridge, U.K.: Cambridge University Press, 1990).
Harold Bloom, ed., *Zora Neale Hurston's "Their Eyes Were Watching God"* (New York: Chelsea House, 1987).
Robert E. Hemenway, *Zora Neale Hurston: a Literary Biography* (Urbana: University of Illinois Press, 1977).
Lillie P. Howard, *Zora Neale Hurston* (Boston: Twayne, 1980).
Zora Neale Hurston, *Dust Tracks on a Road: an Autobiography* (1937), ed. Robert Hemenway (Urbana: University of Illinois Press, 1984).
——, *I Love Myself When I Am Laughing . . . and Then Again When I Am Looking Mean and Impressive: a Zora Neale Hurston Reader*, ed. Alice Walker (New York: Feminist Press, 1979).
——, *The Sanctified Church: the Folklore Writings of Zora Neale Hurston* (Berkeley: Turtle Island Foundation, 1981).
Horace Kallen, "Democracy versus the Melting-Pot: a Study of American Nationality," *The Nation* 100 (Feb. 18 and 25, 1915): 190–4; 217–20.

Hutchins, Robert Maynard (b. Brooklyn, N.Y., Jan. 17, 1899; d. Santa Barbara, Calif., May 14, 1977). Educator. The materialism and anti-intellectualism of modern society, in Hutchins's view, had deflected schools and universities from their true purpose: the transmission of important ideas and the development of critical and logical thinking. President of the University of Chicago from 1929 until 1945 (he started at age 30), he argued that specialized vocational instruction, preprofessional training, and athletics had no place in secondary or college curricula, which should provide broad intellectual training through the study of great books. Founder of the Center for the Study of Democratic Institutions (1959) as a place for scholars to discuss social, philosophical, environmental, and human rights issues, Hutchins was editor-in-chief of the 54-volume *Great Books of the Western World* (1952). His writings include *The Higher Learning in America* (1936), *Education for Freedom* (1943), and *The Learning Society* (1968).

See also MORTIMER ADLER; COLLEGES AND UNIVERSITIES.

FURTHER READING
Harry S. Ashmore, *Unseasonable Truths: the Life of Robert Maynard Hutchins* (Boston: Little Brown, 1989).

Hutchinson, Anne (baptized Alford, England, July 20, 1591; d. Pelham Bay, N.Y., Aug. or Sept., 1643). The daughter of a Puritan minister,

Hutchinson's known history begins with her arrival in the Massachusetts Bay Colony in 1634. Accompanied by her merchant husband and their 11 children, Hutchinson may have emigrated in order to follow the much-admired JOHN COTTON, who had fled imprisonment in England the year before. Admitted to the Boston church, her husband elected to the high office of deputy to the Massachusetts General Court, Hutchinson set about establishing herself as a midwife and spiritual adviser to women. But during her first two years in Boston, she began to hold weekly gatherings to review and comment on the sermon of the previous Sunday.

Attended at first only by women, these meetings quickly grew to include men and soon drew a regular attendance of 60 or more, including such notables as governor Henry Vane and other men of prominence. As her following changed, so too apparently did Hutchinson's message. Instead of recapitulating the weekly sermon, she undertook to reproach the Massachusetts clergy for falling into a covenant of works: "legalists" all, they mistakenly took sanctification—the successful struggle of the saint against sin—as evidence of election, failing to understand that works and redemption bear no necessary connection. Hutchinson, on the contrary, spoke for a doctrine of free grace characterized by the inefficacy of works and the saint's absolute assurance of salvation. Until the arrival in 1636 of her brother-in-law, the Reverend John Wheelwright, only John Cotton was spared Hutchinson's criticism.

Convinced that the Massachusetts ministers had fallen from the true way, Hutchinson's followers were moved to action. Efforts were made to replace John Wilson, then pastor of the Boston church, with John Wheelwright. The animosity between Hutchinson's supporters and her opponents grew until, in January 1637, a Fast Day was set aside in an effort to restore the peace. In a conciliatory move, Wheelwright was asked to preach the Fast Day sermon. His highly provocative sermon resulted in a charge of sedition and this charge, in turn, brought petitions on his behalf to the General Court. Accusations of antinomianism —a perfectionist heresy wherein election is witnessed and sealed by the spirit and cannot be tested by outward means—from one side were met with thinly veiled charges of papism from the other. As disruption and contention spread, affecting participation in colonial elections and the conduct of the Pequot War, not even the prominence of Hutchinson's followers could protect her.

The ministers of the Bay convened a synod—the first in the colonies—for the purpose of responding to the errors of the antinomians. The General Court followed with sterner measures: the leaders among the antinomians were variously disenfranchised and banished, their male supporters disarmed. Considered the ringleader, Hutchinson was herself brought to trial by the court in the fall of 1637 and by the church the following spring. (See also PURITANISM.) Exiled and excommunicated, she fled to Rhode Island in 1638, moving five years later to New York where, apparently in providential vindication of her judges, she and all but one of her family were killed in a raid provoked by Willem Kieft's attack on the New Netherland Indians.

Within a year of Hutchinson's death, the first of what would be generations of accounts of the antinomian controversy appeared in New England. JOHN WINTHROP and William Welde, in A Short Story of the Rise, reign, and ruine of the Antinomians, Familists & Libertines (1644), cast the story of Anne Hutchinson in light of the sacred history of the New Israel. No longer a tale of heresy and dissent, A Short Story tells instead of New England's seduction by a new Eve. It focuses less on the theological and political issues at the heart of the controversy than on the figure of Hutchinson as an American Jezebel whose multiple "misconceptions"—what the Puritans understood as multiple deformed stillbirths—lent divine confirmation to the Puritans' judgment of her. In A Short Story as in most of the colonial narratives of the antinomian controversy, the mother of monsters is fatally pitted against the Puritan fathers.

Well into the nineteenth century the story of Anne Hutchinson was recounted by historians and writers alike as a cautionary tale about the dangers variously of female rebellion, spiritual pride, and radical individualism. Likewise, the controversy has captured the attention of a wide range of modern scholars. In a period in which scarcity and inflation were intensified by a steady increase in population, the disproportionate affiliation of merchants with the Hutchinsonians has been explained as a response to the insupportable contradictions faced by those who would be both pious and successful in commerce. The merchants, according to one historian, used antinomianism as a way to rebel against an authoritarian Puritan regime which tended to constrain their economic behavior. Another scholar argues that the special appeal of Hutchinson's new theology lay in its primitive feminism: in the relation it posited between man and God, antinomianism relegated both men and women to the status that women occupied in the Puritan community. Social and intellectual historians have mined the antinomian controversy for information about the limits of Puritan orthodoxy and about social boundary-marking in the colonies. Literary critics have adopted the term antinomian to describe the oppositional quality they find in the classic literature of the American Renaissance, and have argued that the antinomian impulse sparked literary production in a Puritan culture.

What information we have about Anne Hutchinson comes from seventeenth-century trial transcripts, from published histories of the colonies, and from the surviving journals of notables like John Winthrop. The entire absence of any direct record precludes any definitive interpretation of the antinomian controversy; moreover, it lends itself to the mythologizing of the figure of the American Jezebel whose unwillingness to defer to male authority was surely as important as her theological position.

AMY SCHRAGER LANG

See also CALVINISM; PIETY.

FURTHER READING

Emory Battis, *Saints and Sectaries: Anne Hutchinson and the Antinomian Controversy in the Massachusetts Bay Colony* (Chapel Hill: University of North Carolina Press, 1962).

Philip F. Gura, *A Glimpse of Sion's Glory: Puritan Radicalism in New England, 1620–1660* (Middletown, Conn.: Wesleyan University Press, 1984).

David D. Hall, *The Antinomian Controversy, 1636–1638: a Documentary History* (Middletown, Conn.: Wesleyan University Press, 1968).

Lyle Koehler, *A Search for Power: the "Weaker Sex" in Seventeenth-Century New England* (Urbana: University of Illinois Press, 1980).

Amy Schrager Lang, *Prophetic Woman: Anne Hutchinson and the Problem of Dissent in the Literature of New England* (Berkeley: University of California Press, 1987).

I

ideology "It has been our fate as a nation," Richard Hofstadter once remarked of the United States, "not to have ideologies but to be one" (quoted in Kohn, *American Nationalism*, p. 13). The claim by some intellectuals in Hofstadter's time that American history was unique, or at least distinct from Europe's, in its freedom from the constraints and blandishments of ideology bespoke an old political tradition of national self-assertion which, for all its apparent matter-of-fact common sense, might be regarded as an ideology par excellence.

Hofstadter's aphorism reveals how difficult it is to define the concept of ideology with any precision. The malleability of the term is evident in the controversies surrounding its earliest uses. French revolutionary intellectual Antoine Destutt de Tracy (1754–1836) saw "ideology" as a new "science of ideas" that would free the human mind of illusion; Napoleon later attacked Tracy and his followers as impractical, doctrinaire, and subversive "ideologues." In *The German Ideology*, Marx and Engels relied on the pejorative implications of the word to denounce philosophic idealism, insist on the rootedness of ideas in historical circumstances and practical activity, and suggest that in class-riven societies the leading ideas of a particular time, though typically disguised as universally valid, propounded the peculiar interests, values, and dispositions of the class holding power. Besides suggesting deception and domination, "ideology" also served later Marxists as a value-neutral term for the characteristic values and political program of any social class involved in conflict. Most generally, the concept of "ideology" points to connections between politics, ideas, and forms of social solidarity.

Whether treated explicitly or not, with favor or disdain, ideology has preoccupied U.S. intellectuals throughout the twentieth century. Since the national identity and integrity of the country rests less on clear ethnic or ancient associations than on a recent heritage of political acts (colonial rebellion, state formation, civil war and reunification), belonging to the nation has often been defined by subscription to a particular set of political beliefs. "Americanism" has thus been a constant of the national experience. Understood as an ideology, however, it has engaged the country's political leaders and intelligentsia particularly since the end of Reconstruction, in roughly the same period that new social sciences emerged and attempted to analyze the relation between belief and civil order. The desire to secure a national identity, creed, and program (ideological Americanism) coincided and paradoxically meshed with attempts to criticize and "denaturalize" matter-of-fact assumptions of social life and the national experience.

As attempts to foster national harmony and promote the nation's international stature, the brands of PROGRESSIVISM espoused by THEODORE ROOSEVELT and WOODROW WILSON can both be regarded as exercises in ideological Americanism. In *America's Coming-of-Age* (1915), literary critic VAN WYCK BROOKS signaled a new degree of national self-consciousness among those intellectuals devoted to criticizing and cultivating a unique American culture. Meanwhile, landmarks of Progressive-era social thought promoted a more acerbic program of unmasking the partial interests that allegedly underlay the peculiar cultural forms and social doctrines that passed as unremarked conventions of American life. THORSTEIN VEBLEN challenged the claims of abstract, formal economics and demonstrated that prevailing criteria of cultural distinction ratified social status differentials. CHARLES BEARD, who argued that constitutional principles arose as expressions of elite property interests, also suggested an elementary notion of "ideology" as a critical concept.

By the 1930s, prevalent ideals of INDIVIDUALISM, FREEDOM, competition, equal opportunity, and SOCIAL MOBILITY were challenged as illusory images by Marxist critics of "bourgeois ideology," as well as by liberals such as THURMAN ARNOLD, in his book, *The Folklore of Capitalism* (1936). At the same time, ideological Americanism gained new resources, as the holistic concept of "culture," first used in attempts to "denaturalize" settled custom in American society, helped fuel a nationalistic effort to formulate a distinctively American body of TRADITION and ritual.

Concern over the meaning and force of "ideology" reached a new height with the discovery of "totalitarianism" in the late 1930s and 1940s. As the term became identified with the fervent programs of left and right in Europe, "ideology" was described as a system of belief, characterized by absolutism, extreme partisanship, and gross distortions of empirical reality, that possessed an infernal spiritual force capable of welding together violent mass movements. Revulsion from European ideologies led on the one hand to claims that American life had escaped or transcended ideology, and on the other to claims that America itself offered an ideological alternative to the political creeds of European dictatorships. The desire of prowar liberal intellectuals in the early 1940s to promote "national morale"—defined in part as a worldview which gave a nation's people its cohesion and purpose—led to works such as *And Keep Your Powder Dry* (1942), by MARGARET MEAD, which not only offered an ethnography of the United States but also sought to fashion an American political creed of pluralism, egalitarianism, instrumental reform, and social welfare.

This wartime enthusiasm was soon greeted by another intellectual project, rooted in the Marxian critique of ideology, which described the contours of the national mind as constraining limits rather than motivating bonds. RICHARD HOFSTADTER, in *The American Political Tradition* (1948), and LOUIS HARTZ, in *The Liberal Tradition in America* (1955), analyzed and criticized the ideas that kept political debate within the narrow bounds of market individualism and property rights. The 1940s was the age of ideology and its critique.

The multiplicity of meanings in the term "ideology" was bound to complicate the debate initiated by writers who declared the "end of ideology" in the late 1950s. The most prominent, sociologist DANIEL BELL, defined ideologies as political religions, which fostered false hopes for the realization of messianic aspirations in actual time. Bell welcomed the apparent decline in the appeal such messianic mass political doctrines held for Western intellectuals, but he also decried the trend toward bureaucratic rationality and communal decay which made it increasingly difficult for the society as a whole to broach and resolve the ethical issues that lay behind problems of public policy. Neither the technocrat nor the positivist his critics assailed, Bell helped stimulate disputes that raged through the 1960s about the character of prevailing political discourse and the nature of truth and bias in SCIENCE and SOCIAL SCIENCE. By this time, ideas of "American culture" and "national morale" had yielded to the blander concept of CONSENSUS. If one party regarded "consensus" as an inevitable condition of social unity, and considered the American consensus to be both capacious and progressive, the other regarded consensus as a narrow current of permissible political belief confined by dogmatic anticommunism and paeans to corporate power.

The debate over scientific truth was somewhat more complex. The positivism of most academic social science, which assumed that observation untainted by political bias was not only possible but also assured by contemporary technique, was met by radical critics and by THOMAS KUHN, who argued in *The Structure of Scientific Revolutions* (1962) that all scientific practice rested on nonempirical dogmas held by solidary groups of scientists. (*See also* SCIENTISM AND COGNITIVISM.)

By the 1980s, ideology had become virtually inescapable. American life at large was marked by the resurgence of right-wing CONSERVATISM and strident nationalism. Meanwhile, in academic life, the influence of intellectual radicalism, linguistic theory, and French criticism (particularly Michel Foucault's work) combined to demand disclosure of the political presuppositions in all forms of thought. There were, of course, many social scientists who remained indifferent to such concerns and still cited updated experimental and quantitative methods as the key to value-neutral research. Nonetheless, a significant change had occurred in American intellectual life at large. The 1950s view that the pursuit of knowledge might be freed from corrosive bias gave way to a new view that intellectual life was interminably mired in politics, or even that truth beyond the corruptions of power (in its diverse and ubiquitous forms) was impossible. While this new trend brought a salutary degree of historicism and skepticism to the human sciences, it also threatened to overwhelm an older tradition which proposed that the critique of ideological illusion was part of a struggle to determine and make accessible provisional truths about the world. Severed from that aspiration, the critique of ideology ran the risk of losing its critical edge and its social utility.

HOWARD BRICK

See also AMERICAN EXCEPTIONALISM.

FURTHER READING

Sacvan Bercovitch and Myra Jehlen, eds., *Ideology and Classic American Literature* (Cambridge, U.K.: Cambridge University Press, 1986).

Terry Eagleton, *Ideology: an Introduction* (London: Verso, 1991).

Michel Foucault, *Power/Knowledge* (New York: Pantheon, 1980).

Hans Kohn, *American Nationalism: an Interpretive Essay* (New York: Macmillan, 1956).

David McLellan, *Ideology* (Minneapolis: University of Minnesota Press, 1986).

Karl Marx and Friedrich Engels, *The German Ideology*, in Robert C. Tucker, ed., *The Marx-Engels Reader*, 2nd ed. (New York: Norton, 1978).

Warren Susman, "The Culture of the Thirties," in Susman, *Culture as History: the Transformation of American Society in the Twentieth Century* (New York: Pantheon, 1984).

Chaim Waxman, ed., *The End of Ideology Debate* (New York: Funk and Wagnalls, 1968).

imperialism and anti-imperialism Historical interpretations of American imperialism are inseparable from the debates about its existence. The notion of an American empire is a contradiction in terms, according to popular perceptions and scholarly analyses of the democratic nation as inherently *anti-imperialist* in its foreign policy, from its founding AMERICAN REVOLUTION against the British Empire to its COLD WAR against the "evil empire" of the Soviet Union. From this perspective, America's foreign interventions, whether military, economic, political or cultural, have been acts of liberation, efforts to defend the oppressed from the aggressive designs of other imperialists. An opposing viewpoint has considered imperial expansion to be the central driving force that both enabled American economic and social development and depended on the subjugation of others, from the violent conquest of the territories and peoples of North America to the global role of "superpower" in the twentieth century. From the second perspective, the denial of American empire—and its projection onto demonic others—has served as one of imperialism's major ideological justifications, enlisting popular support, undergirding political practices, and providing one of the cornerstones of AMERICAN EXCEPTIONALISM.

The idea of an American empire was openly embraced by the founding generation, who eagerly sought to supplant the ousted British Empire with what George Washington called "the rising American Empire." An early version of American exceptionalism might be found in the defiance of the age-old maxim of political philosophy that held a territorially vast empire to be antithetical to individual liberty, an antithesis resolved in Jefferson's oft quoted phrase, "empire for liberty." Through the nineteenth century, empire building was synonymous with nation building. Whether through the Louisiana Purchase (1803), Andrew Jackson's Indian wars and treaties, or the Mexican War (1846–8), imperial expansion incorporated vast regions and numerous citizens into the republic while relegating nonwhite indigenous populations and African slaves to colonized status. Yet empire building was never a monolithic process in American history. Not only did Indians, Mexicans and competing European empires resist American expansion, it was pursued in different geographic directions, for competing economic and political goals, by people of different regions. The debate over the extension of slavery through territorial annexation was a crucial factor leading to

the Civil War, as competing versions of empire building threatened to dissolve the nation. Not until after the Civil War did the term American empire drop out of general usage (perhaps in part because the South saw the North as an occupying imperial power), as the consolidation of national power made real the potential and the aspirations for transoceanic imperialism.

Most historians agree that the 1890s marked a turning point in the history of American imperialism. At that time the term itself emerged openly in public debates between self-avowed imperialists and anti-imperialists. Those historians who have denied the significance of empire traditionally dismissed as an aberration America's acquisition—in the aftermath of the Spanish-American War—of the Philippines, Cuba, Puerto Rico, and Guam. They saw it as a consequence of moral idealism and hysterical popular opinion. This view, crystallized by GEORGE KENNAN and the school of "realists," depends on a narrow definition of imperialism as the formal annexation of colonies. Yet such historians have tended to characterize this period in terms of America's assumption of world power, when Britain was forced, for example, to recognize U.S. authority in the Western hemisphere through the Roosevelt Corollary to the Monroe Doctrine.

An opposing interpretation, advanced by William Appleman Williams and other "revisionists," has seen at the turn of the century an important shift from territorial expansion to primarily economic expansion, an anxious search for foreign markets for the overabundance of American products and capital to alleviate economic and social crises at home. This shift, according to Williams, was epitomized by the Open Door policy toward China, which became paradigmatic for U.S. foreign policy in that it blocked European colonial designs in order to keep China open to the free activity of American business and missionaries.

A more recent cultural approach to this period, represented by Richard Drinnon and others, views it less as a dramatic turning point than as a new stage in the process whereby continental and transoceanic expansion were always linked, most strongly since the 1840s. Ideologies of the "westward course of empire" brought together continental "manifest destiny" with the transoceanic "passage to India," through the common belief in the racial superiority of Anglo-Saxons and the desirability of subjugating nonwhites. Thus the shift toward overseas empire, which had been signaled by the 1890 census and Frederick Jackson Turner's declaration of the close of the FRONTIER, was also marked by Wounded Knee, which represented the end of a continental imperial process of subduing Indians and the interlinked beginning of expansion abroad, where the U.S. confronted new "Indians" on new "frontiers." (*See also* INDIAN–WHITE RELATIONS.) This perspective of continuity reveals interconnections between the domestic and foreign fronts of empire building. Not only did the Indian wars prepare the American military to fight in Cuba and the Philippines, for example, but the social policy of Indian reservations was also exported to the colonial rule of the Philippines. The domestic/foreign continuum in military and social policy was underwritten by a continuity in racial attitudes which linked arguments about the incapacity of Filipinos and Cubans for self-government to arguments about African Americans in Jim Crow America. Finally, by the beginning of the twentieth century, the term Americanization emerged with both a national and international meaning, referring both to the assimilation of immigrants at home and to the spread of American culture abroad.

In the twentieth century, the notion of an American empire dropped out of mainstream currency and came to be associated with radical ideology. Instead, the protean forms of international domination took on benign popular images: the international policeman imposing order on chaos, the beneficent banker facilitating modernization and development, or the political missionary "making the world safe for democracy." While after WORLD WAR I the US could be seen as anti-imperial in its opposition to European colonialism, it was equally aggressive in seeking economic markets abroad and opportunities for capitalist investment, whether through private corporate initiatives or direct state intervention. Economic domination could not be separated from cultural domination, since both entailed uprooting and transforming the traditional cultures of the world in the image of the U.S. to encourage capitalist development. Markets were aggressively kept open by military and other forms of intervention in the Caribbean and South America during the interwar period traditionally associated with U.S. isolation.

When at the turn of the century the U.S. assumed the role of global power, it confronted a world on the verge of revolution. The U.S. relation to Cuba seems paradigmatic in that America first supported the Cuban struggle for independence from Spain, but then severely limited and controlled Cuba's national independence to maintain U.S. interests. The US similarly supported "self-determination" and the emergent anticolonialist movements in the aftermath of World War I, as it supported the full-blown national independence movements of the 1950s. Yet

fearful of the local autonomy promised by revolution, the US also asserted its right to control the direction of national development, control often in the form of installing and propping up repressive puppet regimes led by local elites with allegiances to the U.S. (as in Nicaragua, Guatemala, Chile, Vietnam, Iran). Indirect economic and political domination through local collaborators, which has been called neocolonialism, requires an understanding of the local conditions, including internal divisions, that contributed to this form of control.

The debate over the existence of an American empire in the years since WORLD WAR II is inseparable from Cold War politics and ideologies. The dominant view (articulated in the well-known National Security Council Paper 68, 1949) denied the existence of American imperialism and explained American foreign policy as primarily defensive, designed to offset and "contain" the global imperial designs of the Soviet Union and to liberate its victims for democracy. The opposing perspective understands the power of anticommunism in part as an effort to control and direct the economic, political, and cultural development of newly emergent nations. According to this interpretation, governments with socialist interests in the reformation of their own communities, whether such governments were democratically elected, such as Allende's in Chile, or forged by revolution, such as Castro's in Cuba, were seen not only as hostile to U.S. economic interests, but also as necessarily controlled by the communist regime of the Soviet Union. Viewed through the prism of anticommunism, any new government hostile to U.S. interests appeared to be the tool of a larger empire.

A domestic consequence of imperialism in the twentieth century has been the increasing centralization of power in the executive branch to coordinate covert and overt interventions abroad. The concomitant development at home involved increasing domestic surveillance of dissent and protest. While advocates of territorial expansion have long claimed that it would guarantee individual liberty at home, the exercise of imperial power abroad instead necessitated a strong national state regulating, at times unconstitutionally, the political activities of its citizens. Thus during the Cold War fighting communists as home was inseparable from subduing communist revolution abroad. During the Vietnam War, the antiwar movement and all forms of social protest movements, including the civil rights movement, became the targets of illegal surveillance. (*See also* CONSENSUS.)

American imperialism has always met lively

resistance abroad and at home, both from within the government and from organized protest movements. From the Mexican War to the recent Gulf War, antiwar groups, often in alliance with progressive social movements in the United States, have opposed military intervention abroad. Outspoken abolitionists opposed the Mexican War and the annexation of Texas because they objected both to the spread of slavery and to the pillage of a war of conquest. Fifty years later, in response to the Spanish-American War, the Anti-Imperialist League, organized nationwide, vociferously opposed the annexation of the Philippines and the deadly three-year war against Filipino nationalists. The anti-imperialists included well-known reformers, intellectuals and writers, such as THOMAS HIGGINSON, CARL SCHURZ, MARK TWAIN, WILLIAM DEAN HOWELLS, JANE ADDAMS, and WILLIAM JAMES, who opposed the acquisition of territories as intrinsically un-American.

The protest movement against the war in VIETNAM, which reintroduced the repressed term of American imperialism to the political vocabulary, was the most widespread U.S. anti-imperialist movement of the twentieth century. While Congressional opposition to the war focused on constitutional issues, the antiwar movement found a major constituency on college campuses, where students and faculty opposed the draft and the immoral nature of a war waged against the Vietnamese people, perceived to be struggling for national liberation. The antiwar movement included veterans' groups, and other reformist and radical organizations of the "old" and "new" left, and reached even greater proportions when it joined forces with the civil rights movement. The widespread dissent against the war in Vietnam has had a lasting impact on subsequent American politics and culture.

It is difficult historically, however, to measure the efficacy of anti-imperialist movements in the United States, in part because their relation to anti-imperialist struggles abroad has not been fully understood. Domestic movements have, however, been bound by a variety of limitations. In the nineteenth and early twentieth century many anti-imperialists shared the dominant national belief in an American MISSION to the world, and some shared a racist opposition to expansion because they opposed incorporating more nonwhites into the republic. In the twentieth century anti-imperialist movements have been limited by the myopia and lack of knowledge they share with imperialists concerning the world outside the United States. Thus protests against U.S. military intervention have not been always been accompanied by a sophisticated understanding of the politics

and culture of those groups the U.S. was attacking. Peace movements have in addition been split when opposition to U.S. militarism has been combined with ambivalence about supporting the politics of those resisting U.S. intervention (for example, Ho Chi Minh or Saddam Hussein). Finally anti-imperialism in the U.S. has most often coalesced around the most obvious form of imperialism, military intervention. Opposition to less dramatic, but more deeply structural, forms of imperial control in the spheres of economics, politics, and culture has been launched more systematically by the foreign subjects of U.S. imperialism in the Third World and their supporters in this country.

Recent global changes, such as the end of the Cold War and U.S. economic decline, have raised questions about the future relevance of U.S. imperialism as a political force and an intellectual concept. Debates revolve around whether the U.S. has emerged triumphantly from the Cold War, or instead has been economically weakened by investing in the military industrial complex that ensured the stability of its empire; whether it will be surpassed by the new economic empires of Japan and Germany; whether transnational corporations can any longer be linked to discrete national interests; whether the imperial paradigm is relevant to evaluating military intervention in cases of famine or nationalist or ethnic conflicts, or to the international concern with the global environment.

Another challenge to the way imperialism is both experienced and studied belies the traditional geographic view of imperialism as the one-way imposition of power from a metropolitan center to the rural periphery. The technology of mass media and information flow has made possible instantaneous global communication in the circulation of capital, work, and images, while massive immigration to major cities in the U.S. has broken down the clear geographic distinction between first, second and third worlds. Global changes are beginning to redefine the way imperialism and anti-imperialism are studied in the academy. Future scholarship may expand beyond a parochial focus on diplomatic history to include comparative perspectives with other empires; to focus on how gender relations worldwide both inform and are shaped by international relations; to examine the complex role of race in foreign policy; and to explore imperialism and resistance as cultural phenomena.

AMY KAPLAN

FURTHER READING
Richard Drinnon, *Facing West: the Metaphysics of Indian-Hating and Empire-Building* (New York: NAL, 1980).

Cynthia Enloe, *Bananas, Beaches and Bases: Making Feminist Sense of International Politics* (Berkeley: University of California Press, 1990).

Philip Foner, ed., *The Anti-Imperialist Reader: a Documentary History of Anti-Imperialism in the United States*, 2 vols. (New York: Holmes and Meier, 1986).

Willard B. Gatewood Jr., *Black Americans and the White Man's Burden, 1898–1903* (Urbana; University of Illinois Press, 1975).

George F. Kennan, *American Diplomacy, 1900–1950* (Chicago: University of Chicago Press, 1951).

Walter LaFeber, *The American Age: United States Foreign Policy at Home and Abroad since 1750* (New York: Norton, 1989).

Robert Rydell, *All the World's a Fair: Visions of Empire at American International Expositions, 1876–1916* (Chicago: University of Chicago, 1984).

William Appleman Williams, *The Tragedy of American Diplomacy* (New York: Dell, 1959).

——, *Empire as a Way of Life* (New York: Oxford University Press, 1980).

Indian identities Bearing the memories and solace of heard stories, Native American tribal identities are inscrutable creations, an innermost brush with natural reason, and, at the same time, unbounded narcissism.

The sources of tribal remembrance, creation, personal visions, tragic wisdom, and the communal nature of the heard are precarious, but the nuances of posted names are burdened more with colonial discoveries, the duplicities of dominance, and simulations than with the menace of silence, the inaccuracies of memories, or the uncertainties of stories out of season.

The distinctive salutations of a personal tribal nature, however, are more than the mere translation and possession of memories and names. Consider the untold influences and choices in specific cultural experiences, and the various sources of identities in public, private, intimate, and sacred circumstances; the choices become even more enigmatic with the vagaries, pleasures, and treasons of cultural contact, and the transvaluations of such wicked notions as savagism and civilization in the course of histories.

The literatures of dominance, the histories, narratives of discoveries, translations, cultural studies, and prescribed names of time, place, and person are treacherous conditions in any discourse on tribal consciousness. The poses of silence are not natural, and other extremes, such as cultural revisionism, the ironic eminence of sacred consumer names, and assumed tribal nicknames, are sources of identities besides the obvious associations; these distinctions, imitations, and other maneuvers are unsure stories heard over and over in common conversations.

Sacred names, those secure ceremonial names, were scarcely heard by missionaries or government agents and seldom translated as surnames; nicknames were assured in tribal stories, but the stories were lost in translation as surnames. Later, most surnames were chosen and dictated at federal and mission schools. Some tribal names endure in stories, and nicknames are identities learned and ascertained in language; moreover, descriptive names seem to be more esteemed in translation, and certain choices of names are mere simulations with no memories or stories.

Snowarrow is but one recent name that has been chosen by a teacher to augment his tribal identities. Youngblood is another; some nicknames are ostentatious, and others are heard with no ascriptions. Names are eschewed and renounced for countless reasons. Thomas Edward Kill, for instance, petitioned a court for legal permission to change his surname because he hoped to become a medical doctor and he did not think his tribal name in translation would inspire confidence.

Some names and associations are chance, to be sure, an ironic observance, or the break-even consciousness of apostates; for all that, tribal stories and natural reason are unanimous, memorable even in translation, and descriptive names are so celebrated in this generation that thousands of people pursue an obscure tribal connection, a passive wisp of ancestral descent in a name; others consume simulations and pretend, for various reasons, to be tribal in the name, blood, and remembrance of those who endured racialism and, with tragic wisdom, decried the literatures of dominance.

Indian identities are created in stories, and names are essential to a distinctive personal nature, but memories, visions, and the shadows of heard stories are the paramount verities of a tribal presence. The shadows are active and intransitive, the visual memories that are heard as tribal stories; these memories are trusted to sacred names and tribal nicknames.

Tribal identities would have no existence without active choices, the choices that are heard in stories and mediated in names; otherwise, tribal identities might be read as mere simulations of remembrance. The literatures of dominance are dubious entitlements to the names in other cultures, simulations that antecede the shadows of the real and then unteach the mediations of tribal names and stories.

Luther Standing Bear, for instance, chose his names, and the stories of the bear are heard even in the translation of his surname. He wrote in *My Indian Boyhood* that the "Indian very seldom bothers a bear and the bear, being a very self-respecting and peaceful animal, seldom bothers a human being." The bear is the shadow in the memories and the trace in his names. The bear is "so much like a human that he is interesting to watch. He has a large amount of human vanity and likes to look at himself." The bear is "wise and clever and he probably knows it." Not only is the bear "a powerful animal in body, but powerful in will also." The bear "will stand and fight to the last. Though wounded, he will not run, but will die fighting. Because my father shared this spirit with the bear, he earned his name," wrote Standing Bear (pp. 48–53).

N. SCOTT MOMADAY, the novelist, wrote in *The Way to Rainy Mountain* that although his tribal grandmother

> lived out her long life in the shadow of Rainy Mountain, the immense landscape of the continental interior lay like memory in her blood. She could tell of the Crows, whom she had never seen, and of the Black Hills, where she had never been. I wanted to see in reality what she had seen more perfectly in the mind's eye, and traveled fifteen hundred miles to begin my pilgrimage. (p. 7)

Aho, his grandmother, heard stories of a migration that lasted five centuries; she could hear and see a landscape, and these stories became the shadows of tribal remembrance.

Momaday honors the memories of his grandmother and touches the shadows of his own imagination; shadows that trace his identities and tribal stories in three scriptural themes in *The Way to Rainy Mountain*.

Tribal nicknames are the shadows heard in stories; the pleasures of nicknames, even in translation, are an unmistakable celebration of personal identities. Nicknames are personal stories that would, to be sure, trace the individual to tribal communities rather than cause separations by pronouns of singular recognition.

Brian Swann and Arnold Krupat, the editors of *I Tell You Now: Autobiographical Essays by Native American Writers*, pointed out that "the notion of telling the whole of any one individual's life or taking merely personal experience as of particular significance was, in the most literal way, foreign to them, if not also repugnant." (p. ix) Nothing, however, is foreign or repugnant in personal names and the stories of nicknames. The risks, natural reasons, and praise of visions are sources of personal power in tribal consciousness; personal stories are coherent and name individual identities within communities, and are not an obvious opposition to communal values. (*See also* COMMUNITY.)

The shadows of personal visions, for instance, were heard and seen alone, but not in cultural isolation or separation from tribal communities. Those who chose to hear visions, an extreme mediation, were aware that their creative encounters with nature were precarious and would be sanctioned by the tribe; personal visions could be of service to tribal families. Some personal visions and stories have the power to heal and liberate the spirit, and there are similar encounters with tribal shadows in the stories by contemporary tribal authors.

Nicknames, shadows, and shamanic visions are tribal stories that are heard and remembered as survivance. These personal identities and stories are not the same as those translated in the literatures of dominance.

"My spirit was quiet there," Momaday wrote in *The Names*, a meticulous memoir of his childhood at Jemez, New Mexico. "The silence was old, immediate, and pervasive, and there was great good in it. The wind of the canyons drew it out; the voices of the village carried and were lost in it. Much was made of the silence; much of the summer and winter was made of it" (p. 154).

"I tell parts of my stories here because I have often searched out other lives similar to my own," wrote Linda Hogan in *I Tell You Now*. "Telling our lives is important, for those who come after us, for those who will see our experience as part of their own historical struggle" (p. 233).

"I was raised by an English-German mother. My father, one-quarter Cherokee, was there also, but it was my mother who presented her white part of my heritage as whole," wrote Diane Glancy in the same collection. "I knew I was different, then as much as now. But I didn't know until later that it was because I am part heir to the Indian culture, and even that small part has leavened the whole lump" (p. 169).

"Facts: May 7, 1948. Oakland. Catholic Hospital. Midwife nun, no doctor. Citation won the Kentucky Derby. Israel was born. The United Nations met for the first time," wrote Wendy Rose. "I have heard Indians joke about those who act as if they had no relatives. I wince, because I have no relatives. They live, but they threw me away. . . . I am without relations. I have always swung back and forth between alienation and relatedness" (pp. 254–5).

The concerted creations of tribal cultures are in continuous translation as stories, and the situation of hermeneutics remains the same in simulations; the silence of heard stories in translations, and the absence of the heard, antecedes a presence in the shadows of names. Has the absence of the heard in tribal stories turned to the literatures of dominance? What are the real names, nouns, and pronouns heard in the fields of tribal consciousness? How can a pronoun be a source of tribal identities in translation? How can a pronoun be essential, an inscription of absence that represents the presence of sound and a person in translation?

Anthony Kerby argued in *Narrative and the Self* that the loss of the

ability to narrate one's past is tantamount to a form of amnesia, with a resultant diminishing of one's sense of self. Why should this be so? The answer, broadly stated, is that our history constitutes a drama in which we are a leading character, and the meaning of this role is to be found only through the recollective and imaginative configuring of that history in autobiographical acts. In other words, in narrating the past we understand ourselves to be the implied subject generated by the narrative. (p. 7)

In other words, tribal identities are heard in names and stories; otherwise the simulations that antecede tribal stories and tragic wisdom would be tantamount to the amnesia of discoveries in the literatures of dominance.

GERALD VIZENOR

See also ANCIENT INDIAN HISTORY; INDIANS.

FURTHER READING

Anthony Kerby, *Narrative and the Self* (Bloomington: Indiana University Press, 1991).

N. Scott Momaday, *The Way to Rainy Mountain* (Albuquerque: University of New Mexico Press, 1969).

——, *The Names* (New York: Harper and Row, 1976).

Louis Owens, *Other Destinies* (Norman: University of Oklahoma Press, 1992).

Luther Standing Bear, *My Indian Boyhood* (Lincoln: University of Nebraska Press, 1931).

Brian Swann and Arnold Krupat, eds., *I Tell You Now: Autobiographical Essays by Native American Writers* (Lincoln: University of Nebraska Press, 1987).

Gerald Vizenor, *Manifest Manners* (Hanover: University Press of New England, 1994).

Indian–white relations Today Indian peoples within the United States enjoy a legal status unique in the Americas. Numerous semisovereign Indian nations exist within the larger sovereignty of the United States. They stand in direct treaty relation with the federal government to whom they have ceded certain sovereign powers characteristic of independent nations, such as the ability to conduct foreign affairs, while retaining others. The citizens of the Indian nations are simultaneously citizens of the United States and the states. Members of federally recognized tribes thus possess a dual national citizenship, and as tribal citizens they may have treaty rights not possessed by other Americans.

Although in one sense partially independent of the United States, in other senses modern Indian nations are clearly dependent on the federal government. The federal government stands as a trustee for their land and resources and often for tribal and individual monies. Also, Congress can limit Indian sovereignty or completely overturn the treaties at any time. Often desperately poor, most Indian nations rely on various government payments for the survival of their own governments and people. This modern, anomalous situation is the result of five centuries of a complicated history.

English antecedents largely shaped Indian–white relations in the United States. The English, far more than the French and Spanish, envisioned Europeans replacing Indians on the continent. Indians were, after all, diminishing in number, often quite rapidly. The main cause was disease. Virgin soil epidemics (that is epidemic diseases from the Old World to which Indian peoples had no resistance), along with war and the deprivation that followed, reduced native populations from an estimated 3,790,000 north of Mexico at contact to under 250,000 in the United States by 1920.

Despite such huge losses, Indian resistance prevented Indian–white relations from the sixteenth century to the nineteenth century from forming a simple pattern of European advance and Indian retreat. Indian peoples, with considerable resilience and imagination, regrouped in new polities and confederacies and allied themselves with one group of Europeans against others. For considerable periods they actually found shelter in the shadow of European empires. Unable, and often unwilling, to banish Europeans, Indians sought new ways to include them in a common world and pursued new methods of containing them. In the Great Lakes region, in the Southwest, in the South, and in the Pacific Northwest, a middle ground of sorts arose in which Europeans and Indians needed each other as allies and trading partners. Particular middle grounds might last for decades or for centuries, but while they endured, Indians mattered both in the daily life of Europeans and in determining the fate of empires.

The English thus faced a challenge more complicated than simply conquering Indians or moving into lands they had vacated. To dispossess Indians by force was often too dangerous in a world of interlocking alliances. Instead, the English often sought to "quiet the Indian title" through treaties that involved purchase of the lands. The English adopted a European doctrine in which the right of discovery bestowed not possession but the right to acquire title from the natives of an area by either purchase or conquest. And in the treaties thus negotiated, the English recognized the sovereignty of Indian nations, a recognition that became a basic principle of American Indian policy.

Americans continued the policy of seeking land sessions by treaties, but they gave the policy a new twist, and they operated in a new context. To the treaties the Americans connected a "civilization policy" designed to mold Indian behaviors and beliefs to American Protestant, agrarian norms. And after the War of 1812, Indian peoples lost the ability to play expanding empires off against each other. The result was accelerating land loss and increasing American domination during the nineteenth and early twentieth centuries.

American Indian policy moved from treating Indian nations as wards whose remaining sovereign rights needed protection, to treating individual Indians as wards who were incompetent to manage their own affairs. So-called "friends of the Indian," largely Protestant reformers who controlled Indian policy, thought rapid acculturation was the only alternative to disappearance. In the words of Richard Henry Pratt, who founded Carlisle Indian School, they sought "to kill the Indian and save the man."

Sovereignty became a mere paper shield for Indians. When the Kiowa chief Lone Wolf objected that the treaties with his people did not authorize the forced division of communal lands, the Supreme Court ruled in *Lone Wolf v. Hitchcock* (1903) that Congress could unilaterally abrogate treaties. In order to save Indians, the Dawes Act (1887) allowed the government to allot communal lands on many reservations to individuals and opened up most of the remainder to white settlement. They took Indian children to boarding schools with horrendous death rates; they banned religious practices, and they dominated tribal governments.

Yet even from 1880 to 1920, years of seemingly absolute control by the Bureau of Indian Affairs, Indians struggled to shape a different future. American officials wanted Indian assent to their policies, and with this slender reed Indian leaders on the reservations found some ways to limit the damage. Off the reservations, educated Indians formed the first pan-Indian organizations, which, although accepting the goal of assimilation, attacked the Bureau of Indian Affairs and demanded reform and Indian rights.

By the 1920s a serious reevaluation of policy had begun. Indians with land allotments had already become U.S. citizens, and in 1924 all Indians were granted CITIZENSHIP. But more crucial was the federal policy toward the tribes. Reform culminated in the Indian New Deal of the 1930s, during the period when John Collier served as head of the Bureau of Indian Affairs. His Indian New Deal was a mixed success, but it began the restoration of the semi-sovereign treaty status of the tribes. A reaction against Collier's policies in the 1950s brought a termination policy that sought to settle U.S. obligations to Indians through a special claims commission, to "terminate" the existence of the tribes and to distribute their property among members. Opposition to termination became the bedrock of tribal politics.

As the tribes beat back termination, they also achieved remarkable success in the federal courts, which upheld existing treaty rights and validated the doctrine that sovereign powers not ceded specifically in the treaties remained in the hands of tribal governments. Tribal gains were real, and particularly in the West, tribal governments attained significant influence in a variety of resource issues affecting the entire region.

But because these political and legal gains were not accompanied by any lasting economic gains among most tribes, the reservations remained poor and dependent on federal programs. By the late twentieth century, a majority of Indians lived off the reservations, seeking to escape the poverty that plagued reservation communities and thus, ironically, leaving the very lands their successes had turned into homelands.

RICHARD WHITE

See also IMPERIALISM AND ANTI-IMPERIALISM; INDIAN IDENTITIES; INDIANS.

FURTHER READING

Vine Deloria Jr. and Clifford Lytle, *The Nations Within: the Past and Future of American Indian Sovereignty* (New York: Pantheon, 1984).

Loretta Fowler, *Arapahoe Politics, 1851–1978: Symbols in Crises of Authority* (Lincoln: University of Nebraska Press, 1982).

Francis Paul Prucha, *The Great Father: the United States Government and American Indians* (Lincoln: University of Nebraska Press, 1984).

Richard White, *The Middle Ground: Indians, Empires and Republics in the Great Lakes Region, 1650–1815* (New York: Cambridge University Press, 1991).

Charles Wilkinson, *American Indians, Time and the Law: Native Societies in a Modern Constitutional Democracy* (New Haven: Yale University Press, 1987).

Indians As the common American term to designate the native inhabitants of the Western Hemisphere, the name "Indians" is a relic of conquest, an identity imposed on indigenous peoples by Europeans who mistakenly thought they had reached the East Indies. The peoples of North and South America had no common self-designation nor, until the recent past, did they think of themselves as a single collectivity.

In the late twentieth century the term itself became

problematic for many North American historians and political activists who substituted the name Native Americans. Historians distinguished between Indians, a white invention designating a set of specific cultural representations (such as noble savages) that treated native peoples as a homogeneous group, and Native Americans, a designation for the actual inhabitants of the continent who possessed a multiplicity of separate cultures, languages, and beliefs. In certain kinds of political discourse Indian yielded to Native American in the same way that Negro yielded to black and then African American. Shedding the word Indian supposedly involved a step toward shedding the colonialism and ignorance the term represented.

Native American, however, had deficiencies of its own, and has taken only a weak hold. One major problem was that most Indians in the United States did not use it to refer to themselves except in very particular situations involving whites. They more often used the term Indian peoples to refer to the inhabitants of the continent as a collective group.

A second major problem arose among historians, for recent research has tended to dissolve the very distinctions the term Native American was created to emphasize. Current scholarship stresses the historicity of Indian peoples as against images of Indians as separate, unchanging, and traditional. And as historic peoples actively defining and redefining themselves, Indians have reacted to images of them held by whites. (See INDIAN IDENTITIES.) It has usually proved analytically impossible to disentangle the creation of Indian cultures by Indians from images of Indians held by whites.

Modern Indian peoples have been created by the same historical developments that have created other national and ethnic groups in the Americas. They are not merely remnants of an earlier world. They are products of the history of the last 500 years. The onslaught of Europeans and their diseases that began in the sixteenth century brought drastic population reductions and created numerous remnant peoples and refugees. As older cultural and political configurations broke up, Indians as much as Europeans have been engaged in creating new cultural and political structures. They did so not in isolation from Europeans but in the midst of new technologies, empires, republics, missionary efforts, sexual unions, trade relations, military conflicts, and bureaucracies that affected both Indian peoples and Euro-Americans. The creation of Indians and the creation of other American identities have been linked.

Many modern tribal groups are the results of these historical changes. Although some tribes have roots that extend deep into the precontact period, very many groups date from well after contact. Some are literally creations of the treaties that their ancestors signed or the reservations upon which formerly separate peoples were placed. (See also ANCIENT INDIAN HISTORIES.) Following their union in the wake of war and epidemics, 20 different languages were spoken by the Catawbas in the mid-eighteenth century. Similarly, the Creeks or Muscogulges really only emerge in the eighteenth century, when a variety of distinct groups coalesced in what is now Alabama and Georgia. The Seminoles, in turn, were a group of Creeks who repopulated sections of Florida emptied by wars and epidemics. Many of the western Washington treaties united separate villages or towns with distinctive cultural practices into a single tribe because they shared a river drainage. The modern Colville of eastern Washington are a new group created from previously distinct peoples who came to occupy a single reservation. This process of creation continues today.

The continuing creation of separate tribes took place even as Europeans and Americans, while aware of differences in language, culture, and practice among Indian peoples, still thought of Indians as a single group with identifiable common traits. Europeans could create the homogeneous category Indian, even as they recognized differences among Indians, because they defined Indians not in terms of qualities they possessed but in terms of qualities they lacked. They understood Indians in terms of deficiency. Creation of the negative category Indian necessarily involved maintaining a positive, non-Indian category into which Europeans and Americans fit. Indians became a single group because they were deficient in whatever the quality Europeans or Americans at a given time used to define themselves.

Older terms applied to North American Indians by the French and the Spanish demonstrate how this process worked. The French, defining themselves as civil, categorized the Indians as savage, as wild men, and referred to them as *sauvages*. The Spanish, defining themselves as Christian, initially referred to the Indians of New Mexico as Turks, because Turks were the available category of nonwhite non-Christians. Latent in these characterizations of deficient Indians was the possibility that as Indian peoples acquired the defining European qualities—Christianity or civility—they could cease to be Turks or *sauvages* and become Spanish or French.

By the early nineteenth century, under the influence of a romantic nationalism, the defining American quality came to be one of RACE, and then the defining Indian quality came to be skin color. Indian

peoples were redskins in nineteenth-century popular speech. A recognition of biological difference in
terms of skin color and hair had, of course, been present from the beginning, and such differences could
be elaborated into the idea of a separate and distinct
race, but race did not become the paramount difference until the late eighteenth and early nineteenth
centuries, and even then it was contested.

Nineteenth-century Euro-Americans defined Indians as a separate race, but they disagreed as to whether
they were inferior, whether they were doomed to be
replaced by people of European descent, and whether
Indians should eventually mix and merge with Europeans on terms of equality, thus disappearing as a
distinct group entirely. Romantic racism may have
made unlikely, from the moment he uttered it,
Thomas Jefferson's view of a future where "we
shall all be Americans," but the goal of eventual amalgamation and ASSIMILATION continued to dominate
American Indian policy. It did so even as the popular
view of Indians as a doomed, inferior, and increasingly degraded race took hold.

Indeed, it would be the early twentieth century
before the view that Indians were a single, separate,
innately inferior people dominated American Indian
policy. Even here the triumph was brief and incomplete. John Collier's reforms in the 1930s make sense
only in terms of a belief in Indian racial equality.
And by the late twentieth century even the deficiency
image was being put to largely antiracist uses. Noble
savagery, the form of the deficiency image in which
Indians lacked white faults, dominated much late
twentieth-century popular culture.

Indians, however, were not just the objects of this
cultural construction. The images the larger society
constructed were too powerful for Indians to ignore,
but not too powerful for them to modify or alter.
Indian peoples began creating their own version of a
common Indian identity.

Various Indian peoples, of course, quickly recognized Europeans as a group distinct from themselves,
but this did not mean that they divided the world
into simple Indian/non-Indian categories. Navajos,
for example, distinguished between two major categories, the diné (Navajo) and the 'ana'í (enemies).
Whites became a subcategory of 'ana'í distinct from
Indian enemies and Mexican enemies. The Navajos
did not unite "Indians" into a single group, nor did
they unite "whites" into a single group; the Spanish
were a subgroup of Mexicans (Gray Mexicans). Similarly other Indian peoples in eastern North America
created categories that did not break down into simple Indian/non-Indian lines. Politically, Indians often
claimed a common identity with one or another

group of whites, proclaiming themselves to be French
or Spanish. Within the French alliance, for example,
Indians and Canadians were both children of Onontio,
the French governor, and stood together against other
Europeans and other Indians.

By the late eighteenth century, however, such declarations of common identity were giving way to
conceptions of separate "roads" or "ways." In the
Northeast and Great Lakes country in particular,
Indian prophets such as Neolin among the Dela-
wares, Handsome Lake among the Iroquois, and
Tenskwatawa of the Shawnees preached doctrines
of innate differences between Indians and whites
and a separate Indian way. God had ordained that
whites live one way and Indians another. This common identity was largely religious and cultural, but
TECUMSEH, at least, tried unsuccessfully to make it
also political.

The rise of nationalism based on race among
Americans fed this growing sense of a common Indian identity, but it also fed a strain of nationalism
among Indian peoples that partially undercut it. The
Cherokees wrestled with their own identity in the
early nineteenth century, and, like white Americans,
became romantic nationalists stressing their differences from other peoples, white and Indian.

The practical hold of ideas of race and nation,
however, remained relatively weak among many
Indian communities into the nineteenth century. Not
only other Indians, but whites could become members of these communities relatively easily. In a sense,
joining many Indian groups was much like becoming a citizen of the United States. Knowledge and
consent—agreeing to live according to the community's norms and be loyal to them—rather than
descent, that is biological ancestry, was most crucial
in determining membership.

It is only in the twentieth century that Indianness
defined as biological descent, and Indianness as a
single identity that transcended specific native communities, really blossomed among Indian peoples.
Again, these developments cannot be separated from
those in the larger society. As the federal government moved toward allotting reservations—giving
land to individuals—and to paying annuities directly
to individuals, it needed reliable tribal rolls. Tribes
had to establish their membership, and, once established, new members could claim membership only
through descent from old members. Indianness as
defined through tribal membership become not only
biological but quantifiable in terms of percentage of
tribal or Indian "blood." So-called blood quantum—
quarter blood, half blood—became a measure of
Indianness.

At the same time as "blood" became the defining quality of Indianness, other federal policies encouraged a pan-Indian identity. By forcing Indian children to speak English at boarding schools, the government made English a lingua franca for Indian peoples. Boarding schools, too, brought children from widely separated groups into contact. They created a sense of common problems and a network for common action among educated Indians that found expression in organizations such as the Society of American Indians in the early twentieth century. Uniform government policies created a common focus for discontent and pantribal organization.

Pan-Indianism was not only political, it was social and cultural. The peyote religion became a pantribal religion institutionalized first in Oklahoma as the Native American Church in 1918. The growth of urban Indian communities, particularly in the years following World War II, mixed Indians from numerous tribes, and like the boarding schools, fostered intermarriage among various groups. These communities, through Indian centers and in political organizations such as the American Indian Movement (AIM), created aspects of Indianness which were not tribally based. Whether culturally in powwows, religiously in the Native American Church, or politically in the activist organizations of urban Indian communities, a pan-Indian identity had emerged in which both tribal members and those who could not claim tribal membership participated. A self-identified category of ethnic Indian that only partially overlapped with tribal Indian, and was more than the image of Indians created by outsiders, had arisen.

RICHARD WHITE

See also CULTURAL PLURALISM AND MULTICULTURALISM; ETHNICITY; INDIAN–WHITE RELATIONS.

FURTHER READING

Robert Berkhofer Jr., *The White Man's Indian: Images of the American Indian from Columbus to the Present* (New York: Knopf, 1978).

Frederick Hoxie, *A Final Promise: the Campaign to Assimilate the Indians, 1880–1920* (Nebraska: University of Nebraska Press, 1984).

Peter Iverson, *Carlos Montezuma and the Changing World of American Indians* (Albuquerque: University of New Mexico Press, 1982).

William G. McLoughlin, *Cherokee Renascence in the New Republic* (Princeton: Princeton University Press, 1986).

James Merrell, *The Indians' New World: Catawbas and Their Neighbors from European Contact through the Era of Removal* (Chapel Hill: University of North Carolina Press, 1989).

individualism Long a staple principle of American culture, individualism is an almost sacred concept signifying the primacy of personal interests and self-determination. Apparently foregrounding the individual, the concept nonetheless defines that individual in relation to social, political, and economic institutions. The term has shifted in meaning as different views of the most beneficial relation between the individual and institutions have emerged and receded. Individualism has thus connoted both an antipathy to and complementarity with institutions.

While the doctrine of the preeminence of individual human life dates at least from Greek democracy, and developed vividly during the Renaissance, a specific discourse about individualism did not emerge until the nineteenth century. The word entered common usage in the 1820s and, by most accounts, owes its indelible association with the United States to ALEXIS DE TOCQUEVILLE. Writing his impressions of American mores in *Democracy in American* (1835), Tocqueville disapprovingly noted that American political economy, in promoting equality of opportunity, encouraged people to "form the habit of thinking of themselves in isolation and imagine their whole destiny is in their own hands" (p. 508). In Tocqueville's critical narrative of individualism, such interiority and self-interest epitomize the egocentrism that leads citizens to abandon civic consciousness and responsibility:

Individualism is a calm and considered feeling which disposes each citizen to isolate himself from the mass of his fellows and withdraw into the circle of family and friends; with this little society formed to his taste, he gladly leaves the greater society to look after itself. (p. 506)

Tocqueville thus located American individualism in the domestic circle, removed from society and its affairs. His pejorative assessment of individualism rests on the assumption that the private sphere was indeed the retreat that the nineteenth-century rhetoric of domesticity often proclaimed. But domestic rhetoric also distinguished the realm of personal life from the policies of self-definition at work in the American political economy, in short, from individualism. Responding to this depiction of home as a refuge *from* individualism, proponents of DOMESTICITY characterized home as a sanctuary *for* a better form of individualism. By this account, home provided individuals a necessary shelter from the recurrent economic storms that threatened the individual's place in society. Nineteenth-century social reformers working for abolitionism, temperance, and women's suffrage regularly politicized this model of domesticity, or imagined it as an alternative political design and even as a social remedy for the ills of individualism. Whereas Tocqueville situated individualism at home, separate from social institutions, American reformers often located individualism in both the private and public realms, and viewed the domestic site as both supplemental to and potentially reparative of the corrosive effects of individualism.

If Tocqueville oversimplified the character of American domestic life, and the topography of private and public domains (*see also* PRIVACY), his pejorative view of individualism coincided with American nervousness about where the principle and practice of self-interest might lead. Yet Americans also could, and did, see individualism favorably. In his celebrated definition of American individualism, RALPH WALDO EMERSON not only changed the evaluative significance of the term but revised the understanding of the relation of the individual to institutions. All the bases for Tocqueville's indictment of individualism dissolve in Emerson's delineation of the virtues of "self-reliance," published in his 1841 landmark essay of that title.

Society may be well worth shunning when considered as a "conspiracy against the manhood of every one of its members" (p. 178). Aware, however, that society is not an abstract force but a creation and composition of persons, Emerson immediately amends his characterization: "Society is a joint stock company, in which the members agree, for the better securing of his bread to each shareholder, to surrender the liberty and culture of the eater" (p. 178). By regarding society as derived from individual consent, Emerson views social constraints as surmountable because subject to individual choices and actions. Because "an institution is the lengthened shadow of one man," society and its institutions reflect the individuals who cast them (p. 185). These emanations and expressions of the self can be oppressive, as the individual inevitably, like all life-forms, moves and changes. Transition is, for Emerson, a physical law of existence and hence nonconformity to customs and institutions is crucial to the individual's balance. For forward progress, the trailing shadow of society must be ignored.

Emerson's physics of the dynamic self and society makes illusory the division between individual and institution that figured so insistently in the anxious visions of Tocqueville and others. Those visions invoked a spatial configuration in which one category appears as an encroachment upon the other. Emerson's defense of the individual posits instead a temporal distinction between individual and institution in which the always moving individuals outdate their prior actions and their effects. Since institutions follow individuals, they too are always being reinvented as individuals continually relocate and

define themselves anew. From an Emersonian perspective, then, individualism cannot be located in any particular place, public or private, since it is the activity of the self. The character of individualism is therefore variable, depending on what an individual does.

Emerson's elastic conception of individualism has provided both a rhetoric and a logic for the American development of two traditions of individualism: the economic individualism identified with the capitalistic tenets of free enterprise, competition, and private property, and the political individualism associated with the liberal concepts of consensual government and natural RIGHTS of individuals. These forms of individualism obviously predate the United States, emerging in the seventeenth century with the burgeoning of the market economy and the rise of the democratic state. Along with these developments a new definition of the individual appeared: a portrait of the (white, male) individual as proprietor of himself. According to this theory of possessive individualism, every man has property in himself, and thus the right to manage himself, his labor, and his property as he wishes. Economic and political interests therefore merge in the individual. In the nineteenth-century American setting, economic and political individualism further prospered under the aegis of laissez-faire political economy.

To this progress, Emerson's eloquent advocacy of self-reliance furnished a ready reminder of the prerogatives of self-possession. Very different self-interests could find Emerson's model of individualism serviceable. Slaveowners as well as slaves, industrialists as well as conservationists, entrepreneurs as well as laborers, Easterners as well as Westerners, could all see their actions manifesting the self-mobility that Emerson stressed. Emersonian individualism has fueled alike suffragettes' claims for women's individual rights and politicians' invocations of rugged individualism. The various uses to which Emersonian ideas have been put bear no necessary relation to Emerson's own beliefs and opinions on social and political issues. His formulation of individualism linked its forms and effects to the individuals who initiated them. The permutations that Emersonian individualism has undergone attest to the mobility which he took to be the immutable law of life.

The movements of twentieth-century American life stemming from the industrial and technological achievements of economic individualism have raised a new anxiety about individualism, a concern more about the difficulties than the dangers of pursuing self-interest. With the rise of a mass society, individuals have come to seem submerged in the large-scale agencies of work, government, and media. Commentators throughout the century have sounded elegiac notes on individualism, declaring its passing or impossibility. "Instead of the development of individualities which [individualism] prophetically set forth," JOHN DEWEY lamented in *Individualism Old and New* (1929), "there is a perversion of the whole ideal of individualism to conform to the pracices of a pecuniary culture" (p. 18). In Dewey's narrative of individualism in America, the individual is overtaken by institutions, superseded by the corporate.

> The United States has steadily moved from an earlier pioneer individualism to a condition of dominant corporateness. The influence business corporations exercise in determining present industrial and economic activities is both a cause and symbol of the tendency to combination in all phases of life. Associations tightly or loosely organized more and more define the opportunities, the choices and the actions of individuals. (p. 36)

Dewey accordingly recommended "an elimination of the older economic and political individualism," in order to spark "a stable recovery of individuality" (p. 72).

Dewey's dichotomy between individualism and corporatism—and his call for a new, restorative individualism—have set the standard for twentieth-century discussions of individualism. The plight of the modern individual, according to David Riesman's *The Lonely Crowd* (1950), is to suffer loneliness and loss of autonomy. By this representation, corporate-directed Americans suffer from isolation, not the deliberate apolitical seclusion Tocqueville imagined but a debilitating severance of self from sustaining institutions. (*See also* COMMUNITY.) Institutions impede rather than support the self-determination of the individual. Reiterating Riesman's scenario, the coauthors of a later prominent meditation on American individualism, *Habits of the Heart* (1985), worry that "individualism may have grown cancerous" (p. vii) and destructive to individuals.

These diagnoses of individualism, with their rhetoric of crisis, terminality, loss and recovery, reflect and contribute to the therapeutic ethos governing late twentieth-century contemplations of the self. The interests of the individual have become identified with psychological processes and solutions, and expressed in terms such as self-actualization and self-help. Hence the psychic well-being of the individual has become a model for the rehabilitation of individualism. Modern health and leisure institutions—psychoanalysis, psychotherapy, counselling, advice columns, talk shows, the diet and fitness industries, and self-healing books and seminars—reiterate individualistic values in narratives of self-restoration through individual effort.

Recent critiques of individualism—including the late twentieth-century intellectual movements of poststructuralism, feminism, and ethnology—target the idealized model of self projected by modern restatements of individualism. Poststucturalists stress the subject's constitution in culture, its interpenetration with cultural symbolic orders. In this view the notion of self-determination is therefore mythological, perhaps a necessary belief but indicative of the impossibility of self-control. This paradoxical characterization of individual identity—seemingly self-controlled but actually beyond the self's mastery—would seem to dissolve the claims and aims of individualism. From one feminist perspective, the poststructuralist highlighting of the cultural construction of identity aptly demonstrates the provisionality and androcentric character of individualism. Understanding identities as "the *effects* of institutions, practices, [and] discourses" of "phallogocentrism and compulsory heterosexuality," Judith Butler argues in *Gender Trouble* (p. ix), undermines the foundations of identity, thereby revealing the "possibilities" of other forms of identity or making intelligible "those possibilities that *already* exist" (p. 149).

From another feminist perspective, however, intelligible alternative versions of self can be found in already existing forms of individuality—in women and their personal styles. Exploring women's viewpoints, as Carol Gilligan does in her study of women's accounts of morality and justice, *In a Different Voice*, can reveal different models of the individual and her relation to institutions. Minority groups defined by race, ethnicity, or sexual orientation have endorsed and conducted similar reclamation projects: excavating the experiences and achievements of individuals not included within the compass of an individualism identified with white males. Patricia Williams thus writes in *The Alchemy of Race and Rights* (1991) on the intersections of commerce, the Constitution, and her black family history. In her vision of "an expanded frame of rights reference," the law which sanctioned the sale of her great-great-grandmother can be revised to encompass and protect black self-possession (p. 161). Though individualism historically has excluded women and racial minorities, it is for Williams an adjustable framework that can include more and different individuals.

While the poststructuralist critique of the subject has challenged the premises and ideals of individualism, the feminist and ethnological extensions of that critique have often striven to widen the boundaries of individualism to include the civic identities and alternative practices of women and minorities. Whether the boundaries of the individual set by individualism prove constraining (as in the elegiac reading of individualism) or fortifying (as in the reformist visions of individualism) is the question each reformulation of individualism attempts to settle.

GILLIAN BROWN

See also FEMINISM; POSTMODERNISM.

FURTHER READING

Robert N. Bellah, Richard Madsen, William M. Sullivan, Ann Swidler, and Steven M. Tipton, *Habits of the Heart: Individualism and Commitment in American Life* (Berkeley: University of California Press, 1985).
Judith Butler, *Gender Trouble: Feminism and the Subversion of Identity* (New York: Routledge, 1990).
John Dewey, *Individualism, Old and New* (1929; New York: Capricorn, 1962).
Ralph Waldo Emerson, "Self-Reliance," in Larzer Ziff, ed., *Ralph Waldo Emerson, Selected Essays* (New York: Penguin, 1982).
Carol Gilligan, *In a Different Voice: Psychological Theory and Women's Development* (Cambridge: Harvard University Press, 1992).
Thomas C. Heller, Morton Sosna, and David E. Wellerby, eds., *Reconstructing Individualism: Autonomy, Individuality, and the Self in Western Thought* (Stanford: Stanford University Press, 1986).
C. B. Macpherson, *The Political Theory of Possessive Individualism: Hobbes to Locke* (London: Oxford University Press, 1962).
David Riesman, with Nathan Glazer and Reuel Denney, *The Lonely Crowd: a Study of the Changing American Character* (New Haven: Yale University Press, 1959).
Alexis de Tocqueville, *Democracy in America*, 2 vols. trans. George Lawrence, ed. J. P. Mayer (1835, 1840; New York: Anchor-Doubleday, 1969).
Patricia J. Williams, *The Alchemy of Race and Rights* (Cambridge: Harvard University Press, 1991).

industrialism　No force played a greater role in shaping the substance and character of late nineteenth- and early twentieth-century American intellectual life than did the rise of industrialism. The rapid growth of large-scale industry in the United States during the post-Civil War period posed fundamental challenges to institutions, values, and modes of governance that had taken form in a rural agrarian society. How best to respond—or for some, adapt—to industrialism became a matter of extraordinarily sharp and lively debate among intellectuals, social critics, populist agitators, labor activists, anarchists, and what some contemporary observers viewed as an all-too-vocal array of "amateurs."

Industrialism posed three especially vexing problems for turn-of-the-century Americans, problems that would, in turn, profoundly shape the content of intellectual life. The vast scale and tremendously expanded power of industrial organizations raised deep concern, first, about the apparently diminishing roles of individuals in modern SOCIETY. "Man" (and woman) against "society"—the struggle of a single human being against the impersonality of cities, the overweening power of concentrated capital, and the crushing pace of new TECHNOLOGY—was the unifying theme in the stark NATURALISM of American literature, the slashing commentary of contemporary criticism, and the empirical research of many academic social scientists.

American fiction especially reflected a preoccupation with the fate of individuals at the hands of urban industrial society. From Rebecca Harding Davis's searing novella, *Life in the Iron Mills* (1861), to Stephen Crane's grim depiction of urban life in *Maggie: A Girl of the Streets* (1893), through Theodore Dreiser's wrenching tale of *Sister Carrie* (1900), Frank Norris's brutal account of cut-throat economic competition, *The Octopus* (1901), and Upton Sinclair's infamous depiction of industrial workers in *The Jungle* (1906), American writers portrayed through the tragic life stories of individuals the greater evils of industrialism. The social surveys conducted by various professionals, academic intellectuals, and settlement house workers—*Hull-House Maps and Papers* (1895) and the Pittsburgh Survey (1909–14) are notable examples—also attempted to locate within vast urban communities people, often impoverished, who were struggling to survive economic downturns and the chaos of urban life. Finally, social critics such as JACOB RIIS felt compelled to describe for middle-class Americans *How the Other Half Lives* (1890), recognizing that in turn-of-the-century America the evolution of industrial society made it all too easy not to know.

Industrialism challenged, as well, the faith many Americans placed in restricted government and a laissez-faire economy. Leading writers and intellectuals only sharpened and heightened this sense of unease. The unrelenting tales of political corruption and economic exploitation constructed by early twentieth-century MUCKRAKING journalists such as LINCOLN STEFFENS and Ida M. Tarbell helped shape public opinion in ways that created a political climate increasingly receptive to government regulation and reform. Economists JOHN R. COMMONS and Selig Perlman stressed the importance of trade unionism to the stability of American capitalism, a message that echoed the sentiments of many labor activists. THORSTEIN VEBLEN painted a devastating portrait of the cultural irrationality of American capitalism in *The Theory of the Leisure Class* (1899), though he avoided reform advocacy. Other intellectuals such as WILLIAM GRAHAM SUMNER responded to the debate by affirming the inherent wisdom of laissez-faire.

Industrialism ultimately forced Americans to consider how the institutions, values, and ways of life of an agricultural society could be harmonized with modern factories, huge business organizations, wide-scale wage labor, and vast cities (*see also* URBANISM). Thoughtful Americans advanced an often bewildering array of solutions to these new problems. Utopian socialists such as EDWARD BELLAMY envisaged a future in which technology and industry were perfectly joined to the human needs of society. Scarcity, "wage slavery," inequality, and social conflict would all be eliminated as the United States underwent a peaceful revolution by the year 2000. Yet the title of Bellamy's novel, *Looking Backward* (1888), betrayed the persistence of rural agrarian values in a future marked by beautiful rolling parks, abundant natural resources, and ample rewards for hard work and individual merit. Future Americans enjoyed the fruits of industry in a society all but devoid of factories.

Reformers who rooted their initiatives in the here and now displayed a similarly ambivalent posture toward industrialism. As is true today, some activists hoped to extend through enlarged social welfare measures the benefits of American industrial capitalism to groups that lagged behind. They debated, however, the wisdom of expanding governmental authority to achieve these aims. Others insisted upon diligent regulation of industry and a strict separation of business from politics. Even as they criticized the worst abuses of modern industry, they admired its efficiency and productivity. Agrarian radicals seemed to recognize the permanence of modern industry and the power of capital, while vociferously championing the rights of the producing classes. But conflict over how those rights could best be realized bedeviled groups such as the Populists who sought to ally farmers and workers, a challenge made no less formidable by the march of modern industry.

The range of reaction to American industrialism was wide; the controversy it inspired ran deep. But what was perhaps most notable in the struggle was the extraordinary prominence and power of ideas. Social research became an agent of change for Progressive reformers intent on transforming public policy. Investigative journalism helped to shape the dynamics of politics. New social scientific theories found their way into legislative initiatives. Academic expertise carried with it new forms of social and political authority. Even the most radical of critics employed the power of the pen to promote their cause. These trends were advanced by vastly improved and increasingly nationalized communication networks. Industrialism shattered forever the boundaries that separated formal ideas about society from the diverse uses political actors might make of these forceful agents of social change.

Scholars have pondered the nature, meaning, and significance of industrialism virtually from its inception. The topic proved to be especially central to the development of SOCIAL SCIENCE, which was undergoing professionalization during the 1880s and 1890s, a critical stage in the evolution of industrial society. Many scholars, including the talented political economist EDITH ABBOTT, attempted at first simply to chart the impact of industrial growth on wages, markets, employment, and the standard of living. An institutional approach to the study of modern industry soon emerged. Labor always formed an important intellectual focus, as in the writings of RICHARD ELY and in the work of John R. Commons and his students, especially their massive *History of Labour in the United States* (4 vols., 1918–35).

Important tensions have characterized the literature on American industrialism. Recent scholars such as Alfred Chandler have illuminated the vital advances made possible through the economies of scale and scope achieved by modern industry. Historians such as Samuel Hays and Robert Wiebe have emphasized the ways in which economic and social change produced a newly "organized" society. They portrayed a complex and variegated "response to industrialism" that mixed progress and defeat. Others have portrayed these developments in a much harsher light. Gabriel Kolko, for instance, has stressed the ways in which even the reforms that shaped modern industry speeded a "triumph of conservatism." Melvyn Dubofsky, David Brody, and Herbert Gutman have revealed the appalling conditions and grueling pace of late nineteenth- and early twentieth-century industrial work, factors that made the work place a living hell for too many industrial laborers.

These debates will continue as powerful monographic research in women's history, labor history, economic history, ethnic history, and African American history continues to enrich contemporary understanding of industrialism's many meanings. As turn-of-the-century Americans understood so well, there is no way to grasp the character of modern America without confronting the complex realities of industrialism.

ELLEN FITZPATRICK

See also MANAGERIALISM.

FURTHER READING

Edith Abbott, *Women in Industry* (New York: D. Appleton, 1910).

Alfred P. Chandler, *The Visible Hand: the Managerial Revolution in American Business* (Cambridge: Harvard University Press, 1977).

Samuel Hays, *The Response to Industrialism, 1885–1914* (Chicago: University of Chicago Press, 1957).

Morton Keller, *Affairs of State: Public Life in Late Nineteenth Century America* (Cambridge: Harvard University Press, 1977).

Gabriel Kolko, *The Triumph of Conservatism* (New York: Free Press, 1963).

Richard P. McCormick, "The Discovery that Business Corrupts Politics: a Reappraisal of the Origins of Progressivism," *American Historical Review* 86 (1981): 247–74.

Dorothy Ross, *The Origins of American Social Science* (New York: Cambridge University Press, 1991).

Robert H. Wiebe, *The Search for Order, 1877–1920* (New York: Hill and Wang, 1977).

intelligence A word of much cultural resonance in late twentieth-century America, to some intelligence is a measure which can be used to assess human beings objectively, without regard to class, race, ethnicity, or gender. To others intelligence has become a symbol, especially as embodied in standardized tests, of the arbitrary imposition of a single cultural standard on a diverse population and of the deleterious social consequences that can result.

Historically, the concept of intelligence became socially charged only during the nineteenth century, after champions of the ENLIGHTENMENT and practical revolutionaries alike had turned to notions of mental capacity as a partial solution to a particular political problem: having either rhetorically or literally toppled aristocratically organized societies, they wondered what basis for social distinction, if any, was to be introduced. For eighteenth-century writers such as Mary Wollstonecraft, Tom Paine, and Thomas Jefferson, the answer was some type of meritocratic republic. VIRTUE constituted one of the preferred foundations for these new enlightened states; mental attributes, though in the form of "talents" rather than "intelligence," served as another.

Beginning in the early nineteenth century with the post-Revolutionary political consolidations, two important changes occurred. First, anthropologists and biologists, including Samuel Morton and the American school of anthropology, constructed a language of mental capacity in the singular, around the concept of intelligence, that they employed to describe and analyze human beings at the level of groups. Created by transforming reason from an absolute into a characteristic that could be manifested in degrees, intelligence and its synonyms provided a new justification for arraying the animal and human worlds in a simple linear order, now according to

level of mental power. The result was a straightforward scientific explanation of two largely uncontested "truths" of late eighteenth- and early nineteenth-century Western thought: that humans, and more specifically white male Europeans, held pride of place in the animal kingdom, and that European civilization was distinctly superior to all others.

Second, the "talents" half of "virtues and talents" was partially eclipsed as the Victorian preoccupation with character began to dominate social discourse and to subsume other modes of analysis. Regarding the world as a moral theater in which virtue was rewarded and venality punished, Victorians in general and American Whigs in particular stressed the independent, self-determining nature of human beings, the visitation of success or failure as a function of personal worthiness, and the maintenance of a social hierarchy reflecting in large measure the degree of individual virtue.

By the late nineteenth century, however, members of the middle and upper classes had begun to alter their understanding of human nature: genetic endowment became essential to character. Responding to the immense social transformations of the period—including the development of more highly differentiated industrial economies, larger and more obviously culturally diverse cities, and expanded electorates—Americans developed new categories for evaluating the actions of human beings. (*See also* INDUSTRIALISM and URBANISM.) "Intelligence" was one of these. The very meaning of the term narrowed over the course of the nineteenth century, as certain senses of intelligence ("news" and "knowledge") dropped out of common parlance, and intelligence as "ability" became paramount. By the early twentieth century this more restricted denotation was also accorded a new explanatory power. Drawing on notions about human difference developed primarily in philosophy/psychology and anthropology, intellectuals on both sides of the Atlantic increasingly argued that intelligence was a measurable, normally distributed trait, biological in origin and genetically transmitted, that served to characterize in some essential way the nature and value of each individual. Criminality, poverty, and vice all became for many the products not of personal moral failure, but genetic mental inadequacy. Particularly in the United States, the degree of an individual's intelligence was used to explain both what that individual did and where he or she fitted within the social order. (*See also* HEREDITY; SOCIAL DARWINISM.)

Central to this shift in the cultural status of intelligence was the creation by psychologists in the early twentieth century of the mental test, which could make visible fine grades of difference between levels of intelligence, while invoking the authority of science to establish the "reality" of such distinctions. Employed on an unprecedented scale by the U.S. Army during World War I, when over 1.75 million soldiers were examined, intelligence testing enjoyed an enormous boom in the postwar period, when it was widely adopted within American education and industry. Although intelligence testing soon underwent a period of sharp retrenchment in fields outside education, the same cannot be said of "intelligence" itself. As the term "I.Q." was popularized by the rapid spread of intelligence testing, by the late 1920s the idea of "intelligence" as a measurable, unilinear quality became a well-established feature of the American intellectual landscape.

One of the strongest attractions of the concept of intelligence has been that it provides an easily comprehensible explanation for why certain people perform better than others at particular tasks, especially those activities deemed to involve some type of higher reasoning. Elite groups in American society have invoked intelligence to justify their privileged status while maintaining allegiance to a language of meritocratic democracy. Because intelligence came to be constructed biologically—as an innate, heritable, differential reasoning ability distributed on a unidimensional scale—it could be represented as transcending class lines and thus as constituting an inherently egalitarian criterion for selection. Because members of privileged socioeconomic groups generally perform better on tests of intelligence, the concept in its twentieth-century form has offered a way to constrain some of the democratizing potential of merit-based decisions. Finally, in a culture in which educational resources and occupational opportunities must be allocated, assessments of intelligence have proven, at least until the 1970s or 1980s, to be a socially acceptable means of justifying such determinations. In recent years, however, controversy has flared over the objectivity of such intelligence-based decisions, especially as claims by Richard Herrnstein, William Shockley, and Arthur Jensen that African Americans are as a group biologically inferior with regard to intelligence have renewed charges that intelligence tests are inherently culturally biased. The politics of intelligence, as a result, expressed in what the term denotes, who measures or controls it, and how it is used, remains a vital issue in the contemporary intellectual world.

JOHN CARSON

See also SCIENCE; SOCIOBIOLOGY.

FURTHER READING

Carl Degler, *In Search of Human Nature: the Decline and Revival of Darwinism in American Social Thought* (New York: Oxford University Press, 1991).
Paula Fass, "The IQ: a Cultural and Historical Framework," *American Journal of Education* 88, (Aug. 1980): 431–58.
Richard J. Herrnstein and Charles Murray, *The Bell Curve: Intelligence and Class Structure in American Life* (New York: Free Press, 1994).
Winthrop D. Jordan, *White Over Black: American Attitudes toward the Negro, 1550–1812* (New York: Norton, 1977).
Daniel J. Kevles, *In the Name of Eugenics: Genetics and the Uses of Human Heredity* (New York: Knopf, 1985).
Michael M. Sokal, ed., *Psychological Testing and American Society, 1890–1930* (New Brunswick: Rutgers University Press, 1987).
Gillian Sutherland, *Ability, Merit and Measurement: Mental Testing and English Education, 1880–1940* (Oxford: Clarendon Press, 1984).
Lewis M. Terman, *The Measurement of Intelligence* (Boston: Houghton Mifflin, 1916).

Irving, Washington (b. New York, N.Y., Apr. 3, 1783; d. Tarrytown, N.Y., Nov. 28, 1859). Writer. While Irving's earliest works were irreverently humorous sketches of New York urban life, he soon turned to the romantic evocation of a picturesque past in England, Spain, and the American frontier. *The Sketch Book of Geoffrey Crayon, Gent* (1819–20) contains the classic stories "The Legend of Sleepy Hollow" and "Rip Van Winkle." *A Tour on the Prairies* (1835) and *Astoria* (1836), accounts of a western journey, along with his *History of the Life and Voyages of Columbus* (1828), establish him in retrospect as an important and innovative celebrant of western expansion.

FURTHER READING

Peter Antelyes, *Tales of Adventurous Enterprise: Washington Irving and the Poetics of Western Expansion* (New York: Columbia University Press, 1990).

J

Jackson, Helen Hunt (b. Amherst, Mass., Oct. 15, 1830; d. San Francisco, Calif., Aug. 12, 1885). Poet, novelist, and reformer. Jackson's *A Century of Dishonor* (1881) chronicled the federal government's repeated betrayals of INDIANS, stimulated a reform movement, and led to her appointment to a federal commission investigating the conditions of Indians in California missions. Her novel *Ramona* (1884) portrayed the Indians' plight even more vividly, while her other writings exalted the idyllic beauty of the Southwest and its Spanish past before Anglo arrivals. Her poetry's precise form and expressive elegance earned her a reputation as the best female poet of her time.

FURTHER READING
Valerie Sherer Mathes, *Helen Hunt Jackson and Her Indian Reform Legacy* (Austin: University of Texas Press, 1990).

Jackson, Robert H. (b. Spring Creek, Pa., Feb. 13, 1892; d. Washington, D.C., Oct. 9, 1954). Supreme Court Justice (1941–54). Jackson entered the Court as a liberal supporter of New Deal policies, a defender of freedom of speech and assembly, and an advocate of judicial restraint: legislation, he argued, represents the people's will. The Nazis' manipulation of the popular will converted him to a belief in immutable principles of law. Appointed the United States Chief Prosecutor for the Nuremberg trials, he argued that German government, military, and industrial officials were criminally responsible for executing Nazi policies. He developed the notion of a crime against humanity in *The Case Against the Nazi War Criminals* (1946) and *The Nuremberg Case* (1947).

FURTHER READING
Charles S. Desmond et al., *Mr. Justice Jackson* (New York: Columbia University Press, 1969).

James, Alice (b. New York, N.Y., Aug. 7, 1848; d. London, England, Mar. 6, 1892). Diarist. Leaving only a brilliant journal that reveals a vigorous intellect reflecting on politics, literature, history, and the people around her, James devoted her life to invalidism, self-subordination, and preparing for her own death. Describing herself as a barnacle, a hard core of selfhood, she embraced her society's image of the passive, sick, and self-sacrificing woman, but converted it into her own energetic labor. She proclaimed her willed resistance to the "strenuous life" celebrated by her brother WILLIAM JAMES.

See also DIARIES.

FURTHER READING
Jean Strouse, *Alice James: a Biography* (Boston: Houghton Mifflin, 1980).

James, Henry, Sr. (b. Albany, N.Y., June 3, 1811; d. Cambridge, Mass., Dec. 18, 1882). Philosopher. A devotee of Swedenborg and Fourier, James used his inheritance to fund his own writing and lecturing and the education of his children. God's highest creation, James believed, is not individual human beings, but humanity as a whole. People need to be redeemed from the illusion of selfhood, in which the individual is separate from the Creator and humanity, into a divine Society in which people love as God loves, impartially. Social democracy frees the spirit from the constraints of tradition and foreshadows the future unity of societal and individual interests. James authored *Society the Redeemed Form of Man, and the Earnest of God's Omnipotence in Human Nature* (1879), but his greatest intellectual work was his contribution, as a gifted conversationalist and thinker, to the education of his sons William and Henry and his daughter Alice.

FURTHER READING
R. W. B. Lewis, *The Jameses: a Family Narrative* (New York: Farrar, Straus, Giroux, 1991).

James, Henry (b. New York, N.Y., Apr. 15, 1843; d. London, England, Feb. 28, 1916). Novelist, critic and man of letters, James spent his boyhood in New York, London, Paris, and Geneva, thanks to his peripatetic and independently wealthy philosopher father HENRY JAMES SR. In his invaluable study *The James Family*, F. O. Matthiessen reports that the philosopher and psychologist WILLIAM JAMES once said of his younger brother Henry, "He's really, I won't say a Yankee, but a native of the James family, and has no other country" (p. 303). The near legendary James family, which also included two younger brothers and an invalid sister ALICE JAMES, whose fascinating diary was posthumously published, did indeed seem a country unto itself. Its intellectual atmosphere was intense to the point of delirium. As Henry recalled in his *Autobiography*, "ambiguity of view and of measure" flourished while "we breathed inconsistency and ate and drank contradictions" (pp. 123–4). Pressured by their father's relentless appetite for speculation and iconoclasm, and for travel, all the children suffered numerous illnesses and anxieties, with William and Alice becoming afflicted nearly to the point of suicide.

The overheated, hermetic quality of life in the James family mirrors the image endorsed by many critics of Henry James as a hermetic novelist of exquisite sensitivity and Olympian detachment who, like his characters, turns his back on an impossibly vulgar modern world to cultivate what critics were once fond of calling redemptive consciousness. Enshrined as a high priest of formalism and genteel aesthete, James was installed in the modernist pantheon by R. P. Blackmur, who in 1934 described him as the "novelist of the free spirit, the liberated intelligence," and the "ideal vision." That essay conveniently marks the official canonization of Henry James, who has been ever since one of the most prestigious, indeed, sacred cultural icons on the altar of American high culture. There is an undeniable and significant measure of truth in the official portrait, even though it purports to be a fixed image of an author who was always skeptical of the static, whose restless mind conceived of the way out as the way through.

The canonized image of James the cultural icon further lacks even a suggestion of the author of *The American Scene*. This work, James's account of his year-long repatriation to America in 1904, after nearly three decades of residence in London, is usually treated as an oddity in the Jamesian canon, the eccentric travelogue of a reactionary, Anglicized aesthete. The work has always had its admirers; Ezra Pound, W. H. Auden and Edmund Wilson all found it remarkable. But only in recent years, under the impetus of a NEW LITERARY HISTORICISM, has *The American Scene* come to be recognized as an indispensable work of American cultural analysis, one that culminates, as it extends, the concerns of James's fiction. Enacting the subtle power of James's profoundly historical imagination, *The American Scene* confronts on the most intimate bodily level the unsettling challenge of urban modernity, most memorably, perhaps, as James finds himself sympathetically, if uneasily, identifying with the "aliens" he encounters while walking the turbulent streets of New York's Lower East Side. The revaluation of *The American Scene* has prompted an increased skepticism of the conventional image of James as antimodernist and anti-immigrant.

While James may be mired in the nativist prejudices of his social class, he is unusual in submitting those prejudices to the tonic shock of total immersion.

With the publication in 1904 of *The Golden Bowl*, his last complete novel, the so-called major phase of James's fiction concludes and the canonical James ends. But James did not. He went on to create, as recent critics realize, a second major phase (1907–14) of autobiography, cultural criticism, and aesthetics. The motto of this cluster of texts might be James's declaration in the preface to *The American Scene*: "I would stand on my gathered impressions. . . . I would in fact go to the stake for them . . . naked and unashamed." This sounds the most characteristic note—intimate, vulnerable, defiant—of his self-representation throughout the late nonfiction. In these works, as in the late novel *The Ambassadors* (1903), James audaciously depicts the complexities of Enlightenment rationalism's ascetic adherence to fixed identity, as he revises the structure of repression that constitutes bourgeois subjectivity.

In a letter of 1903 quoted by Matthiessen, James reported that he looked forward to visiting America "absolutely *for* . . . the shocks in general" (p. 310). The restless urban *flaneur* of *The American Scene*, like the gaping, strolling young boy of the autobiographies, and Lambert Strether of *The Ambassadors*, improvises the rhythms of vagrant motions, as he drifts, untethered. This willed vulnerability to contingency and trauma recalls Baudelaire and anticipates Walter Benjamin. But James's *flanerie* is also deeply American, for his openness recalls his brother William James's (and later John Dewey's) commitment, characteristic of PRAGMATISM, to risk and hazard as the condition of the noncognitive flux of experience. James is immediately assaulted by flux in *The American Scene*; he feels "instant vibrations" of curiosity prompted "at every turn, in sights, sounds, smells, even in the chaos of confusion and change" (p. 1). The stylistic triumph of James's late work resides in his ability to mime in prose the dissonant rhythms of a meandering curiosity preternaturally alive to the vertiginous texture of modernity.

ROSS POSNOCK

FURTHER READING

J. C. Agnew, "The Consuming Vision of Henry James" in Richard Fox and Jackson Lears, eds., *The Culture of Consumption* (New York: Pantheon, 1983).

William Boelhower, *Through a Glass Darkly: Ethnic Semiosis in American Literature* (New York: Oxford University Press, 1987).

Jonathan Freedman, *Professions of Taste: Henry James, British Aestheticism, and Commodity Culture* (Stanford: Stanford University Press, 1990).

Laurence B. Holland, *The Expense of Vision* (1964; Baltimore: Johns Hopkins University Press, 1982).

Henry James, *Autobiography* (New York: Criterion, 1956).

——, *The Art of the Novel*, ed. and with an introduction (1934) by R. P. Blackmur (New York: Scribner's, 1962).

——, *The American Scene* (Bloomington: Indiana University Press, 1969).

——, *Literary Criticism: American and English Writers* (New York: Library of America, 1984).

F. O. Matthiessen, *The James Family* (New York: Knopf, 1961).

Ross Posnock, *The Trial of Curiosity: Henry James, William James, and the Challenge of Modernity* (New York: Oxford University Press, 1991).

James, William (b. New York, N.Y., Jan. 11, 1842; d. Chocorua, N.H., Aug. 26, 1910). "He is just like a blob of mercury," William James's sister ALICE JAMES once remarked about him, "you can't put a mental finger on him." Her image suggests the vitality of James's personality, the elusiveness of his philosophy, and the challenge facing later interpreters who have struggled to produce a stable account of his life and thought.

William James was the oldest son of the independently wealthy Swedenborgian philosopher HENRY JAMES SR., who was well connected in American intellectual circles but frequently uprooted his family for extended trips to Europe. Unlike his younger, equally cosmopolitan brother, the novelist HENRY JAMES, whose expatriation he could never understand, William remained self-consciously American even though he was as much at home in Europe as in the United States.

Trained successively as a painter, a scientist, and a medical doctor, William James was by his late twenties tortured by indecision about what to do with his manifold gifts. Suffering from depression as well as recurring eye, back, and intestinal problems, he experimented with various rest cures commonly offered for relief from the "neurasthenia" that afflicted so many affluent, well-educated Americans, including his sister Alice. During his four years of wrestling with persistent, at times near-suicidal, depression, he continued to read widely in nineteenth-century European and American science and philosophy. He was torn between romantic idealism and scientific naturalism; his inability to reconcile freedom with the logic of determinism left him emotionally paralyzed.

On May 22, 1868, James recorded in his diary "an unspeakable disgust for the dead drifting of my own life for some time past." As he sank deeper, he reached a crisis that has become as familiar as the similar experience of John Stuart Mill. His notebook entry on April 30, 1870, indicates that James found the lifeline he needed in the writings of the French philosopher Charles Renouvier, who defined free will as the conscious decision to sustain a thought when one might choose to have other thoughts. In that primal experience of selective attention in consciousness, "the self-governing *resistance* of the ego to the world," James found strength (*Letters*, vol. 1, pp. 147–8).

From his "collapse" James ascended only slowly. As a scientist, he had to find a way to reconcile his commitment to freedom with Darwin's theory of evolution. The human capacity for choice, he reasoned, must have evolved over time due to selective pressure. He was fortified further by the invitation to teach anatomy and physiology at Harvard beginning in 1872, and even more profoundly stabilized by his courtship of Alice Howe Gibbons, whom he met in 1876 and married in 1878. In that year too James began work on *The Principles of Psychology* (1890), which remains a classic of American thought. Although much of it is now obsolete because so much more is known about the physiology of the brain, the book remains valuable because James wrote so evocatively about aspects of the mind that still puzzle and intrigue cognitive scientists.

James set out in *Principles* to reconceive the problems of epistemology and psychology. He believed that rationalists and idealists depended on the existence of a mysterious and unverifiable something that lay behind conscious experience. Empiricists, according to James, did well to dispense with the rationalists' spooky "mind dust," but they faced another problem. They could not account for the existence of free choices that human beings repeatedly make. James sought to resolve the debate with a single bold stroke: both rationalists and empiricists misconceived experience by separating the mind from the external world. We should instead see that immediate experience precedes the division between subjective and objective that occurs only in reflection on experience, not in the midst of it. By rejecting subject-object dualism, and replacing it with a conception of human experience as the intersection of internal and external, James inspired European phenomenologists such as Edmund Husserl, Alfred Schutz, and Maurice Merleau-Ponty, as well as Americans including James Edie, John Wild, and Bruce Wilshire.

The second, and equally fertile, new idea in James's *Principles* was his conception of consciousness as a stream. Whereas empiricists had tried to explain how the mind associates the bits and pieces of experience, and idealists since Kant had envisioned time and space as the transcendental forms that provide the structure of human experience, James stated flatly that both traditions were mistaken. "No one ever had a simple sensation by itself," he wrote in the *Principles*. "Consciousness, from our natal day, is of a teeming multiplicity of objects and relations, and what we call simple sensations are results of discriminative attention, pushed often to a very high degree." We do not experience the world "chopped up in bits." Consciousness "is nothing jointed." Instead it flows; a "'river' or 'stream' are the metaphors by which it is most naturally described. In talking of it hereafter," he concluded, "let us call it the stream of thought, of consciousness, or of subjective life" (vol. 1, pp. 224, 239). By taking that step, Alfred North Whitehead has observed, James inaugurated the modernist era. James's student GERTRUDE STEIN was among the first to use the now-familiar stream of consciousness as a narrative technique.

James's *Principles* also pointed psychology away from the physiological, laboratory-centered German psychology he started with and toward an eclectic approach to the mind, an approach very different from the BEHAVIORISM that has preoccupied so many American social scientists. When he emphasized the relatedness of phenomena in our perception and insisted that selective attention itself requires voluntary choice, he underscored dimensions of experience often neglected by physiological and behaviorist psychologists. His work inspired rival schools that have worked quietly but persistently in Europe and America to challenge behaviorism. Whether under the banner of the Gestalt psychology developed by the students of Max Wertheimer, Kurt Koffka, and especially Wolfgang Köhler, or in the cognitive psychology inspired by Jean Piaget, or among the disordered ranks of "humanist" psychologists, a number of psychologists have followed James in insisting that perception is not stimulus-bound but relational, creative, and colored by cultural values.

Rich as *The Principles of Psychology* remains, James's writings about religion are perhaps even more widely read today. James advanced most of his ideas in public lectures before audiences of educated nonspecialists; for that reason his formulations are unusually arresting but often vague. He delivered "The Will to Believe" at Yale and Brown universities in 1896, then the lectures that became *The Varieties of Religious Experience* at the University of Edinburgh in 1900–2. In "The Will to Believe," he declared that we must rely on "our passional nature" to make decisions whenever we face a real dilemma, a "genuine option," and we cannot find conclusive evidence for either option. Since religious questions cannot be answered conclusively, he concluded, "we have the right to believe at our own risk any hypothesis that is live

enough to tempt our will" (*Writings, 1878–1899*, pp. 464, 477). In the essay James carefully stipulated what he meant by a "genuine option," a "live" hypothesis, and the "risk" involved in choosing a belief. He stressed that skepticism is more appropriate than belief in many instances, especially in the realm of experimental science, and he emphasized the importance of trying to verify truth claims empirically despite all the obstacles we face.

Those careful qualifications notwithstanding, James was widely misunderstood as arguing that religion is true because it makes believers feel good. Although a bad parody of a subtle argument, such criticism likewise greeted James's *Varieties*, which provided perceptive examinations of religious *experience*, and provocative reflections concerning the consequences of belief, rather than arguments for the truth value of religious doctrine.

James elaborated his theory of truth in the set of lectures published in 1907 as *Pragmatism*. He again cautioned against the notion that whatever feels good is true: our "ideas must agree with realities," he insisted. But where no such process of verification was possible, as in propositions concerning metaphysics, ethics, and religion, James invoked a different standard and indulged his flair for the dramatic: "Truth happens to an idea. It becomes true, is made true by events." James's critics were not amused or persuaded. His Harvard colleague Josiah Royce wondered if a pragmatist would ask a witness in a court of law to tell the expedient, the whole expedient, and nothing but the expedient, so help him future experience. James had emphasized that, in circumstances in which it is appropriate to invoke the pragmatic test, "*The true is the name of whatever proves itself to be good in the way of belief, and good, too, for definite, assignable reasons*" (*Writings, 1902–1910*, pp. 520, 574, 578). Because his critics—and even some of his friends, notably JOHN DEWEY—were not sure what those reasons were, James tried to clarify what he meant.

In *The Meaning of Truth* (1909), he specified three conditions necessary for establishing that a statement is pragmatically true. First, it must correspond to what is known about the natural world. "The notion of a reality independent of . . . us, taken from ordinary social experience, lies at the base of the pragmatist definition of truth." As an "epistemological realist," James explained, he took that condition so much for granted that he did not consider its discussion philosophically interesting. Second, the statement must be consistent with an individual's stock of existing beliefs, "the rest of acknowledged truth," a condition that attached to the verification process a necessary brake obviating the possibility of solipsism or simple-minded wishful thinking. Finally, a statement may be considered pragmatically true if it fulfills the first two conditions *and* yields satisfaction. That satisfaction is irrelevant if the first two conditions are not fulfilled (*Writings, 1902–1910*, pp. 925, 935, 943).

Oddly enough, some of James's most enthusiastic contemporary champions embrace versions of PRAGMATISM that echo his most unsympathetic critics' characterizations of his ideas and overlook James's own clarifications of his meaning. Whereas some postmodernists characterize as pragmatic their denunciations of all claims to truth as illusory, James insisted that the pragmatic test must extend beyond the discursive sphere.

In addition to his philosophical writings, James intervened in political disputes and wrote essays in cultural criticism. He passionately opposed American suppression of the indigenous forces in the Philippines at the end of the Spanish-American War. On March 1, 1899, he wrote to the *Boston Evening Transcript*, "We are now openly engaged in crushing out the sacredest thing in this great human world— the attempt of a people long enslaved to attain the possession of itself, to organize its laws and government, to be free to follow its internal destinies according to its own ideals." The brutality of American intervention revealed that the emerging behemoth of organized, expansionist capitalism was a "big, hollow, resounding, corrupting, sophisticating, confusing torrent of mere brutal momentum and irrationality."

James's social criticism belies the common view that unlike his fellow pragmatists Dewey and GEORGE HERBERT MEAD, James was an individualist unconcerned about the social self or social justice. He did worry that "an irremediable flatness is coming over the world." He feared that "the higher heroisms and the old rare flavors are passing out of life" (*Writings, 1878–1899*, p. 865). But he understood as clearly as Dewey or Mead that immediate experience itself is irreducibly social, all judgments are value-laden, and the pragmatic method requires interpersonal truth testing. As he put it in *Pragmatism*, "We trade on each other's truth." Indeed, James insisted in *The Meaning of Truth*, pragmatism has a "stronger hold on reality than any other philosophy" precisely because it is "essentially a *social* philosophy, a philosophy of 'co,' in which conjunctions do the work" (*Writings, 1902–1910*, pp. 577, 892). Individual voluntary action remained for James the engine driving society, but the social nature of individual consciousness and the necessity of testing ideas by bringing them before the bar of social experience rule out atomistic individualism.

James's observations about politics do not reflect the complacent elitism that has been attributed to him. In *The Varieties of Religious Experience* he applauded the "sound antipathy for lives based on mere having" that motivated much anticapitalist sentiment. He hoped the democratic spirit of egalitarianism would gradually erode human acquisitiveness and enrich the spirit of humanity that "refuses to enjoy anything that others do not share" (*Writings, 1902–1910*, pp. 292, 297). Society, he wrote, must develop toward a "newer and better equilibrium," and the unjust distribution of wealth must change. But even for those whose material circumstances would improve, such change would guarantee neither happiness nor satisfaction (*Writings, 1878–1899*, p. 878). James denied that political or economic reform, important as they were, could solve problems he considered fundamentally ethical and philosophical.

Celebration of diversity was among the central values James embraced. His impassioned defense of difference, whether in the case of rebellious Filipinos or religious eccentrics, made him an awkward member of the refined late-Victorian academic gentry. Today his position makes him an important figure for debates about diversity in American culture. In his essay "On a Certain Blindness in Human Beings," James argued that his philosophical creed "commands us to tolerate, respect, and indulge" those who live differently from ourselves, "however unintelligible" their ways may be to us. "Hands off," James insisted, when dealing with social and cultural diversity, for "neither the whole of truth nor the whole of good is revealed to any single observer" (*Writings, 1878–1899*, p. 860).

James's critics have been troubled by the apparent evasiveness of his politics as much as by the apparent imprecision of his philosophical writings. But his detachment from partisan politics was deliberate. Despite his participation in particular political debates, he argued that in general "the mission of the educated intellect in society" is to remain critical of all popular passions. He realized that this attitude is "generally unpopular and distasteful" to those who want passionate commitment. James was among the first Americans to adopt as a badge of honor the epithet "intellectual" that was hurled as a reproach at those who defended Alfred Dreyfus in France. "The intellectual critic as such knows of so many interests, that to the ardent partisan he seems to have none," James admitted (Perry, vol. 2, pp. 298–9). Yet he persisted in his belief that intellectuals must maintain their intellectual independence. In *Contingency, Irony, and Solidarity* (1989), RICHARD RORTY advises contemporary pragmatists to adopt a similarly detached position as "liberal ironists." The distance between Rorty and such activist intellectuals as Cornel West, Nancy Fraser, and Robert Westbrook, who criticize Rorty for defending the private–public split, indicates that the question of striking a balance between engagement and independence remains equally challenging for intellectuals today. James's own writings and career suggest that cherishing individuality and difference need not inhibit the intellectual's passionate commitment to democratic activism, and that such activism need not erode commitment to independence of mind and to cultural diversity.

JAMES T. KLOPPENBERG

FURTHER READING

James M. Edie, *William James and Phenomenology* (Bloomington: Indiana University Press, 1987).

William James, *The Principles of Psychology*, 2 vols. (1890; Cambridge: Harvard University Press, 1981).

——, *Writings, 1878–1899*, ed. Gerald E. Myers (New York: Library of America, 1992).

——, *Writings, 1902–1910*, ed. Bruce Kuklick (New York: Library of America, 1987).

——, *The Letters of William James*, ed. Henry James, 2 vols. (1920; New York: Kraus, 1969).

James T. Kloppenberg, *Uncertain Victory: Social Democracy and Progressivism in European and American Thought, 1870–1920* (New York: Oxford University Press, 1986).

Henry Samuel Levinson, *The Religious Investigations of William James* (Chapel Hill: University of North Carolina Press, 1981).

R. W. B. Lewis, *The Jameses: a Family Narrative* (New York: Farrar, Straus, Giroux, 1991).

Gerald E. Myers, *William James: His Life and Thought* (New Haven: Yale University Press, 1986).

Ralph Barton Perry, *The Thought and Character of William James*, 2 vols. (Boston: Little, Brown, 1935).

Charlene Haddock Seigfried, *William James's Radical Reconstruction of Philosophy* (Albany: SUNY Press, 1990).

Jameson, Fredric (b. Cleveland, Ohio, Mar. 14, 1934). Literary critic. As America's leading Marxist intellectual in the late twentieth century, Jameson reworked radical social theory with the aid of poststructuralist ideas about the nature of power and representation. His work on *The Political Unconscious* (1981) posited the existence of "ideologies of form" which replicated, in the form of cultural signs, broader systems of production and oppression. Jameson has been a major theoretical influence on the academic left of the 1980s and 1990s. He is also a theorist of POSTMODERNISM, which in his view supplies a cultural form that sustains the power of consumer capitalism.

FURTHER READING

William C. Dowling, *Jameson, Althusser, Marx: an Introduction to the Political Unconscious* (Ithaca: Cornell University Press, 1984).

Jefferson, Thomas (b. Goochland [now Albemarle] County, Va., Apr. 13, 1743; d. Monticello, Va., July 4, 1826). At his home in Monticello, Jefferson the architect successfully accomplished a goal that forever eluded Jefferson the statesman: he made slavery disappear. By locating the slave quarters out of sight, below the hillsides that surrounded the house, and by placing the stables, the kitchen, and the house servants' rooms beneath the terraces that extended beyond the house, Jefferson removed all traces of the slave labor that lay at the foundation of his existence as a refined and enlightened planter and statesman.

Monticello embodies the contradictions of Jefferson's life and his legacy. Jefferson deliberately sited his mansion so that it faced westward, toward the wilderness that he believed would enable America to expand indefinitely as a republic of yeomen farmers; yet he just as deliberately derived its design from the antique architectural models of classicism. (*See also* ARCHITECTURE.) He cherished America's unsettled West; yet he laid on the entire nation a geometric grid that imposed the Enlightenment's vision of rational order, irrespective of the meandering flow of rivers and the unyielding features of the terrain. He wanted Monticello to reflect his enthusiasm for the finest fruits of the eighteenth-century ENLIGHTENMENT in philosophy, science, and aesthetics; yet he made sure that such examples of refinement as a world-class library, a seven-day calendar clock, and a bust of Voltaire by the French sculptor Jean-Antoine Houdon were juxtaposed with elk and moose antlers, the head of a bison, the bones of a mastodon, and various Indian artifacts, all of which demonstrated the untamed grandeur of the New World.

Jefferson prided himself on his commitment to the newest advances in agriculture, smuggling a strain of rice from Italy, inventing a prize-winning plow, and experimenting with the latest ideas on crop rotation; yet he was unable to turn a profit as a farmer. He often railed against the dangers of manufacturing for a republic; yet he experimented with manufacturing nails and spinning cloth at Monticello, ventures that proved as unprofitable as his efforts at commercial farming. He criticized government spending and argued against encumbering future generations through profligate public expenditures; yet he refused to curtail his own lavish purchases and extravagant entertaining, which left him nearly bankrupt for much of his life and saddled his own heirs with a heavy burden of debt.

Jefferson privately expressed his hatred of slavery, and condemned it with such eloquence in his *Notes on the State of Virginia* that his words were frequently quoted by abolitionists; yet his own comfortable way of life depended on slave labor. He often professed his passionate opposition to miscegenation; yet he kept as slaves members of the Hemings family, all of whom were the children of the union of his father-in-law and one of his slaves, and one of whom, Sally, gave birth to children whose father was, according to various (and hotly contested) accounts, an Irish-born overseer of Monticello, Jefferson's nephew, or Jefferson himself.

Such contradictions are not merely intriguing details that can be reconciled within some broader unity; instead they constitute the essentially inconsistent, even contradictory, nature of Jefferson's life and his thought. Despite the efforts of generations of commentators who have sought to reveal beneath the obvious dissonances a deeper harmony, no such harmony exists except through the creative efforts of historians devoted to muting some part of Jefferson and attending closely to another.

Jefferson was, as his contemporaries and later observers have claimed, the central figure in eighteenth-century American culture, so the urge to resolve his contradictions is hardly surprising. As a symbol of the meaning and aspirations of the new nation, for Americans and for others, Jefferson has overshadowed every other figure, including even Washington and Lincoln. For that reason, efforts to construct a coherent image of his ideas have been a constant feature of American intellectual life from the eighteenth century to the present. In *The Jefferson Image in the American Mind* (1960), Merrill D. Peterson traced the ups and downs of Jefferson's reputation, and the ebb and flow of popular and scholarly writing about him, from his death through the 1950s. The 250th anniversary of Jefferson's birth provided the occasion for a scholarly conference that yielded the volume *Jeffersonian Legacies* (1993), a splendid collection of essays edited by Peter Onuf that continues Peterson's account into the 1990s. Just as Jefferson's first memorialists found profound symbolic significance in the coincidence that both Jefferson and his long-time friend and rival JOHN ADAMS died on July 4, 1826, the fiftieth anniversary of the signing of the Declaration of Independence, so have generations of commentators tried to take stock of American DEMOCRACY by coming to terms with the meaning of Jefferson.

Jefferson embodied the ideal of the eighteenth-century enlightened gentleman. Born to a wealthy family, Jefferson received an education as fine as colonial Virginia could provide. When he entered the College of William and Mary at age 16, he could hunt, ride, dance, play the violin, and read Latin and Greek with confidence. After completing his studies and reading law, he practiced law for five years before concentrating his efforts on managing the 5,000 acres and 22 slaves he inherited. He began work on Monticello in 1771; building and rebuilding it occupied much of his energy, and provided an outlet for his considerable creative impulses, for the rest of his life. In 1772 he married a young widow, Martha Skelton. Of their five children, three died in infancy, and Martha herself died after giving birth to their fifth child in 1782. The deaths of three of his children and his cherished wife devastated Jefferson. He never remarried, and apparently only once again felt strongly attracted to another woman, the highly cultivated (but married) English artist Maria Cosway. Despite his own cultural ambitions, Jefferson scorned the pretensions of the dissolute Virginia gentry. Although often and accurately characterized as a paternalist, he insisted that his two daughters be sufficiently well educated to take care of themselves if, as he feared, either should find herself married to "a block-head" (*Papers*, vol. 6, p. 374) and be forced to manage her household and educate her children herself.

Jefferson's public career began with his election to the Virginia House of Burgesses in 1768. His reputation as a writer was established when it became generally known that he had written the anonymous *Summary View of the Rights of British America* (1774). There he proclaimed, in words that have often been cited to demonstrate his commitment to the primacy of individual rights, "The God who gave us life, gave us liberty at the same time: the hand of force may destroy, but cannot disjoin them" (*Writings*, p. 122). But commentators sometimes neglect Jefferson's careful and characteristic placement of rights within the context of his deep and prior commitment to the democratic idea of popular sovereignty: "From the nature of things, every society must at all times possess within itself the sovereign powers of legislation" (p. 118). (*See also* BILL OF RIGHTS.) Jefferson's dual emphasis on popular sovereignty and liberty, both of which he rooted in divine plan, ancient practice, and English tradition, helped provide fuel and a conceptual framework for the American colonists' resentments.

After those resentments had boiled over and war had begun in April of 1775, the Continental Congress, meeting in Philadelphia, selected Jefferson to draft a Declaration of Independence. Jefferson later explained that his aim was neither complete originality nor accurate representation of the ideas of any other political philosopher. Instead he aimed "to place before mankind the common sense of the subject, in terms so plain and firm as to command their assent." As Jefferson put it in 1825, the Declaration "was intended to be an expression of the American mind" (p. 1501). In part because we have become so suspicious of such concepts as "common sense" and "the American mind," few historians have been willing to accept Jefferson's own simple account of what he did.

Instead generations of commentators have interpreted the Declaration as a proclamation of John Locke's individualism, of French or Scottish Enlightenment philosophy, of eighteenth-century enthusiasm for natural science, and of European or British versions of classical republicanism. Studies emphasizing Locke's role include Carl Becker, *The Declaration of Independence* (1922), and Joyce Appleby, *Liberalism and Republicanism in the Historical Imagination* (1992). Adrienne Koch singled out the role of French *philosophes* in *The Philosophy of Thomas Jefferson* (1943). The most prominent studies stressing the importance of (different) Scottish philosophers are Garry Wills, *Inventing America: Jefferson's Declaration of Independence* (1978), who emphasized Francis Hutcheson's sentimentalism, and Morton White, *The Philosophy of the American Revolution* (1978), who stressed Thomas Reid's rationalism. In *The Lost World of Thomas Jefferson* (1948), Daniel Boorstin charted the distance between Jefferson's view of scientific naturalism and our own. Recent studies of Jefferson's ideas include Richard K. Matthews, *The Radical Politics of Thomas Jefferson* (1984), in which Jefferson appears as a partisan of participatory democracy; and Garrett Ward Sheldon, *The Political Philosophy of Thomas Jefferson* (1991), which argues that Jefferson's odyssey carried him from Lockean LIBERALISM to certain kinds of classical REPUBLICANISM and then back again.

Historiographical essays tend to hypostatize such interpretive disagreements, which are usually (although not always) little more than differences of emphasis derived from critical reflection on similar sources. This artificial hardening of critical positions may create the impression among nonspecialists that studies of Jefferson have degenerated from historical scholarship into ideological warfare; the discord instead reflects the apparently contradictory sources upon which Jefferson himself clearly drew. His own immense learning, and his voracious appetite for ideas, have confounded interpreters keen on finding an "essential" Jefferson beneath the wide array of

diverse influences to which the record gives ample evidence. We may consider such sources inconsistent; Jefferson did not. Jefferson was an activist as well as a theorist. In his words, "what is practicable must often control what is pure theory; and the habits of the governed determine in a great degree what is practicable" (*Writings*, p. 1101). If his principal objective in writing the Declaration of Independence was to express the ideas of liberty and popular sovereignty in a form likely to command assent and inspire Americans to achieve their independence, he succeeded brilliantly.

Jefferson's political activities help to illuminate his guiding political principles. From 1775 through 1779, he worked to reform the Constitution and the laws of Virginia, revealing commitments that continued throughout his career. His proposals included egalitarian elements such as a broader suffrage and land grants of 50 acres to all citizens. But he preferred a Senate chosen by the popularly elected Assembly, not by the people themselves. In his view, the people's own choice "is not generally distinguished by its wisdom" (p. 775). Such ideas might seem contradictory, but they reveal Jefferson's lifelong hatred of inherited privilege and his equally characteristic ambivalence about the judgment of the untutored masses.

Jefferson likewise sought to secure the principle of religious freedom, which he introduced in 1777 and the Virginia General Assembly finally enacted in 1786. Because Jefferson's own religious faith was highly unorthodox, his critics branded him an unbeliever. He nevertheless considered himself both a foe of institutionalized Christianity and a fervent Christian; he later compiled extracts from the Gospels to piece together what he considered a pure version— before their corruption by layers of superstition—of the ethical teachings of Jesus, "the most sublime and benevolent code of morals which has ever been offered to man" (p. 1301).

During these creative years Jefferson also advanced an elaborate scheme of public EDUCATION, whereby all citizens would attend free public elementary schools. The most talented would continue through grammar schools, then a few "geniuses" would be selected for advanced studies at a state-sponsored university. Jefferson envisioned a relentlessly meritocratic system resting on a decentralized, democratic commitment to universal education. He had confidence that the people, given a basic education, would develop sufficiently good judgment to select "those persons, whom nature hath endowed with genius and virtue" (p. 365) to serve in government.

In 1779, during the bleakest days of the War for

Independence, Jefferson served a disastrous term as Governor of Virginia. He was forced to flee Richmond to avoid capture, and charges of dishonor dogged him after he left office. He returned to Monticello to care for his wife; while there he produced his only book, *Notes on the State of Virginia*, which he wrote in response to a series of questions posed by the secretary of the French minister in Philadelphia. Jefferson examined at length a number of issues, the most significant of which was slavery. Whereas Jefferson invoked environmental factors to account for the differences between Indian cultures and white cultures, he expressed his doubt that African Americans, whom he considered inferior to whites by nature, could ever achieve equality. He feared slavery's poisonous legacy would feed mutual hatreds and prevent racial harmony; for that reason he proposed forced emigration for all free blacks. Nevertheless, he also admitted that "I tremble for my country when I reflect that God is just; that his justice cannot sleep forever . . . The Almighty has no attribute which can take side with us in such a contest" (*Writings*, p. 289). Jefferson had hoped to keep quiet such explosive sentiments, but when copies of the privately printed *Notes* began to circulate in French translation, he agreed to publish an English version in 1787 to prevent the appearance of a poorly translated, unauthorized edition.

Jefferson's *Notes* appeared while he was serving as United States Minister to France. There his hatred for aristocracy, superstition, cities, industry, and tradition intensified. He collaborated secretly with Lafayette to advance the cause of the French Revolution, which broke out just as he was preparing to return to the United States. After accepting Washington's invitation to serve as the first Secretary of State, Jefferson served as Vice President during the administration of John Adams and quietly helped organize the emerging opposition to the President's policies.

Jefferson's election to the Presidency, which he and his enemies both later called "the revolution of 1800," signaled and consolidated the stability of the national government. Jefferson's second term, however, was stained by his relentless effort to enforce the Embargo Acts of 1807 and 1808. Although the venomous charges leveled by his partisan opponents surely wounded him (an aggrieved Federalist editor was the first to claim that Jefferson was the father of Sally Hemings's children), Jefferson himself contributed to the rough-and-tumble partisanship of American politics through his passionate, self-righteous commitment to his own program and his intemperate criticism of his opponents. Although he continued

until his death to cherish the ideals of deliberation and meritocracy he associated with the Enlightenment, his partisanship helped create the passionate and vulgar world that left Jefferson himself deeply pessimistic about American culture in the 1820s. Of all the contradictions surrounding Jefferson's life and his ideas, perhaps the most profound is his lack of sympathy for champions of the popular, mass democracy that invoked his name but seemed to him bent on destroying, ostensibly on behalf of his ideals of liberty and popular sovereignty, the principles of reason and refinement he cherished.

JAMES T. KLOPPENBERG

FURTHER READING

Noble E. Cunningham Jr., *In Pursuit of Reason: the Life of Thomas Jefferson* (Baton Rouge: Louisiana State University Press, 1987).

Thomas Jefferson, *The Papers of Thomas Jefferson*, ed. Julian P. Boyd et al., 24 vols. to date (Princeton: Princeton University Press, 1950–).

——, *Writings*, ed. Merrill D. Peterson (New York: Library of America, 1984).

Leonard W. Levy, *Jefferson and Civil Liberties: the Darker Side* (Cambridge: Harvard University Press, 1963).

Dumas Malone, *Jefferson and His Time*, 6 vols. (Boston: Little, Brown, 1948–81).

John C. Miller, *The Wolf by the Ears: Thomas Jefferson and Slavery* (New York: Free Press, 1977).

Peter S. Onuf, ed., *Jeffersonian Legacies* (Charlottesville: University Press of Virginia, 1993).

Merrill D. Peterson, *The Jefferson Image in the American Mind* (New York: Oxford University Press, 1960).

Johnson, James Weldon (b. Jacksonville, Fla., June 17, 1871; d. Wiscasset, Maine, June 26, 1938).   Poet, novelist, songwriter, activist. Johnson was one of the leading figures of the African American cultural and political HARLEM RENAISSANCE in the first decades of the twentieth century. A protégé of BOOKER T. WASHINGTON and from time to time active in the Republican Party, Johnson was also an intimate of W. E. B. DU BOIS. He was an exceptional administrative officer of the National Association for the Advancement of Colored People (1916–30), and a vocal opponent of American hegemony in Haiti. As a writer, Johnson is most often remembered for his novel *Autobiography of an Ex-Colored Man*, published anonymously in 1912, and again, under Johnson's name, in 1927. It is the story of a light-skinned African American who infiltrates white society and is able to observe the subtle workings of systematic racism.

Also significant were Johnson's anthologies, *The Book of Negro Poetry* (1922) and, particularly, the two-volume *The Book of Negro Spirituals* (1925–6). Johnson had started out, in partnership with his brother

J. Rosamond, as a writer of light opera and popular songs (including the Jazz Era anthem "Under the Bamboo Tree"). *The Book of Negro Spirituals* argued that African American culture, revealed most fully in music, was the only truly *American* culture, constructed, that is, out of the stuff of New World experience.

FURTHER READING
Robert E. Fleming, *James Weldon Johnson* (Boston: Twayne, 1987).

Jordan, David Starr (b. near Gainesville, N.Y., Jan. 19, 1851; d. Palo Alto, Calif., Sept. 19, 1931). Biologist and educator. One of the leading botanists in nineteenth-century America, Jordan earned a national reputation with his *Manual of the Vertebrates of the Northern United States* (1876). His later pathbreaking studies of fisheries established him as the world's leading icthyologist. After six years as president of Indiana University, he became the first president of Stanford University in 1891. An active writer and lecturer on the dangers of imperialism and war, he opposed the Spanish-American War and, until 1918, America's entry into World War I. He advocated international arbitration as an alternative to war, and economic expansion, not military engagement, as the proper means of establishing America's global presence. His writings include *Imperial Democracy* (1899), *War and Waste* (1914), *Democracy and World Relations* (1918), and his autobiography *The Days of a Man* (1922).

FURTHER READING
Edward Hall Burns, *David Starr Jordan: Prophet of Freedom* (Stanford: Stanford University Press, 1953).

journalism The ideal public sphere of a liberal democracy is not only a conglomeration of civic institutions. It is also a field of speech through which informed citizens engage, debate, and reach consensus. In this ideal form of polity, the journalist serves as arbiter in an exchange of information which produces an enlightened and decisive citizenry.

The near-mythic status of journalism in American public life lies in these basic assumptions about discourse and popular knowledge, assumptions which originated in the press itself. Liberal and republican theories from seventeenth-century England through the American and French revolutions found expression in the newspapers whose own growth mirrored the expanding industrial and ideological hegemony of the North Atlantic democracies. No less an icon of American public values than BENJAMIN FRANKLIN embodied for generations the figure of the colonial printer-journalist—independent, irascible, ironic yet sentimentally populist—an image which set the standard for American journalistic self-fashioning. Well before the revolution, partisan conflict had been waged in the press; the printer-journalist had established himself early on as one of the most politicized individuals in the eighteenth-century American community.

Lofty aspirations for the public role of American journalism were challenged in the 1830s with the rise of the "penny press." Technological innovations and a rapidly-integrating national economy supported cheap, mass-produced and mass-circulated dailies, as well as a boom in periodical literature. This fledgling mass media began the long process of reconstituting information as "news"—one more commodity in the burgeoning market system. As newspapers concentrated on selling their new product, and as readership expanded beyond the restricted eighteenth-century boundaries of either "gentlemen's" journals or artisanal broadsides, journalists began to lose their attachment to party and their self-conception as active participants in political debates. After the Civil War a group of writers tried to preserve the place of the journalist in public life by developing JOURNALS OF OPINION. Foremost among these was E. L. GODKIN of THE NATION, for whom journalists might still aspire to being arbiters of public taste and makers of informed citizens.

These two primary trends in nineteenth-century journalism—toward mass-market news and toward critical opinion—began to converge after the 1880s. A new generation of information entrepreneurs such as Joseph Pulitzer and William Randolph Hearst built on ground prepared by the penny press. As the urban market grew exponentially, they developed a sensational or "yellow journalism" (*see also* CARTOONING), which elevated urban industrial experience to the level of popular entertainment. Sensationalism was accompanied by the hardy image of the journalist as masculine culture hero, exemplified by Richard Harding Davis and Stephen Crane. At the same time, journalists such as the magazine editor S. S. McClure, inspired by the prestige of literary NATURALISM and its theoretical corollary, sociology, developed MUCKRAKING. This publicly engaged reportage was energized by the market-driven sensational style of Hearst and Pulitzer, but also by the high ideals of the Godkin tradition. The American journalist became the mythic protector and watchdog, the defender of the people. Elsewhere, away from the industrial metropolis, small-town editors like William Allen White, continuing the Franklinesque role of local intellectual/community booster, increasingly charged themselves with the duty of tying their provincial readers into a broader, mass-mediated public. Thanks to Hearst, McClure, White, and many others, American public life after the turn of the century was saturated with the power of print media.

WALTER LIPPMANN, the preeminent twentieth-century American journalist, grounded his public philosophy in a sophisticated appreciation of these developments. He understood that American public experience—political, social, ideational—had been transformed by mass media, and he set out, accordingly, to redefine journalism for the twentieth century. In two books, *Liberty and the News* (1920) and *Public Opinion* (1922), Lippmann worked through his experience of the Wilson administration's blatant manipulation of a willing press for propaganda purposes. His emphasis on the relativity and manipulability of all information undermined the view that citizens could, by themselves, use the news to ground a system of self-governance. The period's "crisis in democracy," he argued in *Liberty and the News*, was in fact a "crisis in journalism": the press was engaged in an unregulated "manufacturing of consent" yet did not fully appreciate its power over the public (p. 5). Lippmann proposed a self-conscious restructuring of journalistic practice, featuring apolitical, nonpartisan news agencies, rigorous standards in the identification of sources and the verification of facts, and the professionalization of journalism—as exemplified in the Columbia School of Journalism, which had opened in 1913. While the circulation of information was central to democracy, only experts, in his view, could ensure its objective representation. Editorial columnists would constitute a national opinion elite and bring enlightened skepticism to bear on social and political issues.

After the 1920s the rapid nationalization of wire services and newspaper syndicates, along with the revolutionary innovation of broadcast news, began collapsing the space/time restrictions which had governed the news market. As a consequence Lippmann's vision of expertise-in-command, first criticized by many for its elitism, became a quaint anachronism. Journalism continued to embody its historic tensions between marketing and informing, but radio, newsreels and television exploded the inherited frame. In the 1960s and 1970s rigid conceptions of reporting style faltered before the New Journalism, a movement described by Tom Wolfe, one of its key proponents, as making news "read like a novel." Continuing a tradition of "literary journalism" popular in New York intellectual circles during the previous generation (in the work of such writers as MARY

MCCARTHY), the New Journalism found a vehicle in an "underground" press that grew within the counterculture of the period. Weeklies and magazines such as the national *Rolling Stone* followed a radical press tradition running from *The Masses* in the early century through the *Village Voice* of the 1950s. The best of this new work—by Wolfe, Hunter S. Thompson, Joan Didion, Gay Talese—focused on the lifestyles and political concerns of a generation which felt increasingly alienated from the terms of "establishment" political exchange.

During the same period, the national press found itself in a more adversarial relationship with government. Whereas mid-century journalism by and large celebrated, with Henry Luce of *Time* and *Life*, "the American century," coverage of the civil rights movement and the war in Southeast Asia challenged many journalists' views of "national interests." Walter Lippmann himself became a significant early critic of President Johnson's Vietnam policy. This alienation among mainstream journalists culminated in the Watergate investigations of the early 1970s. Regaining some of the old public-watchdog luster of the muckraking years, investigative journalists crystallized a new, critical distance between the state and some elements of the press.

As the rapid spread of television eroded the readership of newspapers, daily journalism turned all the more eagerly to image production rather than reportage. As the century closes, moreover, there is some indication that the adversarial position of critical journalists is losing force, as criticism takes on more and more the aura of "insider" commentary, and the editorialist becomes a new instance of mass-mediated celebrity. The electronic pundit can cross from journalism to governance and back again. The television-driven careers of Presidential candidate Pat Buchanan and Presidential adviser David Gergen are only the most dramatic recent examples of this new permeability.

In the last decade of the twentieth century, technology once again threatens to destabilize the cultural field in which journalism operates. "Reality programming" and global live broadcast of "events" reshapes, almost moment to moment, both the definition of news and the scope of any particular market. Perhaps even more significantly, rapidly expanding interactive media—with both state and corporate support—threaten to constitute a "virtual public," transcending previous conceptions of time, space, and information access. Polling can be remarketed as electronic "town halls."

Meanwhile, news magazines increasingly mirror the newspapers' efforts to compete with television by repackaging themselves as purveyors of bright gossip on lifestyles. "Serious" reportage still occurs in the news business, but the entertainment industry's power over information production has more and more pushed analysis and investigation into the monthly and quarterly journals of opinion—whose readerships are limited.

PETER HANSEN

FURTHER READING

Sally Foreman Griffith, *Home Town News: William Allen White and the "Emporia Gazette"* (New York: Oxford University Press, 1989).

Walter Lippmann, *Liberty and the News* (New York: Harcourt, Brace, 1920).

——, *Public Opinion* (1922; New York: Free Press, 1965).

Frank Luther Mott, *American Journalism: a History of Newspapers in the United States through 260 Years: 1690–1950* (New York: Macmillan, 1950).

Michael Schudson, *Discovering the News: a Social History of American Newspapers* (New York: Basic Books, 1978).

Tom Wolfe, *The New Journalism* (New York: Harper-Collins, 1973).

journals of opinion If intellectuals as a social category blur around the edges into other groups—scholars, journalists, authors of popular nonfiction —journals of opinion occupy a literary borderland where they compete with newspapers, academic journals, "little magazines," and newsweeklies for readers and influence. What distinguishes journals of opinion from these publications is their interest in the education and formation of public opinion as a moral and political authority distinct from the professions, political parties, and other established institutions. But in seeking to construct and inform the public, the twentieth-century journal of opinion has exhibited all the ambiguities that characterize the relationship between intellectuals and the rest of American society. At its most democratic, the journal of opinion provides a forum where intellectuals can discover one another, explore unconventional political and cultural positions, and work to expand the boundaries of contemporary public debate. That alternative ideal has coexisted in this century with a more mainstream conception of the journal as an organ of publicity offering readers inside information about the machinations of experts and interest groups within the state. Addressing a largely professional, middle-class readership, the journal of opinion has oscillated between the hope of reinvigorating a democratic public sphere and the mobilization of support for specific policies through the dissemination of elite gossip.

Modern journals of opinion have their roots in the nineteenth century, in publications like the *North American Review*, the original *Dial*, *Harper's*, the *Atlantic*, *De Bow's Magazine*, Frederick Douglass's *Monthly*, THE NATION, and the *Independent*, which sought to shape public opinion by publishing articles on current controversies in politics and culture. But these forerunners were limited in scope by a self-conscious appeal to a particular class, creed, or regional elite, and in some cases by only sporadic attention to public affairs, which waxed and waned with the great crises of the Civil War and Reconstruction. The modern journal of opinion came into its own as a self-conscious response to the upheavals of the Gilded Age. The triumph of a nonideological party system and the marginalization of the partisan press, the emergence of a salaried middle class, the expansion of higher education, the rise of the corporation and the state as dominant economic actors, and the waning allegiance of the educated classes to religion and party politics all set the stage for the simultaneous creation of the intelligentsia as a social group and of the journal of opinion as its chief organ of expression.

With the founding of THE NEW REPUBLIC, the *Masses*, and the *Seven Arts* in the 1910s, the journal of opinion emerged as the most important site for a new criticism linking the autobiographical narrative of intellectuals' self-discovery, explorations in artistic MODERNISM, and political and cultural radicalism. Commitment to a form of expression joining the personal, the political, and the cultural sustained the most significant journals of opinion in subsequent decades: the *New Republic* of the interwar years, *Partisan Review* and the *Nation* during the 1940s and 1950s, *Commentary* during the 1960s, and the *New York Review of Books* during the 1960s and 1970s.

Journals of opinion have always attracted politically minded intellectuals, and their history in his century reflects the changing political allegiances of the American intelligentsia. In the absence of ideologically coherent political parties—with their partisan papers and programs for educating cadres—intellectuals attracted to an ideological politics have gravitated to such journals to define a consistent perspective on public affairs. The *Nation* and *New Republic* have dominated the field of liberal opinion by addressing a broad left-of-center constituency which has only provisional affiliations to a particular party or administration. Publishing topical articles on current affairs alongside more ambitious critical essays, these two journals provide an ongoing account of political and cultural power in Washington and New York and offer readers an ideological point of reference for their roles as voters, activists, and intellectuals. In the process, the two liberal stalwarts have marginalized or eliminated publications like the *Progressive*, the *Independent*, *Survey Graphic*, and *Common Sense*, whose liberalism lacked the national scope or elite access of their more powerful competitors. The *Nation* and the *New Republic* occupied virtually the same ideological space for much of the twentieth century, but the widening gulf between the former's left-liberalism and the latter's neoliberalism reflects profound divisions within the liberal intelligentsia since the 1960s over domestic social programs, foreign policy, and cultural politics.

These journals have faced their greatest challenge over the years from the left, but only rarely from publications with an institutional link to political parties. Two socialist journals, the *New Review* of the 1910s and the *New Leader* of the 1940s and 1950s, were exceptional in their ability to serve as both party organs and forums for rich and contentious ideological debate. The same was true, to a limited degree, of the *Liberator* and the early *New Masses*, where during the 1920s and the early 1930s, an orientation toward the Communist Party coexisted with an openness to other ideological positions on the left. The most important theoretical debates about Marxism in the United States have always taken place on the fringes of formal leftist parties and organizations— in publications like *Modern Quarterly*, *Marxist Quarterly*, *Dissent*, the *Monthly Review*, *Socialist Review*, *Radical America*, and *Telos*, which have also addressed topical political issues. Meanwhile, an indigenous tradition of American radicalism has found expression in a small group of short-lived journals, among them the *Seven Arts*, *politics*, *Liberation*, *Studies on the Left*, and *democracy*.

The ascendancy of the conservative movement since the mid-1950s has also challenged the hegemony of liberal journals within the intellectual community. (*See also* CONSERVATISM.) Between the 1920s and the early 1950s, the *Freeman*, *American Mercury*, the *American Review*, the *Southern Review*, the *Modern Age*, and the *New Freeman* opened their pages to conservatives of various stripes—libertarians, southern Agrarians, Burkean traditionalists, and anticommunists —but it was only with the founding by WILLIAM BUCKLEY of the *National Review* in 1955 that conservatives attained a forum comparable to the *New Republic* or the *Nation*. The *National Review*'s fortunes have been even more closely linked to an organized political faction than the liberal weeklies, and it has struggled in recent years to maintain its independence in the face of conservative electoral triumphs. From the heady days of its founding to the triumph of Reaganism, the *National Review* alternated between, on the one hand, sponsoring freewheeling debates between cultural conservatives, isolationists,

free-market libertarians, and advocates of American expansionism and, on the other hand, boosting its favorite candidates from the Goldwater–Reagan wing of the Republican Party. These tensions notwithstanding, Buckley's journal has been extraordinarily successful in making conservative ideas intellectually respectable and politically effective, clearing the way for a host of other journals on the right, from conservative and neoconservative policy journals like the *Policy Review* and the *Public Interest* to journals of cultural criticism, such as *Chronicles*, the *American Spectator*, and *This World*. Conservatives have also benefited from the rightward turn of important liberal journals of opinion since the early 1970s, notably *Commentary* and the *Partisan Review*, which link contemporary conservative thought to an older generation of formerly liberal anticommunist intellectuals and an influential segment of the American Jewish intelligentsia.

Apart from their political function, journals of opinion have been most important as forums for intellectuals from marginalized regions and social groups to articulate their distinct identity in relation to the rest of American society. *De Bow's Magazine* played such a role for southern intellectuals in the antebellum period. (*See also* SOUTHERN INTELLECTUAL HISTORY.) The *Midland*, a midwestern literary review founded in Iowa City in 1915, inspired a host of regionalist journals in the 1920s and 1930s that published literature, criticism, and political polemics defending the art and values of their region from the cultural imperialism of New York and other metropolitan capitals. The *Frontier*, the *Reviewer*, the *Southwest Review*, *Prarie Schooner*, the *New Mexico Quarterly Review*, and *Space* all made claims for the vitality of regional cultures in the Great Plains and Southwest in literature and criticism that contributed to the folkloric and communitarian revivals of the period. Regionalism made its greatest impact as an intellectual movement in the South, where the Agrarian critics played a leading role in a remarkable array of southern literary, critical, and political journals, including the *Fugitive, Double Dealer*, the *Sewanee Review*, the *Virginia Quarterly Review*, the *Journal of Social Forces*, and the *Southern Review*. Like their counterparts in the Midwest and Southwest, southern regionalist journals understood their defense of local cultural traditions as a form of political opposition to cosmopolitan values and the modern liberal state. (*See also* SOUTHERN AGRARIANISM.)

Intellectuals from distinct subcultures have likewise made use of journals of opinion in this century, and these organs have had to serve an even greater number of needs than the mainstream progressive publications. For Jews, Catholics, Protestant advocates of the Social Gospel, African Americans, women, and gays and lesbians, such journals often function as sites for defining the group's identity as well as articulating its public responsibility. Jewish intellectuals have created journals as different as the *Menorah Review*, *Partisan Review*, *Commentary*, and *Tikkun* to negotiate the tensions among Jewish Americans over assimilationism, cosmopolitanism, and ethnic particularism. (*See also* JUDAISM.) Liberal Catholic intellectuals have turned to *Commonweal*, the *Catholic Worker*, the *National Catholic Reporter*, and the *New Oxford Review* for much the same purpose, as forums for exploring Catholic American identity and launching Catholic interventions in progressive politics, while conservatives have gravitated to such magazines as *Catholicism and Crisis*, as well as the *National Review*. (*See also* CATHOLICISM.) The *Christian Century* and *Christianity and Crisis* have been among the most influential journals for intellectuals associated with the Protestant Social Gospel tradition; conservative Protestant intellectuals have been much fewer in number, but now gather in the pages of such magazines as *The Reformed Journal*.

The most important African American journal of opinion of this century remains *The Crisis*, founded by W. E. B. DU BOIS, but Du Bois's firm control of the magazine between 1910 and 1934 placed severe constraints on its openness to the full range of opinions on black cultural identity and politics. A. Philip Randolph likewise made *The Messenger* a vehicle for his own political positions in the second and third decades of the century, while *Opportunity* faithfully reflected the program of Charles Johnson and the Urban League. Political imperatives often combined with genteel cultural tastes in these magazines to preclude the joining of cultural and political radicalism that was common in the journals of opinion of the day. The most important exceptions are *Fire!!* and *Harlem*, two vital but short-lived publications of the twenties' HARLEM RENAISSANCE that collapsed without the patronage of the major civil rights organizations. The civil rights and black nationalist movements after 1945 generated countless small newspapers and black arts magazines, which debuted or folded with the dramatic shifts in African American politics in that period. Among contemporary journals of opinion, *Reconstruction* is the most promising forum for a renascent African American social criticism.

Feminist journals and publications supporting gay and lesbian politics have had to attend to the same diversity of needs as journals representing racial, ethnic, and religious subcultures. The suffragist publications *Woman's Journal* and *Revolution* were embedded in the "woman movement" of the late nineteenth century, while *Mother Earth* of EMMA GOLDMAN foreshadowed the cultural radicalism of the years 1910 to 1930 in articulating a new identity for women. Likewise, the feminism of the late 1960s and 1970s produced newspapers and magazines like *off our backs, The Women's Page, Ms.*, and *Majority Report* that spoke to the immediate needs of different wings of the women's liberation movement while encouraging more theoretical explorations of women's public and private identities. The *Women's Review of Books* offers a feminist version of the *New York Review of Books*. But much of the social criticism written by feminist and gay and lesbian intellectuals today appears in journals that owe their existence to academic programs in women's studies, gender studies, and gay and lesbian studies: *Signs, Feminist Studies, Hypatia*, the *Journal of the History of Sexuality*, among many others. The theoretical preoccupations and scholarly apparatus of these journals limit their access to a public outside the university and often alienate participants in the very social movements that inspired them. Exchanges between activists and feminist and gay and lesbian academics do take place in left-liberal publications such as the *Village Voice*, but intellectuals associated with feminism and the gay-lesbian movement have yet to create journals of opinion of their own on the model of the *Nation*, the *New Republic*, the *National Review, Commonweal, Commentary*, or *Tikkun*.

Feminist and gay and lesbian intellectuals are not alone in this predicament. The current crisis of the independent intelligentsia has profound consequences for journals of opinion. Today's independent journal editors scramble for advertising, academic subsidies, and foundation grants, while relying on a familiar list of celebrity authors who established their reputations in the 1950s and 1960s. Meanwhile, the market segmentation that closed the weekly *Life* magazine in the early 1970s and rid American downtowns of five-and-dimes has had parallels in intellectual life, with journals forsaking the hope of addressing a broad democratic public for the more modest goal of reaching a specific cultural enclave. Television talk shows and newspaper opinion pages likewise have little use for the public moralists and social critics who defined the mission of the journal of opinion in its heyday: their preference is for policy experts, politicians, and journalists. The one hopeful sign for the future is the growing number of younger scholars who are restless with the arid and narrow concerns of their disciplines' refereed journals and seek opportunities to join scholarship to autobiography and social criticism. It remains to be seen, however, whether such restlessness will produce a revival of the journal of opinion as a resource for wide-ranging democratic controversy, or will instead be incorporated, and contained, by new interdisciplinary academic journals, such as the recently founded *Common Knowledge* and *Contention*.

CASEY BLAKE

FURTHER READING

Frederick J. Hoffman, Charles Allen, and Carolyn F. Ulrich, *The Little Magazine: a History and a Bibliography* (Princeton: Princeton University Press, 1947).

Russell Jacoby, *The Last Intellectuals: American Culture in the Age of Academe* (New York: Basic Books, 1987).

John Tebbel and Mary Ellen Zuckerman, *The Magazine in America 1741–1990* (New York: Oxford University Press, 1991).

Judaism Jews in the United States are engaged in a perpetual negotiation over the shape and meaning of American Jewish identity. Although defined by a shared religion, American Jews are not unified by their common faith; the various expressions of Judaism reflect differing and evolving approaches to the question of how to be Jewish in America. The ideas and debates that define Jewish life do not necessarily revolve around religion or around the questions taken up by Jewish philosophers and theologians. Rather, as at most moments in American Jewish history, American Jews, in the choices they make about their religious, cultural, political, and intellectual lives, are continually seeking to balance the often contradictory forces that shape their identity as Jews and Americans.

American Jews are probably more connected and defined by what they do not believe and do not do than by any positive identity. Most American Jews who come from families that are not intermarried know that they are *not* Christian. Beyond this, there is little upon which American Jews can agree. The openness of American society, which has made it possible for American Jews to be less than clear as to whether being Jewish constitutes principally an ethnic or a religious identity, only contributes to the confusion. For new immigrants at the turn of the century, the different religious, cultural, and linguistic aspects of Jewish identity were inseparable. But as settled Americans, many Jews have retained Jewishness as a salient and unambiguous aspect of their identity while divorcing themselves from any connection with Judaism as a religion. Thus for different individuals, Jewishness may consist of the food they eat, the neighborhood they live in, the intensity of their support for Israel, the code of ethics they profess, the God in which they believe, the people they

know, the political causes for which they fight or to which they give money, the way they talk, their identification with the underdog, their concern for group survival, the magazines they read, or the songs they remember. American Jewish identity is so diffuse and multifaceted that it defies generalization.

However they construct their identity, Jews in the United States have often found it tempting to understand American and Jewish values as congruent and American and Jewish identities as reinforcing. This understanding is consistent with the generally accepted saga of Jewish immigrant achievement. In this story, the traditional Jewish investment and faith in education and intellectual achievement were rewarded with success in the United States and translated into rapid upward economic and social mobility. Another version of the story focuses on how the age-old Jewish experience of oppression became transformed in the United States into a commitment to social and civic justice, which translated into firm adherence to a democratic and pluralistic vision for American society.

This rendering of American Jewish history and experience offers a comforting and affirming vision of ethnic pride and achievement totally consistent with the embrace of American identity, but it is not unproblematic. One danger of this perspective is that it might lead to mistaking one's own values for those of the wider community. After all, Jews would be one of the groups with the most to lose if it turned out that America was not the pluralistic, enlightened society on which they have staked so much. Another threat to this comfortable synthesis arises when the assumption of a stable Jewish identity sustainable by succeeding generations is no longer automatic.

The very success of Jews in neutralizing any tensions between American and Jewish identities is embodied in their ever-accelerating diffusion, geographically, residentially, and occupationally, throughout American society. This success, combined with increasing distance from the immigrant generation and from personal memories of a traditional Jewish ethos, has made it increasingly difficult to rely upon the generational continuity of Jewish identity. In addition, for many American Jews, the easy equation of Jewish with American identity has weakened the claims of a distinctive religious identity. The 1955 observations of the Jewish sociologist WILL HERBERG, in *Protestant, Catholic, Jew*, about the homogenization of different American religious identities into slight variations of one American civil religion still illuminate the situation of the contemporary American Jew. Logic would seem to dictate that one does not have to set oneself apart as a Jew in order to exemplify Jewish cultural values—one can simply be a good American. Thus, with the increasing attenuation of the lines of Jewish continuity, the familiar paradigm of American Jewish synthesis suddenly appears less comforting to those concerned with Jewish survival not as individuals but as a meaningful group.

It is a characteristic of the American setting that the greatest threat to group survival is perceived by many Jews not to be persecution but acceptance. Certainly, the threat of anti-Semitism never disappears from the consciousness of American Jews. The recent opening of the United States Holocaust Museum is ample testimony to both the horrors that the museum documents and the need of American Jews to keep the memory of that horror alive. Though the museum, funded by largely Jewish sources, opened to almost universal acclaim, critics worry that the museum may give visitors a false assurance that they now comprehend the HOLOCAUST, as if a museum could convey more than a glimpse of the attempted destruction of European Jewry.

Indisputably, the memory of the Holocaust has, in recent years, been one of the most effective tools in conveying the weight and significance of Jewish history. For some American Jews, commitment to survival amidst persecution remains the central motivation for the preservation of Jewish identity. For them, the Holocaust proves the defining moment of Jewish and human history. Indeed, much of American Jewish support for Israel is premised on the assumption of a world that will always be hostile to Jews. To believe that America really is different would seem to ignore the repeated and deadly lessons of Jewish history. Thus despite the level of success and range of opportunity that so many Jews have enjoyed in the United States, many cannot avoid the question: "Could it happen here?"

Current uneasiness is exacerbated by worries over right-wing politics inspired by Christian fundamentalism as well as by the vociferous proponents of so-called revisionism who claim that the Holocaust never happened. Recurrent conflict with the African American community has proven particularly troubling. Even more unsettling than the eruption of violent ethnic clashes in places like Crown Heights, Brooklyn, have been the assertions of some African American intellectuals and political leaders, most recently Leonard Jeffries, who target Jews as prime movers in the oppression of their people.

While vicious and racist portrayals of the other persist among both groups, neither black nor Jewish attitudes are monolithic. Many outspoken black intellectuals have openly criticized the virulent anti-Semitism that they perceive within their own community. Among Jews, some intellectuals, notably those identified with NEOCONSERVATISM, view the public policy concerns of African Americans and Jews, particularly over issues such as affirmative action and U.S. policy toward the Middle East, as antithetical. Others yearn for the days of the civil rights era, when many liberal Jews found the demand for racial justice a compelling concern that fitted their vision of America's flawed past and promising future.

Negative portrayals of Jews within the black community assign Jews significant responsibility for activities ranging from the slave trade to the degrading representation of blacks by Hollywood, and, ultimately, for the creation of institutionalized racism in American society. The seeming conflict between the political and social visions held by some Jews and some blacks challenges the way many Jews in America would like to understand themselves. Although Jews have clearly "made it" in America and take pride in the disproportionate success of Jews in various influential fields such as the media, politics, academia, law, and medicine, most still take umbrage at suggestions that Jews wield disproportionate influence in American society. Ultimately, the seeming intractability of black–Jewish tensions, the feeling of being misunderstood, and the apparent acceptance of anti-Semitic rhetoric in public discourse add significantly to a Jewish sense of vulnerability in American society.

Although the persistence of prejudice would seem to mandate a wariness even amidst plenty, American Jews remain the only Jewish community of substantial size whose actual survival has never been threatened by anti-Semitism or persecution. Younger American Jews only infrequently encounter anti-Semitism. Meanwhile, more than half (an estimated 52 percent) of all Jews marrying in recent years have chosen to marry non-Jews, creating a much greater danger to American Jewish group survival than anti-Semitism ever has. The central tensions in American Jewish life are fueled more by the dilemmas posed by social acceptance than by the dynamic of exclusion.

Accordingly, the central challenge at work for those in positions of organizational, religious, and intellectual responsibility for American Jewish life is to help define a positive Jewish identity that American Jews will wish to pass on to their children. Much of American Jewish intellectual energy is thus dedicated to constructing an American Judaism that will guarantee both acceptance as Americans and continuity as Jews for a population which is no longer compelled by older patterns of affiliation.

The effort to address the tensions inherent in American Jewish life may best be seen in ongoing attempts to construct relevant religious models of Judaism. Just as Jews as an ethnic group have adapted to the American environment, so has Judaism as a religion. Perhaps the apparent identity of American and Jewish values convinced Jews in the United States that their religious identity needed to comport with their secular identity. They have for the most part been unwilling to accept great discontinuities between Jewish observance and the rest of their lives.

Two responses have historically shaped the construction of American Jewish identity. On the one hand, American Jews have sought a religious expression that would be responsive to the changing values, expectations and realities presented by American society. On the other hand, amidst the confusing array of Jewish and American identities, Jews have looked to their religion as a repository for distinctive Jewish identity. Differing approaches to reconciling tradition and modernity have resulted in the denominational diversity of American Judaism.

In recent years, the desire for distinctiveness has been reinforced by two general social trends, the celebration of ETHNICITY and the growth of religious fundamentalism. Even Reform temples which had earlier attempted to erase the distinctions between the decorous Jewish and Christian worshipper are introducing more Hebrew and encouraging more distinctive attire and movement during worship. Among the orthodox the shift has taken the form of a more exacting observance of Jewish ritual and tradition within and outside the synagogue.

Despite this new stress on what separates Jewish religious practice from that of other Americans, American Judaism continues to be molded by the realities and expectations of American life. Dizzying social change in recent years has challenged all religious cultures derived from a traditional, patriarchal source. No more than the others has American Judaism avoided the troubling questions posed by feminism and by gays and lesbians. Additionally, American Jews have had to cope with the implications of intermarriage, the ultimate Jewish-American synthesis.

The more liberal movements in American Judaism have done much to redefine Judaism in response to these concerns. The Reform and Reconstructionist movements for instance have been ordaining women as rabbis since the early 1970s; more recently they have acted to acknowledge the presence of gay and lesbian Jews as both congregants and rabbis. The Conservative movement ordained its first woman rabbi in 1985; the issue of homosexuality in Conservative Judaism currently remains a contentious and unresolved issue. All of the movements are struggling with the question of whether or how to accommodate, reject, or reach out to those Jews who marry non-Jews and those non-Jews who marry Jews.

Thus even at the points where a traditional, patriarchal Jewish worldview seems to diverge the most radically from evolving modern expectations, American Jews continue to seek a synthetic blend of Judaism and American culture. The inability of the mainstream movements to respond adequately to current dilemmas has sparked alternative movements which have brought a renewed vitality to American Judaism. Two groups which have responded quite differently to the dilemma of synthesizing American and Jewish values appear to be at opposing ends of the Jewish religious spectrum, yet in their energy and in their commitment to taking the demands and centrality of Jewish law and tradition quite seriously, they share common ground.

Ba'alei Teshuvah are a small but symbolically important population of Jews who were brought up within secular society but who have chosen to take on the extremely strict regimen of a religiously orthodox Jewish life. The adopted culture of the *ba'alei teshuvah* neutralizes and rejects many of the challenges posed by contemporary American life. Within their world, homosexuality and intermarriage do not exist. And although many orthodox groups have adjusted to meet the increasing educational and professional expectations of modern women, the emphasis on traditional gender roles simplifies the confusing choices that the blurring of gender definition has created in the secular world.

The second alternative group does not have a precise label but often exists in small communities called *havurot*. The most committed and engaged of *havurot* Jews believe, like the *ba'alei teshuvah*, that authentic existence as a Jew requires a commitment to distinctively Jewish knowledge, behavior, and community. It is among *havurot* Jews, however, that some of the most radical challenges to traditional Jewish categories have emerged. Their approach appears all the more radical because of their commitment to Jewish tradition. Where mainstream Judaism has responded awkwardly to the needs of those who feel marginalized by traditional Judaism, many feminist as well as gay and lesbian Jews have put themselves at the center in their struggle to make the tradition responsive to their needs. In their fight for a place within Judaism, they are seriously engaging and challenging questions of language, ritual, textual authority, and not least, God.

Recent questioning of the nature of God grew out of discomfort with a God that is always referred to as "He." By asking other Jews if the God they want to worship is really male, feminist challengers have introduced the serious question of what one means when one says God. For some, this sort of questioning has interrupted an often mindless recital of praise for an all-powerful, male being and prompted careful reflection about what they truly believe. Similarly *ba'alei teshuvah*, by accepting the impositions of Jewish law, ostensibly accept the authority of a revelation that comes from God. They too are taking God and the existence of God's particular legislation for Jews with renewed seriousness. Both these groups thus present insistent challenges to America's established Jewish institutions where God's presence has too often seemed merely rhetorical.

Ba'alei teshuvah and *havurot* Jews have injected vital intellectual energy into the American Jewish community. While one group appears to reject the equation of American and Jewish values, the other seems determined to create an authentic rendering of Jewish tradition that still seeks points of contact with secular values. Both these positions and the tension between them will help prompt further reassessment of the boundaries around Jewish life in America. By taking Jewish tradition so seriously, adherents of these movements deny an easy American Jewish paradigm of congruence. Yet they also continue the longstanding effort of earlier generations to create an American Judaism powerful enough to preserve itself. Across the broad spectrum of American Judaism, the balancing act of maintaining a distinctive but mainstream American faith continues.

KARLA GOLDMAN

FURTHER READING

Lynn Davidman, *Tradition in a Rootless World: Women Turn to Orthodox Judaism* (Berkeley: University of California Press, 1991).

Arnold Eisen, "Imagining American Jews: Recent Visions and Revisions," *Conservative Judaism* 41 (winter 1988–9): 3–20.

——, "Jewish Theology in North America: Notes on Two Decades, *American Jewish Year Book 1991* 92: 3–33.

David Ellenson, "The Continued Renewal of North American Jewish Theology: Some Recent Works," *Journal of Reform Judaism* 38 (winter 1991): 1–16.

Sylvia Barack Fishman, *Breath of Life: Feminism in the American Jewish Community* (New York: Free Press, 1992).

Sidney Goldstein, "Profile of American Jewry: Insights from the 1990 National Jewish Population Survey," *American Jewish Year Book 1992* 93: 77–173.

Jack Salzman, ed., *Bridges and Boundaries: African-Americans and American Jews* (New York: George Braziller, 1992).

Jack Wertheimer, *A People Divided: Judaism in Contemporary America* (New York: Basic Books, 1993).

justice ". . . with liberty and justice for all." The pledge of allegiance to the flag of the United States of America ends by proclaiming two paramount values in American thought. Although liberty is uncontestedly the dominant value, justice ranks a close second. (*See also* FREEDOM.) For Americans justice has meant primarily justice under the LAW, a value that has come to include the equal treatment of the races and other groups that deserve equal treatment. A second form of justice, democratic justice, appears in calls for "No taxation without representation" and similar demands throughout American history. Finally, at the turn of the twentieth century, American political thinkers and activists began to stress "social justice," that is, justice in the distribution of opportunities for self-development, income, and wealth.

In early American thought, "justice" meant primarily the first ideal, justice as the rule of law. Americans fought the Revolution for the "rights of Englishmen," which included protection from the legal abuses that they associated with monarchical despotism. Phrases from the Magna Carta guaranteeing a jury of one's peers and forbidding cruel and unusual punishment, as well as later concepts from English law prohibiting bills of attainder, ex post facto laws and self-incrimination, were incorporated into the United States Constitution and BILL OF RIGHTS as ways of trying to guarantee procedural justice under the law.

The ideal of justice under the law has always implied that in some way, as the ancient Greek maxim had it, "justice is equality." The Greek ideal of *isonomia* meant "equality before the law." In "Equality," Isaiah Berlin pointed out that equal treatment within categories is conceptually integral to the meaning of a rule. All societies have rules; all societies consequently have some ideal of equal treatment within the categories established by the rule. Justice requires equal treatment within categories.

This conception of "formal justice," however, says nothing about the construction of the categories. Challenging a rule under which, say, Native Americans, African Americans, women, or noncitizens are subject to treatment different from that of European Americans, men, or citizens requires appealing to standards of justice above the rule itself. These appeals require struggles over the "boundaries" of the categories, drawing arguments from authority, nature, and experience to contend that past reasons for drawing those boundaries to create unequal treatment are invalid. Those who seek to defend any given boundary, Berlin contends, must demonstrate that the boundary is not arbitrary. The default position is EQUALITY.

In American thought, the boundaries of equal treatment under the law were first dramatically contested on the issue of RACE. ANTISLAVERY thinkers appealed to "justice" in demanding freedom for slaves and the rights of citizenship for all adult males born in or naturalized into the nation. (ABRAHAM LINCOLN and others carefully distinguished these rights from social equality.)

After the Union victory in the Civil War, the United States Congress passed and the states ratified the Fourteenth Amendment to the Constitution, which guaranteed that no state should "deny to any person within its jurisdiction the equal protection of the laws." Although this amendment was intended to assure equal justice to ex-slaves in the southern states, the political triumph of white racism in those states and in the United States Congress nullified this objective for generations. Only rarely before the case of *Brown v. Board of Education* in 1954 (desegregating southern public schools) did the justices of the Supreme Court, the nation's most influential practical political philosophers, begin to apply the equal protection clause to overthrow legal discriminations against African Americans. In the early 1970s the Court also began systematically to use this clause to overthrow laws that discriminated against women. Behind these evolving definitions of "equal protection" lay protracted struggles over what boundaries and categories justly distinguished between one group of people and another.

The ideal of democratic justice has had a parallel and equally complex evolution. In 1776 THOMAS JEFFERSON, in the Declaration of Independence, stated in defining form the idea, evolved from debates reaching back to the tenth century, that governments derive "their just powers from the consent of the governed." Only the justice of its political arrangements, originally defined primarily through a theory of consent, legitimated the new American democracy. Yet the nation has grown increasingly distant from the condition of those pilgrim men who, upon landing on the North American shore, literally signed a social contract creating a government for themselves and the women and children among them. Although all still agree that democracy is legitimated by the justice of its procedures, it has become increasingly unclear exactly what democratic justice entails.

American citizens have considered majority rule relatively just throughout the nation's history only because they have held so many cross-cutting interests

that an individual who lost on any one issue might hope to win on another. When the salient cleavages were segmented rather than cross-cutting, as in the South before the Civil War, simple majority rule became arguably unjust. JOHN CALHOUN advanced his theory of the "concurrent majority," on behalf of the South, to establish that any major region should have a veto over national policy when its vital interests were threatened. He argued that majority rule encouraged mutual hostility, while the requirement of concurrence encouraged a common attachment to one's country. Outside the United States, nations with segmented interests, such as Belgium—where the politically salient features of French language, Catholic religion, an agricultural economy and southern geography coincide—have concluded that in their situations democratic justice requires not majority rule but "consociationalism," a form of sharing power and outcomes proportionally among the major segments of the polity.

Both majority rule and consociationalism are procedural definitions of democratic justice, which are arguably just to the degree, among other criteria, that individual citizens have equal power over outcomes. In contrast, substantive definitions judge democratic justice by the closeness of outcomes to some substantive measure of the common good.

Contests over democratic justice also include struggles over its boundaries. Several states restricted the suffrage to taxpayers or proterty owners until the mid-nineteenth century, with the last property qualification for voting falling in North Carolina in 1856. The U.S. Supreme Court ruled the last taxpaying qualifications unconstitutional in 1966. Civil war, political struggle and debate eventually resulted in constitutional amendments giving the vote to African American males in 1870, to women in 1920, and to people aged 18 through 20 in 1971. "Justice" appeared as an argument in the Congressional debates on all three issues. Few Americans have yet proposed giving noncitizens voting rights on the Swedish model.

Finally, prominent early thinkers in the American tradition never raised the third form of justice, justice in the distribution of income and wealth, except, as JAMES MADISON did in *Federalist Papers* 10, 44, and 51, to propound the injustice of majorities using the political process to undermine the rights of private property. For the landowners and merchants from whose classes the framers of the Constitution were drawn, the viability of the new nation required the sanctity of contract.

Many early Massachusetts towns, often religious communities, held large tracts of land in common.

When the citizens in town meeting divided the common land among individuals, they often did so on the basis of a "proportional" justice: those already possessing large individual holdings were given proportionally higher allocations from the common land than those with smaller individual holdings. But Adam Smith's *The Wealth of Nations* was published in Great Britain in the same year that Jefferson wrote the American Declaration of Independence. As the United States evolved, justifications of inequality in material distribution tended to shift from faith in God to faith in the invisible hand of the marketplace.

Radical populist movements repeatedly challenged the justice of particular institutions, such as banks, free trade or monetary policy. Not until the late nineteenth century, however, did American Progressives, influenced by the Social Gospel, socialist thought on the European continent, Fabian thought in Britain, the ferment of ideas that immigrants had brought to the cities, and American experiences of the misery engendered by INDUSTRIALISM, begin to question systematically the justice of existing patterns of wealth and income. In past contexts "justice" had often had a conservative cast, meaning primarily the protection of existing property rights. With a new prefix signaling the change, the concept of "social justice" began at the turn of the century to play a radical role in the critique of existing systems of production and distribution. As JOHN DEWEY put it, the mutual cooperation of economic, social, and scientific factors had now produced the basis for forms of productivity and security that earlier could be found only in the ownership of land. When public parks, lighting, water works, libraries, and schools generally replaced private provision, questions of justice arose regarding the distribution of these goods.

The phrase "social justice," however, slowly and unsteadily faded as the twentieth century wore on, to be revived only recently. "Justice" had always appeared frequently in titles of pamphlets on issues of race. The CIVIL RIGHTS movement of the 1960s brought to the forefront, in the words of MARTIN LUTHER KING JR., demands for "justice and equality," "justice, goodwill and brotherhood," "freedom and justice." But when, in 1962, the Port Huron Statement of the Students for a Democratic Society (SDS) explained the students' political disaffection, the word "justice" appeared only four times in 45 pages, twice in reference to racial justice. In the same year MICHAEL HARRINGTON, in *The Other America*, awakened the nation to the plight of the nation's poor. Harrington, perhaps influenced by Marxist strictures against abstract moralism, never used the word "justice." The resisters to the war in Vietnam, who made justice

central to their politics, did not ask for economic redistribution. In 1966, Martin Luther King, recognizing that civil rights alone were insufficient to help his people, launched a crusade for "economic justice." But while some political parties in Europe even included in their platforms their ideal differentials between top and bottom incomes, American public opinion resisted egalitarian distribution as a conscious goal of public policy.

Only in the aftermath of the activism of the 1960s, as American philosophers turned from previously dominant analytic and linguistic concerns to normative theory, did several philosophers, including JOHN RAWLS, explicitly tackle the problem of just distribution. Rawls's magisterial *A Theory of Justice* (1971) attempted to construct on liberal premises a universally applicable theory of distributive justice. His intuitive idea follows the example of a parent with two children and one cookie who lets one child divide the cookie and the other have first choice. Realizing that he or she will get the smallest piece, the cutter will try to divide the cookie as equally as possible. Rawls asks us to participate in a thought experiment in which individuals hypothetically agree upon a distribution of "primary" goods (such as rights and liberties, income and wealth, and even self-respect) without knowing in what position they will end up in the world created by the distribution to which they agree. Rawls advances this thought experiment as a procedure for determining what distributions are just: if one would agree to a distribution knowing one might find oneself on the low end of that distribution, it is just.

As Rawls himself later recognized, this conception of procedural justice is not universal but rooted in the liberal tradition. It assumes at the outset that the hypothetical individuals choosing in this thought experiment are free, equal, and self-interested, and Rawls argues subsequently that in choosing, these individuals would make liberty (particularly liberty of conscience and of citizenship) "lexically" (absolutely) prior to all other goods.

In *Anarchy, State and Utopia* (1974), Robert Nozick, a philosopher of LIBERTARIANISM, challenged Rawls's theory on the grounds that, like utilitarianism, it took into account only the "pattern" of any given distribution of goods at a particular time (as a snapshot might), and not the history of how that distribution came about. Goods do not arrive as manna from heaven, he argued, but are produced by individuals who have rights in what they have produced. Nozick considers "just" a distribution in which individuals keep whatever goods they can accumulate through just production and just transfers. Assuming a right to everything one produces, Nozick ignores Rawls's arguments that we do not deserve our talents because they are the result of a "natural lottery" in genes, and that because any one individual's production depends on the contributions of the larger society, no one is solely responsible for, or has a full right to, his or her product. Feminist philosopher Susan Okin has argued against Nozick that all possession is socially constructed. Women produce children through hard labor, but do not conclude that they have property rights in their product.

The appropriate boundaries for distributive justice also remain contested. In *Political Theory and International Relations* (1979), Charles Beitz notes that Rawls's theory of justice assumes a nation-state, but it could—and he argues should—apply globally. Susan Okin notes that Rawls does not apply his theory within the family: he gives no reason why one might choose to give up the protections of justice in this highly vulnerable realm, particularly if one is a woman.

Against Rawls, Michael Walzer argues in *Spheres of Justice* (1983) that no one form of distributive justice is appropriate for all kinds of goods. Power, money, security, education, and other different kinds of goods should be distributed according to different criteria. The criteria in each "sphere" of justice evolve from shared social meanings, so that "a given society is just if its substantive life is lived in . . . a way faithful to the shared understandings of the members" (p. 313). But women philosophers from Susan Okin to Judith Shklar point out that those "shared understandings" cannot serve as the sole criteria for justice when some members of society have had disproportionate influence in producing those understandings and other members have had little access to informed alternate understandings of themselves or their societies.

Some theorists of FEMINISM argue further that the Western philosophical and societal privileging of RIGHTS and justice undermines attention to responsibilities and relationships. Lawrence Kohlberg, in *The Philosophy of Moral Development* (1981), gives what he considers an objectively higher value to moral judgments based on concepts of rights and universalistic justice than to judgments based on relationships of care. But Carol Gilligan, in *In a Different Voice* (1982), suggests that societal values in the United States encourage rights and justice language among highly educated men and allocate concern about relationships to women. She argues against Kohlberg that concerns for preserving and enhancing relationships have a moral value equal to concerns for universalistic justice and rights.

Feminist theorists also criticize the standard of "impartiality" in justice, which always masks the power of whatever dominant group implicitly sets the norm for what is perceived to be standard human behavior. Catharine MacKinnon, in *Feminism Unmodified* (1987), points out that when workplaces are designed for workers with wives, health policies for individuals who will not become pregnant, and sports events for athletes who excel in upper body strength, "neutral" laws that allow women to compete "equally" perpetuate domination. Similarly, African American feminists reveal how in a society in which the majority are European American, the very word "women" implicitly encodes experiences typical of European American, but often not of African American, women. Seemingly impartial standards aimed at protecting "women workers," for example, may silently exclude many African American women, a majority of whom before 1960 worked as domestic servants outside the reach of most protective labor legislation.

As contemporary American thinkers struggle with the ways patterns of language and thought maintain and foster patterns of domination, permeating the very ideas of neutrality and fairness that make up our concept of justice, some social critics have begun to adopt again the word "oppression," which FREDERICK DOUGLASS used to describe race relations before and after the Civil War. As Iris Marion Young argues in *Justice and the Politics of Difference* (1990), the word "oppression" expresses the concrete harms of exploitation, marginalization, powerlessness, cultural imperialism, and violence, while theories of justice tend to be abstracted from the particular circumstances of everyday life. But justice entails more than ending oppression or closing the gap between the desire for happiness and obstacles to that desire. People's gut senses of injustice, and their hopes for rectification in the name of justice, reflect the appeal of abstract principles that social actors carry from the context in which they were generated to other contexts, in which their new application can convince people to change. Once principles such as justice under the law, democratic justice, social justice, distributive justice, racial justice, and gender justice become legitimate parts of political debate, they persist even when popular support for greater justice declines.

JANE MANSBRIDGE

See also CONSERVATISM; CRITICAL LEGAL STUDIES; CRITICAL RACE THEORY; FEMINIST JURISPRUDENCE.

FURTHER READING

Isaiah Berlin, "Equality," *Proceedings of the Aristotelian Society* 56 (1955–6): 301–26.

John C. Calhoun, *A Disquisition on Government* (1853; Indianapolis: Bobbs-Merrill/Liberal Arts Press, 1953).

Patricia Hill Collins, *Black Feminist Thought* (Boston: Unwin Hyman, 1990).

John Dewey, *Ethics*, in Jo Ann Boydston and Barbara Levine, eds., *John Dewey: the Later Works*, vol. 7 (1932; Carbondale: Southern Illinois University Press, 1985).

Martin Luther King Jr., *Why We Can't Wait* (New York: Harper and Row, 1963).

Susan Moller Okin, *Justice, Gender and the Family* (New York: Basic Books, 1989).

Judith N. Shklar, *Faces of Injustice* (New Haven: Yale University Press, 1990).

Students for a Democratic Society, "The Port Huron Statement," reprinted in James Miller, *Democracy is in the Streets* (New York: Simon and Schuster, 1987).

Michael Walzer, *Spheres of Justice* (New York: Basic Books, 1983).

K

Kallen, Horace (b. Berenstadt, Silesia, Aug. 11, 1882; d. Palm Beach, Fla., Feb. 16, 1974). Philosopher. Drawing on the Judaism he inherited from his father, a German-born rabbi, and the pragmatism of his Harvard mentor WILLIAM JAMES, Kallen constructed an influential early version of what we currently call cultural pluralism. An ardent Zionist, Kallen sought to emphasize the contributions of Judaism to Western culture by contrasting the particular virtues of "Hebraism" to the "Hellenism" derived from Greek and Roman civilizations. Kallen believed that each ethnic group should cultivate its own cultural traditions but also appreciate the other traditions that together constitute the "symphony" of American democracy. He considered efforts to eliminate ethnic differences in a single melting pot undemocratic and coercive. Kallen's writings include *Culture and Democracy in the United States* (1924), *The Education of Free Men* (1949), and *Cultural Pluralism and the American Idea* (1956).

See also CULTURAL PLURALISM AND MULTICULTURALISM.

FURTHER READING
David Hollinger, "Democracy and the Melting Pot Reconsidered," in Hollinger, *In the American Province: Studies in the History and Historiography of Ideas* (Bloomington: Indiana University Press, 1985).

Kaplan, Mordecai (b. Švenčionys, Lithuania, June 11, 1881; d. New York, N.Y., Nov. 8, 1983). Religious leader. Shaped by the functionalist sociology of Émile Durkheim and the philosophical PRAGMATISM of WILLIAM JAMES, Kaplan founded the Reconstructionist movement in American Judaism. As a professor at the Jewish Theological Seminary in New York City, in books such as *Judaism as a Civilization* (1934), *Judaism in Transition* (1936), and *The Future of the American Jew* (1948), and in the periodical *Reconstructionist*, which he founded in 1935, Kaplan downplayed the role of religious doctrine and emphasized cultural community, Zionism, and revitalized Jewish social traditions.

FURTHER READING
Rachel Libowitz, *Mordecai M. Kaplan and the Development of Reconstructionism* (New York: E. Mellon, 1984).

Kazin, Alfred (b. Brooklyn, N.Y., June 5, 1915). Writer and literary critic. With *On Native Grounds* in 1942, Kazin established himself as a leading interpreter of American literary history and an important cultural critic among the NEW YORK INTELLECTUALS. He insisted on the significance of the American (as opposed to the European) literary tradition and dissociated himself from PROLETARIANISM, which he believed subordinated art to politics. Much of his cultural commentary has appeared in the form of memoirs. *A Walker in the City* (1951) evokes his childhood in the Brownsville section of New York. *Starting Out in the Thirties* (1968) exemplifes his romantic cosmopolitanism, which turns away from ideological prescription and yearns for the warmth and vitality of human relationships. *New York Jew* (1978) brings his story into the postwar years of increasing prosperity and assimilation.

FURTHER READING
Alexander Bloom, *Prodigal Sons: the New York Intellectuals and Their World* (New York: Oxford University Press, 1986).

Keller, Helen (b. Tuscumbia, Ala., June 27, 1880; d. Westport, Conn., June 1, 1968). Writer and lecturer. Keller was rendered blind and deaf by illness in infancy; her struggle to overcome her disabilities has become one of the heroic sagas of modern American culture. Although she was involved in a wide range of activities, including the Socialist Party, labor organization, militant suffragism, birth control, and the movement for racial equality, she was best known as a symbol of triumph over adversity. In a series of magazine articles and in *The Story of My Life* (1902), she explained how she learned to read, write, and speak. In many later books and lecture tours, she worked to erase the stigma of blindness and deafness, to free blind and deaf people from asylums, to obtain federal funding for readers and recorded books, and to secure Social Security coverage for disabled Americans.

FURTHER READING
Joseph P. Lash, *Helen and Teacher: The Story of Helen Keller and Anne Sullivan Macy* (New York: Delacorte, 1980).

Kelley, Florence (b. Philadelphia, Pa., Sept. 12, 1859; d. Philadelphia, Pa., Feb. 17, 1932). As head of the National Consumers' League (NCL) from the time of its founding in 1899 until her death in 1932, Florence Kelley did much to shape the emerging

American welfare state. By orchestrating the agenda and channeling the activism of more than 60 local consumer leagues, she left a strong imprint on the Progressive era.

Kelley's political leadership began where that of her father, William Durrah Kelley, and her Quaker great aunt, Sarah Pugh, ended. A Scottish-Irish Presbyterian, William Kelley helped found the Republican Party and became one of the foremost proponents of a biracial Republican Party in the post-Civil War South. Between 1860 and 1890, he was reelected to 15 consecutive terms in the U.S. House of Representatives. Seeking to embrace the interests of both capital and labor, his advocacy of protective tariffs for American industry earned him the nickname of "Pig Iron Kelley" and his championship of working people the appellation "the conscience of the House."

Through her father, Florence Kelley came to reflect on social injustice and political remedies for it. Her autobiography notes that he taught her to read using a book illustrated with woodcuts of gnome-like children at work in British brickyards, "balancing with their arms heavy loads of wet clay on their heads" (p. 26). She began to read government reports at the age of ten and to use the Library of Congress at the age of twelve. When she graduated from Cornell in 1882, her honors thesis, "On Some Changes in the Legal Status of the Child since Blackstone," was published in a prestigious public policy journal. In an age noted for laissez-faire government, her thesis argued that the state had the power to intervene in family relationships to defend the rights and interests of women and children.

Florence's mother, Caroline Bonsall, came from a Quaker and Unitarian family, and insofar as she received religious training it combined these two dissenting faiths. Her great-aunt Sarah Pugh was a close friend of LUCRETIA MOTT and a lifelong supporter of radical social causes, serving as the president of the Philadelphia Female Anti-Slavery Society for most of its existence between 1833 and 1873. To Florence, Pugh became "conscience incarnate," exemplifying the ability of women's leadership and women's organizations to mold the forces of social change.

Florence Kelley's theoretical framework for social criticism deepened considerably when, as a postgraduate student at the University of Zurich, she underwent a conversion to SOCIALISM, a belief she maintained the rest of her life. In 1884 she married a Russian Jewish socialist medical student, Lazare Wischnewetzky, and gave birth to three children during the subsequent three years. Believing that the processes of industrial capitalism were generating social revolution, Kelley-Wischnewetzky thought that

the impending uprisings could be made more temperate and politically fruitful if working people became familiar with the writings of German scientific socialism, especially those of Frederich Engels and Karl Marx. In 1886 she completed the first English translation of Engels's classic, *The Condition of the English Working Class in 1844*. Hers is still the translation that most scholars prefer.

Moving with her family to New York City in 1887, Kelley tried to find a place for herself in the shifting American political scene. She and Lazare joined but were expelled from the Socialist Labor Party, largely because Kelley scorned the utopianism of its German-speaking membership. After this rupture she shifted her intellectual and political energies to the question of child labor and the inadequacy of efforts by state bureaus of labor statistics to study or regulate child workers. When Lazare's medical practice failed in 1891 and he began battering her, she fled with the children to Chicago, where she soon joined JANE ADDAMS at Hull House.

Hull House was already, only two years after its founding, the nation's preeminent social settlement. Sustained by this stream of vibrant reform activism, Kelley's political effectiveness vastly increased. Establishing herself and the settlement at the head of a spirited attack on sweatshop labor in the city's garment industry, she was appointed Chief Factory Inspector of Illinois by reform governor John Altgeld in 1893. Assisted by 12 deputies, half of whom were required (in legislation drafted at Hull House) to be women, Kelley enforced pathbreaking eight-hour day legislation for women and children. Although the Illinois Supreme Court in 1895 declared the law unconstitutional for women workers, and although she was dismissed by Altgeld's successor in 1896, her three years as the state's chief enforcer of industrial regulations made Kelley one of the nation's most knowledgeable experts on the reform of the industrial workplace.

In 1899 Kelley returned to New York City to head the newly created National Consumers' League, made up of middle-class and trade union women, which spearheaded the expansion of state responsibility for the WELFARE of working people, especially women and children. Until her death in 1932, she coordinated a broad effort among men's and women's reform groups to formulate progressive industrial regulations. She traveled extensively among local consumers' leagues to gain their commitment to the national program, and oversaw the defense of the NCL's legislative strategies in state and federal courts.

Particularly notable was the NCL's successful defense before the U.S. Supreme Court of a state law limiting the working day for women to ten hours (*Muller v. Oregon*, 1908), and a similar law for men (*Bunting v. Oregon*, 1917). (*See also* LOUIS D. BRANDEIS.) Thanks to Kelley's initiative between 1909 and 1923 the NCL also pioneered the establishment and judicial defense of state minimum wage legislation, laying the groundwork for the creation of a federal minimum wage in the Fair Labor Standards Act of 1938. Kelley also devoted herself to an unsuccessful campaign for an amendment to the Constitution prohibiting child labor, and in 1921 she played a key role in the passage of the Sheppard-Towner Maternity and Infancy Protection Act, which first allocated federal funds for human health.

Kelley believed that the best way to overcome the substantive inequalities that women encountered in the paid labor force was to pass compensatory gender-specific legislation. Always an energetic supporter of equal access to the vote and of the woman suffrage movement, she also insisted that promoting the equality of men and women required special legislation for women. When, after the passage of the suffrage amendment in 1920, a small group of suffragists organized the National Woman's Party and advocated the passage of an Equal Rights Amendment, Kelley led the opposition. She feared that this "blanket" approach to WOMEN'S RIGHTS, by eliminating special protections and benefits for women, would subject women to renewed exploitation. For example, legislation limiting hours and providing a minimum wage for women workers might, in the wake of an Equal Rights Amendment, be declared unconstitutional.

Florence Kelley's success was rooted in nineteenth-century social strategies, especially local, grass-roots activism, and nineteenth-century social values—especially the belief that women, whose lives were rooted in the daily practice of taking care of others, could introduce a different and superior vision of social justice into the polity. This belief diminished sharply in the 1920s with the erosion of Progressive reform generally, and the emergence of modern feminism, which stressed individual fulfillment more than social service. Between 1930 and 1960 many of Kelley's legislative accomplishments were used to discriminate against working women as well as to protect them from exploitation. For example, state laws limiting the amount of weight that employers could require women to lift (usually 25 pounds) prompted unscrupulous companies and unions to exclude women by misrepresenting the weight-lifting requirements for many jobs.

In the 1970s the National Organization for Women, determined to push again for equal rights, successfully dismantled state labor laws for women. Yet that position is now contested among feminist legal theorists. For example, legal theorist Christine Littleton has argued in "Equality and Feminist Legal Theory" (*University of Pittsburgh Law Review*, 1987) that substantive equality can sometimes be better achieved through a recognition of gender differences than an insistence on formal equality. The question of how to assist women in overcoming social inequalities is once again being debated in open-ended fashion. Strategies based on equal rights are understood to put women at risk of being subjected to male norms—a risk earlier attributed only to strategies based on "difference." Renewed attention to Florence Kelley's long career as a militant defender of equality through difference can help advance the debate.

KATHRYN KISH SKLAR

See also PROGRESSIVISM.

FURTHER READING

Dorothy Rose Blumberg, *Florence Kelley: the Making of a Social Pioneer* (New York: Augustus M. Kelley, 1966).

Josephine Goldmark, *Impatient Crusader: Florence Kelley's Life Story* (1953; New York: Greenwood, 1976).

Florence Kelley, *The Autobiography of Florence Kelley: Notes of Sixty Years*, ed. Kathryn Kish Sklar (Chicago: Charles Kerr, 1986).

Kathryn Kish Sklar, *Florence Kelley and Women's Political Culture: "Doing the Nation's Work," 1830–1900* (New Haven: Yale University Press, 1995).

Kellor, Frances (b. Columbus, Ohio, Oct. 20, 1873; d. New York, N.Y., Jan. 4, 1952).   Sociologist and reformer. Kellor was the first sociologist to articulate a coherent environmental explanation for criminal behavior and persistent unemployment. In articles for popular and scholarly journals and in *Experimental Sociology* (1901), she explored the sources of deviancy and recommended far-reaching penal reforms. In *Out of Work* (1901), she traced unemployment to systematic discrimination on the basis of race, ethnicity, and gender. In the 1920s and 1930s she helped establish the American Arbitration Association and wrote the first *Code of Arbitration* (1931), outlining ways to resolve commercial, industrial, and international disputes outside the legal system. She was also the author of *Immigration and the Future* (1920).

FURTHER READING

Ellen Fitzpatrick, *Endless Crusade: Women Social Scientists and Progressive Reform* (New York: Oxford University Press, 1990).

Kennan, George (b. Milwaukee, Wis., Feb. 16, 1904).   Diplomat and Sovietologist. In his influential anonymous article "The Sources of Soviet Conduct"

(*Foreign Affairs*, 1947), Kennan articulated the policy of containment. Since the Soviets were inherently paranoid, unreasonable, and aggressive, he argued, the United States must use a consistently and strategically applied counterforce to confine communism to its current boundaries. Later, however, he adopted a more supple position of "disengagement" and criticized COLD WAR inflexibility, the arms race, and the extension of containment to Indochina. A gifted writer, he has published important works of history, including *American Diplomacy, 1900–1950* (1951), and a multivolume *Memoirs*.

FURTHER READING
Walter L. Hixson, *George F. Kennan: Cold War Iconoclast* (New York: Columbia University Press, 1989).

Kent, James (b. Fredricksburgh, N.Y., July 31, 1763; d. New York, N.Y., Dec. 12, 1847). Jurist. As chancellor of the New York Court of Chancery (1814–23), Kent shaped common law into a workable system. Supplementing English common law with ideas of natural law and comparative studies of international law, Kent created a unified system of American equity jurisprudence. His *Commentaries* (1826–30) emphasized property rights: although the state could legitimately regulate the ownership or use of property, he believed that the judiciary should monitor state infringement of individual property rights. An opponent of universal suffrage and universal education, Kent resisted the redistribution of political or economic power.

FURTHER READING
John Theodore Horton, *James Kent: a Study in Conservatism* (New York: Appleton, 1939).

Kerouac, Jack [born Jean-Louis] (b. Lowell, Mass., Mar. 12, 1922; d. St. Petersburg, Fla., Oct. 21, 1969). Writer. Kerouac's *On the Road* (1957), with its frenetic, footloose wanderers and its impulsive sensuality, is a classic of the BEAT GENERATION. Condemning the alienation produced by American social conformity, Kerouac celebrated an exhilarating freedom from middle-class propriety. His search for pure experience and sensation undergirded his principle of never rewriting a text: only a direct record of thought and perception can embody raw, unmediated truth. Kerouac's other writings, all autobiographical, include *The Dharma Bums* (1958), *The Subterraneans* (1958), and *Desolation Angels* (1965).

FURTHER READING
Dennis McNally, *Desolate Angel: Jack Kerouac, the Beat Generation, and America* (New York: Random House, 1979).

Keynesianism As a major school of macroeconomic thought, Keynesianism represents a particular way of understanding the behavior of the aggregate economy (or macroeconomy), as distinguished from the economic behavior of individual households, businesses, and government agencies. The Keynesian approach contains many variants, all of which originate in the work of John Maynard Keynes, a British economist best known for his 1936 book *The General Theory of Employment, Interest, and Money*.

Keynes's theory marked a fundamental departure from orthodox, or "classical," economics, which purported to demonstrate that market forces—namely, wage, product price, and interest rate adjustments—could be relied upon to produce full employment of society's economic resources. When the *General Theory* was published, empirical reality was already testing orthodoxy's explanatory limits, since the world economy was mired in a Great Depression that had lasted for six years and would continue for another three.

One of Keynes's main contributions to economics was to explain how there could be persistent underemployment of society's labor and capital resources in modern capitalist economies, and to explain why society could not rely on market forces to rectify the problem. Keynes's explanation centered around a breakdown of the capital investment mechanism caused by inadequate market outlets (or aggregate demand) for firms' products. When firms do not adequately invest in new capital equipment, national income falls and unemployment levels rise. In Keynes's view, market forces—be they in stock and bond markets, product markets, or labor markets—would not only fail to produce the appropriate adjustment, but they would behave perversely by reinforcing the investment failure. For example, when product prices fall during a recession to correct an excess of supply over demand, this depresses firms' ability and incentive to invest in plant and equipment.

The public policy implications of Keynes's ideas are straightforward. The government should address the underlying cause of investment failures by supplementing private sector spending with public sector spending, by supporting private consumption levels with public income supports (including WELFARE programs such as social security and unemployment compensation), and by exercising more social control over investment decisions and international capital movements.

In many respects Keynes's theory was fundamentally conservative, insofar as it pointed to ways that the government could preserve the basic institutions of capitalism, including private ownership of capital. But his ideas were regarded as heresy by many economists because they cast fundamental doubt on orthodoxy's central tenet, the self-adjusting capacity of markets. While British Keynesians worked to expand on Keynes's break with orthodoxy, mainstream U.S. Keynesians worked to reconcile Keynes's ideas with orthodox macroeconomics, and left many of Keynes's most important insights behind.

The 1950s and 1960s marked the heyday of Keynesianism in the U.S. policy arena. Public confidence in economists' ability to "fine-tune" the macroeconomy over the business cycle was bolstered by the U.S. economy's generally strong record of noninflationary growth during this period (which arguably had more to do with the federally financed expansion of the U.S. defense industry than with Keynesian business cycle policy).

However, U.S. Keynesianism's policy victory was to be short-lived. During the escalation of the Vietnam War, the appropriate economic policy was to raise taxes to prevent excessive aggregate demand growth. But political will failed, and elected officials refused to ask citizens to pay higher taxes for an unpopular war. The result was inflation. Public confidence in Keynesianism eroded in the 1970s with the emergence of "stagflation," simultaneous inflation and unemployment.

As U.S. macroeconomic performance deteriorated in the 1970s, Keynesianism faded from grace in the mainstream of the U.S. economic profession, to be replaced by the "rational expectations" approach. According to this view, government efforts to increase output and employment with Keynesian policy will fail because they will be negated by countervailing private sector agents acting on the basis of "rational" expectations. "Rational" expectations means that households and firms understand the underlying structure of the economy and are therefore able to anticipate how government policy will affect the economy. For example, the government's attempt to stimulate output by increasing the money supply will be stymied as wage-earners, anticipating that real-wage-eroding inflation will result from the money supply growth, refuse to work more hours and demand higher wages to keep their real wages constant. The result? Higher wages and higher prices, but no more output or employment.

Mainstream U.S. Keynesians responded to the rational expectations attack in the 1980s with an approach called "New Keynesianism." New Keynesians accept that expectations are "rational," but argue that government policy will still be effective in the short run because the prevalence of long-term contracts in labor and product markets makes wages and prices "sticky" (slow to adjust). In the above example of expansionary monetary policy, New Keynesians would argue that wage-earners are unable to increase their money wages instantly because their money wages are set in multiyear contracts. As a result, higher money wages and prices will not frustrate policy-makers' goal of higher output and employment —for a while.

While mainstream U.S. Keynesians were preoccupied with neutralizing the rational expectations attack, a new school of U.S. Keynesianism was born outside of the mainstream, Post-Keynesianism. This approach revived Keynes's fundamental skepticism about the market mechanism, stressing the pervasive and destabilizing role of expectations in capital investment decisions and in financial markets. Post-Keynesianism is perhaps best known for its theory of inflation as a struggle among earners of different kinds of income over the distribution of income and for its advocacy of income policies to control wage and price inflation.

Meanwhile, on the 1980s U.S. policy front, the Reagan administration turned neither to rational expectations nor to New Keynesianism, but to "supply-side" economics, which called for lower tax rates to encourage thriftiness, industriousness, and growth. (See also CONSERVATISM; Neoconservatism.) Because a defense buildup was thrown into the mix, the result, ironically enough, was a classic military demand-driven Keynesian boom, with an exploding federal government budget and trade deficits to boot. At the outset of the 1990s, bipartisan political fear of the federal deficit seriously constrained the spending and taxation options of the federal government at the same time that the U.S. economy was mired in a growth crisis not unlike that of the 1930s.

The obsession of mainstream macroeconomics in the U.S., Keynesian and non-Keynesian alike, with policy effectiveness or ineffectiveness in the short run has rendered it singularly irrelevant to the modern economic condition. U.S. Keynesians who value policy relevance in academic work would be well advised to return to the basic ideas put forth in the *General Theory*. Then, as now, the problem of long-run sustainable growth demands critical thinking about the basic social framework of U.S. economic development, not endless debate over the short-term effects of government policy within a social framework the rationality of which is erroneously taken for granted.

JANE KNODELL

See also LAW AND ECONOMICS.

FURTHER READING

Alfred S. Eichner, ed., *A Guide to Post-Keynesian Economics* (White Plains, N.Y.: M. E. Sharpe, 1978).

Robert J. Gordon, "What is New-Keynesian Economics?" *Journal of Economic Literature* 28 (Sept. 1990): 1115–71.

John Maynard Keynes, "The General Theory," *Quarterly Journal of Economics* 51 (Feb. 1937): 209–23.

Arthur Okun, *Prices and Quantities: a Macroeconomic Analysis* (Washington, D.C.: The Brookings Institution, 1981).

Wallace C. Peterson and Paul S. Estenson, *Income, Employment, and Economic Growth*, 7th ed. (New York: Norton, 1992).

King, Martin Luther, Jr. (b. Atlanta, Ga., Jan. 15, 1929; d. Memphis, Tenn., Apr. 4, 1968).   The pre-eminent leader of the modern CIVIL RIGHTS movement in the United States, Martin Luther King Jr. was a charismatic dissenter who both embodied and transformed the African American social gospel tradition. A privileged insider within the largest African American religious denomination, he chose to reject black Baptist fundamentalism in favor of liberal European American theological and philosophical ideas. He was paradoxically a conciliatory revolutionary, battling to overcome entrenched racism and economic oppression while struggling to preserve possibilities for social reconciliation. A cosmopolitan advocate of racial integration, he remained rooted in enduring family relationships and religious ties. He attended Crozer Theological Seminary in Pennsylvania and Boston University, spent five years as minister of Montgomery's Dexter Avenue Baptist church, and traveled widely as an internationally known advocate of Gandhian nonviolence, but his worldview was shaped by, and his life stayed centered in, the Atlanta black community where his forbears had played prominent roles since the 1890s. King's dual grounding in African American and European American cultural and intellectual traditions made him a unique transracial leader.

Until he was 12, King lived in the two-story home on Auburn Avenue where he was born, and where his grandparents had resided since early in the century. A block away was another focus of his childhood, Ebenezer Baptist Church, which his grandparents, Jennie Celeste and Adam Daniel (A.D.) Williams, had transformed from a small congregation without a building in 1894 into one of the city's major African American institutions. The Reverend Williams was one of the organizers of the National Baptist Convention, held many leadership roles in local and state Baptist affairs, and helped establish Atlanta's chapter of the National Association for the Advancement of Colored People. After King's father married the Williams's only child, Alberta, and then succeeded as Ebenezer's pastor when his father-in-law died in 1931, the elder King continued the family tradition of forceful preaching and civil rights activism, leading campaigns for black voting rights and equal salaries for black teachers.

In an autobiographical statement written while a student at Crozer, King Jr. described the "noble example" of his father as "the great moving factor" in his decision to become a minister, but he also wavered between acceptance of and rebellion against the religious traditions his father represented. His persistent doubts about Baptist tenets were not allayed until his undergraduate years at Morehouse College (1944–8), when he came under the influence of President Benjamin Mays and Professor George Kelsey, men he saw as "deeply religious" yet "learned"— "the ideal I wanted a minister to be." During subsequent theological studies at Crozer (1948–51) and Boston University (1951–5), King gradually reconciled teenage skepticism with his "inner urge . . . to serve humanity" through the ministry. His academic papers, flawed by plagiaries, displayed his determined effort to appropriate modern theological and philosophical ideas that would be useful to him in his role as an activist preacher. In one of his papers he explained that his goal was to synthesize the best in liberal theology with the best in neo-orthodox theology, and many of his later writings and speeches would display this characteristic eclecticism. King's 1953 marriage to Coretta Scott, who shared many of his dissenting views on politics and religion, strengthened his capacity to embrace his inherited calling while transcending it.

Once Rosa Parks's refusal to give up her seat in the "white only" section of a bus thrust him into a leadership role in the Montgomery boycott of 1955 and 1956, King's leadership gradually shifted from the religious to the political realm, but his worldview remained constant. Although family connections contributed to his rapid emergence as a national spokesperson for the civil rights movement, he challenged educated and affluent blacks to revive the African American prophetic tradition. Publicly criticizing Cold War liberalism and capitalist materialism, while also rejecting communism, King admitted in *Stride Toward Freedom: the Montgomery Story* (1958) that reading the works of Karl Marx had reinforced his long-held concern about the gap between "superfluous wealth" and "abject poverty." He charged that capitalist materialism always prompted people to prefer "making a living" to "making a life." King's evolving eclectic radicalism mixed his Christian and Gandhian nonviolent civil disobedience with the socialist tradition and with anticolonial currents flowing out of the successful independence movements in West Africa.

King's growing influence resulted not from his intellectual originality but from his political and moral leadership. Yet his public role was always undergirded by his thinking, just as his incomparable oratory drew its power not only from his training as a preacher, but from his study of theology and philosophy. His key legacy for Christian ethics and for American political thought was his reassertion—in the face of mid-century Niebuhrian skepticism about ideals such as pacifism—of the doctrine of nonviolent resistance. Drawing on the African American social gospel precepts instilled in him as a child, as well as the ideas of Gandhi, Jesus, and the early REINHOLD NIEBUHR of *Moral Man and Immoral Society* (1932), King argued that unwarranted suffering was redemptive—and in the particular case of African Americans, the only politically effective strategy in the struggle for rights. King was restating the longstanding liberal Protestant tenet that the law of love should rule all spheres of life, private and public. But he gave that doctrine new saliency by insisting that the preaching of love had to be combined with nonviolent resistance to social evil. A community grew in solidarity as it joined in struggle. And that travail became redemptive when the members of that community eschewed bitterness, when they forgave the enemies against whom they struggled. What Niebuhr had called "the spiritual discipline against resentment" became an essential feature of King's militant resistance to injustice. It permitted a minority community to deepen its inner life while invoking God's judgment upon the failure of the wider community to live up to its own avowed moral standards. Embarking on the path of suffering prepared the way for a reconciliation that could follow the period of crisis and conflict.

President of the Southern Christian Leadership Conference (SCLC) after its establishment in 1957, King experienced difficulty maintaining a middle course between older national civil rights leaders, who generally stressed litigation and lobbying efforts to achieve civil rights reform, and the grassroots leaders who moved toward mass militancy early in the 1960s. Many of the black college students who launched a series of desegregation sit-ins in 1960 initially looked to him for inspiration but not for tactical direction. In particular, young organizers affiliated with the Student Nonviolent Coordinating Committee were increasingly influenced by the emergent ideas of their own local movements, especially those in Mississippi and elsewhere in the deep South. Most SNCC activists agreed with King's broad conception of the objectives of the southern struggle,

and they drew upon the same ideological sources that had influenced King, but SNCC's organizing efforts emphasized the development of sustained movements under local leadership. By the time of the massive desegregation campaign in Albany, Georgia, during 1961 and 1962, some SNCC workers openly derided King's hierarchical leadership style, believing that it reinforced traditional patterns of deference and dependence.

As the African American struggle expanded from desegregation protests to mass movements in the North as well as the South, the news media often depicted King as controlling events, but he limited his active involvement to a few highly publicized civil rights campaigns—notably Birmingham in 1963, and Selma in 1965—that secured popular support for the passage of the Civil Rights Act of 1964 and the Voting Rights Act of 1965. King's ability to focus national attention on orchestrated confrontations with racist authorities, combined with his stunning oration at the 1963 march on Washington, strengthened his effectiveness as the leading African American spokesperson of the first half of the 1960s. In 1964 he was awarded the Nobel Peace Prize. Nevertheless, even as King came to symbolize the entire black struggle, he became less able to influence its course. His authority among African Americans declined after 1965, because of his reluctance, in the face of the escalating black insurgency of the period, to alter his firmly rooted beliefs about racial integration and nonviolence. A product of black institutions and the head of a group comprised of black clergymen, he was nevertheless unpersuaded by black nationalist calls for racial uplift and institutional development in black communities. In his last book, *Where Do We Go from Here: Chaos or Community?* (1967), King dismissed the claim of Black Power advocates to be the most revolutionary force in the United States, but he acknowledged that they responded to a psychological need among African Americans he had not previously addressed. "Against the long night of physical slavery," King affirmed, self-esteem was the most potent weapon, the means of the Negro's "own emancipation proclamation."

King's ambivalence about the course of black militancy in the 1960s was most apparent in his response to the growing influence of MALCOLM X and other ideologues of the African American consciousness movement. While sympathizing with the upsurge of racial militancy symbolized in the Black Power slogan, King saw the rhetorical militancy of Stokely Carmichael and other firebrands as counterproductive. Although his strong ties to the African American church ensured that his black following would remain sizable during the final years of his life, King's continued commitment to Gandhian nonviolence and racial reconciliation led some black critics to paint him as too dependent upon white support. Ironically, even as insular black militants undermined his influence, especially in northern urban areas, King also lost the support of many whites when in 1967 he publicly opposed the Johnson administration over the war in Vietnam.

Yet, even as his popularity declined, King became ever more insistent that his version of Gandhian nonviolence and social gospel Christianity were the most appropriate response to the problems of black Americans. Recognizing the need to build his following among alienated and powerless urban blacks, King garnered only modest support when he led an open-housing campaign in Chicago during the summer of 1966. Late in 1967 he announced plans for a multiracial Poor People's March on Washington designed to prod the federal government to strengthen its antipoverty efforts. King's outspokenness made him unwelcome at Lyndon Johnson's White House and a target of FBI investigations. In March 1968, press criticism of him intensified after he became involved with a strike of Memphis garbage workers that turned violent. At the time of his assassination in Memphis on April 4, 1968, King's popularity was at the lowest point of the decade, but he remained steadfast in his views. In his final public statements, he seemed resigned to his political isolation and perhaps even to his death, while continuing to speak out against exploitation and oppression. Major violent insurgencies in northern cities during the last three years of his life did not undermine his conviction that the nonviolent strategy was not only morally superior to other alternatives but also the most effective one available to African Americans. The setbacks of his final years made him increasingly fatalistic about his personal future, but did not deprive him of the larger hope that issued from his faith. The night before he died he told an audience of Memphis strikers that he had been to the mountaintop and seen the promised land. He might not get there with them, he said, but God would deliver His people.

His final posthumously published essay was titled "A Testament of Hope," and it joined his religious inspiration to the radical political message which he had adopted at the end of his public career. Justice for black people would require radical social changes. The black revolution was more than a civil rights movement: it was a broad-gauged effort to confront America's interrelated failings of racism, poverty, militarism, and materialism.

CLAYBORNE CARSON

FURTHER READING

John J. Ansbro, *Martin Luther King, Jr.: The Making of a Mind* (Maryknoll, N.Y.: Orbis, 1982).

Taylor Branch, *Parting the Waters: America in the King Years, 1954–1963* (New York: Simon and Schuster, 1988).

Clayborne Carson, *In Struggle: SNCC and the Black Awakening of the 1970s* (Cambridge: Harvard University Press, 1981).

David J. Garrow, *Bearing the Cross: Martin Luther King, Jr., and the Southern Christian Leadership Conference* (New York: W. Morrow, 1986).

Martin Luther King Jr., *Stride toward Freedom: the Montgomery Story* (New York: Harper, 1958).

——, *Where Do We Go from Here: Chaos or Community?* (New York: Harper and Row, 1967).

——, *A Testament of Hope: the Essential Writings and Speeches of Martin Luther King, Jr.*, ed. James M. Washington (New York: HarperCollins, 1986).

David L. Lewis, *King* (1970; Urbana: University of Illinois Press, 1978).

Kingston, Maxine Hong (b. Stockton, Calif., Oct. 27, 1940).   The eldest of six children, Kingston is the daughter of Chinese immigrants. Her mother, Ying Lan Chew, a doctor/midwife in China, became a laundress and fieldhand in the U.S.; her father, Tom Hong, a scholar/teacher in China, could find work in the U.S. only as a laundryman and gambling-house manager. Kingston majored in English and graduated from the University of California, Berkeley, in 1962. That same year she married fellow classmate Earll Kingston, an actor, and they have a son, Joseph. After living more than a decade in Hawaii, she is now a professor of creative writing at her alma mater, the University of California, Berkeley.

Maxine Hong Kingston's first book, *The Woman Warrior: Memoir of a Girlhood among Ghosts* (1976), created a sensation in literary and scholarly circles. Although hers was not the first writing by an Asian American, the civil rights and women's liberation movements had prepared readers for her particular blend of ethnic ambivalence and pride and feminist anger. Kingston's voice is strong and angry in its protest against sexism and racism, though it speaks of being weak because continually devalued, both by a patriarchal Chinese culture and by the white-dominated society in the United States. *The Woman Warrior* is an experiment in genre, a collage of seemingly unrelated chapters, an autobiography that crosses into fiction. It tells outlandish Chinese stories and describes strange customs and superstitions in everyday American English, and it makes ready reference to Euro-American authors and traditions. It glides swiftly between locker-room slang and breathtaking poetic metaphor. It is a deeply intimate story of one young woman's confusion in sorting out her Chinese American identity, as well as a universal account of the second-generation immigrant experience. (*See also* ASIAN AMERICAN IDENTITY). It expresses an attitude that is simultaneously exasperated by and proud of its Chinese American heritage, in the voice of a daughter both angry and loving towards her mother. "I learned to make my mind large, as the universe is large, so that there is room for paradoxes," wrote Kingston, and her text itself is composed of such paradoxes.

After *The Woman Warrior* won the National Book Critics Circle award for the best nonfiction of 1976, Kingston won numerous additional awards, including the rare title of Living Treasure of Hawaii bestowed by a Buddhist group in 1980. Her second book, *China Men* (1980), won the American Book Award for 1981; her novel *Tripmaster Monkey* (1990) won the Pen West Award for fiction. She holds honorary doctorates from several colleges. During much of the 1980s, her first two books were so widely taught in colleges that she was the most frequently assigned living American author.

Though greatly admired by feminists and most Asian American women scholars and teachers, others' responses to Kingston's work have been divergent. Some Euro-American reviewers have found her work "exotic" and Chinese. Some readers from China have found it one-sidedly American, while others are dismayed that Kingston so blatantly discloses embarrassing ancient Chinese customs. Some Chinese Americans, most notably playwright Frank Chin, have denounced it for being unfaithful to Chinese legends, unloyal to Chinese traditions, and assimilationist in catering to white stereotypes. (*See also* ASSIMILATION.) This wide spectrum of reactions reveals the peculiarities and difficulties of the position of Chinese American women, having to navigate between the Scylla and Charybdis of others' expectations.

In *The Woman Warrior*, Kingston sought to understand her personal upbringing, beset by conflicting standards of behavior: the self-sacrificial filial obligations demanded of Chinese girls versus the independence and self-fulfillment promised to American children. How was she to fit her mother's Chinese ghost stories and legends into the American world of neon and plastic? How was she to find her own voice and realize her worth when her mother claimed to have cut her daughter's frenum, and the wider society devalued daughters? How was she to develop her own storytelling powers when faced with a mother whose storytelling powers and domineering spirit were so formidable, even threatening?

As *The Woman Warrior* is focused on female experience, Kingston's second book, *China Men*, is devoted to men's stories. In this book Kingston "claims America" by presenting an alternate story of the Founding Fathers. For Chinese Americans, the founding fathers did not land in New England but in Hawaii and California. They were the strong men whose backbreaking labor cleared jungles to create sugar plantations and broke through granite mountains to lay tracks for the transcontinental railroad; who, though scholars, took in laundry to support their families; who, though pacifists, served as soldiers in Vietnam. Again her text is a collage, mixing myth and history, fictional elaboration and biographical fact. Hers are composite, communal stories, the voice of a people as well as stories of her own family. To set the context for these tales of heroism, a contrasting section, called "The Laws," occupies the center section of her book. This section lists the discriminatory laws passed against Chinese men in the United States, an unheroic history of racial hatred and fear.

Kingston's most recent work, *Tripmaster Monkey* (1990), is an ambitious satiric novel about a Berkeley graduate of the 1960s, a loudmouthed, raging Chinese American playwright, Wittman Ah Sing. The novel is wildly humorous and richly textured. Like Kingston's earlier books, it interweaves Euro-American literary allusions with images from Chinese tradition, in this case the classic text *Journey to the West*, also called *Monkey*, by Wu Ch'en-en. Some Asian Americans read the novel as Kingston's portrait of Frank Chin, a long-time outspoken critic of her work. In capturing the voice and personality of this "monkey on her back," she controls, manipulates, and thus overpowers him. *Tripmaster Monkey* is a comic/tragic/surrealistic portrait of a complex young spokesman for a developing Asian American consciousness. Fully aware of racism and its humiliations, Wittman Ah Sing screamingly asserts himself, uninhibitedly expresses his contempt for conventions, seeks validation in personal relationships, and finally channels his passion and fury into a theatrical extravaganza.

Maxine Hong Kingston is a brilliant writer of quiet courage and deep conviction. Among contemporary American women writers, she is in the foremost rank; in fact, she may justifiably be said to be one of the major world authors writing today.

AMY LING

FURTHER READING

King-Kok Cheung, "'Don't Tell': Imposed Silences in *The Color Purple* and *The Woman Warrior*," *PMLA* 103 (1988): 162–74.

Shirley Lim, ed., *Teaching Approaches to Maxine Hong*

Kingston's *The Woman Warrior* (New York: Modern Language Association, 1991).

Amy Ling, *Between Worlds: Women Writers of Chinese Ancestry* (New York: Pergamon, 1990).

Leslie Rabine, "No Lost Paradise: Social Gender and Symbolic Gender in the Writings of Maxine Hong Kingston," *Signs* 12 (1987): 471–92.

Linda Ching Sledge, "Oral Tradition in Kingston's *China Men*," in A. LaVonne Brown Ruoff and Jerry Ward, eds., *Redefining American Literary History* (New York: Modern Language Association, 1990).

Sau-ling Wong, "Necessity and Extravagance in Maxine Hong Kingston's *The Woman Warrior*: Art and the Ethnic Experience," *MELUS* 15 (1988): 4–26.

Kinsey, Alfred (b. Hoboken, N.J., June 23, 1894; d. Bloomington, Ind., Aug. 25, 1956). Sexologist. Trained as an entomologist, Kinsey turned to sex education at Indiana University. Under the auspices of the Institute of Sex Research, which he founded in 1947, Kinsey and his colleagues compiled more than 17,500 case histories of the sex lives of Americans. That research became the empirical foundation for *Sexual Behavior in the Human Male* (1948) and *Sexual Behavior in the Human Female* (1953), which were unexpected bestsellers. Kinsey's evidence revealed a surprising incidence of masturbation, adultery, and homosexuality, practices at odds with culturally mandated norms of respectable conduct. Although his methods were criticized by sociologists as inadequate, his documentation of the actual habits of American adults opened sexuality to serious scientific inquiry for the first time in a generation, and contributed a scientific tone to the reconfiguration of sexual values in the 1960s and 1970s.

FURTHER READING

Paul Robinson, *The Modernization of Sex: Havelock Ellis, Alfred Kinsey, William Masters, and Virginia Johnson* (New York: Harper and Row, 1976).

Kissinger, Henry (b. Fürth, Germany, May 27, 1923). Political scientist and public official. Kissinger arrived in America in 1938, and after military service in World War II attended Harvard, where he rose quickly and became a member of the Department of Government. A significant contributor to COLD WAR geopolitical thought, Kissinger countered John Foster Dulles's concept of "massive retaliation" with a new view of deterrence and limited nuclear conflict in *Nuclear Weapons and Foreign Policy* (1957). *The Necessity for Choice* (1960) argued for an increased capability to wage conventional as well as nuclear war. As national security adviser in the first Nixon administration, and Secretary of State in the second, Kissinger moved the rhetoric of Cold War engage-

ment away from ideological polarization and toward *Realpolitik*, a shift marked most notably by the diplomatic recognition of the People's Republic of China in 1973. In negotiating the U.S. withdrawal from Southeast Asia, in conducting "shuttle diplomacy" in the Middle East, and in the opening of China itself, Kissinger elaborated a style of secret diplomacy based upon a foreign-policy apparatus inside the White House, an extraconstitutional mechanism the roots of which lay in the imperial presidencies of Democratic as well as Republican administrations of the twentieth century.

FURTHER READING

Robert D. Schulzinger, *Henry Kissinger: Doctor of Diplomacy* (New York: Columbia University Press, 1989).

Kristol, Irving (b. New York, N.Y., Jan. 22, 1920). Journalist. Repudiating his early Trotskyist leanings, Kristol became a leading anticommunist and neoconservative. America is in danger of succumbing to hedonism and self-doubt, he holds, because it lacks a clear vision of virtue, of the good life and the good society. People's efforts to do good frequently result in evil, as demonstrated by the failure of the liberal social programs that have overloaded the government. The solution is patriotic loyalty, retrenchment in domestic programs, and a diplomatic and military commitment to restabilizing the world order and protecting American interests. Kristol's writings include *On the Democratic Idea in America* (1972), *Two Cheers for Capitalism* (1979), and *Reflections of a Neoconservative: Looking Back, Looking Ahead* (1983).

See also NEOCONSERVATISM.

FURTHER READING

David Burner and Thomas West, *Column Right: Conservative Journalists in the Service of Nationalism* (New York: New York University Press, 1988).

Krutch, Joseph Wood (b. Knoxville, Tenn., Nov. 25, 1893; d. Tucson, Ariz., May 22, 1970). *More Lives Than One* (1962) was the title of Krutch's autobiography, but an alternative title could have been "More Books Than One." Although he wrote over 20 books, Krutch's place in American thought is generally held to depend on a single philosophical work published in 1929, *The Modern Temper*. It was the American "Dover Beach," a prose version of Matthew Arnold's classic Victorian poem, but Krutch's feelings about his celebrated book became increasingly ambivalent. Long before his death, he had distanced himself from the work for which he was best known.

A native of the South, Joe Krutch left it for good when he took a Ph.D. in English at Columbia University. After a brief stay in the academic world, he joined the *Nation* as associate editor and drama critic in 1924. While Krutch participated in the cultural liberation of the 1920s, living in Greenwich Village, swimming nude with Max and Eliena Eastman, and reporting from the Scopes trial on the controversial status of DARWINISM in the benighted rural South, he also retained a strong legacy of VICTORIANISM. The tension between the old culture and the new gave *The Modern Temper* its memorable tone.

This moving book explored the consequences of the waning faith in absolutes. According to Krutch, traditional value systems had collapsed as science revealed to Western man unsettling facts about himself, nature, and the universe. What remained as strong as ever was the need to believe that morality, free will, and other grand notions which gave meaning to life were truly real. Regrettably, "Man is left more and more alone in a universe to which he is completely alien" (p. 10). A society of the faithless was doomed, its ebbing vitality making it certain to be vanquished by more robust primitive types, people who did not question and did not doubt.

But there was no turning back. Against those who hoped to restore absolutes, Krutch insisted that modern iconoclasm constituted the only attitude that did not involve self-deception. *The Modern Temper* bordered on arrogance in its prideful acceptance of the harsh realities of modernity. Compellingly written, the argument clever yet accessible, the book provoked much contemporary discussion and later became a major source for the standard portrait of the disillusioned 1920s. If ever a text established its own context, it was *The Modern Temper*.

As a liberal humanist, Krutch was out of step with the 1930s. He battled Marxists in *Was Europe A Success?* (1934), and pursued literary studies, writing on European novelists in *Five Masters* (1930), on theory in *Experience and Art* (1932), and on the theatre in *The American Drama since 1918* (1939). His finest research piece, *Samuel Johnson* (1944), examined a man with whom he felt a particular affinity. All of these books were distinguished by fine wit, measured good sense, and a style that could equal E. B. White's in clarity and grace.

In 1937, Krutch accepted an appointment as Professor of English at Columbia. Like other men of letters, he was joining the academy. Again, though, Krutch went his own way. He resigned from Columbia in 1952 and moved to the desert near Tucson, Arizona, a latter-day Thoreau. Much of the impetus had actually come from his biographical study *Henry*

David Thoreau (1948). In addition, he had often toured the Southwest (whose climate alleviated his many ailments), and had already written about his growing passion for nature in *The Twelve Seasons* (1949).

Krutch throve in Arizona, an exception to F. Scott Fitzgerald's famous maxim that "there are no second acts in American life." In his sixties and seventies, Krutch was remarkably prolific, turning out essays and books celebrating nature, critiquing society, and reevaluating the views set forth a generation earlier in *The Modern Temper*. Krutch's nature books, like *The Voice of the Desert* (1955) and *Grand Canyon* (1958), helped spread Aldo Leopold's seminal ideas about ecology and ENVIRONMENTALISM and have had a wide readership. His social criticism, collected in *If You Don't Mind My Saying So* (1964) and *And Even If You Do* (1967), could be trenchant as it examined America's consumerist-materalist fixations. It could also be simply an old man's gripes about the younger generation, and it could be blind, especially on popular culture.

The two full-length statements of the changes in his philosophy since *The Modern Temper—The Measure of Man* (1954) and *Human Nature and the Human Condition* (1959)—were well received, but, lacking the earlier book's depth and poignancy, have not had the same staying power. No longer the ambivalent observer of MODERNISM, Krutch had become an out-and-out antimodernist, attacking the behavioral sciences for robbing man of his dignity and calling for a reaffirmation of absolute values. He attempted to bridge the gap between his humanism and his increasingly pantheistical naturalism by making the most of whatever evidence he could find that some of man's ideals might be inherent in NATURE itself.

H. L. Mencken once accused Krutch of having a nostalgia for God, and there is much truth in the jibe. Unable to believe in a traditional supernatural order, Krutch had spent a lifetime trying to compensate. He managed to die a cosmic optimist, at odds with his divided younger self and with materialistic contemporary society. As he wrote in his *American Scholar* column, he had found "Faith in wildness, or in nature as a creative force. . . . It is even, if you like, a religion."

This embrace of nature is usually interpreted as an advance from the alienation of *The Modern Temper*. It might just as easily be judged an evasion. *The Modern Temper* had looked deeply into the existential abyss of the twentieth century. In his later life, Krutch chose to treat this abyss as a chimera, but without making a full demonstration of its illusiveness. By drawing back from the edge, he gained the freedom to immerse himself in a solacing nature. As elsewhere in American culture, an outlook emphasizing fortitude gave way to one favoring the therapeutic.

PETER GREGG SLATER

FURTHER READING

Gerald Green, *An American Prophet* (Garden City: Doubleday, 1977).

William Holtz, "Homage to Joseph Wood Krutch: Tragedy and the Ecological Imperative," *American Scholar* 43 (Spring 1974): 267–79.

Joseph Wood Krutch, *The Modern Temper: a Study and a Confession* (New York: Harcourt, Brace, 1929).

John D. Margolis, *Joseph Wood Krutch: a Writer's Life* (Knoxville: University of Tennessee, 1980).

Roderick Nash, *The Rights of Nature: a History of Environmental Ethics* (Madison: University of Wisconsin, 1989).

Peter Gregg Slater, "The Negative Secularism of *The Modern Temper:* Joseph Wood Krutch," *American Quarterly* 33 (summer 1981): 185–205.

Kuhn, Thomas S. (b. Cincinnati, Ohio, July 18, 1922). Through his writings in history and philosophy, Kuhn has helped change the way many people think about SCIENCE. In 1962 he published a book about the dynamics of change in the physical and biological sciences that was taken by many readers to be relevant to a host of issues in philosophy, social theory, and historical scholarship. Thirty years later, *The Structure of Scientific Revolutions* had found more than 750,000 purchasers in English, and had been translated into 19 additional languages. Kuhn's interest in the history and cultural significance of science was generated at Harvard University in the 1940s. While completing a Ph.D. in physics, Kuhn worked with Harvard President James B. Conant in developing a history of science course for undergraduates. Kuhn later taught history and philosophy at the University of California, Berkeley, where he wrote *The Structure of Scientific Revolutions*. Kuhn left Berkeley for Princeton University in 1964, and in 1980 moved to the Massachusetts Institute of Technology, where he taught until his retirement in 1992.

Kuhn argued in *The Structure of Scientific Revolutions* that scientific ideas change in two distinctive but related modes, best understood through the concepts "normal science," "paradigm," and "revolutionary science." Kuhn called "normal science" the preponderance of the work scientists do. This work, according to Kuhn, consists in trying to explain newly scrutinized or anomalous phenomena in terms of the conventional wisdom of a community of specialists. Success in this setting comes not by questioning conventional wisdom but by following it, demonstrating that its principles work even in cases where its explanatory power had been uncertain. The principles that guided "normal science" Kuhn called a "paradigm."

The central element in any paradigm is a concrete problem-solution—such as Newton's optics or Darwin's natural selection—mapping domains of nature well enough to create credible expectations for the behavior of natural phenomena, and thereby authorizing programs for research. But a "paradigm" also includes a range of habits and values shared by the community of practitioners. (*See also* IDEOLOGY.) It was the periodic inability of these paradigms—these embodiments of the conventional wisdom of a given scientific community—to predict in large measure the behavior of salient phenomena that opens the way for "revolutionary science," the name Kuhn gave to the second mode of scientific change.

The "scientific revolutions" of Kuhn's title are made when a community agrees upon a new paradigm to guide its work. The atmosphere in which this agreement is reached is radically different, Kuhn argued, from the atmosphere of "normal science." Instead of the steady development of inherited theories, one finds, in "revolutionary science," the questioning of foundations, the proliferation of alternative theories, competition between paradigm-candidates for the role of conventional wisdom, and the somewhat authoritarian imposition of a new paradigm on recalcitrant members of a community.

Kuhn's account of scientific change was an immediate challenge to the prevailing image of the history of science. In the standard view, the story of scientific success was best told as a sequence of individual, heroic, nonconformist acts of intellect yielding an accumulation of increasingly true ideas (a view given its most compelling expression in Charles Gillispie's *The Edge of Objectivity*, 1960). Several features of Kuhn's account quickly brought *The Structure of Scientific Revolutions* to the attention of philosophers and other intellectuals. First, Kuhn emphasized the power of preconceived ideas (as embodied in "paradigms") to control the perception of phenomena on the part of both individual investigators and entire communities. Second, he insisted that outdated scientific ideas could be construed as "valid" for the time and place in which they had been accepted by communities of specialized investigators. Third, he claimed that in choosing between various paradigm-candidates, scientists doing revolutionary science based their judgments upon a combination of utilitarian and aesthetic considerations that could not be translated into the terms of any "scientific method" displayed in textbooks. Finally, he concluded that there did not exist any theory-independent natural order against which ideas could be definitively tested, and which could serve as a goal for the scientific enterprise.

All four of these arguments threatened popular notions of the OBJECTIVITY of science. Although Kuhn had directed his attention exclusively at the most technically developed of the sciences, his historicization of these sciences was understood to have implications for SOCIAL SCIENCE, and for all of learned discourse. If even the most widely confirmed theories of physicists and chemists were to so large an extent culture-bound—dependent upon the historically specific practice of distinctive communities of human beings—what could be said about the ideas of "softer" disciplines, whose ability to get beyond opinion and prejudice had always been precarious and contested? Kuhn appeared to have "politicized" all thought, by showing that even the process of warranting truth-claims in the physical sciences was a deeply social activity, involving conflicts best described with a vocabulary inspired by such noncerebral events as the French Revolution. The extent to which Kuhn had rendered scientific knowledge "relative" or "irrational" was much disputed in a debate in which Kuhn himself played a smaller and smaller part.

Kuhn did publish a collection of essays, *The Essential Tension: Selected Studies in Scientific Tradition and Change* (1977), that addressed some of the issues being taken up in his name, but after *The Structure of Scientific Revolutions* Kuhn's philosophical and historical interests diverged. On the historical side, he wrote a narrowly focused, highly technical contribution to the history of physical theory, *Black Body Theory and the Quantum Discontinuity, 1894–1912* (1978). In this book, Kuhn returned to the practice of the history of science as he had engaged it earlier in his career, as the author of *The Copernican Revolution: Planetary*

Astronomy in the Development of Western Thought (1957). On the philosophical side, Kuhn published less, but in a series of conference papers explored a question he had raised in *The Structure of Scientific Revolutions*: to what extent can contrasting paradigms be translated into the terms of each other, and to what extent are they, in Kuhn's controversial 1962 formulation, "incommensurable"? In these philosophical writings, Kuhn also dealt with the constructions of his work offered by "Kuhnian" thinkers throughout the world who had tried to claim *The Structure of Scientific Revolutions* on behalf of an enormous range of projects about which Kuhn himself proved ambivalent. Kuhn found himself being soberly instructed on the meaning of his own work (was Kuhn not a true "Kuhnian"?), and, like other authors of protean works, was caught in a discourse about himself over which he had lost control.

DAVID A. HOLLINGER

FURTHER READING

Barry Barnes, "Thomas Kuhn," in Quentin Skinner, ed., *The Return of Grand Theory in the Human Sciences* (New York: Cambridge University Press, 1985).

Steve Fuller, "Being There with Thomas Kuhn: a Parable for Modern Times," *History and Theory* 31 (1992): 241–75.

Gary Gutting, ed., *Paradigms and Revolutions: Applications and Appraisals of Thomas Kuhn's Philosophy of Science* (Notre Dame: University of Notre Dame Press, 1980).

David A. Hollinger, "T. S. Kuhn's Theory of Science and Its Implications for History," *American Historical Review* 78 (1973): 370–93.

——, "Free Enterprise and Free Inquiry: the Emergence of Laissez-Faire Communitarianism in the Ideology of Science in the United States," *New Literary History* 21 (1990): 897–919.

Paul Hoyningen-Huene, *Reconstructing Scientific Revolutions: Thomas S. Kuhn's Philosophy of Science*, trans. Alexander T. Levine (Chicago: University of Chicago Press, 1993).

L

La Follette, Robert M. (b. Primrose, Wis., June 14, 1855; d. Washington, D.C., June 18, 1925). Governor of Wisconsin (1901–6) and United States Senator (1906–25). A leader of the Progressive movement, La Follette sought social, economic, and political democracy through practical measures such as higher income and inheritance taxes for the rich, regulation of railroads and public utilities, worker's compensation, and public management of natural resources. He saw state universities as an important source of information, advice, and administrative expertise. Supporting labor unions, La Follette championed "the people"—workers, consumers, and taxpayers—against the selfish elite that he believed dominated American life and government. Founder of *La Follette's Weekly Magazine* in 1909 (it later became *The Progressive*), he sparked hope among liberal intellectuals by running for president on the Progressive ticket in 1924.

See also PROGRESSIVISM.

FURTHER READING
David Thelen, *Robert M. La Follette and the Insurgent Spirit* (Boston: Little, Brown, 1976).

La Follette, Suzanne (b. Pullman, Wash., 1893; d. Palo Alto, Calif., Apr. 23, 1983). Journalist. La Follette's *Concerning Women* (1928) described women as a subordinate class enslaved by the legal and economic order. The institution of marriage, she argued, protects society and the state at the expense of the individual. Men are enchained as breadwinners, while women suffer economic, legal, and social degradation. Both need true economic freedom: the elimination of monopolies and universal access to natural resources. As her antistatist position swung from left to right, La Follette became a founding editor of the *National Review* (1955).

FURTHER READING
Nancy Cott, *The Grounding of Modern Feminism* (New Haven: Yale University Press, 1987).

language If the world is a text, what is language? Language constitutes the social space between conventional objects of historical study, defining them. It is at once intellectual, social, cultural, political. As such it offers historians ways to explore relationships between past and present, among institutions, places, things, ideas, and persons.

As most practitioners of the "linguistic turn" have witnessed, assertions about the "power" or even "authority" of language can be tremendously upsetting to positivists of every political community: the philosophical claims on which the linguistic turn hinges seem to undermine "objective truth," "facts," or "material experience." Rightist positivists rightly recognize that discussions of language may be subversive of the social order status quo, insofar as language can erode otherwise strong hierarchies.

Leftist positivists rightly recognize that an argument which threatens to relegate material conditions of pain, deprivation, and coercion to the realm of "fiction" as it is commonly construed, that is, commercialized spectacular fantasy, is a dangerous one for anyone specially, systematically, or historically subject to pain, deprivation, and coercion. The linguistic turn—here a term of convenience, not a coherent school of thought—has coincided with revisionist denials of the most heinous crimes against humanity that modern history and memory have recorded, such that its best skepticism has appeared as dangerous reaction, while its worst nihilism, perversely, is celebrated as liberation. Recognizing that memory is a key to political power, critics of the linguistic turn fear with good reason an amnesiac philosophy of history enthralled with a single metaphor: "the world is a text"; or "history is fiction." When language, construed in conventional terms as a narrow, personal, ephemeral, and epiphenomenal realm of words in contrast to the ostensibly durable kingdom of deeds, becomes the all-encompassing trope for history, it does indeed set a political snare in which political analysis itself becomes entangled, and politics becomes impossible since discourse is artificially uncoupled—amputated—from its material sources and effects.

Notice here how difficult it is to construct a powerful image of language organically bound to material experience, in which separation appears unnatural! Language is no mere mirror, tool, weapon, that we can turn from, lay down, or bury at will. Language is our skin. It is the wind in our sails. It is a wave. It is the water in the river that was the rain. It is the fetus. It is the warp. It is the egg, before and after the chicken. It is the mouthful that builds strong bones. It is sticks and stones.

Among the social sites—other than the playground—in which the material powers of language are easiest seen are the sites of professional activity. (*See also* PRO-FESSION.) In courts of law, speech is work and even a pause can carry life-and-death import. A favorite ploy of Russian language teachers, illustrating the fluidity of Russian word-order in contrast to the English, is the lesson of "Execute not pardon." In each language the meaning of the phrase, and the prisoner's fate, is entirely dependent on the placement of a comma, either after "execute," or before "pardon." This juridical example is matched in each profession—by medical prescriptions, military orders, scripture, in which life and death, sin and salvation, guilt and innocence hang upon usage and interpretation.

Yet for historians there are further implications that stem from a material understanding of language, a semantic notion of power. First, language is a collective form of long-term memory. It bears the past into the present, and the present into the past. (*See also* ANCIENT INDIAN HISTORY.) Secondly, language is portable, moving in and out of social contexts sometimes independently of its creators and owners, only rarely under their control. Fundamentally metaphorical, language always reinvents the new in terms of the familiar, and thereby reinvents the familiar. As metaphor, language is an engine of social change, creating distinction everywhere it attempts identity, preserving likeness where it invents the novel. It moves, even as people cannot, across time and space, apparently and deceptively detached from both but always somehow embodying its origins. It can create and destroy fragile social consensus, political alliance, emotion. It is inextricably radical and conservative, as Marx observed in "The Eighteenth Brumaire of Louis Bonaparte" (1852):

> The tradition of all the dead generations weighs like a nightmare upon the brain of the living. And just when they seem engaged in revolutionizing themselves and things . . . they anxiously conjure up the spirits of the past to their service and borrow from them names, battle slogans, and costumes in order to present the new scene of world-history in this time honored disguise and this borrowed language. (Tucker, p. 437)

Consider the ways that language is borrowed for all sorts of political purposes: it is borrowed metaphorically, from unlike domains, in order to change the terms of debate within a particular political domain. Politicians borrow sports metaphor. Physicians speak of war. Teachers speak of gardens. Urban social workers speak of natural disasters. Generals speak of surgery.

The language of profession is frequently—perhaps typically—borrowed from explicitly unprofessional realms, from that which constitutes the "lay" practices outside a given profession. In certain political contexts of the United States, in which both capitalism and democracy are made to accommodate one another, at least in theory, this continual self-demotion serves an important function of IDEOLOGY. It maintains the illusion of classlessness and of the permeability of hierarchies.

Talk is cheap, can rarely be wholly owned, and is in some senses therefore affordable to the poor, the disenfranchised, the minority, the oppressed. This affordability is contingent upon the means of production, but not determined by it. This affordability moreover has its absolute limits in the ability of totalitarian regimes to use violence to silence their opponents, and is always constrained by the economies of technique. There is however, as Perry Anderson has pointed out, enormous political leverage in the margin between absolute totalitarian controls over speech, and repressive or unjust social and economic orders that systematically and historically constrain oppositional speech. It is as important not to confuse cultural authority with absolute power, as it is to recognize their connections. (*See also* HEGE-MONY.) There is room, in other words, for hope.

A dominant philosophical vocabulary that insists at every level on the separation between word and deed, thought and action, object and representation, image and reality is one which precludes the creative, historical exploration of a powerful cultural mechanism of social change: emulation. Emulation, conceptually, can help account at once for event and record, object and representation, memory and memorial, while recognizing their mutual dependency. Emulation, a more capacious view of metaphor, emphasizes the concrete "base" of the semantic "superstructure" without requiring that the historian stand on one to study the other.

The authority of powerful political organizations is predicated on a translation of coercive power into hegemonic authority. That translation is a historical process that is fundamentally semantic: it is about the creation of meaning, the extension of force through persuasion, intimidation, and "consent." AUTHORITY is reproduced through semantic emulation, through language borrowed from past or distant reservoirs.

The semantic study of emulation may help historians understand, for instance, looking back on the front-page debates of the 1990s on "professionalism" in the U.S. military services, why the admission of women, the disciplining of heterosexual crime, and the denial of homosexuality are such important issues to military leadership and to some of the rank-and-file. It is not enough to say that the military reflects the biases of the larger society; if that were the case, racial issues arguably would still be front and center. Nor is it enough to say that military men hold ultimate powers of authority because they point the guns (which, in any case, is no longer true). Rather, a semantic argument would hold that the culture of military professionalism—of learning to kill well—is laden with sexual metaphor that is aggressively, violently heterosexual. The morale of the Army as it is currently constituted culturally is *dependent* on these exclusionary practices. It is the military's metaphor of sexual "conquest," borrowed from a violent heterosexual culture, that makes the ostensible threat of all women and openly homosexual men to military order palpable. Heterosexual misconduct actually reinforces rather than undermines this equation of military "discipline" with masculine heterosexual domination, while the presence of (straight) women or (male) homosexuals upsets it. The enemy—Iraq, most recently—is the feminized sexual object of masculinized offensive nationalism. The jingoistic language of "penetration" suffused journalistic constructions of the Gulf War. Conversely, the American nation, through surrogate Kuwait, was the imagined innocent feminized object of masculine, alien aggression, of "rape." Yet the study of professional and rank-and-file military language tells only half the story, for there is a civilian tradition of sexuality-as-combat that continually informs the military usages.

The language of a particular domain (of sexuality, work, family life, battle, profession) cannot be understood historically by reference exclusively to that domain. Generative, metaphorical language is always borrowed from somewhere else—another place, another person, another time. By filling in the spaces between conventional objects of study, it maps the relations among them historically as well as socially. Historians need a vocabulary for language which captures this space-in-between, the interstitial, tense nature of language, in the way the painter Morandi, or Carravaggio, or Vuillard, or Mary Cassatt captured the space in between and made it define, with exquisite sensitivity to the moment as well as to the object, the ostensible solid subject of the work.

JOANNE BROWN

See also DECONSTRUCTION; SEMIOTICS

FURTHER READING
Jean-Christophe Agnew, *Worlds Apart* (New York: Cambridge University Press, 1986).

Perry Anderson, "The Antinomies of Antonio Gramsci," *New Left Review* 100 (1976–7): 5–78.
JoAnne Brown, *The Definition of a Profession* (Princeton: Princeton University Press, 1992).
Arthur Danto, *Narration and Knowledge* (New York: Columbia University Press, 1985).
Murray Edelman, *Political Language* (New York: Academic Press, 1977).
George Lakoff and Mark Johnson, *Metaphors We Live By* (Chicago: University of Chicago Press, 1980).
Susanne Langer, *Philosophy in a New Key* (1942; New York: New American Library, 1951).
J. G. A. Pocock, *Politics, Language and Time* (New York: Atheneum, 1971).
Donald Schon, *Displacement of Concepts* (New York: Humanities Press, 1963).
John Toews, "Intellectual History after the Linguistic Turn," *American Historical Review* 92 (1987): 879–907.
Robert Tucker, ed., *The Marx-Engels Reader* (New York: Norton, 1972).

Larcom, Lucy (b. Beverly, Mass., Mar. 5, 1824; d. Boston, Mass., Apr. 17, 1893). Writer, editor, and educator. Larcom gained a taste for both literature and independence as a Lowell millworker, where she published in the *Operative's Magazine* (later the *Lowell Offering and Magazine*). A woman's true vocation is to serve others, she believed, and one form of service particularly appropriate for women was the creation and dissemination of literature that embodies immortal truths. Author of numerous works, including *Similitudes from Ocean and Prairie* (1854), *Poems* (1869), *Childhood Songs* (1873), and *A New England Girlhood* (1889), she also edited *Songs of Three Centuries* (1883) with JOHN GREENLEAF WHITTIER. Her poems reflect a Christian transcendentalism in which beauty, truth, and morality are one.

FURTHER READING
Shirley Marchalouis, *The Worlds of Lucy Larcom, 1824–1893* (Athens: University of Georgia Press, 1989).

Lasch, Christopher (b. Omaha, Nebr., June 1, 1932; d. Pittsford, N.Y., Feb. 14, 1994). Having long desired to become a writer of fiction (an aspiration shared by his Harvard roommate John Updike), Lasch decided after college to follow the course of RICHARD HOFSTADTER: producing historical scholarship designed as a contribution to intellectual debate. Professor of History for two decades at the University of Rochester, Lasch wrote books and essays widely read outside the academy and exerted a profound influence upon many historians who entered the profession during the Vietnam era. The book for which he is best known, *The Culture of Narcissism* (1979), had a deep impact on public discussion, even before President Jimmy Carter spoke to some of its themes in a speech on cultural "malaise." Often misunderstood as a jeremiad against selfishness and consumerism, the book actually presented an extraordinarily wide-ranging discussion of what Lasch considered an erosion of selfhood in modern America.

From the beginning Lasch's work insisted upon the interpenetration of political and cultural issues, and argued for CULTURAL CRITICISM as the indispensable foundation for a democratic politics. His book *The New Radicalism in America* (1965), along with his frequent contributions to the *New York Review of Books* and other journals in the late 1960s, defined his distinctive brand of historically based cultural criticism. *The New Radicalism* offered an assessment of the liberal intelligentsia of the twentieth century, and called for intellectuals to reject the new radicals' characteristic confusion of culture and politics. Preoccupied in Lasch's view by the failure of their parents' generation to prepare them for "real life," such new radicals as MABEL DODGE LUHAN were apt to offer cultural solutions to political problems, to reinterpret political oppression as psychological repression. New radicals tended toward anti-intellectualism, toward putting the intellectual vocation at the service either of a quest for experience—immersion in the allegedly "real life" of outcast groups—or a campaign for power as social experts.

The intellectuals should have contented themselves, Lasch contended, with doing their own cultural work as the clarifiers of values and the defenders of truth. The now-forgotten Benjamin Ginsburg, a minor thirties' writer, became the hidden hero of Lasch's account. Ginsburg understood, in Lasch's words, that

> instead of trying to save culture through politics, intellectuals should first reform culture itself, over which, in any case, they had more power than they had over politics. He was not advocating a retreat to an "ivory tower" or "art for art's sake." He himself was a socialist . . . fully as "committed" as the men he attacked . . . Ginsburg's radicalism involved . . . a recognition that intellectuals had more influence over politics as *intellectuals* than as political activists in their own right (pp. 295, 298).

Himself drawn in the 1960s and early 1970s to the socialist critique of capitalism, Lasch soon became disenchanted with the usual demarcations of "left" and "right." As he reflected in the late 1970s upon the fate of the family and other social institutions, he concluded that neither socialists nor defenders of capitalism were confronting the glaring problem that faced advanced industrial society: selfhood and community alike were atrophying in a world that subordinated honor, craft, loyalty, or responsibility, to profit, efficiency, fashion, or amusement.

Lasch's book *Haven in a Heartless World* (1977), an examination of the rise of the idea of the family as an island of private solace, marked the beginning of his move not so much from left to right as from the left–right spectrum to a new spectrum altogether, one that he was still in the process of conceiving when he died. *Haven* was a critique of the "helping professions," of the social scientific experts who proposed in the early twentieth century that the family would flourish in the modern world only if it redefined itself as a center of emotional succor. Aided by the growing army of social workers, child guidance professionals, and psychologists, social scientists in effect, according to Lasch, launched an assault on paternal authority, regarded by the experts as arbitrary and irrational authority.

But in Lasch's view the attack on the father, far from empowering women or children, merely put external advice-givers in the father's place. The erosion of the family—and of individual selfhood and communal solidarity, since both, he believed, had always been dependent upon strong families—had been set in motion. So had the ignoring of the problem by intellectuals of left and right, who preferred to trade accusations of "fascism" or "communism" while American life lost its moorings. Conservative appeals to "family values" were no better in Lasch's mind than liberal advocacy of individual self-fulfillment or no-fault divorce. Most conservatives pontificated about their love of family, while cheerfully endorsing the corporate commitment to efficiency, to mobility of capital, and to mechanization of work—all of which undermined stable selves, families, and communities.

The True and Only Heaven (1991) continued Lasch's effort to define a new cultural-political standpoint by tracing the three major intellectual traditions that since the eighteenth century have offered alternatives to liberal progressivism: CALVINISM, REPUBLICANISM, and POPULISM. Sometimes schematic, the analysis nevertheless made a strong case for a new populism informed by Calvinist realism about the limits surrounding human life and republican realism about the fragility of human accomplishments in history. The book also revealed that Lasch had moved beyond his earlier conviction that useful political analysis presupposes cultural criticism, to a perception that useful cultural critique itself presupposes moral inquiry. The pressing question for Lasch at the end of his career was how to ground hope when it was no longer possible to follow the progressives and put one's faith in history. In a striking departure from his earlier work, *The True and Only Heaven* turned to the theology of JONATHAN EDWARDS, the spiritual musings of RALPH WALDO EMERSON, and the religious teachings of REINHOLD NIEBUHR and MARTIN LUTHER KING: gratitude and forgiveness, Lasch suggested, lie at the foundation not only of religion, but of politics and culture.

RICHARD WIGHTMAN FOX

FURTHER READING
Michael Fischer, Larry D. Nachman, Janice Doane, Devon Leigh Hodges, and Christopher Lasch, "A Symposium: Christopher Lasch and *The Culture of Narcissism*," *Salmagundi* (fall 1979): 166–202.
Richard Wightman Fox, "Lasching Liberalism," *Christian Century*, Mar. 11, 1992, pp. 277–82.
Adrienne Harris and Edward Shorter, "Besieging Lasch," *Theory and Society* 6 (Sept. 1978): 279–92.
Stephen Holmes, *The Anatomy of Antiliberalism* (Cambridge: Harvard University Press, 1993).
Jeffrey Isaac and Christopher Lasch, "Modernity and Progress: an Exchange," *Salmagundi* (winter 1992): 82–109.
Michael Kazin, Barbara Ehrenreich, and Christopher Lasch, "Current Debate: the Politics of Populism," *Tikkun* 6 (Sept.–Oct. 1991): 37–44.
Roger Kimball, "The Disaffected Populist: Christopher Lasch on Progress," *New Criterion* (Mar. 1991): 9–16.
Christopher Lasch, *The New Radicalism in America* (New York: Knopf, 1965).

Latino and Latina cultures In 1988 *Time* magazine featured a series of articles on U.S. Latino artistic productions and cultural practices—music, art, cinema, food, fashion, architecture, and language—recognizing, perhaps for the first time in official North American discourse, the impact of the Latino and Latina presence on what has been termed "American culture." The appearance of Mexican American actor Edward James Olmos on the *Time* cover can be read as a belated recognition of Latinos in the United States, an act of symbolic inclusion. The title of the issue, "Magnífico: Hispanic Culture Breaks Out of the Barrio," signaled a new historical stage beyond the paradigms of working-class ethnic identity and nationalism common to the 1960s and 1970s. This trend has continued into the 1990s, and today Latinos and Latinas are appearing in print, on film, and within the music world, in addition to the arena of public service and politics, as seen in the appointments of two Hispanics to President Clinton's cabinet.

There is no question about Latino and Latina penetration of the mass media: John Leguízamo's "Mambo Mouth" on Home Box Office (HBO) and Luis Valdez's "La Pastorela" on the Public Broadcasting System (PBS), and films such as *La Bamba*, *Born in East L.A.*, *Mambo Kings*, and *The Milagro Beanfield War* distributed nationally; the proliferation of Spanish cable-programming throughout the United States (with "Sábado Gigante" as the most popular show in the world); the cult status of Juan Luis Guerra, Rubén Blades and Gloria Estefan. Of course the success of Latino and Latina artists stems in large measure from the support of the growing Spanish-speaking population, but there is also much evidence of wider interest. North American consumer culture has plainly found a high profile stage for the exhibition of Latino and Latina cultural products. But this new development did not spring to life full-blown in the last decade. It was prepared during the long period of American hegemony in Latin America, when Americans developed a "tropicalized" image of the cultures "south of the border." That view of Hispanic peoples as distinctively warm, vibrant, carefree, and exotic continues to mark the attitudes of other Americans—and even of some Hispanics—even in this day of greater inclusiveness. Mainstream acceptance is accompanied by mainstream misrepresentation, a process well known to many ethnic groups.

For all the current visibility and marketability of some Latinos and Latinas, their cultures are still marginalized in many ways. In the academic context, it is revealed in the continued second-class status bestowed upon Chicano and Puerto Rican Studies programs—a fate shared by Asian American and Native American, and to a lesser degree, African American curricula. Within the community of literary critics, mainstream U.S. scholarship has only recently begun to catch up with foreign scholars in giving serious treatment to the literary corpus developed by Chicanos/as and other Latinos/as.

Recent fervor for multiculturalism and for diversity in the academic world has not yet successfully integrated Latino/a works and cultural products into the American canon. Little recognition has been given to the active participation of Chicano/a and U.S Puerto Rican writers, artists, and scholars in redefining America as a multicultural society, or to their pioneering efforts at interdisciplinary inquiry, especially in the emergence of the field of cultural studies. Moreover, issues of ethnicity, race, class, and gender have been explored by Latino/a writers since the turn of the century. The material cultures of the working-class Latino/a produced cultural and artistic products—Salsa, Tex-Mex and corrido music, murals, and other visual arts—which have expressed resistance to the dominant society and are central to understanding historical change in the United States. Exclusionary forces, however, have kept these contributions on the margins of accepted knowledge.

When we speak about the cultures of U.S. Latinos and Latinas, we refer mainly to three geocultural entities. First, the Mexican Americans and/or Chicanos in the Southwest, including their historical contributions to the formation of the entire West over a period of several centuries. Second, the Cubans, Puerto Ricans, and Dominicans, along with a variety of Afro-Caribbeans who moved into the South and urban Northeast after the mid-nineteenth century. Third, the Central Americans, primarily Salvadorans, Nicaraguans, and Guatemalans who have arrived during the last decade. It is too early to assess their cultural impact, but given their rapid increase in numbers and their rich cultural tradition, it is bound to be enormous. In Miami, for instance, linguists are already noting the influence of Nicaraguan Spanish. In San Francisco, Salvadoran religious processions have become an annual event in the Mission District. Salvadoran *pupusas*, music of protest, indigenous crafts and textiles, and an infusion of liberation theology are leaving a mark in what had been predominantly Mexican areas of U.S. urban centers in the West.

Considering the diverse histories of each of these groups, and the political, cultural, geographical, racial, and ethnic specificities of each, it would be a big mistake to conflate them into one cultural paradigm. While Mexican American folklore of the mostly rural Southwest can be traced back to the sixteenth and seventeenth centuries, prior to the expansion of the western frontier by Anglo settlers, the impact of Afro-Cuban and Puerto Rican popular music in the urban Northeast began to be felt in the early twentieth century. Moreover, the racial and ethnic elements—indigenous and mestizo as well as Hispanic—that form the basis for the construction of a Chicano cultural paradigm bring this group closer to Native Americans than to the African-based and mulatto Caribbean identities forged by many Puerto Ricans in New York and Cubans in Florida. The political stances and the historical motives that inform the migration and immigration of Chicanos, Puerto Ricans, and Cubans have created diverse sociocultural and political configurations in which very different artistic productions have emerged.

For instance, the cultural and political resistance to mainstream American culture mounted by Chicanos and Puerto Ricans during the cultural nationalism of the 1960s and 1970s was not matched by the Cubans, who defined themselves as political refugees, exiles, and not as an ethnic minority. The wide spectrum of Spanish and English fluency and linguistic identification among Latinos/as of different generations, social classes, and educational experiences also inform their complex cultural practices and everyday life experiences. Latino and Latina cultures must be approached as plural sites of multicultural subjectivities.

It is precisely this heterogeneity that U.S. institutions—educational, cultural and political—have attempted historically to erase. In the study of American musical traditions, this process is particularly obvious. John Storms Roberts, in his important book *The Latin Tinge: the Impact of Latin Music in the United States* (1979), recovers the numerous unrecognized influences that Mexican, Cuban, and Afro-Caribbean musical forms, rhythms, lyrics, composers, and singers have had on the development of U.S. popular music since the nineteenth century. According to Roberts, very little attention has been given to the Cuban subtexts in the works of classical pianist Louis Gottschalk from Louisiana, or to the participation of Mexican and Cuban musicians in the development of early jazz and rhythm and blues in the New Orleans area.

Hollywood, moreover, has led the way in constructing tropicalized icons of Latin identity through such figures as Carmen Miranda and Desi Arnaz, and most recently in the production of *The Mambo Kings*. This tropicalizing and depoliticizing of Latino/a culture—representing it as essentially frivolous, primitivist, fruity, sensual and erotically desirable—shows no signs of abating, despite the efforts of some contemporary Latino and Latina artists, writers, and cultural workers to reappropriate these stereotypes so as to problematize and dismantle them. John Leguízamo's sketches in "Mambo Mouth," and the works of Chicano, Nuyorican and Latino/a performance artists and comedy groups—Culture Clash, Chicano Secret Service, Marga Gómez, Encarnita Figueroa, and others—constitute a common attempt to challenge the stereotypes by exposing them as unidimensional and fixed images imposed from without.

Ironically, the fixing of ethnic identity and delineating of clear boundaries around a uniform, alternative Latino/a culture was also practiced by Latinos themselves in the cultural nationalist period of the 1960s and 1970s, when many of today's art forms emerged out of political struggles. Luis Valdez's "teatro campesino" and "actos" began as theatre used by Chicano fieldworkers and *braceros* during the strikes of the early 1970s and the formation of the United Farm Workers under the leadership of César Chávez. The denunciatory urgency of the political activism informed the constructions of ethnic identity that would form the basis for much theatre, poetry, fiction, and essays. From a position of pronounced marginalization, Chicano, Chicana and Nuyorican writers and cultural workers proclaimed sharp dualities between a dehumanized and oppressive Anglo-America and a humanist, spiritual, affiliative, and nonmaterialist Latino ethos: the mythical space of Aztlán for Chicanos and the rural paradise of the island of Puerto Rico became the metaphorical spaces for these ideal nationalist constructions. As Alurista wrote in his innovative and revolutionary bilingual poetry, "chicano heart / tú vives tu idea, amerika piensa la suya" ("chicano heart / you live your idea, amerika thinks hers"). Chicano spirituality, as construed during the Movement, countered the rational paradigms of the European Enlightenment by recovering the erased pre-Columbian cultures of Mexico. Nonmaterialist Chicano spirituality was put forth as a critique of a capitalist and imperialist United States whose historical record of invasion and co-optation in Latin America was unrelenting.

Yet for all their own oversimplified constructs of Latino character, the poetry, the popular theatre, the music, the essays, and the novels of the nationalist phase were a precondition for the recent impact that Latino/a cultural products have had on discussions about U.S. culture. This early corpus proposed new cultural forms not seen before. Alurista, for instance, was the first Latino poet to publish bilingual poetry despite continued opposition on the part of editors and publishers. The legitimizing of bilingual or interlingual texts, the switching between English and Spanish, and the use of colloquialisms drawn from the local communities of the authors produced new dynamics between readers and texts. For instance, Tato Laviera's early poem "The Song of an Oppressor" (included in Barradas and Rodríguez, Herejes y mitificadores) capitalizes on the title of a popular soap opera "Simplemente María" (Simply Mary) to create an interlingual and bicultural text about the economic needs of Puerto Rican women in the United States and the labor exploitation to which they have been subjected:

> Doña Eusebia's knees were eliminated
> simple
> her head an army boot upside down
> mente
> her tongue was out from exhaustion
> maría

This interlingual literature not only validated the speech acts of the working-class Chicano and Puerto Rican communities, but challenged the authority of the monolingual literary written text and of the monocultural American literary and cultural canon. These early inscriptions of hybrid cultural spaces—Spanish and English, European and indigenous, mulatto and mestizo, oral and literate, the rural past and the industrial urban present—paved the way for the postmodern pan-Latino cultural and artistic productions of the 1980s and 1990s.

The newer generation of Latino and Latina scholars is more prone to a pan-Latino consciousness than to nationalism, and has therefore found the decentering and de-essentializing theoretical tools of postmodernism, poststructuralism, and discourse theory very useful. Critics in literature and American Studies programs, such as Héctor Calderón, José Saldívar, Chon Noriega, Norma Alarcón, and Angie Chabram, have noted the complexity of the relationship between poststructural theory and Latino/a cultures. Poststructuralism likes to speak of the death of the subject, a stance which poses a conundrum for those Latino and Latina writers whose own literary projects seek to construct a newly integrated historical subject out of the diverse traditions and memories of the past. From Rodolfo "Corky" González's foundational poem of Chicanismo I am Joaquín (1972) to Judith Ortiz Cofer's Silent Dancing (1990), a collection of essays and poetry about growing up between New Jersey and Puerto Rico, the "I," the cultural and individual self, is articulated and redefined in the context of colonialism and of resistance to it. Cofer's collection begins by reaffirming the voices of the women in her family and their impact on tradition and on the poet's own making:

> At three or four o'clock in the afternoon, the hour of café con leche, the women of my family gathered in Mamá's living room to speak of important things and to tell stories for the hundredth time, as if to each other, meant to be overheard by us young girls, their daughters. (p. 14)

Latina and Latino writers have chosen autobiographies, testimonios, and novels of development as literary forms to challenge the historical invisibility of their communities, to speak, as it were, from their "center." As Ramón Saldívar has concluded in Chicano Narrative: the Dialectics of Difference (1990), for Chicanos and Latinos "the act of knowing and writing the self is an act of critical consciousness, an act of knowing oneself as a product of historical processes that can be interrogated, interpreted, and perhaps even changed" (p. 170). Today, the contributions of Latino and Latina voices to the tradition of the American autobiography are being reassessed, with special attention to the ways they have problematized the "ideology of individualized self-interest" (as Saldívar puts it) that characterizes the Anglo-American tradition.

Thanks to this critical and theoretical effort to imagine a pan-Latino identity, the concept of borderland, a paradigm for the study of a hybrid, multicentered subjectivity, has become a commonplace in American Studies. Yet long before that it was a lived experience, geographically, spiritually, psychologically, and socially, for Chicanos/as and Latinos/as. As Latino and Latina cultures have become more visible, their historical experience has been appropriated by postmodern theory. Still, the growing importance of the concept of multiple subjectivities in academic circles has not been accompanied by general recognition of the intellectual and cultural contributions that Latinos have made to postmodern consciousness. Ironically, Latino and Latina artists, writers, and musicians—postmodern *avant la lettre*—are now frequently positioned as followers of the tenets of POSTMODERNISM. The attempt to "apply" postmodern theories to Latino/a cultural practices and products becomes a neocolonial gesture in which Latino and Latina cultures are once again viewed as outsiders from the standpoint of the European and "American" center.

Latina and Latino cultural critics—José Saldívar, Norma Alarcón, Rosalinda Fregoso, Juan Flores, Raúl Fernández, Gustavo Pérez Firmat, George Yúdice, Sonia Saldívar, Tomás Ybarra Frausto, Norma Cantú, María Herrera Sobek, Ramón Saldívar, Tino Villanueva, Teresa McKenna, Alberto Sandoval, Charles Ramírez Berg, Chon Noriega, and many others—are proposing in multi- and interdisciplinary ways theoretical approaches that employ postmodernism and deconstruction in their analyses of Latino and Latina cultures in the United States. Like the artists, filmmakers, and musicians, the critics have striven not to lose the resistance and oppositionality that have infused Latino/a cultural products since the 1960s. Their challenge has been to explore and reaffirm identity from multicentered perspectives, building on the cultural, historical, and linguistic specificities that have informed their lives and their art. The concept of borderland in Chicano and Chicana criticism—and of the *guagua aérea* ("air bus") among Puerto Ricans—has brought to the foreground the complexities of cultural hybridity for Latinos and Latinas. The borderlands project, often identified with the work of Gloria Anzaldúa, is actually a collective effort on the part of Chicanas and Chicanos to decenter and problematize fixed ethnic identity. The borderland is not an abstract construct, but an articulation of the shifting cross-currents of identity that people of color experience in a daily situation of continued colonization. Border identities need to be re-presented via stories, personal narratives, heterogeneous voices in the process of becoming and being, so as to avoid the perennial pitfalls of essentializing. This plural model for cultural identity has deep implications for our definitions of culture, as it does for our traditional habit of distinguishing high and low cultures. There is good reason to hope that Latino and Latina cultural criticism can play a central part in the continuing campaign to complicate our understanding of American identities.

FRANCES R. APARICIO

See also CULTURAL PLURALISM AND MULTICULTURALISM.

FURTHER READING
Frances R. Aparicio, "Salsa, Maracas and Baile: Latin Popular Music in the Poetry of Víctor Hernández Cruz," *MELUS* 16 (spring 1989–90): 43–58.
Efraín Barradas and Rafael Rodríguez, *Herejes y mitificadores: Muestra de poesía puertorriqueña en los Estados Unidos* (Río Piedras, Puerto Rico: Ediciones Huracán, 1980).
Héctor Calderón and José Saldívar, eds., *Criticism in the Borderlands: Studies in Chicano Literature, Culture, and Ideology* (Durham, N.C.: Duke University Press, 1991).
Cherríe Moraga and Gloria Anzaldúa, *This Bridge Called My Back: Writings by Radical Women of Color* (New York: Kitchen Table, 1981).
"Música: Alma del Pueblo," special issue on popular music, *Centro de Estudios Puertorriqueños Bulletin* 3 (spring 1991).
Chon A. Noriega, ed., *Chicanos and Film: Representation and Resistance* (Minneapolis: University of Minnesota Press, 1992).
Gregorio Rivera and Edward Chávez, "Arte Chicano" special issue, *Imagine: International Chicano Poetry Journal* 3 (summer-winter 1986).
Luis Rafael Sánchez, "The Air Bus," in Asela Rodríguez de Laguna, ed., *Images and Identities: the Puerto Rican in a Two World Context* (New Brunswick, N.J.: Transaction, 1987).
John Storm Roberts, *The Latin Tinge: the Impact of Latin American Music on the United States* (New York: Oxford University Press, 1979).

law It is perhaps indicative of our "postmodern" culture that this discussion of the concept of law in American thought begins by noting that the concept itself is "essentially contested." It is as if an entry on the automobile in American thought began by asserting that the basic issue is deciding what in fact an automobile is. There are circumstances in which one might be perplexed about the referent of the term "automobile," but, for most of us most of the time, there is in fact no such perplexity. This is not the case with law. What one decides to call "law" is itself the product of, rather than source material for, self-conscious theoretical reflection. The question facing any author quickly becomes, therefore, precisely what one should write about when writing about law.

Consider, as one approach, the 1832 definition of William Rawle in *A Discourse on the Nature and Study of Law*: "Law, in all its divisions, is the strong action of *Reason* upon wants, necessities, and imperfections." It is "the act of those on whom it has pleased divine Providence to bestow the attribute of reason, as distinguished from those who are guided only by instinct, and can make no rules for themselves" (p. 4). Law is defined in terms of the search for the transcendent and timeless truths that a capitalized Reason can teach those who are willing, by disciplining the emotions, to submit to it. Anyone attracted by this approach might well be tempted to deny the appellation "law" to anything that does not conform with the perceived requirements of JUSTICE or morality. This might be especially important in any culture that treated anything termed "law" as presumptively worthy of respect and, indeed, obedience. A tradition extending at least from St. Augustine to Martin Luther King Jr. has suggested, however, that what is unjust cannot, simply by virtue of being unjust, be law, but only a perversion of legality. Otherwise, we could not meaningfully distinguish between the demand of the armed robber and that of the armed state. What legitimizes the claims of the latter is not that it speaks through institutional officials, but, rather, that these claims accord with what reason describes as moral or just.

Though it has had some distinguished proponents, this wedding of law and morality has not fared well in the United States, for at least two reasons. One is the general, and pervasive, skepticism about the philosophical claims made either about the ontological reality of moral norms or about the epistemological claim to comprehend with any degree of confidence the teachings of these norms, even if one assumes that they exist. A quite different reason, though, is provided by the pragmatic necessities of working within the highly particularized legal system(s) found in the United States. (It is worth mentioning, incidentally, that some theorists would reject the assumption that law is manifested only in "public" organizations—countries, states, cities, etc.— rather than identified as well with the systematic practices of "private" organizations; many sociologists and anthropologists would have no trouble writing about the law of such organizations, though this essay focuses only on public law.)

A mixture, then, of philosophical skepticism and sheer immersion in the actualities of American life have led most American theorists of law to be considerably less ethereal than Rawle. Lawyers (including judges) and ordinary citizens alike are more interested in trying to figure out the practical implications of legal claims than with trying to construct self-consciously systematic philosophies of law.

Almost certainly the most important discussion of law in American history was delivered by OLIVER WENDELL HOLMES JR. in his 1897 speech, "The Path of the Law." Almost a full century later it is still the keystone of distinctively American approaches to, and controversies about, the meaning of law. It includes one of the most frequently quoted sentences in the history of American jurisprudence: "The prophecies of what the courts will do in fact, and nothing more pretentious are what I mean by the law" (p. 173). "Pretentiousness," for Holmes, was any assertion that what courts "do in fact" was *necessarily* linked with the teachings of Reason or in conformity with any other particular standard of evaluation. What allowed one to recognize something as an assertion of law was not its moral attractiveness, but, rather, its accuracy as a prediction of the actual behavior of particular public officials called judges. "Nothing but confusion of thought," Holmes told his audience of Boston University law students and faculty, "can result from assuming that the rights of man in a moral sense are equally rights in the sense of the Constitution and the law" (pp. 171–2). Law and morality are two quite different analytical domains, though one might certainly hope that, by happy coincidence, they make the same demands.

Though Holmes's voice is probably the most influential in our national history on behalf of the analytical separation of law and morality, he was surely not plowing wholly unturned ground. No less a figure than JOHN MARSHALL, in *The Antelope* (23 U.S. (10 Wheat.) 66), an 1825 case involving slavery, distinguished very sharply between the roles of what he termed the "moralist" and the "jurist," with the judge, of course, confined to the latter role. It is no coincidence that he made this observation in a slavery case: the presence of America's "peculiar institution" within the fabric of American law brought home to many thinkers the gap between what most viewed as the undoubted law of the land, protecting slavery, and the teachings of morality or justice. Marshall, like almost all "jurists," readily admitted that slavery violated both natural justice and specifically Christian morality; that was, however, beside the point, given a legal tradition that protected the rights of slaveholders. Legal positivism, the identification of law as the command, which might or might not be moral, of some identifiable sovereign or other political authority, thus came naturally to those elites faced with the task of rationalizing the legal legitimacy of slavery within the American republic.

In many ways, the true originality of Holmes's argument lay in his attack on viewing law as what he elsewhere called a "brooding omnipresence in the sky" instead of "the articulate voice of some sovereign or quasi-sovereign that can be identified" (*Southern Pacific Co. v. Jensen*, 244 U.S. 203, 222 (1917)). Thus Holmes counseled that legal analysts pay close attention to the mundane *behavior* of public officials faced with deciding whether or not to order the public use of force that for Holmes was the foundational reality of a legal order. Holmes was much influenced by the English jurist John Austin, who identified law with the existence of sanctions attached to disobedience. A state lacking the ability to impose force upon recalcitrants was also lacking anything that should be called "law" instead of, say, "requests" that could be rejected with impunity.

Another important early twentieth-century jurist, ROSCOE POUND, wrote a famous article distinguishing between "Law in Books and Law in Action" (1910). It was, Pound argued, wrong to believe that one could grasp the law of a given social order by simply reading and analyzing its formal legal rules found in statute books or even judicial reports. Instead, one had to find out which among these rules were actually taken seriously and routinely enforced by officials with state power. No enforcement, for Pound as for Holmes, meant in effect no law. (One might also discover that certain operational rules were enforced even in the absence of explicit legislative or constitutional authority.)

One's understanding of law could vary greatly depending on the particular officials one studied. Consider, for example, the implication of accepting Holmes's court-centered approach to law. Most legal academics have chosen to focus almost entirely on the decisions of appellate courts (especially, in the case of constitutional law, the United States Supreme Court) rather than, say, the behavior of the far more numerous local courts that resolve the overwhelming number of disputes that go to a court at all.

However, some analysts, the most influential of whom was KARL LLEWELLYN, advised going beyond courts and studying in addition the behavior of all sorts of officials involved in what he called "law jobs"; these included, among others, police, bureaucrats, and, indeed, lawyers themselves. This difference in the definition of "law" could obviously lead to divergent potrayals of legal reality. A person seeking to grasp the American system of criminal law by reading (and predicting) only the decisions of the United States Supreme Court would have a very different understanding from a person who looked for predictive purposes at the behavior of police departments, prosecutors, and local judges. The former might be quite impressed by the legal rights possessed by criminal defendants; the latter might quickly suggest that these formal legal rights are merely "law on the books." Most criminal defendants, represented by grossly overworked and too-often inept attorneys, end up pleading guilty through negotiated plea bargains rather than exercising their constitutional right to go to a trial where formal rights might be most relevant.

Holmes and Pound were the forerunners, and Llewellyn a principal practitioner, of American LEGAL REALISM, the most important American contribution to general jurisprudence (though Pound in particular became quite unhappy with what he viewed as the excesses of some realists). "Realism" took several different forms. Perhaps its most pervasive influence was the displacement of emphasis on the impersonal "formalities" of legal analysis with attention to the personal and political views of the specific persons occupying law-related offices. Legal categories were sufficiently open-ended to allow significantly different interpretation depending on the predilections of the individual decision-makers. For this reason, among others, realists were often viewed as critics of the notion of an impersonal "rule of law" distinguishable from "politics," which is invidiously dismissed as the domain of "instinct" or otherwise base special interest. For realists, though, the "rule of law" could not easily be distinguished from "the rule of men" (or, as we would say today, "of persons"). As FELIX FRANKFURTER put it, judges, especially Justices of the Supreme Court, are shapers of policy, not "impersonal vehicles of revealed truth." Although Frankfurter focused on constitutional interpretation, he could have extended to law in general his point that what judges "'interpret' is to a large measure *their own experience*, their 'judgment about practical matters,' their 'ideal pictures of the social order'" (p. 120). Frankfurter in fact went on to emphasize the duty of judges to discipline themselves and, most importantly, to defer much of the time to the decisions of electorally accountable legislatures, but he never recanted his basically realist insight about the relevance of a judge's particular experience. One form of realism, then, put great stress on the role of judicial personality and ideology; JEROME FRANK, perhaps the most extreme of the legal realists, suggested that judges be psychoanalyzed in order to ascertain the hidden wellsprings of their political ideologies.

American legal realism flourished in the 1920s and 1930s; its various critiques of legal formalism and the claims of judges to be merely impersonal vessels of the law reached fruition in the New Deal, in which many legal realists actively participated. The rise of fascism, however, helped to bring legal realism into disrepute insofar as its critique of the rule of law was thought to scant all-important differences between liberal and autocratic regimes. There was even a revival, led by Harvard's Lon Fuller as well as by Catholic jurists, of approaches to law that emphasized its necessary connection with morality or justice.

The social and political disruptions of the 1960s brought in their wake a reinvigoration of much of the legal realist critique. Various scholars, many of them attached to so-called CRITICAL LEGAL STUDIES, emphasized both the indeterminacy of legal concepts and the importance of ideology for explaining how any particular judge filled in the vague contours of any given concept with specific meaning. "Law" was simply the conduct of politics by other means. The principal work of law, according to some of these scholars, was to legitimate the ideological status quo by justifying it as purportedly required by preexisting legal norms. In response, many of these scholars took as their mission the demystification of law. As before, other scholars issued very strong responses condemning such views as "nihilistic" and articulating the importance of maintaining belief in the rule of law.

Much of this debate has focused on whether there exists a "legal hermeneutics," defined in his *Legal and Political Hermeneutics* (3rd ed., 1880) by FRANCIS LIEBER, a significant nineteenth-century writer on the law, as "[t]hat branch of science which establishes the principles and rules of interpretation and construction" (p. 52). Lieber emphasized the necessity of finding "safe rules" (p. 53) that guarded against the temptation of judges to go beyond the fair sense of the text and to read into the materials their own political predilections. There are both right-wing and left-wing critics of the indeterminacy thesis and of the ensuing skepticism about what Ronald Dworkin, in *Law's Empire* (1986), has termed the "integrity" of the law (pp. 95–6). Robert Bork, for example, has argued in *The Tempting of America: The Political Seduction of the Law* (1990) that the meaning of texts is derived from the discernible intentions of their authors or, just as importantly, the initial audience of the text. Legal hermeneutics, therefore, consists of an inquiry into those original intentions, followed by their application. Dworkin, a vigorous critic of Bork and of "intentionalism," nonetheless argues that legal analysts, especially judges, have as their hermeneutic task the rationalization of the vast plethora of case law and other legal materials by reference to "the principles of justice, fairness, and procedural due process that provide the best constructive interpretation of the community's legal practice" (p. 225).

Also increasingly prominent in the last quarter of the twentieth century have been various "law and" movements, of which by far the most influential has been LAW AND ECONOMICS. Though identified largely with the Right (just as critical legal studies is identified with the Left), Law and Economics, like its left-wing counterpart, expresses skepticism about the practical meaningfulness of much traditional legal thinking. Instead, many of its practitioners call for the conscious injection of economic insights, designed to assure maximum efficiency in the allocation of resources, into legal analysis. Although most legal analysts reject the single-minded focus on economic efficiency, few have rejected entirely the lessons of applying a variety of economic insights to law.

As we enter the twenty-first century, perhaps the most pervasive debate in American thought about law concerns its (at least relative) autonomy from other sectors of the social order. Is there a body of techniques, sometimes summarized as the skills involved in "thinking like a lawyer," that constitute a distinctively professional subculture within wider American culture? Are lawyers (and judges), as the result of their professional education and self-discipline, sufficiently socialized into the norms of that subculture so that major influences generated by what might be termed contingent aspects of the self—political views, race, religion, gender, and the like—are sufficiently "bleached out" to warrant respect from those who lose specific legal disputes? Such a professionalist vision, it might be argued, is crucial to taking seriously the enterprise of law and, concomitantly, the rule of law as truly distinctive social enterprises.

SANFORD LEVINSON

FURTHER READING

Andrew Altman, *Critical Legal Studies: a Liberal Critique* (Princeton: Princeton University Press, 1990).

Ronald Dworkin, *Law's Empire* (Cambridge: Harvard University Press, 1986).

Oliver Wendell Holmes Jr., "The Path of the Law" (1897), in Holmes, *Collected Legal Papers* (Boston: Little, Brown, 1920).

Morton Horwitz, *The Transformation of American Law* (vol. 1, Cambridge: Harvard University Press, 1977; vol. 2, New York: Oxford University Press, 1992).

John T. Noonan Jr., *The Antelope: the Ordeal of the Recaptured Africans in the Administrations of James Monroe and John Quincy Adams* (Berkeley: University of California Press, 1977).

Richard Posner, *The Problems of Jurisprudence* (Cambridge: Harvard University Press, 1990).

Roscoe Pound, "Law in Books and Law in Action," *American Law Review* 44 (1910).

Wilfrid E. Rumble Jr., *American Legal Realism: Skepticism, Reform, and the Judicial Process* (Ithaca, N.Y.: Cornell University Press, 1968).

Bernard Schwartz, *Main Currents in American Legal Thought* (Durham, N.C.: Carolina Academic Press, 1993).

Judith Shklar, *Legalism: Law, Morals, and Political Trials*, 2nd ed. (Cambridge: Harvard University Press, 1986).

G. Edward White, *The American Judicial Tradition* (New York: Oxford University Press, 1976).

Law and Economics   In the mid-1960s a small group of American law teachers began to draw upon economic theory to explain the shape of—or to advocate changes in—legal doctrines. Traditional legal scholars were initially skeptical of the approach, and its viability as a school of legal thought was far from clear. In the 1970s and 1980s, however, the entry into law teaching of many professionally trained economists, combined with an increase in the receptivity of judges and legislators to economic analysis, led to a surge in the popularity and credibility of the method. Today, the influence in legal scholarship of economics is rivaled only by that of CRITICAL LEGAL STUDIES.

Almost all of the work produced by the lawyer-economists has taken one of three forms. Scholarship in the first vein seeks to explain how and why particular legal rules came to assume their current forms. For example, in an important early article, Richard Posner reexamined from an economic standpoint the rise during the late nineteenth century of the negligence principle—the proposition that an actor must compensate a person he has unintentionally injured if and only if the injury resulted from the actor's carelessness or fault. Neither of the two competing conventional explanations for the widespread acceptance of this doctrine (that it reflected the desire of upper-middle-class judges to subsidize industry at the expense of workers and consumers, and that it was motivated by a desire to indemnify the victims of accidents) is plausible, Posner contended. Rather, the doctrine (and all of its myriad refinements and corollaries) derived from judges' semiconscious efforts to use the law of torts to induce private parties to take no more and no less than the economically efficient level of safety precautions, in other words, "to bring about, at least approximately, the efficient—the cost-justified—level of accidents and safety."

Scholarship in the second vein tries to predict the economic impacts of alternative ways of reforming particular fields of doctrine in hopes of aiding policymakers obliged to choose among them. Many examples of this approach can be found in the large body of writing analyzing from an economic standpoint the constitutional principle forbidding governments to "take" private property "without just compensation." Frank Michelman's seminal essay in this field argued that, *if* a judge wished to employ the insights of utilitarianism to decide whether to uphold a statute that might be considered violative of the "takings" principle, he should estimate the following economic impacts: (1) the net efficiency gains secured by the statute in question; (2) the cost of measuring the injuries sustained by adversely affected parties and of providing them with monetary compensation; and (3) the "demoralization costs" incurred by not indemnifying them. If (1) is the smallest figure, the judge should contrive some way to enjoin the action contemplated by the statute—for example, by declaring it to be violative of the constitutional requirement that private property may be expropriated only for a "public use." If (2) is the smallest figure, he should not enjoin the action but should require that the government compensate the parties hurt by it. If (3) is the smallest figure, he should allow the government to proceed without indemnifying the victims. Michelman did not suggest that courts should rely exclusively when resolving difficult "takings" cases on calculations of these sorts; on he contrary, he went on to suggest how the theory of distributive justice advanced by JOHN RAWLS might provide an alternative approach. Michelman's ambition was merely to clarify the implications of adopting an economic approach to the problem.

The third and most influential brand of law-and-economics scholarship, by contrast, openly advances a normative theory. Scholars who take this tack contend that legal rules should be designed and interpreted to maximize the total output of all goods and services in the society, measured by the prices consumers are willing and able to pay for them. The article that, in retrospect, is generally seen as the inspiration for this approach is "The Problem of Social Cost," published in 1960 by Ronald Coase. Coase observed that if no "transaction costs" prevented two persons from entering into a contract determining their respective entitlements, it would not matter from the standpoint of allocative efficiency what rule the legal system selected to govern their affairs, because they would agree on and abide by the socially optimal rule. The effect (though, it seems, not the intention) of Coase's essay was to provoke an ever-growing cadre of legal scholars to try to identify the legal rules that would advance allocative efficiency in situations in which transaction costs did prevent the achievement of optimal solutions through free bargaining. Some doctrinal fields—such as contracts, torts, property, and antitrust law—seemed to invite economic scrutiny. But the lawyer-economists soon brought their tools to bear on such seemingly unlikely fields as criminal law, family law, environmental law, landlord–tenant law, civil procedure, and constitutional law.

From the outset, this third style of economic analysis has been plagued with several methodological difficulties. For example, the developers of the method have never been able to resolve satisfactorily the so-called offer-asking problem: when measuring the "wealth" fostered by a particular legal rule, should the value of the goods or states of affairs it affects (such as habitable apartments or protection against sexual assault) be priced on the basis of the amount of money consumers would be willing and able to pay to obtain them or the amount of money consumers would demand in return for surrendering them? At least as troublesome is the problem of "general indeterminacy." When an analyst must apply the method to two or more legal problems, it often makes a difference which problem is addressed and reformed first. The wealth-maximization criterion, unfortunately, provides no guidance in determining the order of inquiry.

But the most serious of the methodological difficulties concerns not technical problems of these sorts but the weakness of the justification for using wealth maximization as the legal system's principal objective. Had they contented themselves with advocating "Pareto-superior" doctrinal reforms, the lawyer-economists would have had a relatively easy justificatory job; few would oppose the adoption of rules that make some people better off without making anyone worse off (by their own lights). The large majority of lawyer-economists, however, go further, urging lawmakers to adopt reforms that would make some persons worse off, but would confer upon others benefits that, in toto, exceed those losses. Defending the latter, more ambitious, criterion is no easy job.

One of the few scholars to have ventured such a defense is Richard Posner, the most prolific and prominent member of the movement. The heart of Posner's argument is the contention that because all (or almost all) persons are sometimes benefited and sometimes burdened by most legal rules, it is in the long-term best interest of everyone to select the rules that will maximize net social welfare. Among the weaknesses of this argument, the most obvious is that many persons do not stand an equal chance of being benefited and being burdened by a given legal rule. Unless the persons disproportionately benefited by the choices of optimal over extant legal rules compensate persons burdened by such choices (a corrective device few lawyer-economists advocate), the persons burdened have no reason to agree to the adoption of the wealth-maximization criterion. The difficulty is plain enough for most lawyer-economists to eschew Posner's theory.

What explains, then, the substantial and apparently still growing popularity of this approach? The most plausible answer, as Arthur Leff has suggested, is that the wealth-maximization criterion, whatever its problems, offers some relief from the anxieties that have plagued the American legal profession since the early twentieth century. The wealth-maximization criterion, shaky as it is, appears to provide a neutral, apolitical, scientific standard of judgment—a standard that legal scholars can use in differentiating good rules from bad, and that judges can use in making the innumerable hard choices they now realize they must make.

WILLIAM W. FISHER III

See also JUSTICE; LAW; LEGAL REALISM.

FURTHER READING

Ronald Coase, "The Problem of Social Cost," *Journal of Law and Economics* 3 (1960): 1–44.

Jules Coleman and Jeffrey Lange, eds., *Law and Economics*, 2 vols. (New York: New York University Press, 1992).

Robert Ellickson, "Property in Land," *Yale Law Journal* 102 (1992): 1315.

Duncan Kennedy, "Cost–Benefit Analysis of Entitlement Problems: a Critique," *Stanford Law Review* 33 (1981): 387–445.

Arthur A. Leff, "Economic Analysis of Law: Some Realism about Nominalism," *Virginia Law Review* 60 (1974): 451–82.

Frank Michelman, "Property, Utility, and Fairness: Comments on the Ethical Foundations of 'Just Compensation' Law," *Harvard Law Review* 80 (Apr. 1967): 1165–258.

Richard Posner, "A Theory of Negligence," *Journal of Legal Studies* 1 (1971): 29–96.

——, *Economic Analysis of Law*, 4th ed. (Boston: Little, Brown, 1992).

Steven Shavell, *Economic Analysis of Accident Law* (Cambridge: Harvard University Press, 1987).

Lazarsfeld, Paul (b. Vienna, Austria, Feb. 13, 1901; d. New York, N.Y., Aug. 30, 1976). Sociologist. Careful quantitative studies are, Lazarsfeld argued, the best way to study human decisions. Sociology should aspire to be a predictive science relying upon both quantitative and qualitative methodologies. As director of the Bureau of Applied Social Research at Columbia University (1940–50), Lazarsfeld developed rigorous statistical and sampling methods in the course of conducting research for paying clients, who sought to grasp such imponderables as consumer decisions, voting behavior, or the influence of advertising and mass media. His writings include *Radio and the Printed Page* (1940, with Hadley Cantril and Frank Stanton), *The People's Choice* (1944), and *Voting* (1954).

FURTHER READING

Robert Merton, James Coleman, and Peter Rossi, eds., *Qualitative and Quantitative Social Research* (New York: Macmillan, 1979).

Le Conte, Joseph (b. Liberty County, Ga., Feb. 26, 1823; d. Yosemite, Calif., July 6, 1901).   Geologist and natural historian. Evolution, Le Conte argued, is God's will in action. The natural laws of biological evolution parallel the moral laws of social evolution: both tend towards increasing differentiation and culminate in the devout human soul. Recognizing the deficiencies in Darwin's theory of natural selection, Le Conte believed that an organism's interactions with its environment produce inheritable adaptations. His many scientific articles described the formation of mountain ranges, explored the physiological bases of psychology, and argued for the transmutation of physical, chemical, and vital forces.

FURTHER READING

Lester D. Stephens, *Joseph Le Conte: Gentle Prophet of Evolution* (Baton Rouge: Louisiana State University Press, 1982).

Lee, Ann (b. Manchester, England, Feb. 29, 1736; d. Watervliet, N.Y., Sept. 8, 1784).   Religious leader. Lee had four children who died in infancy before she joined the "Shaking Quakers," who taught that God is androgynous—both father and mother—and believed a female Messiah would soon appear. Recurrent visions convinced others, then Lee, that she was that Messiah. Another vision identified sex as the cause of Adam and Eve's expulsion from Eden, and thereafter Lee considered celibacy a prerequisite for salvation. After emigrating to America in 1774, she founded a communitarian, perfectionist, and Pentecostal community near Watervliet, N.Y.

FURTHER READING

Nardi Reeder Campion, *Mother Ann Lee: Morning Star of the Shakers* (Hanover, N.H.: University Press of New England, 1990).

legal realism   An interwar movement of legal intellectuals, legal realism was concentrated at Columbia Law School in the 1920s and at Yale Law School and the short-lived Johns Hopkins Institute for Legal Research in the 1930s. At its height around 1930 it had 30 to 40 affiliates. Those most conspicuously identified with realism were KARL LLEWELLYN, JEROME FRANK, Walter Wheeler Cook, Herman Oliphant, Underhill Moore, Leon Green, THURMAN ARNOLD, WILLIAM O. DOUGLAS, Charles Clark, Walton Hamilton, Max Radin, Felix Cohen, Wesley Sturges and Hessel Yntema; more loosely affiliated were ADOLF BERLE, Robert Lee Hale, Thomas Reed Powell, and James Landis.

What defined and united realism was a negative program, its opposition to the "formalist" or "clas-

sical" jurisprudence that in the 1920s still dominated judicial opinions and legal commentary. Formalism, as the realists saw it, rested on three false premises: (1) *conceptualism*, that the whole system of private-law rules could be rationally derived from a few abstract principles induced from decided cases; (2) *doctrinalism* or *legal autonomy*, that judicial decisions both were and ought to be the products of reasoning from cases and categories wholly internal to the legal system (doctrine), immune from any outside social influences; and that policy, fairness, and likely social effects were proper only for legislatures to consider; and (3) *naturalization of a private sphere* of common law rules of private property and free contract that supposedly merely recognized natural rights and voluntary choices, as opposed to the public sphere of legislative and administrative action that coercively regulated and limited those rights and freedoms. Between 1880 and 1937 formalist judges turned the common law rules into principles of Constitutional limitation, striking down legislation such as protective labor laws which they thought excessively interfered with natural rights of the private sphere.

The realists attacked conceptualism with Justice Oliver Wendell Holmes's aphorism that "general propositions do not decide concrete cases" (*Lochner v. New York*, 1905, 198 U.S. 45, 76). They broke down concepts like "property" into a bundle of subconcepts whose implications pointed in different directions. A property right might give the owner a legal power to restrain infringers by injunction. Yet sometimes a property right gave only a remedy in damages, allowing the infringer to keep on infringing so long as he paid. For some injuries to property the law gave no recourse at all: A may have a property in the profits of his business; but if B starts a competing business that ruins A, A has no remedy. The law's varying treatment of these situations, argued the realists, depended on particular policy judgments—hidden and inarticulate in the cases—about the competing social utility of A's and B's activities. Thus (as Cook argued), when the courts decided that a labor action was an injury to employer's property that demanded an injunctive remedy, instead of a legitimate form of economic struggle like competition that required no remedy, their decision concealed an unanalyzed and debatable policy judgment about the value of labor organizing.

Similar insights fed the realist critique of legal autonomy. Doctrine (the "paper rules") had some effect on results, but a small effect relative to other factors—such as custom, dominant-class opinion, the personal or political biases of judges, latent policy judgments, or irreducibly particular responses to specific fact-situations. Doctrine was anyway too manipulable to determine outcomes: concepts were overgeneral; precedents, principles and statutes could be read narrowly or broadly, and often conflicted. To this "rule skepticism" Frank added "fact skepticism": the "facts" assumed as objective realities by appellate courts were messy, contested, constructed artifacts of the trial process.

By blasting away the conceptual and doctrinal bedrock of formalist law, the realists, who were mostly Progressive-liberals in politics, also sought to undermine the naturalization of common law rights that had led courts to immunize laissez-faire property and contract rules from legislative modification, by enshrining such rules as Constitutional rights. Realist critics, most powerfully Hale, insisted that property and contract rights were not natural but contingent creations of public policy, delegations of legal authority to some persons to use public force. Since all legal regimes, including the common law status quo, were regulatory and coercive, the only useful debates could be not over whether law *should* regulate the market, but over which regulatory powers the law should distribute to what interests for the sake of overall social benefit.

Though often united in their critique of formalism, realists differed in their constructive aims. Like other Progressive social scientists, most thought law ought to be "functional" to "social purposes"; and that knowledge of functions and purposes must be acquired by immersion in social-contextual particulars ("the facts"). Some thought judge-made law was already covertly functional under its formal masks and that its latent (policy) rationales should merely be made more explicit in judicial reasoning. Others sought to reconstruct doctrine around observable regularities in court decisions or the customary behavior of groups, as the Uniform Commercial Code drafted by Llewellyn between 1942 and 1952 instructed courts to apply "merchant" trade norms to contract disputes. Still others such as Arnold and Landis placed their hopes for functional law in the Progressive instrument of the expert administrative agency. Cook, Douglas, Oliphant and Moore constituted an empirical wing of realism. They sought to defer value questions, urging priority for the disinterested scientific study of the social determinants and effects of legal decisions and enactments, the "law in action."

The realists came under sharp attack after the rise of fascism: their skepticism about legal determinacy was widely characterized as a "relativist" or "nihilist" assault on the rule of law. The legal philosopher Lon Fuller charged that their empiricism merely nor-

mativized the conventional status quo. Traditionalists on law faculties resisted realist efforts (notably at Columbia in the 1920s) to redesign the law curriculum along "functional," nondoctrinal lines. The Depression starved the empirical enterprise and the Hopkins Institute of funds. The movement finally dissolved as leading realists, including Douglas, Arnold, Frank, Landis, Hamilton, and Berle, went off to serve the New Deal.

Nonetheless realism's influence has been lasting and profound. Contextualism, policy analysis, and a sense of the open-endedness of legal texts are now commonplace in law teaching and (to a lesser extent) adjudication. Every major school of modern legal thought still seeks either to carry on realist projects or to rebut realist critiques, by reestablishing determinate foundations for legal reasoning. Law and Society continues the empirical project of studying the "law in action." The CRITICAL LEGAL STUDIES school carries on the project of critique, extending it to policy analysis as well as to doctrine. Finally, LAW AND ECONOMICS carries on the project of reconstructing doctrine around its latent function of efficiency. Despite its relatively short life, legal realism thus established the terms of debate that continue to shape contemporary legal scholarship.

ROBERT W. GORDON

See also LAW.

FURTHER READING
Morton J. Horwitz, *The Transformation of American Law, 1870–1960: the Overthrow of Legal Orthodoxy* (Cambridge: Harvard University Press, 1992).
Laura Kalman, *Legal Realism at Yale, 1927–1960* (Chapel Hill: University of North Carolina Press, 1986).
Edward Purcell, *The Crisis of Democratic Theory* (Lexington: University Press of Kentucky, 1973).
William Twining, *Karl Llewellyn and the Realist Movement* (London: Weidenfeld and Nicolson, 1973).
William W. Fisher III, "The Development of Modern American Legal Theory . . . ," in Michael J. Lacey and Knud Haakonssen, eds., *A Culture of Rights: the Bill of Rights in Philosophy, Politics and Law, 1791 and 1991* (Cambridge: Cambridge University Press, 1991).
John Henry Schlegel, "American Legal Realism and Empirical Social Science: From the Yale Experience," *Buffalo Law Review* 28 (1979): 459–586.
Joseph William Singer, "Legal Realism Now," *California Law Review* 76 (1988): 465–544.
G. Edward White, "From Sociological Jurisprudence to Realism: Jurisprudence and Social Change in Early Twentieth Century America," *Virginia Law Review* 58 (1972): 999–1028.

Leggett, William (b. New York, N.Y., Apr. 30, 1801; d. New York, N.Y., May 29, 1839). Journalist. As assistant editor of the New York *Evening*

Post (1829–36) and editor of the *Plaindealer* (1836–7), Leggett was a fiery advocate of the libertarian wing of Andrew Jackson's Democratic Party. Committed to working people's political and economic rights and to labor associations, Leggett argued against government intervention in the market. He endorsed Jackson's assault on the national bank and paper money, attacked chartered monopolies and speculators, and insisted that free trade was the remedy to America's ills. Leggett proclaimed a radical version of laissez-faire in the interest of "producers of the middling and lower classes." Any government activity posed the threat of incipient autocracy; unregulated trade promised freedom and prosperity for all. His perspective reveals the broad sway of free market ideology and the deep fear of public authority in antebellum America.

FURTHER READING

William Leggett, *Democratic Editorials: Essays in Jacksonian Political Economy*, ed. Lawrence H. White (Indianapolis: Liberty Press, 1984).

Edward Williamson, *American Political Writers: 1801–1873* (Boston: Twayne, 1981).

Levertov, Denise (b. Ilford, England, Oct. 24, 1923). Poet. Levertov built her reputation as a writer of meditative poems, but VIETNAM provoked her to write political poems, collected in *Relearning the Alphabet* (1970), that grieved over the war. In *The Poet and the World* (1973), Levertov insisted on the complementarity of "inner" and "outer" worlds, of aesthetic quality and political content. Her later work, such as *Breathing the Water* (1987), became more overtly spiritual, exploring mysticism and women's experience.

FURTHER READING

Audrey T. Rodgers, *Denise Levertov: the Poetry of Engagement* (Rutherford, N.J.: Fairleigh Dickinson University Press, 1993).

Lewis, [Harry] Sinclair (b. Sauk Centre, Minn., Feb. 7, 1885; d. near Rome, Italy, Jan. 10, 1951). Writer. Author of *Main Street* (1920), *Babbitt* (1922), and *Elmer Gantry* (1927), among a score of other novels and plays, Lewis was the first American to receive the Nobel Prize for Literature (1930). *Main Street* and especially *Babbitt* were widely hailed in the 1920s, and have been saluted ever since, for their allegedly unanswerable put-down of bourgeois provincialism. Yet viewed from another angle, his debunking of the "average" American represented a stylized convention in its own right—that of the enlightened observer immune to the blandishments of MASS CULTURE. Moreover, his literary technique, in its devotion to breathless documentation, drew

abundantly on the publicity methods of the bourgeois culture—the culture Lewis's books are supposed to have savaged.

FURTHER READING

Christopher P. Wilson, *White Collar Fictions: Class and Social Representation in American Literature, 1885–1925* (Athens: University of Georgia Press, 1992).

liberal Protestantism Since the early nineteenth century liberal Protestantism, centered in such denominations as the Methodists, Presbyterians, Episcopalians, and Congregationalists (now part of the United Church of Christ), has exerted extraordinary social and intellectual power in American culture. Originating in the revolt of UNITARIANISM against orthodox CALVINISM, liberal Protestantism was instrumental in the nineteenth century in reconciling Americans to worldly values and practices that Calvinism held in deep suspicion. Intellectually, liberal Protestantism promoted the naturalistic assumptions, whether rationalistic or romantic, that stemmed from the ENLIGHTENMENT. Socially, many liberal Protestants pushed for a radical transformation of American institutions in the interest of greater justice for all (thus preserving, while secularizing, the Calvinists' own missionary impulse to reorder human society). Culturally, liberal Protestantism gradually endorsed the pleasures of the burgeoning domain of commercial amusements, thereby helping to cement a firm base for the twentieth-century culture of consumption.

Overall, liberal Protestantism performed a crucial legitimizing function for modern, cosmopolitan, secular habits of mind as they contended for supremacy in a deeply religious culture. It would not be too far-fetched to suggest that in such a profoundly religious society, secular modernism (including scientific empiricism, free-wheeling entrepreneurialism, and a deep-seated consumer ethic) could attain respectability only through religious sponsorship. Liberal Protestantism was scarcely uncritical about secular society, the moral reform of which it continuously and ardently preached. But the stance of reform was part of the broader embrace and validation of the secular world.

Not only did liberal Protestantism put an indispensable stamp of approval on humanism, naturalism, and commercialism, it also helped determine their distinctive American character. The consumer ethic of twentieth-century America, for example, is not simply a propensity to accumulate and enjoy more and more things, a practice observable well before the twentieth century in the United States and elsewhere. It is most distinctively the ceaseless pursuit of therapeutic satisfaction through the personal "growth" made possible by purchased goods, services, and lifestyles. It is a quest for this-worldly fulfillment which nevertheless retains much of the language and bearing of a religious quest for salvation. And liberal Protestantism prepared the cultural path for it by challenging the older orthodox limitation of salvation to the afterlife. Salvation, for the liberals, was not a final reward but a lifelong process of growth in love, service, and well-being. By making salvation an earthly endeavor, one never fully accomplishable, liberal Protestantism opened the way for a secularization that preserved the shape of an unending personal quest for fulfillment. Liberal Protestantism thus gave the consumer culture much more than legitimation; it gave that culture an animating form and ethic.

Although there has been much talk recently about the "decline" of liberal Protestantism in the face of a resurgent EVANGELICALISM—and the decline in liberal church membership since 1970 is very real—liberal religion still exercises substantial cultural power because it is very strong in the upper reaches of American social life, among leaders in business, government, the professions, broadcast and print journalism, universities, and foundations. And although over the last generation liberal Protestantism (like liberal Judaism and liberal Catholicism) has indeed given way to some extent to a humanistic secularism, that shift is ironically a sign of its success as well as its failure. For it has been one of the historic missions of liberal Protestantism to validate commitment to, and immersion in, the everyday human world.

By the early twentieth century liberal Protestantism had reached its peak. As a social and cultural force it was unrivaled in the religious community. At that point it was still both "liberal" and "evangelical," a potent combination of attitudes and beliefs that became less and less plausible by the end of the 1920s. In the half-century between 1875 and 1925, liberal evangelical Protestantism held nearly undisputed sway, even if the tensions that would thereafter produce an irrepressible conflict between "modernists" and "fundamentalists" were already apparent in the late nineteenth century.

To grasp the fundamental character of the liberal Protestant outlook, it helps to remember what it rebelled against: the Calvinist insistence upon God's awe-inspiring sovereignty. The Calvinists worshipped a God of power and might; he kept his own counsel and his decrees were unanswerable. Salvation was of course only for those whom he chose; human efforts to affect his decisions were, in the nature of the case, unavailing. The (self-labelled) liberals, beginning with the well-heeled Boston Uni-

tarians at the start of the national period, shook their heads at what seemed to them an unenlightened denial of human potency and RESPONSIBILITY. In their view individual human beings plainly possessed the capacity to overcome sin and live a life of reason and love. It was inconceivable, indeed blasphemous, to imagine that God would ever choose to punish a person of demonstrated virtue. Human nature was not irreversibly tainted by the Fall. It was wholesome at its center; if human society had not yet reached full enlightenment, there was no reason to doubt that, with education and good will, unbounded progress could be made.

The liberal Protestant insistence on the capacity of human beings to master themselves and to mold the social world produced the "social gospel" movement of the late nineteenth and early twentieth centuries. Not all liberal Protestants became Social Gospelers, active proponents of a restructured, post-laissez-faire political economy. But beginning in the 1880s the Social Gospelers, along with many secular reformers (themselves often raised in and informed by liberal Protestant convictions), built a far-reaching Progressive movement. Such leaders as WASHINGTON GLADDEN, a Congregationalist minister based in Columbus, Ohio, and RICHARD T. ELY, a lay economist at the University of Wisconsin, urged Christians to pursue "social salvation" by rebuilding basic institutions. Indebted to German precedents in social legislation and scientific scholarship, they advocated increased government regulation and professional management of economy and society. Along with other progressives, they also promoted a new social role for people like themselves: morally attuned and scientifically trained experts poised to mediate between the warring parties of labor and capital, parties thought by many late nineteenth-century middle-class Americans to be selfishly subverting the body politic.

It was the liberal Protestants' desire to overcome conflict in every arena of personal and public life that gave a particular moral tone to their thought and action. Some secular liberals, such as LESTER FRANK WARD, shared common ground with liberal Protestants in their devotion to scientific expertise, to the quest for justice, to the rebuilding of institutions, and to a future of progress and enlightenment, but departed from the Protestant liberals by being much more resigned to social and psychological conflict. Some secularists even imagined, following Darwinian and Spencerian assumptions, that progress depended upon conflict. Although few social thinkers actually followed Herbert Spencer or WILLIAM GRAHAM SUMNER in endorsing anything close to the notion of the survival of the fittest, some secular liberals did celebrate the character-building stringency of the marketplace struggle. Liberal Protestants, by contrast, preached the glories of fellowship and solidarity, and imagined that progress could ultimately produce a society of friends and comrades, not competitors or strangers. By the twentieth century American liberalism was often distinguished from Marxism and Freudianism—both premised on the idea of deeply rooted and inexorable conflict, social or psychological—by its faith in the essential harmony of individual and group life. That sentimental assumption came into American liberalism as much from the hopeful hearts of the liberal Protestants as it did from Enlightenment rationalism.

The great liberal Protestant texts of the late nineteenth century, whether written by churchmen like Charles Sheldon (*In His Steps*, 1892) or by unchurched secularists steeped in liberal Protestant assumptions like EDWARD BELLAMY (*Looking Backward*, 1888), dwell above all on the goal of eradicating conflict from human life and erasing the lines between classes. Sheldon's Reverend Henry Maxwell, a mediocre burned-out minister of a respectable Chicago parish at the start of *In His Steps*, is transformed into a peerless charismatic leader when he wakes up to the social challenge facing the middle classes and their churches. The emotional culmination of the story is his crossing the tracks to speak to a working-class gathering, which listens attentively and is galvanized by his sincerity and ardor. Here middle-class readers could vicariously experience the overcoming of their own isolation from the immigrant working class. Edward Bellamy had a simpler solution: eliminate the immigrant working class from his imaginary Boston of the year 2000, and restore social tranquillity by banishing not just exploitation but competition itself from economic life. Both texts illustrate the profound yearning in liberal Protestantism, and in much secular liberalism shaped by it, to reconfigure social life as caring, efficient, unruffled.

Most historians have treated the religious PROGRESSIVISM of the Social Gospelers as the "response" of conscientious men and women to the social and political emergency of the late nineteenth century. But this view tends to reduce religious ideas and practices to afterthoughts; it sees economic and technological change as "basic," ideas and beliefs as secondary. In fact, by proposing to mediate between groups in conflict, and to reform the new large-scale structures of corporate enterprise, such progressives as Ely and Gladden helped to solidify and legitimize the new order, precisely by insisting on its reformability. Their ideological efforts performed indispensable spadework in the construction of the new corporate industrial society; those efforts were not just a humanitarian response to displacements provoked by INDUSTRIALISM.

The most original and influential thinker of the Social Gospel broadly conceived may have been JANE ADDAMS, who like Bellamy moved intellectually along the boundary line between secularism and liberal religion, but the most significant religious thinker of the movement was certainly WALTER RAUSCHENBUSCH (1861–1918), author of such works as *Christianity and the Social Crisis* (1907) and *A Theology for the Social Gospel* (1914). He had become a theological liberal as a seminarian—biblical inerrancy and the old "substitutionary" atonement, for example, no longer made sense to him—but it was not until he took a parish on New York City's West Side in 1886 that he woke up to poverty and became a social liberal. The unsuccessful New York mayoral campaign of HENRY GEORGE in that year was instrumental in turning Rauschenbusch toward the Social Gospel. But his shift did not entail a rejection of prayer or individual piety; with him as with most liberal Protestant Social Gospelers of his generation, liberalism did not conflict with evangelicalism. He could at one and the same time appeal for radical political transformation, laud the scientific analysis of social problems, and praise the revivalistic effusions of famed Bible-preacher Dwight Moody.

Pragmatic in his devotion to "scientific" reform (in the Deweyan sense of open-ended, carefully tested, and democratically administered change), Rauschenbusch was also typically liberal Protestant in his Romanticism. Following the example of liberal preachers HORACE BUSHNELL and HENRY WARD BEECHER in the mid-nineteenth century, Rauschenbusch imagined the spread of Jesus's kingdom as the gradual, organic growth of human character and personality. Social transformation in his view was always a dual process: the makeover of social institutions and the conversion of individual persons. Like Addams, Dewey, Randolph Bourne, and many other secular as well as religious progressives, Rauschenbusch took for granted that any social revolution worth having would be one that encouraged individuals to grow in "personality."

This commitment to personality was at the heart of liberal Protestantism, and it must not be confused with what often passes for devotion to personality in the late twentieth century: surface winsomeness or cosmeticized glow. For the liberal Protestants personality was a spiritual attainment of human beings. They achieved it when they paradoxically both fulfilled themselves and "died to self" by putting the interests of others ahead of their own. Personality was a capacity for love, the self-sacrificial affection which religious liberals believed should rule social relations as well as private life. And personality was a place of deep encounter with the spirit of God, who made himself human in the man of personality par excellence, Jesus Christ. Men and women developed personality as they prayed and acted together, achieving self-realization in the very same commitments that produced vibrant communities.

Until recently the 1920s was widely thought to have been the decade of final victory for religious liberalism, when it vanquished FUNDAMENTALISM at the Scopes trial (even though Scopes was found guilty of teaching evolution, the argument goes, liberalism won the larger war by making WILLIAM JENNINGS BRYAN and religious traditionalism look ridiculous). But as Garry Wills remarks in *Under God*, the deeper meaning of the Scopes trial was that liberalism and evangelicalism, previously wedded, were rent asunder, to the great loss of each. H. L. MENCKEN, star commentator, and CLARENCE DARROW, star defense attorney, were not just attacking fundamentalist religion, but all religion; Mencken made a career out of satirizing the weak-kneed pieties of the bourgeois middle class as well as the hick primitivism of the rural fundamentalists. By the late 1920s young liberal Protestant leaders such as REINHOLD NIEBUHR were also assaulting the sentimental pretensions of the liberal church. Although liberal Protestantism did not suffer major membership losses until the 1970s, it was already suffering internal ideological dissension a half-century earlier.

In the 1950s and 1960s the civil rights activism of the southern black church, and the magnificent oratory of MARTIN LUTHER KING JR., gave liberal Protestantism a second wind. As the twentieth century ends, liberal Protestantism is down in numbers, but retains the allegiance of many strategically placed individuals and continues to offer an institutional home for those testing the boundaries of faith and social action. The women's movement is especially potent in the liberal churches: a majority of ministerial students at the leading seminaries are now women, and such varied thinkers as Carter Heyward, Beverly Harrison, and Sallie McFague have emerged in feminist theology and ethics. Liberal Protestantism will always attract a socially militant vanguard who resonate to Jesus's uncompromising message that the law of love must be extended to the whole of human life. But it will also attract believers who applaud its paradoxical insistence that science and faith are equally deserving of commitment. Faith need never fear critical reason, in the liberal Protestant view, because, beneath all the encrusted and dispensable traditions

that have piled up over the centuries to serve one interest or another, there lies the inspiring, transforming force of personality.

RICHARD WIGHTMAN FOX

FURTHER READING
Sydney E. Ahlstrom, *A Religious History of the American People* (New Haven: Yale University Press, 1972).
Taylor Branch, *Parting the Waters: America in the King Years, 1954–1963* (New York: Random House, 1989).
Richard Wightman Fox, "The Culture of Liberal Protestant Progressivism, 1875–1925," *Journal of Interdisciplinary History* 23 (winter 1993): 639–60.
William R. Hutchison, *The Modernist Impulse in American Protestantism* (1976; Durham, N.C.: Duke University Press, 1992).
C. Eric Lincoln and Lawrence Mamiya, *The Black Church in the African American Experience* (Durham, N.C.: Duke University Press, 1990).
Wade Clark Roof and William McKinney, *American Mainline Religion: Its Changing Shape and Future* (New Brunswick, N.J.: Rutgers University Press, 1987).
Garry Wills, *Under God: Religion and American Politics* (New York: Simon and Schuster, 1991).
Robert Wuthnow, *The Restructuring of American Religion: Society and Faith since World War II* (Princeton: Princeton University Press, 1990).

liberalism Representing an individualistic political language that has been central to American political thought and practice, the term first appeared in Western European politics in the early nineteenth century, where it designated programs opposed to aristocratic privilege and favorable to representative political institutions and free market capitalism. Tracing their principles back to such thinkers as Thomas Hobbes, John Locke, and Adam Smith, liberals constructed a pre-nineteenth-century history. In response to changing political experience and reflection, the liberal tradition has been continually reconstructed ever since.

In the Anglo-American liberal tradition, John Locke is the exemplary figure. Forced by the English Civil War and the collapse of medieval intellectual authority to rethink the bases of political society, Locke drew on several sources. Modern science led him to resolve society into its simple elements in a state of nature and to place the motive force of politics in individuals and their natural mode of functioning. Locke's INDIVIDUALISM also had religious roots. Persons stand in a state of nature, as before God, free and equal. A devoted partisan of reformed Christianity, he urged in his "Letter Concerning Toleration" that "the care . . . of every man's soul belongs unto himself" (p. 129).

Locke also drew on a long judicial tradition that defined liberty as a specific right bestowed by law and that invoked the law of nature to invest the individual with natural rights. Thus, in his *Two Treatises on Government*, he claimed that men are endowed by nature with rights to life, liberty, and property; that they establish a sovereign government to protect those rights by free consent; and that whenever the sovereign breaks the contract by violating those rights, the people are free to overthrow the sovereign and reestablish government on a legitimate basis.

Finally, Locke emphasized the propertied basis of liberty. He anchored in natural right both the goods acquired by one's own labor and those acquired by money. The protection of property from the depredations of those who had none became the central reason men agreed to form a government. Thus his *Treatises* legitimated not only government by consent and a limited government whose purpose was the protection of RIGHTS, but also private property and the accumulation of property characteristic of capitalism. Adam Smith's *The Wealth of Nations* later solidified the economic strand in liberalism by its defense of the public beneficence of individual self-interest. Government became a policeman and facilitator for a free economy and a last resort for needful functions which could not be performed better under the master principle of individual energy and responsibility. The nineteenth-century intersection of Lockean and economic liberalism gave liberalism its "classical" form.

This story of liberal origins, and every other, has been contested by those within and outside the liberal tradition throughout the nineteenth and twentieth centuries. How the multiple strands of liberal theory should be weighted, what historical consequences they have produced, and what theoretical and practical implications can be drawn from them, have become important topics of debate.

Before turning to those debates, it is important to note the historical development of liberal politics. In Europe, liberal political parties, based in the middle class and its classical liberal values of individual responsibility and opportunity, reached their greatest power in the late nineteenth and early twentieth century and were then eclipsed by the rise of working-class socialist parties. In the United States, however, the term liberal was rarely used in the nineteenth century to denote an indigenous political position. During the 1910s and 1920s it came to stand for the reform liberalism of PROGRESSIVISM; since the 1930s, when it was popularized by Franklin D. Roosevelt for his New Deal program, liberalism has meant welfare state liberalism. Hence, during the twentieth century, classical liberalism has become the preserve of political CONSERVATISM, while the generic term

has been captured by reformist liberals who, adapting their individualist tradition to social democratic politics, extended the domain of rights and the government's responsibility to ensure EQUALITY more deeply into civil society.

Liberalism first became a focus of serious intellectual debate in the United States during the late 1930s. Observing the rise of fascism and communism in Europe and fearing that these doctrines might take root in the United States, or conquer it from without, liberal writers began to identify liberalism as the root political philosophy of the Western democratic polities, especially of the United States. From that point through the 1960s, questions about the strengths and weaknesses of liberalism were often subsumed in the question of whether modern Western societies, and America in particular, conformed *in fact* to the ideal set forth in liberal theory. Accordingly, the debate was largely carried on by historians, social scientists, and political intellectuals.

LOUIS HARTZ gave notable expression to one major line of thinking in *The Liberal Tradition in America*. He argued that the American political tradition had been exclusively a liberal tradition in the classic Lockean mold. Reorienting the classic analysis of American democracy by ALEXIS DE TOCQUEVILLE to the categories of liberalism, Hartz claimed that the absence of an aristocracy and the pervasiveness of small-producer capitalism had assured the easy triumph of liberalism in the nineteenth century and the failure of socialism in the twentieth. With its premises so widely accepted, there was thus no need for a specific liberal party in nineteenth-century America. Where socialism was not a viable political force, reform liberalism could dominate the leftward half of the political spectrum. There was sometimes an edge to Hartz's portrayal of acquisitive liberalism, and he feared that a monolithic liberal consensus did not prepare Americans to live in the postwar world, but these darker observations were coupled to Hartz's satisfaction with the classlessness of American politics and his conviction that America's liberal heritage was in any case the only heritage available.

Political scientists reconfigured the American liberal consensus around the idea of pluralism. Because their empirical studies had concluded that the rational deliberation and participation necessary for democracy did not exist in the United States, political scientists had been seeking a way to legitimate the American polity since the crisis of the 1930s. Pluralism turned to liberal models. In modern American society, it was argued, individuals exercised their political will through the many voluntary and functional groups to which they belonged. In the polity, as in the market economy, they advanced their interests through a competitive group process from which a fluid order and rough justice emerged. Like the classic liberal marketplace of ideas, or its purer analogue, the scientific community, the liberal polity guaranteed that all voices would be heard, mistakes corrected, and progress maintained. Under the ideological pressures of the Cold War, pluralism, even more than Hartz's liberal vision of American exceptionalism, identified the actual political practice of the United States with the liberal ideal.

During the 1960s, the rise of the CIVIL RIGHTS movement and of political protest on the left shattered the belief in an American liberal CONSENSUS and challenged the idealized description of American liberalism. Some critics on the left emphasized the disproportionate power of large business corporations and the unequal distribution of income shares. A NEW LEFT, associated with Students for a Democratic Society, focused on racial as well as economic inequality and on the redistribution of political power. They urged the revitalization of community politics and values and the restoration of genuine power to all citizens through "participatory democracy."

A historical reexamination of the liberal tradition also began in the 1960s and bridged the move from the issue of America's conformance to liberalism to a substantive reexamination of the theoretical and practical resources of the liberal tradition. The key text was *The Political Theory of Possessive Individualism: Hobbes to Locke* by C. B. Macpherson, a Canadian political theorist, who believed that modern liberal theory was inadequate to deal with "the centrifugal forces of a possessive market society." The problem, he argued, was that liberalism was itself founded on the model of market society: individuals were conceived as self-possessed, owing nothing to society, and society was conceived as nothing but relations of exchange between proprietors. Macpherson's argument was soon countered by readings of Locke and other liberal sources that emphasized their Christian and natural law foundations.

Simultaneously, historians of America's founding political culture and of Anglo-American political theory were discovering the existence and salience of a republican political language whose Aristotelian premises were very different from those of liberalism. Promising a heritage concerned for the public good and a participatory conception of citizenship, the discovery of REPUBLICANISM was an immediate counter to Hartz's exclusively liberal reading of American politics. It also reopened inquiry into the character of liberalism in the United States, an enterprise augmented by bicentennial stocktaking. Historians of

liberalism moved on two fronts: like Joyce Appleby, who located the impulse toward democracy in America's classical liberalism, they reinterpreted the historical implications of liberal principle; or, as in the work of James Kloppenberg, they showed how liberalism absorbed the moral impulses of adjacent religious and republican traditions. In both cases, the aim was to expand the resources of liberal political culture beyond merely possessive individualism.

That aim has also been at work in the revival of liberal political philosophy since the 1970s. The discussion was set in motion, and has been largely dominated since, by the publication in 1971 of *A Theory of Justice* by JOHN RAWLS. Writing at a moment when liberalism was under political and critical attack, Rawls fashioned an imposing justification of the liberal principles embedded in American political culture and institutions. The issues he raised have been taken up by political, moral, and legal philosophers and have influenced subsequent work in social science and history.

Rejecting the utilitarian theory that had formed the basis for modern liberalism, Rawls made his ideal liberal citizen a Kantian autonomous moral agent and constructed a spare "original position" from which individuals contract basic constitutional arrangements. Such moral agents, stripped of all particular characteristics, would choose justice as the highest good, maximize basic liberties for all, and distribute social goods so that any inequalities benefited the least advantaged, choices that are within the discursive reach, if not the practical grasp, of modern, pluralist, social democratic regimes.

Subsequent discussion of liberalism has taken many paths, of which several can be noted. Communitarian theorists, drawing on the communitarian and participatory themes that had emerged in the 1960s and in the republican revival, argue that liberal theory assumes and promotes an impoverished conception of the self and of the solidaristic needs of modern communities. Theorists of FEMINISM urge that the disembodied rational self and the classic liberal separation between public and private spheres reaffirm the traditional patriarchal distinctions and disabilities of gender. Some liberal theorists have responded to these communitarian and feminist concerns by working to deepen the conception of VIRTUE and CITIZENSHIP in liberal theory and by discussing ways to extend the requirements of justice to the gender system and family life.

An intersecting debate revolves around whether liberalism stands neutral regarding the different, incommensurable goods held by individuals, as Rawls and others argue, or whether liberalism should affirm a substantive conception of the good, as communitarian liberals such as William Galston believe. This debate has been fueled by the revival of conservative politics in the 1980s, with its base of LIBERTARIANISM, and by the increasing political salience of social and cultural diversity.

Given the demise of communism and widespread suspicion of SOCIALISM, and given the proven strengths of the liberal tradition and the possibility of correcting its proven failings, current political aspiration and reflection cannot help but center on liberalism.

DOROTHY ROSS

See also DEMOCRACY; FREEDOM; HEGEMONY.

FURTHER READING

Joyce Appleby, *Capitalism and a New Social Order* (New York: New York University Press, 1984).

Norman Daniels, ed., *Reading Rawls: Critical Studies on Rawls' A Theory of Justice*, 2nd ed. (Stanford: Stanford University Press, 1989).

William A. Galston, *Liberal Purposes: Goods, Virtues and Diversity in the Liberal State* (New York: Cambridge University Press, 1991).

James T. Kloppenberg, "The Virtues of Liberalism: Christianity, Republicanism, and Ethics in Early American Political Discourse," *Journal of American History* 74 (June 1987): 9–33.

John Locke, "A Letter Concerning Toleration" (1685), in Conrad Waligorski and Thomas Hone, eds., *Anglo-American Liberalism: Readings in Normative Political Economy* (Chicago: Nelson Hall, 1981).

Susan Moller Okin, *Justice, Gender and the Family* (New York: Basic Books, 1989).

Carol Pateman, *The Sexual Contract* (Stanford: Stanford University Press, 1988).

Edward A. Purcell Jr., *The Crisis of Democratic Theory: Scientific Naturalism and the Problem of Value* (Lexington: University Press of Kentucky, 1973).

Andrzej Rapaczynski, *Nature and Politics: Liberalism in the Philosophies of Hobbes, Locke, and Rousseau* (Ithaca: Cornell University Press, 1987).

Dorothy Ross, "Liberalism," in Jack P. Greene, ed., *Encyclopedia of American Political History*, vol. 2 (New York: Charles Scribner's Sons, 1984).

Michael J. Sandel, *Liberalism and the Limits of Justice* (Cambridge: Cambridge University Press, 1982).

libertarianism The doctrine has had two rather distinct existences, the first in the nineteenth century, and a second in the past two decades; how far the libertarianism of the recent past resembles the libertarianism of the nineteenth century remains an open question. Certainly, nineteenth-century libertarianism was exclusively the province of radicals, while that of the past quarter of a century has appealed to laissez-faire economists and has been embodied in a movement largely paid for by rich businessmen.

During the nineteenth century several varieties of "individualist anarchism" flourished both in Europe and in the United States. Marx's rival for the allegiance of French radicals, Pierre Proudhon, derived his condemnation of both the state and private property from a belief in the timeless principles of justice and the sanctity of individual human rights. It was his belief that every individual had an inalienable right of access to the means of life and labor that led him to conclude that "property is theft." His contemporary, Max Stirner, was briefly famous as the author of *The Ego and His Own* (1844), and more lastingly and inspiration to individualist anarchists in Italy. Earlier than both of them, William Godwin (1756–1836) in his *Enquiry Concerning the Principles of Political Justice* (1793) had defended the sanctity of each individual's right of private judgment, and the consequent illegitimacy of coercive institutions.

In the United States, credit for first bringing individualist anarchism to American consciousness probably ought to go to Lysander Spooner (1808–1887), who argued for the substantial unconstitutionality of most American law—including the Constitution itself—on grounds that most Americans could take seriously. Spooner held that society ought to be governed by natural law rather than congressional law. In his most famous work, *Trial by Jury* (1852), Spooner argued that juries should be chosen by lot, in order to eliminate government influence over them, and that they should be able to judge of law as well as fact. His slightly older contemporary, Josiah Warren (1798–1874), subscribed to similar views; he came to them by a process with which it is easy to sympathize. His first allegiances were to Owenism; but the experience of life in the Owenite community of New Harmony, Indiana, turned him into an extreme individualist. Warren's vision of a society in which exchange should take place on the basis of "no gain, no loss" had much in common with Proudhon's.

The most articulate and energetic expositor of individualist anarchism was Benjamin Tucker (1854–1939). In *Liberty*, the journal he published from 1881 to 1908, Americans could discover not only the ideas of Proudhon and Stirner but those of the Russian anarchists Bakunin and Kropotkin, and of William Morris and George Bernard Shaw. He wrote much of *Liberty* himself, and published a collection of his most interesting essays, *Instead of a Book: By a Man too Busy to Write One* (1893). Like Spooner and Warren (who converted him to individualist anarchism), Tucker was essentially a nonviolent revolutionary. He was, as other anarchists have been, more than ready to lose his friends for the sake of his principles; Tucker outraged feminists by insisting that "equal pay" movements were misguided because as workers women were inevitably inferior to men. Tucker was the most articulate defender of what is sometimes called "property-rights anarchism" in his day, and along with Spooner is today the hero of defenders of the same ideology.

Even more than its close relations, LIBERALISM and anarchism, libertarianism defies tidy analysis. The leading dictionary definition of "libertarianism" refers to a belief in the FREEDOM of the will; the secondary, political meaning is not distinguished from liberalism generally. No encyclopedia of the social sciences gives libertarianism a distinct entry. It remains in fact obscure where the boundaries lie that distinguish libertarian thought from its near competitors. Among contemporary libertarians we find both "anarcho-capitalists" and libertarian socialists, ardent secularists and Christian fundamentalists, and this is not new. Benjamin Tucker was an individualist, property-right based anarchist, but EMMA GOLDMAN, an anarchist of a socialist, antiproperty stamp, called herself a "libertarian" as well.

The relationship of libertarianism to democracy is clearer. Since libertarianism has either no place for government or a very limited place, a government's democratic legitimacy is irrelevant to its larger illegitimacy. If a single other individual has no right to use my person or property for any purpose for which I have not given my free and unfettered consent, neither does any larger number of individuals. What it is illegitimate for one person to do, it is equally illegitimate for any number of associated persons to do. Even so, very diverse grounds have been given for repudiating democracy. Emma Goldman saw the "mass" quality of democracy as inimical to freedom, a surprisingly elitist thought in an anarchist. More commonly, the thought is that of Robert Nozick's *Anarchy, State and Utopia* (1974), that allowing other people the right to dictate my behavior for anything other than the defense of their own persons and property is in effect to make me to that extent their property. In a democracy each is the partial slave of all.

Libertarianism is best understood as an extreme liberalism. An abiding thought of liberalism is that "that government is best which governs least"; the libertarian corollary is Spooner's inference that that government is best which governs not at all. The antigovernment case may be put in different ways that readily run in harness. One is to point out how much damage governments do. Compared with the misdeeds of governments, individual crime is insignificant. No individual rivals twentieth-century governments in mass murder, torture, and oppression, and the greatest evils done by individuals have been done in their capacity as heads of governments.

Submitting to government to escape the "war of all against all" that Hobbes described as our natural condition, we submit to an entity that launches larger wars itself.

Libertarians hold that forms of association and cooperation can exist that do not have the evil aspects of governments as we know them. The basis for this claim is the other argument against the legitimacy of every actual state. Appealing to Locke's account of our "property in our own persons," libertarians have held that we are essentially self-owning creatures; our bodies, our thoughts, our actions, and whatever we can create by employing our efforts on things we have either acquired in an unowned state or have acquired from their prior owner, are ours. They are ours outright. We have in them what A. M. Honore has described as "full liberal ownership," that is, an indefinite freehold.

The only restraint upon our ownership of ourselves, our talents, our actions, and our external possessions is that which stems from everyone else's similar proprietorship in themselves. As the old tag to the effect that "my freedom to swing my fist ends where the freedom of your nose begins" so inelegantly puts it, I may do what I like with what is mine so long as it does not damage your property or person, and does not violate your similar rights. I may stand where I like, but not if your foot is there before mine; I may drive where I like but not if you are standing where I might otherwise wish to drive.

Since all persons are the sole proprietors and outright owners of themselves, there is one legitimate form of social cooperation and many illegitimate forms. The legitimate form is built on voluntary exchange; the illegitimate forms are in one way or another extractive. That is, they rest on the supposed right of others to take what is mine for purposes to which I have not assented. It does not matter whether these are good purposes or bad.

It is irrelevant whether the persons taking them have benevolent or malevolent motives. All conscription of my efforts, person, or possessions is a form of theft. Saint Augustine observed many centuries ago that a state without justice is only a "large band of robbers [*magna latrocinia*]" and Murray Rothbard has echoed him. Libertarians think that justice is to be defined as "to each their own" and thus that every state that goes beyond securing each of us "our own" is illicit, or even that every state is illicit, *tout court*, because every state, in demanding that we do what we have not consented to, is taking what is "our own." (*See also* JUSTICE.)

Divisions among libertarians are many; as observed before, the line between a libertarian perspective and its near neighbors is all but invisible. FRIEDRICH A. HAYEK (1901–1992) greatly influenced libertarianism, but was not himself a libertarian. He allowed a limited role to the welfare state, and thought that a certain cultural conservatism was necessary for a capitalist system to work well. Nor did he think property rights were "natural" rights. Yet he encouraged libertarians in his antipathy to the very idea of "social justice." Hayek's conception of justice was a libertarian conception, based on the idea that "each should have his own," and this is essentially an antiredistributive conception of justice.

The difference between Hayek and Nozick over the question of how to justify the distribution of goods at the end of a process of exchange indicates one of the ways a free market liberal may differ from a libertarian. Hayek argues that when people exchange goods and services in the marketplace, they improve their position relative to the *status quo ante*, so the final state achieved after a series of exchanges is superior to the opening state before the exchanges took place. This is the familiar voice of the liberal economist. Nozick responds that this is beside the point. All that matters is that the parties to the exchanges *chose* to engage in the exchange. We may give to someone we like a book from which they will get less enjoyment than we do, or sell to someone we pity a valuable object for much less than its market price. That is neither here nor there. Varying the Marxist cliché, Nozick describes the principle of justice as "from each as he chooses, to each as he is chosen."

Contemporary libertarians appeal to Spooner and Tucker in the same spirit that conventional politicians appeal to the memory of Lincoln and Jefferson. Of more recent writers, Alfred Jay Nock, the prewar critic of Roosevelt's New Deal, Ludwig von Mises, Hayek and MILTON FRIEDMAN have been influential in linking opposition to government intervention in the economy to a more general distrust of government. The title of Hayek's 1944 attack on the welfare state, *The Road to Serfdom*, expresses this general anxiety; even a benevolent state will reduce its citizens to the condition of slaves if it takes too large a part in securing their welfare.

The two most significant figures in making libertarianism publicly visible have been the economist Murray Rothbard and the novelist Ayn Rand. The latter publicized a philosophy labelled "objectivism" in her novels *The Fountainhead* (1943) and *Atlas Shrugged* (1957); these defended a form of egoism not unlike Stirner's. Rothbard's *For a New Liberty* (1978) argued for the abolition of government with a verve that alienated conservatives who deplored Rothbard's

hostility to American imperialism and to governments that engaged in "moral legislation" against drugs, prostitution, and sexual deviance as much as his seeming unconcern for the losers in the marketplace alienated welfare state liberals. Rothbard's conviction that there will be a libertarian president by the year 2000 takes the topic into the realm of speculation and out of that of a history of thought.

ALAN RYAN

FURTHER READING
A. M. Honore, "Ownership," in A. G. Guest, ed., *Oxford Readings in Jurisprudence* (Oxford: Clarendon Press, 1961).
Jan Narveson, *The Libertarian Idea* (Philadelphia: Temple University Press, 1988).
Stephen Newman, *Liberalism at Wit's End* (Ithaca: Cornell University Press, 1984).
Robert Nozick, *Anarchy, State and Utopia* (New York: Basic Books, 1974).
Murray Rothbard, *For a New Liberty* (New York: Collier Books, 1978).
Hillel Steiner, "Liberty and Equality," *Political Studies* (1981): 555–69.
Jeremy Waldron, *The Right to Private Property* (Oxford: Clarendon Press, 1988).
Jonathan Wolff, *Robert Nozick* (Stanford: Stanford University Press, 1991).

Lieber, Francis [born Franz] (b. Berlin, Germany, Mar. 18, 1798; d. New York, N.Y., Oct. 2, 1872). Political philosopher. A German emigré, Lieber achieved national renown as a political theorist at Columbia College in the 1850s and 1860s. Warning against the tendency of unchecked democracy to infringe on individual freedom, Lieber asserted that civil liberties are preserved by mediating institutions —including government, family, and religion. His organic model of the nation as a population sharing a common language, territory, and traditions made him a strong Unionist. He was as much an internationalist as a nationalist, however, and promoted the growth of international institutions, especially international law. His *Code for the Government of Armies in the Field* (1863) became the basis for international conventions of war that attempted to protect civilians and prisoners of war. Lieber's other works include a *Manual of Political Ethics* (2 vols., 1838–9) and *On Civil Liberty and Self-Government* (1853).

FURTHER READING
Frank Friedel, *Francis Lieber: Nineteenth-Century Liberal* (Baton Rouge: Louisiana State University Press, 1948).

Lincoln, Abraham (b. Hardin [now Larue] County, Ky., Feb. 12, 1809; d. Washington, D.C., Apr. 15, 1865). Millions of Americans carry about with them images of Abraham Lincoln, his profile imprinted on the pennies they carry in their pockets or purses—the most profuse and portable monuments yet made of any American. There is both honor and debasement in such commonness. Lincoln's face and figure have become visual clichés, obscuring the man by their very familiarity; and so, like the virtually worthless coins that bear his image, he is becoming a symbol without a referent.

Yet for Americans living at the end of the twentieth century, there are reasons to try to get Lincoln back. To retrieve him is difficult because there stands between us and him a larger body of myth than that surrounding any other figure in American history. This mythologizing process began almost immediately after his death, when he was made by northern eulogists into a martyr who had died for the nation's sins. He had, in the words of Joseph Thompson, a Union pamphleteer, disseminated "his philosophy in parables," and had gone "through life bearing the load of a people's sorrows upon his shoulders" (Freidel, vol. 2, pp. 1160, 1162). Then, as the generation that had known him first-hand grew old, Lincoln became obscured beneath a mass of lore (given biographical shape by writers like William Herndon and Ida Tarbell), until he ultimately emerged as the saving prairie giant in the brilliantly imagined multivolume biography by Carl Sandburg, *The Prairie Years* (1926) and *The War Years* (1939). In the 1950s there arose a Cold War version of Lincoln, who taught Americans an exemplary lesson in how to stand up to blustering and brutal frontier outlaws. In the 1960s he became an object of contention between those who claimed him as the father of the civil rights movement, and those who dismissed him as just another white racist throwing crumbs to blacks for whom he had paternalistic contempt.

This process of reimagining Lincoln continues today, when public doubt as to the stability and legitimacy of our civic institutions seems to have risen higher than at any time since the 1850s, when Lincoln came of age politically and intellectually. Then, as now, the central institutions of American life—churches, courts, Congress—seemed to many Americans brittle if not broken. The intractable political issue was, of course, slavery—and in the face of it, the people whose allegiance these institutions claimed were growing uncertain of what, if anything, linked them together as one nation. What Lincoln called the American "political religion"—the revolutionary idea of EQUALITY and individual RIGHTS secured by a voluntary Union—seemed hopelessly compromised by the fact that the holy scripture of this religion, the CONSTITUTION, contained an endorsement of the institution of chattel slavery.

By 1850, as conflict between North and South began to break out into violence, the political development of the United States seemed at an impasse, and the prospect of its dissolution grew. Lincoln, who had served briefly in Congress in the late 1840s, withdrew, discouraged, from public life. But in 1854 he was "aroused" as never before by the Kansas-Nebraska Act, whose passage opened the way for slavery to expand into territories from which it had been excluded since the Missouri Compromise of 1820. This event seemed to Lincoln an act of treason against the Founders themselves; they, he believed, had intended to place slavery "where the public mind [shall] rest in the belief that it was in the course of ultimate extinction" (*Portable Abraham Lincoln*, p. 117). In his speech on the Act he began to describe slavery not only as a form of human cruelty, but as a betrayal of the principles upon which the republic had been founded:

This declared indifference [on the part of Senator Stephen A. Douglas], but, as I must think, covert real zeal, for the spread of slavery, I cannot but hate. I hate it because of the monstrous injustice of slavery itself. I hate it because it deprives our republican example of its just influence in the world; enables the enemies of free institutions with plausibility to taunt us as hypocrites; causes the real friends of freedom to doubt our sincerity; and especially because it forces so many good men among ourselves into an open war with the very fundamental principles of civil liberty, criticizing the Declaration of Independence, and insisting that there is no right principle of action but self-interest. (p. 50)

This kind of talk was received as "black Republican" poison in the South, where Lincoln was reviled as a snake, a buffoon, a friend of niggers. Yet unlike most of his abolitionist critics (who condemned him with equal rancor for moving too slowly against the slaveholders), Lincoln had a tragic sense of history as a web of contingencies in which all men were ensnared. Although his crusade gave him new spiritual as well as political life, he never conflated the evil with the evildoers. "When Southern people tell us," he said in 1854, that "they are no more responsible for the origin of slavery, than we; I acknowledge the fact," and in respect to the ultimate abolition of slavery, he admitted that "I surely will not blame them for not doing what I should not know how to do myself" (pp. 50–1).

Even as he carried the nation closer to the breaking point, Lincoln tried to remain a conciliator. His first Inaugural Address is full of reassurance to the secessionists. He was, however, fully capable of whipping up his supporters with fears of the slave conspiracy, as he had done by portraying the Kansas-Nebraska Act and *Dred Scott* decision as complementary pieces in an infernal Democratic plot. Also capable of pandering to racial hatred, he acknowledged in a speech on the *Dred Scott* decision (collected in his *Speeches and Writings*) the "natural disgust in the minds of nearly all white people, to the idea of an indiscriminate amalgamation of the white and black races" (vol. 1, p. 397). Lincoln knew, in other words, that free-soil politics were in part a politics of fear—fear of the slaves as well as of the slaveowners, fear that wageless blacks would rob white men of the value of their own labor, as well as the more visceral fear of blacks as brutes whose potency was sexual as well as economic. But as he rose first to the leadership of the Republican Party, and then of the nation, Lincoln managed to hold in balance this persistent American fear of racial contamination with a quite different sort of emotion.

This other source of ANTISLAVERY feeling, to which Lincoln gave unrivaled expression, may be called the republican theodicy. It was the deep-seated conviction that degradation and social failure must, in a democracy, be understood as self-wrought punishments, and that inherited servitude was a violation of this principle. Antislavery feeling drew upon the indispensable democratic faith that if you were at the bottom of the ladder, it was not because you had been born low, but because you had gotten yourself there. Lincoln was committed, in other words, to the individual's right to rise or fall according to his own merit. In attacking slavery, he tapped the same emotion—aimed downward rather than upward—as the traditional American hatred of a social order based on primogeniture or any other form of advantageous inheritance. He became chief spokesman for the principle that every man must be free to fashion his own social fate: "I *like* the system," he declared in 1860, speaking not far from the site of a bitter shoeworkers' strike, "which lets a man quit when he wants to, and wish it might prevail everywhere." He went on:

> One of the reasons why I am opposed to Slavery is just here. . . . I want every man to have the chance—and I believe a black man is entitled to it—in which he *can* better his condition—when he may look forward and hope to be a hired laborer this year and the next, work for himself afterward, and finally to hire men to work for him! (vol. 2, p. 144)

Along the way to the presidency, Lincoln articulated with unprecedented fervor this American ideal of SOCIAL MOBILITY as the just reward for honest labor.

He made it clear that slaveholders were right to fear him. His vision of a nation based on free labor would not exclude anyone because of color or previous condition of servitude, and his name for this ideal nation was the Union.

Driven, as his opponents sensed, by something deeper than political ambition, Lincoln seemed to feel himself appointed by fate to be the Union's savior. He spoke, for instance, in the Second Inaugural Address, on March 4, 1865, with an eerie combination of ecstasy and resignation about the terrible war that his ascension to power had unleashed:

> if God wills that [this war] continue, until all the wealth piled by the bond-man's two hundred and fifty years of unrequited toil shall be sunk, and until every drop of blood drawn with the lash, shall be paid by another drawn with the sword, as was said three thousand years ago, so still it must be said "the judgments of the Lord, are true and righteous altogether." (*Portable Abraham Lincoln*, p. 321)

Despite this righteous thunder, Lincoln was, as some historians have recently emphasized, a reluctant abolitionist who resorted to emancipation only when forced to do so by the exigencies of war. To the fury of the abolitionists, he would have preferred to let slavery die of its own accord, and was content to let "the public mind . . . rest in the belief" that slavery was destined for "ultimate extinction." Yet the end of slavery, whether one considers it timely or belated, was the inevitable fulfillment of Lincoln's political vision. He always understood politics as a struggle for public belief, and he recognized that the crisis of his time was the collapse of belief in the Union as a worthy object of public faith, precisely because the presence of slavery defiled it.

Lincoln's great contribution to American life was, as Alexander Stephens, Vice President of the Confederacy realized, to elevate this discredited Union "to the level of religious sublimity" (quoted in Edmund Wilson's *Patriotic Gore,* p. 422). The perpetuity of the Union was such an axiom to him that he claimed in 1863 to be amazed when he heard "the theory of the general government being only an agency, whose principals are the States" (*Portable Abraham Lincoln*, p. 296). He refused, in effect, to accept that some Americans found it conceivable that the United States could actually cease to exist. Such an idea was blasphemy to him, and to have entered into dialogue with those who believed such heresy would have been tantamount to surrendering to a kind of insolent nihilism. Against this threat, Lincoln secured for his own generation and for his posterity a vision of the Union as divine creation, brought into being not by the tainted Constitution, but by the sublime Declaration of Independence—"the sheet anchor" of the republic (p. 63)—in which was inscribed the doctrine of what his contemporary, Herman Melville, called "our divine equality."

This is a vision from which the modern imagination—in part because of the horrors wrought in our century in the name of God-sanctioned nationalism—tends to recoil. Yet the distinctive feature of Lincoln's imagination was his insistence, amid the rancor and hatred that burgeoned with the war, on a vision of evil not in the usual nationalist form of a demonic enemy, but as a failure of spiritual sight—a failure to see the beauty of a Union of free and equal citizens. As his countrymen achieved new heights of invective and recrimination, Lincoln expressed only a revulsion at the absence of the good of human freedom.

Lincoln's mind reveals itself most clearly in his greatest single utterance, the Gettysburg Address, in which the enemy, despite the ferocity of the unfinished war, is never mentioned. The speech builds upon the word "dedicate," which is used in varying forms four times, and rises to a greater and greater sense of bound humility and transcendent possibility. The verbs with which he frames the main body of his message—"endure" and "perish"—are intransitive. They depend on no resistant object for their meaning. And the force of the whole is not to inspire or maintain enmity, but to foster a new measure of positive devotion to the principle invoked by the opening invocation of Genesis—the equality principle of the Declaration. This is a universalist vision, and one that posits no Satan. It is truly Augustinian in the sense that the only evil it understands—with a singleness of purpose that is both appalling and sublime—is the evil of incompleteness.

Fifteen years after Lincoln's death, in his essay, "Great Men and Their Environment," William James (in a phrase that finely registers his own sense that reality exists somewhere between subjectivity and the objective world) said that great men are those "individuals whose genius was . . . adapted to the receptivities of the moment . . . [who] became ferments, initiators of movement . . . or destroyers of other persons, whose gifts, had they had free play, would have led society in another direction." In his time, Lincoln was all these things. In our time, he remains indispensable because he identifies the ongoing challenge of American history: the challenge of retaining a sense of evil in a post-theistic world without resorting to demons. Through this privative sense of evil—evil as incompletion of the good—he makes it still possible to believe in the United States as an idea capable of continual evolution toward the fulfillment of its original promise.

ANDREW DELBANCO

See also CIVIL WAR; DEMOCRACY; MISSION.

FURTHER READING

J. David Greenstone, *The Lincoln Persuasion: Remaking American Liberalism* (Princeton: Princeton University Press, 1993).

Abraham Lincoln, *The Collected Works of Abraham Lincoln*, ed. Roy P. Basler et al., 9 vols. (New Brunswick: Rutgers University Press, 1953)

——, *Supplement* to *The Collected Works*, ed. Roy P. Basler (New Brunswick: Rutgers University Press, 1974).

——, *Speeches and Writings of Abraham Lincoln*, ed. Don E. Fehrenbacher (New York: Library of America, 1989).

——, *The Portable Abraham Lincoln*, ed. Andrew Delbanco (New York: Viking-Penguin, 1992).

Frank Freidel, ed., *Union Pamphlets of the Civil War*, 2 vols. (Cambridge: Harvard University Press, 1967).

James M. McPherson, *Abraham Lincoln and the Second American Revolution* (New York: Oxford University Press, 1991).

Merrill D. Peterson, *Lincoln in American Memory* (New York: Oxford University Press, 1994).

Benjamin P. Thomas, *Abraham Lincoln* (New York: Knopf, 1952).

Garry Wills, *Lincoln at Gettysburg: the Words that Remade America* (New York: Simon and Schuster, 1992).

Edmund Wilson, *Patriotic Gore: the Literature of the American Civil War* (New York: Oxford University Press, 1962).

Lippmann, Walter (b. New York, N.Y., Sept. 23, 1889; d. New York, N.Y., Dec. 14, 1974). The career of Walter Lippmann resonates with many of the aspirations and tensions of American intellectual life in the first three-quarters of the twentieth century. Starting out assuming that modern scientific intelligence would help bring forth a world of truth, beauty, and justice, he went to his grave worried about the human condition and wondering whether America as a democratic society was committed to CITIZENSHIP and capable of self-government. One of the first to move from the Ivy League into the rough and tumble of city politics and news JOURNALISM, Lippmann was also one of the last "public intellectuals," the journalist as reflective "pundit" who could pronounce on a variety of subjects with philosophical and moral acumen.

Lippmann attended a select boys' academy before entering Harvard University in 1906. Here he wrote essays and verse together with the rebellious JOHN REED and the solemn T. S. ELIOT. He also came under the influence of two mentors, the philosophers WILLIAM JAMES and GEORGE SANTAYANA. From the former Lippmann learned to look upon life as an open-ended experiment that could be directed by the exercise of will and conscious scientific control. But Santayana's influence, which proved to be deeper and more enduring, sensitized Lippmann's mind to the need to discover the basis of ideals beyond the flux of experience. He would later remark that although he had loved James, he found Santayana "inescapable."

Lippmann's reputation as the nation's philosopher-journalist began with the publication of *A Preface to Politics* (1913), written when he was only 23. Santayana's influence shows in the attempt to define politics as an aesthetic pursuit answering to the deepest human feelings rather than as a search for the "laws" of civil society. In *Drift and Mastery* (1914) Lippmann tempered his enthusiasm for sheer emotional expression and called for mastery and control. His PRAGMATISM disciplined his Romanticism: politics was a matter of will, purpose, and effort; experiment could guide action and experience would spotlight the mistakes to be avoided in the future.

Armed with such hopes, Lippmann defended America's entry into WORLD WAR I as a means of curbing Germany's military power and allowing President Woodrow Wilson to be present at the peace conference. But the war to "make the world safe for democracy" turned into a tragedy as many of Wilson's Fourteen Points for a just peace settlement were frustrated by European statecraft. Attempting to account for Wilson's thwarted idealism, Lippmann had to face his own misplaced expectations, and henceforth in his career he would be increasingly critical of the two assumptions that had earlier inspired his hopes—that democracy could do the right thing without a theory of AUTHORITY, and pragmatism could do what had to be done without a theory of truth.

In *Public Opinion* (1922) and *The Phantom Public* (1925), Lippmann demonstrated how the press as the medium of political communication made modern DEMOCRACY problematic if not impossible. Historically democracy derived its legitimacy from the consent of the governed; in modern times such consent may have no basis in rational knowledge since the press interprets the "news of the day" and shapes mass attitudes with stereotypes and sensation at the expense of fact and analysis. Readers respond to "episodes, incidents, and eruptions" so that politics is experienced but not necessarily understood. Not only did Jefferson's ideal of the "omnicompetent citizen" seem as difficult to sustain as the idea of popular sovereignty, but even the concept of a "public" became a figment and phantom since in a pluralistic society there exists no authority to render it by defining and articulating the common good. (*See also* PUBLICITY.)

The philosopher JOHN DEWEY responded to Lippmann's thesis in *The Public and Its Problems* (1927). Dewey tried to answer Lippmann's doubts about democracy by suggesting that Americans could live in "the great community" instead of an arena of competing interest groups. How? By seeing social relations as interdependent and drawing upon the cooperative methods of scientific intelligence as laid out in the philosophy of pragmatism. But Lippmann had earlier concluded that pragmatism was part of the problem it purported to solve because it refused to subordinate the self and its demands to a public philosophy.

At the end of the 1920s Lippmann wrote his most poignant book, *A Preface to Morals* (1929), which registered the alienation of the "lost generation" and its search for meaning and value. Here Lippmann goes beyond politics to discuss such institutions as marriage and to probe the mysteries of love and the wisdom of the classical ideas of VIRTUE. All along haunted by the thought that liberalism meant the overthrow of authority and the futile search for its substitute, Lippmann wondered how doubt, skepticism, and the "acids of modernity" would sustain modern civilization. The book is a moving account of the perennial modern dilemma of the moralist in an immoral and unbelieving world.

In the 1930s Lippmann continued his philosophical explorations but his efforts were interrupted by the rise of European totalitarianism and the threat of another world war. As a result Lippmann shelved a book he had been working on in moral philosophy and turned his attention to the threat of collectivist dictatorships in *The Good Society* (1937). He also grew disenchanted with President Franklin Roosevelt and the New Deal. Influenced by Austrian economists, Lippmann became convinced that national planning threatened freedom and paved the road to dictatorship.

Some writers, including Dewey and biographer Ronald Steel, believe that Lippmann's concealed Jewish heritage had something to do with his politics: his conservative sensibility may have been tied to a desire to shun ethnic loyalties and attain a cosmopolitan respectability. Whatever the truth of that claim, it is noteworthy that he did fail to raise his voice about the plight of Jews in Hitler's Germany and remained conspicuously silent when news of the HOLOCAUST emerged at the end of World War II.

Although an interventionist in WORLD WAR II, Lippmann surprised many of his readers when he opposed America's involvement in the emerging COLD WAR in the late 1940s. In several books beginning with *The Cold War* (1947), Lippmann challenged

GEORGE KENNAN, author of the "containment" theory, by insisting that nationalism would prove stronger than the mystique of international communism and that America could not afford to overextend its commitments and resources by becoming the world's policeman.

Lippmann remained skeptical of President Truman's decision to commit troops to South Korea in 1949, a move he predicted would bring communist China into a war with America. A decade after the end of the Korean War he protested even more vigorously America's increasing intervention in the civil war in VIETNAM. He became particularly disillusioned since he had trusted President Johnson's promise to end the war by gradual deescalation and negotiation. When he retired from journalism at the end of the 1960s, he said of the future: "I think its going to be a Minor Dark Age."

Lippmann's last major book was *Essays in the Public Philosophy* (1955). Here he returned to the theoretical concerns that had preoccupied him in the 1920s and 1930s. But now he was even more convinced that America needed some higher philosophical guidance than an improvisational pragmatic experimentation. Recalling how difficult it was for Roosevelt to lead the country into war against Hitler, Lippmann argued that the executive branch had been enfeebled by pressure groups and responsiveness to public opinion rather than to the true national interests. Lippmann advocated a return to the "traditions of civility" that once gave coherence and direction to society because its members believed they were being ruled by transcendent, universally valid principles. Specifically, Lippmann invoked the old medieval Catholic idea of "natural law" that supposedly resides in the realm of "essence" untouched by the contingent world of change and experience. Lippmann's last book represented his final, valiant effort to oppose the implications of the very pragmatism and RELATIVISM he had espoused in the early part of the century. Natural law commanded authority, he contended, because only that which can be discovered, as opposed to that which is made and produced, can elicit our obedience. But he did not suggest how it was to be discovered.

JOHN P. DIGGINS

FURTHER READING

John Patrick Diggins, "From Pragmatism to Natural Law: Walter Lippmann's Quest for the Foundations of Legitimacy," *Political Theory* 19 (1991): 519–38.

Charles Forcey, *The Crossroads of Liberalism: Croly, Weyl, Lippmann and the Progressive Era, 1900–1925* (New York: Oxford University Press, 1961).

Walter Lippmann, *The Essential Lippmann*, ed. Clinton Rossiter and James Lare (New York: Random House, 1963).

Ronald Steel, *Walter Lippmann and the American Century* (Boston: Atlantic Monthly Press, 1980).

Benjamin F. Wright, *The Five Public Philosophies of Walter Lippmann* (Austin: University of Texas Press, 1973).

literacy The meaning of literacy, in the past as in the present, emerges only in reference to its opposite, "illiteracy." This dichotomy defines a hierarchy, literacy representing the "high," illiteracy the "low." How such a hierarchy has been deployed constitutes not only the history, but also the politics of literacy. The politics of this word within Western culture concerns its role in shaping the forms of cultural and social order.

In its root sense *literate* has to do with the knowledge of letters, or EDUCATION; literacy was a category relative to learned culture, and, more narrowly, to the knowledge of Latin. When the founders of Harvard College declared in 1642 that they were moved to establish that institution by their fear of an "illiterate ministry," they had this conjunction of meanings in mind: the classical languages, and particularly Latin; learnedness, that is, the distinctive methods and skills acquired in a formal school; and, secondary to these, the ability to write and read in the vernacular language. Similarly, when the minister JONATHAN EDWARDS paused in the midst of a treatise to explain a particular term to his "illiterate" readers, he meant a cultural hierarchy having to do with a knowledge of rhetoric, logic, and philosophy, and, by extension, with learning and civilization. The pairing of literate and illiterate could be appropriated in any polemics against presumed disorder. It was characteristic of established religious groups to accuse insurgencies—examples in the seventeenth century include the Baptists and Quakers—of being "illiterate," thereby connoting a defiance of the customary authority vested in learnedness, and specifically, the authority of a learned clergy.

The Protestant reformers of the sixteenth century introduced another dimension of literacy by asserting that everyone should have access to Scripture in the vernacular. In countries such as Lutheran Sweden this proposition became the basis of an educational system directed at teaching everyone to read. The same impulse lay behind practices and policies in other Protestant regions, including early New England, where most men and women acquired the ability to read. Rejecting the authority of TRADITION, early Protestantism also asserted the primacy of Scripture as a text that any spiritually enlightened person could understand: the "eye of faith," Protestants declared, sufficed to comprehend and receive the

Word of God. As the insurgencies of the early Baptists and Quakers indicate, this principle was easily turned against the hierarchy of learnedness.

ROMANTICISM, originating in the late eighteenth and early nineteenth century, further complicated the hierarchy of high and low by its "discovery of the folk" and their "oral culture." (*See also* FOLKLORE.) As constructed by the Romantics, the "folk" lived according to traditions that were communicated via song, speech, and oral poetry. By implication, the oral was natural, while the written was artificial or distorting. Hence the call to reform language by restoring its connections to everyday life, myth, and the primitive: "wise men pierce this rotten diction and fasten words again to visible things," wrote Emerson in *Nature*. Out of the linked dichotomies of oral/natural/folk and literate/artificial/learned there also emerged the assumption that the culture of the people, or "popular culture," was autonomous, separate from the culture of the "elite." This assumption has shaped a wide range of practices in the twentieth century—most notably the widespread evocation and celebration of "the people" in the culture and politics of the 1930s, a tendency very much alive today not only in political campaign rhetoric but in historical writing.

Yet in an ironic counterpoint, literacy in the sense of knowing how to read and write began to assume an ever greater importance in the nineteenth and twentieth centuries. Not until the nineteenth century did the civil state become crucially engaged in promoting literacy. It did so via the creation of a standardized, bureaucratized system of "common" or primary schools organized in levels according to age, and staffed by professional teachers who received their formation at special institutions ("normal schools"). The goal of erasing illiteracy via the public school was part of a larger program aimed at creating a unified national culture that overrode regional, class, religious, and other differences. At once conservative and liberal, the advancement of literacy in public schools furthered the process of secularization and helped meet the needs of an economy where credit and debit relationships, the rationalizing of production, and the reorganization of work drew ever more heavily on the tools of literacy. In the context of massive immigration to the United States, literacy also became synonymous with Americanization, or the transformation into "Americans" of diverse, and "alien," groups. Some of these newcomers, notably Catholics, accepted the imperative of becoming literate, but created parochial schools in an effort to preserve the relationships among religion, ethnicity, and learning.

Bureaucratic schools worked well as agents of Americanization, but imperfectly as means of teaching reading and writing, in part because the literacy made normative in these institutions was severed from the literacy of the household, the street, and the workplace. The discovery in the post-World War II years that "Johnny can't read" despite having spent a decade or more in a public school elevated the apparent illiteracy of many Americans into a national problem. This problem became intertwined with the explosive growth in the consumption of TV and pop music, and the concomitant "decline of the book." Here again, hierarchy becomes visible; resisting this hierarchy, some defenders of ethnic and racial groups among whom illiteracy seemed especially evident invoked romantic arguments about the vitality of the "folk" to legitimize vernacular "street talk."

A new term, "cultural literacy," emerged in the 1970s among critics of MASS CULTURE and multiculturalism. Drawing both on liberal and conservative values, critics such as E. D. Hirsch argued that a civic and civilizing national culture required a certain level of common knowledge, dubbed "cultural literacy." In a related critique, Allan Bloom's bestselling *Closing of the American Mind* (1991) expressed disgust with the Dionysian strategies of release that were powerfully advanced by mass culture; "cultural literacy" symbolized self-control, or perhaps social control. But who had the authority to define, much less impose, cultural literacy? While the civil state, the university, and the bureaucratized school have been actively legitimizing "diversity," traditionalists have generated a new system of alternative schools, colleges, and church programs designed to preserve "core values." Whether or not these latter institutions will manage to sustain their announced "culture war" against the forces of diversity, there is no question that literacy will remain a touchstone of public debate.

DAVID D. HALL

FURTHER READING

Arthur Bestor, *Educational Wastelands: the Retreat from Learning in our Public Schools* (Urbana: University of Illinois Press, 1953).
David D. Hall, "The Uses of Literacy," in William L. Joyce et al., eds., *Printing and Society in Early America* (Worcester, Mass.: American Antiquarian Society, 1983).
E. D. Hirsch Jr., *Cultural Literacy: What Every American Needs to Know* (Boston: Houghton Mifflin, 1987).
Carl Kaestle et al., *Literacy in the United States: Readers and Reading since 1880* (New Haven: Yale University Press, 1991).
Diane Ravitch and Chester E. Finn Jr., *What Do Our Seventeen-Year-Olds Know? A Report on the First National Assessment of History and Literature* (New York: Harper and Row, 1987).

David Vincent, *Literacy and Popular Culture, England, 1790–1914* (Cambridge: Cambridge University Press, 1989).

Llewellyn, Karl (b. Seattle, Wash., May 22, 1893; d. Chicago, Ill., Feb. 13, 1962). Legal scholar. A legal realist, Llewellyn argued that LAW is neither mechanical nor formal, but contextual (*see also* LEGAL REALISM). The process of making justice always occurs in a particular place, which manifests specific traditions and aspirations. Jurisprudence should study how decisions, in all their complexity, and nonrationality, are actually made. Jurists should eschew universal laws and principles, yet they should seek out general working theories which help to identify the contingencies of each unique situation. Llewellyn's writings include *The Cheyenne Way: Conflict and Case Law in Primitive Jurisprudence* (1941, with E. Adamson Hoebel), *The Common Law Tradition: Deciding Appeals* (1960), and *Jurisprudence: Realism in Theory and Practice* (1962).

FURTHER READING

Morton J. Horwitz, *The Transformation of American Law, 1870–1960: the Crisis of Legal Orthodoxy* (New York: Oxford University Press, 1992).

Lloyd, Henry Demarest (b. New York, N.Y., May 1, 1847; d. Chicago, Ill., Sept. 28, 1903). Journalist. Made famous by his attacks on the Standard Oil Company and other large corporations, Lloyd was the epitome of the crusading investigator. In his famed *Wealth against Commonwealth* (1894), he exuded faith in the people's determination to battle evil once it was exposed. In the interest of free trade, and for the good of both workers and consumers, he advocated government regulation of monopolies: since competition among individuals was already only a memory, government action could not undermine it. Lloyd was instrumental in popularizing the image of the intellectual reformer as nonpartisan defender of the public interest, an image central to the Progressive generation that built on his example.
See also PROGRESSIVISM.

FURTHER READING

John L. Thomas, *Alternative America: Henry George, Edward Bellamy, Henry Demarest Lloyd, and the Adversary Tradition* (Cambridge: Harvard University Press, 1983).

Locke, Alain (b. Philadelphia, Pa., Sept. 13, 1886; d. New York, N.Y., June 9, 1954). Philosopher, art and literary critic, and long-time professor at Howard University, Locke was also "midwife" (his term) to the HARLEM RENAISSANCE. He has long been recognized by historians and literary and art critics for his contributions to the development of a politically assertive African American art. Recently his philosophical work, now recognized as the grounding for his commitment to a race-conscious artistic movement, has sparked renewed interest among scholars.

An undergraduate at Harvard, Locke was the first African American to win a Rhodes scholarship, which took him to Hertford College at Oxford University. After further study at the University of Berlin he returned to Harvard to receive his Ph.D. in 1918. Locke's philosophy, rooted in PRAGMATISM, was profoundly shaped by his teachers and mentors, including JOSIAH ROYCE, HORACE KALLEN, Ralph Barton Perry, Christian Freiherr von Ehrenfels, Alexius Meinong, and WILLIAM JAMES (although it is not clear Locke ever studied directly with James). Locke, whose primary interest lay in the study of culture, was an exponent of the sort of cultural pluralism associated with Horace Kallen (who first used the term) and FRANZ BOAS. In distinction to the then-dominant view that universal assimilation to a white European culture was the only way to ensure national stability, the cultural pluralists argued that every ethnic and national group could make a valuable cultural contribution to the American nation (*see* CULTURAL PLURALISM AND MULTICULTURALISM).

Locke made the pluralist position more rigorous and complex by placing culture in history. He insisted that cultures could only be understood as a product of a people's environment and historical experience. Each culture deserved respect because it uniquely embodied the needs and goals of its people. Locke called this position "critical relativism." (*See also* RELATIVISM.) Furthermore, since Locke understood culture to be dynamic rather than static, a constant blending and reblending of disparate elements, no culture could be properly viewed as purer than any other. Indeed, cultural reciprocity was a goal to be actively sought; active exchange was a sign of vibrancy and productivity.

Locke was aware of the dangers of extreme relativism. Like the pragmatists, he was looking for "some normative principle . . . of objective validity for values," a normative principle attainable "without resort to dogmatism and absolutism . . . [or to] their corollaries . . . intolerance and mass coercion" (Harris, p. 36). Cultural positions that reconciled differences between groups were superior, he argued, to those that intensified differences. World peace itself might emerge through the spread of such "value relativism." In Locke's formulation, cultural pluralism and cultural reciprocity contributed to a world of fluid and ever-changing identities, but also a world in which values, though never fixed and absolute, were firmly rooted in ethical practice.

Unlike most pragmatists, Locke did not ignore RACE. Indeed, as an African American, Locke was particularly concerned with the relation of culture to race and it is here that he made both his most important contributions and his most contradictory statements. In a radical challenge to the widely held assumptions of his time, Locke posited race as a culturally constructed, rather than a biological category, one lodged in historical experience. Race, he wrote, was "primarily a matter of social heredity." It was "a fact in the social or ethnic sense . . . [but] it has been very erroneously associated with race in the physical sense" (Harris, pp. 191–2). Yet he also occasionally embraced arguments that appeared to weaken his cultural understanding and gravitate back toward a biological viewpoint. In *The New Negro*, his pathbreaking anthology of 1925, he held that "the American Negro brought over [from Africa] as an emotional inheritance a deep-seated aesthetic endowment" (p. 254). Elsewhere he wrote that the "primitive" style of early black artists reflected "the African or racial temperament" (Washington, p. 194). The language of inherited predisposition threatened to undo Locke's careful distinction between biology and culture. This conceptual slippage is of course not unique to Locke. It has marked much of the national political debate about the nature of race from his time to ours.

A certain tension also emerged in Locke's ideas about the relationship of African Americans to pan-Africanism. Like W. E. B. DU BOIS, Locke felt a cultural "two-ness." He contended that African Americans were thoroughly European in their cultural attitudes, but rejected assimilation as a goal. Instead, he criticized Western imperialism and stressed the importance of connections between peoples of African descent all over the globe. Race consciousness, he argued, although only a cultural construct, raised self-esteem, created solidarity among its members, and was therefore crucial for group advancement. As he put it, "To be 'Negro' in the cultural sense, then, is not to be radically different, but only to be distinctively composite and idiomatic, though basically American" (Harris, p. 213).

In Locke's view, the Harlem Renaissance embodied these seemingly contradictory impulses of African American culture by embracing both an African and an American heritage. In the pragmatic tradition, Locke also believed the Harlem Renaissance would establish the legitimacy of black culture in the eyes of whites; art would serve as the vehicle for African American progress. In *The New Negro* Locke

gathered the poetry, stories, essays, and art of a new generation of black artists, including COUNTEE CULLEN, ZORA NEALE HURSTON, Aaron Douglas, CLAUDE MCKAY and LANGSTON HUGHES. Together they spoke for the "New Negro," simultaneously race proud and eager to integrate fully into American political and social life. In his introduction he called the movement the product of a "renewed race-spirit that consciously and proudly sets itself apart," its spokespeople "acting as the advance-guard of the African peoples" (pp. xi, 14). Yet Locke also reminded readers that the goals of the New Negro "are none other than the ideals of American institutions and democracy" and insisted that turning attention to the black experience would reinvigorate American art. Thus the New Negro carried the dual responsibility "of rehabilitating the race in world esteem," and of revitalizing American culture (pp. 10, 14).

To some extent Locke came to recognize the ambiguities and contradictions of the New Negro movement, which in many ways reflected the contradictions of his own position. In a 1949 lecture he lamented that the movement commodified culture and demonstrated an unfortunate "racial chauvinism" which by shifting attention from the "substance of Negro life" to "its complexion" discredited it as a legitimate artistic endeavor. Instead he urged "full integration. . . . [This is] as right as it is inevitable" (Harris, pp. 232, 234). Racial distinctiveness had ceded ground to a powerfully integrative political vision.

Locke is rightly heralded as spiritual father to the Harlem Renaissance and the Black Aesthetic Movement in the 1960s, and his work played an important role in the emergence of black pride movements in the African diaspora, and in the development of African philosophy. His commitment to pluralism, his celebration of racial pride, his critique of imperialism, and his vision of interracial and international peace through cultural reciprocity and respect still deserve serious consideration today. His inability to separate heredity from character, and his simultaneous claims for race as cultural production and biological inheritance, are not flaws distinctive to him. They remain firmly entrenched in the debate over race and culture in American.

CHERYL GREENBERG

FURTHER READING

Everett Akam, "Community and Cultural Crisis: the Transfiguring Imagination of Alain Locke," *American Literary History* 3 (summer 1991): 255–76.

Leonard Harris, ed., *The Philosophy of Alain Locke: Harlem Renaissance and Beyond* (Philadelphia: Temple University Press, 1989).

Russell Linnemann, ed., *Alain Locke: Reflections on a Modern*

Renaissance Man (Baton Rouge: Louisiana State University Press, 1982).

Alain Locke, *Race Contacts and Interracial Relations: Lectures on the Theory and Practice of Race,* ed. Jeffrey Stewart (Washington, D.C.: Howard University Press, 1992).

——, ed., *The New Negro* (1925; New York: Johnson Reprint Corp., 1968).

Johnny Washington, *Alain Locke and Philosophy: a Quest for Cultural Pluralism* (Westport, Conn.: Greenwood, 1986).

Loeb, Jacques (b. Mayen, Germany, Apr. 7, 1859; d. Bermuda, Feb. 11, 1924). Biologist. After beginning his research career in Germany and Italy, Loeb moved to the United States in 1891 and held positions at a number of institutions, including the University of California at Berkeley and the Rockefeller Institute for Medical Research. His entire career was devoted to showing that science offered sure explanations for animal, and by extension human, behavior. He argued in particular that chemical variations could account for (and therefore perhaps control) behavioral events previously explained by such "unscientific" notions as instinct or natural law. His mechanistic approach to biology resembled the efforts of such contemporary psychologists as EDWARD L. THORNDIKE and JOHN B. WATSON to lay the groundwork for a science of human behavior. His writings included *The Dynamics of Living Matter* (1906) and *The Mechanistic Conception of Life* (1912).

FURTHER READING

Philip J. Pauly, *Controlling Life: Jacques Loeb and the Engineering Ideal in Biology* (New York: Oxford University Press, 1987).

London, Jack (b. San Francisco, Calif., Jan. 12, 1876; d. Glen Ellen, Calif., Nov. 22, 1916). Well known in our day as a novelist and short-story writer, London was also well known in his own day as a political essayist, journalist, lecturer, and socialist. He was an illegitimate child who was given his stepfather's last name. He grew up in poverty along the Bay waterfront, and was a newspaper boy, cannery worker, sailor, oyster pirate, longshoreman, tramp, janitor, and gold miner in Alaska before he turned to writing as his career, trade, and business in 1900.

London received an uneven education, finishing only a semester at the University of California, but he was reasonably well read in literature, philosophy, and economics, especially favoring Nietzsche, Marx, Darwin, and Herbert Spencer. Life, for London, meant battle and war, a drama of primitivism, a struggle to the death, and he frequently depicted superhuman heroes engaged in violent combat and feats of strength and endurance. He modeled his literary craft on Rudyard Kipling and Robert Louis Stevenson, adventure tales, and popular magazine fiction, and his best work influenced many later writers, including George Orwell and Ernest Hemingway. A staunch radical, London attacked big corporations, supported trade unions, backed the Industrial Workers of the World (IWW), fought on behalf of the poor and lowly, and preached world revolution (signing his letters, "Yours for the Revolution").

London is often portrayed as an American tragedy: great gifts gone to waste in the production of mediocre books. Maxwell Geismar has referred to London's career as "a dark chronicle in our literary annals," "a case history—very often ironical, morbid and illuminating—of thwarted ambition and moral corruption" (pp. 139, 143). This judgment has been echoed by Warner Berthoff, who names London as "perhaps the most gifted prose talent" of his generation, and "certainly the most prodigally squandered" (p. 245).

There is no denying that London's 19 novels and many collections of short stories and essays (he wrote 50 books in all) contain much negligible prose. And these writings, as well as his letters, are marred by lurid expressions of racism, anti-Semitism, Anglo-Saxon chauvinism, and sexism. But a sizable portion of his work merits serious reading and study: a dozen or so first-rate stories; one superb, hugely popular animal and adventure novel, *The Call of the Wild* (1903, later translated into 68 languages); two compelling books, *The People of the Abyss* (1903) and *The Road* (1907), that blend social commentary and reminiscence; a graphic indictment of American individualism and industrial capitalism, *The Sea-Wolf* (1904); a terrifying rendering of rebellion and counter-revolution, *The Iron Heel* (1908); and two unsparing accounts of personal despair and social corruption—the novel *Martin Eden* (1909), and a memoir about the ruination caused by alcoholism, *John Barleycorn* (1913).

When London is at his best, particularly in such adroit, economical stories as "The Law of Life," "The Apostate," "The Strength of the Strong," and "War," his workmanship is on a par with that of Edgar Allan Poe, Nathaniel Hawthorne, or Hemingway. In these stories, and in *The Call of the Wild*, he practices an unmistakable artistry in what has usually been called the "naturalistic" vein. But it is misleading to lump him with Theodore Dreiser and Frank Norris and Stephen Crane as a representative of NATURALISM, as if these writers shared an ideological program based on the "scientific," unsentimental rendering of human behavior. It is better to see London as a mythologist of "real," vital, dynamic experience, of the sort that many middle- and upper-class Americans by the 1890s feared was being squeezed out by the florid conventions of Victorian America. Like H. L. Mencken, who admired him, London was more the disciple of Nietzsche than of Zola.

Moreover, the variability of his work suggests the importance of seeing his oeuvre as the product of a particular sort of literary career that came into being in his day: the professional writer marketed by a new generation of publishers and editors who prized hard-hitting, "masculine" prose. As Christopher Wilson has shown, London the "popular naturalist" (and first American literary millionaire) helped create and sustain a new system of literary production: "his aesthetic meshed with a new editorial universe geared, as [publisher] Frank Munsey said, to 'real stories'—stories of clear, direct artifice which gripped the reader emotionally and controlled his responses" (pp. 104–5). *Martin Eden* can be seen, among other things, as a creative retelling of his embrace of the market—and of the market's embrace of him as "the fad of the hour." As Wilson notes, the book is a striking account of a working-class writer's encounter not just with a commercialized literary culture, but with "the logic of the factory" itself (p. 105).

In his own writing life London became entrapped by that logic. His successes led to tempting advance payments for future projects, which he executed in frequently formulaic fashion. He grew obsessed with money, lavishing funds on his yacht and sprawling ranch (destroyed by fire in 1913). A vigorous critic of capitalism in his political work, he was nonetheless an active participant in the industrialization and mechanization of literary production. Unable to free himself from this contradiction, of which he was very conscious, he became intensely bitter, prone to self-loathing, and spitefully disdainful toward others. At age 40 he was dead of a drug overdose. "This working out one's soul," he had written to an editor in 1899, "is not a pleasant task" (Wilson, p. 92).

WILLIAM E. CAIN

FURTHER READING

Warner Berthoff, *The Ferment of Realism: American Literature, 1884–1919* (New York: Free Press, 1965).
Maxwell Geismar, *Rebels and Ancestors: the American Novel, 1890–1915* (Boston: Houghton-Mifflin, 1953).
Joan D. Hedrick, *Solitary Comrade: Jack London and His Work* (Chapel Hill: University of North Carolina Press, 1982).
Earle Labor, Robert C. Leitz, and I. Milo Shepard, eds., *The Letters of Jack London*, 3 vols. (Stanford: Stanford University Press, 1988).
Joan London, *Jack London and His Times: an Unconventional Biography* (1939; Seattle: University of Washington Press, 1968).
Christopher P. Wilson, *The Labor of Words: Literary Professionalism in the Progressive Era* (Athens: University of Georgia Press, 1985).

Longfellow, Henry Wadsworth (b. Portland, Mass. [now Maine], Feb. 27, 1807; d. Cambridge, Mass., Mar. 24, 1882). Poet. The most popular poet of his day, Longfellow wrote carefully crafted verse that celebrated the American people. His romantic legends of the American past preached a simple moralism and praised American virtues, but rarely addressed contemporary political and social issues. A talented translator who claimed all of Europe as his cultural inheritance, Longfellow introduced many Americans to European literature. His writings include *Hyperion* (1839), *Voices of the Night* (1839), *Ballads and Other Poems* (1841), *Poems on Slavery* (1842), and *The Song of Hiawatha* (1855).

FURTHER READING

Edward Wagenknecht, *Henry Wadsworth Longfellow: Portrait of an American Humorist* (New York: Oxford University Press, 1966).

Lovejoy, Arthur O. (b. Berlin, Germany, Oct. 10, 1873; d. Baltimore, Md., Dec. 30, 1962). Philosopher and historian. As a "critical realist," Lovejoy recommended, in *The Revolt Against Dualism* (1930), a philosophy modeled on the empirical sciences. More significantly, he helped found the modern discipline of the history of ideas, tracing the paths of broad discursive tendencies—or "unit ideas"—that develop over time and through various intellectual communities. His best-known work, *The Great Chain of Being* (1936), though criticized for its lack of attention to social and political context, was an elegant assertion of the complex "interior" of philosophical ideas.

FURTHER READING

Daniel J. Wilson, *Arthur O. Lovejoy and the Quest for Intelligibility* (Chapel Hill: University of North Carolina Press, 1980).

Lowell, Amy (b. Brookline, Mass., Feb. 9, 1874; d. Brookline, Mass., May 12, 1925). Imagist poet and critic. Author of *Sword Blade and Poppy Seeds* (1914), *Men, Women, and Ghosts* (1916), and *What's O'Clock* (1925), Lowell led a revolt against poetic conventions. In her critical works, such as *Tendencies in Modern American Poetry* (1917), she called for hard, clean poetry freed from traditional constraints of meter, rhyme, and subject material: poets should use the common language to create precise, detailed images, not vague abstractions or sentimental moralisms. While this form is often known as "free verse," Lowell argued that it is actually tightly controlled by the poet's discipline of language.

See also MODERNISM.

FURTHER READING
Jean Gould, *Amy: the World of Amy Lowell and the Imagist Movement* (New York: Dodd, Mead, 1975).

Lowell, James Russell (b. Cambridge, Mass., Feb. 22, 1819; d. Cambridge, Mass., Aug. 12, 1891). Poet and scholar. Often described as a genteel romantic poet, Lowell was accomplished at combining satire with political passion. Early in his career, he supported abolitionism and condemned the Mexican War. Later, he was a partisan of the North, and hoped the war would spur a national moral regeneration. He articulated these positions humorously in *The Bigelow Papers* (two series, 1848, 1867). Though Lowell fostered American literary institutions, especially as co-editor of the *North American Review* (1864–72), he asserted that aesthetics and morality know no national boundaries.

FURTHER READING
C. David Heymann, *American Aristocracy: the Lives and Times of James Russell, Amy, and Robert Lowell* (New York: Dodd, Mead, 1980).

Lowell, Robert (b. Boston, Mass., Mar. 1, 1917; d. New York, N.Y., Sept. 12, 1977).   Poet. Lowell's early poems, collected in *Land of Unlikeness* (1944) and *Lord Weary's Castle* (1946), were rich, allusive, and complex in form and meter. His later works, including *For the Union Dead* (1964), *Notebook 1967–68* (1969), and *The Dolphin* (1973), were more consciously political and autobiographical, using his personal experience to illuminate the confusions of his society. A descendant of an eminent Boston family, Lowell was always interested in the relationships between history and the present, communities and individuals, authority and freedom. A pacifist, he was a imprisoned as a conscientious objector in World War II and was a vocal protester against the Vietnam War.

FURTHER READING
Robert Von Hallberg, *American Poetry and Culture, 1945–1980* (Cambridge: Harvard University Press, 1985).

Luhan, Mabel Dodge (b. Buffalo, N.Y., Feb. 26, 1879; d. Taos, N.Mex., Aug. 13, 1962).   Writer, patron, salon hostess, and cultural catalyst, Mabel Dodge Luhan was the only child of upper-class parents. Following the death of her first husband in a hunting accident and the termination of an affair with her family doctor, she went to Europe, where she married the architect Edwin Dodge in 1905. They purchased a Florentine villa, in which she entertained

émigré royalty and expatriate artists such as Leo Stein, GERTRUDE STEIN, and Eleanora Duse.

In the fall of 1912 Mabel moved to New York City, separated from Dodge, and launched what is arguably the most famous salon in American history at 23 Fifth Avenue. Eschewing "the dead forms of the past" she had cultivated in *fin-de-siècle* Europe, she set about making herself the mistress of a revolutionary age, cultivating friendships with EMMA GOLDMAN, LINCOLN STEFFENS, ALFRED STIEGLITZ, and numerous other modernists, whose debates over anarchism, psychoanalysis, postimpressionist art, and sexuality brought her gatherings national fame. A leading exemplar of the "new woman," Mabel was nonetheless convinced that she could create only through men, as their muse or mentor. When she ended her on-and-then-off-again affair with JOHN REED in 1915, she married the postimpressionist artist Maurice Sterne, with whom she moved to Taos, New Mexico, in 1918.

In 1923, Mabel divorced Sterne and married Antonio Luhan, a Pueblo Indian. Envisioning a messianic role for herself as a bridge between Anglo and Indian cultures, Luhan spent much of the rest of her life as a publicist for Taos as "the beating heart of the universe." Here, she believed, a community-minded people, a healthful climate, and a land of primordial beauty could serve as the center of spiritual and cultural redemption for an anomic and deracinated Western civilization, with her home and its several guest houses as headquarters.

Luhan called others to Taos to help celebrate and preserve the utopian paradise she believed she had discovered. Among them were painters Georgia O'Keeffe and John Marin, to immortalize the landscape; reformers John Collier and MARY AUSTIN, to protect the Indians' land, rights, and culture; and writers D. H. Lawrence and WILLA CATHER, to help publicize the gospel of her new world vision. In the Indian Southwest, Luhan found her own creative voice, publishing seven books, among them her thousand-page, four-volume autobiography, *Intimate Memories*. Here she constructs a symbolic self, a "twentieth-century type," whom she offers to her readers as a paradigm for the decline and fall of Anglo civilization and its potential for rebirth in the American Southwest.

In the early 1920s, a Chicago newspaper reporter claimed that Mabel Dodge Luhan was "the most peculiar common denominator that society, literature, art, and radical revolutionaries ever found in New York and Europe," Luhan was indeed a "common denominator" whose life connects germinal social and intellectual issues in late nineteenth- and early twentieth-century European and American life. Through her own writings and activities and the works of scholars, newspaper reporters, painters, photographers, poets, and fiction writers (in well over a dozen novels, short stories, poems, and plays), Luhan's character and life have become a leading and highly contested paradigm of America's coming-of-age in the twentieth century.

To some of her contemporaries, like Gertrude Stein, Luhan's undammable and discontinuous feminine vitality was particularly suited to express the dynamism of American MODERNISM. To others, like D. H. Lawrence, Luhan represented the questing spirit of the New World, whose lust for "knowing" violated the mysteries of nature and threatened to devour the bedazzled male. When Luhan's memoirs were published in the 1930s, the radical press indicted her as the very personification of bourgeois degeneracy that had brought on the Depression. Ironically, they missed the radical implications of her own self-construction as an epitome of the Anglo-American culture that produced the will to power and domination: the men seeking to master the earth, the women seeking to master the men.

More recent critics have brought a new set of agendas to an evaluation of Luhan's life and work. In *The New Radicalism in America* (1965) by CHRISTOPHER LASCH and in Emily Hahn's *Mabel* (1977), Luhan is viewed as a culture carrier rather than as an originator, one who did not do "her own work," but depended for her identity on the work of creative artists. Because she did not achieve in the masculine realms of public activity, she has been, in their view, justly relegated to historical near-oblivion. This view misses the central point that Luhan was an artist of life, whose realm of work has been undervalued (like that of many other women, going back to MARGARET FULLER and beyond), whose time and energy has been invested in the creative use of space and place to nurture the genius of others, and who have provided arenas for the rich and contrapuntal discourse of the avant-garde.

In the 1980s, the scholarship of POSTMODERNISM has further problematized Luhan's life and work, as she has come to be criticized for her class and race privilege and for her "essentialist" commodifying of Native American culture, which she marketed to the nation. It is true that Luhan ignored the complexities of the construction of racial identity. But as recent scholars have noted, she (like other Anglo writers, such as Mary Austin and Willa Cather, also criticized for racial essentializing) was instrumental in challenging masculinist and imperialist myths of the frontier, and in contributing to an environmentalist and multiethnic ethos of American literature and culture.

LOIS PALKEN RUDNICK

FURTHER READING
Charles Briggs, *The Woodcarvers of Córdova, New Mexico: Social Dimensions of an Artistic "Revival"* (Knoxville: University of Tennessee Press, 1980).
Michael Castro, *Interpreting the Indian: Twentieth-Century Poets and the Native American* (Albuquerque: University of New Mexico Press, 1983).
Mabel Dodge Luhan, *Intimate Memories: Background* (New York: Harcourt, Brace, 1933).
——, *Intimate Memories: European Experiences* (New York: Harcourt, Brace, 1935).
——, *Intimate Memories: Movers and Shakers* (1936; Albuquerque: University of New Mexico Press, 1985).
——, *Intimate Memories: Edge of Taos Desert: an Escape to Reality* (1937; Albuquerque: University of New Mexico Press, 1987).
Vera Norwood and Jan Monk, eds., *The Desert Is No Lady: Southwestern Landscapes in Women's Writing and Art* (New Haven: Yale University Press, 1987).
Lois Rudnick, *Mabel Dodge Luhan: New Woman New Worlds* (Albuquerque: University of New Mexico Press, 1984).
——, "The Male-Identified Woman and Other Anxieties: the Life of Mabel Dodge Luhan," in Sara Alpern et al., eds., *The Challenge of Feminist Biography* (Urbana: University of Illinois Press, 1992).

Lynd, Robert (b. New Albany, Ind., Sept. 26, 1892; d. Warren, Conn., Nov. 1, 1970) Sociologist; and **Helen** (b. La Grange, Ill., Mar. 17, 1896; d. Warren, Ohio, Jan. 30, 1982), Writer.   In *Middletown: a Study in Contemporary American Culture* (1929), the Lynds produced a widely read assessment of the public and private life of a "typical" small American city. The formerly self-reliant and democratic white Protestant heartland was losing its soul. The "pecuniary" values of modern urban civilization, institutionalized in advertising and commercial entertainments, were reshaping habits across the whole cultural terrain. The Lynds pleaded for more social control of life to combat what they considered the disarray of modern experience—a conviction that led them, in the 1930s, to an ever-growing enthusiasm for the Soviet model of an engineered society. After coauthoring *Middletown in Transition* (1937), they wrote separately: Robert issued *Knowledge for What?* (1939) and Helen published *Shame* (1958), among other books.

FURTHER READING
Richard Wightman Fox, "Epitaph for Middletown: Robert S. Lynd and the Analysis of Consumer Culture," in Richard Wightman Fox and T. J. Jackson Lears, eds., *The Culture of Consumption: Critical Essays in American History, 1880–1980* (New York: Pantheon, 1983).

Lyon, Mary (b. near Buckland, Mass., Feb. 28, 1797; d. South Hadley, Mass., Mar. 5, 1849). Educator. Founder of Mount Holyoke Seminary (1837), Lyon insisted that women can meet the same academic standards expected of their male peers. Closely modeled on men's colleges, her curriculum emphasized advanced study in both sciences and humanities. The school was strongly evangelical, though nondenominational; it stressed the intellectual cultivation requisite to producing good wives, mothers, teachers, and missionaries. While students performed all of the domestic work themselves in order to minimize expenses, Lyon refused to include instruction in domestic activities.

FURTHER READING

Elizabeth Green, *Mary Lyon and Mt. Holyoke* (Hanover, N.H.: University Press of New England, 1979).

M

McCarthy, Mary (b. Seattle, Wash., June 21, 1912; d. New York, N.Y., Oct. 25, 1989). Writer and critic. Passionate about language and well known for her acerbic wit, McCarthy believed that literature at its best is about ideas, especially public issues such as politics and religion. Beginning in the 1930s, her range of literary production was impressive: a decade of drama criticism for the *Partisan Review*, the autobiographical *Memories of a Catholic Girlhood* (1957), several novels, including *The Group* (1966), and innumerable important essays, such as her antiwar articles collected in *Vietnam* (1967). McCarthy was a prototypical writer-as-public-intellectual, at a time when the NEW YORK INTELLECTUALS provided a moral and political center for American thought.

FURTHER READING
Carol Brightman, *Writing Dangerously: Mary McCarthy and Her World* (New York: C. Potter, 1992).

McCosh, James (b. Ayrshire, Scotland, Apr. 1, 1811; d. Princeton, N.J., Nov. 16, 1894). Philosopher. President of the College of New Jersey, now Princeton University (1868–88), McCosh was a common sense realist. He was the author of *Intuitions of the Mind Inductively Investigated* (1860), *Christianity and Positivism* (1871), and *First and Fundamental Truths* (1889). He believed that the mind directly grasps a real order that exists outside the mind. Rejecting idealism and TRANSCENDENTALISM, he insisted that perceived facts can be trusted, as can the self-evident principles of causation, moral obligation, and orthodox theology. Despite his conservative defense of orthodoxy, McCosh was one of the first American theological advocates of DARWINISM: God's design, he believed, is revealed in the "special providences" of variation and selection.

See also SCOTTISH COMMON SENSE REALISM.

FURTHER READING
J. David Hoeveler Jr., *James McCosh and the Scottish Intellectual Tradition: From Glasgow to Princeton* (Princeton: Princeton University Press, 1981).

Macdonald, Dwight (b. New York, N.Y., Mar. 24, 1906; d. New York, N.Y., Dec. 19, 1982). A leading figure (and one of the few non-Jews) among the coterie of NEW YORK INTELLECTUALS who held center stage in mid-twentieth-century American intellectual life, Macdonald was the wittiest, the most open-minded, and the most accessible of the bunch. This led many within and without this circle (and some historians) mistakenly to doubt his seriousness and to underestimate the force of his wide-ranging, iconoclastic, political and cultural criticism.

Son of a modestly successful lawyer (whose modesty he admired) and the status-minded daughter of a wealthy family, Macdonald enjoyed a happy childhood and a fine education. He attended Phillips Exeter Academy, where he flourished as a dandyish aesthete, and Yale, where he was a good deal less happy. He was nearly expelled for writing an article in the college humor magazine, satirizing professors (such as William Lyon Phelps) whom he considered pretentious, but he managed to graduate in 1928. After a brief stint in the retail trade as an executive trainee at Macy's, he went to work on the staff of Henry Luce's new business magazine *Fortune* in 1929, joining a talented stable of young writers who included ARCHIBALD MACLEISH and Macdonald's friend JAMES AGEE.

Under the impact of the Great Depression and his marriage to Nancy Rodman, a silk-stocking radical, Macdonald began to take an interest in politics, and by the mid-1930s he was a Communist Party fellow-traveler. Increasingly restless at *Fortune*, he resigned from the magazine following a dispute with his editors over a series of articles he wrote attacking the U.S. Steel corporation, one of which he prefaced with a quote from Lenin's *Imperialism*. Appalled by the Moscow trials, in which Stalin made his opponents confess to their "crimes," he gravitated to the Trotskyists, enlisting on the committee to defend Leon Trotsky from the charges made against him in the trials and eventually signing up with the Socialist Workers Party in 1939. He also joined the editorial board of the leading anti-Stalinist radical journal *Partisan Review*, where in the late thirties he led the attack on the cultural nationalism of MacLeish and VAN WYCK BROOKS (which he termed *Kulturbolshewismus*).

Macdonald left the SWP in 1940, joining the faction led by Max Shachtman which challenged Trotsky's contention that the Soviet Union was a "degenerated workers' state" and argued instead that it was a new and nasty form of "bureaucratic collectivism." In 1941 Macdonald departed from sectarian socialism altogether: he left Shachtman's Workers

Party after protesting the constraints on free debate imposed by the Leninist orthodoxy to which the party leadership continued to adhere. Macdonald's political views also created tension at *Partisan Review* in the early 1940s. When it became clear in 1943 that editors PHILIP RAHV and William Phillips would no longer countenance his opposition to World War II—which in typical Trotskyist fashion he regarded as a struggle between competing imperial powers—he departed.

A year after leaving *Partisan Review*, Macdonald began publication of his own magazine *politics*, which would become the most significant political venture of his career. Although *politics* was to a great degree a one-man journal, Macdonald also attracted an extraordinary roster of contributors, including Americans then largely unknown such as PAUL GOODMAN, IRVING HOWE, MARY MCCARTHY, DANIEL BELL, and C. WRIGHT MILLS and European émigrés and exiles such as BRUNO BETTELHEIM, Andrea Caffi, Nicola Chiaromonte, Lewis Coser, Victor Serge, and Simone Weil. The presence of the Europeans lent *politics* the aura of an American outpost of the European resistance movements.

Although Macdonald would later admit that his Trotskyist position on the war was a mistake, it was a creative mistake that freed him and other *politics* contributors to criticize all sides in the conflict and, especially, to offer a penetrating inquiry into the morally catastrophic means of total war. It was in the analysis of these horrors—the HOLOCAUST, terror bombing, the atomic bomb, and others—that the *politics* circle was at its best. During the war and its immediate aftermath, as Daniel Bell noted in *The End of Ideology* (1960), "*politics* was the only magazine that was aware of and insistently kept calling attention to, changes that were taking place in moral temper, the depths of which we still incompletely realize" (p. 307).

Macdonald remained resolutely anti-Stalinist in the 1940s, struggling to formulate a radical, "third camp" alternative to Soviet communism and American liberalism. He particularly despised HENRY WALLACE and other Soviet sympathizers (terming them "totalitarian liberals"), and he contributed a riotous and destructive portrait of Wallace, in *Henry Wallace: the Man and the Myth*, to the presidential campaign literature of 1948: "Wallaceland . . . is a region of perpetual fogs, caused by the warm winds of the liberal Gulf Stream coming in contact with the Soviet glacier" (p. 24). As the Cold War crystallized, Macdonald's third-camp hopes dimmed and his political energies flagged. He shut down *politics* in 1949 and in 1952 he "chose the West," though he did

so with a heavier heart than most other anticommunist intellectuals.

In the 1950s he devoted himself to criticism of mass culture, savaging such targets as James Gould Cozzens, the Book-of-the-Month Club, and the Revised Standard Version of the Bible in essays reprinted in *Against the American Grain* (1962). He reserved special contempt for what he termed "midcult," commodities like the new Bible that "pretends to respect the standards of High Culture while in fact it waters them down and vulgarizes them" (p. 37). Macdonald did retain an affection for the movies which dated from his boyhood, and he never abandoned all hope for this popular art form. In the early 1960s he wrote a film column for *Esquire* magazine (collected, with his other film criticism, in *Dwight Macdonald on Movies* (1969)). There he both wreaked havoc on Hollywood schlock (Doris Day: "as wholesome as a bowl of cornflakes and at least as sexy") and played a leading role in introducing European "new wave" filmmakers to American audiences.

The war in VIETNAM moved Macdonald to return to political activism. He was an early and vigorous opponent of the war, circulating an antiwar petition at a White House garden party in 1965 and joining the march on the Pentagon in 1967. He was among the few New York intellectuals to lend his support to the NEW LEFT and student radicalism. In the late 1960s he developed an insurmountable writer's block and published little thereafter. In his last years he earned much of his living by means of periodic college teaching, offering film courses and classes on Edgar Allan Poe and his other favorite writers.

When asked to characterize his career, Macdonald labeled himself a "literary journalist," an identity that ironically suggests the blurring of distinctions between high and low culture that he so vigorously denounced. As his friend John Simon observed in his introduction to the 1981 reprint edition of *On Movies*, "Macdonald is that rare, if not unique, critic who combines the highest, most uncompromising standards with an ease and felicity of expression that everyone, high and low, can thoroughly enjoy" (p. 1). Unlike the producers of most of the "midcult" he deplored, Macdonald managed to find a style that rendered difficult ideas accessible without debasing them. Though it would have horrified him to think so, he might even be said to have unwittingly offered in the example of his own work an argument for the virtues of criticism that traffics freely across the aesthetic boundaries he sought so diligently to erect.

ROBERT B. WESTBROOK

See also CULTURAL CRITICISM; MASS CULTURE; MIDDLEBROW CULTURE.

FURTHER READING

Daniel Bell, *The End of Ideology: On the Exhaustion of Political Ideas in the Fifties* (Glencoe, Ill.: Free Press, 1960).

Dwight Macdonald, *Against the American Grain* (New York: Random House, 1962).

——, *Henry Wallace: the Man and the Myth* (New York: Vanguard, 1948).

——, *On Movies* (1969; New York: DaCapo, 1981).

Alan Wald, *The New York Intellectuals: the Rise and Decline of the Anti-Stalinist Left from the 1930s to the 1980s* (Chapel Hill: University of North Carolina Press, 1987).

Robert B. Westbrook, "The Responsibility of Peoples: Dwight Macdonald and the Holocaust," in Sanford Pinsker and Jack Fischel, eds., *America and the Holocaust* (Greenwood, Fla.: Penkevill, 1983).

Stephen Whitfield, *A Critical American: the Politics of Dwight Macdonald* (Hamden, Conn.: Archon, 1984).

Michael Wreszin, *A Rebel in Defense of Tradition: the Life and Politics of Dwight Macdonald* (New York: Basic Books, 1994).

MacIntyre, Alasdair (b. Glasgow, Scotland, Jan. 12, 1929). From Oxford to Essex to a passel of American universities, most recently Notre Dame, Alasdair MacIntyre is a peripatetic in more senses than one. The ease and expertise with which he moves from religion to action theory to the critique of Western culture brought him widespread admiration in the three decades before the 1981 publication of *After Virtue* brought celebrity, and even notoriety. For many it seemed a revelation, a new way of construing our moral and social ills. But MacIntyre's central concerns are already visible in his first volume, *Marxism and Christianity*, with its critique of LIBERALISM and historicist situating of both Marxism and Christianity, all motivated by a compelling interpretation of "the Marxist project" as "the only one we have for reestablishing hope as a social virtue" (p. 116). His subsequent studies in religion and the social sciences, ethics and politics, and the philosophy of science, all point to *After Virtue*.

What makes *After Virtue* engaging to some distresses others, for MacIntyre calls into question not just fashionable philosophical procedures and views, but entire institutions thought to define the progressive, modern world. The social and institutional upheavals that characterized Europe from the late Middle Ages through the mid-nineteenth century drove a wedge between the public and the private self and created an ideological vacuum. This vacuum the marketplace filled, its ideology being the utilitarianism of Bentham and the Weberian dream of maximizing the fit of the worker to his job. It became unclear that there was any natural shape to human life. And so life in the modern world became an arena of desires for private fulfillment, to be achieved not through VIRTUE or moral regeneration, but through the release from anxiety provided by the therapist.

For MacIntyre this transformation of our moral expectations is finally self-destructive. What makes a life choiceworthy is its ability to sustain the claim that its virtues and practices are truly, as opposed to apparently, good. At least in the precursor cultures to modernity, a rough sense of how to describe the virtues could focus debate on what mattered and why. But modern INDIVIDUALISM, codified in the liberal commitment to tolerating positions as long as they don't make a difference to the status quo, isn't an alternative moral vision so much as the refusal to consider one. When a community systematically refuses to acknowledge binding standards, then anything goes and no long-term vision of the human good can be socially sustained. There is no good reason to sacrifice anything for the greater good.

Implied in MacIntyre's argument is the complicity of the academy in undermining the moral community, and this charge intensified the reaction to *After Virtue*. G. E. Moore and the aesthetes of Bloomsbury exalted the judgments of the educated elite beyond critical evaluation, a move canonized in the emotivism of recent Anglo-American moral philosophy. Ironically, the teaching of ethics in the academy now subverts moral community, leaving us, MacIntyre insisted, with the almost impossible choice between Aristotle and Nietzsche (pp. 103–13).

MacIntyre promised a sequel to *After Virtue* and supplied it with *Whose Justice? Which Rationality?* This sprawling volume argues that the competing standards of various moral visions are ultimately incommensurable. Thomas Aquinas's synthesis of Aristotle and Augustine, rather than the procedural justice of liberal pluralism, is, for MacIntyre, the tradition of moral understanding most capable of sustaining an interpretation of the choiceworthy political life. This is not the neoconservativism of George Will, William Bennett, or the late Allan Bloom. Theirs is, ironically, little more than a parochial liberalism, identifying Christian American Democracy with the goal of the ENLIGHTENMENT programme. When, in *After Virtue*, MacIntyre juxtaposed Trotsky and St. Benedict, he signaled his hope for a vision of COMMUNITY carried by a practical reformer capable of implementing ideals in a way that generates institutions and practices that can sustain a way of life. Yet Trotsky is not really viable, because when "Marxism does not become Weberian social democracy or crude tyranny, it tends to become Nietzschean fantasy" (p. 244). So we are left "waiting not for a Godot, but for another—doubtless very different—St. Benedict"

(p. 245). The conclusion of *Whose Virtue? Which Rationality?* would seem to call for some way of adjudicating between the claims of future saints and prophets.

This is the task of *Three Rival Versions of Moral Enquiry*, MacIntyre's most recent volume. He characterizes the nineteenth-century liberal tradition as "Encyclopedic," selectively interpreting everything worthwhile as pointing toward its own achievement. MacIntyre is surely right to see that strategy as unduly biased in favor of the encyclopedists' own perspective. Nietzsche is the father of "Genealogy," the subversion of authority through uncovering its origins and limitations. But in the process Nietzsche's heirs, champions of DECONSTRUCTION and disciples of Foucault, cannot help but subvert themselves, for "among the purposes to be served by both theater and genealogical commentary will be the undermining of all traditional forms of authority, including the authority of the lecturer" (p. 233). "Traditionalists," among whom MacIntyre locates Aristotle and his own version of St. Thomas, are committed to self-criticism and revision, which makes it all the more crucial to acknowledge "the importance of the task now imposed upon us, of continually trying to devise new ways to allow these voices to be heard" (p. 236). For it is only when we can situate ourselves within an ongoing TRADITION of mutual acknowledgement and cooperation in pursuing shared goods that we can give good reasons for preferring, and working toward, one future as opposed to another. The leveling of goods achieved by liberal pluralism makes such choices unintelligible and thus work for a common future impossible. This, for MacIntyre, makes the critique of such liberalism a moral imperative.

G. SCOTT DAVIS

See also CATHOLICISM; JUSTICE.

FURTHER READING

Stanley Hauerwas and Alasdair MacIntyre, eds., *Revisions: Changing Perspectives in Moral Philosophy* (Notre Dame: University of Notre Dame Press, 1983).
Alasdair MacIntyre, *Marxism and Christianity* (1953; New York: Schocken, 1968).
——, *A Short History of Ethics* (New York: Macmillan, 1964).
——, *After Virtue: a Study in Moral Theory* (Notre Dame: University of Notre Dame Press, 1981).
——, *Whose Justice? Which Rationality?* (Notre Dame: University of Notre Dame Press, 1988).
——, *Three Rival Versions of Moral Enquiry: Encyclopedia, Genealogy and Tradition* (Notre Dame: University of Notre Dame Press, 1990).
Jeffrey Stout, *Ethics After Babel: the Languages of Morals and Their Discontents* (Boston: Beacon, 1988).

McKay, Claude (b. Clarendon, Jamaica, Sept. 15. 1890; d. Chicago, Ill., May 22, 1948).   The work of Claude McKay as a poet, novelist and essayist heralded several of the most significant moments in African American culture. His poetry in the late 1910s and early 1920s was the most powerful literary expression of the "New Negro" in the United States. His novels of the late 1920s and early 1930s were sophisticated considerations of the problems and possibilities of pan-Africanism during the last decades of European colonialism. These novels were also meditations on the relation of the black intellectual to the "masses" of black people, and helped inspire the Francophone African and Caribbean writers of the Negritude movement. His poetry and nonfiction prose works had an important impact on the Left-influenced literature and politics of the 1930s and 1940s. And his early vernacular poetry and later stories and novel set in Jamaica were landmarks in the development of modern Anglophone Caribbean literature.

McKay's early Jamaican vernacular poetry sounds the thematic and formal concerns which reappear in much of McKay's later work: the opposition of the rural landscape and the city, and the natural and the civilized; the peasant as the "authentic" representative of black culture; the poetic "voice" of a speaker who is both insider and outsider; the problem of exile; the relation of the black intellectual to the black masses, of class and race within a colonial context. This poetry emerged largely out of McKay's experience as a member of the Jamaican constabulary in Kingston. McKay, who was born to a farm family and educated primarily by his elder brother, a free-thinking school teacher, found the urban life of Kingston oppressive. And he found his identity as a "Constab" alienating, locating him between the urban elite and the great mass of the urban poor.

McKay further developed these concerns in the poetry he wrote after his immigration to the United States in 1912 to attend Tuskeegee Institute. After a short period at Tuskeegee and a somewhat longer stay at Kansas State University, McKay ended up in Harlem, where he worked at a series of menial jobs while he wrote. This period of McKay's work is best remembered for his protest sonnets, which are regarded today as the beginning of the HARLEM RENAISSANCE. In their own day, these poems were used by black intellectuals to promote black literary production. For example, the critical and popular repute of McKay's work was crucial to JAMES WELDON JOHNSON in his project in *The Book of American Negro Poetry* (1922), a seminal anthology which not only proposed a tradition of modern African

American poetry starting with Paul Laurence Dunbar, but also announced a new moment of black writing, of which McKay, in Johnson's view, was the chief progenitor.

But the focus on McKay's protest poetry has often obscured his identity as a poet of exile. In poems such as "Flame-Heart" and "The Tropics in New York" in *Harlem Shadows* (1992), McKay nostalgically invokes a tropical landscape—often opposed to a racist urban North America—and the desire of the poem's speaker to return to a site of communal wholeness. Even in the protest sonnets, the rupture between the poem's speaker and an organic community, often figured in a landscape, is at the root of the speaker's anger. This opposition is also posed structurally with the black intellectual-artist-speaker anxiously mediating between the representation of the black subject and the received poetic forms—sonnets, iambic pentameter, quatrains, etc.—of the metropole. Thus the "conservative" form of McKay's poetry is not, as scholars have often suggested, at odds with the content of the poetry. Rather the form structurally reprises the thematic concerns of the poems.

Thus McKay's engagement with the communist movement in the late 1910s and early 1920s, particularly after his 1919 move to London where he joined the staff of Sylvia Pankhurst's *Worker's Dreadnought*, can be seen not only as a logical extension of the militant antiracism of the protest poems, but also as a potential solution to what McKay, anticipating Harold Cruse, saw as the identity crisis of the black intellectual. Like Cruse in *The Crisis of the Negro Intellectual*, McKay protrayed this crisis as one of the alienation of the intellectual from the black community. But where Cruse, following in the footsteps of McKay's later work, saw the Communist Party as the root source of this alienation, McKay in the 1920s laid the blame on the bourgeois culture of the colonial metropoles. McKay saw an alternative in the communists, who promoted a vision of a world in which distinctions of nation, class and race would become less important as markers of power and in which black intellectuals would have an organic relationship to society. In McKay's speech as a delegate to the Fourth Congress of the Communist International (Comintern) in 1922 he argued that the "Negro question" was central to the world revolutionary movement and took the movement to task for ignoring the struggles of black people in Africa and the diaspora.

McKay's speech helped spark the Fourth Congress's "Theses on the Negro Question," which declared African Americans to be "in the vanguard of the African struggle against oppression." McKay therefore had a hand in moving the struggles of African Americans from a relatively peripheral issue for the Communist Party of the United States of America (CPUSA) to becoming the party's preeminent concern by the early 1930s.

In his novels *Home to Harlem* (1928) and *Banjo* (1929), McKay questions notions of RACE and CLASS within a world divided up by European and American capitalism. McKay posits a connection between the situation of black people in Africa and those throughout the diaspora, but aside from the general link of a common oppression by racism and colonialism, the nature of the connection remains elusive.

In *Home to Harlem* one sees again the opposition between the black intellectual Ray, a Haitian expatriate, and the "natural" representative of the black masses, Jake Brown. Ray agonizes over everything and feels alienated from the black community by his absorption of European "high" culture; Jake is spontaneous and direct, acting without reflection or self-doubt. Ray is a sort of cultural "mulatto," while Jake is purely "Negro." Ray is implicitly effeminate and Jake virilely masculine, suggesting that this joining of opposites might be a productive pairing. Ray and Jake do become close friends, though it is an uneasy friendship, particularly for Ray. Thus *Home to Harlem* and *Banjo*, in which Ray reappears paired with the "natural" black musician Banjo in the old port of Marseilles along with a shifting cast of black dockers, sailors and drifters from Africa, the Caribbean and the United States, propose a new type of intellectual, not unlike Gramsci's notion of the "organic intellectual." This intellectual would be produced by and remain a part of the black masses rather than attempting either to rise above these masses or lead them from above as suggested by W. E. B. Du Bois's notion of the "talented tenth."

McKay's last two books, the autobiographical *A Long Way from Home* (1937) and the sociological *Harlem: Negro Metropolis* (1940), are interesting for their critique of the CPUSA. Historians of the anti-Stalinist Left have not noted McKay's condemnation of the CPUSA for what he saw as its frustration of initiatives that arose from within the black community itself, such as cooperative movements and demands for jobs for African Americans in white-owned Harlem businesses. McKay also pointedly attacked the vast majority of black intellectuals for following the CPUSA, thereby severing their ties to black workers.

McKay's overly simple opposition between (effeminate) intellectuals/metropolis and (virile) black workers and peasant/nature certainly "essentializes" categories that need to be historicized. But this criticism, which also applies to many of McKay's contemporaries, both black and white, should not be allowed to obscure the basic point that McKay made one of the earliest attempts to explore the contradictions of race, class, nationality and ETHNICITY, and the place of the black intellectual in that complex of identities that has continued to provoke modern African and African American authors.

JAMES SMETHURST

See also PROLETARIANISM.

FURTHER READING

James S. Allen and Philip S. Foner, eds., *American Communism and Black Americans: a Documentary History, 1919–1929* (Philadelphia: Temple University Press, 1987).

Wayne Cooper, *Claude McKay: Rebel Sojourner in the Harlem Renaissance* (Baton Rouge: Louisiana State University Press, 1987).

James Weldon Johnson, ed., *The Book of American Negro Poetry* (New York: Harcourt, Brace, 1922).

Tyrone Tillery, *Claude McKay: a Black Poet's Struggle for Identity* (Amherst: University of Massachusetts Press, 1992).

Jean Wagner, *Black Poets of the United States: From Paul Laurence Dunbar to Langston Hughes* (Urbana: University of Illinois Press, 1973).

MacLeish, Archibald (b. Glencoe, Ill., May 7, 1892; d. Boston, Mass., Apr. 20, 1982). Poet and playwright. Trained as a lawyer, MacLeish spent most of the 1920s among the expatriate writers in Europe, where he devoted himself to poetry. With the rise of fascism he abandoned his art-for-art's-sake position ("A poem should not mean / But be," as he wrote in his "Ars Poetica," 1928) and pleaded for putting intellectual work at the service of democracy (in *The Irresponsibles*, 1940). American literature, he insisted, should reinforce traditional principles, affirm and defend American culture, and create a sense of solidarity among the people. Recipient of three Pulitzer Prizes, for *Conquistador* (1932), *Poems 1917–1952* (1952), and *J. B.* (1958), MacLeish developed his critical theory in *Poetry and Opinion* (1950) and *Poetry and Experience* (1961).

FURTHER READING

Scott Donaldson, *Archibald MacLeish: an American Life* (Boston: Houghton Mifflin, 1992).

Madison, James (b. Port Conway, Va., Mar. 16, 1751; d. Montpelier, Va., June 28, 1836). Political theorist, statesman, fourth President of the United States, James Madison is generally regarded by scholars as the principal architect of the United States CONSTITUTION and among the most gifted and influential of America's so-called Founding Fathers. His reputation rests largely on his talents as a thinker, displayed most conspicuously in his contributions to the *Federalist* papers, in which he analyzed and defended the framework of government that he had played such a large hand in drafting at the Constitutional Convention of 1787. These essays, which continue to be scutinized for their nuances and larger meaning by seemingly countless scholars, rank among the most original and profound expression of political thought in American history.

The range of modern scholarly interpretation of Madison's political ideas is vast. For a time during the 1950s and 1960s political scientists enshrined him as an early proponent of a twentieth-century interest-group theory of politics. This "pluralist" reading of Madison's writings, appropriately emphasizing the tenth *Federalist*, was soon dismissed as ananchronistic by historians—particularly those who were developing during the 1960s and 1970s a fresh appreciation of REPUBLICANISM as a distinctively eighteenth-century ideology—and by political theorists, many working under the influence of LEO STRAUSS, who were seeking to understand Madison and his fellow Federalists in the light of a Western tradition of political thought rooted in classical antiquity. If Madison is no longer perceived as a prophet of twentieth-century pluralism, however, the debate over the "modernity" of his political thought, recast in the more historically sensitive terms of critics of that view, remains very much alive.

Outside the rarified circles of specialized scholarship, where consideration of his ideas is paramount, Madison is much less well known and appreciated; his vivacious and much younger wife Dolley may well enjoy as much name recognition among twentieth-century Americans as he. Diminutive in physical stature, modest, even self-effacing in his public demeanor, and generally shy to the point of being withdrawn, Madison remains today, as he did to a considerable extent in his own time, in the shadow of his more colorful, versatile, and commanding political colleague, THOMAS JEFFERSON, whom he first served as Secretary of State (1801–9) and then succeeded as President for two terms (1809–17). Many modern scholars understand clearly what was seen by at least some of the two men's contemporaries: that Madison was the steadier, more disciplined, more incisive, and hence more profound thinker of the two great Jeffersonians. In general, biographers of Madison have enjoyed much greater success in illuminating the sources and context of his ideas and the trajectory of his political career than they have in portraying his character and inner life. Yet the complexity and intrinsic tragedy of this man's career as a republican theorist and statesman is probably most richly revealed in the intersection of his private and public experience.

Madison was the first-born son of the wealthiest planter in Orange County, Virginia, a prosperous provincial outpost of the British empire noted for its tobacco-growing economy based on slave labor. His father had the means and good sense to seek for his intellectually curious son the best education available in such a raw, isolated environment. After five years at a local private school and two more years of tutoring at home, the young Madison journeyed in the late 1760s to the College of New Jersey (later Princeton University), where he studied under the demanding and inspiring direction of President JOHN WITHERSPOON, a Scottish clergyman who introduced his American students to what has come to be known as the Scottish ENLIGHTENMENT. Madison studied the writings of David Hume, Adam Ferguson, and Adam Smith, among others, immersing himself in the moral philosophy of a group of creative thinkers who were seeking to establish a science of human nature and social development. After returning home from Princeton, and sorely missing its rich intellectual ambience, Madison suffered through several years of unhappy isolation and indecision regarding his future. Then, abruptly, came the AMERICAN REVOLUTION—an event that defined to a remarkable extent not just Madison's subsequent career in politics, but his mature sense of his own identity. For the next 60 years, amid considerable emotional urgency, he avidly pursued a republican dream that gave meaning to his life.

The twentieth-century poet Robert Frost once mused that the best dreamer of the American dream was not some wild-eyed enthusiast, but rather the meticulous, soft-spoken Madison, whose dream, Frost perceptively inferred, was "of a new land to fulfill with people in self-control"—people like Madison himself, he might have added (cited by LaFeber, p. 22). In temperament and character the mature Madison who emerged from the Revolution became a model of neoclassical self-command. His admirers came to understand and appreciate the extent to which his characteristic modesty, temperance, and perseverance represented a triumph of reason over passion in a man whose concern for the public good generally overrode petty considerations of personal vanity or partisan advantage. Believing that unrestrained passion threatened moral order within individuals as well as in society, Madison placed the appropriate premium on balance and restraint not only in his own character and behavior, but in the American republic that he came to regard as an extension of himself. In doing so he caught the animating spirit of the enlightened, neoclassical world of the American Revolution, which in turn raised the question and the challenge that became the focus of this provincial Virginian's life: could men as they actually were in modern commercial society—and not as visionaries imagined or wished them to be—govern themselves?

Madison can fairly be characterized as a conservative optimist and a cautious idealist. He believed that republicanism could be made to work in America—certainly a radical idea in an age when monarchical or at least aristocratic authority was widely assumed to be the necessary basis for social order—but only if prudent statesmen took into sufficient account the dangers posed by human nature and also acknowledged the importance of custom and TRADITION in stabilizing a republican regime. Above all, as Madison wrestled with the problems that arose during the years just after the war for American independence, he came to understand that republicanism and nationalism in America were inextricably linked. Passionate, self-interested men and the factions they formed inevitably endangered the measure of civilized stability necessary for justice and good government, even in America, where a revolutionary people had turned out not to be as virtuous as Madison and others had originally hoped.

But Madison, drawing on the insights of Hume, now hoped that by extending the sphere of republican government from the state level, where it was not working well, to the federal or national level, the new Constitution offered a novel remedy for the diseases most incident to popular governments. Contrary to conventional wisdom, which suggested that republics must be geographically small in order to remain stable and survive, Madison suggested that an extended republic offered certain advantages. It would contain so many different interests that oppressive majorities would be much less likely to form and then harass minorities and perpetrate injustice. Madison also hoped that in a larger republic a filtration of talent, by which the most virtuous, prudent statesmen would likely prevail in elections at the federal level, might provide the kind of wise, dispassionate leadership necessary for good government. In both respects, the new Constitution offered a potential vehicle for promoting both national integration and republican stability.

To some meaningful extent the history of the early American republic amply fulfilled Madison's cautious optimism. The Constitution survived several major crises, most notably in the late 1790s and then again during the War of 1812. In both cases Madison was instrumental in securing the republic, first by organizing and leading opposition to a political faction whose vision and policies lacked broad-based support and then by leading the country through an extraordinarily trying second war for independence against England. When Madison retired from public life in 1817 following his second term as President, both he and the republic seemed triumphant after decades of stress and turmoil. In truth, and certainly for Madison in retrospect, all was not well with the great American experiment. Several of Madison's initial hopes—for instance, that the federal government under the Constitution would somehow be insulated from the demagoguery and partisan politics common at the state level—had been abruptly and almost immediately dashed. Popular DEMOCRACY and everything that came with it, including fierce partisanship, were forces emerging from the Revolution that proved impossible to contain. Indeed, if the Constitution managed to serve as a source of national integration during these tumultuous decades, it did so in ways often quite different from what Madison had expected and intended. And the experience of the War of 1812—when, with Madison at the helm, the federal government and the American war effort virtually dissolved under the force of partisan pressure and local resistance—amply demonstrated the weaknesses of the governing framework Madison had helped devise at the Constitutional Convention.

If the survival of the United States during the War of 1812 represented a political triumph for the Jeffersonians that momentarily obscured the deeper sources of trouble, Madison survived long enough to confront fully the ambiguities and shortcomings of his own legacy. Characteristically eventempered and optimistic, he managed to keep a stiff upper lip through the almost two decades of his retirement, during which his beloved republic entered a new and explosive phase of its history. But Madison's equanimity was severely tested. He fretted openly as new approaches to constitutional interpretation threatened the stability of a regime that he believed must remain anchored to the precedent and tradition established during its founding. If Madison's character and vision had been formed in an eighteenth-century, neoclassical world in which reason was enjoined to discipline the unsettling effects of passion, he spent his final years accommodating to a more modern, Jacksonian world of Romantic democracy in which passionate individualism threatened to overturn all restraints of custom, tradition, and history. He especially feared for the stability of a Union precariously founded in a tradition of regional compromise that passionate factions now failed to understand or respect. And above all, events in his own life and in the public arena would not let him forget that the American republic, which he passionately wished to have offer the world the full benefit of its moral and political example, was in fact a regime that included, in more than an incidental way, the abominable and retrograde institution of chattel slavery.

Madison was a principled opponent of slavery for all of his adult life—which is to say, he categorically condemned the institution as intrinsically unjust, indeed inimical to the fundamental principles of a republican revolution rooted in the logic of natural right. That belief in turn generated Madison's commitment to abolishing slavery in the United States; for him, the question was never if, one might say, but only when and how. At the Constitutional Convention he was complicit in the linguistic legerdemain that kept the word slavery out of the document, both because he believed that it would be wrong to admit in fundamental law that there could be property in men and also because he expected, or at least wished, that the Constitution would in the not-too-distant future operate in a republic without slaves. But Madison also understood that abolishing the institution posed an immense challenge to a society in which it had taken such deep root, and above all, in which racial differences had such powerful psychological and cultural resonance (*see* ANTISLAVERY). Although Madison, unlike his friend Jefferson, never articulated a personal belief in the inferiority of blacks, he accepted as permanent his white countrymen's prejudice against African Americans, which prompted him to embrace the popular idea that the abolition of slavery must be accompanied by the departure of the former slaves from the republic. Hence Madison fervently supported the colonization movement that emerged during the early nineteenth century and which resulted in the founding of the colony of Liberia on the west coast of Africa.

Madison's faith in colonization as a practical and just means of promoting an end to slavery, and perforce of resolving his country's racial dilemma—a faith that he obstinately clung to in the face of all logic and fact—struck one of his English admirers, Harriet Martineau, as incongruously naive and misguided (as indeed it does virtually all modern students of Madison). Martineau could explain her hero's shortsightedness only as an ironic reflection of his larger, irrepressible faith in the American experiment in self-government. In one sense, as Martineau so shrewdly inferred, Madison could not admit to himself, much less to others, that the republic he had invested so much of himself in building was in fact fatally flawed in both principle and practice and likely headed for disaster. He was no more successful in resolving his personal dilemma as a slaveholder. Contrary to his own early hopes and expectations in the years just after the Revolution, when as a young man disillusioned with his native state of Virginia he had sought ways to escape his inheritance as a planter and master of slaves, Madison had gradually accommodated himself to his inherited status and home. He owned approximately one hundred slaves at the time of his death, none of whom apparently had any interest in Madison's vision of a new life for them in Liberia.

Madison's republic somehow managed to outlive him by several decades until, a scant quarter-century after his death, the holocaust of civil war that he had come to dread initiated a long overdue national reckoning with the tragic underside of his legacy.

DREW R. MCCOY

See also BILL OF RIGHTS; CITIZENSHIP; VIRTUE.

FURTHER READING

Trevor Colbourn, ed., *Fame and the Founding Fathers: Essays by Douglass Adair* (New York: Norton, 1974).

David E. Epstein, *The Political Theory of "The Federalist"* (Chicago: University of Chicago Press, 1984).

Walter LaFeber, "Foreign Policies of a New Nation: Franklin, Madison, and the 'Dream of a New Land to Fulfill with People in Self-Control,'" in William Appleman Williams, ed., *From Colony to Empire: Essays in the History of American Foreign Relations* (New York: Wiley, 1972).

Drew R. McCoy, *The Last of the Fathers: James Madison and the Republican Legacy* (New York: Cambridge University Press, 1989).

Marvin Meyers, ed., *The Mind of the Founder: Sources of the Political Thought of James Madison*, rev. ed. (Hanover, N.H.: University Press of New England, 1981).

Jack N. Rakove, *James Madison and the Creation of the American Republic* (Glenview, Ill.: Scott, Foresman, 1990).

Magnes, Judah Leon (b. San Francisco, Calif., July 5, 1877; d. New York, N.Y., Oct. 27, 1948).   Rabbi and educator; first chancellor and president of the Hebrew University of Jerusalem (1925–48). An important institution builder who strove to unify New York's German and Eastern European Jewish communities, Magnes left New York for Palestine in 1922. A committed Zionist, he argued for a binational state comprised of both Jews and Arabs. He believed that Jewish life and culture could thrive without a Jewish state, which could not be achieved peaceably. During World War II he urged support of the war against Hitler, in spite of his pacifist beliefs.

See also JUDAISM.

FURTHER READING

William M. Brinner and Moses Rischin, eds., *Like All the Nations?: the Life and Legacy of Judah L. Magnes* (Albany: State University of New York Press, 1987).

Mahan, Alfred Thayer (b. West Point, N.Y., Sept. 27, 1840; d. Washington, D.C., Dec. 1, 1914).   Military strategist and historian. Naval power, Mahan explained, is the key to national power: both military and commercial transportation require ocean routes and ports, which can only be secured by a strong navy. In *The Influence of Sea Power upon History* (1890) and *The Interest of America in Sea Power, Present and Future* (1897), Mahan argued that international relations inevitably express a struggle for power. Prosperity in competitive world markets requires a willingness to use force. Elected president of the American Historical Association after his retirement from the navy, Mahan lived to see his writings contribute to the sizable increases in naval strength around the world before World War I.

FURTHER READING

William E. Livezay, *Mahan on Sea Power* (Norman: University of Oklahoma Press, 1980).

Mailer, Norman (b. Long Branch, N.J., Jan. 31, 1923).   Writer. Accomplished both as essayist and novelist, Mailer became a public figure at an early age with the publication of *The Naked and the Dead* in 1948. His *Dissent* essay on "The White Negro" (1957) celebrated the existentialist "hipster" and exhibited his emerging voice—socially and politically engaged, like the previous generation of NEW YORK INTELLECTUALS, but riveted by his own personal experience, about which, in his later works, he was eloquent. *The Armies of the Night* (1968), based on a 1967 march on the Pentagon, and *Miami and the Siege of Chicago* (1968), an account of the Republican and Democratic national conventions, combined political JOURNALISM and AUTOBIOGRAPHY with the imaginative richness of fiction.

FURTHER READING

Nigel Leigh, *Radical Fictions and the Novels of Norman Mailer* (New York: St. Martin's, 1990).

Malcolm X [born Malcolm Little; later adopted the name El-Hajj Malik El-Shabazz] (b. Omaha, Nebr., May 19, 1925; d. New York, N.Y., Feb. 21, 1965). Malcolm X has been called a lot of things: pan-Africanist, father of Black Power, religious fanatic, closet conservative, incipient socialist, and a plain menace to society. The meaning of his public life

—his politics and ideology—is contested in part because his entire body of work consists of a few dozen speeches and a collaborative autobiography whose veracity is often challenged. Gunned down three months before his fortieth birthday, Malcolm X's life was cut short just when his thinking had reached a critical juncture.

Malcolm's life is a kind of HORATIO ALGER story with a twist. His is not a "rags to riches" tale but a powerful narrative of self-transformation from petty hustler to internationally known political leader. The son of Louisa and Earl Little—a Baptist preacher active in Marcus Garvey's Universal Negro Improvement Association—Malcolm and his siblings experienced dramatic confrontations with racism from childhood. Hooded Klansmen burned their home in Lansing, Michigan; Earl Little was killed under mysterious circumstances; welfare agencies split up the children and eventually had Louisa Little committed to a state mental institution; and Malcolm was forced to live in a detention home run by a racist white couple. By the eighth grade he left school, moved to Boston to live with his half-sister Ella, and discovered the underground world of African American hipsters.

Malcolm's entry into the masculine culture of the zoot suit, the "conked" (straightened) hair, and the lindy hop, coincided with the outbreak of World War II, rising black militancy (symbolized in part by A. Philip Randolph's threatened march on Washington for racial and economic justice), and outbreaks of race riots in Detroit and other cities. Malcolm and his partners did not seem very "political" at the time, but they dodged the draft so as not to lose their lives over a "white man's war," and they avoided wage work whenever possible. His search for leisure and pleasure took him to Harlem, where petty hustling, drug dealing, pimping, gambling, and viciously exploiting women became his primary source of income. In 1946 his luck ran out; he was arrested for burglary and sentenced to ten years in prison.

Malcolm's downward descent took a U-turn in prison when he began studying the teachings of the Lost-Found Nation of Islam (NOI), the black Muslim group founded by Wallace Fard and led by ELIJAH MUHAMMAD (Elijah Poole). Submitting to the discipline and guidance of the NOI, he became a voracious reader of the Koran and the Bible. He also immersed himself in works of literature and history at the prison library. Behind prison walls he quickly emerged as a powerful orator and brilliant rhetorician. He led the famous prison debating team that beat MIT, arguing against capital punishment by pointing out that English pickpockets often did their best work at public hangings! Upon his release in 1952, he was renamed Malcolm "X," symbolically repudiating the "white man's name."

As a devoted follower of Elijah Muhammad, Malcolm X rose quickly within the NOI ranks, serving as minister of Harlem's Temple no. 7 in 1954, and later ministering temples in Detroit and Philadelphia. Through national speaking engagements, television appearances, and by establishing *Muhammad Speaks*—the NOI's first nationally distributed newspaper—Malcolm X put the Nation of Islam on the map. His sharp criticisms of CIVIL RIGHTS leaders for advocating integration into white society instead of building black institutions and defending themselves from racist violence generated opposition from both conservatives and liberals. He was called "violent," "fascist," and "racist" by his opponents. To those who claimed that the NOI undermined their efforts toward integration by preaching racial separatism, Malcolm responded: "It is not integration that Negroes in America want, it is human dignity."

Distinguishing Malcolm's early political and intellectual views from the teachings of Elijah Muhammad is not a simple matter. His role as minister was to preach the gospel of Islam according to Elijah. He remained a staunch devotee of the the Nation's strict moral codes and gender conventions. Although his own narrative suggests that he never entirely discarded his hustler's distrust of women, he married Betty Shabazz in 1958 and lived by NOI rules: men must lead, women must follow; the man's domain is the world, the woman's is the home.

On other issues, however, Malcolm showed signs of independence from the NOI line. During the mid-1950s, for example, he privately scoffed at Muhammad's interpretation of the genesis of the "white race" and seemed uncomfortable with the idea that all white people were literally devils. He was always careful to preface his remarks with "the honorable Elijah Muhammad teaches . . ." More significantly, Malcolm clearly disagreed with the NOI's policy of not participating in politics. He not only believed that political mobilization was indispensable but occasionally defied the rule by supporting boycotts and other forms of protest. In 1962, before he split with the NOI, Malcolm shared the podium with black, white, and Puerto Rican labor organizers in the left-wing, multiracial hospital workers union in New York. He also began developing an independent pan-Africanist, and in some respects "Third World," political perspective during the 1950s, when anticolonial wars and decolonization were pressing public issues. As early as 1954, Malcolm gave a speech comparing the situation in Vietnam with that of the

Mau Mau rebellion in colonial Kenya, framing both of these movements as uprisings of the "darker races" creating a "tidal wave" against U.S. and European imperialism. Indeed, Africa remained his primary political interest outside of black America. He toured Egypt, Sudan, Nigeria, and Ghana in 1959, well before his famous trip to Africa and the Middle East in 1964.

Although Malcolm tried to conceal his differences with Elijah Muhammad, tensions between them erupted. They were exacerbated by the threat Malcolm's popularity posed to Muhammad's leadership, and by Malcolm's disillusionment with Elijah upon learning that the NOI's moral and spiritual leader had fathered children by two former secretaries. The tensions became publicly visible when Muhammad silenced Malcolm for remarking after the assassination of President John F. Kennedy that it was a case of the "chickens coming home to roost." (Malcolm's point was that the federal government's inaction toward racist violence in the South had come back to strike the President.) When Malcolm learned that Muhammad had planned to have him assassinated, he decided to leave the NOI. In March 1964, he announced his resignation and formed the Muslim Mosque, Inc., an Islamic movement devoted to working in the political sphere and cooperating with civil rights leaders. That same year he made his first pilgrimage to Mecca and took a second tour of several African and Arab nations. The trip was apparently transformative. Upon his return he renamed himself El-Hajj-Malik El-Shabazz, adopted Sunni Islam, and announced that he had found the "true brotherhood" of man. He declared that he no longer considered whites to be devils, though he still remained a black nationalist and staunch believer in black self-determination and self-organization.

During the summer of 1964 he formed the Organization of Afro-American Unity. Inspired by the Organization of African Unity made up of independent African states, the OAAU's program combined advocacy for independent black institutions (such as schools and cultural centers) with support for black participation in mainstream politics, including electoral campaigns. Following the example of Paul Robeson and w. e. b. Du Bois, Malcolm planned in 1965 to submit to the United Nations a petition that documented human rights violations and acts of genocide against African Americans. His assassination, carried out by gunmen affiliated with the NOI, intervened, and the OAAU died soon after Malcolm was laid to rest.

Although Malcolm left no real institutional legacy, he did exert a notable impact on the civil rights movement in the last year of his life. Black activists in the Congress on Racial Equality and the Student Non-Violent Coordinating Committee who had heard him speak to organizers in Selma in February 1965 began to support some of his ideas, especially on armed self-defense, racial pride, and the creation of black-run institutions. He also gained a small following of radical Marxists, mostly Trotskyists in the Socialist Workers Party. Malcolm convinced some SWP members of the revolutionary potential of ordinary black slumdwellers, and he began to speak more critically of capitalism. Was Malcolm about to become a civil rights leader? Could he have launched a successful pan-Africanist movement? Was he turning toward Marxism? Scholars and activists have debated these issues, but no firm answers are possible.

Ironically, Malcolm made a bigger impact on black politics and culture dead than alive. The Watts rebellion occurred and the Black Power movement emerged just months after his death, and his ideas about community control, African liberation, and self-pride became extremely influential. His autobiography with Alex Haley became a movement standard. Malcolm's life story proved to the Black Panther Party, founded in 1966, that ex-criminals and hustlers can be turned into revolutionaries. And arguments in favor of armed self-defense—certainly not a new idea in African American communities—were renewed by Malcolm's narrative and the publication of his speeches. Even after the death of Martin Luther King Jr., when the civil rights leader was celebrated as an American hero by many blacks and whites, Malcolm's image loomed much larger in inner city communities, especially among young males.

Despite the collapse or destruction of black nationalist organizations during the mid-1970s, Malcolm X continued to live through the folklore of submerged black urban youth cultures, making a huge comeback thanks to hip-hop music, tiny black-oriented bookstores, and Afrocentric street vendors. The 1980s were a ripe moment for a hero like Malcolm X, as racism on college campuses increased, inner cities deteriorated, police brutality cases seemed to rise again, and young black males came to be seen as an "endangered species." Malcolm's uncompromising statements about racism, self-hatred, community empowerment, and his background as a "ghetto youth," made him the undisputed icon of the young. (*See also* YOUTH.)

The recirculation of Malcolm as icon during the late 1980s and 1990s got its biggest boost from the commercial marketplace, as retailers, publishers and Hollywood cashed in on the popularity of hip-hop music and culture. And as Afrocentrism achieved respectability among black urban (and suburban) professionals, Malcolm's face and name became a central staple among the "Afro-chic" products that made up their casual attire. The rush to purchase "X" paraphernalia affected not only African Americans but suburban whites, Latinos, and Asian Americans fascinated with black youth cultures. Ad agencies boldly marketed "X" products to "the 'X' generation" without even mentioning Malcolm. "Malcolmania" reached its high point with the release of Spike Lee's cinematic rendering of Malcolm's autobiography in 1992. Following Lee's lead, retailers sold millions of dollars worth of "X" caps, T-shirts, medallions, and posters emblazoned with Malcolm's name, body, or words.

Not surprisingly, the selling of Malcolm X in the 1990s generated pointed debate among African Americans. Some argued that marketing Malcolm undermined his message, while others insisted that the circulation of his image has prompted young people to search out his ideas. Some utilized his stress on black community development to support a new African American entrepreneurialism, while others insisted on seeing him as a radical democrat devoted to social justice. His anti-imperialism has dropped out of public memory, whereas his misogyny has been ignored by his supporters and spotlighted by his detractors. However these disputes evolve, it appears that Malcolm X's place in U.S. history, and in the collective memory of African Americans, is secure. Ironically, some of his centrality can be attributed to the mutability of his own viewpoint. Because his ideas were constantly being renewed and rethought during his short career, Malcolm has become a sort of tabula rasa on which people of different positions write their own interpretation of his politics and legacy. Chuck D of the rap group Public Enemy and Supreme Court Justice Clarence Thomas can both declare Malcolm X their hero.

ROBIN D. G. KELLEY

FURTHER READING

James Cone, *Martin and Malcolm and America: a Dream or Nightmare* (Maryknoll, N.Y.: Orbis, 1991).
Ferrucio Gambino, "The Transgression of a Laborer: Malcolm X in the Wilderness of America," *Radical History Review* 55 (winter 1993): 7–31.
Malcolm X, with Alex Haley, *The Autobiography of Malcolm X* (New York: Grove, 1964).
Bruce Perry, *Malcolm: the Life of a Man Who Changed Black America* (Barrytown, N.Y.: Station Hill, 1991).
Eugene Victor Wolfenstein, *The Victims of Democracy: Malcolm X and the Black Revolution* (Berkeley: University of California Press, 1981).
Joe Wood, ed., *Malcolm X: In Our Own Image* (New York: St. Martin's, 1992).

managerialism Both an assertive worldview and an uneasy claim to social authority, managerialism took shape early in the twentieth century in recognition of the sudden emergence of "white collar" men and women situated somewhere between the older populations of capitalists and workers. Salaried, technical, college-trained, and vital to a burgeoning corporate capitalism, these new technocrats promised to recast American life in terms of a new religion of science, productivity, and Progress. They dedicated their lives to the propagation of an organizational faith, one in which the meaning and shape of planning, technical expertise, and efficiency remained to be worked out, but in which their own ultimate role in guaranteeing mass abundance was not in doubt.

Such a self-conscious sense of managerial destiny soon animated the rise of the scientific management movement, collegiate business education, and the fields of public administration, personnel management, industrial psychology, and institutional economics. More, by the 1920s the managerial romance had spilled over national borders to take its place as one of the century's organizing principles. Visions of a world made abundant through Technology and the intervention of technical elites animated the thinking of novelists and revolutionaries, as well as engineers and businessmen. Lenin, H. G. Wells, and Herbert Hoover were among its acolytes. And much that has been built in the name of socialist as well as capitalist Progress owes to the aggressive managerial utopianism they and others embraced.

Proponents and critics of the managerial idea have enjoyed a long run in American social thought. From Thorstein Veblen through C. Wright Mills, and from Adolf Berle through John Kenneth Galbraith, the nature of the manager and his relation to capitalism has been a continual source of debate. Veblen gave first shape and lasting impetus to this argument with his scathing appraisal of the cleavage between businessmen and managers, between those who organize their enterprises to make money and those whose training and spirit drives them to make useful things. He was among the first to indicate the inherent conflict between the manager's dedication to economies of scale, mass production, and consumption, and the businessman's willingness to "sabotage" productivity in pursuit of profit.

Frederick Taylor and the scientific management movement that would bear his name built upon Veblen's favorable view of the new manager. In their hands, the managerial gospel turned decidedly toward social redemption as it posited the manager as the key agent in establishing harmonious class relations. It was in the interests of both workers and owners, converts to TAYLORISM argued from 1910 on, to cede industrial authority to those technically trained and spiritually disposed to seek efficiencies of production sufficient to provide both rising wages and profits. In the bargain, managers could portray themselves as disinterested social arbiters deserving of a respected place at the national table. And following the wide promotion of these notions from 1917 through 1923, the idea that a New Capitalism had emerged, one whose prosperity depended upon managerial intervention between owners and workers, became a commonplace of the 1920s.

Managerialism's impact was compounded early in the 1930s by the discovery that recent structural changes apparently had placed capitalism's fate more firmly within managerial hands. Widespread public ownership of corporate securities, argued Adolf Berle and Gardiner Means, had sundered the historic ties between property and power. Having been widely dispersed, ownership allegedly was losing effective control of large enterprises, whose day-to-day operations were now in the hands of the salaried managers. Increasingly, this "managerial revolution" was viewed as a good thing. Beholden to the superior values of science and blessed with a wide social vision, America's managers were now in a position to build a more rational and abundant society. This was the vision that Berle, Edward Mason, Galbraith, and others would elaborate well into the 1960s.

The enforced scarcities of the Great Depression and World War II, however, were bound to provoke a skeptical view of such claims, and the progress of managerialism in the postwar era revolved around arguments over the "revolutionary" extent of the managers' ascension, and the extent of the divorce between ownership and control. Radical critics Ferdinand Lundberg, C. Wright Mills, and G. William Domhoff, among others, viewed managerialism as an exaggeration, a smokescreen obscuring ruling-class domination of an allegedly pluralist society. Most great fortunes and founding families had never relinquished control of their enterprises, they argued, and even where managers did hold sway they, too, tended to hold large ownership stakes. By the late 1960s, in any case, the idea of a managerial revolution and the utopian gospel of managerialism upon which it was based had lost whatever explanatory or moral capacity they had once enjoyed. Even Galbraith's attempt to revive the idea through an analysis of the "technostructure" of modern capitalism sounded oddly quaint.

That this was so derived in no small measure from the accretion of doubt that increasingly hung over the larger culture of expertise after World War II. By the 1960s, a growing awareness of poverty's persistence, of the mounting public cost of environmental "externalities," and the large role of former academic and business managers in the creation and prosecution of the Vietnam War all had a corrosive effect on the hope that was always crucial to managerialism. Whether representing a resurgence of common sense, or a dangerous descent into a "crisis of authority," a sobering skepticism wore against the American faith in "progress" throughout the 1970s and 1980s. And one of the first, perhaps fatal, casualties was the capacity to take seriously the claims to transcendent authority of experts and managers.

GUY ALCHON

FURTHER READING

Adolf Berle and Gardiner Means, *The Modern Corporation and Private Property* (New York: Macmillan, 1933).

J. Kenneth Galbraith, *The New Industrial State* (Boston: Houghton-Mifflin, 1971).

C. Wright Mills, *White Collar* (New York: Oxford University Press, 1951).

——, *The Power Elite* (New York: Oxford University Press, 1956).

Daniel Nelson, ed., *A Mental Revolution: Scientific Management after Taylor* (Columbus: Ohio State University Press, 1992).

Thorstein Veblen, *The Theory of Business Enterprise* (New York: Charles Scribner's Sons, 1904).

——, *The Engineers and the Price System* (New York: B. W. Huebsch, 1921).

Olivier Zunz, *Making America Corporate, 1870–1920* (Chicago: University of Chicago Press, 1990).

Mann, Horace (b. Franklin, Mass., May 4, 1796; d. Yellow Springs, Ohio, Aug. 2, 1859).   Reformer. A central figure in the common school movement, Mann was at the storm center of debates between those who hoped public schools would guarantee civic VIRTUE and those who feared state-sponsored autocracy. He was opposed by contemporaries who viewed universal public EDUCATION as money wasted on the rabble, and by champions of local autonomy who feared the homogenizing effects of state-run education. In 1838, during his tenure as secretary of the newly formed Massachusetts Board of Education, Mann founded the *Common School Journal* as an organ for reformers' ideas. His *Lectures on Education* (1848) and *A Few Thoughts for a Young Man* (1850) preached universal public education as the only means to transform America's disorderly masses into a disciplined, judicious republican citizenry, thereby removing the dangers of anarchy and class warfare.

FURTHER READING

Jonathan Messerli, *Horace Mann: a Biography* (New York: Knopf, 1972).

Marcuse, Herbert (b. Berlin, Germany, July 19, 1898; d. Starnberg, Germany, July 29, 1979). The circumstances that enabled Marcuse, born into an upper-middle-class Jewish German home, to occupy a place in an account of American thought were created by the Nazi seizure of power in 1933. That event forced into exile the members—Marcuse among them—of the small, highly unorthodox Marxist think tank, the Institute for Social Research. Organized in the mid-1920s, it was affiliated with the university in Frankfurt-am-Main, and would become known in discussions of social theory as the FRANKFURT SCHOOL. After brief sojourns in Geneva and Paris, the Frankfurt producers of "critical theory" settled in the United States in the mid-1930s. Supported by Columbia University, the Institute for Social Research reopened on Manhattan's Upper West Side, from which vantage point its associates examined fascism, war, mass murder, anti-Semitism, Stalinism, Marxism, America, and what the institute's director, Max Horkheimer, termed the eclipse of reason. Unlike most of his associates, who returned to their native Germany after the war's end, Marcuse remained in the United States. He would be the decisive, if not the only, importer of critical theory.

In the late 1960s a remarkable linkage was forged between Marcuse's writings and the explosive youth movements of that decade. Many observers spoke of Marcuse as the guru of the NEW LEFT. While his public, political visibility was sudden, his impact on American intellectual life had already been considerable. Indeed, his ties to the 1960s movements were mediated in part by people who had been students in his own classes during the previous decade. Marcuse taught for several years at Columbia, then for more than a decade, beginning in the early 1950s, at Brandeis University, and finally, from the late 1960s through the mid-1970s, at the University of California at San Diego.

Marcuse was not a system-creating or school-generating intellectual. Always an admirer of Nietzsche, as well as of Hegel, he neither had nor sought disciples. In the late 1960s, however, he certainly found plenty of admirers. In 1968–9, Marcuse was denounced by both Soviet ideologues and the Vatican as the intellectual progenitor of the youth revolts of that year. He was discussed as such in *Time* and *Newsweek*. Student demonstrations in Europe did include placards reading "Marx, Mao, Marcuse" and, both there and in America, the elderly philosopher addressed a number of mass meetings of young radicals who were notoriously wary of anyone over 30. Although notions of his pied piper status are among the (not ineffective) myths of the sixties, they are also indicators of a real Marcusean moment in recent history. That, however, is different from scholarly or general intellectual influence.

Marcuse affected American intellectuals in a wide range of fields. His impact was largely concentrated among members of the generation that came of age in the 1960s. In that cohort, he had students (see the writings of Jeremy J. Shapiro, William Leiss, and Andrew Feenberg), and inspired much social theory and criticism (Russell Jacoby's work; the studies of American consumerism by Elizabeth and Stuart Ewen). He was also of great interest to such feminist critics as Jessica Benjamin and Margaret Cerullo, and, in the late 1960s and early 1970s, to theorists (Dennis Altman, most notably) of the emergent gay liberation movement. The New Left journal *Telos*, founded in 1968, published the first English translations of Marcuse's essays from the late 1920s and early 1930s, and nearly every issue of this quarterly publication contained some discussion of his work.

These samples of Marcuse's influence, however, are themselves pieces of the sixties. In his writings, which were not necessarily studied with care or even read, but which took on a certain political-cultural glow, the New Left found coherent expression of some of its own deepest impulses. Central here was the critique not only of capitalism, but of technological rationality itself; a critique of capitalism not only for failing to deliver the goods, but for succeeding. This was a major component of Marcuse's *One-Dimensional Man* (1964), the work that clinched the link between Marcuse and the student movement. Some saw irony in this: just when Marcuse had claimed that "advanced industrial society" had foreclosed critique and rebellion by literally consuming that dimension of human experience—imagination—on which the realization of a good life depended, America was awash with criticism and revolt. Actually, Marcuse's analysis anticipated the rejuvenation of critical imagination; indeed, it participated in it.

The elective affinities between his thinking and the student movement were also visible in their common focus on the sexual-moral components of both domination and emancipation, their common conviction that revolution must be for pleasure as well as for justice, a theme developed in what may be Marcuse's finest work, *Eros and Civilization: a Philosophical Inquiry into Freud* (1955). (*See also* FREUDIANISM.)

Like the student movement and the New Left in particular, Marcuse was preoccupied with culture, consciousness, and aesthetics as vital dimensions of revolution. (*See also* CULTURAL CRITICISM.) This impulse was present in Marcuse's earliest writings in Germany and was central in his first (and still influential) American publication, *Reason and Revolution: Hegel and the Rise of Social Theory* (1941). Against those who saw Hegel as a philosophical godfather of fascism, Marcuse presented the Hegelian dialectic as the lifeblood of Marx's revolutionary humanism, an argument aimed also at Marxists of the positivistic and mechanistic sort. In 1958, *Soviet Marxism: a Critical Analysis* turned that latter critique on the social contradictions underlying the conundrums of official Marxist ideology in the Soviet Union. It enabled New Leftists to refine their own opposition to Stalinist forms of Marxism.

Pessimism is a notorious feature of Marcuse's work. It is, however, part of an unquenchable will to criticism and, moreover, often appears in the presence of unabashed utopianism. This seemingly paradoxical sensibility is another of the strands linking Marcuse and the student movement. His "Repressive Tolerance" (1965), which troubled many of his admirers, extends the arguments of *One-Dimensional Man* into a criticism of the prevailing notion of tolerance as one that, in practice, erases the idea of a truth beyond the established power structure and thus fortifies that structure. The essay's defense of revolutionary violence and of intolerance toward fascistic and racist ideas played a role in the thinking of some of the violent and cultic currents that emerged from the student movement at the turn of the 1960s.

An Essay on Liberation (1969), which highlighted Marcuse's enthusiasm for a gentler politics than that evoked in "Repressive Tolerance," reflected the ecstasies of 1968 and is among the finest documents of that moment. *Counter-Revolution and Revolt* (1972) is a more sober reflection. Although combative, it returns to the bleaker themes of *One-Dimensional Man*, highlighting the power of what Marcuse liked to call the given and the limits of efforts to transform it.

Prior to the 1960s, he was accustomed to the intellectual and political margins. That was his situation in the late 1920s and early 1930s, for example, when he sought, nearly two decades before Jean-Paul Sartre, to put Marxist theory into conversation with Martin Heidegger's *Being and Time* (1927). Marginality was also a feature, indeed it was an enlivening principle, of the Frankfurt School's Hegelian-Marxist critical theory, of which Marcuse became a practitioner in 1932. As his writings of the 1940s and 1950s make clear, Marcuse was also an eccentric thinker in relation to socialism, and to Marxism in particular.

Those writings, especially *Eros and Civilization*, can now be seen as substantial pieces of the intellectual prehistory of the 1960s New Left, joining in that regard such works as Norman Brown's *Life Against Death* (1955), Paul Goodman's *Growing Up Absurd* (1960), the English translation of Simone de Beauvoir's *The Second Sex* (1953), the writings of c. WRIGHT MILLS, Beatniks, rock 'n' roll music, the early civil rights movement, and so forth. All initially marginal, these texts and social-cultural currents were elements of unsettlingly novel forces-in-formation that would burst on to center stage in the 1960s.

Since the mid-1970s, discussions of Marcuse's ideas have appeared more and more infrequently. His last book, *The Aesthetic Dimension* (1978), which displays the Romantic sensibility that marked his first writings in Weimar Germany, marked a turn away from the social theorizing that had engaged him for decades. Only in aesthetic pursuits, he suggested, could one-dimensionality be transcended.

The Aesthetic Dimension elicited little response. In addition to the New Left's dissolution, and the Reagan era generally, poststructuralist criticism of "master narrative" radicalism, which Marcuse is said to have represented, has helped to push his ideas onto far more impacted margins than those of the 1950s. As the younger intellectuals he inspired two-and-a-half decades ago enter late middle age, there are signs that reappraisals of his work are in the offing. Of a Marcuse renaissance, however, there seems little prospect.

PAUL BREINES

FURTHER READING

John Bokina and Timothy J. Lukes, eds., *Marcuse Revisited* (Lawrence: Kansas University Press, 1994).

Paul Breines, ed., *Critical Interruptions: New Left Perspectives on Herbert Marcuse* (New York: Herder and Herder, 1970).

Barry Katz, *Herbert Marcuse: Art of Liberation* (London: Verso, 1982).

Douglas Kellner, *Herbert Marcuse and the Crisis of Marxism* (Berkeley: University of California Press, 1984).

Sidney Lipshires, *Herbert Marcuse: From Marx to Freud and Beyond* (Cambridge: Schenkmann, 1974).

Paul Robinson, *The Freudian Left: Wilhelm Reich, Geza Roheim, Herbert Marcuse* (New York: Harper and Row, 1969).

Morton Schoolman, *Imaginary Witness: the Critical Theory of Herbert Marcuse* (New York: Free Press, 1980).

Kurt H. Wolff and Barrington Moore, eds., *The Critical Imagination: Essays in Honor of Herbert Marcuse* (Boston: Beacon, 1967).

Marshall, John (b. near Germantown, Va., Sept. 24, 1755; d. Philadelphia, Pa., July 6, 1835). Federalist, Virginia legislator, diplomat, Secretary of State, and author of a *Life of George Washington*, John Marshall is best known as Chief Justice and eponym of the United States Supreme Court from 1801 to 1835. Edward Corwin labeled Marshall the founder of "the American system of constitutional law." He earned that designation as the principal architect of the sacred triumvirate of American constitutionalism: judicial review, vested rights, and federalism.

Appointed by President JOHN ADAMS in 1801, Marshall took the position of Chief Justice, a position traded by John Jay for the New York governorship, and molded it into a seat of unprecedented national influence and power. Marshall abandoned the traditional practice of seriatim opinions, prodding the Court to speak decisively with a single voice (Marshall's in half of the opinions during his tenure). For the next 34 years, that voice articulated a series of authoritative pronouncements on judicial power, property rights, and national supremacy.

In *Marbury v. Madison* (1803) and *Cohens v. Virginia* (1821), Marshall established the Supreme Court as the ultimate arbiter and interpreter of the CONSTITUTION with power to declare Acts of Congress and state legislatures unconstitutional. Marshall's contract clause decisions *Fletcher v. Peck* (1810), *Dartmouth College v. Woodward* (1819) and *Sturges v. Crowninshield* (1819) presaged modern notions of substantive due process by prohibiting states from interfering with vested property and contract RIGHTS. *Dartmouth College* is sometimes seen as Marshall's paean to liberal individualism and (quite anachronistically) corporate capitalism. Finally, in *McCulloch v. Maryland* (1819) and *Gibbons v. Ogden* (1824), Marshall adopted an expansive view of the powers of the federal government and fashioned the commerce clause into a negative check on state legislative intrusions on interstate trade. *McCulloch* is also the *locus classicus* of the notion of a "living" constitution adapted by judicial interpretation to changing conditions. As Marshall put it, "We must never forget that it is a *constitution* we are expounding." Taken together, a strong argument can be made that these opinions were nothing less than the legal prerequisites for a national capitalist economy, a strong Union (prior to the constitutional sabotage of the Taney Court), and a government of laws not men. Hence Marshall's status as a national icon.

Despite an air of consensus about the Marshall Court that has made this litany of "great cases" standard fare for history textbooks, modern assessments of the meaning and significance of John Marshall's jurisprudence have been uneven. On "Marshall Day" in 1901, OLIVER WENDELL HOLMES JR. could muster only the veiled compliment that Marshall's greatness consisted "in his being there" at an opportune moment in history. Holmes extolled Marshall's importance as a national symbol by comparing him to the flag, a simultaneously exuberant and critical image

that reflected Holmes's restrained enthusiasm for Marshall's law.

A survey of the multiple uses made of Marshall's legacy by subsequent judges and scholars validates Holmes's impression of a Marshall perhaps more acted upon than acting. Marshall's reputation soared with the "cult of Constitution" that followed the Civil War. His "nationalist" opinions meshed well with the Fourteenth Amendment and helped brand the states' rights constitutionalism of ROGER TANEY and JOHN C. CALHOUN as aberrant. Since then Marshall has been called both a conservative and a revolutionist. In an effort to reform Court and Constitution, progressives emphasized Marshall's Federalism, property-consciousness, and "landedness" in portraying him as a defender of moneyed interests against a more democratic Jeffersonianism. In *United States v. Darby* (1941), by contrast, Justice Stone summoned Marshall to legitimate the New Deal. Advocates of both judicial activism and judicial restraint have likewise invoked the Marshall mantle. For decades, constitutional historians described Marshall's political philosophy as fundamentally Lockean. With the recent historical revival of classical republicanism and Machiavellian civic humanism, G. Edward White has reinterpreted Marshall again to yield a modicum of concern for public virtue and citizenship.

These shifting sands of scholarly and public opinion leave legal historians (like Justice Holmes) a bit uneasy. Marshall's cultural significance as the symbol of American constitutionalism has produced extraordinary histories similar to the kind that have grown up around the French Revolution and the American Civil War. Such histories often have much more to do with the needs, aspirations, and rationalizations of a given author or era than the subjects they purport to depict.

To get beyond this iconographic historiography, historians must begin to appraise John Marshall's constitutional achievement from a wider and more realistic perspective. A survey of early American regulatory legislation, for example, casts doubt on the overarching significance of Marshall's contract clause as a bulwark of vested property rights. Similarly, Marshall's commerce-inspired nationalism is qualified when his more ordinary utterances on state power, internal police, and eminent domain are exhumed from cases like *Brown v. Maryland* (1827), *Willson v. Blackbird Creek Marsh Co.* (1829), and *Barron v. Baltimore* (1833). One may legitimately wonder, "Why all the fuss about *Dartmouth College*?" when it is learned that state legislatures routinely reserved the power to amend subsequent corporate charters. Investigations of these more ordinary, usual, and timely aspects of Marshall's jurisprudence may help temper some extraordinary, unusual, and presentist interpretations. No one questions the long-term significance of *Marbury v. Madison*, but a better historical perspective is obtained by remembering that no other Act of Congress fell victim to judicial review until *Dred Scott*.

The isolation of Marshall's constitutionalism from the rest of early American Law has only exacerbated a tendency to view his jurisprudence as exceptional and the product of extralegal factors, such as Federalist politics, economic interests, or transatlantic political philosophies. But the power of the Marshall Court in the early nineteenth century (as opposed to its power in the Gilded Age and Progressive and New Deal eras) lay squarely in its commensurability with contemporaneous trends in American law and legislation. Only when we have succeeded in holding Marshall's jurisprudence in proper legal and historical context can we hope to replace the John Marshall of present Mythology—a Marshall stymying redistributive legislatures, counterfeiting American nationalism, and inventing judicial supremacy —with the historical John Marshall.

WILLIAM J. NOVAK

FURTHER READING
Albert J. Beveridge, *The Life of John Marshall*, 4 vols. (Boston: Houghton Mifflin, 1916–19).
Edward S. Corwin, *John Marshall and the Constitution* (New Haven: Yale University Press, 1919).
Philip B. Kurland, ed., *James Bradley Thayer, Oliver Wendell Holmes, and Felix Frankfurter on John Marshall* (Chicago: Chicago University Press, 1967).
Max Lerner, "John Marshall and the Campaign of History," *Columbia Law Review* 39 (1939): 396–431.
R. Kent Newmyer, *The Supreme Court under Marshall and Taney* (Arlington Heights, Ill.: Harlan Davidson, 1968).
William J. Novak, *Salus Populi: American Law and the Well-Regulated Society, 1787–1877* (Chapel Hill: University of North Carolina Press, forthcoming).
G. Edward White, *The Marshall Court and Cultural Change, 1915–1935* (New York: Oxford University Press, 1990).

Marshall, Thurgood (b. Baltimore, Md., July 2, 1908; d. Bethesda, Md., Jan. 24, 1993). Supreme Court Justice (1967–91). As legal counsel to the National Association for the Advancement of Colored People, Marshall insisted that the Constitution already guaranteed blacks full CIVIL RIGHTS and must be enforced even against community opinion. Arguing the famous case *Brown v. Board of Education of Topeka* before the Court in 1954, he developed a psychosocial argument that schools cannot be "separate but equal"—the mandate of *Plessy v. Ferguson* (1896)—since separate schools instill a sense of inferiority in black children. After his appointment to the Supreme Court, Marshall became known as a liberal activist for his support of defendants' rights, affirmative action, abortion access, freedom of speech, and freedom of private sexual behavior.

FURTHER READING
Mark V. Tushnet, *Making Civil Rights Law: Thurgood Marshall and the Supreme Court, 1936–1961* (New York: Oxford University Press, 1994).

masculinity Until recently, masculinity as a category of being has not found itself the topic of widespread cultural or critical inquiry. Not that men and women have failed to write about it; they have. But it has not garnered the status of enigma, has not been posited as the kind of enticing riddle that could provoke psychoanalysts, poets, and others to endlessly ponder it as they have the nature and meaning of FEMININITY. Instead, masculinity has most often existed as though its construction and social function were transparent, indeed quite simple and commonplace. But upon closer inspection, masculinity actually appears terribly remote, almost inaccessible for exposition. Because it is shielded from sexual specificity through its ability to ventriloquize the universal, masculinity remains seriously obscure within the linguistic and philosophical humanism that casts it as the generic myth of "man." To remove the generic fallacy, to unveil masculinity as a particularized ontology: this is the task that FEMINISM in recent years has pursued as a necessary political intervention.

But such an undertaking has not been without its detractors, as the turn toward examining masculinity carries with it a decided rearticulation of earlier feminist assumptions. In the first, heady decade of the contemporary women's movement, for instance, masculinity often assumed an undifferentiated position alongside concepts such as patriarchy, oppression, and the common enemy. Its fuzzy collapse into a generalized "man" and the wholesale melding of men with the organizational practices and privileges of patriarchy had a way of unproblematically linking maleness, men, and the social order of masculine supremacy. The most sustained critique of this homogenization of cultural power came from feminists of color who repeatedly demonstrated the inaccuracy of ahistorical accounts of male domination, especially since men of nondominant races not only have been historically denied the rights and privileges accorded other men, but are often oppressed by women of the prevailing race and class as well. The monolithic assumption of a clear division of power based on sexual difference has given way to a more nuanced approach to the complexities of social power arrangements, and various theorists, male and female, have begun articulating the intricacies underwriting contemporary masculinities. (*See also* RACE and CLASS.)

A key aspect of some of the earliest approaches to the study of masculinity revolved around the meaning and significance of distinguishing between sex and GENDER. This distinction, appropriated from academic work on femininity and highlighting the difference between biology and culture, enabled scholars to cite masculinity as the complicated process of social scripting through which inhabitants of male bodies (sex) were transformed into masculine beings (gender). Through this process, masculine subjectivity emerged as the culmination of the male's engendering in cultural practices and institutional relations, a psychological interiorization of the way maleness was narrated. By studying masculinity as the narrativization of the male body that had deep psychological implications, the movement from sex to gender could be understood as a complex act of translation: here, the body's specificity (its possession of a penis) was the precondition for masculinity's articulation, and underwrote the seemingly universal status accorded to man by the patriarchal logic of masculine supremacy. (*See also* FREUDIANISM.) In this regard, anatomy did become destiny as masculine power legitimated itself by returning to the seemingly natural origin of the BODY. By forging the distinction between sex and gender, however, scholars sought to disrupt this corporeal foundationalism, calling into question any assumption of bodily essence by framing masculinity as social construction.

But the distinction between sex and gender fails to take into account the social constructionism through which the male body is itself crafted as male, cast as the definitive ground for masculinity's fashioning. For how can we understand the positioning of the male body as masculinity's primary referent outside of or apart from masculinity itself? As with any act of translation, the relationship between the first text and its subsequent interpretation is not finally one of original to secondary meaning. Instead, in the very process of translation, the "original" is irreducibly consumed, its meaning now contingent upon, if not replaced by, the primacy of the translation itself. In the case of sexual difference, this suggests that the seemingly original site, maleness, ultimately secures its meaning from gender and not the other way around. Sex and gender—as well as the differences they are intended to elucidate—are thus bound to the same symbolic mechanism, a mechanism that reveals the divide between biology and gender ideology as always constituted on the side of sexual difference.

But if we jettison the distinction between sex and gender in favor of an overarching social constructionism, does feminist theory once again threaten to replicate patriarchal logic by reiterating the equation between maleness and masculinity on which hierarchies of sexual difference depend? The answer to this is yes, but only if our conceptual framework for understanding masculinity cannot envision subversive or contestatory formations that undermine the normative imperatives—of heterosexuality, paternity, and soldiery, for instance—that both establish and govern the cultural meaning of maleness. For this reason, in the wake of dismantling the distinction between sex and gender, scholars have increasingly turned away from their previous emphasis on masculinity as a singular and programmatic process to conceive instead of its multiple and contradictory production. Taking "masculinities" as their object of study, those engaged with issues of sexual difference are now involved not only in tracing the various routes through which discourses of masculinity make claims on male being, but in articulating the political value of locating the contradictions and incoherencies that inevitably divide this being against itself. The fact that a singular, final, and noncontradictory masculinity is impossible to achieve becomes one of the most politically significant insights that contemporary theory can offer.

For Lynne Segal, the shift from masculinity to masculinities contains the possibility for fracturing the consolidation of male bonds that underwrites patriarchal investments in sexual difference. As she explains in *Slow Motion*, "by looking not at 'masculinity' as such, but at certain specific '*masculinities*,' it is . . . *differences* between men which [become] central to the struggle for change" (p. x). By focusing on differences in race, class, and sexuality among men, Segal is interested in disrupting the seemingly seamless relationship between maleness and masculinity on which patriarchal culture routinely depends. This disruption is made possible by establishing differences among men as the countering force to the mythology of masculine *sameness* that grants the category of maleness its most powerful social meaning. Such a mythology is in fact one of the primary ways that dominant discourses and patriarchal institutional relations hail the male into his gendered subjectivity, giving him a vision of essential sexual difference with which to resist contrary intellectual and political claims, particularly those based on race, class, and sexuality.

In her analysis of contemporary representations of the war in VIETNAM, Susan Jeffords pays particular attention to the way that sexual differences are mobilized to discount and repress the panoply of social hierarchies that organize relationships among men. Popular films and television in the past decade, she contends, repeatedly stress the significance of masculine bonds as the ideological counter to the feminizing influences of both a corrupt, betraying government and an enemy who refuses to fight, in Western parlance, "like a man." These representational formations importantly rely upon a broader cultural discourse of masculine sameness in which the heightening of differences between men and women serves as the necessary precondition for establishing a commonality of gender among men. "The masculine bond," writes Jeffords, "insists on a denial of difference—whether black or white, wealthy or poor, high school or college-educated, from north or south, men are the 'same'—at the same time that the bond itself depends for its existence on an affirmation of difference—men are not women" (pp. 59-60). In the post-Vietnam era, the strenuous reassertion of the masculine bond can best be understood as a response to the feminist, civil rights, and gay rights struggles, since these political movements quite forcefully criticized the exclusionary practices on which traditional structures of power were built.

In reaffirming men's difference from women, dominant discourses in the contemporary period offer to men a narrative of power, privilege, and exclusivity based on the singular and seemingly irrefutable fact of maleness. This narrative not only demands and guarantees the excision of the feminine (and its representative, woman), but represses those hierarchical differences among men that might expose the race, class, and heterosexist elitism that organizes social power arrangements. From this perspective, the continued hostility toward female integration into the military seems hardly coincidental, since such hostility actually aids the process of assimilating racial, class, and religious differences among men, while constructing and emphasizing physical and emotional disparities between men and women. As the most contested site of gender's rearticulation in U.S. culture, the struggle over women's participation in warfare, according to Jeffords, brings into crisis the historical functioning of war as the exclusive scene of masculinity's performance. As she suggests, allowing women into the theater of war threatens to disrupt, at a variety of levels, this masculine arena—threatens, in short, to steal its central and most dramatic scene.

The language of theatricality and performance used here underscores the artificiality and constructedness that theorists of sexual difference have come to regard as a predominant feature of contemporary masculinity, thereby making visible the constitutional performativity of a variety of masculinities, from their dominant heterosexual forms to the more subversive gay, black, or antisexist articulations. By reading masculinity as engaged in masquerade, mimicry, and at times parody, scholars are eschewing an older formulation of masculinity as the legacy of social rites and roles that usher little boys uniformly toward "manhood." Instead, the seeming naturalness of adult masculinity—heterosexuality, FATHERHOOD, family governance, soldiery, and citizenry—must be viewed as a set of prescriptive norms that contain the potential contradictions within and between men. These norms repress the male subject's constitution along multiple lines of the social: race, class, and sexuality in addition to gender. In unleashing masculinity from its assumed normativity and reading its function and structure as one of continued performance, the new "masculinity studies" moves toward political intervention in the practices of masculine domination, while locating the possibilities for men to challenge their constitution as men.

ROBYN WIEGMAN

FURTHER READING

Rowena Chapman and Jonathon Rutherford, eds., *Male Order: Unwrapping Masculinity* (London: Lawrence and Wishart, 1988).

Jeff Hearn, *The Gender of Oppression: Men, Masculinity and the Critique of Marxism* (Brighton: Wheatsheaf, 1987).

Paul Hoch, *White Hero, Black Beast: Racism, Sexism, and the Mask of Masculinity* (London: Pluto, 1979).

Alice Jardine and Paul Smith, eds., *Men in Feminism* (New York: Methuen, 1987).

Susan Jeffords, *The Remasculinization of America: Gender and the Vietnam War* (Bloomington: Indiana University Press, 1989).

Michael Kaufman, ed., *Beyond Patriarchy* (Toronto: Oxford University Press, 1987).

Lynne Segal, *Slow Motion: Changing Masculinities, Changing Men* (New Brunswick, N.J.: Rutgers University Press, 1990).

Robert Staples, *Black Masculinity: the Black Male's Role in American Society* (San Francisco: Black Scholars' Press, 1982).

Mason, George (b. Fairfax County, Va., ca.1725; d. Fairfax County, Va., Oct. 7, 1792). Political leader. A Virginia planter and anti-Federalist, Mason shared the traditional republican view that states and nations tend to evolve toward complexity, corruption, and vice. He warned that the United States would deteriorate into a monarchy or aristocracy unless the Constitution explicitly guaranteed the people's rights. The primary author of Virginia's 1776 Declaration of Rights, Mason insisted on a federal BILL OF RIGHTS. He also opposed the compromise allowing the slave trade to continue until 1808: slavery, he believed, undermined democracy by training slaveowners in tyranny.

See also ANTI-FEDERALISTS.

FURTHER READING
Josephine F. Pacheco, ed., *The Legacy of George Mason* (Fairfax, Va.: George Mason University Press, 1983).

mass culture A phenomenon of modern industrial experience, mass culture and its artifacts include advertising, popular music and literature, radio, movies, television, and the mass spectacles of sport. In the U.S. particularly, mass culture is a matrix of technology, public opinion, and image-making that defines the public lives of most Americans. It is a national market which constructs for consumers what Amy Kaplan has called "a shared reality of both information and desire" (p. 13). The popular and commercial expressions articulated in mass culture can be seen as rhetorical navigations of this reality, and as pervasive strategies of public understanding.

The history of ideas about mass culture is a history of debates about the relative worth of technological modernity and its political ramifications. Perhaps the dominant view of mass culture among educated Americans has been one which demonizes popular/commercial expression as the most glaring aspect of "mass society"—the dehumanizing and vulgar colonization of social life by scientific rationality, standardized production techniques, and bourgeois capitalism. Ideologically useful to both right and left, this "highbrow" position has identified mass culture as the detritus of modernity that buries aesthetic and social distinctions alike.

A second view of mass culture has put more stock in the rhetorical potential of technology and the "shared reality" it might foster. Political economist SIMON PATTEN argued in *The New Basis of Civilization* (1907), for example, that mass culture helped undermine social and political inequity by standardizing public expression. The qualified valuation of "lowbrow" culture by VAN WYCK BROOKS in *America's Coming-of-Age* (1915), and Philip Johnson's *Machine Art* exhibition at the Museum of Modern Art in 1934, further exemplify a mood that arguably reached its peak at the 1939 New York World's Fair, where the marriage of commerce and mass culture was projected as the key to a better tomorrow.

Debates about "high" and "low" art, and about mass culture as a visual system, helped legitimate popular/commercial expression in American intellectual life. The most important document in these debates is "Avant-garde and Kitsch" (1939) by CLEMENT GREENBERG, the first thorough, and still one of the more perceptive, critical analyses of the subject. Greenberg claimed that in the mid-nineteenth century the industrial West produced two new cultural forms: an experimental "avant-garde" of modern art, which grew progressively alienated from and critical of its parent bourgeois class, and mass culture on kitsch, "the epitome of all that is spurious in the life of our times." Whereas avant-garde was "the only living culture we now have," kitsch was "debased," mechanical, and formulaic. Kitsch played to "vicarious experience and faked sensations"; it was the West's "deceptive" simulacrum of "genuine" cultural experience, and it had "gone on a triumphal tour of the world [to become] a universal culture, the first universal culture ever beheld" (pp. 11–14).

While Greenberg's assertions about mass culture's origins or ubiquity were rarely challenged, his judgment of its value was increasingly rejected in the postwar period. It was the phenomenon of POP art that more than anything else transformed cultural perception regarding mass production and popular/commercial expression. Since cubism at the turn of the century, modern art had permitted mass-culture images into its own visual systems, particularly in the pivotal figure of French artist Marcel Duchamp (1887–1968). Duchamp's American progeny—artists like Stuart Davis, JOHN CAGE, Robert Rauschenberg, and Jasper Johns—had an appreciation not only of the validity of popular/commercial expression, but of its depth and diversity, its aesthetic interest.

Andy Warhol completed the elision of the avant-garde/kitsch distinction by aestheticizing not only commercial form but mechanized production technique as well. For Warhol, mass culture was the only true source of modern identity, the common base of images and responses. SUSAN SONTAG wrote in the mid-1960s of a "New Sensibility" in which sensory response to all kinds of cultural expression was "experienced without condescension" (p. 303). This openness was shared by the Canadian critic Marshall McLuhan, who followed Patten in seeing mass culture and mass communication as opportunities for the reform of social relations. In McLuhan's *Understanding Media* (1964), Greenberg's insidious "universal culture" was transposed into a "global village." Likewise, Robert Venturi and his colleagues (*Learning from Las Vegas*, 1972) formulated an approach to "postmodern" architecture that accepted the vernacular of mass culture as our "natural" conceptual landscape. Looking for "popular symbols" where Greenberg had found only deception, many postmodernists elaborated Pop's appreciation of mass culture as a prime locus of creativity in late twentieth-century life. (*See also* POSTMODERNISM.)

Such enthusiasm was unpersuasive to those critics who continued to work in the tradition of "mass society" theory. For cultural conservatives like DANIEL BELL, as for the German critical theorists Theodor Adorno and Walter Benjamin, whose work became popular with young American intellectuals in the 1970s and 1980s, the productions of the "culture industry" eroded the spiritual life of the community. Mass culture was industrial pollution, wrecking "genuine" folk or native expression, homogenizing experience, and, contrary to McLuhan, destroying the "citizen" as an active, critical subject. Indeed, many critics of mass culture in the 1940s and 1950s, particularly Adorno and DWIGHT MACDONALD, emphasized the link between mass culture and totalitarianism —an argument supported by the evident philistinism of Hitler, Goebbels, Stalin, and their kind. Greenberg resisted such conspiratorial readings: to him, mass culture was at most merely *useful* to totalitarian demogogy, "another of the inexpensive ways in which totalitarian regimes seek to ingratiate themselves with their subjects" (p. 20).

Recent theorists have continued to roll back not only the conspiratorial judgment, but Greenberg's own highbrow outlook—either by positively celebrating the rich textures of popular culture, or by portraying it more neutrally as a form of public space novel to the twentieth century. At least since the marketing of World War I by the government's propaganda bureau, the Committee for Public Information, a national public sphere has been shaped by distinctively mass-cultural processes. The complexity of these processes has been stressed by scholars such as Lizabeth Cohen, who has shown how Americans adapted themselves at the local level to the nationalizing imperatives of mass culture. Twenty-first-century publicity may simply be a cybernetic overlay on this preexisting domain of image production and consumption.

PETER HANSEN

See also CARTOONING; CINEMA; MIDDLEBROW CULTURE; PUBLICITY.

FURTHER READING

Christopher Brookeman, *American Culture and Society since the 1930s* (London: Macmillan, 1984).

Lizabeth Cohen, *Making a New Deal: Industrial Workers in Chicago, 1919–1939* (New York: Cambridge University Press, 1990).

——, "The Class Experience of Mass Consumption: Workers as Consumers in Interwar America," in Richard Wightman Fox and T. J. Jackson Lears, eds., *The Power of Culture: Critical Essays in American Culture* (Chicago: University of Chicago Press, 1993).

Clement Greenberg, "Avant-Garde and Kitsch," in Greenberg, *The Collected Essays and Criticism*, vol. 1: *Perceptions and Judgments, 1939–1944*, ed. John O'Brian (Chicago: University of Chicago Press, 1986).

Amy Kaplan, *The Social Construction of American Realism* (Chicago: University of Chicago Press, 1988).

Dwight Macdonald, *The Responsibilities of Peoples, and Other Essays in Political Criticism* (1957; Westport: Greenwood, 1974).

Bernard Rosenberg and David Manning White, eds., *Mass Culture: the Popular Arts in America* (New York: Free Press, 1957).

Susan Sontag, *Against Interpretation* (New York: Farrar, Straus, Giroux, 1966).

Mather, Cotton (b. Boston, Mass., Feb. 12, 1663; d. Boston, Mass., Feb. 13, 1728).   Best known for his worst moment, this Puritan minister serves, inside and outside the academy, as the villain of the Salem witch trials. But this greatly distorted portrayal of Mather as a filiopious crank obsessively hunting the devil obscures a richly complex career. The grandson of two distinguished ministers—Richard Mather and JOHN COTTON (from whom he derives his first name)—the son of the equally distinguished INCREASE MATHER, his long life chronicles many important intellectual and political changes in the early history of the United States.

Before Salem, Mather played a prominent role in the political revolt against the royal governor in 1689. After the Restoration, Charles II reclaimed some of the privileges previously enjoyed by the New England colonies, especially the right to their own charter and the right to elect their own governor. While Increase Mather negotiated a new charter in England, Cotton helped to displace the court-appointed Edmund Andros. At this early stage of his career, Mather reached the height of his political influence. He gained prestige and respect internationally; he was awarded an honorary Doctor of Divinity from the University of Glasgow and elected a Fellow of the Royal Society in London. Events at Salem, however, irreparably damaged his reputation at home.

Although Mather did not participate in the witch trials, his writings on witchcraft contributed indirectly to the public fascination with the issue. Mather's behavior at Salem has been misrepresented largely due to a misunderstanding of cultural and intellectual contexts. For example, today we may judge his fascination with the wonders of the invisible world as an irrational preoccupation with superstition, but in his own time the boundaries between science, religion, and the supernatural were not so rigidly drawn. In fact, Mather's belief in witches—a belief he shared with the learned and unlearned both at home and abroad—followed from his interests in scientific experimentation as well as from the inexorable logic of his own faith: "Since there are Witches and Devils," he wrote, " we may conclude that there are also Immortal Souls." Moreover, Mather's behavior was motivated by genuine political and religious threats. Charter problems with the crown, inroads made by the Church of England, the looming presence of Roman Catholics in the form of the French, and conflicts with the Native Americans all indicated to Mather that a diabolical plot had been hatched against the Bay Colony. This conspiracy, however, was ultimately interpreted as part of God's plan for New England: the ordeals reaffirmed the special status of the Puritans, and signaled the millennium soon to come.

In these contexts, Mather's actions during the witch trials may be considered representative at worst and comparatively moderate at best. Mather opposed the more extreme tactics of the court, especially the use of spectral evidence (or apparitions), which he felt led to the conviction of innocent people. Moreover, he demanded extreme caution in the identification of witches because he suspected (as modern-day scholars have confirmed) that people were using the accusation of witchcraft against enemies to settle personal grievances. Nevertheless, Mather's protests extended only so far. Although he voiced serious objections, he did nothing to put an end to the trials and, in fact, urged their continuation against the wishes of many other ministers, including his own father.

The loss of respect and political influence that Mather suffered after Salem led him to pursue more vigorously two other areas of interest: science and social reform, For Mather, scientific inquiry was not in opposition to, but rather an extension of, his religion. Much like Jonathan Edwards and Ralph Waldo Emerson later, Mather thought of the study of nature as a form of worship, a way to discover and comprehend the divine order of the universe. His work in the sciences had practical benefits as well. A lifelong dedication to medicine (as a youth he had considered becoming a physician instead of a minister) culminated in his promotion of a smallpox inoculation, against widespread opposition. Moreover, he used his knowledge of natural science as a form of cultural exchange between the colonies and Europe in order to change the New World's reputation for intellectual provincialism. He proved the colonies worthy of serious scientific attention by submitting his observations to the Royal Society, and he popularized the new science in the colonies—including the Copernican view of the universe and the works of Newton —in books such as *The Christian Philosopher* (1721).

Like his interest in science, Mather's dedication to social reform is best understood as an extension of his religious beliefs rather than as a declension from the intense piety of his forefathers into a secularized moralism. Active in almost every aspect of colonial life, he advocated charity for the poor and the infirm; he founded reform groups; he formulated rules of conduct for lawyers and physicians. In works such as *A Family Well Ordered* and *Ornaments for the Daughters of Zion* he discussed the role of the family and the education of children. In other books he addressed issues such as the slave trade and the rights of Native Americans. In his programmatic—almost meddlesome—civic-mindedness, Mather recalls BENJAMIN FRANKLIN. Indeed, the two near-contemporaries did cross paths: Franklin's character, Silence Dogood, parodies—and derives her name from—Mather's *Bonifacius: Essays to Do Good.* But for Mather, good works remained an effect, never a cause, of spiritual salvation; it is Franklin's more secularized version of doing good that serves as the model for the Protestant work ethic.

Mather's masterpiece—*Magnalia Christi Americana* (1702)—has most frequently been read as the greatest jeremiad ever written: a meandering, nostalgic lament for the glory days of the Founders meant to revive the sluggish souls of the present generation. The *Magnalia* works on many other levels as well. By ranging across a wide variety of material and literary styles—from church history to sermons to biography to verse—Mather attempted once again to elevate the provincial colonies to a place of cultural and political importance. Thus, through his use of learned allusions and the epic mode, Mather located New England in the grand tradition of world history. At the same time, however, he removed PURITANISM from history altogether. The typological implications of the MISSION to the New World depicted the Puritans as a mythic chosen people, harbingers of the end of history and the beginning of the millennium. (*See also* APOCALYPTIC LITERATURE.)

Scholarship for the last two decades has concentrated on the representative role Mather plays in the formation of an American ideology. For Sacvan Bercovitch, arguably the best explicator of Mather's work, Mather serves as the *locus classicus* of an "American self" that conflates sacred and secular history, uses self-denial as a means to self-assertion, and turns personal trial into public triumph through the belief that all persecution ultimately reaffirms one's chosen status in the eyes of God. Although Mather has been the subject of some of the best critical analysis in Puritan studies, and of two outstanding biographies, much work remains to be done beyond questions of Salem and selfhood. The author of almost 400 separate titles, as well as thousands of pages of unpublished manuscript, Mather provides an entry into virtually every area of the colonial experience. Since he had so much contact with all levels of society at home and abroad, his works offer valuable insights into issues such as the development of the New World from colony to province to nation, and the relationship between the learned theology of sermons and treatises to popular practices of folklore and superstition. His works on the family and on education shed light on gender relations and the domestic scene. Finally, his writings on American Indians and on slavery—at times progressive (he denounced the slave trade), at times troubling (he advocated the extermination of unconverted Indians)—constitute some of the earliest chapters in the racial politics of the New World.

MICHAEL KAUFMANN

See also AMERICAN EXCEPTIONALISM; BIBLICAL CRITICISM.

FURTHER READING

Sacvan Bercovitch, "Cotton Mather and the Vision of America" (1972), in Bercovitch, *The Rites of Assent: Transformations in the Symbolic Construction of America* (New York: Routledge, 1993).

——, *The Puritan Origins of the American Self* (New Haven: Yale University Press, 1975).

Mitchell Breitweiser, *Cotton Mather and Benjamin Franklin: the Price of Representative Personality* (New York: Cambridge University Press, 1984).

David Levin, *Cotton Mather: the Young Life of the Lord's Remembrancer, 1663–1703* (Cambridge: Harvard University Press, 1978).

Kenneth Silverman, *The Life and Times of Cotton Mather* (1984: New York: Columbia University Press, 1985).

Mather, Increase (b. Dorchester, Mass., June 21, 1639; d. Boston, Mass., Aug. 23, 1723).   Clergyman and educator. Among the last defenders of Puritan theocracy, Mather first opposed, then endorsed, the Halfway Covenant that loosened the requirements for church membership. Called as minister to the Second Church of Boston (Old North) in 1664, he remained there for the rest of his life, and also served as president of Harvard for 15 years. In addition to works of theology, he wrote many books on politics, history, and science, a subject that interested him profoundly yet did nothing to weaken his belief in supernatural wonders. *An Essay for the Reading of Illustrious Providences* (1684) has been blamed for stimulating interest in witchcraft, but Mather was among the first to question testimony given at the Salem witch trials. He insisted in *Case of Conscience Concerning Evil Spirits Personating Men* (1693) that "spectral evidence"—the appearance of a person in disembodied form—is unreliable. Active in politics, he led protests against the revocation of the Massachusetts charter in 1688 and helped win the new

charter of 1691. His oldest son, COTTON MATHER, was among America's most distinguished Puritan divines.

See also APOCALYPTIC LITERATURE; PURITANISM.

FURTHER READING

Michael G. Hall, *The Last American Puritan: the Life of Increase Mather, 1639–1723* (Middletown, Conn.: Wesleyan University Press, 1988).

Mayhew, Jonathan (b. Martha's Vineyard, Mass., Oct. 8, 1720; d. Boston, Mass., July 9, 1766).   The outspoken Reverend Mayhew was one of the most controversial figures in colonial New England. In *Seedtime of the Republic* (1953), Clinton Rossiter called Mayhew's pulpit "the storm center of Boston theology." Probably the boldest disciple of the ENLIGHTENMENT in America, Mayhew heralded in rough voice a new day for religious and political liberty. The standing order of Puritan clergy frowned on his brash claims regarding reason and human FREEDOM, but Mayhew was undaunted. Throughout his short career, he was a vigorous preacher with a no-nonsense approach, one who embraced reason and the rights and duty of private judgment. As such, this proto-Unitarian and bold religious liberal espoused political views that helped lead toward the AMERICAN REVOLUTION. Through correspondence with English dissenters as well as through printed copies of his sermons, Jonathan Mayhew became one of the best known Americans in Britain.

Born a fifth-generation American and a descendant of Thomas Mayhew (1593–1682), the first governor of Martha's Vineyard, Jonathan was the son of a missionary preacher to American Indians. After graduating from Harvard College (1744), Mayhew became the pastor of Boston's West Church (1747), where he led a loyal congregation until his death. Young Mayhew had a mind of his own, and he expressed it without artifice. In college, he was swept up by the GREAT AWAKENING, the popular religious movement of his day. By graduation, however, he had become openly critical of the emotional excesses of the revivals and the way religious enthusiasm undermined rational thought.

Ordination brought conflict with other Boston clergy, who shied away from Mayhew's liberalism. From 1747 on, Boston's four weekly newspapers fanned the flames of controversy, and added to Mayhew's notoriety, as a way of boosting sales. The Boston Thursday Lecture provided a forum for local clergy to discourse upon points of theology too fine for weekly sermons. Despite the efforts of his friend the Rev. Charles Chauncy to secure an invitation for him, Mayhew was left out. In response, beginning in the summer of 1748, Mayhew gave his own series of lectures, on alternate Thursdays, which gave the people of Boston a chance to hear the controversial new minister of West Church. The audiences at Mayhew's lectures dwarfed those of the weekly series sponsored by the Calvinists. (It is said that Paul Revere was punished by his strict father for having gone to one of Mayhew's Thursday performances.) Printed as *Seven Sermons* (1749), these sermons show the influence of John Locke on Mayhew's thinking about the natural human right to examine all questions, despite the claim of religious creeds and traditions. His reputation grew in England as a result of these sermons, which fast became a guide to religious liberals on both sides of the Atlantic.

In theology Mayhew was Arminian, that is, on salvation he emphasized human agency more than Puritans ever could. Rather than asserting the utter dependence of the creature upon God in fear and trembling, Mayhew argued that the divine will became manifest in the power of love. For Mayhew, religious truth was to be found in the individual, where the creator had implanted the self-regulating principle of reason. This God-given gift guided human action, and so, ultimately, human reason and divine revelation harmonized. Mayhew's theology also fitted well with the political philosophy of REPUBLICANISM.

On January 30, 1750, the anniversary of the beheading of Charles I by English Puritans (a day celebrated by Anglicans as a day of martyrdom), the Reverend Mayhew composed the third sermon in a series about human liberty and the rights of people ruled by a tyrant. Throughout the English-speaking world, his provocative words rang out louder and clearer than the language of Whig political theory. In *A Discourse Concerning Unlimited Submission and Non-Resistance to the Higher Powers* (1750), Mayhew warned:

> For a nation thus abused to arise unanimously and resist their prince, even to the [point of] dethroning him, is not criminal, but a reasonable way of vindicating their liberties and just rights; it is making use of the means, and the only means, which God has put into their power for mutual and self defence. (p. 40)

This was Mayhew's finest hour. His pulpit exploded with a message that stirred the colonies 25 years before the American Revolution. In an 1818 letter to journalist Hezekiah Niles, JOHN ADAMS recalled that the sermon "was read by everybody; celebrated by friends, and abused by enemies"; Adams himself considered Mayhew a "transcendent genius." Arminian theology, a liberal view of human nature, and a republican view of society led Mayhew to

zealously oppose the Stamp Act of 1765. In fact, his sermon *Snare Broken* (1766) was so powerful that he was accused of inciting the Stamp Act riots.

Jonathan Mayhew advanced the cause of human freedom from his pulpit at West Church by opening minds, challenging deferential attitudes, and coaxing Americans toward self-government. His sermons provided religious warrant for the colonial movement toward independence. Although perhaps less profound than some of his contemporaries, his intensity was brilliant and his timing perfect.

JOHN KLOOS

See also PURITANISM.

FURTHER READING

Charles W. Akers, *Called unto Liberty: a Life of Jonathan Mayhew 1720–1766* (Cambridge: Harvard University Press, 1964).

Alden Bradford, *Memoir of the Life and Writings of Rev. Jonathan Mayhew, D.D.* (Boston, 1838).

John Corrigan, *The Hidden Balance: Religion and the Social Theories of Charles Chauncy and Jonathan Mayhew* (Cambridge: Cambridge University Press, 1987).

Jonathan Mayhew, *A Discourse Concerning Unlimited Submission and Non-Resistance to the Higher Powers* (1750; New York: Arno Press, 1969).

Conrad Wright, *The Beginnings of Unitarianism in America* (Boston: Starr King, 1955).

Mead, George Herbert (b. South Hadley, Mass., Feb. 27, 1863; d. Chicago, Ill., Apr. 26, 1931).   Born at a time when fervor for laissez-faire capitalism knew few bounds in the United States, Mead died at the dawn of the New Deal Era, when most Americans accepted government interference in the marketplace as the only way to cope with the nation's problems. This remarkable transformation owed much to the efforts of Mead, JOHN DEWEY, JANE ADDAMS, CHARLES BEARD, and other intellectuals affiliated with PROGRESSIVISM. Mead was powerfully influenced by socialist thought, to which he was exposed in Germany, where he went to study philosophy and psychology with Wilhelm Wundt. So strong was social democracy's appeal to Mead that he seriously contemplated a career as a professional reformer. Even though in the end he settled into academia, first at the University of Michigan and then at the University of Chicago, he retained a lifelong commitment to progressive causes. Whether Mead marched with Jane Addams down Michigan Avenue to show his support for women's suffrage, surveyed immigrants' homes on behalf of the Immigrants Protective League, wrote editorials on school reforms for the Chicago Educational Association, gave public support to beleaguered reformers at the University of Wisconsin, or served as community representative on strike settlement committees—he combined scholarship not only with policy analysis but with advocacy, a plural vocation still eminently respectable in the early twentieth century (*see also* OBJECTIVITY).

Mead's involvement with reforms stemmed from his perception that America had strayed from the founding fathers' ideals. THOMAS JEFFERSON envisioned a community of well-informed, politically active citizens consciously shaping their destiny under state-enforced constitutional guarantees. The reality turned out to be less benign. INDUSTRIALISM, child labor, half-literate immigrants, women excluded from the political process, a virtually nonexistent system of welfare programs, and the ever-increasing gap between wealth and poverty seemed to Mead a far cry from the DEMOCRACY celebrated by the framers of the Constitution.

While decrying the "chasm" dividing theory from practice in American democracy, Mead rejected Marxism and other forms of orthodox socialism because in his view they subordinated democracy to the search for JUSTICE. At least in the short run, leftist radicals were ready to sacrifice FREEDOM to EQUALITY. By contrast, Mead and other progressives urged that efforts to regulate the market and socialize opportunity should leave the core of civil liberties intact. Bourgeois democracy and its political institutions were essential to any lasting social reconstruction.

Mead's political writings can be seen as an attempt to accomplish the socialist humanitarian agenda by moderate constitutional means. His theory is anchored in the premise that public discourse, rather than state power and professional politicians, is central to social reconstruction. For social reforms to succeed, community members from all walks of life must contribute to public discourse. Minimal economic standards must be guaranteed so that all individuals can have the chance to exercise in fact the participatory RIGHTS promised them in theory.

Mead's political agenda found its way into his philosophical and sociological work. The philosophy of PRAGMATISM, to which Mead devoted much of his professional life, was tailormade for an age of reform. According to this creed, the world is neither fully determined nor purely chaotic; rather, it is enlivened with competing perspectives and desires brought forward by historically situated communities of purposeful beings. Human transformative activity routinely falls short of intended results, but communal actions infuse the world with meaning, and allow people to mold an indeterminate situation for the public good. Mead shared many of these insights with other progressive thinkers, most signally with his lifelong colleague and friend, JOHN DEWEY.

Together, they were responsible for articulating a sociologically grounded and radically democratic version of pragmatism that is currently experiencing a renaissance in the United States and Europe, where, owing particularly to the works of Jürgen Habermas, a concerted attempt is now being made to fuse the European project of critical theory with American pragmatism.

Mead deserves much of the credit for developing the concept of SOCIETY, seeing the social as an ontological, primordial quality permeating our universe. Sociality or the capacity to have several identities at once—each reflecting different reference frames and time passages—is at the heart of the evolutionary process in the physical, biological, and cultural worlds. Human intelligence elevates sociality to the highest plane, to a point where one can "take the role of the other," survey the situation from several perspectives simultaneously, and ultimately judge the matter at hand from the standpoint of an entire community or "generalized other." The individual self, for Mead, is a quantum of social reality, a microcosm of the social macrocosm. The self may be "inner" and inescapably "private," but it is social to the core, an embodiment of social-historical conditions (*see also* PRIVACY). This insight, which brings mind, self, and society into one continuum, transcends the dualism of classical sociology. By joining these phenomena in a single hermeneutical circle, Mead helped shape the vision of totality that has dominated much SOCIAL SCIENCE in the twentieth century. We owe especially to Mead and his progressive colleagues the perception that social reconstruction and self-reconstruction must together inform any viable theory of historical PROGRESS.

DMITRI N. SHALIN

FURTHER READING

Mitchell Aboulafia, ed., *Philosophy, Social Theory, and the Thought of George Herbert Mead* (Albany: State University of New York Press, 1991).

Andrew Feffer, *The Chicago Pragmatists and American Progressivism* (Ithaca, N.Y.: Cornell University Press, 1993).

Hans Joas, *G. H. Mead: a Contemporary Reexamination of His Thought* (Cambridge: Polity, 1985).

George Herbert Mead, *Mind, Self, and Society* (Chicago: University of Chicago Press, 1934.)

——, *Selected Writings: George Herbert Mead*, ed. A. J. Reck (New York: Bobbs-Merrill, 1964).

Dmitri N. Shalin, "G. H. Mead, Socialism, and the Progressive Agenda," *American Journal of Sociology* 93 (Jan. 1988): 913–51.

——, "Critical Theory and the Pragmatist Challenge," *American Journal of Sociology* 98 (Sept. 1992): 237–79.

Mead, Margaret (b. Philadelphia, Pa., Dec. 16, 1901; d. New York, N.Y., Nov. 15, 1978). Born into an academic family, educated at DePauw, Barnard, and Columbia, Mead was one of the second generation of anthropologists trained by FRANZ BOAS and RUTH BENEDICT. After writing a Master's thesis on the psychology of Italian immigrants, Mead turned to anthropology when Benedict persuaded her of the importance of the work. By the time she died, Mead had achieved a professional and public stature held by no one else in her field. Her position at the American Museum of Natural History increased her public responsibilities, but sexism within the institution limited her: she spent almost 20 years as assistant curator; another 20 as associate curator, and was only promoted to curator five years before her mandatory retirement in 1969.

When Mead received her doctorate in 1929, Boasian CULTURAL ANTHROPOLOGY was well on its way to establishing the importance of culture in human societies and the importance of tolerance for human differences. Turning away from the study of cultural diffusion, Boas was increasingly interested in the makeup of individual cultures, especially the assumptions and biases that make people resistant to change. At the same time, Ruth Benedict's work on cultural configurations influenced Mead's own research on the relationship of individuals to their cultures, and the two influenced one another in their studies of national character. Mead extended Boasian anthropology by focusing on gender and sexuality and by consistently examining Americans themselves. At a time when many Americans were revolting against the prescriptions of cultural gentility that characterized VICTORIANISM, Mead's work also made her a celebrity.

From the beginning, Mead's research focused on the cross-cultural comparison of sexuality, gender roles, and intergenerational relationships. So central was this theme that she used it as the organizing principle of her autobiography, *Blackberry Winter* (1972), framing a discussion of her anthropological research with discussions of her childhood, motherhood, and grandmotherhood. "I have spent most of my life studying the lives of other peoples, faraway peoples, so that Americans might better understand themselves," she wrote in the prologue. "In much the same way, I bring my own life to throw what light it may on how children can be brought up so that parents and children, together, can weather the roughest seas" (p. 1).

In *Coming of Age in Samoa* (1928) Mead showed that the adolescent crisis so constant in American society was culturally, not biologically, determined. *Growing Up in New Guinea* (1930) continued her interest in the cultural determinants of intergenera-

tional relationships and cultural change, while *Sex and Temperament* (1935) explored the variations of cultural definitions of male and female. In 1949, after she had become a mother herself, Mead wrote *Male and Female*, examining the cultural variations of GENDER roles as founded in the biology of primary sex differences, reproductive functions, and anatomical differences. Aside from illustrating her changing emphasis on the balance between cultural and biological factors, Mead stressed reproduction, mothering, and the family as the determinants of gender identity. She contributed to the rise of an essentialist FEMINISM emphasizing not equal rights but gendered difference. Reacting to Mead, BETTY FRIEDAN, in *The Feminine Mystique* (1963), argued that although Mead's anthropology might have provided evidence for the malleability and diversity of social practices, more often it supported traditions linking woman's social role to her biological function.

Mead's interest in American culture extended the usual cross-cultural comparisons, which were the mainstay of anthropological cultural critique, to full-scale studies of American national character. In this respect, she shared with contemporaries such as Helen and Robert Lynd a preoccupation with applied anthropology, but she advanced her arguments in light of the culture and personality movement of the 1930s and 1940s. *And Keep Your Powder Dry* (1942), "a social scientist's contribution to winning the war and establishing a just and lasting peace" (p. xi), examined American child-rearing practices and aggressiveness. At times her assessment of American institutions mirrored the project of anthropology itself:

> The democratic assumption is to say: all cultures are equal in that each is a complete whole . . . There is no hierarchy of values by which one culture has the right to insist on all its own values and deny those of another . . . But though all cultures have the dignity of wholes, some of them may be utterly incompatible with living on a world scale. (pp. 239–40)

Mead hoped a self-critical United States could contribute to this egalitarian project. Although she was not usually so sanguine about American life, especially after Hiroshima, assessments of national character were to become a mainstay of the postwar years, at least temporarily sustaining the Columbia Research on Contemporary Cultures, which Mead published (with Rhoda Métraux) as *Culture at a Distance* (1953).

Mead's success at bringing anthropology into the mainstream of public discussion about American life is exemplified by the publicity surrounding the publication of Derek Freeman's *Margaret Mead and*

Samoa: the Making and Unmaking of an Anthropological Myth (1983). Freeman argued that Mead had been wrong all along about Samoa, and therefore wrong entirely about the importance of culture. Beginning with a critique of the rise of Boasian arguments against eugenics and racialism, Freeman reasserted the importance of biology. In carrying out the Boasian agenda, Freeman argued, Mead was misled by her informants and consequently misrepresented Samoan society; Freeman insisted that Samoa was not a sexual paradise but a society replete with violence and rape. Although Freeman merely substituted one interpretation of the nature of Samoan culture for another, his contentious argument about the Boasians was part of the revival of biological and evolutionary interpretations, especially SOCIOBIOLOGY, in the 1970s and 1980s. Rarely do internal academic debates—especially about books over 50 years old—generate so much attention, which suggests not only the currency of the issues Freeman addressed but also the power of the image surrounding Mead herself. A woman who "assumed the role of public moralist," as Richard Handler has written (p. 268), Mead got the last laugh: anthropology does indeed tell us most about ourselves.

JULIA E. LISS

FURTHER READING
Mary Catherine Bateson, *With a Daughter's Eye: a Memoir of Margaret Mead and Gregory Bateson* (New York: William Morrow, 1984).
Derek Freeman, *Margaret Mead and Samoa: the Making and Unmaking of an Anthropological Myth* (Cambridge: Harvard University Press, 1983).
Richard Handler, "Boasian Anthropology and the Critique of American Culture," *American Quarterly* 42 (June 1990): 252–73.
Jane Howard, *Margaret Mead: a Life* (New York: Simon and Schuster, 1984).
"In Memorium Margaret Mead (1901–1978)," *American Anthropologist* 82 (June 1980).
Margaret Mead, *Blackberry Winter: My Earlier Years* (New York: Washington Square Press, 1972).
——, *And Keep Your Powder Dry: an Anthropologist Looks at America* (1942; New York: William Morrow, 1965).
Rosalind Rosenberg, *Beyond Separate Spheres: Intellectual Origins of Modern Feminism* (New Haven: Yale University Press, 1982).

medicine Sometime in the mid-1960s, the bloom began to fall from the rose of modern medicine. American physicians then had little reason to anticipate the coming assaults on their prestige, income, and moral authority. Since the late nineteenth century a newly scientific medicine had made unprecedented strides in reducing infectious disease and prolonging life. New public health measures, the rise of bacteriology, the reform of medical education, a virtual explosion of new hospitals, the development of specialized laboratories, diagnostic techniques, pharmacological therapeutics, and life-saving technology—all pointed toward a seemingly limitless horizon of medical progress.

By the early 1990s, vast and unsettling changes had taken place and a new sense of limits had emerged. Almost every aspect of modern medicine had been challenged or altered. Women had entered the profession in record numbers. Revelations of abuse in medical experimentation had led to new federal regulations for the protection of human and animal subjects. Hospitals were often perceived as strange places, dominated by technology, where patients' rights were ignored and bureaucracy prevailed over compassion. Decisions at the bedside were no longer the exclusive concern of an individual physician and patient. Physicians' authority had become subject to debate and review by ethicists, lawyers, and hospital ethics committees. Courts were called on to adjudicate fiercely contested issues such as ABORTION, genetic engineering, euthanasia, and assisted suicide. A rapidly aging population, spiraling health care costs, and growing numbers of the medically indigent combined to make healthcare reform a potent political issue.

The triggering events of medicine's recent turmoil occurred between the mid-1960s and the mid-1970s. This decade revealed that scientific medicine—a profession which had explicitly detached itself from broader frameworks of meaning and value—was not intellectually equipped to handle the moral and existential questions produced by its own technological power. Entirely new fields of academic inquiry and professional practice, known as bioethics and the medical humanities, arose to grapple with problematic issues such as the protection of research subjects, the goals of medicine, the definitions of death, the rights of patients, the cessation of treatment, the meaning of illness, and the distribution of healthcare resources. At first, these fields resolved many problems by emphasizing the moral principle of autonomy and its procedural requirement, informed consent. More recently, however, it has become clear that the principle of autonomy, derived from the commitment of LIBERALISM to protecting the individual, offers little guidance for an aging society marked by a preponderance of chronic illness and an unequal distribution of limited healthcare resources.

In June 1966, Harvard anesthesiologist Henry Beecher published a scathing indictment of clinical research in the *New England Journal of Medicine*. Beecher revealed that leading biomedical researchers commonly performed experiments on human subjects without their consent, often on vulnerable, poor, or minority populations. Beecher and others revealed, for example, that residents at the Willowbrook State School for the Retarded had been purposely infected with hepatitis in the 1950s, and that penicillin —which had been available since the mid-1940s— was withheld until the early 1970s from black men in Macon County, Georgia in a long-term Public Health Service syphilis study.

These and other scandals grew largely out of the dramatic postwar expansion of federally financed laboratory research, an expansion that took place without attention to principles of accountability or mechanisms of peer review. Neither the traditional literature of medical ethics—written with the outmoded assumption that medical research was undertaken by physicians for the direct benefit of their patients—nor the conscience of individual researchers proved adequate to handle the moral problems that arose with so many careers, lives, and federal dollars at stake.

Problems were also brewing in clinical medicine, created by the very same forces that seemed to promise unlimited progress. Increasingly, medical care took place in offices and hospitals, where patients had access to the latest technological advances in diagnosis and treatment. Institutionally based medical care was more efficient and more lucrative, even as it eroded the intimacy and trust of the doctor–patient relationship. The growth of specialization and the continuing transformation of many hospitals into academic referral centers meant that medical practice often took place between strangers.

At the same time, new technological advances (such as kidney dialysis, organ transplantation, artificial respiration and feeding) generated ethical and conceptual questions that had no precedent in the literature of professional ethics. Was an irreversibly comatose person, breathing on a respirator, alive or dead? Who should receive scarce vital organs? Was it ever permissible to turn off a respirator or withdraw a feeding tube?

In 1968, the Harvard "brain death committee" advocated a definition—irreversible coma and two flat EEG readings—that became widely (though not universally) accepted and cleared the way for increased organ donation from people previously considered alive. But this definition did not resolve the conundrum of Karen Ann Quinlan, a young woman brought into a New Jersey hospital emergency room in April 1975 and diagnosed as permanently comatose but not brain dead. In 1976 the New Jersey Supreme Court ruled in favor of her parents' request

to remove the respirator. Ironically, Karen Ann Quinlan survived for another nine years, breathing on her own but nourished by a feeding tube.

David Rothman's *Strangers at the Bedside: How Bioethics and Law Transformed Medical Decision-making* (1991) is the only account of these controversies and changes in American medicine between Henry Beecher's revelation of abuses in clinical research and Karen Ann Quinlan's public tragedy. Rothman's major claims—that medical decision-making became more collective, formal, and public, and that outsiders (ethicists and lawyers) framed the normative principles guiding the doctor–patient relationship—are roughly on target, though oversimplified and sometimes misleading because they ignore the links between cultural history and the new bioethics.

Future scholars of the recent history of medicine will need to work from oral histories and convey a feeling for medical practice as lived experience in order to appreciate why many thoughtful physicians felt confused and sometimes even alienated from their own practice. This confusion was not a personal failing of individual physicians; nor did it result from institutional and technological change alone. Rather, medicine's ethical confusions reflected the erosion of widely shared understandings of human and social well-being. As Protestant moral theologian Paul Ramsey pointed out in *The Patient as Person* (1970), medical ethics no longer had any secure cultural corroboration.

Paradoxically, medicine was the first social institution to confront the failure of its own success in a therapeutic culture. All ethical dilemmas about decisions of life and death could no longer be resolved by appealing to the standard of prolonging life indefinitely for everyone. Leading physicians (such as Edmund Pellegrino, Willard Gaylin, André Hellegers) who acknowledged medicine's moral uncertainties often took the initiative in building institutions, professional associations, and journals to address moral and existential questions in medicine. They opened the door for theologians, lawyers, philosophers, historians, literary critics, and other humanists who developed the new fields of bioethics and medical humanities.

The late 1960s and early 1970s witnessed the birth of the Hastings Institute of Society, Ethics, and the Life Sciences as well as the Kennedy Institute of Ethics at Georgetown University—"think tanks" which have supported many of the influential philosophers who have shaped bioethics. Within a decade, programs in eithics or medical humanities were established at most academic health science centers. The Society for Health and Human Values was formed by ministers, humanists, lawyers, physicians, and other health care providers. In the mid-1980s several prominent centers began offering graduate degrees in bioethics or the medical humanities. By the 1990s, new associations—the Society for Consulting Ethics and the American Association of Bioethics—had been formed and began staking out claims for expert knowledge, standards, and credentials in the professionalizing fields of bioethics and medical humanities.

The rapid emergence and prestige of the new bioethics represented a startling turnaround for moral philosophy, which had become moribund by the mid-twentieth century. In the nineteenth century, moral philosophy had been the capstone of a college education. It was a required course usually taught in the senior year by the college president, who emphasized the central tenets of Victorian morality—that individuals would be rewarded or punished depending on how their lives accorded with the moral and natural laws created by a benevolent God. By 1925 the old requirement of moral philosophy had been jettisoned, a casualty of the modern research university, whose scientists discerned no hierarchy of value or harmony of goals inscribed upon the world by its maker. (*See also* COLLEGES AND UNIVERSITIES.)

When the moral turmoil of modern medicine first surfaced in the 1960s, college ethics had become a rarely chosen elective that paid scant attention either to normative questions or to practical problems. Academic philosophers, then seeking the precision of the natural sciences, were preoccupied by metaethics, the search for a rational grounding of morality, and the analysis of LANGUAGE. Work in medical ethics (largely indistinguishable from medical etiquette) was still written entirely by physicians. The first non-physician writers to enter the terrain of medical ethics were Protestant, Catholic, and Jewish theologians —including Joseph Fletcher, Paul Ramsey, Richard McCormick, and Abraham Jacobovitz. However, theological voices and concepts (the covenant, the virtues, the sanctity of life) were quickly pushed aside by the secular philosophical ethics that rose to prominence in the 1970s and 1980s.

The new bioethics was designed around two pillars of liberal secular thought: respect for the freedom of individuals, and recognition of the impossibility of establishing any particular vision of the moral life by rational argument or common assent. As exemplified by Beauchamp and Childress's popular textbook, bioethics in a secular society was an analytical and procedural enterprise. It aimed only at conceptual clarification of the issues involved in any moral dispute and at methods of resolution that did not impose a particular moral view on any person.

Bioethicists and lawyers figured prominently in both the National Commission for the Protection of Human Subjects (1973–8) and the President's Commission for the Study of Ethical Problems in Medicine and Biomedical and Behavioral Sciences (1978–83). The sudden growth of articles, books, courses, public interest, and careers in this new field seemed to justify Stephen Toulmin's quip that "medicine saved the life of ethics."

The dominant model of bioethics fitted hand-in-glove with administrative and legal methods of resolving conflicts in large institutions. It operated on a decontextualized, contractual view of the doctor-patient relationship, as opposed to the theologians' covenantal model. Bioethics typically began on the high Kantian ground of universal principles (usually autonomy, beneficence, and justice) and derived action-guides or rules that could be applied to particular cases. Any given quandary was to be resolved by ordering or reconciling the relevant moral principles and following the appropriate action-guide or rule. The principle of autonomy, for example, led to the rule that competent patients have the right to refuse treatment, even if their physician considers such treatment necessary.

Ironically, the American bioethicists' quest for fundamental principles and moral certainty betrays considerable continuities with Victorian moralists who postulated absolute, universal truths and clear moral choices in a divinely ordered universe. This irony—and the need for socially accountable, intellectually respectable moral inquiry in medicine—offers engaged scholars a rich and uncharted terrain of pressing public concern. Recent critics argue that the exclusive emphasis of mainstream bioethics on analytic skills and formal procedures is creating a new species of experts who believe falsely in their own neutrality and ignore the complex webs of relationships and values within which ordinary people make moral decisions.

Indeed, feminists, casuists, and interpretive ethicists make a strong case against universal principles and in favor of maxims, circumstances, motives, intentions, and habits in the moral life. They argue for a recovery of practical reasoning about particular, often intractable and ambiguous situations, and suggest that we aim for reasonable opinions rather than certainties. The moral world, as Michael Walzer argues, is neither given from on high (religion's revealed truth) nor deduced by reason (philosophy's universal principles). It is rather the world we all inhabit, a world constituted in part by our prior experiences and judgments of value. Moral philosophy becomes a hermeneutic enterprise—filled with thick descriptions, conversations, and arguments aimed at discerning the morally fitting thing for particular people to do in concrete situations.

The notion of ethics as interpretation is part of a more general reconfiguration of late twentieth-century social thought, in which previously accepted disciplinary boundaries and unifying ideas are giving way to blurred genres—forms of knowledge that accept (rather than erase) the intractable contradiction, paradox, irony, and uncertainty in any explanation of human activity. The new focus on meaning—on the ways that people make sense to themselves—has fundamental implications for medical education and practice. The dethroning of academic philosophy as privileged arbiter of ethical issues has opened up a fluid space in which the interdisciplinary field of medical humanities is flourishing.

In *Doctors' Stories: the Narrative Structure of Medical Knowledge*, Kathryn Montgomery Hunter, for example, has argued forcefully that medicine is an interpretive practice, the art of constantly adjusting scientific abstractions to the needs of individual patients. In spite of all modern scientific and technological development, clinical medicine still relies on the narration of cases for the preservation and advancement of its practical knowledge. Literary and historical inquiry into the voices, forms, erasures, conflicts, and confusions of the "case history" has generated a school of narrative ethics, which has already made clear that a patient's story of illness and her doctor's story of the same disease are often incommensurable, in need of mutual translation. Feminists argue that these stories must be set in a larger context of power and gender relations.

Contemporary medicine's deepest problems originate not in clinical medicine or technology *per se* but in our culture's manic pursuit of individual health. The high cost of and widespread dissatisfaction with health care, for example, are not only due to the usual suspects (an aging population, physician greed, technological medicine, inefficiency, drug companies) but also to our inability to define reasonable goals and limits for medicine. Many Americans unthinkingly regard health as the *summum bonum* of life rather than as a means for living well. Our reluctance to acknowledge that dying is the inevitable price of living, as Daniel Callahan points out, creates a demand that physicians perform endless miracles of life extension. Every death becomes a failure of medicine rather than a fact of life.

It is therefore not surprising that modern medicine's technical power created great confusion about the standards and goals guiding its use. Recently, prominent physician humanists (Eric Cassell, for example) have proposed prevention of disease and relief of suffering as the central goals of medicine. These goals could be given some social and economic backbone if health-care reform in the mid-1990s rewards primary care, guarantees universal access, and caps expenses for high-technology procedures. The establishment of the Park Ridge Center for the Study of Health, Faith, and Ethics, along with a resurgence of theological voices in medical ethics in the 1990s, suggests a strengthening of religion's contribution to these issues. It seems likely, however, that a good deal more economic stringency, social criticism, public dialogue, and cultural dis-ease will be needed to challenge liberal culture's pursuit of individual health as a form of secular salvation.

THOMAS R. COLE

See also PSYCHOTHERAPY.

FURTHER READING
Tom L. Beauchamp and James F. Childress, *Principles of Biomedical Ethics*, 3rd ed. (New York: Oxford University Press, 1989).
Daniel Callahan, *What Kind of Life: the Limits of Medical Progress* (New York: Simon and Schuster, 1990).
Eric J. Cassell, *The Nature of Suffering and the Goals of Medicine* (New York: Oxford University Press, 1991).
Helen Bequaert Holmes and Laura M. Purdy, eds., *Feminist Perspectives in Medical Ethics* (Bloomington: Indiana University Press, 1992).
Kathryn Montgomery Hunter, *Doctors' Stories: the Narrative Structure of Medical Knowledge* (Princeton: Princeton University Press, 1991).
Phillip Rieff, *The Triumph of the Therapeutic: Uses of Faith after Freud* (New York: Harper and Row, 1966).
David J. Rothman, *Strangers at the Bedside: a History of How Law and Bioethics Transformed Medical Decisionmaking* (New York: Basic Books, 1991).
Alan Verhey and Stephen E. Lammers, eds., *Theological Voices in Medical Ethics* (Grand Rapids, Mich.: Eerdmann's, 1993).
Michael Walzer, *Interpretation and Social Criticism* (Cambridge: Harvard University Press, 1987).

Melville, Herman (b. New York, N.Y., Aug. 1, 1819; d. New York, N.Y., Sept. 28, 1891).   Son of an importer of French goods, grandson of two Revolutionary War heroes (Thomas Melvill, participant in the Boston Tea Party, and Peter Gansevoort, defender of Fort Stanwix), Melville was 10 when his father's business failed, 12 when his father died. Family poverty forced him to look for work at 18, and he tried his hand at clerking, manual labor, and teaching before going to sea in 1839 as a common sailor aboard a merchant ship, the *St. Lawrence*, on a four-month voyage to Liverpool. On his return he visited an uncle in Galena, Illinois, but stayed only long enough to get impressions of the Mississippi River.

On January 3, 1841 he sailed for his most fateful and famous voyage, on a whaler, the *Acushnet*, out of New Bedford. In June 1842, disenchanted, he and a friend jumped ship in the Marquesas and wound up living with the Typees, a tribe thought to be cannibal. After four weeks he was rescued by an Australian whaler but found conditions even worse than aboard the *Acushnet* and joined a mutiny. The mutineers were jailed on Tahiti but soon released, and Melville became a beachcomber (or "omoo"). In November of 1842 he signed on with a third whaler, from which he was discharged in the Hawaiian Islands. From there he enlisted in the U.S. Navy for the duration of the voyage of a frigate, the *United States*, to her home port of Boston, where she arrived on October 3, 1844.

These three-plus years of adventures at sea provided nearly all the raw material for Melville's entire career as a writer, beginning with *Typee: a Peep at Polynesian Life* (1846). Controversy over its authenticity and its depiction of the misdirected zeal of Christian missionaries helped to make *Typee* a popular book, and with a career seemingly secured at last, Melville married Elizabeth Shaw, daughter of Lemuel Shaw, Chief Justice of the Massachusetts Supreme Court. *Typee* was followed by other sea adventures—*Omoo* (1847), *Mardi* (1849), *Redburn* (1849), and *White-Jacket* (1850). The writing of his next novel, *Moby-Dick*, was transformed by his rising literary ambitions, which were further encouraged by his meeting Nathaniel Hawthorne in July of 1850; when it was published in 1851 Melville expected to be recognized as a great American writer. Instead the book was attacked by befuddled critics and ignored by a public who only wanted more in the vein of *Typee*, which Melville had come to despise.

The failure of *Moby-Dick* and difficulties in his marriage combined to produce the aggressive nihilism of *Pierre: Or, the Ambiguities* (1852), a novel Melville had characterized as "a rural bowl of milk" but which critics immediately (and properly) recognized as blasphemous, vitriolic, incestuous, and hysterical ("Herman Melville Mad," read the title of one incredulous review). Though he published two more novels (*Israel Potter*, 1854–5, and *The Confidence-Man*, 1857), Melville turned to short fiction for magazines for their surer income and between 1853 and 1856 produced such masterpieces as "Bartleby, the Scrivener," "The Paradise of Bachelors and the Tartarus of Maids," and "Benito Cereno." By 1856, however, his family was so alarmed at his deteriorated mental health that his father-in-law supplied the money for a trip to Europe and the Holy Land. After his return Melville tried to establish himself

as a lecturer, but again he failed to connect with the public. A protracted search for employment finally ended when he took a job as a customs inspector in New York in 1866, but little improved in the Melville household. The following year Elizabeth Melville deflected her minister's desperate proposal that her brothers pretend to kidnap her in order to remove her from the Melville home, and their oldest son Malcolm committed suicide at 18 years old. Melville worked at his new career and concentrated on poetry that he published at his own expense until his retirement in 1886, when *Billy Budd* occupied him. Unfinished at his death in 1891, this last novel was unpublished until 1924, during the Melville revival.

Melville's unquestioned masterpiece, *Moby-Dick*, is an encyclopedic fiction of epic ambition and accomplishment. Interlacing a dazzling array of quest plot, experimental form, philology, epistemology, hermeneutics, cosmology, cetology, *Bildungsroman*, philosophical and theological speculation, labor history, and sociological and political analysis of American life, the novel is also vivid with the tragedy of Ahab's defiance, the genial humor of Ishmael's narrative voice, the comedy of manners of his "marriage" to Queequeg, and the vitality of Melville's search for that "bold and nervous lofty language" to contain his theme. In its generous skepticism and its symbolic method, *Moby-Dick* seems more the contemporary of Joyce's *Ulysses*, Mann's *Der Zauberberg*, and Faulkner's *Absalom, Absalom!* than of *Uncle Tom's Cabin* (1852) or even *The Scarlet Letter* (1850), and indeed it was rarely read until the apologists of modernism had prepared an appropriate audience.

Pierre, with its hints of incest, its Freudian portrayal of the protagonist's mother, its warped portrait of the artist, its relentless exposure of the self-interest, hypocrisy, meaninglessness, and ennui of human life, and its vertiginous nihilism, was unpalatable for most nineteenth-century (and many twentieth-century) readers, but in recent years it has found favor among those modern skeptics, the deconstructionsts. The conundrum of *Billy Budd*, Captain Vere's extralegal execution of the inadvertent murderer, still elicits as much attention and argument as it did in the first wave of Melville criticism. *The Confidence-Man*, though not so favored by critics, is a complex, subtle, and cunning devil's device of a novel that deserves more strenuous analysis. Several of the stories have established themselves, one by one, as pivotal to wider cultural discourses: "Bartleby" as an existentialist parable; "I and My Chimney" and the other tales of wounded masculinity as akin to Hemingway and Faulkner; "Benito Cereno" as an exploration of a society divided by signs of racial difference; "The Tartarus of Maids" and other stories as meditations on the condition of women's lives. Through most of these developments, Melville has been seen as profoundly opposed to the Emersonian optimism of his culture, as possessed by that "great power of blackness" which he admired in Hawthorne's work.

In recent years several studies have portrayed Melville as more representative of the main political and social themes of his culture than oppositional to them—"trapped in the prison-house of the fathers," as Michael Rogin puts it in his psychohistorical biography. Joyce Warren found him so obsessed with "the preservation and assertion of the self" that he "could not recognize the selfhood of the other, least of all the female other," and Wai-chee Dimock added that Melville could not free himself from the American "faith in the self-contained and self-sufficient." For these critics, Melville represents the failure of liberal ideology, the omnivorous indifference of what Sacvan Bercovitch (writing about Hawthorne) has called the "A-morality of compromise."

But Melville is larger than that. No other writer in the American tradition could match the tragic density, the corrosive irony, the Olympian humor of Melville's best work. Even at his worst, as he dashed off *Omoo*, *Redburn*, or *Israel Potter*, the piecework he professed to despise, or as savage indignation choked him into a strangled rage in *Pierre*, Melville was one of the most acute observers and adroit manipulators of symbolic effects in Anglo-American literature. No one else in the nineteenth century was capable of the combination of outrage and restraint displayed in "Norfolk Isle and the Chola Widow" from *The Encantadas* or in "The Tartarus of Maids"; no one else saw so clearly that categories of race, gender, nation, class, and rank were artificial constructs of language and custom; no one else had the sexual awareness or honesty of "Cock-a-Doodle-Doo!" or "After the Pleasure Party." Disappointed or thwarted by practically everything in his life, willful, moody, extravagant, and impractical, Melville nonetheless looms like Moby-Dick himself over the assorted sharks, dolphins, and cuttlefish of our literature.

JAMES D. WALLACE

FURTHER READING

Warner Berthoff, *The Example of Melville* (Princeton: Princeton University Press, 1962).

Wai-chee Dimock, *Empire for Liberty: Melville and the Poetics of Individualism* (Princeton: Princeton University Press, 1989).

T. Walter Herbert Jr., *Marquesan Encounters: Melville and the Meaning of Civilization* (Cambridge: Harvard University Press, 1980).

Carolyn L. Karcher, *Shadow over the Promised Land: Slav-ery, Race, and Violence in Melville's America* (Baton Rouge: Louisiana State University Press, 1980).

Jay Leyda, *The Melville Log: a Documentary Life of Herman Melville, 1819–1891*, 2 vols. (New York: Harcourt, 1951).

Michael Paul Rogin, *Subversive Genealogy: the Politics and Art of Herman Melville* (New York: Knopf, 1983).

Neal L. Tolchin, *Mourning, Gender, and Creativity in the Art of Herman Melville* (New Haven: Yale University Press, 1988).

Joyce W. Warren, *The American Narcissus: Individualism and Women in Nineteenth-Century American Fiction* (New Brunswick, N.J.: Rutgers University Press, 1984).

Mencken, H[enry] L[ouis] (b. Baltimore, Md., Sept. 12, 1880; d. Baltimore, Md., Jan. 29, 1956). Any number of labels fairly describe H. L. Mencken, that most controversial of social commentators. Mencken was both a cultural progressive and a social conservative, an artful rebel and a cantankerous traditionalist. Frequently a sophisticated literary critic, he was just as often an opinionated newspaperman. Such elusiveness accounts in part for his central role in American intellectual history of 1920s America. Though never formally educated, he may have influenced more literate Americans than any other cultural critic of the era.

Mencken was brought up to be conscious of his European lineage. His father, a manufacturer of cigars, and his mother, a homemaker, helped foster the romantic attachment to Germany that would anger Mencken's patriotic readers during World War I and raise questions about his judgment after the United States entered World War II. Singling out leaders from Woodrow Wilson to Franklin D. Roosevelt for special vituperation, Mencken was highly critical of American democratic ideals throughout his career. "For all I know," he once wrote, "democracy may be a self-limiting disease, as civilization itself seems to be" (Cooke, p. 174). Mencken also criticized religion in America, lambasting the "Puritanism" he believed to be endemic in the United States. His satires of WILLIAM JENNINGS BRYAN and religious FUNDAMENTALISM during the 1925 Scopes trial (over the teaching of evolution in Tennessee) are among his most famous writings.

From Mencken's employment at the Baltimore *Morning Herald*, to his editorship of the *Smart Set* and the *American Mercury*, and on through his long affiliation with the Baltimore *Sun*, he amassed an immense power in literary circles. Even those few writers not captivated by his inimitable prose style reveled in (or feared) his blistering judgments. He rankled many of his literary contemporaries by dismissing most of American literary history. "Our literature," he observed in 1920, "despite several false starts that promised much, is chiefly remarkable, now as always, for its respectable mediocrity" (Cooke, p. 89). Yet Mencken, who corresponded with and published dozens of promising novelists and poets, helped elicit a literary renaissance from the southern United States and became a mentor to a number of writers of the HARLEM RENAISSANCE.

Mencken's influence on authors from THOMAS WOLFE to RICHARD WRIGHT is not a tribute to the power of the editor's thought, but to his command of the written word. Wright, for instance, wrote in his autobiography *Black Boy* (1945):

I was jarred and shocked by the style, the clear, clean, sweeping sentences. Why did he write like that? And how did one write like that? I pictured the man as a raging demon, slashing with his pen, consumed with hate, denouncing everything American, extolling everything European or German, laughing at the weaknesses of people, mocking God, authority. What was this? I stood up, trying to realize what reality lay behind the meaning of the words . . . Yes, this man was fighting, fighting with words. He was using words as a weapon, using them as one would use a club. (pp. 217–18)

Mencken's style in periodicals is identifiable by its pungency and sarcasm, as in his squib "The Good Man," where he wrote:

Man, at his best, remains a sort of one-lunged animal, never completely rounded and perfect, as a cockroach, say, is perfect. If he shows one valuable quality, it is almost unheard of for him to show any other. Give him a head, and he lacks a heart. Give him a heart of a gallon capacity, and his head holds scarcely a pint. The artist, nine times out of ten, is a dead-beat and given to the debauching of virgins, so-called. The patriot is a bigot, and, more often than not, a bounder and a poltroon. The man of physical bravery is often on a level, intellectually, with a Baptist clergyman. The intellectual giant has bad kidneys and cannot thread a needle. In all my years of search in this world, from the Golden Gate in the West to the Vistula in the East, and from the Orkney Islands in the North to the Spanish Main in the South, I have never met a thoroughly moral man who was honorable. (Cooke, pp. 126–7)

Behind such rhetoric was an inquiring intellect ever reading theorists of human behavior. Carl Bode, one of Mencken's biographers, has traced Mencken's moral relativism, agnosticism, and antiauthoritarianism to his somewhat idiosyncratic reading of thinkers as diverse as George Bernard Shaw, Friedrich Nietzsche, Thomas Huxley, and WILLIAM GRAHAM SUMNER.

In addition to his early books on Shaw and Nietzsche, and the voluminous essays and memoirs that followed, Mencken completed important work in philology. His magnum opus *The American Language*, published in various editions between 1919 and 1948, was a major contribution to cataloguing the American idiom. Yet the career of this brilliant social critic and philologist was also marked by his tendency to reduce individuals to demeaning racial labels. His honored position in American intellectual history has been tainted in recent decades by the release of his private papers. Since the 1989 publication of his diaries, which contain degrading references to African Americans and Jews, even Mencken's greatest defenders have had to confront the bigotry partially obscured by his public opposition to racial oppression.

Mencken's influence and reputation had, however, already begun to shrink during his lifetime. Between the premature death of his wife Sara Haardt in 1935, and a debilitating stroke that ended his own career in 1948, his opinions became increasingly idiosyncratic. Ultimately, Baltimore's renowned "sage" owed much of his prominence in the 1920s to the desire of educated Americans for an intellectual antihero. At the height of his fame in that decade, Mencken capitalized on a new skepticism about the value of unexamined patriotism and the nobility of America's work-obsessed bourgeoisie, whom Mencken memorably termed the "booboisie." Hardened by World War I and revulsed by a commercialism that had its origins in the Gilded Age, many authors, including SHERWOOD ANDERSON and SINCLAIR LEWIS, satirized American complacency and provincialism. Yet only Mencken, who mocked the middle-class intelligentsia and reviled the uneducated masses, won his fame by insulting the intelligence of all Americans.

THOMAS A. UNDERWOOD

FURTHER READING

Alistair Cooke, ed., *The Vintage Mencken* (1955; New York: Vintage, 1990).
Fred C. Hobson Jr., *H. L. Mencken: a Life* (New York: Random House, 1993).
H. L. Mencken, *The American Language*, ed. Raven I. McDavid Jr., with supplements 1 and 2, abridged (1919–48; New York: Knopf, 1963).
——, *Prejudices: a Selection*, ed. James T. Farrell (New York: Vintage, 1958).
——, *The Diary of H. L. Mencken*, ed. Charles A. Fecher (New York: Knopf, 1989).
Louis D. Rubin Jr., "The Mencken Mystery," *Sewanee Review* 99 (summer 1991): 445–63.
Charles Scruggs, *The Sage in Harlem: H. L. Mencken and the Black Writers of the 1920s* (Baltimore: Johns Hopkins University Press, 1984).

Richard Wright, *Black Boy: a Record of Childhood and Youth* (New York: Harper, 1945).

Merriam, Charles (b. Hopkinton, Iowa, Nov. 15, 1874; d. Rockville, Md., Jan. 8, 1953). Political scientist. The first member of the political science faculty at the University of Chicago, Merriam outlined in *A History of American Political Theories* (1903) the progressivism that won him a seat on the Chicago city council in 1909. Defeated in campaigns for mayor in 1911 and 1919, Merriam returned to academic politics, organizing the Social Science Research Council in 1923, serving as president of the American Political Science Association in 1925, and writing *New Aspects of Politics* (1925), which called for cooperative efforts to marshal social scientific research to solve political problems. Merriam's confidence that science could overcome partisanship inspired his work for Franklin D. Roosevelt's National Resources Planning Board. The board framed ambitious plans for a welfare state, but they were already dead politically by the time FDR proposed them in his "Four Freedoms" address of 1941.

FURTHER READING
Barry D. Karl, *Charles E. Merriam and the Study of Politics* (Chicago: University of Chicago Press, 1974).

Merton, Thomas (b. Prades, France, Jan. 31, 1915; d. Bangkok, Thailand, Dec. 10, 1968). A profoundly important spiritual teacher of the American Catholic Church, Merton was born in France and became a citizen of the U.S. in 1951. He lived abroad in adolescence and then entered the cloistered Cistercian (Trappist) monastery of Our Lady of Gethsemani in Kentucky, from which most of his many writings streamed. His autobiography *The Seven Storey Mountain* (1948) records his lonely life in French and English schools, his early literary efforts in New York, and his discovery of philosophy at Columbia University. Here he experienced an intellectual awakening and then a religious conversion to Roman Catholicism. (*See also* CATHOLICISM.)

The autobiography (still in print) was an enormous success and was followed by essays, poems, books, journals, and reviews, many offering further autobiographical reflection. They all displayed a spiritual orientation that derived from intense study of the Christian monastic and mystical traditions, but cast in the vivid language of a talented writer who made nearly forgotten ideas about the practice of prayer and the experience of God accessible to contemporary readers, Catholic and non-Catholic. He brought asceticism, contemplation, silence, and solitude to an audience accustomed to either legalistic or sentimental moralism. He voiced a prophetic resistance to what he saw as the corruptions of American culture: consumerism, racism, and war-making. He became a leader in the peace movement in the 1960s, even though his antiwar writings often had to be clandestinely circulated since his ecclesiastical superiors had forbidden him to publish his views about the war in Vietnam.

The monastery Merton chose was cenobitical, centered on scheduled communal life and prayer. His personal search for greater solitude in this setting led him to appreciate the eremetical monks, hermits like the Camaldolese or Carthusians, and he considered transferring to one of these orders. But he also discovered, through study of early sources, that the hermit's life was not inimical to Cistercian tradition. Merton was permitted to live temporarily, then permanently, as a hermit in a small cottage in the monastery grounds. Some of his finest writing was done in the hermitage (*Raids on the Unspeakable* and *A Vow of Conversation*) where he spent his last years. He also succeeded in making eremetical life a part of renewed Cistercian monasticism after Vatican Council II. Although Merton sought greater solitude in his later years, he also widened his circle of contacts, maintaining friendships through frequent visits and letter-writing. (His collected letters have been published in three thick volumes, with promise of more to come.) This period was also marked by a romance with a nurse he met during a hospital stay, commemorated in *Love Poems* and other poetry. Despite this experience, he chose to remain a monk. Even as he undertook various travels in his last years—including his final visit to Asia, where he died by accidental electrocution—he maintained his monastic identity, writing affectionate letters to his Kentucky brothers from "Louie." His monastic name was Brother Louis.

Merton had intended to cease writing when he became a monk (believing it a distraction from contemplation), but his first abbot encouraged him to write his autobiography. He did some writing for his Order's internal purposes (lives of Cistercian saints, pamphlets) and then various pieces on Christian spirituality, monasticism, and mysticism for which he is best known. His brief essay "Day of a Stranger" is a good example of his spiritual writing in its simplicity, concreteness, and longing for transcendence.

One might say that I had decided to marry the silence of the forest. The sweet dark warmth of the whole world will have to be my wife. Out of the heart of that dark warmth comes the secret that is heard only in silence, but is at the root of all the secrets that are whispered by all the lovers in their beds all over the world. (p. 215)

After rituals of washing the coffee pot, spraying for bugs, and approaching the outhouse cautiously because of the king snake who often rests there, Merton describes his contemplation:

> I sit in the cool back room, where words cease to resound, where all meanings are absorbed in the *consonantia* of heat, fragrant pine, quiet wind, bird song, and one central tonic note that is unheard and unuttered. This is no longer a time of obligations. In the silence of the afternoon all is present and all is inscrutable in one central tonic note to which every other sound ascends or descends, to which every other meaning aspires, in order to find its true fulfillment. To ask when the note will sound is to lose the afternoon: it has already sounded, and all things now hum with the resonance of its sounding. (p. 218)

Although not a theologian in the technical sense, Merton exhibited a developing theology. Some of his earlier work was marked by the triumphalist spirit of pre-Vatican II Catholicism, while his later work centered on the experience of prayer and the concrete dimensions of lived faith, especially as faith leads to mysticism. His best work reveals his concern to grasp the experiential heart of Christian monasticism and mysticism. His writings about other traditions—Hinduism, Buddhism (especially Zen), Confucianism, Islamic Sufism—elaborate cross-cultural analogies in the life of the Spirit, and confirm his preference for experience over doctrine. Ultimately Merton's theology is autobiographical, the story of a particular life in all its contingencies. Himself formed by existentialist currents of the 1940s and 1950s, he anticipates the narrative turn in contemporary theology: faith itself is the telling and hearing of sacred stories.

ANNE CARR

See also AUTOBIOGRAPHY.

FURTHER READING

Anne E. Carr, *A Search for Wisdom and Spirit: Thomas Merton's Theology of the Self* (Notre Dame: University of Notre Dame Press, 1988).

Lawrence S. Cunningham, ed., *Thomas Merton: Spiritual Master: the Essential Writings* (New York: Paulist Press, 1992).

Thomas Merton, "Day of a Stranger," *Hudson Review* 20 (summer, 1967): 211–18.

Michael Mott, *The Seven Mountains of Thomas Merton* (Boston: Houghton Mifflin, 1984).

Anthony Padovano, *The Human Journey: Thomas Merton, Symbol of a Century* (Garden City: Doubleday, 1982).

Edward Rice, *The Man in the Sycamore Tree* (Garden City: Doubleday, 1970).

William H. Shannon, *Silent Lamp: the Thomas Merton Story* (New York: Crossroads, 1992).

Michelson, Albert A. (b. Strelno, Prussia, Dec. 19, 1852; d. Pasadena, Calif., May 9, 1931).   One of the most artful experimentalists of all time, Michelson contributed significantly to the great revolutionary shifts in physics in the early twentieth century. In 1907 he was the first American to win the Nobel Prize in physics. In the same year he also won the Copley Medal of the Royal Society, the first American winner since Benjamin Franklin. These awards made headline news throughout America, while Michelson became a symbol of the belated coming of age of American SCIENCE.

In 1855, at the age of three, young Albert emigrated from Prussia to New York with his Jewish parents. His family moved soon after to the gold camps of Calaveras County, California, and eventually to Virginia City, Nevada. As a youthful high school graduate in 1869, Albert almost won Nevada's one appointment to the Naval Academy, and then in a desperate trip east finally secured a slot created especially for him by the Superintendent. In the rigorous training at Annapolis he excelled in mathematics and optics. As part of a student project, he began experiments to determine the speed of light.

After a required two years at sea, Michelson returned to teach physics and chemistry at the Naval Academy, where he soon married the daughter of the Commander. Handsome, musical, Michelson was also stiff and formal. Self-absorbed, impossibly demanding of himself and his colleagues, he could be cold and even cruel to associates, most of whom he eventually alienated. His first wife divorced him, and he gained few enduring friendships. He also moved frequently from one academic post to another—from the Naval Academy to Case Institute to Clark University and finally, in 1894, to an enduring position at the Ryerson Physical Laboratory at the University of Chicago. As the demanding admiral of that famous lab, he helped train several gifted students and colleagues, including two winners of the Nobel Prize, Arthur Compton and ROBERT MILLIKAN.

All Michelson's greatest experimental work involved light waves and the interference patterns created by two converging beams of light. While at his first teaching post at the Naval Academy, he dramatically improved upon techniques for measuring the speed of light. In an 1880–2 visit to Europe he met the great names in physics in both France and Germany, and in Germany expanded his speed-of-light experiments into other problems involving light transmission. More important, he perfected his one great instrument—the interferometer. He used semitransparent mirrors to separate light into two beams, transmitted the beams over different paths of approximately equal distance, and then reconverged them. He used exact screws to move one reflecting mirror, thus enabling him to change, in infinitesimal intervals, the distance traveled by one of his beams. Such small changes caused minute shifts in convergence patterns, which he observed through a micrometer. In time, he could detect shifts that reflected a change of one-hundredth of a single wave length.

By 1880 experiments had suggested that the earth's motion had no physical effect upon an elusive ether, and thus that it did not drag an envelope of ether with it. But such motion, everyone assumed, would create an ether wind. The obstacle to testing the effects of an assumed ether wind, and thus ascertaining the absolute speed of objects moving through space, was technical—the level of accuracy demanded in measuring infinitesimal effects had long seemed unachievable. With his interferometer, Michelson now had a device of the necessary accuracy. In Germany in 1881 he first used his interferometer to check for ether wind effects on light beams separated, projected, and then reconverged. He found no shifts. But the margin of error was high and some of his earlier calculations mistaken. He redid this experiment in 1887 at Case, assisted by his then-valued colleague Edward W. Morley. They placed the interferometer on a revolvable concrete platform floating on mercury in an iron trough anchored in a brick pier dug to bedrock. Taking readings in all directions, they did not find even one-twentieth the calculated and expected shifts in interference patterns. In a typically terse report, Michelson and Morley simply reported the results, with no attempt at interpreting the significance. Michelson then assumed that, in some way, the earth dragged the ether along with it.

The Michelson–Morley experiment became famous after Einstein announced his special theory of relativity in 1905. Einstein made a conceptual breakthrough in denying the existence of ether and the meaningfulness of absolute movement in space. Michelson accepted the experimental aspects of the special theory, but never really gave up on the wave theory of light.

In 1882 Michelson accepted a prestigious assignment from the International Bureau of Weights and Measures in France—to establish a new, more exact measure of the meter. This turned out to involve years of work. It began with tedious work in spectrography. He first found a suitable, monochromatic light—the red band of cadmium. Projecting this light through what amounted to four parallel interferometers, he tediously counted every wave along a bronze bar only 0.39 mm long, and used this bar to measure a progression of longer bars. He concluded that the existing platinum-iridium bar was 1,553,163.5 wave lengths of the red line of cadmium, with an estimated error of one in 10 million. Actually, he was more accurate than he thought, and his measurement long remained the world standard. In addition, he used his interferometer to detect minute changes in the shape of the earth's surface (earth tides), to increase spectrographic resolution by etching an unbelievable number of lines (117,000 on a ten-inch glass plate) on a diffraction grating, and even to ape a telescope in calculating the diameter of distant light sources.

Michelson lived until 1931, long beyond his most significant experiments. He had become a legend, largely for work completed decades before. The profession had passed him by. He was by then a bit old-fashioned, famous for his brilliant experimental designs, still master of light waves in an ether that did not exist. Fittingly, he was at the time of his death hard at work on an elaborate project to measure the speed of light, exactly the same problem that enticed him into physics at the Naval Academy almost 60 years earlier. Because of his experimental genius, the theoretical significance of the Michelson–Morley experiment, his widespread recognition in Europe, and his impact upon a brilliant generation of students, Michelson is still honored as the father of American physics.

PAUL CONKIN

FURTHER READING
Stanley Goldberg and Roger H. Stuewer, eds., *The Michelson Era in American Science, 1870–1930* (New York: American Institute of Physics, 1988).
Thomas Parke Hughes, *Science and the Instrument-Maker: Michelson, Sperry, and the Speed of Light* (Washington: Smithsonian Institution Press, 1976).
Bernard Jaffe, *Michelson and the Speed of Light* (Garden City: Doubleday, 1960).
Albert A. Michelson, *Light Waves and Their Uses* (Chicago: University of Chicago Press, 1903).

middlebrow culture   Describing the body of literature, art, and humanistic discourse positioned between avant-garde or learned expression ("high" or "highbrow" culture) and popular amusement ("lowbrow" culture), the phrase encompasses as well the book clubs, publishing projects, radio shows, and similar undertakings that, especially between 1917 and 1950, aimed to make elements of high culture available to a broad public.

The classification of intellectual levels by brow height indirectly derived from the pseudoscience phrenology, which connected behavior to the shape of a person's skull. Even before "highbrow," "middlebrow," and "lowbrow" entered the language in the late nineteenth and early twentieth centuries, however, commentators on the American scene had begun developing the hierarchical view of culture those terms eventually encapsulated. Remarking on the nature of the arts in a democratic, practical society, for example, ALEXIS DE TOCQUEVILLE warned that American authors, writing for a "motley multitude" with little time and patience for subtlety or erudition, would sacrifice taste for passion and compromise aesthetic standards for the sake of material success. Similarly, as the technological changes of the post-Civil War era facilitated the spread of print and the reproduction of images, figures such as E. L. GODKIN, CHARLES ELIOT NORTON, and other representatives of the "genteel tradition" in American literature recommitted themselves to Matthew Arnold's definition of culture as "the best that has been thought and said in the world"; they saw their task as shielding genuine refinement from the "chromocivilization," as Godkin put it in 1874, of gossip, sensationalism, and imitation (*see also* PUBLICITY).

Yet as many genteel writers themselves believed, the same commercial forces that jeopardized the survival of "the best" could also be harnessed to enhance it. Anthologies, Chautauqua lectures, and sets of books sold by subscription operated throughout the nineteenth century to diffuse and desacralize high art by making it accessible. Such efforts—nascent forms of middlebrow culture—existed in tension with the evolution of a rigid cultural hierarchy.

The rise of amusement parks, movies, and other forms of mass entertainment challenged the authority of genteel taste-makers, pitted consumer values against aesthetic ones, and thus intensified the debate about the place of art in a democracy. (*See also* CINEMA.) In 1915, VAN WYCK BROOKS appropriated the terms "highbrow" and "lowbrow' to argue that the combination of desiccated idealism and mindless practicality had severely inhibited American cultural life. Between those extremes, Brooks declared, "there is no genial middle ground." Beginning in the late 1930s, however, DWIGHT MACDONALD, CLEMENT GREENBERG, and other observers located an all-too-evident middlebrow terrain very different from the artistic community Brooks had in mind. Pointing to the emergence since the 1920s of ventures like the creation of the Book-of-the-Month Club and the development of "great books" discussion groups, Macdonald and his colleagues attacked such examples of "midcult" for pretending to uphold high culture while in fact diluting it and contaminating it with commercial motives. Together with sociologists like Leo Lowenthal, they also excoriated MASS

CULTURE as manipulative, homogenizing, and commodified. More recently, literary scholars have added to those charges by implicating middlebrow critics in a process of "canon formation" that excluded all but white male writers in the Western tradition. Yet its assailants have typically overlooked both the complex sources and competing assumptions middlebrow culture encompassed.

Agencies of middlebrow culture proliferated in the three decades after World War I for several reasons. First, the specialization of knowledge and the rise in high school and college graduates made Americans especially receptive to books that offered comprehensible, up-to-date information. Second, the prosperous postwar economic climate encouraged investment in new ways to sell culture. Third, a bewildering increase in books published heightened the appeal of figures who could define what cultured people should know. Fourth, the emphasis in modern America on becoming a successful personality accentuated the demand for culture in order to enhance social performance. Nevertheless, at the same time, Americans wary of pervasive consumerism, desirous of the prestige traditionally associated with liberal learning, or committed to ideals of character and aesthetic training embraced middlebrow culture for a fifth reason: to bolster values threatened by the transformation of the United States into what a contemporary observer labeled a "business civilization."

That agenda informed such developments as Harry Scherman's creation of the Book-of-the-Month Club in 1926. The club furnished members advance information about new books, chosen (along with alternate selections) by an accomplished board of judges. Advertising for Scherman's scheme enhanced its attractiveness by promising to assist those who frequently defaulted on their intention to stay *au courant*. The club equated self-realization with projecting a winning image; it substituted time management and expertise for procrastination and confusion; and it made culture synonymous not with disciplined understanding but, rather, with consumable news. Yet those features of the Book-of-the-Month Club coexisted with others that rested on countervailing tenets. The most powerful figures on the first board of judges, Henry Seidel Canby and Dorothy Canfield Fisher, resembled genteel authorities more than they did modern personalities. They also believed that every reader deserved access to "the best," and conceived of their purpose as democratic and educational. Canby and Fisher's emphasis on character and self-reliance reverberated in advertisements which counseled purchasers that the best books each month were the ones subscribers would have chosen anyway.

The tensions marking the Book-of-the-Month Club in its early years demonstrate that the club mediated between sets of values as well as intellectual strata. This historically derived "middleness" characterized other middlebrow enterprises as well. For example, the "outline" volumes that flooded the book market after the appearance of H. G. Wells's *The Outline of History* (1919) in part accommodated the modern emphasis on social performance and consumption by implying that acquiring secondhand information about scholarly disciplines obviated the need to read primary texts themselves. Yet the career of WILL DURANT, whose bestselling *The Story of Philosophy* (1926) made him the most popular American "outline" writer, revealed Durant's protest against the fragmentation of selfhood that American consumer culture also entailed. In the 1930s and 1940s, the spectrum of educational radio programs suggested middlebrow culture's mediating function: quiz shows such as "Information, Please!" simultaneously revered and deflated literary experts; professors both delivered conventional reviews and appeared on variety shows to tout new books; and "Invitation to Learning," a version of the "great books" curriculum, evolved from a generally erudite exploration of classic writings into a simplified summary for listeners who wanted to hear about books they would find unreadable.

The advent of television and the specialization of publishing were among the factors that, after 1950, altered the conditions in which American middlebrow culture had flourished. By intensifying the preoccupation with personality and image, television helped undermine definitions of the cultured self based on ideas of character and discipline. Meanwhile, the splintering of media markets made less plausible the assumption that middlebrow culture could command a broad audience of ordinary readers and listeners. What the middlebrow writer Clifton Fadiman called "the decline of attention"—the increased reverence for fact rather than insight, the premium on the packaging (as opposed to the substance) of ideas —favored consumerist elements of culture at the expense of contemplation and learning. The middlebrow effort to popularize cultivation came to appear stodgy, even highbrow. The historian's challenge is to complicate that image, to show that the middlebrow advocates' view of themselves as fully democratic cannot be dismissed out of hand. An even-handed analysis of the middlebrow phenomenon can contribute potently to debate in our own day over cultural literacy and the canon.

JOAN SHELLEY RUBIN

See also VICTORIANISM.

FURTHER READING

Van Wyck Brooks, *Three Essays on America* (1915; New York: Dutton, 1970).

Clifton Fadiman, *Party of One* (Cleveland: World Publishing, 1955).

E. L. Godkin, "Chromocivilization," in *Reflections and Comments, 1865–1895* (New York: Charles Scribner's Sons, 1895).

Lawrence W. Levine, *Highbrow/Lowbrow: the Emergence of Cultural Hierarchy in America* (Cambridge: Harvard University Press, 1988).

Dwight Macdonald, "Masscult and Midcult: II," *Partisan Review* 27 (fall 1960): 589–631.

Janice Radway, "The Scandal of the Middlebrow: the Book-of-the-Month Club, Class Fracture, and Cultural Authority," *South Atlantic Quarterly* 89 (fall 1990): 703–36.

Joan Shelley Rubin, *The Making of Middlebrow Culture* (Chapel Hill: University of North Carolina Press, 1992).

Millay, Edna St. Vincent (b. Rockland, Maine, Feb. 22, 1892; d. Austerlitz, N.Y., Oct. 19, 1950). Poet. A member of the Greenwich Village intellectual community during and after World War I, Millay embraced a combined cultural and political radicalism. Her poems, traditional in form, were often described as flippant or hedonistic because of their explorations of femininity, masculinity, and sexuality. She actively protested the conviction of Sacco and Vanzetti, as did many of her peers. Her poetry and her life have come to be taken narrowly as expressions of the New Woman who is straightforward, irreverent, and free from traditional sexual and behavioral codes, even though she was attentive to wider issues. Some of her best-known poems are collected in *Renascence and Other Poems* (1917), *A Few Figs from Thistles* (1920), and *Fatal Interview* (1931).

FURTHER READING

Anne Cheney, *Millay in Greenwich Village* (University, Ala.: University of Alabama Press, 1975).

millennialism   Derived chiefly from the twentieth chapter of Revelation, millennialism denotes belief in the thousand-year reign of Christ at the close of history, or emphasizes other events at the end of time such as the Second Coming of Jesus and the Last Judgment. By extension, secularized or non-Christian visions of a radical transformation of history are also sometimes styled millennial.

PURITANISM was the taproot of American millennialism. Although the first Puritan settlers of the 1630s were primarily interested in restoring primitive Christianity and did not initially believe that New England had a unique mission to inaugurate the last days, millennial hopes became more prominent after

1640. New Englanders shared the expectant mood of many of their English coreligionists during the Civil War and Cromwell's Protectorate. Thus, for example, Edward Johnson, in his *Wonder-Working Providence*, written in 1650–1, declared: "For your full assurance, know this is the place where the Lord will create a new Heaven and a new earth . . . , new Churches and a new Commonwealth together." Such notions were not the dominant motifs in the thought of Johnson and his contemporaries, but they took a major step toward the forward-looking millennialism so characteristic of subsequent religious thought.

In the eighteenth century, diverse trends gave increased vitality to millennialism. A series of religious revivals in various colonies culminated in the GREAT AWAKENING of the 1740s. JONATHAN EDWARDS saw in the revival a sign of the latter days and even dared to hope that the millennium might begin in America. Although he may have later retreated from that optimistic assessment, Edwards set the pattern for American Protestants who would interpret subsequent revivals, stretching well into the nineteenth century, as tokens of God's coming kingdom. Political crises also enlivened the millennial tradition. During the French and Indian War (1756–63) and again during the struggle for independence (1776–83), many ministers infused republican ideology with apocalyptic symbolism. (*See also* AMERICAN REVOLUTION.)

The antebellum period brought millennialism to flood tide. Numerous sectarian and communitarian ventures promised to build the new heavens and new earth. Mormons sought to erect Zion in successive communities in Ohio, Missouri, Illinois, and Utah. Shakers averred that the Kingdom had already come in the person of their founder ANN LEE and that the millennial life was being lived in their various villages scattered from New England to Indiana. William Miller, a Baptist preacher, won nationwide attention and a following numbering perhaps in the hundreds of thousands by predicting that Christ would return about 1843. After the failure of his prediction, remnants of the movement coalesced into several small denominations, of which Seventh-Day Adventism was the most notable. (*See also* APOCALYPTIC LITERATURE.)

Among antebellum clergy of the major denominations, postmillennialism was the dominant opinion. This view, which held that the Second Coming would occur after the millennium, had predated the nineteenth century; but until then it did not become the key to a distinct philosophy of history. After about 1800, however, postmillennialism came to denote an understanding of history as gradual improvement according to rational laws that human beings could learn and use. Postmillennialism often merged with other ideas: belief in PROGRESS, the Enlightened stress on the reasonableness of the universe, and the perfectionist confidence in the possibility of eradicating sin. This explosive amalgam of ideas motivated evangelical efforts to reform American society through revivals, temperance, and antislavery. During the Civil War, many religious leaders, especially in the North, used the prevailing postmillennial faith to proclaim the struggle an apocalyptic battle preparing the way for God's kingdom. (*See also* EVANGELICALISM.)

In the decades after the Civil War, various forms of premillennialism—or belief that the Second Advent of Christ would occur before the millennium—grew in popularity in conservative sectors of Protestantism. In the 1870s, Charles Taize Russell, an independently wealthy clothier, founded a movement, later to be known as the Jehovah's Witnesses, on the prediction of Christ's early return. Within the major denominations, premillennialism frequently assumed a dispensational form. Dispensationalism, usually attributed to the Englishman John Nelson Darby, was premised upon biblical inerrancy and literalism. Pronouncing the current age hopelessly corrupt, dispensationalists scoffed at the postmillennial dream of humankind inaugurating the millennium. Most looked for the Rapture, Jesus's removal of true believers from the earth prior to the tribulations near the end of the age. Wars, increasing decadence, and the restoration of the Jews to their homeland were among the anticipated signs of the end. Through annual Bible study conferences meeting for a quarter-century after 1875, through Bible institutes, and through the widely disseminated Scofield Reference Bible (1909), dispensationalism created a vast subculture which influenced the rise of both FUNDAMENTALISM and Pentecostalism.

In the post-Civil War era the once dominant postmillennial view gradually lost its distinct biblical moorings and inadvertently contributed to the decline of the view that history moved toward a transcendent end. Theologians of LIBERAL PROTESTANTISM such as William Newton Clarke and Williams Adams Brown no longer spoke of a Second Coming (either before or after the millennium). Rather they saw the Kingdom of God as a process of virtually unbounded progress in this world. Advocates of the Social Gospel such as WASHINGTON GLADDEN, Josiah Strong, and WALTER RAUSCHENBUSCH sought to use this vision of the kingdom to reform the inequities of American society. A secularized postmillennialism also contributed to the rise of the experimental, activist, and open-ended search for truth so characteristic of many social theorists in the Progressive era—for example, JOHN DEWEY, RICHARD ELY, and ALBION SMALL.

Since the 1920s, premillennialism has persisted in a large conservative subculture. The tradition's continuing vitality is attested by the extraordinary success of Hal Lindsey's *Late Great Planet Earth* (1970), of which 28 million copies had been printed by 1990. The enduring appeal of dispensationalism reflects, as Paul Boyer had argued, a popular revolt against the apparent "aimlessness of secular history" and an assertion that time does have a predetermined goal. Postmillennialism as a distinct biblically grounded eschatology has virtually disappeared, but its secular remnants remain in invocations of the American Dream, material progress, Ronald Reagan's vision of America as a shining city on a hill, or in George Bush's "new world order." Perhaps, too, portrayals in science fiction of a future golden age—witness the popularity of *Star Trek* in movies and on television—also represent contemporary versions of the millennial hope.

JAMES H. MOORHEAD

FURTHER READING

Sacvan Bercovitch, *The American Jeremiad* (Madison: University of Wisconsin Press, 1978).
Paul Boyer, *When Time Shall Be No More: Prophecy Belief in Modern American Culture* (Cambridge: Harvard University Press, 1992).
Theodore Dwight Bozeman, *To Live Ancient Lives: the Primitivist Dimension in Puritanism* (Chapel Hill: University of North Carolina Press, 1988).
Nathan O. Hatch, *The Sacred Cause of Liberty: Republican Thought and the Millennium in Revolutionary New England* (New Haven: Yale University Press, 1977).
James H. Moorhead, *American Apocalypse: Yankee Protestants and the Civil War, 1860–69* (New Haven: Yale University Press, 1978).
——, "Between Progress and Apocalypse: a Reassessment of Millennialism in American Religious Thought, 1800–1880," *Journal of American History* 71 (Dec. 1984): 524–42.
Ernest R. Sandeen, *The Roots of Fundamentalism: British and American Millenarianism, 1800–1930* (Chicago: University of Chicago Press, 1970).
Ernest Lee Tuveson, *Redeemer Nation: the Idea of America's Millennial Role* (Chicago: University of Chicago Press, 1968).

Miller, Henry (b. New York, N.Y., Dec. 26, 1891; d. Pacific Palisades, Calif., June 7, 1980).   Writer. Miller expatriated to France in the 1930s, a decade later than most of the well-known American literary exiles of his generation. His *Tropic of Cancer*, an account of the inner and sexual life of an American expatriate in Paris, was published there in 1934. Banned in the United States as obscene, it was, like much of his work, an autobiographical celebration of un-inhibited impulse and feeling. *Tropic of Capricorn*, a treatment of his adolescence in New York, was released in Paris in 1939 and similarly banned in America. The two books were not issued in the United States until 1961–2, and their publication was followed by a series of OBSCENITY trials leading to a Supreme Court decision that supported Miller's right to publish. Among his other important writings were *Air-Conditioned Nightmare* (1945), a reflection on American culture, the *Rosy Crucifixion* series (*Sexus*, 1949, *Plexus*, 1953, and *Nexus*, 1959), a continuation of his autobiographical rumination (published in the United States in 1965), and several volumes of letters exchanged with such friends as Anais Nin and Laurence Durrell.

See also EXPATRIATION.

FURTHER READING

Robert Ferguson, *Henry Miller: a Life* (New York: Norton, 1991).

Miller, Perry (b. Chicago, Ill., Feb. 25, 1905; d. Cambridge, Mass., Dec. 9, 1963).   Trained as a scholar of literature, Miller was the leading figure in two major events in the academic history of the twentieth century. The first was the emergence of PURITANISM as a subject-matter for rigorous study. Miller rescued the writings of the religious leaders of colonial New England from the flippant put-downs of H. L. Mencken, and from the filiopietistic antiquarianism of Puritanism's genteel descendants. Miller defined the terms of discourse about Puritanism from the 1930s to the 1990s. The second event was the emergence of intellectual history as a subdiscipline. Miller did more than any other single individual to indicate the promise for American historiography of the study of ideas as developed in formal argumentation by theologians, philosophers, and others who lived what Miller liked to call "the life of the mind." His influence as a methodological exemplar increased with time, and 30 years after his death no American scholar's name was invoked more frequently than Miller's in discussions of the virtues and limitations of "intellectual history."

Impetuous, brooding, and sometimes difficult, Miller was a legend at Harvard University, where he taught in the Department of English from 1931 until his death at the age of 58. He had come to Harvard from the Midwest, where he completed both a B.A. and a Ph.D. at the University of Chicago. For a brief period in his early twenties he was an actor in Greenwich Village and a stevedore in the Belgian Congo, experiences he later made much of when trying to distance himself from his upper-middle-class origins —he was a doctor's son—and from the relatively conventional professorial life he actually lived for most of his days. During World War II he served as an officer in the United States Army's Office of Strategic Services, and he participated in the liberation of Strasbourg and in the occupation of Germany.

When Miller died he was writing a book on the intellectual history of the era from the Revolution to the Civil War, fragments of which were published posthumously as *The Life of the Mind in America* (1965). He did complete one book devoted to aspects of this period's literary culture, *The Raven and the Whale: the War of Words and Wit and the Era of Poe and Melville* (1956), and he edited the influential anthologies *The Transcendentalists* (1950) and *American Thought: Civil War to World War I* (1954). But it was his studies of seventeenth- and eighteenth-century New England that made Miller the preeminent historian of American thought.

Miller addressed the divines of New England as intellectuals of the Reformation, animated by "the Augustinian strain of piety" while working within the conventions of post-Renaissance Europe. In his most commanding work, *The New England Mind: the Seventeenth Century* (1939), Miller treated as a synchronic whole the belief system he found in the writings of the leading preachers in the Massachusetts Bay Colony, especially Samuel Willard. In an earlier book, *Orthodoxy in Massachusetts* (1933), Miller had attended less to the intellectual dynamics of Protestant Europe than to the doctrinal and church-political peculiarities of the Massachusetts Puritans within the narrow context of English Puritanism, and to the process by which an English "heterodoxy" became, after migration, an "orthodoxy" in the colonial setting. How that "orthodoxy" was in turn challenged and transformed by two generations of novel experience became the theme of Miller's most diachronic book, *The New England Mind: From Colony to Province* (1953). This account of how New England thinkers from 1660 to 1730 selected tools from the intellectual inventory bequeathed to them by the founders, used these tools to cope with contingent economic, political, and social-psychological experience, and eventually reshaped or discarded these tools has proved to be Miller's most enduring contribution.

Throughout his engagement with the New England Puritans, Miller was conscious of his own position as an American intellectual of the twentieth century. This self-consciousness was the most fully displayed in two books written in the midst of the liberal professorate's earnest effort to construct a viable intellectual tradition for an America embroiled in the struggles of the Cold War and McCarthy-

ism. *Roger Williams: His Contribution to the American Tradition* (1953) was written in this familiar and (in recent years) much-patronized genre, but *Jonathan Edwards* (1949) was a more idiosyncratic, if more impassioned attempt to endow his society with suitable heroes. This intellectual biography of the greatest of the New England divines has been the most roundly criticized of all Miller's works. It tended to mystify JONATHAN EDWARDS, whom Miller presented as a prophet of modernity, as a cultural hero for a generation steeped in Franz Kafka, T. S. Eliot, and Paul Tillich, all of whom were quoted portentously in the text. This book's meditations on the themes of RESPONSIBILITY and sin invite comparisons between it and another American classic of virtually the same moment, the novel by ROBERT PENN WARREN, *All the King's Men* (1946).

Miller's most direct reactions to the issues of the 1940s and 1950s are recorded in essays collected 16 years after his death, *The Responsibility of Mind in a Civilization of Machines* (1979), but Miller was less distinctive and creative as a commentator on contemporary culture than he was as a historian. His quarrels and enthusiasms about American culture, present as well as past, most repay reading as encoded in the historical essays collected in *Errand into the Wilderness* (1956) (*see also* MISSION) and *Nature's Nation* (1967), and in the book-length studies cited above.

The extent of Miller's empathetic identification with the antirationalist Edwards—the leading theorist of the anti-Enlightenment GREAT AWAKENING—and the warmth of Miller's simultaneous appreciation for the contemporary theologian REINHOLD NIEBUHR led many to regard Miller as a "counterprogressive." But as Francis Butts has shown, Miller's sympathy for the Promethean element in secular humanism was deep, and his critical engagements with modernity were complex. The last line of his 976-page, two-volume construction of the *New England Mind* allowed that the old Puritans had paid insufficient attention to "the greatness of man."

DAVID A. HOLLINGER

FURTHER READING

Francis T. Butts, "The Myth of Perry Miller," *American Historical Review* 87 (1982): 665–94.

David A. Hollinger, "Perry Miller and Philosophical History," in Hollinger, *In the American Province: Studies in the History and Historiography of Ideas* (Bloomington: Indiana University Press, 1985).

James Hoopes, "Art as History: Perry Miller's *New England Mind*," *American Quarterly* 34 (1982): 3–25.

David Levin, "Perry Miller at Harvard," *Southern Review* 19 (1983): 802–16.

Robert Middlekauff, "Perry Miller," in Marcus Cunliffe

and Robin W. Winks, eds., *Pastmasters* (New York: Harper and Row, 1969).

Donald Weber, "Historicizing the Errand," *American Literary History* 2 (1990): 101–18.

Millikan, Robert A. (b. Morrison, Ill., Mar. 22, 1868; d. San Marino, Calif., Dec. 19, 1953). Physicist.

After receiving the Nobel Prize in physics in 1923 for determining the electron's charge and interpreting the photoelectric effect, Millikan went on to cosmic ray studies that helped unfold the structure of matter. Son of a Protestant minister, he argued in *Evolution in Science and Religion* (1927) that science and religion manifest unexpected kinship: both are traditions in the course of development, and both are committed to service. The service performed by science is its contribution to technological progress. A primary organizer of government science during World War I, Millikan participated in jet and rocket research during World War II. In addition to his *Autobiography* (1950), he published *Science and the New Civilization* (1930).

FURTHER READING

Robert H. Kargon, *The Rise of Robert Millikan: Portrait of a Life in American Science* (Ithaca: Cornell University Press, 1982).

Mills, C[harles] Wright (b. Waco, Tex., Aug. 28, 1916; d. West Nyack, N.Y., Mar. 20, 1962). Some

of the most important modern American public intellectuals—Robert Lynd, David Riesman, Daniel Bell, Alan Wolfe—have been sociologists. Yet within their own profession such figures have often been prophets without honor, misfits who have won the ear of a broad public yet suffered indifference, condescension, or even contempt from their academic colleagues. C. Wright Mills, the discipline's legendary "lone wolf," offers perhaps the most telling case in point.

Raised in Dallas, Mills came by his alienation early in life. The son of an insurance agent (one of those "new little men" Mills would describe in *White Collar*) and a devout Catholic housewife, he found himself a choirboy amidst a sea of Baptists. His parents hoped he would have a career in engineering, but after a dismal year of disciplinary problems as a cadet at Texas A & M, he took up the study of philosophy and transferred to the University of Texas in Austin. After compiling a stellar undergraduate career in courses on philosophy, economics, and sociology, Mills graduated in 1939.

After briefly considering a career as a car salesman, Mills entered graduate school in sociology at the University of Wisconsin. His philosophical interests remained strong, and he gravitated toward one of the more theoretically-inclined members of the department, émigré Hans Gerth, with whom he immersed himself in study of the work of Max Weber. In 1946 Gerth and Mills would edit one of the most influential translations of Weber's writings, *From Max Weber*. He completed his Ph.D. degree in 1941 with a dissertation analyzing the social context of American pragmatism (published posthumously in 1964 as *Sociology and Pragmatism*). No sooner had he finished his doctorate than he began, in one of his earliest publications, "The Professional Ideology of Social Pathologists" (1943), to distance himself from the orthodoxies of his profession. He attacked the mainstream leaders of American sociology as little more than backward-looking defenders of the norms of rural, small-town, middle-class Protestantism.

In 1941 Mills secured his first teaching job at the University of Maryland, where he found intellectual companionship with historians Frank Friedel, RICHARD HOFSTADTER, and Kenneth Stampp. But eager to be at the center of intellectual and cultural life, he left a tenured position at Maryland in 1944 for a part-time job at Columbia. In New York, Mills became part of the circle gathered around *politics* magazine (so named by its founder and editor DWIGHT MACDONALD at Mills's suggestion). *politics* was the most important forum for those intellectuals alert to the moral and political quandaries and disasters of World War II, and Mills's appearance in its pages signified his fresh interest in radical politics and his outrage at a war that he privately referred to as "a goddamned blood bath to no end save misery and *mutual* death to *all* civilized values."

Mills eventually won a permanent position at Columbia, where he remained for the rest of his two-decade career. But he was never comfortable with his colleagues (many of whom came to despise him) nor with the NEW YORK INTELLECTUALS, and he targeted many of them—Jacques Barzun, DANIEL BELL, PAUL LAZARSFELD, Seymour Martin Lipset, LIONEL TRILLING—in his work. Feeling unwelcome as a provincial outsider amidst cosmopolitan sophisticates, Mills played up the role of the rebellious Texan. Commuting to Morningside Heights on his BMW motorcycle, he adopted the pose of the sociologist as leather-jacketed Wobbly, which horrified many button-down Columbia professors and endeared him to a later generation of radicals.

From the mid-1940s onward, Mills's work centered on themes of power and powerlessness: the growth in modern societies of massive structures of bureaucratic, rationalized power which were rendering most human beings powerless. These structures weakened the authority of substantive reason (as opposed to technical reason) and undermined the independent intellectuals who should have been its guardians. He pressed these themes in a memorable trilogy anatomizing key sectors of American society: *New Men of Power* (1948), on labor and its leaders; *White Collar* (1951), on the "new middle class" of middle managers, bureaucrats, and salaried employees; and *The Power Elite* (1956), on the "higher circles" of corporate, political, and military power. Drawing on theoretical resources from both European and American thinkers—Marx, Weber, Freud, Dewey, Veblen, Mead—Mills advanced a rhetorically powerful vision of an encroaching "postmodern" society in which democratic "publics" had been replaced by manipulated "masses" and critical intellectuals had been supplanted by technicians, experts, and ideologues in the employ of the "knowledge industry."

Beneath the deep pessimism of Mills's analysis of the dynamics of American society, lay an unexpungeable optimism about the residual power of critical intellectuals such as himself who mobilize reason and conduct what he termed the "politics of truth." Believing that public life could be renewed and the insularity of academic social science overcome, he conceived of himself as a latter-day Balzac and his books as "sociological poems." And despite his conviction that the mass media were on the whole subverting rather than fostering public debate, Mills himself resorted to these media in the late 1950s, publishing two polemical potboilers, *The Causes of World War Three* (1958) and *Listen, Yankee* (1960). The latter, a shortsighted defense of the Castro regime, sold 400,000 copies. At the end of his life, Mills was calling for a NEW LEFT centered among dissident intellectuals, an appeal that found ready ears among young activists such as Paul Booth, Tom Hayden, and Bob Ross—all of whom wrote college theses on Mills.

Mills's exaggerated faith in the power of intellectuals shows that the anti-intellectual pose of his renegade gunslinger image was very deceptive. For all the hostility he elicited and solicited from other sociologists, Mills remained wedded to the classical traditions of his discipline. In *The Sociological Imagination* (1959), one of his best books, he attacked both "grand theorists" (such as TALCOTT PARSONS) and "abstracted empiricists" (such as Paul Lazarsfeld), but against these prevailing models of sociology he juxtaposed another, richer conception of "intellectual craftsmanship" in which, as his friend Richard Hofstadter put it in *Anti-Intellectualism in American Life* (1963), the life of the mind was a life of "piety." Mills, as Hofstadter said, was "pledged, committed,

enlisted. What everyone else is willing to admit, namely that ideas and abstractions are of signal importance in human life, he imperatively feels" (p. 28). Reflecting in a 1961 letter to his parents on the heart disease that would a year later take his life, Mills himself summed up with characteristic bluntness the craftsman's ethic that guided his career as a public intellectual: "I know that I have not the slightest fear of death; I know also that I have a big responsibility to thousands of people all over the world to tell the truth as I see it and tell it exactly and with drama and quit this horsing around with sociological bullshit."

ROBERT B. WESTBROOK

FURTHER READING

Peter Clecak, *Radical Paradoxes: Dilemmas of the American Left, 1945–1970* (New York: Harper and Row, 1973).

Richard Gillam, "C. Wright Mills and the Politics of Truth: *The Power Elite* Revisited," *American Quarterly* 27 (1975): 461–79.

——, "Richard Hofstadter, C. Wright Mills and the 'Critical Ideal,'" *American Scholar* 47 (1977–8): 69–85.

——, "*White Collar* from Start to Finish: C. Wright Mills in Transition," *Theory and Society* 10 (1981): 1–30.

Richard Hofstadter, *Anti-Intellectualism in American Life* (New York: Knopft, 1963).

Irving Louis Horowitz, *C. Wright Mills: an American Utopian* (New York: Free Press, 1983).

James Miller, "Democracy and the Intellectual: C. Wright Mills Reconsidered," *Salmagundi* 70–1 (spring/summer 1986): 82–101.

Rick Tilman, *C. Wright Mills: a Native Radical and His American Intellectual Roots* (University Park: Pennsylvania State University Press, 1984).

mission Self-interest, commercial ambitions, and religious motivations were intermingled in the earliest migrations of Europeans to America. Idealists who wanted to convert the indigenous peoples sailed on the same ships with those who wanted to make their fortunes or to plant European cultures on foreign shores. In 1523 the emperor Charles V declared that the principal reason for Spanish incursion into North America was to bring the "holy Catholic faith" to the "natives." French Canada was founded partly by missionary priests whose passage was paid, at the king's insistence, by investors in the new colony. The Russian Orthodox trappers who entered Alaska in 1741 evangelized the Aleuts themselves until the church could send missionaries 50 years later. The charter granted to English Puritans in 1629 mandated that they evangelize the indigenous inhabitants. An exception to colonial fantasies of religious purity was the Dutch: investors in the Dutch West India Company insisted on religious freedom in their colony, believing that to require religious orthodoxy would undercut successful trade and colonization. Accordingly, the colony accepted the first Jews to New Netherland (New York) in 1654, refugees whose beliefs were suspect but whose credit was good.

The separation between religious belief and economic self-interest exemplified in the Dutch model of colonization ultimately triumphed as North American society became more tolerant. Yet after the separation of church and state was enshrined in the United States BILL OF RIGHTS, the colonialist mission objectives did not so much disappear as become contextualized: the history of the United States came to be seen as a march of progress propelled by American republicanism, democracy, and economic opportunity. Early nineteenth-century Americans believed that in distinction to class-ridden and morally bankrupt Europe, God's purpose in founding the United States was to exemplify individual FREEDOM and public VIRTUE (see also AMERICAN EXCEPTIONALISM). As the United States gradually forced or bought out the Europeans, confined the aboriginal Americans to reservations, and freed the slaves during the Civil War, the national mission took on the appearance of a "manifest destiny." The United States was not only intended to rule North America from shore to shore, but was to spread Western morality, political self-government, and free market capitalism around the world.

When the field of American intellectual history emerged between the two world wars, historians anchored the meaning of America to its concept of national mission. Unable to base their unity on common ethnic backgrounds, Americans had apparently drawn their identity from common purpose—shared commitment to DEMOCRACY, individual RIGHTS, and free enterprise. When the United States entered the fray against both fascism and communism, Ralph Gabriel published The Course of American Democratic Thought. To Gabriel and his followers, the public function of the mission idea was so compelling that they believed American Protestant missions to non-Christians flowed from it.

By the mid-twentieth century, most intellectuals had followed Gabriel in subsuming the specifically religious manifestations of the American mission impulse under the umbrella of national identity. In 1952 historian PERRY MILLER, who in the 1940s had single-handedly rescued the intellectual life of American Puritans from oblivion, published the important essay "Errand into the Wilderness." Here he traced the origins of American identity to the Puritans' desire to preserve pure RELIGION through emigration from Europe. The abundance of land, however, worked against rigorous communal discipline and a national

mission emerged from the failure of the religious one. Miller's essay symbolized for a generation of thinkers the essential unity of American tradition and identity, and the replacement of religious conceptions and motivations by secular ones.

After consensual interpretations of American history were challenged by the social upheavals of the 1960s, mission became a metaphor not of national virtue but of imperialistic excess. (See also CONSENSUS.) To many intellectuals, the failure of American intervention in VIETNAM implicated both Christian mission and national mission as mere rationales for the oppression of minorities, weaker nations, and non-Christian religions. Mission no longer represented America's virtue, but its fatal flaw. (See also IMPERIALISM AND ANTI-IMPERIALISM.) Historian Arthur Schlesinger Jr., in "The Missionary Enterprise and Theories of Imperialism," captured in 1974 the reigning disgust with mission when he equated American missions with cultural imperialism. Missionaries may not have personally wielded economic or political power, he argued, but they represented the purposeful aggression of American culture against the ideas and cultures of other people.

From the 1940s through the 1960s, mission remained a powerful intellectual construct representing American identity, either as the hero or the villain of the world. But the idea of a uniform American identity lost validity as social historians emerged, stressing ethnic, regional, class, religious, and gender differences. The mission that had seemed national was instead depicted as middle-class, white, male, and northeastern Protestant. Catherine Albanese, in a popular undergraduate textbook published in 1981, drew on the new sensibility in arguing that mission was a means by which the dominant religion approached the "other" out of "fear of being swept away" (p. 355). Under the influence of social history, mission has become neither unifying nor normative, but rather a rearguard action by groups struggling to maintain their own dominance.

Paradoxically, the severing of mission from its role as symbol of national identity, a development that appears to herald victory for secular interpretations of American destiny, actually permits a deeper understanding of the significance of religion throughout American history. The missional activities of conservative evangelical Christians, sectarians, women, Catholics, and African Americans can now be taken seriously as sincere manifestations of religious belief, not as mere captives of an American national consciousness or economic self-interest. Because of the voluntaristic nature of religious affiliation in a country where church and state are separated, mission is indeed a very American and very necessary activity for the vitality of religious faith. But in an age in which pluralism is celebrated, the existence and meaning of a unified American mission can no longer be taken for granted.

DANA ROBERT

FURTHER READING

Sydney E. Ahlstrom, *A Religious History of the American People* (New Haven: Yale University Press, 1972).

Catherine L. Albanese, *American Religions and Religion* (Belmont, Calif.: Wadsworth, 1981).

Ralph Gabriel, *The Course of American Democratic Thought* (New York: Ronald Press, 1940).

John Higham and Paul K. Conkin, eds., *New Directions in American Intellectual History* (Baltimore: Johns Hopkins University Press, 1979).

William Hutchison, *Errand to the World: American Protestant Thought and Foreign Missions* (Chicago: University of Chicago Press, 1987).

Frederick Merk, *Manifest Destiny and Mission in American History* (New York: Knopf, 1963).

Perry Miller, *Errand into the Wilderness* (Cambridge: Harvard University Press, 1956).

Arthur Schlesinger Jr., "The Missionary Enterprise and Theories of Imperialism," in John K. Fairbank, ed., *The Missionary Enterprise in China and America* (Cambridge: Harvard University Press, 1974).

Mitchell, S[ilas] Weir (b. Philadelphia, Pa., Feb. 15, 1829; d. Philadelphia, Pa., Jan. 4, 1914). Neurologist and writer. An early investigator, during the Civil War, into the physiology of neurological trauma, Mitchell became well known in the 1870s for his "rest cure" for neurasthenics. Sharing the common belief of his day that people possess a finite quantity of nervous energy, he prescribed extended periods of bed rest designed to conserve energy by removing all stimuli. In addition to *Fat and Blood* (1877), a widely read volume on nervous ailments, Mitchell published poetry and fiction, especially such historical romances as *Roland Blake* (1886) and *Hugh Wynne, Free Quaker* (1897).

See also CHARLOTTE PERKINS GILMAN.

FURTHER READING

Tom Lutz, *American Nervousness, 1903: an Anecdotal History* (Ithaca: Cornell University Press, 1991).

modernism The current status of modernism within historical scholarship presents a paradox. People writing on twentieth-century culture in a variety of fields employ the term regularly. Few would disagree that something called "modernism" has played a major role in shaping virtually all areas of artistic and intellectual endeavor on both sides of the Atlantic during the present century. Moreover, it is obvious that "modernism" represents the precursor to POSTMODERNISM, one of the hottest topics in scholarly discourse today. Yet, despite modernism's unquestionable significance, we currently have almost no agreement on how to define it.

Many factors help to account for this peculiar situation. One problem has been contemporaneity: until recently we have simply been too close to modernist culture to get sufficient perspective on it. Another problem has been modernism's origins. First appearing as an "adversary culture" that came into being in the bohemian quarters of various European cities during the final decades of the nineteenth century, modernism began its existence by staging spectacular assaults on the pieties and aesthetic tastes of the bourgeoisie. Whether those assaults took the form of the radical poetic innovations of the French Symbolists, the startling visual experiments of the Fauves and Cubists, or the manifestoes and antics of the Dadaists, early modernism was designed to shock. As a result, a seemingly indelible impression was created that modernism was a phenomenon limited essentially to the *fin-de-siècle* avant-garde with only occasional intrusions into mainstream society. Were that impression true, however, it would be impossible to account for the vast number of staple items in contemporary culture that are conventionally described as modernist, including the "International Style" architecture that adorns the Chicago skyline or the montage technique so abundantly employed in Hollywood films and television advertising.

Our present understanding of modernism has become particularly confused because of the advent of postmodernism. Though postmodernism itself represents a concept very much in flux, interest in it has grown so rapidly in recent years that modernism has become almost entirely overshadowed. Worse still, some explicators and advocates of postmodernism have dramatically distorted the historical record in regard to modernism, saddling it with the very elements of nineteenth-century positivism and formalism against which it originally rebelled. The modernist culture that such critics conjure up is essentially a straw man; it rests, they claim, on the fundamental assumption that human beings can muster enough objectivity to acquire direct, verifiable knowledge of reality. Postmodernism, the presumption goes, has at last delivered us from this illusion. The problem, of course, is that the cultural revolution that the postmodernists assume took place in the 1970s in fact occured 60 to 70 years earlier. It was precisely the early prophets of modernism such as WILLIAM JAMES who first underscored the limitations of empiricism, just as it was the initial cadre of modernist artists who overthrew the longstanding practices of REPRESENTATION in art.

How, then, can we arrive at a more accurate conception of modernist culture? The first step is to differentiate it sharply from MODERNIZATION. While modernism exists almost entirely within the ideational realm of culture, modernization represents a process of social and economic transformation from the traditional world of peasant agriculture toward a style of life marked by INDUSTRIALISM, URBANISM, novel TECHNOLOGY, and bureaucracy. Those writing on the subject disagree as to whether any deep-rooted relationship exists between modernist culture and modernization. While some modernist writers have been fierce opponents of MASS CULTURE and bureaucratic government, others have welcomed these developments as part and parcel of the spread of DEMOCRACY, and still others have approached modernization with considerable ambivalence. Clearly, "modern" and "modernist" are in no way synonymous.

The origins of modernism are usually traced to the small contingent of Symbolist poets and Impressionist painters who started gathering in and around Paris in the 1870s and 1880s. During the ensuing decades the number of cultural rebels living in the Latin Quarter continued to grow, with the addition of figures like Picasso, Matisse, Braque, Breton, Satie, and Stravinsky. Paris remained the headquarters, but by the start of the new century similar centers of artistic and cultural ferment had sprung up in other major European and American cities. In New York a diverse band of talented men and women met at the Greenwich Village salon of MABEL DODGE LUHAN and at the Little Gallery of the Photo-Secession run by ALFRED STEIGLITZ. In this group one could find the radical journalists JOHN REED and Louise Bryant, soon to become famous for their coverage of the Bolshevik Revolution in Russia; the brilliant but troubled young playwright EUGENE O'NEILL, whose most notable works would include *The Emperor Jones*, *The Iceman Cometh*, and *Long Day's Journey into Night*; the dancer Isadora Duncan, a rebel against classical ballet engaged in pioneering the new genre of "modern dance"; and such writers and activists as MAX EASTMAN, MARGARET SANGER, and WALTER LIPPMANN. In due course the movement would spread beyond these quasi-bohemian enclaves, penetrating academia and a number of important literary circles and, in time, mainstream culture.

The early modernists were engaged in overthrowing the culture of VICTORIANISM they had inherited by breaking all of the moral and epistemological rules that Victorians treasured. The Victorians had sought above all to create a stable, predictable, middle-class world in which social status and acceptable behavior would be clearly defined and the forces of nature

kept at bay. Within that world, an unmistakable dividing line separated what was "moral" and "true" from what was not, and civilized persons stayed on the right side of the line. Especially disapproved of was any traffic with the "baser" human passions or the lower social orders.

To modernists, this Victorian *mentalité* seemed unbearably restrictive, hypocritical, and false. Their aim, to borrow one of their favorite images, was to break down the walls that the Victorians had tried to erect between human beings and the "real world"— especially those painful, imprisoning walls that existed within the self. The "real world," modernists believed, was entirely unpredictable and thus beyond hope of firm human control or understanding. Where the Victorians had clung to the comforting assumption that the universe was governed by some kind of benevolent deity who imposed moral order on it, modernists accepted the post-Darwinian view that nature was ruled primarily by chance and incessant change. There were no "natural laws" for human beings to discover, only empirical regularities to observe and codify into provisional theories that doubtless would not stand the test of time. In a word, modernism decreed that we must henceforth learn to live without any form of epistemological or moral certainty. Anything less would be dishonest and self-defeating.

While the first modernists concentrated on liberating themselves from the constraints imposed by nineteenth-century culture, those who followed turned to the more positive task of building a new basis for social order and knowledge. If the Victorians had tried to perfect society by separating people and things into distinct categories in order to maintain stability and control, modernists sought to integrate all facets of existence. Hierarchies and barriers of all sorts came under attack, especially those dividing social classes, nationalities, races, and genders. Every conceivable duality was challenged, including those of subject and object, body and mind, mass and energy, art and reality, and intellect and emotion. Because nature has no inherent order, the modernists' guiding assumption ran, human beings must create order themselves, relying on experience for whatever imperfect knowledge they can obtain. The task became one of creating what Eugene Lunn in *Marxism and Modernism* calls "contingent syntheses" in order to "remake the world" (p. 51). These new unities were always considered provisional, for experience shows that historical conditions will shift, rendering the synthesis that was successful in guiding human endeavor in one era a detriment in the next. Given the incessant flux in which we live, the gravest danger, modernists claimed, is to conceive of any belief or value as an absolute.

Such is the essential structure of modernist culture, but at this point many additional questions arise, especially in regard to the range of modernism. The primary debate centers on whether modernism should be seen as an influential but nonetheless comparatively small-scale movement, one of several that have appeared on the American cultural landscape during the last hundred years, or, as Stephen Kern writes in *The Culture of Time and Space*, as "a cultural revolution of the broadest scope . . . that involved essential structures of human experience and basic forms of human expression" (p. 6). There is also the matter of where to draw its temporal boundaries. Was modernism principally a phenomenon of the first few decades of the twentieth century, reaching its high water mark in the work of t. s. ELIOT and WILLIAM FAULKNER, or has it persisted as a major cultural movement into the middle decades of the century and beyond?

Putting together evidence from many different realms of discourse, it appears desirable to follow the advice of Peter Gay, who insists in *Freud, Jews and Other Germans* on the need for "enlarging the territory of modernism" (p. 21). Modernist culture has fundamentally transformed our modes of perception, leading to radical changes in painting, sculpture, architecture, literature, photography, film, drama and dance. Modernism has likewise transformed natural SCIENCE, changing the way that physicists view the universe and biologists see the natural environment, as well as totally recasting the epistemological assumptions on which scientists proceed when forming their basic concepts. Finally, one finds heavy modernist influence in SOCIAL SCIENCE in, to take one example, the relativistic conception of culture that suffuses twentieth-century anthropology and sociology. In Gay's words, modernism represents nothing less than "a pervasive cultural revolution, a second Renaissance" (p. 26).

Of course, modernism never gained a monopoly hold, determining every facet of American thought and existence. No culture ever does that. Rather, the key presuppositions of modernism—its beliefs in an ever-changing, unpredictable cosmos, in epistemic and moral relativism, and in the values of integration and authenticity—have become the prevailing assumptions in most areas of intellectual endeavor and, to a somewhat lesser extent, in American social mores and policy.

To be sure, one can easily locate any number of writers or cultural movements in twentieth-century America that do not share those assumptions, or that may even have arisen in reaction to them. It is also possible to point to an array of voices within modernism itself that inevitably developed as the culture spread through American society. The variant of modernism that flourished in New York City, for instance, has sounded quite different at times from those of Chicago or the deep South. Just as pronounced is the variation found across academic fields of inquiry. One prominent strain of modernism located primarily in the arts and humanities stems from the work of William James and tends to emphasize imagination, creativity, and artifice, while another strain more characteristic of the social sciences descends from JOHN DEWEY, is far more empirically oriented, and focuses on social and political pluralism. Similarly, modernists have occupied the entire political spectrum, ranging from protofascists such as EZRA POUND to counterculture radicals of the 1960s such as Abbie Hoffmann. Indeed, charting this medley of voices and discourses within the culture is one of the most pressing tasks now facing historians of modernism as they examine this extraordinarily rich subject, which holds the promise of illuminating so many facets of American life in the twentieth century.

DANIEL J. SINGAL

FURTHER READING

Malcolm Bradbury and James McFarlane, eds., *Modernism, 1890–1930* (New York: Penguin, 1976).

Peter Gay, *Freud, Jews and Other Germans: Masters and Victims in Modernist Culture* (New York: Oxford University Press, 1978).

Stephen Kern, *The Culture of Time and Space, 1880–1918* (Cambridge: Harvard University Press, 1983).

Robert Kiely, ed., *Modernism Reconsidered* (Cambridge: Harvard University Press, 1983).

Eugene Lunn, *Marxism and Modernism: an Historical Study of Lukács, Brecht, Benjamin and Adorno* (Berkeley: University of California Press, 1982).

Dorothy Ross, ed., *Modernism in the Human Sciences* (Baltimore: Johns Hopkins University Press, 1994).

Sanford Schwartz, *The Matrix of Modernism: Pound, Eliot and Early Twentieth-Century Thought* (Princeton: Princeton University Press, 1985).

Daniel J. Singal, *The War Within: From Victorian to Modernist Thought in the South, 1919–1945* (Chapel Hill: University of North Carolina Press, 1982).

——, ed., *Modernist Culture in America* (Belmont, Calif.: Wadsworth, 1991).

modernization Although the precise origins of the concept are far from clear, any consideration of modernization points inevitably to the late eighteenth-century acceleration of economic and technological change. Yet the term appears to be less a synonym for industrialization than a summation of its concomitants, ranging from urbanization, secularization, and increased literacy to the replacement of inherited privilege with market relations and broad political participation. Theories of modernization can be traced to the work of classical social theorists such as Max Weber, Émile Durkheim, and Ferdinand Tönnies. In these thinkers one discerns the relentless and sometimes reckless typologizing characteristic of modernization theory in its mature form. By the turn of the century, ALBION SMALL, Hugo Muensterberg, ROBERT E. PARK, LESTER F. WARD, EDWARD ROSS, and other American social scientists were beginning to disseminate European social theory among their colleagues and students, the latter of whom were to transform these ideas by mid-century into a peculiar theory of social change.

Perhaps the earliest use of the term came with the publication of social anthropologist Robert Redfield's study of the Mexican village of Tepoztlan in 1930. Using ideal types derived from Tönnies by way of Park, Redfield described the village as an intermediate point on a universally applicable evolutionary "folk–urban continuum." By identifying the slow diffusion of "city ways" into the lives of rural peoples as the primary impetus for social change, Redfield sought to explain what he thought of as a series of secondary but interrelated processes, including secularization, increased literacy, and the gradual disintegration of community-based life. Although he revised his conclusions in 1955, arguing that elements of *Gemeinschaft* and *Gesellschaft* coexisted in all human settlements, Redfield's original analysis, by emphasizing one of many ostensibly interdependent processes of social change, and by treating such change as a purely internal phenomenon, anticipated the approach of mature modernization theory. (*See also* COMMUNITY; INDUSTRIALISM; URBANISM.)

Full-blown modernization theory arose in the 1950s and 1960s out of attempts to extrapolate a theory of social change from the static postulates of Parsonian structural functionalism, the dominant school of American sociological thought at the time. In its unrevised form, modernization theory imprudently introduced a Eurocentric bias into the emerging debates over the "development" of decolonized nations in the wake of World War II. Social scientists such as W. W. Rostow, Daniel Lerner, and Clark Kerr mounted a multidisciplinary effort to construct a developmental sequence based on the British model, and then applied this sequence to "traditional" societies with little or no regard for their widely divergent historical trajectories and value systems. Revisions emerged as political conflicts began to sweep across the globe in the 1950s. Reinhard Bendix and S. N. Eisenstadt, for example, retained the same

basic typological scheme as earlier theorists, while achieving a greater interpretive flexibility by rejecting teleological claims of unidirectional development and by taking into account Alexander Gershenkron's notion of the advantages of backwardness, which recognized that effective emulation of "developed" nations invariably required significant deviations from the original process, some of which offered shortcuts. Acknowledging the irrelevance of the British sequence for many non-Western societies, Bendix remarked in his 1967 article on "Tradition and Modernity Reconsidered" that multiple models would be preferable to "forcing all types of social change into the Procrustes bed of the European experience" (p. 323).

Although the bulk of modernization theory was developed and utilized by sociologists and economists—who are inclined toward theoretical generalization to begin with—American historians also found the concept of modernization useful. FREDERICK JACKSON TURNER, RICHARD HOFSTADTER, Samuel Hays, Robert Wiebe, and Alfred Chandler, among others, loosely incorporated its typological dichotomies into their work. This casual, implicit use of modernization typology, which is still evident, for example, in the most recent work of Gordon Wood, should be distinguished from the self-conscious application of modernization theory among American historians, which came (and went) only in the 1960s and 1970s. Just as other social scientists were refining or abandoning the theory, historians such as Richard D. Brown, Robert Gross, and Richard Jensen, eschewing the idiographic propensities of their discipline, were beginning to apply the framework in their various explanations of American social change, often without regard for the theory's difficulties and corrective revisions.

Criticism of modernization theory has come from three main sources. Marxist scholars such as Perry Anderson and Eric Wolf have explored the consequences of clashing modes of production, while others so inclined have followed the lead of Immanuel Wallerstein's world systems approach, which attributes the rise and stability of Western capitalism in large part to the lack of European political unity, enabling greater freedom of movement for economic actors and ensuring the persistence of regional inequalities necessary for the generation of profits. Cultural anthropologists and historians, including Eric Hobsbawm, Jay O'Brien, William Roseberry, and Micaela Di Leonardo, have concentrated on the modern construction of cultural "traditions." "Traditional radical" CHRISTOPHER LASCH viewed the hubris of modernization theory as symptomatic of the impoverished ideology of PROGRESS ascendant since the eighteenth century. To this worldview, which is currently subscribed to by Marxists, liberals, and neoconservatives alike, he attributed a destructive commitment to unmitigated economic expansion and technological domination of nature.

These and other critics have made it clear that the mature expression of modernization theory did not emerge in a political vacuum. Inextricably bound up with Cold War polarization, it provided a convenient ideological spectrum on which to situate the world's nation-states, one that arrogantly placed the positive connotations of "modernity" in the exclusive service of "First World" countries, while consigning the rest of the world to various stages of "underdevelopment." By insisting that developing societies have followed (and should continue to follow) a progression of predetermined stages in the march toward modernity, and by declaring that this progression is driven solely by the internal dynamics of these societies, modernization theorists substituted abstract processes for real political struggles, obscuring the frequently brutal conquest, colonization, and exploitation of non-Western peoples that played a central role in the emergence and consolidation of Western dominance. In the name of progress and anticommunism, for example, the United States government and major foundations created an interventionist rationale in Africa, Asia, and Latin America during the COLD WAR era, hoping to stimulate one or more of the allegedly interrelated variables of social change.

Having succeeded in unhitching a useful set of typologies from their originally ambivalent expression in classical social theory, modernization theorists proceeded to recast them in a celebratory evolutionary progression. Modernizationists ignored Weber's earlier warnings concerning the hypothetical character of ideal types, mistaking them for concrete social and historical realities. This is doubly unfortunate, since oppositional ideal-types—community and society, tradition and modernity, and folk culture and urban culture—can be valuable tools of comparative analysis if handled with precision.

JORDAN KLEIMAN

See also MANAGERIALISM; TECHNOLOGY.

FURTHER READING

Reinhard Bendix, "Tradition and Modernity Reconsidered," *Comparative Studies in Society and History* 9 (Apr. 1967): 292–346.
Dwight Hoover, "The Long Ordeal of Modernization Theory," *Prospects* 11 (1986): 407–51.
Christopher Lasch, *The True and Only Heaven: Progress and Its Critics* (New York: Norton, 1991).
Jay O'Brien and William Roseberry, eds., *Golden Ages, Dark Ages: Imagining the Past in Anthropology and History* (Berkeley: University of California Press, 1991).
Martin Sklar, *The United States as a Developing Country: Studies in U.S. History in the Progressive Era and the 1920s* (Cambridge: Cambridge University Press, 1992).
Theda Skocpol, "Sociology's Historical Imagination," in *Vision and Method in Historical Sociology* (Cambridge: Cambridge University Press, 1984).
Dean C. Tipps, "Modernization Theory and the Comparative Study of Societies: a Critical Perspective," *Comparative Studies in Society and History* 15 (Mar. 1973): 199–226.

Momaday, N[avarro] Scott (b. Lawton, Okla., Feb. 27, 1934). A truism of canon formation: unrecognized literatures need breakthrough events to gain attention and legitimacy. For American Indian literatures, the key event occurred in 1969 when a young, unknown Kiowa painter, poet, and scholar won a Pulitzer Prize for his remarkable novel *House Made of Dawn* (1968). This event is filled with ironies offering revealing insights about the way Native American literatures have gained acceptance, about the nature of N. Scott Momaday's writing, and about the significance of contemporary Native American literature.

The most obvious irony is the great delay in recognition of literatures in several hundred languages that include centuries-old, even millennia-old oral narratives, ceremonial liturgies, and autobiographical accounts, as well as histories, essays, autobiographies, poetry, and fiction written in English. The delay reflects not only the power of cultural blinders, but also a nineteenth- and twentieth-century disciplinary territorialism that placed Indians within the anthropologist's and, occasionally, the historian's camp. Of course, the breakthrough suggests the importance of the 1960s commitment to civil rights and ethnic studies. It also reflects another truism: literary critics and teachers of literature tend to recognize examples of "new" literatures that are different enough to seem Authentically Other but familiar enough to be incorporated into current interpretive discourses. *House Made of Dawn* fulfilled these two requirements wonderfully. The authentically different quotient was provided by the focus on an Indian protagonist and two significant types of Indian settings (a Western pueblo, Jemez, and an urban relocation center, Los Angeles); by the use of English re-creations of oral literatures, both specific (Kiowa narrative, Jemez ritual, Navajo song) and general (the circular structure of the novel); and by the authority of an Indian author who looked Indian, had a seven-eighths Kiowa birth certificate, and a marvelous performance voice. Accessibility came from the use of a familiar and popular genre (the novel) and from beautifully crafted sentences that could echo Hemingway's compactness, Faulkner's stream of consciousness, and the Bible (the protagonist's name is Abel).

House Made of Dawn's rich integrations of oral and written literatures suggest another irony of the 1969 Pulitzer Prize, one that offers insights into all of Momaday's works and into the significance of contemporary Native American fiction and poetry. *House Made of Dawn* is routinely associated with "Indian" or "Native American" literatures. These labels, though useful and appropriate, tend to obscure two dimensions of the multiculturalism (multitribalism, multiethnicity) expressed in Momaday's major works and in the best contemporary literature by Indian writers.

Momaday's background certainly fostered multicultural perspectives. He was born in 1934 in Kiowa country—southwestern Oklahoma—and his autobiographical books, *The Way to Rainy Mountain* (1969) and *The Names* (1976), emphasize the importance of the Kiowa landscape and his father's tribal heritage. But his mother was one-eighth Cherokee and seven-eighths Euro-American blends, so his birth certificate is misleading. Young Scott spent his childhood in several different southwestern communities (Gallup, Shiprock, Tuba City, Chinle, San Carlos, Hobbes), where he was in close contact with Navajo and San Carlos Apache, as well as Hispanic and Anglo children. When Momaday was 12 his parents took teaching jobs at Jemez Pueblo. In his book *In the Presence of the Sun* (1992) Momaday recalls that his childhood experiences made him fall in love with Kiowa, Navajo, pueblo, Spanish, and English words. After studying at a Virginia military academy, Momaday attended the University of New Mexico (B.A. in political science), the University of Virginia (briefly to study law), and Stanford (M.A. and Ph.D. in English). At Stanford he was strongly influenced by Ivor Winters, who supervised his dissertation, a critical edition of the poetry of Frederick Goddard Tuckerman that was published by Oxford University Press in 1965. Momaday has won a Guggenheim fellowship and the Academy of American Poets Prize and has taught at Berkeley, Stanford, and, most recently, the University of Arizona. Emblematic of his varied achievements and background are the two honors he received in 1969: a Pulitzer prize and election into the Kiowa Gourd Clan.

Momaday's fiction makes abundant use of the diversity of his multicultural background. *House Made of Dawn* focuses on a returning Jemez Pueblo World War II veteran sent to prison and then relocated after he kills an albino he perceives as a witch. Indian viewpoints are not, however, limited to Jemez perspectives. In their own (sometimes self-serving, sometimes more altruistic) ways, a Kiowa preacher and pan-Indian peyote man, a relocated Navajo, a white rural farmer's daughter, and an urban doctor's wife all try to heal Abel from their perspectives. In Momaday's second novel *Ancient Child* (1989), the protagonist is Set (Kiowa for bear), an adopted Kiowa-Anglo. He is a successful San Francisco artist going through a painful mid-life crisis. Set's primary healer Grey nurtures him toward an understanding of his Kiowa identity and the exhilarating and terrifying encounter with bear power that comes with that recognition. Grey is one of Momaday's finest multicultural creations. She is mostly Navajo and Kiowa but also Mexican, French Canadian, Scottish, Irish, and English.

Momaday's poetry—as collected in *Angle of Geese and Other Poems* (1974), *The Gourd Dancer* (1976), and *In the Presence of the Sun* (1992)—again communicates the multiculturalism of contemporary Indian literature. In the latter, for example, the third section offers 16 drawings of Plains shields each accompanied by a corresponding prose poem based primarily on Kiowa oral and written history. This section is framed by a gathering of Momaday's Billy the Kid poems (adolescent fantasies of Billy captivated both Momaday and Grey) and by recent poems and drawings that range from celebrations of his Kiowa grandmother expressed in the cadences of a Navajo prayer ("Prayer") to cryptic couplet poems reminiscent of the wit of Alexander Pope and Benjamin Franklin.

Even *The Way to Rainy Mountain*—Momaday's intricate collection of Kiowa tribal and family stories, Kiowa history, and personal memories of Kiowa landscapes and people—is a multicultural reading experience. It grew out of stories Momaday had heard since childhood into a privately published collection of Momaday's English versions of tribal and family narratives (*The Journey of the Tai-me*, 1967) into a brilliant modernist experiment in juxtapositions of public oral and written literatures and private memories.

For scholars and critics in search of pure tribal "Indian" literature, Momaday's Pulitzer and his books may be viewed as contaminated frauds rather than Native American breakthroughs. Of course, these readers ignore the fact that intertribal relations made Indian literatures multicultural long before Columbus labeled our native peoples "Indians." Certainly today, as the best Indian authors repeatedly remind us, the Native American experience is a complex multiethnic, multicultural experience. And since, with each generation, "American culture" is becoming more multicultural, Momaday's breakthrough in 1969 was more than an exciting foreshadowing of recognition for centuries-old literatures and the emergence of Native American writers as powerful as LESLIE MARMON SILKO, James Welch, Gerald Vizenor, Louise Erdrich, and Michael Dorris. The appearance of and favorable response to *House Made of Dawn* was also a foreshadowing of central multicultural issues that will challenge all serious late twentieth-century American writers and thus signaled one of the most significant contributions of contemporary Native American literature.

KENNETH M. ROEMER

See also CULTURAL PLURALISM AND MULTICULTURALISM; INDIAN IDENTITIES.

FURTHER READING

Larry Evers, "Words and Place: a Reading of *House Made of Dawn*," *Western American Literature* 11 (Feb. 1977): 297–320.

Kenneth M. Roemer, ed., *Approaches to Teaching Momaday's "The Way to Rainy Mountain"* (New York: Modern Language Association, 1988).

Susan Scarberry-Garcia, *Landmarks of Healing: a Study of "House Made of Dawn"* (Albuquerque: University of New Mexico Press, 1990).

Matthias Schubnell, *N. Scott Momaday: the Cultural and Literary Background* (Norman: University of Oklahoma Press, 1985).

Martha Scott Trimble, *N. Scott Momaday* (Boise, Idaho: Boise State University Press, 1973).

Charles Woodard, ed., *Ancestral Voice: Conversations with N. Scott Momaday* (Lincoln: University of Nebraska Press, 1989).

Moore, Marianne (b. Kirkwood, Mo., Nov. 15, 1887; d. New York, N.Y., Feb. 5, 1972). Poet. As influential editor of *The Dial* (1925–9) and in her own writing, Moore maintained a strong presence in the male-dominated world of high MODERNISM. Her poetry joined an ironic eye for everyday experience, an interest in formal experimentation, and an ethical sensibility that linked her to such contemporaries as T. S. ELIOT, WALLACE STEVENS, and her close friend Elizabeth Bishop. Her most important volume, *Observations* (1924), exhibited Moore's understanding of poetry as a means of insight into both the moral and natural worlds.

FURTHER READING

Judith Merrin, *An Enabling Humility: Marianne Moore, Elizabeth Bishop, and the Uses of Tradition* (New Brunswick, N.J.: Rutgers University Press, 1990).

More, Paul Elmer (b. St. Louis, Mo., Dec. 12, 1864; d. Princeton, N.J., Mar. 9, 1937). Critic. An accomplished literary editor in New York before taking a teaching position at Princeton on the eve of World War I, More preached a New Humanism that looked to the classical era for models of order, harmony, and morality. He condemned both RoMANTICISM and NATURALISM, upheld property rights as the foundation of a cultured aristocratic class, and deplored democracy's debased standards. Along with his fellow humanist IRVING BABBITT, he rested authority—the source of order in art and life—in the common sense of a finely trained mind. In addition to his articles and reviews, collected in *Shelburne Essays* (11 vols., 1904–21), he authored such texts as *Nietzsche* (1912) and *The Religion of Plato* (1921).

See also CONSERVATISM.

FURTHER READING

J. David Hoeveler, *The New Humanism: a Critique of Modern America, 1900–1940* (Charlottesville: University of Virginia Press, 1977).

Morgan, Thomas Hunt (b. Lexington, Ky., Sept. 25, 1866; d. Pasadena, Calif., Dec. 4, 1945). Geneticist. Morgan developed the chromosomal theory of inheritance by studying mutation patterns in fruit flies. Discovering that certain traits almost always occur together and knowing that chromosome pairs can be seen in the nucleus, he guessed that the genetic elements that cause linked traits are clustered on the same chromosome. Finding that linked traits do occasionally occur separately, he further concluded that chromosome pairs must be able to exchange genetic material. Statistical analysis of these exchanges allowed him to map the distance between genes. First summarized in *The Mechanism of Mendelian Heredity* (1915, with A. H. Sturtevant, C. B. Bridges, and H. J. Muller), Morgan's discoveries provided the first physical basis for the controversial theory of genetic inheritance.

FURTHER READING

Garland Allen, *Thomas Hunt Morgan: the Man and His Science* (Princeton: Princeton University Press, 1978).

Morgenthau, Hans (b. Coburg, Germany, Feb. 17, 1904; d. New York, N.Y., July 19, 1980). Political scientist. Morgenthau's *Politics among Nations* (1948) asserted the basic principle of political realism: that all human relations are based on a struggle for power. The best hope for world peace is an international balance of power, since nations will not sacrifice their own interest to follow international law or opinion. Ethics are not irrelevant to international relations, but abstract moral rules must give way to fact-based analysis, and idealistic intentions must be subordinated to the realistic assessment of actual consequences.

FURTHER READING
Greg Russell, *Hans J. Morgenthau and the Ethics of American Statecraft* (Baton Rouge: Louisiana State University Press, 1990).

Morris, George Sylvester (b. Norwich, Vt., Nov. 15, 1840; d. Ann Arbor, Mich., Mar. 23, 1889). Philosopher. After studying philosophy in Germany, Morris returned home a convert to absolute idealism, which he taught at Johns Hopkins and Michigan. As the principal American champion of the ideas of Hegel and T. H. Green, he asserted that subject and object exist in an organic relation: neither has reality apart from the other. Knowledge of an object requires knowledge of a connected whole to which that object is related, and relation is a function of consciousness, so there must exist a single, permanent, and all-inclusive self-consciousness—an Absolute, or God. Morris criticized philosophy's overemphasis on logic and empiricism: thought is a form of motion, and understanding it requires a "science" of lived experience. This idealism attuned to experience was a major formative influence on JOHN DEWEY. Morris's writings include *Philosophy and Christianity* (1883) and *Hegel's Philosophy of the State and of History: an Exposition* (1887).

FURTHER READING
Marc E. Jones, *George Sylvester Morris: His Philosophical Career and Theistic Idealism* (Philadelphia: D. McKay, 1948).

Morrison, Toni (b. Lorain, Ohio, Feb. 18, 1931). With works translated into 21 languages, Toni Morrison is the most renowned black woman novelist to date. Author of six novels, a collection of essays, and dozens of articles and reviews, she is often favorably compared to writers like William Faulkner, Thomas Hardy, and James Joyce. Critics especially applaud her achievements in voice, narrative movement, and dialogue, her control of verbal nuance, metaphor, image, and point of view, and her ability to transpose black orality into the written word. In addition to the Nobel Prize for literature (1993), her awards include the Pulitzer Prize for *Beloved* (1987), the Modern Language Association's Commonwealth Award in Literature (1989), City College of New York's Langston Hughes Festival Award (1988), and the American Academy and Institute of Arts and Letters Distinguished Writers Award (1978).

Although she is well educated in Western literary conventions and recognizes the value of comparisons of her work to the works of white male literary giants, Morrison insists that her novels derive from certain ineffable elements exclusive to black culture.

Born to parents whose families migrated from the South in search of better life opportunities for their offspring, Morrison was nurtured in childhood by life stories of her elders that kept her close to her ancestors. The world of the black community, with its well-defined codes, superstitions, fables, myths, family quarrels, and songs, is always at the heart of her works. Committed to upholding the integrity of black American cultural aesthetics, she believes that the best art is political but also beautiful. Her main purpose in writing, she says, is to keep alive some of the stories that kept black people alive through centuries of Western oppression, stories which are now endangered as black communities fragment and disperse. Her animating goal of preserving traditions threatened by modern life is conservative in the richest sense of the word.

A teenager who studied Latin and read widely in English, French, and Russian literature, Morrison earned a B.A. (1953) and M.A. (1955) from Howard and Cornell universities. In graduate school her thesis explored suicide in the works of Virginia Woolf and Faulkner. Her writing career, following faculty positions at Texas Southern and Howard universities, and editorial work at Random House, began in earnest with the publication of *The Bluest Eye* in 1970. This book helped inaugurate the decade when black women writers emerged as a group to claim literary territory. Until then, in spite of their astonishing publication record since the early nineteenth century, black women had received little individual or collective public acclaim, even in black literary circles. In the 1970s, with the civil rights and women's movements mobilized to attack the nation's racial and patriarchal assumptions and practices, black women writers gained a place of their own. Along with Morrison, Toni Cade Bambara, Angela Davis, Paule Marshall, Octavia Butler, June Jordan, Audre Lorde, Alice Walker, and Gayl Jones were among the most visible and talented writers of that generation.

The Bluest Eye, the story of a young black girl from a dysfunctional family who craved blue eyes in a search for beauty and happiness that ended in incest and madness, did not bring instant fame to Toni Morrison. Neither did her second novel, *Sula* (1975), the story of a black woman who refused to conform to the social conventions approved for her group. While many black women hailed these works for their skill in conveying painful black female experiences in a direct, moving, and sympathetic way, the white literary establishment tended to dismiss them for provinciality. However, *Song of Solomon* (1977) met an enthusiastic general response. It caught the public's imagination and instantly propelled Morrison to a fame that grew monumentally thereafter. Here a male at center stage plays out familiar themes of flight, journey, and the search for male identity. In *Tar Baby* (1981) Morrison brought together the invasion of an exotic Caribbean locale by wealthy white Americans, the sophistication of Paris, the excitement of New York City, the traditionalism of Philadelphia, and the backwoods sensibility of rural black Florida in a fusion of fantasy and realism rooted in a black folktale.

Beloved, perhaps the most widely read of her novels, is a meditation on the legacy of slavery that grew out of an antebellum newspaper report of a black mother who killed her child to save her from a life of bestial servitude. With an uncommon capacity to render the pain of her characters and of her own encounter with them, Morrison presents and questions a mother love so powerful that it displaces self. The story is a monument to the "60 million and more" lost in slavery, and to the others who, each day of their lives, endured its terrible agonies. *Jazz* (1992), a story of love, jealousy, and death, is set in Harlem in the 1920s and examines the lives of its players across time in the South and the North. In language that captures the rhythms of jazz, the novel is especially praiseworthy for its rendition of a vast array of human emotions.

In each of these works, Toni Morrison is a superb storyteller whose facility with language and style has few equals in twentieth-century American literature. For all the magnificent artistry that sets her apart from most other practicing writers, she has not produced in isolation. Her success in evoking the inner lives of black women and men has made an enormous contribution to opening up literary space and recognition for black and feminist texts. She is also a talented critic and theorist, as evidenced by her outstanding collection *Playing in the Dark* (1992) and her path-breaking essay "Unspeakable Things Unspoken: the Afro-American Presence in American Literature" (1989). The multitalented Morrison currently holds an academic position at Princeton University, where she engages in the important work of revising the critical history of American literature.

Toni Morrison often speaks of black music, especially jazz, as the repository of the black cultural element she most desires her writing to emulate: an articulation that comes to an end without a final chord, so that it leaves listeners on the edge—waiting, wanting more. In this her fiction resembles the most challenging and evocative poetry. The unforgettable concluding exchange between Paul D. and Sethe in *Beloved* in one prime example. "'Sethe,' he says, 'me and you, we got more yesterday than any-body. We need some kind of tomorrow. . . . You your own best thing, Sethe. You are.' His holding fingers are holding hers. 'Me? Me?'"

NELLIE Y. MCKAY

FURTHER READING

Jane S. Bakerman, "Failures of Love: Female Initiation in the Novels of Toni Morrison," *American Literature* 52 (1981): 541–63.

Karla F. C. Holloway and Stephanie A. Demetrakopoulos, *New Dimensions of Spirituality: a Biracial and Bicultural Reading of the Novels of Toni Morrison* (New York: Greenwood, 1987).

Nellie Y. McKay, ed., *Critical Essays on Toni Morrison* (Boston; G. K. Hall, 1987).

Toni Morrison, "Rootedness: the Ancestor as Foundation," in Mari Evans, ed., *Black Women Writers* (New York: Anchor, 1983).

——, "Unspeakable Things Unspoken: the Afro-American Presence in American Literature," *Michigan Quarterly Review* 28 (winter 1989): 1–34.

Gloria Naylor and Toni Morrison, "A Conversation," *Southern Review* 21 (July 1985): 567–93.

Wilfred D. Samuels, *Toni Morrison* (Boston: Twayne, 1990).

Robert Stepto, "'Intimate Things in Place': a Conversation with Toni Morrison," *Massachusetts Review* 18 (autumn 1977): 473–89.

motherhood Mother earth. Mother nature. Mother tongue. The Mother of God. For centuries our language has insisted on the stability and succor offered by maternity. In all cultures motherhood is, among other things, the provision by women of the tender comfort craved by all human beings, who, Freud speculated, yearn for the "oceanic feeling" of belonging acquired in the womb. But in modern American culture, where the ideal of motherhood still conveys the notion of gentle, sacrificial nurture, mothering has been forced into a constricted institutional and ideological matrix. It is not that women are forced to be mothers; on the contrary, women are increasingly encouraged to pursue independent careers apart from or without being mothers. The constraint operates more subtly. In a traditionally and still heavily patriarchal society, motherhood is delimited by a boundary of such apparent naturalness that it is scarcely perceived: women are to mother only their own biological children, the offspring of their husbands.

In the rest of the world, biological mothers are much more commonly joined by other women (and by some men and older children) in caring for their children. In America, women are expected to be able to mother alone, while also pursuing careers or at least jobs outside the home. In the liberal middle class, fathers are increasingly doing some of the "mothering," as fatherhood is redefined to encompass sensitive nurture in addition to the provision of discipline and material sustenance. "Maternal thinking," as Sara Ruddick argues, need not be limited to women. Yet the emergence of domestic FATHERHOOD often complicates the practice of motherhood, since many women feel deprived of the one sure thing that the old ideology of bourgeois motherhood had allowed them: a distinctive responsibility for the care of their offspring. Among American working-class and especially minority women, mothering is much more communal (as well as more frequently unmarried) than it is in the middle class, yet mothers often struggle not just with poverty and a lack of social services, but with the widely disseminated middle-class ideal, which ties status and happiness to the independence (and greater isolation) of the suburban dwelling.

Motherhood has been a deeply contested institution for well over a century. Middle-class feminists argued heatedly in the late nineteenth century for extending the bourgeois liberal revolutions of the late eighteenth century to their logical conclusion: full equality for women. The men who had revolutionized the political and economic worlds of Europe and the United States between 1750 and 1850 had had no interest in transforming motherhood or family relations, aside from encouraging women to help instill republican virtues in their young. Turning the public world upside-down, calling into question long-established patterns of public authority, these revolutionaries had a great stake in preserving a stable private sphere: the unchanging practice of paternal authority at home, the unceasing support offered by self-abnegating women. As the nineteenth-century bourgeoisie turned its attention more and more from political commitments to economic opportunities, as the republican ideal of citizen solidarity was eclipsed by the militant INDIVIDUALISM of liberal culture, motherhood lost some of its political character-building role and became centered in the provision of emotional services for those (mostly male) family members subjected to the numbing demands of the marketplace. Mothers at home were angels of mercy in the capitalist maelstrom.

It was this circumscribed position that women reformers challenged in the nineteenth century: first (with CATHARINE BEECHER) arguing that as mothers women were called to use their influence outside as well as inside the home, to become teachers, nurses, spokeswomen for harmonious social relations; second (with feminists such as CHARLOTTE PERKINS GILMAN) protesting the denial to women of equal access to the means of self-development. Gilman's work, especially her classic volume *Women and Eco-*

nomics (1898), summed up and pushed forward the feminist debate. Indeed, the book is still compelling in its formulation of the perennial dilemma facing FEMINISM: how can feminist theory and practice best take account of the fact that (in Gilman's view) women are (or should be) equal to men and that women are also superior to men (and may always be) in their capacity to dispense care. For Gilman motherhood was the culmination of existence for a woman, as fatherhood was for a man, but only if motherhood was liberated from economic dependence on men and only if parenting was "socialized," only if men and women learned to care for the larger "race" as they cared for their own biological offspring. As the work of Kathryn Kish Sklar (*Florence Kelley and Women's Political Culture*, 1995), Theda Skocpol (*Protecting Soldiers and Mothers*, 1992), and others has recently made clear, the rise of the American welfare state in the late nineteenth and early twentieth centuries was made possible in part by the concerted campaign of women reformers who viewed social policy through the lens of maternal care. (*See also* FLORENCE KELLEY.)

Ann Snitow has noted the recent upsurge of interest in mothering on the part of feminists, who had in the 1970s (as in Shulamith Firestone's influential tract *The Dialectic of Sex*, 1970) taken the lead in challenging the idea of a necessary link between mothering and female fulfillment. Snitow suspects that motherhood reemerged as a paramount goal for feminists in part because the baby-boom generation of women was forced to confront the final ticking of its biological clock. The turn to motherhood may also be a part of a more general reaction against liberal individualism, a reaction led by neoconservative defenders of "family values," but not limited to them. It is also visible among many liberals who believe, with Robert Bellah and the other authors of the best-selling *Habits of the Heart* (1985), that liberalism must transcend individualism if it is to flourish. Motherhood, along with a newly nurturant fatherhood, may be riding a wave of approval among liberals as well as conservatives because it can stand for cross-generational and intragenerational connectedness in a world dominated by temporary, fragile, contractual relationships. (*See also* NEOCONSERVATISM.)

Yet the inherited ideological and cultural framework of motherhood—its traditional capacity to symbolize continuity and care—may be eroding. And not because of feminism, which, far from trying to undermine motherhood as many conservatives imagine, is itself increasingly boosting motherhood as the special site of female fulfillment (although growing numbers of middle-class women, heterosexual as well as lesbian, choose a motherhood without men). The threat to motherhood as a privileged institution, as a symbolic locus of psychic and emotional sustenance, now comes less from feminist agitation than from technological change, economic necessity, and legal innovation. New technology has given rise, for example, to surrogate motherhood, widely publicized in the Baby M case (in which a woman hired to produce a baby for another couple sued unsuccessfully to retain the child after giving birth). Surrogacy has permitted everyday commercial and contractual values to invade what Phyllis Chesler calls the "sacred bond" of the maternal relation. Gilman noted long ago that male commerce in women had already adulterated the family relation, but surrogacy has made the commerce unmistakable.

Meanwhile, economic duress in the middle class as well as the working class has forced many women into the workforce even when they would prefer to stay at home as mothers. Since the early nineteenth century, working-class women have commonly worked outside the home, especially before marriage. After marriage, many continued to work, often by joining family-based groups in factories or by performing piecework at home. As the century progressed, middle-class status was confirmed and signaled by the attainment of a nuclear family life in which the wife was uninvolved in, and unbesmirched by, either the marketplace in general or the wage relation in particular. The wife's protected position became all the more crucial as the industrial era developed: ever larger units of industrial production made it harder and harder for men to attain independence in the world of work, to reach the traditional goal of being their own bosses. White-collar employment for men, for all its promise of greater material rewards, provided a poor symbol of middle-class superiority: no less than blue-collar labor, it represented a state of dependency, as C. WRIGHT MILLS noted in his influential *White Collar* (1951). The "independent" mother, free to oversee her children and to engage in *voluntary* activities from the charity societies and reform organizations of the nineteenth century to the Parent–Teacher Association and the Junior League of the twentieth, was a much more potent symbol of middle-class success. (*See also* SOCIAL MOBILITY.)

The historic importance of the work of BETTY FRIEDAN, especially her bestselling *The Feminine Mystique* (1963), lay in her insistence (following Charlotte Perkins Gilman) that suburban independence was no independence at all, that middle-class women could find true fulfillment only if they were free to enter the marketplace alongside men. But her vision

of female autonomy through careers amounted to a "Super Mom" scenario in which women could have rewarding work outside the home while also diligently succoring their families. Many middle-class women have recently come to doubt their capacity to nurture their families while enduring the treadmill of modern professional WORK. In their belief that career and family may be zero–sum options, they are not unlike the large group of Friedan's female readers in the 1960s who, according to her, resisted the strong judgment *The Feminine Mystique* contained: that home-bound mothers were immature, stuck in the psychological evasion that had led the post-World War II generation of women (and men) to embrace suburban isolation as an emotional salve following the searing decades of the Great Depression and World War II.

In addition to technological change and economic stringency, court decisions are slowly helping to transform family relationships, and with them our idea of what constitutes motherhood. In 1993, for example, 14-year-old Kimberly Mays won the right not to have any contact with her biological parents, and another court upheld a lesbian's right to become the adoptive parent of her partner's child. Kimberly Mays's "father," with whom she had lived since being accidentally switched at birth, was judged to be her legal parent because of the bond that had arisen between them. In the adoption case, Joan G., the adoptive parent, was given parental rights because it was, according to the judge, in the best interest of the three-year-old child. "We cannot continue to pretend," he said, that "there is one formula, one correct pattern that should constitute a family in order to achieve the supportive, loving environment we believe children should inhabit." As motherhood and fatherhood float free of old ideas and practices, they may lose some of their commanding symbolic importance in American culture, some of their capacity to represent permanence in a world of flux, self-sacrificial care in a world of egocentric success-seeking.

That symbolic erosion does not mean that motherhood is coming to an end, only that its particular cultural significance is shifting. Motherhood and fatherhood are rooted in biology as well as culture, even though most scholars now agree that it is impossible to make a clean distinction between the two realms. Indeed, as Thomas Laqueur notes in *Making Sex* (1990), biology itself evolves as culture changes. The fact remains that women and men are instinctual mammals as well as products of social and historical change; the perennial cultural power of motherhood is mysteriously lodged in deep physiological and psychological subsoil. Cultural forms of motherhood will always be regenerated because biology interacts with culture to produce in women as it does in men an urgent call to propagate and protect a new generation. "Natality," as Hannah Arendt suggested at the conclusion of *The Human Condition* (1958), will always confound "fatality." A prime example in our day is the spread of "political motherhood," from the struggle of mothers in Argentina to recover the "disappeareds" (a campaign evoked unforgettably in Lawrence Thornton's 1991 novel *Imagining Argentina*) to the battles led by mothers in the United States against drunk drivers, nuclear weapons, and toxic wastes. If American women continue to mobilize politically as mothers, they will be recreating a movement with deep roots in their own past, from the radical labor agitation of Mother Jones to the indefatigable local and national organizing of Florence Kelley.

RICHARD WIGHTMAN FOX

FURTHER READING

Phyllis Chesler, *Sacred Bond: the Legacy of Baby M* (New York: Random House, 1988).

Nancy Chodorow, *The Reproduction of Mothering: Psychoanalysis and the Sociology of Gender* (Berkeley: University of California Press, 1978).

Angela Y. Davis, "Outcast Mothers and Surrogates: Racism and Reproductive Politics in the 90s," in Linda S. Kauffman, ed., *American Feminist Thought at Century's End: a Reader* (Cambridge, Mass.: Blackwell, 1993).

Faye Ginsburg and Rayna Rapp, "The Politics of Reproduction," *Annual Review of Anthropology* 20 (1991): 311–43.

New York Times: "Court Backs Lesbian's Right to Adopt a Partner's Child," Aug. 11, 1993, p. B5; "Florida Girl, 14, Wins Right Not to See Biological Family," Aug. 19, 1993, p. A16; "Single But Mothers by Choice," Aug. 5, 1993, p. C1.

Barbara Katz Rothman, *Recreating Motherhood: Ideology and Technology in a Patriarchal Society* (New York: Norton, 1989).

Sara Ruddick, *Maternal Thinking: Towards a Policy of Peace* (Boston: Beacon, 1989).

Ann Snitow, "Feminist Analyses of Motherhood," in Barbara Katz Rothman, ed., *Encyclopedia of Childrearing: Critical Perspectives* (Phoenix, Ariz.: Oryx Press, 1993).

Mott, Lucretia (b. Nantucket, Mass., Jan. 3, 1793; d. near Abington, Pa., Nov. 11, 1880). Preacher and social reformer. A gifted speaker as a young woman, Lucretia Mott became a Quaker minister and traveled widely, lecturing on religion and social issues such as slavery and intemperance. Excluded from the 1840 World Anti-Slavery Convention in London because she was a woman, she joined ELIZABETH CADY STANTON in organizing the first women's rights convention (1848, in Seneca Falls, N.Y.).

Meanwhile she continued to fight for the antislavery cause, and in the 1850s helped mobilize the Underground Railroad for escaping slaves.

FURTHER READING

Otelia Cromwell, *Lucretia Mott* (Cambridge: Harvard University Press, 1958).

muckraking   Commonly referring to a diverse body of writing published between 1900 and 1912, muckraking was a "literature of exposure" (as contemporaries called it) that self-consciously unmasked contradictions and inequities in American public life. The name "muckraker" was drawn from Bunyan's *Pilgrim's Progress* by Theodore Roosevelt (1906) in a critique of what he saw as the excesses of a JOURNALISM bent on showing only the worst of industrial institutions and experiences. More generally, "muckraking" also connotes a style of public knowledge-production, initially developed in this literature, and a steady presence in subsequent reform discourse.

The literature of exposure arose from a convergence of two major cultural events in the decades around the turn of the century. The first was a complex revolution in rhetorical technologies opening out from technical, commercial, and aesthetic responses to industrialization (*see* INDUSTRIALISM and URBANISM). Mechanized publishing and expanding commercial distribution fostered rapid growth in the size and reach of the popular press from the middle of the nineteenth century. A national media market transformed the institutions and practices of journalism itself, putting increased focus on competition for consumers (as opposed to the servicing of narrowly designated locales or special-interest audiences). Reportage became standardized around such innovations as sensational or "yellow" journalism, the construction of the reporter as a modern culture hero, and the rise of the editor as "idea man" engaged in the aggressive configuration and promotion of events and non-events as "news" commodities. S. S. McClure (1857–1949), perhaps the greatest entrepreneur of muckraking, was an exemplar of this new editorial type. With institutional changes came a new approach to the *writing* of news. The Olympian sentences of Victorian periodical literature gave way to terse, masculine tones. The news industry helped extend the representational agenda of aesthetic REALISM—in which the industrial commonplace was granted the prestige of the "literary"—into the arena of MASS CULTURE. (*See also* REPRESENTATION.)

The ability of this new medium to generate and direct public opinion was revealed at the time of the Spanish–American War of 1898. Muckraking itself, however, was brought to life by those reforms and social theories conventionally designated by the term PROGRESSIVISM. Muckraking has long been considered a signature of this moment in American political culture: RICHARD HOFSTADTER looked to muckraking for a trace of the epoch's "characteristically journalistic mind" (p. 186); Gabriel Kolko saw in it a vehicle for typically "opportunist" reformers, by nature conservative and "incapable of serious or radical critiques" (p. 161); Robert Wiebe considered it another function of the rationalizing imperatives of "MODERNIZATION" (pp. 198–9). If its presence is less revealing of a Progressive *Geist* than these three influential interpretations suggest, we can still view muckraking as an attempt to mold a new public discourse at a time of widely perceived instability. Events of the 1880s and 1890s provoked an increased awareness of plurality and discord, of unequal distribution of wealth, and of government's inability and/or reticence to address or even recognize the magnitude and character of social conflict. In the multiplicity of public actions called Progressivism, all devoted to coping with this crisis, muckraking played a descriptive role, using information to energize public opinion *for reform*. The literature of exposure provided an accessible lexicon of civic crisis, a type of knowledge about industrial life consonant with the moral impatience and ideological scruples of its bourgeois readership. Exposing the most deeply hidden "realities," the most well concealed plots of bosses and bigwigs to defraud the "public," muckraking confirmed its audience's conviction that the real world was available to be known, and ripe for improvement.

The sensibility of this liberal bourgeoisie was shaped by the affective emplotment of sentimental literature, which drew upon an ethic of "feeling" or sympathetic responses to pain and injustice with roots in LIBERAL PROTESTANTISM. It was also shaped by a cult of practical "efficiency" that linked the Victorian esteem for mechanical science to a newly charged social instrumentalism. These sometimes contradictory modalities could often meet and operate together in common vocabularies, particularly around that nexus of Victorian subjectivity called "character." The popularity of this formula was confirmed by contemporary instructive literature: the stories of HORATIO ALGER, for instance, brought together "practical" doxa and the dramaturgy of sentimentalism into inspirational treatises on how to develop one's character and image for presentation to the world.

Muckrakers appropriated Alger's value code as a bar of popular justice. For example, they isolated the "character" of individuals or institutions operating in public life, then called down a judgment as moralistic as it was political. This was evident even in muckraking's prehistory, in texts such as Charles Francis Adams's *Chapters of Erie* (1869), an elite chastisement of the robber barons' parvenu buffoonery. In the full flush of muckraking, the code of good character could be transferred from the individual to the corporate organization. Institutions increasingly treated as persons in law were afforded that same status of personification and subsequent moral culpability: they were depicted as animated "interests" potentially or really at odds with the public weal. With the pioneering "Story of a Great Monopoly" by HENRY DEMAREST LLOYD (*Atlantic Monthly*, 1881), and again with Ida Tarbell's *History of the Standard Oil Company* (1904), the unethical financial-industrial combination or "trust" became a commanding trope in representations of industrial public life, in much the same way as certain sinister, yet ultimately reformable, characters in sentimental fiction had erected obstacles for a virtuous protagonist. In this case, the call for "uplift" referred less to personal regeneration than to regulation and, by extension, to reform of the polity itself. In this manner, muckrakes of "trusts" could signal a state of moral and analytical crisis while stopping short of pointed indictments of monopoly capitalism as such: there was always the safety-valve of meliorative action by the "informed" public.

This conjunction of popular moralism and practical political analysis provided a workable, if troubled, marriage of sentiment and utility. The ethic of "feeling" had dominated the critical sensibility of such muckraking urtexts as Rebecca Harding Davis's "Life in the Iron Mills" (1861) and, most potently, *Uncle Tom's Cabin* (1852), by HARRIET BEECHER STOWE, but for a variety of reasons (not least its gender connotations), sympathy in itself was ill-suited to the hardy mobilization of public opinion in the twentieth century. What was valuable in sympathy, its emotional thrust, could, in the muckraker's representation of industrial culture, be preserved in the far more hard-edged and tough-minded notion of "practical" self-interest. Supplying "facts" to satisfy popular demand for knowledge, creating a new information marketplace to contain that demand, writers and editors of the literature of exposure broke new political ground. As public experience came increasingly to bourgeois Americans as commodified text rather than lived participation, "citizens" came increasingly to perceive that experience through the mediation of "news," and in so doing they brought the identity of the consumer into the public sphere. This development often caught muckrakers themselves in an irony they could not fully grasp. UPTON SINCLAIR, whose muckrake of the food-processing industry appeared as the novel *The Jungle* in 1906, found himself lodged in this gap between traditional moral didacticism and the consuming subject. Employing the best of the sentimentalist's art, he succeeded not in motivating Christian piety against the appalling conditions of workingmen's lives, but rather in prompting a call for regulation of the food industry; quality control rather than the Good Life. Aiming at his citizen's heart, Sinclair would complain, he hit the consumer's stomach.

Some muckrakers found further evidence of social crisis in this very irony of public identity, converting investigations of the polity into an exposure of the character of "the people." Here, as in the fetish of "trusts," we find another ideological modality at work in muckraking: a kind of etiolated REPUBLICANISM that maintained some of the rhetorical power, if few of the communitarian convictions, of a prolonged discourse on public VIRTUE in American social thought. What this last residue of eighteenth-century speech could offer the late-Victorian critic, aside from a reassuring semblance of tradition, was a scheme of sociopolitical interpretation governed by stories of "interest" and "corruption." Once again, this representation of public life found a receptive audience, one primed by Pulitzer's and Hearst's sensationalism and looking excitedly for the horrid worst. As a young WALTER LIPPMANN noted, muckrakers "spoke to a public willing to recognize as corrupt an incredibly varied assortment of conventional acts" (p. 25).

This "yellow republicanism" was particularly strong in *The Shame of the Cities* by LINCOLN STEFFENS, originally a series he had written for McClure in 1902–3. According to Steffens' *Autobiography*, his exposure of municipal corruption revealed systemic moral "weakness," a "freed people that have not the will to be free." This "civic shamelessness" was the sign of a "natural process," one "by which a democracy is made gradually over into a plutocracy" (p. 413). Cathartic as the jeremiad in a work like *Shame of the Cities* could be, it remained essentially anachronistic, appealing somewhat plaintively to the eighteenth-century romance with virtue while seeking to grasp and shape a twentieth-century polity. But as the citizen was giving way to the consumer, so public morality was moving from "civic humanism" to municipal boosterism, or to a simple desire for government to "run" cleanly and responsively. Steffens himself acknowledged, as he began his subsequent transit toward the political left, that his readers saw government as a product that must "work" like any other.

Nevertheless, Steffens, along with other journalist-critics of the period, held fast to a belief in an information-based communitarian Epiphany, whereby exposure of the Truth about hidden machinations in public life would awaken a "pride in the character of American citizenship," as he put it in *The Shame of the Cities*, a self-respect that "may save us yet" (pp. 16, 18). In such assertions of the socially regenerative nature of exposed fact, typical of public argument in the Progressive years, we can catch a glimpse of muckraking's deepest mark on twentieth-century American liberalism. In muckraking, as in no other contemporary writing, the Victorian prestige of Science—with its privileged locutions of unveiling and demystifying, and its commitment to a seamless representation of reality—was introduced to a vast readership as a primary vocabulary in debate over the nation's collective future. More "believable" than the fiction of NATURALISM (by virtue of its usually nonfictive character), and more strongly part of mass culture than emergent academic SOCIAL SCIENCE (by virtue of its roots in the popular media), muckraking claimed the rhetorical power of "looking objectively" and turned much public opinion against corporate America. Journalistic investigation would henceforth become the most valued form of public knowledge-production; the reformer's lexicon of crisis would be encoded as reportage, in which form it would find its greatest popular resonance; and the rhetoric of American LIBERALISM would take its characteristic (if often disingenuous) "anti-business" tone.

Muckraking has endured as a genre of mass-cultural writing about political and economic institutions. If it has tended to underwrite a fantasy of the media as an instrument of moral mobilization, and if it forever reinvigorates a mythos of conspiracy in many representations of modern American experience, it has also buttressed a critical sensibility in which PUBLICITY serves as an essential antidote to "concealment"—that is to say, information constitutes in itself a sort of public morality, a standing judgment upon violations of the terms of consensus and open-ended speech important to the theory of bourgeois democracy. Muckraking, and the mass-mediated contagion of exposure through which it grew, thus helped form a modern American public sphere governed by the spectacle of "controversy."

PETER HANSEN

FURTHER READING

Louis Filler, *Crusaders for American Liberalism* (New York: Harcourt, Brace, 1939).
Richard Hofstadter, *The Age of Reform, from Bryan to FDR* (New York: Vintage, 1955).
Gabriel Kolko, *The Triumph of Conservatism* (New York: Free Press, 1963).

Walter Lippmann, *Drift and Mastery* (New York: Mitchell Kennerley, 1914).

Richard McCormick, "The Discovery that Business Corrupts Politics: a Reappraisal of the Origins of Progressivism," *American Historical Review* 86 (Apr. 1981): 247–74.

Lincoln Steffens, *The Shame of the Cities* (New York: McClure, Phillips, 1904).

——, *Autobiography* (New York: Harcourt, Brace and World, 1931).

Robert H. Weibe, *The Search for Order, 1877–1920* (New York: Hill and Wang, 1967).

Arthur Weinberg and Lila Weinberg, eds., *The Muckrakers* (New York: Simon and Schuster, 1961).

Christopher P. Wilson, *The Labor of Words: Literary Professionalism in the Progressive Era* (Athens: University of Georgia Press, 1985).

Muhammad, Elijah [born Elijah Poole] (b. Sandersville, Ga., Oct. 7, 1897; d. Chicago, Ill., Feb. 25, 1975). Religious leader. Muhammad exhorted his followers in the Nation of Islam to moral probity, separation from white people, education, economic development, and unquestioning obedience to religious leaders. Imprisoned during World War II for resisting the draft (he said he would not kill for anyone but Allah), Muhammad thereafter focused on converting prisoners, drug addicts, prostitutes, pimps, and the unemployed. Such social evils, he preached, were caused by degenerate white devils who aimed to destroy black people.

FURTHER READING

C. Eric Lincoln, *The Black Muslims in America* (Westport, Conn.: Greenwood, 1982).

Muir, John (b. Dunbar, Scotland, Apr. 21, 1838; d. Los Angeles, Calif., Dec. 24, 1914). Naturalist. An ardent preservationist, Muir wrote lyrical descriptions of nature's beauty in such books as *The Mountains of California* (1894), *Our National Parks* (1901), *My First Summer in the Sierra* (1911), and *The Yosemite* (1912). Not categorically opposed to commercial or governmental resource development, Muir lobbied energetically to keep Sequoia, Yosemite, and other national parks in their natural state. His claim was not only that NATURE should be respected, but that the natural world was the handiwork of God.

FURTHER READING

Michael P. Cohen, *The Pathless Way: John Muir and American Wilderness* (Madison: University of Wisconsin Press, 1984).

Mumford, Lewis (b. Flushing, N.Y., Oct. 19, 1895; d. Amenia, N.Y., Jan. 26, 1990). An influential historian of architecture and theorist of technology and urban development, Mumford was also a moral, social, and cultural critic. As such he has come to embody the ideal of the twentieth-century independent or "public" intellectual. Throughout his long career, Mumford urged Americans to renounce what had become by the twentieth century, in his view, a Promethean worship of power. He sought to retrieve and reinvigorate an ethic of self-fulfillment through civic participation and artistic creation. "I believe in a rounded, symmetrical development of both the human personality and the community itself," he declared in 1930 in "What I Believe" (p. 267). The reciprocal reconstruction of self and culture was the critical vantage-point from which Mumford fashioned a wholesale indictment of modern civilization.

The illegitimate child of a German-American housekeeper, Mumford grew up in modest circumstances on Manhattan's Upper West Side. At an early age, Mumford chafed against what he saw as the emptiness of his mother's lower-middle-class social life and escaped into books and the streets of New York. In an erratic college education punctuated by illness and military service in World War I, Mumford read widely in classical literature and philosophy and in contemporary CULTURAL CRITICISM, but never received a formal degree. His classical studies at City College led him to the Greek agora as the model public space for the creation of a collective civic identity. The agora ideal formed the backdrop against which Mumford read the American Transcendentalists and pragmatists, such Romantic and republican critics of capitalism as John Ruskin, William Morris, and HENRY GEORGE, and the "Young American" cultural critics writing for *The Seven Arts*.

Meanwhile, the chance discovery of the writings of Scottish evolutionist Patrick Geddes led to correspondence and collaboration with the man who became his mentor, and who convinced Mumford that a new postindustrial civilization was emerging that would achieve a holistic synthesis of art, science, and technology. Geddes's efforts in regional planning in turn led Mumford to Ebenezer Howard and the English Garden City movement. Together these early influences left Mumford with an abiding hostility to the capitalist division of art and labor and, indeed, to dualistic thinking and practices of any kind.

Mumford returned throughout his career to the idea that capitalist industrialization had divided culture from practical life, undermining individuals' capacity to find fellowship in the social world. His criticism probed the historical origins of that modern crisis while gesturing prophetically toward a new culture, one dimly visible in emerging artistic symbols and values. Mumford's first books of literary and architectural criticism in the 1920s and early 1930s—from *The Story of Utopias* (1922) to *The Brown Decades* (1931)—recapitulated the Romantic critique of the industrial division of labor and followed the call by VAN WYCK BROOKS for "a usable past" that would give historical roots to a collective democratic life. Despite his polemic in *The Golden Day* (1926) against "the pragmatic acquiescence," Mumford drew as much on JOHN DEWEY as he did on William Morris in advocating a reintegration of aesthetic and practical experience in everyday work and life.

The ambitious volumes Mumford published in the thirties, *Technics and Civilization* (1934) and *The Culture of Cities* (1938), carried this project forward, but also revealed a significant shift in his thinking. These books—the first contributions to the "Renewal of Life" series that also included *The Condition of Man* (1944) and *The Conduct of Life* (1951)—joined a veneration for local cultures and a Morrisite indictment of the factory system to a utopian program based on new technology and modernist architecture. But the implicit managerialism of his technocratic prophecy clashed with the democratic implications of his defense of regional cultures, and disregarded his own sharp insights into the ways that technology inevitably shapes social values and vice versa. In the scintillating historical chapters of those books, he argued that commercial and military imperatives—not the internal logic of TECHNOLOGY or URBANSIM—had driven the design of machines, cities, and society itself. Yet both books concluded by endorsing the technocratic politics derived from Geddes, a politics which had also informed Mumford's own work in the 1920s as the intellectual leader of the Regional Planning Association of America. With its reliance on planning by technicians and professionals, Mumford's "neotechnic" program was not only undemocratic but unsatisfactory as an aesthetic or moral ideal. The documentary that Mumford helped produce for the 1939 New York World's Fair, *The City*, depicted an antiseptic future that was every bit as sterile as the INDUSTRIALISM he decried.

It was only when Mumford confronted the horrors surrounding World War II that he surrendered his hopes for a new society planned from above by experts. During the late 1930s Mumford embarked on a campaign for early American intervention in the European conflict. He penned manifestos against isolationists, resigned from the editorial board of the *New Republic* in 1940, and befriended REINHOLD NIEBUHR, whose realist critiques of liberal "innocence" returned Mumford to the meditation on "the tragic sense of life" that informed his 1929 biography of Herman Melville. Mumford now taunted liberals for their moral shallowness and praised religion (along with the family and rural life) for the encouragement it offered to moral realism. By comprehending human sinfulness, religion could stand as a bulwark against the cult of limitless power that he identified as the driving force behind fascism and progressivism. But with the death of his son, Geddes Mumford, in combat in 1944 and the use of nuclear weapons against Japan, Mumford became despairing about liberal society. War against Nazism had made the democratic nations totalitarian, he bitterly concluded; Hitler's ethics had prevailed, despite Germany's defeat.

The war's outcome forced Mumford to rethink his understanding of urbanism and technology. His postwar "Skyline" columns for the *New Yorker* condemned the geometric asceticism of modernist architecture since the Bauhaus and argued for a return to the democratic humanism of Louis Sullivan and Frank Lloyd Wright. Mumford also campaigned against Robert Moses's urban renewal schemes and the division of a once-thriving urban culture into skyscraper downtowns and bedroom suburbs. *The City in History* (1962) sealed Mumford's abandonment of modernist design, and even of the Garden City ideal: he portrayed the modern city as a "necropolis" laid waste by the automobile and the bulldozer.

The two-volume *Myth of the Machine* (1967, 1970), Mumford's last major work of social criticism, offered a sweeping history of the conflict between "authoritarian" and "democratic" technics since the neolithic revolution. Fueled by his fury at the Vietnam War, he compared the modern military-industrial complex to the human "machines" of slaves that built shrines to rulers in ancient Egypt and Mesopotamia. Critics complained that the optimism of Mumford's early work had given way to a hysterical pessimism. But such readings missed Mumford's interest in subterranean cultures—women's traditional handicrafts, above all—that encouraged an ethic of self-transcendence through cultural creation. Mumford never lost faith in the creative power of personality, once freed from the pursuit of limitless power and control. Citizens could withhold consent from the modern "megamachine" and withdraw into communities governed by radically different values.

Neither Mumford's earlier "neotechnic" utopianism nor his later call for withdrawal were meant to offer political guidance; they were prophecies, not programs. But the political implications of his work, first managerial and elitist, then quietistic, make it difficult to imagine a wholesale revival of Mumford's social criticism. Nonetheless, there are indications of growing interest in his prophetic perspective, as communitarians and advocates of ENVIRONMENTALISM discover that Mumford long ago articulated an uneasiness akin to theirs about modern technology and the direction of cultural life.

CASEY BLAKE

FURTHER READING

Casey Nelson Blake, *Beloved Community: the Cultural Criticism of Randolph Bourne, Van Wyck Brooks, Waldo Frank, and Lewis Mumford* (Chapel Hill: University of North Carolina Press, 1990).

Robert Casillo, "Lewis Mumford and the Organicist Concept in Social Thought," *Journal of the History of Ideas* 53 (Jan.–Mar. 1992): 91–116.

Agatha C. Hughes and Thomas P. Hughes, eds., *Lewis Mumford: Public Intellectual* (New York: Oxford University Press, 1990).

Christopher Lasch, "Lewis Mumford and the Myth of the Machine," *Salmagundi* 49 (summer 1980): 4–28.

Donald L. Miller, *Lewis Mumford: a Life* (New York: Weidenfeld and Nicolson, 1989).

Lewis Mumford, "What I Believe," *Forum* 84 (Nov. 1930): 263–8.

——, *My Works and Days: a Personal Chronicle* (New York: Harcourt Brace Jovanovich, 1979).

——, *Sketches from Life: the Autobiography of Lewis Mumford, the Early Years* (New York: Dial Press, 1982).

Murray, John Courtney (b. New York, N.Y., Sept. 12, 1904; d. New York, N.Y., Aug. 16, 1967). A Jesuit theologian and political philosopher, Murray was born of a Scottish father and Irish mother. He joined the Society of Jesus at the age of 16, received his B.A. from Weston College in 1926 and his M.A. from Boston College in 1927. After teaching in the Philippines for three years, he returned to the United States to study theology at Woodstock College. He was ordained in 1933. Afterwards, he attended the Gregorian University in Rome and received his doctorate in theology in 1937. He returned to Woodstock, this time as a professor, with his course offerings focusing on the Trinity and grace. He continued in this position until his death. In 1941 he became both the editor of the scholarly journal *Theological Studies* and the religion editor of *America*, a publication for educated laypeople and clergy.

Murray's early writings (1942–5) focused on the problem of intercredal cooperation. A debate arose within Catholic circles concerning whether Catholics could cooperate with Protestants in the building up of society that would have to follow the war. The primary concern for those who argued against cooperation, Joseph Fenton and Francis Connell, was the maintenance of the purity of Catholic doctrine. They charged that Catholics who cooperated with Prot-

estants were risking "indifferentism" regarding doctrine. Murray countered that Roman Catholics could cooperate with others and that they were morally bound to so cooperate. He argued that cooperation took place on the temporal plane of social interaction, and need not affect the spiritual dimension, which is the realm of doctrine. If one carefully distinguished between the two planes, then indifferentism could be avoided.

It was a short step from the issue of building up society through intercreedal cooperation to the problem of church and state, which remained Murray's central focus for the rest of his life. While his writing on this topic began as early as 1945, the key series of articles appeared in the early 1950s in *Theological Studies*. In what are now generally referred to as the "Leonine articles," Murray argued that Pope Leo XIII accepted the basic distinctions necessary for constitutional democracy and religious liberty even though, appropriately, he did not condone religious freedom *per se*. The crucial distinction is that between state and society. Society as a whole is responsible for the common good. The state is responsible for the public order that makes pursuit of the common good possible in the first place.

Religious communities contribute to the common good by forming persons in the virtues necessary to support society. Both for this reason and for reasons internal to each religion's faith, the freedom of religion ought to be protected. The precise relationship between church and state that best protects religious freedom depends upon historical circumstances. Murray argued that Leo was wise not to support the disestablishment of religion because the historical circumstances did not warrant it. Society—the "illiterate masses," in the Leonine phrase which Murray often cited—could not sustain the religious practices necessary to advance the common good without the paternalism of the state. The flipside of this argument is that with the rise in literacy and people's awareness of their human dignity, contemporary society allows for and even requires a constitutional arrangement like that in the United States.

The first four articles in the Leonine series appeared in *Theological Studies* in 1952–4. Vatican censors informed Murray's superior, Vincent McCormick, that the fifth article was unsuitable for publication. Murray's silencing came in the form of an indirect request from McCormick: "It seems to me a mistake to wish to carry on with that controverted question under present circumstances." In response, Murray turned his focus to the broader question of religion and American public life in general, and to international affairs. In 1960 he brought together a collection of articles under the title *We Hold These*

Truths: Catholic Reflections on the American Proposition.

The vindication of Murray and his view on the church–state question began in 1963 when, at the request of Cardinal Spellman, he was invited to attend the second session of the Second Vatican Council as a *peritus* or expert. From this position, he went on to play a key role in the writing of the Council's *Declaration on Religious Freedom.* One bishop was said to have said, "The voices are the voices of United States bishops; but the thoughts are the thoughts of John Courtney Murray!"

Following the Council, Murray extended his argument on religious freedom by applying it to the case of atheists on the one hand and to the internal practice of the Catholic Church on the other. His death in 1967 prevented him from pursuing these topics in an extended fashion.

Events since the Vatican Council have solidified the hold of Murray's theory on church–state doctrine. The election of the Polish John Paul II in 1978 brought to the papacy a person who had experienced firsthand the repression of religious practice. In the ensuing years, John Paul would make religious freedom the cornerstone of his rights doctrine. Beneath this doctrine is Murray's distinction between state and society. This distinction gives religious communities considerable scope to articulate their beliefs in the public forum under the rubric of "society."

Two debates now dominate commentary on the Murray literature. First, at least up through *We Hold These Truths,* Murray held that religious communities ought to speak in the language of natural law when entering the public forum, and leave specifically confessional beliefs out of the conversation. The question now is whether this restriction on confessional speech is either possible or desirable. Leon Hooper has argued that Murray himself abandoned this view in his later writings. Second, in setting out his understanding of the right of religious freedom, Murray emphasized that it was strictly a negative protection against intrusion by the state or other groups and thus has no substantive content. The question now being raised is whether more attention must be paid to the positive conditions for religious practice.

TODD WHITMORE

See also CATHOLICISM; CULTURAL PLURALISM AND MULTICULTURALISM; TOLERANCE.

FURTHER READING

David Hollenbach, "Public Theology in America: Some Questions for Catholicism after John Courtney Murray," *Theological Studies* 37 (1976): 290–303.

——, ed., "Theology and Philosophy in Public: a Symposium on John Courtney Murray's Unfinished Agenda," *Theological Studies* 40 (1979): 700–15.

J. Leon Hooper, *The Ethics of Discourse: the Social Philosophy of John Courtney Murray* (Washington, D.C.: Georgetown University Press, 1986).

Robert W. McElroy, *The Search for an American Public Theology: the Contribution of John Courtney Murray* (New York: Paulist Press, 1989).

John Courtney Murray, *We Hold These Truths: Catholic Reflections on the American Proposition* (New York: Sheed and Ward, 1960).

Donald Pelotte, *John Courtney Murray: Theologian in Conflict* (New York: Paulist Press, 1975).

Murray, Judith Sargent (b. Gloucester, Mass., May 1, 1751; d. near Natchez, Miss., July 6, 1820).   The period immediately following the AMERICAN REVOLUTION was crucial in shaping the new nation's attitudes toward women's role and women's place. Some historians have argued that because the Revolution was based on the ideals of equality and opportunity, it accorded American women their first real chance to transcend the domestic sphere, and to claim the promise of the Revolution for themselves. Others have insisted that new political and economic opportunities for men in the postwar world only exacerbated gender differences, making women's exclusion from the male sphere deeper and more permanent, and preparing the way for the "cult of true womanhood" that would characterize the women's world in antebellum America.

The experience of Judith Sargent Murray provides support for the claims of both camps. In her essays, poems, and plays, as well as in her private correspondence, Murray examined and criticized the customary treatment of women in her own society. Her advocacy of political and economic rights for women was more thoroughgoing than that of any of her better-known contemporaries. Her three-volume miscellany, the *Gleaner* (1798), in particular, contains a number of essays that vigorously and unapologetically defend women's rights.

Central to her philosophy was her belief in the equal intellectual capacity of women. If women were silly or less knowledgeable than men, she said, it was not the result of inherent frailty, but of a male-dominated power structure that had systematically denied women the experiences accorded men. GENDER differences, Murray claimed, were attributable "to a false method of cultivation, or perhaps to a total want of advantages, to which, as human beings, [women] are entitled." Thus women needed to be educated and accorded the same opportunities as men if they were to assume their rightful place in a new, presumably enlightened republic. Murray attacked various forms of gender inequality, including the all-male jury system. She espoused egalitarian marriage based on "mutual esteem." While she agreed that in brute strength men were generally women's superiors, she could cite enough historical examples of women who were brave warriors to prove that women could hold their own on the battlefield as well as in the classroom. She even boldly imagined that there might one day be a "female Washington" exercising "sovereign power" in America. No other American woman, not MERCY OTIS WARREN, not, surely, ABIGAIL ADAMS, went so far.

Given her belief that environment shaped character, Murray was especially interested in enhancing women's educational experience. Women, she thought, should be schooled in math and the sciences, in geography, astronomy, history, and literature. They should also learn Latin and Greek—traditionally an exclusively male province. Murray agreed with BENJAMIN RUSH that educated women made good wives and good "republican mothers." But she was even more interested in the value of education for women. She had experienced enough of life's vicissitudes to know that women might be left, at some point, to fend for themselves. Her first husband, John Stevens, had died a debtor. Her second husband, John Murray, was an itinerant minister for the Universalist Church and hopelessly incompetent in economic matters. Thus Murray became obsessed with the need to give women the ability to be economically self-sufficient. While she valued marriage, she thought there was no worse fate than to be wed to an unsuitable companion. Better, she thought, to be "independent" and an "old maid" than to be bound in a loveless relationship. Marriage should be a matter of choice, not necessity.

Murray's advocacy of WOMEN'S RIGHTS was far-reaching—but she remained a product of her times. She was not a twentieth-century feminist. She was not a radical. Her views reveal the limits as well as the possibilities that women confronted in post-revolutionary America. Murray firmly believed in a hierarchical and deferential society, where inferiors obeyed and superiors treated those beneath them with benign "complacency." She also agreed that men and women should occupy separate spheres; she claimed to have no desire to upset the "naturally" gendered social order. Women were sympathetic and loving, men strong, brave, and resolute. PIETY and DOMESTICITY were the hallmarks of women's identity, and their special destiny was MOTHERHOOD. Men were suited to the ranks of laborers, soldiers, and professionals.

Despite her conventionalism, Murray was more willing than most to see the spheres separating women and men as less rigid, more permeable than "custom" permitted. Men, she argued, could take on the "feminine" qualities of compassion and gentleness without losing their "masculinity." Women could invade the public sphere, becoming teachers and farmers, politicians and even warriors. Differences between men and women, she often argued, were largely the result of habit, not of nature. And women might, with practice, even be "fashioned into rational beings." They would, she insisted, gladly exchange their "elevation of sentiment" for that "equality to which [they] were born."

The forces shaping Murray's views were both general and specific. Like many of her contemporaries, her imagination was captured by the egalitarian rhetoric of the American Revolution, and she sought to make the promise of the new nation apply to her own circumstances. Her experience as a widow with few resources served to illustrate the dependent, even "degraded" economic position that women occupied. Lack of education and career opportunities, she discovered, reduced single and widowed women to a state of "artificial imbecility." And married women enjoyed no independent legal or economic position at all. Finally, Murray's conversion to the Universalist faith sometime between 1774 and 1778 was crucial. It was her first, and in many ways her most profound rebellion against the values of her society. Moreover, Universalist theology was more egalitarian, less patriarchal than the Calvinist faith she rejected. It gave her the moral courage to defy convention and to question the very foundations upon which that convention rested.

Murray was an extraordinary woman. She freely admitted that she hungered after "fame," that literary immortality was her ultimate goal. Well-educated, ambitious, and unwaveringly committed to securing a measure of equality for women, she demanded that women and men alike be treated, above all else, simply as humans.

SHEILA L. SKEMP

FURTHER READING

Ruth Bloch, "The Gendered Meanings of Virtue in Revolutionary America," *Signs* 13 (1987): 37–58.

Joan Gunderson, "Independence, Citizenship and the American Revolution," *Signs* 13 (1987): 59–77.

Ronald Hoffman and Peter J. Albert, eds., *Women in the Age of the American Revolution* (Charlottesville: University Press of Virginia, 1989).

Linda K. Kerber, *Women of the Republic: Intellect and Ideology in Revolutionary America* (Chapel Hill: University of North Carolina Press, 1980).

Judith Sargent Murray, *The Gleaner: a Miscellaneous Production in Three Volumes* (1798; Schenectady, N.Y.: Union College Press, 1992).

Sheila L. Skemp, *Judith Sargent Murray* (Boston: Bedford Books, forthcoming).

N

Nader, Ralph (b. Winstead, Conn., Feb. 27, 1934). Lawyer and consumer advocate. In *Unsafe at Any Speed* (1965), Nader exposed the dangers of the Corvair built by General Motors and made a general attack on the secrecy and safety record of the automotive industry. Beyond contributing to legislation leading to new federal safety standards for automobiles, Nader's work revived the MUCKRAKING ethos of earlier reformers and sparked consumer outrage at corporate arrogance and government complicity. He founded the Center for Study of Responsive Law (1969) to ensure the safety of consumer products and to reform outmoded forms of taxation, health care, and environmental regulation. Relying on fact-finding missions, lawsuits, and lobbying to mobilize public opinion, his strategy has been adopted by many consumer groups and by political activists across the ideological spectrum. His intellectual style, based on systematic exposure of the "truth" and on moral outrage at the gap between cultural ideals and cultural realities, has deep roots in the tradition of American PROGRESSIVISM.

FURTHER READING

Robert N. Mayer, *The Consumer Movement: Guardians of the Marketplace* (Boston: Twayne, 1989).

The Nation As rambunctious *Nation* columnist Heywood Broun wrote in 1929 when he wanted to tweak its publisher, "Oswald Garrison Villard is the product of an interesting experiment. His grandfather was an abolitionist and his father a railroad magnate. As far as the researches of science have gone, the rule seems to be that when you cross abolitionist blood and railroad stock you get a liberal." And indeed *The Nation*, founded in 1865 by a group of abolitionists and sold 26 years later to the owner of the *New York Evening Post*—where it survived as a weekly, mostly literary supplement until 1918, when Villard took it over—has from day one been enmeshed in a dialogue/debate between the radicals and the liberals.

In fact, before *The Nation*'s first year was up, its founding editor E. L. GODKIN complained (to *Nation* contributor Charles Eliot Norton) that one of the magazine's radical-reconstructionist shareholders was pressuring him to make it "a mere canting organ of the radical wing," and that "too close an identification with a factional or partisan cause is bad journalism as well as bad policy." Godkin's solution: a new corporate structure which guaranteed that it would be nobody's house organ (although it would continue sympathetically to chronicle the plight of the freedmen). The happy result was that Godkin's *Nation* is more quoted in the histories of the period than any other periodical; and in the longer run, his legacy of editorial independence enabled his successors to write (and perhaps to a modest degree, shape) the history of the left-liberal tradition in America—its values, schisms, personalities, and institutions.

Under the leadership of Villard, a militant pacifist, *The Nation* championed a number of controversial causes: it protested the hysterical denunciations, arrests, and mass deportations of radicals that followed World War I, fought for an executive pardon for the unjustly jailed labor organizer Tom Mooney (a departure from the stance of Godkin, who had opposed organized labor), and commemorated the execution of the anarchists Sacco and Vanzetti with the front-page banner "MASSACHUSETTS THE MURDERER."

But Villard broke with *The Nation* over an issue which split the left-liberal community in the late 1930s. As contributing editor NORMAN THOMAS wrote in an article titled "The Pacifist's Dilemma," there were two real evils in the world—war and fascism—and when the magazine's new editor, Freda Kirchwey, decided that resolute opposition to fascism required war, Villard, who had already relinquished his ownership, quit writing his weekly column.

Although Kirchwey's dominant concerns included WOMEN'S RIGHTS, sexual freedom, and the Spanish civil war, the magazine became best known under her editorship for its refusal to chorus in on the COLD WAR. *The Nation* had found the Nazi-Soviet pact "menacing" and criticized the purge trials and the brutal Soviet invasion of Finland, but her biographer, Sara Alpern, probably has it right when she concludes that Kirchwey, "a relativist toward the Soviet Union," was "a moralist against fascism" (p. 119). The mindset undoubtedly contributed to her famous decision in 1951 to sue the *New Leader* magazine for libel when it published a letter she had refused to print from former *Nation* art critic CLEMENT GREENBERG accusing her friend and political editor J. Alvarez Del Vayo of being "an instrument of Stalin." In the overheated atmosphere of the Cold War the dispute led the respected theologian REINHOLD NIEBUHR, among others, to resign from *The Nation*'s masthead. And Carey McWilliams agreed to serve as Kirchwey's successor only on condition that she drop the case.

Carey McWilliams always insisted that he was not an innovator, that *The Nation* he ran from 1955 to 1975 was informed primarily by his study of Godkin's pluralistic conception of a journal of critical opinion. But the magazine that this rebel-radical produced took sides in the two civil wars which split the liberal community on his watch. First, in the battle between the Cold War liberals and those they liked to label the anti-anticommunists, McWilliams sided with the latter, and beyond that went on to identify the role of Cold War liberals in rationalizing such embarrassments as the Bay of Pigs fiasco and the disastrous involvement in VIETNAM. McWilliams's *Nation* went out of its way to defend victims of what it saw as a domestic witchhunt, and to take on such sacred cows as the FBI (Fred Cook's lengthy exposé helped earn *The Nation* nine volumes in the bureau's surveillance files). Such subversive activities made fundraising so difficult that the magazine was briefly forced to print at a plant in Alabama, where credit was as liberal as *The Nation*'s heretical politics.

Second, by the late 1960s McWilliams's *Nation* had to deal with a generational split between the NEW LEFT and the old. While sympathetic to the oppositional impulse of the counterculture and its bottom-up, community-based politics, *The Nation* had little use for the hippie rejection of politics ("One Cheer for the Hippies," wrote Jack Newfield) or those New Left factions that romanticized violence. A fair gauge of the position of *The Nation*, a strong supporter of the peace and CIVIL RIGHTS movements, is McWilliams's hiring of a still relatively unknown MARTIN LUTHER KING JR. to write its annual civil rights audit.

It has been said that those who at any time have been responsible for upholding *The Nation*'s good name have found themselves to some extent captives of the tradition. By and large it is a good tradition to be captive of. Gore Vidal's "Requiem for the American Empire" (1986) is a direct descendant of W. P. Garrison's "The Pesky Anti-Imperialist," (1902), E. P. Thompson's calls to "Protest and Survive" make urgent sense as the nuclear age equivalent of Villard's militant attack upon militarism. Elinor Langer's special issue on "The Neo-Nazi Movement in America" (1990) is a tribute to Freda Kirchwey's profound resistance to fascism and anti-Semitism, and Ben Bagdikian's meticulous documentation of the dangers of media concentration in an era of transnational conglomerates is an update of the magazine's long-standing commitment to the free flow of information and the values underlying the First Amendment to the U.S. constitution.

But as we move from Cold War verities to post-Cold War multipolarities and ethnic strife, from the culture wars of the 1980s to the multicultural conundrums of the 1990s, from life under the magazine's declared enemy (Reagan, Bush) to life under an administration that received its (very lukewarm) endorsement (Clinton, Gore), *The Nation*'s letters pages once again reflect deep cleavages on the liberal left. Unlike THE NEW REPUBLIC or *Dissent*, other JOURNALS OF OPINION considered, respectively, neoliberal and left, the *Nation* opposed the war in Iraq as a misguided imperial adventure; was divided on how best to protect human rights and life in former Yugoslavia; has disputed the neoconservative charge that "political correctness" has become an orthodoxy on the left, but has nevertheless regularly hectored its readers on the virtues of unbridled free expression; has retained an unfashionable belief in the United Nations as the best hope for settling international disputes; and persists in trying to establish an outsider stance toward an administration whose cabinet and White House include former *Nation* contributors.

VICTOR NAVASKY

See also JOURNALISM.

FURTHER READING
Sara Alpern, *Freda Kirchwey: a Woman of The Nation* (Cambridge: Harvard University Press, 1987).
Katrina vanden Heuvel, ed., *The Nation: 1865–1990, Selections from the Independent Magazine of Politics and Culture* (New York: Thunder's Mouth Press, 1990).
Carey McWilliams, *The Education of Carey McWilliams* (New York: Simon and Schuster, 1979).

naturalism   Both an early twentieth-century American literary movement and, not coincidentally, a broad-gauged tendency in American philosophy throughout the twentieth century, naturalism, whether in the novels of STEPHEN CRANE, FRANK NORRIS and THEODORE DREISER, or in the philosophies of WILLIAM JAMES, GEORGE SANTAYANA, and JOHN DEWEY, is a response to the intellectual reformations that resulted from the late nineteenth-century triumph of Darwinian methods of investigation and assumptions about the world. All of these writers abandoned transcendental providentialism for variations on the natural historical account of human life associated with DARWINISM.

But more broadly, literary naturalism interprets the cultural, social, and political changes that accompanied the industrial "incorporation of America" (ca.1870–1900). Agrarian Protestant narratives, picturing Christian civilities and republican rectitude triumphing over lust, greed, and imperial power, continued to capture American imaginations well into the third quarter of the nineteenth century. Emerson and his transcendentalist epigones Thoreau and Whitman struck the chord: apparent disorder is inevitably on the mend; one providential design, in Emerson's phrase, energizes "the farthest pinnacle and the lowest trench" (p. 78).

The "realism" of WILLIAM DEAN HOWELLS in the *Rise of Silas Lapham* (1885) or *A Hazard of New Fortunes* (1890), while attempting to portray—without moralistic airs—the destructive potential of both producer and consumer capitalism, still maintained this fable instructing culture that private conscience and public virtue held off ever-present sexual, economic, and social demons. Howells hung onto the old ideals. He continued to celebrate what he called in *Criticism and Fiction* (1891) "the more smiling aspects of life, which are the more American," in his "American poetry of vivid purpose." His stories left heroic individuals soaring above the threats of financial and social disaster and the horrors of mass life, even as he was decrying the utter entrapment of laboring conditions and the unswerving brutality of strike-breaking in magazine editorial after editorial.

Some literary critics, like Richard Chase, have interpreted the literary naturalists as turning the tables on the old Christian republican culture, showing that vice prevails. Others, like Donald Pizer, have claimed that the naturalists are actually somewhat more open-eyed and pessimistic Howellsian moral realists, still working to secure "an affirmative ethical conception of life" (p. 14). And still others, like Larzer Ziff and Walter Benn Michaels, demur from this debate on the grounds that the forces of industrial capitalist culture render the terms of the old legend irrelevant. I tend to agree with Ziff and Michaels: unlike Howells, naturalists such as Crane, Norris, and Dreiser assumed that the traditional picture of virtue and vice was beside the point. In the exchange culture of industrial capitalism, distinctions between sexual satisfaction, personal domination, economic gain, and public morality became otiose. The dynamics of insatiable desire determined conduct and outstripped individual character. Humanity must be portrayed in bulk terms; any particular person's story was pretty much controlled by a decisively brutal and repetitively banal set of chances and forces working internally to (mis)shape character and externally to constrain it.

In Crane's *Maggie* (1893), typical urban misery and human cruelty determine the dumb protagonists' destiny. Maggie may yearn for a semblance of Christian joy, but her purposeless circumstances dispose of her dreams as so much false pretense. *The Red Badge of Courage* (1895) unmasks the deceit of chivalry, the lie of spiritual victory over loss, which hung nostalgically over genteel America after the Civil War: Henry Fleming's personality is not set by any conflict of right against might, but rather by balancing irrational anxiety against silly sham; neither reason, virtue, decision, nor action play any role in the life of any character in the book.

Norris combined Joseph Le Conte's deterministic brand of popular Darwinism, which fueled racist resentment of the poor as it rationalized the superiority of the corporate rich, with an equally Darwinian penchant for variation, or "romance." Norris found the latter "in the unplumbed depths of the human heart, and the mystery of sex, and . . . the black, unsearched penetralia of the soul of man" (*Works*, vol. 7, pp. 164, 167–8). *McTeague* (1899) unmasks the duplicitous desolation of the capitalist exchange economy and society—including the economy and society of sexual exchange—to which humankind has doomed itself or, more ironically, is simply doomed. In Norris's vision, a "life force" controls all of history. This force appears as "wheat" in *The Octopus* (1901) and *The Pit* (1903), where it supervenes on all other powers, rendering ferocious battles between farmers and the railroad, or between managers and speculators, incidental and epiphenomenal. Ultimately, for Norris, it is impossible to distinguish vitality or production from inexorable destruction: the life force kills.

Dreiser looked to Spencer's determinism for his understanding of Darwin, as Norris had to Le Conte, but came away far less sanguine than his mentor about the unidirectionality and irreversibility of liberal civilization: Spencer's quest to display a principle of moral and spiritual equilibrium at work in nature was self-deceived. Indeed *Sister Carrie* (1900) portrays sex as a marketable commodity far more advantageous than (other sorts of) common labor, as a value functioning selectively in a culture and economy empowered by perpetual and relentless dissatisfactions that permit no stability at all.

Regarding twentieth-century American philosophy, naturalism has been so pervasive that calling a philosopher a naturalist does little to define her. Most broadly described, philosophical naturalists invoke "nature" or "the natural" as the most general explanatory, interpretive, or normative notion. But there's the rub. Surely it has been the odd ones out, idealists like Josiah Royce, for instance, or theists like the Niebuhr brothers, who have not been regarded as naturalists in this broad sense. Still, great disputes over what to consider natural, how to determine what counts, and what to make of philosophy itself as a consequence, have split the philosophical profession in the United States multiple ways (into logical positivists and empiricists, new and critical and scientific and internal realists, instrumentalists, and pragmatists) for a hundred years.

For the least Darwinian among Darwin's philosophical interpreters, like Herbert Spencer (Dreiser's inspiration) and his American disciples John Fiske and Joseph Le Conte (Norris's teacher), the great lesson taught by Darwin's account of evolution in terms of spontaneous variation and natural selection was that, finally, science's last holdout, the history of humankind, could be subsumed under general laws, invariant structures, and deterministic principles. Philosophers could now proceed with the architectonic unification of the natural sciences, ordered from physics up.

But for Darwin himself, along with his sharpest readers, like William James, the message was not tragic determinism or fatalism so much as comic chance. Life certainly was the result of causes, always fragile, and inevitably mortal. Darwin's novelty lay in showing that the current order of things, including human intelligence and moral life, was the consequence of one funny or incredible thing happening after another. As George Santayana put it, the nature Darwin leaves us does not have "a nature" or an essence or an invariant structure; even necessity is a conspiracy of accidents; evolution itself evolves. This realization even showed up as a recessive counterpoint in the narrative works of the literary naturalists: sparks of spontaneous variation lend whatever color or humor or humane character is evident in the doggedly dog-eat-dog world of Crane's *Maggie*, Norris's *McTeague*, or Dreiser's *Sister Carrie*. Indeed, a far more ironic and comic Darwinian sense of chance and variation still informs late twentieth-century American novelists as diverse as Joseph Heller, Don DeLillo, John Irving, Kurt Vonnegut, Max Apple, or Fred Chappell.

The first reactions to Darwin's achievement were the most radical. James's *Principles of Psychology* (1890), which may well be the best naturalist novel, set the tone and pace by placing a whole nest of issues about human emotions and intelligence within the context of organism–environment interactions. Mind was not a mirror but a bunch of behaviors that let death-haunted humans flourish by managing difficulties and solving problems impeding human joy. Nor was mind simply adaptive, because people reconstructed environments to suit their own vari-

able and modifiable interests. Reason was not simply a set of logical forms or methods but a thoroughly affective social life that let people realize intentions. Moral claims, in particular, emerged out of mutually held desires and instituted ways to satisfy them. As Alexander Bain and C. S. Peirce had already argued, knowledge, whether about comets, comedy, or communion, was an open-ended web of beliefs, or dispositions to act, that best facilitated this kind of life. People required nothing above, below, behind, or outside the natural world to account for, or practice, any of these things. The old philosophical splits between spirit and nature, soul and body, thought and action, word and world, presumed a difference that made no difference: spiritual life was a function of psyche which, in turn, was a structure of material behaviors.

James himself slipped back toward supernaturalism in his efforts to defend belief in inexplicable powers that could help people who could not help themselves. The sort of naturalism his *Principles* inaugurated, however, found diverse and somewhat conflicting champions, first in Santayana's *The Life of Reason* (1905–6), which characterized that life in terms of cultural institutions; most decidedly with the pragmatic works of John Dewey (paradigmatically in *The Quest for Certainty*, 1929) and his circle; and in the work of mavericks like Roy Wood Sellars.

Especially in the 1930s and 1940s, logical empiricists and positivists (many of them German emigrés like Rudolf Carnap, Herbert Feigl, and Hans Reichenbach), and realists (like Morris Cohen) overshadowed Darwin-inspired pragmatic naturalism. These thinkers rejected metaphysics, but otherwise tended to see themselves in traditional philosophical terms, trying to decode the ways fixed mind knows fixed nature according to fixed principles of knowledge.

Though logical empiricists and positivists lost their punch by mid-century, when their verificationist theory of meaning was shown to undercut itself, their philosophical quest to show how words objectively latch onto the world still informs much of the profession. This, despite powerful arguments by figures like W. V. O. QUINE and Wilfrid Sellars refuting basic dogmas on which the tradition rested.

Currently, Quine defines his own naturalism as abandonment of the goal of a first philosophy. For him, natural science still takes its place, revealing the true and ultimate structure of reality. But just as new literary historicists like Michaels have shown that Darwinian images found in naturalistic novels are embedded in a far more pervasive cultural discourse, radical naturalists like RICHARD RORTY have embraced a cultural holism which drops Quine's notion that natural science is the domain of privileged inquiry. For Rorty, one part of cultural discourse is as natural as another, literature and manifesto as much as science: cultures shape up contingently and present open-ended webs of belief that help people get around the world in which they live.

See also REALISM.

HENRY SAMUEL LEVINSON

FURTHER READING

Richard Chase, *The American Novel and Its Tradition* (New York: Doubleday, 1957).

Ralph Waldo Emerson, *Selections*, ed. Stephen Whicher (Boston: Houghton Mifflin, 1957).

Michael Ghiselin, *The Triumph of Darwinian Method* (Berkeley: University of California Press, 1969).

Yervant Krikorian, ed., *Naturalism and the Human Spirit* (New York: Columbia University Press, 1944).

Henry Samuel Levinson, *The Religious Investigations of William James* (Chapel Hill: University of North Carolina Press, 1981).

——, *Santayana, Pragmatism and the Spiritual Life* (Chapel Hill: University of North Carolina Press, 1992).

Walter Benn Michaels, *The Gold Standard and the Logic of Naturalism* (Berkeley: University of California Press, 1987).

Frank Norris, *Works*, vols. 1–10 (Garden City, N.Y.: Doubleday, Doran, 1928).

Donald Pizer, *Realism and Naturalism in Nineteenth-Century American Literature* (Carbondale: Southern Illinois University Press, 1966).

Richard Rorty, *Contingency, Irony, and Solidarity* (Cambridge: Cambridge University Press, 1989).

Larzer Ziff, *The American 1890s* (Lincoln: University of Nebraska Press, 1966).

nature Although trees, plants, animals, rocks, and a variety of other beings and phenomena have a clear existence independent of human thought and perception, nature is a human construct. Nature posits a unity, a specific set of relationships, that links together all material beings and objects on the planet that are not of direct human creation. In the Western European tradition from which American conceptions of nature largely derive, a fundamental distinction is made between natural, "original" things and things that are creations of human artifice. Nature is, at the minimum, the aggregate of these original or natural things. At the extreme, the entire planet is, as in James Lovelock's Gaia hypothesis, an organism with a life of its own.

Nature has always been a problematic concept in American thought and culture, and it has grown more problematic in recent years. There are two basic issues. The first is whether human beings are themselves part of nature. Humans are biologically "original" things, but culturally they are creations of their own artifice. They possess "human nature," but their thought and labor create the category artifice against which nature is defined. The second problem is related to the first. Natural objects such as trees once seemed unproblematically natural, but as human beings first through selective breeding and then through genetic engineering change other beings, the line between original things and products of human artifice increasingly breaks down. Is the domesticated ANIMAL part of nature or culture? And to cut things even more finely, the current disputes in ENVIRON-MENTALISM make distinctions between wild salmon and hatchery salmon. The first is natural, the second is presumably something less than natural.

William Cronon has attempted to resolve these disputes by resorting to Hegelian distinctions between first and second nature, both falling within a larger category of nature. First nature retains the old connotation of original things; second nature are those original things altered by human artifice. Such distinctions, however, tend only to displace the original problem. Wild animals and plants clearly exist, but it is their larger relationship to each other that we call nature. More and more studies have reflected older and older human influences on the natural world through, for example, fire, which helps to determine which and how many plants and animals inhabit a given area. It has become increasingly hard to find environmental relationships unaffected by human artifice and thus a nature as a set of environmental relationships clearly separate from human history.

Despite current academic controversies, Americans in writing and talking about their relationship to nature have often maintained a sharp distinction between nature and culture. The conventional phrasing of this relationship has often been quite simple. It has been one of conquest. Many Americans have defined their national progress in terms of the conquest of nature by civilization. Even Henry David Thoreau, who rejected such a version of progress, demanded the conquest of nature in another more personal sense. "Nature," he wrote in *Walden*, "is hard to overcome, but she must be overcome."

But nature has had a deeper significance in American thought than as a mere obstacle. For American thinkers as diverse as THOMAS JEFFERSON, JOHN MUIR, and FREDERICK JACKSON TURNER, nature was not so much an obstacle to American culture as its true source. Assessments of the state of nature have tended to reflect assessments of the current state of the American republic. American nature has explained and justified American culture. In the late eighteenth and early nineteenth century the bleak assessment of American nature by the French naturalist Buffon had prompted a nationalistic American response apparent in Jefferson's *Notes on the State of Virginia* (1787) and seconded by American naturalists. They replaced Buffon's degenerative nature with a progressive nature whose laws presaged a republican society. In mid-century George Perkins Marsh in *Man and Nature* (1864) detailed how humans ravaged the natural world and the price they paid, but he blamed this on despotism. Nature would yield to the republican yoke without deleterious effects. John Muir gloried in the Sierras as a place of human renewal which restored those engaged in development and progress. In this tradition Frederick Jackson Turner could celebrate open, or wild land, as the source of democratic values and lament the loss of such land as potentially threatening American progress and democracy itself.

Turner's pessimism was not consistent, nor was it characteristic of the late nineteenth and early twentieth century. Some Americans adopted a popular, progressive DARWINISM in which the "laws of nature" itself guaranteed human PROGRESS, albeit at a social cost to be borne largely by the "unfit." Evolution became the reigning cultural and historical metaphor. History itself became naturalized, and nature insured American progress. Nature, to be sure, had to be tamed, harnessed, and managed (as favorite metaphors had it), but under proper management it would ensure a prosperous human future. John Muir and other advocates of wild nature sought its preservation only within quite precise boundaries.

As late twentieth-century Americans have become less certain of progress, they have tended to reevaluate nature and the human relationship to it. Nature no longer guarantees progress. It increasingly seems at once vulnerable and capable of exacting terrible retribution. The coin in which the price of progress is to be paid has become environmental, and beginning with RACHEL CARSON and her *Silent Spring*, environmentalist writings have tallied the debt owed.

The result by the late twentieth century has been rather contradictory. Americans have, for example, marked off areas of supposedly untouched nature as wilderness and made them into virtually sacred spaces. At the same time historians have tended to stress how even apparently pristine lands show the consequences of past human actions and how wilderness and nature are contingent and shifting cultural categories and not real things. Ecologists have stressed that the attributes that culture ascribes to nature—balance, stability, and self-correction—are hard to find in actual ecological systems which also seem shifting and contingent. Meanwhile, even as environmentalists seek to preserve a separate, pristine nature, Bill McKibben in his bestselling *The End of Nature* lamented that with ozone depletion and global warming there is no nature untouched by human beings.

Very real environmental problems aside, Americans seem confused as to the human place in nature. Environmental writers such as Carson, McKibben or the deep ecologists Bill Devall and George Sessions offer conflicting prescriptions. Sometimes humans belong to a category opposed to nature. Sometimes people are urged to be part of nature even as their actions are denounced as "unnatural." Culturally as well as physically, what nature is and what the proper human relationship to it ought to be remains a dilemma at the end of the century.

RICHARD WHITE

FURTHER READING
Daniel Botkin, *Discordant Harmonies: a New Ecology for the Twenty-First Century* (New York: Oxford University Press, 1990).
William Cronon, *Nature's Metropolis: Chicago and the Great West* (New York: Norton, 1991).
Charlotte Porter, *The Eagle's Nest: Natural History and American Ideas, 1812–1842* (University, Ala.: University of Alabama Press, 1986).
Donald Worster, *Nature's Economy: a History of Ecological Ideas* (New York: Cambridge University Press, 1985).

neoconservatism This highly charged label indicates the worldview or ideological stance of conservatives who were once liberals, but who turned to the right during the late 1960s and early 1970s. From the start, neoconservatism has been largely a reactive phenomenon, defining its own positions in relation to the leftward drift of American LIBERALISM—within the Democratic Party, the news media, the universities, and the cultural and literary worlds. Initially, the term "neoconservative" was used as an epithet by the movement's enemies, and most of its proponents resisted the designation, insisting that they, not their ideological foes, were the *true* liberals. Eventually, though, as they began to perceive a continuity between liberalism and radicalism, most "neocons" reconciled themselves to the idea of being part of a larger political CONSERVATISM rather than a dissident liberalism. In the 1980s they were among the most spirited and effective defenders of Reagan administration policies. UN Ambassador Jeane Kirkpatrick, Education Secretary William Bennett, Assistant Secretary of State Elliott Abrams, and Congressman Jack Kemp were prominent administration figures associated with the neoconservative movement. For the most part, though, neoconservatism has been an affair of intellectuals and writers, two of its godfathers being IRVING KRISTOL, editor of the journal *The Public Interest*, and NORMAN PODHORETZ, editor of *Commentary*.

Many neoconservatives were early opponents of America's war in VIETNAM, but then had second thoughts when, in the late 1960s, liberal opposition to the war began widening into a comprehensive attack on the foreign policies of the U.S. government. Increasingly, liberals borrowed, even appropriated wholesale, from the radical theories and critiques of the NEW LEFT, which saw American power, rather than Soviet expansionism or communist ideology, as the main threat to global peace and justice. In response, neoconservatives argued that American power is, all things considered, a relatively safe and benign force in a dangerous world. They tried to restore the anticommunist consensus and containment policies of the early COLD WAR period, and to rebuild confidence in the international leadership of the United States.

Domestically, neoconservatives opposed what they saw as the corruption of the civil rights movement, the overreaching tendency of big government, and the emergence of the "counterculture." CIVIL RIGHTS understood as equality of opportunity and equality before the law had been a noble cause, the neocons said. But once those goals were achieved, they contended, the civil rights movement became corrupted by calls for EQUALITY of result, which required the institution of racial quotas and preferences in hiring and university admissions, the lowering of standards, the enactment of forced school busing to achieve racial balance, and an indulgent attitude toward lawbreakers. By the 1980s these and similar arguments were being voiced by black conservatives and neocons such as Thomas Sowell, Walter Williams, and Glenn Loury, thus provoking new intellectual ferment within the black community and challenging the old civil rights establishment.

While neoconservatives accepted the welfare state established by the New Deal and Fair Deal administrations of the 1930s and 1940s, they opposed (at least retrospectively) the vast expansion of programs and expectations inaugurated by the Great Society's "war on poverty" in the 1960s. For whites as well as blacks, neocons argued, big government discourages enterprise and instills an attitude of dependency. Moreover, it shifts to the federal government many charitable and support functions that properly belong to society's "little platoons"— family, neighborhood, parish, ethnic association— rather than to society at large.

Neoconservatism also defined itself by its opposition to the barbarization of culture engendered by the youth revolt, or "counterculture," of the 1960s. Long after the counterculture's initial and most conspicuous excesses had passed, neoconservatives continued to decry the influence of sixties-style radicalism in American life. As neocons explain it, the erstwhile rebels of the 1960s, far from dropping out of the society they denounced, penetrated the country's major institutions and professions, forming a permanent "adversary culture" within government, law, the press, the entertainment and communications industries, universities and schools, and the arts. With the Cold War over, neoconservatives have found themselves increasingly embroiled in a domestic "culture war." They seek to uphold the norms of a traditional, commonsensical majority against the innovations of a shrewdly ideological "cultural elite" whose commitments, in the neocon view, include: FEMINISM and the elimination of distinctions in custom and law between the sexes; value RELATIVISM in education and intellectual life; vulgarity and OBSCENITY—or at least an elimination of standards— in literature, art, and entertainment; multiculturalism that identifies Western civilization as nothing more than one worldview among others, and an oppressive one at that; therapeutic intervention in place of personal RESPONSIBILITY; and recognition of GAY AND LESBIAN IDENTITIES as morally acceptable. (*See also* CULTURAL PLURALISM AND MULTICULTURALISM.)

Not surprisingly, debates between neoconservatives and their left-liberal opponents continue to be as bitter in the 1990s as they were in previous decades. Neocons are often reviled by left-liberal polemicists for being heartless and "lacking compassion." Curiously, some opposition to neoconservatism has arisen on the right, mainly among the so-called "paleoconservatives," right-wingers of older pedigree who see the neocons as big-city upstarts, sometimes even implying that they are a cabal of unpatriotic Jewish intellectuals, more interested in the fate of Israel than the United States. Though many of neoconservatism's leading lights happen to be Jews, there is nothing inherently Jewish about the movement, which in fact has many Christian (especially Catholic) proponents.

Neoconservatism was anticipated by, and to some extent borrowed from, earlier strains of American liberalism, for instance, the "revisionist liberalism" of the 1950s and the "end of ideology" liberalism of the 1960s. It continues to draw inspiration from thinkers who, in their own day, considered themselves men of the left—the American theologian REINHOLD NIEBUHR, for instance, who expressed a tragic sense of the limits of political redemption, and the British writer George Orwell, who saw the potential for tyranny even in what begins as a relatively mild socialism. Though its package of policies places it in the conservative camp of *American* political thought, neoconservatism, because it stresses free markets and personal liberty over governmentally enforced equality, is very decisively liberal as that term is understood in Britain and on the continent. However neoconservatism is finally classified in American terms—as liberal or conservative—its influence in recent history has been to give American conservatism a hitherto unprecedented intellectual respectability and coherence.

MATTHEW BERKE

FURTHER READING

Peter L. Berger and Richard John Neuhaus, *To Empower People: the Role of Mediating Structures in Public Policy* (Washington, D.C.: American Enterprise Institute, 1977).

Midge Decter, *The Liberated Woman and Other Americans* (New York: Coward, McCann and Geoghan, 1971).

Jeane J. Kirkpatrick, *Dictatorships and Double Standards* (New York: Simon and Schuster, 1982).

Irving Kristol, *Reflections of a Neoconservative* (New York: Basic Books, 1983).

Glenn C. Loury, *One by One from the Inside Out: Race and Responsibility in America* (New York: Free Press, 1995).

Michael Novak, *The Spirit of Democratic Capitalism* (New York: Simon and Schuster, 1982).

Norman Podhoretz, *Breaking Ranks: a Political Memoir* (New York: Harper and Row, 1979).

Peter Steinfels, *The Neo-Conservatives: the Men who Are Changing America's Politics* (New York: Simon and Schuster, 1979).

neo-Freudianism Fierce debates occurred among psychoanalysts in the 1930s concerning Freud's revision of metapsychology to include the death drive as an innate psychic force. Analysts also disagreed about the importance of cultural factors in constituting subjectivity, about the scientific status of psychoanalysis, and about the proper training for and purposes of practicing psychoanalysis.

The term neo-Freudian emerged to mark those who rejected important aspects of Freud's thought. Early neo-Freudians including Karen Horney (*The Neurotic Personality of Our Time*, 1937) and ERICH FROMM (*Escape from Freedom*, 1941) rejected Freud's drive theory. They found its emphasis on aggression and its relatively fixed notion of human nature especially objectionable. They and other dissidents also claimed that psychoanalysis was a critical social theory instead of (or as well as) an empirical science.

Contention about these questions subsided during World War II, but in the postwar period debate reemerged in two waves, the first during the 1950s to late 1960s and the second in the late 1970s. During these periods the term was extended to authors such as HARRY STACK SULLIVAN, HERBERT MARCUSE, Norman O. Brown, Nancy Chodorow, and Dorothy Dinnerstein. The ideas of these authors often conflict, and none would use the term to define themselves. However, they share at least one common position.

Some of their ideas contradict the ego psychology which dominated official American psychoanalytic institutes from the 1950s until the mid-1970s. Ego psychologists stress drive theory and the adaptive capabilities of the ego and its defenses. They also assume a positivistic idea of science. Since psychoanalysis is an empirical science, political questions are outside its domain. From the perspective of "orthodox" analysts such as Heinz Hartmann or Charles Brenner, writers like Herbert Marcuse or Norman O. Brown who consider psychoanalysis a social and political theory and those like Horney or Clara Thompson who reject drive theory would all be neo-Freudians.

A central text for these debates is Freud's *Civilization and Its Discontents* (1930). Freud argued that humans are driven by a need for the satisfaction of instinctual demands. Happiness is drive satisfaction; its absence causes unpleasant tension. There are two primary drives, Eros and death. Eros drives us toward relations with others, death towards the destruction of these relations and of life itself. These drives are innate and invariant across cultures. Their demands and those of culture cannot be fully reconciled. Drives are generally indifferent to the object from which they seek satisfaction or to the consequences of their quest for gratification. Hence, they are a- or antisocial, although their expression may be channeled (sublimated) or affected by social relations.

Modern Western culture, according to Freud, required excessive renunciation of Eros, and consequently left too much of the energy of the death drive unbound. An effect of this imbalance, Freud wrote presciently in 1929–30, was that societies would become increasingly aggressive and violent. Societies tended to demand more instinctual renunciation as they developed; human misery intensified as civilization progressed. Even the most rational societies, however, would require some renunciation, repression, or sublimation of eros. Aggression could not be completely eradicated from civilized life.

Horney and Fromm argued that drive theory was a relic of Freud's attraction to mechanistic models of explanation derived from nineteenth-century physics. Freud's view of human beings, they contended, ignored the role of interpersonal relations in determining human "nature." People were highly responsive to environmental change as well as therapy. Given a reasonably good personal and political environment, unhappiness and conflict are not inevitable. Aggressive behavior was a symptom of neurosis or social problems, not an inescapable expression of an innate drive or energy.

Herbert Marcuse in *Eros and Civilization* (1955)

scornfully used the term neo-Freudianism to attack this rejection of drive theory and the belief that true happiness was possible within contemporary culture. Marcuse, like Norman O. Brown in *Life Against Death* (1959), considered drive theory a source of hope. If the environmentalists were right, no force was available in a period of conformity and repression to provide impetus for rebellion. If drives were innate, they could provide both energy for resistance and an instinctual ground for the demand for pleasure. Marcuse's rejection of Fromm's and Horney's hopeful humanism did not lead him to identify with official ego psychology. He insisted that despite the inevitable limits on happiness in any society, psychoanalysis must critique the surplus misery caused by irrational, unnecessarily repressive forms of social organization.

In the mid-1970s feminist scholars such as Nancy Chodorow in *The Reproduction of Mothering* (1978) and Dorothy Dinnerstein in *Mermaid and the Minotaur* (1976) joined debates about psychoanalysis, culture, and politics. Unlike orthodox analysts, feminist psychoanalytic theorists stress the importance of family structures, power relations, and other cultural factors (rather than biology) in the construction of identity and especially in the organization of subjectivity into distinctive realms of MASCULINITY and FEMININITY. However, as in earlier debates, feminists disagree on the relative importance of social relations and innate or impersonal factors in the constitution of subjectivity. Writers influenced by Jacques Lacan, such as Juliet Mitchell in her introduction to *Feminine Sexuality* (1982), criticize theorists such as Chodorow, claiming they ignore the effects of language and desire in the constitution of subjectivity and construct an excessively socialized account of it.

The arguments of orthodox analysts, of neo-Freudians like Horney, and of their radical critics are equally inadequate. The recurring debates over such questions as nature versus culture and the scientific status of psychoanalysis are symptoms of problems arising from the ambiguous location of psychoanalysis both within and outside ENLIGHTENMENT thinking. Rather than map the constitution of subjectivity along nature/culture lines, we need more fluid and multiple accounts of it. Our subjectivity is constituted through heterogeneous and unfinished processes that are composed of quite disparate and often conflicting elements. These include embodiment, sexuality, fantasy, reason, language, idiosyncratic inner worlds, non-object-related drives, object-related drives, and historically variable social relations of all sorts (family, work, politics, race, gender, class, ethnicity, among others). Each of these elements is also mul-

tiply determined by social, somatic, and discursive forces.

Given its fluid and overdetermined qualities, the best approaches to subjectivity will be those that construct contextual and delimited genealogies. Attempts to build universal theories of "human nature," to attribute certain behaviors or qualities to culture and others to nature, and to define these terms as mutually exclusive are theoretically and practically counterproductive.

JANE FLAX

See also FREUDIANISM; PSYCHOTHERAPY.

FURTHER READING
Charles Brenner, *An Elementary Textbook of Psychoanalysis*, rev. ed. (New York: Anchor, 1974).
Jane Flax, *Disputed Subjects: Essays on Psychoanalysis, Politics and Philosophy* (New York: Routledge, 1993).
Heinz Hartmann, *Ego Psychology and the Problem of Adaptation* (New York: International Universities Press, 1958).
Juliet Mitchell and Jacqueline Rose, eds., *Feminine Sexuality: Jacques Lacan and the École Freudienne* (New York: Norton, 1982).
Harry Stack Sullivan, *The Interpersonal Theory of Psychiatry* (New York: Norton, 1953).
Clara Thompson, *Psychoanalysis: Evolution and Development* (New York: Heritage House, 1951).

Newcomb, Simon (b. Wallace, Nova Scotia, Mar. 12, 1835; d. Washington, D.C., July 11, 1909). Astronomer and mathematician. Newcomb developed a system of equations for predicting the position of all the planets, thus replacing previous theories that could account for only one planet at a time and needed recurrent adjustments. He then developed an accurate theory of the moon's motion. Encouraging astronomers around the world to coordinate their observations and use common constants, tables, and fundamental stars, he fostered global cooperation in astronomical work. Among his popular works were *Popular Astronomy* (1878) and *The Stars* (1901). He also published a memoir, *The Reminiscences of an Astronomer* (1903).

FURTHER READING
Albert E. Moyer, *A Scientist's Voice in American Culture: Simon Newcomb and the Rhetoric of Scientific Method* (Berkeley: University of California Press, 1992).

New Left Radicals of the 1960s termed themselves the New Left to underscore a generational and ideological break with their immediate left-wing predecessors. The term originated in the New Left Clubs of Great Britain and their allied journal, *New Left Review* (1969–present), which undertook the ideological task of freeing radicalism from the Stalin–Trotsky–Social Democratic debates that had held sway for decades. The first American journal to adopt this approach was *Studies on the Left* (1959–67), based at the University of Wisconsin and heavily influenced by historian William Appleman Williams.

The New Left would remain rooted on college campuses. Students for a Democratic Society (SDS), launched in 1960 by a handful of young social democrats, became the largest New Left organization, reaching a peak of 150,000 loosely defined members. Unlike the Marxist-Leninist organizations of the Old Left, SDS was purposely decentralized, with most decision-making at the base. The organization directly expressed the estrangement many young people felt from the government, university, corporate and media nexus commonly referred to as "the establishment." Rather than trying to organize the proletariat as the 1930s radicals had attempted, the New Left sought to mobilize the very poor and racial minorities under the framework of "participatory democracy." Characteristic of this approach were the Newark Community Project, the Educational Research Action Program, and Chicago Jobs-or-Income Now.

The nearly anarchic DEMOCRACY espoused by the New Left stressed the unity of ends and means. Magazines such as the anarchistic *Liberation* and pacifist thinkers like David Dellinger were particularly influential during the early phases of the New Left. The Port Huron Statement, SDS's assertion of principles, owed more to Jefferson, Thoreau, and Dewey than to Marx, Lenin, or Mao. Subsequent movements which had many roots in the New Left elaborated similar democratic and organizational concepts. "Second-wave" feminist thought was rooted in the idea that the personal is political and the ecological movement embraced the injunction to think globally while acting locally.

Seeking a viable revolutionary ideology, the New Left frequently evoked the ideas of Rosa Luxemburg, Antonio Gramsci, HERBERT MARCUSE, and others who believed that not only political injustice or oppression, but the hegemonic culture itself must be combatted. Consequently, a serious effort was made to retrieve indigenous American radical traditions. This effort was most evident in journals such as *Radical America* (1967–present), *Socialist Revolution*, later retitled *Socialist Review* (1970–present), and *Radical History Review* (1977–present). Oral history as practiced by Studs Terkel and Staughton Lynd was a hallmark of this work. The Oral History of the American Left, comprising hundreds of interviews, came to be housed at New York University's Tamiment Library. New Left journals also supported Frantz Fanon's linkage of psychological

disorders with colonialism and critical analysis of the mass media by NOAM CHOMSKY.

In addition to the profusion of New Left printed works, there were documentary films such as *Union Maids* and *The Wobblies*, which recovered past radical history, and *Harlan County* and *Attica*, which treated current problems from a radical perspective. New Left filmmakers became the backbone of the American documentary, winning numerous international awards as well as American Oscars. The New Left also bred more than a dozen literary magazines, but few lasted more than a year. No single theme or style emerged, and there was a marked tendency for blacks, women, and gays to create their own separate literary journals and presses.

Complicating any assessment of New Left thought is the considerable overlap with the counterculture and youth movements. The hard core counterculture, highly influenced by BEAT GENERATION writers, was oriented to recreational drugs, uninhibited artistic expression, sexual liberation, and personal enlightenment. The youth movement adopted many New Left and counterculture ideas but in modified forms usually expressed in music and lifestyle changes. Events like the Stop-the-Draft week of October 1967 and the contemporaneous counterculture Be-Ins drew on common pools of the alienated young. A similar overlap occurred in the new local newspapers dubbed "the underground press." Whether leaning to the New Left or the counterculture, these weeklies promoted cultural and political rebellion. Their combined weekly circulation peaked at about two million readers heavily concentrated in colleges and urban centers. (*See also* YOUTH.)

The individual who best exemplified the interaction of the New Left and the counterculture was the irascible and irrepressible Abbie Hoffman. Although his satirical antics often irritated members of the politicized New Left as much as they did the establishment, Hoffman kept his focus on antiwar, ecological, and antiracist themes. His counterculture counterpart was poet ALLEN GINSBERG. Among Ginsberg's antiwar activities was the attempt to levitate the Pentagon with a Buddhist mantra during the massive 1967 March on Washington.

Among the more conventionally political actions of the New Left was its support for social change movements throughout the Americas. The widely read work of C. WRIGHT MILLS, *Listen, Yankee!*, a book friendly to the Cuban Revolution, along with Fair Play for Cuba Committees, were among the first manifestations of the New Left. Similar sentiments led to the establishment of support groups for various national movements advocating parliamentary reform, liberation theology, or armed revolution. Many of these groups still exist.

Events in China also sparked major interest and commitment. The pro-Maoist books of Edgar Snow, William Hinton, and Felix Greene were broadly influential, and pro-China groups formed in some of the antiwar coalitions. The Maoist upsurge reflected the frustration felt within the movement as the 1960s were ending. Years of militant protests had failed to halt the war in VIETNAM and had only dented institutionalized racism. The establishment seemed more responsive to rioting in the streets than to peaceful marches, however large. The assassinations of MARTIN LUTHER KING JR. and Robert Kennedy, followed by the police riot at the 1968 Democratic convention, led some in the New Left to think the hour of armed struggle had arrived. The group most loudly espousing this view was the small Weatherman faction of SDS which began agitation "to bring the war home" with acts of terrorism on American soil. Paralleling this development was the rise of the Black Panther Party, whose fiery slogans included the police-provoking injunction to "off the pig."

Rather than ushering in a new phase of the movement, the various groups advocating "revolution now" perished in a series of political novas. The New Left began to disintegrate, with many individuals becoming politically inactive or flowing into the burgeoning women's, gay, antinuclear, and ecology movements. A few early SDS leaders like Tom Hayden went into conventional politics, a path later followed by some former Black Panthers as well. More common were academic careers. New Left and formerly New Left scholars soon came to reshape and sometimes dominate academic and intellectual discourse on mass media, revolutionary movements, ethnic communities, racial identity, the construction of gender, and the development of colonialism and imperialism.

Twenty years after the demise of the New Left, it is mostly remembered for its role in the movement against the Vietnam War. Although New Left alumni are still found in leadership roles in many activist groups, they are most visible on college campuses as professors and administrators. These New Left academics have figured prominently in heated national debates on affirmative action, curriculum revision, and the fate of the university. Future historians are liable to judge the New Left to have been extremely influential not only in reshaping culture and politics in the 1960s, but in remaking the intellectual arena of the last quarter of the twentieth century.

DAN GEORGAKAS

See also SOCIALISM.

FURTHER READING

Mari Jo Buhle, Paul Buhle, Dan Georgakas, eds., *The Encyclopedia of the American Left* (Urbana: University of Illinois Press, 1990).

Todd Gitlin, *The Sixties: Years of Hope, Days of Rage* (New York: Bantam, 1987).

James Miller, *Democracy is in the streets: From Port Huron to the Siege of Chicago* (New York: Simon and Schuster, 1987).

Kirkpatrick Sale, *SDS* (New York: Random House, 1973).

Michael Steven Smith, *Notebook of a Sixties Lawyer: an Unrepentant Memoir and Selected Writings* (New York: Smyrna Press, 1992).

Thomas Waugh, ed., *Show Us Life: Towards a History and Aesthetics of the Committed Documentary* (Metuchen, N.J.: Scarecrow Press, 1984).

new literary historicism In literature departments, the new literary historicism is called simply "the new historicism," a label that both causes confusion and helps to situate it historically. Confusion results from historicism's imprecise meaning. Sometimes it refers to a specific brand of historical analysis called *Historismus* in German. Taking off from Otto von Ranke's desire to free the discipline of history from moral philosophy and philosophical systems, *Historismus* relied on empirical data to describe the past "as it really was." But "historicism" can also refer generally to any historically oriented mode of inquiry. The general meaning predominates in literary studies. The new literary historicism, therefore, promises to produce a new sense of literature's relation to the past. The label serves to register shifting claims to newness in literary studies.

On the one hand, "the new historicism" evokes the New Criticism, a formalist mode of analysis that it would displace. On the other, it distinguishes itself from late nineteenth- and early twentieth-century historicism in literary studies against which the New Critics of the mid-twentieth century reacted. The most widely cited difference between the new historicism and the old is its engagement with poststructuralism, which for a while seemed—and still seems to some—the true inheritor to the throne once occupied, successively, by the older historicism and by the New Criticism.

One challenge posed to the old historicism by the new concerns the former's reliance on distinct eras with a homogeneous *Zeitgeist*. The present period bears out the new historicism's perception of overlapping discourses in any era, since the "new" historicism has itself not completely displaced the "old." There may still be more practicing old historicists than new. "New" merely indicates a later arrival on the scene. Poststructuralism's contribution to that arrival leads to another confusion, since it is scarcely monolithic. On the contrary, it consists of many different, often competing, theories, such as those of Michel Foucault, Jacques Derrida, and Gilles Deleuze. Similarly, there are several new historicisms. But the writers associated with the journal *Representations*, including Catherine Gallagher, Walter Benn Michaels, and most notably Stephen Greenblatt, comprise the most prominent group.

Greenblatt's exemplary status derives from the way in which he relates literature and history, particularly his challenge to the distinction traditionalists make between a text and its historical context. By placing a text in its historical context traditionalists have tried to ward off the threat of both the New Criticism and of the various versions of poststructuralism that insist upon the multiplicity of meanings in a text. For instance, E. D. Hirsch, while admitting in *Validity in Interpretation* that the language of any text is indeterminate, insists that its proper meaning is the meaning it had at the moment it was produced. Only by restoring a text to its historical context, he argues, can that meaning be reproduced. In contrast, Greenblatt appeals to the contingency of history to question the assumption that a text has a stable, unitary context. The traditionalists' appeal to context to fix a text's meaning ignores the fact that we cannot reconstruct a context without interpreting yet other texts, texts whose context, in turn, includes the original text being examined. Texts and contexts are always in a relation of reciprocal determination.

This interplay between text and context causes problems not only for those trying to stabilize a text's meaning, but also for older historicists, like Georg Lukács in *Studies in European Realism*, who claim that certain great texts can reflect the totality of their eras. Embedded in an interrelated network of complex social practices, a literary text cannot, in the view of new historicists, achieve a transcendental position outside its context, a position from which to reflect that context. As a result, a typical Greenblatt essay does not begin with historical background material and then move to the analysis of a text. Instead, it challenges the very notion of historical background by employing the technique of montage. Starting with the analysis of a particular historical event, it cuts to the analysis of a particular literary text. The point is not to show that the literary text reflects the historical event, but to create a field of energy between the two so that we come to see the event as a social text and the literary text as a social event. As Louis Montrose puts it in an essay collected in a volume entitled *The New Historicism*, Greenblatt's version of the new historicism examines both the "historicity of texts and the textuality of history" (p. 20).

Greenblatt prefers to call his analysis "cultural poetics," and much of the new historical work done in his specialty, the English Renaissance, could fit under that label. It is a method devised by American scholars to stress the otherness of a distant culture, while also constructing a bridge between that culture and their own. But in other historical periods quite different versions of historical analysis have arisen. Two prominent examples are British Romanticism and nineteenth-century American literature. Scholars of British Romanticism begin with a profound sense of continuity between themselves and romantic writers. Recognizing the romantic origins of their own historicism, they have turned, following Jerome McGann, to a dialectical strategy in order to establish a critical distance from romantic assumptions through techniques of ideological critique. American scholars of nineteenth-century American literature feel even closer to their object of study than students of Romanticism do. But rather than work to establish a historical distance, they have typically attempted to show how these texts constitute the prehistory of our own time. Some emphasize the pre-twentieth-century dynamics of liberalism or consumer capitalism. Others dwell on nineteenth-century voices of previously marginalized ethnic and women writers, such as FREDERICK DOUGLASS and Harriet Jacobs. The different voices within the new literary historicism itself is a sign both of its strength and of the influence upon it of a society that has diverse and often conflicting questions to ask about its literary past.

BROOK THOMAS

See also READING; REPRESENTATION; TEXTUALITY.

FURTHER READING
Catherine Gallagher, *The Industrial Reformation of English Fiction* (Chicago: University of Chicago Press, 1985).
Stephen Greenblatt, *Renaissance Self-Fashioning: From More to Shakespeare* (Chicago: University of Chicago Press, 1980).
——, *Shakespearean Negotiations: the Circulation of Social Energy in Renaissance England* (Berkeley: University of California Press, 1988).
E. D. Hirsch, *Validity in Interpretation* (New Haven: Yale University Press, 1967).
Georg Lukács, *Studies in European Realism* (New York: Grosset and Dunlap, 1964).
Jerome McGann, *The Romantic Ideology* (Chicago: University of Chicago Press, 1983).
Walter Benn Michaels, *The Gold Standard and the Logic of Naturalism* (Berkeley: University of California Press, 1987).
H. Aram Veeser, ed., *The New Historicism* (New York: Routledge, 1989).

The New Republic   For 80 years *The New Republic* has been a journal of record for American LIBERALISM, reflecting in its pages the twists and turns of that ideology. Founded in 1914 under the direction of the editorial troika of HERBERT CROLY, WALTER LIPPMANN and WALTER WEYL, the magazine was bankrolled until the early 1950s by financier Willard Straight and his wife Dorothy (Whitney) Straight, who unlike the journal's subsequent owner-publishers seldom meddled in editorial affairs. *The New Republic* was an immediate success, attracting 40,000 subscribers by 1918 as well as such contributors as CHARLES BEARD, JOHN DEWEY, W. E. B. DU BOIS, and THORSTEIN VEBLEN. Croly was the dominant editorial voice in the magazine's early years, and he used it to advance the vision he had laid out in *The Promise of American Life* (1909) and *Progressive Democracy* (1914) of a new American nationalism in which a regulatory state would make use of its power to control corporate power, advance social welfare, and foster political and economic democracy.

Although Croly's thinking was closer to that of Theodore Roosevelt's "new nationalism" than to Woodrow Wilson's "new freedom," he and the other editors steadily warmed to the Wilson administration, and they were enthusiastic supporters of American intervention in WORLD WAR I. Their ardent endorsement of Wilson's war to make the world safe for democracy led many to believe that the magazine spoke for the administration and provoked such critics of the war as RANDOLPH BOURNE to denounce the "new republicaners" for abandoning their critical intelligence and crucifying democratic values on the altar of "war technique."

In the wake of the Versailles treaty and the suppression of radical dissent at home, *The New Republic* came to rue its support of the war. It found itself embattled both politically and financially in the 1920s. Weyl died in 1919, and Lippmann moved on to wider influence as a newspaper editor and columnist. A dispirited Croly soldiered on, but with the return of the Republican Party to the White House, he announced "the eclipse of progressivism" and increasingly devoted himself to religious speculation until his death in 1930.

The onset of the Great Depression rejuvenated the political energies of the magazine. Under the leadership of editors Bruce Bliven and George Soule, *The New Republic* staked out a position to the left of the New Deal and became a leading proponent of national economic planning and social democracy. Initially critical of Franklin Roosevelt's efforts to save American capitalism from itself, the editors, like many left-liberals, warmed to the President after he launched the social welfare programs of the mid-1930s and won a massive electoral victory in 1936.

In the late thirties, led by literary editor MALCOLM COWLEY, the magazine joined the Popular Front alliance of liberals, socialists, and communists in supporting FDR, condemning Hitler, and suspending judgment on the terrors of Stalinism.

The Popular Front collapsed with the Nazi-Soviet pact of August 1939, but *The New Republic* joined the communists in opposing American entanglement in WORLD WAR II, which began in Europe a month later. Bliven's reluctance to commit the magazine to what he feared would be a repeat of the debacle of World War I provoked bitter criticism from such longtime contributors as Waldo Frank and LEWIS MUMFORD, who charged the editors with fostering a corrupt and morally flaccid liberalism unable to meet the challenge of fascism. The addition of Michael Straight, son of the magazine's benefactors and a vigorous interventionist, to the editorial board in 1941 initiated a decided change in its editorial line on the war, and by August 1941 *The New Republic* was calling for an American declaration of war against the Axis powers. With Stalin, after the Nazi invasion of Russia, once again on the side of the angels, the magazine also settled back into the pieties of the Popular Front. This stance persisted into the early months of the COLD WAR with the appointment as editor of HENRY WALLACE, leading critic of Truman's increasingly hardline posture toward the Soviet Union. But by 1948 and the debacle of Wallace's third-party campaign for President, *The New Republic* was well within the fold of Cold War liberalism, coming to the defense of Truman's anticommunist foreign policy while neglecting the threat to civil liberties posed by the right-wing anticommunism of Senator Joseph McCarthy and his allies.

In 1953 the financially troubled magazine was purchased by Gilbert Harrison and his wealthy wife Nancy (Blaine). Under Harrison's editorial direction, the journal marched in step until the mid-1960s with the liberalism of Adlai Stevenson, John Kennedy, and Lyndon Johnson. But as the war in Vietnam deepened, *The New Republic* joined the opposition to Johnson, and contributors such as GEORGE KENNAN and REINHOLD NIEBUHR offered searching criticism of the premises of American foreign policy. While the magazine's editors shrank from antiwar radicalism and countercultural "freak-outs," they supported the civil rights movement and the left-liberal politics of Eugene McCarthy, Robert Kennedy, and George McGovern.

In 1974 Martin Peretz bought *The New Republic* from Harrison, and over the course of the next two decades he and his writers moved the magazine away from the pieties of left-liberalism toward views that flirted with neoconservative positions on foreign policy (especially in the Middle East and Central America), race relations, and the welfare state. As one former editor told a *New York Times Magazine* reporter, "TNR was about not being easy on blacks, not being easy on Communists and not being tough on Jews."

The New Republic has always been more than a political magazine. Over the course of its long history, the magazine has welcomed an extraordinarily distinguished roster of contributors to the cultural pages at the "back of the book" edited by writers such as EDMUND WILSON, Malcolm Cowley, and ALFRED KAZIN. Current literary editor Leon Wieseltier has sustained this tradition and, like his predecessors, contributed several memorable pieces on such topics as religious fundamentalism and the Holocaust museum to the front of the book as well.

In its current incarnation, Peretz's *New Republic* is led by self-styled "postideological" editor and Gap T-shirt model Andrew Sullivan and features such writers-cum-television-pundits as Fred Barnes, Michael Kinsley, and Morton Kondracke. Under Wieseltier's leadership, the cultural criticism in the magazine consistently surpasses its political commentary. But books such as senior editor Mickey Kaus's *End of Equality* (1992), with its call for a "civic liberalism" oriented less toward income equality and the redistribution of wealth than toward the revitalization of a public realm of social equality and shared citizenship, are worthy successors to the work of the magazine's founders and an indication of the continuing capacity of the journal's writers to make bold contributions to American social thought.

ROBERT B. WESTBROOK

See also JOURNALS OF OPINION.

FURTHER READING
John P. Diggins, "The New Republic and Its Times," *New Republic*, Dec. 10, 1984, pp. 23–73.
Charles Forcey, *The Crossroads of Liberalism* (New York: Oxford University Press, 1961).
Walter Kirn, "The Editor as Gap Model: the New *New Republic* and the Politics of Pleasure," *New York Times Magazine*, Mar. 7, 1993.
Christopher Lasch, *The New Radicalism in America* (New York: Knopf, 1965).
David Levy, *Herbert Croly and "The New Republic"* (Princeton: Princeton University Press, 1985).
David Seideman, *"The New Republic": a Voice of Modern Liberalism* (New York: Praeger, 1986).

New York Intellectuals Modern life is so complex, Isaac Rosenfeld suggested in an "Under Forty" symposium in 1944, that "the outsider often finds himself the perfect insider" (p. 35). There was pleasure in the paradox for Rosenfeld, and a good deal of personal meaning. The New York Intellectuals over several decades cherished the idea that their position was difficult, their outlook sophisticated, their thought both substantive and subtle. Much of their collective history took shape around the creative tensions between persisting on the margins and claiming a central place; between mounting a critique of American society and defending many of its fundamental values; between ratifying aesthetic experimentation and seeking the continuity of tradition. The effort to balance these antinomies without resolving them, to remain both outsiders and insiders, in time invested a particular experience with wide intellectual resonance.

The circle of writers, critics, and scholars who would come to be known as the New York Intellectuals emerged during the 1930s when political principles and literary values led a relative few on the left, including PHILIP RAHV, SIDNEY HOOK, LIONEL TRILLING, DWIGHT MACDONALD, and William Phillips, into vehement opposition to Stalinism. Younger intellectuals coming of age in the 1940s or slightly later would expand the New Yorkers' range and maintain the circle as an identifiable presence in American social and cultural thought at least through the 1970s. For all their durability, the New York Intellectuals never formed a cohesive group or a common school; yet they shared a sense of which were the important questions of a given time, and they found their greatest stimulus (and foremost audience) in one another. Not all of them came originally from New York, and not all of them were entwined in the ethnic ties that linked the majority. Some were distinctly less political than others, and some lacked a developed sensitivity to literary and aesthetic concerns. Even so, the circle in each instance had a center of gravity, and the tensions that gave the New York Intellectuals their edge operated conjointly across the spheres of ethnicity, politics, and culture.

For the most part they were Jewish, commonly the children of immigrants, taking up the shifting challenge of defining their cultural identity. In a pattern established during the 1930s, they generally rejected both assertions of ethnic particularism and the denials implicit in assimilation. Their vision of a worthy intellectual and social life revolved instead around the balancing of specific inheritance with shared tradition: the goal was a cosmopolitan culture in which individual and group differences would contribute to the richness of the whole. Satisfied with neither the provincialism of the immigrant neighborhood nor the nativism of the larger culture, the

New York Intellectuals of the 1930s and 1940s helped turn the tensions between ethnicity and national identity into a generative force, creating opportunities for entering into American society by changing it.

World War II and the Holocaust compelled a more open and explicit consideration of Jewish ethnicity, even as the impact of the war produced a sharp decline in anti-Semitism and an expansion of opportunities. Working from values that were already established, New York Intellectuals like CLEMENT GREENBERG and HAROLD ROSENBERG rejected the extremes of dissolving Jewish consciousness or embracing Jewish chauvinism. Greenberg insisted on the right to be both Jew and American, while Rosenberg reflected broadly on the complexity of modern identity and warned against all ideologies of narrow commitment. Others used Jewish heritage to evaluate dominant traditions, or secular analysis to explore Jewish beliefs. Alfred Kazin turned from literary analysis to memoir by making his ethnic experience an organizing theme. Through bursts of heated debate spanning four decades, writers and critics in the New York circle found a part of their intellectual bite in the doubleness of being both Jews and Americans. The identity thrust upon them as the "New York Intellectuals" recognized both their inclusion in American cultural life and their vibrant distinctiveness.

Most of the young New Yorkers cut their teeth politically on the radicalism of the 1930s, with organizational affiliations that varied. Pulled together after 1937 by their opposition to Stalinist dictatorship and communist tactics, they made the rejection of "totalitarianism" in its various guises a permanent badge of honor within their camp. This position was not simply negative. The incidents and issues that defined their opposition to the Communist Party, including the defense of Leon Trotsky against Stalin's charges in the Moscow trials, most commonly involved questions of democratic process, civil liberties, and free debate. Their anti-Stalinism contained an affirmation of liberal principles as essential to a progressive social vision and a meaningful intellectual life. Their criticisms of the NEW LEFT in the 1960s would echo that affirmation.

Elements of broad agreement thus helped define the circle, yet they did little to establish where the balance between critique and justification should lie. Passionate debates and internal divisions over political and intellectual responsibility became a hallmark of the New York Intellectuals: a shifting fault line divided those drawn more strongly to a radical ideal, with its power of social critique, from those more thoroughly engaged by the need to defend American practices and institutions against external and internal threats. Such tensions helped define the periodicals that provided characteristic outlets for the New York circle. Differences over political and intellectual values framed the decision by Philip Rahv and William Phillips to move *Partisan Review* away from the Communist Party in the 1930s. When Rahv and *Partisan Review* supported American involvement in World War II, Dwight Macdonald stepped away in 1943 to explore radical alternatives in politics. When *Commentary* (a successor to the *Contemporary Jewish Record*) became too wrapped up in Cold War affirmations for some, Irving Howe took the lead in founding *Dissent* in 1954. A set of later JOURNALS OF OPINION staked out positions on the issues of the 1960s and 1970s. Postwar differences over just how vigorously communists and their sympathizers should be pursued as a cultural and political threat, a pursuit for which Sidney Hook provided intellectual leadership and IRVING KRISTOL a sharp polemical voice, created frictions within the New York circle that were among the most enduring.

The contest between critique and affirmation within the New York circle seemed to stimulate rather than dampen a multifaceted engagement with art and ideas during the postwar decade, and to spur the development of newer voices. MARY MCCARTHY launched her career in fiction, and Delmore Schwartz tied *Partisan Review* to an impressive group of young poets. William Barrett helped introduce French existentialism to America, and Nathan Glazer assisted DAVID RIESMAN in writing *The Lonely Crowd*. The rising novelist SAUL BELLOW counted as a cousin among the New Yorkers as did the historian RICHARD HOFSTADTER, and the circle maintained strong intellectual and social links with the German emigré HANNAH ARENDT as she constructed her compelling analysis of totalitarianism.

Politics overlapped substantially with cultural concerns among the New York Intellectuals; for some, culture was primary. Throughout their history, literature provided a principal arena for the assertion of aesthetic and social values. From the earliest disputes of the 1930s between the *Partisan Review* circle and the communist mainstream on the left, two touchstones remained constant: the insistence on high aesthetic standards and the expectation of continuity within an evolving tradition. Such tenets supported a particular interest in literary MODERNISM for its thematic sophistication and indisputable craft, as well as for modernism's complex relationship with a tradition it stood both within and against. The same propositions informed a general (though not universal) critique of the shallowness and commercialism of MASS CULTURE in the 1940s and 1950s that prompted some critics to brand the New York circle as elitist.

The belief had also developed early that, as Rahv once put it, genuine innovation in literature and the arts must not simply take the recognizable world apart but put it together again in a new order. By the later 1950s this expectation was leading toward growing doubts about modernism and about what Lionel Trilling identified as a strain of hostility toward civilization running through it. In the attacks of the 1960s on authority, tradition, and learning itself, many of the New York Intellectuals detected nihilism, not reconstruction. Cultural issues fully as much as political pushed a segment of the New York circle, including Glazer, Kristol, DANIEL BELL, and NORMAN PODHORETZ, toward identification with NEOCONSERVATISM during the 1970s, and by the 1980s Kristol acknowledged himself a "conservative." Although Bell continued to label himself a socialist in economics and a liberal in politics, he made it clear that the legacy of modernism and capitalism had helped over time to make him too a conservative on matters of culture.

For four decades the New York Intellectuals had located themselves within an "intellectuals' tradition" in modern Western culture that depended upon an ongoing tension between innovation and propriety, the writer and the literary past, the critic and the community. This indispensable tension was the engine of their thought. They worked, at their best, to defend the imaginative prospect of intellectuals standing both inside and outside their culture, themselves invested in what they were helping to transform.

In addition to studies of individuals and memoirs by several of the principals, a number of works offer a collective interpretation of the New York circle. Alexander Bloom emphasizes Jewish identity as a theme; Alan Wald strives to make Trotskyism seem central; and Russell Jacoby creates an image of the "last intellectuals" for immediate polemical use. Using a wider lens, Terry Cooney explores the emergence of the circle and its cultural and political commitments through World War II, and Neil Jumonville examines the postwar period by concentrating on struggles over the intellectual's role. Perceptions of the New York Intellectuals may change with time, but their history will remain fertile ground for questions about the ethnic and religious diversification of American intellectual life; the integration of contemporary European ideas into American discourse; the reception and definition of modernism; and the principles and practices essential to intellectual integrity.

TERRY A. COONEY

FURTHER READING

Alexander Bloom, *Prodigal Sons: the New York Intellectuals and Their World* (New York: Oxford University Press, 1986).

Terry A. Cooney, *The Rise of the New York Intellectuals: "Partisan Review" and Its Circle* (Madison: University of Wisconsin Press, 1986).

James Burkhart Gilbert, *Writers and Partisans: a History of Literary Radicalism in America* (New York: John Wiley, 1968).

Russell Jacoby, *The Last Intellectuals: American Culture in the Age of Academe* (New York: Basic Books, 1987).

Neil Jumonville, *Critical Crossings: the New York Intellectuals in Postwar America* (Berkeley: University of California Press, 1991).

"The New York Jewish Intellectuals," *American Jewish History* 80 (spring 1991): 323–96.

"Under Forty: a Symposium on American Literature and the Younger Generation of American Jews," *Contemporary Jewish Record* 7 (Feb. 1944): 3–36.

Alan M. Wald, *The New York Intellectuals: the Rise and Decline of the Anti-Stalinist Left from the 1930s to the 1980s* (Chapel Hill: University of North Carolina Press, 1987).

Niebuhr, H[elmut] Richard (b. Wright City, Mo., Sept. 3, 1894; d. Greenfield, Mass., July 5, 1962). Little known today outside the field of theology and ethics, H. Richard Niebuhr was, with his older brother REINHOLD NIEBUHR and PAUL TILLICH, one of the big three of twentieth-century American religious thought. During his lifetime, inside and outside of his family, he was almost completely overshadowed by Reinhold. But in the generation since his death, Richard has, for those in the discipline of religious studies, come into his own as Reinhold's peer. Many observers consider him the more original and lasting figure in the history of American Protestant thought, in part for the reason that his work was much less topical than Reinhold's, much less closely tied to the social and political events of mid-century.

Son of a leading preacher in the German Evangelical Synod of North America, H. Richard Niebuhr followed his older brother into the ministry and the professoriat, becoming a professor of Christian ethics at Yale Divinity School in 1931 (after Reinhold had turned the position down). In his three decades at Yale he trained some of the most significant Christian ethicists and theologians of our time, including James Gustafson and Hans Frei.

By the 1920s Richard Niebuhr, like Reinhold, had become alarmed by the sclerotic state of LIBERAL PROTESTANTISM, which seemed to them uncritically devoted to both capitalist social relations and a shallow humanistic theology. Richard, more deeply immersed than his brother in church affairs, was also more engaged as a young man in theological currents. He tried to bring together the liberal theology of the German Ernst Troeltsch and the "crisis" theology of the Swiss Karl Barth, whose pivotal *Epistle to the Romans* had appeared after World War I. Barth insisted, in good Calvinist style, that God was not to be "understood" in human moral or philosophical categories, but "stood under" in repentance and humility. He objected to the humanizing of God, the subjection of God to human standards of right and wrong. This insistence on God's autonomy and sovereignty went against the grain of American as well as German liberal Protestantism, both of which had come to stress the companionability of God (at the expense of God's unanswerable judgment) and the "natural" capacity of the human mind to attain knowledge of God (in addition to obtaining such knowledge from God's own revelation in the Bible).

For Niebuhr, Barth was a welcome critic of the relativizing and subjectivizing of the faith, a modern-day JONATHAN EDWARDS. American Christianity was trivializing itself, he thought, by turning itself into a form of therapeutic psychology. Psychology, he argued in 1927, "has substituted religious experience for revelation, auto-suggestion for communion with God in prayer and mysticism, sublimation of the instincts for devotion, reflexes for the soul, and group consciousness or the ideal wish-fulfillment for God." But for all his criticism of the shallowness of much American Christianity and psychology, Niebuhr was much more open than Barth to the "natural" knowledge provided by the human sciences—knowledge not so much, Niebuhr thought, of God himself as of the encounter between God and human beings.

In *The Meaning of Revelation* (1941), Niebuhr took strategic theological advantage of one of the main claims of modern social science: that human existence was circumscribed by interlocking social and psychological conditionings. By showing that human action and knowledge were strongly delimited by culture, history, and biology, the sciences had struck a liberating blow against the pretensions of humanism, against the false belief that human beings could fulfill themselves by exercising their (supposedly) boundless human powers. The sciences helped unintentionally to carve out a terrain for modern theology—by establishing that if there was to be redemption for human beings, it would proceed not from action of their own but from a higher source. Yet Niebuhr was also, in his strong endorsement of scientific investigation, giving substantial credit to the same human powers whose conditioning he stressed. Although in his strong critique of humanism he had moved far beyond the liberal tradition,

he was still linked to the liberal intellectual world of Ernst Troeltsch.

It was the model of Troeltsch, early master of the sociology of religion, that informed Niebuhr's first book, *The Social Sources of Denominationalism* (1929). Along with its follow-up volume, *The Kingdom of God in America* (1937), it is a work of permanent value for the general student of American culture. *Social Sources* is a profound analysis of the history of American religion in relation to the social forces of CLASS, RACE, and region. The central contention of the book is that spiritual developments are inseparable from, though never reducible to, social developments. For example, the Methodists and Baptists, whose growth was exponential in the nineteenth century, had to be grasped in part as class movements, movements of the "disinherited." Like the Diggers and Levellers in the sixteenth century and the Quakers in the seventeenth, they preached the priesthood of all believers, the authority not of the learned scholar or elite minister but of ordinary believers, whose immediate inner experience tied them directly to God.

In *The Kingdom of God in America*, often regarded as his classic, Niebuhr rejected the "social" focus of *Social Sources*, on the grounds that it impeded a full understanding of the spiritual dynamics of American Christianity. That formulation was unfair to his own earlier book, which was very subtle in protecting spirit from reduction to society. But the ideological wheel had turned between 1929 and 1937, and social explanations seemed increasingly implausible to scholars in many fields. Although the *Kingdom of God* is dissatisfyingly uninterested in social forces, it is an extraordinary work that combines intellectual-cultural history and theology. Niebuhr reversed the usual progressive-minded presentism of intellectual history, which labelled each thinker of the past as either a liberal (like ROGER WILLIAMS) or a conservative (like Jonathan Edwards). He saw both of them as premodern Protestant "monastics" and warned twentieth-century interpreters not to press them into service in twentieth-century ideological battles.

For Niebuhr seventeenth- and eighteenth-century preachers spoke for a different culture, one that had had its own distinct (and in some ways superior) conversation with God. As a "radical monotheist," Niebuhr was insistent about relativizing all cultural approaches to God. All human cultures make unavailing attempts to collar the divine; none embodies the Truth any more completely than any other. In "the darkness of the surrounding night which envelops all human efforts in futility" (p. 9), human beings were cast adrift, kept at a distance from their maker, but invited to meet the God of power and love in faith. This stringent faith was not appealing to many American believers of the mid-twentieth century, but for Niebuhr it offered paradoxical relief from the pieties of bourgeois culture. He wanted nothing of the liberal religion which, as he put it in *Social Sources*,

> simplified out of existence the problem of evil and . . . substitut[ed] for the mysterious will of the Sovereign of life and death and sin and salvation, the sweet benevolence of a Father-Mother God or the vague goodness of the All.

In such a religion "the Puritan passion for perfection has become a seeking after the kingdom of health and mental peace and its comforts" (p. 105).

RICHARD WIGHTMAN FOX

FURTHER READING

James W. Fowler, *To See the Kingdom: the Theological Vision of H. Richard Niebuhr* (Nashville: Abington, 1974).
Richard Wightman Fox, "H. Richard Niebuhr's Divided Kingdom," *American Quarterly* 42 (Mar. 1990): 93–101.
Jerry Irish, *The Religious Thought of H. Richard Niebuhr* (Atlanta: John Knox Press, 1983).
H. Richard Niebuhr, *The Social Sources of Denominationalism* (1929; New York: Meridian, 1957).
——, *The Kingdom of God in America* (1937; New York: Harper and Row, 1959).
Paul Ramsey, ed., *Faith and Ethics: the Theology of H. Richard Niebuhr* (New York: Harper and Row, 1957).
Ronald F. Thiemann, *The Legacy of H. Richard Niebuhr* (Minneapolis: Fortress, 1991).

Niebuhr, [Karl Paul] Reinhold (b. Wright City, Mo., June 21, 1892; d. Stockbridge, Mass., June 1, 1971). Rising from the obscurity of a provincial midwestern church, Reinhold Niebuhr became one of the major public intellectuals of mid twentieth-century America. He was the greatest preacher of the twentieth-century northern liberal church, a master of intellectual oratory—an ancient art still widely practiced and appreciated in the first half of the century, but one rapidly undermined in the television age that followed. Niebuhr's influence within LIBERAL PROTESTANTISM was colossal from the 1920s to the 1960s, and in the last half of that period, from World War II until Vietnam, he stood alongside such figures as MARGARET MEAD and WALTER LIPPMANN as a cultural sage of broad stature.

The paradox of Niebuhr's career is the paradox of liberal Protestantism itself: his *religious* mission was both to preach the Gospel and to help relocate the Christian life within the *secular* arena. As a young seminarian in the German Evangelical Synod of North America, Niebuhr was already a liberal Christian, for whom religion was not about obedience to dogma or a literal reading of the Bible, and for whom God was not the distant Calvinist judge but the nearby companion Jesus Christ. Religion was about imitating Jesus, spreading self-sacrificial love through all human relationships, personal and social. Two years at Yale Divinity School deepened his liberalism by "naturalizing" it; the "modernism" that he embraced discarded supernaturalism altogether and "divinized" the natural. Within the human world, the modernists thought, there lay deep and unrealized potential for building an ever-closer approximation of the Kingdom of God on earth. Human personality, threatened by the impersonality of modern machine processes, could nevertheless transform the world by asserting its spiritual power.

But Niebuhr was not, for the time being, interested in the fine points of theology or philosophy. As a budding Social Gospeler, he wanted to have an impact in the social and political world. He turned down a chance to pursue a Ph.D. and took a small, German-language, middle-class parish in Detroit in 1915. During World War I he wrote and traveled widely on behalf of "loyalty" to the Anglo-American cause, a stance that provoked furor in his heavily German immigrant denomination. As a second-generation German American, whose recently deceased father had himself been a well-known minister in the synod, Niebuhr had a great personal stake in rooting out disloyalty, proving his denomination's and his own Americanness. In his later writing Niebuhr would often praise the "particularist" commitments to family, ethnic group, or nation that cosmopolitan, internationalist liberals and Marxists disparaged. But during WORLD WAR I he was a bellicose advocate of liberal universalism, who could justify patriotic obedience to a particular nation only because he believed the American nation, under the leadership of WOODROW WILSON, embodied the universal ideal of democracy. He campaigned hard to rout pro-German war sentiment, and thereby contributed unintentionally to the destruction of German culture in the United States.

After the war Niebuhr worked on expanding the membership of Bethel Church, which became a center of liberal progressive Protestantism in Detroit. He also became an antagonist of Henry Ford, who combined liberal idealism with what Niebuhr considered a reactionary, anti-union labor policy. His encounter with Ford helped turn him against liberal idealism in the social arena, and helped lead him, by the end of the 1920s, to SOCIALISM. Establishing justice meant, in Niebuhr's eyes, supporting labor in its struggle with capital, and supporting labor meant endorsing the "force" and "coercion" contained in such strategies as boycotts and strikes. This was difficult doctrine for liberal Protestants, die-hard believers in the universal applicability of the law of love, to assimilate. Yet Niebuhr's tireless stream of charismatic preaching and hard-hitting prose was instrumental in turning the tide toward "realism" in the social struggle. He single-handedly pushed liberals by the thousands to embrace in good conscience the hand-dirtying endeavor of power politics.

He had the same effect in the international arena. Liberal Protestants continued to preach the power of love and goodwill to transform the relations between nations. But Niebuhr, who followed postwar events in Germany very closely, would have none of it: it was too easy for citizens of the wealthiest nation on earth to proclaim the virtue of nonviolence to the starving masses in the rest of the world. Pacifism was a laudable ideal, he conceded, but only if it was kept relatively supple; justice might in some situations require the resort to violent force, including war. After the rise of Hitler, Niebuhr emerged as one of the most powerful voices in the Protestant community calling for Lend-Lease to the British, even at the risk of American involvement in the war. He was responsible for persuading thousands of Christians to join the military fight against fascism. In international affairs as in domestic politics, Niebuhr promulgated a new "realism" about strategies and goals. JUSTICE, not love, was the proper end of responsible Christian action: force and coercion, violent if necessary, must be added to the legitimate repertoire of the Christian in politics. Thanks to his firsthand experience of labor–capital conflict in Detroit and his intimate knowledge of Germany, Niebuhr was able to place his voice at the center of major debates about the relation between religion and politics.

He remained at the center of those debates into the 1960s. Always first a preacher (to secular as well as religious audiences) and teacher (he left Bethel Church in 1928 to become a professor of Christian ethics at Union Theological Seminary, where he remained until his retirement in 1960), Niebuhr was also an original and influential writer. His major works— *Moral Man and Immoral Society* (1932), *Beyond Tragedy* (1937), *The Nature and Destiny of Man* (2 vols., 1941 and 1943), *The Children of Light and the Children of Darkness* (1944), and *The Irony of American History* (1952)—attracted large readerships in nonreligious as well as religious circles. His thought evolved considerably over the two decades of his major intellectual production, as he gradually turned away from socialism, took an increasing interest in theological

questions, attempted (in the 1930s) to join left-liberal politics with theological and cultural conservatism, and subsequently (in the 1940s) warmed up to the distinctive virtues of New Deal-style democracy.

Moral Man and Immoral Society, with *The Nature and Destiny of Man*, is a classic of American religious and liberal thought. Ostensibly an indictment of liberalism for its gradualism, its prating about education and goodwill as the keys to social advance, *Moral Man* in fact went much further than that in assaulting the liberal social vision. Niebuhr forthrightly rejected the central belief that had inspired liberal reform movements in America over the previous century: American society could in principle become a vast fellowship of like-minded, loving citizens. Niebuhr had no patience for such "sentimentality," as he labeled it. "We are merely," he wrote in *Harper's* in 1932, "a vast horde of people let loose on a continent with little to unify us by way of common cultural, moral, and religious traditions."

After *Moral Man*, Niebuhr withdrew increasingly from the socialist politics and religious organizing that had consumed him in the early years of the Depression (he ran for office twice on the Socialist ticket), and turned toward theological and political reflection. In the mid-thirties he effected an unstable but very provocative joining of radical politics and Augustinian theology. Along with such thinkers as LEWIS MUMFORD and Waldo Frank, he was trying to put radicalism on a new intellectual basis, one that rejected the sunny view of human nature native to American liberalism and that transcended the dry "scientific" rationalism which they associated with Deweyan liberal reformers. Radicalism, they thought, needed the instinctual drive of a vital faith—one grounded in the warm loyalties of family, locality, and workplace, as opposed to the abstract connections among cosmopolitan individuals—if it was to propel masses of Americans to rebuild their society.

By the end of the thirties, with the general decline of radical hopes, Niebuhr devoted himself to his masterwork, *The Nature and Destiny of Man*, delivered as the Gifford Lectures in Scotland in 1939. *Nature and Destiny* was an elegant work of Christian apologetics, designed to demonstrate the superiority of the Christian view of human nature and destiny. Non-Christian faiths, he argued, could not match the depth of Christian insight into the human condition. Human beings were sinners: the doctrine of "original sin," he suggested, might be the most unpopular doctrine among liberal Christians, but it was the one doctrine that received daily empirical validation. Yet human beings were more than sinners: they were made in the image of God. They were capable of virtuous action to create sustaining communities which embodied (more or less) the ideal of justice. For all their creativity, however, human beings were inveterately self-aggrandizing, tempted by pride, always prone to undercut their achievements through their incessant "will to power." Niebuhr thought that Lord Acton was right, in the face of formulaic ideologies of PROGRESS, to caution that all human things, given enough time, go badly. But Niebuhr turned that sentiment around, in one of his oft-repeated phrases, so that it combined realism and the tragic sense of life with a persistent hope for the future: "Nothing that is worth doing can be achieved in one generation."

The perspective of *Nature and Destiny* informed Niebuhr's work for the rest of his career. Human society was a site of indeterminate possibility, not guaranteed progress. The human self was a site of struggle—as the apostle Paul put it, a law in his members warred against the law in his mind—not a blank slate or a benign source of good will. But with humility and forgiveness, and God's grace, fragile and prideful human beings could build communities in which justice could, for periods of time at least, be embodied. Niebuhr was very insistent that the Christian life was of necessity (except for a few saints) a political life. He made a lasting contribution to the question of how politics and RELIGION should be linked, and his voice deserves to be heard again at a time when this issue has become pressing.

The world of secular politics needed the spark of religion, Niebuhr contended, but paradoxically it also needed to be protected against religion. On one level Niebuhr's position was a thoroughly secular one. There could be no explicitly Christian politics. Alarmed during the 1930s by the fanaticism he detected in Nazi and communist "religions," he was thereafter suspicious of *any* religion operating in the public arena. He was hypersensitive about religious or moral militants seeking to impose their particular moral viewpoints. He implicitly endorsed a kind of cultural Madisonianism: no moral or religious perspective should be permitted to monopolize the public square. This cultural pluralism did not strike Niebuhr as disintegrative. Having grown up German American, he was never smitten by the desire to build a "common culture" of the sort that appealed to many Anglo-Protestants. Like the Jewish Walter Lippmann and the Catholic JOHN COURTNEY MURRAY, Niebuhr imagined an American nation held together by its commitment to the culturally neutral procedures of political democracy, not by its cultural uniformity. He was a liberal not because he considered all viewpoints equally valid (Christianity provided a true assessment of the human condition, he believed), but because he thought FREEDOM, whether of thought or of religion, was best assured when the public arena was protected from domination by any one faith.

Niebuhr's strong advocacy of secularity as a protection against religious fanaticism (and as an antidote to the infuriating complacency and pretentiousness of many religious believers) was matched, however, by his paradoxical insistence on the need for a potent "prophetic" religion to keep the secular world honest, to impel that world toward the quest for justice. Left to itself, secularity might descend into merely opportunistic jockeying for power, or even worse, into smiling passivity in the face of the blandishments of a therapeutic, consumerist culture. Secularity could, in other words, become a religion in its own right: a fanatical (though always grinning) faith preaching the all-sufficient beneficence of the world of goods. Those goods included the services offered by religious and nonreligious providers to enhance the "growth" and marketability of one's own personality. Secular ideology was so pervasive, Niebuhr thought, that it was on the verge of excluding other "religious" perspectives from the public arena. For this reason he was not sure that prayer should be disallowed in public schools. Permitting prayer in schools might be one means of pluralizing religious experience in the public sphere.

The main thing was to protect democracy by subjecting the secular world to prophetic, critical judgment upon social institutions and practices in light of the ideal of justice. That judgment, in turn, depended upon a prior "divine" judgment upon the sinful arrogance of all human beings. The great danger of movements for justice was their inclination to demonize their opponents, deprive them of humanity. Fully persuaded of their own virtue, militant reformers were liable to anathematize others, to point a righteous finger at the splinters in others' eyes while ignoring the beam in their own. Niebuhr regarded Lincoln as a model of how to battle to the death for justice while keeping oneself as well as one's enemy under divine judgment. He regarded MARTIN LUTHER KING JR. as another model, since King stressed the common humanity he shared with even the most heinous racists. The example of King demonstrated further that Christian prophecy, based on the conviction that all human beings were sinners as well as creatures made in the image of God, did not erode striving for social justice—as some secular liberals feared it would. On the contrary, in a century marked by the unimagined suffering of two world wars, Christian prophecy was the indispensable foundation for the attitude and practice of hope. Prophetic Christianity could spark the quest for justice even in an age eerily marked by both cynicism and complacency.

RICHARD WIGHTMAN FOX

FURTHER READING

June Bingham, *Courage to Change: an Introduction to the Life and Thought of Reinhold Niebuhr* (New York: Scribner's, 1961).

Richard Wightman Fox, *Reinhold Niebuhr: a Biography* (New York: Pantheon, 1985).

Gordon Harland, *The Thought of Reinhold Niebuhr* (New York: Oxford University Press, 1960).

Charles W. Kegley, ed., *Reinhold Niebuhr: His Religious, Social, and Political Thought* (1956; New York: Pilgrim, 1984).

Christopher Lasch, *The True and Only Heaven: Progress and Its Critics* (New York: Norton, 1991).

Dennis McCann, *Christian Realism and Liberation Theology* (Maryknoll, N.Y.: Orbis, 1981).

Donald Meyer, *The Protestant Search for Political Realism, 1919–1941* (Berkeley: University of California Press, 1960).

Cornel West, *The American Evasion of Philosophy: a Genealogy of Pragmatism* (Madison: University of Wisconsin Press, 1989).

Norris, [Benjamin] Frank[lin] (b. Chicago, Ill., Mar. 5, 1870; d. San Francisco, Calif., Oct. 25, 1902). Writer. A San Francisco journalist and foreign correspondent, Norris is best known for his novels *McTeague* (1899), *The Octopus* (1901), and *The Pit* (1903). His novels are conventionally labeled "naturalistic," though the vast impersonal forces they portray are both natural and economic. *The Octopus*, on one level a bowing to the raw power of the railroad, also expressed a populist disdain for that power. In the essays collected in *The Responsibility of the Novelist* (1903), Norris argued that writers should champion the good of the people against the abuses of power.

See also NATURALISM; REALISM.

FURTHER READING

Daniel H. Borus, *Writing Realism: Howells, James, and Norris in the Mass Market* (Chapel Hill: University of North Carolina Press, 1989).

Norton, Charles Eliot (b. Cambridge, Mass., Nov. 16, 1827; d. Cambridge, Mass., Oct. 21, 1908). Son of an eminent biblical scholar, Norton grew up in a household frequented by Boston's literary elite. After graduation from Harvard College in 1846, he spent the next three decades searching to fulfill his intellectual inclination. A generation earlier, he would likely have become a cultivated minister. A generation later, he would probably have settled quickly as a professor. But he was stranded in the transition from the old clerically dominated, religion-based culture to the new university-oriented, secular intellectual life: a vocational nomad who made distinguished contributions as an art historian, a literary scholar, an academic reformer, and a cultural critic.

A few years in the East India trade were punctuated by sporadic literary and political publications and by projects to improve education and housing for Boston's impoverished Irish immigrants. There followed two years of travel and desultory study in England, France, Germany, and especially Italy. The richness of European culture, especially its art and architecture, appreciated before at second hand, overwhelmed Norton on direct experience.

Returning home in 1857, he accelerated his literary production, including in 1859 the first English translation of Dante's *Vita Nuova*. From 1863 to 1868 he edited America's weightiest quarterly, the *North American Review*, and in 1865 helped E. L. GODKIN to found the weekly journal THE NATION, which immediately became the authoritative American voice in transatlantic liberalism. But centrifugal curiosity and the absence of any vocational lens helped keep Norton's own writing obstinately unfocused.

In 1868, restless with journalism, Norton set out again for Europe, remaining there until 1873. During these years he devoted himself to the study of medieval and Renaissance art and literature, burrowing in Italian archives and spending day after day in galleries, slowly transforming himself into a scholar of literature and an expert art historian.

And in this work he found a glimmer of light in an increasingly dark view of humanity's immediate prospects. Norton despaired at the extremes of wealth and poverty in Europe; news from home of political corruption soured his belief that Civil War idealism had regenerated the republican principles of the American Revolution. He more and more pitched his hopes in the distant future. By now an agnostic in religion as well, Norton found in art and in the glacially slow evolution of humanity the "spiritual" ideals and consolation once provided by faith in God.

In 1874 Norton accepted an invitation to teach at Harvard, becoming the first professor of art history in America. He brought his faith in art to bear on his anxieties about republican democracy. Exposure to great art and literature, Norton believed, provided an antidote to the creeping materialism and self-seeking that infected America's leadership classes. He helped to forge a new vision of liberal-arts education: a morally enlivening and intellectually broadening "liberal culture," set against both the old classical education and a newer vocationalism. His work outside the university—magazine articles, public lectures, art exhibitions, editions of poets, advice to art collectors, support for civil-service reform and opposition to United States imperialism—reflected the same insistence that the fate of the republic depended on its moral tone. By the late 1880s Norton was the most prominent cultural critic in the United States, an analogue to his English friends Matthew Arnold and John Ruskin.

He also tried to shape a new, democratic vision of liberal scholarship, akin to his educational ideal: committed to serious research, equipped with technical expertise, impatient with dilettantism, yet accessible to a generally educated public and aimed at enriching general culture. His best students (who included the art historian Bernard Berenson, the critic IRVING BABBITT, and the Dante scholar Charles H. Grandgent) shared his broad-gauged vision.

And, indeed, Norton had far-reaching influence on academic knowledge. He legitimated art history as a university-based discipline. *Historical Studies of Church-Building in the Middle Ages: Venice, Siena, Florence* (1880) helped to found medieval studies in the United States. Two of his creations, the Archaeological Institute of America (1879) and American School of Classical Studies at Athens (1882), became respectively the major professional body for American classical archaeologists and their chief training ground. The Dante Society (1880), his teaching of Dante, his critical writings, and his own prose translation of the *Divina Commedia* (1891–2) transformed Dante studies from a genteel avocation to a professional subspeciality.

Ironically, the very institutions Norton created acted as midwife to the new "German model" scholarship that he detested. Its triviality and narrowness of focus appalled him, and Norton never directed a Ph.D. dissertation. Yet he had scarcely retired from Harvard in 1898 before his scholarly ideals were swept away by the tide of specialized professionalized research that became the norm of the modern university.

At his death in 1908 Norton was still America's priest of high culture. But his ghost was exorcised from American scholarship almost before he was cold in his grave. Much emaciated, it still haunts American college classrooms—a faint and mournful reminder of the fragmentation of knowledge that continues to debilitate American intellectual life.

JAMES TURNER

See also AESTHETICS; COLLEGES AND UNIVERSITIES; PROFESSION.

FURTHER READING

John Lewis Bradley and Ian Ousby, eds., *The Correspondence of John Ruskin and Charles Eliot Norton* (Cambridge: Cambridge University Press, 1987).

Martin Green, *The Problem of Boston: Some Readings in Cultural History* (New York: Norton, 1966).

Sara Norton and M. A. DeWolfe Howe, *Letters of Charles Eliot Norton, with Biographical Comment*, 2 vols. (Boston: Houghton Mifflin, 1913).

Kermit Vanderbilt, *Charles Eliot Norton: Apostle of Culture in a Democracy* (Cambridge: Harvard University Press, Belknap, 1959).

Noyes, John Humphrey (b. Brattleboro, Vt., Sept. 3, 1811; d. Niagara Falls, Canada, Apr. 13, 1886). Reformer. In 1837 Noyes founded the Oneida Community, a perfectionist group that forbade individual attachment to property or persons. Noyes taught that the human–divine relationship is like that between women and men: humans are passive and receive divine life. Sex reunites the human with God if it is motivated not by a procreative urge but by the desire for transcendence. At Oneida, therefore, Noyes insisted on male continence in a closely regulated "complex marriage" that allowed only a few eugenically selected offspring. His many writings include *Bible Communism* (1848), *Male Continence* (1848), and *History of American Socialisms* (1870).

See also UTOPIAS.

FURTHER READING

Spencer Klaw, *Without Sin: the Life and Death of a Utopian Community* (New York: Viking, 1993).

O

objectivity The term carries a number of different meanings, some acquired as early as the seventeenth century, others only in the nineteenth century. In the English language, it was only between the 1820s and 1850s that the word came into wide use, and by the closing decades of the century, there were three different usages. The first, originating in the nineteenth century, distinguished objectivity from subjectivity. Here objectivity signaled the effort to remove all merely human judgment from the realm of SCIENCE, usually with the aid of some appropriately rigorous methodology. This understanding of objectivity was central to the rise of POSITIVISM.

The second meaning of objectivity conveyed the idea of disinterestedness. Scientists had argued since the seventeenth century that research would yield better results if the inquirer had no stake in the outcome. In the late nineteenth century this preoccupation with neutrality led to a sharp demarcation of SOCIAL SCIENCE from political activism. In the 1880s, for example, WILLIAM GRAHAM SUMNER sharply separated economic laws, based on scientific observation, from public policy, which might or might not make use of such laws. The opposite of this objectivity was not so much judgment or subjectivity as advocacy or action, which were seen as inevitably saturated with bias. At the turn of the century a string of ACADEMIC FREEDOM disputes on American campuses brought this distinction between advocacy and objectivity to the attention of a wide public.

The third sense of objectivity was associated with CHARLES PEIRCE and the philosophy of PRAGMATISM. It opposed subjectivity not in the name of a pure methodology but out of respect for the power of communal judgment. For Peirce, unlike the positivists, judgment was not a function of individual subjectivity. In a truly scientific community, Peirce claimed, judgment was part of a collective decision. Concepts were invented by scholars and then tested; the community of the competent was the proper arbiter. Pragmatic objectivity was not completely novel, since communal judgment as a guide to truth was also sometimes stressed in eighteenth-century SCOTTISH COMMON SENSE REALISM, as it was in Goethe's writings on science.

In the twentieth century each of these approaches to objectivity has persisted and developed, sometimes incorporating elements of the other two. One of the most important strains in social science thinking during the 1920s and 1930s was the Chicago School of sociology, whose leading figures included ROBERT E. PARK and Ernest Burgess. These intellectuals strongly defended objectivity against political activism; they often made fun of what they called "do-gooders." At the same time, however, these scholars rejected social theories which defined objectivity as the absence of all traces of the subjective. Chicago sociology is famous for pioneering "participant-observer" research. Chicago sociologists urged scholars to enter into the lifeworld of those they were studying; through "empathic observation," they could try to piece together the values and behavior of those studied. This injected "subjectivity" into research in two ways: first, by asking scholars to imagine themselves in the place of the observed; second, by focusing on the subjective values and meanings (as well as actions) of those studied. Still, Park, Burgess, and other leading Chicago sociologists viewed their work as objective. They were disinterested observers, not advocates.

A different position, however, understood objectivity as the fruit of a rigorous methodology that excluded all subjectivity, not only of the scholar when doing research, but also of those who were being studied. In the 1920s and 1930s this viewpoint went under the names of "objectivism," "BEHAVIORISM," "positivism," or "operationalism." Thus JOHN WATSON wanted psychologists to look only at the external physiological reflexes; no assessment of feelings was permissible. Leonard Bloomfield in *Language* (1933) argued that all meaning could be gleaned from physiological responses to words. Luther Bernard made similar claims for sociology. These scholars disputed the Chicago sociologists' claim to objectivity. At the same time, these objectivist scholars were far less reticent about connecting their work to politics. Convinced that their methods were objective, they thought they had "truths" that should be listened to. The notion that "objective" scholarship ought to inform public policy appeared in many forms during the 1920s and 1930s, and received one classic expression by ROBERT LYND in *Knowledge for What?* (1939).

In the twenties and thirties, the most visible developer and defender of Peirce's communitarian objectivity was the pragmatist philosopher JOHN

DEWEY. Dewey, like the Chicago sociologists, stressed the active role of the inquirer in the making of knowledge. Unlike the behaviorists or objectivists, Dewey argued that knowledge was the process of ongoing interaction between subject and object. It was a form of active experience, not a disinterested methodology. Moreover, knowledge came from an active community of inquiry in which individuals tested themselves against and contributed to an evolving collective understanding. Despite these differences, Dewey shared with objectivist sociologists the sense that knowledge should be socially ameliorative. And while Dewey thought knowledge was contingent on the circumstances, he was not a proponent of RELATIVISM. He defended "objective" truth, although he claimed truths had to be constantly rethought in each situation.

In the 1940s the constellation of American social thought shifted dramatically. World War II and the start of the Cold War, the arrival of émigré scholars from Nazi Germany, the fading of the Chicago School of sociology, the softening of behavioral dogmas, the arrival of the "action theory" of society developed by TALCOTT PARSONS—all combined to create a new terrain on which the issues of objectivity were debated anew.

MILTON FRIEDMAN restated the positivist position in *Essays in Positive Economics* (1953), where he defended the fact/value split, and research divorced from policy, in ways similar to those of William Graham Sumner in the 1880s and defenders of "objectivism" in the 1920s and 1930s. In post-World War II sociology and political science, the work of Max Weber became extremely important. His *The Methodology of the Social Sciences* appeared in English in 1949. While there were many differences between the inter-war Chicago sociology and postwar Weberian sociology, in respect to objectivity they were very similar. Both were in the tradition of empathic understanding, and both argued against injecting politics into social science. While Weber denied that absolute objectivity could be achieved in the scientific study of society, he still thought researchers should struggle toward "value neutrality," a position resembling Park and Burgess's efforts to separate research from advocacy.

The most creative thinkers in the years after World War II—among them Karl Polanyi and Ludwig Wittgenstein in Europe and HANNAH ARENDT in the United States—regarded the pursuit of value neutrality as misguided. Knowledge, practice, experience, and value were all interwoven in human life. Knowledge was interpersonal and communal, not the product of detachment or suspension of subject-

ivity. Wittgenstein in his *Philosophical Investigations* (1953) and Polanyi in *Personal Knowledge* (1958) stressed that LANGUAGE and knowledge were deeply structured by the patterns of ordinary living. Arendt, in *The Human Condition* (1958), warned that the world of "common sense" was threatened both by abstract modes of knowledge and by excessive emphasis on people's subjective feelings, a theme recently explored by ALASDAIR MACINTYRE, among others.

Arendt, Wittgenstein, and Polanyi all explored issues addressed by Dewey in the 1920s. Experience was the key to knowledge. Knowledge was the product of the ongoing interplay of a subject with other subjects as well as objects. A rigid demarcation of subject and object made no sense. Yet while Dewey hoped that science would correct the limitations of common sense in managing an ever more complicated world, Arendt, Polanyi, and Wittgenstein distrusted the so-called meliorative power of science. Arendt feared the imperial potential of science, its capacity to diminish the very possibility of a commonsensical world, a process that would end in deep alienation at best, totalitarianism at worst. For Wittgenstein, everyday experience and science were two very different sorts of language games, each legitimate in its own realm. Polanyi, who considered natural science a product of communal enterprise, remained closest to Dewey. But Polanyi also thought that Dewey's meliorative dreams for social science might slide into totalitarianism. Instead, prescientific tacit understandings had to be respected, for they were what made science possible in the first place. While Dewey stressed the limitations of common sense, Polanyi stressed its enabling function.

Objectivity has always had its enemies. The upheavals of the 1960s and their aftermath in the academy have tended to increase the respect accorded those distrustful of scientific pretensions to knowledge. By the 1970s, two broad anti-objectivist trends emerged. First, the "experiential" strain of social thought took hold with the growing prominence of hermeneutics and interpretive social science. Many of the attitudes of Wittgenstein and Polanyi were summed up in two books that became extremely important by the late 1960s, Peter Winch's *The Idea of a Social Science* (1958) and Thomas Kuhn's *Structure of Scientific Revolutions* (1962). When Hans Georg Gadamer's *Truth and Method* appeared in English translation in 1975 it became a critical text in this movement, one that seconded Arendt's assault on the imperialism of science. Kuhn's book was influential because it could be read as saying that scientific paradigms developed no differently than any other social beliefs. Science did not discover "reality," but mobilized the collective opinion of scientific communities.

The second anti-objectivist trend was that of critical theory, derived from early twentieth-century Marxists like Georg Lukács, Antonio Gramsci, or the FRANKFURT SCHOOL scholars Theodor Adorno, Max Horkheimer, and HERBERT MARCUSE. This strain, expressed in Alvin Gouldner's widely read *Coming Crisis of Western Sociology* (1970), tended to attack supposed value neutrality for lending support to the status quo. Gouldner argued that passion, knowledge, and interest should be combined to further emancipatory ends. Gouldner's book bore some similarities to Robert Lynd's 1939 *Knowledge for What?*, but while Lynd thought that neutrality was a form of benign neglect that left the political system intact, Gouldner saw neutrality as an ideological cover that provided crucial service for the legitimation of the established political order.

Beginning in the late 1970s a postmodern attack on objectivity emerged. Advocates of POSTMODERNISM contend that the very terms subject and object are meaningless. Instead, we should see ourselves as caught in our own linguistic webs. Language is neither objective (describing what is "really" there), nor subjective (flowing out of some core of "self"). Selfhood, like all other social realities, is itself shaped at the outset by language and discourse. Objectivity and subjectivity are both functions within a particular system of discourse.

Postmodernists follow Dewey in abandoning the subject/object distinction, but their starting point is not Dewey's vision of the perennial interplay of experience and inquiry. Science, Jean-François Lyotard argued in his influential *Postmodern Condition* (translated 1983), was simply one of many kinds of language games. Unlike Wittgenstein, Lyotard saw these language games as free-floating through a media-saturated computer culture. He made no mention of "forms of life," the experiential category that for Wittgenstein was the very root of different language games. Nor does he see science, with Dewey, as a moral-aesthetic and intellectual enterprise in which individuals both solve problems and come together in communities of knowing.

Postmodernists also reject the Weberian presumption that we should war against our passions or strive for disinterestedness. For Weber, perfect neutrality might not be possible, but it was still the ideal standard. Postmodernists, by contrast, stress "free play," "the sublime," "paralogy," and "transgression," all concepts meant to promote imaginative leaps outside conventional frames of reference. The work and life of Michel Foucault have come to be seen as a paradigmatic instance of transgression as self-expression. Postmodern assumptions have made considerable headway within the American academy in recent years, but the size and complexity of American higher education make sweeping claims about its dominance suspect. Defenders of the ideal of objectivity remain, along with proponents of an experiential interplay between subject and object.

KENNETH CMIEL

FURTHER READING
Robert Bannister, *Sociology and Scientism: the American Quest for Objectivity, 1880–1940* (Chapel Hill: University of North Carolina Press, 1987).
Richard Bernstein, *Beyond Objectivism and Relativism* (Philadelphia: University of Pennsylvania Press, 1983).
Lorraine Daston and Peter Galison, "The Image of Objectivity," *Representations* 40 (1992): 81–128.
Mary Furner, *Advocacy and Objectivity: a Crisis in the Professionalization of American Social Science, 1865–1905* (Lexington: University Press of Kentucky, 1975).
Allan Megill, ed., *Rethinking Objectivity* (Durham: Duke University Press, 1994).
Peter Novick, *That Noble Dream: the "Objectivity Question" and the American Historical Profession* (New York: Cambridge University Press, 1988).
Theodore M. Porter, ed., "The Social History of Objectivity," *Social Studies of Science* 22 (1992): 595–652.
Dorothy Ross, *The Origins of American Social Science* (New York: Cambridge University Press, 1991).

obligation   American political theorists have had relatively little to say about obligation. Constitutional and theoretical debates have generally been focused around claims for RIGHTS. This emphasis is congruent with English political theory, which has stressed claims which subjects can make against the prerogatives of the Crown and which has therefore had much more interest in rights than in obligation. Much American thinking on the subject developed in the late eighteenth century when the relation of the citizen to the state was theorized by revolutionaries who were asserting claims of rights against the state. Arguments were modeled on those expounded by Whigs during and after the English Civil War, and also on those developed by Baptists, Quakers, and other groups in their struggle against compulsory church taxes in colonial Massachusetts and elsewhere. These political and religious rebels pushed the defense of rights in the direction of protecting freedom of thought and conscience and of resisting taxation without representation.

Considerations of rights drove the polemical encounters of the founding era—notably the pamphlet literature of the ANTI-FEDERALISTS and the Federalist responses to it. The word obligation rarely appears in *The Federalist*. Hamilton uses it in the general sense of the obligation to keep one's word as a moral person ("the obligations that form the bands of society," in *Federalist* no. 85), and in the specific obligation to pay one's debts (Rhode Island's paper money as an example of "atrocious breaches of moral obligation and social justice," in no. 7). Madison invokes it in a rhetorical flourish (legislators' "obligations to . . . constitutents" in no. 62) and Jay writes that "all constitutional acts of power," whether they emerge from the legislature, the judiciary, or the executive, have the same weight of "legal validity and obligation" (no. 64).

The federal CONSTITUTION was remarkably silent on obligation. The framers restricted the document to a succinctly outlined set of specified powers. The first ten amendments activated a set of limits on those powers, limits enforced by the act of *claiming* rights. The strategy infused constitutional and legal thinking; in the *Dred Scott* case of 1854, Justice ROGER TANEY defined noncitizenship as a lack of rights, not an absence of obligations. The development of mediating bodies like the American Civil Liberties Union and the National Association for the Advancement of Colored People early in the twentieth century made the aggressive claims of rights even more common. A government born in revolution understood itself to be one created by and obligated *to* the people; in Lincoln's terms, "of the people, by the people, for the people." This formulation made little space for the obligations which people might owe *to* the government.

Avoiding the term "obligation," with its implication of a binding and perhaps transcendent moral duty, American constitutional argument, like the political theory of LIBERALISM in general, has by and large rested on the confidence that individuals can be authentically bound only by rules which they themselves have chosen, and that authentic government is shaped by freely chosen agreements among the ruled. Consent theory makes all obligation in some way an obligation to oneself, "there being," Thomas Hobbes wrote in *Leviathan*, "no obligation on any man, which ariseth not from some act of his own" (part 2, ch. 21). Much American constitutional talk proceeds as though the Revolution had created a state of nature and as though the Constitution were a social contract; having consented to the political order, all obligation becomes individually elected obligation.

The obligations of CITIZENSHIP, in liberal theory, rest on all citizens alike. Once the powers of government are properly framed, a binding obligation, impersonally imposed on all citizens, ensues. Carole Pateman has argued, however, that men and women are differently situated in relation to consent

theory: men are imagined as free agents, but most women enter the social contract already bound by marriage and by antecedent obligations to their husbands. Pateman's argument helps us solve the riddle of why American revolutionaries did not change the law of domestic relations at the same time that they radically changed other civic relations.

Obligation is implicit in all discussion of what constitutes legal AUTHORITY or what powers the central government might justifiably claim, since statutes or administrative decisions impose duties on citizens. In a political culture "dominated by the rhetoric of individualism," Thomas Haskell has observed, "rights are the principal means by which duty is smuggled back [in]" (p. 984n). Robert Westbrook has similarly argued that obligation persists in the midst of rights talk but it is commonly expressed as private obligation to oneself and one's family. The demand that one be willing to risk one's life for public or community purposes has generally been associated by twentieth-century Americans with autocratic or totalitarian governments. In wartime mobilization in America, the obligation to the state and community has been smuggled back in through the language of protecting one's own family. Defending the polity has been graspable only when envisioned as the defense by men of wives and mothers.

Theories of social and political obligation flourished in the culture of the slave South before the Civil War; a society that understood itself to be made up of free men who controlled a slave population was obsessed by the need to develop a theory which would honor FREEDOM and slavery simultaneously. Southern theorists such as GEORGE FITZHUGH claimed that the obligations of slaves and masters were reciprocal. They also described obligations among a wide range of dependents and care-takers, particularly wives and husbands, and children and fathers. Southern apologists regarded northern society as chaotic and degenerate because the web of obligation had been rent in it; the owners of capital felt no duty to care for the poor, the old, or the sick. Of course the southern theory of personal obligation as the basis of stable COMMUNITY did not guarantee that obligations would be carried out in practice, any more than northern avoidance of the idea of obligation entailed a complete disregard for it in the concrete. Yet the antebellum southern fixation on obligation highlights the absence of attention to it in the rest of American history and in the liberal theory that has dominated that history. Southern efforts to sustain the language of obligation persisted after the Civil War, but without the structural base they had once enjoyed. (*See also* PROSLAVERY THOUGHT.)

Except for naturalized citizens, there is no liminal moment when most individuals can be said to assume obligations to the state; their consent is taken to be implied by their failure to refuse (to pay taxes, for example, or to pledge the flag), and by their continued acceptance of services that the state provides. As Michael Walzer has remarked, liberalism has leaned on "a kind of silence that may be construed as consent" (Pennock and Chapman, p. 402). But silence raises its own problems. In his classic essay on civil disobedience, written when he refused to pay a poll tax to support the Mexican War in 1848, HENRY DAVID THOREAU considered the question of whether individuals are obligated to obey a law they considered unjust. Most Americans thought they should obey the law in each instance, and endeavor to persuade the majority to alter an unjust one. But Thoreau was skeptical; there were times when individuals should refuse to be bound by a majority's unethical choices. A century later, African Americans resisting segregation also refused to be bound by obligations they understood to be unethical; unlike Thoreau's, their resistance was collective. As A. Philip Randolph put it in testimony to the Senate Armed Services Committee in 1948, when the Congress was considering a peacetime draft, "Negro youth" had a "moral obligation" *not* to serve. Serving would make them "carriers" of the "evil and hellish doctine" of the racial segregation that still marked the armed forces and the wider society. A similar spirit infused the nonviolent passive resistance campaigns led by MARTIN LUTHER KING JR. in the late 1950s and early 1960s. Refusing to respect the obligations imposed on them by segregation laws, African Americans and others mounted massive public demonstrations designed, like the Montgomery bus boycott of 1955–6, to put a spotlight on both the social cost of segregation and the violence that was always contained in its imposition.

Although the language of obligation has usually spoken generically of all citizens, the practice of both obligations and rights has been multiple and gendered. There are four basic types of civic obligation in American history: allegiance and its counterpart, the obligation to refrain from treason; the obligation to pay taxes; the obligation to serve on juries; and the obligation to risk one's life in military service. In every case the obligation has been applied unequally. In the Revolutionary era, the law of domestic relations gave husbands such extended control over their wives' bodies and property—a system known as coverture—that married women's independent civic obligation seemed an oxymoron. Indeed, since wives were understood to owe allegiance above all to their

husbands, the Revolutionary government took the position that the wives of Tories could not have freely consented to the loyalist position. The government protected their dower rights, and the property they held outright, even when seizing their husbands' property. Obligation varied by gender in later years as well. In 1855 alien women who married American men were automatically granted citizenship, but the status of American-born women who married alien men was unclear; their obligation to their alien husbands was taken to override their rights of American citizenship. A statute of 1907, upheld by the Supreme Court in 1915 (*Mackenzie v. Hare*), provided that American women forfeited their citizenship when they married alien men; that situation was not fully rectified until 1934.

The obligation of allegiance has also been interpreted along racial lines. During World War II American-born citizens of Japanese descent were relocated to internment camps; American-born citizens of German descent were not. American women were largely disfranchised until 1920 and African Americans in many regions until the 1960s, yet for generations they were obligated to pay taxes without representation.

Qualifications for jury service generally matched voting qualifications in the colonial period and in the early republic. In 1879 the Supreme Court ruled, in *Strauder v. West Virginia*, that the Fourteenth Amendment meant that black men might not be excluded from jury service; in the same opinion, the Court sustained the exclusion of women from jury service as reasonable. But the wide discretion enjoyed by jury commissioners allowed them to exclude African Americans, who were also barred from voting in the Jim Crow era; not until the Jury Reform Act of 1966 was race discrimination generally forbidden. Only a few states required women to serve on juries after they achieved suffrage; what was understood to be an obligation for men was treated as a privilege for women, and a wide range of gender-related exemptions characterized jury service throughout most of the twentieth century. Not until 1975 did the Supreme Court rule that men's and women's names must be placed in jury pools on an equal basis.

The most extensive reconsideration of the appropriate limits of obligation has occurred during wartime. Civil disobedience has flourished when conscription makes the boundaries of individual obligation a life or death matter. Draft riots tore through New York City during the Civil War. During World War I more than 300,000 men—10 percent of those drafted—avoided or resisted the draft, and EMMA GOLDMAN and Alexander Berkman were imprisoned for counseling resistance. Opposition to the draft was integral to public criticism of the war in VIETNAM.

The obligation of military service has rarely, if ever, rested evenly on the whole population. Until World War II, African Americans were more likely to be rejected by the military as unfit. In the Vietnam War, the obligation of military service rested disproportionately on working-class men, both black and white. In the early stages of the war, before 1967, African Americans were killed at rates considerably higher than their proportion in the total American population. As Christian Appy has noted, the policies of the Selective Service Administration and the practice of student deferments combined to create a military force that, over the course of the war, was about 80 percent poor or working class (p. 27).

Women have been recruited by the military, but never drafted or required to serve in combat. During the Gulf War of 1991, however, military women were required to accept postings into the theater of war. As of 1995, the development of plans to remove combat exemptions for female pilots and to establish a gender-blind physicians' draft puts into question the permanence of female exemption from the obligation of military service. These changes are the perhaps inevitable climax of the slow erosion of coverture over the last two centuries; as women's independent rights to property, suffrage, and bodily integrity were slowly established, the complementary practices of substituting family duties for civic obligation eroded.

If "obligation" is implicit in the concept of a social contract, it is also implicit in the law of contract and of tort, which traditionally assumed that statutes rested on the firm foundation of fixed and transcendent moral obligation. Theoretical challenges to this consensus arose in the nineteenth century among German "scientific" theorists, and in the United States they were articulated in major treatises beginning with *The Common Law* (1881) by OLIVER WENDELL HOLMES JR. Holmes denied that obligation had any source other than the law itself. His argument, which owed much to Herbert Spencer and to SOCIAL DARWINISM, contended that as the law developed it slowly got rid of the religious and metaphysical constraints it had inherited from antiquity. Modern law, especially contract law, floated free of moral obligation. Its boundaries were none other than those set by the state, in the statutes provided by the legislature. In the century since Holmes wrote, this skeptical line of argument has been expounded with particular energy by advocates of LEGAL REALISM, such as Karl W. Llewellyn and JEROME FRANK, in the 1930s,

and, more recently, by legal theorists in the LAW AND ECONOMICS community, among them Richard Posner, and in the CRITICAL LEGAL STUDIES movement, among them Duncan Kennedy.

But from Holmes's time to our own, other theorists have sought to give moral obligation some rational grounding. In Holmes's time his colleague James Barr Ames, and subsequently ROSCOE POUND, proposed what Pound called a "theory of values" as a supplement to legal realism. In our own time, the influential treatise *A Theory of Justice* (1971) by JOHN RAWLS developed a theory of social contract based on equal rights to basic liberties. Rawls proposed the principle of JUSTICE as fairness, both as a preferred social ideal and as an essential requirement of a rational society.

Even the most relativistic utilitarians have historically recognized the possibility of an "unconscionable" contract, a contract into which one is obliged not to enter. The Thirteenth Amendment forbids permanent labor service; state laws bar payment in exchange for adopted children. But the scope of contractual obligations remains hotly contested; as the Baby M case of 1987 demonstrated, the biotechnology of surrogate MOTHERHOOD undermines the exclusion of babies from the economic marketplace.

In contract as in political theory, systems of thought describing the obligations of abstract "individuals" often subvert themselves by making indefensible assumptions about gender and race. The principle of justice as fairness may offer the firmest foundation for a theory of rights and obligations. But it will do so only if it is truly race- and gender-blind. A persuasive theory of obligation must be supple enough to take account of everyone's rootedness in historically constructed bodies and communities, while also generalizing about the obligation we all owe to others.

LINDA K. KERBER

FURTHER READING

Christian G. Appy, *Working-Class War: American Combat Soldiers and Vietnam* (Chapel Hill: University of North Carolina Press, 1993).

Mary Ann Glendon, *Rights Talk: the Impoverishment of Political Discourse* (New York: Free Press, 1991).

Thomas Haskell, "The Persistence of Rights Talk in an Age of Interpretation," *Journal of American History* 74 (Dec. 1987): 984–1012.

Carole Pateman, *The Problem of Political Obligation: a Critique of Liberal Theory* (Berkeley: University of California Press, 1985).

——, *The Sexual Contract* (Stanford: Stanford University Press, 1988).

J. Roland Pennock and John W. Chapman, eds., *Political and Legal Obligation* (New York: Atherton Press, 1970).

Michael Walzer, *Obligations: Essays on Disobedience, War,*

and Citizenship (Cambridge: Harvard University Press, 1970).

Robert Westbrook, "Fighting for the American Family: Private Interests and Political Obligations in World War II," in Richard Wightman Fox and T. J. Jackson Lears, eds., *The Power of Culture: Critical Essays in American History* (Chicago: University of Chicago Press, 1993).

obscenity The subject ignites much heated disagreement in contemporary America, but remarkably little genuine debate. This is because both proponents and opponents of government regulation argue in a historical vacuum, which prevents them from seeing what is at stake in the concept of obscenity. The fundamental issue is not free speech versus censorship, as opponents of regulation would have it, or proper morality versus sexual perversity, as proponents typically claim. Rather, the issue at the deepest level is how we as a society are to determine the tone, texture, and substance of our public life and culture. Today, disputes over the quality and character of our common world are largely left to the courts, and they have constricted the conceptual range of the debate over obscenity by hunting in usual legal fashion for individual victims whose RIGHTS and interests have been violated. This near obsession with individual rights, especially free speech, has virtually banished from current discussions the notions of common sense, taste, and judgment—concepts that have become practically as empty as obscenity itself.

It is striking to note that before the 1950s free speech was rarely invoked as a defense in obscenity litigation. Not until *Roth v. U.S.* (1957) did the Supreme Court address the constitutional status of obscenity, only to find that it was *not* protected by the First Amendment. For almost 80 years, obscenity trials had proceeded within a conceptual framework that had almost no place for free speech. Throughout the nineteenth century there existed a widespread social practice of reticence among the middle and upper classes, a practice described by such then-current terms as common sense, taste, judgment, refinement, politeness, reserve, propriety, tact, discretion, and decency. Knowing which things were capable of flourishing in public and which things were so fragile that they required the shade of PRIVACY if they were to retain their meaning depended on a highly modulated sense of the sacred and the desecrated, of HONOR and SHAME.

From the 1870s through the 1920s the majority of obscenity prosecutions were for pamphlets or public lectures advocating free love or birth control. Judges presiding over these trials spoke the language of reticence, defining obscenity as the "indecent," by which they meant "the wanton and unnecessary expression or exposure, in words or pictures, of that which the common sense of decency requires should be kept private or concealed," that which is "unbecoming, immodest, unfit to be seen or heard" (*U.S. v. Bennett*, 1879). They also defined the harm resulting from obscenity in the same moral and aesthetic register: "familiarity with obscenity blunts the sensibility, depraves good taste, and perverts the judgment" (*U.S. v. Harmon*, 1891).

While policing private morality was a component of nineteenth-century obscenity law, the quality of public life was an equally pressing concern for advocates of reticence. Opponents of public discussions of sexual matters joined critics of fictional REALISM and invasive JOURNALISM in defending the public sphere against "pollution," "contamination," or "desecration." They believed that open or casual discussion about intimate experiences would erode their meaning and vitality, and give rise to a world that was shameless in the literal sense that nothing was considered sacred or worthy of awe and reverence.

This broad understanding of obscenity was reflected in the law until the 1930s. Then the capacity of the law to take account of the public, moral, and aesthetic dimensions of harm began to wane. In *U.S. v. Dennett* (1930), "The Sex Side of Life" by the birth-control advocate Mary Ware Dennett was exonerated on the grounds that its serious and high-minded style "tends to rationalize and dignify . . . [sexual] emotions rather than to arouse lust." In 1934, the Supreme Court acquitted James Joyce's *Ulysses* on the grounds that the book taken as a whole had no "libidinous effect" on "the reasonable man." In both trials, the Court's singular emphasis upon obscenity's effects on individuals effectively diverted legal attention from earlier concerns about public pollution.

The legal shift took place because the cultural consensus on the virtue of reticence had largely eroded. During the first three decades of the twentieth century, sex reformers, feminists, anarchists, free-speech advocates, journalists, realist novelists, and cultural critics won a crucial ideological battle by converting the longstanding and widely practiced discourse of reticence into "the conspiracy of silence." With the aid of FREUDIANISM, those advocating birth control as well as those defending realist fiction created a catalogue of sexual pathologies, neuroses, and perversions, the origins of which they traced to the repressiveness of silence. This linkage enabled them to discredit reticence not only for spawning personal misery and disease, but also for stunting artistic imagination and producing a sterile, parochial national culture. In addition, free-speech advocates and cultural radicals used the findings of the new anthropology to argue that obscenity and other moral questions were always shaped by time and place, and therefore naturally evolved. Once advocates of exposure could confidently claim that PROGRESS was on their side, they were able to dismiss their opponents as irrational or old-fashioned.

From the 1930s through the 1950s, as legal debates narrowed to questions about the effects of obscenity on a person's behavior, educated liberals came more and more to share the view that if obscenity encouraged lewd thoughts or sexual activity, no harm was done because people were entitled to do as they pleased so long as no one else was hurt. While most researchers concluded that no link between obscenity and "antisocial behavior" could be demonstrated, others claimed that sexually explicit writing and images actually promoted "healthy sexual attitudes" or acted as a "safety valve" for potentially harmful behavior. In the 1960s legal theorists completed the dismantling of the earlier broad view of obscenity by redefining it—along with prostitution, homosexuality, the selling and taking of drugs, and gambling —as a "victimless crime." "Consenting adults" might depart from general community standards of morality, but if they did not interfere with the rights of others, their behavior should not be regulated by the state. Obscenity was reduced to a "lifestyle" issue, in keeping with the emerging liberal consensus that moral and aesthetic questions were matters of personal preference. In *Ginzburg v. U.S.* (1966), a trial concerning publications designed to appeal to masochists, the dissenting opinion by WILLIAM O. DOUGLAS revealed how thoroughgoing this relativism had become. Describing the needs of masochists as "somewhat offbeat, nonconformist, and odd," he nonetheless pointed out that

> we are not in the realm of criminal conduct, only ideas and tastes. Some like Chopin, others like "rock and roll." Some are "normal," some are masochistic, some deviant in other respects . . . if the communication is of value to the masochistic community or to others of the deviant community, how can it be said to be "utterly without any redeeming social importance"? "Redeeming" to whom? "Importance" to whom?

Justice Douglas's remarks point to the decay of a shared moral and aesthetic language, a condition that made speaking about community standards increasingly difficult by the 1960s. Once thinking people abandoned the hope of arriving at any consensus about the nature and meaning of obscenity or of art, debates shifted necessarily to the issue of free speech. Since all standards of judgment were open to dispute, decisions about what should appear in public were increasingly left to the "marketplace of ideas." As a result, liberal theory no longer attempts to distinguish between the untrammeled expression of ideas essential to a free society and the expression that exists for the sake of commercial exploitation. While the preeminent liberal legal theorist Ronald Dworkin is willing to grant that pornography is "offensive," he contends that it cannot be banned for that reason "without destroying the principle that the speech we hate is as much entitled to protection as any other. The essence of negative liberty is freedom to offend, and that applies to the tawdry as well as the heroic" (p. 13). (*See also* FREEDOM; LIBERTARIANISM.)

Since the 1970s feminists identified with the group Women Against Violence Against Women have attempted to remove pornography from the innocuous status of victimless crime by seeing it in relation to male subordination of women. As Susan Brownmiller puts it in Laura Lederer's volume *Take Back the Night*, "Pornography is the undiluted essence of anti-female propaganda" (p. 32). Writers of this persuasion argue that pornographic movies not only chronicle degradation of and violence against actual women, but encourage misogyny and even incite rape. While their rallying cry, "pornography is the theory, rape the practice" (p. 139), is limited by the individualistic search for actual victims who need protection, these writers have revitalized the older conception of obscenity, which posited an inextricable link between things private and public. (*See also* FEMINIST JURISPRUDENCE.)

Efforts to move beyond individual rights and to reinvigorate our sense of the broader significance of obscenity have typically been dismissed as "conservative." But such efforts defy simple classification. David Holbrook assembled a number of them in his 1973 volume entitled *The Case Against Pornography*. George Steiner argued that pornography constitutes an invasion of privacy. IRVING KRISTOL contended that pornography depersonalizes sex, reducing it to an animal activity. And Walter Berns charged that it wears away feelings of shame that are essential for protecting the deepest experiences of love and that promote the self-restraint necessary to democracy. The public dimension of obscenity had also been addressed by Harry Clor in his *Obscenity and Public Morality* (1969), where he insisted that it not only erodes community moral standards, but destroys the faculties that permit an individual to develop character by practicing ethical and aesthetic discrimination.

While these late twentieth-century writers echo the most persuasive contentions of the nineteenth-century reticent sensibility, their claims languish in the present social and intellectual atmosphere. Whereas the reticent sensibility held refinement as its highest ideal, and unhesitating shockability as the true mark of cultivation and delicacy, the late twentieth-century cult of exposure venerates sophistication, the world-weary sensibility that has seen everything and consequently is shocked by nothing. The modern sophisticate can savor the aesthetic value of the "centrality of the forearm" in an image of startling sexual violence ("fisting") in a Robert Mapplethorpe photograph, or appreciate the "allegorical" and "parodic" codes of "vernacular traditions" in the graphically violent misogynist songs of 2 Live Crew. The exhibitors of both 2 Live Crew and Mapplethorpe were cleared of obscenity charges in 1990, which suggests that virtually anything can now appear in public and that the legal concept of obscenity is effectively dead in America. It remains to be seen what kind of culture will survive in a society deeply intolerant of age-old distinctions between private and public, sacred and shameful.

ROCHELLE GURSTEIN

FURTHER READING

Paul S. Boyer, *Purity in Print* (New York: Scribner's Sons, 1968).
Harry M. Clor, *Obscenity and Public Morality: Censorship in a Liberal Society* (Chicago: University of Chicago Press, 1969).
Ronald Dworkin, "Liberty and Pornography," *New York Review of Books*, Aug. 15, 1991, pp. 12–15.
Morris L. Ernst and William Seagle, *To the Pure . . . A Study of Obscenity and the Censor* (New York: Viking, 1928).
Rochelle Gurstein, "Misjudging Mapplethorpe: the Art Scene and the Obscene," *Tikkun* 6 (1991): 70–7.
David Holbrook, ed., *The Case against Pornography* (New York: Library Press, 1973).
Laura Lederer, ed., *Take Back the Night: Women on Pornography* (New York: William Morrow, 1980).
Theodore Schroeder, *"Obscene" Literature and Constitutional Law* (New York: Privately Printed, 1911).

Olmsted, Frederick Law (b. Hartford, Conn., Apr. 26, 1822; d. Waverly [now Belmont], Mass., Aug. 28, 1903). Landscape architect and writer. Well known for such travel accounts as *A Journey in the Seaboard Slave States* (1856), Olmsted took charge of New York's Central Park development in 1857. A well-designed park, he argued, uses the curved lines of NATURE, fits the local topography, and provides a pastoral retreat that calms the soul and invites reflection and peaceful sociability. Communities should therefore set aside centrally located land in order to create aesthetic spaces that cultivate desirable social and moral qualities. Among Olmsted's other noted designs are Boston's Emerald Necklace, the grounds of the Capitol in Washington, D.C., Stanford University, and the parks at Yosemite and Niagara Falls.

FURTHER READING

Laura Wood Roper, *FLO: a Biography of Frederick Law Olmsted* (Baltimore: Johns Hopkins University Press, 1973).

Olsen, Tillie (b. Omaha, Nebr., Jan. 14, 1912 or 1913). Born Tillie Lerner to left-wing Russian-Jewish immigrant parents, Olsen spent her youth in the mining villages, farmlands, and factory towns of the Midwest. She began publishing fiction, reportage and poetry in the *Partisan Review* and other left journals in 1934, and joined the Young Communist League in 1931 and the Communist Party later in the decade; for many years political activism, wage-earning, housekeeping, and parenting precluded sustained attention to her writing. While her oeuvre is small, it has earned her a devoted following, particularly among those sharing her premise that most people's lives are "largely circumstanced by . . . sex, class and color" (Yalom, p. 60) and that "there is so much more to people than their lives permit them to be" (Pearlman and Werlock, p. 133).

The autobiographical novel *Yonnondio*—begun in the 1930s and published in unfinished form in 1974 —exemplifies several traits of Olsen's work: dense imagistic style, impassioned narratorial address, revolutionary political vision, and close attention to working-class women's lives. This account of the Holbrook family's struggles with poverty and alienation is a landmark of 1930s proletarian fiction, especially valuable for its portrayal of the sphere of reproduction and its correlation of sexism with capitalist exploitation. Jim Holbrook's hands—with which he both labors and brutalizes his wife Anna—mediate oppression and emancipation alike: "the things in his mind, so vast and formless . . . cannot be spoken, will never be spoken—till the day that hands will find a way to speak this: hands" (p. 79). Combining densely textured stream-of-consciousness narration with italicized authorial interventions and a continually shifting point of view, *Yonnondio* weds experimental narrative techniques to a stark proletarian realism.

Olsen's masterwork is acknowledged to be the series of short stories in *Tell Me a Riddle* (1961). The widely acclaimed first story, "I Stand Here Ironing," presents the monologue of a mother who, as she simultaneously irons, cares for her youngest child, and speaks to a school caseworker, attempts to understand—to "total"—the multiple forces that have estranged her from her firstborn daughter. While the story painfully details the lacks—of money, of time—accompanying working-class parenthood, it represents the resiliency of both daughter and mother, who concludes, "Only help her to know . . . that she is more than this dress on the ironing board, helpless before the iron" (p. 12).

The second story, "Hey Sailor, What Ship?" details the experiences of Whitey, a homeless alcoholic sailor visiting the home of his friends Lennie and Helen. Dedicated to Jack Eggan, a comrade of Olsen's who died in the Spanish civil war, the tale counters the pathos of its hero's plight by affirming Whitey's warm friendship with Lennie and Helen and his commitment to proletarian internationalism. The third story, "O Yes," depicts the coming-of-age of Helen's and Lennie's daughter Carol. Alienated from her black friend Parialee by the "sorting" taking place in junior high school and by her own sense of cultural difference at Parialee's baptism, Carol awakens to the realities of U.S. racism. By stressing the enduring friendship between Helen and Parialee's mother Alma, however, "O Yes" suggests that racial division is neither universal nor inevitable. Carol's question to Helen is posed to the reader as well: "Oh Why is it like it is and why do I have to care?" (p. 61).

"Tell Me a Riddle," the volume's final tale, focuses on Eva and David, the grandparents in the family. Rendered primarily through Eva's increasingly disjointed thoughts as she approaches her death by cancer, the narrative exposes the resentments building up within her over the 47 years of marriage and motherhood that have "drowned" her selfhood. By summoning up memories of her youth when she and David were participants in the 1905 Russian Revolution, however, and by insistently locating their lives amidst key events of the twentieth century, Eva's monologue testifies to the "springs [that] were in her seeking" (p. 84) and compels David to see himself and her as both creatures of history and the lovers they once were. When read by Olsen, "Tell Me a Riddle" moves audiences to tears. The tale enacts Olsen's dictum that—quoting Blake—"'a tear is an intellectual thing.' To move people to comprehension, the tear, the emotion, which includes the intellect, must be present" (Yalom, p. 63).

Olsen's more recent works include the prize-winning short story "Requa I" (1971) and the book Silences (1978), an extended meditation on all the books of genius that have not been written—by women, people of color, workers, anyone lacking "fullness of time." "Where the claims of creation cannot be primary," laments Olsen, "the results are atrophy, unfinished work; minor effort and accomplishment; silences" (p. 13). While Silences was generally greeted with enthusiasm and has played a significant role in redirecting attention to neglected women writers—especially the nineteenth-century American writer Rebecca Harding Davis—it has been criticized by Joyce Carol Oates for "glib and superficial . . . thinking" and by others as an apologia for Olsen's own scant productivity (Pearlman and Werlock, p. 132).

Olsen is routinely applauded for her FEMINISM and for what Burkom and Williams call her "passionately committed" humanism (p. 66). While Olsen's work, in her own words, "verifies the presence of great capacities in human beings" (Martin, p. 41), critics tend to be apologetic about Olsen's past membership in the Communist Party and her conviction that SOCIALISM "is, must be, the future." By minimizing Olsen's Marxist commitments, critics overlook the extent to which her fiction is shaped by a profoundly dialectical conception of process. "You can't talk about loss without talking about gain," Olsen has declared (Pearlman and Werlock, pp. 8, 25). When she portrays her characters attempting to "total" their past lives, to speak with their hands, to seek springs even as they drown, Olsen manifests her conviction that change results primarily from the struggle to achieve the "not yet in the now" (Yalom, p. 63).

Olsen is a significant figure in American letters because she demonstrates the compatibility of the narrative technique of MODERNISM with social REALISM and moral commitment. Moreover, her narratives easily bridge what is often seen as a gulf between feminist and working-class concerns. Literary PROLETARIANISM is deepened by her explorations of gendered subjectivity; feminism is extended through her insistence upon the CLASS basis of experience.

BARBARA FOLEY

FURTHER READING
Selma Burkom and Margaret Williams, "De-riddling Tillie Olsen's Writing," San Jose Studies 2 (Feb. 1975): 64–83.
Constance Coiner, "'No One's Private Ground': a Bakhtinian Reading of Tillie Olsen's Tell Me A Riddle," Feminist Studies 18 (summer 1992): 257–82.
Abigail Martin, Tillie Olsen, Western Writers Series, no. 65 (Boise: Boise State University, 1984).
Tillie Olsen, Silences (New York: Delacorte, 1978).
——, Tell Me a Riddle (1961; New York: Delta, 1989).
——, Yonnondio: From the Thirties (New York: Delacorte, 1974).
Mickey Pearlman and Abby H. P. Werlock, Tillie Olsen (Boston: Twayne, 1991).
Christopher Wilson, "Unlimn'd They Disappear: Recollecting Yonnondio: From the Thirties," in Richard Wightman

Fox and T. J. Jackson Lears, eds., *The Power of Culture* (Chicago: University of Chicago, 1993).

Margaret Yalom, ed., *Women Writers of the West Coast* (Santa Barbara: Capra, 1983).

O'Neill, Eugene (b. New York, N.Y., Oct. 16, 1888; d. Boston, Mass., Nov. 27, 1953). Since the early 1920s Eugene O'Neill has often been called America's greatest dramatist. He has also been one of the most influential: the dramas of TENNESSEE WILLIAMS, Arthur Miller, Lorraine Hansberry, Edward Albee, and David Mamet are all indebted to his work. The winner of three Pulitzer Prizes in the 1920s, and the only American dramatist to have been awarded the Nobel Prize (1936), O'Neill was a self-conscious intellectual as well as a playwright. O'Neill professed anarchist and socialist beliefs as a young man, and the 1910s Provincetown Players to which he belonged included radicals such as JOHN REED, MAX EASTMAN, FLOYD DELL, Mary Heaton Vorse, and MIKE GOLD. Greenwich Village bohemians as well as his Provincetown colleagues were thrilled because O'Neill made sailors—the working class—the subject of tragedy in his naturalist *Glencairn* cycle (1916–17). But 1930s left commentators criticized his *Glencairn* plays and *The Hairy Ape* (1922) as the work of a middle-class tourist fascinated by an "exotic," instinctually "primitive" working class, of a romantic who lost his taste for slumming as he grew prosperous staging "Sunday-supplement Freud" for the middle and upper classes.

LIONEL TRILLING argued in 1936 that the modern "moral and psychical upheaval of the middle class" made it receptive to O'Neill's work—"it wanted certain of its taboos broken and O'Neill broke them." Critics on the left in the 1930s began to shift their attention from what O'Neill broke up to what he helped design and put in place—a new middle-class psychological self that conceives of "liberation" as the individualized resistance of a desiring self to a culture reductively defined as systems of taboos. Left critics saw O'Neill's dramatization of "depth" as a strategy to absorb CLASS alienation into a universal malaise—we're all "hairy apes" frustrated by "life." For Larry Slade, the angst-ridden ex-anarchist in *The Iceman Cometh* (1940), true revolution is a "pipe dream" because human nature is made up of "mud" and "manure." Trilling's cultural analysis and the radical critiques jointly suggest that the therapeutic "exploration" of personal "depth" and a preoccupation with breaking taboos became, thanks to "vanguard" writers like O'Neill, the culturally approved form of middle-class "radicalism." While in *Marco Millions* (1926) O'Neill satirized bourgeois economic INDIVIDUALISM as culturally and emotionally shallow, plays like *Welded* (1924) and *Strange Interlude* (1928) promoted bourgeois psychological individualism as "deep."

O'Neill's representation of blacks is as intriguing as his representation of depth. In both instances his art exposes middle-class ideologies at work while also helping to constitute and develop them. African American intellectuals such as W. E. B. DU BOIS and LANGSTON HUGHES were on target in lauding O'Neill for putting controversial racial issues on the white cultural agenda and for the opportunity he gave black actors to perform in tragic roles, not minstrel, "blackface" caricatures. *The Emperor Jones* (1921) was the Provincetown Players' most financially successful production and catapulted O'Neill onto Broadway. Yet dissenting black critics like CLAUDE MCKAY saw *Emperor* as a "comic grotesque" (saved only by prize-winning actor Charles Gilpin); others pointed out that middle-class white audiences enjoyed seeing a depiction of black psychological primitivism. The fact remains that O'Neill courageously staged *All God's Chillun Got Wings* (1924)—about an emotionally ravaged interracial marriage—despite death threats to himself, his infant son, and his stars, Paul Robeson and Mary Blair. He argued that race was incidental in the play, which simply centered on the psychological interaction of two human beings. But race was more than incidental. O'Neill penetratingly examined how racist ideologies were internalized by blacks and whites alike, leading to devastating psychological damage. It did not go far enough to criticize him, as JAMES WELDON JOHNSON and other critics did, for racial stereotyping. It was the characters, in response to their culture's relentless demand, who stereotyped themselves.

Some of O'Neill's portraits of women—in *The Personal Equation* (1915), *Ile* (1917), and *Long Day's Journey into Night* (1940)—suggest that such mass cultural forms as pop psychology, romance novels, and confession magazines are responsible for packaging notions of "woman," "wife," "mother" which, once internalized, contribute to the formation of FEMININITY. In *Long Day's Journey* O'Neill questions the role that theatre itself has played in producing feminine "depth" and "madness," connecting Mary Tyrone's familial predicament to images of women in Shakespeare and to her husband's nineteenth-century career as a swashbuckling matinée idol. This masterpiece of psychological realism offers subtle insights into the cultural forces that inform and deform the psychological webbing of this Irish American family.

O'Neill's work will remain of intellectual interest in part because of the powerful ideological cross-currents he channeled into drama. Some of his most intriguing plays acted out a modern pop psychological "depth" for the urban, college-educated middle class, and sometimes, in the same plays, understood this "depth" as a dubious cultural invention. As the forms of middle-class subjectivities, and the codes, metaphors, and narratives used to convey these subjectivities, continue to shift and multiply, audiences will find O'Neill's plays strikingly provocative: not because they expose the workings of some natural or timeless self, but because they probe the ways in which modern ideologies of the self took root in us.

JOEL PFISTER

FURTHER READING

Doris Alexander, *Eugene O'Neill's Creative Struggle: the Decisive Decade, 1919–1933* (University Park: Pennsylvania State University Press, 1992).
Eric Bentley, "The Life and Hates of Eugene O'Neill," in *Thinking about the Playwright: Comments from Four Decades* (Evanston, Ill.: Northwestern University Press,1987).
Joel Pfister, *Staging Depth: Eugene O'Neill and the Politics of Psychological Discourse* (Chapel Hill: University of North Carolina Press, 1995).
John Henry Raleigh, *The Plays of Eugene O'Neill* (Carbondale: Southern Illinois University Press, 1965).
Louis Sheaffer, *O'Neill: Son and Artist* (Boston: Little, Brown, 1973).
——, *O'Neill: Son and Playwright* (Boston: Little, Brown, 1968).
Lionel Trilling, "Eugene O'Neill," in John Gassner, ed., *Eugene O'Neill: a Collection of Critical Essays* (Englewood Cliffs, N.J.: Prentice-Hall, 1964).
Charmion Von Wiegand, "The Quest of Eugene O'Neill," in Herbert Kline, ed., *New Theatre and Film 1934 to 1937: an Anthology* (San Diego: Harcourt Brace Jovanovich, 1985).

Oppenheimer, J[ulius] Robert (b. New York, N.Y., Apr. 22, 1904; d. Princeton, N.J., Feb. 18, 1967). Physicist. Known as the father of the atomic bomb, Oppenheimer directed the Los Alamos laboratory (1943–5) and the Institute for Advanced Study at Princeton University (1947–66). After World War II he called for international civilian control of atomic weaponry and led a movement for bilateral arms limitations. He opposed the development of the hydrogen bomb: not only is mass killing inherently immoral, he argued, but bombs with such massive power are unnecessary. Oppenheimer's political stands led to a 1954 Atomic Energy Commission hearing that revoked his security clearance. He authored such works as *Science and the Common Understanding* (1954) and *Some Reflections on Science and Culture* (1960).

FURTHER READING
Peter Goodchild, *J. Robert Oppenheimer: Shatterer of Worlds* (Boston: Houghton Mifflin, 1981).

Owen, Robert Dale (b. Glasgow, Scotland, Nov. 9, 1801; d. Lake George, N.Y., June 24, 1877). Reformer and writer. Son of the famous English reformer Robert Owen, Robert Dale Owen emigrated to America in 1825 and joined the community at New Harmony, Indiana, where he edited the *New Harmony Gazette*. Associated for a time with FRANCES WRIGHT as editor of the *Free Enquirer* in New York, he entered Indiana politics as an advocate of public schools, liberal divorce legislation, and property rights for women. An active opponent of slavery (although not an advocate of immediate emancipation), Owen also, like many nineteenth-century reformers, displayed a keen interest in SPIRITUALISM, about which he wrote such works as *Footfalls on the Boundary of Another World* (1860) and *The Debatable Land between This World and the Next* (1872).

See also UTOPIAS.

FURTHER READING
Anne Taylor, *Visions of Harmony: a Study in Nineteenth-Century Millenarianism* (New York: Oxford University Press, 1987).

P

Paine, Thomas (b. Thetford, England, Jan. 29, 1737; d. New York, N.Y., June 8, 1809). This English political essayist and revolutionary lived and wrote in America from 1774 to 1789 and from 1802 to his death. He was the son of a Quaker corset-maker, and left school at 13; after three years of working in his father's shop and an unsuccessful effort at running his own, he became an excise collector. In 1774 he sailed to Philadelphia, where he turned to political journalism and pamphleteering.

His *Common Sense*, published in January 1776, played a dramatic role in galvanizing colonial opinion in favor of Independence. Marshalling biblical and historical precedent, the self-educated Paine urged Americans to repudiate what he called England's corrupt and tyrannical rule. His arguments were grounded in the ideas of John Locke, the seventeenth-century English writer whose discussions of individual natural rights and the consensual origins of government deeply influenced America's founding generation, as well as in the anti-aristocratic anger of English radicalism. Locke described men abandoning "natural liberty" through the voluntary creation of governments in order better to protect their rights. People retained, however, the capacity to change their government should it cease to defend their liberty and property. Paine's message for the colonists insisted that when the British government violated their natural rights they were justified in replacing it with their own republican government free of monarchic and aristocratic privilege. The message was heard; in 1776 alone, over 100,000 copies of the pamphlet were sold.

Having helped bring about the AMERICAN REVOLUTION, Paine then enlisted in the American army. For the remainder of the war he combined soldiering with writing, producing a remarkable set of pamphlets later published together as *The Crisis*. The first of these appeared on December 23, 1776. It was addressed to all Americans, as well as to Washington and his troops huddled in the New Jersey cold. Its opening lines have remained the most frequently quoted of all that Paine wrote.

> These are the times that try men's souls: The summer soldier and the sunshine patriot will, in this crisis, shrink from the service of his country; but he that stands it now, deserves the love and thanks of man and woman. (*Paine Reader*, p. 116)

After the Revolutionary War, Paine played an active role in the politics of Pennsylvania while also pursuing such scientific ventures as designing an iron bridge. Pursuit of sponsors for this project brought him back to Europe in the late 1780s. Paine exulted in the revolutionary fervor then emanating from France. When Edmund Burke wrote his famous denunciation of the French Revolution in 1790, Paine fired back in 1791 with his most enduring work, *The Rights of Man*. While Burke urged reverence and respect for the traditional, hierarchical social order embodied in the age-old structures of aristocracy, monarchy, and the church, Paine defended the revolutionary ideals of DEMOCRACY and social EQUALITY. Having dispensed with the absurdities of aristocracy and monarchy, Republican England, Paine announced in part two of *The Rights of Man*, would introduce radical social policies. He envisioned state subsidies for the poor and elderly and free education for all children.

The British government responded by charging Paine with sedition; when he was brought to trial Paine fled to France. He served as a delegate to the National Convention and helped draft the French revolutionary constitution. Eventually Paine was caught up in the unpredictably changing mood of the revolution. His disapproval of Louis XVI's execution and his association with the Girondins led Robespierre in late 1793 to have Paine imprisoned. Paine turned to drink and writing. The sometime scientist produced in jail the first draft of *The Age of Reason*, a bitter deist diatribe against supernatural religion. With Robespierre's downfall a year later Paine was freed and he continued to write. His *Agrarian Justice*, which appeared in 1797, developed more precisely the redistributive proposals of part 2 of *The Rights of Man*, suggesting, for example, that governments pay 15 pounds to every person at the age of 21 and 10 pounds per year to all over 50 years of age.

Paine returned to America in 1802, a cranky old man given to drunkenness. His attack on Christianity alienated old friends in Federalist America. Among his former allies, only Jefferson renewed his ties with the man who had helped convert America to the cause of independence.

Two themes pervade Paine's writings, his belief in the liberating mission of America and his commitment to equality. In *Common Sense* he described the independence of the 13 colonies as an event of momentous importance. Like the Hebrews, the Americans were invested with a messianic mission. American independence was a flood which would wipe clean the slate of history. America had it in her power, Paine wrote, "to begin the world over again . . . The birthday of a new world is at hand" (*Paine Reader*, p. 109).

The second theme, equality, dominated *The Rights of Man*. Paine's every reflex was egalitarian, bent on undermining what he considered the "quixotic age of chivalric nonsense." Kings were useless and unproductive, as was hereditary privilege. Is there anything more absurd than the hereditary principle, Paine asked in *The Rights of Man*, "as absurd as an hereditary mathematician, or an hereditary wiseman, and, as ridiculous as an hereditary poet laureate"? Society should be led by men of "talents and abilities," yet its offices of privilege and power were filled by a nobility that, according to Paine, really meant "no-ability" (*Paine Reader*, pp. 211, 229, 242, 257).

Paine represents LIBERALISM at its most democratic moment. His Lockean INDIVIDUALISM was expressed with an egalitarian fervor found in no other liberal theorist of the revolutionary era. His populist ideals endeared Paine to the simple farmers and plain mechanics of 1776 as they were to do to the London journeymen of 1791. His democratic ideals have endured to this day as has his reading of America's special God-given purpose. Paine's brilliant and blunt rhetoric is enlisted in the late twentieth century by Americans of divergent political views. In the 1970s and 1980s his defense of individualism against government was repeatedly invoked in speeches by Ronald Reagan even as this eighteenth-century revolutionary's egalitarian assault on privilege had him consistently head lists of radical counterheroes put forth by nonofficial and alternative "people's bicentennials." Not bad for a self-taught former corset-maker who had arrived in Philadelphia in 1774 at the age of 37 with little else but a way with words.

ISAAC KRAMNICK

FURTHER READING

Gregory Claeys, *Thomas Paine: Social and Political Thought* (Boston: Unwin and Hyman, 1989).
Eric Foner, *Tom Paine and Revolutionary America* (New York: Oxford University Press, 1976).
Thomas Paine, *The Thomas Paine Reader*, ed. M. Foot and I. Kramnick (London: Penguin, 1987).
Audrey Williamson, *Thomas Paine: His Life, Work and Time* (London: Allen Unwin, 1973).

Paredes, Américo (b. Brownsville, Tex., Sept. 3, 1915). Born along the "bloody border" where his Hispano-mestizo ancestors had originally settled in 1749, Paredes became a folklorist, ethnographer, poet, and novelist, as well as a talented guitarist, pianist, and corrido-singer. As a teenager he won a literary contest sponsored by Trinity College in Texas, and he began contributing poetry to *La Prensa*, the major Spanish-language newspaper of San Antonio, Texas.

From 1936 until 1943, Paredes wrote for both the English- and Spanish-language editions of the *Brownsville Herald*, contributing feature articles on culture and society. Called into the army during World War II, he served as a war correspondent in the Pacific, and later as editor of *Stars and Stripes*, the military newspaper. As editor, Paredes reported on the postwar trials of Japanese generals accused of war crimes, and, according to José E. Limón, he "became convinced of their general innocence and deeply suspicious of American racist motives with which he had no small acquaintance in his South Texas past" (p. 111). After the war, he briefly lived in Japan, working as a journalist for the American Red Cross, visiting Korea, and witnessing the communist revolution in China. In 1950, Paredes returned to Texas, completed work on his college degree, and received highest honors in English.

The following year, while he was a graduate student in English at the University of Texas, his unpublished collection of short stories *Border Country* won a literary contest in Dallas. "Over the Waves is Out," one of the stories, takes its title from Juventino Rosas's famous Mexican waltz "Sobre las olas," and is a magical allegory of a young boy's aesthetic desires:

> And finally [the music] came, faintly at first, then more distinctly, though never loud, splashing and whirling about, twisting in intricate eddies of chords and bright waterfalls of melody, or falling in separate notes into the night, like drops of quicksilver, rolling, glimmering.

In 1957, Paredes (with his Ph.D. in hand) joined the English department at the University of Texas at Austin, where he taught creative writing and FOLKLORE for many years and currently holds an emeritus professorship. An award in 1989 from the National Endowment for the Humanities for lifetime achievement in the arts was followed in 1990 by his induction into Mexico's Orden de Águila Azteca, in recognition of his role in preserving Mexican culture in the United States.

Paredes is best understood as a border-crossing intellectual, equally at home as a folklorist, a cultural anthropologist, a creative writer, and a social historian. For example, in *With His Pistol in His Hand* (1958), his classic study of the legends, *cuentos*, and corridos catalyzed by the social struggles of Gregorio Cortez, he begins with a lengthy chapter on border culture—Nuevo Santander—and on the musical aesthetics of South Texas. He then writes an intellectual biography of Cortez. This legendary border hero, falsely accused of horse stealing and murdering an Anglo sheriff, outran and outsmarted a posse of Rangers across half of the state of Texas. The book ends with a rigorous rhetorical and cultural analysis of the corrido proper, which, he argues, broke down the usual white supremacist hierarchies. The Texas Rangers were not brave and invincible, but foolish and cowardly ("All the rangers of the county / Were flying, they rode so hard . . . But trying to catch Cortez / Was like following a star"). The writing of *With His Pistol in His Hand*, like the corrido itself, is wildly creative, a decided alternative to conventional academic discourse, and a self-conscious critique of it.

There can be no denying that Paredes has always been haunted by his "bloody border" country. In his lyrical and vernacular poetry written in the late 1930s and 1940s (republished in *Between Two Worlds*, 1991), he often writes of the border Chicano: "He no gotta country, he no gotta flag / He no gotta voice, all he got is the han' / To go work like the burro; he no gotta lan'." For Paredes, the history of the South Texas borderlands is inaugurated by the loss of local place, of locality. Geographical and cultural identity must be searched for and recovered through the poetic imagination. Of the many striking examples of this cartographic mapping is a poem entitled "The Rio Grande": "I was born beside your waters / and since very young I knew / That my soul had hidden currents / That my soul resembled you." Alert to the dizzying Rio Grande's "swirls" and "countercurrents," to its contested territoriality, the poem struggles to recover the author's sense of place: "We shall wander through the country / Where your green banks are clad / Past the shanties of rancheros / By the ruins of old Bagdad."

Throughout his multifaceted career, Paredes has never doubted the value of the intellectual tools of which his border people have been largely deprived. He takes the literary and scholarly instruments he has been given and turns them against the disciplinary rigidities of the academic mainstream. He has also used them to create what is perhaps the best historical novel of twentieth-century South Texas: *George Washington Gómez: a MexicoTexan Novel* (1990). He has also explored the rich and nuanced folklore, border music, and transcultural jests and

jokes of what he calls "Greater Mexico" in his classic studies, *Folktales of Mexico* (1970), *A Texas-Mexican Cancionero: Folksongs of the Lower Border* (1976), and *Uncle Remus Con Chile* (1993).

In a working career of over 40 years, Paredes has pursued his intellectual and critical concerns across an astonishing range of cultural forms. With the publication of *Folklore and Culture on the Texas-Mexican Border* (1993), Paredes provides readers with a sample of his lifelong interest in the borderland traffic between cultural anthropology and cultural studies. Traditional anthropological research ("The Folklore of Groups of Mexican Origin in the United States" and "On Ethnographic Work among Minority Groups") mixes with essays on everyday life in the border contact zone. Fundamentally, the U.S.-Mexico border, as he theorizes in "The Problem of Identity in a Changing Culture" is defined by contestation: conflict as a way of life, between individuals and cultures. By far the most commanding figure in Chicano Studies, Paredes's work consistently insists on social relations, connections, and complex affinities—crossing the border-patrolled boundaries drawn between discourses and cultures alike.

JOSÉ DAVID SALDÍVAR

FURTHER READING

José E. Limón, "Américo Paredes: a Man from the Border," *Revista Chicano-Riqueña* 8 (1980): 1–5.
——, *Mexican Ballads, Chicano Poems: History and Influence in Mexican-American Social Poetry* (Berkeley: University of California Press, 1992).
——, *Dancing with the Devil: Society and Cultural Poetics in Mexican-American South Texas* (Madison: University of Wisconsin Press, forthcoming).
Américo Paredes, *Folklore and Culture on the Texas-Mexican Border*, ed. and intro. Richard Bauman (Austin: CMAS Books and University of Texas Press, 1993).
José David Saldívar, "Chicano Border Narratives As Cultural Critique," in Héctor Calderón and José David Saldívar, eds., *Criticism in the Borderlands: Studies in Chicano Literature, Culture, and Ideology* (Durham, N.C.: Duke University Press, 1991).
Ramón Saldívar, *Chicano Narrative: the Dialectics of Difference* (Madison: University of Wisconsin Press, 1990).

Park, Robert E. (b. Harveyville, Pa., Feb. 14, 1864; d. Nashville, Tenn., Feb. 7, 1944). Sociologist. After a career as a journalist, Park taught philosophy at Harvard and then, in 1913, became a professor of sociology at the University of Chicago, where he led the "Chicago School" investigations of URBANISM and "human ecology." Author of such volumes as *The Immigrant Press and Its Control* (1922) and *The City: Suggestions for the Study of the Urban Environment* (1925), Park promoted community studies, which allow detailed study of social groups and their interaction. He was a strong advocate of empiricism at a time when the sociology profession was split between reformers in the "social survey" tradition and professionalizers seeking legitimacy for SOCIAL SCIENCE.

See also OBJECTIVITY; SOCIETY.

FURTHER READING

Fred H. Matthews, *Quest for an American Sociology: Robert E. Park and the Chicago School* (Montreal: McGill-Queen's University Press, 1977).

Parker, Dorothy (b. West End, N.J., Aug. 22, 1893; d. New York, N.Y., June 7, 1967. Writer. One of the mainstays of the "Algonquin Round Table," a lunchtime gathering of renowned conversationalists in New York in the 1920s, Parker was a prolific and wide-ranging writer especially known for her wit. Drama critic for *Vanity Fair* and book reviewer for the *New Yorker*, she also wrote verse (*Enough Rope*, 1926, *Sunset Gun*, 1928, and *Death and Taxes*, 1931), short stories (*Here Lies*, 1939), and screenplays (*A Star Is Born*, 1937). Her style, though always spare and precise, was varied: from bitterly sardonic satire to light-hearted flippancy to sentimental pathos. Ever fascinated by wealth, Parker admired workers' strength and honesty, condemned exploitation by class or gender, and satirized the complacent pretensions of the middle and upper classes.

FURTHER READING

Marion Meade, *Dorothy Parker: What Fresh Hell Is This?* (New York: Villard Books, 1988).

Parker, Theodore (b. Lexington, Mass., Aug. 24, 1810; d. Florence, Italy, May 10, 1860). Born on a farm, the last of 11 children, Theodore Parker became one of the most popular and controversial preachers and social activists in the two decades preceding the Civil War. Arguably the most learned man in antebellum America (he was said to know more than 20 languages), Parker was primarily self-educated. Although too poor to enroll formally at Harvard, he passed all the examinations with distinction, after which he spent two years at Harvard Divinity School, where he edited a small journal of biblical criticism, *The Scriptural Interpreter*. Known as "America's preacher," Parker burst onto the public stage in 1841 with the delivery, virulent public criticism, and subsequent publication of his "Discourse of the Transient and Permanent in Christianity," a sermon preached at the ordination of Charles Shackford on May 19 of that year. Although much more popular as a lecturer than RALPH WALDO EMERSON, Parker has been remembered (or not) as only a minor figure in American cultural history. But more interesting than the fluctuating status of Parker's legacy for American culture is the way in which the reinterpretations of his historical legacy conform to, and are in turn illuminated by, the narrative economy of transience and permanence at the heart of his thought.

Shortly after preaching the "Transient and Permanent" sermon, the most compelling account of the Transcendentalist claim that the truth of Christianity (or any religion) depends not on institutional authority but on the intuitive authority of individual religious consciousness, Parker came under attack from Trinitarian as well as Unitarian ministers. Many Unitarians subsequently refused to exchange pulpits with him, and eventually voted to expel him from their association. Throughout the next two decades, Parker continued to consider himself a Unitarian, but his radical theological doctrines, coupled with his virulent abolitionism and his powerful moral and social critiques of poverty, crime, education, and intemperance, prevented his fellow Unitarian ministers from accepting him as one of them.

Theologically, Parker developed a system of "absolute religion," set forth most fully in *A Discourse of Religion* (1842). He grounded three fundamental doctrines—morality, immortality, and the existence of God—in the intuitive facts of consciousness. Parker's social discourse, like his theology, employed the epistemological strategy perfected in the "Transient and Permanent." In this sermon on Luke 21:33 ("Heaven and earth will pass away; but my words shall not pass away"), Parker drew on his extensive knowledge of the "higher criticism" of the Bible to gloss the sermon's text as an assertion of historical relativism. Parker's sermon made clear that because we can have only our own transient notions of intuitive truth, the process of distinguishing between transient institutional truths and permanent intuitions was therefore never-ending. Similarly, Parker grounded his social activism in the permanent authority of intuition, arguing that social injustices were produced by transient institutions that would inevitably give way to those founded on the more permanent intuitive truths furnished by God to the soul. But his sermons also reveal the ways in which those truths which seem to be intuitive turn out to be merely transient notions so deeply institutionalized as to appear to be innate.

Parker's theological legacy has manifested a similar economy of transience and permanence. Although virtually excommunicated from Unitarianism during his lifetime, by the end of the century Parker had been canonized (along with Emerson) as one of the two apostles of American Unitarianism. Parker's canonization was marked in 1907 with the publication of the centenary edition of his works by the American Unitarian Association. Parker's place in American cultural history has also had its transient and permanent elements. In the 1930s Henry Steele Commager posed what he called "The Dilemma of Theodore Parker," his confusion of intuition and experience. Why, Commager asked, did Parker feel the need to ransack the archives of history in support of truths that were grounded in every person's intuition? Commager's dilemma, however, failed to take into account Parker's conviction that intuition and experience were not mutually exclusive but inextricably entwined. Thus, although Parker consistently argued for the permanence of the intuitive truths of absolute religion, he just as consistently argued that historical experience was not inimical to, but constitutive of, intuitive truth. This commitment to the transient circumstances of historical experience was similarly overlooked in the 1950s. Perry Miller advanced Parker's "Transient and Permanent" as paradigmatic of the antinomianism that connected Puritanism to Transcendentalism; R. W. B. Lewis portrayed Parker as one of his American Adams. Parker's subversion of conventional, institutional authority in the name of the individual authority of intuition placed him squarely within the post-World War II reading of American literature as inherently radical, a reading reproduced in a different form by the revival of interest in Parker as an abolitionist prophet, brought about in the context of the civil rights movement.

For at least two decades the oppositional quality of the American literary tradition has been called into question by an ongoing revisionism, in which the critique of American institutions set forth in the classic texts has been shown to be implicated in the very ideological structures these texts would critique. In spite of this revisionism Parker's radical intuitionalism remains pertinent to our cultural history. His criticism of slavery, poverty, and domestic problems such as intemperance and crime, resonates with current academic interest in questions of race, class, and gender in American cultural history. Indeed, in tracing an implicit parallel between Parker's increasing concern for social and political issues and the transformation in American literary history from the epistemological concerns of poststructuralism to today's concerns with the problem of ideology, I have meant to suggest the way in which Parker can warn us to do more than merely substitute ideological concerns for epistemological ones. We must rather (taking a cue from Parker's logic of intuition) seek to recognize the way in which our critical discourse should seek continually to produce, elide, and reproduce the epistemological and ideological distinctions that run through America's permanent and its transient literatures.

RICHARD GRUSIN

See also ANTISLAVERY; TRANSCENDENTALISM; UNITARIANISM.

FURTHER READING

Robert C. Albrecht, *Theodore Parker* (New York: Twayne, 1971).

Henry Steele Commager, "The Dilemma of Theodore Parker," *New England Quarterly* 6 (June 1933): 257–77.

——, *Theodore Parker* (Boston: Little, Brown, 1936).

——, ed., *Theodore Parker: an Anthology* (Boston: Beacon, 1960).

John Edward Dirks, *The Critical Theology of Theodore Parker* (New York: Columbia University Press, 1948).

Richard A. Grusin, *Transcendentalist Hermeneutics: Institutional Authority and the Higher Criticism of the Bible* (Durham, N.C.: Duke University Press, 1991).

R. W. B. Lewis, *The American Adam: Innocence, Tragedy, and Tradition in the Nineteenth Century* (Chicago: University of Chicago Press, 1955).

Vernon L. Parrington, *Main Currents in American Thought*, vol. 2 (New York: Harcourt, Brace, 1927).

Parkman, Francis (b. Jamaica Plain, Mass., Sept. 16, 1823; d. Jamaica Plain, Mass., Nov. 8, 1893). Historian. Combining careful use of sources with a love of drama and heroic narrative, Parkman created a national history that focused on powerful personalities and praised the virtues of Anglo-Protestant civilization. His popular *England and France in North America* (7 vols., 1865–84) chronicled the imperial contest between France and Britain, while *The California and Oregon Trail* (1849, reprinted as *The Oregon Trail*) recounted his own experiences while traveling in the American West. The purpose of history, Parkman believed, is to breathe life into the present by recapturing the spirit and vitality of the past.

See also ROMANTIC HISTORIANS.

FURTHER READING

Wilbur R. Jacobs, *Francis Parkman, Historian as Hero: the Formative Years* (Austin: University of Texas Press, 1991).

Parrington, Vernon Louis (b. Aurora, Ill., Aug. 3, 1871; d. Winchcombe, Gloucestershire, England, June 16, 1929). Literary historian. Parrington, who taught American literature at the University of Oklahoma from 1897 until 1908, and at the University of Washington until his death, published a remarkable two-volume opus, *Main Currents in American Thought: an Interpretation of American Literature from the Beginning to 1920*, in 1927. His unfinished volume *The Beginnings of Critical Realism* *in America* was published posthumously in 1930. In the 1940s and 1950s, historians and literary critics alike judged Parrington's the most influential historical work published in the twentieth century. Inspired by the English critics John Ruskin and William Morris on the one hand, and by American populists and progressives on the other, Parrington presented the history of American thought, viewed through literature and popular political writing, as an uninterrupted battle between DEMOCRACY and elitism. Parrington's unabashed partisanship and colorful characterizations edged his scholarship toward JOURNALISM and CULTURAL CRITICISM. His cheerleading for Jeffersonian idealism contrasted with widespread dismissals of popular democracy in the 1920s.

FURTHER READING

H. Lark Hall, *V.L. Parrington: through the Avenue of Art* (Kent, Ohio: Kent State University Press, 1994).

Parsons, Talcott (b. Colorado Springs, Colo., Dec. 13, 1902; d. Munich, Germany, May 8, 1979). The son of Edward S. Parsons, Congregational minister and college administrator, and Mary Augusta Ingersoll, Talcott Parsons attended Colorado public schools and the Horace Mann School for Boys in New York City before entering Amherst College in 1920 to study biology and prepare for a medical career. His interests shifted to SOCIAL SCIENCE under the influence of two teachers, Walton Hamilton and Clarence Ayres, who introduced Parsons to Thorstein Veblen's "institutional" economics, and to anthropology, sociology, and moral philosophy. Parsons actively supported college president Alexander Meiklejohn, a reformer friendly to liberal and left-wing intellectuals who was forced to resign in June 1923, and chaired Amherst's chapter of the Student League for Industrial Democracy. From 1924 to 1926, Parsons studied abroad at the London School of Economics and the University of Heidelberg. After completing a German doctoral degree with a thesis on the theories of capitalism propounded by the sociologists Max Weber and Werner Sombart, Parsons assumed a position at Harvard University, first as an instructor teaching economics and sociology. He remained at Harvard as professor of sociology until his 1973 retirement.

Parsons's work persistently emphasized the positive attributes of modernity as a system of social life open to change and developing steadily toward a more secure, egalitarian order. Modernity, for Parsons, was neither an "iron cage" of bureaucratic control nor an order of unloosed, acquisitive INDIVI-DUALISM. In response to a political culture strongly biased against institutional regulation of individual action, Parsons insisted on the significance of social institutions in shaping personality and motives—a view which led him in the 1920s and 1930s to challenge laissez-faire economics and advocate social democratic reform. On the other hand, Parsons combated the nostalgic CONSERVATISM that condemned modern individualism as the harmful consequence of the decline of traditional communities. He aimed to find forms of COMMUNITY adequate to assure order in a society open to individual achievement and argued that it was possible to construe individualism in ways not corrosive of collective concern. He took the collegial organization and service ethics of the learned professions, along with their standards of personal achievement, as a model of social action under modern conditions.

In his first book, *The Structure of Social Action* (1937), which highlighted his debts to Max Weber and Émile Durkheim, Parsons tried to demonstrate that the bare "utilitarian" framework of orthodox economics—assumptions regarding the autonomy of the sovereign individual, the unanalyzed "randomness" of the ends or goals individuals pursued, and the primacy of rational efficiency as a standard in human behavior—could not adequately explain the phenomenon of social order. Citing "nonrational" and collective forces at work, Parsons concluded that societies cohered in large part due to "common value integration," or the existence of certain ultimate values shared by human actors and knit together in an organized system of sanctioned ends and norms. After a long interlude marked by personal engagement in support of U.S. intervention and mobilization in World War II, and a major entrepreneurial effort to build a new, interdisciplinary Department of Social Relations at Harvard University, Parsons presented a more elaborate "structural-functional" theory of SOCIETY in his second major work, *The Social System* (1951). Based on the notion of society as a system tending toward equilibrium, as endemic "control mechanisms" checked deviations from established roles and redirected action toward conformity with commonly accepted norms, *The Social System* became the work most commonly identified as an exemplar of "Parsonsian theory." Nonetheless, it was soon outmoded as Parsons reached a more comprehensive and coherent theory summed up in his "four-function model," where economy, polity, social solidarity, and means of socialization were depicted as interacting, and interpenetrating, subsystems of society as a whole.

In a pair of short books, *Societies: Evolutionary and*

Comparative Perspectives (1966) and *The System of Modern Societies* (1971), Parsons described modernity as a social order destined to become increasingly open, inclusive, flexible and powerful. Strong liberal values informed his hostility to racial prejudice and exclusivism, his opposition to prescriptive moral orthodoxies, and his embrace of enlightened secular values, but by this time Parsons was routinely criticized as a deeply conservative thinker by Lewis Coser, Ralf Dahrendorf, c. WRIGHT MILLS, and a growing movement of "radical sociology" among younger practitioners in the field. Though Parsons supported the antiwar campaigns of Eugene McCarthy and George McGovern, his benign view of Western social development, deep confidence in the fundamentally sound and progressive character of American society, lack of interest in disruptive popular social movements as agents of progressive change, and antipathy toward Marxism could not but offend the new academic radicals. His liberal and professional biases often led him to idealize current conditions, as in his essay "The Distribution of Power in American Society," written in response to C. Wright Mills, in which Parsons suggested that power was both widely dispersed and allocated to individuals as a function of their efficiency in serving social needs.

Still, Parsons's perspective on the direction of modern social development retained a social democratic character and suggested the possibility of dramatic social change. While doubting the workability of SOCIALISM and centralized state planning, and insisting that markets as well as income differentials inevitably played a part in modern life, he also expected and advocated a steadily growing role for public control and intervention in economic affairs. He stood firm in promoting development of a genuinely inclusive "societal community"—a common body of people, of diverse groups, whose belonging as citizens to the community brought with it wide-ranging political and social rights. Furthermore, Parsons defined the real productive force of contemporary life as the "socialized capacity" of the educated individual rather than accumulated private wealth. In principle, Parsons's defense of the socialized individual and the inclusive societal community supposed the extension of social provision and a more concrete realization of equal opportunity. In this context, he recognized, the problem of striking a balance between egalitarianism and stratification (in differential rewards for performance) grew more acute and had yet to be adequately resolved. It was undoubtedly due to these reformist elements that the "revival of Parsons," led by writers such as Jeffrey C. Alexander, David Sciulli, and Mark Gould (in *Neofunctionalism*, edited by

Alexander) after Parsons's death, had a faint leftist tinge. In the 1980s, as the possibility of progressive change under modern conditions was denied on the right and mocked on the postmodern left, the resolutely optimistic view of reform that Parsons upheld gave his work continued value and vitality.

HOWARD BRICK

FURTHER READING
Jeffrey C. Alexander, *Theoretical Logic of Sociology*, vol. 4: *The Modern Reconstruction of Classical Thought: Talcott Parsons* (Berkeley: University of California Press, 1983).
——, ed., *Neofunctionalism* (Beverly Hills: Sage, 1985).
Charles Camic, ed., *Talcott Parsons: the Early Essays* (Chicago: University of Chicago Press, 1990).
Leon Mayhew, "Introduction," in Mayhew, ed., *Talcott Parsons on Institutions and Social Evolution* (Chicago: University of Chicago Press, 1982).
Talcott Parsons, *The Structure of Social Action: a Study in Social Theory with Special Reference to a Group of Recent European Writers* (1937; New York: Free Press, 1968).
——, *The Social System* (New York: Free Press, 1951).
——, "The Distribution of Power in American Society," in Parsons, *Structure and Process in Modern Society* (New York: Free Press, 1960).
——, *Societies: Evolutionary and Comparative Perspectives* (Englewood Cliffs: Prentice-Hall, 1966).
——, *The System of Modern Societies* (Englewood Cliffs: Prentice-Hall, 1971).

Parton, Sara Payson Willis [pen name Fanny Fern] (b. Portland, Maine, July 9, 1811; d. New York, N.Y., Oct. 10, 1872). Writer. Parton produced popular, entertaining, and sometimes scathingly satirical assaults on pretentiousness and power. She particularly scorned the repressive nature of families: her heroines frequently repudiate family and marriage to find pleasure and satisfaction in an independent life. Her dry wit and colloquial language contributed to her popularity as she claimed for women the ethos of INDIVIDUALISM. Parton's sketches, first published in periodicals, were collected in *Fern Leaves from Fanny's Portfolio*, which sold 100,000 copies in its first year. Her other writings include the novel *Ruth Hall* (1855) and *A New Story Book for Children* (1864). Her third husband, the biographer James Parton, wrote her life story the year after her death.

FURTHER READING
Joyce W. Warren, *Fanny Fern: an Independent Woman* (New Brunswick, N.J.: Rutgers University Press, 1992).

Patten, Simon (b. Cossayuna, N.Y., or DeKalb County, Ill., May 1, 1852; d. Browns Mills, N.J., July 24, 1922). Economist. Society, Patten argued in *The New Basis of Civilization* (1907), has advanced from an economy of scarcity to an economy of abundance. Social harmony will be achieved only if the working masses participate in that abundance. Poverty, the result of excessive competition, can be eliminated through more efficient TECHNOLOGY. Work hours should be reduced, education and culture made cheap and accessible, and differences of class and ethnicity eliminated through shared consumption in a MASS CULTURE. Patten's other writings include *The Premises of Political Economy* (1885) and *Essays in Economic Theory* (1924), edited by future New Dealer REXFORD TUGWELL.

FURTHER READING

Daniel M. Fox, *The Discovery of Abundance: Simon N. Patten and the Transformation of Social Theory* (Ithaca: Cornell University Press, 1967).

Pauling, Linus (b. Portland, Ore., Feb. 28, 1901; d. Big Sur, Calif., Aug. 19, 1994). Chemist and physicist. A major contributor to knowledge of quantum mechanics, medicine, and biology, as well as chemistry itself, Pauling's pivotal book *The Nature of the Chemical Bond* (1939) led to his reception of the Nobel Prize for Chemistry in 1954, and placed the field on a new footing. Earlier in his career Pauling had developed a comprehensive interpretive/predictive framework for the study of minerals; still later, he demonstrated the chemical nature of congenital disease, as well as the allopathic properties of vitamin C. Pauling was also a significant public intellectual, especially as an opponent of nuclear testing in the 1950s, when he published *No More War!* (1958). In 1962 he received the Nobel Peace Prize.

FURTHER READING

John W. Servos, *Physical Chemistry from Ostwald to Pauling: the Making of a Science in America* (Princeton: Princeton University Press, 1990).

Peabody, Elizabeth (b. Billerica, Mass., May 16, 1804; d. Jamaica Plain, Mass., Jan. 3, 1894). Writer and educator. Associated with Emerson's Transcendental Club, Bronson Alcott's Temple School (which she described in *Record of a School*, 1835), and Brook Farm, Peabody ran a Boston bookshop and printing press, where the Transcendentalists' *Dial* was printed (1842–3). Turning to education, she wrote several textbooks, including *Chronological History of the United States* (1856), edited the *Kindergarten Messenger* (1873–5), and promoted Indian education and the kindergarten movement. Religious feeling grows, she explained, through personal interactions and the influence of one spirit upon another. The model for all religion, therefore, is the relationship between mother and child. A child's pure nature is a more reliable guide to religious truth than adults' flawed readings of Scripture. Teachers should therefore try to permit the untrammeled unfolding of a child's relationship to Spirit.

See also TRANSCENDENTALISM.

FURTHER READING

Ruth M. Baylor, *Elizabeth Palmer Peabody: Kindergarten Pioneer* (Philadelphia: University of Pennsylvania Press, 1965).

Peirce, Charles Sanders (b. Cambridge, Mass., Sept. 10, 1839; d. near Milford, Pa., Apr. 19, 1914). Arguably the greatest thinker in American history, Peirce was and remains undervalued. This is indicated by the fact that this volume devotes only a comparatively brief essay to him. Underestimation of Peirce is due in part to his difficult personality and lack of academic success, which in his lifetime denied him the audience he deserved. Also, Peirce was a polymath whose writings in chemistry, geodesy, mathematics, logic, semiotic, and metaphysics have lain scattered in dozens of journals. This situation is being rectified by an ongoing, 30-volume edition of Peirce's *Writings* published by Indiana University Press.

Although Peirce was employed as a working scientist by the U.S. Coast and Geodetic Survey for much of his adult life, his first love was philosophy, a field in which he failed to earn a living except for five years (1879–84) at Johns Hopkins. This appointment ended after the university's trustees learned that Peirce had shared accommodations with his second wife prior to their marriage in 1883. Subsequently, in 1891, Peirce was pressured into resigning his position with the Coast Survey and ended his days living on the charity of relatives and friends such as WILLIAM JAMES.

Thanks to James's generosity in crediting Peirce with having founded PRAGMATISM, that achievement remains Peirce's best-known contribution to philosophy. Yet Peirce's pragmatism is poorly understood, partly because it has passed down the generations through the filter of James. Peirce's notion that the meaning of an idea could only be made clear by considering the consequences of acting on it was interpreted by James's critics as indicating that the test of truth lies in whether our thoughts, once acted upon, help us to achieve our desires. This RELATIVISM was erroneous in its subjectivism, according to Peirce, who late in life called his philosophy "pragmaticism" to indicate the difference between himself and James, his belief that knowledge is *both* objective and relative. (*See also* OBJECTIVITY.)

Peirce's pragmatism was based in his rejection of Cartesian dualism. Descartes, observing that physical events seem to occur in space and thoughts do not, posited two substances—matter and mind. The essence of matter was spatial extension and the essence of mind was thought, which left modern philosophy with the conundrum of how unextended mind and dumb matter are brought into relation with each other. Whereas many modern idealisms and materialisms are attempts to resolve this issue by explaining one of Descartes's substances in terms of the other, Peirce's more thorough monism rejected Cartesianism altogether.

According to Peirce the phenomenal difference between thoughts and physical events is due to two different kinds of *relations* within one substance. Never questioning the externality of objects, which he categorized as *firsts*, Peirce therefore opposed Berkeleyan idealism. He categorized physical events as *seconds*, the dyadic relation that occurs when one object strikes another. Yet Peirce did not believe that the phenomenal world can be explained solely in terms of physical events, and he was therefore no traditional materialist. In addition to physical events there is another kind of relation in which one object is represented to a second by a *third*, a sign. Thirdness or thought requires dyadic relations between firsts, so thought is as external as any physical event. But thought is distinguished from strictly physical events by its being also a representational event, which is why it seems to occupy no space. (*See also* SEMIOTICS.)

By accounting for thirdness or thought as an external event as objectively real as any strictly physical event, Peirce's system does not require the postulation of a preconstituted, subjective self or soul to contain and know thought after the fashion of Cartesianism. Rather, the self is created by thought. There is nothing ethereal in such an assertion, for it is the body's processes that represent the self in thought. An infant, inferring no self, infers no distinction between its body and that of a hot stove. The child may therefore touch the stove. From the resulting pain the child realizes that its body is discrete and constitutes itself.

Just as it is no denial of the human body to hold that the self is created in thought, so too it is no denial of objective truth to hold that our knowledge of any material body is relative to thought. Peirce's relativism ran no risk of subjectivism. The question of truth cannot be settled simply by seeing whether thoughts lead to actions that satisfy desires but requires ascertaining whether signs accurately represent their objects. Yet the fact that there is objective truth does not mean that objects are independent of thought. Objects which are known in thought doubtless exist apart from thought, but it is a very different existence than they have in thought. Apart

from thought, objects have a brute, meaningless existence. It is fruitless to seek the thing in itself that exists apart from thought, for although thought does not create objects, it gives them the meaning and qualities we rightly know them to have.

The complexity and power of Peirce's philosophy is almost impossible to summarize in a small space, which is one reason why, despite a growing interest in Peirce, he will likely long remain America's least understood and most undervalued major philosopher. Although there is some affinity between Peirce and the semiotic that now flourishes in departments of language and literature, his realistic emphasis on the constraining logicality of all relations, both physical and semiotic, makes him a natural enemy of the linguistic imperialism that attracts many contemporary critics to semiotic. Similarly, the increasing antipositivism of the social sciences does not imply receptivity to Peirce, because of the influence of antifoundationalists who prefer the ad hoc pragmatism of James and JOHN DEWEY to categorical metaphysics of any sort. Peirce's philosophy continues to face the challenge of an unsympathetic intellectual environment which is admirably suited to test its author's confidence that thought is a force as objectively real as any other.

JAMES HOOPES

FURTHER READING

Karl-Otto Apel, *Charles S. Peirce: From Pragmatism to Pragmaticism* (Amherst: University of Massachusetts Press, 1981).

Vincent Colapietro, *Peirce's Approach to the Self: a Semiotic Perspective* (Albany: State University of New York Press, 1989).

Max Fisch, *Peirce, Semeiotic, and Pragmatism: Essays*, ed. Kenneth Laine Ketner and Christian J. W. Kloesel (Bloomington: Indiana University Press, 1986).

Christopher Hookway, *Peirce* (London: Routledge and Kegan Paul, 1985).

Charles S. Peirce, *Collected Papers of Charles S. Peirce*, ed. Charles Hartshorne and Paul Weiss (vols. 1–6) and Arthur Burks (vols. 7–8), 8 vols. (Cambridge: Harvard University Press, 1931–58).

——, *Writings of Charles S. Peirce: a Chronological Edition*, ed. Christian J. W. Kloesel (Bloomington: Indiana University Press, 1982–).

——, *Peirce on Signs: Writings on Semiotic by Charles Sanders Peirce*, ed. James Hoopes (Chapel Hill: University of North Carolina Press, 1991).

David Savan, *An Introduction to C. S. Peirce's Semiotics* (Toronto: Toronto Semiotic Circle, 1988).

Phillips, Wendell (b. Boston, Mass., Nov. 29, 1811; d. Boston, Mass., Feb. 2, 1884). The St. Louis *Dispatch*, a newspaper by no means friendly to Wendell Phillips, described him in 1867 as "the man who as a private citizen, has exercised a greater influence upon the destinies of this country than any public man or men of his age" (quoted by Bartlett, p. 307). Phillips was one of the half dozen or so most prominent American abolitionists. As a theoretician and writer for the ANTISLAVERY cause, he was unequaled among members of the abolitionist circle that remained identified with WILLIAM LLOYD GARRISON from the mid-1830s through the coming of the Civil War. He was generally regarded as the most effective and distinguished antislavery orator, with the possible exception of Frederick Douglass. Phillips virtually defined the role of professional agitator in America; no other individual moved so actively and prominently among a host of nineteenth-century reform movements, from the antislavery crusade to women's rights, prohibition, penal reform, and the eight-hour workday for laboring people, to cite but a few.

Phillips was born to a Boston family of wealth and social distinction. The Reverend George Phillips had emigrated from England to Massachusetts in 1630 with John Winthrop; since then the Phillips family had played a leading role in the cultural life of New England. John Phillips, Wendell's father, was a Harvard graduate, a successful lawyer, and the holder of several Massachusetts political offices, including the first Boston mayoralty, in which capacity he gave expression to his staunchly conservative and Calvinist, Federalist Party leanings.

Through his own graduation from Harvard and his early years as an attorney, there was nothing to suggest that Wendell's career would deviate from the straight and narrow. But in late 1835 he met his future wife, Ann Greene, whose intense antislavery convictions attuned the privileged Phillips to a whole new world of abolitionist "cranks" and "fanatics." Ann's account of the Boston mob that nearly killed William Lloyd Garrison in October 1835 helped initiate the process by which Phillips's initial ignorance of, or indifference to, the slavery issue, would evolve first into passive sympathy for the slaves and their abolitionist defenders, and finally into active commitment to the antislavery cause. The November 1837 mob killing of the abolitionist newspaper editor Elijah Lovejoy in Alton, Illinois, assured and finalized Phillips's abandonment of the more conventional life his family had envisioned for him. The enthusiastic response to his eloquent speech in defense of Lovejoy's civil liberties, delivered at a Massachusetts meeting, convinced Phillips that he had found his true calling: using his reasoning and elocutionary powers to agitate against and reform a corrupt public opinion.

Phillips, though, exercised selectivity when defending the sanctity of the federal Constitution. Indeed, he would later have no truck with those abolitionists who denied that the Constitution contained provisions violating the natural rights of slaves; after the abolitionist schism of 1840, Phillips was prominent in fleshing out the Garrisonian position that the Constitution was a proslavery document and that for this reason alone no true enemy of slavery, the abolitionist Liberty Party notwithstanding, could vote or take office under it.

For all his gratitude and loyalty to Garrison as an antislavery prophet, and despite his subscription to disunionism and other specific positions that distinguished the Garrisonian "Boston clique" of abolitionists up to the Civil War, Phillips's thinking always deviated in significant respects from Garrison's. He never shared his leader's intoxication with the moral and ethereal forces of the human will that, working outside and against repressive institutions, would eradicate chattel slavery and otherwise regenerate society. While noting in a letter to George Thompson in 1839 that "our enterprise is eminently a religious one," Phillips in particular welcomed developments, such as the movement to grow cotton in India, which might render southern slave labor "valueless," and thereby have a real, practical impact upon the slaveholders and others of "that large class of men with whom dollars are always a weightier consideration than duties" (in *Speeches, Lectures, and Letters*, Second Series, pp. 8, 11). Nor did Phillips ever dabble in the religiously grounded pacifism and perfectionism embraced by Garrison, not merely because he regarded these as extraneous to the thrust of the antislavery enterprise, but because he always retained too much of the lawyerly realpolitik, as well as a sense of man's moral limitations derived from CALVINISM, to countenance them.

As James Brewer Stewart and other historians have observed, Phillips was less intent than Garrison and some other abolitionist jeremiahs on morally redeeming souls for Christ; he was more generally concerned with exposing slavery's nationwide dominance as a political, social, and economic institution, including, most notably, the subservience it induced in northern and even foreign political leaders. Richard Hofstadter's reminder is as relevant now as it was over 40 years ago: that Phillips consciously conceived his role as agitator to be vitally different from that of the so-called responsible politician. His primary intention was never to be moderate, patient, or even literally accurate in his argumentation, but rather to prod, educate, and elevate public opinion.

The differences between Phillips and Garrison grew more pronounced in the late 1850s and especially following the Emancipation Proclamation; from this point it became particularly evident that Phillips' self-defined role as agitator transcended his commitment to a single cause. In contrast to Garrison's growing eagerness to close up antislavery shop, Phillips led another group of abolitionists in insisting that the mission of the antislavery enterprise extended well beyond the formal extirpation of the institution. In the American Anti-Slavery Society's original "Declaration of Sentiments" (1833), calling for equal opportunities for American blacks, Phillips found ample rationale for maintaining the existence of the society, and for working above all to secure the political and civil rights of the freedmen.

If not quite so insistently, Phillips also favored the governmental breakup of plantations and their distribution among the ex-slaves to ensure their independence from their former masters. In so aligning himself with the vanguard of radical reconstructionists, Phillips was manifesting more than vengeful hostility to the social and political order of the Old South. He was also expressing antipathy to the condition of dependent wage labor everywhere in America. By September 1871, at the Labor-Reform Convention in Worcester, Massachusetts, Phillips was offering resolutions declaring "war with the wages [and profits] system, which demoralizes alike the hirer and the hired, cheats both, and enslaves the workingman." He later added, in "The Foundation of the Labor Movement," "That's the meaning of the Labor movement—an equalization of property," and described his "ideal of a civilization" as best approximated by "a New England town of some two thousand inhabitants, with no rich man and no poor man in it" (*Speeches, Lectures, and Letters*, Second Series, pp. 152, 163).

Phillips's pronounced postbellum disaffection with northern economic and labor conditions, a disaffection that induced, among other things, his campaign for the Massachusetts governorship on the Labor Reform Party ticket, was conspicuously absent from his consciousness for most of the antebellum period, although a related antagonism to the influence wielded by northern moneyed power did increasingly manifest itself during the 1850s. Phillips's postbellum alternative idea of the good society, in which every individual combined the identities of capitalist and laborer as well as enjoying comparable wealth, defined a "preindustrial" reform mentality common to the mid-nineteenth century and was not in itself incompatible with his own antebellum thinking. What had changed most of all was Phillips's declining confidence that the northern social order yielded the opportunities to generate equalizing conditions for

industrious and temperate wage-earners. With the struggle for the slave's self-ownership won in 1865, the criticisms of labor conditions in the free states shedded much of their adversarial, threatening character for Phillips. He was free to adopt them as his own, and to focus upon northern capitalist interests as somehow analogous to the defunct Slave Power. Many of the positions Phillips embraced in the 1860s and 1870s—from his dismissal of strikes as ineffective and undignified labor weapons, through his support for greenbackism, to his overall faith in the power of the ballot to effect or reverse fundamental structural changes—were lacking in economic realism and prescience; but there remains much that is admirable in Phillips's virtually compulsive need, after the death of slavery, to continue the fight against social injustice.

JONATHAN A. GLICKSTEIN

FURTHER READING
Irving H. Bartlett, *Wendell Phillips: Brahmin Radical* (Boston: Beacon, 1961).
Thomas Bender, ed., *The Antislavery Debate: Capitalism and Abolitionism as a Problem in Historical Interpretation* (Berkeley: University of California Press, 1992).
Richard Hofstadter, "Wendell Phillips: the Patrician as Agitator," in *The American Political Tradition* (New York: Vintage, 1948).
The Liberator (Boston), 1831–65.
Robert. D. Marcus, "Wendell Phillips and American Institutions," *Journal of American History* 46 (June 1969): 41–58.
Wendell Phillips, *Speeches, Lectures, and Letters*, First Series (Boston: Lee and Shepard, 1863); Second Series (Boston: Lee and Shepard, 1891).
James Brewer Stewart, *Wendell Phillips: Liberty's Hero* (Baton Rouge: Louisiana State University Press, 1986).

philosophy The development of philosophy in America can be understood as a series of negotiations between the claims of religion and the claims of science. The debates among seventeenth-century New England theologians over PURITANISM, a British American variant of CALVINISM, filtered into American culture through many channels but into systematic thought largely through the work of America's first major philosopher, JONATHAN EDWARDS. The American version of ENLIGHTENMENT was distinctive because of the continuing preoccupation with questions of religion, but an increasing distrust of religious dogmatism, a growing appreciation of the capacity of human reason, and increased interest in science also manifested themselves in eighteenth-century American philosophy.

The characteristic American attempt to mediate between faith and reason lies behind the eighteenth- and nineteenth-century enthusiasm for SCOTTISH

COMMON SENSE REALISM, which claimed to ground religious and ethical truths in empirical scientific inquiry. Another such compromise was offered by UNITARIANISM, significant historically both in its own right and because of the opponents it generated. Preeminent among them were the advocates of TRANSCENDENTALISM, one of the several varieties of ROMANTICISM that gave nineteenth-century Americans alternative strategies for accommodating science and faith.

By the end of the nineteenth century, philosophers working in the tradition of common sense realism found themselves challenged from two directions. Champions of various kinds of POSITIVISM advocated science as the successor to faith, and proponents of idealism such as JOSIAH ROYCE offered a return to traditional ideals of loyalty and community, but grounded them in metaphysics rather than in revealed religion.

PRAGMATISM emerged as an effort to resolve the conflicts between positivists and idealists. It suggested the testing of propositions in practice as the means of ending otherwise interminable philosophical disputes. Rather than quieting raging controversies, however, the competing philosophies of CHARLES S. PEIRCE, WILLIAM JAMES, and JOHN DEWEY provoked widely discordant responses. Thanks also to the infusion of new ideas from British and Continental philosophy, American philosophers developed versions of NATURALISM, critical realism, logical positivism, and the style of linguistic analysis that has dominated professional American philosophy since the 1940s and found its most visible champion in W. V. O. QUINE. By placing questions of value outside the realm of philosophical inquiry, analytic philosophers, even when they thought of themselves as pragmatists, as Quine did, transformed American philosophy into a narrowly focused, technical enterprise. Analytic philosophy, like BEHAVIORISM in psychology and the social sciences, ignored ethics, politics, and other questions of value and meaning traditionally addressed in the humanities.

Much recent work in American philosophy has built on linguistic analysis but has expanded its focus. Ordinary-language philosophers followed the later Wittgenstein in rejecting the attempt to pattern philosophy after empirical science. STANLEY CAVELL urged philosophers to return to the unscientific, eruptive insights of imaginative writers and thinkers such as RALPH WALDO EMERSON and HENRY DAVID THOREAU. JOHN RAWLS showed that analytic philosophers could still coherently address questions of ethics and politics. THOMAS H. KUHN challenged the presumed stability of scientific knowledge, thereby rocking the foundations of a philosophical enterprise that took the natural sciences as its model. RICHARD RORTY advised his colleagues to discard science as a paradigm for disclosing philosophical truths and recommended that they look instead to novels and poetry for models of truth-telling. ALASDAIR MACINTYRE challenged philosophers frustrated by the limits of linguistic analysis to appreciate and undertake the discipline of sophisticated traditions of inquiry rooted in Aristotle and Aquinas. MacIntyre's work, along with that of many other twentieth-century American thinkers from William James and John Dewey to REINHOLD NIEBUHR and PAUL TILLICH, demonstrates that the seventeenth-century American fascination with religion has not disappeared. Some postmodernists such as Rorty do confidently predict the eventual disappearance of religious faith along with all forms of superstition. But other American philosophers, including some working in the tradition of pragmatism such as John E. Smith and Cornel West, persist in the now centuries-old attempt to join empirical inquiry and religious faith.

JAMES T. KLOPPENBERG

FURTHER READING
Elizabeth Flower and Murray Murphey, *A History of Philosophy in America*, 2 vols. (New York: Putnam, 1977).
John R. Rajchman and Cornel West, eds., *Post-Analytic Philosophy* (New York: Columbia University Press, 1985).

piety At least three types of piety have marked American religion, two characterized by devotion to God, and a third by devotion to ritual. Historians of American religion have often granted preeminence to the tradition of piety represented by the New England Puritans and their heirs, but this tradition is intertwined with a Continental pietism that has been at least as influential as, and in some respects at odds with, Anglo Puritan piety. The third type, devotion to ritual, can be found in a variety of religions practiced in America, including Roman CATHOLICISM, JUDAISM, Hinduism, and Islam. In many instances, this devotion to ritual is merged with forms of devotion to God that are related to pietism.

A defining work in the Puritan tradition is Lewis Bayly's *The Practice of Piety*, which was first published in London about 1611, and reached 60 editions by 1735, including the 1665 translation by JOHN ELIOT into the Massachusetts Indian language. This manual of religious instruction emphasized the importance of transcending worldly pleasures in order to devote oneself every waking moment to the practice of piety, which Bayly defined as loving God. Loving God was a moral activity that fostered the conversion of others and the regeneration of society, as well as that individual "Agility, whereby our bodies shall be able to ascend [to] heavenly life after death."

Especially as it developed in America, the piety of PURITANISM was often associated with female imagery; Puritan ministers encouraged everyone to become yearning brides and devoted wives in their relationship to God. This female imagery reinforced women's submissiveness to men even as it subverted that submissiveness by establishing women's reputations for piety and intimacy with God.

In the late seventeenth and early eighteenth centuries, the Puritan exercise of piety was altered and revitalized by a more mystical Continental tradition associated with the Reformed Protestants Philipp Jakob Spener and August Hermann Francke, which had roots in the medieval spiritual practices of Thomas à Kempis and Bernard of Clairvaux. This pietism also drew on female imagery and appealed to many women, but was more emotionally expressive than Puritan piety, and less oriented toward moral activism. In America and in Europe it exerted much influence on both the Dutch Reformed church and the Lutheran Church. It also contributed to the emergence of Methodism, which has been described as a wedding of Puritan piety and Continental pietism; John Wesley's meeting with a company of Moravian pietists while crossing the Atlantic in 1735, and his subsequent visit with their leaders in Georgia, led to his religious experience at Aldersgate in 1738, which led in turn to that blend of emotional technique and moral activism that came to be known as Methodism.

The GREAT AWAKENING in the American colonies during the early 1740s was part of the larger movement of pietistical enthusiasm sweeping the Western world in the seventeenth and early eighteenth centuries. It was also a defining event in the cultural history of America: grace became more accessible than before by being defined not as God's unmerited gift but as a cultivated state of emotional receptivity. This receptivity was the central doctrine broadcast through a rapidly expanding network of newspapers and itinerant preachers. The fervor for self-expression characteristic of the Great Awakening contributed to the spirit of independence in 1776 and typifies the hospitality to religious enthusiasm that has marked American cultural life to the present day.

Perhaps the most careful critique of pietism is still the 1746 work of JONATHAN EDWARDS, *A Treatise Concerning Religious Affections*. Edwards was a prominent supporter of the Great Awakening, but he was troubled by the emotionalism of the Awakening and sought to understand its relationship to piety. He argued that piety was always characterized by heartfelt emotion, but that heartfelt emotion was not in itself a certain sign of piety. For Edwards, piety was essentially a matter of having the will to love God. He argued that the will incorporated both feeling and cognition, and that the will to love God was a heartfelt and fully rational transcendence of self-love.

Ironically, Edwards's concept of piety has sometimes been interpreted as being in opposition to his disciples' emphasis on moral activity. In *Piety versus Moralism* (1932), Joseph Haroutunian argued that piety in America declined after Edwards because his followers reduced devotion to God to an abstract moral obligation. Haroutunian's plea for a return to the experience of piety—repentance and submission to a sovereign God—formed part of the wave of existential idealism that became popular in America after World War I. This idealism had roots in German Romanticism, which in turn had important antecedents in the Continental pietism of the seventeenth and early eighteenth centuries. But Haroutunian's existentialism made him slight the rationalist and moralistic components of Edwards's own balancing act, components that tied him closely to his disciples and to the Puritan tradition.

Continental pietism has mingled with Puritan piety throughout American religious history, and has also impinged upon those religious traditions in which devotion to ritual is central. Both Hasidism and Jansenism emerged as part of the trend toward pietistical enthusiasm in Europe during the seventeenth century, and heirs of these movements have contributed to Judaism and Catholicism in the United States. For American Jews, Hasidism has stood as a conservative force against modernism, preserving worship of God's mystical presence through obedience to ritual law. For American Catholics, the Church's encouragement of ritual devotion to the Blessed Sacrament of the eucharist has played a key role in its centralization of patriarchal authority and its stand against modernism and liberalism.

Although devotion to the eucharist has not led to women's leadership in the hierarchy of the Catholic Church, it has encouraged them to become mainstays of religious devotion. In contrast, ritualized piety in Orthodox Judaism and in Islam is heavily dominated by men, and women are excluded entirely from some of the central practices of religious life. In recent years, feminist Catholics have challenged the conservative attitudes of their church, and Reformed, Conservative, and Reconstructionist synagogues and yeshivas have set out to reverse the traditional exclusion of women in Jewish ritual.

Devotion to ritual in Islam has long been associated with "bhakti," or devotion to God, and bhakti has been a point of commonality between Muslims and people of other faiths; for example, the presence of Islam in India since the seventh century contributed to the proliferation of bhakti movements in Hinduism. Bhakti also has roots in some of the mystical traditions of ancient Hinduism, which influenced the development of neoplatonism in the ancient Mediterranean world. Neoplatonism in turn contributed to the development of Islam and, later, to the emergence of pietism in Europe. In America today, similarities between Hinduism, Islam, and Christianity are emphasized by teachers of religious studies, who point to common experiences of devotion to God in these religions. Many of these teachers rely on the idea that RELIGION is essentially the experience of the holy, an idea that owes much to the existential interpretations of Platonic philosophy nurtured by Continental pietism. Piety in America has widely dispersed roots and manifestations, but they are often historically intertwined and, as they evolve, mutually reinforcing.

AMANDA PORTERFIELD

FURTHER READING

John Corrigan, *The Prism of Piety: Catholic Congregational Clergy at the Beginning of the Enlightenment* (New York: Oxford University Press, 1991).
Klaus K. Klostermaier, *A Survey of Hinduism* (Albany: State University of New York, 1989).
Rudolph Otto, *The Idea of the Holy* (New York: Oxford University Press, 1958).
Amanda Porterfield, *Female Piety in Puritan New England: the Emergence of Religious Humanism* (New York: Oxford University Press, 1992).
Rodney Stark and Charles Y. Glock, *American Piety: the Nature of Religious Commitment* (Berkeley: University of California Press, 1968).
F. Ernest Stoeffler, ed., *Continental Pietism and Early American Christianity* (Grand Rapids: William B. Eerdmans, 1976).

Pinchot, Gifford (b. Simsbury, Conn., Aug. 11, 1865; d. New York, N.Y., Oct. 4, 1946). Conservationist and government official. A member of the National Forest Commission beginning in 1896, Pinchot believed that natural resources are best preserved if federally controlled private development in wilderness areas makes them economically productive. As head of the Division of Forestry (later Forestry Service) from 1898 to 1910, he supported the establishment of vast national forests available for scientific management and regulated commercial use. Favoring large companies over smaller operations—which could not afford selective cuttings or replantings—he forged an intimate working relationship with the few corporations selected to operate on federal lands. He published such works as *A Primer of Forestry* (1899) and *The Fight for Conservation* (1909). *See also* ENVIRONMENTALISM.

FURTHER READING
M. Nelson McGeary, *Gifford Pinchot: Forester-Politician* (Princeton: Princeton University Press, 1960).

Plath, Sylvia (b. Boston, Mass., Oct. 27, 1932; d. London, England, Feb. 11, 1963). Poet. Plath's poems, collected in *The Colossus* (1960), *Ariel* (1968), and *Crossing the Water* (1971), vividly express the conflict Plath felt between her poetic vocation and the demands of FEMININITY. Often referring to splits within the self, her poems explore themes of MOTHERHOOD, DOMESTICITY, the flux of life, and the static perfection of death. Plath's autobiographical novel *The Bell Jar* (1963) describes a superachieving college student descending into madness under expectations of feminine beauty, purity, and conformity. Both show women's distorted socialization turning inward as self-destructiveness.

FURTHER READING
Jacqueline Rose, *The Haunting of Sylvia Plath* (Cambridge: Harvard University Press, 1992).

play At once utterly simple and conceptually elusive, play is an animal and human activity that touches on a host of fundamental intellectual issues. Simply to define "play" has proven inordinately difficult. Dutch historian Johan Huizinga's seminal *Homo Ludens* defined it as

a voluntary activity or occupation executed within certain fixed limits of time and place, according to rules freely accepted but absolutely binding, having its aim in itself and accompanied by a feeling of tension, joy and the consciousness that it is "different" from "ordinary life."

Subsequent writers have wrangled endlessly over various elements in Huizinga's definition, while largely accepting his basic argument about play: that a play element lies at the foundations of law, war, science, poetry, myth, philosophy, and art. Anthropologists have studied play not only as behavior common to all cultures and many animal species, but also as a representation of the specific values most important to particular cultures. Psychologists have considered children's play as a necessary stage in biological development and as a rehearsal for negotiating the complex interactions of adult life. Sociologists have explored the uses of play as both resistance to control and as replication of society's structures of dominance. Literary and art critics have identified play with the impulse behind aesthetic creation. Philosophers have explored play as the realm of ontological or existential freedom. "Play" ultimately can stand for everything that is not Work, not necessity, not rational, not structured.

The most fruitful way to think about play is to focus on the cultural history of its Representation, an approach that has increasingly characterized studies of play and of many other topics across the humanities and social sciences. The serious interest in play in the United States is little more than a century old; play was not widely "discovered" until after the Civil War. Before that Americans had largely taken play for granted. Insofar as they considered it noteworthy, they simply worried about its abuses: excessive time spent playing was a vice to be corrected, a flaw on the order of gluttony.

The widespread "discovery" of play in the second half of the nineteenth century resulted in part from a sense of loss caused by Industrialism. The debilitating conditions of factory work and urban life led social and health reformers to prescribe play as an antidote. In one sense the separation of work and play into distinct days and hours subordinated play to work, by conceiving of play as a restorative preparation for more efficient work. Yet in another sense the separation of leisure from labor allowed for an eventual reversal of the hierarchy, as the belief grew in the twentieth century that play is the true source of human fulfillment, work merely a means to that end.

The intellectual history of play in the United States is thus inseparable from the history of work, and from a history of the values Americans have invested in both work and play. Over the past century play has increasingly usurped work's place in popular American ideas about happiness and fulfillment. That usurpation has not progressed steadily, however, but in fits and starts. The major thinkers who have contributed to the public discourse about work and play have not so much directed this development as sought to catch up with social practice. A crucial enabling factor in the elevation of play during the nineteenth century was a transformation of Protestant orthodoxy. Although Puritanism was not nearly as antagonistic toward play as we usually think, it remains true that colonial Protestantism was unambiguously committed to the values of work. While Liberal protestantism is often receptive to play, conservatives tend to fear it as idleness or temptation, and theological conservatism remained dominant in American popular religion until the middle of the nineteenth century. One measure of the liberalization of the Protestant mainstream, in fact, can be found in the at first grudging, then gradually more enthusiastic

embrace of play by orthodox ministers. Perhaps the most important figure in this reversal was Horace Bushnell, a Congregationalist minister in Connecticut, whose influential ideas about "Christian nurture" gave unprecedented allowance for children's play. Bushnell's 1848 address, "Work and Play," is thus a landmark text in the cultural history of play.

The first systematic analysts of play in the United States were the leaders of the "playground movement" during the Progressive Era, a group of social reformers such as Henry Curtis, Joseph Lee, and Luther Gulick, who sought to organize children's play for both personal development and social control. They followed the pioneering American psychologist G. Stanley Hall, whose *Adolescence* (1904) argued that the child's development "recapitulated" the history of the race: the stages of a child's development corresponded to stages in human development from primitive to civilized states. Organized play, therefore, was granted an important place in children's lives, for its lessons in controlling instinctual behavior and its nurturing of an embryonic sense of morality. Recent critics of the playground movement have noted that the very idea of organizing play is problematic, since it violates play's essential freedom and spontaneity. Efforts to organize play—in the playground movement, in intercollegiate and interscholastic sports, in physical education programs— have been motivated in part by a social need to control impulses that are inherently spontaneous, irrational, anarchic—in other words, fundamentally threatening to stable social structures. Contemporary American culture is marked by a strong tendency toward deregulation, in play as in other social activities, yet institutional resistance inevitably persists.

Alongside the history of what we might call the "official" public discourse on play, we must place an alternative history: a cultural history of play as the ideological emblem of middle-class desire and countercultural rebellion. In the United States, historically committed to work and Progress, play has expressed perennial resistance to the official culture. The myth of the Old South, which emerged during the sectional rivalry of the antebellum period, then flourished spectacularly in the decades following the Civil war, saw life in the South as gracious leisure and innocent play, in contrast to the demoralizing life of dollar-drunk Yankees in the urban North. In this southern myth, developed by plantation romancers from John Pendleton Kennedy to Margaret Mitchell, and by southern polemicists from antebellum secessionists to the Southern agrarians of the 1930s, play has been invested with a powerful ideological critique of industrial capitalism.

Similarly, the three major countercultural movements of the nineteenth and twentieth centuries— TRANSCENDENTALISM in the 1830s and 1840s, Greenwich Village bohemianism before World War I, and the youth movement beginning with the BEAT GENERATION and flourishing in the 1960s—were deeply imbued with utopian ideas about play. American thinking about play has always been strongly influenced by European intellectuals: by Schiller, Marx, Fourier, Nietzsche, Freud, Ortega, Heidegger, Sartre, and Derrida as well as Huizinga. But major American writers and thinkers about play have also contributed importantly to each of the episodes of countercultural convulsion. Reacting against both the Puritan tradition and the nation's frantic pursuit of material wealth, RALPH WALDO EMERSON and HENRY DAVID THOREAU used the rhetorical figure of the child or animal at play to express an alternative kind of holiness and way of living in the material world. According to the American Transcendentalists, "salvation" lay not in earnest striving after virtue but in spontaneously expressing the divine within. In their journals Emerson envisioned life as a "May game" (June 6, 1839), and Thoreau as energetic "play and frolic in this bower God has built us" (December 29, 1841). Thoreau's Walden (1854) in particular can be viewed as a long meditation on the possibility of transcending the work/play dualism created by modern industrialism, of living life as a kind of earnest play.

Emerson and Thoreau interpreted play in essentially spiritual terms; for the Greenwich Village bohemians play was aesthetic and erotic. Reacting to what they viewed as a dead civilization, cursed by "puritanism," young intellectuals such as FLOYD DELL, VAN WYCK BROOKS, and Harold Stearns called for a spirit of play in the arts and in uninhibited sexual freedom. Greenwich Village bohemians wrote of sex as "play," of women as "playfellows," of Greenwich Village as a "happy playground." For a new generation of countercultural rebels in the 1950s and 1960s, "play" continued to suggest creativity and sexual freedom, but the spiritual dimension of play was also resurrected, most conspicuously in a "theology of play" in such books as The Feast of Fools by Harvey Cox, In Praise of Play by Robert Neale, Gods and Games by David Miller, and To a Dancing God by Sam Keen. And the political possibilities in play were addressed for the first time by leaders within the NEW LEFT such as Abbie Hoffman and Jerry Rubin, who urged "play power" as a strategy of resistance both to American militarism and oppression, and to the oppressive seriousness of the Old Left. The writings of such 1960s gurus as PAUL GOODMAN, Timothy Leary, and particularly Norman O. Brown (Life

Against Death) and HERBERT MARCUSE (Eros and Civilization) in different ways envisioned utopia as a state of play.

The concept of play as the expression of utopian desire has generally been held by relatively privileged white male writers. Nineteenth-century progressive women writers such as HARRIET BEECHER STOWE and LOUISA MAY ALCOTT explicitly rejected the relegation of women to a world of leisure and social play, advocating instead their right to fulfillment through work. And for minorities and the working class during this period, the need for basic economic security tended to repress longings for play. The utopian vision of play in America since the time of Emerson and Thoreau has belonged to the materially satisfied but spiritually unfulfilled. Each of the countercultural movements "failed" in the sense that it did not transform American life, yet each ironically succeeded in unexpected ways, as the radical challenge was appropriated by the mainstream culture. The Transcendentalists' celebration of children's play as an emblem of innate perfection was absorbed into late nineteenth-century Protestant and secular liberalism, the aesthetic and sexual revolution of Greenwich Village bohemians into 1920s consumerism and hedonism, the spirit of the youth movement in the 1960s into the human potential movement of the 1970s and 80s. The current preoccupation with play, not just in the various disciplines of the humanities and the social sciences (where play has become a fundamental feature of POSTMODERNISM), but also in the popular writing on entrepreneurship (the entrepreneur as a brilliant "gamesman") and on the human potential movement (play as joyful, and productive, self-expression), is the consequence of a long transformation of fundamental American ideas about human worth and the possibilities of fulfillment. As play has increasingly usurped work's place in American life and thought, the need to move beyond dualistic ideas about work or play, and toward a dialectical synthesis of work and play, has engaged our best thinkers on the subject. A society in which work is playful and play is serious has emerged as the new ideal.

MICHAEL ORIARD

FURTHER READING

Norman O. Brown, Life Against Death: the Psychoanalytical Meaning of History (Middletown, Conn.: Wesleyan University Press, 1959).

Dominick Cavallo, Muscles and Morals: Organized Playgrounds and Urban Reform, 1880–1920 (Philadelphia: Temple University Press, 1981).

James S. Hans, The Play of the World (Amherst: University of Massachusetts Press, 1981).

Johan Huizinga, Homo Ludens: a Study of the Play Element in Culture (1938; Boston: Beacon, 1955).

Drew A. Hyland, *The Question of Play* (Lanham, Md.: University Press of America, 1984).

Herbert Marcuse, *Eros and Civilization: a Philosophical Inquiry into Freud* (Boston: Beacon, 1955).

David L. Miller, *Gods and Games: Toward a Theology of Play* (New York: World Publishing, 1970).

Michael Oriard, *Sporting with the Gods: the Rhetoric of Play and Game in American Culture* (New York: Cambridge University Press. 1991).

Podhoretz, Norman (b. Brooklyn, N.Y., Jan. 16, 1930). Writer. Initially a left-leaning critic of liberalism, Podhoretz came to view the left in the 1970s as an intellectually coercive orthodoxy. Editor of *Commentary* since 1960, he has led the neoconservative attack on the "Vietnam syndrome," which in his view undermined a strong Untied States defense. His *Making It* (1976) and *Breaking Ranks: a Political Memoir* (1979) are important contributions to the history of the NEW YORK INTELLECTUALS. A strong defender of Israel, Podhoretz is also the author of such works as *The Present Danger: Do We Have the Will to Reverse the Decline in American Power?* (1980) and *Why We Were in Vietnam* (1982).

See also NEOCONSERVATISM.

FURTHER READING

Alexander Bloom, *Prodigal Sons: the New York Intellectuals and Their World* (New York: Oxford University Press, 1986).

Poe, Edgar Allan (b. Boston, Mass., Jan. 19, 1809; d. Baltimore, Md., Oct. 7, 1849). The significance of Edgar Allan Poe as a thinker lies in his talent for mocking, with a vexing mixture of disdain and approval, other writers' systems of thought. Constructing an aura of massive erudition in his fiction and critical prose, Poe draws on the sundry intellectual traditions of British empiricism, German idealism, and American TRANSCENDENTALISM to explore various puzzles of thought. Even from beyond the grave Poe, embraced in recent years as a key precursor to French poststructuralism, seems able to mock our current philosophical interests. Those critics who see Poe as a profound thinker on a par with Leibniz, Locke, or Lacan would do well to consider the improvised, overheated, often farcical rhetorical contexts for his philosophizing. Those readers who would dismiss him simply as a bogus name-dropper, the most pretentious author in all of American letters (which he very well might be), would do well to consider how Poe's philosophical posturing manages over and over again to raise crucial questions that continue to haunt us today: the limits of method and rationality, the bonds between cognition and identity, the confused relation of mind to BODY, the secret links between writing and death.

Any account of Poe's thinking must begin with Poe's life, sad to mythic proportions. Born to itinerant actors in 1809, he was orphaned by the age of three, expelled from the University of Virginia for gambling debts, and discharged from West Point. By his early twenties he had broken permanently with his wealthy foster father John Allan and married his 13-year old cousin Virginia. Then he bounced up and down the East Coast—Baltimore, Richmond, Philadelphia, and New York—working as an editor for a succession of literary magazines, writing book reviews, stories, and poems, drinking heavily at times, and picking quarrels with famous authors (accusing some of plagiarism). He lived his life for the most part in abject poverty. Four years after achieving a minor sensation in New York with his poem " The Raven," he showed up in Baltimore wandering in a feverish stupor. A few days later he was dead at the age of 40, to be notoriously reviled as an erratic drunkard by his literary executor Rufus Griswold, and quickly thereafter championed by Charles Baudelaire in France as a melancholy and misunderstood visionary genius.

The mythologizing of Poe by Griswold and Baudelaire inaugurated a long romantic tradition of conflating the author's works with his melodramatic life. The grim facts of the life became less important than the various roles that Poe fashioned from them and invited his readers to contrive along with him: suffering Byronic hero, southern gentleman, uprooted aristocrat, savage critic, lover of ideal beauty, unappreciated artist victimized by the banalities of American democracy. Although Poe as a professional journalist failed to capitalize on these various postures he assumed for himself, he is perhaps the first American author to understand how the writer gets turned into a vulnerable commodity under the changing conditions of the modern marketplace. The writer is transformed into a public image or celebrity or mere set of gestures subject to the whims of an anonymous readership bent on sensation and amusement. Seeking to attract such an audience yet retain control of his person, Poe in his writing thus continually mystifies himself: he insists on his absolute originality, yet also pretends to demystify, to expose, these same compositional procedures and the process of thinking that underlies them.

Poe's most elaborate and ambitious attempt to define a "philosophy of composition" governing all thought is his late *Eureka: a Prose Poem* (1848), a rather strange treatise subtitled "an Essay on the Material and Spiritual Universe." One of the last attempts in

English to write a cosmology, *Eureka* shifts tone from the somber to the comical, histrionic, and portentous as it draws on a host of philosophers and scientists to trace the universe—"a plot of God," Poe calls it—back to its original unity. More secular and more immediately accessible endeavors to calculate the metaphysical can be found in Poe's tales of ratiocination, where C. Auguste Dupin, Poe's theoretician/detective par excellence, effortlessly solves sensational crimes, only to leave larger mysteries about human agency and mastery intact. Of particular note is the story "The Purloined Letter," which in recent years became the ostensible subject of an important debate about the language of the unconscious between the French poststructuralist thinkers Jacques Lacan and Jacques Derrida.

Causality also remains a mystery throughout Poe's well-known tales of gothic horror. Fantastic crimes, dark doubles, and weird occurrences are detailed with neurotic precision by paranoid first-person narrators, but central questions about motivation remain untouched and untouchable in these dramas of self-betrayal. Perhaps Poe's most philosophically interesting tale is his only completed novel, *The Narrative of Arthur Gordon Pym* (1838). A narrative of uncanny power, *Pym* has been variously read as a rousing sea adventure, a lurid parody of travel tales, an allegory about race relations in the American South, and a search for the linguistic origins of the self.

Lately critics have turned from these standard works to consider lesser-known writings of Poe: his voluminous critical prose, curious angelic colloquies, science fiction, landscape sketches, early burlesques, and obscure late hoaxes (many of which border on self-parody) that exploit his magazine readers' thirst for information. There has also been a renewed interest in his poetry, particularly in relation to the practices of women poets of his day such as Frances Osgood, whom Poe highly regarded. Like the rest of Poe's productions, these works are marked by an extraordinary but uneasy intellect—intense, theatrical, fragile, guarded, perversely self-lacerating—in desperate search of some medium in which to express itself.

JONATHAN AUERBACH

FURTHER READING

Michael Allen, *Poe and the British Magazine Tradition* (New York: Oxford University Press, 1969).

Daniel Hoffman, *Poe Poe Poe Poe Poe Poe Poe* (New York: Doubleday, 1972).

John Irwin, *American Hieroglyphics* (New Haven: Yale University Press, 1980).

John P. Muller and William J. Richardson, eds., *The Purloined Poe: Lacan, Derrida, and Psychoanalytic Reading* (Baltimore: Johns Hopkins University Press, 1988).

Edgar Allan Poe, *Poetry and Tales*, ed. Patrick F. Quinn (New York: Library of America, 1984).

——, *Essays and Reviews*, ed. G. R. Thompson (New York: Library of America, 1984).

Kenneth Silverman, *Edgar A. Poe: Mournful and Never-Ending Remembrance* (New York: HarperCollins, 1991).

political theory American political thought has always reflected the diverse cultures and conflicting aspirations that have shaped the nation. Old assumptions about America's "liberal tradition" stubbornly persist despite new evidence that discloses not only a multitude of dissenting voices outside LIBERALISM, including those of many women and members of racial and ethnic minorities, but also fundamental disagreements within liberal political thought. Beginning with the contrasts between the Reformation-based political ideas of PURITANISM and Southerners' PROSLAVERY THOUGHT, which conditioned the liberty of propertied white male citizens upon the enslavement of African Americans, such tensions have been a constant feature of American political thought. Claims for a static liberal CONSENSUS can be sustained only by refusing to confront a series of deeply contested concepts at the center of American public discourse. Americans have disagreed about the origins and the exercise of legitimate AUTHORITY, about the nature of the RIGHTS and the OBLIGATIONS attached to CITIZENSHIP, and about the proper extent of TOLERANCE in a society marked by CULTURAL PLURALISM AND MULTICULTURALISM.

Moreover, despite the confidence displayed by THOMAS JEFFERSON in the Declaration of Independence and by the countless thinkers who have echoed its phrases, the meaning of the central "truths" that Americans claim to cherish is hardly "self-evident." Some Americans have prized FREEDOM because it protects them, and their property, from government; others have conceived of freedom primarily as the prerequisite to civic VIRTUE. Some Americans have understood EQUALITY to mean only equal access to opportunity; others have rejected that narrow conception in favor of various ideals of JUSTICE that require greater equality of outcomes. American versions of CONSERVATISM, such as SOCIAL DARWINISM, and of INDIVIDUALISM, such as LIBERTARIANISM, have had their champions, as have the ideas of SOCIALISM articulated by nineteenth-century radicals and by some members of the NEW LEFT.

The fundamental principles of American government, DEMOCRACY and REPUBLICANISM, have proven equally protean. For many Americans, especially although not exclusively in the seventeenth and eighteenth centuries, democracy was a nightmare of mob rule, while republicanism was a settled prospect of legitimate popular government attained by the balancing of distinct social orders. Others have championed democracy, and called for extending it from the political to the economic and social spheres, in order to remove the constraining legacies of privilege, hierarchy, racism, and sexism—inequalities often challenged, but also acquiesced in, by many republicans.

The defining document of American public life, the CONSTITUTION, itself embodied these conflicts and ambiguities. By incorporating the BILL OF RIGHTS, and even more profoundly by allowing for its own future amendment, the Constitution encouraged Americans to treat their most fundamental political principles as provisional, thereby contributing to and legitimating continued debate about the meaning and implications of the nation's political ideals.

JAMES T. KLOPPENBERG

FURTHER READING
Edmund S. Morgan, *Inventing the People: the Rise of Popular Sovereignty in England and America* (New York: Norton, 1988).
J. R. Pole, *The Pursuit of Equality in American History*, 2nd ed. (Berkeley: University of California Press, 1993).
Daniel T. Rodgers, *Contested Truths: Keywords in American Politics since Independence* (New York: Basic Books, 1987).

Pollock, [Paul] Jackson (b. Cody, Wyo., Jan. 28, 1912; d. East Hampton, N.Y., Aug. 11, 1956). Painter. The dominant figure of ABSTRACT EXPRESSIONISM, Pollock was the archetype of the passionate bohemian. Trained by the regionalist Thomas Hart Benton, he moved on in his mature work to a seemingly random "drip" style named by critic HAROLD ROSENBERG "action painting." This style exhibited the influence of the French Surrealists, as well as Pollock's preoccupations with myth and psychoanalysis. His aggressive lifestyle and accidental death at the peak of his popularity added to his legendary status in American artistic and intellectual life.

FURTHER READING
Claude Cernuschi, *Jackson Pollock: Meaning and Significance* (New York: Icon, 1992).

Pop Primarily concerned with formulating new aesthetic approaches to the images of MASS CULTURE, Pop flourished in the art world from the late 1950s through the 1960s. Although first developed on a theoretical level by English intellectuals in the early 1950s, Pop was based in New York City. Following the pioneering work of Stuart Davis, Robert Rauschenberg, and Jasper Johns, significant Pop artists included Roy Lichtenstein, Claes Oldenburg, James Rosenquist, and, most importantly, Andy Warhol—all of whom challenged modernist attitudes about the sanctified nature of both art and artist. By admitting an endless plurality of images into serious aesthetic production, and by often negating, through mass production, the "genius" of the individual artist, Pop was an early manifestation of the general cultural movement of POSTMODERNISM.

See also CARTOONING.

FURTHER READING
Lucy Lippard, *Pop Art* (1966; New York: Thames and Hudson, 1985).

populism In recent years, journalists and politicians have spoken so loosely about "populism" that the term seems compromised beyond hope of redemption. It has been applied to Joseph McCarthy, George Wallace, George McGovern, Jimmy Carter, Ronald Reagan, Jesse Jackson, and Bill Clinton, among others. If nothing else, this elastic use of the term suggests that populism defies conventional classification.

A democratic impulse that belongs neither to the right nor to the left, populism tends to reject ideologies as such. Impatience with IDEOLOGY explains both its enduring appeal and its characteristic weakness, a certain lack of intellectual rigor and programmatic clarity. Populists have never been able to formulate a coherent political philosophy, a comprehensive analysis of the economy and the state, or a program designed to prevent either the market or the state from wiping out the last vestiges of a self-reliant citizenry. Their admirable resistance to the encroachments of these centralizing institutions is unsupported by an authoritative body of social and economic analysis that would tell us what is to be done.

The history of American populism has been distorted both by efforts to assimilate it to some other tradition and by ridicule and condescension. For John D. Hicks, the populist uprising of the 1890s stood squarely in the liberal tradition stretching from Jacksonian DEMOCRACY through PROGRESSIVISM and the New Deal. Richard Hofstadter took a more critical view of the reform tradition—which neglected hardheaded economic analysis, he thought, in favor of vague moral pieties—and saw populism as the epitome of middle-class reform at its worst. According to Hofstadter, whose work has influenced historians and journalists alike, populists were full of resentment against foreigners and Jews, addicted to conspiracy theories, willfully ignorant of economics, and consumed by nostalgia for a yeoman ideal that had no meaning in the urban, industrializing nation of the late nineteenth century. Norman Pollack tried to rescue populists from these strictures by stressing the congruence between populist ideology and Marxism—not a very convincing line of argument, considering Marxists' longstanding condemnation of petty-bourgeois movements aiming, in their view, merely to restore the regime of small property.

Lawrence Goodwyn's *Democratic Promise* was the first full-scale study to take populism seriously and to praise it not as an approximation of LIBERALISM or Marxism but precisely as a more democratic alternative to those modernizing, centralizing ideologies. Attempts to reorganize agriculture on a cooperative basis, Goodwyn argued, furnished agrarian radicals with a first-rate political education, by means of which they began to break the habits of deference that usually discourage popular initiative. The collapse of the People's Party in 1896, often treated merely as the prelude to the Progressive movement, led to the weakening of the democratic impulse in American politics, according to Goodwyn. His interpretation forces us to see welfare liberalism and social democracy not as an advance but as a retreat from a more vigorous civic practice. It also forces us to reexamine time-honored assumptions about the historical inevitability of large-scale production—assumptions that have always been central to the disparagement of populism as a backward-looking movement seeking to reverse the march of PROGRESS.

In order to identify what was specific to populism, Goodwyn had to distinguish very sharply between the radicals who came to the People's Party by way of the Farmer's Alliance, and the "shadow Populists" who diverted the movement from the campaign for producers' cooperatives into the free-silver crusade. Since the populist label continues to be used too loosely, this restriction of its scope remains an important prerequisite of conceptual clarity. At the same time, we need to recognize that nineteenth-century populism found other outlets besides the People's Party and took other than purely agrarian forms. It found its way into various workingmen's movements, the antimonopoly and greenback movements, and the Knights of Labor. Broadly construed, it stood for the defense of endangered crafts, opposition to the new class of public creditors and to the whole machinery of modern finance, and opposition, above all, to wage labor, which was transforming artisans into slaves of routine. Populists inherited from earlier political traditions, liberal as well as republican, the principle that property ownership and the personal independence it confers are essential preconditions of CITIZENSHIP. In the second half of the nineteenth century most Americans continued to pay lip service to this principle, but populists took it more seriously than their fellow-countrymen. They tried to preserve it, under the conditions of modern production, not by anachronistically clinging to the rights of small property-owners but by experimenting with new forms of cooperation. Modern-day democrats can learn more from the populist tradition than from the socialist and social democratic alternative, which was based on the cheerful assumption that the socialization of large-scale production was enough to assure the survival of democratic citizenship. Experience having refuted this assumption, we need to explore the history of populism with renewed respect.

CHRISTOPHER LASCH

See also DEMOCRACY; SOCIALISM.

FURTHER READING
Margaret Canovan, *Populism* (New York: Harcourt Brace Jovanovich, 1981).
Lawrence Goodwyn, *Democratic Promise: the Populist Moment in America* (New York: Oxford University Press, 1976).
Steven Hahn, *The Roots of Southern Populism* (New York: Oxford, University Press, 1983).
John D. Hicks, *The Populist Revolt* (Minneapolis: University of Minnesota Press, 1931).
Richard Hofstadter, *The Age of Reform* (New York: Knopf, 1955).
Christopher Lasch, *The True and Only Heaven: Progress and Its Critics* (New York: Norton, 1991).
Norman Pollack, *The Populist Response to Industrial America* (Cambridge: Harvard University Press, 1962).
C. Vann Woodward, *Tom Watson: Agrarian Rebel* (New York: Rinehart, 1938).

Porter, Katherine Anne (b. Indian Creek, Tex., May 15, 1890; d. Silver Spring, Md., Sept. 18, 1980). Writer. Lauded for her mastery of the short story and praised for her careful crafting of language, character, and structure, Porter probed individual subjective experience of particular times and settings. While she warned against subordinating literature to political or theoretical agendas, her treatments of violence and despair, hopelessness and bitterness convey profound insight into the social dimensions of individual experience. Some of Porter's best-known works are *Flowering Judas* (1930), *Pale Horse, Pale Rider* (1939), and *Ship of Fools* (1962).

FURTHER READING
Robert Brinkmeyer, *Katherine Anne Porter's Artistic Development: Primitivism, Traditionalism, and Totalitarianism* (Baton Rouge: Louisiana State University Press, 1993).

positivism One of the most important and novel developments in nineteenth-century thought, positivism originated with the European thinkers Claude-Henri de Saint-Simon, Auguste Comte, and Herbert Spencer; by mid-century systematic positivism was flourishing. Later, Thomas Henry Huxley and Ernst Mach developed critical positivism. Both positivisms found adherents in the United States among scientists, social scientists, and philosophers. One legacy of critical positivism was logical positivism, developed in Vienna in the 1920s and 1930s and brought to the United States before World War II.

All positivists reject metaphysics on the grounds that we can know nothing about ultimate principles, forces, or entities. Explanations or interpretations are derived only from direct observation. Any attempt to transcend the directly observable to an ultimate reality is futile. The epistemology of positivism establishes the methods of SCIENCE as the ideal in all fields of inquiry. Finally, the most advanced sciences are those which have most fully freed themselves from metaphysical assumptions and base their explanations only on directly experienced empirical observations and correlations.

Nineteenth-century positivism developed two branches, systematic and critical. Systematic positivism represented a novel idea. Saint-Simon, Comte, and Spencer were the first to conceive of philosophy as a synthesis of the sciences. The positivist philosopher's task was to build on the empirical results of science, to identify the general laws of the sciences and to integrate these specific laws into an even more general conception of knowledge. Philosophy provided the more general knowledge lacking in the specific sciences. Systematic positivism had a wide impact on nineteenth-century thought that is not completely explained by the growing prestige of contemporary science. Systematic positivism also held out the hope that the principles and methods of science could be brought to bear on social problems. The greatest influence of systematic positivism was on sociology and in the belief that social reform could be guided by scientific principles; it had far less effect on practicing scientists and academic philosophers.

By the late nineteenth century the new discoveries in biology, physics, chemistry, and psychology undermined the search for a grand synthetic general law. Scientists increasingly adopted the methodological principles of positivism—empirical observation and limited generalization—but dispensed with the effort to systematize the results from the different sciences. Among some scientists and philosophers, however, critical positivism developed into a new philosophical movement. Critical positivists subjected the foundations, assumptions, and generalizations of science to critical analysis. In addition, they critically analyzed all claims and generalizations claiming to provide reliable knowledge by scientists and laymen

alike. Practicing scientists increasingly wanted to free science of all taint of metaphysical influence, and critical positivism offered a method of liberation. Finally, critical positivism grew in association with the development of a pragmatic conception of the human mind. Among the leading figures associated with critical positivism were the English evolutionist Thomas Henry Huxley, the German psychologist Hermann von Helmholtz, and the Austrian physicist and philosopher Ernst Mach.

Positivism first became known in America largely through the works of Comte, Spencer, and John Stuart Mill. It first found adherents in the emerging disciplines of social science and sociology. Systematic positivism was attractive because it provided a basis for generalization without resort to religious or metaphysical beliefs. Early social scientists such as LESTER FRANK WARD found positivism most helpful in generating theories and methods of secular social meliorism. Positivism also allowed American thinkers to recast the debate between religion and science on scientific grounds. It encouraged the divorce of religion and science and the development of a purely natural science.

CHAUNCEY WRIGHT, a slightly older contemporary of Charles S. Peirce and William James, was a disciple of Mill and one of the first Americans to employ the methods of critical positivism. His scientific philosophy emphasized neutrality with regard to metaphysical and theological systems, suspension of judgment until all the data were collected, and development of a rigorous scientific method. In rejecting Wright's narrow positivism, Peirce sought a scientific methodology appropriate for all inquiry, but thought that science, philosophy, and religion were compatible so long as one did not mix them. James, too, argued for a science-based philosophy, as well as for the possibility of belief that was not strictly scientific, such as religious faith and belief in psychic phenomena. The pragmatisms of Peirce, James, and John Dewey drew on critical positivism, but their emphasis on the potential value of beliefs that were not generated or validated by scientific method carried them beyond the critical positivists.

In the 1930s a new variant of positivism, logical positivism of the Viennese school, was brought to America by Albert E. Blumberg, Herbert Feigl and RUDOLF CARNAP. The work of the pragmatists had prepared fertile ground for this new philosophy. As phenomenalists, logical positivists reduced all knowledge of fact to knowledge of immediate experience. As conventionalists, they argued that the truths of logic and mathematics were due to language conventions. Finally, as verificationists, they believed that any statement which was neither phenomenally nor conventionally based was metaphysical, without meaning, and at best a feeling. Although logical positivism had only a brief existence as a philosophical movement, it had considerable impact on the development of the analytic tradition which became the mainstream of academic American philosophy from the 1930s to the 1970s.

Positivism was thus an important philosophical movement in nineteenth-century Europe and in America after the Civil War. In both Europe and America it contributed to the attack on religion begun in the Enlightenment and to the growing faith in science and scientific method. In America, positivism influenced the pragmatists and, in its logical variant, the development of analytic philosophy.

DANIEL J. WILSON

FURTHER READING

Thomas L. Haskell, *The Emergence of Professional Social Science: the American Social Science Association and the Nineteenth-Century Crisis of Authority* (Urbana: University of Illinois Press, 1977).

Bruce Kuklick, *The Rise of American Philosophy: Cambridge, Massachusetts, 1860–1930* (New Haven: Yale University Press, 1977).

Maurice Mandelbaum, *History, Man, and Reason: a Study in Nineteenth-Century Thought* (Baltimore: Johns Hopkins University Press, 1971).

Dorothy Ross, *The Origins of American Social Science* (Cambridge: Cambridge University Press, 1991).

Daniel J. Wilson, *Science, Community, and the Transformation of American Philosophy, 1860–1930* (Chicago: University of Chicago Press, 1990).

postmodernism Like the other cultural movements of modern Western history that precede it (ENLIGHTENMENT, ROMANTICISM, MODERNISM), postmodernism is best understood as a plurality, a constellation of ideas, actions, and processes. This is only fitting in the case of postmodernism, since one of its connecting tissues is a sense of "decentered" multiplicity and perpetual regeneration.

Even as the aesthetic and philosophical codes of mature or "high" modernism came to be accepted as the official vocabulary of American cultural life in the 1950s, these codes were being unsettled and reordered. Early postmodernists like JOHN CAGE, Robert Rauschenberg, and WILLIAM S. BURROUGHS did not reject modernism in toto, but drew on such countertraditions of modernist expression as Dada and Surrealism, where the focus was on formal rupture, discontinuity, irrationality, and the radical potential of an imaginative avant-garde disdainful of "establishment" institutions, whether cultural or moral. Another significant aspect of early post-

modernism was an aesthetic interest in MASS CULTURE, challenging the increasingly academic elitism of high modernism. This interest flowered into the POP movement of the 1960s, a particularly important example of the crucial association (sometimes playful, sometimes oppositional) of postmodernism with a "postindustrial" capitalism invested in mass consumption and information processing. There was also a notable congruence with the "counterculture" of the 1960s through a populist cultural RELATIVISM and a shared distrust of theoretical and institutional centralization. Indeed, many early theorists of the American postmodern approached the topic as an entrée in support (Leslie Fiedler, SUSAN SONTAG) or criticism (DANIEL BELL) of radical sensibilities.

In the years after 1968, with much of the fun gone from iconoclasm, postmodernism in America began to change. An important theoretical locus of this transformation was the intellectual world of Paris, which had been caught up in its own intense crisis during the 1960s. Negotiating the doctrinal battles of their Communist Party, French thinkers turned to the modernist countertradition of Dada and Surrealism as well as to structuralist anthropology and linguistics to produce "poststructuralist" critical theories—theories concerned with disrupting normative modes of REPRESENTATION, and "deconstructing" texts to unveil a world of power, dominance, and signification. Thinkers such as Jacques Derrida, Michel Foucault, Jean Baudrillard, Jean-François Lyotard, and Jacques Lacan launched a critique of traditional "master narratives" of Western historical and philosophical development. Influenced by the hitherto suspect anti-philosophies of Nietzsche and Heidegger, they showed human interiority split apart, fragmented beyond the simple conscious/unconscious dichotomy of Freud into a decentered, dispersed and fluid subject, not so much speaking as being *spoken by* language. Without a "genuine" or essential being, individuals were seen as constructed by the texts surrounding them.

As poststructuralism entered American thought in the late 1970s, and postmodernism (or postmodernisms) came to dominate academic discourse in the United States, postmodern ARCHITECTURE developed the concerns of the earlier phase: "futurist" attachment to postindustrial technologies, the hybridization of historical and mass-cultural styles in often ironic combination, and challenges to the programmatic, steel-and-glass utopias urged by the high modernists. These same attributes were often illustrated in other forms of American cultural production, such as the music of Philip Glass and the punks, the films of David Lynch, the literature of Thomas Pynchon and Kathy Acker, the performances of Robert Wilson and Laurie Anderson, and the visual art of Joseph Kosuth, Cindy Sherman, and Eric Fischl.

During the 1980s theorists began to differentiate a "postmodern condition"—symptomatic of consumer capitalism and "the death of the subject"—from a "postmodernism of resistance" which would use the insights of the new theory and aesthetics to subvert the status quo. In the midst of what many intellectuals felt to be a general period of reaction in the West centered around the Reagan, Thatcher, and Kohl regimes, the "cultural Left" emerged as a heterodox resistance movement centered in major universities and the New York art world. In this context, the "liberation" efforts which had effectively balkanized the NEW LEFT were sympathetically engaged by postmodernists enthusiastic for CULTURAL PLURALISM AND MULTICULTURALISM, and resistant to the theoretical totalizing of previous leftist doctrine. Critics such as Rosalind Krauss and Craig Owens employed postmodern ideas about representation and cultural power to destabilize the supposedly "natural" categories of RACE, GENDER, and sexuality. (See also GAY AND LESBIAN IDENTITIES.) Postmodern artists of the eighties likewise moved from stylistic playfulness toward new forms of agitprop. Inspired by early avant-gardist ideals that art could be a catalyst of a general transformation in social, political, and cultural experience, these artists, led by feminists like Judy Chicago and Barbara Kruger, worked on an "anti-aesthetic" which explored, disrupted, and reconfigured not only the conventions of social "difference," but also the validity of any aesthetic categorization.

By the late eighties, postmodern provocations in the art world and elsewhere added to increased awareness, across the political spectrum, that "culture" had become a key field of social conflict in the United States. In the academy, the DECONSTRUCTION of universal reason contributed to a crisis of the disciplines used to produce cultural knowledge, and the very idea of general education was called into question. The epistemological relativism of postmodernism troubled many liberals as well as conservatives, who saw in it a *bête noire* undermining all versions of CONSENSUS.

PETER HANSEN

See also LATINO AND LATINA CULTURES.

FURTHER READING

Hal Foster, ed., *The Anti-Aesthetic: Essays on Postmodern Culture* (Port Townsend, Wash.: Bay Press, 1983).
Linda Hutcheon, *The Politics of Postmodernism* (New York: Routledge, 1989).
Andreas Huyssen, "Mapping the Postmodern," *New German Critique* 33 (fall 1984): 5–22.

Christopher Jenks, *Post-modernism: the New Classicism in Art and Architecture* (London: Academy, 1987).
Margaret Rose, *The Postmodern and the Post-Industrial: a Critical Analysis* (Cambridge U.K.: Cambridge University Press, 1991).

Potter, David M. (b. Augusta, Ga., Dec. 6, 1910; d. Palo Alto, Calif., Feb. 18, 1971). Historian. Potter's writings reflect his acute awareness of the tragic dimensions of history. In *Lincoln and His Party in the Secession Crisis* (1942), *The South and the Sectional Conflict* (1968), *History and American Society* (published posthumously in 1973), and *The Impending Crisis, 1848–1861* (published posthumously in 1976), Potter emphasized the importance of slavery in the sectional crisis and scrupulously avoided passing judgment on those whose actions he sought to understand and explain. Impatient with moralizing in historical writing, he nevertheless provided a model of history as moral inquiry since he strove to listen attentively to his historical subjects and convey in his writing the drama of their existence. Potter's best-known and most influential work was *People of Plenty: Economic Abundance and the American Character* (1954), which argued that abundance, deriving from uniquely rich natural resources developed through innovative TECHNOLOGY, was decisive in shaping the American character.

FURTHER READING

Dennis Brogan, "David M. Potter," in Marcus Cunliffe and Robin Winks, eds., *Pastmasters* (New York: Harper and Row, 1969).

Pound, Ezra (b. Hailey, Idaho, Oct. 30, 1885; d. Venice, Italy, Nov. 1, 1972). Poet, critic, journalist, amateur economist, promoter of MODERNISM in literature, art, and music, translator of work from Chinese, Greek, Italian, Provençal, French, and German, Pound was such a protean and long-lived figure in American culture that his work defies summary in brief compass. Arguably the single most important figure in literary history in the twentieth century and one of the century's greatest and most controversial poets, he virtually created modernist poetry through his insistence on modern subject-matter, innovation in form and technique, and concision and precision in the language of poetry. He was also one of the only significant American writers of the century to attempt to extend his influence beyond literature to the political sphere. And for Pound, political commitment was always a matter of thought as well as action. The most dramatic instance of his political project—his support of Benito Mussolini and the Axis in World War II—was the product, he claimed, of his faithfulness to the ideas of the Founding Fathers, particularly THOMAS JEFFERSON and JOHN ADAMS.

Pound's importance for the history of American thought—as opposed to American literature—lies here, in his exploration of eighteenth-century American civilization and his arguments for its relevance to twentieth-century America. By the end of the nineteenth century, the history of American literature was generally told as the history of New England literature. This privileging of New England has in recent years been criticized for the way it obscures the contributions of non-Protestant, non-English, and nonwhite writers while supposedly promoting Eurocentrism. But Pound found fault with the dominant perspective for being insufficiently Eurocentric, too parochially American. His vision was inspired by Mediterranean and classical rather than English or Anglo-Saxon culture. Pound, though born in Idaho, grew up in Philadelphia and was educated at the University of Pennsylvania and at Hamilton College in New York, a Middle-Atlantic upbringing that inoculated him against New England pieties. Though he was to live in London from 1908 to 1920, his favorite place of residence in Europe was Italy, where he lived from 1924 to 1945 and again from 1958 until his death.

Pound's attempt to intervene in American culture began very early, in a series of essays published in 1912–13 called "Patria Mia." The title comes from Giacomo Leopardi's 1818 poem "All'Italia," a reflection on the fallen state of Italy. Pound sees his own country both as needing a Risorgimento or Renaissance, key terms in "Patria Mia," and as possessing the potential for such a Renaissance. His effort in "Patria Mia" and a related essay of 1915, "The Renaissance," was to pinpoint what needed to be done. His simple answer was patronage: America needed people like the Medici, like his hero Sigismundo Malatesta, who would buy the great art of the present, unlike the typical American millionaire of Pound's day who bought mostly art of Malatesta's time and therefore brought no new art into being.

This concern with patronage permeated the early part of The Cantos, the epic poem Pound worked on from 1917 until his death. Across the Early Cantos, one figure from America's past is linked to Malatesta and the Medici—Thomas Jefferson, for Pound a model American patron of the arts. In Pound's eyes, Jefferson's America was the naissance, the original burst of American creativity, whose values had to be recaptured. However, by the time of the Jefferson Cantos, Cantos 31–4, and even more clearly by the publication of Jefferson and/or Mussolini in 1935,

Pound's interest in Jefferson had expanded. His vaunted modern Medicis had failed to materialize, leading him to critique the culture of contemporary plutocracy for its irresponsibility, and to think that only a strong central figure could impel society toward civic responsibility. In the classical Aristotelian terms still dominating political discourse in Jefferson's time, society needed a strong "one" to protect the "many" from the abuses of the "few." Pound not only became convinced that Italy had found this leader Il Duce, Benito Mussolini; he thought that Mussolini was comparable to Thomas Jefferson in his commitment to action and his capacity to jump-start the cultural life of the nation. Yet as the 1930s progressed, Pound came to suspect that Jefferson's theory of government was insufficiently committed to order. He came to see John Adams, a classical republican exponent of VIRTUE and order, as the true American analogue to his imagined Mussolini. Adams is the central figure of Cantos 62–71, published in 1940, generally known as the Adams Cantos, and he is the only figure given so much space in the entire poem.

America's entrance into World War II pushed Pound's identification of America with fascist Italy beyond the breaking point. He chose Mussolini's Italy over Roosevelt's America and broadcast pro-Axis messages over Rome Radio throughout the war. Nonetheless, he insisted that he was not repudiating the heritage of the Founding Fathers. The radio broadcasts led to his being indicted for treason and staying from 1945 to 1958 in an insane asylum as the only alternative to standing trial for treason. The Late Cantos, written mostly in this period, do occasionally refer to figures from American history such as Thomas Hart Benton and John Randolph of Roanoke, but rely on American material much less than the Middle Cantos.

Pound cannot be said to have had a comprehensive or balanced vision of America, and it is hard to say what influence his stress on the civic culture of the revolutionary period has had. But Pound was certainly ahead of his time and anticipatory of ours in his insistence on the political character of American literature. Ironically, of all the major writers of American modernism, he was probably the most involved in the study of American thought and political culture, even though he spent very little time in his native country. His distance from America had tragic consequences for Pound's own life, as his remoteness from America meant that he utterly failed to grasp the depth of hostility his radio broadcasts would create. However noxious his particular linkage between European and American developments, he remains a significant instance of the ongoing effort to place American culture in a comparative and global framework.

REED WAY DASENBROCK

FURTHER READING

Reed Way Dasenbrock, *Imitating the Italians: Wyatt, Spenser, Synge, Pound, Joyce* (Baltimore: Johns Hopkins University Press, 1991).
Leonard Doob, ed., *"Ezra Pound Speaking": Radio Speeches of World War II* (Westport, Conn.: Greenwood, 1978).
Hugh Kenner, *The Poetry of Ezra Pound* (Norfolk: New Directions, 1951).
——, *The Pound Era* (Berkeley: University of California Press, 1971).
Ezra Pound, "Patria Mia," in *Selected Prose, 1909–1965*, ed. William Cookson (New York: New Directions, 1973).
——, *Jefferson and/or Mussolini: L'idea statale; fascism as I Have Seen It* (New York: Horace Liveright, 1935).
——, *The Cantos* (New York: New Directions, 1989).
Noel Stock, *The Life of Ezra Pound* (New York: Pantheon, 1970).

Pound, Roscoe (b. Lincoln, Nebr., Oct. 27, 1870; d. Cambridge, Mass., July 1, 1964). Legal scholar. After an early career as a botanist in Nebraska, Roscoe Pound became a law professor and eventually Dean of Harvard Law School from 1916 to 1936. He articulated the theory and practice of "sociological jurisprudence," rooted in the philosophy of PRAGMATISM. He believed that LAW should be formulated not in accordance with abstract principles, but with actual human needs. The entire legal system, from legislators to judges and enforcers, should use sociological insights to create a just society. A prolific writer, Pound published such books as *The Spirit of the Common Law* (1921), *Law and Morals* (1924), and *New Paths of the Law* (1950).

FURTHER READING

Edward B. McLean, *Law and Civilization: the Legal Thought of Roscoe Pound* (Lanham, Md.: University Press of America, 1992).

Powell, John Wesley (b. Mount Morris, N.Y., Mar. 24, 1834; d. Haven, Maine, Sept. 23, 1902). Anthropologist and geologist. Author of *Exploration of the Colorado River in the West and Its Tributaries* (1875) and *Report on the Lands of the Arid Region of the United States* (1878), two formative works in geology and conservation, Powell also wrote the influential *Introduction to the Study of Indian Languages* (1877) and was the first director of the Bureau of Ethnology (1879–1902). SCIENCE, he believed, is the key to human PROGRESS. Cultures evolve through progressive stages to become individualist democracies. Religion, philosophy, folklore, and superstition belong to earlier stages of cultural evolution, and are finally replaced by scientific knowledge of the world. A truly scientific understanding of Indian cultures, he believed, would eliminate white prejudice against and exploitation of INDIANS.

FURTHER READING

William H. Goetzmann, *Exploration and Empire: the Explorer and the Scientist in the Winning of the American West* (New York: Norton, 1978).

pragmatism   A collection of diverse ideas usually associated with philosophers and social theorists such as CHARLES SANDERS PEIRCE, WILLIAMS JAMES, JOHN DEWEY, and GEORGE HERBERT MEAD, pragmatism is currently undergoing a revival. From philosophy to social science, from literary studies to ethnic studies, from feminism to legal theory, varieties of pragmatism are attracting attention and sparking debate.

For much of the twentieth century, American philosophers thirsted for certainty. They found in the natural sciences a compelling model for rigorous inquiry that yielded firm results. Students of society and politics, unhappy with merely descriptive accounts, struggled to construct a SOCIAL SCIENCE that would produce quantifiable, verifiable, and, above all, value-free knowledge useful to social engineers as well as scholars.

By the last third of the century, however, the quest for certainty lost much of its appeal for a variety of reasons. First the natural sciences, whose hold on solid knowledge had seemed so secure, fell before the historicist analysis of THOMAS KUHN. Then social scientists such as the anthropologist CLIFFORD GEERTZ echoed Max Weber's earlier acknowledgement that because human experience is meaningful, understanding both behavior and expression requires interpreting the shifting systems of symbols through which individuals encounter and cope with the world. Instead of seeking timeless principles and truth, many scholars began to speak of revolutionary paradigm shifts, incommensurable forms of life, the complexities of thick description, and competing communities of discourse.

These changes contributed to the renewal of interest in pragmatism. Just as Peirce, James, Dewey, and Mead developed their versions of pragmatism to provide alternatives to the failed projects of POSITIVISM and idealism in nineteenth-century philosophy, so more recent pragmatists have built upon ground cleared of the rubble left after the collapse of the grand edifice designed by Anglo-American analytic philosophers and empirical social scientists in the mid-twentieth century.

For some contemporary thinkers, such as the

most widely read pragmatist philosopher, RICHARD RORTY, pragmatism is attractive primarily as a species of antifoundationalism. Just as earlier pragmatists toppled versions of absolutism by denying that truth can be known with certainty, so for some postmodernists pragmatism provides the desired leverage against rigid ideas of AUTHORITY, identity, and universality. Rorty has dismissed as wishful thinking all claims to OBJECTIVITY, arguing that our standards and our practices are cultural conventions, not something embedded in—or mirroring—the world outside ourselves. In *Philosophy and the Mirror of Nature* (1979) and *The Consequences of Pragmatism* (1982) Rorty advised contemporaries to give up the fruitless attempt to ground our beliefs on something lying beyond our own cultural conversation. Rorty pointed out that these battles had been fought by earlier pragmatists, and that he was restating many of James's and Dewey's arguments. Given the enthusiasm of twentieth-century Americans for science and their confidence in objectivity, however, his writings had an explosive force. In *Contingency, Irony, and Solidarity* (1989), he argued that historical comparison—nothing as solid or imposing as either analytic logic or varieties of metaphysics purported to be—is the court of highest appeal for all cultural arguments.

In literary studies, critics such as Richard Poirier have followed Rorty, invoking pragmatism as a version of antifoundationalism that justifies their own "strong readings" of the texts they interpret. In *Pragmatism and Poetry* (1992), Poirier announces that the number of pragmatisms equals the number of pragmatist philosophers. Whereas that diversity had troubled earlier critics such as ARTHUR LOVEJOY, Poirier delights in it; pragmatism underwrites his own linguistic skepticism. James's pragmatism, Poirier insists, is a way of calling attention to the vague, to the extravagant, to the superfluous, and it works in and through language, not beyond it. Poirier argues that pragmatism works

> the way poetry does—by effecting a change of language, a change carried out entirely within language, and for the benefit of those destined to inherit the language. Pragmatism, as I understand it, is not essentially addressed to—indeed it shies away from—historical crises. (p. 132)

Poirier's conception of pragmatism differs from the pragmatism of James and Dewey. Although both were sensitive to the slipperiness and imprecision of language, they insisted that immediate experience is prior to, and cannot be contained by, linguistic expression. Giles Gunn, another literary critic who

invokes pragmatism, stresses this dimension of James's and Dewey's writings in *Thinking Across the American Grain* (1992). According to Gunn, Dewey's ideas of aesthetic and religious experience both depended on what "cannot be expressed in language, and hence conceptualized in ideas, but what can be experienced imaginatively, and thus comprehended as intuition or insight" (p. 114). A similarly expansive conception of AESTHETICS consistent with Dewey's has recently been advanced in Richard Shusterman's *Pragmatic Aesthetics* (1992), which brings the pragmatic tradition to bear for the first time on the analysis of such popular artistic expression as rap music.

James was even more explicit than Dewey about the inadequacy of language to capture experience, and about the importance, nevertheless, of using language not merely to express ourselves but to communicate our meanings as clearly as possible to one another. In James's words, quoted by Gunn, "Something forever exceeds, escapes from statement, withdraws from definition, must be glimpsed and felt, not told" (p. 113). In *Pragmatism* (1907), James acknowledged that "all human thinking gets discursified," and "all truth gets verbally built out," but his point was quite different from Poirier's:

> we must *talk* consistently just as we must *think* consistently; for both in talk and thought we deal with kinds. Names are arbitrary, but once understood they must be kept to. We mustn't call Abel "Cain" or Cain "Abel." If we do, we ungear ourselves from the whole book of Genesis, and from all its connexions with the universe of speech and fact down to the present time." (pp. 102f.)

Although signifiers may be arbitrary and meanings imprecise, they alone enable us to connect with the past meanings that constitute our heritage. Moreover they enable us, however imperfectly, to connect with each other. Thus James insisted both that language is an inadequate medium for conveying the ineffable character of experience, and that language nevertheless allows us, however imperfectly, to communicate shared meanings. The importance of democratic conversation is rightly acknowledged as central to Dewey's pragmatism; the idea of conversation was equally important for James, despite his clear awareness of the limits of language.

Rorty's and Poirier's versions of pragmatism have been widely influential, but they have also attracted critics. The most penetrating has been RICHARD J. BERNSTEIN. Whereas Rorty invokes earlier pragmatists primarily as forerunners for his antifoundationalism, Bernstein has stressed the importance of a community of inquiry, on the one hand, and social action, on the other, as the twin pillars of his pragmatism. He has argued that we can reject foundationalism without embracing RELATIVISM if we return to earlier pragmatists' "fallibilism," the idea that there are no certain truths but plenty of workable, contingent ones. An "engaged fallibilistic pluralism," he writes in *The New Constellation* (1992), is consistent with the most attractive aspects of POSTMODERNISM but capable of moving beyond critique toward constructive social theory (p. 336).

Bernstein shares with Rorty the commitments to antifoundationalism, fallibilism, contingency, and pluralism. But he emphasizes more forcefully than Rorty does the grounding of pragmatism in social, political, and ethical experience. Rorty is concerned to demarcate a zone for individual creativity and what he calls "liberal irony," the awareness of the contingency of all commitments. Bernstein believes that because experience itself is social, our private selves cannot be cordoned off in that way from our ethical or political responsibilities. Any lasting individual fulfillment must be the product of engaging in communal conversation.

Although Rorty and Bernstein are hardly alone among philosophers in returning to pragmatic themes —one might emphasize as well the influential work of NELSON GOODMAN and Hilary Putnam—the contrast between them suggests some of the tensions that have marked pragmatism since its origins. In response to James's writings, Peirce renamed his own philosophy "pragmaticism," a term ugly enough, he hoped, to keep it safe from kidnappers. Peirce aimed to provide a method whereby philosophers could move toward stable, objective truth, an aspiration different from those of James or Dewey, Rorty or Bernstein.

As a weapon often directed against traditional mindsets, pragmatism has appealed to many intellectuals seeking social change. While the appeal of rival approaches such as Marxism, structural functionalism, and liberal pluralism has faded, the importance of pragmatism for contemporary social and political theory has grown. Recent studies that highlight the connections between progressive social action and the pragmatism of Dewey and Mead include Hans Joas, *Pragmatism and Social Theory* (1993); Timothy Kaufman-Osborn, *Politics/Sense/Experience* (1991); and Robert Westbrook, *John Dewey and American Democracy* (1991). Cornel West, a public intellectual who links African American religious traditions with the concerns of the academic left, has advanced what he calls a "prophetic pragmatism" in his book *The American Evasion of Philosophy: a Genealogy of Pragmatism* (1989). Building on the work of W. E. B. DU

BOIS, who studied with James and called himself a "realist pragmatist," West surveys American thought from Emerson to Rorty to establish a philosophical and political position that accents "human powers" in order to transform "antiquated modes of social hierarchies in light of religious and/or ethical ideals" (p. 4).

Feminist philosophers such as Nancy Fraser and Charlene Seigfried, editor of a special issue of *Hypatia* (spring 1993) on the subject of FEMINISM and pragmatism, have pointed out that James and Dewey rejected all dualisms, including those between subjectivity and objectivity, and between emotion and reason. If all cultural norms, including those concerning GENDER, are seen as historical constructs rather than absolutes, feminists can do more than push for access to the "male" world or for the spread of "female" nurturing; they can critique and modify such gender "essentialism." Contemporary feminist-pragmatists find much more in early twentieth-century pragmatism than antifoundationalism and antiessentialism. They also find in James and Dewey a pronounced interest in an ethic of care, and a keen appreciation for the place of empathy in the exercise of judgment.

A similar turn to pragmatism is apparent in legal theory, where a number of writers have sought relief from the increasingly shrill debates raging between champions of the LAW AND ECONOMICS movement and partisans of CRITICAL LEGAL STUDIES. Morton Horwitz's major reinterpretation of legal realism, *The Transformation of American Law, 1870–1960* (1992), illustrates the tendency among legal scholars to adopt an explicitly pragmatist perspective. Thomas Grey's essay on the pragmatism of OLIVER WENDELL HOLMES JR. in the *Stanford Law Review* (1989), and the collection of essays edited by Robert Gordon, *The Legacy of Oliver Wendell Holmes, Jr.* (1992), clarify the crucial difference between Holmes's hardheaded, occasionally cynical pragmatism and the ethical concerns and democratic ideals of James and Dewey.

Pragmatism in Law and Society (1991), an important collection edited by Michael Brint and William Weaver, further illustrates the diversity of the current pragmatic revival. Essays by Hilary Putnam, Joan Williams, and Thomas Grey distinguish between the instrumental aspect of pragmatism, which has troubled critics from JOSIAH ROYCE to A. J. Ayer and Theodor Adorno, and the more radical philosophical insights and political ideas advanced by James, Dewey, and Mead. Margaret Jane Radin calls for a pragmatist and feminist middle way in legal theory that deconstructs gender and CLASS categories along with timeless conceptions of reality and static conceptions of law. Other essays in *Pragmatism in Law and Society* show how thinkers with dramatically different perspectives, including not only Rorty but also the literary critic turned law professor Stanley Fish and even the staunchly conservative jurist Richard Posner, have likewise appropriated aspects of pragmatism—often deliberately opposed to the progressive and social democratic pragmatism of James and Dewey—for their own purposes.

Contemporary pragmatism has several faces. For some thinkers pragmatism is a version of postmodern antifoundationalism attractive to Americans because of its heritage, important primarily as a way of promoting Rorty's ironic aestheticism and undermining all claims to authority. For others, pragmatism (or pragmaticism) holds out the very different goal of stable, objective knowledge to be reached through Peirce's SEMIOTICS. For still others, among whom I count myself, pragmatism originates in the conception of social experience found in the writings of James, Dewey, and Mead, and culminates in their ideal of mutual understanding and open-ended democratic social action. Given such differences, it is important to distinguish those versions of pragmatism oriented toward irony or objectivity from the "engaged fallibilistic pluralism" of Bernstein.

JAMES T. KLOPPENBERG

FURTHER READING

Richard J. Bernstein, *The New Constellation: the Ethical and Political Horizons of Modernity/Postmodernity* (Cambridge: MIT Press, 1992).
Giles Gunn, *Thinking Across the American Grain: Ideology, Intellect, and the New Pragmatism* (Chicago: University of Chicago Press, 1992).
Sidney Hook, *Pragmatism and the Tragic Sense of Life* (New York: Basic Books, 1974).
William James, *Pragmatism* (1907; Cambridge: Harvard University Press, 1975).
James T. Kloppenberg, *Uncertain Victory: Social Democracy and Progressivism in European and American Thought, 1870–1920* (New York: Oxford University Press, 1986).
——, "Pragmatism: an Old Name for Some New Ways of Thinking," *Journal of American History* (forthcoming).
Richard Poirier, *Poetry and Pragmatism* (Cambridge: Harvard University Press, 1992).
H. S. Thayer, *Meaning and Action: a Critical History of Pragmatism* (Indianapolis: Hackett, 1981).
Cornel West, *The American Evasion of Philosophy: A Genealogy of Pragmatism* (Madison: University of Wisconsin Press, 1989).
Robert B. Westbrook, *John Dewey and American Democracy* (Ithaca: Cornell University Press, 1992).

privacy The positive concept of privacy is a relatively recent formulation, indebted to the modern bourgeoisie and the modern state. This is not to deny ancient and, it may be, universal human designation of some practices or habits (usually pertaining to bodily orifices) as appropriately or necessarily private, meaning concealed or held back from general scrutiny. In stateless societies based on kinship there may be rituals reserved to a group defined by sex or age, or transactions withheld from the eyes of others. (*See also* OBSCENITY; SHAME.) Yet such practices do not constitute a realm of privacy as we know it, which depends on its corollary—the recognition of a public realm—and therefore on a formalization of civil society.

The Western political tradition has long harbored a distinction between public and private, a hierarchical distinction promoting the public as the arena of citizenship, political participation, and governance, and demoting the rest as "merely" private, the realm of satisfaction of personal needs. In ancient Greek thought, what was outside the civic institution of the *polis* belonged to the *idion* (root of the English word idiot), a realm of privation and unfreedom. Its characteristic institution was the *oikos* (household), to which women, children and slaves were consigned; only adult free men ranged between and reigned in both the *oikos* and the *polis*. In Latin, similarly, the word *privatus*, meaning withdrawn from public life, derived from the verb *privare*, to bereave or deprive. The vaunted Roman state was literally "the public thing," *res publica*. In contrast to the attention given to the *polis* or *res publica*, the private was a residual category, not elaborated; both by intention and by neglect classical political philosophy made clear that greater goodness, HONOR, worth, and status attached to transactions that were public or political—in the realm of free men—and in the name of the common rather than a private interest.

The American revolutionaries' reverent study of Greek and Roman states was but one indication of their participation in the Western political tradition that honored public exertions above private interests. The founders heralded the commonweal and expected men's active civic life and display of public VIRTUE to be essential to a successful American republic. Yet moderating or complicating this classical heritage were two extremely important characteristics of the American polity: avid appreciation (undergirded by the labor theory of value) for ownership of private property as the hallmark of independent citizens; and a strong Protestant emphasis on unmediated communication with God. If the question was, where was virtue to be found, the revolutionary generation would have acknowledged that it lay not only in civic commitment but also in the security of private property and the assurance of clear conscience.

Moreover, the founders of the American political tradition clearly articulated links between private and public. True, they were contractualists, siding with parliamentarians who (as against royalists) refused to envision government on a patriarchal family model. But the founders nonetheless saw the private realm of family government, property-holding, and moral upbringing as the nursery of public virtue. Their concern with the character of republican citizens even led them to envision a political role for women as wifely and motherly inculcators of virtue in men. (*See also* MOTHERHOOD.)

In Anglo-America prior to the Revolutionary era, there was no strong association between notions of privacy and family life: family residences hardly afforded seclusion, or private spaces. The households of the rich were highly populated locations for both business and pleasure, where individuals of all ages, genders, and social strata were likely to interact; while the households of the poor were small, cramped, and thin-walled. Sociability and surveillance, not privacy, marked the household. One went outdoors, to field or wood, to be alone. Nor did people, unless bent on something denoted shameful, express strong need for personal privacy: the habit of sleeping several to a bed (whether at home with kin or lodgers or in an inn with strangers) is perhaps the single clearest indication of the difference in need for personal space between that time and ours.

Before the Revolution, "private" had two principal inflections: one, etymologically related to "privilege," meant reserved for a select few (as in "the Privy Council"); the other meant covert, shameful (as in "the privy"). By the late eighteenth century, however, social and economic change as well as political philosophy began to make possible a firmer, more elaborated definition of privacy centered around the domestic site of the household. Along with greater emphasis on INDIVIDUALISM and a rise in the proportion of middle-class households with more space and comfortable trappings, a third and more positive valuation of privacy began to emerge. It combined withdrawal from the world with privileged status. The crusading zeal of evangelical Protestantism (at the end of the eighteenth and into the nineteenth century) was instrumental here, in tying spiritual integrity to rejection of worldly delights and relying on household religion to educe PIETY.

As Emerson indicated in "The American Scholar," describing the genius as "the one who raises himself from private considerations and breathes and lives on public and illustrious thoughts," nineteenth-century American norms still placed public-spiritedness above private-mindedness. More than ever before,

however, privacy and the domestic arena to which it was now presumed to attach were positively valued as an alternative to the glare, the competition, the soul-destroying machinations of public life. Even though a hierarchy between public and private was maintained (as between male and female), their reciprocal necessity and complementarity were emphasized. (*See also* DOMESTICITY.)

In the nineteenth century, the cultural opposition between private sentiment and public spirit was doubled by the tension between private property and public regulation, a tension inevitably growing with the expansion and bureaucratization of government power. By that time two different readings of the public/private divide were visible, as they still are today. In one reading, the division between public and private lined up with the difference between work and home: the public included business and politics—all the doings of men; the private was the domestic arena, where men got involved with women. But in a second and also prevalent reading, all private gain (money-making along with family and household) was set off from the public—the commonweal, the state. Sentiment enshrined the one division, the law the other. Both readings of the public/private divide (especially the first, which had no constitutional translation) were normative, ideologically maintained, even sacralized. Despite such contradictory signs as government subsidies for business enterprise, statutory regulation of "obscene" practices, state intervention into family life (especially child-raising by the poor), and the actual presence of women in public life, dominant discourse upheld the inviolability and sacredness of private property and the home.

Indeed, defense of the "sacred precincts of private and domestic life" took center stage in a pathbreaking *Harvard Law Review* article by Samuel Warren and Louis Brandeis in 1890 which first articulated a "right to privacy." Warren and Brandeis were mainly concerned with the capacity of modern media such as photography and mass-distribution newspapers to invade personal affairs and assault domestic relations. They argued that protection of personal privacy was a principle to be found (if one looked for it) in common law, not so much in analogy to private property as in connection with the "general right of the individual to be let alone," a principle of "inviolate personality." Focusing on individual RIGHTS, their argument tied individuality to domestic privacy, with a knot that has persisted in modern privacy doctrine. (*See also* PUBLICITY.)

Mid-twentieth century privacy doctrine emanating from the U.S. Supreme Court articulated a principle limiting not only the media's intervention but most importantly the state's regulation, and it did so by defining and insulating a domestic zone. In the landmark cases of the 1960s concerning sexual and marital choice—intimate and bodily expressions of individuality—the Court stressed the location or exercise of privacy rights in the home, even in the marital bedroom. Modern privacy doctrine, following the language of a 1944 Supreme Court decision, *Prince v. Massachusetts* (321 U.S. 1966), has affirmed that there is a "private realm of family life which the state cannot enter." Connecting the right to privacy with domestic location or institutions such as marriage and childbearing did not, of course, mean that all acts occurring at home or between family members were protected: for instance, murder, incest, adultery, and, as *Bowers v. Hardwick* (478 U.S. 186) made clear in 1986, consensual acts of sodomy, although taking place at home, are not protected from the state's proscription.

The reliance of the right to privacy on the "sacred precincts" of the home, while crucial to definition of the right, also limited its scope. *Eisenstadt v. Baird* (405 U.S. 438 [1971]), which eliminated a Massachusetts statute making it illegal for druggists to sell or doctors to prescribe birth control to unmarried adults, and *Roe v. Wade* (410 U.S. 113 [1973]), which struck down state laws preventing a woman from obtaining an ABORTION during the first trimester of pregnancy, indicated a new tendency. Neither decision focused on the domestic site itself, and both articulated the individual's right to be free from "unwarranted governmental intrusion" (*Eisenstadt*, 405 U.S. 453) in deciding whether to bear a child, thus envisioning a privacy that was portable, so to speak, that belonged to the individual rather than being tied to the home. The concurring opinion of Justice WILLIAM O. DOUGLAS in *Roe* went beyond the majority's assertion of the right to avoid state regulation, to a positive affirmation of privacy as a dimension of FREEDOM.

Late twentieth-century defenses of privacy rights, while indebted to nineteenth-century forbears, face circumstances vastly different from those that brought bourgeois conceptions of public and private into being. The extent and techniques of surveillance, record-keeping, and publicity wielded by government, medical authorities, marketing agencies, and telecommunications media overwhelm inherited expectations of a divide between public and private. Actual differences are erased as state agencies, directives, incentives, and regulations interpenetrate virtually all forms of private enterprise, as headlines (or talk-show hosts) daily scream out the intimate sexual and medical practices of public figures, as formerly hidden orifices of the body become a principal subject for public performance and artistic expression, and outerwear looks like underwear. The actual attainment of privacy, as in "the general right of the individual to be let alone," has become relinked to privilege—economic privilege—since those who are poor and in greatest need of assistance from the state are those whose domestic and personal lives are most pervaded by public oversight. Public scrutiny of the economic and child-rearing conduct of single mothers, especially those who receive public welfare payments, for example, makes a mockery of their having a "private realm of family life where the state cannot enter." As can be seen from the difference between *Griswold v. Connecticut* (381 U.S. 479 [1965]), which affirmed the privacy of the bedroom for heterosexual couples, and *Bowers v. Hardwick*, which denied it to homosexual ones, the right to privacy has been formed around a normative version of two-parent heterosexual marriage and family life, and those who do not conform do not benefit equally.

The apparent breakdown of what used to be seen as a clear distinction between public and private raises the question whether the divide between the two, which has always been as much ideological as descriptive, has strutted its part on the historical stage and should be retired. While the division has been made to seem natural, to have the same implications for all individuals, the tendentiousness of such claims has become clear. Feminist critics in particular have stressed how the formulation that life is divided into public and private spheres (with characteristic institutions and attributes in each) has served to solidify GENDER hierarchy, to corral and limit women to the private sphere only, and to erase the interdependency of household and market. Refusing to honor such a divide between private and public, the feminist statement of 1970 that "the personal is political" recognized power politics in the domestic realm. In the movement to combat wife-battering, for example, feminists confronted the male privilege lurking in the private realm, where a "man's home is his castle," its residents his subjects.

Yet in the era of powerful modern states, erasure of the boundary between private and public seems an imminent threat to personal freedoms. Even defenders of women and children who would dismantle the protected zone of privacy in order to confront domestic violence and father–daughter incest have to acknowledge that the "right to privacy" has been essential in advancing toward the goal of reproductive freedom. At the end of the twentieth century an understanding of privacy as a dimension of liberty—indeed, reconfiguration of the private as the realm of particular freedoms—amounts to a near-complete reversal of the classical view, which located freedom (for men) in public.

NANCY F. COTT

FURTHER READING

Stephanie Coontz, *The Social Origins of Private Life* (New York: Verso, 1988).

Jean Bethke Elshtain, *Public Man, Private Woman: Women in Social and Political Thought* (Princeton: Princeton University Press, 1981).

Martha Albertson Fineman, "Intimacy Outside of the Natural Family: the Limits of Privacy," *Connecticut Law Review* 23 (summer 1991): 955–72.

Isaac Kramnick, "The 'Great National Discussion': the Discourse of Politics in 1787," *William and Mary Quarterly* 45 (Jan. 1988): 3–32.

Carole Pateman, "Feminist Critiques of the Public/Private Dichotomy," in S. I. Benn and G. F. Gaus, eds., *Public and Private in Social Life* (London: Croom Helm, 1983).

Jed Rubenfeld, "The Right of Privacy," *Harvard Law Review* 102 (Feb. 1989): 737–807.

Elizabeth M. Schneider, "The Violence of Privacy," *Connecticut Law Review* 23 (summer 1991): 973–99.

Carole Shammas, "The Domestic Environment in Early Modern England and America," *Journal of Social History* 14 (1980): 3–24.

Samuel D. Warren and Louis D. Brandeis, "The Right to Privacy," *Harvard Law Review* 4 (Dec. 15, 1890): 193–218.

Raymond Williams, "Private," in Williams, *Keywords: a Vocabulary of Culture and Society* (New York: Oxford University Press, 1976).

profession Our primary source for the history of professions in the United States has been a literature of self-presentation, written by successful competitors in the intellectual market. The historiography of the professions also participates in the cultural construction of professional AUTHORITY, and implicates its authors in traditional hierarchies of masculine power. The close identification of the field with intellectual history continually fortifies the exclusive boundaries of the professions that are its subjects. But by taking into account the cultural negotiation of social power, some historians of the professions are locating their subjects in mediating positions between civil society and the state, or between established professions and a fractious clientele.

Just as professions historically have been self-fulfilling and self-limiting institutions, so is the historiography of professions riveted in front of a mirror, encouraged by the beauty of its own image. But to see professions in their social-historical contexts and political complexity, historians have to permit what is not professional to define what is. What would a historiography of professions look like that was drawn with attention to interstices? It would

be, to begin with, a historiography of relationships, of power, of language, of representation. Rather than reinforcing the cherished professional pretenses of political neutrality and epistemological objectivity, this move includes as subjects people and projects heretofore marginalized.

If professional self-definitions are not to be taken at face value but as maneuvers within contexts of social negotiation over social problems, as translations of one form of power into another, then the history of professions becomes a study of cultural authority and power relations. The importance of professions is specified and deepened, not erased, by historical reintegration of professional lives into the cultures of the civil society in which they play a vital mediating role. As Antonio Gramsci suggested, it is the production of intellectual work (including the production of history by—among others—professional historians) that translates civil social experience into state power and explains that power to the populace. What are the historical sites of this translation?

Gramsci's observations on intellectuals suggest the importance of the larger political culture—language, memory, and ostensibly private institutions—for making sense of professional authority. The classical professions, each directly concerned with immediate matters of life and death, form one of the primary social and historical links between the material "base" of lived experience and the cultural "superstructures" of institutions. This linkage is constituted by professional discourse, the vast institution of LANGUAGE that translates authority into power, force into persuasion.

A generation ago, sociology dominated research on the professions. Skepticism toward sociological approaches to the history of professions has arisen in resistance to both the powerful typology set forth by TALCOTT PARSONS, and the positivist materialism of neo-Marxian sociology of professions. The Parsonian approach, in which professions epitomize processes of MODERNIZATION, has fared poorly in the disillusion of postmodernism—above all the loss of confidence in the very idea of PROGRESS; the neo-Marxian approach has tended toward a preference for economic explanation that seems to diminish the cultural forms of authority and power. In reaction to this material determinism, other scholars have abandoned the concrete, the temporal, in favor of a metahistorical "discourse." The subtler insights of both Marx and Weber on the mediation of economy through culture, and the contradictory aspects of authority and consent, have not figured greatly, so powerful has been the rhetorical force of the linguistic turn on academic discourse.

Further, the historiography has been constrained by the overweening effectiveness of the very archetypes of "profession" that historians want to discover. That is, a common notion of "the" professional (a singular, abstract, unattached white Anglo-Saxon Protestant gentleman of a past century) works not only in the history of the professions to preserve and consolidate professional knowledge, authority, and power among a traditional class, gender, and race, but in the present, to reify and reinforce this process through the writing of its history. We have seen the archetype, and he is us.

A more skeptical understanding of the roles of memory, of history, of language, of race, and of classed and gendered archetypes in the formation of professional authority might begin to unhook historians from naive complicity in this authority. It may allow historians to acknowledge our participation in the construction of social authority among the professions, including our own.

The classical professions—medicine, law, the ministry, the military—in Gramsci's vocabulary are both coercive and hegemonic. The degree to which other professional and political groups rhetorically borrow authority from these older professions can account for the otherwise inexplicable power of minor professions. Newer or lesser professions linguistically emulate older and (literally) stronger professions. This is a cumulative, historical process; it is often not a consciously adopted strategy but a "verbal inheritance," elaborated and applied to a particular sociopolitical task.

The fact that this emulative process is verbal does not mean that it is *merely rhetorical*. This is most evident in the verbal, yet exquisitely powerful, nature of the law, where coercion and persuasion meet. Yet it ought to be evident as well—and surely is to subjects of coercive authority—that powers of life and death are conferred also (both legally and informally) by class membership, gender, ethnicity, nationality, age, family, creed, and race, as mediated through professional agency.

Because professions mediate between civil culture and the state, they function along the cusp between coercion and legitimation, between discipline and punishment, persuasion and force. Most of the time professionals are engaged in maintaining order through cultural, semantic, political means, but backing these is the continual threat of force, power over life and death. Professionals are not only mediators between state and society but between language and violence. Thus the vigorous arguments over language lately upsetting so many American historians are central to the historiography of professions.

A semantic approach to the social, intellectual, and political history of the professions raises questions about definition. Our narrow definitions of profession preclude, in advance, much historical study of relationships among inchoate professions, of competing jurisdictions, of "failed" professions, of marginalized and disenfranchised people.

The historical sense of the term profession is itself linguistic: the word denotes the verbal affirmation of a commitment, originally religious, to a particular way of life within a community of peers. Practitioners of MEDICINE and LAW subsequently borrowed the term "profession," linking their increasingly secular enterprises to religious devotion and divine authority, and maintaining the importance, in their self-definition, of the verbal nature of their work. Although "lay," "lay fee" and "laite" were terms used from the middle of the thirteenth century to distinguish the common people from the clergy, it was not until the 1810s in the United States that practitioners of law and medicine conventionally borrowed the terms "lay" and "laity" from the clerical vocabulary, to distinguish themselves from their nonprofessional clientele and from competing professional groups. This usage furthered specialization, for anyone not wholly devoted to a given profession was by definition a "layman," though belonging to another profession. Thus, a lawyer was a layman in a discussion of medicine, a physician a layman in a legal dispute, and so on.

Yet professionals are not only professionals; they are variously and simultaneously children, followers, neighbors, colleagues, debtors, rivals, friends, strangers, employees, clients, owners. Though the "family history" of a given profession is most easily traced through notable forbears, that is, other professions (and here historians together have produced a pretty good genealogy), professions are also enmeshed in social relations of all sorts, many of these significant to professional achievement. Through these social relations, professionals (like everyone else) are linked to a pervasive semantic system of authority that is symbolically constituted as masculine and generative—and not especially "professional." That is, patriarchal authority is replicated not only, not even primarily, through direct and crude coercive exercise of professional power by men, but subtly at the everyday cultural level, outside the contexts of formal professional activity, through a series of metaphoric truisms.

These metaphoric truisms are located in some primitive social sites: in bed, on the farm, in the battlefield. They equate the archetypal father within the home with absolute social authority outside; they equate male sexual "conquest" with martial conquest, and they equate the natural (as against the human) world with the feminine. The ultimate patriarch is the almighty supernatural, linked theologically and explicitly to these worldly orders. The self-replenishing sources of legal, medical, clerical, or military authority are found not only in patriarchy itself as a system of material power and coercive force, but are coded into everyday speech about seemingly unrelated activities such that masculine power is continually celebrated and furthered, and feminine power continually contained and diffused. This argument would be reductionist if it were predicated on a bifurcated concept of "language" versus "reality," but it is instead based on a historical view of language as a collective form of memory, a public fund of evanescent, private, material experience.

Just as the threat, spectacle, and recounting of corporal punishment, rather than the stark statistical likelihood of its infliction, has undergirded the authority of slaveholders over enslaved people, the diffuse—even trivialized—threat of sexual coercion, violence or advantage undergirds the masculine construct of professional authority with such thoroughness that it rarely needs to be explicit in professional contexts. An example is the prevalence of sports metaphor (itself framed in martial and sexual terms) in corporate business, political, and military discourse, language widely shared among men across class and ethnic lines, and significantly less familiar to women, whose exclusion from combat and play creates semantic exclusion within an integrated workplace. Such trivial-seeming equations are always at work in the formation of professional authority, driven by a metaphorical dynamic in which everyday hierarchies are written into the political languages of professional activity.

The language of professions is not borrowed alone from other professions, but frequently taken from the expressly nonprofessional, even antiprofessional culture. This is in part because the professional project is self-contradictory, entailing both popularization and monopoly. In the United States, where professionals are bound both by ideals of democracy and the demands of capitalism, the borrowing can as often take the form of rhetorical populism—hearty metaphorical denials of elitism, monopoly, even of professionalism itself. Combat metaphor is one such pseudo-democratic vehicle, reinforcing gender and sexual hierarchies while denying racial, class, and professional distinctions among men.

The habit of mutual emulation among the learned professions forms a historical succession of authority, in which one already-established profession becomes the model for another. Thus secular law genealogically succeeded divine law; medicine was reinvented as the "laws" of nature were revealed

through science, and so on. In this strict genealogy, however, a complex matrix of cultural authority is reduced to imitation of the static and ahistorical Parsonian archetype. Historians would do better to think about professional emulation as historically specific hierarchies of authority being located also in extraprofessional institutions. Emulation transcends those institutions through the "portable" borrowed languages in which medical, sexual, military, economic, legal, familial authorities stand in for one another, in complex but decipherable ways. A genealogy of successful, established professions will de facto exclude extraprofessional sources of cultural authority, and will leave questions of power only superficially explored: there are no mothers in this family.

The interstices of the professions *have* been explored in works on the "quasiprofessions," on inchoate professions, and on antiprofessionalism. Although it is difficult to miss the gendered character of professional, lay, and antiprofessional pursuits, the question of gender and authority, and the literature on women in the professions, remains largely a separate enterprise from the history of the professions as it has most recently been marked off by nonfeminists. In this field, only women who made it into the professions appear; the other social and political ways that women outside the professions defined professional authority barely figure. These would include women's antiprofessional activities that challenged medical domains, legal institutions, and spiritual authorities; the penumbra of women in the "semiprofessions"; the uses of women as icons in the evocation of professional authority; women as both clientele and subject, and the feminization and deprofessionalization of particular social tasks. The "professions" literature barely engages pertinent works in the histories of nursing, social work, education, domestic medicine, physiology, psychiatry, the natural sciences, public lecturing, anthropology, public health, psychology, philanthropy, popular religion.

Linda Kerber and Joan Scott have pointed out that for professional as well as political reasons, when the "peripheral" territory of women's relations to the professions is explored, it is often without sustained reference to the "metropolitan" centers of masculine power that help explain its marginality. Conversely, when women professionals are the subject of women's history, they are too often segregated from the context of masculine power relations that prevail in the professions historically. There have been exceptions, yet much writing about the professions has been a contained history of a predetermined group of self-described professionals, its boundaries too neatly defined and skirmishes across them too easily seen, in retrospect, as ultimately insignificant because apparently unsuccessful.

JOANNE BROWN

See also ACADEMIC FREEDOM; HEGEMONY.

FURTHER READING

JoAnne Brown, The *Definition of a Profession* (Princeton: Princeton University Press, 1992).

JoAnne Brown and David Van Keuren, eds., *The Estate of Social Knowledge* (Baltimore: Johns Hopkins University Press, 1991).

Jacqueline Goggin, "Challenging Sexual Discrimination in the Historical Profession: Women Historians and the American Historical Association, 1890–1940," *American Historical Review* (June 1992): 769–802.

Jan Goldstein, "Foucault among the Sociologists: the 'Disciplines' and the History of the Professions," *History and Theory* 23 (1984): 170–92.

Evelyn Brooks Higgenbotham, "African-American Women's History and the Metalanguage of Race," *Signs* 17 (winter 1992).

Linda Kerber, "Separate Spheres, Female Worlds, Women's Place: the Rhetoric of Women's History," *Journal of American History* 75 (1988): 9–39.

Philip Pauly, "Summer Resort and Scientific Discipline: Woods Hole and the Structure of American Biology, 1882–1925," in R. Rainger et al., eds., *The American Development of Biology* (New Brunswick: Rutgers University Press, 1988).

Martin Pernick "Medical Professionalism," in *Encyclopedia of Bioethics*, vol. 3 (New York: Free Press, 1978).

Barbara Gutmann Rosenkrantz, "Cart before Horse: Theory, Practice and Professional Image in American Public Health, 1870–1920," *Journal of the History of Medicine and Allied Sciences* 29 (1974): 55–73.

Joan Wallach Scott, *Gender and the Politics of History* (New York: Columbia University Press, 1988).

Nancy Tomes and Joan Jacobs Brumberg, "Women in the Professions: a Research Agenda for American Historians," *Reviews in American History* 10 (1982): 275–96.

progress From the perspective of millennia, the idea that history marches onward and upward is a recent invention, barely 200 years old. Until the end of the eighteenth century, most people would have ridiculed such an idea. If historical events fell into any pattern at all, it was assumed to resemble a series of cycles, not a straight upward line. Dynasties came and went; civilizations rose and fell; growth was always followed by decline.

"Time marches on," we say today, meaning that the future will look like a heightened version of the present—more labor-saving machines, more comforts, more choices. But the future did not look so reassuringly familiar to our ancestors. During most of history, people were more impressed by the destructive effects of time than by the good things it held in store. Time, they thought, doomed everything to decay.

What our ancestors sought was stability, not progress. Was it possible to devise institutions, political institutions in particular, that would resist the corrosive effects of time? That was the great question confronting political theory before the ENLIGHTENMENT; but the historical record did not encourage confidence that it could ever be answered, with much confidence, in the affirmative. Not until the scientific revolution made it possible to envision the conquest of scarcity did the world begin to think of time as an ally.

Belief in progress takes two forms, utopian and incremental. In eighteenth-century France, the apostles of Enlightenment drew the most extravagant conclusions from the advancement of scientific knowledge. Their nineteenth-century offspring, Hegel, Comte, and Spencer, spun out variations on the theme of irresistible progress: history as the universal triumph of reason. Marx contemptuously dismissed "utopian" socialism as the product of wishful thinking, only to promise his followers the classless society, the withering away of the state, and the end of alienation. Marxism was the last of the nineteenth-century UTOPIAS to crumble in our own century of total wars and "final solutions." Yet the idea of progress lingers on. Indeed the death of communism has breathed new life into a conception of progress that associates it not with the creation of an earthly paradise but, more modestly, with the blessings of the free market—with a general increase in productivity, a rising standard of living, rising levels of LITERACY and political awareness, and the replacement of autocratic regimes with parliamentary regimes based on respect for human RIGHTS.

The notion of progress as an open-ended process of gradual and steady improvement, because it allows for intervals of regression and seems to respect the limits of reasons, has proved more durable than the utopian verson. It too derives from the Enlightenment—from the political economy of Bernard Mandeville and Adam Smith rather than from airy speculation about the wonders to come. Smith's analysis of the division of labor and its beneficial effects appeared to root progress in the prosaic details of economic life. The productive forces unleashed by capitalism, Smith explained, encouraged a revolution of rising expectations. The abundance of goods made available by modern industry generated a steadily rising level of demand. Goods formerly defined as luxuries came to be seen as necessities. The appetites unleashed by modern productivity created an inexhaustible market and thus opened up the prospect of economic development without any foreseeable limits.

It was the new political economy, widely popularized during the course of the nineteenth century, that made the idea of progress compelling to sober, practical men and women—not the prospect that history would come to a happy ending in a classless society or some other steady state. The theorists of the market appeared to have solved the problem that baffled their predecessors: how to build a political order resistant to change. Change itself, once it was understood as cumulative and irreversible, assured continuity. Sometimes this progressive view of history, as it was elaborated by liberals and social democrats—the true heirs of Adam Smith—was advanced quite explicitly as a refutation of cyclical theories of change. To prophets of doom and decline, the party of progress replied that the old rhythm of rise and fall had been broken by the invention of abundance—the "new basis of civilization," in the words of SIMON PATTEN, an economist writing at the beginning of the twentieth century. The emergence of a "pleasure or surplus economy," according to Patten, annulled the "ancient tragic model" of civilization and decay. Those who attempted to "predict tomorrow's economic states from a study of the economic states of Rome or Venice" overlooked the unprecedented abundance made possible by the modern productive system. Their apprehensions belonged to a "vanishing age of deficit" (pp. 9, 14, 184).

The history of the twentieth century might be taken to support Patten's qualified optimism. The same wars and calamities that undermined utopian theories of progress promoted economic growth and the integration of a world market and thus appeared to vindicate those who linked progress to an indefinitely expanding process of economic, political, and cultural development. It was no longer possible to claim that history was marching toward the promised land of truth, justice, peace, and love; but more limited claims—those advanced, for example, by students of "modernization"—seemed more plausible than ever. It was hard to deny that MODERNIZATION was both cumulative and, in the long run, irresistible, if only because modern communications opened people's eyes to the possibility of a better life. Nor did it seem utterly fanciful to suppose that the "demonstration effects" of modernization were so clearly visible, even in backward countries governed by tyrants, that tyrants could not hold out indefinitely against the rising clamor for goods and FREEDOM. The promised land was not yet in sight, but the course of events seemed to justify a belief in modest, incremental improvement.

Those who argue in this way are always ready to admit that progress has its price. Constant change tears down old landmarks, undermines old systems of belief, gives rise to widespread nervousness and anxiety. Affluence does not assure happiness or peace of mind, as the affluent know better than most. Still, it is clearly preferable to poverty. Who can deny that the benefits of progress, on balance, outweigh its costs? As long as the question of progress is posed in this way, the question answers itself. The price may be high, but few would seriously choose not to pay it. Progress is an offer we have been unable to refuse.

The real question today is whether progress has built-in limits. When the environmental effects of industrial TECHNOLOGY began to be seriously investigated, the debate about progress entered a new stage. Proponents of ENVIRONMENTALISM argue that the earth will not support indefinite economic expansion along the old lines. Recent evidence of global warming, damage to the ozone layer, and long-term atmospheric shifts caused by deforestation have raised further doubts about unlimited growth. Even though much of this evidence remains controversial, it has already transformed our political discourse. For the first time we find ourselves asking not whether progress is desirable but whether it is even possible, as we have known it in the past.

The global distribution of wealth raises the same question in a more urgent form. Experts may disagree about global warming, but if we consider the effect of extending Western patterns of consumption to the rest of the world, the prospect is truly staggering. Imagine the populations of India and China equipped with two cars to a family, air conditioning in private houses, electrical appliances galore, and the ability to participate in a consumer economy that already makes heavy demands on the environment even when it is confined to a mere fraction of the world's population. It is obvious that the wasteful, heedless life now enjoyed by the West cannot be made available to everyone without stretching the earth's energy resources and its adaptive capacity beyond the breaking point.

The idea of progress loses all meaning if progress no longer implies the democratization of affluence. It was the prospect of universal abundance that made progress a morally compelling ideology in the past. But affluence for all now appears unlikely, even in the distant future. The emergence of a global economy, far from eliminating poverty, has widened the gap between rich and poor nations. The revolution of rising expectations may not be self-generating, as we had thought. It may even be reversible. Famine and plague have returned to large parts of the world. Poverty, moreover, is spilling over into the developed nations from the Third World. Desperate migrants pour into the cities of the richer countries, swelling the vast army of the homeless, unemployed, illiterate, drug-ridden, derelict, and effectively disfranchised.

Progress and DEMOCRACY, we used to think, go hand in hand. Today this proposition is no longer self-evident. A continually rising standard of living for the rich, it is now clear, means a falling standard of living for everyone else. Forcible redistribution of income on a massive scale, which can be achieved only by a state armed with dictatorial powers, is an equally unattractive alternative. The best hope of reducing the gap between rich and poor lies in the gradual emergence of a new consensus, a common understanding about the material prerequisites of a good life. Hard questions will have to be asked. Just how much do we need to live comfortably? How much is enough?

Such questions challenge the notion of progress, which is usually taken to mean that there is no such thing as enough. The prospect of a world in which people voluntarily agree to set limits on their acquisitive appetite bears little resemblance to what is conventionally understood as progress. But then neither does the prospect of a world in which unparalleled affluence coexists with frightful depths of misery and squalor.

CHRISTOPHER LASCH

FURTHER READING

Edward Hallett Carr, *What Is History?* (New York: Vintage, 1961).

Christopher Dawson, *Progress and Religion: an Historical Enquiry* (New York: Longmans, Green, 1929).

Charles Frankel, *The Faith of Reason: the Idea of Progress in the French Enlightenment* (New York: Columbia University Press, 1948).

Michael Ignatieff, *The Needs of Strangers* (New York: Viking, 1984).

Christopher Lasch, *The True and Only Heaven: Progress and Its Critics* (New York: Norton, 1991).

Karl Löwith, *Meaning in History: the Theological Implications of the Philosophy of History* (Chicago: University of Chicago Press, 1949).

Simon N. Patten, *The New Basis of Civilization* (1907; Cambridge: Harvard University Press, 1968).

J. G. A. Pocock, *The Machiavellian Moment: Florentine Political Thought and the Atlantic Republican Tradition* (Princeton: Princeton University Press, 1975).

progressivism Like the monster in some science fiction movie from the 1950s, the concept of progressivism apparently cannot be killed. All powerful, the creature loomed over American historical writing after World War II. In tribute, historians labeled the period of reform from the late nineteenth century to World War I the "Progressive Era." During the 1950s and 1960s, they produced a tidal wave of books and articles about progressivism—its nature, its adherents, its achievements. But all that scholarship had an ironic outcome: the flood engulfed the monster. Historians could not agree on what progressivism was or what it meant—a popular movement to preserve democracy, an earnest attempt to reorganize society on bureaucratic lines, a passionate crusade to tame big business, a canny scheme to protect large-scale capitalism. Nor could historians agree on who the progressives were. By the 1970s, just about every social group—professionals, farmers, urban workers, middle-class women, consumers, small businessmen, big businessmen—appeared to have been progressive. The monster sank beneath the churning waters of definition and redefinition. In 1972, Peter Filene pronounced the obsequies in "An Obituary for 'The Progressive Movement.'" That should have been it—the creature should have been dead. But instead progressivism almost miraculously reemerged to live on in American historiography. The question is why.

Despite the difficulty in defining progressivism, the concept endures for two main reasons. First, the "Progressive Era" seems clearly different from the Gilded Age and the 1920s, the less reformist periods before and after it. More important, the liberal brand of reform that dominated the Progressive Era differed clearly from the laissez-faire liberalism of the earlier nineteenth century and from the New Deal liberalism of the later twentieth century. Progressivism survives because it represents a crucial stage in the evolution of liberal ideology and practice.

For all the historiographical disagreements of the 1960s and 1970s, progressivism seems to have originated in the late nineteenth-century crises of a single social group, the Victorian middle class. By the 1880s and 1890s, professionals, white-collar workers, and petty proprietors found themselves trapped in a hostile world made by their own values. Victorian culture—laissez-faire individualism, nurtured by domesticity and disciplined by self-control—had spurred the industrialization of the United States. Now the middle class was caught between two alien, warring classes—big business and workers—with troubling economic, political, and cultural power. At the same time, the Victorians' domestic life was threatened by growing consumerism, a new immigration, and, above all, by tension between the sexes. Challenged externally and internally, the middle class tried to reform both itself and the wider society. The Victorians needed to redirect their own lives, to control and reshape other classes, and to halt social conflict. The result was a new middle-class ideology, progressivism.

At its core, this ideology recast Victorian notions of DOMESTICITY and INDIVIDUALISM. The middle class groped its way toward a kind of sexual peace between women and men: women should be able to find more freedom and opportunity outside the home; men should be willing to find more fulfillment within the home. More broadly, progressivism entailed the restriction of traditional individualism. Now troubled by a society based on untrammeled individual will, progressives endorsed what some came to call "social control," the external regulation of human beings.

This ideological transformation gave late nineteenth- and early twentieth-century reform its particular character. Given the breadth of the middle-class crisis, progressives necessarily addressed strikingly varied issues, from the economic and political to the social, cultural, and philosophical. Two generations of men and women reconsidered the relationship of knowledge and values, ideas and action, faith and reform. Such thinkers as JOHN DEWEY, JANE ADDAMS, HERBERT CROLY, WALTER LIPPMANN, E. A. ROSS, CHARLOTTE PERKINS GILMAN, WALTER RAUSCHENBUSCH, and RICHARD T. ELY particularly explored the nature of human ties, the relationship of individual, family, community, nation, and state. To deal with labor relations, consumer protection, prostitution, corruption, and other matters, progressives created new vehicles of private action—settlement houses, most notably. But ultimately, these reformers looked to government to solve private and public problems. Progressivism, most fundamentally, shifted authority from the individual and the family to the group and the state.

This new middle-class ideology did not dictate the precise character of the shift. Progressivism was an ideology, not a set of specific policy guidelines. Historians have gotten into trouble when they have tried to isolate uniquely "progressive" measures. Progressivism was expressed in different, even contradictory cultural languages—evangelical Protestant, pragmatist, scientific, racist, and so forth. It was not inherently democratic or repressive. It dictated no firm answers to some crucial questions—above all, whether large-scale business corporations should be dissolved.

That vagueness helps explain progressivism's power. It did not place tight restrictions on reformers. Moving in different directions, they created no single, unified progressive "movement." They could—and did—make common cause with members of other groups and classes on particular issues. Specific aspects of progressivism had wide appeal; the very word "progressive" had great cultural cachet by the 1910s.

THEODORE ROOSEVELT, still wedded to individualism like so much of the upper class, wrapped his political fortunes in the progressive mantle in 1912. But the political uses of progressivism should not obscure its class basis. Progressive ideology was rooted in the crises of the middle class—in the Victorians' distinctive domestic predicament, in their position between labor and capital, in their acute problem with individualism.

In some sense, progressivism was conservative. Although influenced by socialism, progressive ideology, like all brands of LIBERALISM, remained firmly committed to the preservation of the capitalist economy. This was a reformist creed intended to avert conflict, to stabilize unsteady situations at home and at large. But progressivism was not primarily backward-looking: to save themselves, the Victorians exchanged old values for new.

The radical implications of this transformation became clear during WORLD WAR I, when President WOODROW WILSON pursued perhaps the most ambitious statist design of this century. To win the war, the Wilsonians sought to control not only the economy, but ideas and pleasure as well. The effort helped to win the war but undermined progressive ideals. Such policies as labor mediation, income taxes, censorship, propaganda, and prohibition spurred popular revulsion towards the state. Progressivism was doomed.

After World War I, there would never again be quite so much blind faith in social control, in external regulation of human life. During the Great Depression, New Deal liberals sought increased control over the economy but were much less interested in regulating private social relations. In World War II, the government of Franklin Roosevelt was hardly as audacious as the Wilsonians had been in their efforts to control popular opinion.

Progressivism, then, would seem to be a relic of the past, superseded by other forms of liberalism. But the evolution of liberal ideas and policies after 1960 makes progressive ideology more relevant. Since the Great Society, the liberal state seems increasingly compelled to regulate private behavior, to control race relations, abortion, smoking, speech, and so on. Progressivism, not the New Deal, may well be the most useful analog to liberalism at the end of the twentieth century. That is one more reason why the creature will live on.

MICHAEL MCGERR

FURTHER READING

Robert M. Crunden, *Ministers of Reform: the Progressives' Achievement in American Civilization, 1889–1920* (New York: Basic Books, 1982).

Benjamin Park DeWitt, *The Progressive Movement* (1915; Seattle: University of Washington Press, 1968).

Peter G. Filene, "An Obituary for 'The Progressive Movement,'" *American Quarterly* 22 (spring 1970): 20–34.

Richard Hofstadter, *The Age of Reform: From Bryan to F.D.R.* (New York: Knopf, 1955).

James T. Kloppenberg, *Uncertain Victory: Social Democracy and Progressivism in European and American Thought, 1870–1920* (New York: Oxford University Press, 1986).

Arthur S. Link and Richard L. McCormick, *Progressivism* (Arlington Heights, Ill.: Harlan Davidson, 1983).

Jean B. Quandt, *From the Small Town to the Great Community: the Social Thought of Progressive Intellectuals* (New Brunswick: Rutgers University Press, 1970).

Daniel Rodgers, "In Search of Progressivism," *Reviews in American History* 10 (Dec. 1972): 113–32.

Robert Wiebe, *The Search for Order, 1877–1920* (New York: Hill and Wang, 1967).

prohibition   Excessive drinking—and the belief that it is both an abuse of the self and a threat to society—is as old as history. But the idea that the remedy to this evil lay in government prohibition of the production, sale, and use of alcoholic beverages, rather than in individual self-restraint, or sanctions (public or religious) for intemperance, did not appear until the nineteenth and early twentieth centuries. Prohibition, ironically, is a product of modern times. And although the prohibition of drink now is marginal and anachronistic, that of drugs is not, and restrictions on tobacco are very much a growth industry.

Before the prohibition of alcohol there was temperance; or, more accurately, the disapproval of intemperance. Colonial America like early modern Europe had laws and ordinances regulating the liquor trade and penalizing drunkenness. The first outright prohibition was directed at particular classes of people—slaves, Indians, indentured servants, apprentices—who were perceived as social risks. These early restrictions reflected the desire for "social control" that would mark the modern prohibition movement.

The first general assault on the consumption of alcoholic beverages came during the era of American reform that flourished between 1820 and 1860. Like its counterpart in England, the American temperance crusade was part of a general humanitarian (and evangelical) movement to improve the treatment of prisoners and the insane, to secure EQUALITY for women, and to end black slavery.

The American temperance movement at first concentrated on individual moral-religious reformation rather than the general proscription of alcohol. But a rising American nationalism and Protestantism EVANGELICALISM combined to fuel a chiliastic stress on social perfection, which by the 1850s called for outright prohibition as the appropriate goal of the antidrink crusade, and for the immediate and unconditional abolition of slavery (*see also* ANTISLAVERY).

Some historians have stressed the element of social control in the pre-Civil War temperance-prohibition movement. They see lying behind it a growing bourgeois belief that unrestrained drink, like unrestrained sex, undermined social stability and industrial efficiency. But it is important to recognize that the capacity of evangelicalism to set the moral agenda of the time was not contingent upon bourgeois social and economic needs, but stemmed from much larger cultural necessities. It was the congruence of a number of values and objectives—to attain godliness through the rejection of bad habits; to demonstrate the higher morality of the American Republican citizen; to assure an upright, morally cleansed social order—that gave the antidrink movement what authority it had.

Maine was the first state to enact prohibition, in 1851, and some others followed. But the preponderance of social forces during the second half of the nineteenth century worked against prohibition. The Civil War, hostility to strong government, the decline of evangelical reform, new immigration and urban life, the pace of an industrial order that made drink a balm for workers and managers alike: all tended to marginalize the campaign against drink. The Women's Christian Temperance Union (founded in 1874) was more important for the experience in political mobilization that it gave to thousands of women than for changing the drinking habits of males. By 1900 the few remaining state prohibition laws were virtually dead letters.

The lesson of experience seemed to be that the problem of drink, as a contemporary put it, "cannot be dealt with by general enactments or at long range." In any event, liquor consumption appeared to be declining. Why, then, did national prohibition succeed by 1920, precisely when American INDUSTRIALISM, URBANISM, secularism, consumerism—all presumably harmful to the cause—were in full flood?

Certainly rural and small-town American Protestants, anxious about the new immigration and other features of the modern urban-industrial world, found in prohibition (as they did in immigration restriction) an evocative expression of their desire to preserve an older social order. But their efforts would have been unavailing if they had not formed an unlikely alliance with urban reformers who in other respects stood for the modern society that traditionalists abhorred. Progressive social reformers such as John R. Commons and E. A. Ross were drawn to prohibition not because of its evangelical appeal, but because medical and social scientific studies documented the physical and social harm wrought by drink. Women's organizations picked up the old theme of liquor's baleful impact on family life; white southerners (and BOOKER T. WASHINGTON) argued that prohibition would lessen interracial violence and lynching; labor reformers linked liquor to poverty; political reformers identified saloons with party machines; economic reformers attacked the liquor interest as another uncontrolled trust.

True, it required American entry into World War I, and the special boost the war gave to xenophobic nationalism (the liquor interests were widely seen as "German") to ensure the passage in 1919 of the Eighteenth Amendment and the enabling Volstead Act. But the coalition that made prohibition was already in place. Prohibition, like the contemporaneous movements to restrict or outlaw immigration, drugs, and prostitution and red-light districts, was both a modern reform and a reaction by an older American culture threatened by change.

Yet little more than a decade later there was comparably widespread agreement that national prohibition had failed, and had to be ended. Communally enforced behavior, it turned out, had little more chance of success in the 1930s than communally enforced economic or social planning. Liberals and conservatives, workers and businessmen, turned against it, and prohibition was repealed in 1933.

The distaste of Americans for government restrictions on personal behavior is as strong in our own time as it has ever been. At the same time, the continuing prohibition of drugs, and the rise of a campaign against smoking whose scientific rationale and moral fervor bear more than passing resemblance to early twentieth-century liquor prohibition, suggest that the prohibitionist impulse will continue to be a significant component of American public life. It remains to be seen whether advocates of restrictions on drugs and tobacco, or proponents of limits on forms of expression (pornography, "obscene" art, racial or sexual slurs) that many Americans find to be offensive, can mount a compelling intellectual case.

See also OBSCENITY.

MORTON KELLER

FURTHER READING

Jack S. Blocker Jr., *Retreat from Reform: the Prohibition Movement in the United States, 1890–1913* (Westport: Greenwood, 1976).

John C. Burnham, *Bad Habits: Drinking, Smoking, Taking Drugs, Gambling, Sexual Misbehavior, and Swearing in American History* (New York: New York University Press, 1993).

Norman H. Clark, *Deliver Us from Evil: an Interpretation of American Prohibition* (New York: Norton, 1976).

John A. Krout, *The Origins of Prohibition* (New York: Knopf, 1925).

W. J. Rorabaugh, *The Alcoholic Republic* (New York: Oxford University Press, 1979).

James H. Timberlake, *Prohibition and the Progressive Movement* (Cambridge: Harvard University Press, 1963).

proletarianism In the American context, proletarianism as a cultural movement led a short and conflicted existence from about 1921 to the end of the 1930s. Historically, "proletariat" referred to the lowest CLASS of ancient Rome, and through much of the nineteenth century the term was used, in rather a hostile sense, to characterize poor wage workers. But just as originally derogatory words like "protestant" and "dyke" have been affirmatively redeployed by those they were meant to denigrate, so "proletarian," especially in the wake of the Bolshevik revolution, began to accrete positive implications, primarily that of a class-conscious radicalism.

Many of these elements emerge in the well-known *New Masses* editorial by MIKE GOLD entitled "Go Left, Young Writers," published in January 1929.

A new writer has been appearing; a wild youth of about twenty-two, the son of working-class parents, who himself works in the lumber camps, coal mines, harvest fields and mountain camps of America. He is sensitive and impatient. He writes in jets of exasperated feeling and has no time to polish his work. He is violent and sentimental by turns. He lacks self-confidence but writes because he must—and because he has real talent.

Gold's paean, drawing as much upon WALT WHITMAN and JACK LONDON as upon Marx and Lenin, represents a widely shared conception on the left not only of the proletarian artist but of the idealized proletariat. It poses the male worker, fresh from his labor, as the new breed of writer. It validates his unpolished, perhaps undisciplined, but deeply felt writing as central to the formation of class consciousness, signified here as "exasperation," presumably with capitalist forms of production.

By 1929, a complex and shifting debate over proletarian art had been raging for a decade in the Soviet Union. Some, like Trotsky, argued that the working class had to build a culture on the basis of what it had taken over from the bourgeoisie; it could transcend bourgeois culture only by learning it first. Others, however, asserted that a true workers' revolution required the immediate transformation of all social institutions, including those, like schools and the arts, in which culture was produced and used.

Any delay would invite those with cultural power to blunt and roll back the authority workers had gained. Both sides held that art needed to serve the revolution, but that accord only made the debate over strategy more savage, since artists bore such heavy responsibility for helping bring a new society to birth. The debate ended only in the early 1930s, when the Stalinists enforced a rigidly proletarian line.

Soviet developments did not control but significantly influenced American ideas about proletarianism through conferences, books, and periodicals. Obviously, the situation in the United States in 1921, when Gold first called for a proletarian art, was quite different from that of revolutionary Russia. And even with the 1929 stock-market crash and subsequent depression, the objectives, forms, and even appropriate writers of a proletarian literature in America remained a contentious matter. At first, in the early 1930s, the American Communist Party—key to the development of proletarian art—encouraged the formation of "John Reed clubs," basically worker-writer discussion groups; the clubs published radical magazines with titles like *Cauldron*, *Hammer*, and *Partisan Review*, and provided opportunities for participants to discuss each other's work and relevant criticism. Other magazines of the Left like *Anvil* and *Blast* also printed writers active in the communist movement, and party-related publishers, bookstores, and libraries circulated the works that were created.

The Communist Party additionally encouraged development of workers' theater groups, which staged agitational plays like Clifford Odets' "Waiting for Lefty" and other forms of agitprop and political drama by writers like LANGSTON HUGHES, Albert Maltz, and Bertold Brecht. The proletarian movement in the United States also generated considerable new interest in reportage, especially accounts of strikes, rallies, and other direct actions by class-conscious workers. Such writing seemed appropriate to proletarian concerns because of its direct, unadorned style, its engagement with "real" people, and its aim of moving the masses forward. (*See also* JOURNALISM.)

The best-known proletarian literature in the United States has always been the fiction, though recent critics have begun to recover long-buried poetry of the period by writers such as Edwin Rolfe and Genevieve Taggard. Initially, the most successful fictional works were semi-autobiographical novels about coming-to-consciousness, like Gold's *Jews Without Money* (1930), Jack Conroy's *The Disinherited* (1933), and *Daughter of Earth* (1929) by AGNES SMEDLEY. Other novels focused on strikes, especially the communist-led struggle at Gastonia, N.C., in 1929; still others

on those whom Edward Dahlberg termed *Bottom Dogs* (1930), the men on the bum, those who were, in Tom Kromer's title, *Waiting for Nothing* (1935).

Thirties' critics debated the propriety and utility of modernist formal experiments in works at least part of whose audience would be unfamiliar with and perhaps unsympathetic to such departures. Novels like Robert Cantwell's *The Land of Plenty* (1934) and Clara Weatherwax's *Marching! Marching!* (1935) provide more or less successful examples of efforts to adapt modernist narrative tactics. Critics also contested the often exclusive focus on WORK: since far fewer women worked in what were taken to be true sites of proletarian struggle (mines, mills, and camps), did that not marginalize women's participation in the revolution? And could not the concentration on work limit revolutionary transformation to economic issues, ignoring basic social questions, like family structure and male supremacy? Such issues have reemerged in recent years with the publication of works like *Yonnondio* (1974) by TILLIE OLSEN and Meridel Le Sueur's *The Girl* (1978), works written largely during the thirties but not published until long after. Recent critics looking back at proletarianism have questioned whether the novel form, which by historical precedent tended to center on the development of a single protagonist, did not inevitably contradict the purposes of a radically collectivist movement.

By 1935, the Communist Party had ceased to support the John Reed clubs and, with the emergence of the "popular front" against fascism, placed less emphasis on the more agitational aspects of proletarian art. Nevertheless, the movement's emphasis on the struggles of working people, on class, on the workplace continued to influence writer like RICHARD WRIGHT, William Attaway, Nelson Algren; and Ruth McKenney.

During the COLD WAR, critics largely dismissed proletarian art as a contradiction in terms, formulaic, propagandistic, and shallow. Recent criticism and the reprinting of some significant proletarian texts have begun to question such judgments as uninformed and themselves artifacts of Cold War culture.

PAUL LAUTER

FURTHER READING
Daniel Aaron, *Writers on the Left* (New York: Harcourt, 1961).
Ralph B. Bogardus and Fred Hobson, eds., *Literature at the Barricades: the American Writer in the 1930s* (Tuscaloosa: University of Alabama Press, 1982).
Barbara Foley, *Radical Representations: Politics and Form in U.S. Proletarian Fiction, 1929–1941* (Durham: Duke University Press, 1994).

James F. Murphy, *The Proletarian Moment: the Controversy over Leftism in Literature* (Urbana: University of Illinois Press, 1991).

Cary Nelson, *Repression and Recovery: Modern American Poetry and the Politics of Cultural Memory, 1910–1945* (Madison: University of Wisconsin Press, 1989).

Paula Rabinowitz, *Labor and Desire: Women's Revolutionary Fiction in Depression America* (Chapel Hill: University of North Carolina Press, 1991).

Walter B. Rideout, *The Radical Novel in the United States, 1900–1945* (Cambridge: Harvard University Press, 1956).

Jon Christian Suggs, *American Proletarian Literature* (Detroit: Gale, 1993).

proslavery thought The antebellum South produced an ideological defense of slavery that was unique among New World slave societies. Though justifications for human bondage had appeared during the eighteenth century and proslavery arguments had been penned by a few South Carolinians during the 1820s, the intellectual defense of slavery emerged fully when immediate abolitionism appeared in the North in the early 1830s. The proslavery argument was initially a response to the contention of northern abolitionists that slavery was a moral wrong and hence slaveholding was a sin. Consequently, proslavery thinkers during the 1830s based their defense of slavery largely on religious grounds. They turned to the Bible to show that Old Testament prophets like Abraham and Isaac had held slaves. They demonstrated that a strict reading of the New Testament disclosed that Jesus and his disciples had never mentioned slavery as sinful. History as well as religion was a mainstay of proslavery thought in the 1830s. Southern defenders of slavery showed that slavery had flourished in the ancient societies of Greece and Rome and insisted that human bondage had provided the foundation for the great civilizations in Western history.

During the 1840s, arguments of racial inferiority were added to the proslavery arsenal. Slavery was now justified on the additional grounds that blacks were inherently inferior and thus well suited for subordination in slavery. Therefore, slavery was the best social system for the coexistence of inferior blacks and superior whites. Ethnology, the scientific study of racial differences, provided an additional theoretical foundation for proslavery arguments on behalf of racial inferiority. Perhaps the South's most prominent defender of slavery on ethnological grounds was the Mobile physician and racial theorist Josiah Nott. Using cranial measurements and statistical data, Nott sought to demonstrate that blacks had different and inferior capabilities. Ethnologists like Nott also argued that the black and white races were created separately. Since this theory of the plural origin of races conflicted with the biblical version of the unity of the human race, the ethnological defense of slavery met with some resistance in the highly evangelical culture of the antebellum South.

The increasing sectional strife of the 1850s stiffened the southern defense of slavery. There was a drive in the lower South to reopen the African slave trade and expand the "peculiar institution" to Central and South America. Proslavery thought during this decade moved toward an aggressive culmination as slavery came to be advocated as a superior social system. Some proslavery thinkers, notably GEORGE FITZHUGH of Virginia and Henry Hughes of Mississippi, suggested seriously that slavery might become a model for all social relations, suitable for whites as well as blacks. Proslavery polemicists also placed greater emphasis during the 1850s on the basic incompatibility between the slave society of the South and the free labor order of the North.

The ideological defense of slavery occupied a prominent place in the intellectual and political life of the Old South. Enlisting the efforts and talents of politicians, scholars, journalists, and writers, the proslavery argument nurtured the intellectual life of the Old South. As a central expression of the growth of southern sectionalism, it was consequently instrumental in the coming of the CIVIL WAR. Despite its centrality to antebellum southern history, proslavery thought has posed peculiar problems of interpretation. To modern liberal thinking, the intellectual justification of human bondage appears morally repugnant and intellectually retrogressive. (*See also* ANTISLAVERY.) Historians have thus been inclined to label proslavery thought as a peculiarly southern aberration from mainstream American liberal and democratic thought. They have accordingly tended to portray southern defenders of slavery as maladjusted outsiders. In recent decades, however, the changing concerns of intellectual history and new approaches to the history of the South have brought fresh perspectives to proslavery thought. (*See also* SOUTHERN INTELLECTUAL HISTORY.)

The increased interest in the relationship between IDEOLOGY and society has led historians to see in proslavery thought a broader articulation of the deepest values of a slaveholding society. Viewed in this context, the southern defense of slavery was not only a justification of human bondage but a legitimation of a social order that valued tradition, an organic view of society, and a particularistic approach to human relations. Historians have thus sought to explain proslavery ideology within the peculiar social context of the antebellum South. It provided southern slaveholders with a set of ideas that helped mediate their relationships with black slaves, white yeoman, and women. The proslavery argument helped justify paternalism and subordination not only on the plantation but in the family and society as well. (*See also* HONOR.)

The study of proslavery thought has also been influenced by recent efforts to emphasize the similarities between the South and the rest of the nation. Viewed from this perspective, proslavery is no longer seen as distinctly southern but rather as a variant of a conservative, antidemocratic strain of thought that emerged in the wake of the American and French revolutions. Religious and political conservatives in the North contributed significantly in a variety of ways to the proslavery argument. Some of those who accepted a literal interpretation of the Bible adhered to the scriptural vindication of human bondage. Other conservative northern evangelicals fiercely opposed the efforts of abolitionists to bring the slavery issue into the church. Proslavery reflects the "Americanness" of the antebellum South in yet another way. The intellectual defense of slavery reveals the use of shared American values and ways of thinking in the creation of a distinctly sectional ideology. In their debate with northern abolitionists over the morality of slavery, for example, southern clergymen drew upon the most common intellectual resources of their time—the Bible, evangelicalism, natural law, and moral philosophy—to demonstrate the rectitude of slavery.

Proslavery was thus shaped simultaneously by the distinctive social strains of the antebellum South and larger currents of American thought and the distinctive social contours of the slaveholding South. This essential ambivalence points to the larger contradictions which plagued a slaveholding society in a liberal, democratic, and capitalist nation.

MITCHELL SNAY

See also RACE.

FURTHER READING

David Brion Davis, *The Problem of Slavery in the Age of Revolution, 1770–1823* (Ithaca: Cornell University Press, 1975).

Drew Gilpin Faust, ed., *The Ideology of Slavery: Proslavery Thought in the Antebellum South, 1830–1860* (Baton Rouge: Louisiana State University Press, 1981).

George M. Fredrickson, *The Black Image in the White Mind: the Debate on Afro-American Character and Destiny, 1817–1914* (New York: Harper and Row, 1971).

Eugene D. Genovese, *The World the Slaveholders Made: Two Essays in Interpretation* (New York: Pantheon, 1969).

Stephanie McCurry, "The Two Faces of Republicanism: Gender and Proslavery Politics in Antebellum South Carolina," *Journal of American History* 78 (Mar. 1992): 1245–64.

Mitchell Snay, *Gospel of Disunion: Religion and Separatism in the Antebellum South* (Cambridge: Cambridge University Press, 1993).

Larry Tise, *Proslavery: a History of the Defense of Slavery in America, 1701–1840* (Athens: University of Georgia Press, 1987).

psychotherapy This catch-all term encompasses a bewildering number of approaches to emotional anxiety and mental anguish which share little beyond the promise of help and change. Practiced by increasing numbers and types of professionals, psychotherapy today is available to more people for more reasons then ever before. It usually refers to professional services, but self-help movements like Alcoholics Anonymous or co-counseling are sometimes included. Frequently shortened to "therapy," it includes most forms of Freudian and post-Freudian healing in individual and group forms: from psychoanalysis, gestalt, and Rogerian therapy to psychodrama and behavior modification. Before mid-century, somatic techniques were important components of therapy, largely because therapeutic practice was monopolized by physicians. In recent decades, however, talking cures have developed a reputation as humane alternatives to such primitive procedures as electroshock and psychosurgery.

Talking cures are not new. At least since Freud, they have been recognized as legitimate treatments for a range of mental maladies. Before World War II, most Freudian psychoanalysts (a small subgroup within American psychiatry) treated mostly well-to-do clients who were curious about "being psyched." Freud was both gratified and exasperated by the enthusiastic reception his analytic method received in America. His tragic philosophy of life contrasted sharply with American meliorism; he held that psychoanalysis could do little more than turn "hysterical misery into common unhappiness." (*See also* FREUDIANISM and NEO-FREUDIANISM.)

In contrast to the elite practice of office psychoanalysis, most psychiatrists before 1940 worked in state hospitals devoted to custodial care; professionals without medical degrees were not licensed to offer therapeutic services. Prodded by innovative experiments like the private Menninger Clinic (founded in 1919), analytic and other therapies became more common in work with hospitalized mental patients after World War I. But little treatment was available to the public, which still associated clinical services with institutions and insanity. Therapy was a stigma.

World War II changed that. It brought therapy to the masses and opened clinical fields to nonpsychiatric professionals. Determined to contribute to victory, psychiatrists launched aggressive military screening and treatment programs that exposed the extent of mental instability among supposedly normal men. Psychiatrists rejected two million recruits (38 percent of all rejections) and gave over half a million additional discharges—statistics so alarming that they were censored in 1943. The outcry over "war neuroses" temporarily curbed professional rivalries and brought psychologists, nurses, and social workers onto therapeutic teams. After the war, new training programs, funded by public agencies like the Veterans Administration, aided allied professionals in their attempt to practice therapy independently of psychiatric supervision.

Wartime publicity about millions of "normal" but maladjusted individuals caused a radical reassessment of basic clinical terms. Perhaps mental health and illness were a continuum and not fixed states. Perhaps treatment could improve anyone's health, or at least obstruct a possible slide toward illness. Confident that every human relations problem required their attention in the name of "prevention," postwar clinicians moved from the asylum into the community, dramatically expanding the scope of their authority and the potential market for therapy. Mental illness was no longer the principal qualification for therapeutic treatment, nor was mental health a disqualification. Therapy, clinicians acknowledged, worked best with the "normally neurotic."

According to major national studies, by the mid-1970s one-third of all adults routinely sought therapeutic aid when facing distress or crisis, and many viewed psychotherapy as an opportunity for ongoing personal growth rather than as a way of keeping anguish in check. A robust postwar economy, the dissolution of extended families through geographic mobility, disenchantment with organized religion, and the depersonalization of corporate and bureaucratic workplaces all played a part in transforming therapy from a shameful secret into a highly regarded source of comfort, friendship, even meaning. Popular demand for therapy since the 1950s has taken very definite demographic forms, however. People with high incomes and decent educations are more likely to seek out therapists than are the poor. Disproportionate numbers of clients are white, young, and female.

Despite the growth of the therapeutic enterprise, detractors have stubbornly pointed out that little agreement exists about what therapy is and whether it is therapeutic. Some, like psychologist Hans Eysenck in the 1950s, heretically suggested that no tangible benefits had been scientifically proven. A few others have gone further, challenging intentions as well as achievements. Jeffrey Masson, in several books, has decried therapy's negative consequences for a democratic way of life. Masson argues that psychoanalysis—and therapy in general—are classic forms of victim-blaming. Because the therapist always knows best, therapy is authoritarian. In it, ordinary people learn to defer to experts and experts deliver emotional tyranny in the name of health and happiness.

Historians critical of therapeutic practice have found inspiration in the writings of Thomas Szasz, R. D. Laing, and Michel Foucault. Often more sympathetic to therapy than Masson, such writers as Robert Castel, Joel Kovel, and Andrew Scull nevertheless share his concerns: Are clinical practices liberating or repressive? Has humanitarianism or a sinister drive for domination been more salient in the evolution of mental health institutions, professions, and policies? No consensus exists on these questions.

What therapy is and whether it helps or hurts are unanswered—and perhaps unanswerable—questions. Efforts to understand therapy's historical logic and cultural reach need to move beyond the framework of repression versus liberation, or social control versus progress. Such dualistic paradigms cannot fully explain why people have sought therapeutic assistance so tenaciously and for reasons they consider so compelling. If future inquiries describe in more complex detail how cultures have organized the provision of psychological care, they will move us closer to understanding why human subjectivity and its management have been so sensitive to historical change.

ELLEN HERMAN

FURTHER READING

Robert Castel, Françoise Castel, and Anne Lovell, *The Psychiatric Society*, trans. Arthur Goldhammer (New York: Columbia University Press, 1982).

Donald K. Freedheim, ed., *History of Psychotherapy: a Century of Change* (Washington, D.C.: American Psychological Association, 1992).

Lawrence J. Friedman, *Menninger: the Family and the Clinic* (New York: Knopf, 1990).

Gerald N. Grob, *From Asylum to Community: Mental Health Policy in Modern America* (Princeton: Princeton University Press, 1991).

Joel Kovel, *A Complete Guide to Therapy: From Psychoanalysis to Behavior Modification* (New York: Pantheon, 1976).

Jeffrey Moussaieff Masson, *Against Therapy: Emotional Tyranny and the Myth of Psychological Healing* (New York: Atheneum, 1988).

Andrew Scull, *Social Order/Mental Disorder: Anglo-American Psychiatry in Historical Perspective* (Berkeley: University of California Press, 1989).

Joseph Veroff, Elizabeth Douvan, and Richard A. Kulka, *Mental Health in America: Patterns of Help-seeking from 1957 to 1976* (New York: Basic Books, 1981).

publicity The history of the word during the last two centuries reveals a narrowing of scope from the idea of making something known to the public to the idea of the business of promotion, though there was a late nineteenth-century detour in this development in which publicity became synonymous with shamelessness. During that time, the ENLIGHTENMENT commitment to flooding light into dark places was extended to matters previously believed to be either private or not worthy of public notice (*see also* PRIVACY). Three new agencies of exposure were largely responsible for creating modern publicity: mass-circulation JOURNALISM specializing in gossip, scandal, personal interviews, sensational accounts of crime and divorce trials, and advertising; public discussions of and pamphlets about sexual hygiene and morality; and fictional REALISM, which in the United States took the form of novels representing everyday domestic life and on the Continent the form of novels depicting adultery and the life of the demimonde.

The older meaning of publicity as making something open to public knowledge or observation took a characteristic grammatical form: publicity *of* something, that is, publicity about or regarding something. HENRY JAMES employed this older form— even as he gave the word its negative connotation of brazenness—when he described the role of the prying newspaperman Matthias Pardon in *The Bostonians*:

One sketches one's age imperfectly if one doesn't touch on that particular matter: the invasion, the impudence, the shamelessness of the newspaper and the interviewer, the devouring *publicity of* life, the extinction of all sense between public and private. (p. 82)

In her "Décolleté in Modern Life" (1890), Elizabeth Stuart Phelps used the term in the same way:

It is probable that the great increase of physical weakness in our times and the *publicity of* physiological discussions have led to a certain blunting of delicacy in speech which our Brahman lady of the earlier day knew not of. (p. 676)

During this same period, the meaning of publicity dramatically contracted: while it retained its negative connotation, it became synoymous with promotion (especially self-promotion), celebrity, and advertising. Accompanying this localization of meaning was an important change in the grammatical usage of the noun. Publicity no longer required an object; instead it became a realm, condition, or state unto itself. In 1888, CHARLES ELIOT NORTON, in a letter chastizing his friend John Ruskin for making public their first meeting, employed publicity in this self-contained sense: "I, the one man in America who have kept myself private, who have hated the *publicity* and advertising and notoriety which, in these days even our poets have sought" (Vanderbilt, p. 170). Henry James also provides an example of the new grammatical and conceptual status of publicity as an independent condition when he deplored

that mania for *publicity* which is one of the most striking signs of our times. She [a young woman upon whose actions he based *The Reverberator*] was perfectly irreflective and irresponsible, and it seemed to her pleasant and natural and "chatty" to describe, in a horribly vulgar newspaper, the people she had been living with and their personal domestic arrangements and secrets. (p. 82)

Critics of the new publicity claimed that mass-circulation newspapers bore the brunt of responsibility for the growing irreverent tone that defined modern American life. In his account of his lecture tour, "Civilization in America" (1888), Matthew Arnold declared, "If one were searching for the best means to efface and kill in a whole nation the discipline of respect, the feeling for what is elevated, one could not do better than take the American newspapers" (p. 56). Proponents of reticence held that reserve, reverence, and a sense of SHAME were essential for the conduct of civilized life, and that private experiences were so delicate that they could not withstand scrutiny by the public or even by a trusted intimate. Resistance to the new publicity was not a matter of elitism, prudishness, or squeamishness, as apologists of the new journalism charged. Advocates of reticence believed that personal experiences required the shade and security of privacy lest they become degraded or dehumanized. George Eliot expressed this fundamental tenet of the reticent sensibility:

We are bound to reticence most of all by that reverence for the highest efforts of our common nature, which commands us to bury its lowest fatalities, its invincible remnants of the brute, its most agonizing struggles with temptation, in unbroken silence. (Lilly, p. 291)

Proponents of journalistic exposure attempted to justify their assaults on privacy by appealing to their alleged democratic character—candor and openness were true indicators of a democracy, hence citizens had a right to know whatever they wanted about anyone. (*See also* MUCKRAKING.) Advocates of reticence replied that the new journalism represented not the democratic ethos, but a passion for lowering, for exposing the most vulnerable aspects of people's private lives so as to eliminate all distinctions of social, cultural, or intellectual attainment, thereby reducing everyone to the level of the BODY. Critics also charged that commercial journalism trivialized experiences that could be meaningful only in private and debased the character of public discussion by treating strictly personal affairs as if they merited public attention. The new publicity, according to defenders of reticence, progressively wore away people's sense of proportion and their ability to discern the right ordering and true measure of things appearing in public, which, in turn, made for an increasingly distorted and insubstantial common domain. The public sphere, from their perspective, was deteriorating into a chaotic jumble where all things, regardless of scale or seemliness, vied for public notice all at once.

Once the battle to preserve reticence had been lost, in the first decades of the twentieth century, publicity began to shed its association with shamelessness. It then came to signify the commercial enterprise of promotion and was employed as an adjective modifying a new range of activities and occupations—publicity agent, stunt, tour, hound. In modern consumer society, traditional agencies of AUTHORITY have been drowned out by the clamoring of proliferating products, "information," and "personalities" for public attention. Consequently, the original mission of publicity to make something known to the public has been largely taken over by publicists intent on selling their product. Because modern publicity has come to be the primary agency of making distinctions among the hodgepodge of things cluttering our common space, all things—toothpaste, cars, movies, books, art, and presidents—have tended toward a common leveling to the rank of commodity, where they become subject to the caprice of fashion.

The narrowing compass of the idea of publicity reveals the distinctive quality of the public sphere in our own time: it has increasingly lost its former place as the stage where people, through great actions or works, win public acclaim and help build a durable common world. Whereas publicity in the older sense of making something known to the public held out hope that a community could preserve its achievements in historical memory—thereby allaying the seeming futility of human striving in a world bounded by mortality—modern publicity, always anxiously hunting for "news," erases memory and TRADITION.

Instead it offers to those who seek it the hollow prospect of evanescent celebrity, exemplified by Andy Warhol's prescient quip that everyone will be famous for 15 minutes.

ROCHELLE GURSTEIN

FURTHER READING
Matthew Arnold, "Civilization in America" (1888), in Kenneth Allot, ed., *Five Uncollected Essays of Matthew Arnold* (Liverpool: University Press of Liverpool, 1953).
Daniel Boorstin, *The Image: a Guide to Pseudo-Events in America* (1961; New York: Atheneum, 1987).
E. L. Godkin, "The Rights of the Citizen—to His Own Reputation," *Scribner's Magazine* 8 (July 1890).
Henry James, *The Notebooks of Henry James*, ed. F. O. Matthiessen and Kenneth B. Murdock (New York: Oxford University Press, 1947).
W. S. Lilly, "The New Naturalism," *Fortnightly Review* 38 (Aug. 1, 1885).
Elizabeth Stuart Phelps, "The Décolleté in Modern Life," *Forum* 9 (1890).
Ferdinand D. Schoeman, ed., *Philosophical Dimensions of Privacy* (Cambridge: Cambridge University Press, 1984).
Kermit Vanderbilt, *Charles Eliot Norton: Apostle of Culture in a Democracy* (Cambridge: Harvard University Press, 1959).

punishment   The idea of punishment has evolved historically as religious, political, and social beliefs have changed. In colonial New England, crime was viewed as sin, and punishment as its retribution. The theology of CALVINISM offered a stern, judgmental God and the threat of eternal punishment. The seventeenth-century state, as an extension of God's domain, claimed the authority to inflict corporal and capital punishment. Parents punished their children physically in the belief that it was necessary to break a child's will; the state hanged criminals for numerous crimes and punished others with fines, confinement to stocks and pillory, and whippings. The mildest criminal code in colonial America, punishing only murder with death, could be found in Pennsylvania where Quaker religious beliefs, pivoting on benevolence, reform, and universal salvation, held sway. The South, as a consequence of a social system geared to slavery and HONOR, preserved public corporal and capital punishments long after other regions has abandoned them.

Despite some differences among the colonies, punishment in colonial America generally reflected longstanding European practices and beliefs. Between the mid-eighteenth and mid-nineteenth centuries, however, the whole transatlantic world experienced a seismic shift in the philosophies and rituals of punishment. Rejecting public, external, and physical forms of punishment, the state instituted private, internal, and psychological modes of discipline.

Instead of punishing the BODY, legislators and parents began to focus on cultivating the wrongdoer's conscience (*see also* GUILT). Following the American Revolution, efforts to reform punishment proliferated, including movements to reduce the number of capital crimes and even to abolish the death penalty entirely, to eliminate the use of corporal punishment against prisoners, sailors, students, women, and children, to expand the uses of the penitentiary, and to put an end to chattel slavery.

Scholars differ in their accounts of how and why these changes occurred. Some, such as David Rothman, emphasize shifts in intellectual currents: Lockean epistemology, SCOTTISH COMMON SENSE REALISM, ENLIGHTENMENT jurisprudence, REPUBLICANISM ideology, and LIBERAL PROTESTANTISM fundamentally altered notions of sin and severity. Other scholars, while agreeing that new ideas stressed the influence of environment on human behavior, argue that shifts in punishment must be seen in relation to the emergence of INDUSTRIALISM and the capitalist state. Rather than explaining changes as the product of humanitarian reform, writers such as Michel Foucault and Michael Ignatieff argue that new institutions such as the penitentiary advanced the worldview or served the needs of the capitalist state by inculcating prisoners with the values of silence, temperance, and work.

By the late nineteenth and early twentieth centuries, the reformist assumptions of the previous decades had become bureaucratized. SOCIAL SCIENCE turned its attention to crime and punishment. The culture of scientific expertise led to the establishment of parole authorities and probation officers. The correctional system became characterized by indeterminate sentencing, probation, and new forms of incarceration such as reformatories and detention centers. A separate juvenile justice system emerged as experts reexamined the causes of crime and purposes of punishment. The emergence of new methods of capital punishment, such as the electric chair, gas chamber, and lethal injection, embodied twentieth-century transformations in MEDICINE and TECHNOLOGY.

Debates on punishment in recent years have continued to range across the ideological spectrum as commentators discuss the place of retribution, utility, and JUSTICE in justifications for punishment. Conservatives such as Ernest van den Haag and James Q. Wilson insist that rehabilitation should not be the primary purpose of punishment. Focusing on the individual's RESPONSIBILITY for criminal activity, they insist that maintaining social order and achieving justice should be the central aims of punishment. By comparison, a diverse group of commentators, many

of them building upon the insights first outlined by Georg Rusche and Otto Kirchheimer, articulate a theory of punishment that emphasizes the connections between crime and social structure and balances the desire for deterrence with the rehabilitation of the criminal.

The terms of these debates are not new. Discussions of punishment in every era have been characterized by a fundamental conflict in visions of humanity and society. For some, human beings are sinful, corrupt, and damned, even if ultimately redeemable; children must be taught fear and submission to authority, while criminals must be severely punished to deter crime and exact revenge. For others, human beings are moral, educable, and beneficent; children should be raised through love and nurture, while criminals should be reclaimed through instruction and by attacking the social conditions that help create crime. Historical traditions continue to exercise authority when it comes to punishment. Upholding the constitutionality of corporal punishment in public school, the Supreme Court, in *Ingraham v. Wright* (1977), observed that the practice dates back to the colonial era. And while the Court momentarily declared capital punishment unconstitutional in *Furman v. Georgia* (1972), most jurists do not view the death penalty as a violation of the "cruel and unusual punishment" clause of the Eighth Amendment to the Constitution.

Invoking a discourse centered on social RIGHTS and legal protections rather than religious and humanitarian ideals, activists continue to challenge corporal and capital punishment and advocate the reconstruction of the penal system. These efforts have been resisted by evangelicals and conservatives who continue to argue that children should be physically punished and criminals should be incarcerated and executed. As old debates persist in our own day, the number of prisoners continues to mount, and the pace of executions has continued to accelerate. Recent research has demonstrated, moreover, that discrimination by race, still evident in daily life, is also prevalent in state-mandated death. Holding other variables constant, a criminal is more likely to receive the death penalty if the victim was white than if the victim was a person of color. Most of the corporal and capital punishment inflicted in the United States occurs in the southern states, part of the traditional Bible Belt. On the eve of the twenty-first century, more than half of the states permit corporal punishment in public schools and the United States remains the only Western industrial nation that continues to execute its citizens.

LOUIS P. MASUR

FURTHER READING

Michel Foucault, *Discipline and Punish: the Birth of the Prison* (New York: Pantheon, 1977).

Philip Greven, *Spare the Child: the Religious Roots of Punishment and the Psychological Impact of Physical Abuse* (New York: Knopf, 1991).

Michael Ignatieff, *A Just Measure of Pain: the Penitentiary in the Industrial Revolution: 1750–1850* (New York: Columbia University Press, 1978).

Louis P. Masur, *Rites of Execution: Capital Punishment and the Transformation of American Culture, 1776–1865* (New York: Oxford University Press, 1989).

David J. Rothman, *The Discovery of the Asylum: Social Order and Disorder in the New Republic* (Boston: Little, Brown, 1971).

Georg Rusche and Otto Kirchheimer, *Punishment and Social Structure* (New York: Columbia University Press, 1939).

Ernest van den Haag, *Punishing Criminals* (New York: Basic Books, 1975).

James Q. Wilson, *Thinking About Crime*, rev. ed. (New York: Vintage, 1985).

Puritanism   As commonly used by historians of early America and Tudor-Stuart England, Puritanism refers to a religious movement that arose in the reign of Elizabeth I (1558–1603), came into power in England during the 1640s and 1650s, and crossed the Atlantic to New England via emigrants who founded the colonies of Plymouth (1620) and Massachusetts (1628–30). Institutionally, Puritanism in England was transformed into "Nonconformity" after 1662, when ministers of this persuasion were excluded from the Church of England. Puritanism in New England remained in power much longer, though the movement was in decline, or undergoing important redefinition, by the close of the seventeenth century. American and English Puritanism (or Nonconformity) shared much common ground, and the two movements also developed within the wider context of international CALVINISM.

For the past 200 years, whenever Americans have tried to make sense of their national experience, they have regarded the Puritan movement as central. Indeed, an entire history of American culture since independence could be constructed out of the evolution of American attitudes toward and reflections about the Puritans.

The discourse about Puritanism originated in reflections on political independence, REPRESENTATION, and DEMOCRACY. Edmund Burke and JOHN ADAMS in the period of the AMERICAN REVOLUTION attributed to Puritanism the spirit of liberty that moved the colonists to reject British sovereignty. Adams argued that, in leaving England, the Puritans had enacted a rupture with old world "tyrannies." Puritanism thus became the source of our national uniqueness as a pathbreaking republic and exemplary society. This was the myth that orators like DANIEL WEBSTER appropriated to weave around the landing of the Pilgrims at Plymouth Rock.

Yet this myth was complicated by an alternative reading of the past. In the early decades of the nineteenth century a slowly evolving rejection of religious orthodoxy broke into the open in the "Unitarian controversy." The anti-Calvinists who founded what came to be called UNITARIANISM construed Puritanism as intolerant and oppressive. They denounced the ministers and magistrates of the seventeenth century for banishing ROGER WILLIAMS from Massachusetts, executing Quakers on Boston Common, and persecuting witches. For these critics, the PROGRESS that made America so uniquely promising was progress by way of emancipation from the errors of orthodoxy. (*See also* GUILT.)

The debate over whether Puritanism promoted liberty or authoritarianism agitated the mid nineteenth-century literary community of antiquarians, historians, poets, churchmen, and orators, where controversy fixed on such matters as the responsibility of the minister COTTON MATHER for the Salem witch-hunt of 1692. The contradictory views of Puritanism were never resolved, but were creatively elaborated, as in the novels and stories of NATHANIEL HAWTHORNE, where a character such as Hester Prynne could be forced to wear a scarlet letter as a sign of her shame, yet become a model of service to her community.

The old accusations against Puritanism were renewed at the turn of the century by two descendants of John Adams, Charles F. Adams and BROOKS ADAMS, who denounced the "filiopietism" of New England historians willing to overlook acts of intolerance. But it was the mocking, iconoclastic voice of the journalist H. L. MENCKEN that influenced many younger writers of the early twentieth century to perceive American culture as suffering from the blight of a repressive parochialism stemming from the founders of New England. Angered by certain instances of literary censorship and hostile to all forms of Protestant moralism, Mencken defined Puritanism as "the haunting fear that somewhere, someone might be happy." The writers and artists who marched under the banners of "liberation" and MODERNISM were more directly bothered by the allged hypocrisies of VICTORIANISM than with anything that occurred in the seventeenth century. But Puritanism served them well as a shorthand symbol for the America they rejected. In *Main Currents in American Thought* (1927), the Progressive literary historian VERNON L. PARRINGTON summed up all of what he called "the inhibitions of

Puritan dogma" (p. 3), including its presumed anti-democratic principles.

At the very moment when Mencken and Parrington reigned intellectually, a young literary scholar from Chicago, PERRY MILLER, undertook to reverse the prevailing wisdom. He did so by reopening the question of whether the Puritans should be termed "Calvinists." Inheriting from liberal theologians and writers such as Parrington a portrait of Calvinism as focused on the "arbitrary" doctrine of predestination, Miller uncovered a hidden vein of "rationalism" within the Puritan mind, a rationalism embodied in what he termed the "covenant" or "federal" theology, which reconciled divine rule and human initiative. He also detected rationalism in the academic curriculum at Harvard College (founded 1636), which reconciled "piety" and "intellect," or divine revelation and human reason. Miller's essays (some attacking Parrington directly), his comprehensive anthology of documents, *The Puritans: a Sourcebook of Their Writings* (1938), and his magisterial study, *The New England Mind: the Seventeenth Century* (1939) restored intellectual complexity to the Puritans and shattered any possibility of connecting them to the religious FUNDAMENTALISM of the early twentieth century.

Of more importance, Miller drew on the emerging theological movement known as Neo-Orthodoxy to affirm the contemporary significance of the ideas of sin, tragedy, and inherent human limitation. (See also REINHOLD NIEBUHR.) Himself an atheist, Miller deployed the "realism" of the Puritans against what he regarded as the overly optimistic, facile liberalism of Parrington and his ilk. In a sequel, *The New England Mind: From Colony to Province* (1953), Miller traced the Americanizing of the Puritan mind in the course of the seventeenth century, a process that dissolved the fusion of piety and intellect. As Puritanism weakened—Miller called the process "declension" —Calvinist notions about the dividedness and brokenness of the self were discarded. Declension produced a splintered movement. By the mid-eighteenth century, Puritanism flowed in two separate channels, the orthodox but radical EVANGELICALISM that JONATHAN EDWARDS and his heirs articulated, and the rationalism (headed toward Unitarianism) that catered to the middle-class culture of business. Situating himself as a critic of an American culture which, like the Puritanism he chronicled, wore two faces, Miller turned history into prophecy in order to denounce the complacency of a liberal and materialistic society.

The imaginative power of *The New England Mind* gave new energy and importance to Puritanism within the academic disciplines of history and literature. With the burgeoning of early American history and early American literature as fields of study in the 1960s came the emergence of "Puritan Studies": monograph fed on monograph in a sequence that continues to this day. The irony was that, as academic work blossomed, Puritanism was losing most of its significance in the wider debate about the shape and direction of American society. Younger scholars turned away from Miller's interest in using Puritanism to critique American culture as a whole. Returning to the original sources, they began to quarrel with Miller's interpretation. Putting to test the many parts of the story that he told, these scholars have concluded that its relationship to "real" Puritanism is at best ambiguous, and at worst a severe distortion.

Nowhere did the distortion appear greater than in Miller's understanding of Puritan aesthetics. Literary and cultural historians have reclaimed the richness of a "Puritan imagination" that employed the method of figural or typological interpretation. In the hands of these critics, the Puritan imagination becomes the basis of our national literary culture: the Puritanism that draws on the prophetic and apocalyptic books of Scripture to assert the exemplary importance of the "errand" to America is the source of an "exceptional" American national identity. (*See also* AMERICAN EXCEPTIONALISM.) In this respect, the revisionists underscored Miller's own emphasis on the uniqueness of American Puritan thought. A plausible alternative to this description of the rhetoric and intentions of the colonists, however, is to see them as Christian primitivists reclaiming the authority of the New Testament and enacting a return to the "first times" of the Apostles.

New themes have also supplemented the old discourse on the topic of radicalism. The rediscovery of Puritan radicalism was initiated by the English historian Christopher Hill in the 1960s. The question then became: did this mode of Puritanism, which emerged in force during the period of the English Civil War and Commonwealth (ca.1642–60) articulate a vision of EQUALITY and TOLERANCE? And was it absorbed into or suppressed by the mainstream? The debate in America has focused in particular on a charismatic woman, ANNE HUTCHINSON, who criticized the preaching of some of the ministers; her protest, which for a short while had the sympathy of JOHN COTTON, minister in Boston, inspired the "Antinomian controversy" of 1636–8, which ended with her being exiled to Rhode Island. The famous "Examination" she underwent before the magistrates and ministers in Massachusetts reveals that the male leaders of the colony resented a woman's challenge to their authority. Hutchinson has thus become important to women's historians and feminists. As for the broader story, the historian Edmund S. Morgan argued in *The Puritan Dilemma* (1958) that radicalism was contained, and that moderation held sway in Puritan New England. More recently, so-called ideological criticism has thrown a different light on moderation by exposing its "patriarchal" and "colonizing" dimensions as manifested in policies toward Native Americans, the uses of the land, and witch-hunting. (*See also* INDIAN–WHITE RELATIONS.)

Contrasting and contradictory interpretations of Puritanism stem in part from fissures and paradoxes in the movement itself. Historians recognize that in the Elizabethan period the Puritan reformers, though aspiring to run a uniform, established church, nurtured local action to achieve reform against the will of the monarch and the bishops. When a handful of Puritans broke with the Church of England, the more moderate within the movement quickly denounced these "separatists." Almost from the moment of its origins, therefore, Puritanism was at once moderate and sectarian.

The turmoil in Massachusetts during and after the 1630s arose from this tension. Setting up churches of their own for the first time, the emigrants adopted a "congregational" structure for the church that was codified in a formal statement, the Cambridge Platform (1648), written mainly for an English audience. In New England Congregationalism, church membership was voluntary for adults; each ecclesiastical unit, or congregation, had the power to elect to office its own minister, admit members, and handle cases of church discipline. The civil state was responsible for maintaining uniformity and order. In matters of doctrine, the colonists acknowledged the authority of the Westminster Confession, a Calvinist creed drafted in England in 1646.

Uniformity was elusive, challenged from one side by Roger Williams and the Antinomians, from another by conservatives who feared the colonists had gone too far toward "democracy" in their church government. Others protested when, in 1662, the ministers modified the basis for church membership by allowing the right of baptism to descend in those families which were in church covenant (a procedure later nicknamed the "half-way covenant"). Traditionalists, who insisted on a conversion experience as the precondition for baptism, were shocked, but reformers successfully argued that the voluntary, pietistic structure of congregationalism had to be adjusted to take account of the spiritual responsibilities of families. The second and third generations of ministers attempted various strategies of revitalization, including appeals to an idealized, near-mythic past. The "invention of New England," as some historians have termed this effort, may rightly be understood as the opening phase of our long engagement with Puritanism and its consequences.

DAVID D. HALL

FURTHER READING

Sacvan Bercovitch, ed., *The American Puritan Imagination: Essays in Reevaluation* (New York: Cambridge University Press, 1974).

T. Dwight Bozeman, *To Live Ancient Lives: the Primitivist Dimension in Puritanism* (Chapel Hill: University of North Carolina Press, 1988).

Lawrence Buell, *New England Literary Culture from Revolution through Renaissance* (New York: Cambridge University Press, 1986).

Stephen Foster, *The Long Argument: English Puritanism and the Shaping of New England Culture, 1570–1700* (Chapel Hill: University of North Carolina Press, 1991).

David D. Hall, ed., *The Antinomian Controversy, 1636–1638: a Documentary History* (1968; Durham, N.C.: Duke University Press, 1990).

Robert Middlekauff, *The Mathers: Three Generations of Puritan Intellectuals, 1596–1728* (New York: Oxford University Press, 1971).

Perry Miller, *The New England Mind: the Seventeenth Century* (1939; Cambridge: Harvard University Press, 1954).

Vernon Louis Parrington, *Main Currents in American Thought*, vol. 1 (New York: Harcourt, Brace and World, 1927).

Q

Quine, W[illard] V[an] O[rman] (b. Akron, Ohio, June 25, 1908).   One of the most influential thinkers in the Anglo-American analytic tradition, logician and philosopher W. V. O. Quine was raised in Ohio and entered Oberlin College in 1926. There he combined his interests in mathematics, philosophy, and philology. After encountering the writings of Bertrand Russell, he majored in mathematics and read mathematical philosophy for honors. Graduating from Oberlin in 1930, Quine entered graduate study at Harvard University. He completed his Ph.D. in two years, writing his dissertation, "The Logic of Sequences: a Generalization of *Principia Mathematica*," under Alfred North Whitehead's direction. Quine spent the next four years in postdoctoral study, including a year in Europe working with leading logicians and philosophers. He returned to Harvard in 1933 as one of the first junior fellows in the new Society of Fellows.

In 1936, Quine began his long tenure on the Harvard faculty as an instructor in philosophy and logic. Following the publication of *Mathematical Logic* in 1940, he was promoted to associate professor with tenure. Quine joined the Navy as a lieutenant in 1942. Working in radio intelligence for the Atlantic antisubmarine campaign, he had risen to lieutenant commander by the time he left the service in 1945. Quine returned to Harvard in 1946, and he has remained there except for visiting appointments, including those at Oxford, Princeton, and Stanford. In 1948, he was promoted to professor and elected a senior fellow of the Society of Fellows. Quine retired from Harvard in 1978, but has continued to teach and write.

Quine's influence on American thought has been evident in both logic and philosophy. His major contributions in logic have come in the development of set theory. Continually reworking his own contributions and those of others, Quine has sought to simplify logic and to make it more economical. In books following *Mathematical Logic*, such as *Set Theory and Its Logic* (1963), and *Philosophy of Logic* (1970), Quine has elaborated his evolving logical theories.

As a philosopher, Quine can be seen as partaking of the empiricist, pragmatic, and analytic tradition in Anglo-American philosophy. His work falls within the empiricist and analytic tradition because of his efforts to use logical analysis to understand the workings of the world and the language we use to describe it. The pragmatic strain enters in Quine's argument that our values and interests shape our behavior and understanding as we construct theories about the world.

Quine contends that there can be no philosophy more fundamental than science. Philosophy and science jointly attempt to discover how the world is made. They differ in the generality of their inquiries; science asks the narrower questions, philosophy the broader ones. There is not, however, a sharp distinction between the two. Quine sought the most economical account of the world and used the pragmatic standard of usefulness as a means to justify that economy.

A central task of Quine's philosophy is to establish a theory of meaning consistent with his PRAGMATISM. He takes a relativistic approach, arguing that there can be a variety of empirically equivalent but ontologically distinct theories that will explain the working of the world or of some part of it. Quine's significant claim is not the existence of a variety of theories, but that there is a variety of equally good ones. We choose our theories on the basis of certain criteria, such as conservatism, generality, or simplicity. Quine holds that we can never achieve a standpoint external to all theory; we must choose a theory within which to operate—in his case, science. Quine's relativism need not undermine our confidence in science, since along with mathematics and logic, science provides the most economical way of understanding and manipulating the world we live in. Thus we choose science as our central theory on pragmatic grounds; it is the most economical theory that works. As CHARLES SANDERS PEIRCE did, Quine holds that science and philosophy do not give us final answers, but they do give us the best currently available answers.

In developing his philosophy, Quine attacked one of the crucial distinctions in philosophy, that between analytic and synthetic statements. Analytic truths are those which cannot be falsified; they are true by definition or by virtue of their meaning. A familiar example is the statement: all bachelors are unmarried. Synthetic truths are the truths of science; they are contingent and can be falsified. The difference between statements of these kinds is one of degree, for both kinds are embedded in language and cannot be completely separated from their larger linguistic context. Quine draws on the analogy of a spider's web, suggesting that the sentences of our theories, whether analytic or synthetic, are tied to one another and to the web as a whole, so that any change anywhere in the web will have some effect throughout the entire structure. Quine's holism draws on Peirce's claim that the meaning of a sentence is determined by its pragmatic consequences and Pierre Duhem's claim that only theories, not individual sentences, have pragmatic consequences.

Given the multitude of theories possible in the web of belief, Quine faced the problem of translating between them. Having lectured in six languages, he knew firsthand the problems of translation. Quine argued that any process of TRANSLATION—children learning their first language, translating between English and French, or comparing two different theories of the same phenomena—involves considerable uncertainty. Ultimately, there is no "right" translation, only ones that seem to work better than others for particular purposes. On pragmatic grounds, if there is no practical difference between the translations or the theories, then Quine would accept their equivalence.

Quine's present influence is greatest within the field of logic and within the academic community of analytic philosophers. RICHARD RORTY, in *Philosophy and the Mirror of Nature* (1979), cites Quine's work as contributing to his own post-analytic and post-representational project, but faults Quine for failing to escape completely the lingering legacies of a scientific, analytic, and representational philosophy. In spite of Rorty's dissents, Quine's status within the American intellectual community is likely to increase so long as the concerns which animated him remain contested.

DANIEL J. WILSON

See also NATURALISM.

FURTHER READING

Donald Davidson and J. Hintikka, eds., *Words and Objections: Essays on the Work of W. V. Quine* (Dordrecht: Reidel, 1969).

Lewis Edwin Hahn and Paul Arthur Schilpp, eds., *The Philosophy of W. V. Quine*, Library of Living Philosophers, vol. 18 (La Salle, Ill.: Open Court, 1986).

W. V. Quine, *From a Logical Point of View* (Cambridge: Harvard University Press, 1953).

——, *Word and Object* (Cambridge: MIT Press, 1960).

——, *Ontological Relativity and Other Essays* (New York: Columbia University Press, 1969).

——, *The Time of My Life: an Autobiography* (Cambridge: MIT Press, 1985).

R

Rabi, Isidor Isaac (b. Rymanów, Austria-Hungary, July 29, 1898; d. New York, N.Y., Jan. 11, 1988). Physicist. Rabi developed a method for measuring the magnetic moment of an atom, thus opening the path to magnetic resonance technologies, and was also instrumental in the development of radar. He believed that science, respected across national and ideological boundaries because of its practical benefits, could undergird world understanding. An advisor to the Manhattan Project, which developed the first American atomic bomb during World War II, Rabi fought the development of the hydrogen bomb: such a powerful means of devastation, he argued, necessarily targets civilians and is inherently immoral. Rabi received the 1944 Nobel Prize for Physics. He authored *My Life and Times as a Physicist* in 1960.

FURTHER READING

John S. Rigden, *Rabi: Scientist and Citizen* (New York: Basic Books, 1987).

race Dominick LaCapra's remark that race is "a feeble mystification with formidable effects" (p. 1) conveys the dominant wave of recent intellectual opinion. In the past decade, scholars in various disciplines, including literature, philosophy, history, and jurisprudence, have brought new insights to the study of race. As a result, we have a new appreciation of the contingency of racial categories. For traditionalists, race is rooted in nature, and may embody unchangeable attributes of a population. Against such assumptions, recent scholars have pointed to the historical specificity of each construction of racial identity, and have tried to locate the social processes that forged these categories. (*See also* ETHNICITY.) Beyond debunking racial myths, scholars have also exposed racial assumptions in a wide range of texts, practices, and institutions that were previously thought to be neutral or unconcerned about race.

This research departs from the old practice of seeing racism primarily as a problem of prejudice. Racism, in the older view, is a feeling of revulsion that causes racists to dislike those of another race. The convenience of this viewpoint for those who feel no prejudice is that they are then not implicated in racism; they can see themselves as educators or mediators between victims and victimizers. This emphasis on attitudes, however, discourages inquiry into those racial inequalities that are built into social structures. Often, discrimination is not an aberration or the product of intense passion, but the result of the "normal" workings of law and institutional rules. Looking at racism only through the lens of prejudice allows those who believe themselves unprejudiced to distance themselves from the effects of racism.

This kind of distancing is widespread. Cornel West, commenting on the public silence in the aftermath of riots in Los Angeles over the verdict in the trial of policemen accused of beating Rodney King, a black motorist, put it well:

> To engage in a serious discussion of race in America, we must begin not with the problems of black people but with the flaws of American society—flaws rooted in historic inequalities and longstanding stereotypes. . . . As long as black people are viewed as a "them," the burden falls on blacks to do all the "cultural" and "moral" work necessary for healthy race relations. The implication is that only certain Americans can define what it means to be American and the rest must simply "fit in." (p. 3)

The problem is how "we" draw the boundaries of "our" community and who constitutes "we." Yet Cornel West's simple demand for a more inclusive and egalitarian understanding of COMMUNITY identifies one of the core problems of race relations in American society. Encouraged (as the majority population) to think of themselves as the norm, many white Americans believe, often without reflection, that only those who bear the mark of difference have a race. In order that racism and the implication of racial categories be relevant to everyone, white Americans must understand how they, too, are constituted as a race. "Whiteness," as a set of privileges and entitlements, must become visible so that it is not taken for granted.

Although race should be eliminated as a relevant factor in building political community, one cannot accomplish this goal simply by creating the public fiction that race does not exist. Principled assertions of nondiscrimination, while laudatory, do not redress the long history of oppression and its legacy of material and structural effects. This embedded history continues to reinforce longstanding inequalities and create new ones. For people who have been victims of racial discrimination, race is the most salient fact in defining identity and life chances. A socially enforced "polite" silence on race threatens to erase the experiences and histories of those who have suffered the most under racist structures and practices. Instead, race must be put at the center of political discourse. We need to understand how racial discourses have been central to the ways we conceive of social relationships. To find a new way to build political communities, we must first examine why many existing forms of community building have tolerated and promoted racial thinking.

To believe in the reality of race does not require reasoning that is peculiar to racists. Racial thinking developed historically out of the reasoning people did about the solidarities they held closest to their hearts. According to the *Oxford English Dictionary*, "race" is first "a group of persons, animals, or plants connected by common descent or origin." As an example, the dictionary lists "the offspring or posterity of a person." Second, "race" is "a limited group descended from a common ancestor; a house, family, kindred"; as examples, the *OED* offers "a tribe, nation, or people, regarded as of common stock," or "a group of several tribes or peoples regarded as forming a distinct ethnic stock."

The *OED* makes clear that ideas about descent, blood ties, or common substance are basic to the notion of "race." It is striking that "house, family, and kindred" are synonyms for race. Louis Flandrin, in his book, *Families in Former Times*, made the inverse discovery when he looked up "family" in a French dictionary, *Petit Robert*. "Family" refers to "the entirety of persons mutually connected by marriage or filiation," or "the succession of individuals who descend from one another," that is to say, "a line," "a race," "a dynasty." Only secondarily does *Petit Robert* define family in the way we usually mean it, as "related persons living under the same roof," "more specifically, the father, the mother, the children."

These dictionary definitions suggest that race as a social category is intimately linked to one of the basic ways human beings have organized society, that is, by kinship. As Flandrin points out, the use of "race" in England and France to refer to kinship, usually to denote the "patronymic" or "family name"—called literally, the "name of the race" or "le nom de race"—predated the current use of "race" to denote distinct large populations. Race began with kin, and when kinship became a key element in stratified social orders, as in dynastic or caste systems, the concept of race took a decisive turn.

European societies, before actual contact with non-European peoples, were societies organized by racial principles. But the operating definition of race was not based on external physical characteristics. It was based on "blood ties"—or more precisely, some socially construed notion of common substance. In early modern Europe, political power, social station, and economic entitlements were closely bound to blood ties and lineage. Thus race also encompassed the notion of CLASS. But class in this society was an accident of birth: either according to birth order (determining which rights and privileges the child inherited) or more generally to the family into which one was born (noble or common, propertied or not). The privileges or stigmas of birth, in this system, were as indelible and as discriminatory as any more modern racial system based on skin color, facial feature, or any other trait. The purity of bloodlines was a fiction maintained to limit access to elite status.

Maintaining the boundaries of lineage, of class, depended on the control of sexual behavior. The very notion of legitimate and illegitimate birth indicates that "blood ties" did not mean any and all sharings of genetic materials, but rather a cultural definition of "common substance" as "that which is passed on by fathers." In a male-dominated system, social reproduction entails not only regulating the sexuality of women in one's own group, but differentiating between women, dividing them according to legitimate access and prohibition. Race, class, GENDER, and sexuality are not simply discrete aspects of experience; they constitute principles of social organization deeply enmeshed in one another.

In the eighteenth century, systematic inquiry into the differences between populations, defined in terms of physical appearances, capabilities, and temperaments, began to replace the dynastic notions of race (common blood/lineage) prevalent in early modern Europe. But these views did not so much supersede as assimilate and transform earlier kin-based ideas. The older formulation gave emotional power to newer schemes of racial organization. In the colonial societies that Europeans created around the world, the older notion of race, articulating a lineage-based system of entitlements and privileges, was expanded and became the organizing concept through which Europeans attempted to rule subjugated populations. It was only in this context of colonization that skin color became the mark of common substance, the line differentiating colonizers from the colonized and in many cases freedom from enslavement. In other words, only when they defined themselves against a subjugated other, could Europeans unite as "whites." (*See also* PROSLAVERY THOUGHT.)

Of course, these qualities had power only because they could draw on the military force and other forms of coercion that reinforced the political and social privileges accompanying these distinctions. Colonial societies in the Americas, Africa, and Asia differed greatly in the taxonomy of racial categories. They also differed in the degree to which they tolerated sexual unions between colonizers and colonized. Miscegenation laws varied dramatically, as did the status of mestizos. But the underlying problem of creating a hierarchal system of differentiation was similar in each instance. The function of race in this context is to define commonality, to unite those who possess that "common substance" in a special, privileged community. Metaphors of common substance simultaneously articulate the quality of relationship among the members of a group, and specify who belongs and who does not.

The power and utility of notions of common substance lie in their malleability. Racial and kinship metaphors—family, brotherhood, sisterhood, la raza, each with its own specific analogical meanings—are often invoked to create a sense of group affiliation. Such metaphors have been central to nationalist movements and nation building; nationalists called on family bonds as a metaphor for binding heterogeneous populations. In linking common language and culture to blood and soil, such invocation of common substance described relationships within the group as natural and organic, and thus indelible and nonvoluntary. When Alexander Crummel, one of the founders of Black Nationalism in the United States in the nineteenth century, said that "race feeling, like family feeling, is of divine origin. . . . Indeed, a race is a family" (Appiah, p. 17), he did not invoke kinship to call forth lineage hierarchies but to borrow an ethic of mutual caring from a sentimental nineteenth-century view of family bonds. Actual families may rarely live up to the sentimental domestic ideal, but "family feelings" remain a potent representation of enduring love, disinterested commitment, and unconditional obligation. (*See also* DOMESTICITY.)

But is it a contradiction for people who share common features that we normally call "race" to mobilize on that basis to fight racism? Can the oppressed fight against their oppression without reaffirming their oppressor's categories? Is "anti-racist racism," to quote Jean-Paul Sartre, possible? Philosopher Kwame Anthony Appiah responds to this challenge by distinguishing between "intrinsic" and "extrinsic" racism. While both forms are premised upon the belief that human beings are divided into distinct subgroups, a belief which Appiah labels "racialism," intrinsic and extrinsic racists differ in their assessments of other races and in how they act upon these judgments. Extrinsic racists believe that the inferiority of other races is inherent and unredeemable. By contrast, intrinsic racists such as Alexander Crummel view races as distinct but not hierarchically ordered. Appiah concedes that intrinsic racists sometimes imply that members of their own race merit better treatment than those of another, but insists there is still a crucial moral difference between the two forms of racial thinking. Whereas intrinsic racism may in practice be prejudicial or based on faulty biological-genetic assumptions, extrinsic racism is always reprehensible.

This distinction is valid but can offer false hope. Appiah grants that intrinsic racial thinking drifts easily into an insidious exclusiveness, but the point needs to be extended. Extrinsic racial thinking is exceedingly agile: it slips easily into other conceptual landscapes—"nation," "people," "culture"—and takes on protective coloring. Paul Gilroy makes this point about postcolonial Britain, where racial division is evident but "race" is rarely spoken. The populist racism of an Enoch Powell focuses instead on culture and the meaning of "Englishness." Culture becomes a fixed property of social groups, a pseudobiological unit into which one is born and which others cannot join. Invoking English folk traditions, an innocent and laudable activity in another context, does the work of racial exclusion by subtly fusing culture, nation, and race.

It is only in recognizing that racial reasoning can exist in contexts that we consider benign that we can begin to see why race has an ever-present potential to exploit, or why seemingly nonracial conflicts become racialized. Although we may never completely purge our social reasoning of the logic on which virulent racial ideologies rely, we can become more self-consciously critical of how we draw the boundaries of our communities. Some communities, we must remember, draw their sense of commonness not from ideas of common substance, biological or historical, but from the choice of common goals. In these communities, solidarity is the result of conscious political effort, not the fruit of an affinity supposed to reside naturally in the members of the group.

TESSIE P. LIU

See also CRITICAL RACE THEORY; HEREDITY.

FURTHER READING

Kwame Anthony Appiah, *In My Father's House: Africa in the Philosophy of Culture* (New York: Oxford University Press, 1992).

Jean-Louis Flandrin, *Families in Former Times: Kinship,*

Household, and Sexuality in Early Modern France, trans. Richard Southern (Cambridge: Cambridge University Press, 1979).

Henry Louis Gates Jr., ed., *"Race," Writing, and Difference* (Chicago: University of Chicago Press, 1985).

Paul Gilroy, *There Ain't No Black in the Union Jack* (London: Hutchinson, 1987).

David Theo Goldberg, ed., *Anatomy of Racism* (Minneapolis: University of Minnesota Press, 1990).

Dominick LaCapra, ed., *The Bounds of Race: Perspectives on Hegemony and Resistance* (Ithaca: Cornell University Press, 1991).

Cornel West, *Race Matters* (Boston: Beacon, 1993).

Iris Marion Young, "The Ideal of Community and the Politics of Difference," in Linda J. Nicholson, ed., *Feminism/Postmodernism* (New York: Routledge, 1990).

Rahv, Philip [originally Ivan or Ilya Greenberg] (b. Kupin, Ukraine, Mar. 10, 1908; d. Cambridge, Mass., Dec. 22, 1973).   One of the gifted literary men who emerged as if out of nowhere in the 1930s, Philip Rahv was born to a poor Jewish family in the Ukraine; he emigrated with his parents to Palestine but left in 1922 for America. He attended public schools in Providence, Rhode Island, but did not go to college. Instead, he appears to have traveled across the country and then made his way back to New York. The communist movement became his Harvard and Yale. Like many other intellectuals, he assumed a new name when he joined the Communist Party. Few, however, would have thought to name themselves "Rahv," which is Hebrew for "rabbi." Rahv's name is indissolubly linked with that of the journal *Partisan Review*, founded in 1934 as an organ of the New York branch of the Communist-sponsored John Reed Club (*see also* JOURNALS OF OPINION). Its aim was to combat fascism and, on the literary side, to encourage a new PROLETARIANISM in literature, that is, a body of fiction by working-class writers that aimed to promote a revolutionary CLASS-consciousness among their peers. A shift in the party line away from working-class writing to established "bourgeois" writers was responsible for the cessation of publication in the fall of 1936.

When the journal resumed publication, in December 1937, it did so with an entirely new committee of editors and a new agenda: support for cultural MODERNISM (including T. S. ELIOT, Franz Kafka, Thomas Mann, and André Gide) and an independent (that is, non-Communist) radical line in politics. Whereas the old *Partisan* had published obscure working-class writers from the hinterlands, the new *Partisan* led off, in its first year, with such figures as WALLACE STEVENS, EDMUND WILSON, James T. Farrell, JOHN DOS PASSOS, Elizabeth Bishop, R. P. Blackmur, and E. E. Cummings.

Rahv was the leading figure among the editors, who also included William Phillips, DWIGHT MAC-DONALD, F. W. Dupee, and MARY MCCARTHY. As an editor, Rahv is given credit for discovering many new writers, including SAUL BELLOW, Randall Jarrell, John Berryman, and Bernard Malamud. But his major editorial contribution may have been the *Partisan Review*'s symposia, which appeared at crucial turning points in the history of the American intelligentsia. Two representative symposia which reveal traces of Rahv's interests at the time concerned "Religion and the Intellectuals," which appeared in three successive issues in 1950, and "Our Country and Our Culture" two years later. The former asked about the significance of the "religious revival" among writers and intellectuals who had heretofore been ardent secularists and, in many instances, political radicals. The latter symposium wondered anxiously whether the period of the "alienation" of American intellectuals might now have come to an end.

Rahv was also a strong-minded critic in his own right, although the body of his work is small. The best of that work was published in a posthumous collection, *Essays on Literature and Politics, 1932–1972* (1978). This volume differs from the earlier collections he assembled himself, like his first book, *Image and Idea* (1948), because it includes a representative selection of his political pieces. Judging by his own selections, Rahv saw himself chiefly as a literary man, but the posthumous collection accurately reflects the view of some of his contemporaries that his deepest commitments were political.

His best writing appeared in the decade between 1939 and 1949, when he and other so-called NEW YORK INTELLECTUALS were working their way free of sectarian political commitments and turning more wholeheartedly to literature. Rahv's two best-known essays appeared in 1939 and 1940. These are "Paleface and Redskin" and "The Cult of Experience in American Writing." The main idea is that American writing, unlike that of Europe, is handicapped by a needless split between two opposites: a semiclerical, genteel literature and an egalitarian literature immersed in raw experience. Genteel writing "discriminates"—admirably in its devotion to excellence, dangerously in its willingness to exclude. Egalitarian writing is undiscriminating—what it gains in openness it sometimes loses in avoiding judgments of comparative value. The archetypal paleface was Henry James; the ideal-type redskin was Walt Whitman.

Unlike VAN WYCK BROOKS, who had formulated a similar critique of American writing some 25 years earlier, Rahv was most at home with Continental writing. Although he praised Hawthorne and James, he put them a rung below Dostoevsky and Proust. Rahv's several essays on Dostoevsky are among his best. Some of these essays tease a politically radical tendency out of a body of work that rejects social radicalism in the name of Russian Orthodoxy. Much more ingenious than most Marxist critics of his time, Rahv could invoke D. H. Lawrence (trust the tale and not the teller), Freud (the true, or latent, content masked by the manifest content in dreams), and the Marxist "law of combined development"—all to show Dostoevsky to be modern and critical despite living in a preindustrial society and drawing on reactionary Romantic and religious ideas. As Rahv put it in his essay on *The Possessed*: "reactionary in its abstract content, in its aspect as a system of ideas, [Dostoevsky's] art is radical in sensibility and subversive in performance."

Rahv differed from garden-variety academic critics in that he consciously pledged nearly all his essays to a political aim. Thus in the 1950s he argued against critics such as Cleanth Brooks and ALLEN TATE who were popularizing T. S. Eliot's call for TRADITION. As Rahv saw it, the New Critics of the 1940s and 1950s were better understood as conservative apologists for the past than as art-for-art's-sake formalists. He specifically attacked JOHN CROWE RANSOM and F. R. Leavis for an approach to the novel in which the author's historical-social intentions were ignored in favor of close attention to image patterns and "local texture." In addition to depreciating the overvaluation of symbolism in literature, Rahv attacked the emphasis on myth, which was most effectively set forth in Northrop Frye's influential *Anatomy of Criticism*. In these various polemics, written against the grain of post-World War II criticism, Rahv was arguing for attention to history. His last collection, *Literature and the Sixth Sense* (1969), derives its title from Nietzsche's perception that in the modern period the sense of history has become as indispensable as the senses we are born with. But as Rahv shed most of the specific doctrines of Marxism, the appeal to the sense of history in his own essays came to seem abstract and ideological.

In the 1960s Rahv had little to say about the Vietnam War, which was the central preoccupation of other politically minded intellectuals, until it seemed to him that the NEW LEFT and the student movement in general had brought about a situation in which social revolution seemed conceivable. In short, Rahv saw the late 1960s as a replay in many respects of his own seedtime, the 1930s. In 1970 he began publishing *Modern Occasions*, a new quarterly of politics and ideas. After a promising start, that journal, and Rahv himself, became mired in a spirit of negativism, which combined despair over the self-destructive irrationalism of the antiwar movement and disgust with nearly all new movements in literature and thought. The journal ceased after six issues.

Rahv and his contemporaries tend to be patronized by many contemporary Marxist theorists, above all FREDRIC JAMESON. To be sure, Rahv lacks the philosophical range and power of Jameson and Jameson's major European precursors such as Lukács, Adorno, Ernst Bloch, and Sartre. But Rahv's directness in addressing a broad range of moral, historical, and political issues in literary criticism is a quality academic Marxist criticism has lost, particularly as it has surrendered to the gods of POSTMODERNISM. Marxism is more influential as a voice in criticism nowadays, when it has no roots in any indigenous political movement or party, than it was in the 1930s. It would take an observer of the Zeitgeist as unillusioned as Rahv himself to spell out the manifold ways in which contemporary Marxist criticism has paid for its current prestige by accommodation to the spirit of the age.

MARK KRUPNICK

FURTHER READING
Terry A. Cooney, *Rise of the New York Intellectuals: Partisan Review and Its Circle* (Madison: University of Wisconsin Press, 1986).
Andrew J. Dvosin, "Literature in a Political World: the Career and Writings of Philip Rahv," Ph.D. diss., New York University, 1977.
Arthur Edelstein, *Images and Ideas in American Culture: Essays in Memory of Philip Rahv* (Waltham, Mass.: Brandeis University Press, 1979).
James B. Gilbert, *Writers and Partisans* (New York: Wiley, 1968).
Mark Krupnick, "A Memoir of Philip Rahv: 'He Never Learned to Swim,'" *New Review* (London) 2 (Jan. 1976): 33–9.
Alan M. Wald, *The New York Intellectuals: the Rise and Decline of the Anti-Stalinist Left from the 1930s to the 1980s* (Chapel Hill: University of North Carolina Press, 1987).
René Wellek, *A History of Modern Criticism, 1750–1950*, vol. 6: *American Criticism, 1900–1950* (New Haven: Yale University Press, 1986).

Ransom, John Crowe (b. Pulaski, Tenn., Apr. 30, 1888; d. Gambier, Ohio, July 4, 1974). Poet and critic. One of the Southern Agrarians who grieved over the spread of a frenetic industrial culture to the South, Ransom held that LIBERALISM and PRAGMATISM erred in ignoring the limits that circumscribe human endeavor. In the 1940s he turned from CULTURAL CRITICISM to literary criticism. He believed its analytical method could provide a sound AUTHORITY at a time of cultural disarray, since poetic forms disclose a moral and aesthetic order within the contingencies of life. Author of *The New Criticism* (1941), Ransom joined other New Critics in downplaying social context or authorial intention in understanding the meaning of a text. Ransom's poems feature careful meter and precise language while exploring such dualities as order and chaos, reason and imagination, ambition and defeat, love and impermanence.

See also SOUTHERN AGRARIANISM.

FURTHER READING

Kieran Quinlan, *John Crowe Ransom's Secular Faith* (Baton Rouge: Louisiana State University Press, 1989).

Rauschenbusch, Walter (b. Rochester, N.Y., Oct. 4, 1861; d. Rochester, N.Y., July 25, 1918). Clergyman and theologian. Intellectual leader of the Social Gospel, Rauschenbusch brought together the nineteenth-century tradition of evangelical reform and the twentieth-century commitment to scientific reform. In *Christianity and the Social Crisis* (1907), *Christianizing the Social Order* (1912), and *A Theology for the Social Gospel* (1917), he asserted that an ethical stance in the industrial era must combine a realistic assessment of social power relations with a prayer-based commitment to the spread of "personality"— which he grasped as both an individual self-giving and a communal fellowship. Closely tied to the gradualist SOCIALISM of the pre-World War I period, Rauschenbusch urged support for industrial workers in their struggle with capitalists.

See also LIBERAL PROTESTANTISM.

FURTHER READING

Paul M. Minus, *Water Rauschenbusch: American Reformer* (New York: Macmillan, 1988).

Rawls, John (b. Baltimore, Md., Feb. 21, 1921). Harvard University Professor Emeritus, Rawls is America's most prominent contemporary political philosopher, and the many translations of his work are spreading the influence of American political theory abroad. Many readers of his 1971 masterpiece *A Theory of Justice* have noted how very American it is. And Rawls himself now emphasizes that he aims, not to occupy some a priori vantage point free of historical entanglement, but instead to weave together more coherently the strongest strands of the Western liberal tradition. Louis Hartz may have been right to regard the United States as a Lockean nation, but Locke clearly needs updating. Despite writing amidst dangerous political turmoil, Locke was confident in shared Christian fundamentals from which to derive needed limits on the oppressive powers of King and Parliament. Rawls develops a social contract theory in the tradition of Hobbes, Kant, Locke, and Rousseau—texts with which he is deeply engaged and on which many of his students have become leading experts—but one that better reflects contemporary conditions. *A Theory of Justice* is most obviously American in the way it tests and illustrates its principles by reference to institutions embodying an American pattern of separated powers, but it also addresses a question even more fundamental for us than for Locke. As Rawls phrases it in his recent *Political Liberalism* (1993), "how is it possible for there to exist over time a just and stable society of free and equal citizens, who remain profoundly divided by reasonable religious, philosophical, and moral doctrines?" (p. 2). While pluralism has deepened since Locke's day, so has confidence in democratic institutions. Thus Rawls focuses not starkly on drawing limits around state power—as Robert Nozick did in his libertarian critique of Rawls —but constructively on designing basic institutions that cope justly with pluralism and with natural and social inequalities of distribution.

There are many ironies in the broad and deep influence of Rawls's monumental work. As first developed, it was cast within substantive moral theory, a field he is widely credited with reviving. Utilitarianism, the comprehensive moral doctrine directing the agent to maximize the aggregate good of individuals, was the opponent. While some philosophers had tried to refute utilitarianism by producing counterexamples, Rawls forswore that approach. He influentially turned his back on the effort, typical of mid-century analytic philosophy, to give necessary and sufficient conditions for the correct use of a concept like JUSTICE. Instead, he would build a theory, recognizing its imperfections, but hoping that the thinking public would come to accept it after taking account of the relevant arguments and "pruning and adjusting" both their concrete political positions and their abstract principles on due reflection. This ideal of "reflective equilibrium" has been adopted by many moral philosophers. Yet, despite having encouraged them by his methods and his example, Rawls has increasingly made clear that he does not view his liberal theory as a contribution to comprehensive moral theory. Since our pluralism is deep, a political theorist, on his view, must not stand within any comprehensive moral conception the way Locke did within Christianity. Our attempt, instead, must be to develop a specifically political LIBERALISM that avoids, so far as is possible, taking any stance on fundamental questions of moral truth.

Where, then, does Rawls stand? The best answer already lies within the ideal of reflective equilibrium:

he builds from principles he claims "we do in fact accept." Yet some of his writing also seems to imply that these need a foundation in a metaphysical conception of the person, which communitarians such as Michael Sandel have argued that Rawls fails to provide. But is Rawls's conception of the person foundational? Persons, on Rawls's view, are to be viewed as free and equal, as capable of framing rational plans and respecting requirements of justice. Such ideas help specify his social contract theory. In an "original position," artificially designed contracting parties are to decide, once and for all, on principles of justice to govern the constitutional essentials of a society. Rawls argues that the parties constructed to embody these ideals would reject utilitarianism in favor of the two principles of "justice as fairness," which in *Political Liberalism* (pp. 5–6) read as follows:

a. Each person has an equal claim to a fully adequate scheme of equal basic rights and liberties, which scheme is compatible with the same scheme for all; and in this scheme the equal political liberties, and only those liberties, are to be guaranteed their fair value.
b. Social and economic inequalities are to satisfy two conditions: first, they are to be attached to positions and offices open to all under conditions of fair equality of opportunity; and second, they are to be to the greatest benefit of the least advantaged members of society.

While the argument for these principles consists partly in showing why the contracting parties, as defined, would prefer them, it also includes the institutional tests mentioned above and an extended and evolving argument that these principles are important for a just, pluralistic society to be stable. The "political, not metaphysical" ideal of persons as free and equal is thus but one of many mutually supporting elements in Rawls's justification.

While Rawls's understanding of justification as a practical task has attracted many academics and intellectuals, the content of his political theory has not had a proportional practical impact. The political challenge that his theory poses lies mainly in its egalitarianism. His principles demand that all individuals have enough resources for their political liberties not to be mere paper promises, and that basic social institutions be designed to harness and encourage the energies of the enterprising so that the inevitable inequalities benefit all. Rawls recognizes that religious and cultural pluralism remains a serious challenge in many liberal democracies, including the United States. He knows that we are a long way from realizing his egalitarian ideal. Rawls nevertheless continues to elaborate his theory of justice, reasonably, as one that we may yet come to accept on due reflection.

HENRY S. RICHARDSON

FURTHER READING
Norman Daniels, ed., *Reading Rawls* (New York: Basic Books, 1975).
Robert Nozick, *Anarchy, State, and Utopia* (New York: Basic Books, 1974).
Thomas Pogge, *Realizing Rawls* (Ithaca: Cornell University Press, 1989).
John Rawls, *A Theory of Justice* (Cambridge: Harvard University Press, 1971).
——, *Political Liberalism* (New York: Columbia University Press, 1993).
Michael Sandel, *Liberalism and the Limits of Justice* (Cambridge: Cambridge University Press, 1982).
"Symposium on Rawlsian Theory of Justice: Recent Developments," *Ethics* 99 (July 1989): 695–994.
J. H. Wellbank et al., eds., *John Rawls and His Critics: an Annotated Bibliography* (New York: Garland, 1982).

reading The notion of "reading" has evolved considerably over the past three decades thanks to theoretical challenges mounted by poststructuralism and reader-response theory. Jacques Derrida has been the most influential figure in this evolution, having turned the formerly obvious meanings of "reading" and "writing" upside down. Derrida has redefined "writing" as the process of differentiation by which we apprehend the world in LANGUAGE. He asserts, moreover, that linguistic categories not only shape our world, but constitute our only versions of it. Likewise, inverting the conventional relation of text to reader, poststructural thinkers argue that a reader writes or constructs a text as she reads it. To be meaningful, a text must be shaped according to the reader's assumptions about language and the world, and like the world, cannot be apprehended directly.

Building on this poststructuralist inversion, reader-oriented theories of interpretation relocate the site of interpretive authority from the text to the reader. The identity of this newly authorized reader has been seen, in turn, to take its shape from what Stanley Fish has called "interpretive communities." Such communities, according to Fish, are made up of readers who share a framework of assumptions and strategies for interpreting texts. These interpretive paradigms are subject to the contingencies of history, to the imperatives of culture, and to the accidents of class, race, and gender, and are themselves parts of a comprehensive network of contending values. This shift of emphasis from text to reader and the subsequent recognition of the reader as part of a larger cultural "text" informs most current thinking about reading, readers, and that which is, or might be read.

Theoretical conceptions of reading and the reader have found their broadest application in the fields of literary and cultural studies. There, for most purposes, "reading" has become synonymous with "interpretation." Thus, when we speak of a Marxist or a feminist reading of a text, we implicitly acknowledge the perspectival nature of reading, even as we may argue for the superiority, based on the potential effects of a particular reading, of one perspective over another. In literary studies, this conception of reading is opposed to the "objective" poetics of the New Criticism. New Critics held that variant readings were always more or less accurate or inaccurate with respect to the univocal meaning of the text. This meaning was theoretically nonparaphrasable, independent of authorial intention, and unaffected by either the history of the text's interpretation, or by the variety of interpretations competing for preeminence at any given time. But belief in the text as an autonomous entity susceptible to objective explication has given way over the past three decades to an understanding of the text as the site of rhetorical struggle—among readers.

In general, formalist and structuralist accounts of reading depend on spatial metaphors, comprehending the text as an artifact or edifice. The effect of such metaphors is to grant the text an identity which is entirely independent of specific historical readers. Reader-oriented accounts, on the other hand, tend to stress the temporal nature of the reading process and to reject the possibility of a single, stable interpretation over time. Proponents of such a position argue that, at the level of the individual reader, the act of reading a text will influence any subsequent reading of that text, making it impossible for the same reader to produce the same reading twice. Moreover, the interpretive communities of which a reader is a part are themselves subject to, even defined by, historical pressures. For the reader-oriented critic, then, the value of any particular reading must refer to its effects within a specific historical and cultural moment, rather than to a posited hierarchy of interpretation existing independently of the historical conditions that bring new readings into being.

The shift from the reader as the passive recipient of a text's meaning to the reader as an active participant in the construction of meaning in the text has contributed less to a validation of subjectivism than to a disappearance of the subject, or self, as it has been conventionally conceived in Western thought. For the active reader is constrained, or given her cognitive shape, by the interpretive communities to which she belongs. Thus consensus about the meaning of a text arises from shared assumptions about what the text *could* mean within the purview of some or another interpretive community at a specific juncture in time, rather than from convergence upon a single meaning which the text projects. While any given meaning of a text therefore is relative, it can never be, strictly speaking, idiosyncratic. Meaning is only enabled in the first place by the interpretive norms of a community and is not only bound by those norms, but constituted by their employment. This is not say that these norms cannot be violated, or departed from, but only to say that such deviations will always be read as "from the norm." Reading is a rhetorical activity, but a rhetorical activity both constrained and enabled by conventions that exist prior to reading.

The extent to which the text actually constrains the meaning produced by the reader remains a point of contention among reader-oriented approaches. In general, reader-response critics entirely subordinate the text to the reader, contending that interpretive strategies inevitably arise from the immediate cultural, professional, and political imperatives that constitute the reader's context. Reception theorists, on the other hand, seek to maintain a tension and continuity between the structure of a text and the possible or "virtual" interpretations that readers may generate from it. In *The Implied Reader* Wolfgang Iser finesses the question of textual constraint by arguing that literary texts imply in their structure an active reader who will seek to "realize" the text in their own consciousness (p. 57). But differences between reader-response and reception theorists may ultimately be said to reflect rhetorical choices, rather than rigorous methodological differences. The "immediate" context of the reader, that is to say the communal imperatives which inform her reading, necessarily share a linguistic past with texts intelligible to the reader. Thus, just as the reader disappears as an individual subject under the aegis of an interpretive community, so does the discrete text become absorbed into the entire history of textual convention. Readers and texts "imply" each other in a seamless dialectic, the representation of which is never disinterested.

In *Rhetorical Power* Steven Mailloux has shown that convincing demonstrations of a work's significance in past contexts lend credence to a critic's stance on current interpretive disputes (pp. 134–5). Mailloux in effect merges the reception and reader-response approaches by arguing that the history of reception is part of the immediate rhetorical field that conditions our response to literary works. The reconstruction of this history of reception is of course always fragmentary, selective, and driven by the imperatives of current critical debate. But to the extent that critics have come to see such conditions as revealing the constraints of their own interpretive contexts, rather than as evidence damning their lack of objectivity, the shift of authority from text to reader has come full circle. The history of reading itself can never be directly exposed, but only read, in turn, according to the norms of one or another interpretive community.

The current reconception of theorists, historians, and critics as readers complicit in the culture they interpret, as opposed to objective professionals who stand outside that culture, has led to broader awareness of the variety of interpretive communities, and thus the variety of readers, that may encounter any given text. Certainly it remains the end of the critic to influence interpretation, but the rhetorical means by which the critic's influence is brought to bear has begun to reflect the shift of authority from text to reader. Generalizations about how an abstract reader will or ought to react to a novel like *The Scarlet Letter*, for instance, are becoming less common than arguments about how particular reading communities, or particular readers as representatives of those communities, might have understood Hawthorne's novel.

A recent example is an essay by Sacvan Bercovitch, "Hawthorne's A-Morality of Compromise" (1988), which argues that Hawthorne's contemporaries would have seen in Hester Prynne an ambiguous and perhaps unsettling symbol of the violent revolutions that had swept Europe in 1848 and which found parallels for some readers in the burgeoning American women's movement, as well as the abolitionist movement. Hester's ultimate acquiescence in bearing her brand signals Hawthorne's desire for compromise rather than radical action on these issues. Bercovitch observes that Hawthorne's representation of this "ideology of liberal consensus" leads *us*, like Hester, toward an accommodation of the novel's multiple perspectives, and perhaps toward an evasion of the moral significance of any particular perspective. To the extent that we find Bercovitch's argument convincing, it constrains our interpretations of Hawthorne as social thinker. In this case, it becomes more difficult to see Hawthorne as the protofeminist that some critics have seen him to be, and easier to see him as a rather conservative accommodationist who construes the good or bad of issues such as women's rights or slavery as matters of perspective, rather than fixed morality.

The multiple incarnations that texts might be said to have, by virtue of the multiple audiences that give them life, has set the stage for a historicist approach that not only acknowledges the co-implication of texts

and readers but recognizes the entire constellation of material and cultural forces that give shape to the activity of reading. Recently critics grounded in both critical theory and the archaeology of the book have begun to condition the text/reader relation against the resistant materiality of the wider world of objects and activities. Doing so, they take us, as Cathy Davidson has put it in the introduction to *Reading in America*, "toward a history of books and readers" (p. 1).

This history, which could more generally be called the history of publication, or even the history of print culture, understands reading as a social and political activity with respect to which readers can no longer be considered epiphenomena. This understanding is one of the defining characteristics that distinguish the relatively new discipline "the history of the book" from the older field of textual bibliography. In 1972, Philip Gaskell, a textual bibliographer, could write in his authoritative *A New Introduction to Bibliography* that "bibliography's overriding responsibility must be to determine a text in its most accurate form." For Gaskell, "accurate" invariably meant "what the author meant us to read" (p. 1). But the historian of print culture today would understand the word "accurate" to be entirely relative to the purposes at hand. An author's intentions for or about the material object she helped produce become but a single facet of a larger social phenomenon that may be approached with any number of goals in mind. A poorly edited, pirated, but widely disseminated edition of a novel would for some purposes be much more valuable than an author's final draft of the manuscript. The former might tell us much more about a book's functions among, say, a class of readers who could not afford to pay full price for the authorized edition; and the latter, rather than being seen as a revelation of the author's original or even final intentions, might be combed for evidence of the manifold pressures brought to bear on the published work by printers, publishers, distributors, retailers, advertisers, libraries, critics, academic institutions, and any of the other constituencies that might ultimately purchase, borrow, sell, burn, or otherwise use the printed artifact.

Whereas poststructuralist criticism, broadly construed, has sought to demonstrate the indeterminacy of the text, of authorship, and of the reading subject, the historian of print culture takes such indeterminacy for granted; it becomes the point of departure for new historical understanding rather than an end in itself. Like other forms of the new social historicism, or the sometimes more sharply defined NEW LITERARY HISTORICISM, the study of books and readers appropriates techniques and insights from any number of fields, including anthropology, sociology, bibliography, critical theory, and literary studies. This interdisciplinary approach reflects not only a willingness to dissolve old boundaries, but a desire to create new narratives that respond to our ongoing relationship with the printed word. If we are not to make the reader a victim in this world where the myth of comprehensive knowledge has been swept away by the overwhelming flux of electronic information, we must now, more than ever, think of her as a poet, as a maker and shaper of her world, not merely its inheritor.

DAVID BARROW

See also LITERACY; REPRESENTATION; TEXTUALITY.

FURTHER READING

Sacvan Bercovitch, "Hawthorne's A-Morality of Compromise," in Nathaniel Hawthorne, *The Scarlet Letter,* ed. Ross C. Murfin (Boston: St. Martin's, Bedford Books, 1991).

Cathy Davidson, ed., *Reading in America: Literature and Social History* (Baltimore: Johns Hopkins University Press, 1989).

Stanley Fish, *Is There a Text in This Class? The Authority of Interpretive Communities* (Cambridge: Harvard University Press, 1980).

Philip Gaskell, *A New Introduction to Bibliography* (New York: Oxford University Press, 1972).

Wolfgang Iser, *The Implied Reader: Patterns in Communication in Prose Fiction from Bunyan to Beckett* (Baltimore: Johns Hopkins University Press, 1974).

James L. Machor, ed., *Readers in History: Nineteenth-Century American Literature and the Contexts of Response.* (Baltimore: Johns Hopkins University Press, 1993).

Stephen Mailloux, *Rhetorical Power* (Ithaca: Cornell University Press, 1989).

Jane Tompkins, ed., *Reader-Response Criticism: From Formalism to Post-Structuralism* (Baltimore: Johns Hopkins University Press, 1980).

realism As a label realism can be applied with some accuracy to many nineteenth- and twentieth-century writers, including (to name a few) HENRY JAMES, MARK TWAIN, Mary Wilkins Freeman, CHARLES CHESNUTT, THEODORE DREISER, SINCLAIR LEWIS, JOHN DOS PASSOS, and ERNEST HEMINGWAY. The rise of this genre in the United States, however, is perhaps best viewed in relation to the career of novelist, editor, and polemicist WILLIAM DEAN HOWELLS. During the 1880s Howells conceived realism broadly as the democratization of literature through a shift in its subject matter, which would be drawn largely from the commonplaces of everyday life; in its producers, who would hail increasingly from outside the ranks of the New England elite; and in its critics, who would be constituted from its reading public. Never crystallizing into a set of aesthetic protocols or a clearly articulated movement, realism, in Howells's novels and essays (and in the writings of others), signaled a critical attitude toward established genres such as sentimentalism and romanticism. This critical stance deemed other modes to be abstract, cliché, and inadequate to the task of representing the new society that had come into being during the industrial and commercial expansion of the post-Civil War years.

This claim to greater mimetic fidelity than rival genres has often exposed realists, particularly Howells, to the charge of naively believing that literature reflected rather than helped constitute reality. And though such naiveté can be found in polemical statements made by advocates for the genre, the case for realism was more sophisticated than such censures have allowed. Keenly aware of the achievements of the foreign novel in the work of Gustave Flaubert, the Goncourt brothers, Émile Zola, Ivan Turgenev, and Leo Tolstoy, Howells and Henry James sought to gain for the American novel a comparable sense of seriousness and aesthetic range. Accordingly they urged American novelists to confront new and uncomfortable realities. In practice, however, reshaping the aesthetic of the American novel was often compromised by financial necessity. In order to realize a profit from their fictions, American writers had to reckon with the genteel expectations of magazine editors. Howells himself, though working assiduously to expand the ambit of the novel, nonetheless argued from the pages of his "Editor's Study" column in *Harper's Monthly* that the novelist who wished to find an audience was forced to compromise with the standards of decency upheld by the monthly magazine.

Positioned as an insurgent form that was yet obliged to honor prevailing social mores, the realist novel has come to be grasped as a crucial manifestation of the tensions that marked Victorian American society, and as an essential part of the Victorian effort to define and transcend those tensions. Striving to speak simultaneously for democratic change and the preservation of social order, the realistic novel of the 1880s and 1890s was a deeply conflicted form. On the one hand these novels widened their representational scope to include political anarchists, labor strikes, feminist reformers, African Americans, immigrants, entrepreneurs, and financiers. On the other hand, this expansion of vision remained centered in a troubled, but still confident Victorian middle class insistent upon stable identities. The novelists' reluctance to break free entirely from respectability has been understood by some later critics as a defensible, realistic strategy for writers who wanted to reform the social order without destroying it. Other critics, however, have charged that the first wave of realism failed to achieve its promise. Adhering to familiar plots and characters, the novelists of the 1880s and 1890s missed a momentous chance to link a new art to a burgeoning social consciousness. In this latter view the realistic novel first lived up to its potential only with the 1900 publication of Theodore Dreiser's *Sister Carrie*, in which the author resolutely refused to condemn a heroine bent on fulfilling a range of material desires that went beyond marriage and respectability.

But in stepping outside the boundaries of social propriety, *Sister Carrie* also appeared to step outside the bounds of realism: in the eyes of many critics, Dreiser is less a realist than an exemplar of NATURALISM because his works are more committed than traditional realistic novels to determinism and to a scientistic account of human activity. But while an earlier generation of scholars devoted considerable energy to drawing generic distinctions that would permit sure labeling of turn-of-the-century authors, contemporary scholars are more interested in mapping a text's strategies of REPRESENTATION, less eager to judge the accuracy of its mimetic gestures. Realism offers a rich terrain for exploring the relationship of literature to the marketplace, the politics and ideology of representation, and the role of LANGUAGE in producing rather than just reflecting reality.

KENNETH W. WARREN

FURTHER READING
Leo Bersani, "Realism and the Fear of Desire," in *A Future for Astyanax* (New York: Columbia University Press, 1984).
Daniel H. Borus, *Writing Realism: Howells, James, and Norris in the Mass Market* (Chapel Hill: University of North Carolina Press, 1989).
William Dean Howells, *Criticism and Fiction*, ed. Clara Marburg Kirk and Rudolf Kirk (New York: New York University Press, 1959).
Amy Kaplan, *The Social Construction of American Realism* (Chicago: University of Chicago Press, 1988).
Eric Sundquist, ed., *American Realism: New Essays* (Baltimore: Johns Hopkins University Press, 1982).

Reed, John (b. Portland, Ore., Oct. 22, 1887; d. Moscow, Soviet Union, Oct. 19, 1920). Writer. A member of Harvard's legendary class of 1910 (which included T. S. Eliot and Walter Lippmann), Reed went on to Greenwich Village, where he joined MAX EASTMAN, FLOYD DELL, and others at *The Masses*. There he developed a radicalism that was equal parts cultural and political. His celebrated accounts of Pancho Villa (*Insurgent Mexico*, 1914) and the Russian Revolution (*Ten Days that Shook the World*, 1919) portrayed social revolution as adventurous and inspiriting. Deeply committed to labor organizing, Reed helped found the Communist Labor Party after World War I. Under indictment for sedition, he fled to Russia. After his death from typhus and burial in the Kremlin wall, he became a cult figure for the American left.

FURTHER READING
Robert A. Rosenstone, *Romantic Revolutionary: a Biography of John Reed* (New York: Knopf, 1975).

regionalism It was only after the Civil War, when sectionalism moved increasingly from political to cultural spheres, that regional literature began to attract critical attention. Much of this literature, variously termed "local color" fiction or "regional realism," appeared in New York's *Harper's Monthly* and Boston's *Atlantic*, ironically consolidating the cultural dominance of a single region in the name of promoting sectional understanding. The term "local color" expressed this attitude of cultural dominance. Reporters for eastern magazines visited particular locales and "mined" regional materials the way the Forty-Niners had panned for gold in the Mother Lode. Even in the best of local color fiction by Bret Harte, HAMLIN GARLAND, and MARK TWAIN, regional differences are still viewed from the perspective of outsiders and become the occasion for literary humor. In retrospect, such urban interest in regional customs, dialects, and folkways seems to have managed to make sectionalism safe, containing diversity by redefining it as local heritage. In effect, local color fiction viewed regional difference as a circus, the regionals themselves as exhibits in a cultural sideshow that subordinated and often mocked not only regional white and black male characters, but also Native Americans and women.

A revisionist perspective has emerged recently to challenge those critics who place regional writing in the margins of some more central canon. Regionalism, revisionists argue, has its own integrity as a literary tradition. The Anglo-Irish writer Maria Edgeworth may have been the first regionalist, but nineteenth-century American writers, particularly women, developed regionalism as a distinct mode of fiction. They enfranchised regional persons instead of setting them up as objects of ridicule, looking "with" their characters instead of "at" them, in effect shifting the center of perception from the urban outsider to the vernacular speaker. Unlike either their contemporary "humorists of the Old Southwest" (regional writers of the 1840s such as George Washington Harris, Thomas Bangs Thorpe, and Johnson Jones Hooper), or the local color writers who began to publish after the Civil War, regionalists such as

HARRIET BEECHER STOWE (*Mayflower Sketches*, 1843, and *The Pearl of Orr's Island*, 1862), Alice Cary (*Clovernook*, 1852, "Second Series" 1853), and Rose Terry Cooke in her early stories (such as "Miss Lucinda," in *Atlantic Monthly*, 1861) avoided reliance on sexist, racist, or classist stereotypes in their depiction of character. While the regionalists did not write free from the casual racism of nineteenth-century American culture, in general they incorporated inclusivity as a cultural value. Character, relationship to place (if not literal geography), and a respectful approach to difference all distinguish regionalism from other modes of regional literature, including local color fiction. MARY AUSTIN (*The Land of Little Rain*, 1903, and *Lost Borders*, 1909) was the only writer who used the term "regionalism" to describe her work (and not until a 1932 essay), but many others—Mary Noialles Murfree, Sarah Orne Jewett, KATE CHOPIN, Alice Dunbar-Nelson—explicitly differentiate in their fiction between the impulses of regionalism and the local color approach to the depiction of regional life.

Most of the earliest regionalists wrote about New England—Stowe, Celia Thaxter in *Among the Isles of Shoals* (1873), Jewett in *Deephaven* (1877) and *The Country of the Pointed Firs* (1896), and Mary Wilkins Freeman in *A Humble Romance* (1887) and *A New England Nun* (1891)—and wrote in full knowledge of each other's work. Jewett served as a literary and personal bridge for some of the regionalists by acknowledging her indebtedness to Stowe and serving as a mentor to the young WILLA CATHER. Yet Cary wrote from the rural suburbs of Cincinnati as early as the 1850s and others shifted the center of regionalist narratives to other regions—to the Cumberlands for Murfree (*In the Tennessee Mountains*, 1884–5), to New Orleans for Grace King (*Balcony Stories*, 1893), Chopin (*Bayou Folk*, 1894, and *A Night in Acadie*, 1897), and Dunbar-Nelson (*The Goodness of Saint Rocque*, 1899), and to the California desert for Austin. Regionalism created openings for both women of color and white women to write narratives about the complexity of minority group experience in America, as well as about gender and class differences. In addition to African American writer Dunbar-Nelson, who wrote about Creoles from various class and racial origins, Zitkala-Sä (Gertrude Simmons Bonnin), in a series of autobiographical sketches (in *Atlantic Monthly*, January to March 1900), and Sui Sin Far (Edith Eaton), in *Mrs. Spring Fragrance* (1912), wrote regionalist narratives that countered pervasive cultural stereotypes about Native Americans and Chinese Americans. (*See also* INDIANS, ASIAN AMERICAN IDENTITIES.)

After 1910 or 1920, arguably because of the emergence of MODERNISM (which looked with Cosmopolitan disfavor on all types of localism) and the victory for woman suffrage (which enabled women to imagine moving toward equality in other spheres as well), regionalism was redefined. Willa Cather, despite her lifelong interest in regional fiction, created characters, including young women, who no longer turn exclusively to regional identification for their source of values. And in the 1930s, a new wave of writers and critics introduced a new regionalism without even noticing their precursors. Donald Davidson's analysis of the origins of regionalism, in *The Attack on Leviathan*, ignores nineteenth-century women writers and views regionalism as a conservative consciousness, the basis for a southern renaissance in literature that he implies will be both the logical extension of and cultural counterpoint to modernism (*see also* SOUTHERN AGRARIANISM).

At the turn of the twenty-first century, revisionist critics have reclaimed regionalism as a literary form and as cultural critique. They add "region" to the categories of analysis (RACE, CLASS, and GENDER) that animate much of literary and feminist theory in the 1980s and 1990s, arguing that regionalism also serves as a point of historical connection between nineteenth-century white women writers and the proliferation of African American writers and women and men from other minority groups in the twentieth century. In the words of Rose Terry Cooke's impoverished, unmarried, rural, and aging protagonist in "Miss Beulah's Bonnet," regionalism is "free to say" that the lives and experiences of adolescent girls matter as much as those of the boys that dominate canonical American fiction. In the context of new historical approaches to the study of American culture and literature, readers and critics are now also "free to say" that regionalism, as practiced by nineteenth-century women writers, raised questions about regional—as well as gender, race, and class—differences that American society has struggled to understand ever since.

MARJORIE PRYSE

FURTHER READING

Mary Austin, "Regionalism in American Fiction," *English Journal* 21 (Feb. 1932): 97–107.
Donald Davidson, *The Attack on Leviathan: Regionalism and Nationalism in the United States* (Chapel Hill: University of North Carolina Press, 1938).
Josephine Donovan, *New England Local Color Literature: a Women's Tradition* (New York: Ungar, 1983).
Judith Fetterley and Marjorie Pryse, *American Women Regionalists 1850–1910: a Norton Anthology* (New York: Norton, 1992).
Judith Fryer, "What Goes on in the Ladies Room? Sarah Orne Jewett, Annie Fields, and Their Community of Women," *Massachusetts Review* 30 (winter 1989): 610–28.
Marjorie Pryse, "'Distilling Essences': Regionalism and

'Women's Culture,' " *American Literary Realism* 25 (winter 1993): 1–15.

Louis Renza, *"A White Heron" and the Question of Minor Literature* (Madison: University of Wisconsin Press, 1984).

Sarah Way Sherman, *Sarah Orne Jewett: an American Persephone* (Hanover, N.H.: University Press of New England, 1989).

relativism The philosophical tradition has construed the doctrine more or less continuously, from the time of Plato's *Theaetetus* and Aristotle's *Metaphysics* to the present, in close accord with the usual (but disputable) interpretation of Plato's dialogue and Aristotle's explicit judgment that relativism is self-contradictory. Both lines of attack are plainly directed against Protagoras, though we lack Protagoras' de-fense of relativism. One can only improvise a plausible theory of what Protagoras may have meant: Plato's (perhaps better, "Socrates'") objection depends primarily on construing relativism as inherently paradoxical or self-defeating. Aristotle's objection treats relativism as flatly contradictory because it violates certain necessary truths about logic and metaphysics (namely, Aristotle's own doctrine). On the conditions given, relativism is indeed self-defeating or contradictory. But, for one thing, it is possible to interpret Protagoras' belief (reported in *Theaetetus*) in a coherent way that makes the defense of relativism both reasonable and philosophically interesting. For a second, the usual interpretation of the *Theaetetus* is not ineluctable, and Aristotle's objection, though very clearly formulated, is demonstrably indefensible (in its modal form). For a third, a form of relativism that could be called protagorean in intent can be shown to be coherent, defensible, even reasonably preferable to competing views for certain domains of inquiry at least.

It may seem curious to confine a topic like relativism to ancient authors. Certainly, there have been relativists in the modern and contemporary literature. Nevertheless, it would not be unfair to say that, in the academic literature, until quite recently, the single modern specimen view of a relativistic ethics nearly all discussants would acknowledge was Edward Westermarck's; and that is more correctly termed a form of subjectivism than relativism, since it treats values as grounded in our emotions and recommends consistency between one's conduct and such sources. Westermarck is, so to say, more nearly committed to (cultural) *relativity* than to (philosophical) *relativism*, that is, to the diversity of individual psychological sources of values and the reasonableness of bringing one's judgments and commitments into line with that. On a current assessment, Westermarck would not be a relativist at all.

Along related lines, however, *if* one supposed that values and norms were incapable of being justified except in terms of the historically variable practices of the different societies in which pertinent questions arise, then relativism *is* nothing but the admission of the diversity of cultures. In that case, even Ludwig Wittgenstein's notion of variable "forms of life" (*Lebensformen*) would be a relativistic theme, one going well beyond questions of value to the very nature of understanding, knowledge, communication, meaning, and truth. But there is no evidence that Wittgenstein did favor relativism, and there is no evidence that theorists prepared to admit cultural relativity (Peter Winch, Charles Taylor, Alasdair MacIntyre, for instance) would be at all willing to countenance an explicit form of relativism.

There are some well-known recent theorists who profess to be relativists, for instance NELSON GOODMAN and Paul Feyerabend. But neither actually formulates a clear sense of how we should understand the application of truth values in the relativistic way—though they are certainly relativists. On the other hand, quite a number who take relativism seriously today, for instance Hilary Putnam and RICHARD RORTY, regard it as incoherent or paradoxical, and, moreover, their objections are difficult to distinguish from the classical objections offered by Plato and Aristotle. So it is a stunning fact that a serious account of relativism cannot fail to be largely confined to ancient sources. There are other recent theorists who are clearly relativists, Hans-Georg Gadamer and Michel Foucault and THOMAS KUHN for instance, who understand truth-claims to be incapable, in principle, of overcoming the horizonal contingencies of historically changing inquiries; but these authors regularly deny that they are relativists or simply demur on the question. It is, therefore, a better strategy to lay out the formal conditions under which a particular view may reasonably be said to be a form of relativism. That way, one may at least canvass the literature and decide, for cause, just who, and in what sense and to what degree, may reasonably be so identified.

On balance, it turns out that there are two distinct versions of relativism, construed alethically, that is, construed as a theory regarding the choice and definition of truth-values. One is indefensible, along the usual lines of interpreting "Socrates'" objection (that is, the view of the dramatic figure of the dialogues); the other is viable but almost completely neglected in the literature. The remarkable thing is that the ancient objections have persisted almost without change or addition down to our own time (witness the views of Hilary Putnam and Richard

Rorty); the viable version has been explicitly formulated (also adumbrated more and more widely) only as we approach the end of the twentieth century, for instance by Joseph Margolis. But it must be said that, in its merely alethic form, relativism cannot be thought to be of very great interest. It is only when it is developed in a suitable epistemic and ontic context (that is, in terms of cognitive and methodological resources and the analysis of reality) that relativism proves an essential ingredient in the bolder philosophies of the end of our century—for instance, in the views of such thinkers as Foucault and Gadamer (who do not venture that far).

The intriguing thing is that Protagoras seems to have been aware of something of this in advancing his own master thesis, "Man is the measure," in the context of supporting a reading of reality as flux and an avoidance of any principled disjunction between (changing) appearances and (changeless) reality (which both Plato and Aristotle favor). There is reason to think that the *Theaetetus* and the *Metaphysics* are largely occupied with combating any and all versions of the flux and any and all failures to admit the disjunction mentioned—and thus, more marginally, to oppose relativism as entailing those two dangers. In our own time, the doctrine of the flux is more favorably regarded; modal invariances of every sort (that is, conceptual invariances taken as necessary) are either now often dismissed or openly challenged; and the historical contingencies of experience, belief, evidence, rational method, the discernment of truth, and the like have come to dominate Western thought so much that relativism cannot any longer be dismissed out of hand. That is, favorable views of the flux are not as such versions of relativism; but a ramified relativism presupposes the doctrine of the flux (the denial of necessary invariances in the world and in our understanding of the world).

The two versions, then, are these: one option (1) may be called *relationalism* and the other (2), tendentiously, *robust relativism*. The first holds that "true" means "true-for-S" or "true-in-W" or "true-in-L" (where "S" ranges over different individuals, "W" over different worlds, "L" over different languages, or the like). This produces the paradox that one cannot then consistently affirm *that*, say, S_1 employs "true" to mean "true-in-L_1" and S_2 employs "true" to mean "true-in-L_2" and so on; that is, (1) produces self-referential paradoxes. On (1), the very *meaning* of "true" is relativized in being treated relationally. (Socrates' charge, then, is, effectively, that truth is what anyone says it is, that what is true for one is false for another.)

Robust relativism holds (instead) to the usual non-relationalized meaning of "true" but admits that bivalence in any of its familiar forms (the principle of excluded middle, the principle of *tertium non datur*) is not a necessary constraint on thought or language involving assertion or truth-claims; it admits that bivalence may be coherently abandoned or restricted in particular sectors of inquiry; and it holds instead that relativistic truth-values may be consistently reconciled with bivalent values if properly segregated. In addition, (2) holds that we may admit (in restricting or abandoning bivalent truth-values: that is, the rule that "true" and "false" are disjunctive values and exhaust the range of values available for well-formed statements) that a many-valued logic is serviceable, and that statements, claims, judgments, or the like—which, on a bivalent model but not now, would be in or would generate contradiction or inconsistency—need not then be construed as doing so. Call such judgments (the latter) "incongruent." For instance, *if* interpretations of Shakespeare's *Hamlet* take truth-values, it is still possible to hold that two interpretations that are clearly incompatible may both be assigned a positive or favorable or "pro" truth-value (for instance, "apt," "reasonable," "valid," "plausible"—*not* "true") with regard to a proper reading of *Hamlet*. They may be jointly valid, incompatible, and neither true nor false or at least not true. (True and false may be treated in quite different ways, alethically.) Aristotle had held that the principle of excluded middle was a necessary rule of reason (that is, the rule that, for instance, for any well-formed statement, what is predicated of any actual thing is either true or false). It is easy to see that if, as for Aristotle, what is real *is* invariant, then if every real particular has an invariant nature (qua real), then any predication is either consistent or inconsistent with that particular's imputed nature; hence, alethically, no indeterminacies arise and bivalence is secured. Admitting the flux subverts that policy.

Beyond these considerations, relativism in contemporary philosophy is centrally concerned with epistemic issues—incommensurabilism, historicism, the insuperable relativity of meaning and evidence, for instance—and, less conspicuously (but not negligibly), ontic issues—for instance, regarding the inherently indeterminate nature of things or perhaps certain things only, the peculiarities of cultural or intentionally qualified entities and phenomena, endlessly interpretable stories or paintings for instance, things that lack natures and have only histories, things that have interpretable "natures," and "constructivist" views of reality in which no principled disjunction arises between the structure of the real world and the structure of language and thought about the way the world is. Doctrines that tend, whether explicitly or implicitly, to conform to (2) and that address some subset of the issues just mentioned are entitled to claim to be potentially viable forms of relativism.

Strategically, the defense of the more ramified forms of relativism must, first, establish the alethic coherence and viability of a many-valued logic (the replacement of bivalence one way or another) and the admissibility of "incongruent" judgments (that is, on formal grounds); and then (and only then) go on to examine the viability of any of the kind of epistemic and ontic issues just enumerated. Many critics of options of the latter sort (for instance, Thomas Kuhn's incommensurabilism, which, if admitted, would confirm the ineliminability of relativism) charge, among other things, that incommensurabilism leads to an abandonment of bivalence or actually entails the relationalist reading of relativism. The first strategy puts the cart before the horse; the second is demonstrably unnecessary: the charge rests on a confusion between alethic and epistemic considerations.

Once this much is clear, the pivotal issue regarding the defense of relativism is readily identified: *the relativity of evidence bearing on any truth-claim is a matter independent of alethic relativism.* Once, however, one retreats from claims of direct or privileged cognitive access regarding any part of reality—which is the view overwhelmingly favored at the end of our century (and which is by no means itself a form of relativism)—the conjunction of *that* admission *and* alethic relativism (as by way of incommensurabilism, historicism, the denial of any principled disjunction between appearance and reality) instantly entails the viability of relativism. The argument is remarkably powerful and straightforward.

Clearly, relativism is not a form of skepticism or anarchism or nihilism or irrationalism (as it is usually said to be, for instance by Karl Popper). On the contrary, it is a natural development within the strongest tradition of philosophical analysis. In reclaiming it, however, it must be seen to favor, and to be favored by, any and all forms of the doctrine of the flux. Hence, ontic options of the sort mentioned (the denial of essentialism, the alterability of the "nature" of cultural entities by interpreting them —artworks for instance) ineluctably lead to a profound form of relativism. One sees, therefore, the plausibility of imputing the original defense of relativism to Protagoras and of putting in question the classic attacks on Protagoras' doctrine. Alternatively put, it would be fair to assume that all attacks on the tenability of relativism are grounded in the assumption of necessities *de re* (essential or invariant

nature, as in the canonical view that the laws of nature are real and changeless) or necessities *de dicto* (the law of contradiction, or excluded middle, or identity). (This contrast needs to be distinguished from that regarding the option of casting putatively necessary connections either *de re* or *de dicto*, that is, in the "material" or "formal" mode of speech.)

The easy accommodation of the law of contradiction requires that one admit that the law is called into play relevantly only when interpreted and that no interpretation of the properties of any sector of the world itself yields a corresponding necessity *de re* or *de dicto*. Excluded middle, on almost every view, is not demonstrably necessary in alethic terms at all. And the fate of the law of identity is the same as that of noncontradiction. The only interesting question that arises, then, concerns those sectors of inquiry, and the reasons, for which we should prefer a relativistic logic over bivalence. But that itself is an empirical (that is, entirely benign) question. Given these distinctions, it is reasonably clear that relativism (in the "robust" sense) is in the ascendant toward the end of our century, but usually undeveloped on its formal side.

JOSEPH MARGOLIS

See also OBJECTIVITY.

FURTHER READING

Aristotle, *Metaphysics*, trans. W. D. Ross, Book Gamma, in *The Complete Works of Aristotle: the Revised Oxford Translation*, vol. 2, ed. Jonathan Barnes (Princeton: Princeton University Press, 1984).

Paul K. Feyerabend, *Against Method* (London: Hewlett, 1978).

Michel Foucault, *The Order of Things* (1966; New York: Vintage, 1970).

Hans-Georg Gadamer, *Truth and Method*, trans. Garrett Barden and Robert Cumming (New York: Seabury, 1975).

Nelson Goodman, *Ways of Worldmaking* (Indianapolis: Hackett, 1978).

Thomas S. Kuhn, *The Structure of Scientific Revolutions*, 2nd ed., enlarged (Chicago: University of Chicago Press, 1970).

Joseph Margolis, *The Truth about Relativism* (Oxford: Blackwell, 1991).

Plato, *Theaetetus*, trans. F. M. Cornford, in *Plato: the Collected Dialogues*, ed. Edith Hamilton and Huntington Cairns (Princeton: Princeton University Press, 1961).

Hilary Putnam, *The Many Faces of Realism* (La Salle: Open Court, 1987).

Richard Rorty, *Consequences of Pragmatism* (Minneapolis: University of Minnesota, 1982).

Edward A. Westermarck, *Ethical Relativity* (New York: Harcourt Brace, 1932).

religion American religion, as a category of thought, is protean. Statistics suggest its complexity.

Compared to organized religion in Western European societies, the disestablished churches of the United States enjoy enviable institutional health. The competition engendered by religious pluralism has been a major stimulus to growth. In the 1850s Philip Schaff observed that the United States presented a "motley sampler of all church history." It still does. The *Yearbook of American and Canadian Churches* lists over 200 religious groups in the United States. Collectively these bodies attract more active participants than most state churches do. The striking numbers indicate that religious thought is important in the United States, and also hint that it needs to be discussed in more than one way.

The most straightforward approach to religious thought treats it as a systematic intellectual construction preserved in theological treatises and the pronouncements of church councils. This approach will never be passé. Rigorous analysis of theological ideas and debates is necessary to understand the doctrinal differences that separate America's many religious faiths. Although histories of specific denominations and sects can be insular and dreary, religious division in the United States is awash with contentious words that articulate distinct points of view. Among other things, we have to be able to distinguish CALVINISM from Arminianism, Pre- from Post-MILLENNIALISM, Higher BIBLICAL CRITICISM from Barthian hermeneutics. These issues apply to Protestants. Similar intellectual disputes divide American Catholics, American Jews, American Muslims, American Buddhists, and American Hindus.

The analysis of systematic religious ideas also allows scholars to integrate religion into general patterns of American intellectual life. For example, the great work of PERRY MILLER on American PURITANISM not only argued the power of religious thought in seventeenth-century Massachusetts Bay. It further indicated that Puritan religious ideas persisted and lurked in every nook and cranny of the "American mind." Economics, law, art, politics, philosophy —Miller left nothing exempted. The goal of tracking the influence of religious ideas is evident in many individual studies of important American thinkers. A canonical core of such people includes JONATHAN EDWARDS, THOMAS JEFFERSON, ABRAHAM LINCOLN, HENRY WARD BEECHER, Felix Adler, REINHOLD NIEBUHR, DOROTHY DAY, and MARTIN LUTHER KING JR.

However, the discussion of religious thought as disputes carried on at high levels of intellectual discourse isn't enough. It omits the way that ordinary people use religious ideas to shape their lives, and it overlooks how religious experience itself organizes thought in nondiscursive ways. SOCIAL SCIENCE encourages us to understand religious thought as something more than a set of ideas embedded in texts. Although often accused of reducing ideas to epiphenomena of deeper social realities, the functionalist sociology of TALCOTT PARSONS helped restore religion to the central place it had in the work of Émile Durkheim and Max Weber. Functionalism emphasized religious commitment as essential to norm maintenance and to the bonds that joined people into SOCIETY. Parsons's attention to integrated social systems tended to give religion a steadying rather than a transformative role in American life, a fact that has given Parsonian sociology a reputation for political conservatism. Even so, functionalism, by rejecting the notion that contemporary religion was a holdover from a prescientific era, an expression of unconscious atavistic feelings, usefully widened the concept of religious thought to include the perennial nonrational components of human action.

Even more than sociology, CULTURAL ANTHROPOLOGY encouraged innovation in the study of American religious thought. In an influential essay, "Religion as a Cultural System," CLIFFORD GEERTZ defined religion as "a system of symbols which acts to establish powerful, pervasive, and long-lasting motivations in men by formulating conceptions of a general order of existence." The attempt to grasp symbol systems nudges us away from reliance on written texts. A cultural system is a web of meanings that gain an "aura of factuality" over long periods of time. People grow up in a cultural system. They learn to enact their religious beliefs through rituals that formal creeds and churches neither contain fully nor control. What people learn as dogma is only part of the story. For the rest we must look to patterned responses that form the habits of their daily life.

Culture of course is partly textual. But the relevant texts include sacramental performance, architecture, tombstone sculpture, and hymnody. Expanding the range of things we take to be crucial artifacts of religious thought throws a different light on questions of religious pluralism. Division is not always about doctrine. Often the attitudes that divide religious Americans are rooted in the general cultural differences among racial and ethnic groups. Cultural division is as important within religious traditions as between them. Robert Orsi's examination of rituals associated with the annual festival of the Madonna of 115th Street in New York City explains more about the difference between Italian and Irish Catholic immigrants than about differences between Catholics and Protestants. It also indicates how Italian immigrants appropriated Catholicism into their family and community life in ways that affronted the official guardians of Catholic religious symbols. Specific historical experience transforms religious thought, outwitting even the strongest obstacles erected by formalism.

New literary theories of READING that recast the putative receivers of thought as the actual producers of meaning have encouraged the tendency of cultural studies to differentiate popular from elite religious expression. They alter the terms of older Marxist CLASS analyses of religion in which "the people" were force-fed the religious opiates prepared for them. In suggesting that ordinary Americans refigure what they are supposed to hear, scholars have shown that popular appropriations of doctrine and practice sometimes subvert the HEGEMONY of respectable religion. Influenced by Carlo Ginzburg's study of a sixteenth-century Friulian miller who confounded his inquisitors with a singular rendering of Christian belief, American scholars have found their own Menocchios among oppressed people. People filter what they read or hear from "official" sources through what they already believe. Thus, according to some historians, a grid of folk beliefs carried from Africa allowed American slaves to "misconstrue" the teachings of white evangelicals and to create their own distinct form of Protestantism.

The case of African American slaves poses a particular challenge to efforts to understand the religious thought of subaltern groups. The slave population was largely illiterate. African religion lacked written creeds. Whatever was passed on about Africa among American slaves was passed on by oral teaching and storytelling. In its dependence upon the spoken word African American culture is like Native American culture. What we know in written form about early efforts to Christianize American slaves comes from unreliable and often confused white witnesses. These documents do, however, describe ritual. The "ring shout" becomes a crucial bit of evidence to estimate the strength of African survivals. So do the emotional performances of black religious meetings and the rhythms of slave spirituals. To recognize complex expression in ritual experience is to recover religious thought as a collective, eclectic creation that sits at the very center of people's lives.

GENDER studies have also widened the definition of what constitutes religious thought. The majority of Protestant church members in America and the overwhelming majority of church attenders at all social levels are women. They have been almost from the beginning. Yet reading sermons and the reports of church conventions doesn't help explain why women invest so much energy in religion. If we look instead at the church work done by women, we can observe them in a process of investing their lives with coherent moral meanings. In the past, the performance of moral duties provided women with a bridge from private DOMESTICITY into public action. Unlike African American slaves, white women often wrote about religion. We do not lack written documents from which to construct their religious thought. However, what women did often undercut or modified the gender stereotypes that they repeated in formal argument. Poststructuralism has usefully reminded us that action, like formal thought, carries many unintended as well as intended meanings.

Recent scholarship dealing with religious thought does not rest on a consensus. Controversy abounds over all of these new approaches. The question of whether it makes sense to distinguish elite and popular expressions of religious thought is a debate, not a settled issue. The degree to which economically subordinate people can invent their own religious faith is a subject that can bring academics close to blows. Many scholars of American religious thought stress the divisions that run along racial, gender, class, and ethnic lines. Others who argue the now unfashionable case for AMERICAN EXCEPTIONALISM tend to interpret American religion as a unifying force. Among the latter, none has been more influential than the sociologist Robert Bellah, who tried to see Americans as united in their adherence to "civil religion." Outside of and above the doctrines of any one religious group, he maintained, civil religion resides in a vision of millennial hope and national destiny, one that American presidents invoke in their major addresses. All Americans participate in it when they visit national shrines in Washington D.C., when they rise to sing the Star-Spangled Banner, when they attend public events on the Fourth of July and Memorial Day.

Scholars concerned with American religious thought face a field that is much larger and more complicated than it was a quarter of a century ago. They must bring a dispassionate curiosity to many movements that older studies dismissed as bizarre and denatured forms of religion. Recent studies take seriously the intellectual constructions of backwoods Methodist preachers, of Millerites, and of revivalists (see also APOCALYPTIC LITERATURE). They place renewed stress on the importance in religious thought of magical and occult systems that affected both the learned and the unlearned. They explore how the ideas of the Theosophists and of SPIRITUALISM informed FEMINISM and other reform movements. They suggest that religiously inspired healing systems like the Christian Science of MARY BAKER EDDY worked as well as so-called orthodox medicine.

Without question, scholarly interest in popular culture has stimulated an appreciation for variety in religious thought and expression. Catherine Albanese sees Americans enshrining their "sacred stories" in the legends of Davy Crockett, the concerts of Elvis Presley, the rituals of professional football, and the pages of *Playboy*. In other discussions, JACK KEROUAC and Madonna become embodiments of Catholic thought. Genuine sympathy is apparent in some of this scholarship, a sympathy that is more than mere suspended judgment. The fascination of contemporary religious scholars with witchcraft, astrology, mind-cure, homeopathy, and the long list of other things labeled "New Age" suggests that expansion of the ways we define religious thought often represents disillusionment with some of the proudest claims of Western civilization.

There is another important implication in the broadened sense of what constitutes religious thought in America. It has to do with secularization theory. In the United States, scholars have often measured secularization by such things as the disaffection of intellectuals from organized religion, the substitution of science for religion in school curriculums, increased legal restrictions on religion in public life, and the involvement of religious groups in "worldly" mass media. The trouble with these measures, which are accurate as far as they go, is that they avoid questions about the social construction of what secular and religious mean. Too many discussions of secularization reflect a normative conception of what religion ought to look like. Since Cotton Mather did not raise funds to build churches with gymnasiums and bowling alleys, we too easily think that pastors who do so now have capitulated to the secular.

With a widened appreciation for the historical specificity not only of formal religious thought but of the many ways religious thought expresses itself as culture, we are less apt to regard the religious claims of Americans in the late twentieth century as secular. Some measures of secularization automatically doom Protestantism to worldliness from the very beginning of Luther's reforms. We should recognize that what changes over time is not a quantifiable balance between sacred and secular but people's perceptions about the relation between the religious and secular. Today, as in the middle of the seventeenth century, people fight about what exactly is religious and what exactly is secular. Conceptually, in fact, a symbiotic connection exists between the two realms. Neither is thinkable without the other. In the mid-1950s the sociologist Will Herberg noted a paradox: contemporary American religious life combined "pervasive secularism with mounting religiosity." What Herberg

didn't see was that this was nothing new: the paradox is a product of social ideation, one that has marked American religious thought for a very long time.

R. LAURENCE MOORE

See also MISSION.

FURTHER READING

Catherine Albanese, *America, Religions and Religion* (Belmont: Wadsworth, 1992).

Robert N. Bellah, "Civil Religion in America," *Daedalus* 96 (winter 1967): 1–21.

Clifford Geertz, "Religion as a Cultural System," in Geertz, *The Interpretation of Cultures* (New York: Basic Books, 1973).

Carlo Ginzburg, *The Cheese and the Worms: the Cosmos of a Sixteenth-Century Miller* (Baltimore: Johns Hopkins University Press, 1980).

Will Herberg, *Protestant-Catholic-Jew: an Essay in American Religious Sociology* (Garden City, N.Y.: Doubleday, 1955).

Charles H. Lippy and Peter W. Williams, eds., *Encyclopedia of the American Religious Experience: Studies of Traditions and Movements* (New York: Charles Scribners, 1988).

R. Laurence Moore, *Selling God: American Religion in the Marketplace of Culture* (New York: Oxford University Press, 1994).

Robert A. Orsi, *The Madonna of 115th Street: Faith and Community in Italian Harlem, 1880–1950* (New Haven: Yale University Press, 1985).

representation   The United States of America was the first modern nation founded on the principle of representation. One legendary motto of the War for Independence was, of course, "Taxation without representation is tyranny." The war was in real ways a struggle over representation: who will establish the procedures for selecting political representatives and define their authority and responsibilities? Since that time, domestic controversies—slavery, suffrage, taxation—have generally concerned who merits representation, what constitutes fair representation, and how fair representation might be achieved.

This nation's persistent conflicts over representation result in part from the paradoxical conception of representation it implemented—that of LIBERALISM, the Enlightenment political philosophy justifying the overthrow of monarchy. As Hanna Pitkin has observed, since the late Renaissance political philosophers have wrestled with a difficulty in the idea of representation (whether symbolic or specifically political). When symbols or representatives stand for or act for that which they represent, they must be different and distant from what they represent, which remains by definition absent: "Being represented means being made present in some sense, while not really being present literally or fully" (p. 153). Nothing can ever be wholly represented, and representatives, to be representatives, possess some degree of independence. Consequently, the precise relation and responsibilities of symbols or agents to the persons, interests, events, or objects represented are difficult to stipulate.

This paradox will sound familiar to contemporary students of the humanities and social sciences, including the LAW, who contemplate generally poststructuralist strains of philosophy and theory. Although by no means uniform, DECONSTRUCTION, FREUDIANISM, French feminism, and the Marxism influenced by the FRANKFURT SCHOOL characteristically explore the nature and structure of representation. These investigations yield an array of results, but share a common axiom: representation is inevitably indirect, mediated, because signifiers must be different from their referents.

The structure of America's liberal political system underscores the mediated nature of representation. The United States, of course, is not strictly a democracy. In ancient Athens, those males who could vote governed directly through their votes; no representation was involved. In America's representative democracy, or republic, representation is proportionate, never direct, and therefore public debate continually mulls how representation—the ability of groups to participate in electoral and governing processes—will be apportioned.

The Federalist papers testify that the American system of government was designed precisely to distance representatives from their constituents and thereby diffuse their OBLIGATION to any single constituency. Such distinctive mechanisms as the electoral college or Senate representation by state rather than population clearly serve this distancing function. (Indeed, until the twentieth century, Senators were not elected popularly, but selected by state legislatures.) The distinction, even competition, between state and federal domains accentuates the indirectness of political representation. The federal system of checks and balances, moreover, is meant to prevent power from becoming concentrated in—and therefore embodying—one individual or faction. The architects of American government famously sought to multiply the diversity of factions represented; for them, the effect of diversity, as JAMES MADISON put it in *Federalist* no. 10, was precisely to "refine" and dilute the influence of any single faction, and therefore ensure that the federal government directly represents no single set of interests.

Representation in America, then, is distributed like other resources. Political conflicts in effect adjust the economy of representation. Disputes about the ballot, and more generally about RIGHTS, exemplify this process. The CONSTITUTION notoriously denied suffrage to women and slaves, not to mention Native Americans. For decades, poll taxes excluded many from voting. The 15th amendment in principle extended suffrage to blacks, but not to women, nor to Indians, who had been explicitly excluded from the "equal protection" and "due process" clauses of the 13th and 14th amendments. These omissions underscore the dependence of supposedly inalienable rights on the apportioning of political representation. Rights would seem to be independent of political processes, but are in fact functions of representation.

The framers' emphasis on mediated representation in the polity has for the most part been echoed in American AESTHETICS, so much so that one might safely say that America is a culture of mediation. When John Trumbull painted panoramas of Niagara (1787–95) or *The Declaration of Independence* (1818), which now hangs in the rotunda of the Capitol, he meant to represent the essence and vitality of the new nation; in both instances, a significant natural attribute (Niagara) or event (the signing of the Declaration) substitutes for the nation and "people," themselves absent. In *The Old House of Representatives* (1822), Samuel Morse portrayed representatives transcending individual interests to serve the nation, depicted as a universal ideal; in Morse's conception, too, the "people" are rendered only by their representatives, and finally by the building housing them.

WALT WHITMAN is America's poet of democracy; yet his epic attempt in *Leaves of Grass* to write (and be) the poem of America is acutely conscious of the disparity between the nation and its representative, the poet. "One's self I sing, a simple separate person," Whitman writes, "*Yet* utter the word Democratic . . ." (italics added). The poet's embodiment of and identity with nation and audience are incomplete here, even contentious ("Yet"). At the conclusion of *Song of Myself*, this identity is no more complete: "I stop somewhere waiting for you."

American writers' abiding preoccupation with the romance is a prominent example of artists' emphasis on the mediations of representation. Although different in many ways, HARRIET BEECHER STOWE, NATHANIEL HAWTHORNE, HENRY JAMES, WILLA CATHER, CHARLES W. CHESNUTT, even EDITH WHARTON, W. E. B. DU BOIS, FRANK NORRIS, THEODORE DREISER, and NORMAN MAILER have characterized their work in the language of romance rather than mimetic realism or transcription. Art feels "valid," James wrote in his Preface to *The American*, when it takes license with the familiar so that it conveys the real without seeming reducible to it. TONI MORRISON offers a variant on this motif with her emphasis on (re)memory as shaper of history. Even America's impresario of REALISM, WILLIAM DEAN HOWELLS, never called for anything like the purportedly direct mimesis of Zola's experimental novel. Howells's definition of realism is the notoriously vague "truthful treatment of material," by which he meant (also vaguely) that realism maintains an "allegiance to the waking world." For Howells, realism is at base an ethical enterprise that effects allegiance to the material world not through transcription but, he wrote, by making "Reality its Romance"—that is, by departing from reality.

America's most prominent photographer of nature, Ansel Adams, scorned the notion that photography is "the duplication of visual reality." What he called the "absolute realism" of photography is achieved through "visualization," involving "interpretation" and "anticipation"; photography "realize[s] a desired image." Adams's idealistic rather than transcriptive account of photographic representation was shared by the acclaimed photographer of urban landscapes, his friend ALFRED STIEGLITZ. Their views of representation continue the legacy of Thomas Cole and his student Frederic Church, two of the nation's founding landscape painters. Both painters believed that painting composes landscape to fulfill foreordained ideals of nationalism and PROGRESS, although Cole, unlike Church, used this idea of aesthetics to criticize developments in American culture.

A few American artists—HENRY DAVID THOREAU, occasionally Henry James, RALPH WALDO EMERSON, even less frequently, JOHN DOS PASSOS—worry the paradox of mediation: because full representation is impossible, representation risks being unfair. EDWARD BELLAMY conceived his utopia in the novel *Looking Backward* (1888) expressly to overcome what he takes to be the inevitable injustice of representation. Nevertheless, American characterizations of aesthetics envision with few exceptions that art represents the nation and its people not directly but through the mediations that constitute art.

Figures in American political culture, conservatives as well as reformers, have called for direct representation more regularly than have artists. JOHN ADAMS, for example, thought Congress "should be an exact portrait" of the people (quoted in Pitkin, p. 60). Americans speaking in this spirit contemplate bypassing the reviled machinery of American political representation. Andrew Jackson's first address to Congress exemplifies this temper. America's elaborate mechanisms for representing "the will of the People" risk frustrating "their wishes." "It is safer for [the People] to express their own will." The frustration Jackson summoned is familiar. Ross Perot exploited this impulse during the 1992 Presidential election,

and some of the demands heard today for more inclusive representation of diverse cultural identities in governmental bodies, the courts, schools, scholarship, literature, film, and other media inherit Jackson's aspiration to overcome the dualism in the liberal account of representation. Recent calls for more diverse representation often expand the scope of Jackson's and Perot's criticisms, seeing the question of representation as not just conventionally political but also broadly cultural and intensely personal. Judith Butler, for example, maintains that identities and processes of identity construction previously "designated as culturally unintelligible" must be made "articulable within the discourses that establish intelligible cultural life" (p. 149). Butler objects here that prevalent definitions of self and community overlook and exclude many of the identities composing a COMMUNITY. For Butler, the mediations of culture obstruct the realization of identity and therefore community.

It is not necessary, however, to think that what Chantal Mouffe calls the "impossibility of achieving full representation" (p. 379) in itself compromises identity and the results of political effort. Instead, in liberalism, this paradox underlies the idea of identity and constitutes the reason for political effort. The paradoxical economy of representation is evident even in the concept that provides the rationale for representative government—rights. The idea of rights is what makes it plausible to think, first, that citizens should be permitted to protect and advance their interests and, second, that government should represent the interests of different groups and individuals. Since its emergence in the seventeenth century, the concept of rights has itself been an idea about representation. The paradigmatic form of rights has been that of property, the term that follows the customary "life, liberty" in the Fourteenth Amendment. The right to property, like all rights, is said to be inalienable and therefore not subject to political processes.

The idea of inalienability invited the hope that representation could be averted, but even as formulated by John Locke it was already an instance of (indirect) representation. In the most famous passage in "The Second Treatise of Civil Government," Locke proposes that "every man has a property in his own person; this nobody has any right to but himself." Each man owns himself. "The labour of his body and the work of his hands . . . are properly his," and we own the phenomena we expend labor on because this activity "hath fixed my property in them" (pp. 134–5). Here, self and inalienability issue from representation. For Locke, the self is not itself a function of representation—it has an "unalienable" property in itself; nevertheless, the self's inalienability is known only through the property and other attributes through which it is identifiable. Although not reducible to its property, the self acquires its definition through property. Selfhood is discernible only through what represents it.

In liberalism, then, identity is a paradoxical form of representation, and mediation is the condition rather than the obstacle to identity and action. America's main contribution to philosophy, PRAGMATISM, begins with this notion. CHARLES SANDERS PEIRCE argued that there are no immediate perceptions of phenomena, and that premise underlay the definition of the self offered by WILLIAM JAMES. The self, for James, consists of the "I," the cognitive faculty, and the "ME," the self's attributes and properties. The "I" constantly seeks full realization, but can apprehend itself only through the networks of attributes perceived as the "ME." The "I," therefore, is always known indirectly and as an object, inferred from the composition of "MEs" representing it. We might call James's logic of the self quintessentially American: the self arises in an economy of representation in which it can never be fully realized, and this condition sparks the continual effort to realize itself directly that is one hallmark of American political culture.

HOWARD HORWITZ

See also SEMIOTICS; TEXTUALITY.

FURTHER READING

Daniel Boorstein, ed., *An American Primer*, 2 vols. (Chicago: University of Chicago Press, 1966).

Judith Butler, *Gender Trouble: Feminism and the Subversion of Identity* (New York: Routledge, 1990).

William James, *The Principles of Psychology*, 2 vols. (1890; New York: Dover, 1950).

John Locke, "The Second Treatise of Civil Government," in *Two Treatises of Government* (1690), ed. Thomas I. Cook (New York: Hafner, 1973).

Chantal Mouffe, "Feminism, Citizenship, and Radical Democratic Politics," in Judith Butler and Joan W. Scott, eds., *Feminists Theorize the Political* (New York: Routledge, 1992).

Hanna Fenichel Pitkin, *The Concept of Representation* (Berkeley: University of California Press, 1967).

Roberto Unger, *Knowledge and Politics* (New York: Free Press, 1976).

republicanism The historically potent form of this term was the adjective: republican. It signified a project still audacious in the late eighteenth century: a government without hereditary king or nobility. Not until long afterwards did historians begin to discover aspects of the republican agenda usable for times when "liberalism," not monarchy, was in the

saddle. Republicanism is thus a term of contemporary historians' art.

Nothing was automatic in the way Americans became republicans. When the crisis over imperial taxation and authority began to heat up in the 1760s, almost no one thought it would issue in the unseating of the king in the American colonies. Up to the eve of 1776, as Willi Paul Adams has shown, "republican" figured primarily as a scare word in the rhetoric of loyalists and imperial officials. Armed with historical memories of the English Civil War and the Cromwellian dictatorship, the bloody collapse of republican Rome, or the corruption of republican Venice, loyalists employed "republican" as a synonym for internal tumult and disorder. Publicly the leaders of the colonial resistance did not challenge the point. In the structure of political assumptions most of them had been taught, it was not easy to imagine jettisoning monarchy with equanimity. Since the 1640s it had been asserted that the genius of the British constitution was its mixture of the three basic, Aristotelian forms of government—monarchy, aristocracy, and DEMOCRACY—each of which alone, unbalanced by the others, was dangerous and unstable. Where the danger inherent in monarchy was arbitrary and tyrannical power, monarchy's virtue, it was said, was unity of action in protecting the nation's essential interests—precisely the needed counterpoise to democracy's tendency, when unchecked, toward disaggregation and individual license. For all the patriots' growing disillusionment with their royal protector, they did not lightly imagine cutting the web of presumptions which made balance the key to liberty, and monarchy essential to balance.

Americans became republicans in the winter and spring of 1776 unexpectedly, in a rush of shifting premises precipitated by the king's proclamation of a policy of suppression and the electrifying clarity of THOMAS PAINE in *Common Sense*. Distance kept the Americans from seriously entertaining the idea of inviting another king into their former one's place— as the British parliament had successfully managed in 1689, or as the Frankfurt assembly was to attempt, disastrously, in 1849. But the impracticality of reestablishing a monarchy did not, in itself, clarify the form stable republican governments should take, or even the force of the term republican. Some, like Paine, visceral in his hatred of hereditary power, threw overboard the whole idea of mixed Aristotelian parts to argue for simple, direct democracy. Those who played a commanding role in the constitution-writing of 1776–87 chose instead, in a dozen rival designs, to try to graft old notions of balanced and divided parts onto the people's new sovereignty. To

JAMES MADISON, one of those who framed the U.S. CONSTITUTION, it was the principle of representation which made the new governments republican. JOHN ADAMS, more eager still than Madison to distinguish a republican from a democratic polity, took the republican touchstone to be balance itself. THOMAS JEFFERSON, prone to see monarchists under every bed, stuck more tightly to republican's historic meaning: resistance to those who, in every clime and era, itched for crowns and coronets.

Large as this range of interpretations was, "republican" remained, at its eighteenth-century core, a structural description of government. In the 1790s, Paine, faced with defense of the wide array of constitutional constructions Americans had created, was to argue that republican did not define a government's form but its object; where in monarchies the nation's weal was engulfed in the private fortunes of the king, the object of a republic was *res publica*, the "public good." But it was not until they looked behind the essence of republican government to the conditions which might, against the historic odds, enable a republic to endure that most Americans moved beyond constitutional forms to ends and ethos. It had been a commonplace since Montesquieu's *Spirit of the Laws* in 1748 that, whereas ambition for place and honor energized monarchies, only the opposite— a spirit of self-denial, love of country, sacrifice of private ends and ambitions, in a word, "virtue"— could successfully sustain republics against their inherent centrifugal tendencies. The patriots did not need Montesquieu to make the point. The struggle between politics and private economic ambition during the embargo of British trade, the exigencies of mobilizing and financing an army in a tax-averse polity, the battle against profiteering in war goods and supplies, the constant wartime problem of sustaining sacrifice and morale—all this joined with the patriot leaders' book learning to emphasize the indispensability of republican VIRTUE to the very survival of their experiment in kinglessness.

So audacious a break with the past seemed in itself, finally, to demand a new culture and public spirit. Into these conjoined needs patriot writers rushed with the exhortations which were later to seem the rhetorical core of their "republicanism." "So shall our nation, form'd on Virtue's plan . . . this great lesson teach—that kings are vain," wrote Philip Freneau, putting the strenuous mood in verse (vol. 3, p. 91). "Every man in a republic is public property," Gordon Wood quotes BENJAMIN RUSH (p. 61). "His time and talents—his youth—his manhood—his old age— nay more, life, all belong to his country." Into the twentieth century, long after kinglessness had lost its

daring, this sense of breasting the ordinary tides of history through morale and sacrifice alone, this sense of momentous choice between self-interest and the public good, was to remain lodged in the core repertoire of American politics.

None of this would have been surprising to the historians responsible for the rediscovery of "republicanism" in the 1970s and 1980s had not the postprogressive historians of the 1940s and 1950s succeeded so well in depicting a Revolution whose social and self-denying side was so weak and inconsequential. Where the progressive historians of the 1910s and 1920s—Charles Beard at their head— had seen a Revolution filled with class and sectional struggles, the postprogressive historians were impressed, to the contrary, with the relatively limited invasions of person and property the American Revolution had entailed, and its limited utopian fervor. Having seen a world truly fall apart in the 1930s and 1940s, they could not rid their imagination of the contrast the AMERICAN REVOLUTION posed. The great liberal project which the Russian revolutionaries had tried to overleap and the German National Socialists to repeal—emancipation of the individual from the authority of prescribed status, custom, and the needs of state; legitimation of a plurality of private interests, spheres, and purposes; acceptance of the barter and friction inherent in a democratic politics and a market-based economy—all this seemed to have come with remarkably little strain to the United States. A Revolution which invoked the rights of individual property ownership as a radical slogan, which eventuated in so democratic (for the times) a structure of governance, which balanced the rights of individuals so heavily (for its day) against the claims of state and society, was surely a liberal revolution— whatever Benjamin Rush might have said in momentary enthusiasm. Not Rush but Madison was the presiding genius of the postprogressive historians' Revolution: that same Madison who, in the move that seemed to capture the ethos of "liberalism," abandoning hope that the people could ever be as virtuous as Montesquieu claimed republicans must be, transferred his confidence to pluralism, law, and skillful constitutional contrivance.

It was against this backdrop that the rediscovery of the anxious, ethically supercharged side of the Revolutionary publicists by Bernard Bailyn in 1967 and, still more eventfully, the anti-individualistic rhetoric of the public good by Gordon Wood in 1969 took on importance. "Republicanism" was Wood's coinage for the utopian, virtue-demanding Revolutionary *mentalité*. To this in 1975, in a work that strode boldly across space and time, J. G. A. Pocock added a historical connection to the classical republican writings of Renaissance and early modern Europe. Pocock initially called his strand "civic humanism" rather than "republicanism." Not sacrifice of private for public interests but active CITIZENSHIP—engagement of the self in public life and politics—was, for Pocock, the touchstone of Revolutionary virtue; but he accepted the conflation of his findings with Wood's and Bailyn's, not the least in the contrast between all three and liberalism's preoccupation with private rights and interests.

Part of the excitement in these works lay in the apparent discovery not merely of an ideational strand in the Revolution but its impelling "ideology" (Bailyn), its core "political culture" (Wood), the very "language" (Pocock) through which late eighteenth-century Americans could even begin to speak about politics. If the mental world in which Revolutionary Americans lived was not liberal, finding the hinge of history on which modern political culture arrived became an intensely important task. Wood, his interests focused on the Constitutional compromise of 1787, took the Constitutional ratification as the moment when most Americans cashed in their "medieval" assumptions of a homogeneous public good for modern pluralism. Pocock, more interested in the idea that virtue could ward off the corrupting effects of history, thought New World republicanism had survived much longer. Into these questions, scores of historians rushed in the late 1970s and 1980s, some to contend that the republican worldview survived into the Jeffersonians' triumph in 1801, the Madison administration, Whig political culture of the 1840s, or the Civil War; others to argue that republicanism found its firmest footing as an artisan-based culture, pitted against an expanding market economy and an ascendant liberal capitalism; still others to deny that republicanism ever effectively disappeared or, conversely, that it ever effectively existed at all.

The momentous aspect of this quest was its implications not for republicanism but for republicanism's shadow concept: LIBERALISM. In a country where medieval survivals were thin and SOCIALISM weakly rooted, the historians' "republicanism" seemed to give the regnant, liberal assumptions of American politics a powerful, oppositional tradition and a profoundly contingent history. A considerable amount of reflexive mirroring between the two concepts accordingly set in, as republicanism was abstracted from a complicated argument about kings and virtue to become a full-blown rival to liberalism, fit to argue point for point across facing pages of a political theory textbook. That the two families of argument were responses to different problematics, organizing different realms of experience, that (as Pocock had insisted at the outset) they were not fully on speaking terms, proved easy to lose sight of. For historians and political theorists struggling to break out of a paradigmatic conception of America as *purely* liberal, the goal was a vigorous, historically rooted oppositional tradition, and in republicanism many thought they had found it.

Just at this moment, however, the structure elaborated around "republican" began to give way. Even as historians of nineteenth-century America were extending the influence of republicanism forward in time, historians of Revolutionary America were beginning to realize that virtually every late eighteenth-century figure of record had, as purpose and occasion demanded, mixed arguments from repertoires republicanism's discoverers had boxed apart as immiscible and contradictory. By the end of the 1980s, historical writing began to stress the multivalence, if not the cacophony of competing tongues and worldviews in the Revolution, the blends and mixtures—the poorness of fit, in short, between both tightly articulated constructs, liberalism and republicanism, and the ideational tools Americans had actually worked with.

Should the historians' republicanism thus unravel without taking the previous certainties about innate American liberalism down with it, the historiographical event will have played itself out to a futile conclusion. Late eighteenth-century Americans did not think in political theorists' systems. As in the unfolding debate over a kingless polity, they thought for occasions. That debate, in turn, left them receptacles for neither Locke nor Machiavelli, no matter how finely mixed, but possessed of certain habits of disputation, certain enduring associations and dichotomies. To most late eighteenth-century Americans it was clear that a kingless polity could not long survive if its citizens looked out only for themselves, without counterweight to their private ambitions for power and accumulation, without public virtue and a sense of common weal. Being a conviction for specific needs and issues, that assumption could cohabit with private ambitions of considerable strength. But it left them with a way of responding to crises to come, with a script, a point of debate, and a powerful family of arguments.

DANIEL T. RODGERS

FURTHER READING
Willi Paul Adams, "Republicanism in Political Rhetoric before 1776," *Political Science Quarterly* 85 (1970): 397–421.

Joyce Appleby, ed., "Republicanism in the History and

Historiography of the United States," *American Quarterly* 37 (1985): 461–598.

Bernard Bailyn, *The Ideological Origins of the American Revolution* (Cambridge: Harvard University Press, 1967).

Philip Freneau, *The Poems of Philip Freneau*, ed. Fred Lewis Pattee, 3 vols. (Princeton: Princeton University Library, 1902–7).

James T. Kloppenberg, "The Virtues of Liberalism: Christianity, Republicanism, and Ethics in Early American Political Discourse," *Journal of American History* 74 (1987): 9–33.

Drew R. McCoy, *The Elusive Republic: Political Economy in Jeffersonian America* (Chapel Hill: University of North Carolina Press, 1980).

J. G. A. Pocock, *The Machiavellian Moment: Florentine Political Thought and the Atlantic Republican Tradition* (Princeton: Princeton University Press, 1975).

Daniel T. Rodgers, "Republicanism: the Career of a Concept," *Journal of American History* 79 (1992): 11–38.

Gordon S. Wood, *The Creation of the American Republic, 1776–1787* (Chapel Hill: University of North Carolina Press, 1969).

responsibility Like "individualism" and "altruism," French imports that entered the English language only in the 1830s, the word "responsibility" plays such a central role in the form of life we inhabit today that it is not easy to imagine how our ancestors ever got along without it. Yet it is as young as America, its first recorded usage having occurred in 1787, during the debate over the Constitution. Federalist paper 63, written by James Madison, speaks of frequent elections as a means of ensuring "a due responsibility in the government to the people," and notes that "responsibility, in order to be reasonable, must be limited to objects within the power of the responsible party." "Responsibilité" first appeared in France during the same year.

Although born under political auspices, the word's meaning has never been confined to politics. This is not surprising, for although the abstract noun "responsibility" was new in 1787, the adjective "responsible" was not. No counterpart either to the noun or the adjective existed in classical Latin, but "responsible" or its equivalents existed in French as early as the thirteenth century, in English by the end of the sixteenth century, and in German by the middle of the seventeenth century. Even these dates seem surprisingly recent, given the primal quality of the values and practices to which the word refers. Once coined, "responsibility" was easily assimilated to philosophical controversies that had been begun in other terms, such as "free will," "accountability," "answerability," and "imputability." Richard McKeon, writing on "The Development and the Significance of the Concept of Responsibility," found the earliest philosophical treatment of it in 1859, when

Alexander Bain mentioned it only to recommend an alternative, "punishability." Bain contended that "a man can never be said to be responsible, if you are not prepared to punish him when he cannot satisfactorily answer the charges against him." John Stuart Mill agreed, declaring in 1865 that "responsibility means punishment." By the 1880s, L. Lévy-Bruhl was using the term in a more ambitious way that made it a touchstone for all moral questions, but McKeon concludes that, precisely because the term could be so easily substituted for older alternatives, its introduction did little to alter the course of philosophical debate (pp. 6–8, 23).

From a historian's point of view, what is most intriguing about the comparatively short etymological lineage of "responsible" and "responsibility" is the thought that our conceptions of morality and human agency, in which these terms figure so prominently today, may be less a timeless feature of human nature and more the product of historical conditions than is commonly recognized. To put the matter pointedly, it raises the possibility that holding people responsible for their conduct is a recent attainment of mankind, and that our ancestors may not have perceived one another as fully responsible agents. Skittish though we have understandably become about claims of moral progress, such claims are not in this case easily dismissed. Even so sophisticated and skeptical a critic of modernity as Friedrich Nietzsche took them seriously.

In *On the Genealogy of Morals* (1887) Nietzsche dramatized the historicity of responsibility, but left its chronology indeterminate. Some stages of the developmental process he described must have occurred in prehistoric times, others early in the Christian era, still others much more recently. The most radical of historicists, he was no historian and cared not at all for dates. Since we lack anything even remotely approaching a complete history of responsibility, no one can specify when the various elements of this form of life came into play, or how fully it has been embraced by different peoples at different times and places. We have only a few scattered landmarks to help us get our bearings in time.

Max Weber, who read and respected Nietzsche, took the Protestant Reformation of the sixteenth century to be the great watershed between "traditional" and "rational" (or modern) ways of life in Europe. If Weber was right, the ascetic values that define responsible conduct in European and American culture today were first cultivated in monasteries and oriented to otherworldly goals, but marched into the marketplace of everyday life and evolved in close conjunction with capitalism from the time of the Reformation forward. Any thought of a link between capitalism and rising standards of responsibility may seem paradoxical, but even though market economies live by the rule of *caveat emptor* (buyer beware) and deliberately shrink responsibility in some dimensions (as in the limited liability corporation), they also depend on a norm of promise-keeping and cannot thrive without an ample supply of calculating, self-disciplined "economic agents," men and women alert to their interests and acutely attentive to the remote consequences of their conduct.

Recent research by social historians suggests that, as a cultural and psychological phenomenon, the ethic of responsibility had not achieved dominion at all levels of Atlantic societies even as late as the mid-nineteenth century. Evangelical Protestants, for example, certainly felt that they were fighting an uphill battle as they tried to inculcate habits of foresight, repression of impulse, and delay of gratification in working-class populations. These habits helped constitute the cultural phenomenon that Nietzsche thought so momentous and which Weber associated with the Protestant Reformation, but the triumph of responsibility may have been more recent than either Nietzsche or Weber recognized—if, indeed, it is complete even today. No doubt middle-class moralists of the Victorian era underestimated the degree to which responsible conduct presupposes economic security, but they were probably not wrong to sense in working-class culture an attitude more fatalistic and more tolerant of irresponsibility than that of their own class.

Nowhere has the developmental chronology of responsibility been more vigorously debated than in the case of ancient Greece. If there is ample room for disagreement about the timing and the uneven spread of the ethic of responsibility in modern European societies, there is nearly a consensus about its absence from the world of Homer. Yet different from us though the ancients were, they did not regard one another merely as playthings of the gods or straws in the wind of fate. For the most part they saw each other as authentic actors and assigned praise and blame accordingly. True, they left many an opening for divine intervention, but they were not in this respect terribly different from the Christians who came after them, who also found it difficult to reconcile human accountability with divine strength. From Pelagius in the fifth century to Arminius in the seventeenth, devout Christians quarreled about responsibility for sin and salvation in a world ruled by a God whose power was immense—so immense that it could seem to crowd human responsibility out of the picture

altogether, depriving humans of any rationale for doing good and threatening to make God the author even of sin. How could one credit human choices with making a difference without seeming to limit the limitless sovereignty of God? The orthodox response, which Aquinas helped devise, was that "providence does not exclude freedom of the will," but words like these only papered over the problem that would finally break the Christian church in two. When Luther and Calvin attacked "good works" and denied that the will could be free, they were recommending in regard to salvation an attitude not unlike that of the Greeks, who expressed grave skepticism about an agent's claim ever actually to *do* anything.

The difference between the Greeks and ourselves is neither the number of gods they had to accommodate nor the fact that some of their beliefs were contradictory. The past two centuries of secular social thought show that, even in the absence of any god, speculation about FREEDOM and fate never escapes contradiction for long. Rather, the difference lies in the absence or seeming immaturity in Greek culture of concepts such as decision, will, intention, and GUILT. Even Nietzsche gave some credence to the widespread impression that, when all is said and done, there is something childlike and premoral about the ancients. In its boldest form the idea is that with a few exceptions such as Plato, Aristotle, Socrates, and some versions of the character Antigone, the Greeks were indeed children in a Piaget's tale of stages of moral development, in which we moderns figure as the adults.

This "progressivist" scenario has come under sharp attack from the philosopher Bernard Williams. In *Shame and Necessity* (1993) he highlights the similarity of modern and ancient thinking by suggesting that all judgments of responsibility consist of some combination of four elements: *cause, intention, state,* and *response.* Williams's four-part scheme of analysis is illuminating, and it helps him show that at the level of "underlying conceptions," the difference between us and the Greeks may not be as great as the progressivists suppose. But in his effort to demonstrate the continuity of responsibility across the ages, Williams empties its constituent elements of any particular content and soars to such a high, philosophical level of abstraction that he loses sight of the lived experience of actual historical actors and gives up any possibility of understanding how conceptions of responsibility have changed.

Consider slavery, for example. Few differences between us and the Greeks feel more profound than our repugnance for slavery and their unquestioning acceptance of it. Williams's abstract categories leave us with no way to acknowledge this profound difference. Repugnance and acceptance entail two different assessments of responsibility for the suffering of others, but for Williams all such judgments merely rearrange the same four elements: "adjustments" vary, but "underlying conceptions" remain the same. This will not do. It is rather like saying that since poker and bridge are just different ways of arranging the same 52-card deck, the two games come to the same thing. If one wishes to compare poker and bridge one must look beyond their reliance on a common deck of cards and take into account the different rules by which the games are played. Likewise, if one wishes to take the historicity of responsibility seriously, one must recognize that abolitionists of the nineteenth century and Greek philosophers of the fifth century BC were playing the game of responsibility very differently, and ask what could have led to such a profound change in the rules. (*See also* ANTISLAVERY; PROSLAVERY THOUGHT.)

I have no quarrel with Williams's principal point. It is indeed self-indulgent of us to formulate the difference between the ancients and ourselves simply as a matter of their "immaturity." I also think he is on to something important when he asserts that Aristotle and his contemporaries construed slavery in a way that made its abolition almost literally unthinkable. But his ad hoc way of accounting for that perception of necessity is not adequate. To say as he does that "considerations of justice and injustice were immobilized by the demands of what was seen as social and economic necessity" is indiscriminately to lump Aristotle together with Robert E. Lee and thousands of less savory slaveowners who sincerely believed, even on the eve of the Civil War, that their entire way of life depended on the perpetuation of slavery. Williams needs more than this tendentious and self-serving sort of "necessity" in order to make good his claim that Aristotle's moral judgment was not inferior to our own. If the constraints that kept Aristotle from seeing in slavery anything worse than a "necessary evil" boiled down to nothing more than this—an ideological blind spot induced by the inconvenience of doing without slave labor—then surely in this regard we moderns would be entitled to feel morally superior.

Williams's cryptic observation that perceptions of necessary evil have not been "eliminated" in modern times, only "shifted to different places," begs for elaboration. He is of course right to insist that we moderns, too, have our "necessary evils." But that must not be allowed to obscure an equally important fact: that the domain of necessity is perceived to be far smaller today than it once was. Its shrinkage is a dramatic difference between past and present, and in that difference, I suspect, lies the grain of truth behind the persistent, but finally misleading, progressivist intuition that we are more mature moral reasoners than the author of the *Nicomachean Ethics*.

How do "necessary evils" such as slavery come to seem remediable, thus shrinking the domain of necessity and expanding the realm within which responsibility can operate? To answer that question we need a way of thinking about responsibility that candidly acknowledges its historicity without falling back on naive notions of progress. Such an approach need not run to the Nietzschean extreme of obliterating distinctions between good and evil, but neither can it embrace a linear narrative of ever-closer approximations to some moral law or ideal of conduct that stands outside human history. We need to admit that moral judgment is only partly systematic (leaving room for equally competent reasoners sometimes to reach conflicting conclusions) and to recognize that even at its most systematic it is largely a historical and cultural phenomenon, a matter of "luck," if you will, for which individual reasoners deserve little in the way of praise or blame. No philosopher in the analytic tradition has done more than Williams to take luck into philosophical account, and his four-element scheme of analysis provides much of what is needed. In the remainder of this essay, I will propose amending his scheme in two ways: by stressing (even more than he already has) the dependence of all judgments of responsibility on perceptions of causal efficacy, and by noting that causal perception, in turn, cannot help but be largely a matter of social convention, subject to all the vicissitudes of history.

Consider a truism of moral philosophy, "Ought implies can." To say that "ought implies can" is, obviously, to say that we do not hold people responsible for what they cannot do. Less obviously, the truism also means that our sense of what people are responsible for extends no farther than our causal perception, that is, our way of sorting through the many effects of a person's acts and omissions, identifying only a small fraction as really "his" or "hers." At most, we hold people responsible only for evils over which we believe they have causal influence (ones about which they "can" do something). Even this is an outer limit, for there are many evils that people obviously *could do* something to alleviate for which we do not hold them responsible.

Convention enters critically into what we think we "can" do, and because it does, the dependence of "ought" on "can" carries with it the further implication that convention necessarily plays a large role in moral judgment. Cause-and-effect relations pervade our thinking at every level, from high theory to the most mundane affairs of everyday life. They constitute, as the British philosopher J. L. Mackie put it in *The Cement of the Universe*, the glue that holds our world together. Everything we do, from checking a book out of the library to calming a frightened child, draws on our fund of knowledge about the relation of present acts to future states of the world, the relation, in other worlds, of cause to effect. But those relations are not given as such in raw experience; causal relationships are something we impute to the people, events, and things around us, and we do so in ways shaped by social convention.

To illustrate the role of convention, imagine that a great earthquake has just occurred, such as that which struck Mexico City in 1985. In a strictly physical sense, I "can" stop writing this esssay, board a flight to Mexico City, and help save at least one stranger's life by lifting debris and performing other emergency tasks. If I took literally the well-nigh universal rule of reciprocity, "Do unto others what you would have them do unto you," this would seem to be the only acceptable thing to do, for if I were pinned beneath a collapsed building, I would certainly want others to drop their daily routines and come to my aid. Yet I continue writing instead of going to the aid of the stranger, and no one accuses me of violating the Golden Rule. Why not? Because, by the prevailing conventions of my time and place, this "can" is not real, not operative. Mexico City is "too far away"; going there would disrupt my life "too much."

Too far and too much by what measure? Convention supplies the measure. Convention authorizes me to say I "cannot" help the stranger, at least not in this direct way, even though, in a purely physical sense, I undoubtedly possess the means of doing so. This shared, tacit understanding that converts the "can" of physical ability into the "cannot" of acceptable moral practice, need not be arbitrary—it may be loosely related to considerations of relative cost, for example—but its rational elements could never be strong enough to anchor it against tides of change or lift it up out of the category of convention altogether. The existence of such conventions is nothing to regret. In the absence of convention, prescriptions such as the Golden Rule would either have to be ignored altogether, or taken literally, which would set standards so high that no one, no matter how scrupulous and compassionate, could live up to them. The world brims over with suffering strangers who, but for our inaction, would undeniably be better off; we cannot literally do for every suffering "other" what we would have others do for us.

If ought implies can, and "can" is conventional in this sense, it follows inexorably that our understanding of moral responsibility—of what we "ought" to do—is deeply imbedded in social practice and cannot help but be influenced, at least in broad outline, by the material circumstances, historical experiences, and technological capabilities of the society in which we live. As our collective circumstances, experiences, and capabilities change, we should expect the conventions of moral responsibility to change as well, though not in any simple or automatic manner. The easiest way to illustrate the point is to imagine a dramatic change in what we "can" do. The invention of technology that would permit us to travel to Mexico City, or any other scene of disaster, instantaneously and at trivial expense would be very likely to alter the conventions governing moral responsibility in our society—making my failure to go to the aid of the earthquake victim morally unacceptable, at least in some quarters. Any change that stretches our causal horizons and expands the sphere within which we feel we "can" act has the potential to transform what we hitherto perceived as "necessary evils" into remediable ones. And once an evil is perceived as remediable, people will be exposed to feelings of guilt and responsibility for suffering that previously was viewed with indifference or, at most, aroused only passive sympathy—like the sympathy we feel today for distant earthquake victims who are "too far away" to help.

This is the sort of development that I believe paved the way for "modern" or "humane" attitudes toward slavery and many other forms of cruelty and exploitation. Hardly anyone condemned slavery before the eighteenth century: in the entire history of responsibility, there is no more sobering or revealing fact than this. For two millennia after Aristotle, the suffering of slaves continued to be perceived as nothing worse than a necessary evil. The first people to go further and condemn the institution outright were isolated religious zealots of the sixteenth and seventeenth centuries, forgotten by history and dismissed by their contemporaries as misfits. With the single exception of Jean Bodin in the sixteenth century, even Europe's most insightful moralists and philosophers did no more than acknowledge that slavery was ethically problematical, until the middle decades of the eighteenth century. Then, in little more than a century, slavery was suddenly transformed from a troubling but readily defensible institution into a self-evidently intolerable relic of barbarism, noxious to decent people everywhere. On a historical time scale, this reversal of opinion occurred overnight.

Most of those who attacked slavery were fired by

religious indignation, but the Christian doctrines they hurled at slaveowners had for centuries been thought compatible with slaveholding. We do not demean the abolitionists' labors, without which emancipation would never have been achieved, by entertaining the possibility that their crusade was made possible by changes in the material circumstances and technological capabilities of the society in which they lived. The historical developments that set the stage for this new attitude toward servitude are extremely complex, but among them, I suggest, was an upheaval in the conventions governing perceptions of causation, human agency, and moral responsibility. Before substantial numbers of people could feel outraged by the very existence of slavery and take action to uproot it, they had to be able to impute to themselves historically unprecedented powers of intervention, and they had to perceive hierarchical social arrangements and institutional structures, not as reflections of God's will or manifestations of nature's own order, but as contingent, malleable phenomena open to human influence and correction. Not until slavery's evil appeared remediable would people feel responsible for it. And not until human agency seemed expansive enough to challenge even such ancient and interest-bound institutions as slavery would people feel the need for new words like "responsibility."

The coinage of the word "responsibility" in the late eighteenth century was one straw in the wind, registering the onset of a major upheaval in the conventions governing causal attribution in Western culture. That upheaval is still underway and gaining momentum. The philosopher Hans Jonas reminds us in *The Imperative of Responsibility* that its implications are by no means entirely favorable. Like the shell of an exploding star, responsibility swiftly expands in all directions under the impulse of man's growing technological virtuosity, but as it expands, the shell grows thinner and more diffuse. The day may come when it collapses back upon itself. Jonas warns:

Modern technology, informed by an ever-deeper penetration of nature and propelled by the forces of market and politics, has enhanced human power beyond anything known or even dreamed of before. . . . But lately, the other side of the triumphal advance has begun to show its face, disturbing the euphoria of success with threats that are as novel as its welcomed fruits. (p. ix)

Sensational events such as nuclear holocaust and ecological catastrophe are not the sole threats. Two of the most insidious concern the way we think and pass everyday judgments upon one another. Some have sensed in modern culture a growing arbitrariness as expanding causal horizons paradoxically make us responsible for everything in principle and nothing in particular. One fears that responsibility may be transformed from a concrete relation into a diffuse quality that floats freely through all relations, ready to be manipulatively imputed to anyone, anytime, for anything. Others have noted that the ethical maxims of the past fail us because they evolved in contexts dramatically different from those in which we now operate. The goods and evils that our ancestors tried to attain or avoid were close at hand, proximate both in space and time. As Jonas says,

The effective range of action was small, the time span of foresight, goal-setting, and accountability was short, control of circumstances was limited. The long run of consequences was left to chance, fate, or providence. Ethics accordingly was of the here and now . . . the agent and the "other" of his action [shared] a common present . . . No one was held responsible for the unintended later effects of his well-intentioned, well-considered, and well-performed act. The short arm of human power did not call for a long arm of predictive knowledge. (pp. 5–6)

Now, as Jonas says, "All this has decisively changed. Modern technology has introduced actions of such novel scale, objects, and consequences that the framework of former ethics can no longer contain them." As we saw above, it has been chalked up to the wisdom of the ancient Greeks that they were skeptical of an agent's claim actually to *do* anything, but it should now be apparent that their modesty was inseparable from the constricted causal imagination that encouraged them to view the slave's misery as a necessary evil. One can only wonder what will pass for wisdom and modesty in the world of the future, in which, as Jonas says, the "lengthened reach" or "causal pregnancy" of our technological deeds puts responsibility at "the center of the ethical stage," with "no less than man's fate for its object" (p. x). The possibilities for both good and ill are immense.

THOMAS L. HASKELL

FURTHER READING

Arthur W. H. Adkins, *Merit and Responsibility: a Study in Greek Values* (Oxford: Oxford University Press, 1960).

Thomas Bender, ed., *The Antislavery Debate: Capitalism and Abolitionism as a Problem in Historical Interpretation* (Berkeley: University of California Press, 1992).

Joel Feinberg, *Doing and Deserving: Essays in the Theory of Responsibility* (Princeton: Princeton University Press, 1970).

H. L. A. Hart, *Punishment and Responsibility: Essays in the Philosophy of Law* (Oxford: Oxford University Press, 1978).

H. L. A. Hart and A. M. Honoré, *Causation in the Law* (Oxford: Oxford University Press, 1959).

Hans Jonas, *The Imperative of Responsibility: In Search of an Ethics for the Technological Age*, trans. Hans Jonas with David Herr (Chicago: University of Chicago Press, 1984).

Arnold S. Kaufman, "Responsibility, Moral and Legal," in Paul Edwards, ed., *Encyclopedia of Philosophy*, vol. 7 (New York: Macmillan, 1967).

Richard McKeon, "The Development and the Significance of the Concept of Responsibility," *Revue internationale de philosophie* 11 (1957): 3–32.

Friedrich Nietzsche, *On the Genealogy of Morals*, trans. Walter Kaufmann and R. J. Hollindale (1887; New York: Random House, 1969).

Bernard Williams, *Shame and Necessity* (Berkeley: University of California Press, 1993).

rhetoric   From the seventeenth to the end of the nineteenth century, rhetoric saturated American culture. It was widely assumed that rhetoric, the study and practice of the arts of persuasion, was critical to the school curriculum, pulpit, political forum, and court of law. From the seventeenth century on, however, there have also been those suspicious of rhetoric, who thought rhetoric was more about ornament and trickery than persuasion and argument. Between the 1870s and 1930s rhetoric went into a deep decline. Since that time, there have been various academic efforts to revive it, but the public at large has remained skeptical.

The Puritans brought from Europe the Protestant distrust of elaborate display. Their sermons were delivered in the "plain style," a straightforward idiom that suppressed linguistic ornamentation. By the mid-seventeenth century, Harvard College was following the teachings of Petrus Ramus, who considered logic central and rhetoric peripheral because of its ornamental character. This sent rhetoric off on its "modern" association with style instead of argument. Most ancient and Renaissance rhetorics had considered ornament and persuasion two complementary dimensions of the same subject. Ramus pulled them apart.

Puritan distrust of verbal display was roughly akin to seventeenth-century attacks on rhetoric by such thinkers as John Locke, Francis Bacon, and René Descartes. Like the Puritans, these philosophers distrusted the "glitter" of words, and hoped to create some crystal-clear language that would (for Locke) accurately reveal the subjective ideas of the speaker. Numerous later philosophers, Immanuel Kant for example, would repeat some variation of this attack on rhetoric in the name of reason.

But rhetoric did not disappear. In the early eighteenth century, as American colleges came under the sway of the ENLIGHTENMENT, Ciceronian rhetorics replaced Puritan texts. Enlightenment culture accommodated more elaborate forms of display than the Puritans had; rhetoric emerged from its subordination to logic and became central to the project of civic persuasion.

At the time of the American Revolution public speaking was considered a key art form. A figure like Patrick Henry could still make a career with dazzling words. As the Revolution drew to a close, Scottish rhetoric took over the college curriculum, particularly George Campbell's *Philosophy of Rhetoric* (1776) and Hugh Blair's *Lectures on Rhetoric and Belles Lettres* (1783). These rhetorics advocated an elegant, refined prose style, although it was somewhat less lofty in tone than Cicero. Many Americans considered it the perfect idiom for the discourse of REPUBLICANISM.

The years between 1820 and 1860 have often been called "the golden age of American oratory." Hugh Blair's rhetoric could be found in the bookshelves of southern gentlemen; names like HENRY CLAY, DANIEL WEBSTER, and EDWARD EVERETT were known throughout the nation for their stirring speech. The elaborately wrought and closely argued speeches of ABRAHAM LINCOLN constitute one of the high points of public oratory. In those same years, rhetoric continued to be a central subject in higher education.

At the same time, however, popular politics increasingly used expressive gestures indicating sympathy with the "common man." Hard talk, slang, and rustic provincialisms all entered public discourse, making it impossible to sustain the ethos of the refined gentleman that all previous rhetoric had demanded. Moreover, *rhetors* like HENRY WARD BEECHER, one of the most popular public speakers of the mid-nineteenth century, asserted that one should not try to prove things too much. Cultivating *pathos* was enough; *logos*, inessential. By the 1870s there were widespread complaints that public speaking was not what it used to be.

In the last quarter of the nineteenth century, rhetoric began its half-century decline. "Scientific" academics attacked rhetoric as genteel and antiquated. The argument introduced by philosophers like Locke and Kant again gained favor—rhetoric taught verbal trickery. At the same time, these academics developed a sparse, lean idiom, one they associated with OBJECTIVITY. Science, it was thought, was content unbesmirched by style. By the early twentieth century the study of rhetoric had been pushed to a corner of the American university, associated with ornamentation instead of persuasive argument.

Outside the academy, rhetoric also became suspect. By the 1920s, writers like H. L. MENCKEN were attacking elaborate oratory as the work of pompous blowhards; and popular educators like Dale Carnegie urged public speakers to adopt an informal, colloquial style, a public idiom expressly designed to mimic face-to-face conversation. Technology helped this change along. Once the microphone was available, speakers no longer had to worry about projection. They could sound more casual. Franklin Delano Roosevelt's Fireside Chats of the 1930s are a good mark of the transition. This style, which can be traced back to mid nineteenth-century opposition to elaborate rhetoric, now colors nearly all public communication, not only that of politicians and ministers, but also that of television newspeople and commentators (see also JOURNALISM; MASS CULTURE).

Since the 1930s, various writers have tried to revive rhetoric. Both KENNETH BURKE and Wayne Booth are associated with a defense of Aristotelian rhetoric. Against what they saw as the tyranny of a scientistic civilization, these writers attempted to use older categories to think through both literary texts and public idioms, arguing that rhetoric, properly understood, was the theory and practice of persuasion, not just ornamentation.

Since the 1970s, a very different revival of rhetoric has occurred in poststructural theory. The category of "tropes" (figures of speech) became central. Writers like Paul de Man, Jacques Derrida, and Hayden White asserted that tropes structure argument. Like the Puritans, these writers associate rhetoric with figures of speech, but they go much further. Their POST-MODERNISM has nothing in common with the Puritan quest for a logic free of ornament. In their view argument becomes secondary, trope primary. In this way, science as much as literature and public speech is the province of rhetoric, governed by its figures more than by argument or evidence. This sort of analysis became a staple of literary study during the 1980s.

Outside the academy, the term "rhetoric" continues to be associated with pretentious language and popular trickery. Ironically, postmodern academic rhetoric comes close to sharing these assumptions. Like the popular complaint that "it's all just rhetoric," postmodern theory asserts that the core of public language is ornament, and that allusions to concepts like truth, logic, reality, or evidence should be treated with deep suspicion. Both express the distrust of words in a civilization with no choice but to continue depending upon words.

KENNETH CMIEL

See also LANGUAGE.

FURTHER READING

Kenneth Cmiel, *Democratic Eloquence: the Fight over Popular Speech in Nineteenth-Century America* (New York: W. Morrow, 1990).

Stanley Eugene Fish, *Doing What Comes Naturally: Change, Rhetoric, and the Practice of Theory in Literary and Legal Studies* (Durham, N.C.: Duke University Press, 1989).
Kathleen Hall Jamieson, *Eloquence in an Electronic Age* (New York: Oxford University Press, 1988).
Albert Kitzhaber, *Rhetoric in American Colleges, 1850–1900* (Dallas: SMU Press, 1990).
Perry Miller, *The New England Mind: from Colony to Province* (Cambridge: Harvard University Press, 1953).

Rich, Adrienne (b. Baltimore, Md., May 16, 1929). An important poet since the 1950s, Rich has become a leading figure in American FEMINISM generally and in discussions of GAY AND LESBIAN IDENTITIES in particular. A child of the Depression era, she was the product of a mixed marriage. Her father was chair of the department of pathology at Johns Hopkins University, a singular achievement for a Jew of his time and one dependent, he believed, on his assimilation into dominantly WASP Baltimore society. His wife, a Christian, abandoned a promising career as a concert pianist to devote her time to rearing Rich and her younger sister, under her husband's direction. An extraordinarily talented and teachable child, Rich more than repaid her parents' investment in her, graduating Phi Beta Kappa from Radcliffe College in 1951 at the age of 21, and publishing her first book of poetry, *A Change of World*, that same year in the celebrated Yale Younger Poets series. Four years later, she produced her second book, *The Diamond Cutters*. In both volumes, she demonstrated her skill at fulfilling the literary ideals of the period. Indoctrinated while at college into the tenets of New Criticism, she treated her poems as closed products. Writing them, as she has since explained, was a matter of perfecting techniques and keeping herself at a safe aesthetic distance from the material she handled. Above all, as a woman poet, it meant keeping her gender at bay.

As Rich now tells this story, the control she achieved in her early poetry came at a high price, one that left her, in her words, "split at the root," divided not only between her Christian and Jewish heritage, but between her gender and occupation, her body and mind, and her self and the society in which she lives. Since the publication of her first two books, she has increasingly used her poetry as the place where she works these divisions out. To an extent unique, perhaps, among contemporary women poets, Adrienne Rich's poetry is intimately bound up with the course of her life. For better or worse, it gives voice to all her swervings—the problems, guesses, dilemmas, triumphs, and obsessions of a "thinking" woman's life.

By her account, the possibility of change entered

Rich's poetry with her marriage in 1953 to the Brooklyn-born economist Alfred Haskell Conrad (born Cohen). Not only did this marriage alienate Rich from her father, who despised Conrad's Ashkenazi background, but as Rich describes in her full-length study of MOTHERHOOD, *Of Woman Born*, wifedom and childbearing led her into an unpredictable world of sensation and feeling for which her rigorously intellectual education had in no way prepared her. "Experience is always greater and more unclassifiable," she said in 1964, "than we give it credit for being." The effect on her poetry was decisive. She found herself dissatisfied with her old poems. Their very clarity—a clarity dependent on her willingness to suppress or even falsify disturbing material—made them seem "queerly limited." "Without for one moment turning my back on conscious choice and selection," she recalled, she became "increasingly willing to let the unconscious offer its materials, to listen to more than the one voice of a single idea." Far from being treated as well-made artifacts, her poems had become vehicles for thought-in-process. (Gelpi and Gelpi, p. 89.)

Although hardly unique to her, Rich's concept of an open poetic, "true" to the raggedness of experience and the actual movement of thought, has led her to take risks in her writing which not many poets of her stature would care to match. Once positioned outside New Critical aesthetics, her work has become an open arena where the multiple and contradictory voices within her have had free play. By the mid-1960s both she and her husband were deeply involved in antiwar activities and in the progressive social movements of the time. Rich's poetry became "politicized" as well, reflecting even in its disjunctures and incoherencies the intensity and social ferment of the time. As one book followed another, *Necessities of Life* (1966), *Leaflets* (1969), *The Will to Change* (1971), Rich moved further and further away from the ideal of the well-made poem, and ever closer to the poem as an index of personal and social revolution. Inevitably, perhaps, her poetry came to reflect the poet's growing awareness of the significance of GENDER.

In 1973, three years after her husband's death, and one year prior to her "coming out" as a lesbian, Rich published her first book of explicitly feminist poetry, *Diving Into the Wreck*. For the women's movement as well as for the author, it was a "breakthrough" text, voicing the hopes and rage of an entire generation of white bourgeois women. It made Adrienne Rich one of the leading poet-spokeswomen for women's liberation virtually overnight. Like a number of other women poets in this period —Marge Piercy, Judy Grahn, and Audre Lorde— Rich was taken to the hearts of ordinary feminist women, achieving an audience appeal quite unlike anything her elite eduction had trained her for. She became what she herself wanted to be: a woman with a mission—a mission that was now specifically dedicated to dismantling the very institutions that had initially instructed her in her craft.

Since *Diving Into the Wreck*, Rich has produced five more volumes: *The Dream of a Common Language* (1978), *A Wild Patience Has Taken Me This Far* (1981), *Your Native Land, Your Life* (1986), *Time's Power* (1989), and *An Atlas for a Difficult World* (1991), each attempting to explore the new location she has assumed and to work out its multiple contradictions and conflicts. If these volumes continue to proclaim her outrage at social oppression and her commitment to speak for those who cannot speak for themselves, they have also grown increasingly introspective, as Rich has contemplated her own internal conflicts and failings. And it may well be that it is in this unrelenting fidelity to her many difficulties that her poetry's ultimate value will lie. While time has rendered a number of the political positions Rich has taken problematic—in particular her idealization of female bonding in *The Dream of a Common Language*— her poems' value as a record of one highly intelligent and sensitive woman's responses to the times in which she lives has no counterpart in contemporary literature. Taken as a single body of work, from a single if multiply-located author, Adrienne Rich's poetry is one of the unique testaments of our time, one whose value is a good deal greater than the sum of its individual parts.

PAULA BENNETT

FURTHER READING
Paula Bennett, *My Life a Loaded Gun: Dickinson, Plath, Rich, and Female Creativity* (1986; Urbana: University of Illinois Press, 1990).
Adrienne Rich, "Interview," *The Island* 3 (May 1966): 2–8.
——, "Poetry and Experience," in *Adrienne Rich's Poetry: Texts of the Poems, the Poet On Her Work, Reviews and Criticism*, ed. Barbara Charlesworth Gelpi and Albert Gelpi (New York: Norton, 1975).
——, *Of Woman Born: Motherhood as Experience and Institution* (New York: Norton, 1976).
——, *On Lies, Secrets and Silence: Selected Prose 1966–1978* (New York: Norton, 1979).
——, *Blood, Bread, and Poetry: Selected Prose 1979–1985* (New York: Norton, 1986).

Richardson, H[enry] H[obson] (b. James Parish, La., Sept. 20, 1838; d. Brookline, Mass., Apr. 27, 1886). Architect. Trained at the École des Beaux Arts in Paris during the Civil War, Richardson returned to Gilded Age America to produce some of the defining cultural artifacts of that period. With prominent collaborators and friends like John LaFarge and HENRY ADAMS he shared an idealistic medievalism which emerged in a weighty, brooding style which came to be known as "Richardsonian Romanesque." For his part, Richardson believed he was developing a design vocabulary appropriate to contemporary American experience, and his perspective exerted important influence on FRANK LLOYD WRIGHT.

FURTHER READING

James F. O'Gorman, *H.H. Richardson: Architectural Forms for an American Society* (Chicago: University of Chicago Press, 1987).

Riesman, David (b. Philadelphia, Pa., Sept. 22, 1909). Lawyer and sociologist. Best known for his million-seller *The Lonely Crowd* (1950, with Reuel Denney and Nathan Glazer), Riesman began his career in the law, clerking for Supreme Court Justice Brandeis and teaching law at the University of Buffalo. In *The Lonely Crowd*, written after he moved to the University of Chicago as a professor of social sciences, he described a decisive shift from the "inner-directed" individual of the nineteenth century to the "other-directed" type of the twentieth. There was no going back to the autonomous "inner gyroscope" of the nineteenth-century self. In the other-directed world of the twentieth century, the path to autonomy had to pass through creative acts of consumption. A professor of social sciences at Harvard after 1958, Riesman became an influential observer of trends in higher education.

See also FREUDIANISM.

FURTHER READING

Seymour Martin Lipset and Leo Lowenthal, eds., *Culture and Social Character: the Work of David Riesman Reviewed* (New York: Free Press, 1961).

rights From the early 1950s through the mid-1970s, reformers and liberal academics urged Americans to take rights more seriously, including, eventually, the rights of African Americans, ethnic and linguistic minorities, aliens, criminals, women, gays, poor people, consumers, environmentalists, juveniles, the elderly, the disabled, the morally conscientious, self-expressive artists and protesters, political participants, and others. At national, state, and local levels, legislatures, executives, and especially courts responded, creating what Cass Sunstein and others term a "rights revolution." From the mid-1970s through the early 1990s many reformers and academics contended that this "revolution" had gone too far, and that themes

of duty, RESPONSIBILITY, and COMMUNITY needed to be more prominent in American public life.

The debate is a central and recurring one in a nation whose political thought has been so permeated with "rights talk" that it seems distinctively American to express grievances by proclaiming, "I've got a right!" Because so many Americans have made so many rights claims through so much of U.S. history, it is likely that the concept of "rights" cannot possibly coherently order all the causes for which it has been drafted. Thus those like Mary Ann Glendon who maintain that individual rights should not be regarded as absolute moral compasses may well have the stronger philosophical case. This same past also suggests, however, that the stronger historical and political case belongs to those who believe claims of individual rights have always been indispensable for efforts to include all in the benefits of American life.

The material of the modern controversy was stitched into the morning clothes of the new nation. Historians generally agree that the U.S. began as the culmination of evolving claims for British recognition of individual and collective American rights. Many colonists felt unduly restricted by British imperial authorities in numerous respects. Not only were they taxed without representation, and heavily regulated as to whom they could trade with and what they could buy and sell abroad, including slaves; they were also hampered by restrictions on their ability to pass local laws, to control local juries and courts, to expunge Indians and acquire western lands, to keep British soldiers out of their homes, and to welcome European immigrants into their colonies. The colonists began their resistance by arguing that these restrictions violated their legal rights, explicitly provided in colonial charters and other documents. Finding those grounds shaky, they shifted to arguing that it was their rights as British subjects, enshrined in the unwritten British Constitution, that had been extinguished. And as a last resort, they claimed that their rights as human beings, illuminated by God and natural reason, marked the king as so oppressive that they had to create a new regime of their own. The Declaration of Independence therefore announced that their new governments would be dedicated to securing the "inalienable rights," endowed in men by the "Creator," that formed the "ends" of all just governments. It then rehearsed all the grievances listed above, impressively beribboned with the rhetoric of basic rights.

In this evolution lay the germs of ongoing conflicts and discontents. What were, after all, the decisive sources of rights: Explicit laws? Established customs? Widely shared beliefs? Human reason? Divine ordinance? What rights were most important: Communal rights to legislative self-governance, or individual liberties? Collective economic liberties and property rights, or personal ones? Individual rights to fair governmental procedures? Rights to freedom from arbitrary invasion of one's privacy? Rights to political, religious, or intellectual expression? Who could legitimately claim such rights: All of humanity, on an equal basis? All men? All men with proper notions of the Creator, that is, all Protestants, or at least all Christians? All nonslaves, or only all Americans of European descent? Americans took all these positions, coming into bitter conflict with each other. But they all tended to argue in terms of rights.

Even so, for most early Americans conceptions of rights were tightly brigaded with notions of duties, and not merely because claims of rights logically implied duties to honor the like rights of others. John Locke had contended in his *Second Treatise* that every man had a right to preserve himself but also a duty to preserve all mankind (*not* merely to forego killing people), so long as one did not thereby greatly endanger oneself. Locke grounded that duty on the fact that all were God's beloved creations and thus sacred. Similarly, early Americans rarely if ever argued that their claims of rights overrode the moral duties they owed in accordance with the laws of God and natural morality. Still, through much of the nineteenth century, claims of duty were often cast in terms of the community's general competing rights. Thus when the Jacksonian Chief Justice ROGER B. TANEY argued in the *Charles River Bridge* case that a prior legislative charter should not prevent Massachusetts from authorizing a new bridge over the Charles River, he explained that while the rights of property "are sacredly guarded, we must not forget that the community also has rights" (36 U.S. 420 [1837]).

Furthermore, throughout the nineteenth century, whenever groups felt themselves to be unjustly treated, they generally relied on the rhetoric of rights to articulate their outrage, usually invoking the Declaration of Independence itself. As historians like Howard Zinn and Hendrik Hartog have shown, Jacksonian workers employed the Declaration's guarantee of equal rights to denounce special economic privileges bestowed by government on elites, and to advocate the promotion of equal opportunity via public schools. Garrisonian abolitionists cited the Declaration to thunder that slavery was fundamentally immoral, despite whatever protection the Constitution might provide. The nineteenth-century women's movement began in earnest with the 1848 Seneca Falls Declaration of Rights, again modeled on Jefferson's handiwork. Later, Greenbackers, Populists, Knights of Labor, lawyers for the National Association for the Advancement of Colored People, and others would again and again claim to stand for equal rights that were being denied them.

Only in the era of PROGRESSIVISM did the very concept of rights come under attack. Politically engaged academics like ROSCOE POUND and JOHN DEWEY were appalled by the courts' mounting assaults on economic regulation in the name of implicit, near-absolute constitutional liberties of contract and managerial discretion (assaults now identified with the famous case invalidating a state law regulating bakers' hours, *Lochner v. New York*, 198 U.S. 45 [1905]). These Progressive architects of more pragmatic legal and political theories contended that rights should be seen strictly as social creations, justified in term of the concrete social interests they served, and only insofar as they did so without countervailing harms. Rights should therefore be viewed not as intrinsic ends but social tools, to be defined and recurrently redefined by democratically elected officials and their expert advisers. Pound's "sociological jurisprudence" of collective interests sought wholly to displace the older jurisprudence of transcendental rights, especially in regard to property rights.

With the coming of the New Deal, this advocacy of a diminished place for rights in political and especially judicial discourse enjoyed some success; but it proved short-lived. The Depression persuaded most Americans that their government should have broad authority to institute economic measures without being hamstrung by judicially protected economic rights. But there were other interests many New Dealers wanted to advance; and because their numbers were not large enough to effect these changes by legislation, they soon found judicial enforcement of broadly defined constitutional rights an attractive vehicle for doing so. In its momentous 1937 term, even as the Supreme Court denied the power of economic rights to check state and national regulatory initiatives, it began asserting that other rights, such as freedom of expression, religious conscience, and rights to fair criminal processes, should be given special weight by judges.

These claims were greatly accelerated by the emergence of the modern African American CIVIL RIGHTS movement in the 1950s. It not only demanded that African Americans receive in reality the political and economic rights titularly provided them after the Civil War. It also generated a range of constitutional controversies, over rights of political expression, offensive speech, libel, rights of accused protesters and minority defendants, and over the proper means of constitutional interpretation, that all pressed for greater recognition of individual rights. It also helped inspire a range of other rights movements, especially by women but eventually by the whole kaleidoscope of other groups listed above, that made rights central to political as well as legal and philosophical discourse from the late 1950s through the late 1970s.

Academic discussions of rights in these years were fundamentally modified, however, by the decline in intellectual influence of the doctrines that placed certain rights beyond dispute in the minds of many early Americans. Rights could no longer be lightly claimed to be gifts of God, or rationally self-evident aspects of a natural moral order, or veridical intuitions of humanity's moral sense. In the wake of nineteenth-century scientific challenges to revealed religion, along with utilitarian and Romantic challenges to notions of rationally ascertained natural rights, American intellectuals, and to a lesser degree all Americans, increasingly insisted with the Progressive pragmatists that rights must be justified as either democratically enacted or as contributing to the achievement of democratically endorsed purposes. Philosophers like JOHN RAWLS and Ronald Dworkin met this challenge by claiming that their rights doctrines represented what people in American society would find they most valued on reflection, or what any rational person would choose in a fairly designed thought experiment. The Supreme Court similarly contended that its activism on behalf of various rights, including implicit constitutional rights of "privacy," upheld either fundamental values embraced by the supermajorities who framed various constitutional provisions or, most often, by the understandings of morality most Americans now accepted.

Unfortunately, those arguments provide unsteady foundations for rights. If the legitimacy of rights rests on their origins in genuine democratic choices, then democratically elected officials have more prima facie claim to define basic rights than appointed judges, tenured philosophers, or even long-dead constitutional ratifiers. Rights have also been increasingly criticized as clumsy social tools. They tend to cast claims in all-or-nothing terms—to present themselves as "trumps," as Ronald Dworkin argued—and thereby to clog the fair and efficient accommodations of conflicting values that many believe communities can and should make. Hence the "rights revolution" has come in the minds of many to be identified with litigious, expensive, ineffectual governance of a society guided by political theories and legal doctrines that encourage individual and group self-seeking.

Women and minorities have also increasingly criticized rights doctrines on different grounds. Standard theories of rights, spun out primarily by white male philosophers, judges, and legislatures, are said implicitly to take WASP men as the norm in defining what count as rights. Hence these theories dismiss or fail to address the different circumstances and needs that most women and members of racial and ethnic minorities experience. All the renowned architects of liberal rights doctrines, from religious precursors like John Calvin through Enlightenment writers like John Locke and John Milton through jurists like JOHN MARSHALL and later liberal philosophers like John Stuart Mill and John Rawls, are thus said to lack diversity—not a bizarre claim. And women and minority scholars have been able to show in particular cases, such as laws defining culpability for rape and policies defining eligibility for loans, how apparently "neutral" rules in fact have built into them biases in favor of men or whites. Some conclude that Americans need fewer universal rights and more laws recognizing how people are differently situated.

Yet other minority and women scholars like Kimberlé Crenshaw insist that securing basic rights for those denied them must remain a fundamental concern of those working to assist disempowered populations. Programs focused on difference may be appropriate once basic rights are provided for all, but they threaten to divert attention from persistent denials of rights and to slacken efforts to secure such rights. (*See also* CRITICAL RACE THEORY, FEMINIST JURISPRUDENCE.)

It is not clear in any case that recognition of universal rights and of particular differences are so incompatible. Logically, we can maintain claims for universal rights but recognize that rights are indeed political creations, inspired by persuasive moral concerns, aimed at achieving certain purposes on behalf of all who are entitled to claim them. If rights are so conceived, then their scope and meaning must be determined by considering whether they actually work to attain those ends on behalf of people whose needs and circumstances may be quite varied. A civic right of physical access to public buildings, for example, might be deemed satisfied only when wheelchair ramps are provided so that everyone, not just the able-bodied, can enter without difficulty. Some would insist that treating wheelchair ramps as rights deters people from making difficult but necessary calculations of whether the ramps' benefits outweigh their costs. But if we recognize that rights are tools, not absolute trumps, we can see that the moral weight of a right depends upon both the value of the goal it serves, and its practical capacity to realize that goal. Rights that are practically counterproductive should clearly be given little weight. Even a right that is useful for achieving an important goal might be overridden if its costs are quite high. And if terming something a "right" makes it difficult for policy-makers to ignore it, if it compels them to show why it is too costly to extend the right to everyone despite their different circumstances, those burdens may be precisely why the right works to advance social goals effectively. In principle, then, rights can be made responsive to different circumstances, and they can be appropriately limited by careful comparison of their moral and economic costs and benefits with those of alternative policies.

But even if rights might logically play such a constructive role, it remains likely that both the rhetoric and content of rights claims will always be politically and philosophically controversial. They will also remain ubiquitous. The value of having an interest recognized as a moral, statutory, or constitutional right is too great for political actors to abandon rights talk in large numbers, even if potent alternative languages were available, which may not be the case. Thus wildly different moral positions will surely continue to be advanced via competing rights claims.

It is possible that, in the wake of the criticisms of the 1980s, American courts may become less willing to discover implicit rights, or to define explicit rights in novel and expansive ways, in the future. Rights may become more matters of legislative or popular discursive definition, with judiciaries following along more strictly than sometimes in the past. It is probable in any case that judges, as well as legislators and other political actors, will come to stress different rights than the ones that were prominent in the 1960s and 1970s. Some of those, like voting rights, are too firmly established to be questioned, while others, such as constitutional rights to WELFARE, have instead lost support.

What rights may prove central in American politics after the mid-1990s? Intriguingly, as the decade began, an odd couple moved toward increased political, legal, and scholarly respectability: property rights and gay rights. Conservative scholars, emboldened by the Reagan–Bush years and by the intellectual weaponry added via new rational choice perspectives in the social sciences, have reemphasized doctrines of property rights of the sort Progressives attacked. Some defend these rights on economic, utility, or wealth-maximizing grounds, others as natural or moral rights. (*See* LAW AND ECONOMICS.) Most see property concepts as useful for clarifying a broad range of apparently noneconomic rights, such as liberties of conscience, expression, and criminal procedure.

The support gay rights received from American courts and legislatures in the early 1990s was, in contrast, not a revival, but remarkably unprecedented. Although advocates of gay rights were still losing some important judicial and electoral battles, the results were usually close, whereas even raising the issues publicly had seemed impossible only a few years before. This pair of developments might be taken to forecast a new social as well as economic LIBERTARIANISM undergirding expansive rights claims in the early twenty-first century.

It would be wrong to conclude, however, that the renewed stress on market-oriented property rights can easily coexist with all the surviving themes of the 1960s "rights revolution." As the work of scholars like Richard Epstein has indicated, the very cornerstone of the modern civil rights movement's achievements, the 1964 Civil Rights Act, is open to assault on economic libertarian grounds. That law, after all, constrains market choices by compelling participants to deal with persons they would prefer to reject on grounds of race. For those who believe that most restrictions on market freedoms are counterproductive, it is presumptively inefficient. Similarly, many advocates of strong property rights contend that new regulations outlawing discrimination against gays are economically unwise, if not morally unjust.

But the fact that the two types of rights claims that were gaining new prestige in the early 1990s thus tend to come into conflict only confirms that the characteristic place of rights in American thought is likely to endure. The particulars will vary. But Americans seem destined to continue to argue over rights, in terms of rights, so long as they have life and liberty and are pursuing happiness.

ROGERS M. SMITH

See also BILL OF RIGHTS; CONSTITUTION.

FURTHER READING

Kimberlé Williams Crenshaw, "Race, Reform, and Retrenchment: Transformation and Legitimation in Antidiscrimination Law," *Harvard Law Review* 101 (May 1988): 1331–87.
Ronald Dworkin, *Taking Rights Seriously* (Cambridge: Harvard University Press, 1977).
Richard A. Epstein, *Forbidden Grounds: the Case Against Employment Discrimination Laws* (Cambridge: Harvard University Press, 1977).
Mary Ann Glendon, *Rights Talk: the Impoverishment of Political Discourse* (New York: Free Press, 1991).
Hendrik Hartog, "The Constitution of Aspiration and 'The Rights that Belong to Us All,'" in David Thelen, ed., *The Constitution in American Life* (Ithaca: Cornell University Press, 1988).
Daniel T. Rodgers, "Rights," in *Contested Truths: Keywords in American Politics since Independence* (New York: Basic Books, 1987).

Cass R. Sunstein, *After the Rights Revolution: Reconceiving the Regulatory State* (Cambridge: Harvard University Press, 1990).

Howard Zinn, *Declarations of Independence: Cross-Examining American Ideology* (New York: HarperCollins, 1990).

Riis, Jacob (b. Ribe, Denmark, May 3, 1849; d. Barre, Mass., May 26, 1914). Journalist, photographer, reformer. Working as a reporter for the New York *Tribune* and *Sun* (1877–99), Riis recorded the living conditions of the modern urban poor as no one had since Gustav Doré in early Victorian London. Through Riis's stories and, especially, through his groundbreaking photographic studies, the inhabitants of New York's Mulberry Bend became emblematic of the crisis of industrial life. In what he considered artless reportage, Riis's *How the Other Half Lives* (1890) constructed an image sensibility which would resonate in various forms of social realism through the next century. In his move from reporter to activist, Riis also became the paradigmatic exemplar of MUCKRAKING, a role amplified by his partnership with then city politician THEODORE ROOSEVELT. Through books such as *The Battle with the Slum* (1902), and *Children of the Tenements* (1903), and as a popular lecturer, Riis became an early saint in Progressive reform iconography.

FURTHER READING
James B. Lane, *Jacob A. Riis and the American City* (Port Washington, N.Y.: Kennikat, 1974).

Ripley, George (b. Greenfield, Mass., Oct. 3, 1802; d. New York, N.Y., July 4, 1880). Editor and reformer. An exponent of an extremely liberal biblical interpretation, Ripley ran afoul of his Unitarian peers and left the ministry. He helped found the Transcendentalist *Dial* and started Brook Farm (1841–7) in the belief that collective life is the soundest basis for true INDIVIDUALISM and social EQUALITY. After 1849 he was an influential literary critic for the New York *Tribune* and *Harper's Monthly*.

See also TRANSCENDENTALISM; UTOPIANISM

FURTHER READING
Charles Crowe, *George Ripley, Transcendentalist and Utopian Socialist* (Athens: University of Georgia Press, 1967).

Rittenhouse, David (b. near Germantown, Pa., Apr. 8, 1732; d. Philadelphia, Pa., June 26, 1796). Astronomer and instrument maker. Interested in both scientific theory and the solution of practical problems, Rittenhouse not only endorsed Newtonian philosophy and developed an accurate explanation of iron's magnetism, but built telescopes, surveyed state lines, and was applauded for creating the world's finest orrery—a clockwork model of the solar system.

Devoted to the revolutionary cause, he was active in the Philadelphia Committee of Safety and served in the Pennsylvania convention that produced the state's constitution. First director of the U.S. Mint, he followed BENJAMIN FRANKLIN as president of the American Philosophical Society.

FURTHER READING
Brooke Hindle, *David Rittenhouse* (Princeton: Princeton University Press, 1964).

Robinson, James Harvey (b. Bloomington, Ill., June 29, 1863; d. New York, N.Y., Feb. 16, 1936). Historian. A primary advocate of the progressive New History, Robinson believed historians should adapt the techniques of SOCIAL SCIENCE, highlight ideas and beliefs as much as wars and politics, and provide insight into current conditions and problems. History does not provide "lessons," since circumstances are always changing. But outmoded ideas and practices can be fought by placing them in the perpetual flow of historical development. Active in the formation of the New School for Social Research (with THORSTEIN VEBLEN, JOHN DEWEY, and CHARLES BEARD), Robinson authored *The New History* (1912), *The Mind in the Making* (1921), and *The Ordeal of Civilization* (1926), among many other writings.

FURTHER READING
John Higham, *History: Professional Scholarship in America* (Baltimore: Johns Hopkins University Press, 1983).

Rogers, Will[iam Penn Adair] (b. near Oolagah, Indian Territory [now Oklahoma], Nov. 4, 1879; d. near Point Barrow, Alaska, Aug. 15, 1935). Humorist. A cowboy turned actor and nationally syndicated newspaper columnist, Rogers sympathetically exposed the foibles of human nature and voiced the concerns of the "common people." His wry comments about national and international politics in the 1920s expressed popular discontent with the incompetence and cupidity of politicians, of the rich, and of easterners in general. Advocating an anti-imperialist, even isolationist, approach to foreign affairs, he ridiculed the conformist superpatriotism of World War I and called for free speech and religious tolerance. Rogers's books include *Rogerisms—the Cowboy Philosopher on Prohibition* (1919), *Illiterate Digest* (1924), and *There's Not a Bathing Suit in Russia* (1927).

FURTHER READING
Ben Yagoda, *Will Rogers: a Biography* (New York: Knopf, 1993).

romantic historians America's famous romantic historians were prolific authors. The ten-volume *History of the United States from the Discovery of the*

American Continent by GEORGE BANCROFT appeared between 1834 and 1875. William Hickling Prescott's *Ferdinand and Isabella, Conquest of Mexico, Conquest of Peru,* and *Philip the Second* extended to 11 volumes (with a twelfth on Charles V) between 1838 and 1858. John Lothrop Motley's *Rise of the Dutch Republic* and related works reached 14 volumes between 1856 and 1874. FRANCIS PARKMAN produced nine volumes on *France and England in North America* between 1865 and 1892. All tried their hands at other forms of literature. Parkman even wrote a book on roses.

These authors did not consider themselves a school, though all were from Massachusetts and their lives intersected at many points. To their contemporaries all that grouped them together was their popular success. By the late nineteenth century, as history became professionalized (and much less popular), praise for their works grew fainter. While lauded for seeking out sources, they were found too moralistic and too literary. In 1959 David Levin showed that their literary techniques and shared attitudes toward moral progress, individual greatness, and national character linked them to European Romanticism. Since then, their names often appear together as exemplars of the style and taste of an earlier era. Bancroft's *History* is little read, though sometimes disparaged for popularizing myths about America's providential MISSION. Prescott receives occasional praise for his "readability," as does Motley for his "clarity" and "wealth of information." Parkman is the only one whose works still arouse much interest, frequently bitter and critical. But as Pieter Geyl remarked in 1956 of Motley's eclipse, "Scholars carry out their investigations . . . without referring to him or to his views" (p. 146).

Geyl, a Buchenwald survivor, was one of this century's most admired historians; his caustic dismissal of Motley's *Rise of the Dutch Republic* illuminates the submergence of romantic history. Geyl knew why it had long captivated readers. It was moral drama, vigorously presented and devoid of subtlety, which depicted Spanish rulers as "forces of Evil" and aligned the Dutch people in a brave tradition with the English of the Glorious Revolution and Americans of 1776. To moderns like Geyl, however, the past was "not made up of struggles between God and the Devil." Human beings were fallible, their intentions were ambiguous, and their actions had unintended consequences. Absolute rulers, though sometimes tyrannical, might also advance principles of unity and law; and "the cry of 'liberty' covered a multitude of selfish interests, local narrowness, class privilege." Motley's history misconstrued religious conflict and political division in the Netherlands so

badly that it retained no value except as "an eloquent and sincere testimony of nineteenth-century liberal idealism" (pp. 147, 151).

It is not just the content of the great multivolume histories that seems untenable in the post-Holocaust world. The style of these histories depended on according authority to the voice of the historian-narrator, who laid out the scenery, described the pageantry, named the moods the reader should feel, and delineated the contrasting characters in the drama. Modern critics lack patience for "the moral certitude, or perhaps arrogance," of authors like Bancroft, who, as Richard Vitzthum pointed out, constantly "stands between the reader and the past, telling him in no uncertain terms what it means, how it should be judged, how much it is worth" (p. 44). Today Parkman's hortatory passages sound overbearing. Prescott's moral judgments strike the contemporary reader as inconsistent: he idealizes Incan civilization in contrast to American corruption, but then justifies conquest as saving generations of the heathen from perdition. The moral universe of antebellum America is in critical ways incommensurate with that of the 1990s, and this gap contributes, to the aura of irrelevancy that surrounds the romantic historians.

Since the 1960s some scholars have urged reconsideration of moral criticism in historical writing, and in the 1990s the ideal of scientific objectivity has been increasingly identified as little more than the historian's quixotic dream. In an age when the well-wrought narrative gains new legitimacy, why have the old masters of moral drama and storytelling not won new audiences? Their equally "romantic" contemporaries in fiction, painting, and religion (such as HARRIET BEECHER STOWE, Frederic Church, RALPH WALDO EMERSON) rise in esteem, but the reputations of Bancroft, Prescott, Motley, and Parkman sink downward. The reason they remain difficult to rehabilitate is that their viewpoint was so resolutely ethnocentric. Despite occasional sympathetic passages, Bancroft scarcely questioned the justice of the colonial American treatment of the Indians. Motley, whose subject had no bearing on racial conflict in the Americas, wrote an essay on "Progress" emphasizing "our" civilization's Germanic heritage and slighting the attainments of Indian and Asiatic races. Prescott and Parkman expressed their ethnocentrism in accounts of conquests that have taken on the standing of earlier Holocausts. Prescott refers to the "standards of the age" to pardon Cortés's cruelty, but he does not condone such relativism when judging the legitimacy of non-Christian belief systems. Parkman's Indians were treacherous savages, the scourge of the forest, to be overcome as Anglo-American civilization marched forward. Parkman's views on blacks, immigrants, and women repel modern critics. The others took less extreme positions, but all four of these canonical male authors saluted "masculine" vigor as a historical force pitted against "effeminate" sensuality and corruption.

Criticizing these authors from a contemporary "multicultural" viewpoint risks assuming the universality of our own version of moral progress and believing that we have escaped from the narrow-mindedness of an earlier era. We might note, therefore, that a romantic contemporary, THEODORE PARKER, considered Prescott an inadequate historian because of his uncritical judgments about the conquistadors and his neglect of the perspectives of ordinary people. Parker also chided Parkman for exaggerating Indian treachery, overlooking the cruelty of whites, and, indeed, using dramatic forms to distort the meaning of his data.

Parker's criticism of the romantic historians' racism was no less stringent than that of today's most critical readers. Where he differs from many of them is in his conviction that historical research should contribute to humanity's moral advance. Most historians of our day would hesitate to take on such a responsibility. Historians in our age often carry out sounder and more comprehensive research than their romantic ancestors, and in that respect we may rightly speak of scholarly progress. But that progress has come at great cost: diminished confidence among historians in their capacity to illuminate moral problems as they investigate the past.

LEWIS PERRY

FURTHER READING

Howard F. Cline, C. Harvey Gardiner, and Charles Gibson, eds., *William Hickling Prescott: a Memorial* (Durham, N.C.: Duke University Press, 1959).

Pieter Geyl, "Motley and His 'Rise of the Dutch Republic,'" in *Encounters with History* (New York: Meridian, 1961).

Lilian Handlin, *George Bancroft: the Intellectual as Democrat* (New York: Harper and Row, 1984).

Wilbur R. Jacobs, *Francis Parkman, Historian as Hero: the Formative Years* (Austin: University of Texas Press, 1991).

Francis Jennings, "Francis Parkman: a Brahmin among Untouchables," *William and Mary Quarterly* 42 (July 1985): 305–28.

David Levin, *History as Romantic Art: Bancroft, Prescott, Motley, and Parkman* (New York: Harcourt, Brace and World, 1963).

Theodore Parker, "Prescott as an Historian" and "Prescott's *Conquest of Mexico*," in *The American Scholar* (Boston: American Unitarian Association, 1907).

Richard C. Vitzthum, *The American Compromise: Theme and Method in the Histories of Bancroft, Parkman, and Adams* (Norman: University of Oklahoma Press, 1974).

Romanticism The term refers first of all to movements in European art and literature, which are contrasted to classicism and REALISM and seen as precursors of MODERNISM. In the United States, romantic literature is mainly associated with the "American Renaissance" from the decades before the Civil War to the end of the nineteenth century, the writings of Emerson, Thoreau, Whitman, Hawthorne and Melville. Romanticism also describes a period in the history of ideas. Centered in Germany where the term originated, it began as a late eighteenth-century reaction against the excesses of ENLIGHTENMENT reason in the realms of art, metaphysics, morals and religion, law and politics. Romanticism championed feeling against analytic reason, imagination and will against calculations of utility and mundane happiness, the concrete against the abstract, flux and plenitude over system and homogeneity; it drew on neo-Platonist and Idealist thought. The most inclusive approach sees Romanticism as a recurrent sensibility. Its premier expression may be in literature, but the romantic disposition of selfhood is widely distributed in the population and not restricted to artists. If European Romantics are often heroic or aristocratic types, in America the romantic sensibility has strong affinities to democratic INDIVIDUALISM.

The romantic sensibility is marked by a sense of its own boundless potential for creativity and expression, by revulsion at constriction and closure and at the very thought of being authoritatively defined. The sensitive soul seeking the infinite and finding only the finite everywhere is a familiar type. Faced with conventions and restraints, the Romantic assumes one of two postures: expressive individualism, which takes the form of solitary defiance or detachment, or expressive holism, the discovery of correspondence between the outside world and this inner life of plenitude and striving. Romantic sensibilities have inclined to revolutionism and reaction, pastoralism and military glory, folk traditions and Promethean creativity. That is one reason why Romanticism is captured less readily by its positive associations than by its aversions. The romantic sensibility is antimaterialistic, hostile to acquisitiveness and to ceaseless getting and spending; HENRY DAVID THOREAU wrote in *Walden*, "The twelve labors of Hercules were trifling in comparison with those my neighbors have undertaken . . . but I could never see that these men slew or captured any monster or finished any labor" (p. 8). It is anticonventional and repulsed by wearisome customs and routines; when NATHANIEL HAWTHORNE wanted to capture the disappointments of America he employed the metaphor of the Salem Custom House. The romantic sensibility is antilegalistic, and would replace a social ethos of impersonal rules and cold calculations of utility with moral intuition and the spontaneous law of the heart.

Opposition to commercial and industrial society is the common thread of European and American Romanticism, and bears a family resemblance to Marxist, conservative, and fascist critiques of modern society. But Romanticism's sentimental and aesthetic longings and preoccupation with expressive individuality are distinctive.

In American thought, Romanticism is often captured by radical individualism; social bonds have shrunk and are replaced by the imperial self or the infinitude of the private man. "I have my own horizon . . . my sun and moon and stars, and a little world all to myself," Thoreau wrote (p. 3). The romantic sensibility calls us to acknowledge our solitude and self-reliance, to cultivate an appetite for introspection and responsiveness to nature. To see the world and creation anew, as Thoreau did at Walden, and with spontaneous freshness of sensation and reflection to feel at home there, is romantic aspiration. RALPH WALDO EMERSON and Thoreau were not escapists or antisocial, and their writings on AN-TISLAVERY and civil disobedience inspired reformers in practice. But they were detached from ordinary politics, perennial outsiders. They shared nothing with Tocqueville's joiners, usefully combining in voluntary associations. Thoreau declared his intention to stand aloof from cooperation even when it aimed at correcting the most enormous wrong, slavery. For him the only truly salutary combination was friendship, with its rare complementarity of excellences.

Yet American romantic individualism is a far cry from Byron's satanic outcasts or the Romanticism of the German *Sturm und Drang*, with its explosive passion, crime and death, and glorification of defiance against the odiousness of any social order. Thoreau's disobedience was "civil," as was Emerson's self-reliance. Detachment was the prelude to self-reform, not reckless rebellion and certainly not arrant social destruction. And there remains the hope that democracy will be what it was meant to be—a company of beautiful, expressive, self-affirming individualists.

American Romanticism is also characterized by the positive desire for correspondence between the inner self and community. Here too the contrast with European Romanticism is instructive. When English and Continental Romantics imagine reintegration, it takes a creative act of genius to transform a disenchanted world and make it palatable: the poet is Shelley's Legislator or prophet. When European

Romantics identify with community, it is with imaginative recreations of a frankly aristocratic past: beautified medieval Christendom or Hellas, Burke's traditionalism whose beautiful plumage covers our "naked shivering natures" or Schiller's ideal Republic of Letters.

American Romantics have always been embarrassed by overtly antidemocratic visions and claims of genius, and they seldom idealized history. An immense gulf opens between Continental Romantics, including Nietzsche, and American writers who did not reject democracy, equality, or the principle of consent of the governed. If they railed against their neighbors, it was for failing to be all that they might be. The extraordinary soul's contempt of the ordinary was not a defining element of American Romanticism; the exemplary figure is often the independent farmer or urban worker celebrated by WALT WHIT-MAN; Thoreau's true Homeric man is the woodchopper in *Walden*. Stifled by his tenure as surveyor in the Salem Custom House, Hawthorne comforted himself with the thought, "I am a citizen of somewhere else," meaning that he was really at home in his imagination. But he instantly takes back this traiterous thought and chastises himself for being unable to find inspiration in daily routine and for his escape into his Puritan past.

Tension between romantic aloofness and democratic appreciation produces a characteristically American set of romantic scenes of belonging that avoid identification with democratic society as it is, without being contemptuous. Thoreau frankly preferred immersion in nature to any regular association, but kept his misanthropy at bay and found language for detachment not only in metaphysics but also in the shared ideology of political independence. He held out the hope that the destiny of Americans was still untransacted. Emerson wrote about "representative men," great individualists once removed from ordinary people but representative rather than objects of worship, which is not something democratic men and women do. The book was his answer to Thomas Carlyle's *Heroes and Hero-Worship*. Representative men introduce us to ideas and to nature; they are receptive channels for spirit and energy. They are simply exemplary, however, and neither mold nor lead us. There is no substitute for each person's own efforts at personal expression and improvement, which is always possible. Whitman had the most extravagant relation to democracy. He imaginatively dissolved the democratic "en masse" into a dazzle of personalities, and saw in society the spectacle of diversity that other Romantics saw in the plenitude of nature. Whitman portrayed himself merging with every single atom of the teeming nation of nations: "I contain multitudes."

Hawthorne cast a cold eye on this romantic propensity to portray the plain face of democracy as sublime. In *House of the Seven Gables*, Clifford, the exquisitely sensitive aesthete, watches a political procession from the balcony and finds the democratic spectacle so enchanting he longs to plunge into the "surging stream of human sympathies" to his death. Hawthorne explains, "by its remoteness, it melts all the petty personalities, of which it is made up into one broad mass of existence—one great life—one collected body of mankind with a vast, homogeneous spirit animating it." Revolted by prosaic, materialistic society but uncomfortable with heroic individualism, American Romantics seem caught between antiworldliness and privatization on the one side and airy, aestheticized democracy on the other.

In American thought, Romanticism does not take a political form. The unique self is not apotheosized into a personified group or nation with its own will to assert and genius to express. There is nothing to match European romantic nationalism, organic community, or the cult of personality. The romantic celebration of concrete group identity in America, as articulated by HORACE KALLEN and RANDOLPH BOURNE, was cultural and perfectly compatible with universal political citizenship. American Romanticism produced a search for an authentic American literature and a striving to fulfill the promises of 1776, but not an aggressive politics of collective will. Personal freedom makes possible detachment from society generally and even from inherited ethnic or religious identity, and gives a moral imprimatur to the romantic preoccupation with individuality. Moreover, the longed-for correspondence between singular self and community has actual outlets; as GEORGE SANTAYANA remarked, in America "this metaphysical illusion has a partial warrant in historical fact."

For American Romantics, democracy is not just a form of government. As government, Thoreau judged, majority rule is always the imposition of superior force, but even he felt that no constitution was better than America's. Beyond that, democracy is a disavowal of the past and of hereditary conditions, an invitation to self-made identity and elective community. For romantic sensibilities, democratic society and institutions are justified as the setting for individuality. Extending Paine's already radical prescription for a revolution in every generation, Romantics insist on personal independence and on consent to every attachment and obligation, which must be not only voluntary but expressive. In fact, there is a discernible correspondence between the romantic unbounded self and the fluidity and sheer variety of American democracy, with its social movement, periodic elections and changeable laws, and revolutionary ideology. However imperfect, American DEMOCRACY complements the Romantic's experience of the self better than any traditional social or political form. The obstacles to self-made identity and elective community are identifiable and, in principle, corrigible: the persistence of hereditary property and conditions, slavery and the condition of women among them.

Striving for perfect correspondence is always a possibility, and one sure outlet exists in the ease of forming romantic UTOPIAS. Experimental communities are a staple of American culture, and in romantic community the usual socialist focus on division of property and labor is eclipsed by pre-occupation with friendship, sincerity, and the law of the heart. Elizabeth Peabody described Brook Farm as "a few individuals, who, unknown to each other, under different disciplines of life, reacting from different social evils," nonetheless aim at the same object, to be "wholly true to their natures as men and women."

Being true to one's self is the romantic answer to one of the central problems of American society— how to form a COMMUNITY from a company of strangers whose backgrounds and values diverge and who do not share religious beliefs or loyalty to traditional authorities. What is the glue if the available alternatives—rights and contracts, impersonal market relations, or electoral politics appear arid and impersonal? For an elective company of friends and for democratic society, the idea is to reassert heart over head—spontaneity, warmth, excitement, vigor, life-giving energy, and imaginative vision. The inner man and woman of imagination and feeling will unite spontaneously with others. This is the peculiarly democratic wish of American Romanticism.

NANCY L. ROSENBLUM

FURTHER READING

M. H. Abrams, *Natural Supernaturalism* (New York: Norton, 1971).

George Kateb, *The Inner Ocean: Individualism and Democratic Culture* (Ithaca: Cornell University Press, 1992).

F. O. Matthiessen, *American Renaissance* (Oxford: Oxford University Press, 1941).

Elizabeth Peabody, "The Original Constitution of Brook Farm" (1842), in John Humphrey Noyes, *History of American Socialisms* (1870; New York, Hillary House: 1961), pp. 113–17.

Nancy L. Rosenblum, *Another Liberalism: Romanticism and the Reconstruction of Liberal Thought* (Cambridge: Harvard University Press, 1987).

Henry David Thoreau, *Walden and Civil Disobedience*, (1854; New York: New American Library, 1958).

Roosevelt, Theodore (b. New York, N.Y., Oct. 27, 1858; d. Oyster Bay, N.Y., Jan. 6, 1919). Twenty-sixth President of the United States, historian and author, Roosevelt was born into a patrician New York family. He graduated in 1880 from Harvard, where he began work on his first substantial historical study, *The Naval War of 1812*, published in two volumes in 1882. It was followed by another major historical work, *The Winning of the West* (6 vols., 1889–96), and eventually by more than 30 additional volumes of biography, autobiography, essays, and lectures, most of them penned while he pursued a phenomenally active career as a New York state assemblyman (1882–4), North Dakota cattle rancher (1884–6), U.S. civil service commissioner (1889–95), New York City police commissioner (1895–7), Assistant Secretary of the Navy (1897–8), Governor of New York (1899–1901), Vice President (1901) and President (1901–9) of the United States. Small wonder that his friend Henry Adams wrote in *The Education of Henry Adams* that Roosevelt "showed the singular primitive quality that belongs to ultimate matter—the quality that medieval theology assigned to God—he was pure act." Insatiably inquisitive, restlessly energetic, competitive, domineering, and flamboyant, Roosevelt, it was said, had a deep psychological need to be the bride at every wedding and the corpse at every funeral.

Roosevelt entered public life at a moment when men of his comfortable and privileged social status shunned political careers. "The men I knew best," Roosevelt wrote in his *Autobiography*, "were the men in the clubs of social pretension and the men of cultivated taste and easy life." They laughed at the young Roosevelt's interest in politics, and

> assured me that the men I met would be rough and brutal and unpleasant to deal with. I answered that if this were so it merely meant that the people I knew did not belong to the governing class, and that the other people did—and that I intended to be one of the governing class. (p. 56)

So began a political career that by example and sheer force of personality energized a generation of Americans, much as John F. Kennedy inspired a later generation.

Much controversy has surrounded the question of the specific ideological content of Roosevelt's visions and ideals. Different commentators have variously described him as radical, conservative, idealistic, and opportunistic. Partly this confusion reflects still unresolved debates about the essential character of PROGRESSIVISM, the early twentieth-century reform movement with which Roosevelt was closely

identified. As a politician, he embraced and shaped the two great issues of the progressive era: in the international realm, the effort to make American weight felt in the scales of international diplomacy in a measure commensurate with the nation's newly acquired economic might, and with the perils and prospects of the new imperialist competition among the great powers; in the domestic realm, the effort to shape instruments of governmental power commensurate with the scale of corporate power and social problems that had emerged during the rapid industrialization and urbanization of the late nineteenth century. On the first front, Roosevelt had to contend with the deeply entrenched legacy of isolationism. On the second front, he faced the no less deeply ingrained heritage of Jeffersonian, laissez-faire ideas that inhibited all attempts to build a positive, interventionist state apparatus. With these issues Roosevelt all his life struggled manfully—a word that he used often; but what ideas animated his efforts?

In the last analysis, it is probably best to describe the complex of ideas, attitudes, and prejudices that informed Roosevelt's policies as romantic nationalism, tinged with the racialist thinking current in his day, and the moralism typical of his class. Clues to his thought are unusually abundant in the prolific writings of this unusually literary politician. Both his major historical works, especially *The Winning of the West*, rely on the Darwinian concept of evolution through struggle to make the case that the Anglo-American "race" (for Roosevelt and his contemporaries the categories of "race" and "nation" were virtually synonymous) was deservedly destined, by reason of cultural and perhaps biological superiority, for world leadership. That outlook lay behind Roosevelt's aggressive support for American overseas expansion in 1898, and for American intervention in WORLD WAR I. It also helps explain his contemptuous disdain for the timid, self-absorbed materialism of what he called the "flub-dubs" and "mollycoddles" of the "business class," who did not share his vision of an imperially triumphant America. (*See also* IMPERIALISM AND ANTI-IMPERIALISM.)

Roosevelt's support for progressive reform measures at home is also best understood as a reflection of his nationalist sentiments. Like his hero Alexander Hamilton, of whom it was said that he loved his country but not his countrymen, Roosevelt, as John Milton Cooper Jr. has written, "worried about problems of wealth and poverty, but he cared about their effects less on the victims than on the nation's strength and unity" (p. 37). Though he was himself an egregious individualist, he nevertheless deplored the selfish excesses of American INDIVIDUALISM, and exhorted his countrymen to subordinate their narrow, private concerns to higher, nationalistic aims. In a thousand speeches and in all his writings he appealed not to the self-interest, enlightened or otherwise, of his fellow citizens, but, as another of his heroes, Abraham Lincoln, said, to the "better angels of our nature." Roosevelt is often mistakenly characterized as a stout realist; but his deep, altruistic faith marked him instead as a thoroughgoing romantic.

DAVID M. KENNEDY

FURTHER READING

John Morton Blum, *The Republican Roosevelt* (Cambridge: Harvard University Press, 1954).
John Milton Cooper Jr., *The Warrior and the Priest: Woodrow Wilson and Theodore Roosevelt* (Cambridge: Harvard University Press, 1983).
William H. Harbaugh, *The Life and Times of Theodore Roosevelt*, rev. ed. (New York: Oxford University Press, 1975).
Richard Hofstadter, "'Theodore Roosevelt: the Conservative as Progressive," in Hofstadter, *The American Political Tradition and the Men Who Made It* (New York: Knopf, 1948).
Henry Pringle, *Theodore Roosevelt: a Biography* (New York: Harcourt, Brace, 1931).
Theodore Roosevelt, *An Autobiography* (New York: Charles Scribner's Sons, 1913).

Rorty, Richard (b. New York, N.Y., Oct. 4, 1931). Born to an intellectually prominent and politically active family, Rorty was educated at the University of Chicago and Yale University. His early work was squarely within the "analytic" tradition, the dominant school in Anglo-American philosophy departments for most of the twentieth century, which focused on the logical and linguistic terms of arguments made about the nature of knowledge. With *Philosophy and the Mirror of Nature* (1979), Rorty broke with this tradition and set out to deconstruct it, that is, to destabilize its basic assumptions and methods.

Following the historiographical innovations of THOMAS KUHN, Rorty described how Western philosophers since the seventeenth century had constructed a metaphor of "the Mind" as a mirror producing accurate representations of "Reality," representations which could then be evaluated by professional scholars—called philosophers—who saw themselves engaged in a progressive, even scientific quest toward a universal *theory* of knowledge, a "final vocabulary" with which to talk about the Absolute. For Rorty, this turn in Western philosophy exhibited an unfortunate, though admittedly powerful, "desire for constraint—a desire to find 'foundations' to which one might cling, frameworks beyond which one must

not stray, objects which impose themselves, representations which cannot be gainsaid" (p. 315). In abandoning the idea that "knowledge" is a thing or a process grounded in more than language, Rorty was elaborating early twentieth-century PRAGMATISM, building on its thesis that "foundations" or understanding are always *made* by the individual subject at any given moment when the need to "know" —the need to establish an operative truth—presents itself. Although Rorty used the ideas of like-minded European thinkers (Wittgenstein, Heidegger, Derrida), *Philosophy and the Mirror of Nature*, and the following *Consequences of Pragmatism* (1982), served as catalysts for an important revaluation of the particularly American pragmatic discourse.

This phase of Rorty's work cleared the ground for his own "antirepresentational" speculations on culture and subjectivity. Most important in this project was *Contingency, Irony, and Solidarity* (1989), a book in the tradition of John Stuart Mill's *On Liberty* (1859) as a critique of contemporary intellectual practice woven into a liberal manifesto. Rorty's idea of liberty, like Mill's, was primarily negative: liberty to do as one chooses so far as no other is harmed. Further, Rorty followed Mill in asserting a necessary division between "public" and "private" spheres of behavior, a move which many critics who had matured in the 1960s and 1970s found problematic because it challenged their own understanding of the political nature of everyday life, the identity of the personal and the political. While Rorty never denied the historicity of private expression—*all* thought is contingent on historical context as well as on the context of specific truth-claims—he did insist that modern Western culture had developed in such a way as to allow for a privatized sphere of intellectual practice that has no bearing on public life, a sphere created and maintained by our aesthetic sensibilities.

In *Contingency, Irony, and Solidarity*, Rorty calls the subject operating in his "poeticized" private sphere a "liberal ironist": a pragmatist who maintains "radical and continuing doubts about the final vocabulary she currently uses" to ground truth-claims, who accepts the responsibilities of moral RELATIVISM, "that anything can be made to look good or bad by being redescribed" (p. 73). The process of redescription was central to Rorty's concept of subjectivity. Crossing the pragmatist's sense of situational-creative truth (exemplified in the work of JOHN DEWEY) with a transformative aestheticism running back through MODERNISM to ROMANTICISM (exemplified in the work of Friedrich Nietzsche), Rorty offered a vision of constructed selfhood based on nothing more or less than the individual's adventurous play with "possible vocabularies," with ideas culled from the ironist's explorations in intellectual history and literary criticism. The model for this subject was the literary critic Harold Bloom's "strong poet," who reads, challenges, redevelops the self-images of his own precursors. Strong poets, Rorty argued, have been the creative vanguard of modern Western culture, much like the special individuals who, for John Stuart Mill, lead by example, "discover new truths," and "commence new practices" (p. 64).

Unquestionably, such individuals are a cultural elite, and "ironism" is hardly a potential condition for all citizens; indeed, Rorty's own antifoundationalism would prevent such a collective generalization. But rather than presenting an idea of subjectivity applicable in all places at all times, Rorty was content to offer ideas about living as an intellectual in a *specific* place (the cosmopolitan West) at a *specific* time (the late twentieth century). As many critics noted, this refusal to universalize led to an essentially "conservative" political outlook, but not one advocating any conservative political movement—any Right, new or otherwise—but one dedicated to the conservation of present forms: Rorty wanted a situation-specific politics, to "defend the institutions and practices of the rich North Atlantic democracies." He clarified this position in an essay called "Postmodernist Bourgeois Liberalism" (1983): "postmodernist" because it refuted any transcendent story or "metanarrative" of social development (such as "the realization of Absolute Spirit in a People," or "the coming Dictatorship of the Proletariat"), and unabashedly "bourgeois" because Rorty acknowledged that these "institutions and practices are possible and justifiable only in certain historical, and especially economic, conditions" (pp. 198–9). Further, in much the same way as the ironist turns to exemplary strong poets for inspiration regarding self-fashioning, the liberal in politics can give up foundational theories of the Good Life and look instead to the history of reform in the West, to the ideals of abolitionism, feminism, civil rights, social democracy, and even some forms of anti-imperialism.

Rorty could not offer extrahistorical or extra-institutional "reasons" for collective interaction any more than he could refer to some subjective or epistemological *essence* as a basis for knowledge. Instead, perhaps fully ironic in the face of his own anti-foundationalism, he pointed to a sense of "solidarity": sympathetic responses to others' pain and humiliation, a humanistic common denominator that compels us to overlook difference without recourse to any binding theory of moral obligation. Bourgeois society, according to Rorty, has historically learned this sympathetic avoidance of cruelty from novels, which again underlines his basic claim for the pragmatic superiority of literary culture to a tradition of philosophical foundations.

PETER HANSEN

See also ENLIGHTENMENT; POSTMODERNISM.

FURTHER READING

Alan Malachowski, ed., *Reading Rorty* (Oxford: Blackwell, 1990).

John Stuart Mill, *On Liberty, and Other Writings*, ed. Stefan Collini (Cambridge: Cambridge University Press, 1989).

Richard Rorty, *Consequences of Pragmatism* (Minneapolis: University of Minnesota Press, 1982).

——, *Contingency, Irony, and Solidarity* (Cambridge: Cambridge University Press, 1989).

——, *Philosophy and the Mirror of Nature* (Princeton: Princeton University Press, 1979).

——, "Postmodernist Bourgeois Liberalism" (1983), in *Objectivity, Relativism, and Truth: Philosophical Papers*, vol. 1 (Cambridge: Cambridge University Press, 1991).

Rosenberg, Harold (b. Brooklyn, N.Y., Feb. 2, 1906; d. New York, N.Y., July 11, 1978). Art critic. One of the most influential of the critics who brought ABSTRACT EXPRESSIONISM to the public's attention, Rosenberg celebrated a new aesthetic based on the perception that art is not a representation of reality, but the reality of an artist's acts. Its significance, therefore, is not only in the artwork but in the activities that precede and follow it: the artist's creation and the viewers' re-creation of it, and by extension the entire historical tradition of production and reception. Art critic for the *New Yorker* (1967–78), Rosenberg also wrote *The Tradition of the New* (1959), *The Anxious Object* (1964), and *The De-definition of Art* (1972).

FURTHER READING

Jerome Klinkowitz, *Rosenberg, Barthes, Hassan: the Postmodern Habit of Thought* (Athens: University of Georgia Press, 1988).

Ross, E[dward] A[lsworth] (b. Virden, Ill., Dec. 12, 1866; d. Madison, Wis., July 22, 1951). Sociologist. Like many Progressives troubled by the individualist excesses of laissez-faire capitalism, Ross argued for social control of the individual for the good of all. Repudiating SOCIAL DARWINISM and unregulated competition, he held that a restrained but fruitful INDIVIDUALISM could still flourish in the midst of the necessary controls effected by public opinion and persuasion. Social sin—those systemic crimes for which no individual is responsible, such as food adulteration or child labor—must be combated by the appropriate legislation. Government and trained professionals should actively manage society through education and other forms of "social suggestion." Ross's major works are *Social Control* (1901) and *Sin and Society* (1907).

FURTHER READING

Dorothy Ross, *The Origins of American Social Science* (New York: Cambridge University Press, 1991).

Rowlandson, Mary (b. probably South Petherton, England, ca.1635; d. probably Wethersfield, Conn., after 1678). Captured by Indians, Rowlandson described the terror of traveling into a wilderness that, despite the Indians' occasional acts of friendliness, seemed to her unremittingly desolate and menacing. Her pervasive use of biblical imagery revealed both an intimate knowledge of Scripture and an interpretation of experience as divine providence. Submitting to God's chastening rod, Rowlandson presented her narrative as a story of redemption through absolute dependence on God. She was the author of *The Sovereignty and Goodness of God, Together with the Faithfulness of His Promises Displayed: Being a Narrative of the Captivity and Restauration of Mrs. Mary Rowlandson* (1682).

FURTHER READING

Mitchell Robert Breitweiser, *American Puritanism and the Defense of Mourning: Religion, Grief, and Ethnology in Mary White Rowlandson's Captivity Narrative* (Madison: University of Wisconsin Press, 1990).

Royce, Josiah (b. Grass Valley, Calif., Nov. 20, 1855; d. Cambridge, Mass., Sept. 14, 1916). The most influential American absolute Idealist, Royce also set the philosophical canon in the United States for decades in *The Spirit of Modern Philosophy* (1892). Troubled by the problem of evil or error, and resting squarely within the Western metaphysical heritage, Royce hoped to crack the code of codes organizing any and all of experience. Indeed, true to his architectonic ambitions, he investigated the latest moves in mathematics and logic in his effort to unlock the structure of consciousness and reality.

Royce was born in a frontier mining town and his life and thinking were indelibly marked by his understanding of moral predicaments in early California life, dilemmas he portrayed in a history, *California* (1886), and a novel, *Feud at Oakfield Creek* (1887). In both, he focused on the struggles of people committed to COMMUNITY trying to overcome threats of personal isolation, possessive individualism, mass mindlessness, and atavistic racism.

After schooling at Berkeley, Leipzig, Göttingen, and Johns Hopkins, Royce accepted an invitation from WILLIAM JAMES and George Herbert Palmer in 1882 to teach philosophy at Harvard. He remained in that post until he died, working alongside James, Palmer, Hugo Münsterburg, and his student GEORGE SANTAYANA during Harvard's philosophical "golden age."

Royce argued for a transcendental metaphysics that accommodated a pragmatic account of ideas as plans of action. Maintaining that humankind could be saved from a "chaos" of conflicting beliefs and purposes by finding an absolute standard of accountability, Royce tried to demonstrate, in *The Religious Aspect of Philosophy* (1885), that extreme skepticism disclosed absolute truth: he argued that, whether "There is error" is true or false, there is error, making the judgment absolutely true. What, then, Royce asked, makes error possible? To make an error, he claimed, is to make a judgment, or plan of action, that does not agree with, or realize, its object. When I make a judgment, I not only have an idea that resembles an object; I propose an idea that resembles an object that interests me. Suppose, more particularly, that I make a judgment about your thought. Given that "your thought" is my idea, don't I already know or possess it? But if this is so, how can I err about it? The answer, Royce claimed, lies in a difference in perspective. Error is possible because I may know your thought partially but not fully. For me to err, there must be some third person who actually has my conception of your thought along with your thought fully in mind and who, then, can check one against the other. Where my perspective on your thought, and vice versa, are partial, this third mind must be "all-inclusive," at once "Absolute Truth" and "Absolute Knowledge."

James was greatly impressed with this argumentation but, eventually, found it wanting, first because it left individuals and their thoughts "really" indistinguishable from "the whole"; second, because it made error or evil an aspect of truth or good; third because its image of knowledge as possession was counterproductive; and finally, because its transcendental claim about an all-inclusive mind added a level of legitimacy to beliefs that appeared to make no practical difference: the Absolute, James maintained, carried no more epistemic freight than a series of finite criticisms or verifications delivered.

Royce's skirmishes with James over "the Absolute," however, obscured the fact that the two men shared important philosophical views—enough for Royce, eventually, to characterize his position as *absolute pragmatism*. For example, both philosophers repudiated the philosophical importance of "the given": experience came interpreted; "ideas" and theories were plans of action which must be tested by the course of experience.

In *The Conception of God* (1897) and *The World and the Individual* (1899–1900), Royce put to use current mathematical and logical inquiries on infinite systems in an effort to do two things: (1) answer the charge that his absolutism provided no adequate account of free individual life, and (2) reconcile science and religion, by showing that the scientist's world of finite descriptions was really a world of appreciation or infinite self-realizing purpose. On the first score, Royce argued, against James and George Howison, that individuals and the Absolute were connected in the same way that portions of a "self-representative system" were connected to the whole system. Individuals were irreplaceable parts or fragments of the Absolute. On the second score Royce argued, against F. H. Bradley's *Appearance and Reality* (1893), that there was a way to comprehend infinite reality. The infinite and divine unifying purpose behind any and all finite scientific descriptions, whether of persons or things, was self-representation or self-knowledge or self-possession. Royce virtually acknowledged, however, that his effort to warrant this view of an actual infinite in terms of the logic of well-ordered series was, on his own grounds, a failure.

In *The Philosophy of Loyalty* (1908), *The Sources of Religious Insight* (1912), and *The Problem of Christianity* (1913), Royce brought his "pragmatism" to the fore by making, first, solidarity rather than objectivity the purpose informing conscious activity, and, second, interpretive community, rather than the Absolute, the key to realizing that end. Utilizing the doctrine of signs introduced by CHARLES SANDERS PEIRCE, Royce pictured divinity as an infinite social process of interpretation that mediates between dangerously opposed pairs (for instance, of opinion or action) by clarifying what they share. Apart from such community, he claimed, individuals are lost or detached or self-willed. He construed this process as operating unidirectionally and irreversibly toward an absolute convergence of purpose (and knowledge) among selves. Moreover, he argued that this "will to interpret," informing communities of memory and hope, was no arbitrary human invention or decision, but was hard-wired into the ways of the world.

Even before the outbreak of the Great War, this communitarian idealism began to seem quaint. While pragmatists like Dewey and naturalists like Santayana joined Royce in construing interpretation as "the main business of philosophy," they accepted the findings of natural scientists about the ways of the world and lost all interest in searching for some supposed metaphysical backup or structure authorizing this or that form of discourse.

Currently, some religious philosophers (notably Cornel West) look to Royce for an account of interpretation that facilitates social solidarity. Otherwise, philosophers now lack all but historical interest in Royce's work.

HENRY SAMUEL LEVINSON

FURTHER READING
John Clendenning, *The Life and Thought of Josiah Royce* (Madison: University of Wisconsin Press, 1985).
——, *The Letters of Josiah Royce* (Chicago: University of Chicago Press, 1968).
Bruce Kuklick, *Josiah Royce: an Intellectual Biography* (Indianapolis: Bobbs-Merrill, 1972).
——, *The Rise of American Philosophy* (New Haven: Yale University Press, 1977).
John J. McDermott, ed., *The Basic Writings of Josiah Royce*, 2 vols. (Chicago: University of Chicago Press, 1968).
Murray Murphey, "Kant's Children: the Cambridge Pragmatists," *Transactions of the Charles S. Peirce Society* 4 (1968): 3–33.
Frank M. Oppenheim, *Royce's Mature Philosophy of Religion* (Notre Dame: University of Notre Dame Press, 1987).
Daniel S. Robinson, ed., *Royce's Logical Essays* (Dubuque: William C. Brown, 1951).
John E. Smith, *Royce's Social Infinite* (New York: Liberal Arts, 1950).

Rush, Benjamin (b. Byberry, Pa., Jan. 4, 1746; d. Philadelphia, Pa., Apr. 19, 1813). Doctor, philosopher, and reformer, Benjamin Rush was one of the most fascinating members of an extraordinary generation of American Revolutionaries. Best known as a pioneer of medicine and psychiatry in the United States, he was also a signer of the Declaration of Independence and physician to the Continental Army. Perhaps more important, Rush was a revolutionary social thinker whose own addition to the ferment of thought about the American future addressed problems relatively untouched by the great Constitution-makers. He emphasized the need not only to create a republican political structure, but also to transform everyday assumptions, manners, and morals so that common Americans would honor and defend the Republic. Toward that end, Rush developed a remarkable agenda for social and personal change: antislavery, temperance, abolition of war, abolition of the death penalty, humane treatment of criminals and the insane, and educational reform.

Born just outside of Philadelphia, Rush was steeped in the vivid providential legacy of the GREAT AWAKENING. He and his mother (his father died when Rush was five) attended the church of the Awakening minister, Gilbert Tennent. At age eight Rush boarded at the school of the Reverend Samuel Finley, whose sermon *Christ Triumphing, and Satan Raging* (1741) argued that the Awakening's revivals and the opposition they engendered signified nothing less than the prophesied battle between the forces of God and the Devil that would precede the millennium. Finally, at age 14, Rush entered the College of New Jersey (now Princeton), presided over by another Awakener, the Reverend Samuel Davies. Late in 1760, after consultation with Davies and Finley, Rush chose a career in medicine. Six years after beginning his apprenticeship, he traveled to Edinburgh for further training in medicine.

Meanwhile, tensions between England and the colonies had erupted in the Stamp Act Crisis of 1765. Rush had supported the colonial position. While in Scotland, fellow students exposed him to doctrines that made sense of the colonial cause—Common Sense philosophy and REPUBLICANISM. He embraced these ideas with religious fervor, forging their insights with those of medicine and millennial Christianity into an increasingly unified social vision. Thus, even before the AMERICAN REVOLUTION, Rush responded to the pleas of his friend Anthony Benezet, a Quaker antislavery activist, with *An Address to the Inhabitants of the British Settlements in America, upon Slave-Keeping* (1773), in which he combined economic and common sense moral arguments with visions of America's republican destiny and threats of God's vengeance should slavery continue.

When independence and war came, Rush worked tirelessly as a member of the Continental Congress and as medical adviser to the army to improve the health of the patriot army. He applied to the patriot cause the same unflinching self-scrutiny that informed his antislavery pamphlet. He sought in the actions of individual Americans a virtue as perfect as his dream of millennial republican revolution.

Thus, when the war was won, Rush only occasionally succumbed to optimism about the future. He worried his way through the years of the Confederation, and even with the Constitution in hand he predicted momentous tasks ahead. "There is nothing more common than to confound the terms of *American Revolution* with those of *the late American war*," Rush noted in 1787. "The American war is over: but this is far from being the case with the American Revolution" (quoted by D'Elia, p. 5). Republican political structures in place, the American people must now be reeducated to their very fiber with the habits and values of republican VIRTUE. Rush devoted much of the remainder of his life to this task.

Rush based his Republican vision on a scientific doctrine that lay at the core of his medical system: environmentalism. He argued that although the capacity for choosing good over evil was innate in humans, its development was deeply affected by the outer environment and the condition of the body in which it was housed. Clarity of thought and, ultimately, the choice for republican virtue instead of profligacy depended upon exposure to correct ideas and upon a disciplined nurturing of those ideas by the proper diet, choice of drinks, style of labor, amount of sleep, and degree of cleanliness. The individual must also be exposed to proper preaching, correct medicine, and moral forms of punishment and government.

In the late 1780s and 1790s Rush drew visionary blueprints for just such a republican environment. He felt that EDUCATION was crucial, and created plans for systems—from the field school to the university level—which were to train "men, citizens, and Christians" rather than "scholars," and indeed to "convert men into republican machines" (*Selected Writings*, p. 92). He argued that schools should teach an "American language with propriety and grace" so as to create pride in the new country (p. 93). He included complementary plans for female education in republican virtue, for he saw women as in some ways the most important educators. He recommended that educational games replace combative ones in the school yard, and that punishments as well move from the corporal to the educational. As for personal habits, Rush combined medical and sociological proofs in arguing against alcohol. He showed that drink might doom the moral fabric of society. Rush produced temperance pamphlets whose influence would stretch through the mid-nineteenth century. And he continued his war against slavery.

Rush predicated his program on the maintenance of selfless commitment to community, a notion sorely tested by the rise of the party system, the debate over the Embargo and the War of 1812. Indeed, Rush died fearing that the republican experiment had failed. Yet he left as his legacy a way of thinking about republican virtue and specific social issues that deeply influenced later nineteenth-century reformers. And he posed questions about the preservation of political and social values in a democracy that still haunt us today.

ROBERT H. ABZUG

FURTHER READING

Robert H. Abzug, *Cosmos Crumbling: American Reform and the Religious Imagination* (New York: Oxford University Press, 1994).

Carl Binger, *Revolutionary Doctor: Benjamin Rush, 1746–1813* (New York: Norton, 1966).

Donald J. D'Elia, *Benjamin Rush: Philosopher of the American Revolution*, Transactions of the American Philosophical Society, n.s., 64, pt 5 (Philadelphia, 1974).

David Freeman Hawke, *Benjamin Rush: Revolutionary Gad-fly* (Indianapolis: Bobbs-Merrill, 1971).

Benjamin Rush, *The Selected Writings of Benjamin Rush*, ed. Dagobart D. Runes (New York, 1947).

——, *Letters of Benjamin Rush*, ed. L. H. Butterfield, 2 vols. (Princeton: Princeton University Press, 1951).

Melvin Yazawa, *From Colonies to Commonwealth: Familial Ideology and the Beginnings of the American Republic* (Baltimore: Johns Hopkins University Press, 1985).

Ryan, John A. (b. Vermillion, Minn., May 25, 1869; d. St. Paul, Minn., Sept. 16, 1945).   Ethicist. Author of *A Living Wage: Its Ethical and Economic Aspects* (1906) and *Distributive Justice: the Right and Wrong of Our Present Distribution of Wealth* (1916), Monsignor Ryan invoked Roman Catholic ideas of natural law and a corporatist society to reform capitalism. He tried to combine a defense of the rights of private property with a campaign for economic justice and the full development of personality. A major proponent of minimum wage laws in the 1930s, he advocated redistribution of income and wealth and envisioned an industrial DEMOCRACY organized by guildlike structures within occupations. Though in principle he supported labor organizations, he relied primarily upon government legislation to achieve justice for working people.

FURTHER READING

Patrick Gearty, *The Economic Thought of Monsignor John A. Ryan* (Washington, D.C.: Catholic University of America Press, 1953).

S

Sandburg, Carl (b. Galesburg, Ill., Jan. 6, 1878; d. Flat Rock, N.C., July 22, 1967).   Writer and poet. Sandburg's early adulthood continued the itinerancy he had known since joining the workforce at age 11. He served in Puerto Rico during the Spanish–American War, worked his way through Lombard College, wrote for newspapers, and was secretary to the Socialist mayor of Milwaukee. In 1913 he moved to Chicago and his poetry, collected in *Chicago Poems* (1916), established him as an original lyric voice in the tradition of Whitman. His later work, poetry and prose, celebrated colloquial speech, folk music, and the virtue of the American people. His most important books were *The People, Yes* (1936) and a six-volume biography of Abraham Lincoln (1926–39). Sandburg's autobiography appeared in two volumes, *Always the Young Stranger* (1953) and *Ever the Winds of Chance* (1983).

FURTHER READING
Penelope Niven, *Carl Sandburg: a Biography* (New York: Charles Scribner's Sons, 1991).

Sanger, Margaret (b. Corning, N.Y., Sept. 14, 1879; d. Tucson, Ariz., Sept. 6, 1966).   Reformer. Early influenced by socialist and feminist thought, Sanger championed the right of all women to control their sexual and reproductive lives. Advocating the diaphragm, which put birth control in the control of women, she founded a magazine, *The Woman Rebel* (1914, later titled *Birth Control Review*), and wrote several pamphlets and books, including the notorious *Family Limitation* (1914) and *What Every Mother Should Know* (1917). She was prosecuted in 1915 for sending birth control information through the mail, and opened a birth control clinic in 1916 as an act of civil disobedience. Angered by the left's lack of interest in the cause, she embarked on a campaign for legalization and founded the American Birth Control League in 1921. She began to attract mainstream support only when she adopted eugenicist arguments about "better babies" and endorsed the idea of physicians dispensing birth control information and supplies.

FURTHER READING
Ellen Chesler, *Woman of Valor: Margaret Sanger and the Birth Control Movement in America* (New York: Simon and Schuster, 1992).

Santayana, George (b. Madrid, Spain, Dec. 16, 1863; d. Rome, Italy, Sept. 26, 1952).   Transplanted from Spain to Boston at the age of eight, and educated at the Boston Latin School and Harvard College, Santayana went on to graduate study in philosophy at Harvard and in Europe. At the age of 25 he was appointed assistant professor at Harvard, joining WILLIAM JAMES and JOSIAH ROYCE in the preeminent philosophy department of the time. Awarded tenure in 1897, Santayana abruptly and permanently left Harvard and America in 1912.

"He was able to laugh at us without despising us, a feat often too intricate for the native-born," remarks Richard Rorty of Santayana in *Consequences of Pragmatism* (p. 60). His Spanish Catholicism and philosophical materialism found little sustenance, spiritual or intellectual, in America's genteel Protestant culture. As Santayana wrote in his famous essay on "The Genteel Tradition in American Philosophy," America combined the "agonized conscience" of a residual Calvinist GUILT with Emersonian idealism's "systematic subjectivism" (pp. 38, 41). The result was an ascetic culture of compulsive work and sexual prohibition that arrogantly believed itself the world's pinnacle of enlightened progress.

One of the most influential men of letters in the first half of the twentieth century, Santayana's reputation went into eclipse for 35 years after his death. But in the last half-dozen years Santayana has enjoyed something of a renaissance, sparked by the ongoing publication of a 19-volume definitive edition of his work and by the still compelling intellectual power of his analysis of the genteel tradition. Besides the seminal essay of that title, his anatomy of the genteel can be found in *Character and Opinion in the United States* (1920), *Persons and Places* (1944–53), and *The Last Puritan*, his bestselling novel of 1936.

Santayana's prolonged, nearly obsessive campaign against the genteel is far from merely a philosophic critique; rather, it is inseparable from his personal sense of suffocation. He was able to find air only by resigning from Harvard and from America and taking up the life of the perpetual stranger. His 1912 EXPATRIATION is perhaps the most elaborately calculated estrangement in American intellectual history: he ended his 23-year professorial career, spending his remaining 40 years in Europe (largely in England

and Italy), never once returning to America. England, France, and Italy would be the scene of his temporary, makeshift residences, usually of one or two rooms in a hotel until, in his last ten years, he lived in a small room with a narrow bed in the Hospital of the Blue Nuns in Rome. Five valises and nine cases of books and papers made up the sum of his worldly possessions. In his autobiography *Persons and Places*, Santayana explains this minimalism as enacting a movement "from the temporal to the eternal," a "platonic transition . . . from the many to the one, from the existent but transitory to the ideal and eternal" (pp. 423, 426).

Given his impenetrable pride and commitment to impersonality, Santayana leaves unsaid the fact that his refusal of the compulsive heterosexuality of the period had forced him into a closeted existence. Instead, in his autobiography he seeks to convince himself and us that his expatriation was the product of perfect equanimity, without a trace of psychological or social coercion.

Santayana's personal investment in lordly, suave, unruffled poise reflects his "hard non-humanistic naturalism" which, as he says in a letter, venerates the greatness of nonpurposive, inscrutable nature, after the manner of "the old Ionians or the Stoics or Spinoza" (*Letters*, p. 408). Santayana's NATURALISM posits as its "forming perception," says Lionel Trilling, "the discontinuity between man and the world" (p. 161). And this antisubjectivism, contends Trilling, in an influential essay of 1956, is what Americans "fear" in Santayana, and explains why dislike of him in America is "endemic and almost inevitable," so that he must be "hustled off into the limbo" we reserve for "'aristocratic critics of American democracy'" (p. 156). Appropriately, our contemporary age of antihumanism has come to appreciate Santayana.

Under Santayana's withering, virtually wholesale indictment, subjectivism, idealism, moralism, transcendentalism, egotism, pragmatism, and absolutism are arraigned as modes of the genteel tradition in philosophy. In his eyes they are all guilty of the intellectual defect he identified, in his essay "Dewey's Naturalist Metaphysics," as the "dominance of the foreground," an imbalance that occurs when "some local perspective or some casual interest is set up in the place of universal nature or behind it, or before it, so that all the rest of nature is reputed to be intrinsically remote or dubious or merely ideal" (p. 115). This mistaking of the local for the universal is not only the source of metaphysics but of humanism. The latter doctrine has driven man to repudiate arrogantly his animal status for the "Satanic

dream that we [are] creators and not creatures," he writes in his important essay "Americanism" (p. 202).

Neither cynical nor relativist, Santayana's non-humanistic naturalism is historicist, for it challenges the narcissism implicit in the romantic or Emersonian effort to make man divine and make nature his mirror. Santayana's suspicion of such arrogant egotism extends to his critique of AMERICAN EXCEPTIONALISM, which remains one of his most lasting contributions to American thought. The particular focus of his critique is the liberal intellectual (beginning with his colleague William James) whose self-pity, impotent self-righteousness and "offended sensibility" lead him to lament the sins of imperialism and capitalism while taking refuge in the moral purity of an oppositional stance. To puncture the delusions of exceptionalism in all its guises is a perpetually necessary task. Because few performed it more brilliantly than Santayana, his epochal critique of the genteel tradition will always be vital.

ROSS POSNOCK

See also AESTHETICS.

FURTHER READING

Henry Levinson, *Santayana, Pragmatism, and the Spiritual Life* (Chapel Hill: University of North Carolina Press, 1992).

John McCormick, *George Santayana: a Biography* (New York: Knopf, 1986).

Richard Rorty, *Consequences of Pragmatism* (Minneapolis: University of Minnesota Press, 1982).

George Santayana, *The Last Puritan: a Memoir in the Form of a Novel* (New York: Scribner's, 1936).

——, *The Letters of George Santayana*, ed. Daniel Cory (New York: Scribner's, 1955).

——, "Americanism," "Dewey's Naturalist Metaphysics," and "The Genteel Tradition in American Philosophy," all in Richard Lyon, ed., *Santayana on America: Essays, Notes and Letters on American Life, Literature, and Philosophy* (New York: Harcourt, Brace, 1968).

——, *Persons and Places: Fragments of Autobiography* (Cambridge: MIT Press, 1986).

Lionel Trilling, "That Smile of Parmenides Made Me Think," in *A Gathering of Fugitives* (Boston: Beacon, 1956).

Sapir, Edward (b. Lauenburg, Germany, Jan. 26, 1884; d. New Haven, Conn., Feb. 4, 1939). Anthropologist and linguist. Sapir's early fieldwork on Native American languages led him to emphasize the importance of native intuition and to formulate the study of phonemes: how native speakers cluster sounds as "same" or "different." People do not, he argued, perceive the world "objectively," but through the categories embedded in their languages. Anthropology should be an interdisciplinary study of human beings that relates psychology and social structure, aesthetics and economics, personality and culture. Also the author of published verse, Sapir is best known for his *Language: an Introduction to the Study of Speech* (1921).

FURTHER READING
Regna Darnell, *Edward Sapir: Linguist, Anthropologist, Humanist* (Berkeley: University of California Press, 1990).

Schlesinger, Arthur M., Jr. (b. Columbus, Ohio, Oct. 15, 1917). Historian. Believing that political and scholarly pursuits are compatible in the life of a citizen, Schlesinger has studied periods of reform in American history and put his insights to contemporary use as a Democratic speechwriter and chronicler of the Kennedys. As an adviser to John F. Kennedy, he called for a pragmatic LIBERALISM that seeks gradual change and rests upon a responsibly chastened view of the limits of human nature and history. In the 1990s he entered the debate over CULTURAL PLURALISM AND MULTICULTURALISM with *The Disuniting of America: Reflections on a Multicultural Society* (1992), a strong plea for cultivating a core tradition of democratic values. His other major works include *The Age of Jackson* (1945), *The Vital Center* (1949), *The Age of Roosevelt* (3 vols., 1957–60), and *A Thousand Days: John F. Kennedy in the White House* (1965).

FURTHER READING
Marcus Cunliffe, "Arthur M. Schlesinger, Jr.," in Cunliffe and Robin Winks, eds., *Pastmasters* (New York: Harper and Row, 1969).

Schoolcraft, Henry Rowe (b. Albany County, N.Y., Mar. 28, 1793; d. Washington, D.C., Dec. 10, 1864). Ethnologist. After serving as Indian Agent in the Lake Superior region and superintendent of Indian Affairs for Michigan from 1836 to 1841, Schoolcraft became one of the leading ethnologists of the nineteenth century. His two-volume *Algic Researches* (1839) presented the myths and legends of the Algonquins, while *Onéota* (1844–5) was an encyclopedic compilation of data on Indian culture. *Notes on the Iroquois* (1846) reflected hopefully on the prospect of bringing white civilization to the Iroquois. But in his richly detailed six-volume *Historical and Statistical Information Respecting the History, Condition, and Prospects of the Indian Tribes of the United States* (1851–7), Schoolcraft concluded that Indian cultures were doomed by their stubborn resistance to Christianity and agriculture.

FURTHER READING
Richard G. Bremer, *Indian Agent and Wilderness Scholar: the Life of Henry Rowe Schoolcraft* (Mount Pleasant: Clarke Historical Library, Central Michigan University, 1987).

Schumpeter, Joseph (b. Triesch, Moravia, Feb. 8, 1883; d. Taconic, Conn., Jan. 8, 1950). Lawyer and economist. An émigré from Germany in 1932, Schumpeter took a position of Harvard upon arrival in America. His important *Theory of Economic Development* (1911) appeared in English in 1934. Though an economy tends toward stasis, Schumpeter explained, intermittent spontaneous innovations cause change. Clusters of innovation create economic booms; depression is a movement toward a new equilibrium. In *Capitalism, Socialism, and Democracy* (1942), Schumpeter argued that capitalism is destroying itself as entrepreneurship becomes bureaucratized and ownership becomes abstracted into shareholding without moral or political allegiances. Government policy has created a managed economy that threatens to slip into a state capitalism largely indistinguishable from socialism.

FURTHER READING
David L. McKee, *Schumpeter and the Political Economy of Change* (New York: Praeger, 1991).

Schurz, Carl (b. Liblar, Germany, Mar. 2, 1829; d. New York, N.Y., May 14, 1906). Political leader, journalist, orator. As a German revolutionary (1848–9), United States Senator (1869–75), Secretary of the Interior (1877–81), and member of the staff of the New York *Evening Post* (1881–3) and *Harper's Weekly* (1892–8), Schurz expressed an ideological commitment to REPUBLICANISM. He campaigned for Lincoln in 1860, argued for freedmen's suffrage, and attacked the Grant administration for corruption. Editor of newspapers in Detroit and St. Louis after the Civil War, he helped form the Liberal Republican movement in 1872. As Secretary of the Interior, he tried to reform Indian policy. As a New York journalist, he pushed civil service reform and joined the ranks of the anti-imperialists in 1898—on the grounds that republican principles of self-determination prohibited such imperial acts as the annexation of the Philippines.

See also IMPERIALISM AND ANTI-IMPERIALISM.

FURTHER READING
Hans L. Trefousse, *Carl Schurz: a Biography* (Knoxville: University of Tennessee Press, 1982).

science Tying science to a specifically American context is a problematic task. Many philosophers and scientists have long asserted that one defining characteristic of scientific knowledge has been its universality. A more historically grounded, yet still powerful, objection to emphasis on national categories in the analysis of science has come from consideration of the longstanding international character of scientific communities and communication networks.

In spite of these doubts, historians have explored the specifically American in science. There have clearly been American sciences—areas of knowledge developed largely in the United States, either because of geographic specificity in subject-matter (as in historical geology or the sociology of ethnicity), or as a consequence of localized intellectual entrepreneurship (clinical biochemistry, experimental psychology, and particle physics, for example). The question of an American "style" of science—marked by empiricism, faith in instruments, or cooperation—has been examined in some depth. Lastly, there is a large genre that could be termed "science and . . . " investigations: examinations of the interactions of science with philosophy, religion, political theory, or other analogous intellectual categories.

These studies of aspects of American science have illuminated much intellectual territory, but they have not successfully countered the arguments—whether philosophical or sociological—that the universality of science has made it an exceptional area within American intellectual history. Such studies have either been limited in chronological or topical coverage, or they have focused on issues professedly incidental to science itself. To appreciate more deeply the national cultural specificity of science we need a chronologically full and conceptually comprehensive history of "American science." We can get further with such a project if, instead of beginning with analytic abstractions about what the characteristics of science were and the degree to which Americans exhibited them, we historicize the category of American science itself as fully as possible.

What follows is a sketch of the career of the meaning of "American science" during the last two centuries. It has always been an important category for those Americans engaged with science, and yet the degree of its articulation was often inhibited by the belief that it was fundamentally an oxymoron. As a result there were quite different assertions both about how real it was and whether it was primarily a matter of ideas, behaviors, or social groups. How broad was the domain of American science, and to what degree was it a single entity? Who were its representatives? Was it something to cultivate, or should its particularity be eliminated? Amidst the wide diversity of opinion on these issues, it is possible to discern four particularly prominent, historically sequential, interpretations of American science. They have provided the focus for much of the professional historical literature in the area during the last generation; together they illuminate the boundaries around

that literature. American science apparently is in the process of entering a new phase; one consequence is that the future for historical writing is unusually open.

Through most of the eighteenth and nineteenth centuries, the most common view was that American science was the sum total of knowledge held by Americans. This perspective motivated Franklin, Jefferson, and the socially mixed membership of the American Philosophical Society during the early years of the Republic. It predominated in the semi-eponymous *Scientific American*, the most widely circulated technical periodical in the decades around 1850. John Harley Warner has explored how it undergirded the behavior of most nineteenth-century physicians. It provided the cultural framework within which middle-class Americans studied, heard lectures, and participated in local learned societies.

Describing this phase of American science as "Baconian" is not inaccurate, but it gives too narrowly philosophical a character to a deeply held but diffuse set of beliefs. Knowledge was fundamentally an individual possession, which could be gained through a range of avenues—from books and formal study to apprenticeship and the lessons of practice. The scientific domain was extensive, encompassing not only mathematics and knowledge of the natural world, but also "mechanical science" and the moral sciences. In spite of this dispersal and breadth, Americans' knowledge gelled into American science through its indefinite exchangeability, whether through personal contacts, publications, or products; this network of transfers was maintained through faith in utility, which ranged from self-improvement and support for religion to increase in individual wealth and aid to national expansion. There were major disagreements—most prominently among medical practitioners—about the value of the various elements of knowledge, and the relative importance of accumulation, systematization, and engagement with particulars, but these did not affect the underlying consensus that Americans did possess knowledge and that such knowledge comprised American science.

In the two decades around 1850, a small, coherent elite developed a conception of American science much narrower than that which was generally accepted. Alexander Dallas Bache, JOSEPH HENRY, and their associates formed the vanguard of American scientific professionalizers. As such they sought secure jobs and recognized status for a small number of "men of science"; they also sought to organize national projects and to participate in, and regulate access to, the international networks they identified with the most important science in Western Europe. The leading professionalizer Bache also had a broader political aim: to build an objectified national hierarchy within the formal egalitarianism of post-Jacksonian society. (*See also* PROFESSIONS.)

The new professionals' highly visible campaign on behalf of American science involved mobilization of financial support, imposition of standards, and creation of national organizations such as the American Association for the Advancement of Science and the National Academy of Sciences. What is retrospectively most remarkable, however, is the lack of intellectual content in their program. They were trapped by their paradoxical provincial belief that American science existed insofar as it was, with the exception of particular facts about the American continent, essentially indistinguishable from contemporary European developments; as a consequence, they had little interest in emphasizing originality, with its attendant problem of singularity. Moreover, in their desire to facilitate the display of distinctions between individuals, they dramatically narrowed the domain and limited the activities associated with science. The result was a privileging of "exact science," characterized by precision measurement of simple quantities by specially trained observers. The culmination of this subordination of content to method can be seen in the career of the astronomer SIMON NEWCOMB: his long-term project to refine the tables of planetary motion, his public articulation of the values of exact science, his destructive critiques of reformist economic ideas, and his extensive international ties combined to make him the leader of American science during the last decades of the nineteenth century.

By the turn of the century, however, a third conception of American science was beginning to take hold: American science as the enterprise centered around original research. By contrast with either knowledge or measurement, research was a difficult basis for an entity with national scope. Something whose value derived from what was not known, whose realization lay in the future, and whose focus was continually in flux could be claimed by anyone and ascertained by no one. The universities, by providing physical plant, tenure, modes of certification, hierarchy, and procedures for teaching discovery, formed the framework necessary to make such a conceptualization persuasive and manageable. They provided the core from which the research ethos spread to government, private foundations, and a few corporate centers.

The identification of American science with the activity of research gave it a focus and an importance it had not had earlier. Research mediated between individual desires and the public good. It sanctioned

moves beyond emulation of European activities and the pursuit of subjects and ideas that were sometimes culturally distinctive. Moreover, it enabled scientists to appropriate crucial late nineteenth-century elements of the national mythology—on the one hand, the recently discovered American tradition of exploration, and on the other the aura of wizardry associated with technical innovators such as Thomas Edison and Luther Burbank.

Both the breadth and potential cultural penetration of American science increased in the early twentieth century. Organizations ranging from the Department of Agriculture to the American Telephone and Telegraph Company placed research at the center of national identity and presented it as the basis for the nation's future. The model of experimental investigation was easily extended from natural sciences to SOCIAL SCIENCE, the technical professions, and even into education. JOHN DEWEY represented the furthest extension of the research ideal in his argument that American science provided the model for all intelligent behavior. Yet as the research ethos tied American science to the promise of American life, it became disconnected from specific claims about the nature of the world. The Scopes trial of 1925 and the controversy over teaching the theory of natural selection, for example, demonstrated how wide was the gap between faith in science's future and acceptance of scientists' statements in the early twentieth century. (*See also* DARWINISM.)

In the middle third of the twentieth century, research was subsumed into a grander framework: the claim that American science was the instantiation of science itself. Foundation patronage for basic projects, the relative decline of the European economies, the migration of prominent central European thinkers to the U.S. in the 1930s, and the new partnership between scientists and the military in the 1940s produced an enterprise of unprecedented scale, scope, and status. The United States became the center for world scientific culture and the focal point for intellectual advancement.

Although anything distinctively American in science remained invisible, science clearly was important for the country's identity and future. It represented, even more effectively than abstract expressionism in art, the arrival of the United States at the forefront of civilization. Science's ability to generate new military technology made it central to the defense of freedom in the Cold War. It offered, in the words of Vannevar Bush, an "endless frontier" in which Americans' exploratory impulses and their search for material improvement could both be satisfied; this image was concretized in the space programs of the

1960s. Scientific communities, Robert K. Merton argued, provided the model for rational democratic decision-making. Yet these benefits derived from universal science realized in the United States. The nation's provincial scientific past was important only insofar as it provided a physical and attitudinal infrastructure.

This universalist vision of American science has been in retreat since the 1960s. The close ties between scientists and the state in the pursuit of military power were increasingly seen as a very particular and problematic situation. The result of controversies over nuclear power and recombinant DNA was the formal subordination of expert decision-making to democratic politics. The public remained indifferent and even hostile to the claim that science formed the intellectual basis for modern culture.

Still, the possibility that a new conception of American science might be replacing its identification with universalism has only become conceivable with the apparent ending of both the Cold War and American global economic hegemony. A more open international regime may result in the decoupling of science and national security, and thence to a smaller, more pluralist image of American science, more explicitly oriented to TECHNOLOGY. Such a change would offer the usual mix of challenge and opportunity to historians. The historiography of American science has revolved around uncovering infrastructure and searching for particularity; as such, it has been tied almost completely to the development and critique of universalism. The future may offer the more constructive project of understanding the multiplicity of possibilities that American science has had and may offer.

PHILIP J. PAULY

See also THOMAS S. KUHN; OBJECTIVITY; SCIENTISM AND COGNITIVISM.

FURTHER READING
Robert V. Bruce, *The Launching of Modern American Science* (New York: Knopf, 1987).
George H. Daniels, *Science in American Society: a Social History* (New York: Knopf, 1971).
Daniel J. Kevles, *The Physicists: the History of a Scientific Community in Modern America* (New York: Knopf, 1978).
Sally Gregory Kohlstedt and Margaret W. Rossiter, eds., *Historical Writing on American Science: Perspectives and Prospects* (Baltimore: Johns Hopkins University Press, 1986).
Philip J. Pauly, *Controlling Life: Jacques Loeb and the Engineering Ideal in Biology* (New York: Oxford University Press, 1987).
Nathan Reingold, *Science, American Style* (New Brunswick, N.J.: Rutgers University Press, 1991).
Charles E. Rosenberg, *No Other Gods: On Science and American Social Thought* (Baltimore: Johns Hopkins University Press, 1976).

John Harley Warner, *The Therapeutic Perspective: Medical Practice, Knowledge, and Identity in America, 1820–1885* (Cambridge: Harvard University Press, 1986).

Scientism and cognitivism Intellectual movements said to partake of "scientism" are usually felt to exaggerate the cultural and social value of the modes of thought developed and prominently displayed by practitioners of the modern physical and biological sciences. The stronger the claim that these attitudes and methods can instruct political, social, religious, and cultural practice, the more "scientistic" the maker of the claim. Although the concept of scientism is occasionally invoked neutrally, to denote confidence in the importance of natural knowledge, the concept owes its currency to a discourse critical of the pretensions of SCIENCE. Some aspects of human life are beyond the scope of science, it is said, or are vulnerable to distortion or destruction if treated scientifically. According to such critics, movements that stretch science beyond its appropriate limits are not truly scientific, but scientistic.

Whatever one may take to be the limits of science, and whatever principles one may invoke to determine these limits, a generous view of science was a vital historical reality in late nineteenth-century and twentieth-century America. The fountainhead of this hopeful perspective on science was the ENLIGHTENMENT of the eighteenth century, with its confidence in the liberating and ameliorating potential of the systematic application of human intelligence to the social as well as the natural world. Among the most powerful vehicles for this confidence throughout the North Atlantic West were the works of a number of European thinkers of the early and mid-nineteenth century, including Auguste Comte, Karl Marx, and John Stuart Mill. But in the United States it was only in the wake of the controversy about DARWINISM that the movements destined to be characterized as scientistic flourished on a formidable scale. Darwin's explanation of the origin of species and of the descent of humankind in terms of purely naturalistic agencies dramatized as no previous event had been able to do the potential of science to address questions previously taken by most American Protestants to be well outside its scope.

Beginning in the 1870s, American intellectuals with a great variety of concerns proclaimed their adherence to a "scientific" way of doing things. Efforts proliferated to put theology, business, and public administration on a scientific basis (*see* MANAGERIALISM). Movements to create social scientific disciplines and to build universities designed to sustain research gained enormous momentum, and by World War I had established the world's most imposing complex of disciplinary organizations, laboratories, and doctoral programs. Although some of the men and women who propelled these movements were disciples of Comte and called themselves "positivists," enthusiasm for scientific remedies and reforms was much broader and more diffuse than the influence of Comtean positivism. Champions of PRAGMATISM in philosophy and PROGRESSIVISM in politics often saw their projects as the flowering, in their own fields of endeavor, of science. The first American writer to win a Nobel Prize, SINCLAIR LEWIS, achieved his greatest critical triumph with a novel of 1925 that offered scientific method as an ethical model for modern society. It was an index of the range and depth of science's appeal that a prophet of social planning as radical as LESTER FRANK WARD and a defender of laissez-faire as conservative as WILLIAM GRAHAM SUMNER could both insist that science provided the unique authority for their opinions.

Although these varieties of enthusiasm for science waxed and waned in a multitude of specific discursive contexts during the remainder of the twentieth century, a difficulty in identifying scientism and in determining its historical significance has been the largely invidious connotation of the very concept of scientism itself. Even if it is easily granted that many strivings toward a scientific culture have been naive by almost any standard accepted by leading thinkers today, the concept of scientism guides historians only toward the most easily ridiculed manifestations of this historic aspiration. Hence some historians have begun to use a noninvidious term, "cognitivism," to refer to this aspiration.

The core of the concept of cognitivism is the human "knower," the person who attends to truths ostensibly discovered rather than divined. The sense of "scientific knowledge" implied here is more that of the broad German notion of *Wissenschaft* than of the more narrow English term, "science." Knowing, in this view, is secular, methodical, and empirical. Excluded are whatever truths one might claim on the basis of religious experience, poetic insight, speculation, common sense, or practical but undisciplined experience in the workaday world. *Wissenschaftliche* knowers draw upon a world of reference, rather than seeking to create culture out of their own subjectivity. It is faith in the potential of such knowers to contribute significantly to culture—rather than simply to provide technical information—that identifies cognitivism.

So considered, cognitivism is broader than, but no less specific than, a host of closely related "isms" that do not quite coincide with it. The various meanings

of NATURALISM, for example, converge in the idea that a given phenomenon is to be explained in terms of the order of nature, rather than in terms of spiritual efficacy or cultural traditions. Many cognitivists are also naturalists, but naturalism takes its sense from nature, not from any distinctive human enterprise. Naturalism, moreover, is often taken to refer to a biocentric reductionism that minimizes the qualities that distinguish humans from other animals. POSITIVISM more directly addresses knowledge as a foundation for culture, but prominent among the many variations of positivism are tendencies to radically restrict the sphere of knowledge, to separate knowledge sharply from any object of cognition, and to associate faith in science with the specific pseudoreligion of Comte. Moreover, positivism is often taken to imply a belief in the absolute certainty of truly verified knowledge; cognitivism, while by definition generous in its assessment of the validity of what scientists at any given time count as knowledge, is limited by no such extravagance.

The diverse efforts of nineteenth- and twentieth-century American and European intellectuals to create a culture organized around the human ability to know can thus be construed as a single, if multitudinous movement, in much the same way that the various efforts of other intellectuals to create a culture organized around the artistic capabilities of humans has come to be known as MODERNISM. Scholars have tended to celebrate art-centered modernism, and to insist on its ultimate singularity, while simultaneously patronizing the comparable science-centered enthusiasm as "scientism," or dividing it up into a host of little "isms"—realism, empiricism, positivism, naturalism, progressivism, etc.—that obscure the magnitude and generality of this major phase of modern intellectual history. The concept of cognitivism promises to correct this imbalance.

The science-centered movement some historians now call cognitivism served to reformulate and bring into the nineteenth and twentieth century some of the great idealistic and optimistic currents of the Enlightenment. Knowledge had traditionally been seen as valuable, but cognitivism developed a sharper definition of knowledge and at the same time placed on the shoulders of knowledge a heavier burden than it had ever been asked to carry. Men and women as knowers were to perpetuate what was most worthy in the Western tradition, while placing under critical scrutiny what was least worthy; they were to create a culture congruent with and ultimately in control of the machines, the bureaucracies, and the system of capital accumulation associated with modernity. Cognitivism was a way of insisting that human beings and their knowledge defined modern civilization, or were capable of defining it. The cultural hero of cognitivism was a major character in the drama of modern history, the professional scientist, who most fully embodies our will to inquire and our belief in our ability to interrogate our world successfully.

DAVID A. HOLLINGER

FURTHER READING
Yaron Ezrahi, *The Descent of Icarus: Science and the Transformation of Contemporary Democracy* (Cambridge: Harvard University Press, 1990).
David A. Hollinger, "The Knower and the Artificer," in Daniel J. Singal, ed., *Modernist Culture in America* (Belmont, Calif.: Wadsworth, 1991).
E. J. Hundert, "A Cognitive Ideal and Its Myth: Knowledge as Power in the Lexicon of the Enlightenment," *Social Research* 53 (1986): 133–57.
Wolf Lepenies, *Between Literature and Science: the Rise of Sociology*, trans. R. J. Hollingdale (Cambridge: Cambridge University Press, 1989).
Dorothy Ross, ed., *Modernist Impulses in the Human Sciences, 1870–1930* (Baltimore: Johns Hopkins University Press, 1994).

Scottish Common Sense Realism   The American philosophical tradition known as Scottish Common Sense Realism has long served a variety of causes as an all-purpose target of criticism. Transcendentalism, German Idealism, phenomenology and other movements have all included it in their demonology and thus contributed to the image of a Scottish scourge that made large tracts of America a philosophical wasteland for much of the nineteenth century. In the process the identity of the culprit has often been blurred to the indistinct "Scottish philosophy," but recent American work has begun to utilize the distinctions of modern scholarship on the Scottish Enlightenment to draw a more nuanced picture.

In America, as in Britain, the common reaction to Berkeley's immaterialism and Hume's skepticism was a more or less naive realism; a distinctly philosophical response was due to the Scottish philosopher Thomas Reid (1710–1796). Reid was regent at King's College, Aberdeen, then professor of moral philosophy, in succession to Adam Smith, at the University of Glasgow. While closely linked with earlier moral sense theories—especially that of Francis Hutcheson—the direct origins of Scottish Common Sense Realism lie in the comprehensive criticism that Reid leveled against most of modern philosophy. From René Descartes via Nicholas Malebranche, John Locke and George Berkeley to Reid's own time, philosophical views of how the human mind acquires knowledge of the world had become, as Reid saw it, more and more at variance with common understanding. In personal life, in society and in science, humanity displays a capacity for knowledge and for being guided by this knowledge. It was the task of philosophy to explain how this was possible, and philosophy had, on Reid's view, failed to do so.

Philosophers had been misled by the triumph of natural sciences into drawing an analogy between matter and mind and thus to using the methods of these sciences to explain both the cognitive and the active faculties of the mind. Although few philosophers were materialists in the strict sense, most tended to understand the connection between ideas, passions, the will, and behavior in causal or quasicausal terms. When driven to its final, absurd conclusions, which Reid found in the work of David Hume (1711–1776), modern philosophy had created a phantom world of so-called "ideas" that sprang from objects of observation; the self was a conglomeration of perceived ideas; and the will as the source of action was nothing but the balance of passionate impulses at any given moment.

Reid considered modern philosophy not only false but dangerous. He saw no empirical evidence to support the analogy between mind and body. On the contrary, it was common experience that mental representation of the external world is inherently different from spatial phenomena, so that the process from sensation to idea must be understood in terms other than those of causation. This was further underlined by the obvious fact that the mind is itself highly active in the perception of both external and internal sensations. All perception is judgmental. It was equally at variance with experience to suggest that the mind perceives only simple, discrete ideas from which it composes complex ones. The mind generally perceives complex objects immediately and only reaches their simpler components through analysis.

The danger that Reid saw in modern philosophy was its skeptical tendency in knowledge and, consequently, in morals. The suggestion that the immediate objects of the mind are ideas led to a hopeless search for guarantees that the supposed ideas adequately represent their objects, but all proposed guarantors—such as God—must themselves be apprehended through ideas. And if the self was dissolved into a sequence of events, then there could be no inherent connection between acts of will and behavior and hence no sense in ascribing moral responsibility.

The characteristic Common Sense approach to these problems is to point out that skeptics like Hume are of necessity inconsistent in their skepticism. In the very living of life and discussion of philosophy with other people, skeptics are affirming what their theories deny or question, namely the existence of a stable external world, of other minds, of the continuity of their own minds, and of their own and other people's ability to ascribe and accept responsibility for actions. We can understand all of this by proper empirical observation and philosophical analysis of the activity of the mind which will yield a detailed account of the various innate powers of the mind. On this basis Reid put forward a theory of free will and rational agency and a moral philosophy that investigates the system of duties which Reid, in accordance with the common natural-law tradition, divided into three areas, duties to God, to oneself and to others. Set within a teleological framework and an ideal of the moral progress of humanity, Reid's moral theory led to a utopian leaning in politics.

The spread of Common Sense philosophy in America owes a great deal to Reid's disciple, Dugald Stewart (1753–1828; professor of moral philosophy at the University of Edinburgh in succession to Adam Ferguson), an eclectic thinker much influenced also by Adam Smith and others. To a greater degree than Reid, Stewart promoted the philosophical treatment of "the fundamental laws of human belief" as a coherent Baconian science, parallel with but inherently different from natural philosophy. Stewart drew historicist implications from the idea of the moral perfectibility of humanity, in contrast to Reid's utopian leanings, and one can see his philosophy of mind as part of an overall defense against political radicalism in the context of British reactions to the French Revolution. He was, however, first of all a fine and most effective popularizer of Common Sense philosophy. While the school—as it came to be seen—became more and more eclectic in its native land (as with Thomas Brown, 1778–1820, and Sir William Hamilton, 1788–1856), it established itself as a semi-official philosophy in France and was the most widespread form of philosophy in America until the third quarter of the nineteenth century.

While Reid's work became known in America immediately on publication, there is little evidence of any major impact during the revolutionary period. Although Garry Wills has traced basic Jeffersonian ideas to Reid, they are nothing but common ENLIGHTENMENT goods. An important precursor of Reid's, Scottish philosopher JOHN WITHERSPOON (president of the College of New Jersey—Princeton—from 1768), provided in his lectures an uneasy combination of evangelical Calvinism and a philosophical realism which he had outlined already in the 1750s. Witherspoon's great influence, not least through his numerous students, including JAMES MADISON, helped

make the American mind unusually receptive to Reid's ideas.

The great significance of Common Sense philosophy in the earliest national period was due to the fact that some Americans saw it as a two-edged sword usable against evangelical enthusiasm as well as Humean skepticism and conventionalism. First, while maintaining a substantive view of the mind as a free-willed agent, Common Sense philosophy was preeminently a theory of the socially fostered culture of the innate powers of the mind. As a philosophy of culture and politeness, it was in sharp contrast to evangelical ideas of a soul spiritually defined only through divine inspiration. Beginning with Witherspoon's compromise and carried on by his successor Samuel Stanhope Smith, the development of Common Sense realism as a curb on religious enthusiasm provides an interesting parallel to Dugald Stewart's simultaneous reaction to the political enthusiasm of the French Revolution.

Second, Common Sense philosophy's central concern with the educability and social integration of the intellectual and active powers was premised on the evident existence of a coherent, continuous mind responsible for voluntary behavior. This was seen to stand in sharp contrast to the Humean dissolution of the mental world into discrete events (the occurrence of isolated perceptions and ideas) and the consequent meaninglessness of responsibility. On such a view the coherence of the individual and the society of the many were nothing but socially induced habits. The American version of this battle was fought with particular valor on behalf of Common Sense by JAMES WILSON.

The progressive conservatism of Common Sense was soon underwritten by its entrenchment as the most pervasive academic philosophy, led by Harvard philosophers such as Francis Bowen (1811–1890), Levi Frisbie (1784–1822), Levi Hedge (1766–1844) and James Walker (1794–1874); prominent outside Harvard were JAMES MCCOSH of Princeton (1811–1894) and Noah Porter of Yale (1811–1892). The significance of Common Sense philosophy in this connection is the extent to which it was a philosophy of science. Taking over the comprehensive Scots syllabus for mental philosophy, the American philosophers strongly promoted the sciences as in effect extensions of natural religion, that is, of the theory of the divine mind. Both the experimental disciplines of natural philosophy and the full range of moral sciences from psychology to political economy were provided with a philosophical home.

Much of the antagonism to Common Sense philosophy is testimony to its importance. The idea of the mind as active and judgmental in its approach to the world led Common Sense thinkers to introduce their students sympathetically to philosophical traditions that might have been ignored by others. The Scots founders had always been interested in Platonism, especially Cambridge Platonism, and in America the similarities between the Platonist soul and the Common Sense mind became significant for unitarian thought, for instance in WILLIAM ELLERY CHANNING (1780–1842). Similarly the Common Sense professors were among the earliest to discuss Kant, Hegel, and other modern German philosophers, as were Stewart and Hamilton in Scotland. A good deal of the material that formed TRANSCENDENTALISM and Hegelianism was thus disseminated by the eventual victims of these movements.

KNUD HAAKONSSEN

FURTHER READING

J. David Hoeveler Jr., *James McCosh and Scottish Intellectual Tradition, from Glasgow to Princeton* (Princeton: Princeton University Press, 1981).

Daniel Walker Howe, *The Unitarian Conscience: Harvard Moral Philosophy, 1805–1861*, 2nd ed. (Middletown, Conn.: Wesleyan University Press, 1988).

Keith Lehrer, "Scottish Influences on Contemporary American Philosophy," *Philosophical Journal* 5 (1968): 34–42.

Thomas Reid, *Philosophical Works*, with notes and supplementary dissertations by Sir William Hamilton; photographic reproduction of the 8th ed. (1895), introd. H. M. Bracken (Hildesheim: Georg Olms, 1983).

——, *Practical Ethics. Being Lectures and Papers on Natural Religion, Self-Government, Natural Jurisprudence, and the Law of Nations*, edited from the manuscripts with an introduction and a commentary by Knud Haakonssen (Princeton: Princeton University Press, 1990).

Samuel Stanhope Smith, *The Lectures . . . on the Subjects of Moral and Political Philosophy*, 2 vols. (Trenton, N.J.: Daniel Fenton, 1812).

Garry Wills, *Inventing America: Jefferson's Declaration of Independence* (New York: Doubleday, 1978).

John Witherspoon, *The Selected Writings*, ed. T. Miller (Carbondale: Southern Illinois Press, 1990).

Scudder, Vida D. [born Julia Davida] (b. Madura, India, Dec. 15, 1861; d. Wellesley, Mass., Oct. 9, 1954).   Writer and reformer. A professor of English at Wellesley College, Scudder was an Episcopalian socialist, active in both the Women's Trade Union League and a semimonastic order called the Companions of the Holy Cross. Though she thought that the church itself should not endorse any specific economic or political program, she believed that the Christian spirit and the church's medieval traditions (especially Franciscan mysticism and voluntary poverty) could spark not only contemplative withdrawal, but also social action. Marxism, she argued, is not contrary to spiritual ideals. Its insight into the social

and economic determination of reality can guide the implementation of spiritual ideals. Scudder's writings include *Social Ideals in English Letters* (1898) and *A Listener in Babel, Being a Series of Imaginary Conversations Held at the Close of the Last Century and Reported by Vida D. Scudder* (1903).

FURTHER READING

Theresa Corcoran, *Vida Dutton Scudder* (Boston: Twayne, 1982).

Sedgwick, Catharine Maria (b. Stockbridge, Mass., Dec. 28, 1789; d. West Roxbury, Mass., 31 July, 1867).   Novelist, autobiographer, and cultural commentator, Sedgwick was the daughter of Theodore and Pamela Dwight Sedgwick, both members of prominent families in Massachusetts's Connecticut River Valley. Sedgwick received only a smattering of academic schooling, combined with social accomplishments, at a series of schools in New York City, Albany, and Boston. This formal education constituted the most advanced then available to women. Arbitrary and unstructured as it was, Sedgwick's reading in history, fiction, philosophy, and drama proved much more important. In a household that valued learning and made the transmission of culture a responsibility, Sedgwick's informal education left her with the sense that cultural enrichment was her birthright.

Formal or informal, Sedgwick's education was not designed to prepare her for a career. Instead, elite families considered female education preparation for the role of wife and mother. Those women who did not marry were expected to reside with parental families or to attach themselves to siblings' families. Whatever the individual circumstances, a woman's life was still defined in the context of DOMESTICITY. Sedgwick challenged prevailing experience and expectation. Unlike nine out of ten women in the nineteenth century, she remained unmarried. Still more strikingly, she pursued a career that made her one of antebellum America's most famous writers.

The elite standing of Sedgwick's family and the gender conventions of her century intersected in the perspective she brought to that career. The daughter of an influential Federalist, Sedgwick nonetheless discarded her father's commitment to the hierarchy, the finely graded stratification, and the deference to a gentlemanly elite that had prevailed in colonial America, coming instead to support a more egalitarian society. Nevertheless, Sedgwick along with others posed a question that resonated through the early nineteenth century: was there a role for individuals of privilege in an increasingly democratic America? Sedgwick maintained that elite status entailed cultural responsibilities to the numerically dominant. Defining the obligations as cultural rather than political, Sedgwick envisioned an elite that might yet be crucial to the success of a society that increasingly defined itself as democratic. Those who could no longer expect to dominate at the polls could maintain power and authority in the domain of culture. But was it possible for a *woman* to invest herself with the obligations Sedgwick accorded an elite? Entitled by her family's standing to enrich herself intellectually and culturally, Sedgwick took a further step and became a participant in the construction of culture. Combining the increasingly popular idea that women should be moral guardians with the long-standing conviction that culture should be informed by moral as well as aesthetic purpose, Sedgwick circumvented barriers based on gender and legitimated herself as a writer.

Throughout a career in which she published six novels and nearly one hundred tales and sketches, Sedgwick sought to create a consciously *American* literature. Ranging from a revisionary depiction of the conflict between Puritans and Indians to a dissection of a Jacksonian America dominated by commercialism, Sedgwick's fiction dealt with issues that were decidedly social and political in character. Portrayals of reform movements, discourses on class relations, doctrinal debates between Congregationalists and Unitarians, all these issues and more were interwoven in a body of literature that spoke to the felt realities of early nineteenth-century Americans. Equally concerned with issues of GENDER, Sedgwick placed strong, independent, and articulate heroines at the center of her fiction. Sedgwick's model of gender relations presumed different roles for women and men. Nonetheless, she accorded women central status as social and cultural actors.

Practically unrecognized until now, Sedgwick's AUTOBIOGRAPHY and journals constitute her second major contribution to American letters. In an autobiography of her childhood and adolescence, Sedgwick wove together a deeply personal narrative and an illuminating portrayal of a newly independent America. Beginning with her entries in the summer of 1821, Sedgwick filled the 12 volumes of her journals with meditations upon herself as an adult and the world she shared with other antebellum Americans. Like her novels, tales, and sketches, Sedgwick's autobiography and journals offer readers a representation of changes and continuities in relations of power that took place in the decades between America's Revolution and its Civil War. More than a century before historians did so, Sedgwick situated power in its broadest context. In all of her writings,

she extended the meaning of power to include gender relations as a central dimension, addressing with equal insight social and political relations.

Throughout the nineteenth century, Sedgwick ranked with WASHINGTON IRVING, JAMES FENIMORE COOPER, and WILLIAM CULLEN BRYANT, all of whom were acclaimed as founders of a distinctively American literature. Until recently, however, her reputation diminished in this century. Published between 1917 and 1921, the four-volume *Cambridge History of American Literature* elaborated upon the achievements of Bryant, Irving, and Cooper but only mentioned Sedgwick as one of Cooper's contemporaries. By the middle of the century, she had become a footnote in Robert Spiller's monumental *Literary History of the United States*. Today literary critics and intellectual historians are recovering the voices of nineteenth-century women. Seen as signal to an understanding of America's culture, Sedgwick's novels are being reprinted, her tales and sketches included in anthologies, and her autobiographies and journals published. This time she is being read with an enlarged sense of her remarkably rich, complex, and insightful legacy.

MARY KELLEY

FURTHER READING

Barbara Bardes and Suzanne Gossett, *Declarations of Independence: Women and Political Power in Nineteenth-Century American Literature* (New Brunswick: Rutgers University Press, 1990).

Lawrence Buell, *New England Literary Culture* (Cambridge: Cambridge University Press, 1986).

Judith Fetterley, *Provisions: a Reader from Nineteenth-Century American Women* (Bloomington: Indiana University Press, 1985).

Mary Kelley, *Private Woman, Public Stage: Literary Domesticity in Nineteenth-Century America* (New York: Oxford University Press, 1984).

Catharine Maria Sedgwick, *Hope Leslie*, ed. Mary Kelley (New Brunswick: Rutgers University Press, 1987).

——, *"The Power of Sympathy": the Autobiography and Journals of Catharine Maria Sedgwick*, ed. Mary Kelley (Boston: Massachusetts Historical Society, 1993).

semiotics The study of signs is one of the leading areas of methodological interest in the humanities and is of increasing interest in the social sciences as well. It flourishes especially in university departments of language and literature where it has sanctioned some ingenious forms of literary theory. This literary semiotic is largely Continental in origin and owes a large debt to the great Swiss linguist Ferdinand Saussure (1857–1913) and the contemporary French deconstructionist, Jacques Derrida. There is also a principally American tradition in semiotic that is less influential, even in the United States, than is the Continental tradition. The American tradition, which has a sounder philosophical base and much broader potential applications, derives from the philosopher CHARLES SANDERS PEIRCE (1839–1914), who focused not merely on the semiotic aspect of language, as does the Continental tradition, but on a general theory of signs.

There is a general and mistaken impression that semiotic is a creation of POSTMODERNISM, but prior to the conquest of Western thought by Cartesian dualism in the seventeenth century, there was a long tradition of speculative semiotic that culminated in the work of John Poinsot (1589–1644). After Descartes, signs became a subject of marginal interest in the philosophy of mind because of the dominance of his model of mind as possessing immediate, unrepresented knowledge of its thoughts; the external world had to be represented to the mind in the form of ideas, but the ideas themselves were known immediately rather than through REPRESENTATION. Both the Continental and the American or Peircean traditions in semiotic reject the Cartesian notion of the immediacy of thought, reject, as Derrida puts it in *Of Grammatology*, "the metaphysics of presence" (p. 50).

The Continental tradition returned semiotic to Western culture more or less through the back door, through the study of LANGUAGE rather than philosophy. Saussure's lectures in linguistics (1906–11) emphasized that verbal signs, words, are arbitrary conventions. Saussure did not mean, however, to suggest an arbitrary relationship between the signifier and the signified. A sign or word might be an arbitrarily chosen convention, but its meaning, its relationship to the signified, was determined by the structure of the language within which the word was employed. Despite the arbitrariness of the signifier, it was bound firmly to the signified by language.

Derrida challenges Saussure's belief in the bond between signifier and signified by arguing in *Writing and Difference* that there is "no transcendental or privileged signified." Rather, there is only the endless and infinite "play" of signification, which is tantamount to rejecting "even the concept and word 'sign' itself—which is precisely what cannot be done" (p. 281). In less paradoxical passages, Derrida makes clear that he has been visited only with prophetic glimpses of what it means to affirm "play" and "pass beyond man and humanism." He is nevertheless confident, even as he finds futility in the notion of choice, that of the "two interpretations of interpretation" his joyful universe of play is superior to the ideal of objectivity, the "saddened, *negative*" dream "of deciphering a truth or an origin which escapes play and the order of the sign" (p. 292).

Some influential literary critics in American universities have understandably found Derrida a liberating force both in their own interpretive relations to texts and in their understanding of the relation or lack thereof of texts to social and historical contexts. But even deconstructionists have begun to find a troubling pattern in their own supposed liberation from the tyranny of the signified. If every text can be read as a commentary on the impossibility of signification, then it seems that texts do have a determinate meaning and a disconcertingly similar one at that. There have of course also been predictable positivist outcries against DECONSTRUCTION as an assault on the concept of objective truth.

The alternate tradition in modern semiotic derives from the philosophy of Charles Sanders Peirce, who believed that all mental or spiritual activity, not just language, is semiotic in nature. Accordingly, Peirce believed that thought is an objective rather than a subjective process and that there is no inconsistency in considering truth as both objective and relative.

One of the reasons that Peirce's semiotic is more realistic and respectful of objectivity than is Derridean deconstruction is that Peirce posited three elements, not two, in the semiotic process. Where Saussure and Derrida see the process as a dyadic relation of signifier and signified, Peirce posited a triadic relation in semiosis: object/sign/interpretant. The sign is interpreted by a subsequent thought (interpretant) as a representation of an object. Because the meaning of the sign is determined by its relation with both the object and the interpretant, Peirce's system allows for realistic recognition of the sign's relativity without an unrealistic withdrawal from the object in the fashion of deconstruction.

Peirce divided signs into three types—icon, index, and symbol—each of them defined by a different relation between the sign and its object. An icon achieves meaning by being interpreted as resembling its object as does a portrait. An index is interpreted as being determined by its object as is a weathercock by the wind. A symbol is an arbitrary or merely conventional representation of an object, as is the octagonal shape of a stop sign. Yet even the symbol has a real relationship to its object. A driver might arbitrarily interpret the stop sign to mean "floor it," but in thus ignoring the sign's object of arresting the car's motion, the driver would put himself at real risk. The American or Peircean tradition in semiotic thus allows for a much broader and more realistic recognition of the role of signs than does the Continental or literary tradition that began with Saussure and has been critically extended by Derrida.

JAMES HOOPES

FURTHER READING

Jonathan Culler, *The Pursuit of Signs: Semiotics, Literature, Deconstruction* (Ithaca: Cornell University Press, 1981).

John N. Deely, *Introducing Semiotic: Its History and Doctrine* (Bloomington: Indiana University Press, 1982).

Jacques Derrida, *Of Grammatology* (Baltimore: Johns Hopkins University Press, 1976).

——, *Writing and Difference* (Chicago: University of Chicago Press, 1978).

Umberto Eco, *Semiotics and the Philosophy of Language* (Bloomington: Indiana University Press, 1984).

Michael Fischer, *Does Deconstruction Make Any Difference? Poststructuralism and the Defense of Poetry in Modern Criticism* (Bloomington: Indiana University Press, 1985).

Charles William Morris, *Foundations of the Theory of Signs* (Chicago: University of Chicago Press, 1938).

Ferdinand de Saussure, *Course in General Linguistics* (New York: McGraw-Hill, 1959).

Sequoya [also known as George Gist or George Guess] (b. Taskigi, N.C. [now Tenn.], ca.1770; d. probably San Fernando, Tamaulipas, Mexico, Aug. 1843). Inventor of the Cherokee syllabary. A Cherokee nationalist, Sequoya sought to preserve the traditional ways of his people by developing a system for recording their history, religion, and new discoveries. Illiterate in English, he released in 1821 the first method for writing a North American Indian language. Although Sequoya was disappointed that few texts other than Bibles and tribal laws were ever printed using the syllabary, handwritten communications were important in strengthening traditionalist resistance to assimilation.

FURTHER READING

George E. Foster, *Se-quo-yah, the American Cadmus and Modern Moses* (New York: AMS Press, 1979).

Sewall, Samuel (b. Bishopstoke, England, Mar. 28, 1652; d. Boston, Mass., Jan. 1, 1730). Merchant and magistrate. Best known for his role as a judge at the 1692 Salem witchcraft trials—a role for which he later repented publicly—Sewall was the author of a vehement antislavery tract, *The Selling of Joseph* (1700), which invoked both God and natural law against slaveholding, and *A Memorial Relating to the Kennebeck Indians* (1721), which called for humane treatment of the Indians. His three-volume diary, covering most of the years between 1673 and 1729, is an incomparable source for understanding popular religion in early New England.

FURTHER READING

David D. Hall, *Worlds of Wonder, Days of Judgment: Popular Religious Belief in Early New England* (New York: Knopf, 1989).

Shachtman, Max (b. Warsaw, Poland, Sept. 10, 1904; d. Floral Park, N.Y., Nov. 4, 1972). Journalist. A founder of American Trotskyism, Shachtman became increasingly critical of the Soviet Union and eventually split with the Trotskyists because he disputed their claim that the Soviet Union was a workers' state. Stalin, he argued, had created an exploitative new class of bureaucratic functionaries. A workers' state must be democratically controlled by the workers; democratic ownership of production is the essence of SOCIALISM. Editor, with JAMES BURNHAM, of *The New Internationalist*, Shachtman remained committed to leftist politics even after he excoriated Stalin in *Behind the Moscow Trials: the Greatest Frame-up in History* (1936) and *The Bureaucratic Revolution: the Rise of the Stalinist State* (1962). Shachtman spent his later years trying to develop ties between the Democratic Party and the labor movement.

FURTHER READING

Gary Dorrien, *The Democratic Socialist Vision* (Totowa, N.J.: Rowman and Littlefield, 1986).

shame Most authorities interpret shame as the painful awareness of failure, as opposed to GUILT, the awareness of having injured someone. Shame, they say, is self-regarding, whereas guilt arises out of our relations with others. But it is not enough to identify shame simply with a sense of failure, a loss of self-esteem. These terms point us in the right direction but miss the all-important link between shame and exposure. Shame is experienced not just as failure but, at a deeper level, as a violation of our PRIVACY, of our very person—an intrusive reminder of our vulnerability, an exposure of things that ought to remain concealed (*see also* PUBLICITY).

It is our bondage to nature, as Erich Heller has observed, that makes us ashamed. Bodily exposure is a source of shame because the body resists our efforts to control it and therefore confronts us with the inescapable limitations of the human condition. Shame implies a decent respect, even a certain reverence for the contingency and finitude of human life—for the mystery at the heart of existence. "Shame," said Nietzsche in his *Human, All Too Human*, "exists everywhere where there exists a 'mystery'" (section 100). There is a close connection, accordingly, between shame and the sense of the sacred.

The secularization of American culture has encouraged a widespread disparagement of shame, now seen as a remnant of Victorian prudery. The secular mind dislikes a mystery. It opens everything to investigation, pries into every secret, drags everything into the light of day. Its ethic of demystification and exposure refuses to acknowledge any limits on the public's "right to know." Journalists insist on full disclosure, therapists declare war on "denial." The prevailing consensus might be expressed in a single sentence: "There is nothing, absolutely nothing, to be ashamed of."

A leveling impulse—not to be confused with democracy, which rests on respect for persons—informs the journalistic and therapeutic assault on shame. The best defense against shameful feelings of weakness and failure, some therapists argue in effect, is a homeopathic dose of the same medicine, designed to prevent us from taking ourselves too seriously. The reminder that no one escapes the "call of nature," as our grandparents used to put it so delicately, serves both to deflate self-importance and to mock false modesty. By reconciling them to their limitations, such therapies might have a good effect on people suffering from an exaggerated sense of their own importance or an obsession with the defense of their "honor." But therapies that merely encourage people to lower their sights contribute to the current debasement of all ideals. There is a crucial difference between the acceptance of limitations and the impulse to reduce everything to its lowest common denominator. "Acceptance"—the watchword of those who deplore a "judgmental" approach to life—becomes shameless, cynical surrender when it can no longer distinguish between nobility and pomposity, refinement of taste and social snobbery, modesty and prudery. The culture of cynicism and irreverence confuses delusions of grandeur, which call for moral and therapeutic correction, with grandeur itself.

The concept of shame survives, nowadays, only in the attenuated form of damaged self-esteem. Deaf to its moral resonance, those who urge more intensive study and treatment of shame—an allegedly neglected pathology—understand it merely as anything that prevents people from "feeling good about themselves." Formerly the word referred not only to a respect for privacy but to the fear of disgrace, which implied a failure to live up to internalized codes of HONOR. Today it is widely believed that people come to grief when they adopt "society's" standards as their own. Therapists and authors of self-help manuals advise them to set their own goals instead of conforming to what others expect of them. A healthy sense of self, according to Gloria Steinem, depends on "seeing through your own eyes instead of through the eyes of others" (p. 44). In earlier times, shame was the fate of those whose conduct fell short of cherished ideals. Now that ideals are suspect, it

refers only to the "negative self-image" that results from misguided attempts to live up to standards set by someone else.

Self-esteem, otherwise known as "empowerment," is held up as the cure for everything that ails us. Schools try to promote it by abolishing failing grades. Churches redefine sin as a failure to live up to "your own potential." In California, a statewide Task Force to Promote Self-Esteem, appointed in 1983, advanced the dubious thesis, unsupported by reliable research, that low self-esteem was a "primary causal factor" in "crime and violence, alcohol abuse, drug abuse, teenage pregnancy, child and spousal abuse, chronic welfare dependency, and failure to achieve in school" (Steinem, p. 28).

A shameless culture, which accepts no limits on human control and "human potential" and teaches its children, as a corollary, that they can become whatever they want to be, finds it hard to explain failure except as the product of defeatist attitudes, the removal of which presumably requires a redoubled insistence that there is nothing to be ashamed of except shame itself.

CHRISTOPHER LASCH

FURTHER READING

"The Curse of Self-Esteem," *Newsweek*, Feb. 17, 1992, pp. 46–52.

Erich Heller, "Man Ashamed," *Encounter*, Feb. 1974, pp. 23–30.

Helen M. Lynd, *On Shame and the Search for Identity* (New York: Harcourt, Brace, 1958).

Donald L. Nathanson, *Shame and Pride* (New York: Norton, 1992).

Friedrich Nietzsche, *Human, All Too Human* (1878, 1886), trans. R. G. Hollingdale (Cambridge: Cambridge University Press, 1980).

Carl D. Schneider, *Shame, Exposure, and Privacy* (Boston: Beacon, 1977).

Gloria Steinem, *Revolution from Within: a Book of Self-Esteem* (Boston: Little, Brown, 1992).

Léon Wurmser, *The Mask of Shame* (Baltimore: Johns Hopkins University Press, 1981).

Shaw, Anna Howard (b. Newcastle-upon-Tyne, England, Feb. 14, 1847; d. Moylan, Pa., July 2, 1919). Reformer. An ordained minister and a physician holding advanced degrees in theology and medicine from Boston University, Shaw was one of the leading orators of the woman suffrage movement. She stressed what she considered the innate differences between men and women, and held that women's unique virtue would promote social reform once they had the vote. Her argument for suffrage was principled as well as practical: full EQUALITY between men and women was implicit in Christianity, which demanded that all souls should be able to develop to their fullest potential. She was president of the National American Woman Suffrage Association from 1904 to 1915. Shaw wrote, in addition to countless speeches, an autobiography, *The Story of a Pioneer* (1915).

See also WOMEN'S RIGHTS.

FURTHER READING
Wil A. Linkugel, *Anna Howard Shaw: Suffrage Orator and Social Reformer* (New York: Greenwood, 1991).

Silko, Leslie Marmon (b. Albuquerque, N.Mex., Mar. 5, 1948). Writer. Drawing on Laguna traditions, myths, and modes of storytelling, Silko portrays the interactions between Euro-American and Native American ways. Her novel *Ceremony* (1977) is the story of a disillusioned mixed-blood veteran who is restored when he recognizes the inseparability of people, rituals, and the land. Silko's works, which also include *Laguna Woman* (1974), *Storyteller* (1981), and *Almanac of the Dead* (1991), show both the cultural debility that results from a history of persecution and the persistent vitality of Indian traditions in modern Indian life.

FURTHER READING
Per Seyersted, *Leslie Marmon Silko* (Boise, Idaho: Boise State University Press, 1980).

Silliman, Benjamin (b. North Stratford [now Trumbull], Conn., Aug. 8, 1779; d. New Haven, Conn., Nov. 24, 1864). Geologist and chemist. One of the new nation's preeminent scientists, Silliman asserted that national pride depended upon a vibrant scientific community. His *American Journal of Science and Arts* (founded 1818), combined with his teaching at Yale and his popular lyceum lectures, did much to promote, organize, and generate public enthusiasm for American science. Science, he believed, confirms Christian faith by unveiling God's order: geological layers, for example, correspond to the six ages, or "days," of Genesis. In addition to his scientific works, including *Elements of Chemistry* (1830), he published *A Journal of Travels in England, Holland and Scotland* (1810).

FURTHER READING
Chandos Michael Brown, *Benjamin Silliman: a Life in the Early Republic* (Princeton: Princeton University Press, 1989).

simplicity   Most of the world's great religions and philosophies have advocated some form of this ancient and universal ideal as a means of ensuring that material desires and activities do not corrupt the priorities of the mind and spirit. Both Greek and Roman philosophers preached the virtues of the golden mean, as did the Old Testament prophets—Amos, Hosea, and Jeremiah. "Give me neither poverty nor wealth but only enough," prayed the author of Proverbs. And of course it was such a life of pious simplicity that Jesus led and preached. He repeatedly warned of the "deceitfulness of riches" and the corrupting effects of luxury.

Simplicity has also been an especially prominent strand in the fabric of American values. From the colonial period to the present, moralists, intellectuals, and common folk, some well-known, others unfamiliar, have rejected the sumptuous life in favor of some version of simplicity. In doing so they have sustained an elevated vision of the good life that has proved both enduring and elusive.

Simplicity is not simple—either to define or to live. Its meaning can never be precisely stated because it is not so much a single idea as it is an omnibus label used to refer to one or more of the following attitudes, ideas, and beliefs: a concern for family nurture and community cohesion; a hostility toward luxury and a suspicion of riches; a belief that the primary reward of work should be well-being rather than money; a desire for maximum personal self-reliance and creative leisure; a nostalgia for the supposed simplicities of the past and an anxiety about the technological and bureaucratic complexities of the present and future; a taste for the plain and functional, especially in the home environment; a reverence for nature and a preference for country living; and a sense of both religious and ecological responsibility for the proper use of the world's resources. What unifies this cluster of attitudes is the conscious desire to purge life of some of its complexities and superfluities in order to pursue "higher" values—faith, family, civic duty, artistic creativity, and social service.

As a way station between too little and too much, the ethic of simplicity encompasses a wide spectrum of motives and behavior, a spectrum bounded at one end by religious asceticism and at the other by refined gentility. In between there is much room for individual expression. Figures as diverse as JOHN WINTHROP, JOHN WOOLMAN, SAMUEL ADAMS, JOHN ADAMS and ABIGAIL ADAMS, THOMAS JEFFERSON, RALPH WALDO EMERSON, HENRY DAVID THOREAU, LEWIS MUMFORD, Scott Nearing and Helen Nearing, Wendell Berry, and many others have viewed America primarily as a spiritual commonwealth and a republic of VIRTUE rather than as a cornucopia of worldly delights and entrepreneurial opportunities. Some proponents of simplicity have been quite conservative in appealing to traditional religious values and or classical notions of republican virtue; others have been liberal or radical in their assault on corporate capitalism and its ethos of compulsive consumerism. In addition, class biases, individual personality traits, and historical circumstances have also combined to produce many differing versions of simple living in the American experience. Consequently, there is no simple life as such that can be universally prescribed or adopted, only an array of different patterns of living that in their own context seem "simpler" than other ways of life.

Although most people tend to associate simplicity with self-sustaining rusticity, such rural contentment has not been the only path to simplicity. Suburban or urban dwellers whose getting and spending are guided by carefully considered choices may also claim to lead simpler lives than their peers. Nor is simplicity merely a joyless program of denial: self-restraint and conscientious consumption do not mandate a primitive or monastic regimen. The essence of simplicity lies not in renunciation but in discrimination. It requires learning to distinguish between the necessary and superfluous, between the useful and wasteful, beautiful and vulgar. Wisdom, the philosopher William James once remarked, is knowing what to overlook. Indeed, the key to mastering the fine art of simple living is discovering the difference between personal trappings and personal traps.

The history of simplicity in the American experience has been a festival of irony, for the ideal of enlightened restraint has always been linked in an awkward dialectical embrace with the growth of abundance and complexity. The nation's phenomenal economic and social expansion has in one sense provoked the desire for simpler living. Only those who have too much can aspire to live on less. Only those surrounded by bigness can decide that smaller is more beautiful.

Yet if America's abundance has made simplicity possible, it has also helped prevent it from being widely embraced. We have become a people increasingly dependent on plenty, frenetic in our pursuit of wealth, conspicuous in our consumption, as notorious for our wastefulness as for our TECHNOLOGY, and often ruthless in our INDIVIDUALISM. The self-indulgent imperatives of an ever-expanding consumer culture have become so deeply embedded in the popular imagination and in the social structure that it has become increasingly difficult to sustain a simpler way of life in the midst of such ubiquitous prosperity.

Since the colonial era, advocates of simple living have been professing a way of life at odds with an American environment full of bountiful resources, entrepreneurial opportunities, and increasingly powerful institutions that combine to exalt the glories of self-indulgence and to war against contentment. Puritan and Quaker settlers who arrived in America during the seventeenth and eighteenth centuries brought with them a delicately balanced social ethic stressing hard work, self-control, plain living, civic virtue, and spiritual devotion.

Their goal was to create model societies in which simplicity of worship, dress, manners, and speech would be practiced and enforced. Yet in both Puritan Massachusetts and Quaker Pennsylvania the champions of collective simplicity soon found themselves waging a losing battle against the corrupting influence of rapid population growth, religious pluralism, secular materialism, and entrepreneurial opportunities. In 1733 a Boston minister bemoaned their fall from grace when he said in a sermon that "the powerful love of the world and exorbitant reach after riches have become the reigning temper in persons of all ranks in our land" and their original spiritual and social ideal was being "abandoned, slighted and forgotten" (quoted by Shi, p. 23).

The lesson in both Massachusetts and Pennsylvania seemed to be that pious simplicity as a *societal* ethic was impossible to sustain in the midst of such a fluid and dynamic American culture blessed with so many opportunities for economic gain and social display. Certainly that was the assumption of the many pietistic sects that settled in America in the eighteenth century and after. The so-called "plain people"—Mennonites, Amish, Dunkers, Brethren in Christ, Moravians, Shakers, and others—shared a strong commitment to communal simplicity and a strict nonconformity to the ways of the larger world.

In the New World these various religious groups set themselves apart from mainstream society by establishing small, isolated, homogeneous, and self-sustaining rural communities. Through mutual aid, intensive agriculture, thrift, and diligence, their settlements prospered. Some required communal ownership of property; others allowed for private property but placed restrictions on its use. Some verged on asceticism, practicing celibacy and renunciation of sensual and material pleasures; others allowed cohabitation and a comfortable sufficiency. But all of them insisted upon the priorities of faith and family and COMMUNITY. In other words, these religious nonconformists required social conformity.

American history is strewn with dozens of other examples of communal efforts at simple living, UTOPIAS ranging from the Transcendentalists' communities at Fruitlands and Brook Farm in the 1840s to the hippie communes of the 1960s and 1970s. Few of them, however, lasted more than a few months. Many of the participants in such alternative communities were naive about the hardships involved and lacked experience in the basic skills necessary for self-reliant living. They were also narrowly anti-urban in outlook and disdainful of the liberating and enlightening effects of prosperity and technology. Any virtue pressed too far can become counterproductive.

Yet the history of the simple life in the United States includes victories as well as defeats. That many of the "plain people" have managed to retain much of their initial ethic testifies to the strength of their spiritual commitment as well as to the rigidity of their social discipline. There have also been many successful and inspiring individual practitioners of simple living. As a guide for individual living and as a myth of collective commitment, simplicity has thus displayed remarkable resilience. No sooner is it declared an anachronism than it undergoes a revival of interest. During periods of war, depression, or social crisis, its merits have been successfully invoked by politicians, ministers, and reformers to help revitalize public virtue, self-restraint, and mutual aid. In this way simplicity has exerted a powerful influence on the complex patterns of American culture.

The ideal of simplicity, however ambiguous, however fitfully realized, has survived in part because there is something ennobling in the attempt to elevate aspirations beyond the material and the mundane. Who has not occasionally yearned for simplicity, for a reduction in the pace and complexity of everyday life and material encumbrances? In the American experience the simple life has remained particularly enticing because it reminds us of what so many of the original settlers and "founding fathers" hoped America would become—a nation of practical dreamers devoted to spiritual, civic, and ideal purposes, a "city upon a hill" serving as a beacon of PIETY, enlightenment, and moderation to the rest of the world.

Today, simplicity remains what it has always been: an animating vision of moral purpose. Thousands of Americans in the 1990s profess and practice an ethic of plain living and high thinking in order to recover personal autonomy and meaning. But as is the case with all noble visions, most people prefer to view it from a distance. "Simplicity," observed the Quaker reformer Richard Gregg in 1936, "seems to be a foible of saints and occasional geniuses, but not something for the rest of us" (p. 1).

Yet even though the ideal of simplicity does not yet move the millions, it still seizes and nourishes sensitive imaginations. Properly interpreted, a modern version of the simple life informed by its historical tradition can be a socially constructive and personally satisfying path to happiness. As

Christopher Lasch observed in his luminous work *The True and Only Heaven*, the conventional notion equating the pursuit of happiness with the growth of the industrial economy and the accumulation of more and more personal possessions is revealing its self-destructive dynamic. There are inherent limits to the conventional notion of PROGRESS. A continually rising standard of living for the affluent few has meant a falling standard of living for everyone else. The best hope of narrowing the gap between the rich and poor, Lasch argues, is for the wealthy to set voluntary limits on their acquisitive appetites.

Precisely. For those living in a press of anxieties, straining desperately, hectically, often miserably after more money, more things, and more status, only to wonder in troubled moments how to get off such a treadmill, the rich tradition of simplicity in the American experience still offers an enticing path to a good life.

But a genuinely simple life, that middle way between excess and deprivation, is difficult to achieve and even harder to maintain. "'Tis a gift to be simple," says the old Shaker hymn, and it indeed requires the gift of transcendent commitment to sustain a regimen of enlightened restraint in our fast-paced world.

DAVID E. SHI

FURTHER READING
Duane Elgin and Arnold Mitchell, "Voluntary Simplicity: Lifestyle of the Future," *Futurist* 11 (1977): 200–9.

Stephen Foster, *Their Solitary Way: the Puritan Social Ethic in the First Century of Settlement in New England* (New Haven: Yale University Press, 1971).

Richard Gregg, *The Value of Voluntary Simplicity* (Wallingford, Pa.: Pendle Hill, 1936).

Christopher Lasch, *The Culture of Narcissism: American Life in an Age of Diminishing Expectations* (New York: Norton, 1978).

——, *The True and Only Heaven: Progress and Its Critics* (New York: Norton, 1991).

David E. Shi, *The Simple Life: Plain Living and High Thinking in American Culture* (New York: Oxford University Press, 1985).

——, ed., *In Search of the Simple Life: American Voices Past and Present* (Layton, Utah: Peregrine Smith, 1986).

Leo Stoller, "Thoreau's Concept of Simplicity," *New England Quarterly* 29 (1956): 443–61.

Sinclair, Upton (b. Baltimore, Md., Sept. 20, 1878; d. Bound Brook, N.J., Nov. 25, 1968).   Born to hard times and Episcopalian piety, Sinclair worked his way through City College of New York as a hack writer, eventually revitalizing the tradition of using popular fiction in the service of reform. At an early age he took Christ and Shelley as models for his own career, and in more than 80 books he fashioned an influential activist style, a crossing of Romantic myth-making and Protestant fervor.

Sinclair's prominence in American intellectual history is largely due to a single work, the novel *The Jungle* (1906), an exposure of contemporary food-processing practices usually considered one of a few central works in the MUCKRAKING genre. Living seven weeks in the Chicago stockyards, Sinclair recorded the lives of immigrant workers, their local cultures, and the systems of exploitation in which they were trapped. The book, Sinclair's comrade JACK LONDON declared, aspired to do for "the wage slaves of today" what HARRIET BEECHER STOWE had done for black slavery in *Uncle Tom's Cabin* (1852), that is, focus broad attention on the human costs of institutional injustice, and thereby mobilize public opinion for change (Harris, p. 81). Sinclair had in fact been inspired by Stowe's example, and the tone and polemical thrust of *The Jungle*—generally consonant with the public speech of PROGRESSIVISM—reasserted the melodramatic affectations of sentimental literature, its ethic of "feeling" and strong sense of social justice.

The book's vivid recreations enraged its bourgeois readership, prompting the earliest food and drug legislation. Sinclair was less than completely thrilled with such a contribution: he had sought to move hearts, he complained, not stomachs. But *The Jungle* did make him famous, affirming his self-image as crusader and putting him squarely at the center of the marketplace of opinion-making that was then forming at the intersection of politics and media consumption. His critiques of industrial life include *King Coal* (1917), *The Profits of Religion* (1918), *The Goose-Step* (1923), and *Oil!* (1927).

Sinclair invested profits from *The Jungle* in the establishment of Helcion Hall, a small community devoted to free love, good diet, and the single tax. Like the use of sentimentalism, these utopian dalliances recall the style of nineteenth-century American radicalism, for which Sinclair had a strong affinity. The bent toward revolution shared by many of his contemporaries was less to his taste. Although Sinclair founded the Intercollegiate Socialist Society in 1905, after joining the Socialist Party the previous year, he remained on the "right" or "independent" wing, finally bolting the party in 1917 to support U.S. intervention in World War I. Despite his postwar recantation and critical treatment of liberal politics—demonstrated in *Jimmie Higgins* and *The Brass Check* (both 1919) and *100%* (1920)—American communists would remain hostile to Sinclair. Faithful to republican institutions, and to change within the electoral system, he began in the early 1930s to build an efficient progressive coalition in the California

Democratic Party under the rubric "End Poverty in California," or EPIC—an acronym appropriate to Sinclair's sense of mission. EPIC's program, an updated Christian Socialism, appeared under a title typical of his messianism: *I, Governor of California, and How I Ended Poverty: a True Story of the Future* (1933). Franklin Roosevelt, already bothered by other regional protest movements, kept EPIC at arm's length, and in the 1934 gubernatorial race Sinclair and his popular following were left to the wolves of the California mass media.

Sinclair's last significant incarnation began in 1940 with the publication of *World's End*, the first of 11 "Lanny Budd" novels. In a manner anticipating Gore Vidal, Sinclair followed his protagonist—the wealthy heir of an arms dealer—around and through the Great Events of the twentieth century, crossing paths with newsmakers in international intrigue before World War I, with high society on the French Riviera during the twenties, and finally involving himself in conflicts with totalitarianism, German and Soviet, wherein Lanny found his true calling as a high-level spy for the Roosevelt administration. The books were very popular; one volume, *Dragon's Teeth*, won the Pulitzer Prize in 1943.

With the Lanny Budd books, as with all of his work, Sinclair brought popular fiction and/or his reputation as a popular writer into the main currents of American public life, whether the heady atmosphere of Progressive reform, or the struggle for national purpose in an international crisis. Lanny's adventures, in particular, revealed some sort of linear sense in the disturbing events of the first half-century, with the inference that there was in fact a worthy, above all defensible, liberal culture coming together for Americans. Constructing narratives which ordered traumatic experiences was a strong program in American public discourse during the 1940s: what Sinclair (and Hollywood) did with male romance, Max Lerner was doing with scholarly social comment, and RICHARD HOFSTADTER with a new historiography of liberal ideas.

Sinclair's most interesting and suggestive work aside from *The Jungle* was an anthology of the "literature of social protest" called *Cry for Justice* (1915). In this hefty volume, Sinclair presented texts from Marx, Thomas More, and Leviticus, from Tolstoy and H. G. Wells, Jefferson, and St. Jerome. Canon-building is always one of the more telling intellectual activities, and Sinclair's shows an attempt to construct a myth-tradition of rhapsodic humanist reform, written through with a Romantic sensibility of moral outrage and individual piety: thus the significant number of entries from thinkers like Thomas

Carlyle and the prophet Isaiah. Sinclair's social thought remained millenarian with unembarrassed enthusiasm and self-importance; indeed, he saw *Cry for Justice* as "a Bible of the future, a Gospel of new hope for the race."

If this enthusiasm was less sophisticated than some readers might hope, it was certainly no less effective in the fashioning of the American left in the twentieth century. For Sinclair and other "literary radicals" who followed, public life *was* romance (his *Boston*, 1928, contributed to the apotheosis of anarchists Nicola Sacco and Bartolomeo Vanzetti, folk heroes of the mythic left), and the evangelical figure of "crusader" was the paradigm of ostensibly secularized and "rebellious" intellectuals. As Alfred Kazin suggested, Sinclair is best seen as a literary counterpart of WILLIAM JENNINGS BRYAN: both exhibited a strong cultural provincialism, and both could assert social leadership by triggering American piety (p. 90). We might add that Upton Sinclair kept alive in the *tone* of twentieth-century activism Bryan's righteousness and evangelical ego. Behind Sinclair's example and within the myths he helped build, a style of pious earnestness and the sense of living an epic of social renewal that had energized the readers of Stowe and *The Jungle* would continue to inspire educated Americans as they listened to King, to Kennedy, or looked elsewhere for political revival.

PETER HANSEN

FURTHER READING
Leon Harris, *Upton Sinclair: an American Rebel* (New York: Thomas Y. Crowell, 1975).
R. N. Mookerjee, *Art for Social Justice: the Major Novels of Upton Sinclair* (Metuchen, N.J.: Scarecrow Press, 1988).
Alfred Kazin, *On Native Grounds: an Interpretation of Modern American Prose Literature* (1942; Garden City: Anchor, 1956).

Skinner, B[urrhus] F[rederic] (b. Susquehanna, Pa., Mar. 20, 1904; d. Cambridge, Mass., Aug. 18, 1990). Psychologist. All human behavior, Skinner believed, occurs in response to stimuli, and positive reinforcement is more effective than deterrence in shaping behavior. Claiming to be aware of the sinister potential of the social control he believed possible through BEHAVIORISM, he nevertheless urged the use of behavioral conditioning in education and other areas of life. Skinner presented his theories in *The Behavior of Organisms* (1938), *Walden Two* (1948), *Science and Human Behavior* (1953), and *Beyond Freedom and Dignity* (1971), which asserted that conventional ideas of FREEDOM should be scrapped as anachronistic.

FURTHER READING
Daniel W. Bjork, *B. F. Skinner: a Life* (New York: Basic Books, 1993).

Small, Albion (b. Buckfield, Maine, May 11, 1854; d. Chicago, Ill., Mar. 24, 1926). Sociologist. One of the original faculty members at John D. Rockefeller's University of Chicago, Small was the first professor of "sociology" in the United States. His work, like that of the discipline as a whole, shifted from the reformist zeal of *An Introduction to the Study of Society* (coauthored with George E. Vincent, 1894)—a work that reflected the shaping influence of the Social Gospel—to the cool empiricism of his *General Sociology* (1905), which emphasized the relative social stability produced by the interaction among various social groups. His later work, in which the ideal of OBJECTIVITY became central, includes *The Meaning of Social Science* (1910) and *The Origins of Sociology* (1924).

FURTHER READING
Vernon K. Dibble, *The Legacy of Albion Small* (Chicago: University of Chicago Press, 1975).

Smedley, Agnes (b. near Campground, Mo., Feb. 23, 1892; d. Oxford, England, May 6, 1950). Journalist and revolutionary. Smedley's struggle for autonomy and belonging was graphically described in her autobiographical novel *Daughter of Earth* (1929), an account of her working-class childhood in the American West, and of her realization that women are ensnared not only by economic dependence, but by their desire for love. The book also traces her immersion in the liberation movement in India during World War I, a movement in which she discovered intellectuals who, unlike her bohemian friends, were not alienated from society, but devoted to their nation. That discovery galvanized her, and led to her subsequent involvement in the Chinese revolution, about which she wrote, among other books, *Chinese Destinies* (1933) and *Battle Hymn of China* (1943).

FURTHER READING
Janice R. MacKinnon and Stephen R. MacKinnon, *Agnes Smedley: the Life and Times of an American Radical* (Berkeley: University of California Press, 1988).

Smith, Joseph, Jr. (b. Sharon, Vt., Dec. 23, 1805; d. Carthage, Ill., June 27, 1844). The founder of the Church of Jesus Christ of Latter-Day Saints (LDS) was born into a rural and downwardly mobile family. His father, who variously worked on farms and sought hidden treasures, moved to Palmyra, New York, in 1816. Here young Joseph grew up. He was a loner, only infrequently involved with churches, and fascinated with occult phenomena (he used a seer stone to search for underground water and hidden money). By his later memory, his first religious vision occurred in 1820 when he was only 15; it was a vision that identified the apostasy of all existing churches.

In Smith's next great vision, in 1823, an angel, Moroni, told him of a history of earlier inhabitants of America written on gold plates. In his earthly life Moroni had helped complete the writing of the plates and had deposited them in their resting place on a nearby hill (Hill Cumorah). These plates contained the fullness of the Gospel as Jesus had revealed it to ancient American inhabitants. After three years, Smith began his alleged translations of these mysterious plates, dictating the contents through curtains to his wife and two disciples. The product would be the *Book of Mormon*, published in Palmyra in 1830.

The *Book of Mormon* provided the impetus to the formation of the LDS. Yet the most distinctive Mormon doctrines came not from it but from the later visions of Joseph Smith (now contained in the equally authoritative *Doctrine and Covenants*). The *Book of Mormon* is in most respects consistent with the Christian Bible. The overall story is complex and confusing. It includes the story of three ancient peoples in America, one pre-Jewish in origins, but the main story involves members of a Jewish tribe who moved to America around 600 BCE. These were the children of Lehi, and particularly the offspring of two sons of Lehi, Nephi and Laman. Soon after arriving in America, the descendants of Nephi and Laman split into two often warring tribes or nations. The Nephites tried to follow the Mosaic law, while the Lamanites generally disobeyed, receiving as a punishment darker skins (they became the American Indians).

The main body of the *Book of Mormon* tells the story of these tribes in America, up until the final destruction of the Nephites by the Lamanites around 384 CE. The last great Nephite ruler, Mormon, wrote the history of his people in Egyptian-like hieroglyphics. A very brief section of the book (III Nephi 11–28) recounts the visit of Jesus to the Jews in America after his ministry in Palestine. As the promised Messiah, he could not neglect them. Here he instructed his people, first meeting them at the Nephite Temple in the city of Bountiful. He referred to the future of certain Gentiles in America who would by repentance and proper baptism join themselves to all the promises of the covenant and thus help build in America the New Jerusalem.

Guided by a divine revelation, Smith selected April 6, 1830 as the time for founding a new church. Its early history involved several small towns in the Palmyra area, but within less than a year most Mormons moved to Kirkland, Ohio, where several members of a Disciples congregation had converted.

This early LDS was much closer to mainline Christian EVANGELICALISM than the church would ever be again. In organization it was patriarchal, eventually with two orders of all-male priests, with most faithful young boys entering the Aaronic priesthood at age 12, but with the spiritual priesthood (of Melchizedek) limited to adult males. Doctrinally, it was eclectic— abstemious, restorationist, and adventist, with a belief in free will, adult baptism for repentance, weekly communion, and early spiritual gifts (prophecy, some healing, speaking in tongues). Eventually, Smith added to this mix some very distinctive doctrines, including a form of corporealism (matter is alone eternal and thus all gods finite), a functional polytheism (the three persons in the Christian trinity each have a distinct identity), a processive theme (the Father God gained his power and wisdom through time), and a humanistic promise (all faithful saints can in time become gods in a celestial kingdom).

Smith saved his most creative and distinctive religious innovations until the last five years of his life (1839–44), when he served in effect as king of the largest Mormon colony at Nauvoo, Illinois, until his death at the hands of an anti-Mormon mob. This final phase followed a turbulent six years in which Mormons had struggled, against great resistance and eventually successful repression, to create their new Zion in western Missouri. In Nauvoo, Smith launched the construction of a great Mormon Temple (much larger than an earlier one in Kirkland), and simultaneously revealed three new, secret Temple rites available to both the living and the dead. Only two were widely known and practiced among Mormons before Smith's 1844 martyrdom—a special anointing ritual called an endowment, and vicarious baptisms, by living Mormons, in behalf of dead progenitors, in order to make available to them the forms of celestial glory otherwise open only to latter-day saints. This practice led Mormons to establish what has become an unmatched archive of genealogical records.

The third rite involved a special, Temple marriage for eternity, a marriage necessary for the highest forms of glory in the afterlife. This marriage, performed both for living couples and vicariously for ancestors, had one troubling and in time for American Mormons almost disastrous implication: Mormon males, like the ancient Jewish patriarchs, could seal themselves to more than one wife. Smith was sealed to a still controverted number of wives, and used his authority as head of the church to seal several elders in plural marriages. Until his death, Smith and the Apostles tried, without great success, to keep plural marriages secret; not until 1852 in Utah did Smith's successor, Brigham Young, announce it to the whole church. Smith was spared the four decades of controversy and near warfare that followed in Utah. After his death, his first wife and a number of midwestern Mormons denied that Smith ever authorized plural marriages. They rejected all the secret Temple rites and eventually formed the Reorganized LDS.

Joseph Smith was one of the most original and inventive religious prophets of the last two centuries. His early, cultlike sect would mature into a large, international religion in one century. For a time the most radical and persecuted sect in America, it is now respected, socially conservative, and wealthy. Joseph Smith never expected such an outcome, but his church still honors him in all ways. Since his death, the LDS has neither deviated from any one of his distinctive doctrines, nor has it added to them.

PAUL CONKIN

FURTHER READING

Fawn McKay Brodie, *No Man Knows My History: the Life of Joseph Smith, the Mormon Prophet* (New York: Knopf, 1971).

Richard L. Bushman, *Joseph Smith and the Beginnings of Mormonism* (Urbana: University of Illinois Press, 1984).

Joseph Smith, *Selected Sermons and Writings*, ed. Robert L. Millet (New York: Paulist Press, 1989).

Ernest H. Taves, *Trouble Enough: Joseph Smith and the Book of Mormon* (Buffalo: Prometheus Books, 1984).

Social Darwinism In a 1903 article the Progressive Era sociologist EDWARD A. ROSS introduced the first printed discussion in the United States of "Social Darwinism." Typically, the reference was negative. Typically, the target was imprecise. Typically, Ross would himself be condemned by historians as a "Social Darwinist."

The phrase arose in Europe as an epithet to be hurled at ideological opponents. Several European socialists and left republicans argued in the 1890s that "social Darwinists" misinterpreted Darwinian theory as an apologia for the economically successful. In the next decade a second definition with completely different objects of criticism arose among pacifists for whom the emphasis on struggle, competition, and survival in DARWINISM seemed to glorify battle. American social scientists like Ross occasionally borrowed one of the possible usages of Social Darwinism, but sometimes confessed an understandable confusion about its ill-defined, amorphous character.

The phrase gradually entered the lexicon of political and intellectual historians, particularly after the publication in 1944 of *Social Darwinism in American Thought* by RICHARD HOFSTADTER. Due primarily to

Hofstadter's work the presumed center of Social Darwinist activity shifted from Europe to the U.S., while its heyday moved back to the 1870s and 1880s. Most critically, Social Darwinism broadened into the reigning social philosophy of the Gilded Age. The term became associated especially with Herbert Spencer and WILLIAM GRAHAM SUMNER, to the point that Social Darwinism was whatever either writer might have written that historians found repugnant. In this scenario, reformist social theorists led by LESTER FRANK WARD launched a counterattack that ultimately culminated in Progressivism. Historians (such as Bernard Semmel, R. J. Halliday, Thomas Gossett, Janet Sayers) also expanded the Social Darwinist rubric to include propagandists for imperialism, eugenicists, and any writers on racial or sexual politics who resorted to biological arguments. However, while this analytical flexibility allowed many figures to be added to the roster of reputed Social Darwinists, it also provided grounds for demands to expunge others because they did not precisely fit the criteria for one or another of the possible definitions (thus Irvin Wyllie on the American businessman, Joseph Wall on Andrew Carnegie, and David Burton on Theodore Roosevelt). At the same time, the assumption that Ward, Ross, and other critics of Sumner and Spencer had presented a real alternative came increasingly under question, especially (although not exclusively) by historians to the left of Hofstadter. As they investigated the Darwinistic rhetoric of liberal reformers as well as conservatives, it seemed to Greta Jones and other scholars that a biological reductiveness existed at the core of mainstream Anglo-American social theory.

Simultaneously the phrase began to reemerge in critiques of current trends, notably the economic and social policies of the Nixon–Ford and Reagan–Bush administrations, that writers found reminiscent and probably derivative of nineteenth-century Social Darwinism. Meanwhile some scholars (such as Allan Chase, Stephen Jay Gould, Steven Rose, and Marshall Sahlins) discerned a revived Social Darwinism in claims of statistical links between race and IQ; in the work of professional and amateur ethologists interpreting important human traits as survivals of animal drives; and above all in SOCIOBIOLOGY, which is literally "social Darwinism" but dares not use a name that has from its inception been reserved for ideas with which an author disagreed.

Nineteenth-century intellectuals certainly believed that the Darwinian revolution had implications for social science, if only because it symbolized the most critical step in the secularization of Western thought. Charles Darwin and the early Darwinians were no exceptions. However, most applications of Darwinized phraseology prior to the mid-1890s did not represent serious efforts to fuse biological and social science, nor did Social Darwinism hold sway as a popular philosophy. The occasional presence of phrases like "survival of the fittest" does not indicate their meaning or significance, for the metaphors that writers choose to employ do not necessarily reflect the underlying structure and sources of their ideas. The best available evidence indicates that Darwinian phrasing even for Sumner represented an effort to engage audiences with current jargon that could be, and was, dropped when it proved counterproductive.

Nevertheless, from around 1890 through the first decade of the new century, theorists of all political orientations felt compelled to situate their views within a Darwinian universe of ideas. The traditional dream of a unitary philosophy of existence and the belief in a hierarchy of sciences, in which sociology built upon (even as it remained distinct from) biology, ensured that social scientists would have to deal with evolution. Moreover, by the mid-1890s natural selection seemed more important to biologically sophisticated social thinkers than in previous decades, as neo-Darwinism called into question liberal hopes for rapid social change through the inheritance of acquired characteristics. By 1920, however, the impetus to relate social and biological science had faltered, primarily due to the specialization within academic disciplines associated with professionalization. An emphasis on environmental rather than innate problems also contributed to the shift, as did the temporary eclipse of natural selection as a factor explaining evolution during the early years of Mendelian genetics.

The advent of sociobiology and similar endeavors suggests that the arguments against seeking common ground between biology and social life have lost much of their potency. Social scientists will of course differ in their attitudes toward the new approaches, which vary in the sturdiness of their foundations and the plausibility of their interpretative frameworks. Invective, however, should not be confused with scholarly debate, nor epithets with analysis. In both historical studies and discourse on contemporary political and scientific issues, it is time to retire "Social Darwinism" from our vocabulary.

DONALD C. BELLOMY

FURTHER READING

Robert C. Bannister, *Social Darwinism: Science and Myth in Anglo-American Social Thought* (Philadelphia: Temple University Press, 1979).

Donald C. Bellomy, "'Social Darwinism' Revisited." *Perspectives in American History*, n.s., 1 (1984): 1–129.

Carl N. Degler, *In Search of Human Nature: the Decline and Revival of Darwinism in American Social Thought* (New York: Oxford University Press, 1991).

John C. Greene, *Science, Ideology, and World View: Essays in the History of Evolutionary Ideas* (Berkeley: University of California Press, 1981).

Richard Hofstadter, *Social Darwinism in American Thought* (1944; rev. ed., Boston: Beacon, 1955).

Greta Jones, *Social Darwinism and English Thought: the Interaction between Biological and Social Theory* (Atlantic Highlands, N.J.: Humanities, 1980).

Robert J. Richards, *Darwin and the Emergence of Evolutionary Theories of Mind and Behavior* (Chicago: University of Chicago Press, 1987).

George W. Stocking Jr., *Victorian Anthropology* (New York: Free Press, 1987).

social mobility "The opportunity for social mobility for everyone," wrote Lloyd Warner in 1953, "is the very fabric of the 'American Dream'" (p. 129). Yet the fact is that the promise of American life came to be identified with social mobility only when more hopeful interpretations of opportunity had begun to fade; that the concept of social mobility embodies a fairly recent and impoverished understanding of the American dream; and that its ascendancy, in our own time, measures the recession of the dream and not its fulfillment.

The assumption that opportunity has always meant what it means today calls for critical examination. Yet historians and sociologists alike have confined their attention to the question of whether mobility rates have increased or decreased over time. A vast body of social research points fairly consistently to the conclusion that rates of mobility have remained more or less constant ever since the Civil War. During that same period of time, however, the concentration of wealth and power has widened the chasm between the affluent classes (no more than the upper 20 percent of the population) and those who struggle to make ends meet, follow orders instead of issuing them, and take little part in the conversation of our culture. It appears that a high degree of social mobility is by no means inconsistent with deep divisions of CLASS. As Wendell Berry has observed, our society is at once highly stratified and highly mobile.

This seeming paradox should make us ask whether social mobility is a good index of DEMOCRACY. Mobility rates tell us something about the recruitment of elites but very little about the distribution of social rewards, the nature and structure of privilege, or the vitality of institutions that promote popular self-government. The Nazis and the Bolsheviks, rising elites eager to break aristocratic control of the military and civil service, encouraged a system of promotion based strictly on merit; yet they can hardly be said to have established democratic regimes. That Americans have embraced social mobility as the very definition of democracy suggests that democracy has come to be understood primarily as a method of choosing our leaders and of regulating access to elite status.

It is the concept of social mobility, then, and not the rate of upward mobility, that most requires historical study. It was only toward the end of the nineteenth century, when the increasingly hierarchical structure of American life became undeniable, that opportunity came to be widely associated with the achievement of superior standing in a stratified, pecuniary, and class-conscious society. In the early part of the nineteenth century it was more commonly associated with the well-being and self-respect allegedly enjoyed by the "workingmen"—an expansive term that included not only those who worked with their hands but anyone who "superintends the employment of capital," as Robert Rantoul put it in 1833, "which diligence and prudence have enabled him to acquire" (p. 223). A broad distribution of property appeared to distinguish the social order of the northern United States from the hierarchical class systems that prevailed in older countries and in the planter society of the South. The force of the contrast depended on the claim that most Americans owned a little property and worked for a living, not that it was easier for Americans to start from the bottom and rise to the top. Citizenship appeared to have given even the humbler members of American society access to the knowledge and cultivation elsewhere reserved for the privileged classes. It was their restless curiosity, their skeptical and iconoclastic turn of mind, their resourcefulness and self-reliance, their capacity for invention and improvisation that most dramatically seemed to differentiate the laboring classes in the North from their counterparts in other parts of the world.

Lincoln's refutation of the "mud-sill theory" advanced by apologists for slavery summed up the view of democracy that prevailed in the first half of the nineteenth century (not without opposition, to be sure, from competing conceptions of the promised land). The mud-sill theorists took the position that every form of civilization had to rest on one or another form of forced, degraded labor. Wage labor, they argued, was far more cruel than slavery, since employers acknowledged no responsibility to feed and clothe hired laborers. Lincoln did not quarrel with his opponents' disparaging view of wage labor, but he maintained that there was no "such thing as the free hired laborer being fixed to that condition for life." His claim that wage labor in the North was a temporary condition leading to proprietorship

has often been misunderstood as a typical statement of the belief in what later came to be called social mobility; but a closer reading makes it clear that Lincoln conceived of property as a means not of escaping from labor but of realizing its full potential for self-culture. When he argued that advocates of free labor "insisted on universal education," he did not mean that education served as a means of upward mobility. He meant that citizens of a free country were expected to work with their heads as well as their hands. Democracy, he said, had abrogated the "old rule" that "educated people did not perform manual labor"; it thus severed the historic link between learning, leisure, and inherited wealth (pp. 478–9).

It is significant that "social mobility" entered the academic vocabulary in the context of uneasiness about the closing of the frontier. Summing up the "contributions of the West to American democracy" in the *Atlantic* in 1903, Frederick Jackson Turner gave a new twist to the opportunity so long associated with the frontier.

> Western democracy through the whole of its earlier period tended to the production of a society of which the most distinctive fact was the freedom of the individual to rise under conditions of social mobility, and whose ambition was the liberty and well-being of the masses. (p. 266)

The last phrase preserved some of the older meaning of democracy, but the rest of the sentence identified the "well-being of the masses" not with the democratization of competence, virtue, and self-respect but with the opportunity to rise in the social scale. In the twentieth century, this interpretation of democracy has completely eclipsed the much richer interpretations that preceded it. Ambition no longer seeks a "competence." "Moving up," as Berry says, appears to be the only prize worth pursuing.

> One does not think to improve oneself by becoming better at what one is doing or by assuming some measure of public responsibility in order to improve local conditions; one thinks to improve oneself... by 'moving up' to a 'place of higher consideration.' (p. 159)

Berry takes this last phrase from a memoir written by Justin Smith Morrill in 1874, in which Morrill explained the purposes behind the 1862 legislation bearing his name—legislation establishing a system of land-grant colleges for teaching "agriculture and the mechanic arts." The Morrill Act, as Berry sees it, can be seen both as the fulfillment of the Jeffersonian tradition and the beginning of its undoing. On the one hand, it was designed to discourage "short occupancy and a speedy search for new homes," practices associated with an exploitative, wasteful pattern of farming and with the "rapid deterioration of the soil." In other words, it was designed to discourage mobility, not to promote it. On the other hand, it also appeared to aim at the elevation of agriculture to professional status. Morrill objected to the "monopoly of education" exercised by liberal arts colleges, on the grounds that it restricted the "number of those who might be supposed to be qualified to fill places of higher consideration in private or public employments to the limited number of graduates of the literary institutions." (*See also* PROFESSION.) As Berry points out, Morrill's intentions were ambiguous. He wished to "exalt the usefulness" of "those who must win their bread by labor," but what he really seemed to exalt was professional status. "Would education exalt their usefulness by raising the quality of their work or by making them eligible for promotion to 'places of higher consideration'?" (pp. 145–7)

Berry's interrogation of Morrill defines the most important choice a democratic society has to make—whether to raise the general level of competence, energy, and devotion—VIRTUE, as it was called in an older political tradition—or merely to promote a broader recruitment of elites. Our society has clearly chosen the second course. It has identified opportunity with upward mobility and made upward mobility the overriding goal of social policy. The debate about affirmative action shows how deeply this pathetically restricted notion of opportunity has entered public discourse. A policy designed to recruit minorities into the professional and managerial class is opposed not because it strengthens the dominant position of this class but because it weakens the principle of meritocracy. Both sides argue on the same grounds. Both see careers open to talent as the be-all and end-all of democracy, whereas careerism tends to undermine democracy by divorcing knowledge from practical experience, devaluing the kind of knowledge that is gained from experience, and generating social conditions in which ordinary people are not expected to know anything at all. The reign of specialized expertise—the logical result of policies that equate opportunity with open access to "places of higher consideration"—is the antithesis of democracy as it was understood by those who saw this country as the "last, best hope of earth."

CHRISTOPHER LASCH

See also EQUALITY.

FURTHER READING

Wendell Berry, *The Unsettling of America: Culture and Agriculture* (New York: Avon, 1977).

Rex Burns, *Success in America: the Yeoman Dream and the Industrial Revolution* (Amherst: University of Massachusetts Press, 1976).

Abraham Lincoln, "Address before the Wisconsin State Agricultural Society," Milwaukee, Sept. 30, 1859, in Roy P. Basler, ed., *The Collected Works of Abraham Lincoln*, vol. 3 (New Brunswick: Rutgers University Press, 1953).

Robert Rantoul, "An Address to the Workingmen of the United States of America" (1833), in Luther Hamilton, ed., *Memoirs, Speeches, and Writings of Robert Rantoul, Jr.* (Boston: John P. Jewett, 1854).

Stephan Thernstrom, *Poverty and Progress: Social Mobility in a Nineteenth-Century City* (Cambridge: Harvard University Press, 1964).

Frederick Jackson Turner, "Contributions of the West to American Democracy" (1903), in *The Frontier in American History* (New York: Henry Holt, 1920).

W. Lloyd Warner, *American Life: Dream and Reality* (1953; rev. ed., Chicago: University of Chicago Press, 1962).

social science   In the United States, since the early twentieth century, social science has referred to a group of disciplines that position themselves between the natural sciences and the humanities and seek systematic knowledge of the human world. Centering on the fields of economics, sociology, political science, and anthropology, the social sciences have at various times also included geography, social psychology, and linguistics, and drawn heavily on history and psychology. This domain of knowledge has been differently constructed in different countries; what the French call the *sciences humaines* and the Germans the *Geisteswissenschaften* are less closely modeled on natural science than is the case in the United States and also less narrowly focused on the practical management of social affairs.

The origins of the social sciences can be traced to the ambitions of the ENLIGHTENMENT. Such thinkers as Montesquieu, Adam Smith, Condorcet, and Herder had as their object of interest the progressive, modern, differentiated society that they believed had come into existence in the eighteenth century; their hope was to use the new scientific methods developed in physical science and philology to understand and guide it. Distinctive intellectual traditions formed during the course of the nineteenth century, first political economy, around the classical paradigm developed by Smith, Malthus, and Ricardo; then more loosely, a science of politics that drew largely from history; and sociology, building on both the speculations of Comte and Spencer and on the social investigation of what were called the dependent, delinquent, and defective classes. Anthropology joined a tradition of investigation of non-Western peoples to progressivist assumptions about Western modernity, in rationalist or romantic counterpoint to the other social sciences.

From the late eighteenth century, when the Constitutional framers utilized Montesquieu's science of politics, and the early nineteenth century, when debates over national economic policy drew on political economy, the social sciences figured in discussion of public affairs in the United States. They also gradually entered the curriculum of COLLEGES AND UNIVERSITIES under the umbrella of moral philosophy. At the end of the century, social scientists were participants in and beneficiaries of the reform of American higher education and established their fields in the new universities.

These disciplines were always diverse, harboring conflicting viewpoints and multidisciplinary impulses, yet it is possible to describe the predominant course or mainstream of American social science. From the outset, economics, sociology, and political science were framed by the idea of AMERICAN EXCEPTIONALISM and the aim of escaping the ills that modernity was inflicting upon Europe. During the Gilded Age, rapid industrialization, class conflict, and then mass immigration and urbanization forced social scientists to join American experience to that of Europe and embrace modernity. Yet exceptionalism continued to shape their idealized vision of American liberal society and their desire to insure it against the vicissitudes of history by scientific control.

From the 1890s through the 1950s, perhaps the highpoint of their influence on American thought, the social sciences played a number of roles in intellectual life. Along with natural scientists, social scientists restructured practical knowledge around the specialized knowledge of experts. Committed to the American MISSION, the duty of leadership, and often, Christian idealism, they were eager to solve the problems of the new industrial society. Specialized bodies of knowledge gave them a basis for practical intervention and served to establish their professional authority. (*See also* PROFESSION.)

Most of the tasks social scientists undertook, however, involved controversial, inherently political, problems. Since demand for their services rested on their ability to provide unbiased information and advice, their professional standing as experts required that they circumvent or repress any radical values inherent in their diagnoses and prescriptions or wear the protective coloration of moderate politics. With few exceptions, social scientists worked along the main ideological lines of American politics, from conservative protection of the market economy to liberal promotion of state-centered economic regulation, social provision, and political reform.

Equally important in American intellectual life were the visions of the individual and SOCIETY that the social sciences purveyed to students and the public. Given their commitment to LIBERALISM, most social scientists constructed their discourses around the functioning of individuals within a social field. They were also conscious of the need to legitimate American society, first against the threat of SOCIALISM, and then, from the 1930s to the 1950s, against the dual threat of fascism and communism. However, there was a decided shift from the liberal worldviews they formulated into the 1930s, focused on socializing individuals and their practices, to the concern for integrated social systems in the 1940s and 1950s.

In economics, the earlier and later liberal paradigms were tied uneasily together. In the economists' marginalist neoclassical paradigm, autonomous individuals satisfied their wants, values tended toward equilibrium, and maximum utility was attained in the capitalist market. According to the macroeconomic theory of KEYNESIANISM that was joined to this individualistic microeconomics, central government manipulation of aggregate factors was necessary to keep the system going at full employment. Sociologists countered the economists' hypertrophy of individual self-interest, but, rooted in liberal theory, many of them also postulated autonomous individuals and discussed the processes that knit them into community and society. In the theories of the 1940s and 1950s, the functional constituents of society and behavior replaced individuals as the focus of analysis, as in the work of TALCOTT PARSONS, and the systemic character of these functional units was stressed as they moved through permeable social structures toward social cohesion and equilibrium. Political science developed in a parallel direction. Increasingly skeptical of ordinary individuals' ability to act as rational deliberative agents in a democracy, political scientists like David Truman reconfigured the polity as a pluralist system of competing interest groups that tended toward an equilibrium of justice and order.

In the hands of FRANZ BOAS and his students, the anthropologists' concept of culture initially served the purposes of a skeptical and egalitarian liberalism, countering traditional biological ideas of RACE and GENDER and encouraging the recognition of cultural relativism. But the concept of culture was also used to solidify the functionalist social systems of the 1940s and 1950s. Hence, if visions of the cooperative order produced by liberal individualism remained at the base of these theories, the individual was now fully integrated into a social system, less a free rational agent than a unit programmed to "choose" the market goods, functional goals, group interests, and cultural values set by system norms. Social science theories achieved their authority in the 1950s by legitimating American liberal society in a period of doubt, but also often by expressing, as did DAVID RIESMAN in *The Lonely Crowd* (1950), deep ambivalence about the transformation of liberal individualism. At the time, social scientists rarely recognized their own complicity in that impasse.

The practical and discursive roles that the social sciences played in American intellectual life were heavily influenced by scientism, the determination to fashion the social sciences on the model of natural science, based on the positivist assumption that scientific knowledge provides privileged access to reality (*see also* SCIENTISM AND COGNITIVISM). The social science disciplines had aspired to the status of sciences since they entered the universities, and the desire to escape ideological controversy and to develop the capacity for prediction and control of society sharpened their intention.

The neoclassical paradigm early allowed economists to claim scientific status. During the 1920s scientism captured or invaded the other social sciences, spearheaded by the movement to BEHAVIORISM in psychology and the adoption of statistical techniques in sociology and political science. A still higher point of scientific aspiration was reached in the 1950s with quantitative modeling, systems analysis, functionalism, and behavioral science. Scientism steered the practical efforts of the social scientists toward technocratic manipulation and reified their liberal worldview as natural process, masking the contingent structures of history and the social scientists' own normative judgments.

Throughout this period, there were dissenters from the expert practice, liberal ideology, and/or scientism of mainstream social science, notably adherents to the historical school of economics, various champions of socialism such as THORSTEIN VEBLEN, and pragmatist nonconformists. In the 1960s a more powerful opposition was mounted from outside as well as inside these disciplines. If mainstream social science had resonated with the CONSENSUS around nationalism and chastened Cold War liberalism of the 1950s, this was not the case in the 1960s, when political and social upheaval helped to amplify longer-standing critical currents.

Opposition to mainstream social science centered on its claim to OBJECTIVITY. An attack from the political left, inside and outside the academy, exposed the liberal biases and conservative purposes within its theory and practice. Although there were defenders of science and expertise, the polarization of opinion in the academy only strengthened the case against objectivity. Another, potentially more serious, challenge came from the philosophical critique of POSITIVISM. While the positivist faith of American social scientists was not always self-conscious or theoretically informed, they had often used positivist philosophy to justify their positions. In the 1960s, however, positivism was severely undermined by philosophers and historians of science like THOMAS S. KUHN; by the 1970s, RICHARD J. BERNSTEIN, CLIFFORD GEERTZ, and others brought these critical reflections home to the social sciences. Soon, theoretical and political critique was joined by feminists, poststructuralists, and others. Besides extending earlier historicist and pragmatist concerns, these heterodox social scientists drew support from the contemporary rise of hermeneutic and linguistic theory in the humanities.

Among many social scientists, however, faith in the privileged status of science did not depend on its philosophical defense, and the discrediting of so much of the theory and practice of the 1950s only encouraged the search for new and better forms of science. These social scientists turned to the natural sciences, particularly evolutionary biology and cognitive psychology, and to the most mathematized of the social sciences, economics, for models of social behavior.

One consequence of this situation has been to deepen fragmentation, as SOCIOBIOLOGY and rational choice theory join a now substantial variety of Marxist, phenomenological, historical, hermeneutic, and feminist explorations. Substantive fragmentation, and the conflict it engenders, has probably gone furthest in anthropology, the social science most open to new currents from the humanities. A second consequence has been to strengthen economics in relation to the other social sciences. Political polarization and the rise of conservative politics left sociology, the discipline most closely associated with the upheavals of the 1960s, weakened by attacks from the left and right. Economics, however, benefited, for since the 1960s it had placed increasing reliance on its individualistic microeconomic theory and was a principal intellectual source of NEOCONSERVATISM and the new CONSERVATISM of the 1970s. Moreover, as it became mathematized, economics had become increasingly abstract, so that it was prepared to extend its reach to any kind of rational choice under constrained conditions. As a result, rational choice theory has colonized considerable areas of sociology and political science, transforming what had been understood as social and institutional bonds into calculations of self-interest.

Whether the social sciences will be dismembered by these shifts, or whether the disciplines will once again simply incorporate their warring factions as independent subdivisions, is, at this writing, uncertain. So too is the extent to which—outside of economics—social scientists devoted to scientism can continue to constitute a mainstream of their heterogeneous disciplines.

DOROTHY ROSS

FURTHER READING

Richard J. Bernstein, *The Restructuring of Social and Political Theory* (New York: Harcourt, Brace, Jovanovich, 1976).
——, *Beyond Objectivism and Relativism: Science, Hermeneutics and Praxis* (Philadelphia: University of Pennsylvania Press, 1983).
Howard Brick, "Society," in Stanley I. Kutler, ed., *Encyclopedia of the United States in the Twentieth Century* (New York: Simon and Schuster, forthcoming).
Burton R. Clark and Guy R. Neave, eds., *Academic Disciplines and Indexes*, vol. 4 of *The Encyclopedia of Higher Education* (Oxford: Pergamon, 1992).
Sandra Harding, *Whose Science? Whose Knowledge? Thinking from Women's Lives* (Ithaca: Cornell University Press, 1991).
Charles E. Lindblom, *Inquiry and Change: the Troubled Attempt to Understand and Shape Society* (New Haven: Yale University Press, 1990).
Peter T. Manicas, *A History and Philosophy of the Social Sciences* (Oxford: Blackwell, 1987).
Dorothy Ross, *The Origins of American Social Science* (Cambridge: Cambridge University Press, 1991).
——, ed., *Modernist Impulses in the Human Sciences, 1870–1930* (Baltimore: Johns Hopkins University Press, 1994).

socialism   Why was there ever any socialism in America? How could anyone have ever believed that America would become a socialist country?

At the close of the twentieth century, these questions seem more pertinent than the older conventional inquiry into why American socialism has not been stronger. The death of Marxism as a serious political force in the world has erased what remained of the once commonplace assumption that some sort of socialism was bound to supplant capitalism in the industrialized countries. Consequently, the old debates about AMERICAN EXCEPTIONALISM—the failure of the United States to follow this path of presumed progress—now seem quaint. The United States, far from exceptional, now appears to have been in the vanguard; socialism, no wave of the future, now looks (at best) like a temporary historical stage through which various nations passed before reaching the great transition to capitalist DEMOCRACY. The strongest challenges to that transition have come not from socialism but from ethnic and national identities, some old, some surprisingly new—just as in America the politics of RACE, ETHNICITY, and region have always superseded the politics of CLASS. More than

ever, socialism looks utterly irrelevant to the history of American ideas.

And yet even a cursory review of American politics and culture shows that a variety of socialist traditions have been deeply embedded in our national life and have surfaced repeatedly. Consider, for example, the importance of socialism (or close encounters with socialism) to many of the canonical American novelists, from NATHANIEL HAWTHORNE, WILLIAM DEAN HOWELLS, and THEODORE DREISER to JACK LONDON, RICHARD WRIGHT, and NORMAN MAILER. Then consider the library of socialist writings by lesser American figures, most of them little read today outside the classroom but once followed closely by huge audiences—the editorials of Horace Greeley, the tracts of Laurence Gronlund, the muckraking novels of UPTON SINCLAIR, and scores of more obscure works. Entire intellectual and artistic movements—TRANSCENDENTALISM, MODERNISM, the Social Gospel, social REALISM—are unintelligible without an appreciation of American socialist ideas. Outside of the intelligentsia, the Marxian socialist vision of comradely EQUALITY once galvanized immigrant workers and native-born dissenters from the sweatshops of the Lower East Side to the lumber camps of the Pacific Northwest. More recently, long after Marxian socialism had retreated to the outer fringes of American politics, one could still find other socialist influences in the pronouncements of various popular movements and spokesmen, not least in the American commonwealth evoked by MARTIN LUTHER KING JR.

Behind this long history of American socialism lies a paradox: socialism's apparent failures in the United States partially stem from a widespread acceptance of some of its key tenets. In Britain and Europe, socialism, with its radical egalitarian ideals, emerged in the nineteenth century as a thorough rejection of the combined forces of monarchy, landed aristocracy, and moneyed power. Only late in the century, when LIBERALISM began to gain the ascendency, did European socialists gain a modicum of intellectual and political legitimacy; after Anglo-European liberalism declined in the era of World War I, laborites, socialists, and (eventually) communists were poised to fill the political vacuum.

The United States, however, was more hospitable to certain lines of socialist thinking at a much earlier date—before, in fact, the term "socialism" had even passed into common English usage. Religious notions of the covenant, the American Revolution's declaration of the natural right to rebellion against oppressive authority, the vaunting of the transcendent common good in the early state constitutions, the ideal of a formally classless state—all marked the new republic's mainstream political culture as a radical departure from the rest of the world (although slavery and other injustices tempered that departure). The central ideal of equality, compatible with purely selfish and privatist understandings, could also be turned—as the Federalists discovered to their chagrin in the 1790s—into blistering political critiques of the exploitative power of the moneyed few over the productive many. Even with regard to property, early nineteenth-century American courts came to enshrine not some fancied absolutism of individual property rights, but the principle that when individual rights were in conflict, the interests of the greater public good should prevail. With these ideas already so much a part of American life, later proponents of socialist politics (and especially revolutionary politics) would always run the risk of sounding redundant, out of touch with American conditions.

This initial paradox of American socialism gave rise to another: despite socialism's difficulties, the United States, with its professions of democracy, became the testing ground for a dizzying array of socialist ideas—the home to what was probably the greatest number of practical socialist projects in the world. Immigrants, many of them refugees from autocratic oppression, brought with them every variety of Marxism, Lassalleanism, communist anarchism, and religious communitarianism. Where immigrants did not do the importing, home-grown intellectuals and activists tried to Americanize socialisms from abroad, producing hybrids that ranged from the American Fourierism of the 1840s to the American Maoism of the 1960s. Still other Americans, drawing on native secular and sacred traditions, forged untold hundreds of socialist communities and campaigns: utopian religious societies, labor-note cooperatives, free-love communes, and political insurgencies. From one angle, the United States may look like the least socialist of nations; from another, it looks like a great hothouse of socialist experimentalism.

The full history of this experimentalism dates back to the émigré German pietists of the seventeenth century. Limiting ourselves to the modern period, there have been three phases of roughly equal length in American socialist development. The first phase, which lasted from the aftermath of the Revolution to the Civil War, was broadly speaking communitarian, and reflected a widely felt spiritual and political disquiet amid the early market revolution. Revivalist churches and a profusion of small radical sects, eager to reestablish the congregation of saints that seemed endangered by selfishness and greed, shaded off into more zealous collections of believers who were determined to live free of sin and to surrender themselves

completely to the Kingdom of Christ on earth. Prophecies of the Kingdom varied widely, from the celibate communism of the United Society of Believers (or Shakers) to the authoritarian complex-marriage régime of the Oneida Perfectionists, led by JOHN HUMPHREY NOYES. The religious communitarians shared, however, belief in a MILLENNIALISM, the conviction that they lived in suspended time, and that by their submergence of self into the communal family they were preparing themselves for the day of reckoning.

The secular communitarians, led by the Owenites and Fourierists, were less interested in salvation than in pursuing happiness on earth, as delineated in the Declaration of Independence. Increasingly, they (like many other Americans after 1815) saw the growing class divisions and inequalities of the market revolution as a threat to the Revolution's legacy. Taking their fears to the logical conclusion, the followers of the British socialist Robert Owen, including his son ROBERT DALE OWEN, constructed cooperative manufacturing villages (most important, the Owenite community in New Harmony, Indiana, founded in 1825). In the 1840s, after the Owenite experiments had failed, Yankee Transcendentalists and reformers found new hope in the principles of associationism and the balanced passions as enunciated by Albert Brisbane, the disciple and self-appointed American promoter of the French utopian Charles Fourier.

The demise of these secular communities, and the marginal existence of their religious counterparts, is hardly surprising. By the 1850s, the costs of mounting such experiments and making a go of it in the rapidly commercializing United States were simply too great to bear. Yet the remarkable thing is that, as long as they lasted, the early communitarians won toleration, even respect. Whereas heretical millenarians in Britain and Europe had faced fierce official persecution, America's Shakers, Perfectionists, and others faced hardly any. Albert Brisbane, assisted by his friend and sometime devotee Horace Greeley, explained his Fourierist teachings to a mass audience for over a year on the front page of the Whiggish *New York Tribune*. More orthodox proponents of land reform, labor reform, educational reform, and antislavery mingled with socialist sympathizers in movements like George Henry Evans's National Reform Association.

Such relatively easy toleration vanished during socialism's second phase, the era of formal socialist politics that coincided with bitter industrial strife from the end of the Civil War to the aftermath of World War I. Socialism gained a harder political edge amid the wrenching economic transformations and violent labor clashes of the Gilded Age and after. Simultaneously, antisocialist assaults intensified, as employers, the courts, and elected officials insisted that the property rights of corporate wealth were, indeed, absolute. Through the 1870s, socialist activity was largely confined to the sectarian Marxists and Lassalleans in and around German immigrant working-class enclaves, who espoused revolutionary doctrines that sounded strangely amoral and authoritarian to most Americans. But as the pretense that the United States boasted a classless state grew unpersuasive, interest in socialist ideas began to spread. Intellectuals and publicists—most notably Laurence Gronlund, EDWARD BELLAMY, HENRY DEMAREST LLOYD and WILLIAM DEAN HOWELLS—proclaimed socialist ideas in moralizing idioms better suited to American politics. And in the aftermath of the momentous Pullman strike of 1894, the socialist movement gained its single most important convert, the railway union leader, EUGENE V. DEBS.

Debs, and the Socialist Party he helped to found in 1901, transformed American socialism from a collection of sects into a popular movement. The Socialist Party spoke the Marxian language of class struggle and revolutionary PROLETARIANISM, but it did so while appealing to the well-springs of American political culture. It presented itself as the idealistic alternative to undemocratic class rule, the living embodiment of the unselfish cooperative commonwealth. With Debs as its great evangelist, the party gathered immigrant and ethnic workers, farmers, ministers, philanthropists, professionals, and intellectuals of widely different persuasions. Although not without their tragic blind spots—especially regarding racism—the Debsian socialists came closer than any other American socialist insurgency, before or since, to combining secular concerns about moneyed power with the sense of spiritual solidarity and transformation that had driven the old communitarians.

The Socialist Party's success was, of course, illusory. Intraparty squabbling sapped its strength after 1912; the combined effects of government repression, the party's opposition to World War I, and the political fallout of the Bolshevik revolution vastly reduced its following. Thereafter, self-designated socialists mainly found themselves relegated to the political wilderness. The surviving Socialist Party, under NORMAN THOMAS, ran well in 1932 and retained a certain moral eloquence, but it was a shadow of its old Debsian self. The Communist Party, which emerged gradually after 1919, expanded its influence in intellectual circles and trade unions during the Great Depression; after 1935, Communists played an important role in the upsurge of industrial unionism and the formation of the Congress of Industrial Organizations. But the Communist Party's dogmatic Marxist-Leninism and its reflexive loyalism to the Soviet dictatorship led to its steady demise, hastened by a series of spectacular episodes, from Stalin's Moscow trials to the Nazi-Soviet pact of 1939 and on to Khrushchev's denunciation of Stalin in 1956. What was left of Leninist thinking, apart from a battered (and, during the McCarthy period, persecuted) band of CP stalwarts, passed into certain militant currents of the NEW LEFT in the 1960s; its last traces survive today in Third World solidary campaigns and anti-imperialist groups. COLD WAR rhetoric and repression, ostensibly directed against a supposed internal communist menace, had far wider implications, as the entire socialist vision became branded in the public mind as a species of conspiratorial anti-Americanism.

Yet what might look, superficially, like the era of American socialism's agonizing death was actually a third phase in its history, the period of social liberalism. To the abiding perplexity of European observers, twentieth-century American liberalism and American socialism (in its more democratic forms) showed a tendency to blur into one another at the edges. Correspondences between liberal and socialist thinking began to appear during the Progressive years before 1917, for example in the urban settlement house movements and the "new liberalism" of HERBERT CROLY and THE NEW REPUBLIC. They grew more pronounced with the coming of the New Deal. To be sure, many social democrats (and not a few liberals) objected to any such identification, asserting that Franklin Delano Roosevelt's major aim was to save American capitalism. Plainly, however, one of the costs of saving capitalism was to alter it with a series of initiatives of socialist lineage, from Social Security to federal protection for workers' organizations. Apart from France's short-lived Popular Front, the U.S. response to the global depression of the early 1930s came closest to adhering to a broadly social democratic agenda.

The full history of social liberalism after 1945 awaits its chronicler, but some pieces of it are plain enough. Social liberalism's most conspicuous backers were in the liberal wing of the Democratic Party, as well as in state parties (like the Minnesota Democratic Farmer Labor party) that carried forward the more social democratic tendencies of the New Deal. The unions formed a major pillar of support, particularly the activist unions like the United Auto Workers under the social democrat Walter Reuther. Leading black civil rights advocates, from the labor leader A. Philip Randolph to the socialist Bayard Rustin, had important ties to the social liberal milieu (and would, in time, bring rising figures like the young Martin

Luther King into closer contact with it). Important intellectual backing came from writers who dwelled at the border of liberalism and socialism, ranging from liberal Democrats like JOHN KENNETH GALBRAITH to the democratic socialists MICHAEL HARRINGTON and IRVING HOWE. Additional support came from an amalgam of clerical and lay religious groups.

During its heyday, from the late 1940s to the mid-1960s, social liberalism could claim significant victories in numerous areas of American life. Labor unions were stronger than at any other time in American history. American workers, overall, enjoyed the highest wages and standard of living in the world. Broadly Keynesian economic ideas held sway. The burgeoning CIVIL RIGHTS movement, combining grassroots defiance of segregation and support from many leading social liberals, attacked the most glaring contradiction of the New Deal coalition, the alliance with the Jim Crow South. By 1965, when a southern Democratic President was openly identifying himself with civil rights and declaring an unconditional war on poverty (partly inspired by Harrington's *The Other America*), social liberalism had apparently come into its own.

Social liberalism's decline and fall came almost as swiftly as that of the Debsians had half a century earlier. A backlash against civil rights, the weakening of the American economy, and the disastrous war in VIETNAM (escalated and then embraced for far too long by many leading social liberals) destroyed the social democratic moment of the mid-1960s; the New Left, born of Whitmanian emancipatory hopes and shocked indignation at racism, poverty, and the war, degenerated into bickering sectarianism and desperate acts of resistance; the civil rights movement, having begun to fracture into competing elements of moderate integrationism, social liberalism, and various forms of black nationalism, continued to lose its direction after King's assassination in 1968. FEMINISM and the gay rights movements of the 1970s and 1980s supplanted other forms of dissent; they also profoundly altered the tone and many of the structures of American life (*see also* GAY AND LESBIAN IDENTITIES). But social liberalism, as it had emerged out of the New Deal, was all but dead, devastated by the Reagan administration's success in shattering old party identifications. By the end of the 1980s, the federal government had run up such huge deficits that any return to a social liberal agenda seemed chimerical. Social liberals themselves began to have second thoughts about some of the main policies they had once endorsed, including affirmative action and urban poverty programs.

The collapse of the Soviet communist empire in the late 1980s and early 1990s had the ironic effect of destabilizing the Reagan coalition, for which Cold War anticommunism had been an important glue. Veteran socialists, who had long been among the most forceful anticommunists in America, could not help greeting Soviet communism's fate with a sense of satisfaction. Yet they could scarcely gloat, since the abject failure of the command economies appeared to discredit socialist ideas once and for all, as newly liberated nations rushed headlong into a romance with unchecked capitalism. The outbreak of ethnic warfare inside and outside of the fallen communist empire testified further to the naiveté of a once-invigorating socialist universalism. Most important of all, the globalization of capital and labor markets, accelerated by the computer-chip revolution, posed problems about competitiveness and innovation to which neither old-line social democracy nor social liberalism had any ready answers. The unexpected victory of the Clinton Democrats in 1992 seemingly marked a widespread revulsion against the old-time capitalist religion as practiced by the supply-side Reaganites. But it also marked a desire to transcend the formulas of social liberalism in the face of changed economic and social circumstances. Initially, the Clinton administration concentrated on universal health insurance, a diluted version of an old social democratic standby. The failure of that campaign, followed by the Republican victories in 1994, cast doubt on the political viability of any kind of social liberalism.

It should surprise no one, however, if at the dawn of the new millennium, it turns out that the history of American socialism, far from being over, has simply entered yet another phase. Since ALEXIS DE TOCQUEVILLE, a long series of observers has noted that American democratic egalitarianism breeds a corrosive INDIVIDUALISM, an egoistic withdrawal into crass material pursuits. Yet repeatedly, when confronted with the consequences of that individualism, some Americans have countered with a social egalitarianism, a larger sense of the common good—an egalitarianism that, more than de Tocqueville and others may have realized, has also been a basic component of our political life. American socialists, with their array of socialisms, have historically operated as the most idealistic proponents of that egalitarianism—sometimes failing completely, sometimes stumbling into moral blindness, but often enough helping to shape the terms and the outcomes of political debate. The label "socialist" may not survive much longer, just as the blueprints of the communitarian utopians, the Debsians, or the New Deal social liberals have not survived. But the political and intellectual impulses that have animated American socialism almost certainly will.

SEAN WILENTZ

FURTHER READING

Donald Drew Egbert and Stow Persons, eds., *Socialism and American Life*, 2 vols. (Princeton: Princeton University Press, 1952).

Albert Fried, *Socialism in America from the Shakers to the Third International: a Documentary History* (Garden City, N.Y.: Doubleday, 1970).

John H. M. Laslett and Seymour Martin Lipset, *Failure of a Dream?: Essays in the History of American Socialism*, rev. ed. (Berkeley: University of California Press, 1984).

Irving Howe, *Socialism and America* (San Diego, Calif.: Harcourt Brace Jovanovich, 1985).

society   Although reflection on the nature of human interaction has classical and Christian antecedents, the concept of society dates from the eighteenth century. It first emerged in the Scottish Enlightenment writings of Adam Ferguson. Francis Hutcheson, John Millar, and Adam Smith, who tried to understand the economic, religious, and political turmoil of the seventeenth and eighteenth centuries that dissolved traditional hierarchical networks of AUTHORITY and identity. Freed to pursue personal ends, economic and otherwise, individuals staked their claims to the satisfaction of wants and asserted personal autonomy. Their activities followed regular, discernible patterns and constituted a new sphere of human activity, which the Scots termed "civil society." Civil society differed from "COMMUNITY" and related terms for associated living in its clear demarcation from the state and church and in its independence from the intentions of any single person or group. Civil society did not degenerate into anarchy, the Scots contended, because it was maintained by exchange and by "natural sympathies." These sentiments of emulation and fellow feeling created the trust that made contracts possible. Personally entered but impersonally enforced, the contract replaced customary OBLIGATION and duty as the primary form of human relationship in civil society.

Having both material and moral foundations, "society" could ideally integrate egoism and altruism, reason and passion, FREEDOM and order. The history of the concept, however, has been the history of the difficulties in sustaining this delicate synthesis. The meaning that Americans have attached to the term has undergone constant revision. At issue in the "society" debate has been the relative weight of moral and material elements, the ability of society to function properly without conscious intervention, the capacity of individual actors in social life, the inherent harmony of collective arrangements, and even the existence of the entity that the concept purports to describe.

Although Europeans have long regarded the United States as the prime example of civil society, Americans were relatively late in developing their own distinctive "society" tradition. Until THOMAS PAINE wrote his famous first paragraph of *Common Sense* (1776), religious and political definitions of collective life prevailed. Paine contended that society

> is produced by our wants, and government by our wickedness: the former promotes our happiness *positively* by uniting our affections, the latter *negatively* by restraining our vices. The one encourages intercourse, the other creates distinctions. (p. 65)

This separation of society from polity remained a minority view in America long after Paine, although elements of his position appeared in anti-Federalist agitation and, indeed, in *Federalist 10*. American state builders, while not oblivious to the existence of private interests, shared little of Paine's faith in the viability of a realm produced by allowing human desire free play, and emphasized instead the centrality of political institutions in uniting affections.

Paine's definition of society gave economic interaction as much significance as political engagement, but it did not identify the arena of "wants" and "intercourse" exclusively with the marketplace. By the second decade of the nineteenth century, emphasis shifted decisively toward the market as the basis of all social life. For a growing number of Americans, the values and assumptions on which economic exchange depended became the predominant ones. Politicians like HENRY CLAY and writers like HENRY C. CAREY made economic productivity and the accumulation of wealth—which colonial divines and revolutionary leaders had regarded as antithetical to ethical behavior—the measure of social health. More often than in previous periods, rational behavior meant advancing one's material interest. Even VIRTUE, which once signified the disinterested service of the public good, came to be compatible with market participation, although the female realm of DOMESTICITY was often regarded as the seat of highest virtue. Many antebellum Democrats in particular treated the liberation of society from government as the true purpose of politics. In his 1834 editorial, "True Functions of Government," WILLIAM LEGGETT offered the archetypal statement of this view:

> As a general rule, the prosperity of rational men depends on themselves. Their talents and their virtues shape their fortunes. They are therefore the best judges of their own affairs, and should be permitted to seek their own happiness in their own way, untrammeled by the capricious interference of legislative bungling, so long as they do not violate the

equal rights of others, nor transgress the general laws for the security of person and property. (p. 5)

Leggett and those who held his notion of society advocated the unfettered play of self-interest because they envisioned society as self-correcting, achieving social cohesion and moral ends through the unintended consequences of individual actions. Yet as ALEXIS DE TOCQUEVILLE noted *Democracy in America* (1835, 1840)—which remains the definitive statement of the organization of collective life around EQUALITY (his term for the absence of hierarchy based on birth and position)—many Americans believed equilibrium was threatened, not guaranteed, by the individual pursuit of interest. Voluntary associations dedicated to the solution of "social problems"—a phrase then coming into prevalent use—proliferated. Rational behavior would become moral, antebellum reformers believed, only through conscious effort and the establishment of such institutions as a compulsory system of EDUCATION and various reformatory asylums to discipline personal habits. Others were shocked by the formation of the CLASS distinctions that accompanied market relations, and troubled by the anomie and nervousness that spread through urban life. Despite their many differences, the utopian socialist followers of ROBERT DALE OWEN and Charles Fourier, such southern defenders of slavery as Henry Hughes and GEORGE FITZHUGH, and the converted Catholic defender of organicism ORESTES BROWNSON, all conceived of "society" not as the self-regulating arena of possessive INDIVIDUALISM but as its collectivist or corporate antidote. Socialists drew on ideas of "community" to define JUSTICE as cooperation, while southerners sought a return to the reciprocity of deference and protection. Both denied the validity or viability of a civil society based upon the self-determining individual.

The self-determining individual did not vanish from investigations of society during the last third of the nineteenth century, but he (and the male was still the referent) appeared less frequently as thinkers turned to a conception that distinguished society from the individuals who constituted it. Reflecting the sense of a new power outside and beyond the self, "society" now connoted a cause as well as a result of human action. Gone was the moral individualism that pervaded earlier formulations. Gone too was the term "civil society," now replaced by the simpler "society." The subtle linguistic change indicated a new emphasis on the unlimited scope and apparently objective, irresistible nature of the social domain. Two harbingers of this transformation in the meaning of society were the founders of American sociology: WILLIAM GRAHAM SUMNER and LESTER FRANK WARD. For all his well-known individualism, Sumner portrayed the history of society as an unfolding, impersonal development that individuals were powerless to deflect. His polemical opponent Ward rejected Sumner's laissez-faire stance, according to which reformers' "effort to make the world over," in the title of a famous Sumner essay, was "absurd." Ward argued that social evolution had produced in the human species beings capable of acting intelligently to shape the very evolutionary process that had produced them. But, like Sumner, he assumed the primacy of the "social" over the "individual."

Between 1880 and 1960 those who refined the holistic view of society implicit in Sumner's and Ward's work were primarily academics. The burgeoning discipline of sociology attracted men and women disenchanted with the individualistic and rationalistic psychology of the society-as-economy school, and convinced that unchecked industrial capitalism destroyed social harmony. Hoping to discover the tools to restore social solidarity, they concentrated their attention on the common moral and ideational elements identified in outline by the Scottish thinkers but slighted by many subsequent students of society. "Society," they postulated, was held together by nonrational bonds; the word denoted a web of connections of which the economy was but one part. Since this web had a reality above and beyond individuals, sociologists suggested, it also had a special power to check the disintegrative tendencies of prevailing economic relations. The work of ALBION SMALL and the social psychologists GEORGE HERBERT MEAD and CHARLES HORTON COOLEY, for instance, explored the implications of their shared belief that the individual was not an isolated monad but a being created and existing in relationship with others. That something so individual as a self was in fact formed through interaction with others led them to conclude that cooperation, not competition and egoism, was the foundation and measure of social well-being. Building upon the rejection of possessive individualism by Small, Mead, and Cooley, EDWARD A. ROSS maintained that a set of management techniques which he dubbed "social control" could restore and preserve social cohesion and keep its biological (racial) sources uncontaminated.

The high point of the polemic against the individualist, market model of society was the "Chicago School" of ROBERT E. PARK, Ernest Burgess, W. I. Thomas, and Florian Znaniecki, which identified the (noneconomic) family, school, church, and neighborhood as the locus of society. Thomas and Znaniecki's *The Polish Peasant in Europe and America* (1918–20) was representative in its stress on the collective normative rules of behavior and on the relation between those social norms and individual dispositions. Despite its accent on moral norms, the Chicago School did not entirely disregard the material aspects of society. Its members sharply differentiated traditional from modern societies, defining the latter as constituted by market relations and interest-seeking rationality. Viewing "disorganization" as the result of the failure of adaptation, they envisioned the creation of new social bonds in activities that were, in the final analysis, heavily economic and self-interested, such as farmers' cooperatives.

Where many of the leading sociologists of the first third of the twentieth century regarded "society" as a corrective to capitalism, those of the middle third stressed the study of the totality of human relations independent of and prior to the economy as such. Jettisoning common assumptions that social investigation was ultimately a reform enterprise, a quest for justice in the economic realm, students of society turned toward a noneconomic view of the social sphere. TALCOTT PARSONS and his student Robert K. Merton viewed societies as organizers of action, and argued that the common orientation of actors toward "basic values," not coercion or self-interest, accounted for social order. Parsonian "structural-functionalism" treated society as the interdependence of four functions: the management of resources, the determination of collective goals, the integration of differentiated social roles, and the replication of basic value patterns.

Parsons's work dominated the field from the mid-1940s to the late 1960s, when such critics as C. WRIGHT MILLS, Ralf Dahrendorf, and Reinhard Bendix offered a conception of society rooted in conflict rather than equilibrium. They contended that Parsons and Merton had no way, given their focus on functional social systems, to account for differential power relationships or to elucidate such persistent social problems as inequality. The new focus on conflict in the 1960s and 1970s returned the material component to the study of society. Barrington Moore's exploration in historical sociology, *The Social Origins of Dictatorship and Democracy* (1966), and Erik Olin Wright's *Class, Crisis, and the State* (1978) were just two of a number of disparate works that took society to be formed by relations between groups with conflicting interests. Not all challenges in this period to the postwar paradigm of society as harmonious integration came from materialists in the strictest sense of the term. The struggles and movements of African Americans and women underscored the saliency of RACE and GENDER in structuring reciprocal human action. Influential works like Frantz

Fanon's *Wretched of the Earth* (1963) and Kate Millett's *Sexual Politics* (1970) argued that race and gender were not simple biological characteristics, but relations of power which continually imposed burdens on people of color and women to the benefit of white males. Too often, these critics charged, the study of society had served to legitimate and normalize these inequalities.

In recent years the concept of society itself has been called into question. Some writers, rejecting the possibility of identifying systematic arrangements in the totality of human relationships, have concentrated instead on small groups or discrete functions. *The International Encyclopedia of the Social Sciences* (1968), unlike its predecessor *Encyclopedia of the Social Sciences* in the 1930s, contains no entry for "society." Others have borrowed from poststructuralist literary theory and CULTURAL ANTHROPOLOGY to dispute the assumption that the meaning of social action can be made definite. Such advocates of "indeterminacy" as the French writers Jean Baudrillard and Jean-François Lyotard, who have significant followings in the United States, and the historian and cultural theorist James Clifford contest the notion of a distinct social entity having an overall structure that impinges on or determines actions carried out within its sphere. "Society," this current of thought asserts, is an intellectual convention and does not exist independently of our discourse about it; the claim that it can depict the totality of human practices is false, disguising relations of power. Poststructuralist views, like earlier Marxist ones, are correct to note that from its inception the concept of society has been put to ideological uses. But the eagerness of poststructuralists to dismantle the idea of society as a time-bound construct is often accompanied by a dangerous complacency about the admirable goal that inspired the concept of society in the first place: grasping the obstacles to and conditions for a fulfilling collective life.

DANIEL H. BORUS

FURTHER READING

Jeffrey C. Alexander, *Theoretical Logic in Sociology*, vol. 4: *The Modern Reconstruction of Classical Thought: Talcott Parsons* (Berkeley: University of California Press, 1983).

Martin Blumer, *The Chicago School of Sociology: Institutionalization, Diversity, and the Rise of Sociological Research* (Chicago: University of Chicago Press, 1984).

William Leggett, "True Functions of Government," in Lawrence H. White, ed., *Democratick Editorials: Essays in Jacksonian Political Economy by William Leggett* (Indianapolis: Liberty Press, 1984).

Thomas Paine, *Common Sense* (1776; New York: Penguin, 1986).

Dorothy Ross, *The Origins of American Social Science* (Cambridge: Cambridge University Press, 1991).

Adam Seligman, *The Idea of Civil Society* (New York: Free Press, 1992).

Quentin Skinner, ed., *The Return of Grand Theory in the Human Sciences* (Cambridge: Cambridge University Press, 1985).

Gordon Wood, *The Radicalism of the American Revolution* (New York: Knopf, 1992).

sociobiology The concept is most broadly and briefly defined as the study of the biological sources of all animal social behavior, including that of human beings. Although the term achieved popular recognition with the publication of entomologist Edward O. Wilson's book *Sociobiology, the Modern Synthesis* in 1975, its usage extends at least as far back as the 1940s. Its scientific roots reach even farther back to Charles Darwin. Ultimately, modern sociobiological thought and practice depend upon Darwin's work for having established the validity of natural selection as the primary explanation for the evolution of all living organisms. (*See also* DARWINISM; NATURALISM.)

Simply because of that dependence, it is necessary to distinguish sociobiology from other, more familiar, if less validated uses of Darwinian evolution. To begin with, sociobiologists recognize that biological or genetic causes for social behavior vary greatly across species; in some it is clearly predominant; in others less so, as in the human species where language and culture obviously play a large role in accounting for behavior. Sociobiology differs from racial explanation for human behavior simply because its object of study is the whole species, not "races" or varieties within the species. For the same reason it is also to be distinguished from SOCIAL DARWINISM and eugenics: it does not seek to account for, or assert the superiority or inferiority of any individual or group within the human species.

Most of the work in sociobiology has dealt with animal, not human behavior. Only 30 pages of Edmund Wilson's *Sociobiology* deal with human behavior; the remaining 550 pages are devoted to the analysis of the behavior of the rest of the animal world. Sociobiology, in short, was in 1975 and is now an established field of inquiry in zoology. The extension of its principles to human behavior is the principal source of the public concern and controversy that has accompanied the concept almost from the beginning. How have its assumptions and principles been used by students of human society?

Sociobiologists assume that human beings are included in the evolutionary system enunciated by Darwin and confirmed by modern genetics, molecular biology, and population genetics. Most people in the modern world accept the idea that their bodies, thanks to the Darwinian principle of natural selection, are descended in fairly obvious fashion from animal ancestors. Many, however, find they cannot accept the related idea that human *behavioral* patterns could have been derived from animal ancestors, even though the genetic transmission of behavior in animals has been well established. (*See also* HEREDITY.)

Among those findings concerning the behavior of animals is the general absence of inbreeding among closely related social animals, a conclusion that provides the most promising explanation for the evolution of the so-called incest taboo among human beings. A similar scientific documentation of hierarchy or dominance among social animals in the wild has suggested that hierarchy, which social scientists have long identified in the great majority of human societies, past and present, is no more a human cultural invention than incest avoidance.

Since sexual reproduction usually exacts higher bodily costs for females than for males, as among human beings, it follows that the two sexes will shape their reproductive behavior around those differential costs. Thus, one would expect males to compete to gain exclusive access to females in order to maximize their reproduction, as in many animal species. The principle helps to explain why a woman's adultery, outside of modern industrial societies, is universally more severely punished than a man's. Under different ecological circumstances, females are often "courted" by males, as in many species of birds. The sociobiological reason is that the female seeks to mate with the male most likely to produce an offspring with high likelihood of survival and reproduction. This is "sexual selection," Darwin's second evolutionary principle, which he enunciated in *The Descent of Man* (1872). Some social scientists have recently found the principle to be useful in accounting for the differential sexuality of human males and females.

Since Darwinian natural selection theory concluded that each organism worked to achieve its own reproductive success, Darwin was not able to account fully for the so-called altruistic behavior of some social animals, as when an individual, despite its vulnerability, gave warning signs, or shared food. The full explanation for the behavior was only possible with the development of modern genetics in the twentieth century when it was recognized that genetic relatedness was the key to "altruistic" behavior. Ethological studies revealed that animals favored relatives who were genetically close to them because they shared the same genes. The principle is commonly referred to as "kin selection" and has been applied by social scientists in accounting for the familiar historical practice of nepotism, and for the support human family members provide for one another. It is, of course, not "altruism" in the usual humanistic meaning—"assistance without compensation"—since the vulnerable individual's danger of not reproducing would be compensated for by the genes it shared with those it was assisting.

Aside from the particular insights that sociobiology and ethology may have already provided in explaining some aspects of human behavior, many social scientists point to an additional and powerful intellectual gain. By bringing to completion the Darwinian evolutionary theory on which sociobiology rests, sociobiologists may at last be able to place the human and the biological sciences under a single explanatory framework, thereby laying a foundation for a truly evolutionary theory of human social behavior, as Darwin originally intended.

CARL N. DEGLER

See also SCIENCE; SOCIAL SCIENCE.

FURTHER READING

Christopher Badcock, *Evolution and Individual Behavior: an Introduction to Human Sociobiology* (Oxford: Blackwell, 1991).

Arthur L. Caplan, ed., *The Sociobiology Debate: Readings on Ethical and Scientific Issues* (New York: Harper and Row, 1978).

Martin Daly and Margo Wilson, *Homicide* (New York: Aldine and Gruyter, 1988).

Carl N. Degler, *In Search of Human Nature: the Decline and Revival of Darwinism in American Social Thought* (New York: Oxford University Press, 1991).

Jared M. Diamond, *Third Chimpanzee* (New York: HarperCollins, 1992).

Philip Kitcher, *Vaulting Ambition: Sociobiology and the Quest for Human Nature* (Cambridge: MIT Press, 1985).

Melvin Konner, *The Tangled Wing: Biological Constraints on the Human Spirit* (New York: Holt, Rinehart and Winston, 1982).

Donald Symons, *The Evolution of Human Sexuality* (New York: Oxford University Press, 1979).

Sontag, Susan (b. New York, N.Y., Jan. 16, 1933). Novelist and critic. Sontag's *Against Interpretation* (1966) established her as an original and influential critic of literature, the arts, and culture. She warned against the tendency of criticism to suck art dry by stressing its "meaning" at the expense of its "transparence" and "luminousness." The conditions of modern life, she held, conspire to produce a withering of the sensory and an imperial expansion of the ratiocinative; criticism, therefore, should strive not to interpret art but to make it real in our experience, to "show how it is what it is, even that it is what it is, rather than to show what it means." Her important chapter "Notes on Camp" extended the argument by showing how one could probe a new

cultural "sensibility" without reducing it to an "idea." Sontag's crusade against overinterpretation was still evident in her *Illness as Metaphor* (1979) and *AIDS and Its Metaphors* (1988), which insisted that illnesses—cancer, tuberculosis, AIDS—do not present moral meaning, despite our perennial urge to bestow such meaning on them. In addition to her fiction, Sontag is the author of such works as *Styles of Radical Will* (1968) and *On Photography* (1977).

See also CULTURAL CRITICISM.

FURTHER READING

Sohnya Sayres, *Susan Sontag: the Elegaic Modernist* (New York: Routledge, 1990).

Southern Agrarianism The term has come to be identified with the Vanderbilt Agrarians and their manifesto *I'll Take My Stand* (1930), but a brief look at the three Agrarian traditions in the South can more adequately place the Nashville group in an appropriate context. The first is a broadly secular, enlightenment-derived tradition, descending from Thomas Jefferson. The second is a conservative, organicist-romantic tradition identified with figures such as the antebellum thinker GEORGE FITZHUGH. The third, largely political, Populist tradition rose and fell in the late nineteenth century, though its legacy has persisted in diffuse ways, particularly in the region's political culture.

More intellectual energy has been expended on analyzing, championing, and denouncing the Vanderbilt Agrarians than on almost any other American community of intellectuals. Its first incarnation was as a group of poets who published a journal, *The Fugitive*, in the mid-1920s. That group, which included ALLEN TATE, JOHN CROWE RANSOM, ROBERT PENN WARREN and Donald Davidson, originally sought to rescue southern literature from the genteel tradition and thus bore witness to the first stirrings of modern writing south of the Mason-Dixon line. Not originally concerned with defending the South, the one-time Fugitive poets responded to attacks on southern culture from H. L. Mencken and others with a polemical counterattack, *I'll Take My Stand*. Comprised of polemical essays (including ones by the four figures named above), this manifesto contained a dozen broadsides directed against developments which they identified with the North (against the South), with modernity (against tradition), and with industrialization and urbanization (as opposed to an agrarian way of life).

But the Agrarianism championed in *I'll Take My Stand* was hardly monolithic. While some contributors seemed to consider their essays to be a continuation of the Civil War by other means, others were just as clearly using "the South" as a trope or metaphor. Several of the Agrarians were serious about preserving an agricultural economy, while others saw Agrarianism as a broadly conceived challenge to the spirit of cultural modernity. Still other contributors modeled their vision of the ideal social order on the plantation version of an organic society. *I'll Take My Stand* also contained truculent defenses of what Paul Conkin in *The Southern Agrarians* (1988) calls the "proprietory ideal" (p. 171), thus suggesting the presence of a kind of depoliticized populism. Of the Jeffersonian tradition of Agrarianism there was little evidence in *I'll Take My Stand*.

Two other aspects of the Agrarian position demand attention. First, except for Robert Penn Warren's essay, race was hardly mentioned in *I'll Take My Stand*. But this did not indicate a progressive or agnostic position on the issue. The Agrarians were thoroughgoing defenders of racial segregation: southern Agrarianism was generally "for whites only." Herman Nixon would later "go over" to the more progressive Chapel Hill Regionalist position, and Robert Penn Warren would later recant his relatively "moderate" defense of segregation. By contrast, Donald Davidson, Frank Owsley and Andrew Lytle of the original contributors remained stalwarts in defense of racial apartheid. The rest of the original contributors largely remained silent about race.

The aspect of Agrarianism uniting the more literary-minded Agrarians was a defense of TRADITION and of poetry (broadly construed) against the positivist spirit of science and technology. Thereby implied was the moral and even cognitive superiority of a literary to a scientific, positivist culture. And it was this position that provided the spiritual foundations for the literary critical position known as the New Criticism which was developed by Tate and Ransom, Warren and Cleanth Brooks in the mid to late 1930s.

The southern version of the New Criticism developed three broad approaches to literature, each of which derived, however indirectly, from the Agrarian ideology. First, John Crowe Ransom developed a poetics which stressed the "texture" of a work of art as an organic whole, aside from the intentions or the effects of that work of art. The aesthetic qualities of the best poetry—hierarchy, complexity, paradox—should mirror the structure of traditional society as it had existed prior to its dissolution by the acids of modernity. Allen Tate, on the other hand, wrote poetry which directly mirrored contemporary spiritual dislocations. For Tate, modern literature in general and the southern

literary renaissance in particular could only have issued from a "Janus-faced" culture, caught between tradition and modernity. For both Ransom and Tate, then, the work of art, despite its atemporal ontological status, had an obliquely mimetic function: as a reminder of what modernity had destroyed or as an exemplification of modern culture's loss of spiritual coherence and meaning. Finally, besides championing the method of practical criticism developed by Brooks and Warren in *Understanding Poetry*, the southern New Critics joined others such as T. S. Eliot who wanted to recast the traditional literary canon to incorporate modern poetry as a kind of metaphysical poetry (in both senses) and to demote the Romantics. Thus, for instance, irony was not simply one literary trope among others; rather, it was elevated to the master trope in the modernist struggle against modernity.

Ironically, the academic triumph of the New Criticism after 1945 was accompanied by the demise of the agricultural economy of the South. Though former Agrarians edited and controlled journals such as *The Southern Review*, *The Kenyon Review*, and *The Sewanee Review*, what began as an ideologically charged poetics became a more or less neutral technique of reading taught to several generations of college students all over the country. Except for Warren, whose literary and critical productivity continued apace, and Brooks, whose influence as an academic critic was pervasive, most of the original Agrarians gradually disappeared from intellectual prominence. Perhaps the one second-generation Agrarian of enduring importance was Richard Weaver (1910–1963). His general defense of the "classical-Christian-medieval synthesis," and his historical analysis of the southern tradition in *The Southern Tradition at Bay* (1963), are major statements in the canon of modern organic, traditionalist CONSERVATISM.

In general, modern Southern Agrarianism can be seen as the most important expression in twentieth-century American intellectual history of hostility to modernization and modern culture. Its attacks on modern capitalist culture and society were often as biting and cogent as those issuing from its dark double, Marxism. (There was also a radical ecological dimension to the Agrarian ideology which was never adequately developed from within the Vanderbilt Agrarian camp.) But superseded by history, Southern Agrarianism lacked a plausible vision of the future. For some interpreters, the Vanderbilt Agrarians retain value insofar as they present a counterideal to MODERNISM and POSTMODERNISM. But for others, the Agrarian vision has been so compromised by outmoded racial and cultural assumptions that it lacks any significant contemporary importance and should be consigned to the intellectual history of the region and the nation.

RICHARD H. KING

FURTHER READING

Cleanth Brooks, *Modern Poetry and the Tradition* (Chapel Hill: University of North Carolina Press, 1939).

Paul Conkin, *The Southern Agrarians* (Knoxville: University of Tennessee Press, 1988).

Richard H. King, *A Southern Renaissance: the Cultural Awakening of the Modern South, 1930–55* (New York: Oxford University Press, 1980).

Michael O'Brien, *The Idea of the Modern South, 1920–1941* (Baltimore: Johns Hopkins University Press, 1979).

Louis Rubin, *The Wary Fugitives: Four Poets and the South* (Baton Rouge: Louisiana State University Press, 1978).

Twelve Southerners, *I'll Take My Stand* (1930; New York: Harper Torchbooks, 1962).

Richard Weaver, *The Southern Essays of Richard Weaver*, ed. George M. Curtis III and James J. Thompson Jr. (Indianapolis: Liberty Press, 1987).

southern intellectual history. The tradition of identifying a distinctive pattern of intellectuality in the American South dates from the early nineteenth century, but the practice of a subdiscipline called "southern intellectual history" is a very recent phenomenon. To understand this, it helps to consider the circumstances under which these terms— "southern" and "intellectual"—converged and became attached to the discipline of history.

There were cultures in what we now call the South for centuries before the category of "the South" was invented in the early nineteenth century. Though many things later named as characteristics of the South—agrarianism, slavery, white supremacy, manners—existed before 1800, these were disparately described; the colonial plantation societies of Virginia and the Carolinas were understood in relation to others of their ilk, like Barbados, as parts of British imperial culture. Only after 1776 and 1789 and the creation of a Federal Union was there anything reliably to be "south" of, and only after the abolition of slavery in the northern states did the South come to have a distinguishing social institution; the tensions implicit in federalism drove many of the ideas formative of southern ideology. Northerners began to criticize slave society as a pernicious social anachronism. Concomitantly southern critical thinkers, partly as a means to understand slave society, began to define a role for themselves as custodians of culture, and thereby invented a culture to guard; they were the equivalent of those romantic thinkers in Europe, like Mazzini in Italy, who rested their case as thinkers upon a mutually reinforcing bond with a nation, imaginatively defined. Up to 1861, the nature of

southern society was in dispute. Controversy centered upon the centrality of slavery, whether it disqualified the South from a role in modern and progressive society, and whether the reality and depth of southern culture necessarily mandated a political independence that alone could guarantee that reality. This discourse, which identified the "South" with historical change, was reinforced by the influence of ROMANTICISM and, in particular, by historicism, with its central claim that human nature assumed different forms in different times and places, and that there were characteristic and evolving social configurations, of which nations and races were the most formative. The South was increasingly nominated and accepted as such a configuration.

At the same time, the words "intellect" and "intellectual" were undergoing a significant change. The adjective had long existed and, by the late eighteenth century, denoted a quality roughly equivalent to "rational" or "pertaining to the understanding"; it was often used by those influenced by the psychological categories of Scottish Common Sense philosophy. Thus Hugh Blair Grigsby of Virginia might write in his diary for 1828 that a debating society was "well designed to whet the intellect and amuse the fancy of those who composed it," and thereby he distinguished separable components of the mind. Professions thought peculiarly to require rationality, especially the law or the academy, were distinguished by a larger admixture of such intellect. By extension, a country might have an intellect, that is, a significant quality of rationality in the conduct and comprehension of its affairs; hence Frederick Grimké in 1838 asked Hugh Legaré, a fellow South Carolinian, to estimate "the intellect" of Germany. By this he meant, what are the significant products of rationality in Germany and how should we appraise them? The South being increasingly regarded as a cultural nation, it too might have such an intellectual quotient. So in October 1847, a writer in the *Southern Quarterly Review* could speak of "the activity of Southern intellect." In 1858 James Johnston Pettigrew of North Carolina, in approved romantic manner, could say that "the intellect of the south is like its land."

It was argued that intellect mattered in the directing of society. In 1854, for example, Oscar Lieber observed to his father Francis Lieber that graduates of the South Carolina College were "above the average of intellect of the country," a good thing since such graduates would come to form the state's elite. Similarly, in 1859 Basil Manly of Alabama argued that cities were peculiarly important because in them congregated "more of the living, controlling intellect of the land." Hence there were increasingly frequent attempts to understand the characteristic pattern of southern intellect. GEORGE FITZHUGH argued in 1857, for example, that 20 years earlier "the South had no thought—no opinions of her own." By this he meant that the South had only recently justified and constructed the educational and literary institutions by which her culture might be sustained. "It is all important that we should write our own books," he said (Faust, ed., *Ideology of Slavery*, pp. 274, 279).

The attempt to define "us," the necessarily circular venture of self-definition, has provided the essential subject-matter of southern thought ever since. Broadly speaking, the movement has been from an exclusive definition to one that is inclusive; at first, in Fitzhugh's usage, "we" were white males of the planting class, though almost simultaneously the circle was extended outwards to white women of the same class; it tentatively reached non-slaveholders before the Civil War, then more successfully whites of every class after Reconstruction and, finally and ambivalently in our own day, African Americans, who now sometimes claim the title of southerner, sometimes refuse it. "Southern" was thus one of the more expansive social identities of modern times. Intellectuals have concerned themselves with administering the processes of the identity, adjusting or exploiting its tensions, negotiating and understanding the many harrowing social transformations that have especially afflicted the South. However, before the Civil War, there was little sense of a usable noun, "the intellectual," or of a class of people called "intellectuals" or "the intelligentsia" who might be the subject-matter of a history: in the South, as elsewhere, that is a later development.

The formal study of southern thought began systematically only after the Civil War. A 12-volume study of *The South in the Building of the Nation* was published in 1909, of which the seventh volume, edited by John Bell Henneman, was entitled *History of the Literary and Intellectual Life of the South*. Its contents define the then-current definition of intellectual life: there are chapters on genre (poetry, historical studies, "English studies," classical scholarship, mathematics, astronomy, the physical sciences, natural history, philosophy), on professions (the law, medicine, music, the press, librarianship), and on a few miscellaneous categories (folklore, humor, Louisiana). There is, by way of an afterthought, a concluding chapter on "The Literary and Intellectual Progress of the Negro." There is a general chapter on the "Intellectual Tendencies of the South," whose emphasis, consonant with the orientation of the volumes toward the "New South," was on accomplishments, the South's return to the nation,

the importance of science, the growth of education and industry; throughout there is a disparagement of "the barrenness of the Old South in the field of literature," which is explained by the tendency of slavery to promote intolerance. But the New South's fracturing of such an "artificial unity of thought and speech" would nevertheless leave the South with an identity, since it would retain customs that mark "its peculiarities as a province" (pp. xxxii–xliv). In short, romantic nationalism would survive, minus separatist politics, but southern culture was now "provincial" or "regional," with the clear implication that there was a metropolitan culture somewhere else to whose status the South should now aspire.

The title of this volume posited a conjunction between literature and intellectual life that has been very important in the South, because literary scholars were the first, and have always been the most zealous, to establish a canon for southern thought-qua-literature. This had been done only fitfully before the Civil War, but the pace became brisk afterwards in books such as James Wood Davidson's *The Living Writers of the South* (1869) and Louise Manly's *Southern Literature from 1579–1895* (1895). This work was summarized in the 16-volume anthology *The Library of Southern Literature* (1907), which was the joint work of academics and "amateurs." Later a more singly academic tradition of southern literary history emerged, culminating in Jay B. Hubbell's *The South in American Literature, 1607–1900* (1954), sustained by many monographs and anthologies, and renewed in our own day by *The History of Southern Literature* (1985). A weaker second to this tradition was that of the history of southern political thought, which flourished most vigorously from the end of the nineteenth century to World War II; its notable landmarks were Ulrich B. Phillips's *Georgia and States Rights* (1920); Frank Owsley's *States Rights in the Confederacy* (1925); and Jesse Carpenter's *The South as a Conscious Minority, 1789–1861* (1930).

The idea of gathering together such discrete enquiries under the rubric of "intellectual history" came slowly, however, and evolved from a very different intellectual genealogy, external to the South. Its ancestor is the systematic history of philosophy, written first by philosophers such as G. W. F. Hegel or Dugald Stewart as a way of understanding earlier and mistaken metaphysics, later by nonphilosophers as a way of conveying the accomplishments of human intelligence. By the mid-twentieth century this latter tradition had transmogrified into the "history of ideas," a term popularized by ARTHUR O. LOVEJOY; in 1938 he had pointed out in *Essays in the History of Ideas* the need to draw together discrete traditions of intellectual inquiry, the histories of philosophy, science, language, religion, literature, fine arts, economic theory, and education, as well as folklore studies, comparative literature, political and social history, and the "historical part of sociology." This school concentrated more on the logical content and relationship of ideas themselves, less on the intellectuals who held them and their social context; philosophy was its core discipline, with social and political history on the periphery.

The precise moment at which "intellectual history" was born has not been satisfactorily established. Perry Miller has been credited with using the phrase first in 1939 in the preface to *The New England Mind: the Seventeenth Century*, when he wrote of "the intellectual history of New England." In fact, it is much older. Hugh Legaré in 1828 wrote of "a philosophical inquirer into the intellectual history of the species." But this was a phrase, not a program for a scholarly discipline, as was the case with Miller. By the 1940s works in southern intellectual history had begun to appear, first with Clement Eaton's *The Freedom-of-Thought Struggle in the Old South* (1940), later with Rollin Osterweis's *Romanticism and Nationalism in the Old South* (1948), written as a Yale dissertation under Ralph Gabriel. Eaton later added other studies: *The Mind of the Old South* (1964) and *The Waning of the Old South Civilization* (1968). Sometimes such books were inspired by the so-called "American Studies" approach, as with William R. Taylor's *Cavalier and Yankee: the Old South and American National Character* (1961). Collaterally, some literary scholars were broadening their methodology to write intellectual history: notable was Richard Beale Davis, whose *Intellectual Life in Jefferson's Virginia, 1790–1830* (1964) was later to be surpassed in length by his *Intellectual Life in the Colonial South* (1978).

However, a self-conscious subdiscipline of "southern intellectual history" is a product of the last 20 years; some of its chief works are listed in the Further Reading. These books have marked characteristics, being poised between the traditional preoccupations of southern history and the discipline of intellectual history. That is, they are influenced by modern theories, many of them nonsouthern in origin (Freud, Geertz, Rorty, Skinner, Gramsci and many others), some of them indigenous (Calhoun, Tate, Weaver); likewise they often employ paradigms—the Enlightenment, Romanticism, Victorianism, modernism—current in European and "American" intellectual history. But these books are also connected to the traditional preoccupations of southern historiography; the nature of slave society and PROSLAVERY THOUGHT, the origins of the Civil War, the problems of bi-

racialism, the broad issues of social and political history. This is so, because those intellectuals who designated themselves as southerners or (more loosely but distinguishably) those who resided in the South were formed by and meditated upon these issues. This preoccupation with political and social history is the more marked because the traditional formative influence upon intellectual history elsewhere, philosophy, has been notably absent in the South, which has not produced a body of abstract metaphysics.

Intellectual history, as a discipline, has never been securely established, mostly because its topics—works of the intellect and people called intellectuals—have been notoriously hard to define and, awkwardly for a democratic culture like that of the United States, intrinsically elitist. The willingness to affirm the existence and significance of intellectual elites, by the culture that surrounds intellectuals and even by intellectuals themselves (many of whom deny the title that others wish to give them), has made intellectual history an uncertain venture. This familiar problem has been compounded for southern intellectual history by two skepticisms, one northern, the other southern. Northerners, the most imperial force in American culture, who compelled the South back into the Union at the point of a bayonet, have been inclined to view southerners as backward and unintelligent and hence to see southern intellectuality as an oxymoron. For their part southerners have evolved a culture that has stressed social unity and organicism, partly driven by the scarring impulses of racism but also by the need to survive together in a world that—with little ambiguity between 1861 and 1865 and thereafter—expressed hostility to the southern way of life. Such a culture has resisted the premise that intellectuals form a distinct class, but has instead striven to make them ideological voices, elaborators of ideas commonly held. Many southern intellectuals have accepted this role, but many others, embracing the familiar modern obligation of alienation as evidence of intellectuality, have resisted it. This tension between being southern and belonging, and being intellectual and singular, has formed a characteristic motif.

MICHAEL O'BRIEN

See also SOUTHERN AGRARIANISM.

FURTHER READING
Richard Beale Davis, *Intellectual Life in the Colonial South, 1585–1763*, 3 vols. (Knoxville: University of Tennessee Press, 1978).
Drew Gilpin Faust, *A Sacred Circle: the Dilemma of the Intellectual in the Old South, 1840–1860* (Baltimore: Johns Hopkins University Press, 1977).
——, ed., *The Ideology of Slavery: Proslavery Thought in the*

Old South, 1830–1860 (Baton Rouge: Louisiana State University Press, 1981).

John Bell Henneman, ed., *History of the Literary and Intellectual Life of the South* (Richmond: Southern Historical Publication Society, 1909).

Richard H. King, *A Southern Renaissance: the Cultural Awakening of the American South, 1930–1955* (New York: Oxford University Press, 1980).

Michael O'Brien, *Rethinking the South: Essays in Intellectual History* (Baltimore: Johns Hopkins University Press, 1988).

Louis D. Rubin Jr. et al., *The History of Southern Literature* (Baton Rouge: Louisiana State University Press, 1985).

Daniel J. Singal, *The War Within: From Victorian to Modernist Thought in the South, 1919–1945* (Chapel Hill: University of North Carolina Press, 1982).

spiritualism. A broad-based movement of alternative PIETY that today would likely be described as "New Age" religion, spiritualism was most influential among Americans from the late 1840s through the 1880s. Influenced by the teachings of the eighteenth-century Swedish mystic and visionary Emmanuel Swedenborg, and by the philosophical meditations of the American Andrew Jackson Downing, spiritualists argued that matter and spirit were essentially one and that the universe contained a multitude of "correspondences" between the physical and the spiritual. Spiritualist visions of a benevolent afterlife (which contained no vestige of hell or punishment) denied orthodox Christian views of a fundamental disharmony between the divine and created worlds, and, by extension, ruled out any disharmony or punitive hierarchy between the sexes.

Offering a "holistic" approach to piety that argued for the materiality of heaven and the divinity of the created world, spiritualists opened "channels" of communication between the two. To become a medium through whom spirits communicated required simply a willingness to try to establish contact with the deceased. Whether through seances, "table-rappings," or the utterances of "mesmerized" mediums (spiritualism absorbed and outlasted the earlier cultural interest in "animal magnetism" or "mesmerism"), spiritualist practice vastly democratized access to the spirit, promising contact if not with the Deity, then at least with the legion inhabitants of the afterlife.

Spiritualism became quickly popular among churchgoers disillusioned with the theological strictures of evangelical Protestantism (specifically, the requirement that one undergo a "saving conversion" and accept a judgmental God who relegated most souls to hell). Resisting any institutionalizing of their faith, spiritualists offered a much more divinized, enchanted view of ordinary reality, while also claiming a firm empirical basis for things invisible (one could hear, converse with, and sometimes see the spirits of the departed).

Saturated with numinous correspondences, daily life enjoyed the loving guardianship of the deceased. Contacting the spirits and listening to mediums perform in intimate parlor seances or large lecture halls became especially widespread during the Civil War years as Americans struggled to assuage their grief by communicating with the war dead. An essential (and still little explored) connection between spiritualism and sentimentalism is evident in such bestselling wartime fiction as Elizabeth Stuart Phelps's *The Gates Ajar* (1869), a novel that offered its principally feminine readership visions of a comfortably material and domesticated heaven where the dead happily dwelled.

Allied in the public mind not only with a sentimental EVANGELICALISM but also with reformist, even radical politics, spiritualism advertised both the reassuring proximity of the spirit world and the urgency of contemporary issues, especially ANTISLAVERY and WOMEN'S RIGHTS. Orthodox Christians were often doubly alarmed: the spiritualists were democratic in politics and antidogmatic in religion. At times they preached a socially utopian form of piety that imagined an impending regeneration of social relations through female emancipation (and more vaguely, the liberation of the feminine principle). The age's most vocal convert to Roman Catholicism, ORESTES BROWNSON, devoted a lengthy fiction entitled *The Spirit-Rapper: an Autobiography* (1854) to exposing the alleged conspiracy between radical socialists and spiritualists: the "connection of spirit-rapping or the spirit manifestation, with modern philanthropy, visionary reforms, socialism, and revolutionism, is not an imagination of my own" (p. 2).

Even such theological skeptics as NATHANIEL HAWTHORNE satirized the movement's confusion of spiritual and political aims under the guise of "philanthropy." In *The Blithedale Romance* (1852), he transforms the exploited female medium into the only slightly less dependent figure of the docile wife. RALPH WALDO EMERSON himself, although deeply influenced by the Swedenborgian theory of correspondences, recorded in his journal that spiritualism (with its dual penchant for the empirical and sensational) was the "Rat-revelation, the gospel that comes by taps in the wall, and thumps in the table-drawer" (p. 327).

Such invective against spiritualism can be understood in part as a reaction against the subversive anti-institutionalism of its claims and practices. The spiritualist belief that Creation was material and continuous and that, consequently, the afterlife was itself material, reachable by sensory exploration from this world, gave amateur folk direct access to visions of the supernatural, a troubling development for the gentry clerical class. Participants in seances not only heard spirits rapping out answers to questions, but as the movement became increasingly sensational in the postbellum decades, "saw" ghostly figures while mediums stayed locked (and hidden from view) in cabinets.

Embracing politically progressive doctrines (derived partially from the radical French Revolutionary heritage of mesmerism), spiritualists inevitably disrupted Victorian American GENDER relations. Women directed seances and spoke as mesmerized orators on such issues as the immortality of soul and body and the necessary emancipation of woman. Like the famous adolescent Fox sisters, who in 1848 in upstate New York began the spiritualist movement by performing a series of "table-rappings" for rural crowds, female mediums forged an improvised public space, one that drew upon the subversive oratory of female abolitionists and women's rights advocates. Many spiritualists were themselves abolitionists and advocates of women's rights; all three movements were deeply influenced by a radical insistence on the sovereignty of the individual (*see also* INDIVIDUALISM).

However docile and spiritually "refined" such mediums might be in outward appearance, they nonetheless fashioned a new form of female personality, one that displayed an alarming ability to blend a "feminine" receptivity with "masculine" performative skills. "The Confessions of a Medium" in the *Atlantic Monthly* (1860) discloses the gender transformations that spiritualism made possible. It records dramatic acts of metamorphosis on the part of a "frail, little" female medium who in her trances becomes various male (usually combative) figures: as "Cribb, a noted pugilist of the last century, she floored an incautious spectator, giving him a black eye which he wore for a fortnight afterwards" (p. 705). This figure of a protean female, who not only communicates with the dead but assuages and avenges herself upon the living, constitutes one of the most provocative cultural legacies of nineteenth-century spiritualism.

JENNY FRANCHOT

FURTHER READING

Ann Braude, *Radical Spirits: Spiritualism and Women's Rights in Nineteenth-Century America* (Boston: Beacon, 1989).
Orestes A. Brownson, *The Spirit-Rapper: an Autobiography* (1854; Detroit: Thorndike Nourse, 1884).
Ralph Waldo Emerson, *Selections from Ralph Waldo Emerson*, ed. Stephen E. Whicher (Boston: Houghton Mifflin, 1960).
Howard Kerr, *Mediums, and Spirit-Rappers, and Roaring Radicals: Spiritualism in American Literature, 1850–1900* (Urbana: University of Illinois Press, 1972).
R. Laurence Moore, *In Search of White Crows: Spiritualism, Parapsychology, and American Culture* (New York: Oxford University Press, 1977).

Spock, Benjamin (b. New Haven, Conn., May 2, 1903). Pediatrician and political activist. Spock's popular child-rearing manuals, notably his *Common Sense Book of Baby and Child Care* (1946), encouraged parents to trust themselves and their affectionate impulses. He was the most influential advocate of greater permissiveness in child-rearing; he urged sensitivity to children's psychological as well as physical needs. Author of *Decent and Indecent: Our Personal and Political Behavior* (1970), Spock sought to contribute to the reform of international as well as family relations. A participant in the antinuclear campaigns of SANE (the Committee for a Sane Nuclear Policy), he also took part in Vietnam War protests, which led to his trial for conspiring to subvert the draft law.

FURTHER READING

William Graebner, "The Unstable World of Benjamin Spock: Social Engineering in a Democratic Culture, 1917–1950," *Journal of American History* 67 (Dec. 1980): 612–29.

Stanton, Elizabeth Cady (b. Johnstown, N.Y., Nov. 12, 1815; d. New York, N.Y., Oct. 26, 1902). The preeminent nineteenth-century political philosopher of women's rights and an important figure in the elaboration of American LIBERALISM, Elizabeth Cady Stanton received the best education available to a young woman at the time—an education which stopped short of college and left her immensely resentful of men's economic, educational, and social privileges. While other women found their salvation from worldly frustrations through religion, Elizabeth developed a lifelong hatred of authoritarian CALVINISM. Instead, she rebuilt her life and hopes around "reform": the semisecular, semispiritual community of social activists dedicated to social and moral change at all levels of American society. Her entry into this world was facilitated by her cousin, Gerrit Smith, her husband, Henry Brewster Stanton, and the woman from whom she learned the basic tenets of women's rights, LUCRETIA MOTT.

In 1848, a year of global revolution, Elizabeth (now the mother of three rambunctious boys) organized the world's first women's rights convention in Seneca Falls, New York; there she articulated more clearly than anyone had ever done before the importance of political rights for women. Three years later, she met

SUSAN B. ANTHONY, a temperance activist, and converted her to the doctrine of EQUALITY of the sexes. Together these two women led the American women's rights movement for half a century.

The most well-known and widely embraced aspect of Stanton's work was the campaign for legal and political equality for women in the public arena. Stanton's women's rights program began with the demand for equal economic rights for wives, which included not only equal rights to own and dispose of real property, but, of much greater significance, equal rights to control of wages earned. Women's rights activists were able to realize legal reforms in married women's economic rights relatively quickly, although judicial decisions and wage-earning realities undermined their achievements. The demand for woman suffrage proved a much more challenging one because of the opposition it engendered and the mobilization it required. Stanton valued the enfranchisement of women so highly because electoral and party politics, over which men had a monopoly, were the key to accomplishing women's many reform goals. She also recognized that the franchise was the ultimate marker of inclusion in American democracy.

Stanton's efforts to extend the blessings of liberal INDIVIDUALISM to women were not limited to winning the same legal and political rights that men enjoyed; because women occupied different social positions than men, she recognized that liberty had different meanings for them as well. She wanted not only to establish women's rights outside the home, but to bring the principles of self-determination and individual rights into the private, or domestic world, where women's most distinctive grievances lay. She championed liberalization of divorce law at a time when other women reformers sought to make the marriage contract more binding, and called for the extension of the principles of liberal individualism to matters of sexuality and reproduction. She advocated want she called "self sovereignty," the right of women to engage in intercourse and become pregnant only when they so chose (thus repudiating the tradition of conjugal rights of husbands), and played an important role in advancing the ability of other reform-minded women to envision changes in women's sexual and maternal conditions (see also MOTHERHOOD).

Stanton's commitment to refashioning liberal DEMOCRACY to include full equality for women made for a more complex attitude toward government power than was characteristic of classical liberalism. Women, unlike men, did not have a private realm of independence and autonomy threatened only by the encroachment of tyrannical government; on the contrary, women suffered tyranny and unjust government *within* the family, and needed the strength and authority of a sovereign state to enact and ensure their individual rights. The Constitutional reforms of the Reconstruction period helped Stanton reconcile her belief in individual rights with her conclusion that government must aid women in overcoming their subordination. Learning from the freedmen, she identified strong national government with protection of the rights of the individual, and government at the state level ("states rights") with the violation of individual RIGHTS.

In the 1880s and 1890s, however, Stanton's commitment to extending individual FREEDOM into the realm of DOMESTICITY led her to oppose efforts to expand legislation for the control of drinking and other personal habits. In the last decades of her life, she became a leading critic of the Christian moral reform movement. She campaigned against Sunday closing laws and warned against a trend toward national legislation to establish a restrictive, uniform federal law regulating divorce. She also directed her energies against the cultural influence of Christian moralism. She wrote extensively about the antidemocratic assumptions of traditional Christian thought and was the author of *The Women's Bible*, a controversial popular critique of the Bible from a women's rights point of view. Many women activists were favorably inclined toward Christian moral reform, and Stanton's aggressive secularism alienated them; even Susan B. Anthony, although not herself a devotee of the movement to spread evangelical rectitude, was ready to make her peace with it to help build the woman suffrage movement.

The political and intellectual reputation of Elizabeth Cady Stanton has changed significantly since her death in 1902. By the time the vote was won, in 1920, the figure of Susan B. Anthony, who had been single-minded in her devotion to building the woman suffrage movement, had come to stand almost exclusively as the heroine of women's rights. With the appearance of a new feminist movement in the 1970s, however, Stanton's historical reputation revived precisely because of the breadth of her concerns. Modern feminist scholars examine her thought for its contribution to the debate over whether "equality" (the view that women have or should have the same capacities and rights as men) or "difference" (the view that women are distinctive in needs and powers) supplies a better framework for women's liberation. But the richness of Stanton's inquiries into the complex matter of women's subordination makes it difficult to claim her for one side or the other. Her understanding of women's emancipation rests on liberal premises even as it pushes those premises far beyond their classic limits.

ELLEN CAROL DUBOIS

FURTHER READING

Ellen Carol DuBois, ed., *Elizabeth Cady Stanton, Susan B. Anthony: a Reader* (Boston: Northeastern University Press, 1992).

Elisabeth Griffith, *In Her Own Right: the Life of Elizabeth Cady Stanton* (New York: Oxford University Press, 1984).

Karen Offen, "Defining Feminism: a Comparative Historical Approach," *Signs* 14 (1988): 119–57; Ellen DuBois, "Reply," *Signs* 15 (1989): 195–202.

Elizabeth Cady Stanton, *Eighty Years and More: Reminiscences, 1815–1897* (Boston: Northeastern University Press, 1993).

——, *The Woman's Bible* (Boston: Northeastern University Press, 1993).

Steffens, [Joseph] Lincoln (b. San Francisco, Calif., Apr. 6, 1866; d. Carmel, Calif., Aug. 9, 1936). As for so many intellectuals of his era, Lincoln Steffens's reputation has often been bound to the mixed legacy of LIBERALISM—and in his case, to the evanescence of what any one generation considers news. Originally, Steffens's bestselling *Autobiography* (1931), not unlike the testament of HENRY ADAMS a decade earlier, draped historical events upon the figure of a willing witness to the loss of Mugwumpish illusions. Indeed, Steffens's memoir so successfully chronicled an event-by-event, decade-by-decade pilgrim's progress of American liberalism that subsequent readers would marvel at Steffens's uncanny ability to have been present at all the watershed events: the raids conducted by Reverend Charles Parkhurst in the early 1890s, exposing the underworld of Tammany Hall's police corruption; the exploits of THEODORE ROOSEVELT as New York City's reform-minded police commissioner; the national battles with the urban boss system, retold particularly in Steffens's *The Shame of the Cities* (1903) series for *McClure's Magazine*; the wreckage of Wilsonian PROGRESSIVISM at the Paris peace conference in 1919; and, of course, the new future that Steffens thought he glimpsed in the wake of the Bolshevik revolution.

But as his future became our past, Steffens's reputation for exposure and prophecy foundered. Since mid-century, the preference has been for muckraking the man. Indeed, Steffens's deeply rehearsed, self-reflexive shame over his own middle-class hypocrisy—a subtext suffusing even his most documentarian of exposés—has been detected by nearly every study since Richard Hofstadter's *Age of Reform* (1955). Following Hofstadter's lead in 1965, CHRISTOPHER LASCH expanded upon this critique, partly by debunking the *Autobiography* itself, in particular by foregrounding Steffens's early quest—as a graduate student under German psychologist Wilhelm Wundt—for an "experimental" basis for ethics. To Lasch, Steffens's early dalliance with Wundt's experiments in physiological psychology betrayed not the loss of liberal illusions, but a search for newer, more manipulative styles of bourgeois governance. In 1974, Justin Kaplan's full-length biography went even further, exposing an often-dispirited private Steffens, beset by a "crippling" disassociation of love from sexuality (p. 289), drawn to political strongmen like Mussolini, often reverting nostalgically to the Golden Rule after publicly tarnishing experiences.

Kaplan also uncloaked the man the memoir had so successfully camouflaged: a "leftist" who found himself ridiculed by the self-styled proletarians of the 1930s, who never joined the Communist Party, who described himself as a *Moses in Red* (1926) unprepared to occupy the promised land. Steffens's temperamental quixoticism has always caused considerable chagrin among those in quest of intellectual consistency—prompting one recent scholar, for instance, to declare Steffens "incapable of clear and precise thought." Challenged on any one idea, Stephen J. Whitfield complains, "like the Cheshire cat, he disappears, leaving behind only a wicked grin" (pp. 90, 103).

In some sense, the alternately hubristic and disenchanted voice of the *Autobiography*, recounting its almost *Candide*-like plot—with a Steffens *naif* functioning, as Kaplan puts it, as the "shadow protagonist" for a lost "American Innocence" (p. 303)—invites all these attempts at decanonization. As Lasch's study argued and then came to exemplify, liberal historiography has been only too ready to debunk the "realism" of past generations—if only, by doing so, to covertly reclaim the ground. Certainly the Archimedean pose of a supposedly experimental temperament, free of moralism and ideology, barraged only by facts, has made Steffens an easy target, a surrogate for liberalism's facile claims; the morality tale of Steffens's fall from the lyrical days of Greenwich Village—his "literary" avocations notwithstanding—into defenses of Stalinism also had predictable uses. Taken solely on ideological or philosophical grounds, this is not a man liable to be redeemed from his own myth-making.

Nevertheless, the focus on Steffens's characteristically hazy ideology and ethical vocabulary often misses the mark. In many ways, the *Autobiography*'s best array of "facts"—destabilizing the boundaries between bosses and reformers, cops and criminals, the clubbers and the clubbed—are those designed to fall outside any explanatory frame and leave you dead in your tracks. And even in these moments, Steffens's example is not, as some might imagine, that of the muckraker, the fact-finder trained under Wundt, the father of exposé. Looking back to Victorian mentors like JACOB RIIS and forward to the scoundrel-hunting of a Dashiell Hammett or a LILLIAN HELLMAN, Steffens's education actually reflects the genesis of a modern, hard-boiled insider: the process by which one liberal newswriter gradually chose to barter knowledge that could be easily exposed, and summarily reported, for an ever-closer look at the darker heart of power. News thus became not public property, but a capital to be hoarded for later, more strategic, use: as Steffens says so tellingly in his memoir (turning the urban boss's bribe against itself) "knowledge was my price."

Even stylistically, the *Autobiography* anticipates the double vision of news writing, with its oscillations between the "hard" and the soft, the comic and the tragic, the blank naiveté of a wide-eyed child and the posture of the disaffected wisdom that—with a wink—really knew all along. This was, after all, a professional logic soon to be legitimated by Steffens's one-time protegé WALTER LIPPMANN, who (in *Public Opinion*, 1922) called for the creation of "intelligence sections" of news elites to stand between managerial politics and the mass citizen. For Steffens, news became not empirically naive fact-gathering, but what Gaye Tuchman calls the modern journalist's "strategic ritual" of OBJECTIVITY, a stance that often puts facts in a labyrinth of attribution, inside stories against a backdrop of public relations—and, so often, the entire world within knowing scare quotes. (*See also* JOURNALISM.)

At his worst, Steffens also forecast the failings of this ritual, in his overconfidence in his mediating role, his recurrent adoration of force and charismatic rule, his growing distrust of the public he proposed to serve. But if the events he exposed are no longer news, the protocols of coverage he established persist. The paradox may be that, though Steffens spoke of himself as always in quest of a *theory* of professional ethics—his synonym for the legitimation of self-interest and sheer ruthlessness—he was in fact always more adept at representing, in literary narrative, the *practice* of power, in the police station, on Wall Street, and in newsrooms themselves. If this practice of power is by its nature elusive or protean, then the experimental method of the *Autobiography*—intent upon tracking its prey, yet also sometimes coming to mirror its habits—is a compelling representation of how the news-hunting game is played.

CHRISTOPHER P. WILSON

See also MUCKRAKING.

FURTHER READING
Richard Hofstadter, *The Age of Reform* (New York: Knopf, 1955).
Justin Kaplan, *Lincoln Steffens* (New York: Simon and Schuster, 1974).
Christopher Lasch, "The Education of Lincoln Steffens," in *The New Radicalism in America, 1889–1963* (New York: Knopf, 1965).
Walter Lippmann, *Public Opinion* (New York: Harcourt, Brace, 1922).
Robert Stinson, *Lincoln Steffens* (New York: Frederick Ungar, 1979).
Gaye Tuchman, *Making News: a Study in the Construction of Reality* (New York: Free Press, 1978).
Stephen J. Whitfield, "Muckraking Lincoln Steffens," *Virginia Quarterly Review* 54 (winter 1978): 87–103.

Stein, Gertrude (b. Allegheny, Pa., Feb. 3, 1874; d. Paris, France, July 27, 1946). Her choice to become an American exile has long been understood by Gertrude Stein's critics as a defining moment of her artistic life. Just short of 30, at the point of embarking on a literary career, she decided, like so many American modernists of her generation, to abandon what she termed "the joylessness of America" and move to Paris. Stein's decision to live as an émigré in a land of another language is for many readers the biographical counterpart to the self-enclosed aestheticism she cultivated in her writings. Both life and work betray a claustrophobic obsession with language, and with the monotonous patterns of Stein's own ego-maniacal psyche.

Yet even the most negative critical assessments of Stein's experimentations affirm that something deep is at stake in them. She is always "going straight to the heart of a subject, to its roots," writes one critic, expressing a curiously persistent conviction of the excavatory quality of Stein's word play. Another critical view augments this image of Stein as an archaeologist trying to exhume the language: "If the name of anything or everything is dead . . . the only thing to do to keep it alive is to rename it. And that is what Miss Stein did and does" (*Selected Writings*, pp. xx, xxi). This critical attention to the problem of reviving language points to what is perhaps the most typical narrative feature of her writing: repetition. Repetition was her mode of resuscitation. It was Stein's means of capturing being in language, the key to what she called an individual's "bottom being." One of her earliest readers intuited this in remarking that Stein "has set down all the repetition and recurrence, the casting back, the weary round of those faint stirrings in the brain which we call human thought" (*Three Lives*, p. xviii). Stein's project of revitalizing words and things, and reconceiving the relationship between them, was not merely a playing with language, but an effort to contribute to a new understanding of the character of the social life partly constituted by language. Preferring to see her as a solipsistic experimentalist, content to toy with words in the isolation befitting an artistic intellectual, critics have neglected her profound interest in probing the patterns of social existence—particularly the range of social "types."

This interest informed her work from the start. Describing the subjects of her first published work of fiction, *Three Lives*, Stein wrote in a letter in 1906, "I don't know how to sell on a margin or do anything with shorts or longs, so I have to content myself with Niggers and servant girls and the foreign population generally . . . dey is very simple and vulgar and I don't think they will interest the Great American Public" (in *Three Lives*, p. xv). Stein's observation not only betrays a characteristic anticipation of rejection by reading audiences, which was invariably combined with provocation designed to ensure it, but can also be taken as representative of her intellectual concerns and methods throughout her 40-year career.

Stein's interests in social heterogeneity, in the collective psychology of CLASS relations, and in the nature of GENDER difference came together in her fascination with what she called "kinds in men and women." Like many intellectuals of her generation, Stein sought, as Nancy Stepan writes in *The Idea of Race in Science*, to "move beyond the variety presented by individuals to some imagined essence or type to which, in abstract, each individual could be attached" (*see also* RACE). Stein was drawn to typological categories as aids in her ambition to catalog "everyone who was or is or will be living" (p. 94). The historical specificity of Stein's methodological devotion to types has been obscured not only by the critical tradition that labeled her an elitist exile, a high modernist whose works lack social referents, but by a more recent tradition that views her as a prescient forerunner of postmodern FEMINISM. The complexity of Stein's peculiar art of social description can only be grasped by an appraisal of its ties to the classificatory passions of her generation, especially those of her contemporaries in SOCIAL SCIENCE. Her typological thinking was part of an international literature on social types (including such writers as W. I. Thomas, Adolf Meyer, Otto Weininger, and Georg Simmel).

Stein's lifelong pursuit of the type—the "normal" as well as the "aberrant"—began with two publi-

cations in the *Psychological Review*, based on experiments conducted under the direction of her teacher WILLIAM JAMES. In these essays (which were published in 1896 and 1898, and continued to be cited by such specialists in the field of gender differences as W. I. Thomas and Helen B. Thompson long after Stein had turned to literary pursuits), she reports the change in her experimental focus, from initial concern with how individuals react to given stimuli ("normal automatism"), to an interest in basic "character types." Stein's medical studies at Johns Hopkins in the late 1890s brought this interest in character types to the domain of hard science. Stein was drawn to the subject of brain anatomy, and proved especially adept at modeling anatomical variations among human types.

Stein is notoriously dismissive of her medical school years in *The Autobiography of Alice B. Toklas* (1933), but her research continued after she left medical school, and she never entirely gave up her scientific interests. The central terms of her scientific sojourn—essentialist paradigms of pathology and normality, theories on the transmission of disease, the classification (and depersonalization) of human subjects, ideals of PROFESSIONALISM and the role of a professional elite, the case study method which follows a subject from birth to death, the interest in cultural and national habits and traits, the view of the lower classes as ideal experimental objects—were not abandoned but aestheticized. Stein's early writings can be seen as a translation of standard psychological and biological types into her own unique characterological system.

In theory, *Three Lives* (1909) represents an incomparable turn-of-the-century confrontation with social difference, since it highlights the lives of three women—two German immigrant maids and a mulatta woman from the lower middle class. Technically, however, these stories are remarkable for the repetitiveness and monotony of their plots, the almost coercive similitude of their categories. Given a writer so alert to the layered meanings of words, it is no accident that Stein is writing about maids. It is an appropriate and characteristically literal joke on Stein's part that each story in a collection whose central action is representing the domestication of social difference, concerns a *domestic*. Stein's subject is the daily theatricalization of heterogeneity as homogeneity: the methods by which differences are reduced to a recognizable domestic code.

Looking back on her writing career in a spirit of triumph following the popular success of *The Autobiography of Alice B. Toklas*, Stein wrote: "My little sentences have gotten underneath their skins"

(*Selected Writings*, p. ix). Stein's observation expresses her modernist fascination with the way in which larger social phenomena are imprinted upon individual minds: her interest in the syntax and rhythms of class distinction, racial discrimination, the struggle between determinism and free will. Stein's sentences could not have penetrated so deeply into the enlightened minds of her generation had those sentences not been invested with that generation's most profound social preoccupations.

SUSAN MIZRUCHI

See also MODERNISM.

FURTHER READING

John Malcolm Brinnin, *The Third Rose: Gertrude Stein and Her Circle* (Boston: Little, Brown, 1959).
Leon Solomons and Gertrude Stein, "Normal Motor Automatism," *Psychological Review* 3 (1896): 492–512.
Gertrude Stein, "Cultivated Motor Automatism: a Study of Character in Its Relation To Attention," *Psychological Review* 5 (1898): 295–306.
——, *Three Lives* (1909; New York: Vintage, 1958).
——, *The Autobiography of Alice B. Toklas* (New York: Harcourt Brace, 1933).
——, *The Making of Americans* (London: Peter Owen, 1968).
——, *Selected Writings of Gertrude Stein*, ed. Carl Van Vechten (New York: Vintage, 1972).
Nancy Stepan, *The Idea of Race in Science: Great Britain* (Hamden, Conn.: Archon, 1982).

Stevens, Wallace (b. Reading, Pa., Oct. 2, 1879; d. Hartford, Conn., Aug. 2, 1955). Poet. While pursuing a career in insurance, first as a lawyer and then as an executive, Stevens was also developing into a distinguished modernist poet. From the publication of his first volume, *Harmonium* (1923), at the age of 44, he produced a body of work which, like that of his friend WILLIAM CARLOS WILLIAMS, attempted to join European traditions of thought to a particular experience of being a modern American. For Stevens, this experience took place primarily in the life of the mind, and in his verse he attempted to convey some of the rhythm and form of a critical and reflective imagination at work. Influenced philosophically by thinkers such as WILLIAM JAMES and Friedrich Nietzsche, and by his Harvard mentor GEORGE SANTAYANA, Stevens's voice was skeptical and relativist. Observing a completely secular universe, Stevens rejected the tragic mindset of many of his contemporaries. He chose instead to esteem the aestheticizing capacities of individual intellect as a moral source in modern life.

FURTHER READING

Helen Vendler, *Wallace Stevens: Words Chosen out of Desire* (Cambridge: Harvard University Press, 1988).

Stieglitz, Alfred (b. Hoboken, N.J., Jan. 1, 1864; d. New York, N.Y., July 13, 1946). The oldest son of German Jews who had emigrated to the United States after the revolution of 1848, Stieglitz spent most of his life pitting art against the encroaching forces of America's business-oriented civilization. That stance drew some of its psychological force from a rebellion against his father, a successful merchant, whom he considered excessively authoritarian. In 1881 the family moved back to Germany, where Stieglitz lived until 1890. He later claimed that the sojourn completed the process of making him unfit for conventional society. Living the life of a bohemian, he pursued his interests in the arts, and never felt compelled to prepare himself to earn a living. He discovered both photography, which was in its infancy and not yet accepted as an art, as well as neo-romantic German culture, with its insistence on liberating the "spirit"—which in the German form, *Geist*, conveyed decided overtones of cultural and spiritual awakening.

Since 1883 Stieglitz had sought to take photographs that would be regarded as art, which to him meant pictures capable of both expressing an inner vision and communicating universal values. In New York City at the turn of the century he became photography's leading advocate, organizing the New York Camera Club in 1897, founding and editing its journal, *Camera Notes*, and arranging photographic exhibits, while also making photographs that extended the new medium's expressive capacity—photographs like "Spring Showers" (1901), "The Hand of Man" (1902), and "The Steerage" (1907). These pictures capture the aggressive, if also wistful, mood of America's new civilization in the first decade of the twentieth century, as well as Stieglitz's own emerging confidence in himself as an artist.

In 1902, drawing upon fin-de-siècle symbolism and the revolt against realism in Germany and Austria, Stieglitz withdrew from the New York Camera Club, and organized an alternative he called the "Photo-Secession." In the same year, with the help of fellow photographer Edward Steichen, he launched an exquisitely produced photographic quarterly, *Camera Work*. Together, the Photo-Secession, which opened a gallery just north of Greenwich Village in 1905, and *Camera Work* soon became focal points for the first American avant-garde, which was responsible for the introduction of modern art in American culture.

Founded originally as a showcase for both photography and painting, the Little Galleries of the Photo-Secession gradually shifted its attention after 1907 away from pictorial photography and toward an advanced exploration of the latest developments in European modern art. 291, as the gallery became known (after its address on Fifth Avenue) introduced August Rodin, Henri Matisse, Paul Cézanne, Henri Rousseau, and Pablo Picasso, laying the groundwork for the ARMORY SHOW of 1913, often credited with unveiling modernism in the United States. While the Metropolitan Museum's curator of painting concluded in 1911 that Picasso's "mad pictures would never mean anything to America," Stieglitz and his circle of critics and artists helped launch the conceptual revolution that led ultimately to a new view of Post-Impressionist painting and to the transformation of American art.

Stieglitz based his understanding of modern art on three then-radical principles: a commitment to pluralism that extended permissible definitions of art to include even a urinal by R. Mutt (Marcel Duchamp), a belief in discovering and expressing the inner self, and, most important, a utopian faith that modern art, since it was based upon uncovering new ways of seeing the inward meaning of external realities, contained the seeds of a new world order. These assumptions enabled Stieglitz not only to appreciate abstract art before most of his contemporaries, but to become the first American exhibitor of African art and children's art. He also published important avant-garde criticism (including Gertrude Stein's). As the columnist Hutchins Hapgood wrote in 1913 about Stieglitz's work, he wanted to "dynamite the baked and hardened earth so that fresh flowers can grow."

But if art could transform life, as Stieglitz argued, American artists could not simply imitate European styles and expect to shape life in the United States. In common with other cultural nationalists of the period, he decided that American artists had to discover their own authentic means of expression. For the next 30 years he sought to make it possible for a select group of American artists to paint as they wished by promoting their work. The promotion was effective in part because of his claim that he was a "revolutionist," not a mere "dealer." John Marin, Arthur Dove, Marsden Hartley, and, finally, Georgia O'Keeffe (who married Stieglitz in 1924), all owed their careers in large part to Stieglitz's efforts both before and after 291 closed in 1917. *Camera Work*, whose last two issues were devoted to the sharply focused, abstract photographs of his young protégé Paul Strand, ceased publication the same year.

The immediate cause of 291's demise was the Lever Food and Fuel Control Act of August 1917, which prohibited the use of foodstuffs in the manufacture of distilled spirits. Income from his first wife's Brooklyn brewery had supported Stieglitz's outpost on the frontiers of art, and its cessation meant that he could no longer finance his forays into experimental art and criticism. But the more basic cause was the demise, after World War I, of Stieglitz's fundamental conviction that by changing consciousness and human relations, modern art could transform society. Although he did some of his best photography after 1917, notably his portraits of O'Keeffe and his "Songs of the Sky," and although he did open two new galleries, Stieglitz introduced no new artists after 1917 and was not in the vanguard of American expression after the war. Following the Depression and the spread of documentary techniques and impulses, his romantic and idealist notion of the artist as prophet seemed ever more remote.

Stieglitz stopped taking pictures in 1937. After his death and the eclipse of socialist realism, photographers, including Ansel Adams and Elliot Porter, rediscovered his contribution to the development of photography as an art. He is remembered today as the father of modern photography, the man who helped introduce modern art in the United States, and the champion of America's first avant-garde in painting, a group that included among others his wife and muse, Georgia O'Keeffe.

EDWARD ABRAHAMS

FURTHER READING

Edward Abrahams, *The Lyrical Left: Randolph Bourne, Alfred Stieglitz, and the Origins of Cultural Radicalism in America* (Charlottesville: University Press of Virginia, 1986).

Alexandra Arrowsmith and Thomas West, eds., *Two Lives: Georgia O'Keeffe and Alfred Stieglitz* (New York: HarperCollins, 1992).

Benita Eisler, *O'Keeffe and Stieglitz: an American Romance* (New York: Doubleday, 1991).

Waldo Frank, Lewis Mumford, Dorothy Norman, Paul Rosenfeld, and Harold Rugg, eds., *America and Alfred Stieglitz: a Collective Portrait* (New York: Doubleday Doran, 1934).

Sarah Greenough and Juan Hamilton, eds., *Alfred Stieglitz: Photographs and Writings* (Washington, D.C.: National Gallery of Art, 1983).

William Innes Homer, *Alfred Stieglitz and the American Avant-Garde* (Boston: New York Graphic Society, 1977).

Sue Davidson Lowe, *Stieglitz: a Memoir/Biography* (New York: Farrar, Straus and Giroux, 1983).

Dorothy Norman, *Alfred Stieglitz: an American Seer* (New York: Random House, 1973).

Stone, I[sidor] F[einstein] (b. Philadelphia, Pa., Dec. 24, 1907; d. Boston, Mass., June 18, 1989). Journalist. An editorial writer for numerous newspapers during the Depression, World War II, and the early Cold War, Stone launched his own four-page newsletter, *I. F. Stone's Weekly*, in 1953. It provided cogent investigative reporting and analysis until 1971, when he began writing regularly for the *New York Review of Books*. The *Weekly* asserted its complete independence not only by refusing all advertising, but by taking potshots at political parties and viewpoints all over the spectrum, though Stone's own perspective was firmly left-of-center. Late in life he taught himself Greek and wrote *The Trial of Socrates* (1988). Among his earlier books were *The Hidden History of the Korean War* (1952) and *The Haunted Fifties* (1964).

FURTHER READING

Robert Cottrell, *Izzy: a Biography of I. F. Stone* (New Brunswick, N.J.: Rutgers University Press, 1992).

Stone, Lucy (b. West Brookfield, Mass., Aug. 13, 1818; d. Dorchester, Mass., Oct. 18, 1893). Reformer. A powerful orator, talented organizer, and moral idealist who worked for abolitionism, WOMEN'S RIGHTS, and universal suffrage, Stone helped found the American Woman Suffrage Association (1869) and the *Woman's Journal* (1870), which she and her husband Henry Brown Blackwell edited after 1872. During Reconstruction she took the position that although women deserved the vote as much as black men, suffragists should nevertheless support freedmen's political rights. She married Blackwell after agreeing with him on her retention of economic and reproductive autonomy after marriage, an arrangement symbolized by her becoming the first American woman to keep her birth name: she was known thereafter as Mrs. Stone.

FURTHER READING

Andrea Moore Kerr, *Lucy Stone: Speaking Out for Equality* (New Brunswick, N.J.: Rutgers University Press, 1992).

Story, Joseph (b. Marblehead, Mass., Sept. 18, 1779; d. Cambridge, Mass., Sept. 10, 1845). Supreme Court Justice (1811–45). Nominally a Jeffersonian Republican, Story shared many Federalist values and goals and thought the judiciary should help forge a stable social order. He wrote the majority opinion in *Martin v. Hunter's Lessee* (1816), which declared the Supreme Court's supremacy over state courts. At Harvard Law School (1829–45), Story organized the curriculum and wrote nine volumes of COMMENTARIES (1832–45) that became of a foundation of American jurisprudence.

FURTHER READING

R. Kent Newmyer, *Supreme Court Justice Joseph Story: Statesman of the Old Republic* (Chapel Hill: University of North Carolina Press, 1985).

Stowe, Harriet Beecher (b. Litchfield, Conn., June 14, 1811; d. Hartford, Conn., July 1, 1896). "So you're the little woman who started this great war," Abraham Lincoln supposedly said upon meeting Stowe in 1863. This apocryphal tale underscores what many remember most about Stowe: her passionate abolitionist writings, most notably *Uncle Tom's Cabin* (1852). Since the novel's publication, critics have argued heatedly about her politics: she has been dismissed as sentimental, cast as racist, condemned as an apologist for domesticity, even charged, by Ann Douglas, with contributing to America's embrace of consumerism. Today, most scholars agree that her work masterfully reveals her generation's ambivalences toward race, gender, religion, and capitalism. This new critical focus, spurred by feminist criticism and cultural studies, has revived our interest in Stowe's remarkably varied corpus: historical romances, novels of manners, regional sketches, household advice columns, biography, children's stories, poetry, hymns, and essays on politics, the "woman question," home decorating, and religion.

Today the most famous of the children of the evangelical LYMAN BEECHER, Stowe was profoundly influenced by a father who candidly wished "Hattie had been a boy," and by the myth of a sainted mother who before her premature death fulfilled every prescriptive maxim of DOMESTICITY. The Bible, John Bunyan, and Puritan theology vied with Shakespeare, Lord Byron, and Sir Walter Scott as Harriet's literary influences. Her formative years were spent in female seminaries run by her older sister CATHARINE BEECHER, and with her father in Cincinnati, a border town split over abolition and secession. In that city she met and married Calvin Ellis Stowe, an unprepossessing biblical scholar with whom she had seven children. *Uncle Tom's Cabin* catapulted her to fame; she supported the family, eventually building a rambling Victorian house in Hartford, Connecticut, next door to Mark Twain. But a poorly conceived biography of Lady Byron in 1869 (which repeated the story of Lord Byron's incestuous relationship with his half-sister) sent her reputation into decline; her later work suffered from her efforts to win back her audience. Stowe's artistic decline was paralleled by the final events in a series of personal tragedies that extended from the loss of an infant in 1849 to Calvin's death in 1886. It was perhaps a blessing that towards the end of her life, her mind was, as she wryly put it, "nomadic."

Stowe's abolitionist works continue to evoke controversy, and to be misunderstood. The contemporary meaning of an "Uncle Tom" as an obsequious black man who caters to whites derives from distorted renderings of her novel in nineteenth-century popular culture. Stowe's Uncle Tom is much more subtle than that: he transcends his enslavement through his Christian belief, which gives him a freedom and a moral center denied him by the logic of slavery. Moreover, Stowe's sentimental style challenges the assumptions that made slavery possible; she establishes moral and psychological equivalences between black slaves and the white middle-class women implied as her readers. These equivalences overcome the distance between black and white by enabling the reader to identify, for example, with the anguish of a slave mother separated from her child.

But Stowe also encourages her readers to assume that their own values are universal, thereby implicitly invalidating much of the black experience. Her radical demands for emancipation are undercut by her reliance upon racialist assumptions of difference, assumptions brilliantly dissected by James Baldwin. Stowe's desire to bridge racial differences and her inability to do so won her comparisons to Zola and Dickens, but they also make the novel a chillingly prescient commentary on contemporary America's earnest confrontations with and evasions of what W. E. B. Du Bois termed "the color line."

Like her sister Catharine, Harriet was preoccupied with domesticity. Indeed, it was slavery's disrespect for the sanctity of the family that helped fuel her antagonism toward it. Yet her letters on domesticity and MOTHERHOOD, where she bemoaned "the smell of sour milk, and sour meat, and sour everything," reveal her ambivalence about female roles, an ambivalence which found its way into her fiction. In the historical New England novels that most critics agree are her best work (*The Minister's Wooing*, 1859, *The Pearl of Orr's Island*, 1862, *Oldtown Folks*, 1869), she delicately balances an endorsement of culturally prescribed GENDER difference with an ideal of EQUALITY based upon what she called the "faculty" of competent, determined women who can do whatever needs doing. The balance collapses in the later New York society novels (*Pink and White Tyranny*, 1871, *My Wife and I*, 1871, *We and Our Neighbors*, 1873), in which her heroines concentrate on decorating and matchmaking, and exchange their claims to political or economic equality for a dubious spiritual superiority.

As a religious thinker Stowe was also ambivalent about her heritage. She celebrates the principled logic of her father's CALVINISM, and what she sees as the moral integrity of its practitioners, but she also judges it harsh and uncompromising. In her fiction, she

emphasizes Christ's love over God's justice; in her life, she turned to the refuge of the theologically liberal Episcopal Church.

For all the passion her politics inspired, Stowe's greatest legacy was as a pioneer of American REALISM. She left a vital literary inheritance for younger writers—Mary Wilkins Freeman, Sarah Orne Jewett, Bret Harte, HAMLIN GARLAND, MARK TWAIN. She taught them to focus on the ordinary, to invest moments of daily life with symbolic meaning. *Uncle Tom's Cabin* did not, contrary to myth, start the Civil War, but Stowe helped launch an aesthetic revolution in American letters.

LISA MACFARLANE

FURTHER READING
Elizabeth Ammons, ed., *Critical Essays on Harriet Beecher Stowe* (Boston: G. K. Hall, 1980).
James Baldwin, "Everybody's Protest Novel," in *Notes of a Native Son* (1955; New York: Bantam, 1964).
Lawrence Buell, "Hawthorne and Stowe as Rival Interpreters of New England Puritanism," in *New England Literary Culture from Revolution through Renaissance* (New York: Cambridge University Press, 1986).
Ann Douglas, *The Feminization of American Culture* (New York: Knopf, 1977).
Joan D. Hedrick, *Harriet Beecher Stowe: a Life* (New York: Oxford University Press, 1994).
Mary Kelley, *Private Woman, Public Stage* (New York: Oxford University Press, 1984).

Strauss, Leo (b. Kirchhain, Germany, Sept. 20, 1899; d. Annapolis, Md., Oct. 18, 1973). An intensely controversial political theorist, Leo Strauss was a Jew who found refuge in America from Nazism. In the United States, he launched a movement to refound Socratic political philosophy. His life story bespeaks the doubtful fate of both Socratic political philosophy and Judaism in the twentieth century.

Leo Strauss was born to a rural, orthodox family. After serving in the German army during World War I, he studied mathematics, natural science, and above all philosophy at the universities of Marburg, Frankfurt am Main, Berlin, and Hamburg. In 1921 he received his doctorate from Hamburg, with a dissertation on the theory of knowledge of Friedrich Jacobi, written under the supervision of the neo-Kantian Ernst Cassirer.

By this time the young Strauss, himself a neo-Kantian, had moved rather far from his orthodox religious roots. But his discovery of the shattering power of Nietzsche's critique of rationalism in all its forms compelled Strauss to abandon Kant and to acknowledge the yet unmet challenge of religious faith. Strauss's subsequent personal encounter with Martin Heidegger and Franz Rosenzweig confirmed for him the deep inadequacy of modern rationalism. On the other hand, postdoctoral study under Edmund Husserl at Freiburg fueled Strauss's consuming need to seek the possibility of a "philosophy as rigorous science" that could withstand Nietzsche's critique and meet the challenge posed by faith.

Meanwhile, in his early twenties, if not before, Strauss had seen more and more urgently the political vulnerability of Jews in Germany. He became an active leader of Zionist youth, while at the same time doubting whether Zionism possessed a coherent alternative to secular liberalism, whose highest philosophic expression was Kantianism. Strauss thus found himself in the grip of a dilemma: he could not simply accept traditional Jewish faith, but he could not find in modern rationalism or science, and in modern liberal society, a foundation or even a strong possibility for a moral and civic life of dignity.

This sketch of Strauss's intellectual biography reveals the basic issues with which he wrestled for the rest of his life. The mature Strauss later came to see the problem of being a Jew as a clue to the insolubly problematic character of all political life, in all times and places. The abiding theme of Strauss's mature philosophic reflection was what he called, following Spinoza, the "theologico-political problem." This problem has several facets. First and foremost is the question whether or not God exists; and, in the second place, what difference His existence or nonexistence makes, above all for our understanding of JUSTICE. Does justice, and hence the good society, ultimately require divine support, and faith in that support, or is there a natural, purely rational basis for justice? If justice rests ultimately on *divine* right and law, how does one decide between the various competing religions? Alternatively, if justice rests ultimately on *natural* right and law, how does "philosophy as rigorous science" discover the principles of natural right? By insisting on these questions, Strauss set himself in radical opposition to almost all the reigning dogmas of the twentieth century. He charged that the most influential thinking in the twentieth century avoided these fundamental questions by such dodges as RELATIVISM, PRAGMATISM, existential commitment, subjective faith, or IDEOLOGY of one sort or another, including uncritical acceptance of the basic norms of modern liberal democratic culture.

To begin to deal with the theologico-political problem, Strauss undertook a study of the original normative foundations of modern SCIENCE. He found those foundations expressed most intransigently in the critique of religion carried out by Spinoza and Hobbes. As research assistant in the Academy of Jewish Research in Berlin (1922–35), Strauss published his first book, *Spinoza's Critique of Religion* (1930), which was to be followed by a sequel, *The Political Philosophy of Hobbes; Its Basis and Its Genesis* (1936). Dissatisfaction with Spinoza and Hobbes led Strauss back to Spinoza's great antagonist, Moses Maimonides. Through Maimonides and his Islamic philosophic teachers, especially Farabi and Avicenna, Strauss rediscovered what he came to believe to be the decisive superiority of classical rationalism as epitomized in Socrates and the Socratic way of life. Strauss's second book, *Philosophy and Law* (1935), announced this discovery to the world and set the agenda for all Strauss's subsequent work, elaborated in some 13 other books, the most important of which are *Persecution and the Art of Writing* (1952), *Natural Right and History* (1953), *The City and Man* (1963), *On Tyranny* (1963), *Liberalism Ancient and Modern* (1968), and *Xenophon's Socratic Discourse* (1970).

Strauss was professor of political philosophy at the New School for Social Research from 1938 to 1949, and then at the University of Chicago from 1949 until 1967. In America he mounted a searing critique of relativistic SOCIAL SCIENCE and of democratic dogmatism. As he insisted in *Liberalism Ancient and Modern*, "precisely because we are friends of liberal democracy we cannot be its flatterers" (p. 24). The primary civic duty of the Socratic philosopher, in Strauss's view, is constructive criticism of the political order, with a view to exposing the specific excesses of the reigning moral dogmas. In the aristocracies and monarchies of the past, it was belief in hereditary privilege that required criticism. In today's liberal democracy, the philosopher's duty is to identify and criticize the constriction of public life caused by narrow INDIVIDUALISM, and the inattention to human excellence caused by excessive enthusiasm for EQUALITY.

Like Socrates, Strauss aroused—and continues to arouse after his death—bitter opposition from almost all established intellectual and cultural authorities. He was an extraordinarily influential teacher, and, like Plato, he left behind a "school" of followers distinguished for their success as teachers, who have since produced two further generations of students, numbering in the hundreds. Most of these—notably Muhson Mahdi and Harvey Mansfield Jr. (at Harvard), Herbert J. Storing and Joseph Cropsey (at the University of Chicago), David Bolotin (at St. John's College), Paul Cantor (at the University of Virginia), and Christopher Bruell and Ernest Fortin (at Boston College)—have chosen the path of scholarship and teaching, in the fields of literature and theology as well as philosophy and political science. Others of Strauss's students or students' students have become influential in journalism and government: prominent examples are William Galston, domestic issues adviser in the Clinton White House and earlier in the Mondale campaign for the Presidency; and William Kristol and Paul Wolfowitz, who held high positions in the Bush administration; Marc Plattner, who has been an editor of the journals *democracy* and *The Public Interest*; and Werner Dannhauser, who was an editor of *Commentary*.

Strauss's revival of the Platonic project of a "school," or a group of dedicated student-teachers, joined by strong bonds of personal friendship, who inspire future student-teachers with the passion for study and debate of the ideas of the great minds of the past, marks a striking departure from conventionally respectable notions of intellectual life and teaching in America. "Straussians" have received the abuse often heaped on those who reject conformity to reigning norms and insist on forging a new set of scholarly mores. The history of "Straussianism" is thus a fascinating commentary on the purported "openness" of the American academy and American mind. It is no accident that Strauss's most famous student, Allan Bloom (John U. Nef Distinguished Professor at the University of Chicago) entitled his bestselling critique of American intellectual life and culture *The Closing of the American Mind*.

THOMAS L. PANGLE

FURTHER READING
Allan Bloom, *The Closing of the American Mind: How Higher Education Has Failed Democracy and Impoverished the Souls of Today's Students* (New York: Simon and Schuster, 1987).
Thomas L. Pangle, ed., *The Rebirth of Classical Political Rationalism: an Introduction to the Thought of Leo Strauss* (Chicago: University of Chicago Press, 1989).
Leo Strauss, *Persecution and the Art of Writing* (Glencoe: Free Press, 1952).
——, *Natural Right and History* (Chicago: University of Chicago Press, 1953).
——, *Liberalism Ancient and Modern* (New York: Basic Books, 1968).

Strong, Anna Louise (b. Friend, Nebr., Nov. 24, 1885; d. Beijing, China, Mar. 29, 1970). Journalist. Radicalized by police killings of workers and the repression of dissent during World War I, Strong investigated worker uprisings throughout the world. Although shocked by the chaos and starvation in postrevolutionary Russia, she maintained her faith in the principle of a worker-run state. Her writings on China in the 1920s reveal an increasing sensitivity to the cultural character of revolution and emphasize the triumph of human consciousness over weapons. Always a pacifist, she reported critically on United States involvement in Indochina. A founding editor of the English-language *Moscow Daily News* (1930–46), Strong also wrote such works as *China's Millions* (1928), *Dawn over China* (1948), and an autobiography, *I Change Worlds: the Remaking of an American* (1937).

FURTHER READING
Tracy B. Strong, *Right in Her Soul: the Life of Anna Louise Strong* (New York: Random House, 1983).

Sullivan, Harry Stack (b. Norwich, N.Y., Feb. 21, 1892; d. Paris, France, Jan. 14, 1949). Psychologist. Human behavior and psychology, Sullivan held, is fundamentally interpersonal. Emotional problems, therefore, often stem from difficulties in relationships between people, difficulties which may be traceable in their turn to cultural problems. Psychoanalysis may be helpful in reducing anxiety, but its basic concepts are metaphors inaccessible to observation or testing. A more practical therapeutic approach examines and intervenes in the basic dynamics of interpersonal relations. Primarily a teacher and clinical researcher, Sullivan outlined his ideas in *The Interpersonal Theory of Psychiatry* (1953) and *The Fusion of Psychiatry and Social Science* (1964).

See also NEO-FREUDIANISM.

FURTHER READING
Helen Swick Perry, *Psychiatrist of America: the Life of Harry Stack Sullivan* (Cambridge: Harvard University Press, Belknap, 1982).

Sullivan, Louis (b. Boston, Mass., Sept. 3, 1856; d. Chicago, Ill., Apr. 14, 1924). Architect. Best known for his dictum that form should follow function, Sullivan designed skyscrapers, beginning with the Wainwright building in St. Louis (1890), whose soaring vertical lines visually reflected their underlying skeletal structures. Rejecting classical styles and historical allusions as impediments to the development of an indigenous American ARCHITECTURE—which would be innovative and expansive—he looked to nature for inspiration as he created an ornamental style based on curved lines and organic forms. His most important written work was *The Autobiography of an Idea* (1924).

FURTHER READING
Robert C. Twombly, *Louis Sullivan, His Life and Work* (New York: Viking, 1986).

Sumner, William Graham (b. Paterson, N.J., Oct. 30, 1840; d. Englewood, N.J., Apr. 12, 1910). For nearly 40 years, "Sumnerology"—his gruff lectures on economics, political theory, political and social history, sociology, and anthropology—made Sumner one of the most popular professors at Yale University. After his death Sumner's writings became the chief source for discussions of so-called SOCIAL DARWINISM in the United States.

Sumner's father was an English emigrant who found work in Connecticut's railroad machine shops. Despite the family's commitment to bettering the children's position through education, early in his teens Sumner was forced to leave school to work in a dry goods store for two years until a Congregational minister persuaded his parents to send him to high school and, in 1859, to Yale. After graduation a classmate's brother lent him money to study theology and biblical criticism for three years in Germany and England. From 1869 through 1872 Sumner was a key figure in American Broad Church Episcopalianism, which comported with his preference for science and modernity over revivalism, ritualism, and sentimentalism. Pastoral duties bored him, though, and he found other issues more engaging. After he left the active ministry, Sumner told Albert G. Keller that he never deliberately rejected his Christian beliefs: "I left them in the drawer, and, after a while, when I opened it, there was nothing there at all" (Keller, p. 103).

The process of secularization was accelerated by Sumner's return to Yale in 1872 to fill its new chair in political and social science. An invigorating classroom presence, he often taught economics from the daily newspaper and tried to lecture in social science from Herbert Spencer's religiously heterodox *Study of Sociology* (1873). His choice of textbooks precipitated one of many clashes with faculty traditionalists led by Noah Porter, Yale's president. A doughty combatant beyond the campus as well, Sumner eagerly sought opportunities to castigate protectionists and soft-money advocates. With the advent of labor turmoil and the reception afforded Henry George's *Progress and Poverty* (1879), Sumner's ideology grew more inflexible and his pithy epigrams more sardonic. "What social classes owe to each other," the question posed in the title of his book of 1883, was nothing. To protect the "forgotten man" from further intrusions on his bank account, Sumner recommended leaving the drunkard to his just deserts: the gutter. The only alternative to the survival of the fittest, he argued, was the survival of the unfittest.

The references to "survival of the fittest" have identified Sumner with Herbert Spencer as the archetypal "Social Darwinists," a misleading term that exaggerates the importance of both Spencer and the *Origin of Species* for Sumner's intellectual development. Despite his enormous respect for Darwin,

Sumner was not trying to formulate a Darwinian social theory. "Survival of the fittest" was a metaphor for economic success through an individual choice to exercise the values of perseverance and delayed gratification. When readers objected to the Spencerian phrase, Sumner dropped it after fewer than ten uses in favor of "competition," "struggle," and "success," since that was what he had meant all along.

Undergirding Sumner's commentary on social and economic issues in the 1880s was an extremely deterministic blend of Malthusian population theory and Ricardian economics. The man–land ratio at a given level of technology was the primary factor establishing economic opportunity, class relations, and political organization. However, no man–land ratio was permanent. Democratic politics and nineteenth-century optimism were epiphenomena of a temporarily propitious ratio that would gradually erode in the years to come.

Throughout this period Sumner was tormented by his wife's attacks of "nerves." He reacted to Jeannie Sumner's frequent absences by driving himself even harder in his work, until in 1890 he broke, both physically and emotionally. Friends paid for extended rests in Europe, but he was not able to resume a full teaching schedule until the mid-1890s. Sumner's personal crisis initiated a professional transition, as he shifted focus from evangelism in economics to scholarship in sociology.

Sumner returned to the political fray in 1899, opposing U.S. annexation of the Philippines as a repudiation of the country's best traditions and principles. However, Sumner eventually acknowledged that if the mores of the American people changed, calls for consistency with the country's past were futile. At this point he began work on *Folkways* (1906), a catalogue of beliefs and practices demonstrating that "in the folkways, whatever is, is right" (p. 28). But he disliked too many aspects of early twentieth-century America to yield completely to relativism or to his argument's implicit determinism. Eager for an escape hatch from mores like expansionism that he abhorred, Sumner advocated, in place of unconscious mores and unintelligent legislation, the authority of the scientific method in the hands of a new modernized elite of trained experts. Faced with choices between custom and change, relativism and modernism, determinism and individual initiative, Sumner tried to have it both ways.

Sumner chose words for directness and clarity. Anything else was, in his favorite epithet, "gush." But he found it difficult to organize his ideas into cohesive paragraphs, probably in part due to unresolved tensions in his personality and ideas. He was among the first to attempt to combine the traditionalism and institutionalism of an Edmund Burke with the economic individualism elicited by the spirit of modern capitalism, to reestablish an orderly world of universal laws and obedient citizens within the turmoil of economic revolution and scientific experimentation. By temperament he was both an iconoclastic rebel demanding change and a pessimistic determinist who felt that he could exercise little control over his destiny. One of the great educators of his generation, beyond the Yale campus he antagonized many more than he converted, and left few disciples in either economics or sociology.

Today historians of SOCIAL SCIENCE such as Robert Bannister and Dorothy Ross are providing fresh evaluations of Sumner's academic and professional activities, but the process of reinterpretation and contextualization has lagged in contemporary political discourse. Even conservatives did not rush to embrace Sumner during the resurgence of the right during the 1980s, if only because Sumner represented an antiutopian strain of CONSERVATISM incompatible with the rhetoric of Reaganism. For most readers today, Sumner remains the figure created by liberal historians in the 1940s and 1950s, a quotable bogeyman with a convenient penchant for brusque, artless statements of a brazen, heartless ideology.

DONALD C. BELLOMY

FURTHER READING

Robert C. Bannister, ed., *On Liberty, Society, and Politics: the Essential Essays of William Graham Sumner* (Indianapolis: Liberty Fund, 1992).

Bruce Curtis, *William Graham Sumner* (Boston: Twayne, 1981).
Richard Hofstadter, *Social Darwinism in American Thought*, rev. ed. (1944; Boston: Beacon, 1955).
Albert G. Keller, *Reminiscences (Mainly Personal) of William Graham Sumner* (New Haven: Yale University Press, 1933).
Dorothy Ross, *The Origins of American Social Science* (New York: Cambridge University Press, 1991).
Harris E. Starr, *William Graham Sumner* (New York: Henry Holt, 1925).
M. W. Taylor, *Men Versus the State: Herbert Spencer and Late Victorian Individualism* (Oxford: Clarendon Press, 1992).

Szilard, Leo (b. Budapest, Hungary, Feb. 11, 1898; d. La Jolla, Calif., May 30, 1964). Physicist. One of the people who created the first nuclear chain reaction, Szilard soon realized it could be used to make a powerful bomb. At first he tried to persuade scientists to keep their results confidential. Once he learned that the Germans were making progress, however, he helped convince Roosevelt to pursue the Manhattan Project. He fought the bomb's first use in Japan: a demonstration of its power, he argued, would be equally effective. Later he tried to ensure civilian rather than military control of nuclear research, protested nuclear proliferation, and promoted peaceful uses of nuclear energy.

FURTHER READING

William Lanouette, *Genius in the Shadows: a Biography of Leo Szilard, the Man Behind the Bomb* (New York: Scribner's, 1992).

T

Taney, Roger (b. Calvert County, Md., Mar. 17, 1777; d. Washington, D.C., Oct. 12, 1864). Supreme Court Chief Justice (1836–64). Taney held that the police power—which he defined as the power to provide for the welfare of the community —belongs to the states, not the federal government. States may therefore regulate whatever does not require national uniformity. In *Ableman v. Booth* (1858), however, he asserted the ultimate authority of the federal courts over the state courts. His most famous decision was his majority opinion in *Dred Scott v. Sandford* (1857), in which he ruled that Dred Scott, a runaway slave, could not sue in federal court because, as a Negro, he could not be a citizen. Taney also ruled that Congress did not have the power to exclude slavery from the territories—a finding that negated the Missouri Compromise and galvanized antislavery opinion in the North.

FURTHER READING
Don E. Fehrenbacher, *The Dred Scott Case: Its Significance in American Law and Politics* (New York: Oxford University Press, 1978).

Tate, [John Orley] Allen (b. Winchester, Ky., Nov. 19, 1899; d. Nashville, Tenn., Feb. 9, 1979). "Man of letters" was his favorite self-description. Allen Tate was the son of a Virginian mother and Kentucky father, who gave him a childhood of marked instability in and around the Ohio Valley. Tate attended a large number of schools before entering Vanderbilt University in 1918. There he was taught by JOHN CROWE RANSOM and Donald Davidson, was a contemporary of ROBERT PENN WARREN, and joined the circle of poets who published *The Fugitive* (1922–5), the most influential southern magazine of poetry in its day. In 1924 he went to New York, to become a freelance poet, book reviewer, and biographer of *Stonewall Jackson: the Good Soldier* (1928) and *Jefferson Davis* (1929). He married the novelist Caroline Gordon in 1924; she was the first of his three wives, though not of his many

lovers. After the publication of his first volume of verse, *Mr. Pope and Other Poems* (1928), he received a Guggenheim Fellowship, spent partly in Britain but mostly in France, where he mingled with the American expatriate literary community. Then he helped to found SOUTHERN AGRARIANISM, participated in *I'll Take My Stand: the South and the Agrarian Tradition* (1930), returned to live in Tennessee, unsuccessfully attempted a biography of Robert E. Lee, coedited with Herbert Agar *Who Owns America? A New Declaration of Independence* (1936), and published a historical novel of Civil War Virginia, *The Fathers* (1938). During the mid-1930s he abandoned the financially precarious life of a freelance writer and started a career as a college professor, variously spent, but most lastingly at the University of Minnesota (1951–68). Between 1943 and 1944, he held the chair of poetry at the Library of Congress, and from 1944 to 1946 he edited the *Sewanee Review*. In his retirement, he returned to Tennessee. Throughout his life, he was notable for the intensity of his care for contemporaries and juniors who were writers; from them he received and deserved a fierce devotion.

Tate began his intellectual career as a proponent of H. L. Mencken, moved to an admiration for the French Symbolist poets (especially Baudelaire), then fell under the influence of T. S. ELIOT, the merits of whose *The Waste Land* Tate was among the first to urge in the South, against the skepticism of Ransom. In the discussions of the Fugitive poets, Tate stood for cosmopolitanism, freedom from inhibition, the impossibility of general truth, and indifference to place. These standpoints he began to reconsider, after having experienced New York and France, though he never completely abandoned them. In "Ode to the Confederate Dead" (1926), which portrays a modern southerner attempting but failing at a Confederate cemetery to touch the reality of past sacrifice, Tate began to explore his mature theme: the delicate and fructifying tension between community and commitment, on the one hand, and alienation and self-awareness, on the other; a doctrine parallel to and fostered by Eliot's doctrine that modern times had witnessed a "dissociation of sensibility" which it was the business of men of letters to define and resist. Beginning with his essay, "The Profession of Letters in the South" (1935) and continuing until "A Southern Mode of the Imagination" (1959), Tate applied this theme to southern literature, especially that of the so-called "Southern Renaissance."

Tate felt that, if modernity was to salvage sanity, the intellectual must by an act of will assert a meaningful social and religious order, almost irrespective of whether or not he accepted the general truth of that order. In the late 1920s and 1930s, Tate gave more attention to the social problem, though even in *I'll Take My Stand* he was drawn to make "Remarks on the Southern Religion." He argued that agrarianism—as opposed to urban industrial capitalism—would better conduce to morality, prosperity, and community. More rapidly than most of his confederates, however, he began to minimize the southern dimension of the cause by reaching out to other cultures, notably to the English Distributists, who were to be represented in *Who Owns America?* His last sustained venture in considering southern culture was *The Fathers*; its theme was the triumph of rapacious modernity over older traditions of noblesse oblige and civility. After 1938 Tate abandoned the attempt to make the South a repository of meaning and turned more strictly to religion; he converted to Roman Catholicism in 1952.

Tate's standing is in flux. He is most often discussed as a critic of southern literature, one whose essays formed the dominant critical interpretation of his day; the essays have continued to have a marked though diminished influence, since the generation which grew up with Tate's writings as a prescriptive guide is now passing. This decline is the more noticeable since he was idiosyncratically associated with the New Criticism, more famously urged by his friends Cleanth Brooks, Warren, and Ransom, which has now been repudiated by critics drawn to DECONSTRUCTION and the NEW LITERARY HISTORICISM. Tate does not find favor with those who see social issues so differently. As a poet, he is often regarded as a significant but minor modernist, whose elaborate, metaphysically learned, and emotionally opaque verse is uncongenial to a blunter time, to whom prose matters more than poetry. His historical standing as a significant molder of American and southern culture, however, is in no doubt.

MICHAEL O'BRIEN

See also SOUTHERN INTELLECTUAL HISTORY.

FURTHER READING

John Tyree Fain and Thomas Daniel Young, eds., *The Literary Correspondence of Donald Davidson and Allen Tate* (Athens: University of Georgia Press, 1974).
Marshall Falwell et al., comp., *Allen Tate: a Bibliography* (New York: D. Lewis, 1969).
Radcliffe Squires, ed., *Allen Tate and His Work: Critical Evaluations* (Minneapolis: University of Minnesota Press, 1972).
Walter Sullivan, *Allen Tate: a Recollection* (Baton Rouge: Louisiana State University Press, 1988).
Allen Tate, *Collected Poems, 1919–1976* (New York: Farrar Straus Giroux, 1977).
——, *Memoirs and Opinions, 1926–1974* (Chicago: Swallow Press, 1975).
——, *Essays of Four Decades* (Chicago: Swallow Press, 1968).

Taylor, John (b. Caroline County, Va., probably Dec. 19, 1753; d. Caroline County, Va., Aug. 21, 1824). Political theorist. Taylor protested what he saw as the corruption of republican ideals. Rather than maintaining a healthy distrust of power, he warned, post-Revolutionary Americans were coming to regard government as an extension of the people. That fatal step permitted powerful individuals to use government for their own ends: corporations and tariffs are endorsed in the "common interest," but enrich only a few. Economic PROGRESS destroys agrarian egalitarianism and sacrifices community. States' rights must become a bulwark against additional federal intrusions. Taylor presented his views in such works as *A Defense of the Measures of the Administration of Thomas Jefferson* (1805), *An Inquiry into the Principles and Policy of the Government of the United States* (1814), and *Construction Construed and Constitutions Vindicated* (1820).

FURTHER READING

Robert E. Shalhope, *John Taylor of Caroline: Pastoral Republican* (Columbia: University of South Carolina Press, 1980).

Taylor, Nathaniel W. (b. New Milford, Conn., June 23, 1786; d. New Haven, Conn., Mar. 10, 1858). Theologian. Architect of the New Haven Theology, Taylor taught at Yale Divinity School from its founding in 1822. He attempted to develop a rationally plausible notion of original sin in order to adjust the CALVINISM of JONATHAN EDWARDS to the liberalizing outlook of the antebellum era, which combined rosier assumptions about human nature with a persistent revivalistic faith in personal transformation. God, Taylor asserted, does not predestine human beings to sin. As autonomous beings with free will, people can choose to follow their better motives, yet frequently do not. Sin is "original" because it is universal. It is not a pre-existing condition, but a state concurrent with the act of sinning.

FURTHER READING

Bruce Kuklick, *Churchmen and Philosophers: From Jonathan Edwards to John Dewey* (New Haven: Yale University Press, 1985).

Taylorism Frederick W. Taylor (1856–1915), a mechanical engineer and business consultant, developed the basis of the dominant ideology of modern management. Taylorism, or scientific management, provided prescriptions for corporate governance, thereby justifying the power of professional managers and helping create the ethos of contemporary bureaucracy.

Taylor contributed to a search for control within turn-of-the-century manufacturing corporations. Leaders of these firms lacked regular procedures for controlling routine operations, scattered work sites, and individualistic workers. Craft workers or harsh foremen controlled the labor process. Through trial and error, corporations replaced arbitrary authority, ad hoc actions, and craft traditions with administrative systems. To improve shopfloor management, Taylor formulated specific techniques for machine operation, incentive wages, and foremanship.

By 1903 Taylor went beyond technical advice to create a general theory of management. Calling for "a mental revolution" at work, Taylor wanted to empower a new elite of industrial engineers. They would study work scientifically, take job knowledge from backward foremen and workers, and then organize tasks to promote efficiency. Such professional managers would then direct the newly deskilled tasks and employ incentive wages to create harmony between labor and capital. In sum, Taylorism prescribed centralization of power, separation of planners and doers, and specialization of tasks as the path to productive efficiency and class harmony.

Before World War I a few dozen firms applied Taylor's entire scheme and discovered that his ideas produced efficiency but not harmony. Craft workers in particular despised their loss of independence. Workers tried to defend themselves by quitting, restricting output, demanding high wages, or forming unions.

Despite such dysfunctions, corporate managers had accepted Taylor's fundamental approach by the 1920s. They believed that scientific management verified bureaucratic trends already underway and legitimized managerial power. It also created an agenda for corporate practice and academic research; further efforts would resolve technical problems. By mid-century, managers and professors had applied BEHAVIORISM and other varieties of psychology, sociology, economics, mathematics, and cybernetics to business problems. The new techniques, however, maintained Taylor's principles of management.

Scientific management was nearly as influential outside corporate circles. Radicals like Thorstein Veblen and V. I. Lenin believed that cadres of engineers could purge Taylorism of capitalist notions and end the exploitation of labor. Professional people from the new middle class eagerly endorsed the notion that apolitical experts could solve problems in government, social work, education, and other areas. No wonder that Peter Drucker, the leading post-World War II management thinker, argued in *The Practice of Management* that Taylorism was "the most powerful as well as the most lasting contribution America has made to Western thought since the Federalist Papers" (p. 280).

Even so, American academics have questioned Taylor's premises and debated the impulses that drove the professionalization of management. Business historians like Alfred Chandler have contended that inexorable imperatives of TECHNOLOGY replaced the invisible hand of the market with the visible hand of professional management. Radical scholars like Dan Clawson have offered contingent interpretations; because managers chose Taylorism and exercised power to implement it, they never explored opportunities to fuse planning and doing and thus minimize class conflicts. Other radicals like Harry Braverman have contended that managerial hierarchies and degraded work were inherent in capitalism.

Perhaps ironically, optimism about the possibility of transcending Taylorism has developed within the management community. Beginning in the 1950s such corporative thinkers as Peter Drucker and Douglas MacGregor argued that scientific management underused skilled professionals and antagonized educated workers. If managers used "democratic leadership" and "participative management" to fuse planning and doing, firms could become communal and labor could become cooperative. In the 1960s and 1970s the prospect of harmony within hierarchy led to experiments with such techniques as management by objectives, sensitivity training, and job enrichment. Most corporate leaders, however, believed that synthesis of planning and doing threatened their power.

The challenge of foreign competition in the 1980s caused managers to reconsider. This time critics of Taylorism changed their focus from psychology to economics and engineering. Robert Reich contended that corporate planners lacked engineering knowledge; isolated from the shopfloor, managers necessarily relied on abstract quantitative methods that overemphasized short-term profits at the expense of long-term growth and innovation. Such arguments helped lead to "quality circles" and other team methods designed to extract production knowledge from workers. Middle managers, however, felt a team approach threatened their jobs and often refused to surrender power. Moreover, a team organization of tasks contradicted the individualistic reward system of Taylorism and business corporations.

Despite managers' reluctance to practice what corporate reformers preached, their language of harmony has influenced historical scholarship. Hindy Schacter and others have sought to rehabilitate Taylor as a prototeam man, spotlighting his rhetoric of class cooperation and overlooking his goal of empowering professional managers. By conflating pseudoteams dominated by managers with cooperative labor among peers, the new mythology masks the continued separation of planning and doing.

While many have tried to transcend Taylorism, few have succeeded. In practice Taylor's ideas have promoted managerial hierarchy without necessarily creating productive efficiency or social harmony.

STEPHEN P. WARING

See also MANAGERIALISM.

FURTHER READING

Harry Braverman, *Labor and Monopoly Capital: the Degradation of Work in the Twentieth Century* (New York: Monthly Review Press, 1974).
Alfred D. Chandler, *The Visible Hand: the Managerial Revolution in American Business* (Cambridge: Harvard University Press, 1977).
Dan Clawson, *Bureaucracy and the Labor Process: the Transformation of U.S. Industry, 1860–1920* (New York: Monthly Review Press, 1980).
Peter F. Drucker, *The Practice of Management* (New York: Harper and Row, 1954).
Robert B. Reich, *The Next American Frontier* (New York: Times Books, 1983).
Hindy Lauer Schacter, *Frederick Taylor and the Public Administration Community: a Reevaluation* (Albany: State University of New York Press, 1989).
Frederick W. Taylor, *Scientific Management: Comprising Shop Management, the Principles of Scientific Management, Testimony before the Special House Committee* (New York: Harper, 1947).
Stephen P. Waring, *Taylorism Transformed: Scientific Management Theory since 1945* (Chapel Hill: University of North Carolina Press, 1991).

technology Diego Rivera once offered a double-edged paean to the Ford River Rouge factory, a verdict that epitomizes an ambivalence characteristic, by the early twentieth century, of the American love affair with technology.

I thought of the millions of different men by whose combined labor and thought automobiles were produced, from the miners who dug the iron ore out of the earth to the railroad men and teamsters who brought the finished machines to the consumer, so that man, space, and time might be conquered, and ever-expanding victories be won against death.

For Rivera technological achievement—wresting resources from nature and transforming them into machines to conquer space, time, death, *and man*—imprisons while it liberates in an uneasy synthesis of promise and threat. Making sense of these powerful conflicting valences requires attention to a century-long history during which the concept of technological practice slowly took on a twentieth-century formulation that proved remarkably durable until the very recent past.

In the late nineteenth century, electric power utilities and other complex systems began to replace mechanical contrivances like the steam engine as the dominant symbols of technology. At roughly the same time, the word "technology" began to replace earlier expressions such as "the mechanical arts." Warnings about new technology can be found as early as Jefferson's famous call to leave factories in Europe lest their vices corrupt a republican citizenry. Throughout the nineteenth century, a handful of critics such as Emerson, Thoreau, Melville, and Hawthorne warned of invention's seductive power to distract from higher purpose. Emerson's 1833 exultation in railroad speed turned somber by 1857: "Machinery is aggressive. The weaver becomes a web, the machinist a machine. If you do not use the tools, they use you. All tools are in one sense edge-tools, and dangerous" (p. 164).

Such wariness, however, was dwarfed by unbridled popular enthusiasm about PROGRESS. For engineers, politicians, preachers, and business leaders, America's destiny to construct a new society through the power of invention was a constant refrain in public rhetoric. The notion of exceptional American inventiveness depended in part on the twinned mythologies of a land free from tradition's constraints and of prior inhabitants lacking legitimate culture. The "empty land" welcomed freewheeling and aggressive creativity, not as conquest of peoples or conflict between classes, but as youthful innocence and civic virtue. To cite one among a host of celebrants, Russell Conwell's enormously popular lecture "Acres of Diamonds" (first delivered in 1861 and subsequently performed more than 6,000 times) exhorted listeners to seize hold of opportunity, to believe that their creative capacities opened a world of boundless possibility where wealth rewarded the virtuous citizens whose private achievements built up the public order. "I say that you ought to get rich, and it is your duty to get rich . . . The men who get rich may be the most honest men you find in the community" (p. 18). Had the term been much in use at mid-century, "technology" would have described the tools, some conventional and some startlingly novel, that this ingenious people used to craft a new society in the wilderness.

During the Gilded Age, however, two seemingly contradictory trends began to coalesce into a new national climate, at once daring and anxious. Americans thrilled to protean technological triumphs transforming what had been a rough frontier life. On the other hand, urban violence frequently seemed to threaten all they held dear. Two decades of bloody confrontations between workers and management police were rushed to readers in lurid, generally antiworker, detail thanks to new communications technologies: the telegraphic wire service, high-speed printing, and half-tone photographic reproduction. Still more unsettling, millions of immigrants from Eastern and Southern Europe flooded the nation; many prior residents saw them as invading hordes who spoke strange languages and affronted a Protestant God.

Contemporary technologies, precisely rational and elegantly complex, stood out for many, especially among the middle class, in welcome contrast to these alarming signs of social disorder. New inventions such as telephones, skyscrapers, and electric utilities showcased experts who could introduce seemingly miraculous systems to solve unimaginably complex problems. What was not immediately obvious was the conformity these same systems demanded from the people who used them. A new technological style, based on standardized systems, was gradually replacing earlier, less efficient techniques that had required more hands-on negotiation. Older types of negotiation—skilled workers with foremen and owners, independent engineers with clients, or local businesses with national companies like the rail lines—were unpredictable and sometimes truculent. Traditional practitioners needed political skill along with technical know-how. The new standardized systems not only replaced these less efficient arrangements; they also modeled a post-political ideal of systemic control in an uncertain time. Not surprisingly, many who feared social chaos looked to technological expertise for answers and, in the process, elevated efficiency and control to the status of essential public values.

Substituting systems designed by experts for more traditional negotiations appealed to middle-class and elite observers in part because the new systems did work much better than many older ones. Railroads rolled past the nation's mostly dirt roads; skyscrapers, hotels, and department stores lit by electricity gave hope of transforming dim filthy tenements; early automobiles evoked the dream of streets free from horse manure. Pronouncements about reorganizing society according to rational laws were made by Progressive Era technocratic heroes such as Thomas Edison, Charles Proteus Steinmetz, Frederick Winslow Taylor (see TAYLORISM), or Henry Ford, and they were treated as hot copy by the popular press throughout the period. Ensconced as General Electric's resident wizard, socialist inventor Steinmetz saw the corporation as the model for social justice. The Socialist Party, he argued in 1915,

> cannot be antagonistic to the corporation principle, since its ultimate aim, socialistic society, may be expressed as the formation of the industrial corporation of the United States, owned by all the citizens as stockholders. (Klein, p. 219)

For the enthusiasts of large systems, whether socialist like Steinmetz or capitalist like Ford, new technologies announced an exciting era of abundance for all. Yet other observers noticed that the new technical systems created an artificial landscape that defined the individual as a tiny figure against imposing, sometimes brutal, and always dynamically changing technological forces. Technology appeared increasingly to mold the world according to its "own" mysterious and inexorable trajectory. Increasingly cut off from its eighteenth- and early nineteenth-century relationship with a republican vision of democratic politics, progress was now guaranteed by impersonal machines and systems. It no longer required the consent of an independent citizenry.

The perception that modern technology imposed cultural passivity occurred to many writers throughout the twentieth century, from LEWIS MUMFORD to the refugee scholars of the FRANKFURT SCHOOL. But it has generated politically significant opposition to the ideology of progress only in the recent past. Antitechnology movements stem in part from technical triumphs of World War II that came to be seen as heinous. Germany, epitome of scientific and engineering sophistication, used its expertise to build death camps; the United States constructed atomic bombs and dropped them on civilian targets. Building on this grim symbolic foundation, several social trends have coalesced in what some observers see as a crisis for the idea of technological progress itself. Since the mid-1960s, ecological consciousness and no-growth notions have achieved significant political power in some localities and are increasingly influential in national debates. They have combined with other currents of thought—from FUNDAMENTALISM and New Age religion to philosophical RELATIVISM and literary POSTMODERNISM—to mount an unprecedented challenge to the ENLIGHTENMENT heritage of scientific rationalism.

Nevertheless, technological determinism continues to exert a powerful influence on public debate. Pervasive popular rhetoric, in such varied contexts as Disney's immensely popular EPCOT Center, advertisements using hi-tech iconography, and Congressional testimony on competitiveness or weapons research, portrays a race toward the future driven by extant technologies which resist critique from any person, place, politics or social vision. Deterministic "Technology," inexorably moving forward, intimidating even as it promises abundance, remains the dominant assumption underlying popular attitudes. The staying power of this definition of technology may be due in part to the abiding allure of the myth of the empty land. When the United States is seen as the fortuitous product of an innocent conquest of open wilderness, when the essentially political work of the Constitution's designers is forgotten, technology, with its restless innovative energies, operates in public consciousness as an omnipotent force, sometimes benevolent, sometimes nefarious, godlike in power and devilish in whim. When, by contrast, technological decisions are seen as part of an unending and necessary debate about allocating resources toward competing goals, in short as politics in the original meaning of the word, technological practice is situated in a hopeful context of chosen human purposes. From this perspective, retrieving the old tradition of civic VIRTUE, achieved through public action and debate, appears to be a primary national agenda.

JOHN M. STAUDENMAIER

FURTHER READING

Russell H. Conwell, "Acres of Diamonds," in Robert Shackleton, *Russell H. Conwell: His Life and Achievements* (New York: Harper, 1915).

Ralph Waldo Emerson, "Works and Days," in Emerson, *Society and Solitude* (Boston: Houghton Mifflin, 1870).

Steven L. Goldman, ed., *Science, Technology and Social Progress*, Research in Technology Studies, vol. 2 (Bethlehem, Pa.: Lehigh University Press, 1989).

Thomas Parke Hughes, *American Genesis: a Century of Invention and Technological Enthusiasm* (New York: Penguin, 1990).

John F. Kasson, *Civilizing the Machine: Technology and Republican Values in America, 1776–1900* (New York: Penguin, 1977).

Ronald R. Kline, *Steinmetz: Engineer and Socialist* (Baltimore: Johns Hopkins University Press, 1992).

Leo Marx, *The Machine in the Garden: Technology and the Pastoral Ideal in America* (New York: Oxford University Press, 1964).

Merritt Roe Smith, ed., *Beyond Technological Determinism* (Cambridge: MIT Press, 1994).

Tecumseh (b. Old Piqua [now Ohio], 1768; d. near Thames River, Canada, Oct. 5, 1813). The story of Tecumseh and his brother, the Great Shawnee Prophet Tenskwatawa, is recounted in popular and official histories of the emergence of the United States. Among a handful of Indians whose stories get told in official accounts of American expansion west, Tecumseh is celebrated as a great patriot chief. These accounts speak of him as a unique orator, a brave warrior, an exemplary Indian whose failed defense of his people's land west of the Ohio River constitutes a noble footnote in the forward march of national destiny. Historical accounts that attempt to restore a narrative of Indian resistance recall Tecumseh's role in promoting unity among Indian nations during the early nineteenth century, and, less often, look to the role of the pan-Indian religion spread by Tenskwatawa in fulfilling this vision of solidarity. In many Shawnee homes in Oklahoma, portraits of Tecumseh hang today, maintaining a popular memory of this story.

Tecumseh was born in central Ohio, a region already marked by 150 years of contact between Indian and European cultures. Responding to the geopolitical changes brought by colonization, the Shawnee had become increasingly migratory prior to the birth of Tecumseh and his younger brother, who was known as Lalewethika prior to his conversion experience. The brothers grew up in an atmosphere charged with political, economic, and cultural changes. As Europeans and Indians competed for diminishing game, the Shawnee economy became more reliant on trade; similarly, alliances with other Indian nations shifted as Shawnees tried to counter European expansion west. The brothers were acquainted with members of these different Indian cultures as well as with Euro-American traders and settlers; one of the most famous accounts of Tecumseh's early years comes from the writings of Stephen Ruddell, a white boy who was captured and adopted by the Shawnee. (*See also* INDIAN–WHITE RELATIONS.)

Drawing on this culturally mobile and diverse background, as well as on 150 years of Indian responses to colonization, Tecumseh and Tenskwatawa called for unified Indian military and cultural resistance to Euro-American encroachments on Indian lands and ways of life. Tenskwatawa preached that a rejection of European cultural influence would ensure the restoration of Indian land and peace, while Tecumseh traveled widely in the midwest and among the Southeastern Indian nations, calling for military and political unity among all Indian people. Whereas traditional native concepts of identity had been based on distinctions of culture and language, Indians in this period responded to Euro-American racial categories of "Indian" and "white" by making strategic use of them. Tecumseh and other Indian leaders drew on the concept of RACE to ground a new pan-Indian movement. This intellectual syncretism mirrored the simultaneous religious syncretism between native and Christian religions. (*See also* INDIAN IDENTITIES.)

After the Treaty of Greenville in 1795 temporarily established a firm territorial boundary between

Euro-American settlements and the land the Indians were told would be theirs "in perpetuity," Tecumseh and Tenskwatawa, along with their allies in the Kickapoo, Potowatomie, Wyandot, and Miami nations, founded a settlement at Greenville, in what is now Ohio, called Prophetstown. Indians from diverse nations east of the Mississippi, as well as some representatives of Dakota and Anishanabe bands from the Plains and Upper Midwest, converged in Prophetstown, awaiting a "Mid Day" when the Indian federation would be complete, and Tenskwatawa's visions of an unimpaired Indian way of life would be realized. These Indians left their traditional homes because they understood that the best hope of defending their land lay in a broadly conceived alliance.

In 1808, the settlement relocated 125 miles northwest to Tippecanoe, in present-day Indiana, on some land that supportive Kickapoo and Potowatamie bands offered to them. A year later, the Treaty of Fort Wayne abridged many of the promises made to the Indians in the Treaty of Greenville. Thereafter relations between Indians, the Euro-American settlers who were encouraged by the U.S. government to act as the first line of territorial encroachment, and the U.S. government declined, with Ohio Territories Governor William Henry Harrison repeatedly asserting that Prophetstown was merely a front for the English to "stir up" the Indians against the new American nation. Meetings in 1809 and 1811 between Harrison and Tecumseh at Vincennes, on the contemporary border between Indiana and Illinois, established an official truce between the two leaders, but failed to dispel the growing hostilities between Indians and Euro-Americans in the Northwest territories. In the fall of 1811, while Tecumseh was in the South, recruiting support, Harrison led a successful campaign against the settlement at Prophetstown, shattering the military, if not the cultural and spiritual, ambitions of the pan-Indian alliance at the Battle of Tippecanoe.

It is significant that this battle is what is most commonly remembered about Tecumseh. Harrison successfully ran for President in 1840, with the slogan "Tippecanoe and Tyler, Too," asserting a virile image of frontier struggle. In official national histories, Tecumseh is portrayed as a "noble savage," fighting a doomed but valiant fight against the progress of American manifest destiny.

There is no such mention, however, of Tenskwatawa, or of the thousands of Indians who were involved in the movement to create Prophetstown and the vision of pan-Indian unity it stood for. Tenskwatawa is often portrayed as a liar and a fanatic, and his religious leadership is discounted. Tecumseh

can be celebrated as a patriot in most standard narratives only because these accounts dismiss the collective resistance embodied in the pan-Indian federation he and his brother organized. Most accounts also neglect or underestimate the reliance of the federation on the popular religious revivals not only of Tenskwatawa, Wovoka, and the Delaware Prophet, but also of the frontier religions of the Euro-American settlers. On the other hand, popular histories, like the portraits in Shawnee homes and the repeated references to Tecumseh in writings of the American Indian movement, circulate throughout the hemisphere, defying national boundaries and histories justifying the Indian's eclipse. These grassroots stories commemorate anticolonial movements like the pan-Indian federation and the Ghost Dance, attesting to the persistence of imaginings of alternative visions of the Americas.

RACHEL BUFF

FURTHER READING

Gregory Dowd, *A Spirited Resistance: the North American Indian Struggle for Unity, 1745–1815* (Baltimore: Johns Hopkins University Press, 1992).
Bil Gilbert, *God Gave Us This Country: Tekamthi and the First Civil War* (New York: Atheneum, 1989).
Jan Pieterse, "Amerindian Resistance: the Gathering of the Fires," *Race and Class* 26 (1986).
Tecumseh Papers, 13 vols., Lyman C. Draper Manuscript Collection, State Historical Society Archives, Madison, Wisconsin.
Richard White, *The Middle Ground: Indians, Empires, and Republics in the Great Lakes Regions, 1650–1815* (New York: Cambridge University Press, 1991).

textuality   Traditionally a text was presumed to be a concrete phenomenological object with a fixed meaning pointing beyond itself. It was thought to describe or reflect some outside reality. But more recently a text has been seen as an open-ended methodological process in which multiple meanings are created through interpretation, an act often focused on the nature of the text itself. Such a definition of text developed as part of structuralist and Poststructuralist theorizing in France and reached the United States as part of the interpretive, linguistic, and rhetorical turns in the human sciences since the 1970s. At its extreme, Jacques Derrida's words, "il n'y a pas d'hors texte" (there is nothing outside a text), were taken to mean that everything could and ought to be interpreted textually. Thus the word text came to embrace paintings, films, television programs, advertising, the spectacle of sports, political rallies, cultures and social systems, even the human body and history itself, in addition to its traditional definition of books and other verbal artifacts. The strong version of textualism presumes to understand life itself as a text. Not only does human behavior and social interaction from this view produce texts, but humans and their societies understand themselves through and as interpretive textualizations. Some see such pantextualism as a latter-day form of philosophic Idealism.

Textualist critics search for the hidden part of the texts, artifacts, or sets of social or cultural acts that their authors, creators, or enactors are unaware of but depend on for the work or event to achieve its effect. These inner workings are displayed as formal structures of rules according to linguistic and semiotic models, as a "process of signification" in Roland Barthes's term, or as "discursive practices" to use Michel Foucault's phrase. (*See also* SEMIOTICS.) Each method seeks to show how human activities and products are constituted as social subjects or cultural objects through these processes or practices, and how they should therefore be interpreted as and through textualization. Under each version of textuality, traditional notions of authorship and intention are absorbed into or superseded by the process of interpretation, whether by supposedly universal formalist structures, by the culturally bound readings of individuals or interpretive communities, or by anonymous but socially and historically specific bodies of rules. Since textualist analysis explores not the seemingly evident part of the textualization but rather its hidden presumptions or prescriptions, its findings point to what is often called the subtext (as opposed to the surface or explicit text).

Textualist criticism has furthered "the crisis of the sign" or the crisis of REPRESENTATION, since it denies any easy connection among words, their meanings, and their objects (that is, what they refer to). Textualism has, in linguistic terms, stressed the arbitrariness of signifiers, signifieds, and referents. In its most extreme forms, deconstructionist critics read a text by creating a countertext that can be submitted in turn to another textualist analysis. Hence some textualists have a reputation for open-ended playfulness, and for glorifying the critic as the equal of any literary author. As a result of the never-ending possibility of further DECONSTRUCTION and demystification, texts are seen as indeterminantly open to revision, just as language is said to be in general.

Textuality also problematizes the distinction between text and context, for much of what was traditionally assumed to be extratextual could be interpreted by and as another text. Thus what was once asserted to be a text's cultural, social, and particularly historical context becomes a web of textual constructions posing as contextualization. Whether contextualization is interpreted as a process of signification or as a discursive practice depends upon one's theory of how well a LANGUAGE can refer to the reality of its world. The less transparent a language is to its supposed referents, the more context reduces to the network of words or signs themselves in a text. What is contextual, according to an extreme version of this view, might better be termed autotextual or, better, intratextual, because the process of contextualization centers on the text itself by comparing one part to another, or a part to the whole.

Less solipsistic is a version of contextualization that constructs the context from other texts. Intertextuality consists of one text drawing upon one or more other texts, or one text being referred to by others through citation, emulation, or parody. A more traditional view of context as extratextual would portray intertextuality as the dialogue of a PROFESSION or other interpretive community, that is, as a discursive practice. In an extreme contextualist view, context is an independent reality, standing completely apart from the social location of the knower and untouched by the process of knowing. To a devoted textualist, such a view seems naive REALISM or objectivism.

Textuality has particularly important implications for theorizing about the practices of historians and those who would historicize their subjects through contextualization. In historical writing, of course, all past behavior is interpreted textually in the simple sense that it is reconstructed only through the examination of texts. In all cases, however, historical context is also constructed through interpretation, and never more so than through such seemingly obvious but complex textualizations as society, culture, polity, gender, race, and nationality. Hence, to place past texts in their specific historical contexts requires constructing histories that are themselves further textualizations.

ROBERT F. BERKHOFER JR.
See also NEW LITERARY HISTORICISM; READING.

FURTHER READING
Richard Harvey Brown, *Society as Text: Essays on Rhetoric, Reason, and Reality* (Chicago: University of Chicago Press, 1987).

Josue V. Harari, ed., *Textual Strategies: Perspectives in Post-Structuralist Criticism* (Ithaca: Cornell University Press, 1979).

Linda Hutcheon, *A Poetics of Postmodernism: History, Theory, Fiction* (New York: Routledge, 1988).

Paul Ricouer, "The Model of the Text: Meaningful Action Considered as Text," in Paul Rabinow and William M. Sullivan, eds., *Interpretive Social Science: a Reader*, (Berkeley: University of California Press, 1979).

Richard   Rorty,   "Nineteenth-Century   Idealism   and

Twentieth-Century Textualism," in *Consequences of Pragmatism* (Minneapolis: University of Minnesota Press, 1982).

Edward Said, "The Problem of Textuality: Two Exemplary Positions," *Critical Inquiry* 4 (summer 1978): 673–714.

Cesare Segre with Tomaso Kemeny, *Introduction to the Analysis of the Literary Text*, trans. John Meddemmen (Bloomington: Indiana University Press, 1988).

Robert Young, ed., *Untying the Text: a Post-Structuralist Reader* (London: Routledge and Kegan Paul, 1981).

Thomas, Norman (b. Marion, Ohio, Nov. 20, 1884; d. Huntington, N.Y., Dec. 19, 1968).   Political leader. Radicalized by the economic injustice he witnessed as a Presbyterian minister in East Harlem, New York, Thomas embraced SOCIALISM. Leaving his church in 1918, he joined the Socialist Party and rose rapidly in its ranks. By 1928 he was its Presidential candidate, a position he accepted every four years until 1948. During the early years of the Depression he garnered impressive support from the intellectual community, which regarded Roosevelt as an opportunist with no coherent plan for putting people to work, much less for establishing justice in labor–capital relations. The Socialist Party made radical proposals for nationalizing banks and some large enterprises, and for redistributing income and establishing a social safety net, but Thomas managed to convey the impression of gradualism and reasonableness—in part by stressing his own and his party's anticommunism. A talented orator, Thomas was also the author of *As I See It* (1932), *A Socialist's Faith* (1951), and *Socialism Re-examined* (1963).

FURTHER READING

Harry Fleischman, *Norman Thomas: a Biography* (New York: Norton, 1964).

Thompson, Dorothy (b. Lancaster, N.Y., July 9, 1894; d. Lisbon, Portugal, Jan. 30, 1961).   Journalist and activist. On her graduation from Syracuse University in 1914, Thompson was active in the woman suffrage movement as a speaker and publicist. In the 1920s and 1930s she was a prominent foreign correspondent for a number of newspapers and wire services, and took the lead in covering the rise of National Socialism in Central Europe. In 1936 Thompson began her regular column in the *New York Herald Tribune*, "On the Record." She became one of the strongest voices advocating U.S. intervention against fascism, and pleading for action to save European Jewry. In syndication, her column had an estimated 8 million readers in the years leading up to World War II. An unfailingly public woman devoted to liberal causes around the world, Thompson continued to attract readers as a columnist in *Ladies Home Journal*—and listeners, via regular radio broadcasts—through the 1940s and early 1950s.

FURTHER READING

Peter Kurth, *American Cassandra: the Life of Dorothy Thompson* (Boston: Little, Brown, 1990).

Thoreau, Henry David [originally David Henry] (b. Concord, Mass., July 12, 1817; d. Concord, Mass., May 6, 1862).   Long after Henry Thoreau's death, American culture enshrined him as an icon. Even to people who have never read his writings, he is familiar as a solitary thinker in the woods, prophet of SIMPLICITY. But this image was slow to develop. During his lifetime, he was considered a minor disciple of Emerson. With the posthumous publication of his abolition essays just after the Civil War, he earned a small reputation in the North as a political moralist. In the late nineteenth century, selections from his journals were published in four volumes—one for each season of the year—and he became known as a romantic rhapsodist of wilderness. Not until the 1930s did he enter the canon as a major figure, the ultimate American individualist.

Thoreau's INDIVIDUALISM has often been understood as a nostalgic and antimodernist plea for natural and simple living. Many, especially in the first half of the twentieth century, have seen him as a precursor to conservative-liberal critics of the welfare state ("That government is best which governs least"). The New Criticism, by contrast, emphasized his originality as a mythologist of NATURE and LANGUAGE. After Indian independence and the civil rights movement, however, his well-known influence on Mahatma Gandhi and MARTIN LUTHER KING JR. helped to revive his reputation as a political radical and prophet of counterculture. More recently, he has been popularly described as the father of ENVIRONMENTALISM. With the significant exception of FEMINISM, most branches of modern culture have been able to develop useful or inspiring versions of Thoreau—though in many contradictory ways.

Originally David Henry Thoreau, he reversed the order of his names only after college. His father John Thoreau had failed repeatedly as a shopkeeper before turning to the manufacture of pencils, a trade in which the son later assisted. Henry attended Harvard, graduating in 1837. For the rest of his life he pursued an unconventional self-education, ranging from the classics to linguistic theory and natural history. He also read widely in English translations of Asian philosophies and religions—not then well known in America—and orientalist themes appear throughout his works.

After college he taught school with his older brother John, whom he loved intensely. When John proposed marriage and was rejected, Henry made the same proposal, to the same woman, with the same result. (Earlier, he had been infatuated with *her* brother, then 12.) When John died of lockjaw in 1842, Henry suffered a hysterical repetition of the lockjaw symptoms. John's death was probably the greatest trauma of Thoreau's life.

From 1841 to 1843, Thoreau boarded with RALPH WALDO EMERSON—his mentor and one of his closest friends—as a family handyman, and for a while tutored Emerson's nephews in Staten Island. For many years thereafter he lectured, worked as a surveyor, and did odd jobs. Cranky, somewhat misogynist, rather unattractive and, in later years, restricted by illness, Thoreau nevertheless maintained important friendships with other Concord area writers: WILLIAM E. CHANNING, ORESTES BROWNSON, BRONSON ALCOTT, NATHANIEL HAWTHORNE, and MARGARET FULLER, not to mention Emerson. After 1843 he remained rooted in Concord, though he left on various travels: nearby lyceum lectures; several expeditions to Maine, Canada, and Cape Cod; surveying business as far away as New Jersey; a famous visit to Whitman with Alcott in Brooklyn; and a trip to Minnesota with Horace Mann Jr. Tuberculosis killed him at the age of 44.

Thoreau built a small house on a plot of land that Emerson owned on Walden Pond, living there from July 1845 to September 1847. His life at Walden was not (and was not intended to be) reclusive, as myth would have it. Indeed, it was on one of his frequent visits to town during his Walden residence, in July of 1846, that he spent a night in the Concord jail for nonpayment of his poll tax. He had had brushes with local authorities before, refusing in 1840 to pay his church tax. He explained his protest in 1846 as a repudiation of a state government complicitous with slavery. Influenced by his politically active mother and sisters (whom he curiously almost never mentions), Thoreau had followed the cause of abolition closely, contributing to the underground railroad and writing for *The Liberator*. Throughout his brief career, Thoreau devoted some of his best efforts to lectures and essays based in abolitionist theory: "Resistance to Civil Government" (1848; better known as "Civil Disobedience," the title assigned to it after his death), "Slavery in Massachusetts" (1854), and three essays on Captain John Brown (1859–60). "Resistance to Civil Government," Thoreau's first major publication, remains the work by which he is best known around the world.

In these works Thoreau adopted a radical posture strongly influenced by WILLIAM LLOYD GARRISON. He advanced not just an opposition to slavery to be expressed through efforts to influence political institutions, but an opposition to the political institutions that he regarded as complicit with an unjust order. Thoreau, in fact, read "Slavery in Massachusetts" at the same antislavery convention before which Garrison burned the U.S. Constitution; in it, he announces, "My thoughts are murder to the State."

Thoreau, however, says little in these essays about race or slaves. When he conspicuously describes FREDERICK DOUGLASS as having a *fair* intellect and a *colorless* reputation, it becomes clear that he is more interested in the moral debate than in the experience of race. (In his later years, however, Thoreau's lifelong interest in Native Americans became a virtual obsession, and he left behind many notebooks based on his readings about and conversations with them.) In the reform essays, slavery serves as an extreme example of a problem in modern political systems. The problem is that a modern state is seldom responsive to ideals of JUSTICE; its white male members may vote, but according to Thoreau they are more subjects than citizens in the classical sense. In a modern administrative state, men find that their political conscience is useless and has no expression in the daily business of government. The institution of government, and its ties to entrenched interests, seem to contradict the promise of representative DEMOCRACY.

Under these conditions, Thoreau urged civil disobedience as a higher version of CITIZENSHIP than mere voting or compliance with the majority. He was no fan of liberal proceduralism: "All voting is a sort of gaming," he remarks in *Civil Disobedience*, "like chequers or backgammon, with a slight moral tinge to it." And he was willing to imagine much more than the nonviolent protest that Gandhi and King were to preach in his name—and that continues to be understood as "civil disobedience." Civil disobedience, in the essay that took that title, primarily means not paying taxes that will support unjust government or war; but Thoreau more broadly endorses any transgression of the status quo. "Let your life be a counter friction to stop the machine." Later, in "A Plea for Captain John Brown," Thoreau argued that even violence against an unjust order was better than peaceful compliance; after all, he pointed out, a state supplied with police and armies and jails is already violent.

In the same year that Thoreau published "Resistance to Civil Government," he also published his first important piece about nature, "Ktaadn and the Maine Woods" (later included in the posthumous volume *The Maine Woods*). Part travel narrative, part natural history, and part moral essay, it contains a famous and sublime cry for contact with the natural world.

The mixed genre of this essay would also be the basis for Thoreau's first book-length work, *A Week on the Concord and Merrimack Rivers* (1849), and *Walden* (1854), the only other book Thoreau published in his lifetime. Both books are conspicuous for defying the conventions of genre; both incorporate large chunks of Thoreau's journal, steering between philosophy and autobiography.

A Week was a failure of legendary proportions. It sold 218 copies in four years. Thoreau had gone to Walden Pond mainly in order to write it, conceiving the book as a memorial to his brother. The book is based loosely on a boating trip made with John in 1839, though Thoreau weaves in a number of digressions, including a long, remarkably homoerotic discussion of friendship in the "Wednesday" chapter.

In *Walden* the mixed generic elements produce a book like no other. Thoreau worked through several manuscript versions between his stay at Walden Pond and the book's publication. He inserted material from journal entries as far apart as 1839 and 1854. Critics have often noted the book's seasonal pattern; Thoreau compressed two years of life at Walden into his narration, presenting in effect one year. Thus *Walden* moves gradually to winter and then to spring. But the book is expansive in other ways. It begins as autobiography, and rapidly becomes an essay on "Economy," the title of the first chapter. Other philosophical chapters punctuate the book, notably "Higher Laws" and the "Conclusion." *Walden* indeed never becomes the narrative that the autobiographical mode seems to invite.

The book is often misunderstood as arguing that everyone should live in the woods without money. Thoreau carefully notes that this is not his point: "I do not mean to prescribe rules to strong and valiant natures." His purpose is to defamiliarize the norms of everyday life, the coercive force of custom. "Strong and valiant natures" may do this already, but "the mass of men," as he writes in one of the book's most famous lines, "lead lives of quiet desperation."

"Economy," therefore, asks a disarming question: why do you work? Thoreau argues that the basic dispositions of life in capitalist culture are taken for granted, thoughtlessly, and with the result that people lead estranged and diminished lives, treating themselves and the world around them as instruments rather than as ends. As he puts it in another work,

the essay "Life without Principle," "I do not need the police of meaningless labor to regulate me." In the same essay he tries to defamiliarize the world more generally: "Why do precisely these objects which we behold make a world?" With this insistence on contemplation, Thoreau resists both the common sense of tradition *and* the instrumental thinking of modernity.

Although Thoreau made a number of contributions to natural history, in works such as *Walden* the natural world is never presented as an object to be mastered by scientific reason. It is an environment to which he submits, as a kind of fate. The same could be said of Thoreau's own self. As he had put it in "Ktaadn": "I stand in awe of my body, this matter to which I am bound has become so strange to me." Thoreau thus typically mingles subjective and objective experience. All the phenomena of the world, insofar as they are perceived, come into view as aspects of subjective experience. At the same time, there is no such thing as a clearly bounded subject or self, because the very contemplative and receptive attitude that makes the world subjective also means that one's self is also encountered as given; it does not simply act in a masterful way.

The strongest expression of this theme appears in "Spring," the penultimate chapter of *Walden*, in a long description of a thawing sandbank. The oozing earth here becomes an excremental metaphor for the grotesque that cannot be refused. "What is man but a mass of thawing clay?" As Thoreau writes in the climax of the chapter, "We need to witness our own limits transgressed." "We are cheered when we observe the vulture feeding on the carrion which disgusts and disheartens us and deriving health and strength from the repast."

This contemplative interest in transgression, which Richard Poirier has called Thoreau's "scatological vision," also forms the basis of Thoreau's aesthetics. (Indeed, the thawing sandbank passage contains an *elaborate* theory of language.) He cultivates awareness of language, not as a mere instrument of communication, but as the given environment of knowledge, experience, and sensation. Sometimes the result of this view is a gnomic density of metaphor, or a relentless but generally inconspicuous habit of punning. "It is a ridiculous demand which England and America make," he writes in *Walden*'s final chapter, "that you shall speak so that they can understand you." Ultimately language, style, and form become, for Thoreau, ways of resisting the coercive force of common sense. "The commonest sense," he explains in the same passage, "is the sense of men asleep."

MICHAEL WARNER

FURTHER READING
Sharon Cameron, *Writing Nature* (Chicago: University of Chicago Press, 1985).
Stanley Cavell, *The Senses of "Walden"* (New York: Viking, 1972).
Walter Harding, *The Days of Henry Thoreau: a Biography* (New York: Dover, 1982).
——, "Thoreau's Sexuality," *Journal of Homosexuality* 21 (1991): 23–44.
Walter Harding and Michael Meyer, eds., *The New Thoreau Handbook* (New York: New York University Press, 1980).
Lyndon Shanley, *The Making of "Walden"* (Chicago: University of Chicago Press, 1957).
Michael Warner, "Thoreau's Bottom," *Raritan* 11 (winter 1992): 53–79.
——, "Walden's Erotic Economy," in *Comparative American Identities: Race, Sex and Nationality in the Modern Text*, ed. Hortense Spillers (New York: Routledge, 1991).

Thorndike, Edward L. (b. Williamsburg, Mass., Aug. 31, 1874; d. Montrose, N.Y., Aug. 9, 1949). Educational psychologist. Thorndike inaugurated the use of quantitative measures of INTELLIGENCE in the assignment of students to classes, and joined the effort during World War I to rank recruits by administering intelligence tests. An early student of animal psychology, he argued that human and animal intelligence are essentially alike. Since learning occurs through the reinforcement of neuronal connections, people have innate tendencies to link situations and responses. While these tendencies can be reinforced or discouraged, they ultimately predetermine each individual's educational capacities. A firm advocate of universal literacy and primary education, Thorndike believed advanced education should be reserved for the gifted. His writings include *An Introduction to the Theory of Mental and Social Measurement* (1904), *Animal Intelligence* (1911), *Educational Psychology* (3 vols., 1913–14), and *Human Nature and the Social Order* (1940).

FURTHER READING
Geraldine Joncich, *The Sane Positivist: a Biography of Edward L. Thorndike* (Middletown, Conn.: Wesleyan University Press, 1968).

Thurber, James (b. Columbus, Ohio, Dec. 8, 1894; d. New York, N.Y., Nov. 2, 1961). Writer and artist. Thurber's writings and drawings are full of odd turns and quirky idiosyncrasies that verge on the surreal. Overwhelmed by daily life in a complicated urban world, his protagonists typically have an almost childlike innocence that belies their underlying confusion or dread. Obsessed with the battle of the sexes, Thurber frequently portrayed big, brassy, assertive women who overwhelm weak, ineffectual men—who survive by escaping into a dreamlike resignation. A frequent contributor to the *New Yorker*, Thurber also published *Is Sex Necessary?* (1929, with E. B. White), *My Life and Hard Times* (1933), *Fables for Our Times* (1940), and *My World—And Welcome to It* (1942).

FURTHER READING
Charles S. Holmes, *The Clocks of Columbus: the Literary Career of James Thurber* (New York: Atheneum, 1972).

Tillich, Paul (b. Brandenburg, Germany, Aug. 20, 1886; d. Chicago, Ill., Oct. 22, 1965). One of the most important and controversial Protestant theologians of the twentieth century, Tillich was raised in the relatively stable and smugly optimistic Germany of the decades before World War I. He experienced with full force the shattering of worlds produced by that conflict. Rather than succumb to nihilism, he sought to revitalize a sense of the sacred by following the course of other modern artists and writers in embracing the perceived chaos of the twentieth century. The broken character of modern life was the starting point of reflection. He lived in America from 1933 on, where he helped to revitalize Protestant thinking by challenging it to face the anomie of the modern age. Some critics felt that he strayed too far from traditional Christianity, and that his unorthodox personal life mocked his pretensions to moral seriousness. Others thought he generalized too often from his own personal *angst* in assessing the spiritual state of most human beings. Yet 25 years after his death, his life and work remain a touchstone of philosophical and theological debate.

Although Tillich's ideas stand as a coherent system, they are best understood within the events and issues of his life. He was the son of a Lutheran pastor, attended university at Berlin, Tübingen, and Halle, and in 1912 was ordained as a minister of the Evangelical (Lutheran) Church. But he felt his talents lay in an academic rather than a pastoral career, and he undertook a major work on the supernatural in German theology. He married and seemed headed for a distinguished but altogether traditional life as a German academic.

World War I changed all that. Tillich enthusiastically enlisted as an army chaplain, only to have his innocence crushed by front-line confrontations with unimaginable scenes of death and mutilation. A battlefield reading of Nietzsche's *Also Sprach Zarathustra* gave him new meaning in life and a new germ for theology. By December 1917, as related by Marion and Wilhelm Pauck, he could write: "I have long since come to the paradox of *faith without God*, by thinking through the idea of justification by faith to its logical conclusion" (p. 54). He meant faith without the God preached by the now (he thought) moribund churches, faith reconceived (in his later formulation) as the "unconditioned" embrace of "Ultimate Concern," a faith in the "God beyond God."

Unsettling events continued as he returned to civilian life. His wife precipitated a divorce and his beloved sister Johanna died in childbirth. In desperation but also with creative exhilaration, Tillich threw himself into the bohemian life of Weimar Germany. He became especially enraptured by expressionist art and dance. Intellectual, artistic, and sexual experimentation only deepened his commitment to forging a new vocabulary for faith, a task he began in his first book, *The Religious Situation* (1924). Recovering a sense of transcendence meant confronting Nietzsche's idea of the *demonic*—the urgent and unified force of creativity and destruction. Tillich saw the *demonic* as the *sine qua non* of all discovery and beauty, but believed its distinctive power must be harnessed by self-critical reason. Human society became a stage upon which men and women struggled with the *demonic*, sometimes triumphing over its destructive elements and sometimes surrendering to its seductive tyranny.

History became society's drama of endless struggle. Because of the destruction and disillusionment wrought by war and defeat, Tillich considered the culture of the 1920s both prone to the *demonic* and poised to experience a new sense of "Ultimate Concern." He appropriated the term *Kairos*, traditionally the time of Christ's coming, to denote just such eras in which intimations of the Kingdom of God allow for radically new directions in human thinking. Indeed, in Berlin he helped create the *Kairos* Circle, a group of intellectuals devoted to reenvisioning life and society in the light of *Kairos*. One important element of Tillich's new thinking was the development of a "religious socialist" position, which he fleshed out in *The Socialist Decision* (1933).

The intellectual excitement generated by Tillich's work assured his success in academia. He quickly advanced to a professorship of philosophy and sociology at the prestigious University of Frankfurt. He became the mentor of Theodor Adorno, who with Max Horkheimer founded Frankfurt's Institute of Social Research (*see also* FRANKFURT SCHOOL). However, Tillich's defiance of Nazi students and ardent defense of Jews put an end to his German career soon after Hitler's takeover in the spring of 1933. The Nazis immediately suspended his professorship, and by November he had exiled himself in New York. Tillich's move had been facilitated by

offers of a temporary lectureship at Union Theological Seminary, where he taught until 1955. He then became a University Professor at Harvard from 1955 to 1962, and ended his career as Nuveen Professor of Theology at the University of Chicago, where he taught from 1962 until his death.

Tillich had a profound influence on religious and secular figures alike, including MARTIN LUTHER KING JR., ERIK ERIKSON, and Rollo May. His search for a common language of faith beyond denominations fitted in well with a pluralistic American religious life and the tradition of LIBERAL PROTESTANTISM, as did his insistence on the centrality of the spiritual life in the midst of a so-called secular era. In addition, his interest in FREUDIANISM was perfectly suited to a postwar period in which Americans turned avidly toward PSYCHOTHERAPY. Tillich's influence reached its height with the publication of *The Courage to Be* (1952), which moved freely through history, psychology, and theology to grapple with peculiarly modern versions of anxiety, GUILT, meaningless, and despair. The book summarized the roots and paradoxes of Tillich's thought, ending with the enigmatic aphorism: "*The courage to be is rooted in the God who appears when God has disappeared in the anxiety of doubt*" (p. 190).

ROBERT H. ABZUG

FURTHER READING

James Luther Adams, Wilhelm Pauck, and Roger Lincoln Shinn, eds., *The Thought of Paul Tillich* (San Francisco: Harper and Row, 1985).

Rollo May, *Paulus: Reminiscences of a Friendship* (New York: Harper and Row, 1973).

Marion Pauck and Wilhelm Pauck, *Paul Tillich: His Life and Thought*, vol. 1: *Life* (New York: Harper and Row, 1976).

Hannah Tillich, *From Time to Time* (New York, Stein and Day, 1973).

——, *From Place to Place: Travels with Paul Tillich and without Paul Tillich* (New York: Stein and Day, 1976).

Paul Tillich, *The Interpretation of History* (New York: Charles Scribner's Sons, 1936).

——, *The Protesant Era* (Chicago: University of Chicago Press, 1948).

——, *The Courage to Be* (New Haven: Yale University Press, 1952).

Tocqueville, Alexis de (b. Paris, France, July 29, 1805; d. Cannes, France, Apr. 16, 1859). A historian, political theorist, and politician, Tocqueville was born in Paris into an aristocratic and royalist family with strong ties, including the family chateau, in Normandy. His sentiments were always in some sense aristocratic, yet he early understood that the future belonged to democracy. He projected his personal journey from aristocrat to ambivalent democrat into a historical abstraction that guided his inquiries. This personal experience, more than books and traditions of political discourse, gave form to his life's work. His objective was always, as he put it, to "abate the claims of aristocrats" and to prepare them for "an irresistible future" (quoted by Smith, p. 182).

Although Tocqueville is often listed among foreign travellers to America who commented upon the conditions and customs of the nation, that miscategorizes him. When he visited the United States in 1831, he came as a political theorist whose interest was the nature of DEMOCRACY. As he wrote in *Democracy in America*, he came in search of "more than America; I sought there the image of democracy itself" (vol. 1, p. 14). Although democracy in its revolutionary guise terrified him—in France it had cost some members of his family their lives—he realized, more clearly than anyone else in the France of the 1820s, that revolution and democracy were not necessarily linked. The United States provided a living example of this more appealing democratic future.

Tocqueville obtained an unpaid commission to investigate the prison system of the United States. With Gustave Beaumont, his co-commissioner, Tocqueville published his report on the prisons (*Du système pénitentiaire aux États-Unis et de son application en France*, 1833). But the real harvest of the trip was *Democracy in America*, published in two volumes, the first in 1835, the second in 1840. This work immediately won him international acclaim and election to the Académie Française. Still pursuing the issue of equality, democracy, and modernity, he wrote a second classic, *The Old Regime and the French Revolution* (1856). His memoir of the revolution of 1848, published after his death as *Souvenirs* (1893), has been appreciated both for its political insight and its literary style.

Tocqueville was captivated by a single idea, the progressive and inevitable leveling of social conditions in Western civilization. "The gradual development of the principle of equality," he wrote in *Democracy in America*, "is . . . a providential fact" (vol. 1, p. 6). Tocqueville, unlike Karl Marx, his near contemporary, was little concerned with understanding the historical process that brought about equality. He accepted equality as fated, and he devoted his inquiry to the implications of this revolution in human identity. He was equally concerned with the sociocultural and the political implications of EQUALITY. His notion of politics and society demanded this approach, for he believed that a nation's social traits profoundly affected its political character. He believed that social and cultural patterns were largely

the product of inheritance and circumstance—in the American case, English traditions and the New World condition. But political character was a product of human choice, and he wrote in the hope that he might help the French choose more wisely.

There is a sharp difference in tone between volume 1 and volume 2 of *Democracy in America*. The first volume, it might be said, is more about America than is the second, which seems to be more about his worries concerning the increasingly anemic condition of democracy in France. The first volume is relatively optimistic. The Americans, blessed with a tradition of local government and fortunate geographical circumstance (abundance and no threatening neighbors), developed institutions (voluntary associations and a free press) that protected them against the worst dangers of democracy. The second volume reflects his fear that materialist INDIVIDUALISM (inward-turning and self-centered) and centralization would produce a new kind of despotism. Democracy, he warned, might supply material needs and facilitate private pleasures, but at the cost of citizenship. Public life would be replaced by private life; such a transformation, although not tyrannical, "compresses, enervates, extinguishes, and stupifies a people" (vol. 2, p. 337).

The contrast of aristocracy and democracy is a consistent theme of *Democracy in America*, and this contrast is both historical and normative. On the one hand, Tocqueville specified the dimensions of change involved in passing from one type of social order to another, from aristocracy to democracy. On the other hand, he used the model of aristocracy as a baseline to evaluate the gains and losses, the strengths and weaknesses, of democracy. Aristocratic society is hierarchical; reciprocal responsibilities between inferior and superior define all social intercourse and determine political authority. In a democracy, by contrast, all legal privileges vanish; the political body and society become one.

Social scientists have from time to time calculated the degree of socioeconomic inequality in Jacksonian America, rather easily amassing evidence of inequality. They assume they have thus undermined Tocqueville's analysis. But because they misunderstand his method, which stresses typological difference, they miss his point. Tocqueville characterized a tendency, and he was more concerned to understand the collective psychology associated with each type than to map their empirical dimensions.

A disciple of Montesquieu, Tocqueville came to America believing that VIRTUE, understood as dedication to the public good as opposed to private interest, was crucial for preserving republics. But in America he discovered a people who were, in his words, "enlightened" but not "virtuous." He discerned in the United States "a new politics" that demanded a new theory of politics. Democracy in America marked the end of classical politics, with its emphasis on virtue. Although interest was acknowledged, even celebrated, in America, the United States remained a republic. What he saw persuaded him that knowledge, particularly in the form of political experience, could be as effective as virtue in sustaining a sufficient commitment to the civil realm.

Tocqueville was not much cited by the progressive historians of the early twentieth century. His portrait of a nonrevolutionary and consensual society did not fit well with their emphasis on conflict, whether of class or section. In the 1940s and 1950s, however, Tocqueville was widely heralded, particularly for his notion of AMERICAN EXCEPTIONALISM; his praise of voluntary associations; his worries about conformity; and his warnings (echoing James Madison) about the danger of majority tyranny. More recently, however, the heart of his work has been taken to be a concern for the future of civic or public life in a democracy. Is liberty secure, and can civic spirit survive, in democratic times? Since, for Tocqueville, liberty meant the positive freedom to participate in public life, not the negative freedom so manifest in our own time to do as we wish in our private lives, he believed that the preservation of FREEDOM required a nurturing of civic spirit.

THOMAS BENDER

FURTHER READING

Seymour Drescher, *Tocqueville and England* (Cambridge: Harvard University Press, 1964).

François Furet, "The Conceptual System of *Democracy in America*," in Furet, *In the Workshop of History* (Chicago: University of Chicago Press, 1984).

Richard Herr, *Tocqueville and the Old Regime* (Princeton: Princeton University Press, 1962).

André Jardin, *Alexis de Tocqueville*, trans. Lydia Davis and Robert Hemenway (London: Halban, 1988).

Lynn Marshall and Seymour Drescher, "American Historians and Tocqueville's *Democracy*," *Journal of American History* 55 (1968): 512–32.

George W. Pierson, *Tocqueville and Beaumont in America* (New York: Oxford University Press, 1938).

James T. Schleifer, *The Making of Tocqueville's "Democracy in America"* (Chapel Hill: University of North Carolina Press, 1980).

Bruce James Smith, *Politics and Remembrance: Republican Themes in Machiavelli, Burke, and Tocqueville* (Princeton: Princeton University Press, 1985).

Alexis de Tocqueville, *Democracy in America*, trans. Henry Reeve, 2 vols. (1835, 1840; New York: Knopf, 1945).

tolerance The United States throughout its history, and even before its founding, has been a society shaped by immigration. Every generation experiences the arrival of new groups, each adding to the rich diversity of nationalities, races, religions, and cultures. This history creates and recreates a society that is dynamic, yet lacking universally shared feelings of harmony or social tolerance. Political tolerance, though, is at the very core of the ethos of American democracy, and assures, at least in part, a voice to people in all groups and constituencies.

In America we understand political tolerance as the requirement of citizens and leaders to secure certain political "inalienable" RIGHTS, and not just for the most powerful or for those with whom "we" agree; securing the political rights of those who contest "our" views presents a far greater challenge, one most essential to the notion of tolerance. This is so because tolerance presumes preexisting feelings of distrust and estrangement among the various groups in society.

In the United States, as in England, the doctrine of political tolerance emerged from two principal concurrent historical trends. First, and most important, the doctrine of religious toleration was advanced in the seventeenth and eighteenth centuries to moderate and control the civic disorder resulting from the proliferation of religious sects in England. Second, following the pattern of religious toleration, the attempt to establish and secure liberal pluralistic representative regimes required that individuals be made secure in their personal political beliefs and actions. Neither development might have been necessary nor desirable had either religious or political authorities been able to hold fast against the decentralizing consequences of modernity. Indeed, ALEXIS DE TOCQUEVILLE, in *Democracy in America* (1840), noted the linkage between modernity, the growth of conformity, and the evolution of liberal democratic practices. He recognized that as institutions of authority weaken, the public is more, not less, subject to conformity. Thus, individuals and minority groups who seek unpopular goals may find it difficult to gain majority support for their efforts.

Political tolerance is warranted by the need to avail the practices of democratic politics to all those who can properly claim the title of citizen, and to safeguard the procedural processes that define a representative liberal regime. Political tolerance seeks to protect specific activities, such as free speech and the right of assembly, and make them available to all citizens. Tolerance is justified by its ability to achieve and secure the existence of the liberal democratic state. And this is assured by several requirements of such liberal regimes: the selection and legitimization of political leaders by the free endorsement of those who are ruled, through democratic competitive elections; and free and unfettered political discussion and criticism.

However, tolerance is not only directed at protecting citizens in their political rights asserted against a powerful state. Tolerance, in a plural and dynamic society, presupposes that individuals will find themselves frequently in conflict with other citizens. FREEDOM, in its various guises, will place people in relationships, one to another, marked by uncertainty, suspicion, and, occasionally, enmity. Freedom does not guarantee or establish a compliant people marked by a high level of courtesy and social harmony, for freedom enables and encourages people to find and follow personal direction. Tolerance requires people to uphold the rights of others, withstanding whatever aversion they may experience toward what may to them be offensive groups.

When the American CONSTITUTION was formulated, the Founding Fathers recognized there are two ineradicable sources of political intolerance: tyranny of the regime, stimulated by the ambition of rulers to secure, maintain, and expand the privileges of power; and, tyranny of faction, driven by the impulse to pursue the interests of one's party. Even before formulating the BILL OF RIGHTS, the Founding Fathers created essential constitutional provisions to limit tyrannical intemperance by the government. Some notable protections from the possible excesses of governmental power afforded to citizens include protection of *habeas corpus* and the establishment of a judiciary generally secure from intrusive meddling by the executive and legislative branches of government (thanks to the life tenure of its jurists). The Bill of Rights further extended the enumeration of rights and the limitations placed on state action.

Of course, such protections, as well as those anticipated from the system of "checks and balances" and "separation of powers" would not prove sufficient. From the outset, the grudging acknowledgment of slavery in the Constitution placed many beyond the protections proffered by these documents. Moreover, both government and popular sentiment soon found effective ways to breach these securities, if only temporarily.

The new government in 1798, under the leadership of the Federalists, passed the Alien Acts, which gave the President the authority to deport or imprison political dissenters who were not as yet citizens. Concurrently, the Sedition Act made it a crime for newspapers to publish malicious or false stories about national elected officials. Throughout America's history, the federal government has found ways to expand its authority to the detriment of the rights of citizens, especially in times of civil unrest and war. The Civil War, World War I, World War II and periods during and following the Korean War and then the Vietnam War all saw efforts by the government to restrict dissent.

Some recent writers on tolerance have apparently forgotten the important insight that intolerance may be initiated either by the public or by the government. Critics of popular government focus on the public as the principal source of tolerance or intolerance. Political conservatives such as Joseph Schumpeter and Giovanni Sartori focus on the intolerance of the people, their ill-suitedness for democracy. They therefore conclude that political elites have the superior ability to rule. By contrast, participatory democrats such as Benjamin Barber and Carole Pateman argue that the people can rule without intolerance if they are given full authority and responsibility. They argue that progress toward greater participation will enable citizens of a fully democratic society to realize their ideal of civic VIRTUE. (*See also* DEMOCRACY.)

Whatever hopes we may have for a tolerant and civil society seem less realizable than those we may have for promoting political tolerance. Social tolerance seems, even in this modern age, less well protected than political tolerance, itself bolstered by the tradition of "rights," the protections of law and political practices. Thus it is likely that the opposition between the values of freedom and privacy and the social pressure of conformity will preserve the tension between popular antagonism toward the eccentric, unfamiliar, foreign, or unpopular and the popular commitment to the "inalienable" rights of the marginal and the minority.

GEORGE E. MARCUS

FURTHER READING

Tyler G. Anbinder, *Nativism and Slavery: the Northern Know Nothings and the Politics of the 1850's* (New York: Oxford University Press, 1992).

Richard M. Fried, *The McCarthy Era in Perspective* (New York: Oxford University Press, 1990).

Richard Polenberg, *Fighting Faiths: the Abrams Case, the Supreme Court, and Free Speech* (New York: Viking, 1987).

John L. Sullivan, James Piereson, and George E. Marcus, *Political Tolerance and American Democracy* (Chicago: University of Chicago Press, 1982).

Toomer, Jean (b. Washington, D.C., Dec. 26, 1894; d. Doylestown, Pa., Mar. 30, 1967). The tragedy of Jean Toomer's life was the debate over his blackness, a debate that engulfed and disabled him. This issue of his status as a black writer still dominates Toomer criticism.

Cane (1923), a superbly crafted impressionist

evocation of the black experience, led critics in his own day to predict a splendid literary future for him as a black writer. That designation helped derail a possibly outstanding career. For his promise never materialized, and later generations of scholars have continued to speculate on the causes of that failure. The culprit consistently fingered is conscious and unconscious American racism.

Toomer was born into a middle-class, mixed-blood family. His maternal grandfather, P. B. S. Pinchback of Reconstruction Louisiana political fame, was a "race" man—one devoted to the uplift of the black race—despite being so fair-skinned that he was mistaken for a white man. Pinchback moved to Washington in the 1880s, and when Toomer was born a few years later, he and his mother, abandoned by her husband, went to live with Pinchback. Although Nina Pinchback Toomer's remarriage in 1906 took mother and son away from Washington and her father's house, Toomer returned in 1909 after her untimely death, and he remained closely tied to his grandparents until their deaths many years later.

Although he came of age in Washington, D.C. at a time of near total segregation in the nation's capital, he did not feel disadvantaged. Toomer's family belonged to the successful black middle class of the city. He attended the M Street High School, where many of his classmates and friends, such as Mary Church (Terrell), later became prominent in education, politics, and letters. Writing about this group early in his life, he observed that although they were segregated, the quality of their lives was as rich as that of their white peers, and that blacks of their class neither envied whites nor wished to intermingle with them, or, in Toomer's case (since he was so fair-skinned), become part of that racial group.

At the same time, for reasons that remain unclear, Toomer chose to attend a college where he was unlikely to be taken as black. In 1914 he enrolled at the University of Wisconsin in Madison. But he remained there only half a year, and though he subsequently attended half a dozen other nonblack colleges, he never graduated. The late Darwin Turner, an early Toomer scholar, surmised that Toomer was so driven by a fear of failure that, as a young man, he found it impossible to complete tasks he undertook. This was the pattern of his life until he began to write Cane.

Toomer decided to be a writer around 1918, and he published a few items in journals and magazines at the beginning of the 1920s. But his inspiration for Cane, a collection of stories, sketches, poems and a drama of black life, in the South and the North,

came when he lived briefly in Georgia in 1921. In this his first encounter with black folk culture he was so moved by what he heard and saw that he immediately wrote about it with energy and enthusiasm. White and black critics hailed the work as the harbinger of a new era in black literature. With Cane, Toomer moved beyond the realism of CHARLES CHESNUTT and JAMES WELDON JOHNSON. His embrace of modernist techniques was a rejection of the view that literature must directly serve the cause of social protest.

Toomer was taken to be the new black prophet, signaling new and exciting possibilities ahead for African American literature.

Yet after Cane was released, its author found that his literary fame was forcing him to embrace a black racial identity. Six years earlier Toomer had decided on a nonracial identity, calling himself the first conscious member of the American race, the amalgam of his seven bloodlines, white, black, and red. Great unhappiness over the public designation of him as a black writer led him to reject art and literature as means to address problems of racism in America. In its place, he began to search for a philosophy to better unite people whatever their race, to create harmony in the self and between the self and the world. This quest occupied him for the rest of his life, and constantly depressed him. For although he followed many paths, he never located the ideas, the system that fully satisfied his needs. The ideas that engaged him longest, from 1923 to the mid-1930s, were the teachings of George Gurdjieff, the Greek-Russian-Armenian mystic who promoted a knowledge by which human beings could achieve internal harmony and a harmonious existence in the world. For more than a decade, Toomer was an avid disciple and teacher of the Gurdjieff philosophy, until he became disillusioned with it too.

Jean Toomer did not give up writing after he published Cane. On the contrary, he wrote copiously until the middle of the 1940s: short and long fiction, poetry, drama, essays, and autobiography. His readers, however, expected him to practice the literary art of Cane. His own path led elsewhere, away from the lyrical expressive style and toward an earnest didacticism. Few readers, and no publishers, cared about his quest for personal harmony within himself and between himself and the world. But contemporary scholars find his failure to fulfill his early promise very intriguing, and a lively debate over his work has centered on the torture his racial ambiguities appear to have caused him, and the role that American racial feeling and categories played in undermining his creativity. Whatever the verdict on those questions, *Cane* remains an unforgettable masterpiece in the national literature.

NELLIE Y. MCKAY

FURTHER READING

Bernard W. Bell, "Jean Toomer's 'Blue Meridian': the Poet as Prophet of a New Order of Man," *Black American Literature Forum* 14 (summer 1980): 77–80.

Rudolph P. Byrd, *Jean Toomer's Years With Gurdjieff: Portrait of an Artist, 1923–1936* (Athens: University of Georgia Press, 1990).

Frank Durham, ed., *Studies in Cane* (Columbus: Charles E. Merrill, 1971).

Cynthia Earl Kernan and Richard Eldridge, *The Lives of Jean Toomer: a Hunger for Wholeness* (Baton Rouge: Louisiana State University Press, 1987).

Nellie Y. McKay, *Jean Toomer, Artist: a Study of His Literary Life and Art* (Chapel Hill: University of North Carolina Press, 1984).

Therman B. O'Daniel, ed., *Jean Toomer, a Critical Evaluation* (Washington, D.C.: Howard University Press, 1988).

Darwin T. Turner, "An Intersection of Paths: Correspondence between Jean Toomer and Sherwood Anderson," *College Language Association Journal* 17 (June 1974): 455–67.

tradition Because questions of identity are paramount in the postmodern world, tradition has become a hot political issue. In the field of education, for example, battles are raging over the content of school curricula. Powerful voices call for a renewed emphasis on traditional values, subjects, and thinkers whose ideas are said to be essential to Western civilization. Ignorance of this legacy is the essence of cultural illiteracy, according to many conservatives. Like other forms of illiteracy, this one has debilitating consequences: students who have not absorbed traditional lessons will not become a part of America, nor will they conduct themselves in ways that continue its greatness in years to come. Thus, for people like William Bennett the future of the nation is at stake in debates over curriculum.

Critics of the canon dismiss Bennett's tradition as the work of "dead white European males." The critics favor a multicultural orientation, one that stresses the diversity of American historical experiences, and condemns the self-aggrandizing tendencies of the so-called dominant tradition or cultural mainstream. Like conservatives, liberals have a distinctive image of America's past, a past built upon the subjection of powerless peoples. Liberals want to convey this image to children in public schools, hoping to encourage more TOLERANCE in the future.

The controversy has spread to politics, where conservatives like Dan Quayle and Pat Robertson seek a return to traditional values, particularly in private life, but also in public affairs, where restraint on government is urged. Contending with this party of the past is a party of the future, which looks forward to the elimination of old-fashioned racism, sexism, and other forms of intolerance and is willing to use government power to accomplish those ends. Between the two parties, cultural warfare looms (and has perhaps already begun, if James Davison Hunter is right).

If war occurs, it will not be the first time in American history. A GREAT AWAKENING in the eighteenth century opposed the increasingly secular ways of settlers in British North America, and aimed to restore religion to a position of preeminence in colonial life. A Second Great Awakening of religious fervor in the nineteenth century combated the moral decline of Americans bent on pursuing their earthly fortunes without regard for the well-being of fellow citizens. And the PROHIBITION movement of the twentieth century hoped to cure some of the worst diseases of modern life (for alcohol was linked to the financial ruin of workers, broken homes, and high rates of juvenile delinquency, that is, the breakdown of the traditional family unit).

The Great Awakening, the Second Great Awakening, and Prohibition are only three previous episodes in the struggle between proponents of restoration and advocates of transformation; many others are less well known. Indeed, it is tempting to describe American culture in historical terms as a more or less continuous dispute over the importance of traditional values in social, economic, and political life. But that description is misleading insofar as it suggests that one side of the debate wants to do away with tradition and replace it with another, more modern kind of social bond, when in fact the party of the future has always been careful to maintain its affiliation with the past.

That is to be expected in a nation that prides itself on political stability as well as progress, and in fact is deeply suspicious of radical change. Continuity is a powerful political theme in U.S. society. The party of the future has always been obliged to present itself in familiar terms, and to portray its actions as part of an ongoing struggle to realize distinctively American values. Certain values, such as those of liberal INDIVIDUALISM, have deep roots in our past, and proponents of change who fail to connect with this liberal tradition risk political marginalization, or in the case of socialist parties in the early part of the twentieth century, outright repression.

By the same token, a successful party of the past must not try to turn back the clock; instead it must show the relevance of traditional values to contemporary problems. The ideologists of the Reagan revolution understood this very well, whereas arch-critics of big government under the New Deal, groups such as the American Liberty League, never grasped the point. Neither did the Federalists, who lost control of a government they created, and contemplated secession in a desperate and ill-fated effort to reestablish the status quo ante. Without some nod in the direction of posterity, a party of the past is as doomed as an amnesiac party of the future.

Thus disputes between American political parties or social movements typically center on which program best combines continuity and change, reassurance and hope, memory and anticipation. In this debate, soldiers from the past are liberally recruited for political purposes. The party of the past consults the teachings of the country's founders for arguments against contemporary big government, while the party of the future recalls Lincoln's vision of a nation free of slavery. Washington's warning against entangling alliances is recalled by traditional isolationists, only to be answered with a remembrance of Woodrow Wilson's internationalism and an endorsement of his efforts to construct a new world order. And the list goes on, for the richness and ambiguity of the past provide ample resources for groups trying to fashion an all-American identity for themselves (and others, too, for that matter).

References to the past are politically effective because generations of people understand themselves as part of an ongoing historical community, even when they have no desire to repeat the lives and actions of their forbears. Slavery was a significant part of American history, but no one seeks to revive it, not even the most ardent supporters of a return to traditional values. Likewise, the political, legal, and economic subjection of women was a part of our past that we all want to escape, some more quickly than others. These parts of our past tend to be quickly forgotten or repressed in shame, while the attractive elements—the patriotism of Patrick Henry, the resolve of the Alamo's defenders, the strength of Susan B. Anthony, the fortitude of Martin Luther King Jr., etc.—are assimilated to a reassuring model of American character.

In that sense, every generation understands tradition selectively, in terms that define its place in the story of America. For some generations, this role is revolutionary; for others it is conservative: Daniel Webster, Henry Clay, John C. Calhoun, and the other great orators of the antebellum generation projected their generation as defenders of the Union. Still other generations make progress toward a New Republic, or a Great Society, appearing as reformers in a Whiggish understanding of history.

Every successive generation is also revisionary. New generations do not blindly adhere to traditional ways of life. They may honor tradition, but they also adapt institutions, practices, and behavior in light of new circumstances and changing aspirations. The tradition or set of traditions handed down from one generation to the next is thereby altered, and as successive revisions of the past accumulate over time, traditions may be materially transformed. So, for example, Fourth of July perorations on independence have given way to parades and speeches that have more to do with town boosterism than patriotism.

Sometimes traditions are reworked to the point of exhaustion. The comfortable idea of America as a "melting pot," which was itself a political invention, is now being recast by those who see in America a seething cauldron of differences and resentments. (See also ASSIMILATION; CULTURAL PLURALISM AND MULTICULTURALISM.) When this happens to central elements of a society's collective self-understanding, the cultural equivalent of an identity crisis may occur, for a people with no sense of a common past is unlikely to see its way toward the future. How could it, since the future is an outgrowth of present possibilities, which are themselves realizations of past contingencies?

Democracies are particularly susceptible to this malady, according to ALEXIS DE TOCQUEVILLE. Because democrats' grasp on the past is often infirm and highly partisan, their sense of common purpose is uncertain. Consequently, Tocqueville concluded that

> not only does democracy make men forget their ancestors, but [it] also clouds their view of their descendants and isolates them from their contemporaries. Each man is forever thrown back on himself alone, and there is danger that he may be shut up in the solitude of his own heart. (p. 508)

Few insights about social life are likely to emerge from a solitude that knows no past, and has no sense of a collective future. It is therefore essential for democrats to maintain an appreciation for their historic differences—and commonalities. Debates about the past serve this purpose well, reminding us that *e pluribus unum*—from many, one—is not simply a motto, but a description of our historical aspiration as well.

RUSSELL L. HANSON

See also CONSERVATISM.

FURTHER READING

John E. Bodnar, *Remaking America: Public Memory, Commemoration, and Patriotism in the Twentieth Century* (Princeton: Princeton University Press, 1992).

Louis Hartz, *The Liberal Tradition in America* (New York: Harcourt, Brace and World, 1955).

E. D. Hirsch, *Cultural Literacy: What Every American Needs to Know* (New York: Vintage, 1988).

James Davison Hunter, *Culture Wars: the Struggle to Define America* (New York: Basic Books, 1991).

Michael G. Kammen, *Mystic Chords of Memory: the Transformation of Tradition in American Culture* (New York: Knopf, 1991).

Edward A. Shils, *Tradition* (Chicago: University of Chicago Press, 1981).

Alexis de Tocqueville, *Democracy in America*, ed. J. P. Mayer, trans. George Lawrence (Garden City: Doubleday, Anchor, 1969).

Transcendentalism   A movement of thought that shaped the ideas and activities of a group of high-minded, mid nineteenth-century intellectuals living primarily in and around Boston, Transcendentalism has, since its heyday in the three decades before the Civil War, provoked enormous scholarly attention. (A recent review of research lists nearly four thousand publications.) The reasons for this fascination are not difficult to discern. The Transcendentalists counted among their principal leaders such familiar authors as RALPH WALDO EMERSON, BRONSON ALCOTT, MARGARET FULLER, THEODORE PARKER, and HENRY DAVID THOREAU. The Transcendentalists were deeply rooted in New England cultural soil, yet were for America unprecedentedly modern and cosmopolitan. They were widely associated with a potpouri of democratic social movements while also producing among the most trenchant critiques of American democracy ever written, and they vitally influenced major thinkers and currents from philosophy, theology, social thought, and politics to literature, painting, and music.

Yet when one tries to go beyond these externals and define the core meaning of the movement, one is left with perplexity. Partly this is inevitable given the Transcendentalists' sprawling intellectual interests, not to mention the daunting range of their Western and non-Western sources. But an even greater obstacle to defining Transcendentalism lies in the word itself. The term is derived from Immanuel Kant's claim that crucial determinants of what we know about God and the world come not from our senses and our reflection upon them, which John Locke had argued was the basis of all knowledge, but from certain "transcendental" categories in the mind that we know intuitively. This hardly made the Transcendentalists Kantians, however. For one thing, Kant made it clear that we have no way of knowing if these concepts correspond to anything outside the mind. This dualistic position was at sharp variance with the Transcendentalists' central monistic philosophical project—to use in various ways intuitively known ideas to *constitute* the world.

The Transcendentalists also borrowed from other idealist traditions to further their enterprise. Radically idealistic Transcendentalists such as Alcott, Emerson, Fuller, and Thoreau exploited a host of Platonic, Neoplatonic, and Post-Renaissance mystical, pantheistic, and romantic authors, especially Coleridge and Carlyle, to establish the correspondences between nature and spirit and the intuitive self that perceives them. Those better versed in German philosophy, like Frederic Henry Hedge and James Freeman Clarke, did the same with post-Kantian philosophers such as Jacobi, Fichte, and Schelling, whom Carlyle and Coleridge popularized. Dipping gingerly into these writers were more social-minded Transcendentalists like GEORGE RIPLEY, Theodore Parker, WILLIAM HENRY CHANNING, and ORESTES BROWNSON, who preferred to take their post-Kantian philosophy from the putatively more "empirical" French Victor Cousin and his followers.

Finally, as many scholars have noted, the Transcendentalists were not principally philosophers. Even those like Hedge and Brownson, who tolerably analyzed philosophical problems, did so primarily to further other intellectual purposes. The most important of these, especially in the beginning, as the intellectual historian Perry Miller once justly argued, was religion.

The starting point for the Transcendentalists' religious consciousness was UNITARIANISM. Even outside of Massachusetts, American adherents of Transcendentalist philosophy came overwhelmingly from Unitarian backgrounds. Plainly Unitarians were not entirely the "corpse-cold" negators stigmatized later by Transcendentalists. On the contrary, Unitarian ministers' enthusiasm for secular literature, human judgment of the Scriptures, and men and women's divinelike capacity for moral growth all helped lay the groundwork for the Transcendentalists' own humanism. But American Unitarian intellectuals were also supernatural rationalists: not only did they believe that Jesus Christ, if less than God, was still partly divine but, as good Lockeans, they were equally strenuous in contending that his divinity was proven by the miracles recorded in the Gospels and empirically validated by critical scholarship. The young Transcendentalist ministers disputed all these claims. The scholarly George Ripley, in a pamphlet war in 1839–40 with Andrews Norton, his former teacher and Harvard's leading biblical scholar, while not challenging the empircal claims for the miracles, argued nonetheless that they had nothing to do with a Christian religious faith, which depended on the believer's inward perception and experience of the truth of Christ's teachings.

More radical still was Emerson who, in his address before the graduating Harvard Divinity School class the previous year, startlingly characterized the Christian concept of miracle as "a Monster" because it suggested that nature was devoid of spiritual animation, declared that any religion that left "God out of me" is dead, and broadly asserted that the entire ministerial profession was mired in formalism on account of its preaching a merely historical, second-hand experience rather than a living faith. The result was inevitable: Harvard, most Unitarian journals, and many Unitarian churches closed their doors to the Transcendentalists. Meanwhile, for their part, the Transcendentalists, including theological moderates like Ripley, Brownson, Clarke, and Hedge, who had serious reservations about what they perceived to be the pantheism and subjectivism of Emerson and the excessive antisupernaturalism of Parker, rallied around their besieged leaders, started their own journals, and constituted, some without and some uneasily within the Unitarian fellowship, their new faith.

While accepting religion as the originating core of Transcendentalism, scholars in recent decades have focused increasing attention on the more broadly cultural dimensions of the movement. One approach, associated with a number of influential historical critics especially active in the 1950s and 1960s, has portrayed the Transcendentalists as variously rooted in or emblematic of broad trends in American cultural life. Some, like R. W. B. Lewis and Leo Marx, have seen in Transcendentalism's spiritualistic NATURALISM a peculiar version of America's Adamic or pastoral myths. Others have interpreted the movement as a modern flowering of New England PURITANISM, either in its antinomian and pietistic phase or, as in the more recent work of Sacvan Bercovitch, in its behemothlike incarnation as America's nationalist self. Still others, like Perry Miller, have construed the movement as a cultivated, bohemian offshoot of the hyperemotional evangelical religious revivals that swept through America in the early nineteenth century. Although the totalistic conclusions of such work have been criticized in the last couple of decades, the best of it has left open—and therefore still interesting—the question of the degree to which the Transcendentalists chimed with or rebelled against their culture.

The other approach to Transcendentalist ideology has been more overtly political, asking, to put the question simply: Were the Transcendentalists democrats? Clearly European ideological categories are not very helpful. Unlike many of their Restorationist era European romantic counterparts, none of the Transcendentalists was a statist or a strong proponent of hierarchy; nor, on the other hand, except for Margaret Fuller in revolutionary Italy, did any of them experience the radical political disaffection of a generation of pre-1848 Romantics. Recognizing this, post-World War II historians like Arthur Schlesinger Jr. and Stanley Elkins depicted the Transcendentalists as perfectionist utopians, either lamentably evasive in the battles between the pro-business Whigs and the working-class-oriented Democrats, as Schlesinger argued in *The Age of Jackson* (1945), or dangerously anti-institutional and therefore incipiently pro-Civil War in their anarchistic attacks on slavery, which was Elkins's assessment in *Slavery* (1959).

One difficulty with these sorts of politicized arguments is their monolithic character. Orestes Brownson, for example, considered his pro-Democratic Party politics thoroughly consistent with the Transcendentalist search for the divine in the common, while Emerson, though a strong supporter of the antislavery cause after 1850, for many years held himself aloof from abolitionism precisely because he thought its supporters too much disregarded men and women's internal psychological shackles. He also feared that strong political commitments threatened the creative autonomy of intellectuals like himself.

Highly politicized interpretations of Transcendentalism often evade or pass over too lightly the question of what, on their terms, the Transcendentalists were *for*. Very generally, they tended to combine the liberal Whigs' preoccupation with social purity with the liberal Democrats' emphasis on individual liberty. More theoretically, they were liberals who accepted the Jeffersonian ideal of an egalitarian democratic state, but one that was sharply circumscribed in its coercive powers in matters of libertarian "principle" (as, most extremely, in Thoreau's 1849 defense of civil disobedience in "Resistance to Civil Government"). Most importantly, they were liberals who yearned for a society enriched by a culture whose romantic purposes went beyond, even if they did not controvert, the traditional Lockean interest in protecting individual security and property. These purposes included fostering introspective self-culture, psychological originality, and, above all, a symbolistic perception of nature and the ordinary.

Such concerns particularly dominated the writings and activities of those Transcendentalists engaged with cultural issues: Alcott's imagination-encouraging conversations with children at his Temple School in Boston, Fuller's feminist-minded conversation meetings with women, Emerson's poetic lecture-dramas of intellectual self-reliance, and, most memorably,

Thoreau's fabulous jeremiads touting, as in *Walden* (1854), the superiority of an economy of SIMPLICITY in self-conscious harmony with NATURE as against a desperate fantasy-life of competition and material acquisition.

Some Transcendentalists tried to pass beyond symbolic words and gestures into social reorganization. Most notably, George Ripley and other Transcendentalists, provoked by the severe economic depression of the early 1840s as well as by romantic utopian hopes to achieve an organic life free of class divisions and alienating work habits, established the socialistic community of Brook Farm. Most leading Transcendentalists, while sympathizing with their ideals, declined to join. Emerson particularly recoiled over what he felt was Brook Farm's mechanism, parochialism, and, worst of all, violation of his belief in spiritual individuality. Its failure after six years, in 1847, was perhaps less a testimony to Emerson's prescience than to the precariousness of cultural radicals like the Transcendentalists as they confronted an expanding democratic capitalist culture to which they were tied more closely than they knew.

The Transcendentalists' most lasting cultural accomplishments, of course, were in literature. Impelled by the movement's romantic-minded philosophy, Emerson, Fuller, and other literary Transcendentalists projected the ideal of the artist as a divinely inspired poet-priest scorning inherited rules, rigid patterns, and mimetic representations in favor of original creations, organic forms, and symbolical invocations of spiritual realities. Concomitant with these values, Transcendentalist critics like Fuller severely judged decorously studied popular poets such as Henry Wadsworth Longfellow and James Russell Lowell less valuable than cruder but more sincere or more mind-stirring writers.

As hostile commentators have frequently pointed out, the Transcendentalists often fell woefully short of their promises. Even friendly critics have conceded that Transcendentalist writing, especially of the lesser figures, was often careless, diffusive, and vapid. Yet in the greatest Transcendentalist writings these characteristically ethereal ramblings are overcome. In the densely packed, metaphorically rich symbolic excursions of Thoreau and the imagistically pungent and dialectically visionary essays of Emerson, critics have found a freshness and power that did, indeed, signify, if not Emerson's "liberating god," certainly new and revolutionary voices in American literature.

By the early years of the Civil War, Fuller, Parker, and Thoreau were dead. Meanwhile most of the other principal Transcendentalists were coming to adjust their ideals to the marching truths of the northern struggle for democratic renewal and war. Since then the Transcendentalists have bequeathed a living—and contentious—tradition of inheritors. Both William James and John Dewey in different ways claimed Transcendentalism's mix of philosophical subjectivism and democratic ethics as the primary American precursor of PRAGMATISM. Writers as disparate as Nathaniel Hawthorne, Herman Melville, Walt Whitman, Emily Dickinson, Henry James, and F. Scott Fitzgerald looked back on the movement's symbolistic strategies and vatic stances as either inspiration for their own literary approaches or—with Hawthorne, Melville, and James—major themes to be dramatized and contested. In the 1960s Transcendentalists like Thoreau were seen as major inspirations for the principle-minded politics of the civil rights and environmental movements, as well as the anticapitalist gestures of the counterculture and the New Left. More recently as unlikely a pair as STANLEY CAVELL, in *In Quest of the Ordinary* (1988), and IRVING HOWE, in *The American Newness* (1986), have looked to leading Transcendentalists for guidance in their search for, respectively, the fantastically ordinary and the post-Marxian socialist.

Transcendentalism, like Thoreau's "time," is a river that many intellectuals continue to fish in, much to their wonderment and ours.

CHARLES CAPPER

FURTHER READING

Lawrence Buell, *Literary Transcendentalism: Style and Vision in the American Renaissance* (Ithaca: Cornell University Press, 1973).

Julie Ellison, *Delicate Subjects: Romanticism, Gender, and the Ethics of Understanding* (Ithaca: Cornell University Press, 1990).

Michael T. Gilmore, *American Romanticism and the Marketplace* (Chicago: University of Chicago Press, 1985).

Philip F. Gura and Joel Myerson, eds., *Critical Essays on American Transcendentalism* (Boston: G. K. Hall, 1982).

Perry Miller, ed., *The Transcendentalists: an Anthology* (Cambridge: Harvard University Press, 1950).

Joel Myerson, ed., *The Transcendentalists: a Review of Research and Criticism* (New York: Modern Language Association of America, 1984).

Anne C. Rose, *Transcendentalism as a Social Movement, 1830–1850* (New Haven: Yale University Press, 1981).

Taylor Stoehr, *Nay-Saying in Concord* (Hamden, Conn.: Archon, 1979).

translation In the absence of any history of translation into or out of American English, a brief essay can only identify some of the themes and subjects such a history should consider.

One special factor influencing translation in America has been the encounter between American English and what ROGER WILLIAMS called "the language of America," that is, the languages of Native Americans. The distance between English and the languages of America—not just the distance between an Indo-European language and a multitude of non-Indo-European ones, but also the distance between a written language and oral ones—forced Euro-American translators of these languages to develop two alternatives to traditional European practice: first, a tradition of radically literalist anthropological translating, as in the work of FRANZ BOAS and the records of the Bureau of American Ethnology, in the linguistic relativism of BENJAMIN WHORF, and in our own time in the ethnopoetics of Dell Hymes and Dennis Tedlock; second, a tradition of free imitation and adaptation, as in the translations of HENRY ROWE SCHOOLCRAFT, in certain of the poems of HENRY WADSWORTH LONGFELLOW and AMY LOWELL, and in our own time in the work of Jerome Rothenberg. On the other hand, the original evangelizing motives of the first translators *into* Native American languages, who saw the goal of translation as the transmission of a converting message, and saw languages simply as convenient or inconvenient instruments of that message, also shaped much subsequent thinking about translation generally; Williams's 1643 language manual, *A Key into the Language of America*, and the 1663 translation by JOHN ELIOT of the Bible into the language of the Massachusetts Indians anticipate the currently influential theories of Eugene Nida and his school.

Until the twentieth century, Americans for the most part took their translations of European and Asian languages from the British, but there are some important exceptions. First among these was the *Bay Psalm Book* (1640), which though it claims in its preface that "God's altar needs not our polishings" (p. 3), in fact inaugurates the great American translational tradition of linguistic annexation, by adapting the rhythms of the Hebrew Psalms to the meters of New England choral psalmody. Also important was the mid nineteenth-century translating done by the New England Transcendentalists and their Boston neighbors; together they spanned the whole spectrum of American translational possibilities. Among their most interesting works are the translation of Dante's *Vita Nuova* by RALPH WALDO EMERSON into what in a letter he called "ruggedest grammar English" (vol. 3, pp. 183–4), and the fluent translations by MARGARET FULLER of Eckermann's Goethe; among their greatest works, and among the first American literary translations of high excellence, are the often brilliant renderings of Pindar and of Aeschylus' *Prometheus Bound* by HENRY DAVID THOREAU, and Longfellow's melodiously plainspoken Dante.

EZRA POUND, in his translational ransacking of all the cultures of the world for their best bits of poetry, resembles the acquisitiveness of the robber barons; his free, commanding reshaping of the poetry he found resembles the industrial conversion of raw material into finished product for a profit. But these similarities diminish neither the importance nor the high quality of Pound's work. The "Sea-Farer" (1912), *Cathay* (1915), and the *Homage to Sextus Propertius* (1917) were simply better poems than were any extant translations or adaptations of those texts. They brought into English poetry important new excellences, often precisely the excellences that scholars had attributed to the poets Pound translated. Pound by his success established linguistic annexation as the dominant tradition of American translation.

The work of the best contemporary American translators of European and Asian languages lies largely within that tradition. A few, like ROBERT LOWELL, hold to that tradition both in theory and in practice. A good many others, like Robert Bly, Richard Howard, Stephen Mitchell, and Richard Wilbur vary from it in practice; they adhere much more closely to the sentences of the original texts than Pound did. In their theory, however, almost all of them celebrate Pound's sovereign freedom, and espouse Bly's forthright claim in *The Eight Stages of Translation* that a translator must "ignore the sentence structure of the . . . original, and try to move all sentences bodily into the genius of English" (p. 24).

Pound gave American translation not only its dominant poetics but also its dominant model of production, namely, collaboration between philologist and poet, with the philologist supplying the linguistic material out of which the poet makes the translation. This quasi-industrial division of labor has troubling implications for American intellectual life generally: that there can be a poetry separate from philology and a philology separate from poetry, that philology supplies raw material for poets to make finished products of, that the translator's necessary encounter with alien languages can be done vicariously. But as in the case of Pound's poetics, the best defense of the collaborative model of translational production is that it works so well, and that its competitors work so badly. The recent collaborative Oxford series of Greek Tragedy in New Translations, for example, is simply better than the older University of Chicago Complete Greek Tragedies, flawed by the mediocre work of unpoetical philologists working unassisted.

A history of American translation would link together stories that have previously been treated separately: American translational encounters with the languages of America and American translational encounters with the languages of Europe and Asia, American translation as art and American translation as economic production.

LAWRENCE ALAN ROSENWALD

FURTHER READING

The Bay Psalm Book (1640; facsimile ed., Chicago: University of Chicago Press, 1956).

Robert Bly, *The Eight Stages of Translation* (Boston: Rowan Tree Press, 1983).

Ralph Waldo Emerson, *Letters*, ed. Ralph Rusk, 6 vols. (New York: Columbia University Press, 1939).

Edwin Honig, ed., *The Poet's Other Voice: Conversations on Literary Translation* (Amherst: University of Massachusetts Press, 1985).

Ezra Pound, *Personae*, ed. Lea Baechler and A. Walton Litz (New York: New Directions, 1990).

Jerome Rothenberg, ed., *Technicians of the Sacred*, 2nd ed. (1968; Berkeley: University of California Press, 1985).

Brian Swann, ed., *On the Translation of Native American Literatures* (Washington, D.C.: Smithsonian Institution Press, 1992).

Benjamin Whorf, *Language, Thought, and Reality*, ed. John B. Carroll (Cambridge: MIT Press, 1956).

Trilling, Lionel (b. New York, N.Y., July 4, 1905; d. New York, N.Y., Nov. 5, 1975). A critic of literature and general ideas of culture and society, Trilling was perhaps the single most influential literary man of the American 1950s. As such he may also have been the last of a type, inasmuch as the Matthew Arnoldian critic of literature and culture has largely been replaced, since the 1960s, by the academic theorist-specialist, on the one hand, and the journalist on the other.

In the years when Trilling was an undergraduate at Columbia College, from 1921 to 1925, its teaching of the humanities bore the impress of John Erskine, a pioneer advocate of the "great books." Trilling was well drilled in the close reading of canonical texts, but he also discovered the soon-to-be classics of MODERNISM. The years 1921–5 have been celebrated by another critic, R. P. Blackmur, as the *anni mirabiles*. These years witnessed the publication of T. S. Eliot's *The Waste Land*, James Joyce's *Ulysses*, Thomas Mann's *The Magic Mountain*, W. B. Yeats's *The Tower*, Wallace Stevens's *Harmonium*, and most of the separate volumes of Proust's *Remembrance of Things Past*. In later years Trilling would be regarded as a conservative by many of his radical students at Columbia, the university where he spent, as student and professor, over five decades of his life. But he started out in the early 1920s as a literary radical, a fellow traveler of the modernist avant-garde.

After 1929 Trilling moved to the political left along with others in his intellectual circle. He even became involved, although very briefly, with a communist front organization. But Trilling was never much of a political activist, and he became disillusioned with the communist movement very early on. By the end of the 1930s he had eliminated most traces of Marxism from his critical writing. Although he was associated with the anti-Stalinist radical journal *Partisan Review*, Trilling was making his way back to the middle-class liberal humanism that, modified by his sympathy for aesthetic modernism, had been his point of departure in the 1920s.

Trilling's Columbia University doctoral dissertation on Matthew Arnold became his first book in 1939. Soon after, in 1943, he published a slim volume in praise of the English novelist E. M. Forster. But the work that established Trilling's reputation among the general reading public was *The Liberal Imagination* (1950), a collection of his essays from the 1940s. All through that decade he had taken one occasion after another to criticize the political-cultural attitudes of the intellectual left. In these reviews and essays Trilling argued for the "literary imagination," with its sensitivity to "variousness and complexity," against the simplifications and self-deception of the "liberal imagination." There was an irony in the title of Trilling's collection, for by it he meant to signal the absence of a true spirit of liberality in the culture of the left. So many liberals, in his view, were narrowly "progressive" or even "Stalinoid," so out of touch with "the deep places of the imagination," that the "liberal imagination" was in practice an oxymoron.

This argument was conducted not in directly political or sociological terms but in the form of literary criticism. Trilling attacked the liberal piety according to which THEODORE DREISER and SHERWOOD ANDERSON were major novelists. Indeed, Trilling attacked nearly all the sacred cows of the new literary realism of the American 1920s and 1930s. Excepting only a few figures, most notably F. SCOTT FITZGERALD, Trilling exposed what he felt to be the softheaded idealism and abstractness of such writers as John Steinbeck, whose work had been coopted for their own ends by the communists. As against the social realism of popular fiction of the 1940s, Trilling offered the "moral realism" of Forster and HENRY JAMES. He presented his own tough-minded awareness of the actualities of money and social class as an alternative to the sentimental left-liberal pieties of other critics like V. L. PARRINGTON and F. O. Matthiessen.

The Liberal Imagination became an intellectual bestseller of the 1950s. It sold nearly 200,000 copies in an Anchor paperback edition and became part of the wisdom literature of the time, along with books like *Escape from Freedom* by ERICH FROMM and *The Lonely Crowd* by DAVID RIESMAN.

Trilling also developed his message in the medium of prose fiction. He had always wanted to be a "writer," and not merely an academic literary critic. But his novel about communism, liberalism, and the moral life, *The Middle of the Journey* (1947), received a mainly negative reception from reviewers, and Trilling never again published a work of fiction. His single novel and his short stories, the latter written in the late 1920s and early 1940s, are worth reading as further explorations of ideas presented in Trilling's critical essays. They are also revelatory of Trilling's personal conflicts and aspirations, as are two of his best essays, on James's *The Princess Casamassima* (1948) and the letters of Keats (1951).

In the 1950s Trilling disengaged to a considerable degree from political issues. The essays in *The Opposing Self* (1955) consolidated his reputation but did not break new ground. These essays, most of them on nineteenth-century figures—Austen, Dickens, Flaubert, Howells, and others—are mainly biographical and reveal Trilling's search for a new moral basis in the aftermath of postwar depoliticization. It was not only draftees who were demobilized, returned to civilian life; political intellectuals, too, struggled to find their footing amidst the new normalcy.

Trilling's next major collection, *Beyond Culture* (1965), includes an important essay, "Freud: Within and Beyond Culture," originally presented at the New York Psychoanalytic Institute. It is explicitly about the quest for a reliable foundation for the self in its struggle with culture. As this essay makes clear, Freud's own self, not his ideas alone, strengthened Trilling in his resistance to the oversocialized, other-directed culture of the postwar period. But it is in another essay in that collection, "On the Teaching of Modern Literature," that Trilling anticipated the stance of his last decade (1965–75). In that essay Trilling mused on the institutionalization, within the universities, of the "adversary culture." Modernist literature had been the passion of a small student avant-garde during Trilling's own college days. By the 1960s, in his view, that literature had become the basis, among a very different generation of students, of an orthodoxy of dissent as philistine in its own way as the old-style philistinism it prided itself on defying.

When in the late 1960s violence broke out on university campuses, Trilling was disposed to regard its causes as broadly cultural and psychological rather than political. Undergraduate radicals might insist on their detestation of the impersonal American "multiversity" linked to an imperial government making war on Vietnam. Trilling, for his part, conceived of the student movement as "modernism in the streets." In his view, the students had fed on modernist literary fantasies of radical authenticity and were now proceeding to act out those fantasies. Trilling urged a distinction between the complex moral imagination of a Yeats or a Lawrence, and the simplifications of left-wing activism. Once again, as in the 1940s, he explored the dialectic of (good) ironic-complex literary imagination and (bad) ideological conformity, the latter married to (even worse) unthinking political action.

Trilling's antagonism to the anti-intellectual, desublimated culture of the 1960s issued in *Sincerity and Authenticity* (1973), his last book and his most influential work since *The Liberal Imagination*. Here Trilling distinguished between his own traditional ego ideal and a newer liberatory ideal preached by Sartre, Marcuse, and others unwilling to accept Freud's or Reinhold Niebuhr's idea of civilization's inevitable discontents.

Altogether, *Sincerity and Authenticity* sums up and affirms the ideals of self and society that had informed Trilling's entire career. These were old, unglamorous ideals, and when Trilling died in 1975 it was generally felt, by admirer and detractor alike, that this quietly decent, honorable man represented the last of his line.

MARK KRUPNICK

See also CULTURAL CRITICISM; FREUDIANISM.

FURTHER READING

R. P. Blackmur, "The Politics of Human Power," in *The Lion and the Honeycomb* (New York: Harcourt, Brace and World, 1955).

Joseph Frank, "Lionel Trilling and the Conservative Imagination," in *The Widening Gyre* (New Brunswick, N.J.: Rutgers University Press, 1963).

Geoffrey Hartman, "Lionel Trilling as Man in the Middle," in *The Fate of Reading* (Chicago: University of Chicago Press, 1975).

Mark Krupnick, *Lionel Trilling and the Fate of Cultural Criticism* (Evanston: Northwestern University Press, 1986).

——, "Lionel Trilling and the Politics of Style," in Ian F. A. Bell and D. K. Adams, eds., *American Literary Landscapes: the Fiction and the Fact* (New York: St. Martin's Press, 1989).

Daniel O'Hara, *Lionel Trilling: the Work of Liberation* (Madison: University of Wisconsin Press, 1988).

Mark Shechner, "Psychoanalysis and Liberalism: the Case of Lionel Trilling," in *After the Revolution: Studies in the Contemporary Jewish Imagination* (Bloomington: Indiana University Press, 1988).

Robert Warshow, "The Legacy of the 30's," in *The Immediate Experience* (New York: Atheneum, 1975).

Truth, Sojourner [originally Isabella Van Wagnenen (or Van Wagner)] (b. Ulster County, N.Y., ca.1797; d. Battle Creek, Mich., Nov. 26, 1883). An itinerant preacher of unusual charisma, Truth was a wide-ranging reformer: feminist abolitionist, spiritualist, Perfectionist, utopian. In 1843 this former slave, performing household labor in New York City, recreated herself as Sojourner Truth and set out to the East—to Brooklyn—preaching. In the following decade, she remade herself once again on the antislavery feminists' lecture circuit into the symbol of the slave mother. As the embodiment of the strong black woman, Sojourner Truth has endured as an American hero for more than a century. Her triumph over the wounds inflicted by slavery, poverty, racism, sexism, and lack of education have inspired those facing adversity, and her gift for plain speaking delights her latter-day counterparts in the battle against bigotry.

Analysis of the figure of "Sojourner Truth" is doubly complicated: first, because she was illiterate, we know nothing of her directly and all source material is mediated; and, second, because her significance as a symbol is not based on any specific experiences as a historical actor. Although we might have learned to honor has as a preacher (along with the rest of her forgotten cohort of some 80 antebellum women preachers), we in fact usually treasure her for a potent rhetorical question—"And ar'n't *I* a woman?"—which she did not actually pose. As a figure who is famous for something she did not say, Truth joins the company of others renowned for what they did not do: George Washington and his fictional cherry tree, Betsy Ross and her imaginary flag, and Chief Seattle and the warning he did not utter about cherishing the environment.

The woman who recreated herself as Sojourner Truth was born a slave in Ulster County in the Hudson River Valley of New York. During her enslavement she worked mostly on Dutch-speaking farms, married, and bore five children. In 1827 she was emancipated under New York state law and a few years later sought work in New York City. She also pursued the Perfectionist brand of Methodism that had attracted her in Ulster County, becoming recognized as a charismatic preacher by the early 1830s. Joining the scores of women who were itinerant preachers in the early nineteenth century, she made a name in camp meetings in and around New York City. She never doubted that the voice she heard in her head was God's; her ability to convince others that God spoke to her lent her power, whether she was preaching on Jesus' redeeming love, the evils of slavery, or women's need for the vote.

Her success in reaching feminist as well as evangelical audiences was crucial in ensuring her historical longevity. Had she not entered the historical sources relating to WOMEN'S RIGHTS published in the late nineteenth century, she would today be as obscure as Rebecca Cox Jackson and Harriet Livermore, who were also gifted itinerants of Truth's generation. Her crossover appeal became crucial as early as the 1840s, as women preachers were encountering increased opposition in evangelical circles and were being silenced unless they could address nonreligious issues.

After several years' stay among the reform-minded utopians of the Northampton Association, Truth began to address antislavery and women's rights audiences, to whom she sold her dictated *Narrative of Sojourner Truth* (1850). In the course of marketing her book, Truth encountered two educated white women, HARRIET BEECHER STOWE and Frances Dana Gage, who spread her fame through published profiles. Gage chaired the women's rights convention in Akron, Ohio, which Truth attended to sell her book. After the phenomenal success of *Uncle Tom's Cabin*, Truth asked Stowe for a statement for use in promoting her own book. Stowe wrote the blurb, which appeared in the 1853 printing of Truth's *Narrative*. Several years later, Stowe published a profile of Truth in the *Atlantic Monthly*, entitled "Sojourner Truth, the Libyan Sibyl." Stowe's 1863 essay moved Frances Dana Gage to publish her own version of a speech that Truth had delivered in Akron in 1851.

Writing 12 years after the fact, Gage invented the memorable line "And ar'n't *I* a woman?" that is now so closely associated with Truth. Both Gage's and Stowe's essays appear in the "Book of Life" included in the 1875/1878 edition of the *Narrative of Sojourner Truth*.

Stowe portrayed Truth as a devout evangelical, but Gage's stylized version of Truth, which accentuated Truth's feminism and downplayed her religion, fixed Truth in an identity that would appeal to secular-minded, twentieth-century audiences. Gage's friend, ELIZABETH CADY STANTON, one of the editors of *The History of Woman Suffrage* (1881), reprinted Gage's essay on Truth rather than Stowe's, for Stowe had never been a feminist and had remained outside woman suffrage networks. *The History of Woman Suffrage* became the main means of perpetuating the figure of Sojourner Truth in American memory, including her concern that the enfranchisement of black men without giving women the vote would perpetuate the prevailing, unjust gender hierarchy among blacks as well as whites.

NELL IRVIN PAINTER

FURTHER READING

Jacqueline Bernard, *Journey toward Freedom: the Story of Sojourner Truth* (1967; New York: Feminist Press, 1990).

[Olive Gilbert], *Narrative of Sojourner Truth* (1850, 1875; New York: Arno, 1968).

Nathan O. Hatch, *The Democratization of American Christianity* (New Haven: Yale University Press, 1989).

Nell Irvin Painter, "Representing Truth: Sojourner Truth's Knowing and Becoming Known," *Journal of American History* 81 (Sept. 1994): 461–92.

——, "Sojourner Truth," in Jessie Carney Smith, ed., *Notable Black American Women* (Detroit: Gale Research, 1992).

——, "Sojourner Truth in Feminist Abolitionism: Difference, Slavery, and Memory," in Jean Fagan Yellin and John C. Van Horne, eds., *An Untrodden Path: Antislavery and Women's Political Culture* (Ithaca: Cornell University Press, 1993).

——, "Sojourner Truth," in *The Oxford Companion to Women's Writing in the United States* (New York, Oxford University Press, 1993).

Tubman, Harriet [originally Araminta Green or Ross] (b. Dorchester County, Md., ca.1820; d. Auburn, N.Y., Mar. 10, 1913). Like other American heroes, Harriet Tubman is only part historical figure. She is also a powerful political idea about African American resistance to slavery, and about female strength, courage, and activism—an idea freshly incarnated in each generation of Americans in ways that reflect its own politics of race, class, and gender.

No general history of slavery, African Americans, or American women could be published in this era without at least a ritualized reference to the "legendary" Tubman, who was born to Maryland slave parents and married in 1844 to the free man John Tubman. Her legend begins with her escape from slavery in 1849, after which she turned Underground Railroad conductor and made repeated clandestine trips to the South in the 1850s; in that capacity she is traditionally said to have helped "at least 300" other slaves to escape. John Brown's respect for her reputation and accomplishments is also "legendary," as indicated in the much-repeated story of his calling her "General" at their first meeting in Canada in 1858. During the Civil War, she served in the Union army as scout (and trainer of scouts), spy, nurse (and herbalist healer), cook, and teacher of newly emancipated slaves. After the war she lived in Auburn, New York, working to support her aged parents and to raise funds for the relief of other indigent ex-slaves. Her activism in the postwar period included speaking on behalf of temperance and woman suffrage.

Despite Tubman's mythic importance to African Americans and others, her life has been surprisingly neglected by the current generation of historians. She is known primarily from a former generation's inspirational biographies, especially Earl Conrad's *Harriet Tubman, Negro Soldier and Abolitionist*, published in 1942, and his fuller *Harriet Tubman* (1943); and two fine young readers' books, Dorothy Sterling's *Freedom Train* (1954) and the novelist Ann Petry's *Harriet Tubman: Conductor on the Underground Railroad* (1955).

One reason for her neglect by modern historians may be the mediated nature of the nineteenth-century sources. During the more than 50 years in which she was a public figure (1860–1913), the illiterate Tubman was dependent on others to record her stories. On several occasions, beginning during the Civil War, she offered partial oral autobiographies to white abolitionist allies, male and female. In choosing her interviewers carefully, and in choosing to tell her stories in certain ways, Tubman was always an active participant in the creation of her own legend.

Her white interpreters also shaped her public history in complex ways related in part to their own gender, class, and racial identities—deciding how to render the sound of her language in writing, which stories to use and which to omit and how to interpret them. In most cases, there is no way to know how much the writer altered the meaning of Tubman's original story in recording it. However, the existence of two versions of one of these nineteenth-century Tubman biographies allows a telling glimpse into the process by which Tubman's self-presentation in storytelling was altered by her collaborator.

At Tubman's request, the children's book writer Sarah H. Bradford created two versions of Tubman's life story: *Scenes in the Life of Harriet Tubman* in 1869, and *Harriet, the Moses of Her People* in 1886. The first is a comparatively disorderly collection of anecdotes collected through several days' interviewing, prepared for publication in great haste. In the second, Bradford took the time to rewrite many of Tubman's original stories, losing important detail and much of what was represented in quotation marks in the first version as Tubman's own language. Bradford's revisions in the later book tempered Tubman's salty personality and erased all references to racial politics. Bradford accentuated Tubman's victimization as a slave, downplayed her expressed pride in outwitting her white oppressors, and omitted jokes and implicit criticism of white liberals such as HARRIET BEECHER STOWE.

One major issue that will confront a modern biographer of Tubman is the shifting meaning of her womanhood to her African American and white admirers, female and male, past and present. Whereas Sarah Bradford seems to attempt to "feminize" her image of Tubman in the revised biography, other contemporaries stressed ways in which she modeled herself on "masculine" virtues. John Brown wrote admiringly of her to his son in just such terms, even to the point of invoking the masculine pronoun: "Harriet Tubman hooked on his whole team at once. He is the most of a man naturally that I ever met with" (Conrad, 1942, p. 24).

Earl Conrad's major biography of 1943 features her military heroism in leading an 1863 expedition of 300 African American soldiers on a nighttime raid against Confederate armaments on the Combahee River—calling it "the only military engagement in American history" inspired and led by a woman, black or white (Conrad, 1943, p. 170). Conrad's account is exemplary in presenting her masculine-sphere activities as praiseworthy while not neglecting her more traditional feminine-sphere war work such as nursing and herbal healing. Yet Conrad, like many of his predecessors, still drew the portrait of a larger-than-life heroine, and his suspicion of religious experience distorts her thinking. Harriet Tubman still awaits the writers of this generation who can accommodate her full range of experience and achievement as a gifted, courageous, and complex African American woman.

JEAN M. HUMEZ

FURTHER READING
Earl Conrad, Harriet Tubman, Negro Soldier and Abolitionist (New York: International Publishers, 1942).
——, Harriet Tubman (Washington, D.C.: Associated Press, 1943).
——, "I Bring you General Tubman," The Black Scholar (Jan.–Feb. 1970).
"Moses," The Freedman's Record [Boston], Mar. 1865.
Benjamin Quarles, Black Abolitionists (New York: Oxford University Press, 1969).
——, "Harriet Tubman's Unlikely Leadership," in Leon Litwack and August Meier, eds., Black Leaders of the Nineteenth Century (Urbana: University of Illinois Press, 1988).
[Franklin B. Sanborn], "Harriet Tubman," The Commonwealth [Boston], July 17, 1863.
Dorothy Sterling, We Are Your Sisters: Black Women in the Nineteenth Century (New York: Norton, 1984).

Tugwell, Rexford G. (b. Sinclairville, N.Y., July 10, 1891; d. Santa Barbara, Calif., July 21, 1979). Economist. An influential member of Roosevelt's "Brains Trust," Tugwell was a partisan of centralized economic planning. He helped write the Agricultural Adjustment Act (1933) before becoming head of the Resettlement Administration in 1936. Tugwell's collectivism antagonized conservatives, who preferred free market solutions, and disturbed those New Dealers like LOUIS BRANDEIS who equated DEMOCRACY with local control. Tugwell advanced his ideas in many books, including *The Trend of Economics* (1927) and *The Battle for Democracy* (1935), a plea for the New Deal. In *The Place of Planning in Society* (1954) and *The Democratic Roosevelt* (1957), he defended his own vision of the New Deal and criticized FDR's shift toward decentralization after 1936.

FURTHER READING
Michael V. Namorato, Rexford G. Tugwell: a Biography (New York: Praeger, 1988).

Turner, Frederick Jackson (b. Portage, Wis., Nov. 14, 1861; d. Pasadena, Calif., Mar. 14, 1932). The son of a local newspaper editor, Turner attended the University of Wisconsin and Johns Hopkins University. At Hopkins he reacted strongly against Herbert Baxter Adams's "germ theory," which held that American institutions derived from German folk models. In Turner's view, the key features of American democracy came not from the Old World but the New, and he began formulating a thesis that would place this exceptionalist argument at the center of American historiography for at least the next half-century. While completing his Hopkins dissertation, he joined the history department at Madison in 1889. There he drafted an essay on "The Significance of the Frontier in American History," which he delivered in July 1893 at the World's Columbian Exposition in Chicago. Although little noted at the time, it would eventually be regarded as the most influential essay ever written by an American historian. Turner produced a series of essays elaborating his thesis of the FRONTIER, collected in a 1920 volume entitled *The Frontier in American History*. He published only one book-length monograph during his lifetime, *The Rise of the New West* (1906), but a long book on *The United States, 1830–1850* was published posthumously in 1935. He moved from Wisconsin to Harvard in 1910, retired back to Madison in 1924, and in 1927 became a research associate at the Huntington Library, where he remained until his death.

"The existence of an area of free land," Turner wrote in *The Frontier in American History*, "its continuous recession, and the advance of American settlement westward, explain American development" (p. 1). As Europeans colonized the eastern seaboard and pushed west across the Appalachians, they encountered lands less "civilized" than they had known back home. In building communities in the West, they supposedly shed the trappings of civilization and invented a new society. Wedded to models of social evolution derived from DARWINISM, Turner argued that frontier communities passed through a sequence of stages in which Indians and fur traders gave way to pastoral livestock raisers, who gave way to subsistence farmers, who gave way to commercial farmers, who gave way in turn to townspeople and factory workers. Turner believed that the encounter with "free land" had transformed the American character, making it restless, inventive, acquisitive, individualist, egalitarian, democratic. The frontier, in other words, and especially the frontier of the Old Northwest, had forged American nationalism and DEMOCRACY. Now, Turner argued, the frontier era was drawing to a close, and the United States must look elsewhere for energy and inspiration if its democracy was to survive. (*See also* AMERICAN EXCEPTIONALISM.)

Few historical arguments have risen so high and then fallen so far in scholarly reputation. Political leaders as diverse as Theodore Roosevelt and Woodrow Wilson hailed Turner's work as a powerful vision linking the nation's past, present, and future. It was invoked in contemporary political debates about American overseas expansion (to create new frontiers), immigration restriction (since new immigrants could no longer be "Americanized" by the frontier), and the creation of national parks (to protect vestiges of America's frontier past). Turner's seminars at Wisconsin and Harvard would train some of the leading historians of the next generation, guaranteeing that his frontier narrative would persist for decades in textbooks and monographs.

Not until after Turner's death in 1932 would a systematic attack be mounted against the frontier thesis. By the 1940s, historians were noting that the frontier as Turner employed it could be a line, a zone, a phase, or a process, rendering it so malleable that it could seem to explain virtually anything while in fact explaining nothing. Many critics pointed to the European and eastern colonial roots of American political institutions as proof that the frontier was far more derivative than Turner claimed. In the 1950s, Turner's arguments looked dangerously materialist; in the 1960s, they looked racist, sexist, and imperialist, making too little room for Indians, Latinos, Asian Americans, women, and others whose histories did not fit neatly into the frontier pageant of civilized progress. Although Turner would continue to serve as a favorite whipping boy for scholars wishing to promote their own arguments at his expense, the scholarly consensus 50 years after his death was that his thesis was without much merit. Rarely have so many nails been pounded into one scholarly coffin.

Not all of this criticism was fair. Turner shared the prejudices of his age, and wrote history as a patriot celebrating what he saw as the special achievements of his nation. Moroeover, he saw American history through midwestern eyes, and regarded the upper Mississippi Valley as the place where American democracy had attained its fullest expression; aside from his chauvinistic habit of overgeneralizing the experience of his region, it hardly seems fair to fault him when arguments originally intended for the Old Northwest do not easily apply to the trans-Mississippi. (Indeed, one could argue that many of Turner's modern critics pay too little attention to the Middle West.)

As a teacher, Turner helped create the academic discipline of history as we know it today. Refocusing the attention of scholars away from centers of national power and the history of "great men," he sought to explore the past lives of ordinary people, the social and economic origins of cultural and political institutions, and the relationship of human beings to the land. As such, he was an earlier practitioner of what a later generation would call "history from the bottom up," and it is also no accident that his field of Western history has helped spawn the field of environmental history. It was both his good luck and his misfortune to attach his work to a central myth of American nationalism, a myth that existed before his birth and that survives to this day. In lending his name to that myth, he achieved a fame unequaled by any other American historian. Then, when the myth itself became suspect, it was probably inevitable that Turner would bear the brunt of the intellectual attack against it.

WILLIAM CRONON

FURTHER READING
Ray Allen Billington, *The Genesis of the Frontier Thesis: a Study in Historical Creativity* (San Marino: Huntington Library, 1971).
——, *Frederick Jackson Turner: Historian, Scholar, Teacher* (New York: Oxford University Press, 1973).
William Cronon, "Turner's First Stand: the Significance of Significance in American History," in Richard Etulain, ed., *Writing Western History: Essays on Major Western Historians* (Albuquerque: University of New Mexico Press, 1991).
Richard Hofstadter, *The Progressive Historians: Turner, Beard, Parrington* (New York: Knopf, 1968).
Howard R. Lamar, "Frederick Jackson Turner," in Marcus Cunliffe and Robin W. Winks, eds., *Pastmasters: Some Essays on American Historians* (New York: Harper and Row, 1969).
Frederick Jackson Turner, *The Frontier in American History* (New York: Holt, 1920).
——, *The Significance of Sections in American History* (New York: Holt, 1932).

Twain, Mark [Samuel Langhorne Clemens] (b. Florida, Mo., Nov. 30. 1835; d. Redding, Conn.,

Apr. 21, 1910). Born to what he once called "poor but dishonest" parents of southern roots and sympathies, Samuel Clemens began his adult years in a seemingly ceaseless pursuit of the "main chance." Adventures as a printer's apprentice, river pilot, Confederate irregular, prospector, and western journalist provided neither permanent wealth nor prominent position. These experiences did, however, furnish the material he was to use to achieve literary success and acclaim as Mark Twain, his celebrated *nom de plume* taken from the calls by which Mississippi rivermen measured the water's depth. Fashioning a unique combination of frontier exaggeration and hardheaded empiricism into a distinctive, lean prose, Twain confronted his and America's ambivalence about money, race, and other morally charged conundrums.

Simultaneously attracted to and repelled by bourgeois society and morality, Clemens lived a life of unresolved contradictions. A lifelong supporter of organized labor, he plunged into bankruptcy as a result of his quixotic investment in the Paige typesetter, which he loved, he said, because it neither got drunk nor joined a union. Critical of the shallow materialism of the Gilded Age, which derived its name from the title of the 1873 novel that he wrote with Charles Dudley Warner, Twain nevertheless ended his days as a friend of ANDREW CARNEGIE and Standard Oil executive Henry Rogers. Capable of transcending his white southern attitudes on race, going so far as to declare that whites owed blacks reparations, he employed only black butlers because he could never force himself to give orders to a white man. Enjoying and cultivating his literary renown, he spent much of his later life entangled in business schemes designed to free him from ever having to write again. Contemptuous of conventional mores and the hypocrisy that they engendered, he rigidly monitored his daughters' behavior, and caused a stir when he reneged on sponsorship of Maxim Gorky's trip to America because the Russian traveled in the company of a woman who was not his wife.

Mark Twain came to national prominence with "The Celebrated Jumping Frog of Calaveras County" (1865), a tale of rogues who load down a champion frog with buckshot. In his early comic stories and in *Innocents Abroad* (1869), an account of his participation in an American expedition to Europe and the Holy Land, and *Roughing It* (1872), the chronicle of his western adventures, Twain established himself as the premier American humorist of his time. While retaining the bravado characteristic of the tradition of frontier HUMOR, he shed the customary practice of getting laughs at the expense of uneducated characters. His uncanny ability to undermine the assumption of a rational and morally ordered world without giving offense was achieved by clothing his complaints in a genial hyperbole that subtly undercut their gravity, a strategy that allowed him to question the values of his audience without directly attacking them. Although recent scholarship has challenged his authorship of such *bon mots* as "everyone complains about the weather but no one does anything about it," those he did originate rank among the gems of American humor. While it was wonderful to have discovered America, he said in *Pudd'nhead Wilson* (1894), it would have been more wonderful to miss it.

Twain's reputation as a comic writer and chronicler of boys—the result of the wildly successful *Tom Sawyer* (1875)—rankled him. Upon his return east in 1866, he took advantage of the patronage of his friend WILLIAM DEAN HOWELLS to publish in such "respectable" magazines as *The Atlantic* and *The Century*. Cherishing the opportunity to write "serious" literature, Twain put familiar subject-matter to new uses. His most sustained work appeared in the 1880s: *Life on the Mississippi* (1883), a telling evocation of his days as a river pilot, and *Adventures of Huckleberry Finn* (1885). Both books used humor to probe profound issues. In the former, Twain expertly explored the joys of craft knowledge, the majesty of American nature, and the threats to American innocence posed by commercialization and by slavery.

Huckleberry Finn, which Ernest Hemingway claimed initiated American literature, was Twain's greatest triumph. Narrated in the voice of the title character, a barely literate 13-year-old Missouri boy who took for granted the righteousness of slavery, the book follows Huck and the runaway slave Jim Turner as they float down the Mississippi trying to escape detection. Their journey on the raft constitutes Huck's sentimental education. When one of his tricks pains Jim, Huck feels like "trash." Contrary to his racist upbringing, he humbles himself and, he tells us, "warn't sorry for it afterwards, neither" (p. 71). Huck's partial recognition of Jim's capacity for human feeling does not completely erase his sense that Jim is property whom he has helped "steal." Driven by this guilt, Huck composes a letter to Jim's owner informing her of his whereabouts. In the book's pivotal and most debated moment, however, Huck recalls Jim's kindness and tears up the letter, resolving to "go to hell" instead (p. 168).

Although critics of the 1950s and 1960s praised the novel as a socially daring work for its vivid presentation of the conflict between prescribed and natural morality and its dissection of the foibles and conceits of Americans, much of the criticism of the last two decades has found Twain supportive of the repressive attitudes of his day. Some have objected to the book's promiscuous use of "nigger" and have rejected all claims that the usage is ironic. The more serious charge about the racial politics of the novel concerns the contrived and drawn-out ending. Huck and Tom Sawyer, who coincidentally meets up with the runaways at Pikesville, enact a fantasy rescue of Jim from bondage in which the portrayal of Jim reverts to degrading stereotype. Jim's actual manumission by his owner's consent only highlights the futility of the second half of the novel, critics charge, and mars the moral majesty and artistic virtuosity of the first. Feminist critics have noted in the novel and in such work as his essays on the founder of Christian Science, MARY BAKER EDDY, Twain's reliance on the Victorian polarity between a feminized and artificial civilization and a realm of masculine freedom from restraint. Nowhere are the negative connotations of the feminine world more pronounced than in *Huck Finn*'s final paragraph, where Huck reacts to Aunt Sally's wish to adopt and civilize him by determining to light out for the Territory.

Twain's inability to resolve his complex and contradictory feelings about civilization and his anger at the intractability of human nature became more pronounced in his later writings. *A Connecticut Yankee in King Arthur's Court* (1889), the fable of the efforts of a Hartford master mechanic transported to feudal England to transform it into a bourgeois, industrial republic, ends with the dream of progress destroyed in a scene of mass destruction. In such political pieces as "To a Person Sitting in Darkness" (1901), a strident condemnation of American imperialist ventures in the Philippines and of the moral fraudulence of politicians and missionaries, and "The United States of Lyncherdom" (1902), his fury and disgust overrode his characteristic humor. Twain's despair permeated *Pudd'nhead Wilson* (1894), which once again addressed the problem of RACE, and his attempt in the novel to demonstrate that training, not natural endowment, determined character ran afoul of an unbreakable determinism. As his pessimism turned to cynicism, Twain was increasingly unable to imagine how a satisfactory human life was possible. His final resignation stood in marked contrast to the official optimism of the nation that hailed him then as its foremost man of letters.

DANIEL H. BORUS

FURTHER READING

Van Wyck Brooks, *The Ordeal of Mark Twain* (New York: E. P. Dutton, 1920).

Laurie Chapman, ed., *The Critical Response to Mark Twain's "Huckleberry Finn"* (New York: Greenwood, 1991).

Guy Cardwell, *The Man Who Was Mark Twain: Images and Ideologies* (New Haven: Yale University Press, 1991).

Wilma Garcia, *Mothers and Others: Myths of the Female in the Works of Melville, Twain and Hemingway* (New York: American University Studies/Peter Lang, 1984).

Justin Kaplan, *Mr. Clemens and Mark Twain* (New York: Simon and Schuster, 1966).

James Leonard, Thomas Tenney, Thadious Davis, eds., *Satire or Evasion? Black Perspectives on "Huckleberry Finn"* (Durham, N.C.: Duke University Press, 1992).

Peter Stoneley, *Mark Twain and the Feminine Aesthetic* (Cambridge: Cambridge University Press, 1992).

Mark Twain, *Adventures of Huckleberry Finn* (1885; New York: Norton, 1962).

U

Unitarianism The Great Awakening which swept New England in the 1740s signaled a crisis in the development of Calvinism, the beginning of an unraveling of the "New England Way" which had held the divergent energies of that theological system in uneasy tension after the Puritan migration. While the aim of the GREAT AWAKENING was a spiritual quickening which would revivify the stress on salvation by grace central to CALVINISM, it unintentionally focused new concern on the role of the will in spiritual development. In a profound historical irony, the Great Awakening thus spawned the two movements that represented the repudiation of Calvinism: revivalistic EVANGELICALISM and Unitarianism. The Unitarian critique of Calvinism can be traced to Charles Chauncy's vigorous criticism of the Awakening in the 1740s, initiating a process of theological reconstruction that eventuated in the emergence of the party of "liberal Christians" in Boston and Eastern Massachusetts.

That emergence can for the most part be described as a "silent advance" during the late eighteenth century, in which ministers of many congregational churches simply ceased to emphasize the distinctive doctrines of Calvinism, thus undermining it without open theological warfare. But the split between the liberals and the "Orthodox," as the Calvinists came to be called, became entangled with the future of Harvard College in 1805, when Henry Ware, a liberal, was elected Hollis Professor of Divinity. Over the next 30 years the "Unitarian controversy" dominated New England theology, until the Unitarians were riven by their own internal challenge, TRANSCENDENTALISM.

The distinctive feature of New England Unitarianism was its construction of the spiritual life as a process of cultivating the inherent spiritual potential of the self. While this doctrine of self-culture was a repudiation of the Calvinist doctrines of innate depravity and election to grace, it was rooted in versions of Puritan "preparationist" theology. RALPH WALDO EMERSON and his Transcendentalist followers would later attack Unitarianism as they had known it, even though their own rebellion was anchored in a radical faith in the spiritual potential of the self that was the legacy of Unitarianism.

WILLIAM ELLERY CHANNING was the most significant figure in the articulation of the Unitarian doctrine of self-culture. He achieved public prominence in 1815 with his *Letter to the Rev. Samuel C. Thacher* which defended the liberal movement against recent Calvinist attacks, and he later codified the Unitarian position with his 1819 sermon "Unitarian Christianity." While Channing and other early Unitarians could be classed as optimists about human nature and possibility, they were by no means sanguine or complacent about the work of cultivating the soul. "Our present state, made up, as it is, of aids and trials, is worthy of God, and may be used throughout to assimilate us to him," Channing preached in his 1828 sermon "Likeness to God" (p. 158). While the tone of the passage is unquestionably affirmative, the phrase "aids and trials" should not be overlooked— Channing did not preach the existence of an unearned spiritual state or automatic sainthood. The point of his emphasis on the culture of the soul, and the closely related doctrine of probation emphasized by his colleague Henry Ware Jr., was to foster the strenuous pursuit of a spiritual perfection, whose foundation was the fundamental "likeness" of the human soul with God. The purpose of religion, Channing averred, "consists in making us more and more partakers of the Divinity" (p. 146).

The Unitarian denomination was formed through the sometimes bitter splitting of the established churches of Eastern Massachusetts, a process in which many of the original churches in Eastern Massachusetts became Unitarian, while "Orthodox" elements of these congregations broke away to form new churches, which came to be known as the Congregationalist churches. Channing's call to sectarian consciousness in "Unitarian Christianity" eventuated in the formation of the American Unitarian Association (AUA) in 1825, although the Unitarians remained oriented primarily to the individual congregation as the essential unit of church governance. The Unitarian doctrine of self-culture fostered a rich literary culture and also emphasized social reform. It provided, in combination with the ENLIGHTENMENT humanism of THOMAS JEFFERSON, a potent foundation for liberal moral reflection in America. Channing's "Remarks on National Literature" (1830) was an important early call for the development of an independent American national literature, and his treatise *Slavery* (1835), placed his considerable influence on the side of the ANTISLAVERY movement.

The literary and reformist currents of the Unitarian ethos rose to overflowing in the Transcendentalist movement, keyed by Emerson's exposition of the moral dynamics of philosophical idealism in *Nature* (1836), and his controversial Divinity School Address at Harvard (1838), in which he rejected the biblical miracles as essential evidence of the validity of religion. That address was castigated by Unitarian theologian Andrews Norton, whose critique marks the most significant moment of the Transcendentalist controversy of the late 1830s and early 1840s. While Emerson would deny that there was any Transcendental party, his theological innovations and literary achievements were supplemented in the political sphere by the antislavery preaching of Theodore Parker, George Ripley's communal experiment Brook Farm, and the early feminist treatise *Woman in the Nineteenth Century* (1845) by MARGARET FULLER. Though not in the denominational mainstream, the Transcendentalists did represent an intellectual vanguard within Unitarianism, and their example was inspirational to succeeding generations of social and religious thinkers.

The Transcendentalist controversy proved to be the first of three major denominational struggles that reflected the growing trend toward an antisupernatural secularism in Unitarian theology. Three decades after the Transcendentalist controversy, Henry W. Bellows's organization of the National Conference of Unitarian Churches in 1865 led to a sharp dissent by younger Unitarian radicals, who saw in the organization the possibility of a denominational creed, and the curtailment of free theological speculation. They formed the Free Religious Association in 1867 as an answer to Bellows, who continued to concentrate his efforts on the formulation of a viable institutional structure for the loosely organized denomination. In the 1910s and 1920s, controversy erupted over the presence of religious humanists in the denomination, exemplified by John H. Dietrich and Curtis W. Reese. The ensuing humanist–theist debate explored the possibility of a religious stance that did not include a belief in God. None of these debates was settled; debates are seldom settled within Unitarian circles. But the denomination continued by enfolding all sides into a consensual affirmation of noncreedalism, resulting in an increasingly diverse spectrum of theological positions, which now ranges from Christian theism through humanism to more recent forms of New Age spirituality. The efforts of Bellows to solidify the institutional structures of Unitarianism, and the influential leadership of Frederick May Eliot, who served as AUA president from 1937 to 1958, were important factors in the stability of the denomination.

In 1961 the AUA merged with the Universalist Church of America to form the Unitarian Universalist Association.

Unitarian theology in the twentieth century has centered on the attempt to formulate a new social ethic. Francis Greenwood Peabody's *Jesus Christ and the Social Question* (1900) was an important articulation of the quest for an ethical code that would do justice to the problem of social equality in the industrial era. Peabody's concerns were extended in the influential work of James Luther Adams, a theologian insistent upon the political relevance of the church. Adams argued that the liberal church, one instance of the "voluntary association" typical of modernity, could play a crucial social role by promoting both personal autonomy and communal responsibility.

In the past 20 years the stress on social ethics has been accompanied by a renewed spirituality. Unitarians have looked both to the Western Christian tradition, and to forms of Eastern spirituality such as Buddhism, to reappropriate and extend the legacy of spiritual culture articulated by Emerson and the Transcendentalists. FEMINISM, and the desire to define a women's spirituality that rejects a gendered hierarchy in religious thinking, has been at the heart of this search, and has accorded well with a growing ethos of ENVIRONMENTALISM within Unitarian Universalism, a development that has sparked a new joining of spirituality and ethical purpose. The campaign for a vital social ethic and a deepened concept of spirituality have situated contemporary Unitarian Universalism as an important alternative to the revival and the politicization of religious FUNDAMENTALISM in the 1970s and 1980s, and indicate its continuing significance in American culture.

DAVID M. ROBINSON

See also LIBERAL PROTESTANTISM.

FURTHER READING

Lawrence Buell, *Literary Transcendentalism: Style and Vision in the American Renaissance* (Ithaca: Cornell University Press, 1973).

William Ellery Channing, *William Ellery Channing: Selected Writings*, ed. David Robinson (New York: Paulist Press, 1985).

Daniel Walker Howe, *The Unitarian Conscience: Harvard Moral Philosophy, 1805–1861* (1970; Middletown, Conn.: Wesleyan University Press, 1988).

Perry Miller, "From Edwards to Emerson," in *Errand into the Wilderness* (Cambridge: Harvard University Press, 1956).

——, ed., *The Transcendentalists: an Anthology* (Cambridge: Harvard University Press, 1950).

David Robinson, *The Unitarians and the Universalists* (Westport, Conn.: Greenwood, 1985).

Conrad Wright, *The Beginnings of Unitarianism in America* (1955; Hamden, Conn.: Archon, 1976).

——, ed., *A Stream of Light: a Sesquicentennial History of American Unitarianism* (Boston: Unitarian Universalist Association, 1975).

urbanism Although sporadic commentary on urban places appeared in earlier phases of American history—as when Thomas Jefferson, an agrarian-republican, complained that cities were "pestilential" to morals, health, and liberty—systematic theorizing about urban living as a distinctive mode of group life is a product of the late nineteenth-century crisis of industrial modernity. The term "urbanism" first appeared around 1889 to describe the kinds of social life apparently new in all human history and manifest in the great industrial cities (*see* INDUSTRIALISM), and to contrast that life with the otherness of rural living.

In this century, cities have presented the raw material for the intellectual crises of modernity and of postmodernity. The central trope of modernity is time; that of postmodernity is space. As these two dimensions of social being are rendered problematic by the industrial (and postindustrial) capitalist city, the successive modern and postmodern discourses of urbanism have selected opposing features of urban living to valorize or fear. The modernist discourse feared diversity and disorder while the postmodern discourse fears uniformity and order.

"Urbanism" the concept was the product of the founders of university-based sociology. ALBION SMALL and Franklin Giddings in the United States, Georg Simmel in Germany, and Émile Durkheim in France simultaneously built the transatlantic discipline of sociology with graduate schools and scholarly journals to explain the fate of human society under industrial urban conditions.

Marking the birth of the American discourse of urbanism was the nearly simultaneous appearance in the prototypical modern industrial city, Chicago, of Frederick Jackson Turner's "Significance of the Frontier in American History," (1893); Albion Small and George Vincent's *Introduction to the Study of Society* (1894); and *Hull-House Maps and Papers* (1895).

The exemplary modernist text of American urbanist thought, widely republished and read until the 1960s, was Louis Wirth's "Urbanism as a Way of Life," published in 1938. Summarizing the perspective of the Chicago School that Wirth had helped to build, the essay stresses demographic variables that disorganize tradition: large population size, high settlement density, and great heterogeneity. "Bonds of kinship, neighborliness, and the sentiments of living together for generations under a common folk tradition are likely to be absent or, at best, relatively

weak in an aggregate the members of which have such diverse backgrounds" (p. 70). Highly segmented roles develop; interaction is mediated through contract relations and the cash nexus; superficiality, anonymity, and anomie also result. Under high population density, work and place of residence are separated and social groups are segregated by "income, racial and ethnic characteristics, social status, custom, habit, taste, preference, and prejudice" (p. 74).

Wirth's essay is, of course, built from the ideas of the great theorists of modernity: Ferdinand Tönnies, Georg Simmel, Émile Durkheim, and Max Weber.

Despite the mountain of urbanist texts that had already accumulated by 1938, Wirth began his essay with a significant complaint: "we look in vain for a theory systematizing the available knowledge concerning the city as a social entity" (p. 67). The urbanist thought Wirth summarized was not really about cities *per se*, but about manifestations of modernity observable in them. Completing a general theory of urbanism would require the demystification of space in the collapse of the metanarrative of temporal progress.

While American urbanist thought is most typically associated with the "Chicago School," there were in fact *two* Chicago schools. The first was typified by ALBION SMALL, JANE ADDAMS, JOHN DEWEY, and W. I. Thomas. Social democratic and pragmatic, it sought to create a new genus of social beings who could adapt to the conditions of modernity through creative participation at work and in public life. The greatest expression of the first Chicago school was achieved in W. I. Thomas and Florian Znaniecki's *The Polish Peasant in Europe and America* (5 vols., 1918–20).

The second Chicago school, headed by ROBERT E. PARK after Thomas's dismissal and Small's death, dominated American urbanist thought until the late 1960s. Park and his colleagues consolidated the normative strands of the MODERNIZATION paradigm, and suppressed the social democratic, pluralist, and feminist pathways explored by their predecessors, to create the "ecological" model of urbanism. Codified in a collection of essays edited by Park, Ernest Burgess, and Roderick McKenzie under the title *The City* (1925), the ecological model drew proudly on plant biology to describe the "natural habitats" of communities, ghettoes, and gangs, and the "natural history" of newspapers. Neighborhoods were ever in the process of becoming the habitats of new social groups which were experiencing upward, downward, or static socioeconomic mobility.

The second Chicago school made its most powerful contribution to American urban practice in the modernist Great Society policy-making of the 1960s.

The leading War on Poverty policy-makers included Leonard Ohlin, who had been trained by Ernest Burgess. They conceived of poverty and its "tangle of pathology" as a mismatch between the progressive forces of modernity and the ill-adapted individual. Oscar Lewis's "culture of poverty" thesis recommended reconditioning the values and behavior of the poor.

A critique of modernist urbanism began *within* that discourse, with dissident voices who attempted to assert the spatial dimension against the temporal. The earliest dissenter was CHARLOTTE PERKINS GILMAN, who proposed, in *Women and Economics* (1898) and more specifically in *The Home: Its Work and Influence* (1903), a feminist spatial theory of urban society. Gilman explained women's lack of freedom as a spatial incarceration in an institution atavistically and even deliberately produced in a "man-made world" so as to extract the maximum labor power from half of the human species.

LEWIS MUMFORD, although quintessentially modernist, nevertheless developed an elaborate urban theory which established the shared spaces of cities as central to urbanism. Almost completely ignored by the second Chicago school, Mumford's spatial critique of industrial cities was an elaboration of the social democratic modernism of the first Chicago school, aiming to achieve the union of "Art and the Machine" voiced first by Frank Lloyd Wright in the latter's 1901 Hull-House lecture of that title. Wright and Mumford sought an urban form within which urbanites could understand the oneness of their social being through shared symbolic meaning inscribed in the aesthetic design and planning of a unified built environment. In his *Story of Utopias* (1922), *The Culture of Cities* (1938), the massive *The City in History* (1961), and innumerable essays (especially his "Skyline" column for the *New Yorker* from 1931 to 1963), Mumford set himself apart from Chicago School modernists by preferring the past (especially the medieval city) over the future in the flow of time. But Mumford's spatial critique only camouflaged capitalist social relations within a manufactured aesthetic of precapitalist social relations.

It was instead the genuinely antimodernist Jane Jacobs who rapidly found an audience in the 1960s with her indictment of American urban planning and business development, *The Death and Life of Great American Cities* (1961). Where the modernists had fought physical deterioration, population concentration, and "social disorganization" in all phases of urban life, Jacobs opened the postmodern urbanist critique by affirming these phenomena as diversity arising spontaneously from below:

City districts will be economically and socially congenial places for diversity to generate itself and reach its best potential if the districts possess good mixtures of primary uses, frequent streets, a close-grained mingling of different ages in their buildings and a high concentration of people. (p. 242)

Intellectuals in the 1960s and 1970s now took their cues from the intense urban social crisis of those decades and inverted modernism's priorities. Los Angeles became the prototype of the postmodernist discourse after the violence and destruction in the black ghetto of Watts in 1965 confirmed Jacobs's verdict on modernist urban thought, design, and public policy. Buried social democratic elements of the modernist discourse—especially those concocted in the Hull-House milieu—now resurfaced in the celebration of multicultural diversity and the search for participatory democracy.

The modernist metanarrative of PROGRESS in defiance of space succumbed to two interrelated, but ultimately contradictory postmodern urbanisms: (1) the aesthetic urbanism of postmodern multiculturalism and urban design, and (2) a critical urbanism which has worked to redefine the city as the spatial product of capitalist political economy.

In the 1990s, postmodern urban design has become commonplace in redevelopment projects from shopping centers to residential complexes, stressing ahistoric eclecticism, geographic dispersal, and encyclopedic polymorphism. In their celebration of all historical styles and the contiguity of all global ethnic groups in constructed space, the aesthetic postmodernists annihilate historical time and deconstruct Progress. (*See also* POSTMODERNISM.) Architects and urban design theorists, inspired by the radical critique of modernism in the work of Nietzsche, Heidegger, and Jacques Derrida, have displaced modernist themes of purpose, design, centering, master codes, determinacy and transcendence with, respectively, the themes of play, chance, dispersal, ideolects, indeterminacy, and immanence.

Critical postmodern urbanism uses the dimension of space to refashion elements of Marxian historical materialism. Manuel Castells in the *City and the Grassroots* (1977) rebuilt Marxian urban theory around the fact of recent social movements. Dolores Hayden, in *The Grand Domestic Revolution* (1981) and *Redesigning the American Dream* (1986), rebuilt Gilman's feminist urban theory on the fact of the recent feminist movement, criticizing twentieth-century urban form as a gendered spatial product of political-economic origins.

Following especially Henri LeFebvre's *La Production de l'éspace* (1967), David Harvey, Edward Soja, and

Mike Davis have forged a space-time critique of both modernity and postmodernity to reach toward an ethical-political praxis for contemporary urbanist discourse. In its heavy reliance on Marx, this recent critical urbanist thought has been burdened by modernist assumptions of order, system, and centering processes. In its reconceptualization of space as an independent, socially conditioning variable, however, it has appropriated postmodernism's central trope to combat capitalist urbanism.

In *The Condition of Postmodernity*, Harvey has developed a theory of urbanism even more encompassing than Wirth's by stressing "the speculative grounding of capitalism's inner logic" (p. 345). Harvey sees *both* the industrial *and* the postindustrial city as spatial products of capitalism's perpetual problem of overaccumulation. Harvey draws on Pierre Bourdieu's theory of "symbolic capital" to follow Fredric Jameson in naming postmodern cultural production (from serious art to mass marketing) as the cultural logic of late capitalism under the regime of post-Fordist flexible accumulation.

In the work of Edward Soja and Mike Davis, Los Angeles is to postmodernism what Chicago was to modernism. Layered archaeologically in the postmodern city is the continuous structuring of consciousness through the spatial fallout of past class (production) struggles and aggregate individual (consumption) freedoms. There is in Los Angeles, Soja observes, a Boston, a Lower Manhattan, a South Bronx, a São Paulo, and a Singapore: "Los Angeles seems to be conjugating the recent history of capitalist urbanization in virtually all its inflectional forms" (p. 193).

The postmodern character of Harvey's, Soja's, and Davis's critical urbanism is especially evident in their revalorization of space in analytical theory and in their advocacy of difference and otherness as central rather than peripheral to the historical process. Some, however, suggest that these authors are not critical enough to break the cycle of domination and exploitation realized in cities modern and postmodern. Harvey, Soja, and Davis all trace the crisis of postmodernity to the encompassing logic of a single economic system and devote very little attention to the dimension of gender. "By insisting on their totalizing and reductionist visions," Michael Dear retorts, "Soja and Harvey squander the insights from different voices and alternative subjectivities" (p. 549).

The challenge posed by critical postmodern urbanism may well be to work from within those "alternative subjectivities" so ruthlessly produced in the space-time configurations of cities. As the 1965 Watts rebellion signaled the end of modernist urbanism, the South Central Los Angeles uprising of 1992 must surely typify the crisis of postmodern urbanism—both as a practice and as an intellectual concept. The "urban problems"—poverty, crime, violence, family disorganization (or reorganization), class, race and ethnic conflict, juvenile delinquency, gender hierarchies and sexual exploitation—that first animated the discourse of modernity in the 1890s continue to worsen. If a "L.A. School" is to emerge from the crisis of the postmodern paradigm, then it, like the Chicago School, must have something to offer in the way of solutions.

PHILIP J. ETHINGTON

FURTHER READING
Manuel Castells, "Theory and Ideology in Urban Sociology," in C. G. Pickvance, ed., *Urban Sociology: Critical Essays* (New York: St. Martin's, 1976).
Mike Davis, *City of Quartz: Excavating the Future in Los Angeles* (London: Verso, 1990).
Michael Dear, "The Premature Demise of Postmodern Urbanism," *Cultural Anthropology* 6 (Nov. 1991): 538–52.
David Harvey, *Social Justice and the City* (Baltimore: Johns Hopkins University Press, 1973).
——, *Consciousness and the Urban Experience* (Baltimore: Johns Hopkins University Press, 1985).
——, *The Condition of Postmodernity: an Enquiry into the Origins of Cultural Change* (Oxford: Blackwell, 1989).
Dolores Hayden, *The Grand Domestic Revolution: a History of Feminist Designs for American Homes, Neighborhoods, and Cities* (Cambridge: MIT Press, 1981).
Lewis Mumford, *The City in History: Its Origins, Its Transformations, and its Prospects* (New York: Harcourt, Brace, 1961).
Edward W. Soja, *Postmodern Geographies: the Reassertion of Space in Critical Social Theory* (London: Verso, 1989).
Louis Wirth, "Urbanism as a Way of Life," *American Journal of Sociology* 44 (1938): 1–24.

utopias "A map of the world that does not include Utopia," Oscar Wilde quipped, "is not worth even glancing at." A history of American thought without discussion of utopia would be similarly useless. To envision an ideal world that is nowhere (*outopia*, from the Greek *ou*, expressing a negative, plus the Greek *topos*, for place) but also somewhere good (*eutopia*, from the Greek *eu*, expressing perfection) and perhaps even attainable, is the essence of the utopian project. Its distinguished genealogy in Western thought recedes beyond *Utopia*, Sir Thomas More's fantasy/satire of 1516 that gave the literary genre its name, to ancient tales of a Golden Age, Greek theories of ideal republics, and Christian visions of the Second Coming. Yet it is no accident that More's traveler's tale followed the Columbian encounter. (*See also* INDIAN–WHITE RELATIONS.) Anxious Europeans imposed myriad utopian dreams upon the New World:

the Garden of Eden; the laboratory for rational, progressive civilization; the home for natural, beloved community; the haven for watchers of the millennium. The very name "America," increasingly fastened specifically upon the United States, became a trope for utopian longings, a connection strengthened by a history of "invented" nationhood, democratic politics, economic and geographic expansionism, and massive immigration.

Whatever metaphor American utopian thought uses—the garden, the machine, the community, the millennium—it has been animated by a unique sense of possibility. Applying a broad definition of utopia, the history of the United States ever since the Puritan "city on a hill" can be described as a contest of utopian ideas and experiments, each claiming a unique ability to realize, reform, criticize, or supplant the one big utopia: America itelf.

Scholars first catalogued American literary and experimental utopias in the 1940s. After World War II the "myth-and-symbol" approach and pervasive AMERICAN EXCEPTIONALISM of the American Studies movement made the utopia/America connection a focal point. Finally, research into specific utopian ideas and movements has accelerated since the social and intellectual ferment of the 1960s. As yet, however, there is no comprehensive history of the subject.

When that history is written, it will have to trace the ebb and flow of American interest in utopia as well as its changing forms of expression. Above the near-constant hum of utopian nationalism, the distinctive but more intermittent voices of utopian social theories, communal experiments, literary utopias and anti-utopias, sometimes arising simultaneously and often echoing one another, have demanded a hearing. Their collective strength correlates roughly with troughs in long-term waves of the economy and with recurrent religious "awakenings." Meanwhile, trends in ideology, social organization, technology, and government have conspired to make certain utopian forms emblematic of their eras.

The years from 1820 to 1880 saw widespread communal experimentation by millenarian sects such as the Shakers, Rappites, Mormons, and Oneidans, or by utopian socialists such as the Owenites and Fourierists. Many were convinced that successful small pilot communities would redirect American development along cooperative lines. But the loose communal movement faded when the individual experiments either collapsed or conformed, the Civil War entrenched individualist capitalism as the American way, and urban-industrial development outmoded ideal villages.

Utopian colonization persisted and would resurface in changed form in New Deal resettlement programs and the communes of the 1960s; but after 1880 socialist theory and technological invention privileged evolutionary, industrialized, and statist models. These found their most appropriate venue in the literary utopia, especially the phenomenally popular *Looking Backward* (1888) by EDWARD BELLAMY, whose vision of Boston in the year 2000 evoked scores of novelistic responses, and whose Nationalist program influenced Socialist Party platforms, Progressive urban planners, and New Deal agencies such as the TVA.

But the socialist/technological utopia gave rise to its own critique. In the twentieth century the dystopia or anti-utopia, prefigured in Mark Twain's *Connecticut Yankee in King Arthur's Court* (1889), split off as a subgenre and dominated public debate. In the context of conformist commercialism, alienating bureaucracy, technological warfare, and especially the development of fascism and communism into totalitarian regimes, Bellamy's state as "The Great Trust" came to resemble the "Big Brother" of George Orwell's *Nineteen Eighty-Four* (1949). Refugee intellectuals such as Karl Popper defined utopia as a collectivist blueprint whose false rationalism led inevitably to dictatorships and concentration camps. By mid-century there were indications that the United States itself had evolved into an anti-utopia, a grotesque emblem of MASS CULTURE, inequality, commercialism, and imperialism. Ugly details of modern America surfaced in Aldous Huxley's *Brave New World* (1932) and formed the backdrop of countercultural critiques by PAUL GOODMAN, HERBERT MARCUSE, and Theodore Roszak.

It is not surprising, then, to find disagreement today about the fate and relevance of utopia. Conservative commentators identifying utopia with the aspirations of socialist or communist ideology point to the collapse of communist regimes to discredit the concept. Cold War predictions of the "end of ideology" have transmuted into procapitalist declarations of the "end of history," and by implication the obsolescence of utopia. In a much less celebratory mood, leftist literary and cultural historians, influenced by linguistic and poststructuralist theory, note how the inextricable binding of utopia to America has induced mass "false consciousness" and reduced would-be subversive critics to the loyal opposition. Yet there are also signs of a revival of the literary utopia as a vehicle for exploring feminist or ecological alternatives. The feminist futures envisioned by Marge Piercy and Joanna Russ revive a tradition dating to *Herland* (1915), by CHARLOTTE PERKINS GILMAN, while Ursula Le Guin's *The Dispossessed* (1974) and Ernest Callenbach's *Ecotopia* novels (1975,

1981) update William Morris's *News from Nowhere* (1890) for an era of global interdependence.

Despite twentieth-century doubts about PROGRESS and reason, as we approach the third millennium we can expect the problems of creating an equitable and satisfying postindustrial, postpatriarchal, and post-national society to engender new utopias. Whether these ecological, feminist, and multicultural blueprints will couch themselves in the traditional but by now damaged rhetoric of America's utopian destiny is far less certain.

CARL GUARNERI

FURTHER READING

Arthur Bestor, *Backwoods Utopias: the Sectarian and Owenite Phases of Communitarian Socialism in America, 1663–1829*, 2nd ed. (Philadelphia: University of Pennsylvania Press, 1970).

Carl J. Guarneri, *The Utopian Alternative: Fourierism in Nineteenth-Century America* (Ithaca: Cornell University Press, 1991).

Krishan Kumar, *Utopianism* (Minneapolis: University of Minnesota Press, 1991).

Frank E. Manuel, ed., *Utopias and Utopian Thought* (Boston: Beacon, 1966).

Iacov Oved, *Two Hundred Years of American Communes* (New Brunswick, N.J.: Transaction, 1988).

Kenneth Roemer, *The Obsolete Necessity: America in Utopian Writings, 1888–1900* (Kent, Ohio: Kent State University Press, 1977).

Lyman Tower Sargent, *British and American Utopian Literature, 1516–1985: an Annotated Chronological Bibliography* (New York: Garland, 1988).

Ernest Lee Tuveson, *Redeemer Nation: the Idea of America's Millennial Role* (Chicago: University of Chicago Press, 1968).

V

Veblen, Thorstein (b. Manitowoc County, Wis., July 30, 1857; d. Palo Alto, Calif., Aug. 3, 1929). Born on the Wisconsin frontier to Norwegian parents, Veblen was educated at Carleton College under the marginalist economist JOHN BATES CLARK and at Yale under the laissez-faire sociologist WILLIAM GRAHAM SUMNER. This sober background did little to restrain his eccentric personal deportment or his iconoclastic teachings, both of which prevented him from holding academic posts for very long. Dismissed from Chicago, Stanford, Harvard, and Missouri, he ended his days unemployed and living alone in a mountain cabin outside Palo Alto. A turgid and often obscure writer, Veblen made his most significant contribution to American social thought by recasting economics as the cultural history of material life. Central to his opposition to the prevailing neoclassical school was his insistence that production and distribution were best understood as the result of the action of evolving institutions—which he defined as clusters of accumulated habits of thought—on the instinctual inheritance of humankind.

Veblen challenged accepted economic wisdom for both its "natural law" foundations and its hedonistic psychology. The metaphysical vestiges of orthodox thought led economists to misconstrue those features of economic life which did not meet the "normal" case. Such phenomena as strikes, lockouts, monopolies, government intervention, and prolonged economic downturns became merely "disturbing factors," inexplicable under the reigning assumptions of the discipline. Nor did he believe that a view of human nature in which economic actors were treated as passive registers of pain and pleasure could account for humanity's active urge to seek outlets for its impulses. The failure of academic economic science to regard economic activity as a cumulative process of human adaptation of means to ends, he concluded in "Why Is Economics Not an Evolutionary Science?" (1898), reduced it to a taxonomic and uncritical pursuit.

Veblen's desire to forge a critical economics was apparent in his best-known book, *The Theory of the Leisure Class* (1899). Usually interpreted as a fierce satire of contemporary mores, a characterization Veblen always rejected, the book actually traced the continued importance in modern economic life of waste—the expenditure of energy that "does not serve human life or human well-being on the whole" (pp. 96–7). During the first stage of civilization ("savagery"), human survival required everyone to work. In the succeeding "barbarian" stage, however, the existence of a surplus allowed a class of men to exempt themselves from actual production and to live off their ability to compel others, particularly women and captives, to toil. This leisure class solidified its status by flaunting signs of its avoidance of WORK—first through such nonproductive behaviors as war and sports and subsequently by ostentatious display of accumulated and wasteful wealth. Although industrial civilization deemphasized the physical prowess venerated in the barbarian period, it continued to disdain labor as irksome and to honor "conspicuous consumption." Industrial society converted the natural human desire to emulate into "invidious" comparison; in meticulous analyses Veblen demonstrated that the norms of conspicuous consumption ("canons of pecuniary repute") infiltrated moral and aesthetic standards, the organization of "devout observances," the "higher learning," and amusements.

Although later critics have faulted Veblen for his reduction of culture to socially validated waste, for his reliance on a narrow, anti-aesthetic standard of usefulness, for his embrace of a now outdated anthropology of racial traits, and for his failure to acknowledge that all consumption was invariably conspicuous (since it takes place under the gaze of others), *The Theory of the Leisure Class* was pathbreaking in its challenge to conventional doctrine. Where turn-of-the-century LIBERALISM celebrated modern life for replacing relations of status with those of contract, Veblen insisted on the persistence of status as a barbarian inheritance. Against the blithely innocent belief that social evolution was the inevitable achievement of peaceful interdependence, he perceived the continuation of force, conflict, and the exercise of power. In place of the fables of neoclassicism in which the distribution of the social product proceeded frictionlessly according to each person's imputed contribution to the production process, Veblen discerned underlying manipulation and coercion. To those economists and theologians who held that labor was naturally unfulfilling, Veblen responded that it was existing institutions that had decreed it so.

In his subsequent work Veblen elaborated his

contention that modern institutions distorted the beneficial instincts of "workmanship," "idle curiosity," and "the parental bent," those "savage" traits which directed humans toward purposive and cooperative activity. At the heart of his arguments in *The Theory of Business Enterprise* (1904), *The Instinct of Workmanship* (1914), and *Engineers and the Price System* (1921) was his famous distinction between "industry"—production that aimed at the satisfaction of needs—and "business"—the maximization of pecuniary values through manipulation of markets, restricted production, and capitalization on expected income. The conflict between the instinctual direction of "industry" and the institutional imperatives of "business" unfailingly eroded the former, he contended. As humans lost touch with their instinctual endowment, such "anthropomorphistic" beliefs as property rights, in which objects were credited with humanlike powers, attained hegemony, ushering in a regime of conservatism, deference, egotism, and "sabotage" (the conscientious refusal to produce efficiently).

Although convinced that humans would always be creatures of habit whose capacity to make sense of events lagged behind actual conditions, Veblen nonetheless foresaw possibilities for the overturn of industrial society. By inculcating an understanding of the material and impersonal laws of causation, "machine discipline" could reveal the anthropomorphistic myths of the leisure class and empower the united actions of "engineers"—an amorphous group characterized by dedication to productivity, not profits—to seize power from the "vested" interests. He also applauded the nascent feminist movement, which renounced women's role as nonproductive trophies of status. Although Veblen's celebration of engineers as disinterested production specialists had technocratic implications, he himself never thought the solution to social problems was the mere application of impartial, specialized knowledge. He never believed that a perfect fit between a machine order and those instincts best suited to human needs could be fashioned. This caution and the critical urge that animated his entire undertaking disappeared in the institutional economics of the 1930s, which laid claim to his legacy. Reduced by many of his erstwhile followers to a neutral chronicler of the business cycle, Veblen was made over into an advocate for a MANAGERIALISM based on the power of government to discipline the market. Shorn of his radicalism and noted primarily for his technical work on the business cycle, Veblen as an intellectual force became by the middle third of the twentieth century what in his own lifetime he had been as a personality: a curiosity.

DANIEL H. BORUS

FURTHER READING

Theodor Adorno, "Veblen's Attack on Culture," in *Prisms* (1941; Cambridge: Harvard University Press, 1981).
John Diggins, *The Bard of Savagery: Thorstein Veblen and Modern Social Theory* (New York: Seabury, 1978).
Joseph Dorfman, *Thorstein Veblen and His America* (New York: Viking, 1934).
Murray G. Murphey, "Introduction," in Veblen, *The Instinct of Workmanship and the State of the Industrial Arts* (1914; New Brunswick, N.J.: Transaction, 1990).
David Riesman, *Thorstein Veblen: a Critical Interpretation* (New York: Charles Scribner's Sons, 1953).
Cynthia Russett, *Darwin in America: The Intellectual Response, 1865–1912* (San Francisco: W. H. Freeman, 1976).
Thorstein Veblen, *The Theory of the Leisure Class* (1899; New York: Penguin, 1979).

Victorianism Monarch of Great Britain for much of the nineteenth century (1837–1901), Queen Victoria had her name appropriated as a general designation for the times through which she lived. By the 1920s, the term had evolved from its benign origins into a pejorative: "Victorian" came to refer to visual ugliness, emotional repression, religious hypocrisy, and the imperialism of a self-satisfied middle class. A key manifesto was *Eminent Victorians* (1918) by the English writer Lytton Strachey. By mid-century in both Britain and America, this representation of Victorianism had spread into popular culture from the avant-garde circles in which it originated. In doing so the term shed most of its specificity, turning instead into a generalized reference to prudery, "old-fashioned" values, and the censorship of culture.

In one of those reversals that so often occur, scholars after World War II began to rethink the standard dismissive approach to Victorianism; an important vehicle for this reappraisal has been the journal *Victorian Studies* (1957–). In the arts a growing revulsion against twentieth-century modernist aesthetics manifested itself in the founding of the Victorian Society (1966 in Great Britain; 1968 in the United States), dedicated to preserving what remained of nineteenth-century architecture and decorative arts. The term Victorian has thus taken on an indeterminacy of meaning and reference: someone who cherishes Victorian-era furniture may also practice a lifestyle contemptuous of "Victorian" values.

In America Victorianism has had less currency in CULTURAL CRITICISM—the discourse about culture, democracy, and nationalism—than in Britain. An alternative phrase, "the Genteel Tradition," became current after GEORGE SANTAYANA coined it in 1910; though never defined with any precision, it may be understood as a moral idealism that became detached from the "practical" or "material" world of everyday life. The term "Puritanism," understood by H. L.

MENCKEN and others as a philistine fear of the beautiful, overlapped with "the Genteel Tradition" in the usage of intellectuals eager to distance themselves from the decorous rigidities they perceived in the past. In *America's Coming-of-Age* (1915), VAN WYCK BROOKS lamented the division in American culture between "high ideals" and "catch-penny realities," and in *The Ordeal of Mark Twain* (1920) he described Twain's blighted career as a product of that fatefully fragmented culture (*see also* MARK TWAIN).

The American reaction against Victorianism (or "the Genteel Tradition") fed on several sources. Some of the early popularizers of Sigmund Freud's ideas turned them into a critique of "repression," attributed in part to Victorian attitudes toward sexuality. MODERNISM in the arts and literature repudiated two crucial tenets of Western culture, the mimetic (representational) function of the arts and literature, and the relationship between the arts and moral or philosophical teaching; in turning against these age-old ideas, the modernists turned most harshly against the writers and artists who immediately preceded them—for example, the novelist WILLIAM DEAN HOWELLS, the "Schoolroom Poets," and Beaux Arts architecture. The crisis of capitalism in the 1930s prompted a critique of the social and economic philosophies of INDIVIDUALISM and "laissez-faire," or LIBERALISM in the nineteenth-century sense of the term. Progressives rejected this Victorian liberalism in favor of social DEMOCRACY and the welfare state; poverty thus passed from being understood as the penalty for insufficient self-control to being perceived as a consequence of "social" or environmental conditions for which individuals bore no RESPONSIBILITY and which the state should remedy.

These several critiques retained their force well past mid-century. Meanwhile, however, the nineteenth century was beginning to be reappraised. A key statement was that of the American literary historian Walter Houghton with his book *The Victorian Frame of Mind* (1957), which construed British Victorianism as composed of contradictory strands (for example, "dogmatism" *and* "the critical spirit"). Houghton recovered the deep strain of "anxiety" that ran like a dark thread through the "optimism" of the period, and pictured the Victorians as affirming the possibility of moral heroism in the face of uncertainty. In so doing he turned the movement into a precursor of the modern situation; the present became an extension of the past, not a repudiation of it.

From another direction came an intriguing reconsideration of the word "culture." The great English critic Matthew Arnold had propounded "culture" as the antithesis of and remedy for the ills of his own century (*Culture and Anarchy*). Arnold had not been spared by the modernists, and the word he so admired became at times a synonym for snobbery. But the English socialist literary critic Raymond Williams demonstrated in *Culture and Society* (1958) that nineteenth-century British critics of advancing INDUSTRIALISM (including its alienating consequences for workers) had used the word "culture" to convey their vision of an organic society in which work was creative and cooperative. His sympathetic interpretation of culture and its leading advocates (Arnold, Thomas Carlyle, John Ruskin) culminated in a portrait of William Morris, who transformed the ideal of culture into the politics of SOCIALISM and the aesthetics of the Arts and Crafts movement.

Other spurs to revision of Victorianism included a reexamination of the history of modernist aesthetics and of women's experience in the nineteenth century. The American architectural historians Henry Russell Hitchcock and Vincent Scully performed for modernist architecture an analysis parallel to Walter Houghton's, locating its roots in such nineteenth-century figures as H. H. RICHARDSON and in movements like the "Shingle Style." But the evident exhaustion of Modernist aesthetics also opened the way in the 1970s for a revival in ARCHITECTURE and the decorative arts of once despised materials, colors, and forms; art museums began again to exhibit furniture, paintings, and sculpture that modernists had rejected—in particular, objects produced by the Arts and Crafts movement. A rethinking of Protestant moralism and of the "cult of domesticity" emerged from women's history, which proposed that Victorian evangelical Protestantism was not a stuffy other-worldliness but a source of power for middle-class women. (*See also* DOMESTICITY.) It led them out of the home into voluntary "reform," and thus gave them a crucial role to play in redeeming the nation.

Victorianism continues to mobilize defenders and detractors, in ways that defy simple ideological categorization. Many conservatives find Victorianism admirable, as in historian Gertrude Himmelfarb's praise for its no-nonsense approach to poverty. Many liberals and radicals, especially literary scholars, find the influence of Victorianism to be pernicious, since in their view the literary "canon" that we inherit from the Victorians legitimizes unacceptable forms of domination. But many feminists and liberals find themselves drawn to the Victorian sensibility, just as many conservatives embrace modernism as their aesthetic faith.

Situated amid these conflicting valences, Victorianism continues to generate powerful responses in those who try to identify and explain the central trends of the last century of American cultural history.

DAVID D. HALL

FURTHER READING

Henry Russell Hitchcock, *The Architecture of H. H. Richardson and his Times* (New York; Museum of Modern Art, 1936).

Daniel Walker Howe, ed., *Victorian America* (Philadelphia: University of Pennsylvania Press, 1975).

Walter Houghton, *The Victorian Frame of Mind, 1830–1870* (New Haven: Yale University Press, 1957).

H. L. Mencken, *A Book of Prefaces* (New York: Knopf, 1917).

Vincent J. Scully Jr., *The Shingle Style: Architectural Theory and Design from Richardson to the Origins of Wright* (New Haven: Yale University Press, 1955).

Lytton Strachey, *Eminent Victorians* (New York: Garden City Publishing, 1918).

Raymond Williams, *Culture and Society, 1780–1950* (New York: Columbia University Press, 1958).

Vietnam For most Americans, Vietnam is the site of the event now listed in libraries as "Vietnamese Conflict, 1961–1975." For many of those who went there, it became a particular nightmare. "'Quakin' and shakin',' they called it, great balls of fire, Contact." So Michael Herr described what he saw as the first actual rock'n'roll war. "There was such a dense concentration of American energy there," he wrote, "American and essentially adolescent, if that energy could have been channeled into anything more than noise, waste and pain it would have lighted up Indochina for a thousand years." "Vietnam," he said, "was where all the mythic tracks intersected": "some unnatural East–West interface, a California corridor cut and bought and burned deep into Asia, and once we'd done it we couldn't remember what for" (pp. 20, 43–4, 63).

For policy-makers at the time, Vietnam was, in William Gibson's words, "the perfect war," technowar: rigorous strategic analysis married to a myth of military invincibility. For many of them it became what Neil Sheehan has called "a bright shining lie": a ten-year binge of true believing, promise after promise of imminent victory masking the bankrupt assumption that an American-supported regime could win the hearts and minds of the Vietnamese.

Americans at home became veterans of the first television war. The actuality of Vietnam merged with the six o'clock news, and thus conflated, in Jean Baudrillard's observation, "the physical bombardment of the enemy" with "the electronic bombardment of the rest of the world" (p. 49). Meanwhile, out in the streets, the country was at war with itself. The March on the Pentagon; the Siege of Chicago; the Moratorium; among young activists, especially,

the stakes mounted, blows against the empire. Reaction became increasingly surreal. President Johnson's administration came tumbling down and then Nixon's. Suddenly, it was 1975; and again, television captured it all. On screens across the country, the last evacuation helicopters lifted off from Saigon, and it was over. The United States of America, for the first time in history, had lost a war.

Understandably, most Americans have now tried to relegate Vietnam to history. Yet the living pain of 58,000 Americans dead and probably more than 2 million Vietnamese killed and wounded lingers as a central fact of the national experience. Americans may think that they have made Vietnam history. In fact, in one sense it has made them part of the general flow of history. For this generation of Americans Vietnam will long remain the geopolitical equivalent of the Fall, the end of national chosenness. What Vietnam made history was the myth of American historical innocence.

At present, America still struggles to heal itself. Vietnam veterans have gone from being pariahs to victims and then onward to something like heroes. Ten years after the Vietnam Wall brought recognition for the sacrifice of Americans who died in Vietnam, that memorial remains the most visited site in the nation's capital. Relations between Communist but increasingly capitalist Vietnam and the American government have warmed considerably. President Bush's attempt to use Vietnam in his campaign against President Clinton got nowhere, despite Clinton's evident discomfort with conflicting reports of his own draft history. Perhaps this is because Clinton stands for a liberalism of the center, one that has abandoned the previous liberal cry of "no more Vietnams" and joined conservatives in calling for an end to "the Vietnam syndrome." In national politics, 1992 may indeed mark the moment when Vietnam passed into history.

In literature and film, the attempt to make sense of Vietnam continues in a steady stream of novels, poems, plays, memoirs, works of documentary and journalism, a landmark PBS television history, and Hollywood productions without number. Pulitzer Prize and National Book Award winners include Frances Fitzgerald's *Fire in the Lake*, Neil Sheehan's *A Bright Shining Lie*, Gloria Emerson's *Winners and Losers*, Robert Stone's *Dog Soldiers*, Michael Herr's *Dispatches*, Tim O'Brien's *Going After Cacciato*, and Larry Heinemann's *Paco's Story*. Provocative memoirs extend from Philip Caputo's *A Rumor of War* and Ron Kovic's *Born on the Fourth of July* to Lewis B. Puller's *Fortunate Son*. Other major works—David Rabe's *Sticks and Bones*, C. D. B

Bryan's *Friendly Fire*, Bobbie Ann Mason's *In-Country*—register with deep understanding the impact of the war at home, not only upon men and women of the Vietnam generation, but upon their parents and children. Oral accountings in Wallace Terry's *Bloods* and poems by Yusef Komunyakaa measure the special price levied upon black Americans in Vietnam. Along with representations of Vietnamese life and consciousness by writers fluent in the language such as the poet John Balaban and the novelist Robert Olen Butler, immigrant Vietnamese Americans have now begun to tell their own stories in works such as Le Ly Hayslip's *When Heaven and Earth Changed Places*.

Vietnam enters contemporary cultural debates over other issues as well. In gender studies, for example, Susan Jeffords has seen in Vietnam literature and film a "remasculinization" of American life. She finds it necessary to contend not only with cartoon fantasies such as *Rambo* or *Missing in Action*, but also with realistic works such as *Platoon* or *Full Metal Jacket* that still, however innovative in film technique, use representations of Vietnam to reaffirm traditional codes of maleness. In another area, the rise of "post-traumatic stress syndrome" as a psychological category of growing significance stems from the experience of Vietnam veterans, and contributes to a major cultural debate over the rights of victims of all sorts of adversity and abuse. Vietnam may recede from the arena of national politics, but its cultural weight will be felt far longer, since as Michael Herr put it in the last line of *Dispatches*, "Vietnam, Vietnam, Vietnam, we're all been there."

PHILIP D. BEIDLER

See also IMPERIALISM AND ANTI-IMPERIALISM; NEW LEFT.

FURTHER READING

John Balaban, ed. and tr., *Ca Dao Vietnam* (Greensboro, N.C.: Unicorn, 1980).

Jean Baudrillard, *America*, trans. Chris Turner (New York: Verso, 1988).

Robert Olen Butler, *A Good Scent from a Strange Mountain* (New York: Henry Holt, 1992).

James William Gibson, *The Perfect War* (Boston: Atlantic Monthly Press, 1986).

Michael Herr, *Dispatches* (New York: Knopf, 1977).

Susan Jeffords, *The Remasculinization of America* (Bloomington: Indiana University Press, 1989).

Stanley Karnow, *Vietnam: a History* (New York: Viking, 1991).

Neil Sheehan, *A Bright Shining Lie* (New York: Random House, 1988).

virtue Today's connotation of virtue as female sexual propriety and vague do-goodery represents a crucial shift in usage. Virtue traditionally was a central political term, associated with masculinity and the public sphere; its depoliticization and its transformation from masculine to feminine highlights the role of GENDER in policing the boundaries of politics. Until well into the nineteenth century, virtue also played a major role in the American religious tradition. This essay follows a different trajectory of the term, for historians in the past 30 years have focused less on virtue in the context of religion *per se* than on the complex interaction of gender, religion, and political discourse.

The most fully developed newer usage plots virtue's role in the tradition of REPUBLICANISM. Republican virtue connoted the ability to act with integrity, rooted in independence. "Dependence begets subservience," noted Thomas Jefferson; subservience precluded men's ability to devote themselves to the pursuit of the public good, which the survival of a republic required. Thus virtue held the key to avoiding a descent into tyranny. A republic peopled by virtuous citizens would sustain itself over time, so the challenge was to ensure the virtue of the citizenry.

The strategies that emerged can be schematized into two alternatives. The elitist strain of republicanism proposed to assure the virtue of the voters by limiting the franchise to the virtuous, that is, those with sufficient property to free them from subservience and allow them to pursue the common good. The late eighteenth- and early nineteenth-century restrictions limiting the franchise to propertied white males reflected this strain of republican theory. Although the position that government should be limited to a few good men had left the mainstream of American thought by the mid-nineteenth century, a softer version—that government office should be held only by men of education and standing—retained considerable force into the twentieth century.

The alternative way to assure the voters' virtue was to distribute property so widely that all white males would attain sufficient independence to allow them to pursue the public good. This egalitarian strain fueled Jacksonian Democracy, in which context "virtue" played a less prominent role than its opposite, the "corruption" of would-be aristocrats who sought government favors.

In the revolutionary era, Ruth Bloch has noted, virtue stood at the center not only of republicanism but of religion. Nonconforming Protestantism emphasized the value of public virtue in prompting otherwise selfish individuals to act for the public good. In this tradition, virtue stemmed not from ownership of property but from one's relationship with God. Political virtue in the Christian tradition was primarily a trait of good rulers, who tended the political order with God's help.

Both the republican and Protestant traditions associated public virtue with MASCULINITY. Women could exercise the private virtues such as PIETY, prudence, temperance, and charity. But public virtue—the active pursuit of the public good—was intertwined with notions of manhood. Christianity's embrace of the mandates of wifely submission and womanly modesty precluded women from participation in the public sphere. Republican virtue's association with masculinity reflected both the Homeric notion of *aretê* (translated as virtue), which stressed physical strength and bravery, and Greek and Roman ideas about the intellectual virtues of CITIZENSHIP. Hanna Pitkin has shown that the association of virtue and manhood continued in the Renaissance, when virtue was set off against fickle *fortuna*, whose feminine unpredictability threatened to sabotage the efforts of virtuous men.

As of 1770, public virtue was understood as clearly masculine. A century later, virtue was firmly associated with FEMININITY. The transformation was both gradual and complex. As early as the 1780s, women had forged for themselves a role in the creation of public virtue. They argued that women needed education so they could play their unique role in preserving the republic by training their sons in the virtues necessary for citizenship. Yet theirs was an auxiliary role; republican virtue remained the province of men. Its association with femininity emerged between 1780 and 1830, with the emergence of the ideology of DOMESTICITY.

Domesticity is best described by comparing it with the gender ideology that preceded it, in which the submission of women to men was viewed as one of a series of hierarchies in the "great chain of being"— of animals to humans, lower to upper classes, children to parents, servants to masters, etc. Hierarchy was part of the natural order of things, and the submission of women to men reflected both God's will and men's greater strength. Women were viewed not only as physically weaker than men; they were also intellectually inferior, and morally weaker, more subject to the temptations of both the flesh and the spirit.

By the mid-nineteenth century, this traditional approach to gender was considered inconsistent with a commitment to equality. Though some (notably the Grimké sisters in the 1830s) argued that women's equality required truly egalitarian arrangements, this remained largely a marginalized, "radical" position until well into the twentieth century. More common was the claim that the sexes "naturally" belonged in separate (but presumably equal) spheres: men in the public spheres of economics and politics, women in the domestic sphere of the home.

The "naturalness" of this allocation rested on a redescription of men and women. The traditional understanding of women as the "weaker vessel" was replaced by a new understanding of virtuous women as the moral superiors of men. MOTHERHOOD became the defining female role, and a focus on motherly nurture replaced the earlier focus on the paternal role in child-rearing. Moreover, the self-sacrifice traditionally demanded of all virtuous Christians (and all virtuous citizens as well) was increasingly redefined as an inherent female quality.

Men, too, found their roles redefined by domesticity. The traditional exhortation to Christian selflessness gradually eroded, and the rival notion emerged that society worked best if men pursued their own self-interest. Although self-interest had long played an important role in liberal thought, before the nineteenth-century liberal thinkers tended to assume that self-interest would be pursued within the bounds of duty as defined by religion, republicanism, and other traditions. Domesticity siphoned off notions of duty that had limited the permissible scope of self-interest in the thought of John Locke and others. By allocating selflessness to women, domesticity helped legitimate self-interest as the appropriate motivation for men. Thus domesticity played an important role in what James Kloppenberg has called the flattening of liberalism into possessive individualism by the second half of the nineteenth century.

The re-gendering of virtue can be interpreted as part of an attempt to purge virtue from its traditional location in the public sphere and confine it to a private, domestic sphere outside public life. This development left a newly reconfigured economic sphere where self-interest reigned supreme. The relation of politics to virtue became ambiguous; yet virtue increasingly seemed "naturally" to belong to the domestic province of women. The strongest version of this story suggests that gender effectively policed virtue out of the public sphere, and relegated it to the realm of female sexual propriety.

Yet the success of domesticity in banishing the "virtues of liberalism" was partial at best. An alternative story emerges if we divide domesticity into two strands: one compensatory, and one public. Compensatory domesticity viewed women's role as providing a haven from a heartless "bank note" world, a realm of noncommodified nurturance to provide solace after men's daily struggles in the competitive marketplace or alienating workplace. This conservative version of domesticity emerges today in the antifeminist insistence that women must maintain traditional roles to protect (liberal, selfish, competitive) society from itself. An alternative strand of domesticity, whose adherents ranged from Catharine Beecher to female moral reformers and Progressive activists, used domesticity's description of women to forge new professional and political roles for women, and to preserve the selfless pursuit of the common good as a continuing strand in American political life.

Kathryn Kish Sklar's studies of CATHARINE BEECHER and FLORENCE KELLEY examine this alternative strand. Beecher, operating within an evangelical frame of reference, invoked domesticity's paeans to women's virtue to claim for women the leading cultural role traditionally played by ministers. Whereas the compensatory version of domesticity, by allocating virtue to women in the domestic sphere, helped enshrine self-interest at the center of public life, female reformers argued that women's higher morality required them to enter the public sphere for the good of the nation.

One concrete result was the capture of teaching and social work as professions suitable for women, yet the impulse to use domesticity's feminization of virtue to forge new public roles for women ultimately reached much further. Women used the notion of their higher morality to launch an "era of association" that included temperance, abolitionism, and female moral reform. These movements, often derided in ways characteristic of the devaluation of women, used women's claim to virtue as an entrée into the political sphere during an era when women still lacked the vote and other political rights. De Tocqueville's comments on the prevalence and influence of voluntary associations in American life dramatize women's success in using domesticity to gain a central public role, despite their exclusion from institutional power in politics and religion.

The activist strain of domesticity ultimately merged with other currents into PROGRESSIVISM. The influence of Progressivism shows the limitations of interpreting domesticity as eliminating virtue from the public sphere. Progressivism challenged the flattened liberalism of the late nineteenth century by presenting a language that drew on religious and republican sources to insist that values other than self-interest were required in public life. When the Progressives began their sustained attempt to inject virtue back into politics, however, they faced a tradition that strongly associated virtue with womanliness, and with female sexual propriety in particular. "Virtue" as a keyword remained in its marginalized feminine domain; the Progressives argued instead that the

pursuit of self-interest had to be tempered with a selfless pursuit of "the public interest." The virile, scientized "public interest" rescued virtue from its marginalized feminine domain, and reinjected the "virtues of liberalism" into public life.

Even today, "public interest" law firms and groups represent consumer and environmental positions and defend civil rights and civil liberties. Yet these claims to represent the interest of the broad public have been hotly contested since the 1980s. Conservatives have sought to undermine these liberal overtures in two ways. First, they have insisted that liberals represent not the "public interest" but "special interests," thus challenging the progressive notion of an objectively known good. Conservatives also have claimed that they themselves represent the "public interest," notably in new "public interest" law firms that represent corporate and business interests. A notable example is the Pacific Legal Foundation, which has played a central role in constructing a vigorous challenge to governmental regulation in the name of property rights.

So successfully have conservatives undermined the progressive rhetoric of "the public interest" that Americans arguably lack a persuasive language in which to speak of the common good. For that reason communitarians such as Robert Bellah, William Galston, and Amitai Etzioni have returned to the older language of virtue, seeking to resuscitate both the traditional linkage of virtue and the common good and the nineteenth-century linkage of virtue with bourgeois family life.

JOAN WILLIAMS

FURTHER READING

Paula Baker, "The Domestication of Politics: Women and American Political Society, 1780–1920," *American Historical Review* 89 (June 1984): 620–47.

Ruth H. Bloch, "The Gendered Meanings of Virtue in Revolutionary America," *Signs: Journal of Women in Culture and Society* 13 (autumn 1987): 38–58.

Nancy F. Cott, *The Bonds of Womanhood: "Woman's Sphere" in New England, 1780–1835* (New Haven: Yale University Press, 1977).

Linda K. Kerber, *Women of the Republic: Intellect and Ideology in Revolutionary America* (Chapel Hill: University of North Carolina Press, 1980).

James T. Kloppenberg, "The Virtues of Liberalism: Christianity, Republicanism, and Ethics in Early American Political Discourse," *Journal of American History* 74 (1987): 9–33.

Mary P. Ryan, *Cradle of the Middle Class: the Family in Oneida County, New York, 1790–1865* (New York: Cambridge University Press, 1981).

Kathryn Kish Sklar, *Catharine Beecher* (New Haven: Yale University Press, 1973).

——, *Florence Kelley and Women's Political Culture: "Doing*

the Nation's Work," 1830–1900 (New Haven: Yale University Press, 1994).

Laurel Thatcher Ulrich, "Virtuous Women Found: New England Ministerial Literature, 1668–1735," *American Quarterly* 28 (spring 1976): 20–40.

Joan Williams, "Virtue and Oppression," *Nomos* 34, ed. John Chapman and William Galston (1992).

Voegelin, Eric (b. Cologne, Germany, Jan. 3, 1901; d. Stanford, Calif., Jan. 19, 1985).   Political philosopher. Ideological movements, Voegelin argued, reflect a psychological and spiritual disorder endemic to the human condition. Painfully aware of the imperfection of earthly life, people are tempted to escape that condition by seeking either release from this world into a transcendent realm, or a transformation of this world into a heaven on earth. Either course is a dangerous oversimplification of the human prospect; each produces a totalizing ideology. Acceptance of the inherent tension between human limits and human transcendence can lead to an authentic humanity. Voegelin's writings include *The New Science of Politics* (1952), *Science, Politics, and Gnosticism (1968)*, and *Order and History* (5 vols., 1956–87).

FURTHER READING

Ellis Sandoz, *The Voegelinian Revolution: a Biographical Introduction* (Baton Rouge: Louisiana State University Press, 1981).

W

Walker, David (b. Wilmington, N.C., Sept. 28, 1785; d. Boston, Mass., June 28, 1830). One of the earliest and most militant voices among black abolitionists, David Walker was born a free black. His early life is obscure. His father was a slave and may have died before David was born; his mother was free. Walker acquired books, read extensively, attended camp meetings, and became intensely religious in the Christian millennial and evangelical manner. By his own testimony he traveled widely throughout the South before moving to Boston during the mid-1820s. Walker had witnessed many of the ravages of slavery and experienced the bitter and anomalous life of a free black in antebellum America. By 1827 Walker operated a small clothing shop near the wharves in Boston, and by 1828 he was an agent and an occasional writer for the first black weekly newspaper, *Freedom's Journal*. During 1829–30, Walker published three editions of his 78-page *Appeal to the Coloured Citizens of the World, but in particular, and very expressly, to those of The United States of America*.

The *Appeal* quickly became the most notorious document in American abolitionist literature to that date. Walker's pamphlet was an impassioned indictment of slavery, slaveholders, and all those, black and white, whom he deemed complicitous with slavery. It was a cry of outrage against black ignorance, Christian hypocrisy, colonization schemes, and the contradictions embedded in the coexistence of racism, human bondage, and American Republican-ism. Walker challenged blacks, slave and free, to seize control of their own lives, develop their own leadership, and shoulder the burden of their own liberation at a time when slavery was expanding in unprecedented fashion. He shocked most Americans who read his pamphlet by appealing directly to the slaves to rise up, rebel, and overthrow slavery by force. Walker's *Appeal* is widely regarded, therefore, as a founding text of black nationalist thought in America.

But the *Appeal* must also be viewed as a product of the Second Great Awakening, of the jeremiadic tradition, and of a pivotal moment in the history of American abolitionism. Under the influence of evangelical religion, and especially of the campaign to end slavery in the British empire, American abolitionists steadily radicalized their tactics in the late 1820s and early 1830s. Abolitionists' increasing awareness of an intransigent southern defense of slavery caused gradualism to give way to "immediatism" in ANTISLAVERY thought. After 1831, when WILLIAM LLOYD GARRISON founded *The Liberator* in Boston, abolitionism became an organized crusade and slavery was attacked as individual and national "sin." Walker's *Appeal* foreshadowed and represented this radical turn in American antislavery thought.

Walker's writing burned with biblical apocalypticism, and a dark, almost deterministic fatalism. The *Appeal* is full of eschatological symbolism, of an angry God entering history and wreaking vengeance upon America for the evil of slavery. Walker's apocalyptic vision was a classic jeremiad, typical of antebellum radical reformers. He worded his claims with absolute certainty:

> Fortune and misfortune, two inseparable companions, lay rolled up in the wheel of events, which have from the creation of the world, and will continue to take place among men until God shall dash worlds together. (p. 19)

He drew his terrible warnings from the book of Revelation, and his sanctions as well as the style of his language from both the Old and New Testaments. Blacks in America were the captive "children of Jacob," and the "enlightened Christians of America" were the "heathen Pharoah" ruling over a vast "Egypt" (pp. 8–9). What set Walker's jeremiad apart in the tradition of APOCALYPTIC LITERATURE is not only its early appearance, but its fierce and violent tone, and its qualities as a black chanted sermon. "I tell you Americans!" Walker seemed to shout, "that unless you speedily alter your course, *you* and your country are gone!!!!!! For God Almighty will tear up the very face of the earth!!!" (p. 39). And in his direct call for violent resistance on the part of slaves, it was as if he was a mysterious adviser to Nat Turner, who would strike in Virginia a year later: "if you commence, make sure work—do not trifle, for they will not trifle with you . . . therefore, if there is an attempt made by us, kill or be killed" (p. 25). Such rhetoric frightened the public as nothing had before. Although prominent abolitionists such as Benjamin Lundy and Harriet Martineau disapproved of the incendiary quality of the pamphlet, Garrison reprinted major portions of it in his paper.

Walker wrote as a self-appointed protector of those blacks he thought were ignorant of their plight, and as prosecutor of those "treacherous creatures" among blacks who were "in league with tyrants" (p. 22). Such doctrinaire self-righteousness has sometimes characterized even the greatest spokesmen of black nationalism. Many echoes of David Walker can be heard in the voices of MARCUS GARVEY, ELIJAH MUHAMMED, or MALCOLM X. The cunning ethos of survival, the peasant consciousness, and the conservative habits of southern slaves, who had the most to lose in rebellions imagined by northern black intellectuals, may have constituted a worldview that Walker simply could not accommodate into his apocalyptic vision. But his sermon was one in which all blacks were called to see a central tenet of black nationalist ideology as it has developed over a century and a half: a shared sense of oppression and bonds of obligation among all peoples of African descent.

One of the most artful aspects of Walker's *Appeal* is his use of and engagement with the discussion of racial capacities by THOMAS JEFFERSON in his *Notes on the State of Virginia* (1789). Jefferson, who had died only three years before the first edition of the *Appeal* was published, provided a rich and strategic symbol of the religious and political hypocrisy that Walker wished to expose. Most importantly, Walker pointed to Jefferson's famous discussion of black slavery as a product of "nature" and not "condition" as the taproot of America's impending doom. Jefferson, and by implication, the very meaning of America, had to be confronted. "Unless we try to refute Mr. Jefferson's arguments respecting us," said Walker, "we will only establish them" (p. 15). Such were the stakes of Walker's conception of the problem of slavery in America. Hence he bitterly chastised Jefferson at the same time that he appropriated and quoted at length from the Declaration of Independence, especially concerning the principles of EQUALITY, natural RIGHTS, and the right of revolution. The deep irony was altogether self-conscious for Walker. In 1820, while considering America's future with slavery, Jefferson had said, "I tremble for my country when I reflect that God is just." Walker repeatedly echoed Jefferson in the *Appeal*, linking dark forebodings with calls to fulfill the promise of American republicanism and to heed the warning that "God is a God of justice" (p. 5). Walker's *Appeal* endures as a pivotal document in the history of race, religion, and reform in America. Students of abolitionism and of the jeremiadic tradition will find in Walker's *Appeal* many anticipations of John

Brown's later deeds and of the rhetoric of HENRY HIGHLAND GARNET and FREDERICK DOUGLASS.

Walker's pamphlet caused fear and severe legal reactions in southern states. At least four states held sessions of their legislatures in order to draft harsher "sedition" laws against such literature, and Georgia placed a significant price on Walker's head when 60 copies of the *Appeal* turned up in Savannah. One of Walker's clandestine methods for distributing his document was to sew copies into the trousers and jackets he sold to sailors destined for the South. Only a few weeks after publication of the third edition of the *Appeal* in June 1830, Walker was found dead in the doorway of his Boston shop, a victim of poison according to the most oft-repeated story.

DAVID W. BLIGHT

FURTHER READING

David Walker's Appeal to the Coloured Citizens of the World, ed. Charles M. Wiltse (New York: Hill and Wang, 1965).

Clement Eaton, "A Dangerous Pamphlet in the Old South," *Journal of Southern History* 2 (1936): 323–34.

Donald M. Jacobs, "David Walker: Boston Race Leader, 1825–1830," *Essex Institute Historical Collections* 107 (Jan. 1971): 94–107.

Leon F. Litwack, *North of Slavery: the Negro in the Free States, 1790–1860* (Chicago: University of Chicago Press, 1961).

Jane H. Pease and William H. Pease, *They Who Would Be Free: Blacks' Search for Freedom, 1830–1861* (New York: Atheneum, 1974).

Benjamin Quarles, *The Black Abolitionists* (New York: Oxford University Press, 1969).

Sterling Stuckey, *The Ideological Origins of Black Nationalism* (Boston: Beacon, 1972).

——, *Slave Culture: Nationalist Theory and the Foundations of Black America* (New York: Oxford University Press, 1987).

Walker, Francis Amasa (b. Boston, Mass., July 2, 1840; d. Boston, Mass., Jan. 5, 1897). Statistician and economist. After the Civil War Walker taught Latin and Greek before joining the U.S. Bureau of Statistics to direct the census of 1870, which he completed while serving as U.S. Commissioner of Indian Affairs. He made his mark as an economist at Yale in the 1870s. Profit is fixed by the market and wages by labor productivity, Walker argued, and their equilibrium must not be disturbed. Competition yields technological, intellectual, and moral progress. Walker also promoted international bimetallism to expand the world money supply, and pushed free trade. President of MIT from 1881 to 1897, he was the author of, among other works, *The Indian Question* (1874), *The Wages Question* (1876), *Money* (1878), and *Political Economy* (1883).

FURTHER READING

Bernard Newton, *The Economics of Francis Amasa Walker: American Economics in Transition* (New York: A. M. Kelley, 1968).

Wallace, Henry A. (b. Adair County, Iowa, Oct. 7, 1888; d. Danbury, Conn., Nov. 18, 1965). Politician, editor, agriculturist. As Secretary of Agriculture during the Depression, Vice President during World War II, and Secretary of Commerce in the early Cold War, Henry Wallace was a central figure in New Deal politics. A geneticist and farm economist of some renown, Wallace had been raised in the tradition of the western Populists and was never quite at home with the managerial style of many New Deal officials. Forced from office by Truman for voicing "Soviet sympathies," Wallace became editor of the NEW REPUBLIC, which he remade into the national organ of liberals disaffected by Truman's apostasy from internationalism and the New Deal social project. In 1947, Wallace created Progressive Citizens of America (PCA), which would subsequently evolve into the Progressive Party behind Wallace's own third-party candidacy in the Presidential election of 1948. The PCA and the Progressive Party brought together—for the last time in a generation—left-wing artists and intellectuals, social democrats, trade unionists, student radicals, and communists around an agenda of an international peace movement, civil rights, and anticapitalism: ideological positions anticipating those of American radicals during the 1960s and early 1970s. Wallace wrote many books, including *America Must Choose* (1934) and *The Century of the Common Man* (1943).

FURTHER READING

Richard John Walton, *Henry Wallace, Harry Truman, and the Cold War* (New York: Viking, 1976).

Walling, William English (b. Louisville, Ky.; Mar. 14, 1877; d. Amsterdam, Holland, Sept. 12, 1936). One of the few innovative thinkers of the American left in the early twentieth century, Walling was born into a wealthy and politically prominent Louisville family, his expensive education leading to the economics and sociology programs at the University of Chicago in the 1890s. From there he built the résumé of a prototypical Progressive Era activist: from factory safety inspector to resident at New York's University House settlement; from muckraking journalist to the editorial boards of *New Review* and *The Masses*; from race riots in the Midwest to revolutionary Russia, where he met Tolstoy and Lenin. Walling was instrumental in the foundation of both the National Women's Trade Union League and the National Association for the Advancement of Colored People, and remained active in the Socialist Party until 1917.

Once celebrated in the salons and editorial offices of the New York cultural scene in the 1910s, Walling's status suffered from the left's typically harsh judgment of his support for American involvement in WORLD WAR I, and his early, very vocal anti-Bolshevism. Sympathetic to prowar factions within revolutionary Russia, Walling was brought into the Wilson administration as an adviser on international SOCIALISM. The twenties found him flacking for Samuel Gompers's voluntaristic industrial democracy, corresponding for the International Labor News Service from Latin America, and standing for Congress in 1924. When Walling died in Amsterdam in 1936, he had been building support for the German anti-Nazi underground.

A prolific journalist and political analyst, Walling's serious intellectual production was largely limited to four books—*Socialism As It Is* (1912), *The Larger Aspects of Socialism* (1913), *Progressivism—and After* (1914), and *Whitman and Traubel* (1916)—the latter two in fact containing only pale developments of ideas put more forcefully earlier. At the center of this work was a critique of the processes by which contemporary social theory and reform/revolutionary practice replicated the historical formations of monopoly capitalism, suffocating democracy and freezing real progress. True "socialism," Walling believed, would push beyond the collectivism legitimated by evolutionary naturalism and "organic" theories of society and systematized in projects of "state socialism" across the political spectrum, from Bismark to Fabianism, from Theodore Roosevelt to the leadership of the American Socialist Party. In these ideational and political agendas, he argued, "the activities of the state are of infinitely greater moment than the self-development and self-government of citizens who use the state as their mere tool" (*Larger Aspects*, p. 122). Only the self-asserting individual subject, operating freely in a democratic context, could challenge the coercive signification of "state as god" shared by reactionaries, Progressives, and socialists alike.

By calling his position "socialism," Walling reminds us of the unstable nature of that term before 1918; placing it in a Marxian tradition is at best problematic. Rather, it was a product of the discursive hybridization in Anglo-American social thought, which also produced a "new liberalism" in early twentieth-century England and in the early work of Walling's young friend WALTER LIPPMANN. More specifically, Walling's ideas were inspired by an atmosphere of enthusiastic cultural radicalism, that moment of relatively free political/epistemological/ aesthetic intercourse we associate with PROGRESSIVISM and the first bloom of American MODERNISM. Indeed, the critical theory developed in *The Larger Aspects of Socialism*, his most mature and interesting work (written in 1913, the same year as the ARMORY SHOW), should be considered an artifact of that avant-garde.

Introducing a socialism in terms of "larger aspects" is itself indicative of the project of total critique Walling and his bohemian contemporaries felt necessary for a truly modern life, reflecting concern not merely with conflict between classes but between "the two civilizations they represent" (p. vii). As early as 1905, looking to instigate an "American Socialism" (also the title of his journal article) grounded in the work of his Chicago teacher THORSTEIN VEBLEN, Walling toyed with a configuration of CLASS struggle as not simply an issue of relations to material production, but a "conflict of minds" structured by the "physical, mental, and moral" differences of socially determined individuals (p. 580).

Walling continued to move beyond rigid class analysis, focusing on "the absolute interdependence of the cultural [with] the economic and political sides of civilization and human progress" and on representations of change as the "creative evolution of man . . . and the adaptation of life to his own purposes," a "psychological evolution" that would foster genuine social *revolution* (*Larger Aspects*, pp. ix, 28, 86). This is typical of the early twentieth-century avant-garde's sublation of rationalized materiality in a total critique of the practice of bourgeois life, as well as its hopeful insistence on moral transformation that Walling characterized as a struggle of "the future against the past" (p. xiv).

Walling's critical program was grounded in a mediation of the "profound and destructive" philosophies of JOHN DEWEY and Friedrich Nietzsche, two thinkers often understood to espouse very different modernisms; he appears to be the first to have attempted a thorough synthesis. For Walling, Dewey's PRAGMATISM destabilized the "paralyzing, narcotizing theory" of evolutionary naturalism and the statism it supported (p. 385), opening traditional structures of social knowledge to the freedom of uncertainty. Yet rather than simply anticipating Dewey's later theory of social democracy, Walling held to a version of subjectivity far more radical. The avant-garde found in Nietzsche a moral philosophy supportive of their own dynamic self-fashioning, directing rebellion through various modes of political, psychological, aesthetic, and sexual "liberation." On this ground Walling constructed a utopian individualism primed

to make use of the field cleared by Dewey's epistemological disruption.

Proposals for radical democracy based on creative egoism, drawn from the works of the late-Romantic thinker Max Stirner (then enjoying a vogue in anarchist circles) and WALT WHITMAN (a guiding spirit of American modernism), led Walling further to sense the real possibility of "practically [creating] a human character if we know what we want" and of reconfiguring society from that point. What he envisioned was a lifeworld constituted of "individuals who vary most widely . . . who require and compel the largest and most rapid development of society; instead of individuals who repress themselves, individuals who assert themselves" (pp. 192, 193).

Like many early modernists, Walling pioneered some *post*modern territory, such as Michel Foucault's sense of the dehumanization of the individual subject by the ideas behind modern institutions; further, his positive reading of Nietzsche suggests those of Alexander Nehamas and RICHARD RORTY. But perhaps most significantly, Walling's best work is an innovative case of the application of modernist sensibilities to critical theory in America. In keeping with his example, the accents of liberal/social-democratic discourse would continue to shift from the material and institutional to ideas about culture and subjectivity. While these insights would rarely suggest the utopian possibility they did for Walling, he nevertheless stands at an auspicious turn in the growth of modern American social thought.

PETER HANSEN

FURTHER READING

Peter Bürger, *Theory of the Avant-Garde*, trans. Michael Shaw (Minneapolis: University of Minnesota Press, 1984).

Leslie Fishbein, *Rebels in Bohemia: the Radicals of "The Masses," 1911–1917* (Chapel Hill: University of North Carolina Press, 1982).

Jack Meyer Stuart, "William English Walling: a Study in Politics and Ideas," Ph.D. diss., Columbia University, 1968.

Anna S. Walling, ed., *William English Walling: a Symposium* (New York: Stackpole and Sons, 1938).

William English Walling, "An American Socialism," *International Socialist Review* 5 (Apr. 1905): 577–84.

——, *The Larger Aspects of Socialism* (New York: Macmillan, 1913).

Ward, Lester Frank (b. Joliet, Ill., June 18, 1841; d. Washington, D.C., Apr. 18, 1913). Sociologist. Ward rejected the laissez-faire argument, associated with WILLIAM GRAHAM SUMNER and Herbert Spencer, that people should not interfere with the natural law of development of human SOCIETY. Indeed, he argued, the human mind was an adaptive tool perfected in the natural evolutionary process; thus it was natural for people to use it to promote both material abundance and psychological well-being. Ward believed that native intelligence is equally distributed among all races, classes, and sexes, and should be developed by egalitarian education, and that government should take an active role in furthering social goals. Ward became a professor of sociology (at Brown University) only in 1906, after a long career as a geologist and paleontologist in the U.S. Geological Survey. His major works include *The Psychic Factors of Civilization* (1893), *Dynamic Sociology* (2 vols., 1883), and *Applied Sociology* (1906).

FURTHER READING
Clifford H. Scott, *Lester Frank Ward* (Boston: Twayne, 1976).

Warren, Earl (b. Los Angeles, Calif., Mar. 19, 1891; d. Washington, D.C., July 9, 1974).   Supreme Court Chief Justice (1953–69). After serving three terms as Republican governor of California, Warren led the Supreme Court in an affirmation of CIVIL RIGHTS and personal liberties. His Court destroyed the "separate but equal" principle in the landmark decision *Brown v. Board of Education of Topeka* (1954), a major turning point in American race relations. His court also established one-person, one-vote representation in *Reynolds v. Sims* (1964), mandated legal representation for suspected felons in *Miranda v. State of Arizona* (1966), and supported freedom of speech and freedom of religion. Warren sought unanimous Court decisions, especially in controversial cases, and asserted the judiciary's right to intervene if the legislative branch fails to fulfill its responsibilities. Despite the pathbreaking decisions handed down during his term as Chief Justice, Warren did not articulate a rationale for the Court's judicial activism.

FURTHER READING
G. Edward White, *Earl Warren: a Public Life* (New York: Oxford University Press, 1982).

Warren, Mercy Otis (b. Barnstable, Mass., Sept. 25, 1728; d. Plymouth, Mass., Oct. 19, 1814). Revolutionary polemicist, poet, and historian. All government, Warren argued, tends to become authoritarian and abusive. Best remembered for her political satires, such as *The Adulateur* (1773) and *The Group* (1775), she excited revolutionary sentiment through her pamphlets, plays, correspondence, and salon. Her detailed, on-the-spot chronicle of the Revolution, published as *History of the Rise, Progress, and Termination of the American Revolution* (3 vols., 1805), emphasizes the ability of heroic individuals to

counter conspiratorial power. Believing that governmental power should be kept to an absolute minimum, Warren became a staunch Anti-Federalist.

FURTHER READING
Rosemarie Zagarri, *A Woman's Dilemma: Mercy Otis Warren and the American Revolution* (Arlington Heights, Ill.: Harlan Davidson, 1994).

Warren, Robert Penn (b. Guthrie, Ky., Apr. 24, 1905; d. Stratton, Vt., Sept. 15, 1989).   Poet, novelist, political essayist, and literary critic, winner of the Pulitzer Prize three times (twice for poetry, once for fiction), Robert Penn Warren was the first Poet Laureate of the United States (an office about which he felt skepticism). Prevented from entering the Naval Academy by an accident that cost him the use of one eye and for years threatened the other, he entered Vanderbilt University, where he joined the circle of poets and thinkers which included JOHN CROWE RANSOM, ALLEN TATE, Donald Davidson, and Frank Owsley, among others. During these years he contributed to (and co-edited) *The Fugitive*, a little magazine whose importance in the development of the Southern Literary Renaissance, and in the importation of literary modernism into the American literary scene, was out of proportion to its slender finances and brief life. Many of this group were later identified with SOUTHERN AGRARIANISM, a defense of the rural economy and traditions of the South against the pressure of what struck them as an amoral and anonymous modernity. Warren's involvement with Agrarianism was tangential, although he contributed to the Agrarian manifesto, *I'll Take My Stand* (1930), an essay on racial segregation which shortly embarrassed him and which perhaps worried him into the maturer reflections on that subject in *Segregation: the Inner Conflict in the South* (1955) and *Who Speaks for the Negro?* (1965). His early, debunking biography *John Brown: the Making of a Martyr* (1929) is, despite its partisanship, an acute analysis of the political crisis of the 1850s and anticipates the more morally sophisticated views he takes of that era as a time when the republic lived out some of the cruxes and contradictions of its founding values in his meditation *The Legacy of the Civil War* (1961).

After graduate education at the University of California at Berkeley, Yale, and Oxford, he taught at Louisiana State University, where he co-edited the *Southern Review*, one of the premier literary quarterlies of that or any other time. With Cleanth Brooks, he wrote a series of influential textbooks, including *Understanding Poetry* (1938), *Understanding Fiction* (1943), and *Modern Rhetoric* (1949), which revolutionized the teaching of literature in the United States by spreading the methods and habit of mind of what is loosely called New Criticism. In Warren's hands, New Criticism is essentially a way of referring to his poet's eye for telling details and for subtleties of argument. Although critical schools since that time have stigmatized New Criticism for its resistance to reflections on history and politics, for its exclusion of considerations about the reader or the author, and for its view of the meaning of texts as unitary and stable, not one of the traits attributed to New Criticism in fact characterizes Warren's criticism or New Criticism as he understood it. In particular, few critics have been more historically literate or politically conscious than Warren. Because it sought to make literature inwardly available to students who brought to it little more than an acute sensibility, New Criticism played a crucial role in adapting the college curriculum to the postwar expansion of educational opportunity.

Also while at LSU Warren published his first book of poems, *Thirty-Six Poems* (1935), which, with *Eleven Poems on the Same Theme* (1942), established his reputation as a highly polished formalist, strongly influenced by Marvell and Donne, coolly skeptical about human nature, bitterly aware of human folly, sinfulness, and moral evasion. The dark narrative poem "The Ballad of Billie Potts" promised a new, more personal, more discursive kind of poetry, but ten years of poetic silence intervened before Warren took up poetry again.

Although Warren wrote fiction throughout his career, his greatest novels date from the period of his poetic silence. Warren is preeminently a novelist of politics and morals. As a sympathetic and unprogrammatic analyst of the tragic contradictions of the political life, the tendency of genuine values to issue in bloodshed or of worldly compromises to set one on the slippery slope to pure expedience, Warren is unsurpassed in American fiction even by Faulkner. Warren's best-known novel, *All the King's Men* (1946), treats of the rise and fall of a dictatorial southern governor loosely modeled on Louisiana's Huey Long. It sees Governor Stark neither as a corrupt hack nor as a cryptofascist, but as a man led astray by an angry hunger for justice and an impatience with legal forms; and as such Stark perhaps has less kinship with the great totalitarians of the 1930s than with the tyrants who, to popular acclaim, subvert popular government, figures who have haunted republican political thought since Machiavelli.

Warren is also interested in how his protagonists' search for personal integrity—his protagonists are typically the hangers-on of tyrants rather than the tyrants themselves—renders extremism of one kind

or another attractive to them. Warren is most in his element when describing how a cause with which he is in sympathy can come unglued when, under the pressure of a political crisis, reformers may adopt extreme measures which seem to them all but inevitable. Examples include Warren's treatment of the failed attempt of Kentucky tobacco growers to resist the power of the large buyers in his first novel, *Night Rider* (1939), and his treatment of the Debt Relief crisis of 1820s Kentucky in his greatest novel of politics, *World Enough and Time* (1950). Warren's most startling political narrative is the book-length poem *Brother to Dragons* (1953), which treats the murder of a slave by two of the nephews of Thomas Jefferson.

The poetry that Warren began writing in the early 1950s, after the end of his turbulent first marriage and his remarriage to the novelist Eleanor Clark, was looser in form and more personal than his earlier work, although it shares with his earlier work a dark distrust of human nature and a fascination with transcendental experiences. His best poems are marked by a tense and sinewy line, roughened with alliteration and with startling rhythmic and syntactical inventiveness. The intellectual ambition and tragic vision of his late poetry brings to mind the work of Thomas Hardy, like Warren both a novelist and a poet, and, like Warren, a poet who joins a dark metaphysics with a narrative poetic bent and a restless metrical energy.

JOHN BURT

FURTHER READING
Calvin Bedient, *In the Heart's Last Kingdom: Robert Penn Warren's Major Poetry* (Cambridge: Harvard University Press, 1984).
Leonard Casper, *Robert Penn Warren: the Dark and Bloody Ground* (Seattle: University of Washington Press, 1960).
Barnett Guttenberg, *Web of Being: the Novels of Robert Penn Warren* (Nashville: Vanderbilt University Press, 1975).
James Justus, *The Achievement of Robert Penn Warren* (Baton Rouge: Louisiana State University Press, 1981).
Victor Strandberg, *The Poetic Vision of Robert Penn Warren* (Lexington: University Press of Kentucky, 1977).

Washington, Booker T. (b. Franklin County, Va., Apr. 5, 1856; d. Tuskegee, Ala., Nov. 14, 1915). Born a slave on a farm (not a "plantation" as he claims in his autobiography), Washington was freed by the Emancipation Proclamation at seven years of age. After the Civil War he moved with his family to Malden, West Virginia to join his stepfather, who had found work in a salt processing plant and a coal mine. Through his mother's efforts he got some education, but it was not until he made his way to the Hampton Institute in 1872 that he was able to study regularly.

The institute's founder Samuel Chapman Armstrong, a former Union officer who commanded African American troops during the Civil War, became Washington's mentor. It was through Armstrong's recommendation that Washington arrived, at age 26, to take charge of a new school for former slaves at Tuskegee, Alabama. Out of virtually nothing and literally with his (and his students') hands, Washington was able to build what was to become Tuskegee Institute and eventually Tuskegee University.

Thanks to his association with the northern philanthropists he encountered through Armstrong, he began in the 1880s to attract national attention. In 1895, just after the death of FREDERICK DOUGLASS, the acknowledged leader of African Americans, Washington delivered an address at the Atlanta Exposition. Known as the "Atlanta Compromise," the label selected by his prime intellectual adversary w. e. b. DU BOIS, the address catapulted Washington into national fame. Northern and southern whites could hardly help admiring him, since he absolved them of moral blame for having supported or tolerated slavery. His moderate tone assured northern whites that African Americans would not cause labor problems in the southern enterprises that northerners owned; and it assured southern whites that blacks sought neither social equality nor political power.

Critics of Washington asked whether his program of vocational education was intended to create among blacks a servant and laboring class and whether it was wise to give up the franchise so easily. Many felt that Washington's educational policies were meant to serve the interests of industrialists who needed a stable labor supply in the South. Other observers believed that Washington acted responsibly within the historical confines of a racist society. Vocational training, on this view, was what the freedman really needed; it was the only basis, in that time and place, for self- and community development.

Historians debate the issue to this day. Defenders of Washington's judgment, eager to note Washington's subterranean militance, emphasize the veiled threat contained in his address: "Nearly sixteen millions of hands will assist you in pulling the load upward, or they will pull against you and the load downward." Critics point to the ameliorative modesty of the address: "We have proved our loyalty to you in the past, in nursing your children, watching by the sickbeds of your mothers and fathers, and often following them with tear-dimmed eyes to their graves . . ." They also fix on the most famous sentence of the address, which when delivered in 1895 produced wild cheers in the the mainly white audience: "In all things purely social we can be as separate as the five fingers, and yet one as the hand in all things essential to mutual progress." It was one year later that *Plessy v. Ferguson* established the rule of "separate but equal," thereby sanctioning racial segregation.

Literary scholars have devoted much attention to the development of Washington's life story as recounted by him in successive autobiographies: the two editions of *The Story of My Life and Work* (1900 and 1901), and *Up from Slavery* (1901). *Story* was plainly designed for a broad popular audience (white as well as black), *Up from Slavery* for a more discriminating one: for a period of time at the turn of the century, therefore, Washington was writing two different life stories at the same time, while of course continuing to live the life he was writing about. Indeed, the revision of *Story* and the writing of *Up from Slavery* was a process by which Washington attempted to regain control of his life by regaining control of his life story, which he felt had been surrendered to the J. L. Nichols company, publisher of *Story*. The double revision of his life story culminating in *Up from Slavery* was a campaign for self-fashioning, one that eventuated in a work of substantial artistic value. It allowed him to create a self—not unreal but nevertheless fictive. "I suspect I must have been born somewhere at some time," he writes on the first page of *Up from Slavery*, and the act of birth was repeated and mimicked in the ongoing text of his life.

DONALD B. GIBSON

FURTHER READING
Houston Baker, *Long Black Song: Essays in Black American Literature and Culture* (Charlottesville: University Press of Virginia, 1972).
Charles T. Davis and Henry Louis Gates Jr., eds., *The Slave's Narrative* (New York: Oxford University Press, 1985).
W. E. B. Du Bois, *The Souls of Black Folk* (1903; New York: Penguin Classics, 1989).
Donald B. Gibson, "Strategies and Revisions of Self-Representation in Booker T. Washington's Autobiographies," *American Quarterly* 45 (Sept. 1993): 370–93.
Louis Harlan, *Booker T. Washington: the Making of a Black Leader, 1856–1901* (New York: Oxford University Press, 1972).
———, *Booker T. Washington: the Wizard of Tuskegee, 1901–1915* (New York: Oxford University Press, 1983).
Robert Stepto, *From Behind the Veil: a Study of Afro-American Narrative*, 2nd ed. (Urbana: University of Illinois Press, 1991).

Washington, George (b. Westmoreland County, Va., Feb. 22, 1732; d. Mount Vernon, Va., Dec. 14, 1799). Commander-in-Chief of the Continental Army and first President of the United States. Known as early as 1778 as the "father of our country," Washington's importance in American thought derives more from his symbolic status than from his own ideas. Having had little education himself, he painstakingly acquired a familiarity with republican ideology and set out to serve as America's Patriot King, a role modeled on Joseph Addison's interpretation of the Roman original in his popular play *The Tragedy of Cato*, with which Washington's writings reveal close familiarity. His legendary reticence masked his uneasiness in the company of men of ideas, many of whom shared John Adams's disdain for his lack of education. But others interpreted his reserve as thoughtful, steely resolve. By refusing a salary as head of the Continental army, and submitting to Congress an account of his expenses, Washington established his reputation as a selfless hero, a modern-day Cincinnatus who put down his plow to serve his country, then returned to his furrows afterwards—an image further bolstered when Washington resisted efforts to make him king. As President he sought to exemplify republican VIRTUE by remaining above partisan disputes. As a symbol of the new nation he hoped to galvanize national feeling and promote national unity.

FURTHER READING

Paul K. Langmore, *The Invention of George Washington* (Berkeley: University of California Press, 1988).

Watson, James D. (b. Chicago, Ill., Apr. 6, 1928). Molecular biologist. Using physical models, Watson and his colleague Francis Crick deduced DNA's double-spiral structure from biochemical and X-ray crystallographical data generated by others. DNA, he argues, is the "master molecule" that alone determines an organism's structure: once we understand DNA, we will understand development. His bestseller *The Double Helix* (1968) portrayed science as a highly individualistic and competitive activity and provoked controversy over the function of scientific communities and the attribution of discoveries. Watson later directed the human genome project (1988–92), which intends to produce a complete map of human genes. Author of *Molecular Biology of the Gene* (1964), he received the 1962 Nobel Prize for Physiology or Medicine (with Francis Crick and Maurice Wilkins).

FURTHER READING

Horace Freeland Judson, *The Eighth Day of Creation: Makers of the Revolution in Biology* (New York: Simon and Schuster, 1980).

Watson, John B. (b. Greenville, S.C., Jan. 9, 1878; d. New York, N.Y., Sept. 25, 1958). Psychologist.

A committed behaviorist, Watson argued that the environment creates the individual. All actions, including language and thinking (that is, subvocal language), can be explained without reference to consciousness, will, or perception; they are all responses to stimuli. Psychology should give up the effort to understand consciousness and become an experimental science with the goal of predicting and controlling human behavior. After World War I, Watson abandoned his academic career at Johns Hopkins and joined an advertising firm, where his talents found immediate application. His writings include *Behavior: An Introduction to Comparative Psychology* (1914), *Psychology from the Standpoint of a Behaviorist* (1919) and, for general readers, *Behaviorism* (1925).

FURTHER READING

Kerry W. Buckley, *Mechanical Man: John Broadus Watson and the Beginnings of Behaviorism* (New York: Guilford Press, 1989).

Wayland, Francis (b. New York, N.Y., Mar. 11, 1796; d. Providence, R.I., Sept. 30, 1865). Educator. President of Brown University from 1827 to 1855, Wayland sought to make higher education serve democratic goals and principles. Grounding ethics in a theistic natural order, he held that the goal of the moral life is the full use of human powers. Since the faculties develop sequentially—first objective observation, then imagination and the inner life, then generalization and abstraction—education should aim to strengthen the evolving faculties through exercises that both increase knowledge and improve the mind. Wayland's *Elements of Moral Science* (1835) was long the most widely used text in the courses on ethics that were the capstone of the nineteenth-century college curriculum. His other works include *The Moral Dignity of the Missionary Enterprise* (1823), *Thoughts on the Present Collegiate System in the United States* (1842), and *Report on the Condition of the University* (1850).

FURTHER READING

Donald Harvey Meyer, *The Instructed Conscience: the Shaping of the American National Ethic* (Philadelphia: University of Pennsylvania Press, 1972).

Webster, Daniel (b. Salisbury, N.H., Jan. 18, 1782; d. Marshfield, Mass., Oct. 24, 1852). Lawyer, orator, political leader. Webster served almost continuously in the House of Representatives, in the Senate, or as Secretary of State from 1813 until his death. The greatest orator of antebellum America, he delivered speeches in political campaigns, in Congress, and before the Supreme Court that helped create consensus among many northerners and even southerners on many matters of justice and nationhood. His orations display remarkable poetic talent, as well as the conventional moral philosophy he learned at Dartmouth College. Webster detested slavery and feared its extension. He treasured REPUBLICANISM as a guarantor of morality and property, and he believed economic growth, by bringing prosperity to all Americans, would promote social harmony.

FURTHER READING

Paul D. Erickson, *The Poetry of Events: Daniel Webster's Rhetoric of the Constitution and the Union* (New York: New York University Press, 1986).

Webster, Noah (b. West Hartford, Conn., Oct. 16, 1758; d. New Haven, Conn., May 28, 1843). Lexicographer and educator. Author of the *American Spelling Book* (1783) and the *American Dictionary of the English Language* (2 vols., 1828), Webster believed that a national language and literature would nurture democratic patriotism and morality. His textbooks and dictionaries defined a specifically American spelling and usage in order to differentiate American from British English and foster a unified and uniform national consciousness. Simplified spelling and inexpensive mass-produced textbooks would, he hoped, promote the universal LITERACY required in a republic. To protect his work, Webster helped institute copyright laws.

FURTHER READING

David Simpson, *The Politics of American English, 1776–1850* (New York: Oxford University Press, 1986).

Weld, Theodore (b. Hampton, Conn., Nov. 23, 1803; d. Hyde Park, Mass., Feb. 3, 1895). Lecturer and writer. A revivalist converted by CHARLES GRANDISON FINNEY, Weld sought to convince a broad audience of the moral evil of slavery. As an agent for the American Anti-Slavery Society, he trained traveling lecturers and wrote abolitionist pamphlets, including *The Bible against Slavery* (1837) and *Slavery As It Is* (1839). While he had little faith in political action or centralized authority, he believed abolitionists should use political tactics as well as the educational and inspirational strategies he favored. He advocated equality of the sexes and supported female abolitionists, but played down the issue so as not to alienate potential supporters.

FURTHER READING

Robert H. Abzug, *Passionate Liberator: Theodore Dwight Weld and the Dilemma of Reform* (New York: Oxford University Press, 1980).

welfare In its current usage the word is a neologism, and its new meaning has almost entirely reversed its traditional one. A term for prosperity and general well-being now connotes the opposite: poverty, ill-being, disreputableness. The trajectory of that transformation reveals much about the history of the U.S. welfare state and the social thought behind it.

In the nineteenth century and before, no one called programs of public or private material aid "welfare." One spoke of charity, the dole, relief, assistance, aid. Yet one aspect of the modern construction of the term "welfare" was present almost from the beginning of European settlement in North America —the fact that some forms of public aid to private individuals and groups were accepted as normal, even honorable, while aid to the poor was suspect and likely to contribute to corruption of character. Colonial governments were in many ways constructed around "giveaways," in particular of land to European settlers. Charity, while an obligation of local governments and private associations, was caught in a paradoxical circularity: European traditions divided the poor into the deserving and the undeserving, and only the former were entitled to receive aid; yet the very receipt of aid functioned also as a sign of possible, even probable undeservingness. The authentically deserving poor, according to this logic, were always reluctant to request assistance. This stigmatizing of relief discouraged the needy from asking for help and justified offering aid only to the very most desperate. That stigma was strengthened by the fear that relief might encourage the poor to lose their work ethic and their "independence."

In accord with these traditions, early U.S. poor relief was organized around a set of principles similar to those of the 1834 British poor law reform; these included (1) the principle of least eligibility—that aid should always be less desirable than work at the minimum available wage, in order not to encourage the poor toward laziness and not to threaten employers' ability to hold down wages; and (2) the opposing principle that the poor would always attempt nevertheless to malinger, and that careful investigation of aid claims was necessary in order to prevent cheating. Charity workers and volunteers believed that the problems of the poor extended beyond the lack of resources to include defects in character or social relationships.

This ideology about welfare (an IDEOLOGY in that a particular set of arrangements was conceived as inevitable and natural) constructed independence as deriving from property or wage labor, and government aid to the independent as an entitlement of

CITIZENSHIP; those without property and unable to support themselves by wage labor were conceived as in danger of dependence, the aid they received as stigmatizing. These tenets prefigured contemporary welfare ideology; indeed, while there have been substantial changes in policy over time, the assumptions underlying welfare ideology have proven remarkably enduring.

In the late nineteenth century, industrialization, urbanization, and immigration together intensified and spread poverty (if we understand poverty as a relative concept) and made it more visible. Reformers responded with public investigations into the "facts" of poverty. Several streams of welfare reform thought arose. The largest such current was that of "scientific" charity, which called for thorough investigation of the circumstances of each claim for help and ongoing supervision of recipients—an approach which came to be called "casework." Scientific charity gave birth to modern professional social work. By the early twentieth century numerous schools offered professional social work training, and increasing numbers of public and private helping agencies hired only professional caseworkers. Until the Great Depression of the 1930s, most reformers of this stream of thought were committed to the principle that all aid should be accompanied by casework to help rehabilitate and reform the poor. In the 1930s, "welfare" was conceived as a branch of social work.

Women were prominent among welfare reformers and newly professionalized social workers, and the field offered an important arena of acceptable public-sphere activity for many women who, despite education and privileged class position, were at this time blocked from most other professions. The woman-dominated charity and social work establishments particularly identified needy women and children, and the immigrant poor, as recipients of humanitarian concern. The first victorious reforms emanating from this network were the state mothers'-aid laws providing limited aid to single mothers, usually widows, passed in most states between 1911 and 1920. This social work approach to welfare can be considered in many respects a feminized, even maternalist, current of thought. Until the Depression, the dominant social work orientation to welfare never entirely lost its heritage of "friendly visiting" and its conviction that the poor needed moral and spiritual as well as economic help. And many women leaders of social work, including some key welfare advocates, defended their suitability for this work on the grounds of their experience and/or destiny as mothers. This women's welfare strategy can be considered (generically) feminist, not only

because women and children were identified as those most in need, but also because, in helping poor single mothers to support their children, the women reformers sought to raise the perceived social value of women's domestic, unpaid labor.

Meanwhile another group of reformers was inventing a considerably different approach, social insurance. Influenced by European governments responding to the growth of workers' movements and socialist political parties, social insurance advocates, primarily male, envisioned and designed programs of public aid which broke decisively with the charity/social work tradition. They sought programs to replace lost wages (for the aged, the unemployed, the disabled, for example) for working men and their dependents. Their first victories were the workmen's compensation laws, providing fixed sums to workers injured on the job, passed by the majority of states in virtually the same period as the mothers'-aid laws. Social insurance advocates wanted programs that would be entirely without the stigma of poor relief. Indeed, they did not even orient their programs particularly toward the poor; they preferred insurance for male wage-earners, including the secure and prosperous. They designed programs in which entitlements to provision would follow automatically from meeting clearly defined eligibility criteria, such as length of employment, as opposed to programs in which caseworkers would have discretion about whether and how much to give. This approach was not "paternalist," because it did not emphasize a parental, personal caretaking dimension. Like social work, social insurance had a social control dimension. Its proponents worried about the potential contribution of poverty and unemployment to social disorder. But this social control relation was distant, not individually supervisory. Nevertheless, while not primarily fatherly, this social insurance strategy was definitely male in content as well as personnel, assuming wage labor to be the fundamental source of entitlement, devaluing unpaid domestic labor, and lacking the women's vision of a personally caring welfare state.

These two visions of welfare did not conflict but proceeded cooperatively throughout the late nineteenth century and early twentieth century. Social work welfare advocates supported social insurance proposals, and social insurance advocates conceded the necessity of personalized, therapeutic programs of help for those not reached by social insurance. Their cooperation was based not only on this division of labor but also on common assumptions which, in hindsight, seem more important than their differences. Most believed in the family wage, that is, a family system in which the male head of household earned enough to support all his dependents, while the wife and mother devoted herself full-time to domestic labor. In providing aid to single mothers, social work reformers believed that single motherhood should and would decline in significance as the wrongs of the industrial system were corrected. While many women welfare reformers supported women's rights to education and to employment, most conceived women's economic independence as impractical among the poor. (*See also* MOTHERHOOD.)

Some dissident streams of welfare thought produced different analyses and recommendations. For example, a long tradition of African American welfare activism—primarily in building private institutions rather than lobbying for public provision since blacks, mostly disenfranchised, lacked political clout—was considerably less wedded to the premise of the family wage. African American women could be said to have presaged late twentieth-century norms in their favorable attitude toward employment and economic independence as a goal for married women. Moreover, they considered child-raising a function of extended as well as nuclear families. For both these reasons, they were less fearful that welfare provision would encourage single motherhood or other unconventional household forms. During the Depression, for another example, several social movements, including not only those of the left but also some right-wing populisms such as those inspired by Francis Townsend or Huey Long, developed proposals that broke with the principle of "least eligibility." Strongly committed to KEYNESIANISM, these groups favored priming the economic pump by getting money into consumers' hands, and were dedicated to the premise that one of the responsibilities of government and RIGHTS of citizenship was public provision. These alternative welfare visions, moreover, did not presume that basic entitlements should be attached to and funded through employment, and might thereby have been less discriminatory against women and minorities than the plans that were adopted.

But the influence of the dissident welfare voices was limited. When the basic federal welfare system—the Social Security Act of 1935—was being debated, the prowelfare public agitation created by these movements served to create pressure for its passage but did not affect its structure and philosophy. Instead, Social Security pasted together a variety of programs representing the two major streams of welfare thought. Two of its titles, Old Age Insurance and Unemployment Compensation, established social insurance programs. Several public assistance titles followed social work principles, creating means-tested, personally supervised aid programs, of which Aid to Dependent Children was to become the most prominent and the program most people refer to as "welfare." There have been reforms and a few new programs, but in general the Social Security Act still defines "welfare" today.

Ironically, in introducing social insurance as a new category of public provision, the Social Security Act, despite the intentions of its authors and supporters, tended to confirm the stigmatization of public assistance. It did so not merely through its inclusions and exclusions but, equally importantly, through its construction of the meanings congealed in our welfare system. Social insurance provided new mechanisms and justifications for government aid without stigma, but did so by defining only certain programs as entitlements, and thus honorable; such aid went primarily to the nonpoor. Eligibility for these social insurance entitlements was exclusive and discriminatory: the original provisions excluded most minorities and most women of all ethnic groups, by excluding the kinds of jobs in which they were clustered (for instance, agriculture; domestic service; seasonal, temporary and/or part-time work; and work for small employers). Later amendments broadened these programs but, since they were based on employment-related eligibility criteria, they continued to serve, disproportionately, nonpoor men. In the late 1930s and 1940s federal officials promoted a two-track welfare system, deliberately separating social insurance from public assistance in order to win support for the former among the prosperous. Indeed, they argued for holding down public assistance stipends in order to create a public preference for social insurance (a preference which did not previously exist). They emphasized wage deductions to fund old age pensions in order to construct a belief that social insurance recipients get their *own* money; this is not the case, as Social Security funds have been pooled with other federal monies, and stipends are not based on contributions. As a result of their success, pejorative concepts such as "welfare" and "dependency" apply today only to public assistance; no one regards old age pensioners as receiving welfare.

In excluding so many from the "entitlement" programs, the welfare system has, perversely, contributed to deepening inequality and poverty. The social insurance programs, for example, have maintained decent stipend levels through cost-of-living increases, while public assistance payments have declined in real terms since three decades ago. Moreover, the vetting and supervision of public assistance recipients encourages them to "cheat" (for example, to hide income, boyfriends, roommates, systems of sharing), thus encouraging the public to view them as undeserving; and these constructions then discourage public political support for more generous "welfare" policies.

Thinking about welfare remains to a remarkable degree bounded by the perspectives of the nineteenth century. Some related assumptions about family responsibility have changed substantially—children are no longer always considered responsible for their aged parents, and woman are expected to earn. But other family- and gender-related assumptions remain: many people continue to believe that single-parent families and families with two full-time workers are irregular, and that the normative family has a father earning a family wage sufficient to raise children without nonmarket economic help. The guiding assumptions in most welfare discourse continue to be remarkably consistent with those of a century ago: that public assistance to the poor is "welfare" while other government provision is not; that depending on welfare for subsistence is regrettable and should be minimized; that welfare recipients should be less comfortable than they might be in the lowest-paid jobs. In current discussions of medical insurance, assumptions made in the Social Security Act remain alive, notably that entitlements should be based on employment, on contributions from both employer and employee, and that tax-funded stipends should go only to the proven poor.

Although many scholars and commentators have interrogated these assumptions, including those whose works are listed below, they have not been able to alter hegemonic assumptions. Policy discourse has been narrowed by its politicization. The "Poverty Program" of the 1960s began to fund poverty/welfare research; since then private foundations, notably conservative ones, have entered the field as well. The product is a poverty/welfare research industry which orients welfare scholarship today to policy-related, technical studies, often quite partisan. Welfare thought which adopts a critical stance—which examines assumptions, long-term historical change, and the social construction of values—has less currency.

LINDA GORDON

FURTHER READING

Mimi Abramovitz, *Regulating the Lives of Women: Social Welfare Policy from Colonial Times to the Present* (Boston: South End Press, 1988).
Jerry R. Cates, *Insuring Inequality: Administrative Leadership in Social Security, 1935–54* (Ann Arbor: University of Michigan Press, 1983).
Kathryn Edin, *There's a Lot of Month Left at the End of the Money: How Welfare Recipients Make Ends Meet in Chicago* (New York: Garland, 1993).
Nancy Fraser and Linda Gordon, "A Genealogy of 'Dependency': a Keyword of the US Welfare State," *Signs* 19 (winter 1994).
Linda Gordon, *Pitied but Not Entitled: Single Mothers and the History of Welfare* (New York: Free Press, 1994).
——, ed., *Women, the State and Welfare* (Madison: University of Wisconsin Press, 1990).
Michael B. Katz, *In the Shadow of the Poorhouse: a Social History of Welfare in America* (New York: Basic Books, 1986).
Sara McLanahan and Gary Sandefur, *Growing Up with a Single Parent: What Hurts, What Helps* (Cambridge: Harvard University Press, 1994).
Charles Murray, *Losing Ground: American Social Policy 1950–1980* (New York: Basic Books, 1984).
Theda Skocpol, *Protecting Soldiers and Mothers: the Political Origins of Social Policy in the United States* (Cambridge: Harvard University Press, 1992).

Welty, Eudora (b. Jackson, Miss., Apr. 13, 1909). Writer. Welty's stories, set in the Mississippi Delta, explore the relationships between individuals and their families and communities. Torn between desires for connection and love on the one hand, and identity and separation on the other, her characters travel and stay home, rebel and grow old, in a world where everything changes yet everything stays the same. Her women especially feel the weight of social sanction: they are the community's backbone, and rarely defy convention to become self-conscious or assertive individuals. *A Curtain of Green* (1941) was Welty's first collection of short stories; her novels include *Delta Wedding* (1946) and *The Optimist's Daughter* (1972). Her moving memoir, which asserts the redemptive force of privacy, storytelling, and memory, is *One Writer's Beginnings* (1988).

FURTHER READING
Peter Schmidt, *The Heart of the Story: Eudora Welty's Short Fiction* (Jackson: University Press of Mississippi, 1991).

Weyl, Walter (b. Philadelphia, Pa., Mar. 11, 1873; d. New York, N.Y., Nov. 9, 1919). Journalist. Trained as an economist, Weyl was an advocate of direct DEMOCRACY, labor organization, and the mobilization of the middle class as consumers to effect broad social and political changes. America's "social surplus" might, he suggested, allow the nation's industry and natural resources to be brought under democratic public control, thus expanding material and social progress to include the poor without depriving the rich. Not the working class, but the middle class, with its broad literacy and freedom from poverty, was the seedbed of such reforms. A founding editor of THE NEW REPUBLIC, Weyl wrote *The New Democracy; an Essay on Certain Political and*

Economic Tendencies in the United States (1912) and *American World Policies* (1917).

FURTHER READING
Charles Forcey, *The Crossroads of Liberalism: Croly, Weyl, Lippmann, and the Progressive Era, 1900–1925* (New York: Oxford University Press, 1961).

Wharton, Edith (b. New York, N.Y., Jan. 24, 1862; d. Saint-Brice-sous-Forêt, France, Aug. 11, 1937). A novelist, intellectual, and cultural critic, Edith Wharton emerged from the upper class of New York society, where WASHINGTON IRVING was accepted as a cultural icon yet the writing of fiction was associated with the equally remote fields of manual labor and the occult arts. In the circles in which Edith Newbold Jones was raised, women were the receptacles of CLASS traditions: emblems of stasis and adversaries of any sign of social change. While men either quietly collected income from real estate or more disruptively entered the competitive world of business, women regulated the home and the hierarchies of social relations; they offered the illusion of stable and unchanging coves in the sea storm of economic escalation and recession which followed the Civil War.

To escape the post-Civil War economy, the Jones family moved to Europe when Wharton was four. They remained for six years, living on the high rents from their homes in America while enjoying the relatively low cost of living in France, Italy, Germany, and other places, where Wharton was introduced to the languages and layers of cultural traditions which made up the Old World. When she returned to America at the age of ten she felt herself to be in exile. Destined to become a debutante and to devote her life to the taxing duties of the responsible society matron, yet determined to become a writer, she was married to the boyish and sports-loving Teddy Wharton for 26 years. After a great deal of conflict (including a nervous breakdown), she emerged as one of the most gifted and productive writers that America has ever produced. Separating from her husband and America in 1911, Wharton became a permanent resident of France and after her divorce in 1913 she returned to America only twice for brief visits. During the Great War, Wharton became a social leader, organizing American-supported relief efforts which provided food, clothing, fuel, and jobs for the many wartime refugees in Paris.

Wharton published over 35 book-length works, including 22 longer works of fiction (almost equally divided between novels and novellas), 86 stories, two collections of poetry, and numerous nonfiction works, including a book about house decoration (which contains many of the most powerful formulations of her aesthetic principles), travel books, treatises on gardens and architecture, a volume of literary criticism, and an autobiography. During her lifetime, Wharton was a more successful writer than her friend and mentor HENRY JAMES—she won the Pulitzer Prize for *The Age of Innocence* in 1921—yet she suffered from critics who, blinded by her social class, chose to see her merely as a lesser Henry James. Like James, Wharton was an expatriate, but unlike him, she continued, even after she had ceased to visit the United States, to write extensively about Americans in America. While she occasionally devoted an entire work (like *The Reef*, 1912) to describing the life of Americans living abroad, or devoted sections of novels to descriptions of European scenes, more often Wharton used her increasing sense of estrangement from her family and her native land to write powerful and often devastating critiques of America.

In 1905, then the author of a two-volume novel on eighteenth-century Italy and two collections of short stories, Wharton published *The House of Mirth*, a bestselling novel which offered readers a rare and revelatory view into the lives of the fashionable elite. In other works which followed, particularly *The Custom of the Country* (1913) and *The Age of Innocence* (1920), Wharton would speak in increasingly anthropological terms of the tribal practices of what she had begun to call "Old New York." Best known for her REALISM in these works, Wharton's detailed depictions of the language and rituals of high society have been regarded as accurate portrayals (and, at least for some of her own contemporaries, painfully insightful betrayals) of the complex inner workings of life among the elite.

Amidst the widespread disputes about realism and the authenticity of cultural description which dominated responses to literature in the early part of the century, MARY AUSTIN tried to put Wharton in her place by declaring that *The House of Mirth* was Wharton's regional novel. This assertion questioned the universality of a novel about New York, as well as the cultural authority of Wharton's New England novels, *Ethan Frome* (1911) and *Summer* (1917), which tried to depict the harsh and derelict lives of the backwoods communities that she claimed had been sentimentalized by Mary Wilkins and Sarah Orne Jewett. New England in Wharton's work represents the past, a place of primitive emotions which play themselves out on what can only be described as a psychic landscape.

In general, Wharton used the regions of America to represent and embody aspects of American social and cultural identity. The Midwest in Wharton's fiction figures a future which takes the form of a vast internal emptiness filled with a seemingly unlimited appetite for acquisition. This flat land, lacking culture, embodied for Wharton the forces which would destroy America from within. Anticipating the critique offered by LEWIS MUMFORD in *Sticks and Stones* (1924), Wharton did not make her heroine in *The Custom of the Country* a pioneer; rather, Undine Spragg embodies the destructive spirit of the miner who is interested in excavating and consuming both material and spiritual interiors. While Wharton's critique of modern America in *The Custom of the Country* and *Hudson River Bracketed* and *The Gods Arrive* is far from a realistic portrayal of a regional culture (her actual experience of the Midwest was limited to a few days in Detroit), these novels pictured the threat that she saw to the traditions of Old New York and European culture. New England, despite Wharton's repeated claims about the shallowness of its cultural soil and her emphasis on the intractability of its "granite outcroppings," offered a more fertile literary ground. With a belief in the importance of the layers of the past, first grasped during her formative childhood years in Europe, Wharton would come to see the New England of *Summer* and of her later novels as a place where valued cultural traditions are preserved.

Whether basing her work in the rock-bound winter or summer landscapes of New England or among the rigidly ranked hierarchies of New York society, whether an insider who betrayed her kind or an outsider who would never be more than a summer visitor among the common folk, Wharton used her fictions to position herself as a critic of American culture. As Wharton clips and incorporates pieces of advertising to form the rich, deceptive surface of modern America, she exposes the ruthless materialist ethos which lies below the surface, threatening to devour cultural traditions not only of Europe but also of a settled America. Her writing benefits from a combination of intimacy and distance which gives her work a fierce wit and sharp critical edge. Arguably one of the most widely read and most profoundly intertextual of American writers in any era, she drew on the work of thinkers like THORSTEIN VEBLEN and Charles Darwin, a daunting range of English, French, Italian and German poetry and prose, the history of painting and aesthetics, and popular sources like advertising circulars, magazine clippings, gothic and crime thrillers, and stage melodrama. There is remarkable variety in the tone, style, and structure of Wharton's most powerful nonfiction and fiction, which ranges from her first bestseller in 1905 to her highly critical but in many ways more elegiac novel, *The Age of Innocence*.

While Wharton continued to compose some of her finest work in the short stories (particularly the ghost stories) which she wrote in the 1920s and 1930s, many of her novels from that period appear to have suffered from her efforts to write marketable fiction suitable for serialization in popular women's magazines. In much of her work Wharton constructs a gendered drama in which she links sentimentalism to feminine efforts at concealment, and realism to a stripping away that would reveal the hard structure underneath. Critics have speculated that since she could no longer understand the social concerns of America after the war, she took refuge in the sentimental vagueness which she had always excoriated in her own critical prose. In her best work, however, repeatedly staging the scene of a revelatory realism, Wharton mounts a complex critique of American society in which even her class biases, cultural prejudices, and anxieties about GENDER are highly instructive. She deserves to be read not only for her insightful portrayals of elites at a time of great change, but also as one of the most perceptive and original cultural critics of the period.

CANDACE WAID

FURTHER READING
Elizabeth Ammons, *Edith Wharton's Argument with America* (Athens: University of Georgia Press, 1980).
R. W. B. Lewis, *Edith Wharton: a Biography* (New York: Harper and Row, 1975).
R. W. B. Lewis and Nancy Lewis, eds., *The Letters of Edith Wharton* (New York: Charles Scribner's Sons, 1988).
Blake Nevius, *Edith Wharton: a Study of Her Fiction* (Berkeley: University of California Press, 1953).
Candace Waid, *Edith Wharton's Letters from the Underworld: Fictions of Women and Writing* (Chapel Hill: University of North Carolina Press, 1991).
Cynthia Griffin Wolff, *A Feast of Words: the Triumph of Edith Wharton* (New York: Oxford University Press, 1977).

Wheatley, Phillis (b. Senegal, West Africa, ca.1753; d. Boston, Mass., Dec. 5, 1784). Poet. As a child Wheatley was enslaved when bought by a Boston merchant, who gave her a literary education. In her day she was noted for her neoclassical verse and celebrated for being an African American woman poet. Her poetry was stylistically conservative and thematically conventional: tributes to American institutions, elegies to dead heroes and dead children, reflections on philosophical abstractions. Nevertheless, Wheatley was one of the few female poets of her century to address political issues, and her relatively few allusions to slavery or Africa, although not outwardly critical, stressed the goal of freedom from "tyrannic sway." Her poems were first collected in *Poems on Various Subjects, Religious and Moral* (1773).

FURTHER READING
William H. Robinson, *Phillis Wheatley and Her Writings* (New York: Garland, 1984).

White, Ellen G. (b. Gorham, Maine, Nov. 26, 1827; d. St. Helena, Calif., July 16, 1915).   The inspired prophetess of Seventh-Day Adventism, Ellen G. White rivals JOSEPH SMITH and MARY BAKER EDDY as a creative founder of a major religion. White was the single most important figure in the development of an apocalyptic, corporealist, and millenarian form of Christianity in America and eventually in the world. Seventh-Day Adventism rivals Mormonism as a successful American export.

Ellen Gould Harmon, born in Gorham, grew up in nearby Portland. As a child, she suffered a broken nose and extended nasal blockage because of a stone thrown by a playmate. Thus a sensitive, isolated Ellen grew up at home. She was still an adolescent when she first heard William Miller preach in Portland in 1840.

Miller, a lay Baptist and self-taught Bible scholar from Low Hampton, New York, began his careful study of the apocalyptic sections of the Protestant Bible about the time Ellen was born. From his interpretation of passages in Daniel, he calculated that Jesus would in all likelihood return to the earth in 1843. Aided after 1840 by the promotional ability of Joseph V. Himes, Miller gained a wide following. After his general prediction proved wrong, his movement gained a great sense of urgency in the summer of 1844 when other adventists redid Miller's calculations and settled on October 22, 1844, as the exact final date for Jesus's return. This prediction provoked two months of preaching and revivals. The failure of this prediction devastated adventists, who soon referred to the Great Disappointment.

Ellen's family became early Millerites. Ellen experienced conversion and joined a Methodist congregation, only to be expelled with her family in 1844 because of their militant adventism. She was particularly devastated by the Great Disappointment. But in its aftermath she experienced the first of what eventually became hundreds of visions or revealing dreams. In this one she was consoled by the sight of advent people travelling toward the city of God, a vision that she used to comfort adventists in Portland. She thus began her unique ministry of visions which she used to instruct other adventists. In 1846, just after she began to have frequent visions, she met and married a Millerite minister and publisher, James White. Another adventist minister, Joseph Bates, persuaded her that Christians were obligated to worship on the Sabbath, not on Sunday.

In her most important vision, White provided special, supernatural authority for Sabbath observance. She was privileged to look inside a heavenly sanctuary and view two tablets of stone which contained the ten commandments. The fourth, on the Sabbath, was bathed in a halo of light. This vision made clear to her that the obligation to honor the Sabbath had a special status among the ten as a direct memorial to creation. It above all others established God's authority and drew the distinction between God and his creatures. She blamed first-day worship on the Roman Catholic Church, and viewed this as the major apostasy of Christian history. Sunday worshipers, if aware of God's demands, jeopardized their salvation.

A small Sabbatarian adventist movement matured in the decade just before the Civil War. Bates spread the gospel west, particularly to Michigan. James White used his printing press to publicize the movement, and at every critical juncture Ellen settled doctrinal issues by means of her prophetic visions. The movement incorporated as a publishing association in 1861 and matured into a full denomination in 1863. Ellen generally worked with the other leaders (all men) in the new movement, and in effect often certified group decisions. She soon developed a popular constituency. After the death of her husband in 1881 she took plenty of initiatives on her own, not without opposition and controversy. By an unstated choice, the church accorded special authority only to Ellen's revelations and would not choose to institutionalize her role after her death.

What Ellen G. White helped establish were the four most distinctive doctrines and practices of American adventism. First in importance was Sabbatarianism. Only slightly less important was the belief that the Christ had indeed begun cleansing a heavenly sanctuary on October 22, 1844 (Miller reinterpreted), a step preparatory to his early return to earth. Joined with this sanctuary doctrine was a denial of any spiritual substance, a corporealism typical of most adventist movements. At death no soul survives the body (soul rest), but individuals will later be resurrected to face divine judgment, with the righteous living on in an earthly kingdom which Jesus will establish here on earth. Those not worthy face a horrible death in a fiery pit but no eternal torment.

The fourth distinctive doctrine involves highly sanctioned rules about health and hygiene. Most Adventist leaders were temperance reformers. Even before 1860 Ellen White launched a crusade against tobacco. During the war years the illness of James White led both Whites to consider available therapies. They also read extensively in the diverse literature on diet and hygiene. From this research, and from a series of visions, Ellen G. White worked out her own regimen and developed a series of health publications. She condemned meats, hot beverages (coffee and tea), and excessive amounts of food. She wrote rules for child care, advocated simple and unrestrictive clothing for adventist women, mandated cleanliness, and endorsed a type of hydropathic or water therapy which involved almost no drugs. Ellen persuaded her denomination to establish the first Battle Creek sanitarium for the "rational" treatment of sickness in 1866. Here gathered the first skilled Adventist physicians and health theorists, led by Dr. John Harvey Kellogg.

After her husband died, and as part of her commitment to foreign missions, White spent several years in Australia. After she returned to America, she agreed in 1903 upon a plan to move the church's headquarters from Battle Creek to Takoma Park, Maryland. Its main medical institutions moved west to Loma Linda, California. Despite chronic illnesses, and her busy role as parent, wife, and seer, she lived to be 88. Ellen G. White died in California in 1915. But her influence continued. Her diet reforms led, indirectly, to the cereal industry that came to distinguish Battle Creek. Her teachings, now published in a series of inexpensive books, remain a source of inspiration and guidance for a worldwide and growing Seventh-Day Adventist movement. Her health reforms led to many Adventist medical schools and hospitals and to an extensive program of medical missions.

PAUL CONKIN

FURTHER READING

Roy E. Graham, *Ellen G. White, Co-founder of the Seventh-Day Adventist Church* (New York: P. Lang, 1985).

Ronald L. Numbers, *Prophetess of Health: a Study of Ellen G. White* (New York: Harper and Row, 1976).

Ellen G. White, *The Great Controversy between Christ and Satan* (Mountain View, Calif.: Pacific Press, 1911).

——, *The Drama of the Ages; the Conflict of the Ages Illustrated in the Life of Christ* (Mountain View, Calif.: Pacific Press, 1940).

Whitehead, Alfred North (b. Ramsgate, England, Feb. 15, 1861; d. Cambridge, Mass., Dec. 30, 1947). Mathematician, philosopher, and educator, Alfred North Whitehead was the son of a schoolmaster and minister who contributed to Whitehead's interest in education, and from whom Whitehead learned the value and interconnectedness of community firsthand. In 1880, Whitehead began his 30-year association with Cambridge University when he entered Trinity College. At Trinity he studied pure and applied mathematics exclusively. Whitehead also read widely in politics, religion, philosophy, literature, and history, engaged in a continuing conversation with his peers, and became an active member of the "Apostles," a society of young intellectuals. Whitehead became a fellow at Trinity in 1885 and began teaching there the following year. He married Evelyn Willoughby Wade in 1890; they had three children. In 1910 Whitehead moved to London to teach at the University of London, and from 1914 to 1924 he was professor of applied mathematics at the Imperial College of Science and Technology. Whitehead then accepted Harvard University's invitation to join its faculty. He retired from teaching in 1936, but continued to write until his death.

Whitehead's philosophy evolved from his early interest in mathematics to his late writings on metaphysics and cosmology. During his tenure at Cambridge, he focused on the logical foundations of mathematics. Following early work on algebra, Whitehead collaborated with his student Bertrand Russell on their pathbreaking work on the logical foundations of mathematics, *Principia Mathematica* (1910–13). The emphasis of Whitehead's work shifted following his move to London. While in London, his writings concentrated on the philosophy of science. The central problem of this phase of his career was to find a connection between logical schemes and empirical interpretations. While at Harvard, Whitehead developed his philosophy of science into a comprehensive metaphysics and cosmology. This later philosophy, especially as developed in *Science and the Modern World* (1929) and in *Process and Reality* (1929), has had the greatest impact on American thought.

Whitehead's metaphysical system is characterized by an emphasis on organism and process. Whitehead developed his viewpoint from youthful experience, from knowledge of modern physics, from work in the logical foundations of mathematics, and from wide reading in history and literature. His metaphysics was also developed in opposition to the scientific materialism prevalent in modern thought. Whitehead believed that all events and objects, regardless of importance or size, are related to one another and to the environments in which they occur. His organism emphasized events over objects; objects were relatively constant "societies" of events. Nature can best be understood as interrelated systems of larger and smaller events, some of which are relatively stable. Whitehead's metaphysics was also a philosophy of process. Events are always changing. Change represents the actualization of certain potentialities and the disappearance of others. The world does not simply exist, it is always becoming. Living entities are those which can provide direction and initiative to the process of change. Although his metaphysics is conceivable without God, Whitehead believed that his cosmology was incomplete without God. His God, however, is not a being separate from and outside of nature. God is the source of creativity, of freedom, and of direction. God is immanent in the world, as well as transcendent, and becomes the sum of the actualized potentialities; God grows with the world. For Whitehead, then, the universe becomes a continually growing and developing organism.

Whitehead's influence on American thought can be seen in four areas: philosophy, religion, education, and social science. Whitehead came to the United States just as the analytic tradition in philosophy was gaining strength. Although his early work with Russell contributed to the Anglo-American analytic tradition, Whitehead's cosmological and metaphysical turn after 1924 set him apart from the philosophic mainstream from the 1930s through the 1970s. Thus Whitehead's influence has been felt more substantially outside academic philosophy. Whitehead's religious influence has been seen most clearly since the 1960s. Theologians concerned with the problems of religion and science, Catholics under the influence of Teilhard de Chardin, and liberation theologians have found useful insights in Whitehead. Whitehead's educational philosophy developed as a protest against dead knowledge and inert ideas. For him, education was a process of guiding the self-development of students. Knowledge was not to be valued for its own sake, but for its usefulness in furthering self-development. Whitehead's emphasis on interconnectedness supports the emphasis on interdisciplinarity in American education. His *Aims of Education and Other Essays* (1929) inspired teachers on both sides of the Atlantic, but his educational philosophy had less direct influence on the shape of American education than that of his contemporary, JOHN DEWEY. In the realm of social thought, Whitehead's concept of a society in process has been especially influential. He also emphasized the organism's selective response to parts of the total environment. Selective response has proven important in understanding how individuals act in a larger social order and how the different elements of the social order interact. Whitehead's work has been a rich source of insight in the sociological investigation of organizations and organizational behavior.

Although he spent only the last 23 years of his life in the United States, Alfred North Whitehead is considered an American philosopher. His early work with Bertrand Russell on the logical foundations of mathematics helped foster the analytic tradition in Anglo-American thought that has dominated American philosophy since the 1930s. His later cosmological and metaphysical work, done largely after coming to the United States, has helped to shape recent religious thought, to deepen our understanding of social organization, and to inspire educational thinkers and practitioners.

DANIEL J. WILSON

FURTHER READING
Victor Lowe, *Understanding Whitehead* (Baltimore: Johns Hopkins University Press, 1962).
——, *Alfred North Whitehead: the Man and His Work*, vol. 1: *1861–1910*; vol. 2: *1910–1947*, ed. J. B. Schneewind (Baltimore: Johns Hopkins University Press, 1985, 1990).
Paul Arthur Schilpp, ed., *The Philosophy of Alfred North Whitehead*, 2nd ed. (New York: Tudor, 1951).

Whitman, Walt[er] (b. West Hills, N.Y., May 31, 1819; d. Camden, N.J., Mar. 26, 1892).   The future poet spent his youth in and around Brooklyn and Manhattan, where he worked at a variety of jobs, ranging from country schoolteacher and printer's assistant to newspaper writer and sometime editor. Active during the same years in the radical wing of local Democratic Party politics, he published a number of tales, a temperance novel entitled *Franklin Evans* (1842), and some conventional verse. Whitman seems to have begun in the early 1850s to write the kind of original and controversial poetry which would make his reputation. This bold departure came in response to a combination of stimuli as varied as the explosive sectional crisis in national politics and a phrenological reading of his skull—which suggested among other things that he was highly "adhesive," that is, strongly emotionally drawn to other persons of his own sex.

Whitman published the first version of *Leaves of Grass* in July 1855. In its initial form the tall, slender volume contained only 12 poems, the first of which, later entitled "Song of Myself," ran to over half the length of the book. The book was elaborately decorated with scrolling, had leafy designs on its cover, and featured inside a frontispiece engraving of the author in worker's garb, his undershirt visible at his neck and his hat cocked at the viewer at a rakish angle. The contents of the book were equally provocative. The poems were written in long, unrhymed lines, and the breadth of their references was extraordinary. The poet endeavored to include in his work all parts of the human body, including the "private" parts, and all kinds of occupations and social conditions—bricklayers, prostitutes, loafers, slaves at auction.

Judging from his long, vatic "Preface" to the first version of *Leaves of Grass*, Whitman hoped the book would move a large popular audience of American readers to "absorb" him as their first fully "democratic" poet. Instead, it sold few copies and evoked complex and generally negative responses from the literary men to whom Whitman directed copies. RALPH WALDO EMERSON made the most positive response, writing to Whitman (previously unknown to him) to "greet [him] at the beginning of a great career" and to congratulate him on "the most extraordinary piece of wit and wisdom that America has yet contributed." The enthusiasm of the preeminent transcendentalist philosopher and poet later cooled, however, after Whitman excerpted this congratulatory letter as a blurb on the spine of the second, expanded version of *Leaves of Grass* (1856) and then subsequently resisted Emerson's advice to make the third version of the book (1860) less insistently sexual.

Whitman was one of the first writers to embrace the TECHNOLOGY of mass production and national distribution ("What is commonest, cheapest, nearest, easiest, is Me," he wrote in "Song of Myself," section 14), along with the literary MASS CULTURE that emerged thanks to these innovations, including cheap, high-volume printing and publication methods. A denizen of the burgeoning working-class boardinghouse, streetcorner, and tavern culture of the new metropolis, and a student as well as (presumably) a practitioner of the novel modes of social and sexual relations among males that it enabled, Whitman was also an early champion of the centrality of sexuality in the lives of the relatively freefloating populations of the big city. "Difficult as it will be," he wrote retrospectively in "A Backward Glance o'er Travel'd Roads" (1888),

it has become, in my opinion, imperative to achieve a shifted attitude . . . towards the thought and fact of sexuality, as an element in character, personality, the emotions, and a theme in literature. I am not going to argue the question by itself; it does not stand by itself.

Many of Whitman's early readers were offended, and others excited, not only by the boldness of his representations of sexual organs and acts but also by his general insistence on recognizing the value of bodily pleasures of all kinds.

In 1860, in the third edition of *Leaves of Grass*, Whitman inserted a section of 45 new poems entitled "Calamus," in which he attempted to represent the full emotional range of male–male desire, from bitter regret to ecstatic union. Aware that these were the most revealing of all his poems, not only of his own "adhesiveness" but of the intensities of same-sex desire in general, Whitman nevertheless staunchly persisted in reprinting "Calamus" in its entirety in all subsequent editions of *Leaves of Grass* published

during his lifetime—with the exception of a couple of poems which he did withdraw after their initial appearance in "Calamus" ("Long I Thought That Knowledge Alone Would Suffice" and "Hours Continuing Long, Sore and Heavy-Hearted").

Whitman made another crucially important addition to *Leaves of Grass* as a consequence of his participation in the Civil War as a volunteer nurse in the military hospitals of Washington, D.C. "Drum-Taps," the section of poems about the war added to the fourth (1867) version of the book, is impelled by the powerful currents of male-homoerotic love which Whitman saw underlying the heroism of the common soldiers. The relation between the desire of one male for another and the extraordinary generosity and courage of the many Civil War combatants he had observed in the hospitals is also an important topic in Whitman's extended essay *Democratic Vistas* (1867–8). In this work, the poet speculated on the nation's prospects in the aftermath of the war, rebutting what he considered the antidemocratic cultural analysis in such works as Thomas Carlyle's "Shooting Niagara" and Matthew Arnold's *Culture and Anarchy*. *Democratic Vistas* reasserted Whitman's faith in the class of persons which he magniloquently calls the

Grand common stock! to me the accomplish'd and convincing growth, prophetic of the future; proof undeniable to sharpest sense, of perfect beauty, tenderness and pluck, that never feudal lord, nor Greek, nor Roman breed, yet rival'd.

In a second prose work, *Specimen Days* (1882), Whitman presented dozens of "memoranda" of episodes of his wartime experience ("Bad Wounds—The Young" and "The Real War Will Never Get in the Books" are characteristic entries), along with his observations about such topics as the pleasures of outdoor life ("Sundown Perfume—Quail Notes—The Hermit-Thrush") and the health benefits of nude sunbathing.

Whitman has long been known to his many readers in the Americas and beyond as "the poet of democracy." His conceptions of the political and of the modern cannot be understood apart from the high valuation of sexuality, especially male homosexuality, that permeates his writing. A working-class autodidact, Whitman learned substantially from such disparate sources as Epictetus' stoic ethics, Hegel's philosophy of history, and the grand nature theory of Alexander von Humboldt and later of Charles Darwin. Whitman seems also to have learned from his participation in the common life of the streets of 1850s New York City and of the Civil War military hospitals that new political and social realities had emerged in his time that demanded responses of a kind that previous generations could hardly have foreseen. Throughout the century since his death, Whitman has continued to inspire readers of many kinds to imitate his full embrace of modernity and to attempt to articulate further the kinds of impassioned visions of emergent conditions that characterize his writing.

MICHAEL MOON

FURTHER READING

Betsy Erkkila, *Whitman the Political Poet* (New York: Oxford University Press, 1989).

George B. Hutchinson, *The Ecstatic Whitman: Literary Shamanism and the Crisis of the Union* (Columbus: Ohio State University Press, 1986).

M. Jimmie Killingsworth, *Whitman's Poetry of the Body: Sexuality, Politics, and the Text* (Chapel Hill: University of North Carolina Press, 1989).

Michael Moon, *Disseminating Whitman: Revision and Corporeality in "Leaves of Grass"* (Cambridge: Harvard University Press, 1991).

Eve Kosofsky Sedgwick, "Toward the Twentieth Century: English Readers of Whitman," in *Between Men: English Literature and Male Homosocial Desire* (New York: Columbia University Press, 1985).

Charley Shively, ed., *Calamus Lovers: Walt Whitman's Working Class Camerados* (San Francisco: Gay Sunshine Press, 1987).

——, *Drum Beats: Walt Whitman's Civil War Boy Lovers* (San Francisco: Gay Sunshine Press, 1989).

Sean Wilentz, *Chants Democratic: New York City and the Rise of the American Working Class, 1788–1850* (New York: Oxford University Press, 1986).

Whittier, John Greenleaf (b. near Haverhill, Mass., Dec. 17, 1807; d. Hampton Falls, Mass., Sept 7, 1892). Poet and reformer. Best remembered for his poem *Snow-Bound* (1866), Whittier wrote poems, songs, and pamphlets that inspired abolitionists and other reformers. Believing that the sufferings of white women were far less than those of black slaves, he protested that the abolitionists' debates over women's rights were a distracting and extraneous issue. After the Civil War he devoted his life to literature, composing numerous hymns and writing bucolic poems about life in the villages and farms of New England's preindustrial past.

FURTHER READING

Edward Wagenknecht, *John Greenleaf Whittier: a Portrait in Paradox* (New York: Oxford University Press, 1967).

Whorf, Benjamin Lee (b. Winthrop, Mass., Apr. 24, 1897; d. Wethersfield, Conn., July 26, 1941). The facts of Benjamin Lee Whorf's life make clear that this most visionary and influential of American anthropological linguists was an amateur, in the great line of American scientific and creative amateurism

that runs from Benjamin Franklin to John Cage. Whorf graduated in 1918 from the Massachusetts Institute of Technology with a degree in chemical engineering. He then took a job with the Hartford Fire Insurance Company as a fire prevention engineer. The field was new then, and Whorf became a pioneer in it, remaining with Hartford in essentially the same line for the rest of his life; he was made Special Agent in 1928 and Assistant Secretary in 1940.

Whorf began his avocational work in linguistics around 1924, under the influence of the French philologist and mystic Antoine Fabre d'Olivet (1768–1825). He took from d'Olivet an interest in deep lexical and phonetic structures, and in pursuit of that interest wrote his early accounts of Nahuatl and of Mayan language and hieroglyphs. Then, under the mentoring influence of EDWARD SAPIR (1884–1939), he turned his attention from deep lexical structures to deep grammatical ones, and began to ask what maps of the world were implied in such structures, how accurate those maps were, and to what extent speakers of a language were constrained to see only the map their LANGUAGE implied. His answers to these questions are given both in his extraordinary technical essays on Hopi and in the more popular essays he wrote on general linguistic questions toward the end of his life.

Whorf's work bears, then, on two related matters: the nature and prestige of certain Native American languages, and the nature of linguistic difference generally. The power of his work is a consequence of his keeping these matters in relation; many of the critiques of his work fail because they separate them.

Abstracted from the individual essays, Whorf's argument consists of three propositions. The first is that languages do, in some cases, differ radically in the map they imply of the natural world. Whorf does not argue that every language differs radically from every other, or that radical differences in mapping are encoded in a language's lexicon. He does argue, with great power, that Hopi in particular differs radically from what he calls Standard Average European (SAE), and differs not in its lexicon but in its deep grammatical structure. The second proposition is based on the assumption that the maps languages imply can be evaluated for accuracy. (Whorf was, as George Lakoff writes in *Women, Fire, and Dangerous Things*, a "relativist with respect to fact" but an objectivist "with respect to value" [p. 324].) On that assumption, Whorf argues that Hopi implies not only a different map of the natural world than does SAE, but also a better one; in particular he argues in *Language, Thought, and Reality* that Hopi does a better job of mapping the natural world described by modern physics: "in this field and in various others, English compared to Hopi is like a bludgeon compared to a rapier" (p. 85). The third proposition is that languages constrain their speakers to see the maps their languages imply. Whorf is of course describing in English the map implied by Hopi, and this fact and others like it may seem to refute this proposition; Whorf's argument, however, bears not on what a speaker *can consciously know about* that map, but on how a speaker *must habitually see by means of* that map.

Critics of Whorf's work object (1) that his argument is falsified by experiment, (2) that he understands language *only* as a map of the natural world, and (3) that his account of linguistic relativity neither makes clear, in Ann Berthoff's phrase, "just *what* is relative to *what*" (p. 9), nor holds to a single description of how constraining the relationship is. The first objection is only partly true. The most elegant and ingenious of the experiments devised to test correlations between language and nonlinguistic behavior, the Kay-Kempton experiment testing relations between color and terminology and color recognition, has tended to confirm Whorf's argument. (That experiment showed that speakers of English, having names both for green and for blue, were, when asked which of three color chips in the blue-to-green range was most different from the other two, likely to "push" colors on the blue side of the blue–green boundary toward blue, and that speakers of the Uto-Aztecan language Tarahumara, which has only one name for the blue-green sector of the spectrum, exhibited no such behavior.)

The second and third objections, on the other hand, are true, and the weak side of Whorf's amateurishness is shown both in his reduction of language to a means of mapping the natural world, without any consideration of its relation to the social world, and in his inconsistent and slipshod diction. But these objections only point to the tasks that anthropological linguists inspired by Whorf's vision of language have before them. George Lakoff's admiring essay on Whorf, for example, responds to the critique of Whorf's diction; Lakoff refines Whorf's terms to produce a more sophisticated and lucid relativism, in which "*systematic* differences in conceptualization" (p. 336), reflected in the grammar of a language, can "affect behavior" (p. 337), but cannot determine it because conceptual systems are not monolithic.

Whorf's linguistic RELATIVISM, with its auspicious mix of fixed natural values and varying linguistic ones, could contribute much to our current debates over cultural relativism. His work legitimately retains a lot of influence, both as a celebration of the intellectual complexity and precision of Native American languages, and as a resonant description of the radical differences between languages and of the constraints languages make on behavior.

LAWRENCE ALAN ROSENWALD

See also INDIAN IDENTITIES; TRANSLATION.

FURTHER READING

Ann E. Berthoff, "Sapir and the Two Tasks of Language," *Semiotica* 71 (1988): 1–47.

Dell Hymes, "On Typology of Cognitive Styles," *Anthropological Linguistics* 3 (1961): 22–54.

George Lakoff, *Women, Fire, and Dangerous Things* (Chicago: University of Chicago Press, 1987).

James H. Stam, "An Historical Perspective on 'Linguistic Relativity,'" in R. W. Rieber, ed., *Psychology of Language and Thought* (New York: Plenum, 1980).

George Steiner, *On Difficulty and Other Essays* (New York: Oxford University Press, 1978).

Benjamin Lee Whorf, *Language, Thought, and Reality: Selected Writings of Benjamin Lee Whorf*, ed. John B. Carroll (Cambridge: MIT Press, 1956).

Wiener, Norbert (b. Columbia, Mo., Nov. 26, 1894; d. Stockholm, Sweden, Mar. 18, 1964). Mathematician. In *Cybernetics: or, Control and Communication in the Animal and the Machine* (1948), Wiener coined the term "cybernetics" to describe the study of information flow in and between living and mechanical beings. Computers and nervous systems, he suggested, use analagous procedures—for instance, feedback loops—to counter entropy and produce a desired result. The danger is that, as computers become more powerful, humans may cede control over their use: computers will become ubiquitous, and the social world will adapt to them instead of the reverse. Wiener's earlier work on harmonic analysis—and on the probabilistic description of physical processes that have an element of randomness, such as Brownian motion—aided in the development of quantum theory.

FURTHER READING

Steven J. Heims, *John von Neumann and Norbert Wiener: From Mathematics to the Technologies of Life and Death* (Cambridge: MIT Press, 1980).

Willard, Emma (b. Berlin, Conn., Feb. 23, 1787; d. Troy, N.Y., Apr. 15, 1870). Educator. Founder of the Troy Female Seminary, Willard believed that young women should learn academic subjects usually reserved for men, along with the usual courses in domestic work, religion and morality, and the ornamental arts that they would need as wives and mothers. Her "Plan for Improving Female Education" (1819), addressed to the New York legislature, argued (unsuccessfully) that states should charter and finance colleges for women as well as men. Educated mothers would raise citizens of better character, she explained, and female teachers would be both more virtuous and less expensive than male teachers. Graduates of the school she founded, now the Emma Willard School, played an important part in the development of American education.

FURTHER READING

Alma Lutz, *Emma Willard, Pioneer Educator of American Women* (Boston: Beacon, 1964).

Willard, Frances (b. Churchville, N.Y., Sept. 28, 1839; d. New York, N.Y., Feb. 18, 1898). Born into an old New England family which migrated in 1846 to an isolated farm in Janesville, Wisconsin, Willard reveled in the freedom of an unconventional girlhood but longed for social contacts. Teaching positions proved her ticket into the wider world, and led her to the presidency of the Woman's College of Northwestern University in 1871. Resigning from this job in 1874, shortly after the Woman's Crusade in Ohio brought temperance into the headlines, she began her lifelong association with the temperance movement. By 1879 she was president of the recently formed Woman's Christian Temperance Union, and for the next 20 years oversaw its development into the first mass national women's movement, boasting a membership of over 150,000. Willard, a noted Methodist laywoman, used her position as head of the most influential woman's group of the 1880s and 1890s to become a nationally known spokeswoman on matters of social policy extending well beyond temperance. During this period "St. Frances" was the most visible woman in American public life.

The WCTU called itself "organized mother love," and its strength lay in a woman-centered organization and a maternal politics. Willard was a charismatic leader whose social life centered around women: except for a brief engagement her most intimate relationships were with her mother and a series of female friends. The union's public face was womanly as well: without challenging nineteenth-century GENDER roles, the movement cast its political initiatives as a defense of the family. More comfortable with duties than RIGHTS, the WCTU constructed a network of obligations in which alcoholism represented not victimless self-abuse, but a breach of familial and social duty. Willard found Robinson Crusoe—the hero of liberal individualists—a pathetic and unrepresentative figure, and she deplored the emphasis on individual FREEDOM at the expense of social accountability. Willard feared that the standard liberal split between public and private spheres posed the danger of allowing the "private" arena of business to function with no moral compass. She preferred to imagine SOCIETY as a set of concentric circles moving outward from the home; thus those engaged in commercial and public life could be judged by the same standard of moral behavior and maternal care that ruled at home.

While temperance remained the union's organizing principle, Willard was instrumental in expanding its agenda to include woman suffrage. The ballot was a goal temperance workers shared with other suffragists, but their rationale relied more on utilitarian good than on abstract right: their suffrage slogan was "Home Protection." Under Willard's leadership the WCTU aggressively entered the male world of politics, both to seek the vote for women and to support the Prohibition Party in national elections.

But it was Willard's genius to lead the union beyond conventional politics, pioneering new forms of governance which circumvented the sphere of law and legislation. Rejecting a narrow definition of temperance, she viewed the movement as a complex of social issues touching the welfare of families. This broad approach translated into the national union's adoption of a progressive social agenda: nurseries and kindergartens, hygiene and nutrition programs, public health and sanitation initiatives, and support for labor's positions on minimum wage and the eight-hour day. Willard made clear that these services should not depend on private charity: her contribution to political theory was the concept of the "maternal state." One of the earliest proponents of state-run WELFARE programs, she saw government as benevolent and omnipotent, tenderly ministering to the needs of her citizens. Unlike many liberal feminists, Willard and her followers were enthusiastic advocates of a theocratic Christian nationalism. The big state held no fears for them, and *Looking Backward* by EDWARD BELLAMY became one of Willard's favorite texts. In pursuit of this vision union members took the lead in creating and staffing new state and local posts in health and education. Her supporters were part of the wave of voluntary groups that parlayed their good works into quasi-official institutions at the end of the nineteenth century, laying the groundwork for the vastly expanded state and federal bureaucracies of the twentieth century.

Willard's thought always outstripped that of her followers, and by the 1890s she had moved well beyond temperance. She spent much of this decade in England, where she became associated with Fabian socialism; and in the United States her overtures to the Knights of Labor and the Populist Party gave pause to some WCTU members who feared that a radical image would weaken their cause. The WCTU's flexible organization, making national initiatives optional for state and local chapters, defused tension over the progressive national platform. But it became clear that the rank and file would not follow Willard far down the path to SOCIALISM, and after her death the union returned to a more conventional temperance platform.

Because she was so closely associated with a movement now regarded as quaint, Frances Willard's fame has not lasted into the twentieth century. Recently, though, historians have made a more positive assessment of temperance, acknowledging the dangers that male alcoholism, a very common nineteenth-century affliction, posed to women and children. Willard's temperance suffragism also represents a valuable "womanist" critique of the individualist, rights-based orientation of liberal suffragists like ELIZABETH CADY STANTON. Some women's historians have continued to interpret Willard's politics as reinforcing the most repressive aspects of patriarchal society; in their view only an insistence on a theory of rights and autonomous selfhood can deliver women from the subordination inevitably contained in a "maternal politics."

Willard's own characterization of the WCTU as providing every American with 100,000 mothers tells both sides of the tale. Certainly the temperance movement had a repressive and elitist thrust in its theocratic agenda of prohibition, censorship, school prayer, Sunday closing, and social purity. In a democratic society, the mother–child relationship is not the best paradigm for the relationship between the citizen and the state, and represents the meddlesome face of a "connective" politics. At the same time, Willard and other temperance women went much further than liberal feminists in imagining the concrete contours of an expanded state that would address the ills of an unregulated, industrializing society; and in emphasizing that individual rights only made sense in the broader context of both private and public RESPONSIBILITY and OBLIGATION.

ELIZABETH B. CLARK

See also MOTHERHOOD; WOMEN'S RIGHTS.

FURTHER READING

Ruth Bordin, *Frances Willard, A Biography* (Chapel Hill: University of North Carolina Press, 1986).

Mari Jo Buhle, *Women and American Socialism, 1879–1920* (Urbana: University of Illinois Press, 1981).

Elizabeth B. Clark, "The Politics of God and the Woman's Vote: Religion in the Suffrage Movement in America, 1848–1895," Ph.D. diss. Princeton University, 1989.

Mary Earhart, *Frances Willard, From Prayers to Politics* (Chicago: University of Chicago Press, 1944).

Barbara L. Epstein, *The Politics of Domesticity: Women, Evangelism, and Temperance in Nineteenth-Century America* (Middletown, Conn.: Wesleyan University Press, 1981).

Amy R. Slagell, "A Good Woman Speaking Well: the Oratory of Frances E. Willard," Ph.D. diss., University of Wisconsin-Madison, 1992; contains a number of texts of Willard's speeches.

Frances E. Willard, *Glimpses of Fifty Years: the Autobiography of an American Woman* (Chicago: Woman's Temperance Publishing Association, 1889).

——, *"Writing Out My Heart": the Journal of Frances E. Willard, 1855–1896, a Selected Edition*, ed. Carolyn DeSwarte Gifford (Urbana: University of Illinois Press, 1994).

Williams, Roger (b. London, England, ca. 1603; d. Providence, R.I., between Jan. 16 and Mar. 15, 1683). Minister, religious dissident, statesman, diplomat, and founder of Rhode Island, Roger Williams was born in England, the son of a prosperous merchant tailor. He was educated at Charterhouse School and later Pembroke Hall, Cambridge, where he received his bachelor of arts degree in 1627. Two years later he accepted employment as chaplain to a prominent Puritan family in Essex, and he soon gained the acquaintance of important and influential members of the Puritan gentry. His prospects for a living in England, however, were bleak, so he and his wife Mary set sail in late 1630 for New England, where he hoped to become a missionary to the Indians. He quickly discovered that his life in the New World would not be what he had supposed.

Williams's uncompromising beliefs set him apart from the mainstream of PURITANISM. He declined the position of teacher in the Boston church, saying he dared not "officiate to an unseparated people," a congregation not formally separated from the Church of England. Over the next five years, Williams's Separatism became a painful thorn in the side of the Massachusetts Puritans. Williams became pastor of the church in Salem, a small community north of Boston, and preached against the right of magistrates to punish breaches of God's first four Commandments. His position revealed his deep conviction that the affairs of church and state should be divided by a "wall of separation"; it also convinced the Boston authorities that Williams was dangerous to the religious orthodoxy of the Massachusetts colony. As a result, Williams was summoned several times to appear before the General Court; in October 1635 the court voted to banish him from the colony. In January, to escape deportation to England, Williams fled from Salem in the dead chill of a winter's night and made his way to Narragansett Bay, where he took refuge in an Indian village. In the spring of 1636, having been joined by a small number of friends and their families, Williams established the settlement of Providence at the head of Narragansett Bay on land that was given to him by two Indian chieftains.

His banishment was the central event of his life, and it became for him like a soldier's wound. Williams never let anyone—particularly his adversaries in Puritan colonies of New England—forget the hardships he and his family suffered as a result of his expulsion from Massachusetts. In a pamphlet war he waged during the 1640s and 1650s against JOHN COTTON, the foremost minister of Massachusetts, and the Puritan leadership, Williams used his banishment as a dramatic example of how intolerance and the unity of church and state violated the teachings of Christ. Although his most famous published work, *The Bloudy Tenent of Persecution* (1644), made no explicit mention of his banishment, his discussion of religious liberty (what he called "liberty of conscience" or "soul liberty") throughout the book was shaped by his direct experience with intolerance and oppression. His later writings castigated the men who had exiled him.

The banishment also enabled Williams to understand the dynamics of his own role as a "witness of Christ," awaiting the appearance of Christ's apostles in the world as an imminent sign of the Second Coming. Although Williams served as a reluctant magistrate in the town of Providence and later in the colony of Rhode Island, he believed his greatest vocation lay within the framework of his own millenarian PIETY. The banishment, as he pointed out, allowed him to hear Christ's call and to understand its importance; he regarded his expulsion from Massachusetts as an act of Christ that permitted him to demonstrate his faithfulness "in any measure to suffer such great and mighty trials for His name's sake" (*Complete Writings*, vol. 1, p. 326).

His own personal suffering gave Williams a fierce commitment to the ideas of liberty of conscience and separation of church and state. Relying on this experience and on his reading of the New Testament, Williams concluded that soul liberty was necessary. No one on earth could know for certain which form of worship God had intended. Only God had the power and the wisdom to judge man in matters of conscience and religion. But Christians, said Williams, had a special duty to refrain from the persecution of others who differed in their religious beliefs. "I must be humbly bold to say," he wrote in 1651, "that 'tis impossible for any man or men to maintain their Christ by the sword, and to worship a true Christ!" (*Correspondence*, vol. 1, p. 344). Williams remained devoted to his principle of TOLERANCE throughout his lifetime, wavering only occasionally in the face of such spiritual threats as Quakerism and the polytheism of the Algonquian Indians of New England.

But he never permitted himself to respond to different forms of belief—or to the very common practice of *unbelief* among his Rhode Island neighbors—by embracing bigotry or coercion.

Scholars have regarded Williams in ways that mirror the opinions of his contemporaries. William Bradford, the governor of Plymouth, once said that Williams was "a man godly and zealous, having many precious parts but very unsettled in judgment" (Winslow, p. 104). A fellow Rhode Islander, William Coddington, declared that Williams was "a mere weathercock, constant only in unconstancy" (Fox, part 2, p. 246). Cotton Mather, the Puritan divine, called him quixotic and dangerous, but he also admitted that Williams had "the root of the matter" in him (Gaustad, p. 200). In the nineteenth century, antiquarian descendants of the Massachusetts Puritans voiced similar sentiments about Williams and his place in history, dismissing him mostly as a crank or a religious crackpot who dared to challenge orthodox opinion. During the early twentieth century, some scholars saw Williams as a progressive democrat, a harbinger of Jeffersonian democracy who happened also to crusade for religious liberty. After World War II, the scholarship of Perry Miller and Edmund S. Morgan focused attention on Williams's religious beliefs and his role as a radical Puritan.

For the past 40 years, scholars have followed the path first laid out by Miller and Morgan; unfortunately the result has been a profusion of studies that examine Williams's theology and piety as if he were a monk living in a monastery, a man possessing only an inner life. But it was the interplay of Williams's pietism and his experience in New England, and not the influence of democratic ideas and principles, that forged his commitment to liberty of conscience. To disembody the man's spirituality from his quotidian experiences is to miss the significance of the part Williams played in shaping not only Puritan New England, but also American culture.

GLENN W. LA FANTASIE

FURTHER READING

George Fox, *A New-England Fire-Brand Quenched* (London, 1679).

Edwin S. Gaustad, *Liberty of Conscience: Roger Williams in America* (Grand Rapids, Mich.: William B. Eerdmans, 1991).

W. Clark Gilpin, *The Millenarian Piety of Roger Williams* (Chicago: University of Chicago Press, 1970).

Perry Miller, *Roger Williams: His Contribution to the American Tradition* (Indianapolis: Bobbs-Merrill, 1953).

Edmund S. Morgan, *Roger Williams: the Church and the State* (New York: Harcourt, Brace and World, 1967).

Roger Williams, *The Complete Writings of Roger Williams*, 7 vols. (New York: Russell and Russell, 1963).

——, *The Correspondence of Roger Williams*, ed. Glenn W. LaFantasie, 2 vols. (Hanover, N.H.: University Press of New England, 1988).

Ola Elizabeth Winslow, *Master Roger Williams: a Biography* (New York: Macmillan, 1957).

Williams, Tennessee

Williams, Tennessee [born Thomas Lanier Williams] (b. Columbus, Miss., Mar. 26, 1911; d. New York, N.Y., Feb. 25, 1983).   Playwright. Author of *The Glass Menagerie* (1944), *A Streetcar Named Desire* (1947), and *Cat on a Hot Tin Roof* (1955), Williams sympathetically portrayed misfits plagued not by social structures or sanctions, but by their own twisted natures. Impossible dreams, misdirected sexuality, psychological imbalance, and uncontrollable violence pervade his characters' lives. Williams's interest in irrationality, delusion, and desire, combined with his powerful dialogue, generated plays rich in symbolism that starkly reveal the unalterable loneliness of life.

FURTHER READING

Donald Spoto, *The Kindness of Strangers: the Life of Tennessee Williams* (Boston: Little Brown, 1985).

Williams, William Carlos

Williams, William Carlos (b. Rutherford, N.J., Sept. 17, 1883; d. Rutherford, N.J., Mar. 4, 1963). Staunchly antiacademic, Williams was a poet, novelist, playwright, essayist, short-story writer, editor, painter, and general medical practitioner. He grew up amidst a profusion of languages and other cultural influences: his mother, who had come to the U.S. from Santo Domingo, surrounded him with French, Spanish, and Caribbean relatives, while his English father regaled him with readings that ranged from Shakespeare to the African American poet Paul Laurence Dunbar. His mixed cultural ancestry led Williams to embrace America as his only possible home, a place "expressly founded for me, personally," as he once put it. In his writings Williams set out to explore and possess that place, the New World, in ways that set him apart from many of his contemporaries.

America's topography was crucial to Williams's poetry from the start, early romantic allegories like "The Wanderer" (1914) notwithstanding. Sherman Paul notes that for Williams, poetry was "the imaginative action of men in contact with their environment" (p. 31), which put him very much at odds with the poetic doctrines of EZRA POUND and especially T. S. ELIOT. Williams's response to *The Waste Land* (1922) was unqualified horror: "It wiped out our world as if an atom bomb had been dropped upon it," he wrote in his *Autobiography* (p. 174). In defense against Eliot's Spenglerian pessimism and his Eurocentrism, Williams, the "poet of reality" who resembles Wallace Stevens's Crispin from "The Comedian as the Letter C," proposed and practiced a poetics of the local and the quotidian, a combination which, according to Ron Callan, amounts to a secular notion of "transcendence rooted firmly in the field of domesticity" (p. 192).

His belief in the New World as, ironically, "the only universal" did not keep Williams from traveling throughout Europe more than once after completing his medical training in 1909. But, unlike his close friend Ezra Pound and so many other American expatriates, Williams was not tempted to relocate. He settled into Rutherford to practice medicine for a living. Despite his New Jersey residence and the constraints of his medical practice, Williams continued to be very much a part of New York's artistic scene, where he mingled with writers such as Alfred Kreymborg, HILDA DOOLITTLE (H.D.), WALLACE STEVENS, MARIANNE MOORE, and Nathanael West. With the latter, he co-edited the short-lived journal *Contact* in 1932. Williams regularly published poems and essays in a number of small-press journals ranging from the *Little Review*, *Broom*, *transition*, and *Others*, to the *Dial*. Ironically, it was from the *Dial*, the same journal that had published *The Waste Land*, that he received a poetry award in 1926 for an embryonic version of what would later become *Paterson*. While literary influences, notably those of Whitman and Keats, are central to Williams's writing, early twentieth-century European and American visual arts also had a decided impact, not only on his shorter lyrics but on longer, collagic texts, such as *Kora in Hell* (1920), *Spring and All* (1923), and *In the American Grain* (1925). Paintings by Juan Gris, Marcel Duchamp, Marsden Hartley, Charles Sheeler, and Pieter Brueghel, and the photographs of ALFRED STIEGLITZ were important inspirations for many of Williams's Imagist poems.

If Williams was possibly the most influential and original American poet of this century, he was also in many ways the most neglected, at least until the early 1950s, when four out of the five books of *Paterson* had been published (1946–51; the fifth followed in 1958). A controversial reaffirmation of Whitmanian plenitude against Eliotic sterility, *Paterson*, that American "epic" which some have labeled "romantic," others "modern," was much more difficult to ignore than Williams's briefer lyrics. Yet, despite the proliferation of critical work on him during the past 40 years, Williams still tends to be excluded from versions of the American poetic canon in which WALLACE STEVENS occupies the place of Whitman's most successful twentieth-century heir.

One of the results of the literary standing Williams

finally acquired with *Paterson* was the recovery of *In the American Grain*, a curious assemblage of 21 "essays" on American history, whose initial critical reception had been spectacularly negative. None of Williams's contemporaries, from KENNETH BURKE to D. H. Lawrence, had much appreciation for the experimental "indigenism" of this book-length appeal to "facing inland" instead of to Europe, and the kind of cultural "regeneration" that was more concerned with Native Americans, outlaws, conquistadors, and Catholic missionaries than with paying homage to Emerson, Thoreau, Hawthorne, and even Whitman. Much like *Paterson*, *In the American Grain* resists literary (and historiographic) conventions as it emphasizes America's *genius loci*, the spirit of the place which Williams designates as "Indian." The place to which Williams lays claim in *In the American Grain* is that of the New World, not just of the United States. He does retrieve EDGAR ALLAN POE as an "authentic" literary forebear. Yet Poe's importance for Williams is not that of a transcendent writer surpassing time and place but that of a beacon of American terrain.

Merging documentary with fictional modes, *In the American Grain* is a tough-minded critique of New England PURITANISM and its cultural legacy. Part of that legacy during the early decades of the twentieth century was the concept of cultural pluralism as pioneered by HORACE KALLEN. Cultural pluralism, formulated at the very time when immigration became subject to national origin quotas, gained currency and acceptance as a liberal alternative to the "melting pot" idea of Americanization. Kallen and others saw cultural pluralism as a way of giving each people its voice, rather than reducing them to a common, standardized type. But Williams suggested that pluralism, far from empowering each ethnic or racial group, was a subtle way of furthering Puritan parochialism and exclusivity: a variety of white ethnic cultural traditions could be celebrated, while certain undesirable "others," notable African Americans and other peoples of color, were excluded from the political and cultural mainstream.

Ironically, *In the American Grain* does its own share of cultural stereotyping—of the Puritans, of Catholicism, of Native Americans (whom Williams reduces to "ghostly souls"), and of African Americans (whose vernacular speech and music he exoticizes). But his sharp critique of North Americans' fear of cross-cultural, and especially of cross-racial, "contact" remains astute in suggesting that what appeared—in the notion of cultural pluralism—to be a culturally inclusive process was actually coercive, a process indeed of internal colonization, to use the language of a later day. Williams's insights can be directly applied to late twentieth-century assessments of CULTURAL PLURALISM AND MULTICULTURALISM in relation to emerging literatures. Traditionalists are well known for resisting the relativistic implications of cultural pluralism. But as Williams understood, what poses as pluralism may well be another form of ghettoization that needs to be resisted by the very groups it purports to empower. As he writes in *Paterson*, Book Four: "Dissonance / (if you are interested) / leads to discovery" (p. 176).

VERA M. KUTZINSKI

FURTHER READING
Ron Callan, *William Carlos Williams and Transcendentalism* (London: Macmillan, 1992).
Joel Conarroe, *William Carlos Williams' "Paterson": Language and Landscape* (Philadelphia: University Press of Pennsylvania, 1970).
Bram Dijkstra, *The Hieroglyphics of a New Speech: Cubism, Stieglitz, and the Early Poetry of William Carlos Williams* (Princeton: Princeton University Press, 1969).
Vera M. Kutzinski, *Against the American Grain: Myth and History in William Carlos Williams, Jay Wright, and Nicolás Guillén* (Baltimore: Johns Hopkins University Press, 1987.)
Paul L. Mariani, *William Carlos Williams: a New World Naked* (New York: McGraw-Hill, 1981).
Sherman Paul, *The Music of Survival* (Urbana: University of Illinois Press, 1968).
Joseph N. Riddel, *The Inverted Bell: Modernism and the Counterpoetics of William Carlos Williams* (Baton Rouge: Louisiana State University Press, 1974).
William Carlos Williams, *The Autobiography of William Carlos Williams* (1951; New York: New Directions, 1967).
——, *Paterson* (New York: New Directions, 1958).

Wilson, Edmund (b. Red Bank, N.J., May 8, 1895; d. Talcottville, N.Y., June 12, 1972). Few American writers defy easy characterization more than Edmund Wilson. He was a literary critic, novelist, poet, playwright, historian, journalist, travel writer, memoirist, and cultural conscience. Above all, he was—as Henry James said of Charles Sainte-Beuve—"the student, the inquirer, the observer, the active indefatigable commentator, whose constant aim was to arrive at justness of characterization." Because he resisted the triumph of the professional in American intellectual life after World War II, Wilson has often been termed the last great American "man of letters"—a title that both pays tribute to his catholic interests and suggests the air of anachronism that hung about him in the last years of his career.

Wilson was born into the local gentry of the Jersey shore. His father was a brilliant trial lawyer and sometime state attorney general, and his mother was a prominent socialite. Bereft of acquaintances beyond the family circle, he suffered a lonely childhood, his isolation compounded by his mother's deafness and his father's periodic bouts of depression and hypochondria. His relationship with his mother would always be a distant one. Having hoped for a son who would accompany her to Princeton football games, she disapproved of his decision to become a writer and never read his work. Wilson was much more deeply attached to his troubled father, who detested the ravages of industrial capitalism and (like his son after him) took his moral bearings from the early nineteenth-century world represented by the family's old stone house in the hamlet of Talcottville in upstate New York. From his father, Wilson received the gifts of intellectual curiosity and social sympathy. His description in *A Piece of My Mind* (1956) of his father's courtroom manner as "a mixture of learning, logic, dramatic imagination, and eloquence" (p. 218) might well stand as a characterization of his own work.

Wilson attended prep school at the Hill School in Pennsylvania, where he received a rigorous classical education and was taught to write with "Lucidity, Force, and Ease." He entered Princeton University in 1912, where he was a classmate and friend of F. SCOTT FITZGERALD and John Peale Bishop. A bookish young man determined to become a writer, he edited the college literary magazine and starred in the classroom of his favorite teacher Christian Gauss, who introduced him to modern European literature and nurtured his lifelong fascination with languages.

After graduating from Princeton in 1916, Wilson worked briefly as a reporter for the *New York Evening Sun* before enlisting as a private in the hospital corps following American entry into World War I. He served in Europe until 1919, transferring to military intelligence in order to distance himself somewhat from the horrors of a war he came to regard as "the abortion of every kindly impulse." Upon returning to the United States, he took up residence in Greenwich Village and landed a job on the staff of *Vanity Fair*. Soon thereafter he began to write regularly for THE NEW REPUBLIC, which would serve as the principal outlet for his writing in the interwar years.

Wilson would later come to think of himself as a "man of the twenties," and his published writing and notebooks provide an unequaled tour of the culture of that decade. His capacity to write well about anything that captured his imagination was quickly evident. He churned out drama and book reviews, reportage of sensational murder trials, and essays on an extraordinary range of subjects including architecture, jazz, and the circus. Unlike many of his contemporaries, Wilson was able to do good work while drinking heavily and sustaining a promiscuous sex life, and he found material for his first novel,

I Thought of Daisy (1929), in love affairs with poet EDNA ST. VINCENT MILLAY and with a woman he picked up on the streets of New York. But it was as a literary critic that Wilson achieved his greatest stature in these years. He championed the cause of such young writers as Fitzgerald and ERNEST HEMINGWAY, and in his remarkable survey of "symbolist" writing, *Axel's Castle* (1931), he guided American readers to the riches of Yeats, Eliot, Proust, Joyce, and other modern masters.

Although Wilson probably did more than anyone else to carry MODERNISM to American shores, he was uneasy about what he saw as the dissociation of modern writers from a critical engagement with the life of their society, and with the onset of the Great Depression he plunged into radical politics. In *American Jitters* (1932) he recorded his travels across an American social landscape laid waste by the collapse of capitalism, and in the pages of *The New Republic* (January 14, 1931) he appealed to progressives to "take Communism away from the Communists." Turning from modernism in literature to modernism in politics, Wilson devoted much of his energy in the 1930s to the study of Marxism and the European revolutionary traditions that lay behind the Russian Revolution. Although Wilson's enthusiasm for Marxism and the Soviet Union cooled in the wake of Stalin's purges, the product of his researches, *To the Finland Station* (1940), was an extraordinary work of historical imagination and arguably his finest book.

The early 1940s were dark years for Wilson. Fitzgerald's untimely death in 1940 was followed by the end of Wilson's stormy, eight-year marriage (his third) to MARY MCCARTHY in 1946. His isolationist convictions led him to oppose American participation in World War II, which brought an end to his association with *The New Republic*. Nonetheless, his productivity did not slacken. Turning from Marx to Freud in the *Wound and the Bow* (1941), he acutely analyzed the relationship between art and neurosis in writers such as Dickens, Kipling, and Hemingway. In 1943 he signed on for a stint as literary editor of the *New Yorker*, and this magazine would be the principal venue for his work for the next 30 years.

After the war literary criticism moved into the hands of academic professionals, some of whom disparaged Wilson's writing as little more than popular journalism and afforded him no place in their critical canon. In this and other respects, Wilson found himself increasingly out of place in his culture. In response, he unleashed a sequence of caustic assaults on the suburban middle class (*Memoirs of Hecate County*, 1946), on the American state (*The Cold War and the Income Tax*, 1963), and on literary pedantry (*The Fruits of the MLA*, 1968). At the same time, as if to reflect his sense of marginality, he devoted himself to traveling in and writing about various "marginal" civilizations and cultures in such books as *Scrolls from the Dead Sea* (1955), *Apologies to the Iroquois* (1959), and *Red, Black, Blond, and Olive* (1956)—an account of his visits to Zuñi, New Mexico, Haiti, Russia, and Israel.

Wilson sought solace in the past as well, and turned in particular to Talcottville and his own family's Jeffersonian past for refuge (memorializing this world in 1971 in his last book, *Upstate*). His criticism took on an elegiac quality, enhanced by his publication of *The Shores of Light* (1952) and *The American Earthquake* (1958), massive collections of old pieces from the 1920s and 1930s. The crowning achievement of Wilson's last years was *Patriotic Gore* (1962), a masterful study of the literature of the Civil War and a register of Wilson's deep ambivalence about his nation's politics, society, and culture. Here penetrating and sometimes moving portraits of figures such as ABRAHAM LINCOLN, HARRIET BEECHER STOWE, Alexander Stephens, and OLIVER WENDELL HOLMES JR. were prefaced by a bitter introduction that stripped the Union cause of any moral claims and drew no distinctions between Nazi, Soviet, and American foreign policy, likening every nation at war to a voracious sea slug. As Alfred Kazin noted in *New York Jew* (1978), this preface was "an effort to deny the love of the American past and [Wilson's] belief in American moral heroism that made the book itself so moving" (p. 246).

Shortly before his death, Wilson began to edit his notebooks for publication, and these volumes, now complete in five volumes covering *The Twenties* (1975) through *The Sixties* (1993), afford an unparalleled view of a life in which nothing mattered more than words, than language. "There is no other critic," Kazin observed in *The Inmost Leaf* (1959), "who so evenly and so hauntingly writes criticism as a work of art." Wilson wrote "like a man whose life hangs on the rightness of each sentence" (p. 95). Such a critic, even when he was wrong, was, and still is, worth reading.

ROBERT B. WESTBROOK

FURTHER READING
David Castronovo, *Edmund Wilson* (New York: Frederick Ungar, 1984).
George H. Douglas, *Edmund Wilson's America* (Lexington: University Press of Kentucky, 1983).
Sherman Paul, *Edmund Wilson: a Study of the Literary Vocation in Our Time* (Urbana: University of Illinois Press, 1965).
Edmund Wilson, *Letters on Literature and Politics, 1912–1972*, ed. Elena Wilson (New York: Farrar, Straus and Giroux, 1977).
——, *A Piece of My Mind: Reflections at Sixty* (New York: Farrar, Straus and Cudahy, 1956).
——, *The Portable Edmund Wilson*, ed. Lewis M. Dabney (New York: Viking Penguin, 1983).

Wilson, James (b. Carskerdo, Scotland, Sept. 14, 1742; d. Edenton, N.C., Aug. 21, 1798). Amid the current revival of scholarly interest in American constitutional theory, Wilson should become a founding father of increasing significance because he personified so many of the complexities and anomalies characteristic of early American civic culture. Throughout the birth and early life of the Republic he proved an aristocratic democrat, a visionary conservative, a brilliant lawyer disinclined to reduce constitutionalism to legalism, and a founder singularly ambitious for fame and fortune who soon lost both, despite contributions to the Founding unsurpassed by all but the foremost demigods of his generation.

Wilson emigrated to America from Scotland in 1765, at age 23. He brought with him not only the aspirations of the humble immigrant but also the resources of a strong university education, at St. Andrews, in the ideas of the Scottish ENLIGHTENMENT. His penchant for copious learning and abstract ideas would become the hallmarks of his public career in his new homeland. He settled in Pennsylvania; there his youthful training in law and his successful law practice served as the springboard to public prominence.

Wilson was too much the man of grand theory to be content for long with the routine of the common lawyer. In 1768 he penned (although he did not publish until 1774) his *Considerations on the Nature and Extent of the Legislative Authority of the British Parliament*, which anticipated the later proto-Revolutionary arguments of THOMAS JEFFERSON, JOHN ADAMS, and others that colonial America's only constitutional tie with the federal British empire was allegiance to the crown.

Wilson's law training and practice also helped launch his career in political office. He was elected several times to the Continental Congress, where he became increasingly identified with nationalist "conservative" financial interests. He was also elected a delegate to the Federal Convention of 1787, to the Pennsylvania Ratification convention, and then to the Pennsylvania constitutional convention of 1790.

Wilson made his greatest mark as a distinctively erudite, cogent, and systematically principled framer and theoretician of American constitutionalism. At the Philadelphia Convention of 1787 he was second only to JAMES MADISON in influence and effectiveness.

He then became one of the earliest nationally prominent advocates of Ratification; and he led the crucial and successful Ratification campaign in Pennsylvania. In all these endeavors as framer and founder he distinguished himself particularly in his visionary appreciation of the importance of the separation of powers; a strong, popularly authorized executive branch; and, indeed, the fundamental idea of popularly authorized government comprehending even an unelected judicial branch of authority fully equal to that of the legislature and executive.

Moreover, Wilson's ideas about the purposes of government were so forthrightly visionary that they isolated him, even as they impressed some of his most insightful collaborators in the Founding. Wilson insisted that the improvement of both private and public life, social and economic, was a central task of government, and that the single most important end of government must be the cultivation of the human mind. It was this conception of active, improving government—supporting and informing private social life, entrepreneurship, and an expansive sense of citizenship—that Wilson invoked largely to justify his theories of federal union, participatory politics, and a constitutionalism that put the rights of persons unambiguously above the rights of property.

Such principles, and the mechanics of constitutional design that would best serve them, became even more evident in Wilson's role as the chief framer of the Pennsylvania constitution of 1790 than they had been in the Federal Convention of 1787.

Nevertheless, by far the most comprehensive exposition of Wilson's vision of American constitutionalism and law—economizing on the seventeenth-century English common-law tradition, but aiming to improve on it in light of American experience and European science and Enlightenment—was Wilson's series of lectures composed for delivery as the first professor of law at the College of Philadelphia in 1790–1. Although left unrevised and unfinished, these extensive lectures stand as Wilson's *summa* as an early American constitutional and legal theorist more systematic, more optimistic—and perhaps harder to categorize—than any other. The profoundest argument of the lectures was that the American Republic had been established on novel principles; that these principles had generated constitutions and other legal institutions of unprecedented promise; but that this promise would be fulfilled only through fidelity to those principles; and that the challenge to Americans was, therefore, nothing less than to formulate and put into practice what Wilson called a "comprehensive" theory of the Republic as a social union of all its citizens.

Despite Wilson's success in law practice, and even greater renown as a legal scholar, his last and most important law job became his greatest disappointment, to himself and his contemporary supporters and later admirers. Passed over for the position of Chief Justice, he was, however, appointed an Associate Justice of the first Supreme Court of the United States. Although he remained in that office from 1789 to 1798, he contributed remarkably little from the high bench to early American jurisprudence. His only landmark judicial opinion, in the case of *Chisholm v. Georgia*, where he espoused so much of his vision of what America should become—a great national DEMOCRACY of popular government and personal RIGHTS—was in effect soon overruled by the Eleventh Amendment and the broad-based nationwide campaign that had led to its adoption.

The principal challenge Wilson presents his students today is to understand his uniquely systematic approach to early American LAW and constitutionalism on its own amalgamated terms, and to understand why his approach variously succeeded and failed in his own day, especially where his initially rejected ideas were later embraced.

During the last few years of his life, Wilson's visionary tendencies led him to professional and, ultimately, physical ruin, on account of overextended investments in land speculation. He died in disgrace, a broken man in hiding from creditors, who was nonetheless unwilling to resign his seat on the bench. His scandalous end is part of the explanation for his relative obscurity among the leading founders; but the more important part of the explanation lies in the yet unsolved problem of appreciating his avowedly "philosophical" view of the new political, legal, and constitutional culture he helped to create in America.

STEPHEN A. CONRAD

FURTHER READING

Samuel H. Beer, *To Make a Nation: the Rediscovery of American Federalism* (Cambridge: Harvard University Press, Belknap, 1993).

Stephen A. Conrad, "Polite Foundation: Citizenship and Common Sense in James Wilson's Republican Theory," in Philip B. Kurland et al., eds., *Supreme Court Review—1984* (Chicago: University of Chicago Press, 1985).

——, "Metaphor and Imagination in James Wilson's Theory of Federal Union," *Law and Social Inquiry* 13 (1988): 1–70.

——, "James Wilson's 'Assimilation of the Common-law Mind,'" *Northwestern University Law Review* 84 (1989): 186–219.

Charles Page Smith, *James Wilson: Founding Father, 1742–1798* (Chapel Hill: University of North Carolina Press, 1956).

James Wilson, *The Works of James Wilson*, ed. Robert Green

McCloskey, 2 vols. (Cambridge: Harvard University Press, Belknap, 1967).

Wilson, [Thomas] Woodrow (b. Staunton, Va., Dec. 28, 1856; d. Washington, D.C., Feb. 3, 1924). Probably the last real intellectual to win the presidency of the United States, Woodrow Wilson is a crucial figure in modern American thought—but not primarily because of his many books on history and government. Wilson's writings, interesting and revealing, were not terribly original. His politics, on the other hand, were distinctly innovative. Through word and act, Wilson marked out the transition from the INDIVIDUALISM and laissez-faire liberalism of the nineteenth century to the statism and interventionist liberalism of the twentieth. Wilson's rhetoric established the cadences of modern LIBERALISM; his policies foreshadowed its troubled future.

Born five years before the Civil War, Woodrow Wilson grew up in a world where religion, class, party, and region reinforced liberal values. He was nurtured in the stern individualist moralism of the Presbyterian church, the self-disciplined striving of the Victorian middle class, the Jeffersonian ideals of the Democratic Party, and the southern states rights heritage of Virginia.

This inherited creed came under intense strain as a result of the industrialization, urbanization, class conflict, and political corruption of the Gilded Age. Like so many of the middle class, Wilson was troubled by the new big businesses that stifled competition, challenged individualism and threatened democracy. And like other Victorians, Wilson offered an ambivalent response to a transformed America. He wanted to save democracy in the name of the people. But to do so, Wilson proposed to strengthen the authority of the state in general, and of high officials in particular. Influenced by the example of Great Britain, he called in his first book, *Congressional Government* (1885), for the transfer of power from Congress to the President. Wilson also had a low opinion of the rights and virtues of at least some of the people: he was unwilling to disturb the segregation and disfranchisement of African Americans in the South; and he wrote disparagingly of new immigrant groups from Eastern and Southern Europe.

Despite his concerns about American society, Wilson was reluctant to advocate dramatic reforms at the start of the twentieth century. But his yearning to leave academia for government forced him toward the middle-class agenda of PROGRESSIVISM, which called for using the state to stabilize industrial society. Elected governor of New Jersey in 1910, he pushed

for such measures as utilities regulation, workmen's compensation, and the direct primary. Running for President in 1912, he could still condemn social welfare legislation and propose the "New Freedom," a program to restore the competitive capitalism of the nineteenth century. In the White House, however, Wilson was persuaded that the state must accept and regulate an economy dominated by giant corporations: instead of the "New Freedom," his administration created the Federal Trade Commission and the Federal Reserve and put controls on the labor of children and the hours of railroad workers.

As President, Wilson also had to come to terms with the implications of American economic power for the nation's foreign policy. At the turn of the century, he had endorsed old-style imperialism. But Wilson ultimately rejected a globe divided into empires for a world of free, self-determining states open to free, unrestricted trade. That vision squared with Wilson's idealistic belief in freedom and democracy and with America's practical need for overseas markets and resources. Yet Wilson violated his own vision: as President, he authorized military intervention in Haiti, Santo Domingo, and Mexico. But in 1917 he was willing to bring the United States into WORLD WAR I in order to protect American shipping and to make the world "safe for democracy."

The war was the apotheosis of Wilsonian progressivism. At home the federal government controlled the economy by organizing production, financing war industries, fixing prices, taking over the railroads, and mediating labor relations; it controlled pleasure by sponsoring PROHIBITION; it controlled thought and speech by arresting dissidents, keeping publications out of the mail, and spewing propaganda from the Committee on Public Information. In Europe, American soldiers fought for Wilson's "Fourteen Points," his prescription for a world of free states and free trade guaranteed by a league of nations. With the Bolshevik revolution in 1917, Wilson's vision loomed as the progressive middle way between old-style imperialism on the right and communism on the left.

Wilson found victory on the battlefield but disaster at home. His wartime state produced chaos instead of stability: there were strikes, inflation, race riots, and the ugly repression of civil liberties culminating in the "red scare" of 1919. The Senate rejected the Treaty of Versailles with its provisions for American membership in the League of Nations. Worn down by the struggle with the Senate, Wilson suffered a paralytic stroke in the fall of 1919. He died in 1924, his leadership seemingly rejected.

Woodrow Wilson necessarily remains a figure of

contention: too much is at stake to let him alone. For many liberals, he is a heroic, even martyr-like figure. For the New Left, he is the archetypical "corporate liberal" dedicated to the preservation and extension of corporate capitalism at home and abroad. The "corporate liberal" tag is hard to accept: Wilson, like THEODORE ROOSEVELT before him, did not care much for business values. And his central commitment to DEMOCRACY seems genuine. But Wilson's rhetoric smoothly meshed together the imperatives of American capitalism and the promise of democracy. After Wilson, the two were so utterly interwoven that it has become almost impossible to separate ideals and interests in American foreign policy. In the same fashion, Wilson also helped bind together democratic values and the activist, modern state. His administration, in peace and in war, offered the cardinal promise of liberalism that a powerful state, run by a powerful executive, can and will protect freedom and equality.

At the end of the twentieth century, after the failure of the Great Society and the Vietnam War, Wilson is a hard figure to embrace. His career presented all the contradictions of modern liberalism: the admixture of idealism and self-interest, the belief in freedom but the resort to military intervention, the call for self-determination but the opposition to revolution, the celebration of the people but the empowerment of the President, the invocation of democracy but the relentless centralization of authority in large-scale institutions. Wilson's liberal successors have struggled with these contradictions, but they persist. That is why Woodrow Wilson remains such a central figure in American life. Looking back at him, we are face to face with the promise and the failure of modern liberalism.

MICHAEL MCGERR

FURTHER READING

John M. Blum, *Woodrow Wilson and the Politics of Morality* (Boston: Little, Brown, 1956).

Kendrick A. Clements, *The Presidency of Woodrow Wilson* (Lawrence: University Press of Kansas, 1992).

Thomas J. Knock, *To End All Wars: Woodrow Wilson and the Quest for a New World Order* (New York: Oxford University Press, 1992).

Arthur S. Link, *Wilson*, 5 vols. (Princeton: Princeton University Press, 1947–65).

Arthur S. Link et al., eds. *The Papers of Woodrow Wilson*, 69 vols. (Princeton: Princeton University Press, 1966–93).

Martin J. Sklar, *The Corporate Reconstruction of American Capitalism, 1890–1916: The Market, the Law, and Politics* (Cambridge: Cambridge University Press, 1988).

Niels Thorsen, *The Political Thought of Woodrow Wilson* (Princeton: Princeton University Press, 1988).

Woodrow Wilson, *Congressional Government* (Boston: Houghton Mifflin, 1885).

Winthrop, John (b. Edwardstone, England, Jan. 22, 1588; d. Boston, Mass., Apr. 5, 1649).   At the moment in Nathaniel Hawthorne's *The Scarlet Letter* when John Winthrop dies, a meteor fills the sky with "the appearance of an immense letter—the letter A—marked out in lines of dull red light." The townspeople imagine the celestial "A" means the Governor has joined the angels, but the self-absorbed Arthur Dimmesdale interprets it as heaven's announcement of his still unconfessed crime. In 1850, Hawthorne saw how easily Winthrop, first governor of Massachusetts Bay Colony, could be turned into a symbol and used for various interpretive purposes. Despite mountains of subsequent scholarship, this is still the case today. It seems impossible to approach Winthrop without expecting to find a fixed and reliable Puritan alpha that will provide clues to the fate of our uncertain American omega.

The most common view of Winthrop falls into this trap. Misreadings of Winthrop's vision for the Massachusetts colony have provided easy means to celebrate AMERICAN EXCEPTIONALISM. In his sermon on "Christian Charity," Winthrop called upon the trope, common at the time, of the colony as a "city upon a hill" with "the eyes of all people upon us" in order to emphasize the embarrassing visibility of the settlers' undertaking should they fail (*Life and Letters*, vol. 2, p. 19). The prevailing belief that this phrase reveals Winthrop to be an ecstatic visionary with a messianic sense of America's future does not square well with the practical magistrate of Winthrop's other writings, and fails to connect with the central issues of his life.

Born in England, Winthrop spent four decades gradually assuming the many responsibilities he inherited as the son of Adam Winthrop, lord of Groton manor in Suffolk, and mastering his unruly self through the slow, uneven process of religious conversion to PURITANISM. These years culminated in his anguished remove from the aspects of English life that would not conform to his developing vision of order, discipline, and authority: an unpredictable economy, a despotic monarchy, and a corrupt Church of England. Together with other like-minded Puritans, Winthrop organized the migration of thousands of settlers to New England. The challenges of governing a colony perfectly matched his temperament and skills. Shortly after his arrival in 1630, with fellow emigrants dying all around him, Winthrop wrote to his wife, "I never fared better in my life, never slept better, never had more content of mind" (pp. 48–9). For most of the next 20 years, until his death in Boston, Winthrop served as governor or deputy governor of the colony. Winthrop presided over the transformation of Massachusetts Bay from a chartered corporation to a virtually independent state, conducted the colony's relations with neighboring colonies, Indian nations, and the mother country, and had a hand in decisions both great and small concerning the colony's domestic affairs.

The best interpretations of Winthrop focus on the issues that framed the major struggles of his career: separatism versus responsibility to the world, the relationship of FREEDOM and AUTHORITY in a voluntary community, and the competing demands of JUSTICE and mercy in a godly society. Edmund Morgan's *The Puritan Dilemma* elegantly treats the first of these, casting Winthrop's career as an ongoing struggle to resist the separatist impulse and harness righteousness to the cause of social reform. The second and third issues were emphasized by several nineteenth-century historians in attempts to make Winthrop into the precursor of later American social and political developments. George Bancroft depicted Winthrop as a pioneer in liberty and representative government, while Brooks Adams and Charles Francis Adams emphasized the authoritarian and persecuting character of the society Winthrop founded. From either perspective, the complexity and coherence of Winthrop's engagement with his world were lost, and were not recovered until Samuel Eliot Morison and PERRY MILLER brought renewed attention to the significance of the religious dimension that underlay Winthrop's social and political thought.

For Winthrop, true liberty was not the natural freedom of man or beast "to do what he lists," but the liberty to know good from evil through God's laws and the ability to do "that only which is good, just, and honest" through Christ's freely bestowed grace (*Life and Letters*, vol. 2, pp. 340–1). For those blessed with this kind of liberty, obedience to divinely sanctioned authority was mandatory. The colony's charter granted freemen annual choice of their rulers, but once chosen, the magistrate's word was law, to be obeyed in love and respect. In return, a ruler owed the same love and respect to his subjects, and if his commands were not good, just, and honest, his was not true authority "but a distemper thereof" (p. 341). Mercy was therefore as important as justice in Winthrop's understanding of the magistrate's role. His own religious experience made Winthrop constantly aware of fallible humanity's sinful inclinations, and he was usually ready to begin with forgiveness as the ruler's proper attitude toward human weakness. Just as Winthrop expected the people to forgive their magistrates for errors in judgment but not for bad faith, so the magistrate could be lenient toward transgressors who were still committed to living by the law.

In the antinomian controversy of 1637, this vision proved to be incompatible with the obliquely expressed beliefs of ANNE HUTCHINSON and her fellow "heretics." At no other time in his career was Winthrop less confident, coherent, and articulate. His befuddlement arose from the difficulty of dealing with members of the community who refused to recognize any connection between grace, the source of Christian liberty, and its fulfillment in obedience to the law. Toward such "offenders" neither justice nor mercy could be exercised, for they acknowledged neither the need nor the right of authority to punish or forgive them.

Winthrop is often criticized for his role in the antinomian controversy, as if he envisioned that New England would become America and deliberately planted an authoritarian seed in the bed of our national character. But this analysis does an injustice to Winthrop's capacity to maintain charitable relationships with other "Americans" like ROGER WILLIAMS, or the separatists of Plymouth, whose ideas of the good society rested on premises different from his own. Winthrop's genius lay in knowing the limits and purposes of the voluntary community he was chosen to lead, and in his commitment to maintaining its highest ideals in the present, not in creating a prescriptive foundation for future glories in communities with unbounded horizons. Hawthorne's linking of Winthrop with the symbol that overshadows his romance does, after all, capture something of the way Winthrop's life was shaped by the tensions between human nature and divine grace, liberty and law, justice and mercy, tensions that continue to be played out in American dramas of sin and redemption.

MARK A. PETERSON

FURTHER READING

Brooks Adams, *The Emancipation of Massachusetts* (Boston, 1887).

Charles Francis Adams, *Three Episodes of Massachusetts History* (Boston, 1892).

George Bancroft, *History of the United States of America: From the Discovery of the Continent*, vol. 1 (New York, 1859).

Perry Miller, *Orthodoxy in Massachusetts, 1630–1650* (Cambridge: Harvard University Press, 1933).

Edmund S. Morgan, *The Puritan Dilemma: the Story of John Winthrop* (Boston: Little, Brown, 1958).

Samuel Eliot Morison, *Builders of the Bay Colony* (Boston: Houghton Mifflin, 1930).

John Winthrop, *The History of New England from 1630 to 1649*, ed. James Savage, 2 vols. (Boston, 1825–6).

——, *Life and Letters of John Winthrop*, 2 vols. (Boston, 1864–7).

——, "A Short Story of the Rise, reign, and ruine of the Antinomians, Familists & Libertines," in David D. Hall, ed., *The Antinomian Controversy, 1636–1638*, 2d ed. (Durham: Duke University Press, 1990).

The Winthrop Papers, 6 vols. (Boston: Massachusetts Historical Society, 1929–92).

Wise, Isaac M. (b. Steingrub, Bohemia, Mar. 29, 1819; d. Cincinnati, Ohio, Mar. 26, 1900). Rabbi. The leader of Reform Judaism, Wise sought to adapt Judaism to its American context by avoiding theoretical argument and building national structures. Believing that Jews should be full members of American society, he argued that outgrown forms should be discarded as unnecessary to the inner spirit of the Jewish faith. His reforms—including family pews and the abandonment of dietary laws—sparked controversy over the essential nature of Judaic law and religion. Wise helped organize the Union of American Hebrew Congregations, the Central Conference of American Rabbis, Hebrew Union College, and the *Union Prayer Book* (1894). He was a prolific author of novels and plays as well as histories of JUDAISM. He published his *Reminiscences* in 1901.

FURTHER READING
Sefton D. Temkin, *Isaac Meyer Wise: Shaping American Judaism* (New York: Oxford University Press, 1992).

Wise, John (baptized Roxbury, Mass., Aug. 15, 1652; d. Ipswich, Mass., Apr. 8, 1725). Minister. Best known for leading a tax revolt against Governor Andros and defending Congregationalist polity against Presbyterianism in *The Churches Quarrel Espoused* (1710), Wise fought for democracy in both secular and church government. God's natural order, he argued, is revealed through reason. Natural law proves human equality: all people inherently possess a capacity for rational thought, a tendency toward self-love, a drive toward sociability, a need for liberty, and a desire for justice. Wise's *Vindication of the Government of New England Churches* (1717) influenced secular as well as religious thought about DEMOCRACY.

FURTHER READING
George Allan Cook, *John Wise: Early American Democrat* (New York: King's Crown Press, 1952).

Witherspoon, John (b. Gifford, Scotland, Feb. 15, 1723; d. Princeton, N.J., Nov. 15, 1794). Minister. Witherspoon was the president of the College of New Jersey, now Princeton University (1768–94). Although he originally believed that ministers should not engage in politics, he was a signer of the Declaration of Independence. His *Dominion of Providence over the Passions of Men* (May 1776) was the first of many sermons that he published in support of the Revolutionary cause. A strong advocate of SCOTTISH COMMON SENSE REALISM, Witherspoon argued that the moral sense is a form of common sense, prior to reason, and its unchanging axioms are teachable. While humans are innately depraved, the moral behavior required in a republic can be achieved if people are instructed in their duties.

FURTHER READING
Martha Lou Lemmon Stohlman, *John Witherspoon: Parson, Politician, Patriot* (1976; Louisville, Ky: Westminster/John Knox Press, 1989).

Wolfe, Thomas (b. Asheville, N.C., Oct. 3, 1900; d. Baltimore, Md., Sept. 15, 1938). Although Wolfe spent much of his adult life based in New York and traveling widely throughout the United States and Europe, he remained haunted by his childhood in North Carolina. His parents' unhappy marriage, exacerbated by his father's alcoholism, made for a chaotic home. In 1906 Wolfe's mother opened a boardinghouse in town and within a few weeks had moved into "Dixieland" with her youngest son, who slept either with her or in whatever bedroom was vacant. Wolfe's father did not move with them, and the other five children lived more or less where they pleased. There was no clear breakup, but the family dissolved.

Wolfe escaped the distress of his family life by means of books. He received one of the best educations of any American writer, attending preparatory school in Asheville, college at the University of North Carolina, and graduate school at Harvard, where he studied drama, intending to become a playwright. He moved to New York in 1924 and in the following year met Aline Bernstein, a successful stage designer who became his mistress and patron. With her help Wolfe discovered that autobiographical fiction was the genre to which he was best suited, and in 1929 *Look Homeward, Angel*, his first novel, was published.

Following the success of *Look Homeward, Angel*, Wolfe wrote voluminously but was unable to complete his second novel to his satisfaction. Finally his editor at Charles Scribner's Sons, Maxwell Perkins, took the manuscript of *Of Time and the River* and informed Wolfe that it was finished. Perkins's decision has sparked considerable disagreement, especially since Wolfe's second long autobiographical novel suffers from unevenness in style and structure. Wolfe's trouble with the book stemmed in good part from his wrestling with memory-dominated novelistic form, experimentation that he did not live to bring to a satisfying conclusion. Some critics, following C. Hugh Holman, have claimed that Wolfe is badly served by overemphasis on his abilities as a novelist, suggesting that he was primarily a master of shorter forms, notably novelettes, stories, and sketches, of which he published many in the years between his first two novels.

Perkins's action in getting *Of Time and the River* to press is one of a number of editorial issues that plagued Wolfe's life and have continued to surface since his death. In fact, Perkins had edited the manuscript of *Look Homeward, Angel* heavily as well, but his work on the second novel became widely known after Wolfe published *The Story of a Novel*, an account of the writing of *Of Time and the River* that acknowledged Perkins's extensive help. In a contemporary review of this volume that has itself assumed a place in Wolfe studies, Bernard De Voto excoriated Wolfe as an undisciplined writer who merely poured forth words that had to be shaped by an editor into artistic shape.

The most serious of the editing controversies concerns Wolfe's last two novels, *The Web and the Rock* and *You Can't Go Home Again*, which were published posthumously. In 1937, Wolfe severed his association with Scribner's and signed a contract with Harper & Brothers. His new editor, Edward Aswell, had courted Wolfe with a large advance that was not contingent upon receipt of a finished work. This seemed lucky for Wolfe, who was having great difficulty once again shaping a large bulk of manuscript into a whole. It has not been lucky for Wolfe's reputation, however, for Wolfe became fatally ill and died in 1938, leaving Aswell with a packing crate full of very rough manuscript and an obligation to publish something out of it.

After Wolfe's death, Aswell tried to follow an outline Wolfe had left and stay within legal and moral editorial limits in preparing the book for publication, but he ended by combining drafts, writing transitional passages, and altering inconsistent and potentially objectionable material as he made the first half of the huge manuscript into *The Web and the Rock*. The following year Aswell used an even heavier hand to make *You Can't Go Home Again* out of four rough novelettes that were among the last pieces Wolfe wrote. Since the four pieces were among the best of Wolfe's writing and have considerable integrity by themselves, this novel is more successful than *The Web and the Rock* despite the piecemeal way in which it was put together.

These editorial issues have dogged Wolfe's reputation because the reading public is not accustomed to a writer willing to admit his faults, and not used to regarding as serious literature works that call into question the image of the full-blown autonomous artist presupposed by romantic AESTHETICS. Wolfe's texts are important precisely because they probe and exhibit unresolved issues of artistic autonomy.

They have as their main project the creation of an artist, in a manner that resembles James Joyce's *Portrait of an Artist as a Young Man*, but they also explore post-Kantian subjectivity in modernist prose that echoes Joyce's *Ulysses* and even *Finnegans Wake* (which Wolfe bought and read as it appeared in serial form). The personal subject of his fictionalized memories may be defined as much by a lack or absence in it, to use Lacanian terms, as by its power to secure for itself a position of dominance and centeredness. Artist, first- or third-person narrator, and reader are effects, projections, within the discourse of Wolfe's novels, not simply full beings who can understand and thus control both the past being narrated and the self that exists by virtue of its extension through time.

The question of who was responsible for writing Wolfe's texts may thus be viewed as part of the larger question of what authorship may be for modern writing (or indeed writing in general). Wolfe wrote on the cusp of the modernist movement, with one part of him in the worlds of the post-Reconstruction South, his classical training, and the conservatism of mass trade publishing, and another in the more experimental and less secure worlds of the new writing and thinking. He was an irrepressible teller of good stories, mimicker of voices, and molder of language into rhythmic and beautiful patterns, but he was equally an experimenter with ideas and literary form, bringing philosophical skepticism about the integrity of the self into artistic shape. It is appropriate that authorship itself should be questioned in a body of work that asserts as well as doubts its power to make a clear entity of the man who wrote it.

Wolfe's corpus includes four novels, two collections (one published posthumously) of short pieces culled from numerous periodical publications and manuscripts, and several essays. Five early plays, other unpublished sketches, notebooks, letters, and a journal of a Western trip have also been published since Wolfe's death. Two collections worth noting are Holman's compilation of *The Short Novels of Thomas Wolfe* and Francis Skipp's edition of *The Complete Short Stories of Thomas Wolfe*, both of which contain pieces that were published separately before being incorporated into the novels.

The most compelling texts from this body of work almost always exist in a tension-ridden middle ground between autobiography and fiction. Wolfe went home again and again, rewriting himself as one fiction after another, charging each story with the rhetorical investment of the autobiographical author and experimenting with structures to encompass both the forward drive of narrative and the widening circles of memory. *Look Homeward, Angel*, the most polished of his novels, brings into a harmonious conclusion the needs of the retrospective narrator and the protagonist of the *Bildungsroman*. Wolfe never attained such balance consistently, since his chosen form is inherently unstable. However, as Louis Rubin has noted, it is suggestive that for all his faults Wolfe has consistently attracted the admiration of other writers. WILLIAM FAULKNER, for example, remarked of the writers of his generation that "we had all failed, but Wolfe had made the best failure because he tried hardest to say the most"; he would "throw away style, coherence, all the rules of preciseness" so that he could "try to put all the experience of the human heart on the head of a pin, as it were" (Walser, p. vii). As long as textual risk-taking is compelling for some readers, Wolfe's grand gestures will continue to find a place in American letters.

MARGARET MILLS HARPER

FURTHER READING
Bernard De Voto, "Genius Is Not Enough," *Saturday Review of Literature*, Apr. 25, 1936.
David Herbert Donald, *Look Homeward: a Life of Thomas Wolfe* (Boston: Little, Brown, 1987).
C. Hugh Holman, *The Loneliness at the Core: Studies in Thomas Wolfe* (Baton Rouge: Louisiana State University Press, 1975).
John Lane Idol Jr., *A Thomas Wolfe Companion* (Westport: Greenwood Press, 1987).
Richard S. Kennedy, *The Window of Memory: the Literary Career of Thomas Wolfe* (Chapel Hill: University of North Carolina Press, 1962).
Louis D. Rubin Jr., *Thomas Wolfe: a Collection of Critical Essays* (Englewood Cliffs, N.J.: Prentice-Hall, 1973).
Richard Walser, ed., *The Enigma of Thomas Wolfe: Biographical and Critical Selections* (Cambridge: Harvard University Press, 1953).
Thomas Wolfe, *The Story of a Novel* (New York: Charles Scribner's Sons, 1936).

women's rights What is the place of "women's rights" in the history of feminism? In 1970, Gerda Lerner argued that the movement for women's rights was only one aspect of the larger history of FEMINISM, because it focused exclusively on formal EQUALITY with men in the public realm and ignored the roots of women's subordination in the family. Lerner's efforts to distinguish an expansive women's emancipation tradition from a limited women's rights one followed closely on that of her predecessor, MARY RITTER BEARD, who argued that the women's rights movement had erroneously asserted women's universal historical powerlessness. For the most part, subsequent historical assessments have emphasized the limitations that "rights thinking" has placed on the organized efforts of American women to elevate and expand their social position. This is an important contribution, and yet tends to underplay the place of the women's rights movement in its own historical setting, as well as its continuing contribution to American feminism.

The American women's rights movement was in its heyday in the middle third of the nineteenth century. From the 1830s through the 1880s, women's rights was the most radical of several approaches for securing higher status and greater public influence for "womanhood." Other perspectives held that women, fundamentally superior to men in spiritual matters, needed not new rights but more individual FREEDOM to develop the distinctive nature of their sex; or contended that their feminine gifts of inspiring, caring, or educating should have greater social weight. In contrast to these romantic and evangelical perspectives, "women's rights" thinkers drew on the natural RIGHTS strain of post-Revolutionary political thought; they challenged the fundamental significance of the "difference of sex," asserting instead that since women's capacities were the equal of men's, their political and economic status should be the same.

In 1790, Mary Wollstonecraft, a British supporter of the French Revolution, first used the term "women's rights," in her passionate manifesto, *Vindication of the Rights of Woman*. Between the publication of Wollstonecraft's *Vindication*, which Americans read and debated, and the rise of the American women's rights movement in 1848, women's rights ideas were advocated by only a few individuals. FRANCES WRIGHT, a leader in the American workingman's movement of the 1820s, and SARAH and ANGELINA GRIMKÉ, abolitionist orators of the 1830s, were widely criticized because they crossed into men's sphere to become public speakers and political figures. Perhaps in response, they also became active advocates of women's rights to education, public advocacy, and the vocation of reformer. Wright was a freethinker while the Grimkés were Quakers, but all three drew on natural rights ideas to effect a link between their women's rights ideas and their labor reform and abolitionist politics. In 1837, Angelina Grimké declared:

> I believe it is woman's right to have a voice in all the laws and regulations by which she is to be governed, whether in Church or State, and that the present arrangements of society, on these points, are a violation of human rights, a rank usurpation of power, a violent seizure and confiscation of what is sacredly and inalienably hers. (p. 119.)

In 1848 women's rights became, for the first time, the basis of an organized movement, when ELIZABETH

CADY STANTON and LUCRETIA MOTT organized a "women's rights convention" in Seneca Falls, New York. The convention condemned "all laws which prevent women from occupying such a station in society as her conscience shall dictate, or which place her in a position inferior to that of man," and passed "A Declaration of Sentiments," an adaptation of that manifesto of natural rights, the Declaration of Independence. "All men and women are created equal," it declared, "they are endowed by their Creator with certain inalienable rights; ... to secure these rights governments are instituted," and when government "becomes destructive of these ends, it is the right of those who suffer from it to refuse allegiance to it." The Seneca Falls convention envisioned itself as the beginning of a movement to right these wrongs. "We shall employ agents, circulate tracts, petition the State and National legislatures, and endeavor to enlist the pulpit and the press in our behalf," it announced (p. 203).

The program of the nineteenth-century American women's rights movement emphasized economic, educational, and political rights for women. Under British law, women's economic position followed the rule of coverture, by which her rights to own or contract for property were forfeited to her husband upon marriage. The women's rights movement fought for married women to retain the rights of ownership, not only to real property but to the disposition of their labor and the wages earned by it. Beginning in New York in 1860, women's rights agitation succeeded in reforming state laws in favor of married women's economic rights. Women's rights to education, especially to training for a profession or a skilled trade, complemented this commitment to economic INDIVIDUALISM; it also reflected the conviction that women were no less capable of rational thought than men.

In 1848, the Seneca Falls Declaration clearly asserted women's right to "the first right of a citizen, the elective franchise," but the demand for woman suffrage did not come into its own until the 1860s, in the wake of Civil War and Reconstruction. Deeply influenced by debates about the political rights of the freed slaves, women's rights advocates argued that the right to vote was not a privilege bestowed by government on those who could be trusted to use it prudently, but a natural, inalienable right, equally possessed by all and underlying the establishment of government. Starting in the late 1860s, the right to vote was recognized as the leading women's rights demand. For the next half century, women pursued enfranchisement through efforts to amend both state and federal constitutions, and through petitioning, legislative lobbying, and direct action at the polls and in the streets.

Ironically, this exclusive focus on enfranchisement began a process by which the general women's rights perspective on inequality lost its prominence. Although its antebellum roots lay in a broadly egalitarian philosophy, woman suffragism after Reconstruction was frequently counterposed to the rights of others—nonwhite and immigrant men, in particular. In addition, as more and more women embraced the call for political rights, the distinctive women's rights argument, that women had the same natural rights as men, was overwhelmed by other claims on the franchise, notably women's moral superiority and special capacity to eradicate political corruption and social impurity. As historian Aileen Kraditor put it, the classic "justice" argument for suffrage was still invoked, but now it was coupled with an "expediency" approach, which focused on what women could do with their votes, not why they had an inherent right to them.

By the early twentieth century, women's rights ideas were displaced by a more "modern" perspective, "feminism." Whereas women's rights had focused on equal access to work, education and politics, feminism turned to more personal aspects of women's lives. EMMA GOLDMAN, who disparaged the organized woman suffrage movement in favor of emotional and sexual emancipation, and MARGARET SANGER, who led the birth control movement, were heralds of the new order. The focus on rights survived primarily in the National Woman's Party's demand for an Equal Rights Amendment, first made in 1923. However, while the ERA movement continued to insist on the fundamental equality of women and men, it lost the women's rights capacity to extend itself to ever new dimensions of human entitlement; the ERA movement only asked that women have the same legal position as men, no matter how reduced or constricted. In the 1970s, the broader, women's rights vision of equality reemerged as "women's liberation," in which feminists, still focused on personal issues, organized for their rights, which they now defined largely in relation to reproduction and sexuality.

ELLEN CAROL DUBOIS

See also FEMINIST JURISPRUDENCE.

FURTHER READING
Nancy Cott, *The Grounding of Modern Feminism* (New Haven: Yale University Press, 1987).

"Declaration of Sentiments" (1848), in Mary Beth Norton, ed., *Major Problems in American Women's History* (Lexington, Mass.: Heath, 1989).

Ellen DuBois, *Feminism and Suffrage: the Emergence of an*

Independent Women's Movement in America, 1848–1869 (Ithaca: Cornell University Press, 1978).

Eleanor Flexner, *Century of Struggle: the Women's Rights Movement in the United States* (Cambridge: Harvard University Press, Belknap, 1959).

Angelina Grimké, *Letters to Catharine Beecher* (1838; New York: Arno Press, 1969).

Gerda Lerner, "Women's Rights and American Feminism," *American Scholar* 40 (spring 1971): 235–48.

Aileen Kraditor, *Ideas of the Woman Suffrage Movement, 1890–1920* (New York: Columbia University Press, 1965).

Mary Wollstonecraft, *Vindication of the Rights of Woman* (London, 1790).

Woods, Robert (b. Pittsburgh, Pa., Dec. 9, 1865; d. Boston, Mass., Feb. 18, 1925).   Reformer. Head of Andover House (later South End House) in Boston (1891–1925) and author of *The City Wilderness* (1898), *Americans in Process* (1902), and *Neighborhood in Nation-Building* (1923), Woods believed that human societies are organic entities whose basic unit is the neighborhood. While internal tensions threaten to tear society apart, settlement houses can promote social reconciliation by guiding the conflicting interests of a particular neighborhood through comprehensive moral and social reformation.

FURTHER READING

Mina Julia Carson, *Settlement Folk: Social Thought and the American Settlement Movement, 1885–1930* (Chicago: University of Chicago Press, 1990).

Woodward, C[omer] Vann (b. Vanndale, Ark., Nov. 13, 1908).   Few American historians have loomed as large in their chosen field of scholarship as C. Vann Woodward has in the study of the modern South. As J. Morgan Kousser and James McPherson have put it,

> Woodward's chosen period and region have become "his" in much more than the usual sense for a historian. It is hard to think of a serious book or an important scholarly article written on the post-Reconstruction South or on modern American race relations in the last generation which does not repeat, take issue with, flesh out, test on other data, or carry out the implications of some idea first adumbrated or at least first fully enunciated by Woodward. (p. xvi)

Born in a small town settled by his great-grandfather, Woodward grew up among middle-class educators and college professors, and family friends included such notable members of the small but distinguished band of liberal southern intellectuals as Will Alexander, Howard Odum, and Rupert Vance. The family moved to Georgia in the late 1920s, and Woodward graduated from Emory University in 1930. After a brief sojourn in the North in which he secured a masters degree in political science from Columbia University, he returned to Atlanta in 1932 to teach at Georgia Tech. He was dismissed from this post in 1933 amidst widespread Depression layoffs, though his fall into the ranks of the unemployed may also have been helped along by a growing reputation as a political radical. Woodward had ventured beyond the pale by forming friendships with LANGSTON HUGHES, J. Saunders Redding, and other black intellectuals, by visiting the Soviet Union, and above all by playing a leading role in the defense committee of Angelo Herndon, a black communist jailed for fomenting insurrection in Atlanta.

Unemployed and intrigued by the radicalism of the past as well as the present, Woodward began research on a book about populist firebrand Tom Watson. Watson had in the 1880s and early 1890s embraced an agrarian radicalism which threatened the hegemony of white supremacy, but he eventually turned to the virulent racial demagoguery that sustained this very hegemony. When Woodward ran out of money, he turned to graduate school as a vehicle for completing this project, enrolling in 1934 in the Ph.D. program in history at the University of North Carolina (where Watson's papers were housed). He earned his degree with a dissertation on Watson, which was quickly published as *Tom Watson: Agrarian Rebel* (1938). In his telling of the story of Watson's tragic struggle against and eventual capitulation to southern racism, Woodward marshalled the deep research, lucid prose, and ironic sensibility that would henceforth be the hallmark of his most distinguished work. This extraordinary book soon earned a place among the finest American biographies, and launched Woodward's long battle against the myths of historical continuity, white solidarity, and black contentment that held sway in southern history.

In the late 1930s and early 1940s Woodward held a series of jobs at the University of Florida, the University of Virginia, and Scripps College in Claremont, California. In 1943 he entered the Navy and served for three years as an intelligence and public information officer, capping his naval career with a fine work of military history, *The Battle for Leyte Gulf* (1947). After the war he joined the faculty of Johns Hopkins University, where he remained for 15 years.

While at Johns Hopkins, Woodward published the books that established his towering reputation among American historians. In *The Origins of the New South* (1951), his masterpiece, he forcefully undermined the prevailing wisdom about the late nineteenth-century South. Rather than a restoration of the antebellum social order by an honorable planter elite of "Redeemers" who rescued the region from the corruption of carpetbaggers, scalawags, and ex-slaves, the New South in Woodward's portrayal was principally the work of a rapacious and often crooked new class of industrial entrepreneurs who mouthed the pieties of the old regime but transformed the region into an exploitative, underdeveloped, low-wage colony of northern capital. Moreover, the book exposed the bitter conflicts that this "modernization" of the South brought in its wake and offered a warmly sympathetic account of the struggles of the defeated Populists who had fought for a more democratic society and had been ignored by most southern historians. Amidst the celebratory CONSENSUS historiography of the 1950s, *Origins* stood out as powerful narrative of class conflict and defeated hopes.

Deeply invested in the battle against racial segregation, Woodward contributed to the brief of the National Association for the Advancement of Colored People in *Brown v. Board of Education* (1954), and followed up on this activism with publication of *The Strange Career of Jim Crow* (1955), which Martin Luther King Jr. later characterized as "the historical Bible of the civil rights movement." The significance of the book to those battling for racial justice lay in its contention that legal segregation in the South was not a timeless folkway but a set of practices that had not emerged until the 1890s and had been preceded by much more fluid race relations after Reconstruction. Subjected to sometimes fierce criticism by other historians (principally for exaggerating the magnitude of the change marked by the legalization of segregation), *Strange Career* found a large and appreciative general audience. But Woodward was chagrined to discover that many readers believed (despite his qualifications and cautions) that he had uncovered a golden age of racial harmony in the 1880s. A presegration period of fluidity did not mean that blacks and whites had equivalent opportunities.

From the outset of his career, Woodward took sustenance from the southern literary renaissance and from such writers as WILLIAM FAULKNER and ROBERT PENN WARREN. In *The Burden of Southern History* (1960) he contributed his own voice to this distinguished chorus, while articulating a "liberal realism" which also owed much to theologian REINHOLD NIEBUHR. Here, in a set of elegant essays provoked in part by the hubris of the rhetoric of the COLD WAR, Woodward advanced the hope that the distinctly un-American character of southern history—a history of defeat, poverty, frustration, failure, and tragedy—might serve as a counter to the dominant myths of American innocence, unending PROGRESS, unlimited material success, and national invincibility. This hope, like that Woodward held for thoroughgoing racial democracy, was to be disappointed. If anything, modern southerners proved especially susceptible to the American myths Woodward imagined they might subvert, and as he later ruefully observed, it was a southern President that led the nation into the quagmire of Vietnam.

In 1961 Woodward left Johns Hopkins for Yale University, where until his retirement in 1977 he continued to train legions of distinguished southern historians. During these years and since, he has remained a central figure in American historiography, urging the virtues of comparative history on his colleagues and defending, reconsidering, and revising his pathbreaking views in essays and lectures collected in *American Counterpoint* (1971), *Thinking Back* (1986), and *The Future of the Past* (1988). But the hallmark of the latter years of Woodward's career is his Pulitzer Prize-winning edition of the extraordinary diary of MARY CHESNUT (*Mary Chesnut's Civil War*, 1981). Her richly reflective journal is the work of one of those loyal southern outsiders with whom Woodward has always identified.

ROBERT B. WESTBROOK

FURTHER READING

Sheldon Hackney, "*The Origins of the New South* in Retrospect," *Journal of Southern History* 38 (1972): 191–216.

J. Morgan Kousser and James M. MacPherson, eds., *Region, Race, and Reconstruction: Essays in Honor of C. Vann Woodward* (New York: Oxford University Press, 1982).

Michael O'Brien, "C. Vann Woodward and the Burden of Southern Liberalism," *American Historical Review* 78 (1973): 589–604.

David M. Potter, "C. Vann Woodward and the Uses of History," in Marcus Cunliffe and Robin Winks, eds., *Pastmasters: Some Essays on American Historians* (New York: Harper and Row, 1969).

John H. Roper. *C. Vann Woodward, Southerner* (Athens: University of Georgia Press, 1987).

Robert B. Westbrook, "C. Vann Woodward: the Southerner as Liberal Realist," *South Atlantic Quarterly* 77 (1978): 54–71.

C. Vann Woodward, *Thinking Back: the Perils of Writing History* (Baton Rouge: Louisiana State University Press, 1986).

Woolman, John (b. Ancocas [now Rancocas], N.J., Oct. 19, 1720; d. York, England, Oct. 7, 1772). Minister and reformer. Woolman's Quaker belief in each individual's direct personal communication with God underlay his conviction that all people deserve to be treated with respect, love, and justice. He criticized great disparities of wealth and poverty, refused to pay war taxes, and became an itinerant preacher calling on slaveholders to emancipate their slaves. His *Journal* (1774) is considered a classic record of the spiritual life.

FURTHER READING
Paul Rosenblatt, *John Woolman* (New York: Twayne, 1969).

work   Beginning in the 1960s, a number of new pressures began to be felt in the American workplace. Women and minorities sought access to jobs which had formerly been unavailable to them, and legal sanctions were brought to bear in their support. At the same time large-scale economic changes stemming from technological innovation and international competition appeared to point to an unfamiliar "post-industrial" era in which skilled manufacturing jobs declined. Since these were the very jobs many women and minorities most desired, an explosive political battle took place in the 1970s and 1980s—most notably over "affirmative action," which also dramatically affected access to jobs in the professional and public sector occupations.

Underlying the political combat was a level of social anxiety about work unprecedented since the end of the Depression, and a renewed debate within unions, among academic scholars, and in the mass media about the nature and value of work itself. There was a new flurry of interest in the history of work, often appearing in fiction and scholarship alike as images of a world which had once been whole, a world of organic villages and urban ethnic communities which were destroyed by INDUSTRIALISM and the intrusive machine. This reassuring representation of past work relations obscured the physical danger and difficulty as well as the CLASS antagonisms of much early labor, but it did point to a set of beliefs and images which have persisted in American ideas about work since the earliest colonial ventures.

Some Renaissance Europeans who contemplated the New World saw America as a garden teeming with bounty, there to be easily plucked, while others, such as Governor JOHN WINTHROP, took it as a new field for taxing, world-creating labor, endeavor which would transform wilderness into a form of European civilization higher than Europe itself. To both of these quite distinct views, work was at the heart of a utopian vision. In the one, work and PLAY would no longer need to be opposed; the ancient mythological traditions of a Golden Age or Isles of the Blessed would be realized. For the other, work would be more relentless than ever, but it would produce a kind of second creation, an immaculate new world unsullied by the sins of the old one. Against this mythic and religious background, the notion that America was "exceptional"—in the condition of its labor as much as in its political and religious condition—continued to mark intellectual debate as

well as practical experiment (*see also* AMERICAN EXCEPTIONALISM).

The strongly utopian side of the American understanding of work has appeared most clearly in the recurrent experimental communities, from the Shakers in the eighteenth century, to such nineteenth-century endeavors as Brook Farm and Robert Owen's New Harmony in Indiana, to the communal experiments of the 1960s. While most of these experiments quickly failed, they occasioned extensive debate about how work ought to be organized, and what its social value ought to be. Though the intellectuals of Brook Farm, for example, seem to have disliked physical labor and to have been rather incompetent farmers, they were committed to the idea of joining manual and mental labor. This question of the division of handwork from headwork has continued to be a crucial focus for discussions of the social consequences of work. For many nineteenth-century intellectuals, such as GEORGE RIPLEY at Brook Farm, it was essential to a democratic nation that class divisions be minimized. Intellectuals should not lose sympathy with the labors of most men and women, and workers, in their turn, could not exercise their proper rights as citizens of the republic if their purely physical work kept them ignorant of public affairs and unpracticed in logic and imagination. Manual work was good for young people preparing to enter the professions because it instilled in them a properly democratic sensibility. Beneath these various social recommendations lay the question of whether work itself had intrinsic value, or was simply instumental—a way of staying alive, or of increasing one's comfort and security. Put in religious terms, as it often was, the question was whether work should be regarded as God's curse on a fallen world, something to be endured as an inescapable condition of life, or whether it was fundamentally redemptive, an opportunity to find salvation.

In arguing about the nature of work, these commentators were, even more fundamentally, arguing about whether men and women are shaped by the work they do, or whether, to the contrary, the work they do merely reflects their essential qualities. This was a hotly contested issue among northern white Protestants, but debate ceased when the workers in question were recently arrived immigrants. For Irish laborers building canals in New York State, or Chinese working on the railroads of the West, or Polish hands in the steel mills of Pittsburgh, the work was generally assumed to fit the type. For successive groups of immigrants, and for those other Americans who watched them adjust to a new life, collective ethnic identity was inextricably bound up with occupation.

Nowhere is the link between work and identity in

American thought more crucial than in the case of slavery. For some of its proponents in the period before the Civil War, slavery was the basis upon which an egalitarian white aristocracy, like that of classical Greece, could be constituted. Such a society would bring the potentialities of civilization to their fullest fruition, since slaves would permit privileged whites to avoid such "lower" occupations as personal service and dirty physical labor. At its extreme, this argument understood the forced confinement of blacks to be a natural consequence of supposed racial inferiority. The reluctance of southern whites to perform certain kinds of work was in fact an indication of how fully work and human identity had been linked. Inferior men and women could be identified by the work they naturally performed. For their part, northern abolitionists had contradictions of their own to confront, as southern defenders of slavery such as GEORGE FITZHUGH were eager to point out. "Free labor" sounded fine in the abstract but in practice might mean the freedom to starve at the hands of greedy capitalists—as the slave owner, St. Clare, explains to Miss Ophelia in Stowe's *Uncle Tom's Cabin*.

If it was African Americans who suffered most grievously by the binding of work to what society supposed to be their essential being, they were not alone in this condition of socially enforced identity. From the earliest colonial period, women too had worked hard and life-long, but only in those kinds of jobs thought appropriate to their feminine natures. Although crucial to the overall economy, women's work, unlike men's, was not recognized as a distinct, market-oriented activity, but consisted of a nearly continuous fabric of many tasks (such as gardening, spinning, preparing food, raising children), each one interrupted by another throughout the day. The question of how women's labor related to the larger economy of market labor and commodity production has persisted to the present day, as in debates over comparable pay for comparable work, and over whether a dollar value can be placed on housekeeping and child-raising—tasks often viewed as outside the realm of "work" altogether. (*See also* DOMESTICITY).

The realization that women do indeed work first came to crisis as large numbers of girls and women entered New England's fabric mills as paid workers in the nineteenth century, and as that experience was recorded by writers like Lucy Larcom, a mill-girl herself in the 1830s. The Lowell girls tended to stay only a short time before marrying and returning home, and they helped solidify the notion that all women's work outside the home was temporary. That idea endured long after it became clear that many women were in the job market to stay. Male union members could use the idea to resist equal pay for women, or female access to unions. In fact, the movement of women out of domestic work and into the marketplace was a threat to the patriarchal family, and women as well as men felt great anxiety about how the work experience of women would affect their identities. By the early twentieth century, as women had begun to arrive in the workforce in great numbers, popular magazines (and even union publications) spoke to this anxiety by publishing reassuring fiction about working women who nevertheless proved their femininity by winning a handsome man. On a more realistic note, Anzia Yezierska, writing about Jewish immigrants in the early years of the century, and Harriette Arnow, depicting Appalachian migrants to the industrial North during World War II, showed how painful it could be for women to alter their traditional relationship to work.

Throughout the late nineteenth century, a process of rationalization shaped American industry, culminating in the work of Frederick W. Taylor and his "scientific management" movement. TAYLORISM began with an attempt to analyze the work process scientifically, to break it down into its basic components in order to specify the most efficient way to do each job. One consequence of this strategy was the "deskilling" of workers, since many factory jobs were reduced to a machine-like regularity requiring little prior training. As Taylor attempted to change work itself, a vast literature devoted to furthering, contesting, or simply understanding the rationalization of work began to appear. In *Middletown,* their classic study of Muncie, Indiana, in the 1920s, Robert and Helen Lynd described the working lives of the business and laboring classes. Using 1890 as a point of comparison, the Lynds presented a picture of profound change in industrial work, and the broader culture. High-speed machines eliminated many kinds of jobs, as well as many older, highly skilled workers, and traditions of working-class community life atrophied, with devastating consequences for democratic politics. Business-class boosterism was itself a poor substitute, the Lynds argued, for the family-based work and leisure of an earlier era. The changing conditions of work in the white-collar ranks was subjected to caustic critique after World War II by C. WRIGHT MILLS. He pointed to the absence among the new middle classes of either the older Calvinist compulsion to work or the historic ideal of craftsmanship. They were left only with their ever more precious leisure as an escape from work's grim necessity.

Leisure was a crucial term in much serious scrutiny of work in the twentieth century, beginning with *The Theory of the Leisure Class* by THORSTEIN VEBLEN.

Veblen argued that ancient systems of social prestige and status based on the notion that labor was ignoble had persisted down to the present day. Half a century later, HANNAH ARENDT also asserted a classical origin for the idea that labor is base, but she noted too that just as TECHNOLOGY seemed poised to liberate men and women from their age-old bondage to toil, industrialism had transformed work into an endless cycle of repetitive labor. For Arendt, the body's "labor" was an aspect of biological survival and the reproduction of the species, while "work" was creativity, the crafting of a cultural legacy of beauty as well as utility.

The alienation of men and women from their labor is a theme which runs through much of twentieth-century social theory and analysis. DANIEL BELL argued that commercialized culture has replaced both work and religion as a means of self-fulfillment in a "post-industrial world." HERBERT MARCUSE proposed that work continues to be repressive because it is organized to perpetuate social domination, and that "the liberation of Eros" could create new and fulfilling conditions of work. Writers from John Steinbeck and TILLIE OLSEN to JAMES AGEE and Edna Ferber have put work at the center of their art, as have photographers such as Lewis Hine and WALKER EVANS. Steinbeck's exploited migrant workers, and Agee and Evans's poor Appalachian farmers have taken on mythic stature. In recent years such writers as MAXINE HONG KINGSTON, in her stories about laboring *China Men*, and Thomas Pynchon, in his fictions about multinational information flow, have added compelling accounts for an era in which an ethnically and racially diverse workforce of men and women confronts a workplace made unrecognizable by technological change.

JAMES F. KNAPP

FURTHER READING

Hannah Arendt, *The Human Condition* (New York: Doubleday, 1959).

Harry Braverman, *Labor and Monopoly Capital: the Degradation of Work in the Twentieth Century* (New York: Monthly Review Press, 1974).

Jonathan A. Glickstein, *Concepts of Free Labor in Antebellum America* (New Haven: Yale University Press, 1991).

Carol Groneman and Mary Beth Norton, eds., *"To Toil the Livelong Day": America's Women At Work, 1780–1980* (Ithaca: Cornell University Press, 1987).

C. Wright Mills, *White Collar: the American Middle Classes* (New York: Oxford University Press, 1953).

David Montgomery, *Workers' Control in America: Studies in the History of Work, Technology, and Labor Stuggles* (Cambridge: Cambridge University Press, 1979).

Daniel T. Rodgers, *The Work Ethic in Industrial America, 1850–1920* (Chicago: University of Chicago Press, 1978).

Christopher P. Wilson, *White Collar Fictions: Class and Social Representation in American Literature, 1885–1925* (Athens: University of Georgia Press, 1992).

World War I In the United States, the Great War of 1914–18 was peculiarly an affair of the mind. The crisis that exploded in the Balkans in the summer of 1914 left Europeans scant time for reflection. But Americans enjoyed nearly three years of neutrality while the guns roared on the far shore of the Atlantic. The neutrality period furnished unique opportunities for deliberation—and disagreement. Even after the United States Congress declared war against Germany on April 6, 1917 (and against Germany's ally, Austria-Hungary, on the following day), most Americans remained distant from the actual fighting and continued to debate, sometimes passionately, the war's meaning for their country. The congressional vote on April 6 vividly reflected the divisions in the country at large; despite open attacks by German submarines on American merchant ships, 50 Representatives and six Senators voted against the war resolution. Indeed, controversy about the war's legacy persisted well beyond the Armistice of November 11, 1918.

The war erupted at a particularly stressful moment in American history, the era of PROGRESSIVISM. It was a time marked by campaigns for women's suffrage, workers' rights, economic regulation, antitrust legislation, and electoral reforms. Sensitive to the war's possible effects on the fresh and therefore fragile accomplishments of progressivism, President Wilson remarked in 1914 that "Every reform we have won will be lost if we go into this war" (quoted in Baker, vol. 5, p. 77). Nor was this Wilson's only worry. The United States in the progressive era was more deeply seamed by ethnic differences than at any other time in its history. The census of 1910 counted over 13 million foreign-born persons in the American population, nearly 15 percent of the total. Fully one-third of the residents of the United States had either been born abroad or had at least one parent born abroad. Of those 32 million people, some 10 million derived from Germany or Austria-Hungary. Their loyalties could not be taken for granted. (*See also* ASSIMILATION.)

The remoteness of the fighting, along with the fractious political and social circumstances of the day, combined to convince the federal government that it had to manufacture a spirit of enthusiasm for the war where little such spirit naturally existed. The government's chief instrument for that task was the Committee on Public Information (CPI), a propaganda agency established on April 14, 1917. Thus the war in Europe begot another war at home, a war for the American mind.

The CPI had first to overcome the legacy of iso-lationism that was a cornerstone of American for-eign policy, and even of American cultural identity. The CPI blanketed the country with pamphlets, posters, films, and war expositions, as well as vol-unteer speakers—"four-minute men"— who exhorted audiences to make common cause with their European brethren in what President Wilson called the "war to make the world safe for democracy." The nation's schools were flooded with "war study course" materials that emphasized America's stake in the fate of Europe. Among the long-lived progeny of such efforts were the "History of Western Civiliza-tion" courses that became commonplace in college curricula for the remainder of the century.

The CPI's prodigious engines of persuasion were matched by other government agencies' no less prodigious engines of repression. Armed with the authority of the Espionage Act of June 15, 1917, the Justice Department and the postal authorities system-atically silenced antiwar voices. Abetted by quasi-official vigilante organizations such as the American Protective League, government authorities harassed pacifists, socialists, radical labor leaders, certain eth-nic groups, and others suspected of "disloyalty." The Supreme Court upheld the constitutionality of the Espionage Act in the case of *Schenck v. United States* (1919), which provided the occasion for Justice OLIVER WENDELL HOLMES JR. to proclaim that speech posing a "clear and present danger" to public order was not protected by the First Amendment. World War I thus initiated a process of limiting First Amendment freedoms that has reverberated through the courts ever since.

Historians have long debated whether the war fulfilled or killed the progressive reform impulse. Much of that argument has focused on a confrontation between the eminent philosopher JOHN DEWEY and the embittered young radical critic RANDOLPH BOURNE. Dewey believed that the conflict might provide the opportunity to temper, in the name of a higher collec-tive good, the chaotic and destructive individual-ism of American life. Bourne countered that Dewey and his allies had abandoned their core principles and gone whoring after influence in the corridors of power. He took them especially to task for their alleged complicity, however indirect and unintended, in the campaigns to snuff out dissenting views.

Bourne's critique of the liberal war supporters has long echoed in the history books, but the complicated truth is that Dewey and many other liberals were always tentative in their support for the war. They conditioned their prowar sentiment on the hope for social reform. In this they were largely disappointed,

as the progressive accomplishments of wartime, such as transient economic controls, precarious gains for labor, and the achievement of women's suffrage in 1920, gave way to decidedly illiberal developments like the great "red scare" of 1919–20, the severe re-striction of immigration in 1921, and the conservative Republican regimes that presided over the postwar decade—not to mention the highly imperfect peace settlement imposed on the Germans by the Treaty of Versailles, a treaty whose punitive features espe-cially galled liberal advocates of a "just peace."

Many liberals, such as the influential journalist WALTER LIPPMANN, were so appalled by the pro-pagandistic excesses and ferocious repressions of the war years, by Wilson's inability to direct the peace negotiations to liberal ends, and by the American Senate's eventual repudiation of the peace treaty that they began to back away from the optimistic faith in human rationality that was a historic hallmark of the liberal creed. Lippmann's *Public Opinion* (1922) testifies eloquently to that disillusionment.

In the last analysis, World War I left a bitter taste in the mouths of many Americans. When Europe again teetered on the brink of war in the 1930s, the memory of the earlier conflict powerfully deepened the traditional isolationist currents in American cul-ture, and contributed directly to the enactment of the Neutrality Acts that hobbled Franklin Roosevelt's efforts to defend the European democracies against Hitler's Germany.

DAVID M. KENNEDY

FURTHER READING
Ray Stannard Baker, *Woodrow Wilson: Life and Letters*, 8 vols. (Garden City, N.Y.: Doubleday, Page, 1927–39).
Robert H. Ferrell, *Woodrow Wilson and World War I, 1917–1921* (New York: Harper and Row, 1985).
David M. Kennedy, *Over Here: the First World War and American Society* (New York: Oxford University Press, 1980).
H. C. Peterson and Gilbert Fite, *Opponents of War, 1917–1918* (Seattle: University of Washington Press, 1968).
Stuart I. Rochester, *American Liberal Disillusionment in the Wake of World War I* (University Park: Pennsylvania State University Press, 1977).
Harry N. Scheiber, *The Wilson Administration and Civil Liberties, 1917–1921* (Ithaca: Cornell University Press, 1960).
Stephen Vaughn, *Holding Fast the Inner Lines: Democracy, Nationalism, and the Committee on Public Information* (Chapel Hill: University of North Carolina Press, 1980).

World War II World War I brought industrial-strength death to millions of soldiers in the trenches. World War II extended the reach of mechanized, im-personal, rationalized destruction to millions of non-combatants. The massive taking of innocent civilian life on all sides was the most distinctive feature of

World War II and that which rendered it a moral watershed in the course of modern civilization. The preeminent symbols of the Second World War are the concentration camp and the mushroom cloud.

These attributes of "total war" were not lost on the civilian populations of most combatant nations, millions of whom were displaced and demoralized by the destruction. The great exception were American civilians, who—unless they were Japanese American—neither suffered nor witnessed the war's terrors at first hand. Indeed, for many Americans the most significant immediate consequence of World War II was the happy renewal of economic prosperity it fostered in the early 1940s. As Richard Pells observes in *The Liberal Mind in a Conservative Age*,

> the American memory of the war is peculiarly parochial, disconcertingly innocent. At the outset of the conflict, Americans seemed incapable of comprehending what was to come. At the end, they remained curiously untouched by what had happened. (p. 7)

Most American intellectuals differed little from their compatriots in this regard—at least in the short run.

During the "defense period" (1939–41) a bitter debate raged between interventionist intellectuals such as MORTIMER ADLER, Waldo Frank, LEWIS MUMFORD, and REINHOLD NIEBUHR, who argued that the fate of civilized values rested with American participation in the war, and opponents such as CHARLES BEARD, JOHN DEWEY, and NORMAN THOMAS, who had been burned by one war for international democracy and were reluctant to commit themselves to another for fear of the consequences for democratic life at home. But with the bombing of Pearl Harbor significant opposition to the war by American intellectuals ceased. Most gave Franklin Roosevelt's war effort their "critical support," which usually amounted to far more support than criticism.

For some, support for the war was direct. Writers such as SAUL BELLOW, Dashiell Hammett, IRVING HOWE, CLEMENT GREENBERG, James Jones, IRVING KRISTOL, and NORMAN MAILER enlisted or were drafted into the armed forces. Others—including Frank Capra, Lewis Coser, John Ford, John Huston, H. Stuart Hughes, ARCHIBALD MACLEISH, and HAROLD ROSENBERG—found work in the Office of War Information, the Office of Strategic Services, and other government propaganda or intelligence agencies. There they were joined by refugees from Hitler such as Otto Kirchheimer, HERBERT MARCUSE, and Franz Neumann. Anthropologists such as Gregory Bateson, RUTH BENEDICT, Geoffrey Gorer, and MARGARET MEAD helped American policy-makers penetrate the mysteries of the Japanese mind, and American scientists joined émigré colleagues in government-funded laboratories from which they emerged bearing their labor's fruits, radar and the atomic bomb.

Other intellectuals supported the war more indirectly, serving as cheerleaders for the Roosevelt administration. Nowhere was this more evident than in the antifascist Popular Front of liberals and communists which was reconstituted following the German invasion of the Soviet Union in June 1941. Thereafter, FDR had no more loyal advocates than American communists and their liberal comrades. In the pages of the leading liberal magazine, THE NEW REPUBLIC, editor Bruce Bliven and his staff backed the President while attacking his adversaries in Congress and the "tories" in the State Department who appeased reactionary regimes in Vichy France, Spain, and Latin America and undermined prospects for a global New Deal. Insistent that the war required "tough managers" and a concentration of power in the executive branch of the government, *New Republic* liberals had few misgivings about Roosevelt's imperial Presidency. Nor did they have much criticism to offer of FDR's wartime ally, Joseph Stalin, whom they viewed as a shrewd, decisive, pragmatic, and tough-minded leader with whom American statesmen of the same stripe could reach a satisfying accommodation. Seldom alert to Roosevelt's own tory proclivities, these liberals imagined that after the war he would lead the nation toward an American-style social democracy marked by full employment, perpetual economic growth, and an activist, Keynesian welfare state. These dreams were brought up short in the Presidential campaign of 1944 when FDR dumped Vice President HENRY WALLACE, the liberal hero, as his running-mate in favor of the lackluster Harry Truman. But even this betrayal did little to cool the liberal ardor for Roosevelt and the war.

Like other Americans, intellectuals were slow to awaken to the implications of the profound moral disasters of the war. To its credit, *The New Republic* published a harrowing report by Varian Fry in December 1942 on "The Massacre of the Jews," followed in August 1943 by a special issue on Nazi genocide. But apart from Reinhold Niebuhr, DOROTHY THOMPSON, Stephen Wise, and a few others, liberal intellectuals had enormous difficulty confronting these events, for the HOLOCAUST mocked their convictions about human rationality and their dreams of social PROGRESS. They rushed to domesticate the Holocaust, to assimilate it to their faith in progress by treating it as a horrible premodern aberration or a peculiarly German frenzy. At the same time, they refused to confront the moral implications of the horrors perpetrated by the Allies, such as the terror bombing of civilian populations, which they defended as militarily necessary and morally just.

There were a few exceptional intellectuals who insisted that the way the war was fought on all sides had produced a defeat for reason, justice, and progress. For example, Catholic writers armed with centuries of reflection on just and unjust wars subjected Allied arguments for terror bombing to withering critical scrutiny. But it was the circle of intellectuals gathered around Dwight Macdonald's *politics* magazine which offered the most profound meditations on the moral costs of the war. As Daniel Bell later wrote in *The End of Ideology* (1960), *politics* was "the only magazine that was aware of and insistently kept calling attention to, changes that were taking place in moral temper, the depths of which we still incompletely realize" (p. 307).

DWIGHT MACDONALD and other *politics* contributors —including BRUNO BETTELHEIM, Albert Camus, Nicola Chiaromonte, PAUL GOODMAN, MARY MCCARTHY, C. WRIGHT MILLS, and the late Simone Weil—repudiated the progressive pieties of other liberals and radicals and examined with uncommon moral imagination the way the war was being waged. Although they offered startling insights into the unique features of Nazi terror, they were equally troubled by Allied terror and by the shared features of what Macdonald termed "their horrors and ours." Both the Allies and the Nazis depended on modern science, bureaucratic organization, and mass production to attain victory. On both sides, the war was a triumph of technical rationality. The death camp paid tribute to scientific management and modern industrial design. In articles later collected in *Politics Past*, Macdonald asserted that at the end of the war two horrors confronted one another:

the dying Nazi horror and the surviving Allied horror; the horror of conscious, rationalized destruction of the fabric of Western culture and ethics; and the horror of vast technological power exerted in warmaking by nations with no positive aims and little social consciousness.

The war had produced "the maximum of physical devastation accompanied by the minimum of human meaning" (p. 159).

The dropping of the atomic bomb deepened this conviction for Macdonald. Hiroshima, he contended, rendered concepts like "Good," "Evil," "democracy," and "progress" obsolete. "Can one imagine," he asked, "that the Bomb could ever be used 'in a good cause'? Do not such means instantly . . . corrupt *any* cause?" In Macdonald's estimation both the atomic bomb and Nazi death camps were the end results of remote technological and governmental processes over which the average individual had no control, but in whose name they were always employed. For this reason, the "Bomb is the natural product of the kind of society we have created": a society in which "vast numbers of citizens can be organized" to create weapons of universal destruction "without even knowing they were doing it" (pp. 169–79).

Views such as this were seldom advanced or appreciated by American intellectuals during World War II, and Macdonald was attacked by liberals for his tender-minded negativism. But in the postwar years, the *politics* perspective seemed a good deal more compelling to many, including Lewis Mumford and Macdonald's friend Hannah Arendt. Her powerful and celebrated portrait of the Holocaust as the rationalization of irrationality in *The Origins of Totalitarianism* (1951) echoed his own. As the nuclear arms race threatened civilian populations with "mutually assured destruction," the decision to drop the bomb no longer appeared as self-evidently justifiable as it had in the euphoria of war's end in August 1945. Some critical intellectuals like Mumford began to treat atomic warfare with what Macdonald had termed the "lively interest of victims." And in the best novels to emerge from World War II—Norman Mailer's *Naked and the Dead* (1948), James Jones's *From Here to Eternity* (1951), and Joseph Heller's *Catch-22* (1961)—the most memorable fascists wore American uniforms. Yet, it still must be said, World War II remains the "good war" for most Americans. Most intellectuals have followed Reinhold Niebuhr and WALTER LIPPMANN in seeing the war, for all its horrors, as a necessary defense of civilization against barbarism. Few have been willing to entertain the possibility that the war may have been fought at great cost to the values they hold most dear.

ROBERT B. WESTBROOK

FURTHER READING

John Morton Blum, *V Was for Victory: Politics and American Culture during World War II* (New York: Harcourt Brace Jovanovich, 1976).

Paul Boyer, *By the Bomb's Early Light: American Thought and Culture at the Dawn of the Atomic Age* (New York: Pantheon, 1985).

John W. Dower, *War Without Mercy: Race and Power in the Pacific War* (New York: Pantheon, 1986).

William S. Graebner, *The Age of Doubt: American Thought and Culture in the 1940s* (Boston: Twayne, 1991).

Barry M. Katz, *Foreign Intelligence: Research and Analysis in the Office of Strategic Services, 1942–1945* (Cambridge: Harvard University Press, 1989).

Dwight Macdonald, *Politics Past* (New York: Viking, 1957).

Richard Pells, *The Liberal Mind in a Conservative Age:*

American Intellectuals in the 1940s and 1950s (New York: Harper and Row, 1985).

Robert B. Westbrook, "Horrors—Theirs and Ours: the *Politics* Circle and the Good War," *Radical History Review* 36 (1986): 8–25.

Wright, Carroll (b. Dunbarton, N.H., July 25, 1840; d. Worcester, Mass., Feb. 20, 1909). Statistician, first Commissioner of Labor (1885–1905). Wright sought to use labor statistics to correct the maladjustments of the industrial system. The factory, he believed, is the beneficent culmination of the human tendency towards association: it increases productivity and enables workers to enjoy culture. Labor unrest arises from ignorance and shortsighted greed on both sides. Disinterested citizens who seek the public good can eliminate such local conflicts by employing impartial and scientific statistics. Wright outlined his ideas in such works as *The Relation of Political Economy to the Labor Question* (1882), *The Industrial Evolution of the United States* (1895), and *Outline of Practical Sociology* (1899).

FURTHER READING

James Leiby, *Carroll Wright and Labor Reform: the Origin of Labor Statistics* (Cambridge: Harvard University Press, 1960).

Wright, Chauncey (b. Northampton, Mass., Sept. 20, 1830; d. Cambridge, Mass., Sept. 12, 1875). Of all mid nineteenth-century American philosophers, Chauncey Wright has worn the best. The revived fascination with American PRAGMATISM and the sustained interest in the sources of Darwin's views on human self-consciousness have both assured Wright's reputation. His prophetic role, not any particular doctrines, gained him this reputation.

Wright lived for only 45 years. He never published a book, never held other than temporary academic jobs, and earned no advanced degrees. In his youth he revealed special talents in mathematics and an aversion to classical languages; by the help of a benefactor, he completed his B.A. at Harvard in 1852. He excelled in mathematics and philosophy, and became fascinated with pre-Darwinian theories about the evolution of species. His only permanent job would be as a human computer, making the endless celestial calculations needed annually by the *Nautical Almanac*.

Personally, Wright was a lovable eccentric. Unmarried, dependent and childlike, he suffered bouts of depression and was an alcoholic. Others cared for his few physical needs, while only conversation (he would argue or talk all night) and the com-

panionship of friends rescued him from complete despair. In two temporary teaching positions at Harvard he proved inept, delivering monotonous lectures that were over the heads of undergraduates. He excelled in direct tutorial instruction, and among friends gained a reputation as the American Socrates. He rejoiced in conversations at a literary club before the Civil War, and after 1865 became the leading catalyst for a philosophical discussion group labeled the Metaphysical Club. In it were WILLIAM JAMES, OLIVER W. HOLMES JR., and CHARLES S. PEIRCE, the architects of a later pragmatism. All were directly influenced, even if at times discomforted, by the detached, rigorous (James later called it tough-minded) empiricism of Wright.

From the war years on, Wright was dependent upon the friendship and almost daily hospitality of the family of Harvard President CHARLES NORTON. When in Europe in 1869–70, the Norton daughters tried to buoy up the spirits of a lonely Wright by letters deliberately loaded with philosophical queries, all of which Wright conscientiously answered. These letters and a series of critical essays in the *Nation* and the *North American Review* make up the corpus of his surviving philosophical works. These came after a bequest freed him from his labors for the *Almanac* and allowed him a trip to Europe, where in the climactic experience of his life he was able to spend some time in the home of his greatest hero, Charles Darwin.

As a philosopher, Wright adhered closely to the views of John Stuart Mill. He rejected all metaphysical systems, and, with almost complete detachment from the religious and moral issues that so absorbed his companions, he tried to understand the foundations of scientific reasoning. He qualifies as America's first philosopher of science. He found the roots of metaphysical speculation in wonder and awe, in the ancient but surviving appeal of animism, and in an infatuation with obscure forces or reified abstractions that was possibly genetic and thus, for most people, irresistible. Such a speculative addiction led to various competing ontological systems, none supported by objective data.

More difficult, dependent upon a rare discipline, and late in the history of human achievement, were the generalizing, empirical sciences which Wright always celebrated. He was most original in exploring both the formal and the experiential aspects of scientific inquiry. He sought a naturalistic and linguistic explanation for the functionally but not transcendental a priori content of scientific theory. He believed intellectual curiosity, not compelling moral concerns or practical needs, provided the indispensable motive for disciplined, objective, self-correcting inquiry, although he knew that the products of such inquiry might serve various human uses. He glorified what people now call "basic" or "pure" SCIENCE, and believed that a restrained Darwin, who eschewed all metaphysical speculation, who never assigned efficacy to mere abstractions, who rejected any ultimate hypotheses, provided the ideal model of a scientist.

It was in response to Darwin that Wright wrote his one great essay, a long monograph on the origins of human self-consciousness which he published in the *North American Review*. Darwin gladly acknowledged the controlling influence of this essay upon his *Descent of Man*. The essay, written in a typically dense style, explored new themes in human physiology and psychology. Wright's goal was to offer a naturalistic hypothesis for the development of higher mental processes in humans, processes that marked a high degree of difference in function, but not a difference of degree, between humans and other mammals. Such a naturalistic explanation was required if one were to assimilate human self-consciousness, and culture, to Darwin's theory of natural selection. This line of argument broached the most revolutionary implications of Darwin's explanation of how new species emerge—that mind is not a cause of natural events but itself a belated outcome of historical processes. It is an emergent, not a prior cause.

Wright's solution to what Darwin saw as the dilemma of self-consciousness is not simple or even completely clear. He was working in new ground. His essay included a rich, complex analysis of the role of internal signs or images in the brain during all learned behavior, or whenever higher mental processes mediate between stimulus and response. By the gradual development of true external signs, such as words, humans were able to isolate and remember internal images present in past experience, and to correlate such images with external signs, those involving hearing and modulated speech. This enabled humans to reflect on the process, reflectively to distinguish subject and object, and thus to become self-conscious in a way denied to animals without such a repertoire of external signs and thus without a symbolic language. All higher mental activities required such self-consciousness. Characteristically, Wright saw scientific generalization as the final and highest outcome of the one greatest adaptive tool—LANGUAGE.

Wright was the ablest nineteenth-century spokesperson in America for a lean and hard empiricism, or a position often called POSITIVISM. He first sought naturalistic sources for the formal aspects of thought, and in his explorations of language and grammar anticipated later functionalist versions of psychology.

PAUL CONKIN

FURTHER READING
Edward H. Madden, *Chauncey Wright* (New York: Washington Square Press, 1964).
Chauncey Wright, *Philosophical Discussions*, ed. Charles E. Norton (New York: Henry Holt, 1877).
——, *Letters*, ed. James B. Thayer (Cambridge: John Wilson and Son, 1878).
——, *Philosophical Writings: Representative Selections*, ed. Edward H. Madden (New York: Liberal Arts Press, 1958).

Wright, Frances [Fanny] (b. Dundee, Scotland, Sept. 6, 1795; d. Cincinnati, Ohio, Dec. 13, 1852). Writer and lecturer. A proponent of sexual, racial, and class equality, Wright argued for women's suffrage, attacked women's subjugation in marriage, and asserted that people should form and break sexual unions as they saw fit. Campaigning against slavery, she maintained that gradual emancipation could be made economically viable and would fully integrate blacks into society. She championed urban workers, advocated a state-sponsored system of free education that would eliminate social class, and insisted on freedom of religion and the press. Well known as an orator, editor, and activist, she wrote voluminously for periodicals and published *Views of Society and Manners in America* (1821).

FURTHER READING
Celia Morris Eckhardt, *Fanny Wright: Rebel in America* (Cambridge: Harvard University Press, 1984).

Wright, Frank Lloyd (b. Richland Center, Wis., June 8, 1867; d. Phoenix, Ariz., Apr. 9, 1959). Architect. Originator of the relaxed, open-plan "Prairie style" that deeply influenced twentieth-century residential design, Wright believed that physical spaces always mold, and should therefore consciously reflect, the social processes within them. A building, he held, should fit both its function and its environment. Blending interior and exterior, his technologically advanced designs emphasize horizontal lines, provide flowing open spaces, and use building materials themselves as the primary decoration. Wright explained his architectural philosophy in "The Art and Craft of the Machine" (1901), *An Organic Architecture* (1939), and *An American Architecture* (1955).

See also ARCHITECTURE.

FURTHER READING
Meryle Secrest, *Frank Lloyd Wright* (New York: Knopf, 1992).

Wright, Richard (b. Roxie, Miss., Sept. 4, 1908; d. Paris, France, Nov. 28, 1960). In *American Hunger* (the longer version of *Black Boy*), Richard Wright records the major stages in his formative years from rural Mississippi to the communist circles of New York. The autobiography of the son of a sharecropper who deserted his schoolteacher wife, herself soon stricken with paralysis, first shows him living in the homes of relatives, mostly at his grandmother's. Her strict Adventist faith, which cast literature as an abomination, alienated him from religious practice; he had been writing stories even as a young teenager. While employed in a Memphis optical company, Wright read H. L. MENCKEN and the American naturalists, and they sustained his vocation. A migrant to Chicago in 1929, he held several menial jobs in order to support his family during the Depression, was forced into unemployment, and finally obtained a position in the Post Office.

His first break as a writer came when the left-wing John Reed Club gave him entry into racially integrated writers' and artists' circles; he became acquainted with progressive authors and published revolutionary verse in little magazines like *Left Front*, *Anvil*, and *Partisan Review*. He joined the Communist Party for political reasons, but also in order to retain his position in the Club, which supported his writing. In 1935, he worked for a Negro Theatre unit of the Works Progress Administration. As soon as he became eligible for the Federal Writers' Project in 1937 he moved to New York to head the *Daily Worker* Harlem bureau. Meanwhile, he wrote forceful short stories dealing with racism and violence in the South. Several of them, starting with "Big Boy Leaves Home," won awards before they were collected as *Uncle Tom's Children* (1938).

Native Son (1940), a hard-hitting novel in the line of Dreiser's *An American Tragedy*, treated the role of racial oppression in shaping a ghetto youngster into the murderer of his millionaire white employer's daughter. Bigger Thomas, the name of the protagonist, has since become synonymous with the rebellious violence of the black underclass in capitalist society. The novel catapulted Wright to national fame, while also making him highly controversial. He adapted it for the stage in collaboration with Paul Green and it was produced by Orson Welles the following year.

Wright married twice within a couple of years. He was a left-wing star, and his *Twelve Million Black Voices* (1941), "a folk history of the Negro in the United States," is a splendid blues text in a Marxist vein. But, while retaining his ideological perspective, he left the Communist Party in 1942 because it tampered with his literary freedom. At that point he started work on his autobiography. In 1945, *Black Boy* (the text being limited to "a record of childhood and youth") brought him lasting international fame. He had become affluent and respected as a writer but still felt the sting of racism. Following vacations in Mexico and Quebec, he spent an initial eight-month sojourn in Paris, and decided to exile himself there in 1947. He was fleeing both racial discrimination and the growing anti-leftist feeling which culminated in the McCarthy witch-hunts. France, he thought, offered an atmosphere conducive to creativity and intellectual growth. Even before becoming acquainted with existentialism as a philosophy, he had written an existentialist parable, "The Man who Lived Underground" (1941) in order "to go beyond stories in black and white." He became a friend of the Paris existentialists—Jean-Paul Sartre, Simone de Beauvoir, and Albert Camus—and completed *The Outsider* (1953), a thesis novel in the form of a thriller. It explored the contemporary human condition while repudiating the ideologies of communism and fascism. Positing human solidarity and questioning the ideal of the Nietzschean superman, it ended in the defeat of unbridled INDIVIDUALISM. It met with only moderate success in the United States.

Hailed as a spokesman for his race, Wright soon became interested in Africa and helped launch the review *Présence Africaine*. But *Black Power* (1954), "a record of a journey in a land of pathos," while commending Pan-Africanism and Kwame Nkrumah's policies in Ghana, also reveals Wright's psychological and cultural estrangement from Africa. *The Color Curtain* (1956), his report on the first conference of nonaligned countries held in Bandung, reveals his growing attention to the problems of Third World countries. At the First Conference of Negro Writers and Intellectuals at the Sorbonne in Paris in 1956, he recommended the discarding of traditional native cultures in the struggle for decolonization. *Pagan Spain* (1958) likewise analyzed the complex impact of the Catholic traditions on European culture, while denouncing the totalitarianism of Franco's regime. Meanwhile Wright's advocacy of justice and freedom for the Third World resulted in several lectures collected in *White Man, Listen* (1959).

The Long Dream (1959) is the first novel in an unfinished trilogy. With it, Wright returned to the Mississippi world of his childhood, while the still unpublished "Island of Hallucinations" covered the lasting psychological effects of racial oppression on the black man in a new, European setting. Wright had hardly recovered from amoebic dysentery when he died of a heart attack. He was under great mental stress at the time, partly from the activities of the CIA in harassing and spying on the African American community in Paris. Rumors surfaced blaming the CIA for poisoning him.

Wright's oeuvre is of the foremost importance in American literature. His outspoken denunciation of American racism, his honest acknowledgement of black complexes, and his baring of black resentment against white society established the necessity of uncompromising writing in the 1940s. It helped to free the next generation of writers, including JAMES BALDWIN, from having to pursue protest against deprivation and discrimination; they could instead explore and celebrate more positive aspects of black life. It also set an example for non-U.S. black writers like novelists Peter Abrahams from South Africa and George Lamming from Barbados. Political theorist Frantz Fanon derived much from Wright's analysis of the fear-hate-fear syndrome and of the liberating value of "revolutionary violence."

Largely self-taught, Wright was in several ways a precursor: not only did he cast the black American as a symbol of the contemporary human being in his transition from rural feudalism to urbanized modernity, he also stressed the relevance of sociology and psychoanalysis for literary creation. His diverse production encompasses his socially and politically committed writing, but also includes thousands of haiku poems. Wright's earnest, rational, Marxist, nonreligious perspective should not hide, either, his spirituality, exhibited in the metaphysical questions he raised in his essays and lectures. And his poignant, often bleak writing is occasionally marked by a strongly comic voice, as in his first novel *Lawd Today* (not published until 1963). Moreover, for all his proclaimed resistance to native cultures, he still makes consistent use, in his devotion to modernity, of African American folk expression. His depiction of women has been roundly criticized by feminist critics, but his textual strategies are receiving increased critical attention and acclaim. And unlike most of the writers of his generation he has remained highly popular among readers throughout the world.

MICHEL FABRE

FURTHER READING
Michel Fabre, *The Unfinished Quest of Richard Wright* (1973; Urbana: University of Illinois Press, 1993).
——, *The World of Richard Wright* (Jackson: University Press of Mississippi, 1985).
Yoshinobu Hakutani, ed., *Critical Essays on Richard Wright* (Boston: G.K. Hall, 1982).
Joyce Ann Joyce, *Richard Wright's Art of Tragedy* (Iowa City: University of Iowa Press, 1986).
Kenneth Kinnamon et al., *A Richard Wright Bibliography: Fifty Years of Criticism and Commentary, 1933–1982* (Westport: Greenwood, 1988).
Edward Margolies, *The Art of Richard Wright* (Carbondale: Southern Illinois University Press, 1969).
Eugene E. Miller, *Voice of a Native Son: the Poetics of Richard Wright* (Jackson: University Press of Mississippi, 1990).

Y

youth The idea that youth is a special and problematic stage of life is not a product of recent American history. "Youth" has always been a crucial category that transcended its significance in individual families to influence public expressions of national identity. The range of meanings of the term has evolved considerably.

Beginning in the 1630s a Euro-American rhetoric invested a "younger" generation with particular responsibility for maintaining community ideals. The concern for youth was more than metaphorical. By the middle of the 1600s and until the late 1700s the median age in America was 16. Socially, early colonial Americans shared with their English forebears a belief that youth represented a significant step on the journey of life, in which a young person was expected to submit to the discipline of the patriarchal family before marriage and the establishment of an independent home. Culturally, youth took on particular significance in New England, where PURITANISM faced a crisis of institutional continuity. A language of generational responsibility created by ministers and cultivated by secular civic authorities identified young people as the crucial agents in maintaining the Puritan errand in the New World. They placed critical importance on transmitting community values to those who followed the founders. As years passed, these inheritors, the "rising generation," became equated with the "young."

In the eighteenth century, America itself, often described as an infant, became associated with youth and growth; patriots depicted themselves as young men ready to stand alone against their parent England. In contrast to colonial sermons' representations of youth surrounded by sin and temptation, Revolutionary and post-Revolutionary spokesmen used the youth image to describe the hopeful possibilities and prospects for the country. Young men and women in mid nineteenth-century cities took their elders' assertions seriously, and made youth the basis for a claim to participate in public life.

Youth in the early nineteenth century described persons aged roughly between 20 and 30. In the antebellum years they comprised about a quarter of the white population in rapidly growing northern cities. The working-class young formed an intricate social network based on leisure and workplace alliances, while the young dwelling in poverty became identified as "dangerous classes," the target for benevolent "child savers." A male member of the rising middle class, meanwhile, was often designated as a "young man." These urbanites formed voluntary associations for self-help, political advancement, and social reform.

The passing of the Republic's founding fathers once again raised the specter of cultural discontinuity, and again the young were singled out. After the late 1820s, young white men in political, antislavery, and temperance organizations claimed affinity with the founders and declared their responsibility for taking action to protect the nation. Free blacks in several northern cities formed their own young men's groups and participated in the same discourse of the responsibility of youth. These organizations provided a means for ordinary men to make a mark in the public sphere. They emphasized particular male qualities of martial courage and aggressiveness, and the obligation of young men to defend the nation against threatening forces—whether the sin of intemperance or the candidate of a rival party. They enshrined notions of brotherhood and loyalty to founding ideals; even conflicts with elders were described as a higher form of obedience. Young women, also active in urban movements for reform, rarely formed groups self-consciously identified by age. While a place at the head of society seemed the likely end for the activist young man, MOTHERHOOD defined the prime OBLIGATION in the young woman's future. The few women's groups organized by age made clear that members would not be young and single for long.

The language of youthful duty and integrity was transformed when it migrated into wider social and political discourse and was used by a range of spokesmen who all employed the same rubric—Young America. Strident advocates of a national literature, inspired by European nationalists or Americans such as RALPH WALDO EMERSON, first launched Young America in the 1840s. The phrase was meant to symbolize a local literature free of foreign influence and representative of youthful, manly virtues—a perfect synthesis of cultural ideals about youth's responsibilities. American Renaissance figures including MARGARET FULLER, HERMAN MELVILLE, EDGAR ALLAN POE, and William Gilmore Simms were associated at various times with the New York editors and writers who promoted Young America. Soon political polemicists absorbed the phrase and reversed the old paradigm. Youth no longer represented a defense of founding principles; instead, the genuine heritage of the Fathers was a readiness to overthrow the past. Deployed in the Presidential campaign of 1852, Young America became shorthand for an expansionist American foreign policy.

In the last half of the century, young men appeared most often in literary portrayals that (following a tradition initiated by BENJAMIN FRANKLIN) described their struggles for success in the city. Popular stories written by authors such as HORATIO ALGER enshrined what historian R. Richard Wohl called "The Country Boy Myth" of honest, hard-working youth. Women writing popular domestic and sentimental literature, meanwhile, took seriously young women's inner lives and aspirations; their stories offered a more complex treatment of their experience than did popular works about young men.

From the Civil War to the first decades of the twentieth century, young people's public roles diminished markedly. Their lives grew increasingly regulated and routinized in state-run institutions. The expansion of mandatory schooling and age-grading in education coincided with increasing PROFESSIONALISM and specialization in the labor market. Soon the only imaginable location for a middle-class young person's activities was in school or in adult-led organizations such as the Young Men's Christian Association or the Boy Scouts, groups that tried to promote behavior appropriate for future professional life. The publication of Adolescence (1904) by G. STANLEY HALL confirmed the association of youth with one stage in a carefully sequenced life course. The path to adulthood would be increasingly structured and subdivided into ever finer units, each under appropriate expert supervision.

A young life led in age-graded schools and peer communities produced the dilemma JANE ADDAMS called the "snare of preparation": the increasing alienation of youth from the "real" world outside school, a bifurcation that produced an inner emptiness. RANDOLPH BOURNE and fellow radical intellectuals such as VAN WYCK BROOKS invoked the old phrase "Young America" to signal their disgust with the catchpenny realities of business civilization and with the tired formalism of Victorian artistic expression: they called for a newly vibrant life symbolized by the culturally diverse Columbia University student body celebrated by Bourne.

Other critics, including ROBERT and HELEN LYND in Middletown (1929), examined the age-specific crisis of youth in a disillusioned age. Social scientific investigation of "normal" as well as delinquent youth proliferated, while literary narratives of youth and the urban ghetto, such as Anzia Yezierska's Bread Givers (1925), brought the full struggles of immigrant and working-class young people to middle-class readers.

In the post-World War II period social scientists sealed their demarcation of youth as the time of "identity" formation. By the middle of the twentieth century, school peer groups and delinquents were identified as members of youth "cultures." Those cultures manifested some resistance to adult norms, a contained resistance memorably evoked by James Dean in Rebel Without a Cause, but most observers offered the reassuring view that bohemianism or rebellion was a "stage" followed by the absorption of appropriate adult behavior.

As baby boomers began entering universities in the 1960s, close scrutiny followed them. Observers from psychologist Kenneth Keniston to social critic PAUL GOODMAN argued in the early 1960s that educated middle-class youth experienced a contradiction between preparation for success in a bureaucratic society and potent youthful ideals that resisted such routinization. The contrast between seeking material prosperity and searching for identity typified the outlook of the student NEW LEFT. A yearning for committed solutions to national problems could be found in both the 1960 inaugural address of President John F. Kennedy—"young" at 43—and the 1962 Port Huron Statement of Students for a Democratic Society. Student protest against inhuman bureaucracy and the demand for a political transformation that satisfied individual needs gained support as the decade progressed.

White and black student activists revived the longstanding tradition that youth had the primary responsibility for saving the nation from itself. Student protesters assailed their universities as knowledge "factories" producing educated cogs for the efficient wheels of state and corporations. Critics might assail protest on the campus and against the Vietnam War as irrational Oedipal rebellion against parental authority, but student radicals and the broader youthful counterculture became symbols of an impending shift in human values. Bestselling books such as Charles Reich's The Greening of America (1970) and Theodore Roszak's The Making of a Counterculture (1969) proclaimed the dawn of a newly expansive consciousness, and advertisers and other marketers began the long campaign to promote and capitalize on the quest for novel lifestyles.

A much bemoaned culture-wide "generation gap"

was actually far from proven. "Countercultural" youth often rejected parental ideals, but most politically radical youths shared their parents' liberal values. Youthful "alienation" as a stage in an eventual integration into society was an option available only to children of the middle and upper classes. Working-class youth were thrust into adulthood at an earlier age.

Scholars examining youth must remain wary of applying contemporary categories of identity crisis and generational conflict to earlier periods, or imagining a transhistorical, essential "youth." The seemingly universal qualities of youth mask its close association with a boisterous, aggressive male character. Scholars are beginning to explore the distinctive experience of young women, although usually in studies devoted primarily to broader subjects—as in recent work on women's leisure, such as Kathy Peiss's *Cheap Amusements* (1986).

The idea of youth played a central role in minority group organizing over the last generation. CIVIL RIGHTS organizations such as the National Association for the Advancement of Colored People developed leaders through separate youth sections, while the Student Non-Violent Coordinating Committee and other groups built explicitly upon the energies and militancy of the younger generation. African American youth leaders, like those from other racial and ethnic communities, came from working-class backgrounds much more often than white youth activists.

After riots in Watts, Detroit, Newark, and other cities in the 1960s, "youth" became indelibly associated with images of city life and decay. Significant memoirs such as Claude Brown's *Manchild in the Promised Land* (1966) and Piri Thomas's *Down These Mean Streets* (1968) provided evidence for social commentators who saw the violent explosions of the ghetto as the essential fact of modern urban life: dark-skinned youths as a ticking time-bomb buried inside the American body politic. Recent accounts of African American and Chicano young men, including Jess Mowry's *Way Past Cool* (1992) and Luis Rodriguez's *Always Running* (1993), as well as such journalistic studies as Alex Kotlowitz's participant-observer work *There Are No Children Here* (1991), reinforced the story of gang and random violence as the dominant narrative of minority youth life and even urban existence in general. Urban youth came to represent a contemporary version of the nineteenth-century "dangerous classes." This kind of mythologizing built upon but also diverted attention from the deeper social reality of late twentieth-century cities: the endemic poverty and unemployment facing inner-city dwellers. The precise relation between poverty and violence is a matter of debate, as is the question how to combat them both. There is no debate about the fact that almost half of all African American children live below the government's poverty line.

White middle-class youth, meanwhile, have provoked widespread puzzlement in social observers seeking to gauge their degree of "commitment." Curiously, cultural critics tend to use the youth movement and campus activism of the 1960s as a normative standard for assessing the next generation, even as they simultaneously have come to view 1960s radicalism as a historically exceptional instance of youthful agitation. Some analysts do detect a resurgence of youthful idealism in social arenas as diverse as rap music and national politics. Whatever the truth of that claim, there can be no doubt that youth remains a symbolic touchstone for those charting social trends or identifying new marketing opportunities. In a country that has always looked to its future for images of fulfillment, the actual or imagined experience of youth will surely continue to guide social and cultural prognostication. And from time to time, as they have throughout American history, young people themselves will assert their primacy as beacons of national purpose.

GLENN WALLACH

See also CHILDHOOD.

FURTHER READING

Anne M. Boylan, "Growing Up Female in Young America, 1800–1860," in Joseph M. Hawes and N. Ray Hiner, eds., *American Childhood, a Research Guide and Historical Handbook* (Westport: Greenwood, 1985).

Howard P. Chudacoff, *How Old Are You? Age Consciousness in American Culture* (Princeton: Princeton University Press, 1989).

Paula S. Fass, *The Damned and the Beautiful: American Youth in the 1920s* (New York: Oxford University Press, 1977).

Kenneth Keniston, *Youth and Dissent* (New York: Harcourt Brace Jovanovich, 1971).

Joseph Kett, *Rites of Passage: Adolescence in America, 1790 to the Present* (New York: Basic Books, 1977).

Michael W. Miles, *The Radical Probe: the Logic of Student Rebellion* (New York: Atheneum, 1971).

John Modell, *Into One's Own: From Youth to Adulthood in the United States, 1920–1975* (Berkeley: University of California Press, 1989).

Glenn Wallach, "Obedient Sons: Youth and Generational Consciousness in American Culture, 1630–1850s," Ph.D. diss., Yale University, 1991.

Index